ALSO BY JOHN FABIAN WITT

*American Contagions: Epidemics and the Law from
Smallpox to COVID-19*

Lincoln's Code: The Laws of War in American History

Patriots and Cosmopolitans: Hidden Histories of American Law

*The Accidental Republic: Crippled Workingmen, Destitute Widows,
and the Remaking of American Law*

To Save the Country: A Lost Treatise on Martial Law
(ed. with Will Smiley)

Scholarship students between classes—and on the cusp of big things—at Brookwood Labor College, 1927.

THE RADICAL FUND

HOW A BAND OF VISIONARIES AND A MILLION DOLLARS UPENDED AMERICA

JOHN FABIAN WITT

Simon & Schuster

NEW YORK   AMSTERDAM/ANTWERP   LONDON
TORONTO   SYDNEY/MELBOURNE   NEW DELHI

Simon & Schuster
1230 Avenue of the Americas
New York, NY 10020

For more than 100 years, Simon & Schuster has championed authors and the stories they create. By respecting the copyright of an author's intellectual property, you enable Simon & Schuster and the author to continue publishing exceptional books for years to come. We thank you for supporting the author's copyright by purchasing an authorized edition of this book.

No amount of this book may be reproduced or stored in any format, nor may it be uploaded to any website, database, language-learning model, or other repository, retrieval, or artificial intelligence system without express permission. All rights reserved. Inquiries may be directed to Simon & Schuster, 1230 Avenue of the Americas, New York, NY 10020 or permissions@simonandschuster.com.

Copyright © 2025 by John Fabian Witt

All rights reserved, including the right to reproduce this book or portions thereof in any form whatsoever. For information, address Simon & Schuster Subsidiary Rights Department, 1230 Avenue of the Americas, New York, NY 10020.

First Simon & Schuster hardcover edition October 2025

SIMON & SCHUSTER and colophon are registered trademarks of Simon & Schuster, LLC

Simon & Schuster strongly believes in freedom of expression and stands against censorship in all its forms. For more information, visit BooksBelong.com.

For information about special discounts for bulk purchases, please contact Simon & Schuster Special Sales at 1-866-506-1949 or business@simonandschuster.com.

The Simon & Schuster Speakers Bureau can bring authors to your live event. For more information or to book an event, contact the Simon & Schuster Speakers Bureau at 1-866-248-3049 or visit our website at www.simonspeakers.com.

Interior design by Paul Dippolito

Manufactured in the United States of America

1 3 5 7 9 10 8 6 4 2

Library of Congress Cataloging-in-Publication Data is available.

ISBN 978-1-4767-6587-7
ISBN 978-1-4767-6635-5 (ebook)

For Beverly

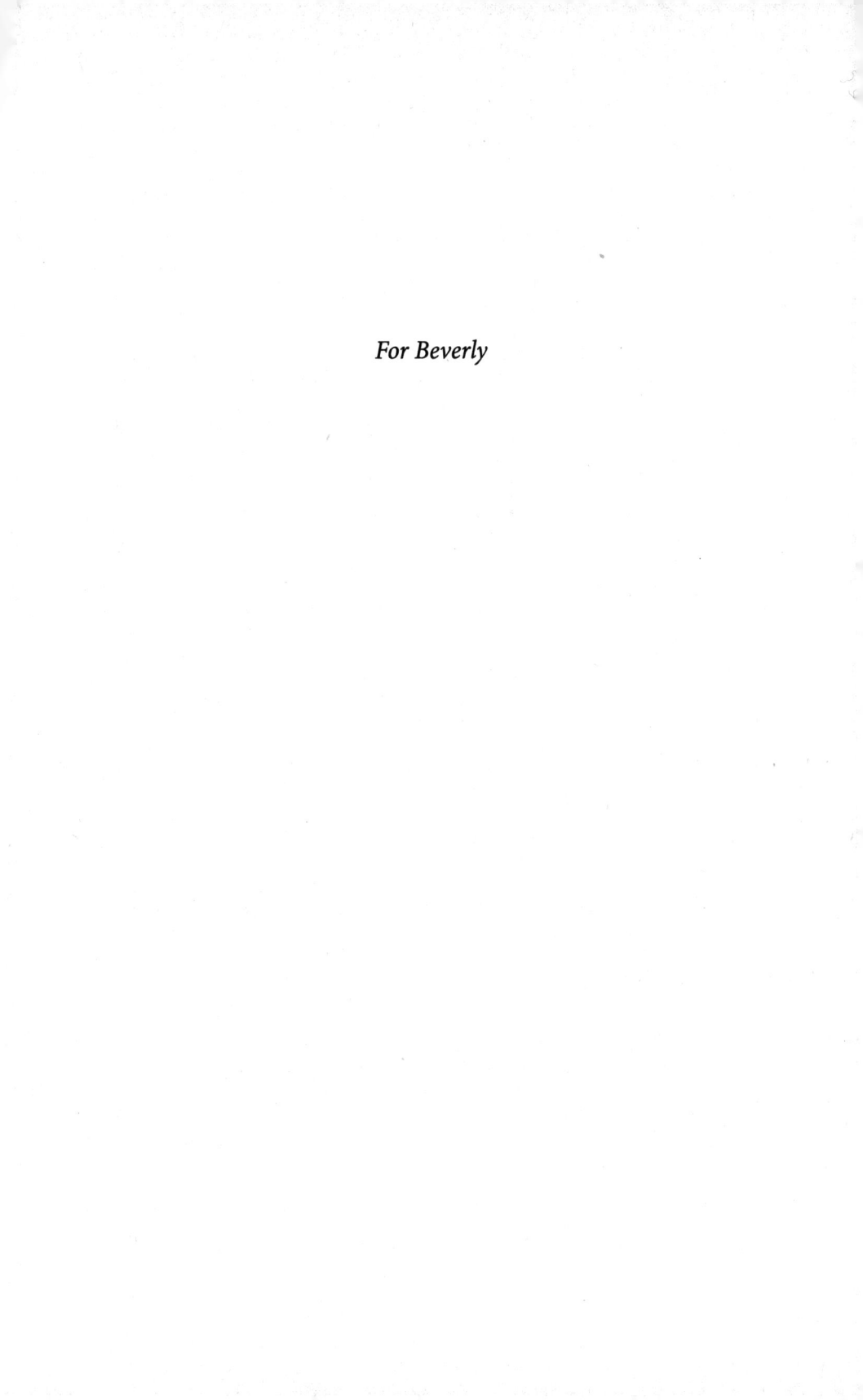

The love of money is the root of all evil.
—1 TIMOTHY 6:10

Money makes the world go round.
—AMERICAN PROVERB

CONTENTS

Cast of Characters: The World of the Garland Fund   xv

Prologue: A Curious Inheritance   1

PART I: MASS DEMOCRACY IN AMERICA

1. Democratic Faith   13
   The Education of Roger Baldwin
   The People Can Rule
   Outrage of the Century

2. Weapons of Truth   39
   You Will Be Suppressed
   Not by Bread Alone
   War Fever

3. The Less We Know   57
   A Preparatory School of Crime
   Blanket of Silence
   The Best Test of Truth?

4. Freedom and Economics   81
   A Civil Liberties Union
   The New Benevolence

5. Garland's Million   99
   Cause of All Unhappiness
   A Trust Fund for Pioneering Enterprises
   The Left Compass

6. Free Love Farm   117

PART II: AGAINST JIM CROW

7. The Usual Crime — 125
The Fury of the Mob
Greatest American Game
Explode the Rape Myth

8. Educate the Masses — 161
Cash Value
Out of Our Field
Fasten Slavery Permanently

9. First Victories — 189
Thunder Bolt from a Clear Sky
The Most Celebrated of Cases
Nothing Except Power

10. Capturing the Captors — 217
Fascinating Perils
Culture for the New Masses
The Vanguard

11. Money Haters and Tax Lawyers — 241

PART III: AMERICAN REVOLUTIONARIES

12. Nothing in Common — 253
A Rebel Girl Smashes the Chains
Sabotage
The IWW Does Not Believe in Violence

13. Industrial Democracy — 291
Sacco and Vanzetti
I Shall Not Leave This Platform
Brookwood

14. The Messenger — 325
The Most Dangerous Negro in America
Upon the Shoulders of Black Abolitionists
A Quitter Never Wins

15. Millennia Don't Just Happen — 357
The Black Belt
A Revolution in Economic Life
Kindergarten Propositions

16. Radical Enterprises — 393

PART IV: OUTSIDERS ON THE INSIDE

17. A Way of Action — 405
The Public and Its Government
Powers of the Hualapai
Evil Eye and Unequal Hand

18. Scottsboro and After — 435
Tactics for Mass Pressure
The Cost of Skin Pigmentation
Outstanding Accomplishment

19. Use This Weapon — 467
Brookwood Unbound
Affirmative Legal Action
Sit-Down Strike

20. Switch in Time — 499
Vanguard of the Black Workers
Power Plays

21. A Rather Astonishing Fund — 527

Epilogue: Legacies — 533

Appendix A: Gifts, 1922–1941 — 543
Appendix B: Garland Fund Outlays, 1922–1941 — 567
Appendix C: Board of Directors, 1922–1941 — 568
Appendix D: Note on Language — 571
Acknowledgments — 573
Notes — 579
Photo Credits — 681
Index — 685

CAST OF CHARACTERS
The World of the Garland Fund

Roger Nash Baldwin. Director of the American Civil Liberties Union, champion of labor and civil rights, pivotal Garland Fund founder.

Edward L. Bernays. Public relations expert, nephew of Sigmund Freud, creator of a Garland Fund–sponsored anti-lynching ad campaign.

John Brophy. Pennsylvania coal miner from the age of twelve, dissident organizer at the United Mine Workers, board member at Brookwood Labor College.

George Creel. Wilson administration propagandist, foil for the Garland Fund's work on democracy.

Clarence Darrow. Trial lawyer, defender of Garland Fund causes.

Madeleine Doty. Author and journalist, specialist in prison reform and pacifism; egalitarian marriage to Roger Baldwin in 1919.

W. E. B. Du Bois. Founder of the National Association for the Advancement of Colored People and editor of *The Crisis* magazine, sometime Garland Fund beneficiary and frequent Garland Fund advisor

Crystal and Max Eastman. ACLU founder and Garland Fund beneficiary, respectively; sister and brother team prominent in the Fund's Greenwich Village world.

Morris Ernst. New York lawyer, specialist in obscenity trials and labor arbitration, liberal director at the Garland Fund.

Elizabeth Gurley Flynn. Fiery labor organizer, roused the Industrial Workers of the World in the 1910s, galvanized the Garland Fund board of directors.

William Z. Foster. Organizer of the great steel strike of 1919, leading Communist Party member, Garland Fund director.

Felix Frankfurter. Lower East Side immigrant turned Harvard Law professor, advisor to the Garland Fund, associate justice on the U.S. Supreme Court.

Lewis Gannett. Editor at *The Nation* magazine, anti-Communist director at the Garland Fund.

Charles Garland. Heir to a Wall Street fortune, critic of inheritance, founder of utopian farming communes.

Benjamin Gitlow. Communist Party founder in the U.S., denounced by Stalin in 1929, member of the Garland Fund board.

Clinton Golden. Child laborer in iron mines, later a machinist and autodidact; member of the Garland Fund board, early organizer for the Congress of Industrial Organizations.

Samuel Gompers. President of the American Federation of Labor, bitter foe of the Garland Fund.

Abram Lincoln Harris Jr. Economist, Garland Fund beneficiary, charismatic Young Turk of the 1930s NAACP.

William "Big Bill" Haywood. One-eyed leader of the Industrial Workers of the World, uncompromising critic of capitalism.

Sidney Hillman. First president of the Amalgamated Clothing Workers, founding director of the Garland Fund, architect of the new unionism, influential New Deal labor leader.

Charles Hamilton Houston. Transformative dean of Howard Law School, director of the NAACP's Garland Fund–supported legal campaign.

James Weldon Johnson. Jacksonville-born polymath, musician, diplomat, and writer; executive secretary of the NAACP, Garland Fund director.

Scipio Africanus Jones. NAACP-affiliated lawyer in Little Rock, lawyer to Black sharecroppers after a murderous 1919 massacre.

CAST OF CHARACTERS

Freda Kirchwey. Editor of *The Nation* magazine, Garland Fund director, stalwart supporter of liberal causes.

Walter Lippmann. Columnist and author, advisor to the Garland Fund, theorist of democracy in mass society.

Alain Locke. Howard University philosopher, intellectual sparring partner of W. E. B. Du Bois, proponent of education for Black Americans.

Robert Morss Lovett. English professor at the University of Chicago; *New Republic* editor; Garland Fund director who later fought the House Un-American Activities Committee and won.

Judah Magnes. New York–based rabbi, pacifist, founding Garland Fund director, first president of Hebrew University.

Nathan Margold. Brooklyn-raised, Harvard-trained immigrant lawyer, solicitor of the Interior Department, director of joint NAACP–Garland Fund legal campaign.

Thurgood Marshall. Transformative civil rights lawyer, counsel to the NAACP, first Black justice on the U.S. Supreme Court.

Mary McDowell. "Angel of the stockyards" in Chicago, peace activist, member of the Garland Fund board.

Clarina Michelson. Wealthy Communist, Garland Fund director, critic of the NAACP and progressive unions.

Frank Murphy. Detroit trial judge, governor of Michigan during the New Deal sit-down strikes, and associate justice on the U.S. Supreme Court.

Pauli Murray. Lawyer and writer, accomplished practitioner of "confrontation by typewriter."

A. J. Muste. Minister, labor organizer, pacifist, chairman of Brookwood Labor College.

Scott Nearing. Left-wing economist, internal critic on the Garland Fund board, counterculture homesteader.

Walter Nelles. New York lawyer, counsel to the ACLU, expert on the use of court orders in labor disputes.

A. Philip Randolph. Florida-raised Black socialist in Harlem, founder of the Brotherhood of Sleeping Car Porters, leader of the March on Washington Movement.

Walter Reuther and his brothers, Roy and Victor. Early leaders at the United Auto Workers, participants in the world of Brookwood Labor College, sit-down strike organizers.

John D. Rockefeller Jr. Son of the Standard Oil founder, philanthropist.

Nicola Sacco and Bartolomeo Vanzetti. Immigrant anarchists, icons of a six-year international publicity campaign arising out of their convictions on murder charges; executed in 1927.

David Saposs. Labor economist with Sidney Hillman's Amalgamated Clothing Workers; faculty member at Brookwood.

Joseph Schlossberg. Cloakmaker, Yiddish-language editor of socialist and labor publications, treasurer of the Amalgamated Clothing Workers.

John Scopes. High school science teacher, football coach, evolution case defendant.

Upton Sinclair. Author of *The Jungle* (1905), socialist, cofounder of the Garland Fund.

Bester William Steele. Locomotive fireman in the Association of Colored Railway Trainmen, litigant at the U.S. Supreme Court.

Ossian Sweet. Black physician, Detroit resident, race riot survivor, murder charge defendant, and Clarence Darrow client.

Norman Thomas. Presbyterian minister, Socialist Party presidential candidate, advocate of industrial democracy, Garland Fund director.

Carlo Tresca. Italian anarchist editor, Garland Fund beneficiary, bon vivant, lover of Elizabeth Gurley Flynn.

Marie Tudor. Mother of Charles Garland, free spirit, patron of writers and artists.

Robert Wagner. German immigrant and U.S. senator, sponsor of eponymous labor legislation that remade American capitalism.

Harold Ware. Founder of a Soviet experimental farm, director of espionage cell in Washington, D.C., comrade of Charles Garland.

Walter White. Executive secretary of the NAACP, author, anti-lynching crusader.

Woodrow Wilson. Wartime president, supporter of draconian speech repression and positive program of propaganda; enforcer of Jim Crow in the federal government.

THE RADICAL FUND

Charles Garland, the reluctant heir, at his farm in 1922.

PROLOGUE

A Curious Inheritance

In November 1920, three weeks after Warren Harding won election to the presidency on a promise to restore normalcy, a restless young man on a farm in Cape Cod, Massachusetts, did something that was not normal at all.

Charles Garland was coming into his adulthood, like many young people, with a growing dismay at the world into which he had been thrust. Just past his twenty-first birthday, he was tall, with dark hair, a soft mustache, and a generous if distant smile. He had a slightly brooding disposition. And he saw grievous inequalities all around him. He recoiled at the gap between the haves and the have-nots. He was a white man who deplored the postwar mob violence against Black communities. He loathed the spread of narrow-minded nativism. Yearning for a more communal and cooperative way of life, he found himself moved simultaneously by the spirit of the New Testament, the pacifism of Leo Tolstoy, and what he dimly understood as the romance of the Russian Revolution. The socialism of his favorite writer, the English novelist and commentator H. G. Wells, inspired him to prize service to others over the selfishness of private property.[1]

But young Garland was also rich. As an heir to a Wall Street banking fortune, he was the beneficiary of several substantial trusts. In addition, he stood to inherit outright more than a million dollars from his late father's estate. And when he came into the bequest, Garland said no. "A system which starves thousands while hundreds are stuffed condemns itself," he announced. Someone, he added, needed to stand against the organized selfishness of society. He decided that he would do his part.[2]

The executors of the estate were perplexed; no one could recall anyone declining such a fortune. Local newspapers took note. And soon reporters from up and down the East Coast and as far away as San Francisco descended on Garland's mother's fashionable Cape Cod farm to get a word with the attractive young eccentric. The *New York Times* reported that Garland invoked the example of Jesus and said he preferred to earn a living with his hands. The front page of the *Boston Globe* explained that Garland, who had recently dropped out of college at Harvard, had chosen a life of "honest toil." Private property, he said, sapped the meaning from life. Newspaper columnists asked their readers what they would do with a million dollars. A jovial janitor told reporters he would buy cigars and automobiles—and then minutes later came into a more modest inheritance of his own, which he assured readers he would keep. "If you really want to know," a comedian quipped, "just leave me a million and I will tell you." Letters to the editor took sides for and against. Onlookers asked if the Bolsheviks had influenced young Garland. (Would the revolution against private property spread to American shores?) Journalists probed Garland's unusual ideas about sex and marriage. (Would collectivist ideas about property lead to free love?) Reactions alternated between scandalized and voyeuristic. Photographers followed Garland and his beautiful young debutante wife as they came and went. Gossip columnists spread rumors about an affair with a paramour. It seemed an episode perfectly tailored to titillate the society pages of the postwar idle rich and their aimless children. From England, Garland's erstwhile hero H. G. Wells deprecated Garland's decision as "depressing news to receive so early in the day."[3]

A few people watching from afar, however, had a more ambitious idea. In Los Angeles, the muckraking author Upton Sinclair, whose bestselling novel *The Jungle* had publicized the horrors of the meatpacking industry, wrote to Garland with a proposal. Don't refuse the money, Sinclair urged. Accept it and give it away. Sinclair recommended that Garland get in touch with a man named Roger Baldwin, who had recently founded the American Civil Liberties Union, and whom Garland knew already through family connections. Baldwin and Garland met on the Cape. And by early 1922, a plan was in place. Garland would accept the bequest. He would transfer several hundred thousand dollars to his wife and their infant daughter. And he would make a nearly $1 million gift—equivalent after inflation to around $18 million today—to endow a philanthropic foundation called the American Fund for Public Service, dedicated "to promote the wellbeing of mankind throughout the world."[4]

Baldwin, a preternaturally energetic New England patrician and self-described "philosophical anarchist," conceived of the endeavor as what he called a "gamble in human nature," a high-risk experimental wager in social change. "We are not reformers trying to patch up the defects of existing institutions," he explained to a friendly journalist. "We are rather a group of those who would assist those forces which are experimenting with new institutions." The premise of the Fund, he asserted, was that basic features of American society—from its ideas and norms, to its laws and most powerful organizations—were not fixed in place, not inevitable or unchangeable. The Fund would aim for fundamental transformations. It would challenge the "present means of producing and distributing wealth," question the "controlling of ideas in education," and protest, if need be, "private property itself." It would support, Baldwin said, organizations that instilled into workers the kinds of "knowledge and qualities" valuable "for carrying on the struggle for the emancipation of their class." Baldwin proposed to test new ideas for what he believed was the central question of his time: how to build democracy for an immense, racially divided country in the age of inequality, mass production, and mass communications. If the "law of percentages" worked out, some of the Fund's efforts, maybe even "a fair proportion," Baldwin guessed, might produce ideas "valuable to mankind."[5]

Skeptics doubted that the Fund would amount to much. "The only result" of Garland's "liberality," sneered the *New York Tribune*, "will probably be to part him from $800,000." Garland's gift paled by comparison to the great endowed foundations already being created by the titans of the American economy—Carnegie, Rockefeller, and Russell Sage among them. Thanks to the booming stock market of the 1920s, Garland's money would ultimately support grants of nearly $2 million, or around $36 million in 2024 dollars. By 1922, the Rockefellers alone had given away enough to amount to a Garland-sized foundation every day for nearly an entire year.[6]

Concerned critics warned that the new philanthropic initiative might act as "a golden transmission belt for Communist propaganda" or as "the life stream of the Red Revolutionary movement in the U.S." The editors of the *New York World* called the Fund a criminal enterprise. Others branded it the "Free Love Fund," scandalized by its participants' unorthodox ideas about marriage and sex. At the new Radical Division of the federal government's Bureau of Investigation, J. Edgar Hoover opened a file labeling the group "revolutionary." In years to come, observers would charge that the Fund was a vital node in a "red network" aiming to subvert America. The red-hunting Texas congressman Martin Dies and his successors in the House Un-American Activities Committee would denounce the Fund as a shadowy threat to American values. After being turned down for a grant, the old-line labor leader Samuel Gompers at the American Federation of Labor dismissed the Fund as quintessential "parlor pinks."[7]

Baldwin and the board of directors he assembled to run the American Fund, however, were after something that even giant sums could not guarantee, and for all but a few of the Fund's directors it wasn't Soviet-style revolution. The Fund's core project came to life in a group of men and women who understood themselves as practical agents of transformative social change. They would seek to remake an unjustifiably unfair society—but they would do so not by smashing the world and building it from a clean slate. Some of the Fund's directors had flirted with violent revolution earlier in their careers; a minority counted themselves, at one time or another, among the Communist Party faithful. But most on the Fund's board aimed to start with people as they existed in the world. The Fund's pivotal efforts drew on the United States' history, its institutions, and its wealth, deploying them as resources in the struggle for something better. Along with Baldwin, key figures in the Fund's orbit included innovative labor leaders, advocates for racial minorities, left-leaning economists and social scientists, liberal journalists, birth control advocates, and progressive reformers. There were anti-Communist liberals and leading socialists. They were a fractious bunch—a "mixture of forces," as Baldwin came to think of it, intentionally designed to take in all points on the left-liberal side of what he called the American political compass. They cooperated and they bickered. They learned from one another. They competed with one another. Sometimes they divided into bitter factions, and at least once they formed romantic connections. Shared beliefs, however, linked them throughout. They believed that American capitalism was broken. They believed that American democracy, if it had ever existed, disserved those who had the least. And they believed that American institutions needed to be radically remade for the modern age.[8]

This book is about the American Fund and its legacies. During a decade in which a Gatsby-tinted haze of jazz and fabulous wealth masked a violent system of Jim Crow segregation and widening economic inequality, the Fund nurtured progressive social movements in exile. What *Time* magazine would later call "Mr. Garland's Million" functioned behind the scenes as the funding wing of the ACLU, sustaining efforts to establish a democratic conception of free speech—no small thing in a nation emerging from draconian wartime speech controls and struggling under an onslaught of war-fueled propaganda and disinformation in the press. The Fund and its circle helped finance a new generation of progressive labor unions, too. Throwing its weight behind unions that sought to transform American capitalism, the Fund supported so-called industrial unions that organized all workers in a given industry, from lowest paid to highest, including workers of all races and all trades. In time, Fund beneficiaries cultivated the fledgling Congress of Industrial Organizations and helped build the federal labor laws of the New Deal. And after years of trial and error, the Fund and the National Association for the Advancement of Colored People, or NAACP, began a campaign for race equality in the law.[9]

Coming just as the Wall Street crash of 1929 devastated the Fund's financial position, the directors' grant for an NAACP legal campaign was the most hotly contested award in the Fund's nineteen-year existence. The campaign produced two landmark decisions in the U.S. Supreme Court. The 1954 decision in *Brown v. Board of Education* ruled racially segregated public schools unconstitutional. *Brown* is how historians remember the Fund, when it is remembered at all. But the Fund's joint campaign set in motion a mostly forgotten parallel case, too. Coming a decade before the famous desegregation case, *Steele v. Louisville & Nashville Railroad* told unions and employers they had to deal fairly with Black workers. *Steele* marked a culmination of the Fund's efforts to shape the racial maldistribution of modern capitalism's spoils. For the directors of the Fund, race emancipation and class liberation traveled together. It is the little-remembered *Steele* that best embodied the Fund's ambitions—and both the power and the limits of its achievements.[10]

Successes for labor, race, and free speech were hard to foresee in the aftermath of the First World War, when democracies on both sides of the Atlantic slid into forms of authoritarianism. In 1920, American voters elected Harding to the presidency on the basis of an impossible promise to restore the greatness of an imagined Anglo-Saxon past, before mass immigration from southern and eastern Europe, before Black migration to the North, before the flu pandemic of 1919, and before the creative destruction of modern capitalism. Harding's campaign platform of normalcy had done nothing to arrest galloping economic inequality. With each passing year, the economy's wealthiest men—oil king John D. Rockefeller, automobile manufacturer Henry Ford, and steel magnate Elbert Gary among them— won preposterous, world-historic riches. Rockefeller's net worth alone amounted to around 1.6 percent of annual American economic output in the 1920s, roughly equivalent to the net worth of Elon Musk a century later if we were to measure his assets as a share of the national economy. By the end of the 1920s, the wealthiest 10 percent of Americans owned 84 percent of the nation's wealth.[11]

Workers in industries like railroads, steel, iron, and agriculture, on the other hand, saw few gains in the 1920s. In a decade of prosperity for many, employees in the sprawling textile industries and in coal's underground archipelago worked long hours in grim conditions. Concerted employer campaigns against labor drove union membership down to levels not seen since the beginnings of the nineteenth century. Huge new industrial firms, making everything from home appliances to automobiles, adopted novel systems of scientific management that exerted tyrannical control over workers' lives. Congress shut down the borders to most immigrants. Meanwhile, lynch mobs murdered hundreds each year, three-quarters of them Black, in unashamed public spectacles. Racial violence in the American West took the lives of Mexican immigrants and people of Chinese descent. States enacted a wave of new laws banning political radicalism, while the courts upheld the arrest and imprisonment of those who spoke out in dissent. Novel strategies of disinformation and propaganda whipped up public opinion into red scares, nativism, and a second Ku Klux Klan, calling into question the capacity of voters to know basic facts about the democracy in which they lived.[12]

The men and women who ran the American Fund for Public Service—also known as the Garland Fund, after its donor, or as the American Fund, or simply the Fund—understood themselves to be in a distinctively modern struggle for democratic power. They did not mean voting procedures or political parties; the Fund supported no partisan political projects. The Fund's directors were concerned with what they saw as the underpinnings of modern political life—the sources of public opinion, most of all. They hoped to dislodge the habitual patterns of thought that, in one of Baldwin's favorite quips, made the country "safe for intolerance." The American Fund aimed its efforts at the sources of what Baldwin called "fear and hate"; it targeted the habits of mind sustaining crying injustices and vast social inequality.[13]

The Fund left its fingerprints on what sometimes seems like nearly every controversial cause of the age. It financed the NAACP's campaign for anti-lynching legislation. It contributed to the defense of radicals and aliens caught up in the Justice Department's indiscriminate postwar raids. Margaret Sanger's American Birth Control League received support for its voluntary motherhood campaign, though the Fund steered clear of her baleful ideas about eugenics. Civil rights firebrand W. E. B. Du Bois consulted regularly with the Fund and relied on its support for projects that turned the Fund's attention toward segregated education. Theologian Reinhold Niebuhr worked on American Fund projects, as did the Black labor leader A. Philip Randolph, who received crucial Fund support at precarious moments early in his career. The pacifist A. J. Muste was one of the Fund's chief beneficiaries, decades before becoming an inspiration to Bayard Rustin and Martin Luther King Jr. in the practice of nonviolent protest. The American Fund supplied the money behind Clarence Darrow's 1925 defense of John Scopes, charged with the crime of teaching evolution in Dayton, Tennessee, as well as Darrow's defense later that same year of Ossian Sweet, a Black doctor charged with murder for defending his family and their home against a mob of white neighbors in Detroit. For much of the decade, the Fund helped pay for the nationwide campaign to free the anarchists Nicola Sacco and Bartolomeo Vanzetti, sentenced to death after a grossly inadequate murder trial in Massachusetts. In the early 1930s the Fund underwrote both the NAACP and the Communist critics of the NAACP in their rival efforts to defend the nine young Black defendants known as the Scottsboro Boys against rape charges in Alabama. Fund resources financed high-profile 1920s labor strikes, subsidized a bold study of rural electrification for the poor, and supported the first generation of twentieth-century civil rights lawyers, men like Charles Hamilton Houston and Thurgood Marshall, as they pressed for an end to Jim Crow.

Garland's inheritance could not sustain so many efforts by itself, to be sure. In a sprawling nation of 100 million people, with a gross domestic product of $74 billion, a foundation with between one and two million dollars at its disposal had modest power at best. Like any organization, moreover, the Fund made wrong turns and foolish investments. Under an onslaught of grant applications from alchemists, from inventors of quack patent medicines, and from makers of novel tooth powders, the Fund's directors financed ill-conceived efforts, hopeless causes, and fraudulent enterprises. On more than one occasion, the Fund's enemies and even its friends charged the directors with corrupt self-dealing, and not without reason. And yet, for all this, Garland's gift offered a shelter in progressivism's wilderness years. While Jazz Age celebrities like F. Scott Fitzgerald and his friends tired of what they disdainfully called "Great Causes," and in an era when historians wondered what had become of America's reform energies, the Fund served as a nursery for fragile new social movements, an incubator in which new ideas could take root and grow in preparation for a more propitious moment. In the decades to come, the quiet work of the Fund and its beneficiaries would bear fruit. More even than its founders could have guessed, the world the Fund sustained helped shake loose what Baldwin called "the bonds of old institutions."[14]

If the Garland Fund and most of its key figures are no longer well-known to American audiences, that is at least in part by design. Even as the men and women charged with administering Garland's gift distrusted money and expressed suspicion of its power, they typically behaved more like the buttoned-down directors of a corporation than members of a radical group. Incorporated inconspicuously in Delaware, the Fund assiduously kept its ratio of overhead expenses to grants low and produced meticulous annual reports documenting its grants and expenditures. It had no formal offices, but it hired accountants to comply faithfully with state regulatory requirements. The Fund's lawyers, in turn, navigated the modern U.S. tax code and even helped develop new tax treatments—loopholes, critics would later call them—for nonprofit foundations.[15]

Such efforts to remain out of view have obscured the Fund's story for observers ever since; in the historians' view, the Fund has retreated behind the movements it supported. But the Fund's disappearing act has made it harder to see the interconnectedness of the core projects of modern American liberalism. The Fund's story illuminates an amalgam of radicalism and practicality at the foundations of some of the signal achievements of the twentieth century.

Today, much of what the Fund's beneficiaries accomplished is under siege. Like the world in which Charles Garland and the Fund's directors lived a century ago, the United States is a wealthy nation in crisis, plagued by unjustifiable economic inequalities, strained by racial divisions, and beset by disinformation campaigns that openly distort the democratic process. Detractors on the left and the right alike have turned on the Fund's legacies.[16] This book is an effort to recover the astonishing world of the American Fund and to tease out the lessons its history holds for our own. The Fund's key figures—men and women, Black and white, working-class and outrageously privileged—were among the first to take up the challenge of remaking a recognizably contemporary mass capitalist society. Their lost struggle is an education in overcoming the injustices of the twenty-first century.

But saying so gets ahead of the plot. The Fund's story begins with what democracy was up against more than a hundred years ago when, in the aftermath of World War I, the young Charles Garland launched a most unusual experiment in democratic change.

PART I

MASS DEMOCRACY IN AMERICA

*Roger Baldwin on his honeymoon, shortly after
the end of the First World War.*

1

Democratic Faith

My democratic thinking was upset when I discovered that a majority can be a tyrant. My too simple theory of democracy changed.

—ROGER BALDWIN

Roger Nash Baldwin was born on January 21, 1884, in Wellesley, Massachusetts, outside Boston. The first of seven children in the affluent New England family of Frank Fenno Baldwin and Lucy Cushing, Baldwin liked to say the family had come over on "the inescapable *Mayflower*." Strictly speaking, none of his forebears had actually sailed on the *Mayflower*. But everyone understood the point. Baldwin's paternal ancestors had been among the first English settlers in the New World. On his maternal side, the Cushings boasted distinguished merchants, statesmen, and soldiers going back to the American Revolution.[1]

Baldwin attended Harvard College, graduating in the Class of 1905 and living in the most exclusive of the so-called Gold Coast buildings constructed for students whose wealth allowed them to buy their way out of the relatively frugal rooms of Harvard Yard. He went to what he called the "proper parties," dined with "the best people," and took part in what he remembered as "swanky dances" with fellow students like Franklin Roosevelt, who was a year ahead of him.[2]

But what is most striking about Baldwin is that the young playboy became one of the most influential American radicals of the twentieth century. Friends from his long adult career remembered him as fairly pulsing with an outsized energy. From the First World War to his death more than six decades later, he championed the causes of the downtrodden and the oppressed. In 1918 he was imprisoned for a year for refusing to comply with the wartime draft. After the war, he joined the Industrial Workers of the World, better known as "the Wobblies," and worked in the lead mines and brickyards of Missouri, on a railroad section gang in Illinois, and in the steel mills of Pittsburgh. In the great steel strike of 1919, he served as an industrial spy for the unions—an experience that nearly got him killed. In 1920 he founded the American Civil Liberties Union, better known as the ACLU. Seven years later he traveled to Soviet Russia and wrote a short book defending revolutionary communism and downplaying its civil liberties abuses. He scandalized his Harvard classmates by championing socialist ideas and free speech for all.[3]

How the patrician became the radical is a parable for American democracy at the dawn of the modern age. It is also the backstory, with twists and turns, of the philanthropic foundation he would run for nearly two decades. In the war years and their aftermath, Baldwin ran headlong into the evils that shaped the American Fund for Public Service's campaigns. Baldwin would himself become an imprisoned dissident. He would see firsthand the autocratic sway of giant capitalist firms over their workers and their communities. And on the cusp of war, his self-assured outlook collided with a harrowing racist massacre—one that sent him scrambling for ways to alter the wellsprings of American life.

The Education of Roger Baldwin

As a child, Baldwin loved walking in Henry David Thoreau's woods on Walden Pond. He spent countless hours in canoes. He took to birdwatching, often with a family friend, who happened to be the executor of Thoreau's estate. Baldwin's childhood friends described him as a sensitive boy. They attributed at least some of his unusually gentle temperament to his fraught relationship with his domineering father.[4]

Frank Baldwin was a successful leather merchant and manufacturer. Some called him "the Grand Duke." He "exuded authority," as Baldwin later remembered. The Grand Duke's children all feared him. Frank's relationship with his firstborn son, Roger, seemed to be the most difficult. Among other things, as the oldest child, Roger must have been the most acutely aware of his father's chronic affairs. Frank kept a nearby farm, where he spent much of his time with a young woman who lived there. While Roger, his mother, and his siblings went on a yearlong European trip in 1906, Frank began another affair with his wife Lucy's niece (and Roger's cousin). Lucy was devastated. A young Roger demanded that his father break off the affair. Frank refused and moved out, relocating to the farm, where soon he was living with still another woman and her three children. He and Roger did not speak for more than a decade.[5]

Roger always denied that his father had any long-term influence on him. Perhaps he was right. But for much of his life, Roger carefully walled himself off from deep romantic attachments. He did not have a child of his own until he was in his fifties. Frank was a spendthrift. "The best money I ever had," he liked to say, "was the money I spent." Roger, by contrast, became notorious for his penny-pinching ways, both in his personal life and in the organizations he ran. He hated spending money as much

Roger Baldwin (first in line at age fourteen) with his siblings in 1898.

as his father loved it. Most of all he developed an abiding rebelliousness toward authority and a deeply ingrained support for the people he called underdogs.[6]

The most searing event of Roger's childhood took place when he was thirteen. His youngest brother, Frank Jr., had been born the year before. Suddenly the infant fell ill with pneumonia. Roger's mother was too distraught to care for the child. Frank Sr. was absent as usual. For three days, Roger tended to him. But there was nothing to be done. The infant died in Roger's arms. Even eight decades later, Roger remembered the boy's last days with clarity. Few things ever shook Roger Baldwin. But right up to the end of his life he would cry when discussing his youngest brother's death.[7]

Baldwin's failed effort to nurse little Frank back to health was his first fight on behalf of the weak and the helpless. And maybe, just maybe, it is one of the reasons why, at the end of college, Baldwin the campus playboy made the otherwise unexpected decision to take up the life of a progressive reformer, lifting up the less fortunate in the New England reform tradition.

"My parents," Baldwin remembered, "were liberal Unitarians, and I was a natural product of a suburban Boston community where Unitarians were among the best people." ("Or *we* thought so," he added with a characteristic grin.) Nineteenth-century Unitarianism summoned an entire moral universe. New England's forbidding Puritan tradition had insisted on the depravity of man and the predestination of the soul. But by the early nineteenth century, a striking new idea was transforming New England Protestantism. Man was not irredeemably depraved. To the contrary, people possessed an extraordinary faculty, one that their Creator had conferred upon them. It was a capacity for moral knowledge. People could tell right from wrong.[8]

For Unitarians of Baldwin's sort, debate over the moral faculty had crystallized nearly a century earlier, when William Ellery Channing, the most important figure in nineteenth-century Unitarianism, had concluded during a youthful stint as a tutor in Virginia that the moral faculty made slavery an unredeemable evil. For the next forty years, Channing preached the gospel of gradual emancipation as pastor of the powerful Federal Street Church in Boston. The self-styled transcendentalists among

Channing's followers insisted that slavery warranted more precipitous action. Men like Ralph Waldo Emerson and Theodore Parker proposed immediate liberation for a people whose souls—like those of all men—were necessarily endowed by God with the same moral faculty that inspired Channing. In 1858, Parker joined a secret committee of abolitionists helping John Brown prepare for the ill-fated assault on Harpers Ferry that aimed to touch off a slave insurrection across the South.[9]

In the Baldwin family, Roger's uncle, William H. Baldwin Jr., carried forward Channing's moderate version of the New England reform spirit. As it happened, Uncle William grew up in the same house that Channing had once occupied near Boston Common. As an adult, William Baldwin served as president of the Long Island Railroad and lived in the wealthy Locust Valley section of Long Island alongside Morgans and Vanderbilts. When the railroad business took him to the South, he became a benefactor and close friend of Booker T. Washington, then the most influential Black man in America.[10]

Born into slavery, Washington had emerged as an influential voice in the Black community just as the hopeful era of Reconstruction was closing. In 1881, Washington founded the Tuskegee Normal and Industrial Institute in Alabama as a vocational high school for Black students, run by Black teachers and administrators. Tuskegee soon became a center of efforts to support Black life in the increasingly inhospitable post-Reconstruction South. The school drilled its students in Washington's distinctive brand of self-help and race uplift, encapsulated in the educator's most famous speech, "The Atlanta Compromise," delivered in 1895, the same year in which William Baldwin Jr. was elected as a Tuskegee trustee. Urging Black people to take up agricultural and industrial labor, Washington promised white listeners that America's 8 million Black people would be a loyal labor force, willing to work "without strikes and labor wars" and without the strange tongues of unfamiliar immigrants. Washington endorsed segregation and promised to forgo the radical claims of equality advanced by Black leaders during Reconstruction. "In all things that are purely social," he famously concluded, "we can be as separate as the fingers, yet one as the hand in all things essential to mutual progress." Washington asked only that Black people be allowed to exercise their basic civil rights, free from the terrors of lynching and race violence. Six months later, in the case of *Plessy v. Ferguson*, the Supreme

Court upheld the emerging southern system of segregation, affirming that laws mandating "separate but equal" facilities were consistent with the Constitution's promise of equality. The justices did nothing to uphold the guarantee of freedom from violence that Washington had asked for in return.[11]

By the turn of the twentieth century, William Baldwin was Washington's closest advisor and the dominant force on the Tuskegee board of directors. "I almost worship this man," Baldwin said of Washington. Later, critics wondered whether the influence was not the other way around. William, they charged, dominated the Black educator and used foundation money to dictate Washington's policies. Either way, William lobbied President Theodore Roosevelt at the White House on Washington's behalf. He defended Roosevelt after Washington's dinner at the White House in 1901 caused an angry backlash in the South. He appealed to Robert Todd Lincoln, president of the Pullman Palace Car Company and son of the great Civil War president, to resist discrimination against Black passengers on the company's railroad cars. He invited Washington to his home as a matter of course whenever the Tuskegee man was in New York.[12]

Like Channing before him, William believed that the natural moral sensibility of men and women in the South, Black and white alike, would gradually express itself, at least if given time and nurtured in the right fashion. Within the minds of Black boys and girls, William asserted, there lay the same "rich deposit" of the human moral faculty—like "gold in a vein," as his biographer put it. But William Baldwin's formulation twisted Channing's faith in individuals' capacity for gradual moral growth into an accommodation of racist segregation. The right kind of education, as William saw it, would draw out the capacities of the Black community, but only over decades. Rash tactics, by contrast, might interfere with the moral faculty's gradual expression by stirring up the passions of the white South. Black critics whispered that William Baldwin's real project was to produce a compliant class of inexpensive nonunion Black labor for his railroads.[13]

William Baldwin's dubious racial enlightenment shaped young Roger's early sensibility. As a child, Roger met Washington at his uncle's New York home. He played with Washington's children when they were enrolled in private schools in Massachusetts. Washington even took a youthful Roger along on a train tour across the South, where Roger met a white man who explained in matter-of-fact fashion how to beat a Black female servant. No record indicates how Washington reacted, if he was present for the episode at all. But the trip left a lasting impression on the teenage Roger, who promptly sent Washington a donation of $20 for Tuskegee's endowment along with an admiring note. The work of the great Black educator seemed to young Roger in line not only with that of his uncle but also with that of John Brown, who had been one of the family heroes of his Unitarian youth.[14]

William's views on race sometimes slid into rank racism. For a time, young Roger picked up the same sensibility. After a short trip to Norfolk, Virginia, in 1898, the fourteen year old Roger wrote a friend to say that the city was "the worst and dirtiest and the most full of lounging niggers that I ever saw." He continued: "When I got off the electric car I was accosted by about five niggers all wanting to carry my bag to the boat but I refused them all and carried it myself."[15]

Harvard College did little to alter Baldwin's callous prejudices. The paleontologist Nathaniel Southgate Shaler, who had an outsized influence on the views of an entire generation of Harvard men, was one of the teachers Baldwin remembered decades later. Born into a slave-owning family in Kentucky twenty years before the Civil War, Shaler had attended Harvard in the early 1860s, where he became the trusted protégé of the charismatic Swiss-born zoologist Louis Agassiz, the United States' most influential believer in polygenesis: the theory that the different human races of the earth had origins as separate species.[16]

Shaler's racial science stopped short of insisting that races were species. But Agassiz's influence stayed with him throughout his career. In one of Harvard's most popular classes, Shaler taught that the races were radically different from one another. The Black race, he asserted, had been "bred in immemorial savagery and slavery." For 10,000 years, Africans had been separated from the benefits of civilization. And so Black people, Shaler said, were not simply whites with a different skin color. To the contrary, members of what Shaler imagined as a single, coherent African race were less intellectual and more passionate than other peoples. They lacked the capacity for effective cooperative action, he contended, and had little family instinct. For the most part, Black people were like "children lost in a wood," utterly unable "to carry the burden of our own civilization." They were best kept out of politics, for their own good and that of others.[17]

Youthful Roger Baldwin's racism was as commonplace among whites in the North as his personal relationship with, and admiration for, Booker T. Washington was rare. For young Baldwin, the latter seems not to have interfered with the former. He had grown up in a privileged nineteenth century of Channing and Thoreau, of Unitarianism and noblesse oblige philanthropy. But events were fast eclipsing the world of his youth. Baldwin was never a theorist and never an abstract thinker as such. He learned by experience, not from texts and not in classrooms. And not long after leaving Harvard, Baldwin experienced a shock, one that altered his views about race and left his callow moral optimism in tatters.

The People Can Rule

In September 1906, Roger Baldwin moved to St. Louis to join the vanguard of a reform movement that was coming to think of itself as "progressivism." At the close of his time at Harvard, he had decided to look for a way of "doing other people good," which, he later reflected, seemed to him the "essence of Unitarianism." With the encouragement of his father's lawyer, the future Supreme Court justice Louis Brandeis, Baldwin concluded that progressivism's self-assured amalgam of moral improvement, efficiency, and social work was the best and most scientific way of doing good. Brandeis, who had grown up not far away in Louisville, recommended St. Louis as a place where a young man could make an impression. Baldwin fairly leapt at the suggestion. At the jurist's urging, he came to think of the city as ideally suited to what he called a project of "democratic experiment." He arrived in the midwestern city full of the "uplift and self-confidence," he later recalled, that his privileged family background and hopeful Unitarian ideals could provide.[18]

As the fourth-largest city in the country, St. Louis had many of the classic problems that attracted progressives' attention. One-fifth of the city's

Baldwin the reformer in St. Louis, 1906.

population was foreign born; fully a majority of its half-million people had either been born abroad or had parents who were. And while St. Louis had long had a German immigrant population, increasing numbers of the city's immigrants were Irish or from Eastern Europe. Many were Jewish. The new immigrants crammed into slum neighborhoods in undesirable sections of the city near the Mississippi River. An infamous section derisively named "Kerry Patch" housed an Irish population in notorious tenements and boardinghouses. It was, one city historian writes, "a place of stark poverty." A late nineteenth-century English visitor found "stinking slums" filled with women and children "as squalid and dirty" as those in

Dickensian England. Newspapers wrote about the city's "begging girls" and its "starving families." Baldwin remembered a neighborhood crowded with fights between Irish Catholics, on the one hand, and Poles and Russian Jews, on the other.[19]

Late nineteenth-century economic growth left city governments across the United States vulnerable to corruption. The party machines of St. Louis had been early to the trough. In 1870, the city's distilleries had been the center of the infamous "Whiskey Ring" scandal, in which officials in Ulysses S. Grant's Treasury Department took bribes in return for allowing distillers to evade the federal whiskey tax. By the turn of the century, longtime local power broker Edward Butler would brag that he had "been stealing elections in St. Louis for 30 years." Indeed, the "blacksmith-politician," as Butler was known, helped foster a system of municipal corruption so pervasive that locals had their own specialized language for it. The ward bosses in the Democratic Party machine were the "Dark Lanterns." The tight-knit alliance of the bosses with powerful business interests was the "Big Cinch." And their corrupt practices made up the art of the "boodle." Corrupt backroom deals awarded lucrative city contracts, natural gas monopolies, and streetcar franchises to wealthy insiders. Dark Lantern fixers like Butler made out like bandits. The Big Cinch controlled the boodle and the people paid for it.[20]

Between its industrial conditions and its political corruption, St. Louis practically cried out for progressive intervention. Baldwin threw himself into the kinds of reform projects with which progressives were experimenting around the country. He moved into one of the city's poorest areas, aiming to be close to the problems on which he would work. He served as a social worker in the settlement house known as Self-Culture Hall, organized as a combination of Jane Addams's famous Hull House in Chicago and Felix Adler's New York Society for Ethical Culture. Baldwin lived in the Hall for two years, alongside poor Irish Catholics and recent Jewish immigrants in one of the city's toughest neighborhoods. The Hall was a natural fit for him, and not only because his uncle William had helped support Adler's efforts. Self-Culture Hall in St. Louis offered services that aimed to deliver to the white urban poor what Booker T. Washington called uplift. The Hall sponsored evening classes for the literary, vocational, and moral elevation of workingmen. It provided childcare for poor mothers and offered a boardinghouse for young workers. The entire Ethical Culture project had been founded on the belief that men had what one contemporary called "the power of knowing right and wrong." The Hall carried forward the conviction that institutions of learning and disciplined care could lift their clients' moral capacity. If poverty and environmental conditions obstructed the moral faculty of the poor, Self-Culture Hall would update the ideas of Channing and the Unitarians with a new generation of modern social science expertise. Progressive social workers would redesign the conditions of the urban poor, liberating their capacities to improve themselves.[21]

Such was the idea of the St. Louis progressives, anyway. Baldwin embraced the project with an energy that would soon be his trademark characteristic. When he noticed that many of the children coming through Self-Culture Hall ended up involved in the city's new juvenile court, he became a volunteer probation officer there. Soon he was the chief probation officer, presiding over a substantial staff and supervising 2,000 children a year, most of them boys. Eight years later, he would coauthor what quickly became a leading book on juvenile justice. Arguing that a child's delinquency was "a result of conditions not of his own making," Baldwin urged judges around the country to keep juvenile proceedings out of criminal courts and "to apply to the delinquent child the same procedure it would apply to the neglected child." The aim of juvenile justice was not to punish but to "protect and educate." Done right, the progressives' scientific adjudication might be able to rescue the moral sense of even the most hard-bitten youth.[22]

The indefatigable Baldwin taught social work in the new sociology department at the city's Washington University. He served as secretary of the city's Civic League. He organized the St. Louis Civic Federation and founded the National Probation Association. He participated in a local interracial civil rights group and on the statewide Committee for Social Legislation. He was president of the Missouri Conference of Charities and Corrections and chair of the Social Service Conference of St. Louis and editor of the *National Municipal Review*, a journal for progressive social work research. Not everyone took kindly to Baldwin's relentless efforts. "He is young, impetuous and not always wise," commented a longtime St. Louis reformer, who added gently that Baldwin had taken on more jobs than he could handle. Baldwin paid such criticisms little mind, if he heard them at all. It was as if he gained strength with each additional project. He fed off his work and soon carved out a substantial role for himself in the nation's fast-growing reform world.[23]

In later decades, Baldwin's stamina, his sheer intensity, would earn him admirers and detractors alike in the ACLU role for which he became best known. That same spirit would make him the principal organizing figure at the American Fund for Public Service. But more than anything in his background, it was Baldwin's experience of democracy and its failings in St. Louis that shaped his ideas about how change in America could be made to happen.

The biggest project of Baldwin's St. Louis years was the progressive attack on Dark Lantern insiders like party baron Edward Butler. Even before Baldwin had arrived, an ambitious young district attorney named Joseph Folk had decided to stamp out the Big Cinch and the boodle. Folk pulled the curtain back on the city's backroom deals. He won thirteen bribery and perjury convictions in 1902 alone, and ten more in the next two years, bringing down the men who had benefited from corruption in the city's contracts for garbage, lighting, streetcars, gas, and more. Butler himself was sentenced to three years in prison. The muckraking journalist Lincoln Steffens made Folk a national figure, and when the people elected Folk governor of Missouri in 1904, Folk wrote triumphantly to Steffens that his "faith in the plain people" had "not been misplaced." The journalist agreed. Politicians, he insisted, would supply whatever kind of government the people demanded. Voters in St. Louis and Missouri had shown that they would demand good government. They had proven, Steffens wrote, "once and for all, that the people can rule."[24]

Folk's celebration and Steffens's optimism proved premature. Butler never served a day of his sentence. Most of the convictions Folk had won, Butler's included, were reversed on appeal to the state's higher courts. Some suggested that the Big Cinch had captured the state judiciary, but one way or another only eight of Folk's defendants ever went to prison. Criminal prosecutions had proven too awkward a tool to pry government away from the alliance of corrupt politicians and their business cronies.

Reform-minded progressives—even those armed with indictments—seemed unable to deliver a knockout blow. What was needed was a better way to run government, a better way to let the people rule.[25]

Beginning in the 1890s, American reformers seemed to have hit upon a way to fight the corruption of government officials and prevent their capture by powerful interests. Basic decisions about government could be referred to the voters for direct decision by the people themselves. Voter initiatives put questions on the ballot and allowed the people to circumvent an unresponsive or corrupt government. Voter referendums let the people approve or reject decisions made by their elected officials. In combination, the initiative and the referendum promised to allow the people to rule directly. The aggregated minds of the people themselves would redeem the promise of democracy from the corrupt party machines and the special interests.[26]

A small group known as the People's Power League, in Newark, New Jersey, organized in support of the remedy in 1892. New such leagues popped up in South Dakota and Kansas in 1894; the next year others joined in Michigan, Colorado, and Nebraska. The direct democracy movement ran close alongside populists' and farmers' movements in western and midwestern states. Advocates of Henry George's crusade for the "single-tax" were also among the most supportive initial backers. Very soon, however, the initiative and the referendum swept the country as the quintessential progressive reforms. In 1907, perennial Democratic Party presidential nominee William Jennings Bryan announced his support, insisting that the initiative and referendum become part of the party's national platform; before long, he was barnstorming through states on special campaign trains advocating for direct democracy reform. Just a few years later, former president Theodore Roosevelt championed the initiative and the referendum in his ill-fated 1912 Bull Moose campaign for president. By then California and Oregon were each submitting between twenty and thirty different questions to the voters every year on issues such as temperance requirements and gambling restrictions. Other groups invoked the initiative to abolish the death penalty and liberalize divorce. Between 1898 and 1918, twenty-two states put initiative and referendum provisions into their constitutions. In 1914, voters nationwide took up a total of nearly three hundred ballot proposals.[27]

Missouri enacted the initiative and referendum at the state level in 1908. St. Louis added initiative and referendum provisions to its municipal charter in 1911. As Baldwin saw it, direct democracy realized the aspirations of men like Folk and Steffens and vindicated Channing's optimistic psychology. Here was a way for the human faculty of the people to express itself in democratic self-government. The state's initiative and referendum, crowed one Missouri voter, was "the only measure which will enable public sentiment to crystallize into just laws."[28]

Yet even as Baldwin lobbied for new direct democracy mechanisms, he began to wonder whether "popular government" might require, as he put it in 1914, "the better organization of public opinion." Direct democracy, he intuited, would place new pressures on how the people came to know what they needed to know to govern themselves.[29]

No one in the first decade of the twentieth century was more practiced in public opinion and its formation than the writers at a new generation of sensational newspapers, and no newspaper staff was more practiced in the art than that of Joseph Pulitzer's *St. Louis Post-Dispatch*. If progressives like Baldwin saw public opinion as a cure-all, Pulitzer's editors understood it as a product. Baldwin relied on it. But the *Post-Dispatch* made it.

Newspapers in the nineteenth century had been part and parcel of political parties. They acted as kingmakers in the party system and, in turn, relied on parties' patronage. But all that began to change in 1878 when Pulitzer—a German-speaking immigrant from Hungary—bought the St. Louis *Dispatch* for $2,500 at a sheriff's sale. After serving briefly in the Civil War, the German immigrant became the daring lead reporter for a German-language newspaper allied with the Republicans in Missouri's rough-and-tumble politics. In 1870, he shot and wounded a political adversary in a hotel brawl. But with the *Dispatch*, Pulitzer broke from the political party system. Combining forces with a fledgling paper known as the *Post*, Pulitzer's new *Post-Dispatch* attracted readers and advertisers with sensational crime stories, investigative local reporting, and a populist editorial stance. Pulitzer himself continued to flirt with politics. But when the Dark Lantern of the Democratic Party machine turned against his congressional candidacy in 1880, Pulitzer adopted an independent editorial posture that aimed to expose the cabal of corrupt politicians who controlled the city.[30]

Pulitzer's formula of sensational stories combined with a crusading editorial stance gave the *Post-Dispatch* a mass commercial circulation at just the moment when declining paper costs and booming advertising revenue made the new business model possible. By 1904, the paper boasted a circulation of 117,943, up from less than 1,000 twenty-five years before. Pulitzer exhorted his editors to "fight for progress and reform," to "oppose privileged classes and public plunderers," to be "drastically independent," and to fearlessly attack the wrongs of a "predatory plutocracy." "The new idea," announced the *Post-Dispatch* in 1904, was "public service through publicity." If Butler's blacksmith shops had been forges for fusing politics and business, Pulitzer hammered out a new politics of public opinion on the anvil of the *Post-Dispatch*.[31]

In 1883, Pulitzer left St. Louis for New York to buy a struggling newspaper called *The World* from the railroad baron Jay Gould. Boasting celebrity writers like Nellie Bly, who feigned insanity to write an exposé of the conditions inside a state mental institution for the poor, Pulitzer's sensationalist formula could whip public opinion into a frenzy violent enough to change the fate of nations. Imitators soon came on the scene; rival newspaper empires soon battled one another with ever more sensational stories in a fierce competition for circulation. Some thought the fight between Pulitzer's and William Randolph Hearst's newspapers had even been responsible for the Spanish-American War in 1898. Hearst grasped the significance for democracy as well as his predecessor. "The force of the newspaper," Hearst said, "is the greatest force in civilization." Most importantly, he explained, in a democratic government, the "newspapers form and express public opinion." They passed legislation. They even declared wars.[32]

In St. Louis, Joseph Pulitzer Jr. carried on his father's work at the *Post-Dispatch*. But having helped create new struggles over public opinion, the *Post-Dispatch* editors now opposed the direct democracy measures favored by Baldwin. Ordinary people, the editors observed, had few opportunities to discuss and evaluate issues of public import. There was no reason to think that they would be good at the things government required. Indeed, in 1907, when the *Post-Dispatch* surveyed public opinion about the impending bribery trials of two municipal officials, it found that many residents were completely unperturbed. "St. Louisans," the editors concluded, "look upon public office as a perfectly legitimate field for graft." The finding was "a stinging indictment of universal suffrage," the editors warned, one that revealed most citizens to be "palpably unfit for self-government or for participation in the government of others."[33]

Undeterred, Baldwin launched two separate initiative campaigns in 1914. One sought voter approval of a new city charter that would authorize broad initiative and referendum provisions.

A second and simultaneous campaign aimed to smash the railroad monopoly over the city's bridges across the Mississippi River. For years, a consortium known as the Terminal Railroad Association had controlled the bridges connecting St. Louis on the west bank of the river to Illinois on the east. The association charged a toll to all who crossed—a toll so unpopular it had become known as "the bridge arbitrary." Freight carriers paid the toll. Passengers paid the toll. Even pedestrians paid the toll. In 1906, the city had approved a bond issue of $3.5 million to build a free "people's bridge." But the association fought back, and when funds ran out with the bridge only partially completed, the project came to a standstill. For six years, the free bridge stood unfinished. The press lampooned the bridge as "the longest bridge in the world" because its construction seemed to have no end. The Big Cinch seemed to have triumphed again.[34]

To restart the bridge project, Baldwin relied (as he later recalled) on "every device known to popularize an issue." His aim, he said, was to "reach the average person." He deployed motion picture shorts and blasted loudspeakers from automobiles. He held outdoor mass meetings among the lunchtime throngs of the busy downtown area. He organized in factories and in public schools. He hired an ad hoc staff of publicity men and organizers to craft and distribute the campaign's message. It was the first of many publicity campaigns in Baldwin's long career. And on Election Day, Baldwin emerged victorious. The new city charter adopted what Baldwin called "the most radical initiative, referendum and recall provisions in effect in any metropolitan city in the union." Most of all, the initiative process had won a new bond issue to finish the people's bridge. Here was proof that the direct voice of the people could break up monopolies of economic and political power. St. Louis, Baldwin concluded, was at last a city where "the people rule." Political "bossism" had been crushed. The Big Cinch, Baldwin wrote, was dead.[35]

But then he got a bitter surprise. The very first initiative under the new city charter turned out not to be a blow to the corrupt party bosses or the city's powerful economic elite. The first initiative proposed to mandate racial segregation in St. Louis's neighborhoods.[36]

In the 1910s, the Black population of St. Louis nearly doubled, rising from 44,000 to 75,000 people. Attracted by the city's expanding industrial labor market, rural migrants from the South increased the Black population from 6 percent to 12 percent of the city's residents. A 1914 report coauthored by Baldwin found that Black workers and their Eastern European immigrant counterparts were stuck in "the hardest and most menial tasks." Nearly half the Black workers in St. Louis earned less than $12 a week at a time when the average bricklayer took in $33 and the average painter $25. Few opportunities for advancement presented themselves. Dismal economic conditions and racist violence in the rural South meant that the city's poorest neighborhoods practically burst at the seams nonetheless.[37]

In St. Louis, Baldwin cut a more progressive figure on race questions than he had in the past. In 1910, he took part in early strategy discussions with the founders of the new National Association for the Advancement of Colored People, which had been founded the year before to offer a new model of civil rights leadership, one that would not be beholden to Booker T. Washington's Tuskegee empire. Beginning in 1911, Baldwin founded a series of interracial groups to coordinate reform work in St. Louis's Black neighborhoods. He won a fight to invite Black community leaders to the regular luncheon meetings of the city's social workers and proposed a new social work degree program for Black students at the city's lily-white Washington University. In one episode, Baldwin invited two Black public school principals to address a mixed-gender audience of students at the university. Local white newspapers reacted with indignation. "Black Teachers Talk" to "Washington University Co-Eds" blared the headlines. Young women, complained the *St. Louis Star*, had been "forced to listen to addresses by two negroes," one of whom "virtually advocated the amalgamation of the white and black races." Scandalized editors at the *Star* quoted Baldwin saying openly that he counted Booker T. Washington as a friend and social equal.[38]

Given whites' reactions to his efforts, Baldwin was implausibly optimistic about trend lines in the politics around race. Writing to a friend, he predicted that residential segregation ordinances would not have much momentum. The election of segregationist Woodrow Wilson to the presidency in 1912 might have warned him otherwise. Cities across the country, and especially in North-South border states such as Missouri, were drawing on ideas like those Shaler taught at Harvard to enact residential segregation laws restricting the areas in which Black people could live. Baltimore enacted a racial zoning ordinance in 1910. Two North Carolina cities followed in 1912. Richmond, Atlanta, and Greenville, South Carolina, added ordinances the next year. Louisville, Kentucky, enacted another in 1914.[39]

The initiative process—Baldwin's favorite progressive reform—turned out to hand segregationists a new tool. Oklahoma used an initiative to adopt its notorious grandfather clause restricting Black voting rights. Arizona voters approved a measure requiring that 80 percent of the employees in any company be U.S. citizens. Initiatives in California strengthened the alien land laws that prevented Chinese and Japanese immigrants from purchasing property.[40]

In 1915, with Baldwin's initiative process in place, a group of white St. Louis residents known as the United Welfare Association launched two residential segregation proposals designed to keep Black migrants out of white neighborhoods. Advocates asserted that when Black people moved in, property values dropped. Others argued that segregation was the modern and humane way to organize a community. (Louisville's law was titled "an ordinance to prevent conflict and ill-feeling between the white and colored races.") But an air of menace haunted the campaign. The association warned of a coming "negro invasion" of white neighborhoods. "How," asked one initiative proponent, "can we afford to let the Negro whip the white man?"[41]

Pulitzer's *Post-Dispatch* opposed mandatory segregation. The city's aldermen overwhelmingly rejected it. The city's tiny Black middle class tried to fight off the proposal, too. A local Black real estate salesman challenged the constitutionality of the city charter's new initiative provision, but the state courts upheld it. A hastily formed "Citizens' Committee Opposed to the Legal Segregation of Negroes," which included Baldwin as one of its ten members, protested racial zoning as "utterly opposed to American traditions and principles, thoroughly undemocratic, and degrading to our city and the people of both races."[42]

Baldwin was certain that the racial zoning initiative would fail. "It will be impossible," he wrote to Booker T. Washington, "to pass the segregation bill." But in a city where whites still outnumbered Blacks by more than nine to one, segregation won in a landslide. In a special election held on February 29, 1916, 52,000 voters endorsed both Jim Crow initiatives, as against some 17,000 opposed. The *Post-Dispatch* mourned the outcome, but reminded its readers that it had warned them that a naive direct democracy would turn into an "instrument of intolerance and prejudice," even if intended by its supporters "to protect the people against injustice and oppression." For his part, Baldwin tried to save face. "In the long run," he said, "the control of legislation by the people is best for all of us." It was only in this single exceptional instance, he insisted weakly, that public opinion would give way to "race prejudice" at the cost of "individual rights and constitutional guarantees."[43]

Outrage of the Century

As it happened, the fight over the segregation initiative was not over yet. And here, too, there would be lessons. St. Louis provided Baldwin's first encounter with a problem that would come to occupy a central role in his future as a funder of left and liberal social movements. In 1917 he learned just how combustible racial hatreds could be when they intersected with competition for jobs.

Around the country, residential Jim Crow ordinances like the one in St. Louis faced legal challenges. Louisville's Jim Crow law had landed at the U.S. Supreme Court in the spring of 1916. Federal judge David Dyer, who had prosecuted the Whiskey Ring corruption cases four decades earlier, halted the St. Louis measure pending the Court's decision.[44]

The Louisville case was set to be among the most important cases of the Court's 1915–16 term. When it was argued in April 1916, Louisville's lawyers asserted that "the races of the earth shall preserve their racial integrity by living socially by themselves." Twenty years earlier, the Court had insisted in *Plessy v. Ferguson* that African Americans themselves were responsible for any perception of inequality arising out of segregation. So, too, the lawyers in the Louisville litigation now snarled, the residents of racial ghettos had no one to blame but themselves: "the shiftless, the improvident, the ignorant and the criminal," they argued in their brief to the Court, "carry their moral and economic condition with them wherever they go."[45]

In November 1917, after a delay arising out of election year politics and transitions in the Court's membership, the justices unanimously struck down the Louisville provision. Judge Dyer followed suit and struck down the St. Louis law. Nearly two years before, the people of St. Louis had voted overwhelmingly for Jim Crow. Now the United States Supreme Court had overruled the voice of the people.[46]

Baldwin for one was grateful. "Majorities," he mused, might "be just as great tyrants as despots." Baldwin's "democratic faith," as he put it, had been upset; his thinking about democracy, he realized, "had been too simple."[47]

For St. Louis, the Court's relief was too little, too late. Across the river, where the eastern end of the new free bridge now finally touched down on the far side of the Mississippi, racist hostility gave way to slaughter.

By 1917, as many as fifty-five industrial firms had set up shop in the city of East St. Louis, lured in part by not having to pay the toll fees of the old "bridge arbitrary" on goods shipped eastward. The city boasted new and growing stockyards, meatpacking plants, steel foundries, aluminum ore processors, and railroad lines. The same forces that had drawn African Americans to St. Louis proper brought them to its smaller sibling city across the river, too. The Black population of East St. Louis essentially doubled in a year; the precise number is unknown, but somewhere around 10,000 African Americans migrated into the city in the second half of 1916 and the first half of 1917, joining an existing population of 10,000 in a city with a total population of just under 100,000 people. Tensions between the newcomers and white workers emerged rapidly; the latter had aimed to use wartime demand for labor as an opportunity to organize unions and raise their wages. Black workers from the South offered employers a new labor source, one that whites-only labor unions excluded from their ranks. The city's Central Trades and Labor Union began to speak of the "growing menace" of "undesirable negroes" and called on its members to act. White strikers at the packing plants owned by firms like Armour & Company and Swift & Company looked on as new Black migrants, barred from membership in the unions, crossed the picket lines to take the strikers' jobs. "Negroes," warned the American Federation of Labor, the country's largest labor organization, were being "imported to lower industrial standards."[48]

Tensions burst in late May 1917 when the anger of white strikers at the Aluminum Ore Company spilled over into violence. For two days roving gangs ransacked Black-owned buildings, smashed the windows of homes, and assaulted Black residents.[49]

A month later, on the evening of July 1, a gang of whites drove an automobile through the Negro district shooting into the homes of Black workers. That night, Black men defending their families fired on another car carrying a group of white men. The whites may have been East St. Louis police or another gang of marauders, or they may have been both. Either way, the shots struck and killed a white police officer. A full-scale race massacre followed the next day. Six thousand whites massed in downtown East St. Louis demanding that Black people be expelled from the city. By early afternoon, the crowd had begun to pull Black men off streetcars to beat them. As evening set in, the rioters moved into the Black districts with torches, guns, and ropes. A white reporter wrote that residents were "shot down by mobs as they fled from their homes, which the whites had set on fire." More than one horrified witness reported a deliberateness to the killing. The *Post-Dispatch* reported "a man hunt, conducted on a sporting basis" in which the slogan was "Get a nigger."[50]

Atrocities filled the city. A mob with a rope hoisted a Black man up a telephone pole to be lynched; when the rope broke, the mob shot him amid laughter at his plight. "Negroes are lying in the gutters every few feet in some places," reported a journalist. White rioters dragged a Black man by an open wound to his skull "up to the rope from which he was to hang." If Black women were too afraid to come outside, white arsonists burned their homes with them inside. White boys armed with revolvers fired with abandon. White girls attacked Black women on streetcars with impunity. Not even infants were immune; "a colored baby was seized from its mother," reported one stunned observer, "and thrown into the fire." Gov-

Mineola McGee of East St. Louis, shortly after losing her arm in the massacre of 1917.

ernor Frank O. Lowden declared martial law and called out the National Guard to bring peace; a regiment charged with fixed bayonets and fired a volley to keep a mob of more than two hundred whites from burning more buildings in the Black district along Third Street. More often, the militia looked on and did nothing. One Black girl who lost her arm to a bullet reported that the militia and the police had been the ones who shot her.[51]

When all was said and done, the white mob had massacred between 100 and 200 Black men, women, and children. White souvenir hunters collected bits of clothing from the dead and displayed them in the city's downtown. Property damage in the Black section of town amounted to as much as $3 million. More than 5,000 people had been driven from their homes.[52]

News of the monstrosity ricocheted around the country. "Race Rioters," screamed an outsized headline in the *New York Times*; "Many Bodies in the Ruins." Shocked editors at *The Nation* wrote angrily of Black men and women "hunted down by white mobs on the streets and in their homes." The *Los Angeles Times* condemned the riot as a disgrace and likened it to the pogroms on Jews in Russia. In the days that followed, African Americans in New York marched down Fifth Avenue dressed in white. Anti-lynching champion Ida B. Wells quickly compiled a record of the atrocities, which she published as *The East St. Louis Massacre: The Greatest Outrage of the Century*. At Carnegie Hall, in an event to celebrate the Russian ambassador, Theodore Roosevelt and Samuel Gompers nearly came to blows when Gompers blamed the events in East St. Louis on employers and Black strikebreakers. The former president accused the labor leader of offering excuses "for the murder of women and children in our own country" and condemned the "appalling outbreak of savagery."[53]

What had produced the worst race riot in two decades? At first, Baldwin (like Gompers) blamed industrial interests, namely the elites who had controlled the bridges over the river. "If the people of East St. Louis really controlled their own government democratically," he insisted, "the recent outrages would have been impossible." But Baldwin's response was implausible. Too many of the working whites of East St. Louis had been directly involved in the riot to blame it on the city's industrial cabal.[54]

The brilliant Black advocate and scholar W. E. B. Du Bois had a different view of what had happened. A founder of the NAACP, Du Bois understood how deeply the racist sentiments of white workingmen and women had shaped the East St. Louis atrocities. *Labor omnia vincit* was the motto of the white trade unions: "Labor conquers everything." In the East St. Louis massacre, Du Bois concluded bitterly, labor had "conquered Liberty" along with Justice, Mercy, Law, Democracy, and nearly every other virtue. Du Bois understood another thing, too. In a democracy, the power of majority sentiment would powerfully shape the response of public officials. The United States attorney for the District of Illinois, Charles Karch, initially reported to Attorney General Thomas Gregory that there were ample grounds for a Justice Department investigation. Gregory and President Woodrow Wilson, however, declined to pursue the matter. Dominant public sentiment in the form of white public opinion did not warrant federal action. Gompers's constituency of white workers blamed Black people. "Excited, undisciplined negroes," Gompers claimed, "intoxicated by higher wages than they had ever known," had brought the violence upon themselves.[55]

The 1917 massacre was only one of a sequence of urban massacres beginning in Wilmington, North Carolina, in 1898, running through Atlanta in 1906, and Springfield, Illinois, in 1908. Within a month of the East St. Louis slaughter, the murder of a white man by an African American touched off riots in the fast-growing industrial town of Chester, Pennsylvania, outside Philadelphia. A month after that, the lawless arrest of a Black soldier by Houston police led 150 of his fellows in the colored 24th Infantry to march on the city; before the night was over twenty people were dead, including four Black soldiers and four white policemen.[56]

Racist massacres were a shock to naive hopes for American democracy. After the Atlanta riots, Booker T. Washington had urged Black Americans to seek accommodation with the white population. Beware, he cautioned, of "lighting a fire which you will have no ability to put out." But white violence seemed to beget more white violence, regardless of the Black response. When Washington died in 1915, his increasingly vocal critics argued that racist violence had revealed the limits of interracial accommodation. "It is nonsense to cry peace," fumed Bishop Alexander Walters of the African Methodist Episcopal Zion Church, "when there is no peace." In the wake of the Springfield riot, Walters and Du Bois joined with white liberals to establish the NAACP as a new civil rights organization. Now in the ugly aftermath of East St. Louis, Du Bois took to the pages of the organization's journal to insist on page after gruesome page that the massacre had revealed the failure of accommodation. As Du Bois saw it, East St. Louis was a call for new ideas and new action.[57]

For Roger Baldwin, East St. Louis badly undermined a nineteenth-century worldview shaped by men like Channing and his uncle William. His New England predecessors had believed that human beings possessed within themselves the capacity to grasp moral truths, to distinguish virtue from vice. Booker T. Washington had taken this advice as confirmation of the conciliatory racial strategy of Tuskegee. Baldwin had seized on it, too, adapting it to progressive reforms like the initiative and the referendum.

When he arrived in St. Louis, Baldwin later reflected, reform had "all looked very simple." Direct appeal to the people had seemed "the very perfection of democracy." But after the double blows of 1916 and 1917,

Baldwin's ardor for the innate moral sensibility of the people cooled. Democracy seemed to require something more. What the situation demanded, he wrote his aunt Ruth, was a "shaping of public opinion." Perhaps engaging people in a new way could yield better results. Maybe public opinion need not devolve into violence.[58]

The challenge was vast. For by the time of East St. Louis, the United States had entered World War I.

Propaganda poster for the U.S. Committee on
Public Information, 1917–18.

2

Weapons of Truth

We were all swamped by the war fever.
—ROGER BALDWIN

On March 16, 1917, off the coast of Plymouth, England, a German submarine torpedoed an American freighter named the *Vigilancia*, killing fifteen. Across the next two weeks, submarines sank four more American vessels and killed nearly fifty sailors. On April 2, President Woodrow Wilson asked Congress to declare war, creating in turn an exquisite dilemma of his own making.[1]

Six months earlier, Wilson had won reelection to the White House on a platform of peace. His campaign had announced as much in its election year slogans. "He Kept Us Out of War," they trumpeted. But now he would have to reverse course. Modern warfare required the mobilization of entire populations. Wilson would have to muster the nation's material resources. He would have to forge support for the war and turn the nation toward winning a conflict he had promised to avoid.[2]

The traditional move of wartime governments had been to repress dissent, and Wilson's administration embraced the time-tested strategy with a campaign of censorship unprecedented in American history. But the president unveiled a more innovative strategy, too, one that drew on the new attention to public opinion in places like St. Louis. Wilson's wartime administration coupled restrictions on what people could say with an affirmative program of saying things it wanted Americans to hear. Its practitioners unashamedly called it "propaganda," a word whose negative connotations had not yet solidified.[3]

Roger Baldwin was buffeted by both sides of Wilson's double-edged campaign. In a year and a half of war, Baldwin witnessed up close the full force of government's coercive power. Before the war's end, he would become one of Wilson's targets. But Baldwin also recognized in the government's propaganda campaign a new front in the struggle over public opinion he had encountered in St. Louis. The war showed a new generation of progressives that the flow of information forming the public's ideas was no more natural than the path of German torpedoes. When the shooting came to a close, Baldwin and a cohort of like-minded peers would set out to fundamentally alter its trajectory.

You Will Be Suppressed

At the age of thirty-four, Roger Baldwin moved to New York City to join the American Union Against Militarism, a group formed to advocate against American entry into the war. Jane Addams, leader of the prominent settlement house in Chicago, was a founder. So was Paul Kellogg, who presided over the unofficial journal of record for progressives known as *The Survey*, for which Baldwin had been the St. Louis correspondent.[4]

Addams and Kellogg sought to accomplish for the war what campaigns for the initiative and the referendum had aimed to do for local government. They set out to harness public opinion against a pell-mell race into armed conflict. Their union produced anti-war pamphlets—some 600,000 in all. It distributed anti-war news stories to papers around the country. It targeted the labor papers and the hundreds of farmer weeklies in the South and Midwest. It built a publicity bureau in Washington, as well as a speakers bureau in New York. With the help of friendly members of Congress, the union arranged hearings at the Capitol and sponsored public meetings at Carnegie Hall and then swung through the Midwest. Posters illustrated "Democracy Controlling the Dogs of War"; a Lady Liberty figure announced "No Militarism Here." Channeling the progressive generation's persistent optimism about public opinion, the American Union called on Congress to hold a "national referendum on peace or war," redeploying for foreign policy questions the direct democracy mechanism being put to work in cities like Baldwin's St. Louis.[5]

U.S. entry into war, however, produced new legislation in Congress that placed the American Union Against Militarism's work, and even its existence, in peril. The Selective Service Act, signed into law in May, created the nation's first modern military draft. The act required all male citizens between twenty-one and thirty to register with local draft boards and authorized the president to draft 1 million men into the military service of the United States. The Espionage Act, passed in June, banned false statements intended to interfere with the military forces of the United States. The measure also prohibited willful efforts to cause insubordination in the military or to obstruct "the recruiting or enlistment service of the United States." The law declared material in violation of the act to be "unmailable" and prohibited the post office from delivering it.[6]

Together, these two pieces of legislation—the Selective Service Act of May and the Espionage Act of June—empowered Attorney General Thomas Gregory and Postmaster General Albert Burleson to wield vast new authority over dissenters around the country. Close friends from their days as state government lawyers in Austin, Texas, the two men had worked under one of the first southern state constitutions to be violently recaptured by white Democrats from Black and Republican voters after Reconstruction. Gregory, who had advised Wilson not to investigate the racist massacre in East St. Louis, observed with pride that during Reconstruction every man in his family had joined the Ku Klux Klan; the Klan, he said, had rescued the South from the "intolerable burden" of a government "sustained by the votes of ignorant negroes."[7]

With the onset of the war, Gregory initiated what the *New York World* called an "intellectual reign of terror" against anti-war dissenters. "May God have mercy on them," Gregory thundered, "for they need expect none from an outraged people and an avenging Government." In Ohio, Gregory's Justice Department prosecuted Eugene Debs, the captivating labor leader and perennial Socialist presidential candidate, for delivering an anti-war address. A federal judge sentenced Debs to ten years in prison. In Chicago, a jury convicted more than one hundred members of the Industrial Workers of the World on over 10,000 separate counts of violating the Espionage Act. Further prosecutions in Sacramento and Wichita led to dozens more IWW convictions. In New York, the United States attorney charged Max Eastman and other editors of the eclectic avant-garde magazine *The Masses*. A hung jury spared Eastman and his colleagues, but few Espionage Act defendants were so lucky. During the course of the war, the federal government indicted more than 2,000 people under the Espionage Act, including a former U.S. senator from South Dakota. In Wausau, Wisconsin, a man was charged under the Espionage Act for expressing the opinion that the conflict was "a rich man's war." Countless more were arrested by state officials, often on baseless charges. Philadelphia authorities arrested a group of men distributing pamphlets arguing that the U.S. Constitution did not permit a compulsory military draft. ("Long Live the Constitution of the United States," read the ostensibly offensive pamphlet.) A man was arrested in Garrison, North Dakota, because he had the temerity to express contempt for the town's "business element."[8]

Burleson's post office was in some respects even fiercer than Gregory's Department of Justice. Within a month of the wartime spy law's enactment, Burleson had prohibited fifteen major publications from passing through the mail. He declared unmailable such periodicals as the mainstream liberal magazine *The Nation*, Eastman's *The Masses*, and the socialist newspaper *The World Tomorrow*. Burleson refused to tell editors which passages had caused their materials to run afoul of the law, making it virtually impossible to know in advance whether a publication had complied with the post office's new strictures. When a federal judge overruled Burleson's determination that a 1917 issue of *The Masses* violated the Espionage Act, Burleson suspended the mailing privileges available to it as a magazine. The delay caused by the post office's seizure, he said, had caused *The Masses* to violate the unrelated requirement that periodicals come out at regular intervals. "Since the magazine had skipped a number," the postmaster general explained, "it was no longer a periodical." By the fall of 1918, Burleson had used such tactics to deny mailing privileges to seventy-five separate newspapers and magazines. Under additional congressional authority granted in October 1917, he shut down dozens of foreign-language publications, too. Countless Americans found their mail tampered with or delayed because of spurious suspicions of radicalism or disloyalty or both.[9]

No publication, Burleson announced, could lawfully say that the government "got into the war wrong," or was "in it for the wrong purposes." No one could legally "impugn the motives of the Government," or call it a "tool of Wall Street or the munitions-makers." Such statements would encourage insubordination in the armed forces by nurturing disloyalty. Anything that might "hamper or obstruct the Government in the prosecution of the war," Burleson believed, could not be allowed. "The instant you print anything calculated to dishearten the boys in the army," he said candidly, "that instant you will be suppressed, and no amount of influence will save you."[10]

At the American Union Against Militarism, Baldwin was a virtual whirlwind of activity in defense of those facing arrest. Baldwin was a "demon for work," remembered one friend. He seemed always to be in motion, working closely with figures who would shape the rest of his career. With lawyers like wealthy Brooklyn Heights liberal Albert DeSilver and the tenacious young litigator Walter Nelles, Baldwin established a team he would later describe as unmatched by any during the rest of his career. A rotating cast of others joined them, including Norman Thomas (later a six-time Socialist Party nominee for the presidency) and the prominent Unitarian minister John Haynes Holmes.[11]

For all Baldwin's energy, his persuasive efforts mostly went for naught. Baldwin had no success lobbying the Justice Department or the post office. Burleson's fiefdom, in particular, was "a graveyard for us," Baldwin recalled. Advocating on behalf of conscientious objectors cleaved the American Union in two when Kellogg and prominent founder Lillian Wald resigned from the group in protest. Supporting wartime dissent, they worried, might fatally compromise the organization's ability to influence the peace.[12]

Defending dissent was quickly proving to be Baldwin's cause, so much so that he and his colleague Crystal Eastman (sister of Max) gave the effort a new label. As one American Union Against Militarism member put it, with the onset of war "there came suddenly to the fore in our nation's life the new issue of civil liberties." In July, Baldwin and Eastman established what they called "the Civil Liberties Bureau" at the Union. The phrase was new in American usage. An older term, "civil liberty," had long served as a call to arms for a certain kind of classical liberalism, a way of thinking about the relationship between the government and the individual in which the government had only limited authority over the rights, and especially the property rights, of its citizens. But the phrase "civil liberties" had never appeared in American politics except as an accident of grammar, occurring when nineteenth-century Americans listed more than one civil liberty—property rights and freedom of religion, for example—and added them up into two or more "civil liberties." The new phrase, which Baldwin and Eastman borrowed from a British anti-war organization, aimed to update the idea of civil liberty for a modern era. What exactly it would mean was not yet entirely clear. In the plural, "civil liberties" could be a way of responding to the many capacities of a modern wartime state. It could stand for a cluster of limits on government power over the individual: freedom from unlawful searches, from censorship, and from arbitrary arrests and convictions, to mention only a few.[13]

Baldwin hoped that civil liberties would serve another purpose, too. He sought to deploy the new rallying cry not only in defense of individual liberty against the state but also in the multifront public opinion battle that raged across the American homeland. But here the prospects for the civil liberties project were more daunting.

Not by Bread Alone

In the war for public opinion, the Wilson administration relied from the beginning on an affirmative strategy alongside its repressive one. Mobilizing a people, administration insider Arthur Bullard noted, required a "loud, clear call to arms," not merely a repressive hammer. Wilson ally and newspaper editor Frank Cobb noted early on that efforts to "conscript public opinion" would rely as heavily on positive strategies as on negative ones. Spreading ideas was more effective than censoring them. Crude efforts to block information drew attention to embarrassing facts and risked stifling important intelligence.[14]

Critics of censorship had a powerful example close at hand. World opinion had condemned the German army's atrocities in Belgium, but had made little note about the British blockade that was starving millions of German civilians. The reason, the critics suggested, was not that one course of conduct was any more or any less barbarous than the other. The difference was that the Kaiser had suppressed news of the Allied blockade to hide the full extent of its success. The German people, of course, learned of the blockade in any event. Censorship, it seemed, was ineffective and counterproductive.[15]

A similar sentiment led members of Congress to remove formal censorship provisions that had appeared in early versions of the Espionage Act on the grounds that speech was an asset in wartime as much as a liability. "If the truth causes disaffection among soldiers," urged Democratic senator Blair Lee of Maryland, "then we should welcome disaffection and try to remove the causes." Censorship insulated leaders from accountability for bad decisions. Writing directly to the president, Upton Sinclair made the point with characteristic flair. The superior strategy, Sinclair told Wilson, was not to suppress dangerous speech with the force "of the policeman's club" but to answer it with counter-speech. "Weapons of Truth," Sinclair insisted, were far stronger than the crude stick of suppression.[16]

The man who wielded Wilson's weapon of truth was a longtime supporter of the president named George Creel. Within a week of Congress's declaration of war, Wilson established a new Committee on Public Information and appointed Creel to be its chairman. A sensationalizing journalist from Missouri like Pulitzer before him, Creel sided with Arthur Bullard against the advocates of censorship. War, he said, would be a struggle over the terrain of the mind. "People do not live by bread alone," Creel said. They hungered for ideas that would give meaning to their actions. Creel reasoned that an effective publicity campaign would draw on the new science of advertising and its dark arts of persuasion. Americans, he concluded, craved what he called "catch phrases": memorable packages that reduced the chaotic stimuli of the world to a simple message. The war effort, he explained with a flourish, would have to be "dramatized and staged" to arouse the "ardor and enthusiasm" of the nation.[17]

With a skeletal staff, Creel's Committee distributed an astonishing 75 million pamphlets during the course of the war. It published a daily newspaper, the first official daily in the history of the U.S. government, and furnished press releases and weekly digests for newspapers around the country. Content supplied by the Committee filled a full newspaper column each day in each of the United States' 2,000 leading newspapers. Committee material appeared in schools and colleges with titles like "How the War Came to America" (5.5 million copies), "The President's Flag Day Address" (6.8 million copies), "Conquest and Kultur" (1.2 million copies), and "The Kaiserite in America" (5.5 million copies). The Committee's Speaking Division coordinated some 10,000 speakers, including military heroes fresh from the trenches. A Division of Pictorial Publicity produced 1,438 drawings and designs on patriotic themes ("the best posters ever drawn," Creel called them). A Film Division produced hundreds of thousands of feet of film per month from the front lines in Belgium and France. Another division sent Committee officials to state fairs with displays of machine guns, trench helmets, gas masks, and carrier pigeons. Captive audiences were even better. One branch specialized in distributing talking points to traveling salesmen on passenger trains. Another, perhaps the most famous, organized the 75,000 Four-Minute Men, who delivered coordinated messages during the reel-change breaks in movie theaters.[18]

By the end of the war, the Committee on Public Information reported that it had delivered 755,190 four-minute speeches to 314,454,514 audience members. The precision of the CPI's numbers was unlikely, but implausi-

George Creel's wartime propaganda inaugurated a new era in the struggle for public opinion.

ble exactitude was part of Creel's storytelling machine. The whole point of Creel's campaign of charismatic "catch-phrases" was to insert them into the way people talked and thought. War propaganda might then free ride on the speech of private citizens, where it would penetrate the parlors and dining rooms of Americans across the country. In all, Creel blustered, the Committee delivered a psychological impact equivalent to the projectile force of the world's first repeating artillery piece, the legendary French 75.[19]

The genius of Creel's mobilization strategy was, among other things, that it produced forces of public opinion so vast as to overwhelm Baldwin's tiny and underfunded band of critics. The Civil Liberties Bureau had been assembled to combat old-fashioned forms of government coercion and force. There was plenty enough of that, thanks to Burleson, Gregory, and Congress's espionage legislation. But in crucial respects the wartime crisis for American democracy was not the repression of opinion but its production. And here the small team at Baldwin's Civil Liberties Bureau could hardly even begin to keep up with the massive effort to sell the war.[20]

Many of the most spectacular episodes of intolerance and repression during the war were not the result of government action at all, at least not directly. On the first day of April, a thousand pro-war protesters raged against David Starr Jordan, former president of Stanford University and a leading light in the prewar peace movement, when he appeared at the Academy of Music in Baltimore. "Hang Dave Jordan to a sour apple tree," they cried, while police formed a cordon to protect the speaker from the rabid crowd. In October, vigilantes assaulted Herbert Bigelow, the gadfly pastor of the People's Church in Cincinnati. Bigelow was a former member of the Ohio House of Representatives and a nationally known critic of the war. A band of masked night riders abducted him, bound him, and drove him across the river into Kentucky, where they stripped the pastor naked, tied him to a tree, and lashed him with a blacksnake whip, cutting off his hair and pouring crude oil over his head. In the spring of 1918, in a little town ten miles from East St. Louis, a crowd of five hundred tied up a German-born young man named Robert Praeger, wrapped him in an American flag, and hanged him from a tree limb until he was dead. Praeger had fallen under suspicion when the local Council of Defense urged the town's citizens to seek out the disloyal. In Arkansas, a mob seized a

Black preacher named J. H. Ellis in November 1917 and pressed local officials to detain him for three months without trial on trumped-up charges of disloyalty and treason. When at last he was released (in part because of the Civil Liberties Bureau's interest in the case), he was beaten mercilessly with clubs by men he called "the leading white citizens of this town."[21]

Civil libertarians at the Bureau documented 164 instances of mob violence during the war. They cited cases of German Americans tarred and feathered, of beatings, and of men driven out of towns or painted yellow. Crowds attacked people caught refusing to buy Liberty Bonds. Mobs forced men and women to kiss American flags in Pine Bluff, Arkansas, in December 1917; in Canton, Ohio, and Trenton, New Jersey, in February 1918; again in Boston and Brooklyn in March; and yet again in Reno, Nevada, and Anaconda, Montana, in April. Private patriotic groups formed, ranging from the Boy Spies of America and the Knights of Liberty, to the Sedition Slammers and the Terrible Threateners. The American Protective League, which boasted some 200,000 members, became so powerful that Attorney General Gregory deputized them to provide added manpower for the Department of Justice's investigations.[22]

President Wilson took little action to stop such attacks and mob actions in practice, even if he condemned them in theory. As in the East St. Louis massacre of 1917, Wilson's Justice Department usually declined even to pursue investigations, typically citing limits on federal power. (In Herbert Bigelow's case, the government brazenly cited the pastor's opposition to the war among the reasons not to prosecute his attackers.)[23]

Baldwin sprang into motion after such mob assaults, but to little effect. Part of the problem was that a civil liberties campaign was awkwardly positioned to respond to the forms of abuse involved in mob violence. Men like Robert Praeger, Herbert Bigelow, and J. H. Ellis were not victims of the Espionage Act or of government repression, at least not in the first instance. They had become targets in a process fueled by the mobilization of millions of American minds, maybe tens of millions. The problem seemed to be one of mass psychology and opinion, arising out of an outpouring of intolerance and repressive sentiment from citizens themselves. Public opinion had helped produce the war's coercive environment.[24]

What Baldwin's Civil Liberties Bureau confronted, then, was not simply a crisis of government overreach to be countered by a modernized version of the old civil libertarian opposition to state coercion of the individual. In despair, Baldwin wrote a friend in April 1918 that "intolerance will get its victims regardless of legislation. If the authorities don't do it, a mob will." Walter Nelles, the dogged lawyer in the Bureau's back office, described the organization's work as an effort to "counteract unjust prejudices in the public mind." But engaging in the struggle for mass public opinion was too big a project for a small, underfunded outfit organized to defend dissenters from the state.[25]

War Fever

It was a twenty-nine-year-old captain in the American army named Walter Lippmann who came out of the trenches of the Western Front with the clearest theory of public opinion and propaganda in modern democracies. The ideas he forged in France would, before too long, help organize Baldwin's thinking in the decade to come.[26]

In truth, Lippmann was a poor soldier if he was a soldier at all. He had grown up in a privileged German-Jewish world on Manhattan's Upper East Side. In 1914, shortly after graduating from Harvard College, he cofounded a magazine called the *New Republic*—a journal of liberal opinion that soon became one of the most influential publications of the age. Lippmann and his fellow editors had opposed American entry into the European war; they had argued that it was not in the United States' interest. But as their magazine grew in prominence, it gradually became one of the administration's most valued channels for communicating its message to the world. Lippmann became a Wilson administration insider. Indeed, President Wilson lifted the aphorism for one of his central war aims—"peace without victory"—from the magazine's cover.[27]

It was hard to tell whether the heady experience of power led Lippmann to shift his views on the war, or whether his increasing support for the war afforded him greater access. The truth was probably some of both. But one way or another, the young journalist increasingly abandoned his opposition to the war and thrilled to the president's vision of a war to end all wars. Signing up to assist in the war effort he had once resisted, Lippmann was assigned along with journalist Heber Blankenhorn, a former reporter on labor relations for the *New York Sun*, to command a propaganda platoon at

American Expeditionary Force headquarters in Chaumont, France. Their aim, as Lippmann put it, was to engage in "a frank campaign of education" for German and Austrian troops.[28]

The group's first challenge arose as the AEF and General John Pershing were preparing an assault on an enemy-occupied pocket of territory—a "salient," as the military men called it—created by an oxbow in the Meuse River at a town called Saint-Mihiel. German officers in the Saint-Mihiel salient were spreading rumors of atrocities by Americans in order to discourage surrender and desertion in their ranks. Lippmann and his colleagues set out to persuade the ordinary German infantryman otherwise. Lippmann drafted a leaflet setting forth the United States' humane treatment of POWs and highlighting the generous daily rations afforded to soldiers and POWs alike in the American trenches. U.S. patrols dropped several thousand copies of Lippmann's message across the barbed wire. Aircraft delivered still more beyond enemy lines.[29]

The leaflet soon proved a great success. Civilians reported seeing German and Austrian soldiers reading Lippmann's words and pocketing the leaflets for later study. Desertions and surrenders accelerated. And when the Allies led an assault on the salient in the middle of September, the weakened German lines gave way. The attack on Saint-Mihiel, under the command of a young colonel named George S. Patton, featured the first important use of tanks in American warfare. In the annals of military history, the clash along the Meuse is known as the battle that foreshadowed Patton's tank campaigns more than two decades later in World War II. But Lippmann believed the victory at Saint-Mihiel demonstrated the power of words.[30]

As a whole, the Allied propaganda campaign was so successful that General Erich Ludendorff of the Imperial German Army credited it with winning the war. "We were hypnotized by the enemy propaganda," the German military leader later said, "as a rabbit is by a snake." Ludendorff exaggerated, but he had seen an important new truth about power in modern statecraft. Words and information traveled alongside tanks and field guns. Americans' words, as Heber Blankenhorn put it with the flair of a wartime propagandist, were "as bitterly honest" as their bayonets.[31]

Lippmann had not only encountered a new way to fight. In the trenches of the Western Front, he had inadvertently stumbled on the science of modern public opinion.

Psychologists on both sides of the Atlantic had studied the sources of collective action as far back as the 1880s, when the philosopher Friedrich Nietzsche had written about what he called the "herd-instinct" of the human race. The movement began in earnest in France in the study of the revolutionary crowd. Taking up the French Revolution and its nineteenth-century aftershocks, an intellectual named Gustave Le Bon contended that collective human behavior could be explained by unconscious suggestibility. A literature quickly sprang up around Le Bon's thesis. His rival, the sociologist Gabriel Tarde, proposed that in the world of modern mass communications, groups were made up of what he called "publics"—powerful modern collectivities whose cohesion was mental rather than geographic. Tarde noted that people in modern societies believed their ideas were rational responses to their environments. But Tarde argued that this was no more than a soothing just-so story. Lockstep thinking and pell-mell rushes into war, not to mention the ebb and flow of fads and fashions, all suggested something very different. In the modern world, Tarde announced, the master logic of public opinion was what he evocatively called "*magnétisation*." The minds of individuals were like iron filaments near a powerful magnet. People's ideas turned together in a collective process of which they were barely aware.[32]

The psychology of the public and the crowd made it into Anglo-American political thought through Graham Wallas, an Englishman who taught at Harvard while Lippmann was a student there. In his 1908 book, *Human Nature in Politics*, Wallas argued that politics arose out of a deep reservoir of impulses, tendencies, and habits—"half-conscious repetitions," Wallas called them. In *The Great Society* (1914), which Wallas dedicated to Lippmann, he asserted that the sources of political action were not merely (as Le Bon had believed) suggestibility or herd behavior. Instead, human behavior arose out of instinct expressing itself through political institutions. A factory owner's pursuit of profits, for example, took on new dimensions when economic policy incentivized indifference toward the lives of his workers. Older and smaller communities had managed such desires and impulses. Community feeling had blunted the excesses of self-interest. The conundrum for modern statesmen, Wallas contended, was that the industrial era had altered the scale and the mechanisms of social solidarity. He believed that modern mass society—which he called "the Great Society"—exerted an influence over its members' thinking akin to Tarde's magnetized publics.[33]

Lippmann the propagandist intervened at precisely this juncture, identifying in Wallas's ideas the hidden levers of modern statecraft. Statesmen, Lippmann believed, came in two classes: the "routineers" and the "innovators." The routineer reproduced existing social habits, and to him, the principal strategy of the state was to prohibit forms of behavior that might disrupt those habits. Lippmann called this "the method of the taboo." The routineer statesman forbade things. He jailed the anarchist. He banned prostitution. He proscribed behavior like narcotics use and gambling. Such a leader, Lippmann wrote, imagined that he could prevent bad con-

Walter Lippmann and his teacher Graham Wallas in England around the time Lippmann was formulating his theory of modern public opinion.

duct if he "forbade the existence of evil by law," "pronounced it damnable," and "threatened to club it."[34]

Lippmann followed Le Bon, Tarde, and Wallas to conclude that the taboo method was folly, at least in the modern world. Leaders could no longer monitor their subjects closely enough to govern by prohibition alone. Indeed, in mass society, prohibitions often had the perverse effect of increasing the prevalence of the practices they promised to stamp out. Efforts at repression, as any good Freudian could see, redirected the energies to those they regulated. In dry states, alcohol abuse increased. Police blotters revealed fewer drunks and more wife-beaters on Mondays in towns where taverns closed on Sundays. Prostitution became more alluring and more dangerous when driven underground. Gambling responded to being outlawed by retreating into private homes, where it exerted bad influence on children. The central and inescapable problem, as Lippmann put it, was that "lust has a thousand avenues." In a panic, the routineer turned to the taboo. But no statesman could possibly shut down the myriad paths of unconscious desire.[35]

Lippmann's hero was the innovator statesman. In the Great Society, Lippmann's innovator statesman put away the club and set aside the taboo. The new move was to redirect dangerous or otherwise unsettling impulses in constructive directions. The aim, Lippmann wrote, was "to find for evil its moral equivalent," or to substitute "the love of heaven for the fear of hell." The innovator statesman would allow the radical and the anarchist to march and to speak. He would even defend their right to do so. Smart regulation, Lippmann predicted, would have "a most disconcerting effect on the anarchists," who would be "suddenly stripped of all the dramatic effect that belongs to a clash with the police."[36]

Lippmann wanted his readers to see that the cure for problems as wide-ranging as anarchist speech, alcohol abuse, and prostitution offered a general strategy for modern statesmanship. At the same time, the very effectiveness of positive social control raised a disturbing prospect. If Lippmann's statesman could turn German soldiers from their trenches, if minds were like filaments before a magnet, then what were the limits on the organized power of the state? Outsized success in shaping public opinion put the very possibility of democratic government at risk.[37]

Indeed, for Lippmann there was an emblematic case even closer than the trenches of Saint-Mihiel. Though he never admitted it, the most conspicuous example of the power of propaganda campaigns for Lippmann was his own conversion experience. In 1915 he had opposed entry into the war. He had done so for good reasons and explained his position at great length. Yet over the subsequent year and a half, the lure of prestige and ever-greater access to power had helped flip Lippmann's views. Like a participant in Le Bon's crowd, or like a member of Tarde's modern public, Lippmann had turned on cue. Once a skeptic of the war, he had become a cheerleader.[38]

Roger Baldwin would spend much of the subsequent few years coming to terms with the implications of Lippmann's studies of public opinion. He would draw on Lippmann's ideas to formulate a rationale for raising the resources to launch propaganda and information campaigns of his own. But for the moment, the jaws of old-fashioned repression began to close on the defenders of civil liberties.

In June 1917, officers of the Department of Justice interrogated Baldwin about his wartime activities. Military intelligence officials planted a mole in the Civil Liberties Bureau to investigate Espionage Act violations. In August, the post office blocked the Bureau's pamphlets from the mail. And at the end of the year Baldwin was called in for questioning by the inspector general of the army about wild rumors that he had engaged in traitorous activities along the Mexican border. A bewildered Baldwin assured his interrogator that he had never traveled to the border, let alone provided support to Pancho Villa.[39]

The greater difficulty was that much of what Baldwin was actually doing came perilously near to violating the broad reach of the Espionage Act. Officials in the Military Intelligence Branch of the War Department recommended already in the winter of 1917–18 that Baldwin be charged. The Justice Department tapped his telephone and transcribed his conversations. On the last day of August, federal officials raided the Civil Liberties Bureau offices and seized its files. Espionage Act and Sedition Act indictments seemed certain to follow.[40]

Baldwin's legal difficulties grew when Congress raised the eligibility age for the draft to forty-five. Registering with his local draft board, Baldwin told them that he would refuse "to perform any service under compulsion"; he was opposed, he explained, "to the principle of conscription in time of war or peace, for any purpose whatever." When the time came for his physical exam, he respectfully declined to appear and presented himself instead to the United States Attorney in New York, where he was arrested and charged with violating the Selective Service Act. Baldwin promptly pleaded guilty.[41]

On October 30, he appeared in a packed federal courthouse in Manhattan for sentencing. Before an audience of friends, well-wishers, and curious onlookers ("all my good friends were there," he wrote), Baldwin delivered a speech that caught the attention of newspapers nationwide. "The compelling motive for refusing to comply with the draft act," he said, "is my uncompromising opposition to the principle of conscription." Citing his New England roots, he said that freedom was the right to "choose one's way of life"; freedom from coercion was "the essence of the liberties brought by those who fled the medieval and modern tyrannies of the old world." What brought these liberties together was the "freedom of the individual from arbitrary external controls." His aim, he proclaimed, was to "maintain the rights of free speech and free press, and the Anglo-Saxon tradition of liberty of conscience." Writing to the judge shortly thereafter, Baldwin emphasized the point. "There is a part of every man," he wrote, that "cannot surrender to law makers."[42]

The press treated Baldwin's courtroom address as impractical. Editors at the *New York Times* scoffed. Physical force, they insisted, was required to achieve "about all the ends there are." The modern state taxed its subjects whether they liked it or not. It vaccinated its people, regardless of their preferences. It set the boundaries of right and wrong and punished those who fell afoul of the lines it drew. The *Times* had a point. Baldwin's courthouse address had summoned a heroic but unrealistic idealism.[43]

A further flaw went mostly unobserved. Baldwin's speech was not so much impractical as it was anachronistic. Baldwin had presented himself at the Manhattan courthouse as a latter-day Henry David Thoreau, summoning a nineteenth-century rejection of brute coercion of the individual by society. Oswald Garrison Villard, whose maternal grandfather had been the uncompromising abolitionist William Lloyd Garrison, saw this as a virtue. "My mother and I," he wrote Baldwin about the courtroom speech, "both think it worthy of the finest Abolitionist traditions." Baldwin's words had harkened back to the freedom of the autonomous soul endowed with a moral faculty. He had voiced the claims of William

Ellery Channing's inner spark of moral genius. These ideas, however, offered no more than a halfway response to the distinctive forms of power in Wilson's wartime machine. Most World War I–era Americans were not so much coerced as they were reoriented like Tarde's magnetized iron filaments or Lippmann's impressionable German soldiers. A country that elected Wilson on a platform of peace had come around in a short six months to full-throated support for war.[44]

Creel and Wilson had helped to reveal that the very structure of thought was a social artifact, not the product of an individual faculty. Minds did not find the world unfiltered, as Channing's Unitarian model had suggested. Instead, people encountered packages of ideas that came preassembled into catchphrases by concerted social projects such as Creel's wartime mobilization. Ideas were, in part, an effect of the information environments in which people found themselves. Those environments, in turn, were the product of more or less self-conscious efforts in the struggle for mass opinion. How else had Europe careened into a war that killed 20 million people in four years? How else had Creel transformed American opinion in only a year and a half of war?

The political ideal of the individual dissenter was as out-of-date in the 1918 courtroom as a Civil War–era Springfield rifle in the age of the French 75. "We were all swamped," Baldwin later recalled, "by the war fever." To change the postwar world, Baldwin would need to summon powers not on offer in the models of his New England past.[45]

3
The Less We Know

Private propaganda is the order of the day.
—THE NEW REPUBLIC, 1919

Madeleine Doty as a journalist shortly before marrying Roger Baldwin.

It was among the most tumultuous peacetime years in the history of American democracy. In 1919, more than two dozen cities around the country were sites of murderous violence that killed hundreds of Black people. The East St. Louis massacre two years earlier had been a prelude. Four days of rioting in Washington, D.C., left six Black residents dead and hundreds more wounded. Crowds of white rioters killed nearly two dozen Black Chicagoans just days later. Prisons swelled with political dissidents. As many as 20,000 people were serving federal prison sentences for refusal to participate in the draft. Hundreds of radicals moldered in much longer sentences for Espionage Act violations. Perhaps 2,000 enemy aliens, most of them German nationals, remained in wartime internment camps. Meanwhile, labor unions launched a wave of strikes like none the United States had ever seen. Four million workers—one out of every five—went on strike. Sixty thousand walked off the job in Seattle alone, led by the city's shipyard workers. Police officers in Boston and steelworkers in the upper Midwest stepped away from their jobs. Four hundred thousand miners refused to go into the coal mines. Yet with the support of mayors, governors, state militia, and President Wilson himself, powerful employers crushed the unions in nearly every strike, defeating (as one recent account puts it) "telephone operators in New England," "blacksmiths in Ohio," and "cigar makers in Baltimore." Strikers went down to defeat at General Electric in upstate New York. Textile workers struck and mostly lost up and down the East Coast.[1]

Roger Baldwin began his 1919 in prison. On Armistice Day in November 1918, he had entered the Essex County Jail in New Jersey to serve his sentence. Baldwin boasted that he looked forward to the experience. He needed a rest, or so he said. Perhaps it was false bravado. What he couldn't have guessed was that one of the most harrowing years for American democracy would be a different kind of whirlwind year in his young life. In the peculiar social laboratory of the American prison, Baldwin came to a new view about the malleability of people. And then, on the outside by the fall of 1919, Baldwin took part in the hardest-fought and most momentous strike of the year's labor stoppages. In Pittsburgh, at the giant United States Steel Corporation, he came face-to-face with the forbidding mix of force and persuasion reshaping people and politics in America. Both experiences would remake the outlook of the wartime civil libertarian. Advocating for civil liberties protections and free speech rights would propel Baldwin to prominence in the 1920s. But the Baldwin who had been through the social experiment of prison, and who had endured the searing steel strike, did not think that negative freedoms alone offered a viable path to a free and equal democracy. The year 1919 led Baldwin and a small group of friends to take up the parallel project he had quietly been developing in his mind: a search for the resources to finance a positive program of social change.[2]

A Preparatory School of Crime

Baldwin's many well-placed friends promised to lobby President Wilson for a pardon, but he discouraged them from advocating on his behalf. He would refuse early release, he insisted, so long as so many others had to "drag out long, lifeless days behind bars" for the crime of resisting Wilson's war.[3]

In truth, Baldwin was not quite as heroic as he seemed. Many who had refused induction into the military found themselves facing courts-martial and long terms in dismal military prisons. Espionage Act convictions produced sentences of ten to twenty years in grim conditions. Baldwin's guilty plea to the lesser offense of violating the Selective Service Act, by contrast, had produced a prison sentence of less than a year in the relatively gentle confines of New Jersey's state jail and prison facilities. Baldwin later claimed to have found prison relaxing and sometimes pleasurable.[4]

In the weeks leading up to his sentencing, Baldwin had been held in New York City's infamous "Tombs," where generations of New Yorkers awaiting trial had dealt with overcrowding and brutal treatment. Baldwin, however, had been treated as a special prisoner, separated from run-of-the-mill offenders. A junior Justice Department official ("a fine young Yale man," Baldwin wrote to his mother) plucked him from the Tombs every morning and brought him to the department's downtown offices to help prosecutors make sense of the disorganized files seized from the Civil Liberties Bureau. For a month, Baldwin spent each day assisting agents in his own investigation—and then dining with the same agents before returning to the Tombs at night. Once, his Justice Department escort even took him to a burlesque show. Baldwin still remembered the show's star by name a half century later.[5]

Special treatment persisted even after Baldwin's sentencing. The Essex County Jail, he reported after his first day, was "a cooker"—"much better than the Tombs." It was clean, with white paint and fresh air. "I will have a fine long vacation," he wrote, assuring friends and family alike that "everybody is extraordinarily decent to me." He was encouraged, too, by the continuing praise pouring in from friends, family, and other admirers of his courtroom performance. Even his difficult father lavished praise on him, much to his son's relief. "I am proud of you," the older man wrote.[6]

Baldwin treated prison as time to think. He had no shortage of books. His correspondence was essentially unrestricted. Prison, a friend wrote to him, would be a chance for the retreat he needed after the maelstrom of his wartime activities. Baldwin confided in his mother that he would "really enjoy the quiet and seclusion of a prison cell." Prison, he added, was a little like the cabins on the steamship he and his family had taken to Europe after his Harvard graduation. "I'd just as soon do several years," he wrote implausibly, "as long as I can read and write and get letters and talk with folks." Friends and family alike agreed that at least some time away—an opportunity for "self-communion," as one put it—might do him good.[7]

Baldwin aimed in particular to make sense of the political landscape the Civil Liberties Bureau had encountered in its struggles over the war. He took modest pride in some of the Bureau's work with conscientious objectors. But in its other efforts, the Bureau seemed to have failed. The nation had been whipped into war frenzy almost overnight. Juries had convicted a thousand Americans for dissenting speech and anti-war activities. Mobs had assaulted war dissenters, labor radicals, and racial minorities.[8]

Sitting down with pen and paper in his cell, Baldwin ran through options for better strategies. He ruled out violent revolution; the bullet, he observed, could not produce the kind of change for which he worked. The ballot seemed no more promising. The state—even the ostensibly democratic state—seemed to have functioned as an engine of mass coercion. The lesson of Baldwin's wartime failures, along with his frustrating St. Louis efforts before the war, seemed to be that public opinion was too easily manipulated by powerful interests for any conventional political program of reform to work. The government's twin campaigns of suppression and propaganda during the war seemed to yield the same lesson. As Baldwin had written to Woodrow Wilson at the time, "American public opinion" on anti-war protesters had guaranteed that "almost any injustice toward them can be perpetrated without protest."[9]

What, then, was a path forward? Never comfortable with the quiet reflection and rest his friends hoped for him, Baldwin decided to use his time in prison as a laboratory for experiments in organizing human beings. He had been an organizer in St. Louis. Organizing people is what he had done during the war, too—and it had worked, at least up to a point. Now prison walls provided Baldwin with a new site for his ongoing project.

In 1914, Thomas Mott Osborne, chairman of New York's prison reform commission, had conducted an experiment of his own. Going undercover into one of his own institutions, Osborne took a page from Joseph Pulitzer's intrepid reporter Nellie Bly. Where Bly had gone undercover for her famous 1890s story on life inside asylums, now Osborne did the same to learn about life in the prisons he oversaw. For a week, he lived in the state facility at Auburn, in a cell four feet by seven and a half. He learned to obey the prison disciplinary rules. He saw prison guards deliver violent punishments. He was even subjected to the prisoner measurements standardized by a French police official named Alphonse Bertillon at the end of the nineteenth century. By the 1910s, the Bertillon system of measurements ("from top to toe") was regular practice in American prisons. Anthropometric measurement, Bertillon had believed, would not only help identify criminals. Biology would reveal a natural basis for the criminal's inner workings, both an explanation and a predictive tool for managing crime.[10]

With each passing day, however, Osborne came to think that Bertillon was wrong. Prison behavior seemed to be the product not of inner tendencies or innate characteristics, but of the environments in which the inmates found themselves. Misfortune and poverty were the reasons most of his fellow prisoners seemed to have turned to crime. Once in prison, environment seemed to shape their behavior more than anything about their supposed criminal disposition or their measurements on Bertillon's scale.[11]

Osborne held a press conference from inside the prison and published a bestselling book about his experience. It was a publicity stunt, to be sure, but one that brought attention to the work of a generation of prison reformers committed to a powerful if controversial idea. Crime, the reformers insisted, was not a product of heredity or inherent vice. It was a result of social choices about the environment in which we live.[12]

Consider the effect of panic on human behavior, Osborne reasoned.

"Raise the cry of 'Fire' in a crowded place," he wrote, "and many an excellent person will discard in the frantic moment every vestige of civilization." As it happened, just such an episode had taken place the previous year at a union hall in Calumet, Michigan, where a Christmas party for striking miners and their families had been interrupted by a false shout of "Fire." Seventy-three people were killed, nearly all of them European immigrants and most of them children, when the partygoers tried desperately to escape down a steep flight of stairs. The miners union blamed the mine owners, alleging that a company man had raised the false alarm. In Osborne's telling, the important point was that environments of terror brought out an "elemental brute" in people. Even the gentlest of men, he asserted, would "trample down women and children" and indeed "perform almost any crime in the calendar" to make good on "his mad rush for safety."[13]

The lesson of human behavior, in or out of prisons, was the same. If any one of us might commit unspeakable acts, then there was "no such thing as 'the criminal'" and "no such group as a 'criminal class'" except one that included us all. Crime was the result of circumstance because human beings were plastic, shaped by their environments, whether that meant the overcrowded city, the impoverished rural town, or the barbaric, brutal, and ultimately counterproductive American prison. Bad prisons practically bred criminality in inmates and guards alike.[14]

Osborne was interested in prisons and their reform, but the phenomenon of environment and behavior was a more general one. When Osborne argued that the superior strategy was to enlist the minds of the prisoners in their own rehabilitation, he was mirroring the same basic ideas as Lippmann. Osborne was an innovator statesman, with Auburn Prison as his public. Before he left Auburn, Osborne had founded a prisoners' organization, the Mutual Welfare League, to be run by the prisoners themselves, enlisting their own interests—their "true interests and welfare"—in the management of the institution.[15]

Baldwin and Osborne were acquaintances; they had first encountered one another in juvenile justice work in St. Louis. Now, as Baldwin entered the Tombs in New York and then the Essex County Jail in New Jersey, he fell back on Osborne's experience at Auburn. "No one," Baldwin asserted, "can really know what prison means until he's been in himself." He had visited juvenile jails as a social worker. But visiting was not the same as really being on the inside. And what Baldwin concluded when he made his own first-person investigation was that Osborne was right. Human beings were exquisitely sensitive to their environs. People were responsible for the conditions under which they lived, to be sure, at least to a degree. But prisons showed that conditions also made people.[16]

As a prisoner, Baldwin turned to the project of converting his surroundings from dens of vice into schools of virtue. During his weeks on the seventh floor of New York's notorious Tombs, Baldwin founded an inmates' association to do for its residents what Osborne's Mutual Welfare League had done at Auburn. A radicalizing Baldwin added a socialist provocation. Adopting a faddish new title to evoke the self-governing collectives of revolutionary Russia, Baldwin's "Seventh Tier Soviet" aimed to give prisoners in the Tombs a voice in the governance of the institution. After his removal across the Hudson, Baldwin founded a Prisoners' Welfare League for the Essex County inmates modeled more directly on Osborne's Auburn group. Deplorable conditions, the new Welfare League charged, led the jail's residents deeper into a life of crime.[17]

Baldwin quickly became a leader among the Essex inmates. The prisoners, he reported, were "a mixed lot, of course." But there were "many interesting characters among them." Prison life, he found, was "packed with dramatic and varied experience, and warm human contacts." Jail, he wrote to one friend, was "getting too interesting to leave." Every day it was "a humming laboratory of new ideas and sentiments."[18]

Baldwin experimented with his own new feelings when he became close to a troubled eighteen-year-old named Harry Bellair. A social worker friend of Baldwin's later diagnosed Bellair as "a very unstable, and nervously poorly organized type." Bellair also seems to have been an addict. Whatever his condition, the young man shared with Baldwin the view that imprisonment only made criminality worse. He insisted that his own case was a prime example. And in Bellair's stilted, grammatically awkward account, the two men grew intimate. "Never in the world" had he "dreamed I would ever feel so affected with your friendship," Bellair wrote to Baldwin. "I never loved my own family so much."[19]

At some point, Baldwin's relationship with Bellair seems to have taken a turn. "Ain't it funny," Bellair wrote to Baldwin, "how a man can love another man?" Bellair worried about what he called his "womanish feelings" for Baldwin, but maybe (he assured himself) such "tender feelings" were "only human." Indeed, Bellair told Baldwin, "I was not human until after I met you." The younger man confided in Baldwin that he wondered "how I'll be when I'm with you steady for three months." But Bellair thought he knew the answer, and he supplied the emphasis himself: "I'll be the biggest fairy that ever walked on solid ground."[20]

What did Bellair mean? In 1919, the term "fairy" was one of a variety of terms used to describe men who several decades later would be characterized as gay. It was not merely a slur, though it was sometimes that. The historian George Chauncey has observed that "fairy" described a gender identity more than a sexual orientation. The fairy was a variation on what the influential English sex writer Edward Carpenter in 1908 called "the intermediate sex." Carpenter, whose ideas circulated widely among Greenwich Village bohemians like those Baldwin had come to know in New York, theorized that sexual orientations existed along a continuum, and that temperaments and orientations were distributed with "immense diversity" between the pure types of female and male. The fairy served as an identity that helped many "conventionally masculine men," Chauncey writes, "to engage in extensive sexual activity with other men without risking stigmatization."[21]

For Baldwin his prison experiments in sexuality produced long-lasting effects. Years after his release, a man named Phil Taft, formerly of the Industrial Workers of the World, spent a weekend at the modest cabin Baldwin owned in the New Jersey woods. Taft later told journalist Joseph Lash that Baldwin asked to get into bed with him. Rumors long circulated about Baldwin's sexuality. He once confided in a female friend about his "unfulfilled desires." But he seems never to have thought he had to choose one or another orientation. He had always enjoyed the company of female admirers. The Justice Department's wiretaps of his telephone conversations in 1918 seem to have confirmed this; he was, one investigator concluded stiffly, "not leading a moral life." Baldwin later remembered himself as "quite a gay young blade." At least one woman who joined him in nude sunbathing during the 1920s and 1930s at an artists' colony on Martha's Vineyard admired his sexual prowess. (With talent like his, she said, laughing, she had never understood why Baldwin pursued so many political causes.) A close friend even credited Baldwin's extraordinary public energies to his partially repressed private appetites. "His inner repulsions against restraint" seemed to have "produced the impetus for his public fights." Regardless of exactly what transpired between Baldwin and Bellair, the intensity of their unusual relationship testified to environment's capacity to shape people's most intimate behavior.[22]

Imprisonment was transformative for Baldwin in more than one way. Writing to his friends, he reported that prison was "one of the most revealing and dramatic experiences of my life." Prison created one of the very few moments in his crowded adult life in which he had an opportunity to step back and think. "Sharing the life of prisoners," he said, opened up "new reaches of understanding." Writing years later he recalled prison as "a dramatic and pleasurable experience" that had produced powerful "attachment to place and people."[23]

If Baldwin had entered prison imagining himself as the investigator in a scientific experiment, he left altered by the prison's effects. Most of all, Baldwin used his nine months behind bars to think about what he called "the social processes toward freedom." He learned for himself what Osborne had come to know at Auburn and what Lippmann had observed in the wartime trenches of France. Opinion and behavior were not rooted in innate ideas. They were produced by social influences and conditions. People were impressionable. And if people could change, then surely the societies in which they lived could, too.[24]

But people's plasticity had worrisome implications as well. Impressionability and the power of suggestion had led Lippmann to worry for the prospects of democracy. The changeability of the mind meant that people might be subject to persuasion for ill as well as for good.[25]

Blanket of Silence

When Roger Baldwin's sentence concluded in July 1919, he embarked on a new series of experiments outside the prison walls.

On August 1, Baldwin tested out a different kind of institution when he married journalist Madeleine Doty. The two had met in St. Louis while working to reform the city's juvenile justice system. Doty was a member of the New York State Commission of Prisons. Two years after Thomas Osborne's adventure in Auburn Prison, Doty and a friend had entered the state's women's prison to run the same experiment. Doty took on the assumed name "Maggie Martin." Like Osborne, she concluded from her week in the prison that incarcerated women were not intrinsically criminal. "No special shape of head or hand marks the convict," she wrote in a book about the experience. Women who became criminals were victims of circumstance. Prisons therefore ought to replace punishment with education. "The collective mind," she said hopefully, had "awakened" to the crying need to allow prisoners to learn "self-control through self-government."[26]

Baldwin and Doty aimed for a marriage that would be a kind of experiment, too. They aimed to reject hierarchical traditions and live up to the bohemian sexual freedoms that were commonplace in Greenwich Village in the 1910s. Norman Thomas, Baldwin's socialist colleague at the Civil Liberties Bureau, performed the ceremony. One of Baldwin's young friends from prison served as an informal best man. The couple drafted defiant vows declaring that marriage was "a grim mockery of essential freedom" and announcing to friends and family that they had rejected "the monogamic ideal" and its "tyranny of emotional repression." Doty, who was friends with the sex theorist Edward Carpenter, professed support for open marriages. Husband and wife continued their careers, and each kept their name. The couple committed to divide the rent and the housekeeping equally. For every hour of housework, Doty told one reporter, "I charge my husband 50 cents."[27]

Yet it was never clear that their vision of egalitarian independence could survive the cooperative endeavor of marriage. Taking their open vows literally, Baldwin had affairs nearly from the start. He urged Doty to do the same; only then, he explained, would he feel comfortable exercising his own "desires to their natural limit." Baldwin began dreaming of having a new wife—a fantasy he openly shared with Doty. Soon, their marriage, as Baldwin later described it, resembled two people trying to "walk a tightrope over Niagara." Doty concluded that the two had an "intellectual compatibility," but not a "spiritual union." She had hoped "Roger would be willing to give up some personal freedom for the sake of a home." But he told her that he could not "concentrate on a great personal love." The relationship deteriorated into daily clashes. Doty began spending summers away with her parents. In 1924, they separated when Doty moved to Switzerland. The two would divorce formally a decade later, when Baldwin decided to marry a wealthy Barnard graduate named Evelyn Preston.[28]

In truth, Baldwin and Doty had begun to part almost immediately after their wedding. After their two-week honeymoon camping trip in western New Jersey, Baldwin left Doty to seek out "first-hand experience," as he put it, of the "essential facts in the struggle of labor." Baldwin aimed to see what life looked like for the mass of working-class Americans—to experience it for himself, as best he could. "I am a crowd man," he told Doty. And so for two months he became a manual laborer. It was too short a time to really come to know the texture of working-class life. But it was long enough, and the fall of 1919 was momentous enough, to confront Baldwin with the ways in which speech and power worked together to favor the strong in peacetime as well as in war.[29]

"You will never understand the labor movement," a labor leader friend told Baldwin, "until you have worked with other men with your hands and known that's your only support." If the comfortable progressive were to go hungry from time to time, that would be "so much the better." Baldwin considered going to the harvest fields of the Great Plains and the lumber camps of the Northwest; he thought about experiencing the mines of the far Southwest or the sharecroppers' farms of Texas. In the end he decided on manual labor in the Midwest. The industrial conflict seemed to be "most tense" there, and by plunging into the center of the conflict, he wrote to his old Civil Liberties Bureau associate Albert DeSilver, he would gain "direct contact" with the heart of the problem. Firsthand experience would peel away the layers of secondhand impressions derived from books and the press. "My whole training," he told Doty, "must be overturned—and my field of knowledge extended."[30]

Baldwin traveled first to Chicago, where he met with IWW leader Big Bill Haywood, who was out on bail pending appeal of his conviction on Espionage Act charges in 1918. Haywood expressed skepticism for whether Baldwin was cut out for manual labor. He doubted, too, whether a man in Baldwin's position could actually experience the condition of the working class. The intrepid Harvard graduate persisted and enlisted in the IWW with Haywood's reluctant blessing. He joined a Cooks and Waiters Union affiliated with the American Federation of Labor as well, but found it to be stuffy and hypocritical as compared to Haywood's Wobblies. He liked the IWW men. "They had guts," he recalled, and "a philosophy," too.[31]

Carrying both Wobbly and AFL cards, Baldwin worked in a lead smelter in southern Missouri. He served as a brickyard laborer until he was fired by a suspicious foreman. He worked on a railroad gang in Illinois and did railroad construction in Ohio. He sent his mother his first industrial wages: $12.90 for four and a half days, a wage that would have put him among the very poorest of the industrial working class, right around the typical wage of a Black worker in St. Louis. And in November, Baldwin moved on to Pittsburgh, where one of the greatest strikes in American history had begun. Baldwin wanted to be in the thick of it.[32]

Organizing the steel industry had been a goal of ambitious leaders in the American labor movement for a generation. In 1892, Henry Clay Frick's armed Pinkerton guards had crushed the unions in a violent clash at the Carnegie steel mills in Homestead, six miles up the Monongahela River from Pittsburgh. The steel mills had seen little union activity since.[33]

Founded in 1901 by J. P. Morgan as a merger of eight of the nation's largest steel companies, the United States Steel Corporation two decades later was responsible for 60 percent of the nation's steel production. The giant firm implacably opposed unionization. Skilled workers had tried to reorganize on a few occasions. But Elbert Henry Gary, the head of U.S. Steel, flatly refused to meet with the representatives of labor. "Industry," he testified in the Senate, "must be allowed to proceed untrammeled by the dictates of labor unions or anyone else." The result was an industry based on twelve-hour shifts, seven-day weeks, and wages that were below subsistence levels for tens of thousands of unskilled workers.[34]

Wartime economic conditions seemed to create a new opportunity to organize for fewer hours, higher wages, and union recognition. Demand for iron and steel increased while the conflict in Europe cut off the inflow of new immigrants, who made up most of the industry's unskilled labor force. The draft reduced the labor supply still further. Workers' market position had rarely been better. Meanwhile, the Wilson administration's wartime labor policy encouraged Samuel Gompers, the longtime head of the American Federation of Labor, to think that the government might lend support to unionization. In the summer of 1918, twenty-four unions in the AFL joined together to form the National Committee for Organizing Iron and Steel Workers, which began recruiting in mill towns across western Pennsylvania and the Midwest. In May and June 1919, Gary refused to meet with union representatives seeking to negotiate on behalf of workers at U.S. Steel. Two months later the unions voted to strike. And on September 22, the strike began. A quarter-million workers, making up half the industry's labor force, walked off the job.[35]

When Baldwin arrived in Pittsburgh six weeks into the strike, he went immediately to the offices of William Z. Foster, the strike's leader. A thirty-eight-year-old veteran of the labor movement, Foster had been a trade unionist in Philadelphia and member of the Industrial Workers of the World in Washington State. By 1919, he was one of labor's leading strategists, and he instantly saw a use for the new arrival. The mills, Foster told Baldwin, were using nonunion scab labor to defeat the strike. The mill

Steelworkers gather around labor organizers as the 1919 steel strike approaches.

owners boasted that they could continue operation of the mills indefinitely regardless of the strike. If this were true, the unions might collapse. But good information about what was going on inside the mills was hard to get. Foster and the National Committee came by their information at a distance. And so Baldwin agreed to serve as a labor-side industrial spy. He would bring Foster news about true conditions inside the mills. Disguised as a laborer, Baldwin took a job in the Homestead mill where Frick had smashed the unions nearly three decades before.[36]

There Baldwin witnessed a stunning replay of the pattern of the war: a potent mix of forceful repression and pervasive propaganda. Even before the strike began, state police and local authorities ran roughshod through union meetings. An ordinance in Allegheny County, which included Pittsburgh and Homestead, prohibited all assemblies of three or more people. State troopers broke up meetings routinely; the day before the strike began, armed state police rode horses through a picnic for strikers' families, scattering women and children. Lawless arrests, imprisonment without charges, and sudden raids on union members' homes were standard occurrences. Magistrates told strikers that they would go to jail unless they promised to return to work. Troopers shot and killed several and wounded hundreds more, arresting men and women alike without provocation. Dozens of affidavits by strikers testified to widespread abuses. Journalist Mary Heaton Vorse observed the "brutality" of the police; she was stunned by their use of "the third degree." In Gary, Indiana—a city named after the leader of U.S. Steel himself—rioting led to the arrival of federal troops under the authority of General Leonard Wood, a veteran of colonial occupations in Cuba and the Philippines. Wood promptly declared martial law, forbade parades, and broke up picket lines.[37]

Just as important, the steel companies directed a vast communications and propaganda campaign. In October, when a coalition of liberal Protestant denominations known as the Interchurch World Movement launched an investigation of the strike, they were shocked to find that it was virtually impossible to come across reliable information, least of all from traditional sources such as the newspapers. Papers, the IWM complained, "did no firsthand independent investigation of the facts." Unmediated reporting would have supplied valuable information. A decade later, the fictional journalist Mary French in John Dos Passos's novel *The Big Money* would nearly give her life trying to deliver "firsthand news" of the police violence on the steel-

A *Pittsburgh Chronicle Telegraph* advertisement from the great steel strike of 1919 illustrates how giant business firms captured the sources of information in communities across steel country.

workers' picket lines. But in 1919 the Pittsburgh press did little more than repackage U.S. Steel news releases. Stories asserted with little basis that the strike was failing, and that steel production was continuing apace.[38]

The Interchurch investigation found that Pittsburgh-area newspaper headlines left readers with "no other impression than that the strike was practically at an end." On September 24, when the number of strikers reached its peak, the *Pittsburgh Leader* ran the false headline "Pittsburgh Mills Running Full." Three days later the *Chronicle Telegraph*'s front page blared, "Report: Laborers Going Back All Through District." Four days after that (and a full three months before the strike's conclusion) the *Chronicle Telegraph* headline read "Strike Crumbling." The city's *Gazette Times* quoted supposed leaders of the strike conceding that the "strike was lost." And in early December readers of the *Pittsburgh Press* encountered reports that the strike would be called off entirely.[39]

All this was false, or at least indifferent to the truth of the matter. The newspapers' editors published such stories even as their business pages were recording steep declines in steel production. But the colossal steel firms aimed to create their own truth. In all the reporting about supposedly dwindling strike numbers, there was nary a word in the Pittsburgh papers about the goals of the strikers, nor about the lawless conduct of the police, nor about the capture of the local governments by U.S. Steel and the other firms in the industry. Mary Heaton Vorse described the area's steel communities as "dark towns" because the light of truth barely reached them. The Interchurch investigators called it a "blanket of silence."[40]

The Interchurch team retained propaganda specialist Heber Blankenhorn to document the phenomenon. Recently returned from his work alongside Lippmann in the Propaganda Subsection of the American Expeditionary Force in France, Blankenhorn's report, titled *Public Opinion and the Steel Strike*, documented across hundreds of pages the ways in which steel company publicity departments maintained an iron grip over the newspapers. Writing in the pages of Lippmann's *New Republic*, journalist Frank Cobb argued that "private propaganda" was now the order of the day. The postwar world, Cobb continued, was like Europe in the era of the Thirty Years War. In the 1600s, "bands of marauding soldiers" had terrorized the countryside. Now "bands of propagandists" were wandering the country and "terrorizing public opinion." The grave difficulty, as Cobb saw it, was that such communication made truth harder to know, not easier. "The more of that kind of publicity we have," he concluded, "the less we know."[41]

With time the steel companies' propaganda helped to produce its own reality. The strike lasted a little more than a month after Baldwin's arrival. Workers had been trickling back into the mills for weeks. And in January, Foster called off the strike, with none of the unions' goals met. The twelve-hour day would remain the industry standard. So would the seven-day week and impoverishing wages for the unskilled.[42]

Baldwin did not make it to the strike's bitter conclusion. Steel company officials soon suspected that the unusual strikebreaker was not who he said he was. Perhaps it was the clumsy "covert surveillance" he tried to perform while (as he later remembered) "pretending to go to the lunchroom or the toilet." Maybe it was his transparent class manners or his education. There's a chance, too, that undercover Department of Justice investigators tipped off U.S. Steel to Baldwin's identity; the government was secretly tailing him for months after his release from prison. One way or another, company officials decided that this implausibly well-spoken scab was not what he seemed. At the end of his first week at Homestead, Baldwin returned to his modest room to find it ransacked by company Pinkertons. The next day he escaped back to Pittsburgh, bringing Foster one last report on conditions inside the mill.[43]

What Baldwin had seen in the Pittsburgh steel strike quickly became for Lippmann and others like Blankenhorn the quintessential case study in the modern mechanics of public opinion formation. "In order to tell the truth about the steel worker in the Pittsburgh district," Lippmann concluded in 1922, "there was needed a staff of investigators, a great deal of time, and several fat volumes of print." But ordinary newspapers could not make such investments. And even if they could, their readers would have been hard-pressed to find the mental resources to come to terms with the steel industry's complex labor dispute. Powerful interests had wielded communications in their own interest and done so with extraordinary success.[44]

The "romantic notion that the People could rule," Baldwin reflected, needed to be abandoned. Baldwin rejected the old "crusades for the initiative, referendum and other devices for popular control." He dismissed the muckraking journalism he had once favored as a tool for fighting the party machines. All these were futile strategies, he concluded, for reasons Lippmann had first articulated. "There is no public," Baldwin wrote in 1919, echoing Lippmann before him. The "people," or at least the people conceived as a whole, seemed unorganizable for purposes of making a better politics. Baldwin made the same point a few years later when he adopted a phrase Lippmann had coined: there was, Baldwin said, only a "phantom public."[45]

In another man, so complete a disenchantment with the progressive theory of democracy might have produced bitterness. Lippmann himself would soon retreat into the deep skepticism of democracy for which he would become famous as a mid-century journalist. Baldwin, by contrast, turned his hard-won intelligence to new experiments in organizing. The public might not be organizable as such. But segments of the public might be organized around projects of particular interest to them. If resources could be brought to bear, campaigns for hearts and minds might win victories. Hadn't German soldiers surrendered with U.S. Army leaflets in their hands? Hadn't Wilson persuaded the country to go to war? The lessons of propaganda campaigns during the war and in its aftermath, not to mention Thomas Osborne's adventures in the prisons, all pointed in the same direction. Human beings' views could be shaped and reshaped if one engaged the struggle in the right fashion. Where Lippmann saw democracy's end, Baldwin saw a new ground on which to fight.[46]

The Best Test of Truth?

A striking thing about the modern law of free speech is that it was born in the aftermath of the wartime propaganda campaigns and Creel's Committee on Public Information, after Lippmann's account of the distorting power of communications in mass society, and in the midst of the steel giants' news blackout.

The First Amendment to the Constitution provides that "Congress shall make no law abridging the freedom of speech." Between its enactment in 1791 and the end of World War I, however, lawyers and judges typically understood the amendment merely to prohibit the restraint of speech or the press in advance of publication. On the eve of the First World War, Justice Oliver Wendell Holmes Jr. had asserted that "the main purpose" of the First Amendment was "to prevent all such previous restraints upon publications," not to "prevent the subsequent punishment of such as may be deemed contrary to the public welfare." And in the spring of 1919, Holmes reaffirmed the long-standing principle, writing three opinions upholding wartime convictions under the Espionage Act, including the conviction of Socialist presidential candidate Eugene Debs for his anti-war speech. "The most stringent protection of free speech," Holmes wrote, "would not protect a man in falsely shouting fire in a theatre and causing a panic." The analogy was to the Calumet union hall fire that Thomas Nott Osborne had cited five years before. So long as speech seemed to pose a "clear and present danger" to the community, Holmes continued, the state had the power to restrict individual freedoms and punish the speaker.[47]

The story of free speech over the subsequent year has been told many times. A cluster of prominent men who had Holmes's ear objected. Roger Baldwin's friend Zechariah Chafee Jr., on the Harvard Law School faculty, was one of them. Federal district court judge Learned Hand in New York, who had rejected the post office's censorship of *The Masses* under the Espionage Act, was another. A brilliant young English political scientist named Harold Laski, who was then teaching at Harvard, was a third. Together the three men lobbied Holmes to take better account of what Chafee called "the social interest behind free speech." Hand suggested to the justice that opinions were "at best provisional hypotheses, incompletely tested" and that free speech might thus be an experimental technology for testing opinions and leading men ever closer to truth.[48]

Under the combined assault of Chafee and Hand, Holmes altered his approach.* In the fall of 1919, while the steel strike raged in the Midwest, five Russian anarchists appealed their Espionage Act convictions on charges that they had distributed leaflets protesting American intervention in the revolutionary conflict in Russia. Baldwin knew the defendants; one of them, Jacob Abrams, had been a member of Baldwin's Seventh Tier Soviet in the Tombs in New York. Abrams had given Baldwin's group its name. In the Supreme Court, the justices upheld Abrams's conviction along with those of his fellow anarchists. But Holmes now dissented. Joined by fellow justice Louis Brandeis (the old Baldwin family friend who had sent young Roger to St. Louis), Holmes drafted a peroration that would become one of the most memorable passages in American law. "Persecution for the expression of opinions," he wrote, "seems to me perfectly logical. If you have no doubt of your premises or your power and want a certain result with all your heart you naturally express your wishes in law and sweep away all opposition." But in a world of doubt, Holmes explained, a different policy recommended itself:

> when men have realized that time has upset many fighting faiths, they may come to believe even more than they believe the very

---

* Whether Holmes changed his view or remained consistent with the spring 1919 opinions is a perennial question of debate. There were some differences between the cases. Holmes himself observed that the *Abrams* defendants were protesting Wilson's Russian intervention, not the war with Germany. Felix Frankfurter emphasized that the early 1919 cases were wartime speech cases, while the later 1919 cases were not. More recently, Robert Post has noted that the Sedition Act charges in the later cases were broader in scope than the Espionage Act charges in the earlier cases. Chafee himself later insisted that Holmes was simply "biding his time." In the end, the case for an alteration in Holmes's approach seems to me to be stronger.

foundations of their own conduct that the ultimate good desired is better reached by free trade in ideas—that the best test of truth is the power of the thought to get itself accepted in the competition of the market, and that truth is the only ground upon which their wishes safely can be carried out.

"That at any rate," Holmes concluded, "is the theory of our Constitution." Its approach was "an experiment," just as "all life is an experiment."[49]

The First Amendment conceived by men like Chafee, Hand, and Holmes between 1917 and 1919 purported to draw on an idea about how people come to know things—an idea the Harvard philosopher William James called pragmatism. Where Channing's Unitarians claimed that human understanding operated through an inner faculty, pragmatists like James started with the pervasiveness of uncertainty and insisted that knowledge was provisional. Ideas were true not because they corresponded with some Truth of the matter nestled in the mind of individual human beings; propositions were true if, when tested, they turned out to work. James put it this way: "the true is the name of whatever proves itself to be good." Perhaps his most famous illustration took up the proposition that there is a God. Was it a true statement? As James saw it, the question came down to whether it was useful to say so. "If the hypothesis of God works satisfactorily," James explained, then "in the widest sense of the word, it is true."[50]

For nearly a hundred years, observers and historians have attributed the rise of the modern First Amendment to James's theory. Truth, Chafee wrote, could be "sifted out from falsehood" only if a question were "vigorously and constantly cross-examined." This is what Holmes said in his 1919 *Abrams* dissent. And though Supreme Court majorities would not accept the idea for another decade, Holmes's dissent would eventually become a canonical statement of the Court's modern position on speech and a touchstone for the American Civil Liberties Union that Baldwin would establish in 1920.[51]

Yet for all this, the pragmatist theory of free speech, at least in Holmes's version, practically disproved itself. Taken seriously, its uncertainty principle meant that judges could never be sure that more speech would produce better truths. This idea about speech would itself have to be subject to pragmatism's uncertainty principle. As Lippmann noted pointedly, if one took the pragmatists seriously, "there could be nothing worth resisting, nothing worth attaining, nothing particularly worth defending"—not even free speech. Only confidence in one's view could sustain the commitment to free speech that men like Chafee, Hand, and Holmes espoused.[52]

In the fall of 1919, with U.S. Steel's news blitz blanketing the upper Midwest, and with Cobb's marauding gangs of propagandists roving the land, there was less reason than ever to think that the market for ideas had produced more or better truths. Holmes's dissent in *Abrams* took no account of two and a half years of opinion-shaping efforts by people like the propagandist George Creel. Speech was not so much a marketplace from which truths emerged as it was a weapons chest for participants in great social struggles. Creel had said as much when he likened propaganda to the repeating artillery pieces of the Western Front. Arthur Bullard said much the same when he objected to Woodrow Wilson's war censorship regime. The philosopher John Dewey—himself a leading pragmatist—argued for free speech not on the ground that it would reveal truths but because it would help the United States win the war. Dewey's onetime colleague at the University of Chicago, the law professor Ernst Freund, wrote that "toleration of adverse opinion is not a matter of generosity, but of political prudence." Free speech was smart government policy for accomplishing goals.[53]

Holmes's *Abrams* dissent thus did not actually reject the position of the Wilson administration as a whole; it took a position in a debate going on within the government, a debate that had split both the White House and Congress. Holmes and Brandeis rejected the position taken by the administration's most thuggish enforcers, men like Burleson and Gregory. They sided with figures who believed that the war effort would benefit from more speech, not less. They sided with men like Lippmann.

Writing privately to Justice Holmes a week after his dissent in the *Abrams* decision, Lippmann questioned whether free speech rights could be justified by the pursuit of truth. Holmes's view on speech, the younger man said, overlooked "institutions such as the press, propaganda, and censorship which block the road to truth." Combined with what Lippmann called "men's natural limitation in apprehending truth about society," it was not clear that speech would inevitably produce better truths. To the contrary, Lippmann suggested, truth "can prevail only if the facts to which they refer are known." Where the facts are distant, "false ideas are just as effective as true ones."[54]

In a series of articles published in the *Atlantic Monthly*, Lippmann developed the idea further. The real problem, he argued, the thing that shaped and constrained people's understanding of the world, was not censorship at all but the much more intractable fact that the human mind dealt in stereotypes and conventions rather than facts. Lippmann began where his teacher Graham Wallas had left off. In modern societies, people come to know things not firsthand, but "second, third, or fourth hand." "News," Lippmann wrote, "comes from a distance." Even worse, it "comes helter-skelter, in inconceivable confusion."[55]

Lippmann likened modern citizens to the prisoners in Plato's cave. We imagine that we understand the forms of things. But all the while we are merely boxing with shadows—with the derivative image of the real thing. As Lippmann put it, the complexity and scale of the modern world create an ever-growing gap between "the world outside and the pictures in our heads." The pictures in our heads are not perfect reflections of Truth; they are not "messengers of truth." Rather, they are themselves produced by the newspapers, writers, and editors—the managers of opinion, whose own opinions are in turn constructed and shaped by prior sets of what Lippmann called "habitual viewpoints" or preconceptions. In the pell-mell rush of information, people in the modern world could hope at best to seize what Creel and now Lippmann called "catchwords" to connect incoming information to systems of beliefs. At the heart of the information landscape lay "stereotypes" and "conventions": premade molds into which we pour the "great, blooming, buzzing confusion" of the world (William James's phrase) in the effort to make sense of it all. The very utility of the stereotype is that it precedes the unmediated stream of reality and thus allows us to organize it. But therein lies a great risk, too, for the stereotype easily becomes a kind of Procrustean bed, doing violence to facts that don't readily fit its template. "For the most part we do not first see, and then define," Lippmann explained, "we define first and then see," selecting out from the profusion of worldly facts "what our culture has already defined for us."[56]

Lippmann's favorite example was newspaper reporting on the Russian Revolution, but he applied the point to the 1919 steel strike, too. For Lippmann, the pseudo-information environments of newspaper coverage turned mass society into an ideal setting for the success of propaganda. Scale and complexity had turned the modern world into an arena for "the quack, the charlatan, the jingo, and the terrorist." The Great Society, it turned out, was Le Bon's crowd, poised perilously between bewilderment and panic, always susceptible to what Lippmann called "the contagion of unreason."[57]

Here, truly, was a crisis for democratic self-government. Freedom of speech, Lippmann saw, was merely "a subsidiary phase of the whole matter." Protecting the rights of dissenters, or blocking the heavy-handed suppression of the Justice Department, would only begin to address the real problem, which lay in the complex and often badly distorted processes by which citizens came to views about the world around them. The new defenders of free speech, men like Chafee, Hand, and Holmes, had little to say about the sources of people's ideas. But relying on free speech to save American democracy, Lippmann quipped, was like "trying to make bricks without straw." If the pictures in people's heads diverge too sharply from the truth of the matter, then the marketplace of ideas would be more like a melee than a debating club; when you have a debate with someone committed to radically different preconceptions about basic facts in the world, Lippmann observed, "you are not arguing, you are fighting."[58]

In New York in December 1919, with the catastrophe of the steel strike and his prison stay behind him, Baldwin turned back to his wartime civil liberties project, but now with a new orientation toward labor and economics. The project would require more resources. Its aim would be nothing less than to alter the systems of habit, convention, and stereotype that produced public discourse among the masses of people in the American working class.[59]

"My two months of miscellaneous labor," he wrote to one friend, were "the most inspiring and most informing experience I ever had." The experience, he confided, had gone "even deeper than jail." He resolved to continue his experiments not merely in the work of defending civil liberties but in the trenches where the war for public opinion was fought. Within months of the steel strike, Baldwin began casting about for funds to finance experiments on a larger scale than his prison laboratories had permitted. And before long, he happened on an unexpected opportunity.[60]

The writer Upton Sinclair, at right, picketing outside the offices of John D. Rockefeller Jr., in 1914.

4

Freedom and Economics

My sense of democracy is alienated by the autocracy, however benevolent, of private trusts.
—ROGER BALDWIN

American radicals have had a long and fraught relationship to wealth. Thomas Jefferson, who insisted that the earth belonged to the living, proposed a constitutional revolution every generation. But he spent so much on luxuries during his lifetime that he left his accounts in bankruptcy; creditors split up his estate's slaves, including his own enslaved children. The abolitionist John Brown was a broker who made and lost a fortune in the wool market before leading his violent assault on slavery at Harpers Ferry in 1859; some of the nation's wealthiest men had financed his failed attack on the slave system. In the early twentieth century, Greenwich Village radicals consorted with fashionable elites. In the late 1960s, Black Panthers would mix with the wealthy in chic Park Avenue penthouses. The motivation is clear. Financial resources permit a path forward for dissenting voices to whom the electoral system offers little hope. But there are risks, too. The wealthy have their own interests, and wealth introduces its own imperatives. Pursuing money is seductive. But it constrains goals and alters means.[1]

Money posed an especially acute problem for dissenters in the 1920s, and it presented a challenge to Roger Baldwin in particular. A close observer once noted that Baldwin seemed both fascinated and disgusted by money. He was the son of a successful merchant who lived most of his life with comfortable wealth. But he was also a self-diagnosed "tight wad"—a "hairshirt" person, as one colleague put it. Baldwin thought of money as corrupting. It was the "one thing you just can't talk to Roger about," observed a friend. Discussing money, Baldwin remarked more than once, was vulgar. He kept fanatical track of his personal spending, right down to individual phone calls and newspapers. He counted his pennies and nickels. His clothes were threadbare. (He was rumored to acquire his wardrobe by barter.) He avoided taxis as an unwarranted luxury and sometimes, when meetings took place in restaurants, he even brought his own food so that he would not have to order pricey items from the menu.[2]

Baldwin was ill at ease around money at least in part because of what money meant in early twentieth-century America—and what it seemed to be doing to American democracy. The vast sums earned by the large business enterprises of the era had produced an inequality like none the United States had ever seen. By the 1920s, the top 10 percent of American income earners took in half the country's handsome yearly national income. The richest 10 percent owned four-fifths of the nation's wealth. Contemporaries estimated that six financial groups on Wall Street owned controlling interests in firms employing more than two and a half million people, more than a quarter of the workforce in America's major industries. One banking syndicate alone controlled firms employing more than three-quarters of a million people.[3]

Such wealth had allowed U.S. Steel to dominate public opinion in Pittsburgh in 1919. It had shaped newspapers' coverage of the Russian Revolution and the war. Money was power. It molded citizens' judgments about the crucial issues of the day. And so, as Baldwin threw himself back into the civil liberties project, he gave it new direction. He turned it toward economics.

A Civil Liberties Union

Upon his return to New York from the Pittsburgh steel strike, Baldwin resumed the directorship of the National Civil Liberties Bureau. Espionage Act defendants still needed assistance. Conscientious objectors languished in prisons. The deportation of radical aliens was underway. The Bureau's wartime work hardly seemed complete.[4]

Baldwin's time on the picket lines, however, led him to insist that the organization's work now had to center on "the cause of freedom of expression in the industrial struggle." The "cause we now serve," he told his colleagues, "is labor." To mark the organization's expanded postwar project, Baldwin renamed it the American Civil Liberties Union. The rechristened organization opened its doors for business in January 1920 with Baldwin as its formal director and organizing center. The ACLU's sixty-person National Committee was made up mostly of liberal lawyers, union organizers, NAACP officials, and a handful of socialists; a New York–based executive committee of seventeen handled most of the deliberations, while a handful of poorly paid staffers and volunteers worked alongside the director. The shell of the wartime Civil Liberties Bureau provided a scaffolding, and Baldwin's tirelessness built the organization quickly. By the time the year was out, the ACLU boasted 1,000 members paying yearly dues of $2. A network of corresponding lawyers gave the fledgling organization the semblance of national reach. Baldwin announced a ringing new mission: "We are fully partisans of labor in the present struggle."[5]

Baldwin's emphasis on labor emerged from a distinctive new way of thinking about the work of civil liberties. "I believe," Baldwin wrote from prison, "that the vote, the State, and majority control in political units are not only ineffective means to freeing mankind, but illusory and therefore dangerous." He even called for "the abolition of the state as we know it." Wartime governments had taken repression to irrational lengths. Postwar officials had helped put down the steel strike. Baldwin had no remaining confidence, he explained to a friend, in what he called "parliamentary" or political remedies.[6]

Durable change required something more than minimum-wage laws, safer workplaces, and expert juvenile courts. Such achievements through electoral politics were all fine things by Baldwin's lights. The kind of change he was after now, however, would require not merely achieving new standards but also some way of "formulating, securing, and holding" them, as one of his allies put it. The real question, Baldwin concluded, was about the "sources of power" for "getting and holding" the desired outcomes. Gaining such power required vital organizations made up of masses of people to push for and sustain new and better ways of life through "direct action" and "organization on the job." It required a form of organizing the people that made them responsible agents of their own destiny.[7]

Policy success without a strong democratic foundation, Baldwin came to think, had been the great failing of prewar progressivism. In juvenile justice reform in St. Louis, he had embraced the idea that the state might serve as a kind of parent to people in trouble. But now Baldwin found this approach "timid, cautious, and philosophically narrow." Only by taking hold of the public's mind and its heart could he and his fellow advocates for the weak and downtrodden reach "the underlying bases" of society's evils. Real change would need to spark the passions of the people themselves.[8]

Baldwin's ACLU reoriented itself to building an infrastructure for democracy. He called on prewar progressives to "socialize and democratize the public service" and to bring the labor movement "into all cooperative efforts for general community service." Drawing loosely on the democratic pragmatism of John Dewey, Baldwin urged the construction of experimental projects in which citizens could develop their own ideas for reform—in which they could "learn by doing," as Baldwin summarized Dewey's ideas on the subject.[9]

Walter Lippmann's influence showed, too. Baldwin had no illusion that free speech rights alone would construct a democratic culture of public opinion. In place of romantic notions about the rule of the people, he tried on a new idea. The "old American faith that the privileged classes could be controlled by the 'Public,'" he proposed, had been revealed as a myth. There was, Baldwin said, following Lippmann, no public at all, for the public was not organizable, at least not as such. But as Dewey contended, there were many smaller publics, each constituted around particular issues and questions. Most obviously, workers could be organized in labor unions. "Of all forms of liberty," Baldwin believed, "the most essential, considering the major conflict of our time, are the rights of labor to organize, strike, and picket." Freedom "to speak and to interpret the facts" would be necessary to challenge existing industrial conditions. Civil liberties, then, would be a way of protecting the preconditions for a better and more democratic society. As Baldwin put it in one debate, civil liberties were "a weapon in the struggle, and an end, too." They were both, because the more they became simple "habits of life," the more likely it was that they would establish more democratic institutions.[10]

In later years, critics would sometimes attack the ACLU for putting individual rights over majority will. Indeed, Baldwin as an older man would remember his organization as always seeming to be "a minority working against the apathy, prejudices and ignorance of a public." But the American Civil Liberties Union began with a powerful (if chastened) democratic vision. In the era of the crowd—in the world of Wallas's Great Society and in the age of Lippmann's public opinion—Baldwin believed that true democracy rested on effective free speech rights for the great mass of the people: the working classes.[11]

The scale of the challenge became clear to Baldwin when he set out across the country in the spring of 1920. Appearing together with IWW organizer Elizabeth Gurley Flynn, Baldwin spoke before audiences across the upper Midwest. He went back to St. Louis, where he was watched carefully by both local authorities and the Justice Department's Bureau of Investigation. And he made it all the way to California and Washington State.[12]

The tour was demoralizing. Everywhere Baldwin went, the prospects for democratic revival seemed bleak. "The lid is on," he reported. Indeed, there seemed "little evidence in the country of free speech and press." "Critical political thinking," he wrote, "is dead." At the core of the problem was a "campaign against free expression" that seemed to be succeeding in its effort "to weaken organized labor." Employers attacked "the right of labor to organize, strike, and picket," and all too often they won. Judges and politicians went along. The idea that "constitutional American rights can be maintained through law," Baldwin wrote, "has been pretty well exploded." Legal rights, it seemed, were "hollow shams without the political and economic power to enforce them." As Baldwin saw it, "the only places in the United States today with free press and free assemblage are where the workers or the farmers are strongly enough organized to take and hold these rights."[13]

What America needed, Baldwin began to think, was not only a defense of free speech but also a campaign to reimagine democracy altogether. This, however, would be a bigger and more expensive venture than he and his ACLU colleagues had contemplated. Such an effort, he noted in 1920, would require a "budget to carry the work on a much larger scale." He would need a fund for the promotion of democratic life.[14]

Yet Baldwin chafed at the prospect of raising money in large sums. In the age of giant industrial fortunes, money seemed to be the problem, not the solution. A particular episode loomed especially large. Only a few short years before, the role of wealth in American democracy had been thrust onto the public stage when America's wealthiest family found itself implicated in a deadly episode in the West.

The New Benevolence

In September 1913, 9,000 coal miners had walked off the job at the Colorado Fuel & Iron Company. CF&I, which was owned principally by John D. Rockefeller Sr. and his son, John D. Rockefeller Jr., operated the largest coal-mining facilities in southern Colorado. Its miners were from some thirty-two countries and spoke twenty-seven languages. ("The League of Nations was there, you might say," remembered one miner years later.) After two decades of frustrated efforts to organize a union, the miners went out on strike, demanding higher wages, safer working conditions, and relief from the exploitation of company stores and company towns. Most of all, they demanded recognition of the United Mine Workers of America as their union, a step that many workers reasonably thought would be the only way for them to have a say in their work lives. Fed up with company autocracy in the isolated coalfields, the miners insisted that the union would serve as a more robust version of the old "pit committees" that miners had long used to communicate grievances to mine operators. Union representation, in the words of the strike's leading historian, was the "miners' vision of industrial democracy."[15]

Like all Rockefeller-controlled firms, however, CF&I was bitterly opposed to recognizing a union. Rockefeller Sr. snarled that unions aimed "to do as little as possible for the greatest possible pay." Trusted Rockefeller family advisor Frederick T. Gates objected that unions aimed to confiscate "the whole wealth of society." Rockefeller Jr., who was taking over much of the day-to-day management of the family's interests in CF&I, followed his elders, defiantly defending the "open shop" system in which the firm negotiated with individual employees, not with a union.[16]

In Colorado's company towns, coal-mine operators like CF&I had powerful leverage over vulnerable workers and their families. Mine guards "hastened to the little huts where miners lived," one contemporary recounted, and "threw their families and furniture into the street," evicting them from their homes and from the company towns in which they had lived. Almost instantly, a series of tent cities sponsored by the United Mine Workers sprang up around southern Colorado's coal mines. Within weeks, ten encampments housed thousands of Colorado miners and their families. All told, 20,000 people settled into makeshift canvas homes to spend a desolate winter on $6 a week in union-provided strike relief, less than half a miner's wages.[17]

Tensions between strikers, mine guards, and strikebreaking miners produced violence from the very start of the strike, especially at the largest and most important tent city at a railroad junction called Ludlow. Miners gathered at the Ludlow junction to watch would-be strikebreakers pass toward the CF&I mines and discourage them from doing so. Rumors abounded that the union was arming for battle. For its part, CF&I hired private detectives, who engineered an early armored car with a machine gun, which they called the "death special." Open battles between strikers and CF&I security detachments soon broke out. Within a month of the strike's beginning, gunfire from recurrent battles had killed more than two dozen, including strikers, strikebreakers, guards, and bystanders. Violence abated over the winter when the state's governor called in the Colorado National Guard to keep the peace. But fighting resumed in March, with more deaths.[18]

On the morning of April 20, 1914, a shot rang out near the Ludlow tent colony. No one is sure who fired first. But it soon made little difference. The National Guard, made up largely of CF&I security, began firing from a machine-gun position in the nearby hills. Canvas tents offered no shelter. Women and children ducked into the primitive adobe cellars some miners had dug beneath their tents. And late in the afternoon, calamity struck. Some reported that the guardsmen lit the tent city ablaze. Others suggested that the militia had been drinking and set a fire by accident. Still others contended that the fire was a result of hidden munitions stored among the canvas tents by the miners themselves. Whatever the reason, the camp caught on fire. The fire burned so fast and so hot that it asphyxiated women and children still hiding in the informal dug-out cellars beneath the burning tents. Two women and eleven children died.[19]

In grief and outrage, striking miners set out to have their revenge. The state Federation of Labor issued a "call to arms," and for more than a week, the coalfields of southern Colorado were the setting for a running gun battle. This time, the miners were committed to getting the better of it.

In the ruins of the Ludlow strikers' tent colony after the militia opened fire.

With few further casualties of their own, the strikers destroyed six mines, smashed company towns, and killed more than thirty company guards, militiamen, and strikebreakers. Only when President Wilson ordered federal troops into southern Colorado did the roaring guns of what locals would come to call the Ten Days War at last fall quiet.[20]

The Colorado strike trudged onward for another eight months before finally collapsing in December. But the massacre at Ludlow produced a public relations crisis for the Rockefellers that would last far longer. It was to solve this problem that John D. Rockefeller Jr. turned to a fledgling institution.[21]

Junior first conceived of a new philanthropic foundation in 1905 as he developed plans for the family's swelling fortune. Philanthropic foundations were an old idea. Benjamin Franklin had created one. In the nineteenth century, rich men endowed institutions such as Philadelphia merchant Stephen Girard's school for fatherless boys. In the early twentieth century, however, the Rockefeller family stood at the forefront of a vast new movement of assets from the great industrial fortunes of the era into nonprofit foundations. In 1870 there had been one hundred millionaires in the United States. By 1916 there were 40,000. The nation's richest men possessed truly staggering fortunes. The senior Rockefeller, who founded Standard Oil, was worth around $1 billion on the eve of American entry in the First World War, equivalent to $26 billion today. In 1901, when Andrew Carnegie sold his eponymous steel corporation to J. P. Morgan, the Scottish immigrant held assets amounting to around half a billion in his day's dollars, or nearly $15 billion in twenty-first-century terms after accounting for inflation. At the height of their wealth, each man's net worth equaled nearly 2 percent of the yearly gross domestic product of the United States. Measured this way, as a share of the American economy, each man's estate would have been worth roughly $450 billion in 2025, equal to or greater than the wealth of Elon Musk and two or three times the size of the giant fortunes owned by Jeff Bezos and Bill Gates.[22]

Such vast sums transformed American life. In 1902, Rockefeller Sr. established the General Education Board to support university endowments and public high schools in the South; across the next eight years he gave the board $53 million. (William H. Baldwin, Roger's uncle, was its first chairman.) Carnegie established the Carnegie Institution of Washington in 1902, endowing it with $12 million principally for research in the sciences. Four years later the Carnegie Foundation for the Advancement of Teaching established a $10 million fund. In 1907, the widow of railroad magnate Russell Sage established a $10 million foundation in her late husband's name. Six foundations chartered between 1903 and 1913 had endowments totaling $325 million, an amount equal to approximately half the annual budget of the federal government. By 1920, John D. Rockefeller alone had given away an estimated $475 million to his various philanthropic foundations; Carnegie had donated $350 million. By 1924, the *Los Angeles Times* could report that $2 billion had been given in philanthropic gifts over the previous decade.[23]

The new foundations inaugurated what the *New York Observer* called "a new era in benevolence." Where old foundations such as Girard's Philadelphia school had limited themselves to specific purposes, the new ones assumed a breathtakingly open-ended authority to improve the welfare of the people. The Rockefeller Foundation, for example, announced a purpose "to promote the well-being of mankind throughout the world." The new philanthropists adopted a philosophy to match their ambitious agenda. Where foundations had once offered charity, the new philanthropists aimed to help govern. Rather than provide alms for the poor, the new philanthropists would identify efficient and scientific ways to get at root causes and reduce poverty. The editors of *Harper's Weekly* called it a transformation "from alms and welfare work to socialized business efficiency." Philanthropy in the modern era, one well-placed editor said, would attack not suffering, but the "evil conditions out of which suffering springs."[24]

The new philanthropy, however, raised concerns alongside opportunities. In particular, it produced novel questions about wealth and power in a democratic system of government. Since at least the seventeenth century, concentrations of wealth in endowments had caused observers to worry about the so-called dead hand problem. A foundation with a particular purpose allowed a wealthy man to control the use of his vast fortune even after his death. The earth, Thomas Jefferson warned, belongs to the living, not to the dead. But charitable foundations ran the risk of allowing people to control the use of resources from beyond the grave.[25]

The general-purpose charters of the big twentieth-century foundations seemed to solve one piece of the dead hand problem. Future trustees would not be bound to any one vision of the good of mankind. But in solving one problem, such charters exacerbated another. The new general-purpose foundation knew no limits at all. It seemed to aspire to supplant the power of government. In an era in which the annual yield on Rockefeller's and Carnegie's gifts alone amounted to twice the federal budget for education and social services, the new nonprofit foundation seemed to turn the dead hand of the past into a threat to democracy itself.[26]

Anxieties about the power of philanthropic interventions nearly prevented the Rockefeller Foundation from coming into being. The family originally intended to establish the foundation and its $100 million initial endowment by an act of Congress, making it a rare federally chartered corporation. A congressional charter, the elder Rockefeller believed, would insulate the foundation from meddling state and local officials. But the proposal quickly ran headlong into powerful objections. Attorney General George W. Wickersham warned President William Howard Taft that $100 million without any corporate limitations on its use "might be in the highest degree corrupt in its influence." Taft privately agreed. Such objections made a federal charter politically impossible, especially given the controversy over the ongoing antitrust case against Standard Oil. In 1913, the family settled for a charter from New York State.[27]

Anger over the Rockefeller fortune surged anew in the aftermath of Ludlow. Upton Sinclair saw the massacre as another outbreak of the horrors of the "wage slavery" he had documented a decade before in the slaughterhouses of Chicago for his novel *The Jungle*. Sinclair organized protests outside the Standard Oil building at 26 Broadway in lower Manhattan. "I intend this night," Sinclair told Junior, "to indict you upon a charge of murder before the people of this country." One speaker exhorted the crowd to repay Junior in kind for the deaths of the women and children of Ludlow; "shoot him down like a dog," he howled. Another was soon arrested trying to get into the Rockefeller offices with a loaded pistol. Protesters appeared at the Rockefeller townhouse on 54th Street, too. Uptown, on Lexington Avenue, a bomb exploded, destroying the upper stories of an apartment building and killing four people associated with anarchism and the Industrial Workers of the World, one or more of whom was apparently making an explosive device to use against the Rockefellers. At the Rockefeller estate in the Hudson Valley, anarchists including Emma Goldman gathered to protest outside the estate's heavily guarded walls. Helen Keller (once a beneficiary of Rockefeller largesse) charged that "Mr. Rockefeller is the monster of capitalism. He gives charity and in the same breath permits the helpless workmen, their wives and children to be shot down."[28]

Privately, Junior spluttered with indignation at such charges; he denied there was a massacre at all, writing in a memo for his files that it was "unjust in the extreme to lay it at the door of the defenders of law and property, who were in no slightest way responsible for it." But the younger Rockefeller felt all too painfully the blows raining down on him in the press and among the protesters. He was slowly coming to think that the family needed a new approach to industrial conflict. The foundation proved to be just the thing.[29]

In the months after Ludlow, Junior announced a new initiative of the Rockefeller Foundation: a study of industrial relations. At the encouragement of Charles Eliot, the president of Harvard, Junior enlisted William Lyon Mackenzie King to direct the new program. King was heir to an old and distinguished Canadian political family; he had served already as Canada's labor minister and he would go on to become prime minister. Junior and his advisors decided that involving King formally in the mediation of the dispute at CF&I would undermine the impartiality of his report; his work for the Rockefeller Foundation was ostensibly independent of the Colorado situation. But in truth, King developed his industrial relations plan for the Rockefeller Foundation while working closely on the management of the Colorado strike.[30]

The solution to labor strife, as King saw it, was to create a mechanism for labor relations "between the extreme of individual agreements," which he said were often exploitative of workers, and the opposite extreme of labor unions, which he claimed interfered unduly in the relations between employers and employees. King proposed a middle ground: bargaining between capital and an organized body of those workers "immediately concerned in

John D. Rockefeller Jr. (right) and Mackenzie King (center) dressed up as coal miners for a Rockefeller Foundation publicity stunt to try to win back public confidence after Ludlow.

any certain industry." Such a system of employee representation, King asserted, would "afford opportunity of easy and constant conference between employers and employed." It would end the old struggles and bitterness and replace them with a framework in which employers and employees could communicate their concerns constructively with one another.[31]

Junior unveiled King's new plan at CF&I in September 1915 during a visit to the Colorado coalfields. CF&I miners, still reeling from the violence of the previous year, approved the "Rockefeller Plan" in a secret ballot by a margin of 2,404 to 402.[32]

A Missouri lawyer named Frank Walsh thought the miners who voted for the Rockefeller Plan had been given no choice. As it happened, Walsh also saw in the Rockefellers' public relations effort a chance to get himself out of a jam. His response would launch the modern critique of philanthropic foundations and their influence in American life.[33]

Walsh had made his name by successfully defending Jesse E. James, son of the famous bandit, against train robbery charges in a sensational 1898 trial. Walsh had gone on to a career as a politically active labor lawyer with a populist flair. And in 1913, Woodrow Wilson picked him to chair the Commission on Industrial Relations, created by Congress a year before.[34]

The commission had struggled to find its way at first. But the Ludlow catastrophe offered the ambitious chairman a chance to reverse the fortunes of his languishing commission and to raise his profile in the process. Walsh called Junior for two separate rounds of testimony, subjecting him to what the *New York Times* described as "the hammer and tongs" method of interrogation. By the time Walsh was done, his investigation into industrial relations had become an inquiry into foundations and their influence.[35]

Walsh's report, which was joined by only a minority of his fellow commissioners, openly warned of the danger of ostensibly "benevolent industrial despots," whose power "is being extended through the creation of enormous privately managed funds." Walsh asserted that in the field of industrial relations, foundations' riches had "the power to influence the entire country" in the determination of one of its most vital policies. With its riches and its claims to expertise, the Rockefeller Foundation in particular was trying to "create a psychological condition among the working people of the nation" that would make democracy impossible. The basis for the Rockefeller-King labor relations plan was not any social-scientific breakthrough; it was the naked "industrial interests of Mr. Rockefeller" himself. And to make matters worse, as Walsh saw it, the Rockefellers financed their foundation with resources gained through the exploitation of workers and consumers alike. Walsh could only conclude, as he said writing separately, that "the huge philanthropic trusts, known as foundations, appear to be a menace to the welfare of society." The "Rockefeller Foundation," Walsh concluded, "can justly be characterized as an attempt to present to the world, as handsome and admirable, an economic and industrial regime that draws its substance from the sweat and blood and tears of exploited and dispossessed humanity."[36]

The chairman's report called for a host of new regulations on nonprofit foundations, including specific limits on their fields of engagement. Most of all, Walsh demanded the dissolution of the Rockefeller Foundation altogether. The commission's report was ultimately splintered by dissents; many of the commissioners found the chairman's tactics unduly aggres-

The Commission on Industrial Relations took up the question of whether great fortunes and vast economic inequality were compatible with democracy. Commissioner Frank Walsh is third from right.

sive. But even the dissenting commissioners called for the imposition of new inheritance taxes to reduce the swelling size of the vast new estates of the industrial age.[37]

The Denver journalist George Creel condemned the Rockefellers and organized local protests against CF&I. The very same Creel who would go on to run war propaganda for the Wilson administration complained that the foundation gave Rockefeller interests the power to distort the truth and bend public opinion to their will. Creel charged that the CF&I public relations campaign, run by a publicity man named Ivy Lee, grossly misrepresented the facts. Lee had designed a series of pamphlets inflating union organizers' salaries. He had fabricated the story about the miners' setting the fire at Ludlow with their own ammunition. Creel was having none of it. The new Rockefeller philanthropy, he charged, was little more than "a carefully premeditated fraud, designed by unscrupulous millionaires to chloroform public opinion." The foundation, he asserted, aimed to "muddy the waters" around the Colorado controversy to obscure its founders' responsibility. When Creel attacked Lee and his fellow flacks as "poisoners of public opinion," Upton Sinclair incorporated the idea into a moniker that stuck. "Poison Ivy" Lee, Sinclair called him. Two years later, Sinclair published a novel—*King Coal*—that aimed to do for coal mining in the Rocky Mountain West what *The Jungle* had done for the slaughterhouses of Chicago.[38]

At bottom, the critics of the Rockefeller initiative lodged a subtle but powerful objection. Talking to reporters from his jail cell after conviction on murder charges in the aftermath of the April fighting, Colorado union organizer John Lawson asserted that "Mr. Rockefeller has missed the fundamental trouble in the coal camps." The real key was "democracy," but "the coal companies have stamped it out." The purpose of unions in the Colorado mines was not merely to ensure better wages and working conditions, though those were vital, too. The more important function of the union was to put workers in a position to be able to participate collectively in governing the mines and governing their own lives. Unions created a kind of democratic infrastructure in the industrial community. The Rockefeller Plan's system of employee representation, by contrast, undercut democracy by removing the unions that presented the only countervailing force to the brute fact of employer power. Employee representation in the Rockefeller Plan was not democracy but rather a cynical paternalism.[39]

Earlier foundation efforts to interfere with democratic politics had been more ham-fisted. When Andrew Carnegie had proposed in 1912 to use his foundation to finance pensions for the country's former presidents, critics howled. Two years earlier the original Rockefeller Foundation charter had proposed an oversight board featuring the sitting president of the United States, plus the speaker of the House of Representatives, the president of the Senate, and the chief justice of the United States. Such proposals would have created blatant conflicts of interest, ensnaring public officials in the networks of the wealthiest Americans.[40]

Sharp-eyed critics saw a disguised effort to co-opt democracy in the Rockefeller Foundation's new efforts, too. The president of the American Federation of Labor, Samuel Gompers, implored reporters to "imagine an organization of miners formed by the richest man in the world, who employs its members!" "What influence," Gompers asked incredulously, "can such a pseudo union have to insist upon the remedying of a grievous wrong or the attainment of a real right?" Even worse, Gompers's *American Federationist* charged, Rockefeller had "corrupted the very springs of public opinion" by which democratic processes operated. Testifying before the Walsh Commission, Gompers contended that the Rockefeller Foundation was either "an all-pervading machinery for the molding of the minds of the people" or a kind of "verbal narcotics" that aimed to "dim" the "perceptive faculties" of the citizenry. Walsh himself called for government takeover of the giant industrial foundations. "Most dangerous of all," he asserted, was "the attempt by the Rockefellers, especially, to become molders of public thought." The "huge philanthropic trusts, known as foundations," he concluded, "appear to be a menace to the welfare of society."[41]

Roger Baldwin told Walsh that the Commission on Industrial Relations' report would "do more to educate public opinion to the truth of existing conditions than any other one document in existence." Baldwin's old mentor Louis Brandeis attested that his "faith in democracy" led him to fear the power of big foundations. Baldwin's friend, the liberal clergyman John Haynes Holmes, testified to the Walsh Commission that giant trusts were "repugnant to the whole idea of a democratic society."[42]

Like Walsh and the commission's witnesses, Baldwin harbored grave fears about money's influence in democracy. His uncle William had taken a lead role in the new age of philanthropy. But by 1918, Baldwin asserted that "no work can be democratic which is supported by one class for the benefit of another." During the war, big money had supported the "professional patriots," who whipped up mobs to attack the Civil Liberties Bureau's clients. Baldwin supported efforts "financed by all for the benefit of all"; only such work "can be truly democratic," he said. Looking back in later years, Baldwin observed that his "sense of democracy" was "alienated by the autocracy, however benevolent, of private trusts."[43]

And yet critics of the big foundations faced a problem. For all the attention given to Walsh's attack on the undue influence of foundations, it was hard not to see that Rockefeller had come out of the episode a winner. By 1920, as Baldwin formed the ACLU, the Rockefeller Plan was fast on its way to becoming the dominant labor relations system of the coming decade. At their height, employee representation plans modeled on Mackenzie King's Rockefeller Plan would boast 3 million members, nearly as many as belonged to unions affiliated with the American Federation of Labor. Company unions going under the name Employee Representation Plan, or sometimes just American Plan, would come to include millions more. Well-funded campaigns to shape the minds of Americans seemed to work. And so, proceeding in parallel at first, and only later coming together as a team, Roger Baldwin and Upton Sinclair turned in earnest to raising funds of their own.[44]

Fund directors Freda Kirchwey (far right) and Lewis Gannett (back row at center with mustache) at a 1925 outing of The Nation *magazine staffers and American Fund insiders to the Connecticut estate of Oswald Garrison Villard, owner of the magazine. Villard stands tall in rear; editor Dorothy Van Doren is at front left with her husband the critic Mark Van Doren, back row second from left. Joseph Wood Krutch at far left; Marcelle Krutch front center; Irita Van Doren front second from right.*

5

Garland's Million

I wouldn't refuse a million from the meanest person in the world.
—GEORGE M. COHAN

James Albert Garland Sr. went from rags to riches not once but twice. Albert, as he was known, grew up in the two decades before the Civil War, the son of a poor Philadelphia shoemaker. As a child, he was skilled with numbers. After graduating from a local commercial college, he became a math tutor at the same institution, a place called Crittenden's. Among his students there was a youth named Jay Cooke Jr. The boy's father, Jay Cooke Sr., was a Philadelphia banker poised to become one of the richest and most controversial financiers in American history. The ambitious tutor with a knack for numbers saw in Cooke's then-modest firm, Cooke & Co., an opportunity to put numbers to work in a way that was more lucrative than training future bookkeepers. Catching the senior Cooke's eye, James Garland landed a job as a clerk in 1862. Before long he worked his way up to partner.[1]

The firm of Cooke & Co. made its name issuing and speculating in Civil War bonds to finance the federal wartime budget. In the postwar years, the firm turned to railroad securities, aiming to make its vast sums into even more vast sums. The firm borrowed heavily to take a big position in the Northern Pacific Railroad, then under construction. But delays in completing the railroad stretched Cooke & Co. too far. In 1873 the firm was unable to meet its obligations. And when it shut its doors, the entire Wall Street market collapsed. The Panic of 1873 closed the New York Stock Exchange for ten days and touched off five years of economic recession. Markets around the globe felt its reverberations. And the newfound Garland fortune was gone.[2]

James A. Garland Sr., the mathematically inclined son of a Philadelphia shoemaker, at the turn of the twentieth century.

Albert clawed his way back to wealth. He moved to the First National Bank of New York, then in the infancy of what would one day become the Citibank empire. There he climbed back into American finance and amassed a second fortune to rival the first. Eventually he owned a seat on the New York Stock Exchange and served as a director of more than thirty companies, including the New York Central Railroad. When Albert died in 1900, he left a substantial estate to two surviving sons. One of those sons, James A. Garland Jr., was a notorious gambler and playboy, known best for having been the first high-society lover of the enchanting celebrity model and ingenue Evelyn Nesbit.[3]

The playboy, as it happened, outlived the financier by only six years. He, in turn, left what remained of his share of the estate to be divided and handed over to his three young sons upon their twenty-first birthdays. Thus came Charles Garland, James Jr.'s middle child, into a million dollars in June 1920.[4]

Cause of All Unhappiness

Compared to the largest fortunes of the day, Garland's bequest was not giant. In one week that November—the same week when Charles Garland's decision to refuse his inheritance hit the news—the Rockefeller family added $64 million to the endowments of its philanthropic foundations. Still, a flat million in 1920 was no small thing, and it was certainly of significance to its intended heir.[5]

Charles Garland was entirely innocent of both his grandfather's hardscrabble origins and his financial wizardry. The younger Garland spent his early years on Cape Cod, coddled in the social world of the Anglophilic East Coast elite. He attended school for a time at Eton, the exclusive English boarding school. He moved on to St. Paul's in New Hampshire. By the time he was sixteen, Charles was over six feet tall and physically striking. People who met him almost always commented on his handsomeness—"one can hardly keep one's eyes off him," said a frequent houseguest.[6]

Friends said that Charles got his looks from his eccentric mother, Marie Tudor, who laid a dubious claim of descent from Henry VIII and the Tudor line of English monarchs. It was Marie who had insisted Charles attend Eton, and it was Marie whose strong-willed example offered her son a model of how to manage bequests. Her late husband James's will had established a generous income for her—but it also specified that she be cut off from its proceeds in the event of remarriage. Rebelling at the control of the dead hand from beyond the grave, Marie had married her gardener in 1912 and forfeited the benefits of James's largesse. The marriage lasted only two years, but there was no sign that Marie regretted the loss of her income. She remarried twice more in the subsequent decade and took lovers along the way. (Roger Baldwin claimed privately to have been among them.) In 1918, she hosted the Lebanese poet and mystic Kahlil Gibran as he began to write his famous poem, *The Prophet*. By the end of the 1920s, Marie was living on a ranch in New Mexico with her new husband, the avant-garde filmmaker Henwar Rodakiewicz, and a long-term guest, the artist Georgia O'Keeffe.[7]

After St. Paul's, young Garland enrolled at Harvard College. But he lasted only a year. Tall, handsome, and wealthy, he was also more sensitive to the world than most. In later years he would suffer from, and be hospitalized for, mental illness. And through his unusual mother and her unusual experience, this emotionally delicate soul encountered the idea that basic institutions like marriage and inheritance were unjust and ought to be abolished.[8]

The notion that inherited wealth was wrong had been around for a long time. The English jurist William Blackstone observed in the middle of the 1700s that "naturally speaking, the instant a man ceases to be he ceases to have any dominion." In the nineteenth century, the utilitarian philosopher Jeremy Bentham argued that states should intervene upon the death of wealthy citizens to prevent "too great an accumulation of wealth." Bentham's student the political philosopher John Stuart Mill defended steep inheritance taxes so as to minimize the influence of one's birth on one's life chances. In the United States, economist Richard T. Ely saw inheritance taxes as a way to achieve "more general prosperity" for all while still preserving the "springs of economic activity" that private property produced. In 1906 and 1907, President Theodore Roosevelt took up Ely's ideas to press for a sharp federal inheritance tax on large fortunes. In defense of such a tax, Roosevelt cited Abraham Lincoln's belief in "equality of self-respect" and "an approximate equality in the conditions under which each man obtains the chance to show the stuff that is in him." Anyway, Roosevelt added forthrightly, the government had "the absolute right to decide as to the terms upon which a man shall receive a bequest or devise from another."[9]

Criticisms of inheritance hardly implied radicalism; Roosevelt, for one, was quick to reject any connection between stiff inheritance taxes and socialism. But socialists criticized inheritance, too. Young Garland encountered criticisms of inheritance in the work of English writer H. G. Wells, whose wildly popular book *New Worlds for Old*, first published in 1908, introduced a generation of Americans to what Wells called "a plain account of socialism." Garland thrilled to Wells's idea of a society based on a "spirit of service" rather than a "spirit of gain." Science-fiction novels like *The War of the Worlds* and *The Time Machine* would make Wells famous for a century and more. But Garland thought there was nothing science fiction about Wells's analysis of inherited wealth. Inheritance, Wells said, sustained "monstrous property" holdings in "a comparatively small body of individuals." Wells's version of socialism advocated a world of actual, rather than merely pretend, equality. "We modern Socialists want everyone to have play for choice and individual expression," Wells explained. And as a result, all but a modest form of inherited wealth—some residual mode of transmission to accommodate the natural "pride of descent" within families—would have to be abolished.[10]

Garland saw his own inheritance as precisely the kind of thing Wells and others had so powerfully criticized. Garland had grown up, as he noted, "among those who did not question the justice of private ownership." At Harvard College, his teachers justified the "injustices of the present economic system," with its "great wealth beside great poverty," by invoking "the argument that everyone has a fair chance to make a living." But Garland knew that this argument was false. By no effort of his own, Garland had become the beneficiary of greater wealth than most Americans would ever have. The argument from fairness was a naked effort to legitimate unjust inequalities rather than "face the facts honestly." And so, in November 1920, he announced a decision. He would not accept his inheritance. He cited Wells along with Tolstoy and Jesus Christ as inspirations. Unearned wealth, he said, was immoral. Private property had produced inequality in the control over basic decisions about the world; it placed undue power "in the hands of the few." Sometimes he went further. "Private property," he suggested, was "the main cause of all unhappiness." The world, he said, was an unjust place. Obscene fortunes existed side by side with grinding poverty. Garland would not go along. The right way to think about man's moral obligations, Garland insisted, was for each man "to hold the welfare of mankind above his or her individual welfare."[11]

Reactions were swift. Most observers thought the whole situation a ridiculous lark. Songwriter George M. Cohan, impresario of popular Broadway musicals, deadpanned that he wouldn't refuse a million "from the meanest man in the world." A lawyer volunteered to pay a hefty commission to anyone who brought him such a princely sum. Even Garland's idol, H. G. Wells, thought poorly of the decision. From across the Atlantic he accused Garland of sheer foolishness.[12]

> ## "MONEY IS NOT MINE" GARLAND DECLARES
>
> ### Youth Who Refused Million Says Present System of Society Condemns Itself

Headline in the Boston Globe, *November 30, 1920.*

To be sure, some were more admiring of Garland's stance. The editors of *Harper's* commended him in a respectful if cautious editorial. The *New York Evening World* pronounced him "America's most extraordinary young man."[13]

Yet there was a deep puzzle about Garland's decision. To criticize inherited wealth put Garland in a long and venerable tradition. But to reject an inheritance altogether, to refuse even to exercise the power to donate it, was another thing entirely. Why not accept the money and give it away?

No one seemed quite to be able to understand what could be wrong with this response. Garland struggled to explain. He wanted nothing to do, he insisted, with a system of property that produced such glaring inequality and such inexcusable poverty in the world. To take the money, he said, would implicate him in that system. But as observers quickly pointed out, this answer did not seem available to the comfortable Garland. He was already implicated. He lived on his mother's expensive farm on Cape Cod, where the wealth supposedly derived from the Tudor kings of England. Moreover, as it turned out, a complex array of trusts already supplied young Garland with a lifetime income of $15,000 annually, and this at a time when a typical family might earn one-tenth that sum for a full year's hard labor. If private property were the problem, well then Garland seemed caught in a set of inconsistencies he could not explain very well. The press had a field day. Newspapers quoted truck drivers, stenographers, and elevator runners gleefully skewering the confused Garland.[14]

Pressed, Garland hit upon a final explanation. In a world of indefensible injustice, he said, his million was a mere drop in the bucket. To pretend as if giving his money to the poor would end hunger, he explained, would be to convey the false impression that the social crises of the postwar world could be solved by modest acts of selfless generosity. There was something to this answer, of course. Maybe his money was not enough. But was it an answer to the question of why not feed a thousand men to observe that many millions more would remain hungry? Garland added another idea. The symbolism of the thing, he said, would legitimate the unrestrained capitalism he rejected. Philanthropy was part of the problem to be solved, not part of the solution. And put this way, perhaps Garland's curious position wasn't a hopeless contradiction at all. Most importantly, it caught the attention of a writer 3,000 miles away, a writer who thought he saw a use for the money that would reveal it not to be too small after all.[15]

A Trust Fund for Pioneering Enterprises

When Upton Sinclair read about Garland's inheritance in the Los Angeles papers, he reached out to the young man with an idea. The self-described propagandist and muckraking novelist conceded to Garland that a million dollars could not feed all the poor and hungry. But the real solution to the social problems that troubled Garland, Sinclair told the young man, lay in people's heads, not in their stomachs. During the war, Sinclair had urged Wilson to use propaganda as a "weapon of truth." And as George Creel had shown, ideas could be cheap.[16]

Sinclair, as it happened, was increasingly preoccupied with the ways in which wealth and power shaped political thought in America. In 1918 he published the first of a series of six novels on the problem in what he called his "Dead Hand" series. The name was in part a play on Adam Smith's "invisible hand" of capitalism. Sinclair, who was a sometime member of the Socialist Party, thought capitalism's influence far more destructive than Smith's invisible hand metaphor had famously suggested. But the name of Sinclair's series had a more specific meaning, too. The dead hand was the influence of the past in the here and now. It was the power of those who had passed into another world to retain control in this one through their wealth. Thomas Jefferson had denounced the idea a century before. And now Sinclair condemned it, too. In his second Dead Hand book, a 1919 bestseller titled *The Brass Check*, Sinclair anticipated in cruder language what Walter Lippmann would bring out in his influential postwar writing on newspapers and public opinion. Sinclair denounced the press as a tool of the powerful and the wealthy. Never before, he said, had the public relied so much on the press to know the world around them. But the press reported the stories its owners and advertisers wanted to hear, not the facts. The "brass check" of Sinclair's title was a $3 token that customers purchased at a brothel and presented to a prostitute in return for her services. The check, in Sinclair's words, was "the price of a woman's shame." American journalism, he argued, should feel the same kind of ignominy, for the newspapers did not present facts so much as propaganda that had been bought and paid for through advertising. Only a newspaper without advertisements and without editorials—a "record of events pure and simple"—would escape the distortions imposed by the imperative of advertising, Sinclair said. *The Brass Check* proposed a paper titled "National News" with an independent endowment overseen by men of distinction in the labor movement.[17]

Sinclair's idea was that the young man underwrite such a paper. "I want to congratulate you upon the very fine propaganda stunt you have pulled off," Sinclair wrote to a startled Garland, "it beats any of mine." But Sinclair warned that the half-life of Garland's ploy would be short. In a matter of days, Sinclair predicted, Garland's sensational rejection of his inheritance would amount to little more than historical trivia. And so Sinclair proposed to Garland that the young man take the money and give it away. If not to Sinclair's "National News" paper, then Garland should give it to well-placed men on the liberal left who would use it to remake public opinion. "You have it in your power," Sinclair urged Garland, "to do more to enlighten the American people than any other man has ever done in our history." Give $100,000 to Max Eastman at *The Liberator*, he suggested, and $100,000 to the *New York Call*—publications that came as close as any to the model newspaper he had sketched out in *The Brass Check*. Sinclair exhorted Garland to give $100,000 to the Federated Press, a news agency opened by the unions to combat the press errors revealed in the Pittsburgh steel strike. He recommended that another $100,000 go to Roger Baldwin at the American Civil Liberties Union. Perhaps Garland could even endow some new publication as the "honest weekly newspaper" Sinclair had contemplated in his book.[18]

Garland had a ready reply. How could he take a million-dollar inheritance and use it to preach the wickedness of million-dollar inheritances, he asked Sinclair, without being a walking contradiction? He admired *The Brass Check*, and pored over the copy Sinclair sent. But the "dumbest of mankind" could see the hypocrisy in such a course of action. The California novelist was unmoved. "Such is the complexity of life," he answered, adapting Emerson's dictum about foolish consistencies and little minds. An "inconsiderate consistency," Sinclair wrote, "is a tragedy to the radical movement." Inheritance was a social process, not an individual one. No one person could abolish it; only society could, and it was therefore Garland's obligation to use his resources to persuade society to do so. Take the million, Sinclair urged, and "use it to establish an honest newspaper"—a "daily newspaper or weekly magazine to convey to the people the truth about our dishonest social system."[19]

For weeks, Garland and Sinclair kept up a correspondence. The young heir insisted on the value of principle. Sinclair cited the imperatives of compromise. He appealed to Garland's wife, Mary. ("I want an honest newspaper to tell the truth to the American people," he wrote her.) Here at last was a chance to address capitalism's excesses through education, "a chance to break down the triple armored wall of poverty which the system has built up about the radical movement." Was Garland to remain pure "while democracy is slowly strangled to death throughout America?" Surely fate had never presented "a more ironical spectacle than this."[20]

Unable to persuade Garland to give the money away himself, Sinclair switched tacks, urging Garland to be in touch with Roger Baldwin. Sinclair proposed that Garland find someone who "would be able to select a group of men and women to administer your money as a trusteeship." Here was a way for Garland "to achieve the maximum amount of public service" without having to do the difficult work of selecting the beneficiaries himself. Sinclair shared the idea with Baldwin, who replied in gratitude: "That letter of yours to Garland is a vote of confidence I don't often get."[21]

In a marvelous coincidence, Baldwin had met young Garland while swimming in a pond near Plymouth, Massachusetts, in the summer before the inheritance story hit the news. Family connections among the Northeast elite offered him an inside track. Baldwin's younger brother had attended Harvard with one of Garland's brothers. Marie Tudor, who had divorced her gardener, was now married to Swinburne Hale, a prominent New York lawyer in the civil liberties world who had been one of Baldwin's college classmates and was a law partner with ACLU lawyer Walter Nelles. There was even a chance Baldwin and Garland were distantly related. One of Garland's maternal great-grandparents was a Fenno; Baldwin's father's middle name was Fenno. Related or not, Baldwin found himself (as he so often did) connected as an insider. Naturally, he got wind of Garland's unusual decision to reject his inheritance even before the story appeared in the papers.[22]

The timing was propitious. In 1920, Baldwin had founded a group called the Mutual Aid Society, inspired by the Russian anarchist Peter Kropotkin's call for voluntary organizations of collective self-help. The society raised $30,000 to support dissidents and radicals who needed lawyers or bail money.[23]

But Baldwin aspired to bigger projects, too, and not merely defensive ones. Even before hearing of the Garland money, Baldwin had been casting about for a new financing source. Writing to ACLU members, Baldwin had proposed a "national Trust Fund" for "pioneering enterprises directed to social and economic freedom." If Garland could be persuaded to accept his inheritance and then donate it, Baldwin's national trust might come into being. Baldwin visited Garland in 1921 in North Carver, Massachusetts, on a cooperative farm the young man had established there. "I found him a serious, philosophical youth," Baldwin later remembered, "handsome and charming, a bit inarticulate." More visits followed. By the beginning of 1922, Baldwin described Garland as a "fairly close" friend.[24]

Under the combined exhortations of Sinclair and Baldwin, Garland's opposition gave way. It didn't hurt that Garland needed money for a personal crisis, too. Upon quitting Harvard he had married his nineteen-year-old sweetheart, Mary. A baby had come soon thereafter. Now Mary was leaving him, with their infant daughter in tow. Charles Garland held unusual ideas about marriage and sexuality, too, not unlike those on which Baldwin had tried to base his own marriage two years before. Living with Mary and their new infant, Garland told her he had fallen in love with another woman, whom he wanted to bring into their marriage. "A man who can love two women deeply," he told one reporter, "is just so much better than a man with only one love." But Mary was having none of it, and with Mary moving out, Garland now needed to support her and their child. And so he agreed to accept the inheritance, giving part of it to his estranged wife and child. The rest went to Baldwin, who acted quickly to secure the gift. "We were taking no chances," Baldwin later remembered, lest time lead the confused young man "to change his mind."[25]

Baldwin established the American Fund for Public Service as a Delaware corporation in July 1922. Initially the plan had been to charter the organization in New York, but the secretary of state in Albany had thrown up roadblocks against incorporation of an organization so closely connected with labor radicalism and civil liberties. Delaware, it seemed, presented no roadblocks to corporations of any kind.[26]

Baldwin rapidly brought the Fund to life. Garland attached virtually no strings to the money. He asked that Baldwin use the money "to the benefit of poor as much as rich" and "black as much as white." He aimed, he said, to put his funds to work for "foreigners as much as citizens" and for those he described as "so-called criminals." Garland also urged that the money "should be distributed as fast as it can be put into reliable hands." The longer you have large amounts of money, the young man asserted, "the harder it is to see straight." But beyond these exhortations, Garland surrendered all say in how the funds were distributed.[27]

As Baldwin saw it, the funds were to be used for "freeing people's minds from the bonds of old institutions." He thought of the money as a resource for smashing the stereotypes and conventions that had such a grip on American life—the storylines and scripts that had dominated news coverage of the war and of strikes like those in Pittsburgh in 1919 and Colorado in 1913. Garland's million would serve "as a fund to finance all sorts of leftist and pioneering causes, nonpartisan and unconventional"; it would finance projects that "no established foundation would dream of touching." Such a strategy meant experimenting with different kinds of grants. The Fund would not "follow rigid rules" in deciding on grant recipients.[28]

Baldwin did adopt some general guidelines. The Fund would focus on American projects rather than international or foreign ones; the Fund's directors seemed best positioned to be able to evaluate the merit of domestic grant proposals. The Fund would not award money to individuals, nor would it support agricultural colonies or mechanical inventions. The Fund would eschew "partisan or sectarian movements." The Fund would not support "social agencies of established conventional types," either. Instead, as Baldwin wrote in the organization's first weeks, the Fund was "more interested in experimental movements in the field of education and industrial organization, particularly those in the interest of the producing classes." The aim would be to identify groups that were "so new or experimental that they do not command general public support."[29]

Baldwin was at pains to avoid the worst features of the big foundations. "We don't want to form a 'trust,'" he explained, "that could dictate the direction of giving to new causes." And so the Fund would not be a perpetual organization. It would spend itself down to zero by gambling on "experiments in new movements" and new ideas. "We are not reformers trying to patch up the defects of existing institutions," Baldwin explained. "We are rather a group of those who would assist those forces which are experimenting with new institutions, new relationships." The Fund would finance cooperative movements, labor colleges and workers' schools, tenant farmer movements, and periodicals spreading new ideas. Most of all, the Fund would take the risk of refusing to be "bound by convention in the pre-judging of men or movements." The results might be uneven, but Baldwin hoped that "by the law of percentages" the outcomes would be "valuable to mankind in a fair proportion of cases."[30]

The Left Compass

The most important step was organizing a board of directors to make funding decisions. Sinclair, who was too mercurial to be relied upon anyway, bowed out of consideration early in favor of seeking funding for his own projects. In his place, Baldwin emerged as the Garland Fund's central figure, its "kingpin," as one insider later put it. And from the start, Baldwin sought out "persons of wide contact" with "a practical point of view" and with what he described as "a knowledge of how best to promote the cause of freedom."[31]

Baldwin identified an evolving group of about a dozen people, "intentionally mixed," as he put it, to include a variety of liberal and left-leaning views. "We were a mixed group," he explained, designed to span what he called "the left compass" of American politics. Among the first people he tapped was James Weldon Johnson, leader of the National Association for the Advancement of Colored People. Johnson was the NAACP's first Black executive secretary and a close associate of its founder, W. E. B. Du Bois.[32]

Baldwin leaned heavily on people in the liberal press and the free speech movement, which made sense given his hopes to alter public opinion. Nine of the first twelve directors were members of the founding National Committee of the ACLU. Six were members of the civil liberties organization's Executive Committee, Frank Walsh of the Commission on Industrial Relations among them. Robert Morss Lovett was an editor at Lippmann's *New Republic* and a professor of English at the University of Chicago whose anti-war stance had been strengthened by the death of his son at Belleau Wood in 1918. Lewis S. Gannett served on the editorial staff of *The Nation*. Two years in, Gannett was joined by his colleague Freda Kirchwey, the magazine's managing editor.[33]

The labor movement took a seat at the table, too. Sidney Hillman, who had emigrated from Eastern Europe as a child, was president of the Amalgamated Clothing Workers of America, an innovative union pressing for a reorganization of labor around industry-wide unions rather than the narrow trade unions of the hidebound American Federation of Labor. Years later, he would be one of the most influential labor leaders in American history, an insider in the administration of Franklin Roosevelt and a key power broker in the new labor politics that industrial unions had helped create. A cluster of Hillman's closest advisors at the Amalgamated Clothing Workers would serve in and around the board for the American Fund's entire nineteen-year existence.[34]

Two directors were members of the Socialist Party. Norman Thomas, a New York minister who had become deeply involved in Baldwin's wartime civil liberties activities, joined the board and served while taking over for Eugene Debs as the Socialist Party's perennial presidential candidate. Scott Nearing was a stern forty-year-old radical economist who had been fired from the Wharton School faculty at the University of Pennsylvania in 1915 for his critiques of industrial capitalism. Nearing (whom Baldwin affectionately called "an errant leftist") had joined the Socialist Party in 1917, only to be indicted (and ultimately acquitted) on charges of violating the Espionage Act. Nearing was especially concerned with what he called "the manufacture of public opinion."[35]

William Z. Foster, who had seen public opinion manufactured by U.S. Steel while directing the 1919 steel strike, served as the sole founding director from the Communist Party. Rabbi Judah Magnes, a wartime member of the Civil Liberties Bureau who would soon depart for Jerusalem to become the first chancellor of Hebrew University, took Frank Walsh's place after the populist lawyer bowed out of the Fund in its early weeks; Magnes joined the board because of his grave concerns for the future of "free political discussion" in a world in which "big business" controlled "the means of communications." Harry F. Ward, a prominent faculty member at Union Theological Seminary, was the founding chairman of the ACLU's board and a leading figure in liberal-left thinking about the relationship between Christianity and the labor movement.[36]

Social worker Mary McDowell was far and away the oldest in the group. Host to Sinclair as he wrote *The Jungle* in 1904, McDowell had founded a settlement house near the Chicago slaughterhouse district, where she was widely known as the "Angel of the Stockyards."[37]

Baldwin added further key figures to the Fund's world as well. Morris Ernst was an unsentimental New York lawyer who represented textile and clothing workers while advocating in favor of civil liberties and Black people's rights. Ernst became treasurer in 1922 and then a director in 1926. Elizabeth Gurley Flynn, who had barnstormed across the Midwest with Baldwin in 1920, was a fierce labor advocate with a longtime role as an organizer for the Industrial Workers of the World; in 1924 she replaced McDowell on the board. Clinton Golden, who had gone into the iron mines at age twelve, and who had taught himself the history and economics of the labor movement while working on railroads and in machine shops, joined the board in the same year as Flynn; a decade later he would become a founder and vice president of the new United Steelworkers of America.[38]

From its earliest days, a cast of carefully selected outside advisors consulted on grant applications and Fund initiatives. Baldwin chose Walter Lippmann to serve on a committee on publications. The philosopher John Dewey took a seat on the Fund's educational committee. Prominent labor economist Leo Wolman of Hillman's Amalgamated Clothing Workers, who briefly served as a director at the Fund, worked for more than a decade on Fund projects relating to the labor movement. Industrial safety expert Alice Hamilton, the first woman to serve on the Harvard faculty, collaborated with Wolman on a committee to evaluate proposals for industrial research. Future Supreme Court justice Felix Frankfurter, then on the faculty of Harvard Law School, offered counsel and advice and his extensive network of connections.[39]

In all, as Baldwin remembered, the Fund was a "reasonably happy family." It was a family with a particular politics, to be sure: a "family on the left," as he put it. But as Baldwin had hoped, the Fund's members were a diverse bunch nonetheless. They were from different backgrounds and had different projects. They proved, Baldwin later recalled, to have an "essential catholicity."[40]

Once a month, beginning in August 1922, the eclectic group gathered for lunch in a small dining room at the Civic Club in New York's Greenwich Village. Their work was to decide how to spend the foundation's money. The procedure was straightforward: a simple majority vote of the directors present at a given meeting, plus the proxy votes of any who were absent. There was no shortage of ideas—499 applications poured in during the Fund's first year, most of them in response to the widespread newspaper coverage of the Fund's inaugural press releases. The board of directors often disagreed about which of these proposals to support. It was too varied, fractious, and outspoken a group to do otherwise. Yet there was no shortage of money. The directors decided early on to accede to Garland's request that they not create a perpetual organization, and that they instead spend down the Fund's principal. Perhaps it was the rare abundance of resources this posture afforded, or perhaps it was the unceasing energy of Baldwin. But one way or another, the directors in the Fund's early years engaged in little of the bitter partisan infighting for which the left is so famous. They found ways to move past their disagreements. And within one month of the Fund's incorporation, it began to disburse money with the aim of remaking how Americans thought about their democracy.[41]

The very first grant by the Fund supported West Virginia members of the United Mine Workers, still reeling from a long and violent strike that had culminated in open warfare with heavily armed sheriffs' deputies. It was precisely the kind of spending Baldwin believed the Fund should do—a grant to sustain the kinds of labor union efforts that the new ACLU was defending in the courts. Baldwin had tapped most of the Fund's directors for their expertise in labor organizing and industrial change. Money for the mine workers was money in pursuit of a vision of economic life Sidney Hillman and his allies described as industrial democracy. The idea meant different things to different people; disagreement over its definition would produce some of the fiercest controversies in the Fund's two-decade history. But the Fund's directors shared a conviction that industrial democ-

The Fund's first grant in 1922 went to dissident miners in the West Virginia coal wars; here pictured turning over weapons to the state militia in 1921.

racy meant defending workers like West Virginia's miners and giving them a say in the basic institutions shaping their lives.[42]

Baldwin cast the Fund's net widely. He aimed, he told the *New York Tribune*, to "survey the entire field in the United States, examining every new movement particularly in industry and economics which is directed to the fundamental evils of our present society." And he imagined that the Fund would invest in "the field of propaganda for free speech and civil liberties," issues that had been "brought to the front by the war and by conditions since."[43]

What Baldwin did not quite anticipate was that, from almost the very start, the problem of race would rise to the forefront of the Fund's agenda and take center stage in its internal controversies. A small grant supported ACLU efforts to block the government's effort to strip Hindu immigrants from South Asia of their citizenship on the basis of their race; a further small award backed legal defense for Native peoples in North America, and several additional projects financed advocacy on behalf of Chinese Americans. But emancipatory efforts in Black communities would ultimately prove to be the defining problem for the Fund's operation, the key to its historical legacy. Labor causes were Baldwin's initial priority; he believed that injustice ran along class lines first and racial ones second. He had included James Weldon Johnson on the Fund board almost as an afterthought. But no one would exert more lasting influence on the Fund than the quiet NAACP leader. Among the very first grant applications were requests for help in unionizing African American workers. And one of the Fund's first and most significant awards went to finance the fight against lynching. If Baldwin thought he had set the race question aside after St. Louis, he was sorely mistaken. For the heart of the Fund board, industrial democracy and racial equality would come to be parts of the same problem.[44]

What Is April Farm?

APRIL FARM
Coopersburg, Pa.

Garland's April Farm recruited members to a utopian commune that rejected private property and marriage.

6

Free Love Farm

*Charles Garland, I am convinced, is a man extraordinary.
Possibly he's a saint.*

RABBI LEWIS BROWNE IN THE *WASHINGTON TIMES*

While Roger Baldwin was incorporating the American Fund for Public Service to change the world, Charles Garland was retreating from it. With a small collection of idealists and disaffected young people, he sought refuge from a competitive society in a utopian communal living arrangement.

Garland had given away his inheritance, but he retained trust accounts yielding $15,000 annually at a time when unionized carpenters in Boston could expect to earn $2,000 in a year. With his money he bought a small sixty-acre farm from a farmer named Joe April in North Carver, Massachusetts, about twenty miles from his mother's home on the Cape. He called it April Farm, simply enough. And he aimed to set up a better way of life.[1]

Utopian communities in the United States stretched back deep into the nineteenth century. In the 1820s, Welsh textile manufacturer Robert Owen's planned socialist community at New Harmony, Indiana, aimed to model "a new moral world." In 1841, a community called Brook Farm, west of Boston, became the first of dozens of American communities designed around French utopian Charles Fourier's system of cooperative social life. John Humphrey Noyes's Oneida Community, established in upstate New York in 1847, featured communal living arrangements for several hundred men and women along with an elaborately spiritual sexual system he called "complex marriage."[2]

The early twentieth century witnessed a little-remembered revival of the earlier utopian commune tradition. If nineteenth-century communities had offered escapes from the exploitation of wage labor and the suffocating hegemony of the nuclear family, their twentieth-century heirs stood for the rejection of consumerism and regimented mass production. In the desert north of Los Angeles in 1914, a socialist politician and minister named Job Harriman established an experimental cooperative called Llano del Rio, aiming, as one historian put it, "to demonstrate the validity and desirability of socialism to a skeptical nation." Within a few years, more than a thousand people had moved in; the colony relocated to Louisiana when its wells ran dry. In Stelton, New Jersey, an anarchist colony sprang up in 1914, made up of several dozen families organized around a progressive, counterculture school called the Modern School. The Stelton colony and its school, which thrived for a decade and a half, aimed to educate a new generation of children to resist the conformist tendencies of mass society. Dozens of other communes appeared in these same years, ranging from evangelical communes like Bethel College in Topeka, Burning Bush in East Texas, and Zion City outside Chicago, to the Nevada Colony (a spin-off from Llano) and the Army of Industry, which set up communal living in spartan conditions in Auburn, California.[3]

Charles Garland visited both Llano and Stelton as he planned April Farm. Back in North Carver, he dynamited stumps from the fields and bought a tractor to remove rocks and debris. He renovated a chicken coop in the farm's barn to serve as low-ceilinged living quarters. And in 1924, when neither the land nor the living arrangements in New Carver turned out to suffice, Garland moved April Farm to a larger, two-hundred-acre farm on fertile agricultural land south of Allentown, Pennsylvania.[4]

The Pennsylvania location of April Farm boasted an orchard of 5,000 trees, mostly apple and peach. Garland designed an informal system of cooperative work-sharing alongside modest $10 cash contributions paid monthly by each of the farm's approximately two dozen residents. Garland himself labored nine or ten hours each day. He ate simple food in a communal setting. "Work to him," wrote one reporter in the *Washington Times* in 1923, was "lovely, beautiful, gloriously cheering." Here, the *Times* concluded, was a "heroic" and "earnest" effort to "point the way to a new social order." Those around him seemed to love it, too. Determined to re-

Charles Garland at April Farm in the early 1920s.

nounce his claims to private property, Garland deeded April Farm to the farm's residents, who ran it as a trust.[5]

Residents at April Farm included a conscientious objector from the First World War, as well as a former member of the Industrial Workers of the World named James Slovick, who had led the Marine Transport Workers in Philadelphia before being sentenced to prison by Judge Landis in the mass Chicago trial of the IWW in 1918. A handful of anarchists from Stelton relocated to April Farm once it moved to Pennsylvania.[6]

Some observers called the residents "philosophical anarchists." But neither they nor Garland hewed to any one view of the world. The farm's members announced that their community was "non-sectarian and strictly non-political." Garland aimed to create a community in which like-minded people would be able to express themselves as they truly were, freed of the encumbrances of social life in the outside world. April Farm "was an experiment in social science," explained the group's application for incorporation to the Pennsylvania secretary of state in 1925. The basic idea of the commune, as a pamphlet published by the group that same year explained, was common ownership: "the elimination of private property within the group." Citing Brook Farm and the Fourierist experiments that had captured the attention of nineteenth-century luminaries like Hawthorne, Emerson, and Thoreau, April Farm described "experimental work in co-operative community life" as its central project: the replacement of individual profit with collective well-being. To the charge that this meant communism, Garland and his fellow residents responded that their form of community undertook to "gather together those who believe in its methods and to build on the strength of their voluntary effort." Newcomers were invited to a six-month probationary period. At the end of six months, April Farm required those receiving permanent invitations to divest themselves of their private property and to devote themselves to the group.[7]

Like many of its nineteenth-century forerunners, Garland's commune experimented with sexual freedoms, too. April Farm adopted a collective arrangement for sexual freedom alongside communal property and cooperative labor. The newspapers called April Farm a "free-love colony for radical college girls and men." But Garland, like John Humphrey Noyes before him, had ideas about sex that were more utopian than they were titillating. Marriage, Garland told one reporter, was "too closely tied up with the idea of private property." In marriage, "a man owns a woman and a woman owns a man," but ownership seemed like the wrong framework. Such arrangements, Garland insisted, amounted to "slavery, and slavery kills love."[8]

Opposition to marriage did not, for Garland, mean surrender to animal passions or indiscriminate desire. Garland pursued what he called "a spiritual interpretation" of marriage. Roger Baldwin, who later recalled days in the apple orchard at April Farm, said that Garland "never did strike me as a fellow who talked about or was much interested in sex." He was, by all accounts including Baldwin's, handsome and physically attractive. He had three or four romantic partners during his time at April Farm. Later in the 1920s, fallout from his love affairs would produce real trouble. But in April Farm's early years, as Garland saw it, sex served as a way for commune members to "surrender their better selves" to one another. It was, Garland insisted, an occasion for connecting to the goodness of people's hearts.[9]

Flapper Visits Garland's Love Farm and Tells of Life She Led in Guise of a Lonely Wayfarer Seeking Aid

GARLAND'S LOVE NEST AND FIRST "SOULMATE" —At the top, the Cape Cod farmhouse where the millionaire put his love theories into practice; at the right, the kitchen; and above, Lillian Conrad.

Society page columnists like the Hearst papers' "Flapper" pursued Garland's commune for salacious stories.

April Farm seemed to thrive. The residents built a packing house for canning fruit from the orchard. They installed electricity to light the farm buildings and power basic machinery. A new irrigation system watered the fruit trees and new cabins housed the residents. One woman who moved to April Farm from Stelton recalled the "beautiful peach and apple orchards," a vegetable garden, and "a communal dining room." Her "first spring there," she added, "was the happiest of my life." Neighbors in Pennsylvania remembered Garland as "easy-going," tall, and intelligent, as the kind of person from whom one could borrow equipment at a moment's notice. Reporters found him baking bread or tending his fields or working his favorite tractor: a Fordson model manufactured by the Ford Motor Company. Garland said he would live indefinitely at April Farm as a "poor but happy farmer, content with his arduous labor, his books and his thoughts." His inheritance had launched a philanthropic foundation. And thanks to his remaining trusts, he had set in motion a community of cooperative farm labor and liberated sexuality.[10]

Onlookers from the surrounding community and in the press agreed for the most part that the young man seemed "supremely happy." It was as if he had displaced his concerns over the brute iniquity of the world. In one large donation, he had delegated his social obligations to men and women better equipped to navigate the politics of social change.[11]

For most Americans, however, and for many Black Americans in particular, injustice was not so easily set aside.

PART II
AGAINST JIM CROW

James Johnson in 1887, age sixteen, in his entering portrait at Atlanta University.

7

The Usual Crime

The American public has had grafted upon its mind ... the idea that the lynching of Negroes and the crime of rape invariably go together.
—JAMES WELDON JOHNSON, 1919

At first, he thought the approaching cries might be a band of hunters crashing through the woods. But as the noise grew closer, twenty-nine-year-old James Johnson realized his peril. The shouts were from hunters, of a sort, but he was the quarry. It was 1901, in Jacksonville, Florida. A party of armed white men had heard rumor of a Black man with a white woman in the secluded park. Soon the men came into view.

"Death turned and looked at me," Johnson remembered, "and I looked at death."[1]

This was not the first time that young James Johnson had found himself the target of a lynch mob. Seven years earlier, coming home to Jacksonville from school in Atlanta, Johnson had insisted on his right to buy a first-class train ticket. Georgia had not yet passed a Jim Crow law for railroad cars; Johnson may technically have been correct about his legal rights. But scandalized white passengers telegraphed word of his affront to the next town up the tracks. By the time Johnson's train arrived there, a crowd had formed with the intention of pulling the brazen young man off the train. A quick-witted Black train porter averted the danger by wrestling the indignant Johnson into the train's second class car.[2]

Nor was Jacksonville the last time Johnson would face a lynch mob. In 1918, newly appointed as an officer of the nine-year-old civil rights organization known as the National Association for the Advancement of Colored People, Johnson traveled to rural Georgia. Eleven African Americans had been killed in what began as an employment dispute between a white farmer and a Black laborer in the town of Quitman. The victims included a woman named Mary Turner, who had been near full term in a pregnancy, and whose only offense was to proclaim her husband's innocence. A white mob strung her upside down, doused her body in gasoline, and set her on fire. They cut the fetus from her belly and killed it, too. And then they riddled her hanging body with bullets.[3]

Quitman was a dangerous place for African Americans who even so much as questioned white supremacy. And sure enough, as Johnson talked to Black residents, a gang of white men ("a pretty tough-looking lot," Johnson remembered) began to follow him. Johnson guessed that the men were among the perpetrators of the Quitman lynchings. They meant to make him their twelfth victim. And so, after a sleepless night, and having gathered the information he needed, Johnson caught the first train out of town.[4]

Of Johnson's three near-lynchings, the Jacksonville mob in 1901 came closest to taking his life. One hundred and eight Black lives ended in violence that year at the hands of white southern lynchers. In the previous decade, such lynch mobs had killed a thousand people, and maybe more, most of them Black men. Now, in a Jacksonville park, the violence of white supremacy was coming for Johnson because of a mistake born of racism and hatred in a moment of turmoil and disorder. A massive fire had destroyed much of Jacksonville just a few days before. Johnson agreed to talk to a female reporter from an out-of-town Black newspaper about the devastating effects of the fire on the city's Black neighborhoods. Johnson wanted to tell her about how the fire department had refused to protect Black homes. He wanted to explain how the department had allowed the conflagration to burn the school where Johnson served as principal. The reporter was so light-skinned, however, as to seem white, at least from a distance. When a white streetcar conductor saw the two walking into a park, their innocent conduct triggered a storyline so deeply etched into southern white habits of mind as to call forth a virtually scripted response. The conductor sounded an alarm. A nearby state militia regiment, already assembled to keep the peace in the fire's aftermath, sprang into action. White militiamen armed with rifles and bayonets rose to the defense of white womanhood.[5]

Finding the pair in a clearing in the woods, the armed white men surged around Johnson, seized him, and began to beat him. They tore his clothes. "Kill the damned nigger! Kill the black son of a bitch," they yelled. Death by lynching seemed certain. Johnson believed that showing even the slightest sign of fear would seal his fate; any attempt to flee would be his undoing. But self-possession and dignity, he thought, might keep him alive. And so he submitted to the beating in hopes that something would intervene and cause it to stop. Johnson made no complaint when a white Jacksonville police officer placed him rather than his attackers under arrest and took him and his journalist companion to the militia's temporary headquarters. The commanding officer there turned out to be a Jacksonville lawyer who knew Johnson's family. He quietly released Johnson as soon as it became clear what had happened. Adrenaline carried Johnson all the way home. Only there did he collapse in a mix of anger, exhaustion, terror, and shame—shame, he wrote a few years later in a partly autobiographical novel, that he "belonged to a race that could be so dealt with," and shame, too, for his country, which claimed to be "the great example of democracy to the world."[6]

W. E. B. Du Bois would later describe Johnson's near-lynching in Jacksonville as the formative event in his friend's life. His brush with danger caused Johnson to move to New York on the verge of the Great Migration. Nearly 6 million African Americans would relocate from the South to the North during the next half century. Johnson would become a prominent figure in the first outpouring of Black creativity it produced, later known to many as the Harlem Renaissance. He would write poems on the violence of white supremacy and publish his influential novel, whose final scene climaxed in a spectacle lynching of the kind to which he himself had nearly fallen prey. As a writer and as a leader of the NAACP, Johnson would speak out about his own near-lynchings and about the thousands of others that turned out far worse.[7]

Johnson's experience also set a path for him into the world of American race politics—a path that would shape the course of his career for the next two decades. Johnson would become known for his elegant and refined manner, for the dignity with which he carried himself, and for the grace with which he treated others. Roger Baldwin described him as an artist and a scholar, someone who on the outside appeared "ill-fitted" for a fight.

Du Bois said that Johnson had "the fine soul of a poet." But beneath his refined surface, Johnson burned with a quiet anger at the violence that enforced Jim Crow. He crafted his own image as an indictment of the lawlessness of the lynch mob.[8]

In the wake of the First World War, Johnson would dedicate his life to ending the scourge of lynching. His work took him to the United States Congress, where tireless lobbying efforts ultimately failed despite an eleventh-hour grant from the new American Fund for Public Service. In the culture, however, Johnson would win important victories. At the very moment in which people like his new friend Baldwin were turning away from the formal politics of the ballot box, the futility of his work in Congress caused Johnson to do the same. Like Baldwin, Johnson stopped campaigning for congressmen's votes, at least for the time being, and took up campaigning for public opinion. Johnson aimed to change what Americans thought. And that effort drew him deep into the world of the American Fund.

The Fury of the Mob

Johnson was born James William Johnson in 1871. He was one of the few Black children in the Reconstruction South not to be the child of a formerly enslaved person. His maternal great-grandfather, Etienne Dillet, had been a white French soldier stationed in Haiti after France abolished slavery in its colonies in 1794. His maternal great-grandmother was a Black woman there named Hester Argot. When Napoleon restored slavery in most of France's American colonies in 1802, Dillet hurried Hester and their son, Stephen (James's maternal grandfather), off the island on a vessel that eventually made landfall in the Bahamas. Johnson's maternal grandmother, Mary Symonett, moved with her daughter Helen (Johnson's mother) to New York City before the Civil War. Mary and Helen fled back to the Bahamas soon after South Carolina fired on Fort Sumter in 1861 out of fear that if the South won the war their freedom might be taken away, even in the North.[9]

On Johnson's paternal side, his father, also named James Johnson, was born a free man in Virginia in 1830 before moving as a child to New York and then to the Bahamas to follow his love interest, Helen. The two married. And meanwhile James thrived as the head waiter at an exclusive hotel in the booming economy of the wartime Bahamas. (Confederate blockade runners and English merchants used the islands as a layover.) During the postwar Bahamian recession, James and Helen moved to Jacksonville, which was fast becoming a winter destination for well-heeled northerners. Harriet Beecher Stowe, the author of *Uncle Tom's Cabin*, wintered there beginning in 1867.[10]

Tourist dollars and a clientele of former abolitionists made the city an unusually appealing place for Black Americans during Reconstruction. The younger James Johnson later remembered that the Jacksonville of the 1870s was "known far and wide as a good town for Negroes." The older James Johnson purchased a large home and found a new job, this time in the exclusive St. James Hotel, where the head waiter held a position of social authority and commanded a good salary. Johnson's mother worked as a schoolteacher at the Stanton Normal School, one of the leading institutions of Black education in the state. The family acquired modest but not insignificant holdings in local real estate.[11]

The Johnson family was part of a thriving Black middle class in postwar Jacksonville. In 1880 there were at least thirty-eight Black-owned businesses in the city. Successful tradesmen and merchants owned leading stores like Abraham Campbell's famous meat and poultry stall in the city market, and Milton Christopher's legendary produce market. Black businessmen ran small manufacturing shops, a real estate agency, clothing and shoe stores, oyster markets, and beauty parlors. Others worked as contractors and home builders. A Black-owned photography studio boasted white and Black patrons. There were four Black doctors in the city. The flourishing economy produced an array of voluntary and civic organizations, too. The Duval Fire Engine & Hose Company started as a volunteer institution in 1876 and was incorporated into the new municipal fire department a decade later. Charitable associations like the Benevolent Association of Colored Folks and the Colored Orphan's Home Association provided aid for needy members of the Black community. The Colored Law and Order League upheld community standards and policed crime. The Colored Medical Protective Health Association and the Colored Relief Bureau looked out for the community's medical needs.[12]

There was racial segregation in the Jacksonville of Johnson's childhood, too. But segregation in Reconstruction Jacksonville was more often a matter of custom than of law. Even then, Jim Crow stopped short of several important areas in the city's life.

Florida's constitution had been written in 1868 by Republicans in a convention at which nearly 40 percent of the delegates were Black. The charter they produced promised equality in voting rights at the state level. In the city of Jacksonville, the political power of African Americans was even greater. Black people made up a slight majority of the population, and the city was a bastion of Republican Party politics. In the year Johnson was born, Black men served in citywide elected office as marshal, as tax assessor, and as justice of the peace. Black men sat on the city council. Johnson's own father served as an official in the small nearby suburb known as LaVilla. In the city proper, elections produced a Black mayor and an interracial city council as late as 1887. That same year saw a Black man appointed to the municipal court and another named to the three-person police commission.[13]

Political participation routinely produced legislative victories for Florida's Black community. In 1873, when Johnson was two years old, the Republican-controlled state legislature enacted a civil rights bill prohibiting discrimination in public accommodations like inns, railroads, and theaters. The bill went even further. It repealed every existing Florida law and local ordinance in which the word "white" was used to discriminate on the basis of "race, color, or previous condition of servitude." The state's Republican governor promptly signed the civil rights bill into law.[14]

Johnson's family took advantage of the freedoms afforded them. The family typically sat in first-class cars when they traveled by rail. Johnson's first two childhood friends were white boys, and the family's friends and neighbors included whites as well as Blacks. As a newborn, when his own mother fell ill, Johnson was nursed by a white neighbor named Mrs. Mc-Cleary. ("In the land of black mammies," an older Johnson liked to quip, "I had a white one.")[15]

From his earliest years, Johnson took part in the basic trappings of middle-class life. His mother trained him on the family piano and read aloud to him from the novels of Dickens. A precocious young Johnson was soon racing through classics of European literature, ranging from the Christian allegory of *The Pilgrim's Progress* and the macabre fairy tales of

James Johnson, at center, as an elementary school student at the Stanton School in Jacksonville.

the Brothers Grimm to the poetry of Sir Walter Scott. As a teen, Johnson played on a baseball team known as "the Roman Cities"; the team was all Black, but it played before integrated Jacksonville crowds. Johnson's parents made sure that he and his brother had the chance to see the world, too. In 1884, the family took a long trip to New York City, where they spent time with T. Thomas Fortune, editor of the nation's leading Black newspaper, the *New York Age*. Fortune's brother lived in Jacksonville, where the editor had been a houseguest of the Johnsons. Johnson also traveled to the Bahamas as a child, where he met the family of his maternal grandfather, Stephen, who had been smuggled out of Haiti as a small child eight decades earlier.[16]

Beginning at the age of five, Johnson attended the school where his mother taught. The Stanton Normal School had been built in 1869 with funds from the Freedmen's Bureau and from the American Missionary Association, an antislavery organization whose money helped build scores of schools across the South after Emancipation. In 1887, Johnson left Jacksonville to continue his studies at Atlanta University, where he attended both high school and college, graduating in 1894. Johnson received a classical education modeled on the academic courses Atlanta University's first three presidents had taken at Yale: classes such as Greek, Latin, and algebra. (Like Stanton Normal, the university was another American Missionary Association school.) Time in Georgia also gave Johnson something like an education in the world outside Jacksonville. He encountered strict racial separation in the city of Atlanta. Even the university's white teachers were shunned by the city's white community for their dealings with Black students.[17]

On graduating, Johnson returned to Jacksonville. His many talents bloomed. He became the young principal of his alma mater, Stanton Normal. Journalism caught his eye, too. In 1895, he founded the *Daily American*, a short-lived but spirited newspaper that served briefly as an antidote to Jacksonville's white-owned and racist *Florida Times-Union*. He read law in the office of a local white lawyer and became the first Black lawyer to be admitted to the Duval County bar. Soon he began practicing law with a friend who was admitted shortly after him. Johnson handled the writing and the office work, while his partner took the courtroom roles.[18]

As if the work as school principal, newspaperman, and lawyer were not enough, Johnson took up songwriting, too. His younger brother, Rosamond, had moved to Boston as a teenager to study music at the New England Conservatory. By the late 1890s Rosamond was in New York performing in the country's most famous African American vaudeville show. Hosted by the legendary mixed-race impresario John Isham, *Oriental America* was the first show to appear on Broadway with an entirely Black cast. Rosamond had a lead role and soon became a prominent songwriter in the city's racially integrated theatrical scene. James joined in, writing lyrics for Rosamond's scores. Together with a prominent Black showman named Bob Cole, the two brothers wrote operettas and highly successful musical theater songs like "Under the Bamboo Tree" and "Congo Love Song." Their work was a hit with Broadway audiences, white and Black alike. In 1900, the brothers wrote a song on the occasion of Abraham Lincoln's birthday. They called it "Lift Every Voice and Sing." Its influence spread. The NAACP dubbed it the Negro National Anthem. It is still sung and celebrated a century later.[19]

Even as Johnson flourished, however, Jacksonville's Black community suffered. Looking back decades later, Johnson would reflect that for at least the first fifty years of his life, conditions for Black people in Florida and all around the South were in precipitous decline.[20]

Johnson was five years old when Florida's white Democrats swept an interracial Republican administration from the statehouse in 1876. Johnson was ten when the state prohibited racial intermarriage. Four years later, in 1885, a new state constitution adopted a poll tax that disfranchised poor Black voters (and often poor white ones as well). In 1887, the newly reconstituted state legislature passed a Jim Crow law requiring railroads to separate passengers by race. (Heading off to Atlanta University that year, Johnson recalled, was his first experience on a Jim Crow car.) The city of Jacksonville remained the state's last haven of mixed-race Republican rule for some time longer. But that could not last in a state dominated by the party of white supremacy. In 1889, Democrats in the state capital rewrote the Jacksonville city charter to eliminate home rule. The new charter authorized the governor to appoint the city council and gave the governor's appointees the power to select the mayor. At the same time, a complex statewide multiple-ballot scheme aimed to make voting as difficult as possible. By 1891, 2,228 of the 2,365 registered voters in Jacksonville's Duval County were white. Two years later, with Jacksonville now made safe for Jim Crow, the state legislature restored home rule to the city. Under white leadership again, the new Jim Crow Jacksonville promptly prohibited mixed-race education and segregated the city's streetcars.[21]

Jacksonville's story was repeated in cities across the South at the end of the nineteenth century. In state after state, the relative freedoms of Reconstruction gave way in the face of Jim Crow's violent onslaught. The Supreme Court's 1896 decision in *Plessy v. Ferguson*, which had followed on the heels of Booker T. Washington's Atlanta Compromise address, confirmed the constitutionality of state Jim Crow laws like the 1887 Florida law requiring racial segregation on the rails. Equally important decisions made it nearly impossible to protect African Americans against private discrimination. The Fourteenth Amendment, ratified in 1868, provided that no *state* could discriminate. The Supreme Court reasoned that private businesses were not states and thus not bound by the amendment. Making matters worse, the Court's *Civil Rights Cases* decision in 1883 struck down Congress's effort to reach private businesses. The Fourteenth Amendment, concluded the Court, did not grant Congress the power to regulate private discrimination. Discrimination by railroads, wrote Justice Joseph

P. Bradley, was beyond Congress's reach. So, too, was discrimination in theaters and hotels.[22]

Nowhere were the declining fortunes of Black Americans more apparent than in the violence of white lynch mobs. "The race," Johnson later observed, had been subjected to two crushing blows—first "Disfranchisement and Jim-Crowism" and then "the fury of the mob." In his adult life, during his time at the NAACP and in his service on the board of the American Fund for Public Service, Johnson would dedicate himself to reversing both.[23]

The half century after 1882 witnessed at least 2,278 documented lynchings in the South, taking the lives of some 2,805 victims. Estimates going back to Reconstruction put the total number far higher; according to one leading student of the phenomenon, the number of deaths at the hands of southern lynch mobs was probably closer to 5,000. Eighty-seven percent of lynching victims were Black. Participants in lynch mobs, by contrast, were nearly all white. And few participants were ever punished for their actions. In 1917, the NAACP estimated that out of more than 2,000 lynching episodes in the previous thirty years—many of them public events in broad daylight—fewer than six men had been convicted on criminal charges.[24]

In Florida, where Johnson grew up, 311 Black Americans were lynched during the era of Jim Crow. The toll of victims began to mount while Johnson was a teenager and young man; some 105 Black men were lynched in Florida during the fifteen years from 1889 to 1903, precisely when Johnson was himself most vulnerable. Leaving Florida for school in Atlanta offered no respite. Georgia witnessed more lynchings than any other state; more than sixty-one of them, according to an NAACP count, took place while Johnson was enrolled at Atlanta University. And as time went by, the brutality of lynchings seemed to grow. A few years after Johnson left Atlanta, a Black man named Sam Hose was lynched not far from the city. Hose, a farm laborer, stood accused of murdering his white employer. Later investigations would suggest that Hose was acting in self-defense. But the posse assembled to track him down was convinced otherwise. By the time the pursuers captured Hose, rumors had spread that he had also raped his employer's wife. Hose admitted to the murder. Even under torture, he denied the rape charge. Nonetheless, the mob took Hose to a public road where some 2,000 whites had gathered. According to a euphemistic *New York Tribune* report, the mob cut off his "ears, fingers, and other portions of his body." As spectators cheered, the mob tied Hose to a stake and burned him alive. When the fire was finished, they cut his charred bones into pieces and distributed the fragments as souvenirs.[25]

Hose's lynching was one of a deadly parade of spectacle lynchings in the South near the end of the nineteenth century. Time and again, mobs of white men took the law—or what they supposed the law to be—into their own hands and executed Black Americans in the most terrible fashion. In Texas in 1897, a Black man named Robert Hilliard was burned to death before a crowd whose cheers grew louder with evidence that he was still conscious during the ordeal. (A local publishing company hawked souvenir photographs of the event.) In Dade County, Florida, in early 1901, a mob of thirty men shot two Black murder suspects dead through the bars of a jail cell when the jailer refused to surrender the keys.[26]

Lynchings were said to be the punishment for Black men who raped white women—this, white southerners insisted, was the "usual crime" to which lynching was the only sufficient response. But the truth was that only one in four lynchings involved even an allegation of rape, and many of those, like the lynching of Sam Hose, were almost certainly fabricated. Approximately eighty lynching victims during the period were women, several of them pregnant. Lynching, as Johnson put it, was thus not really about "punishment for the crime of rape," nor even about "the alleged criminality of the negro." It was instead "a relic of slavery," representing the determination of white southerners to continue to assert the "dominance" of white supremacy "by force." There was one thing that connected the thousands of lynchings, and it was not rape accusations. Lynching was the ultimate expression of the system of Jim Crow and racial subordination that spread across Jacksonville and the South during the last two and a half decades of the nineteenth century. It was a continuation and extension of the Jim Crow state in violent form, a kind of "state-sanctioned terrorism," as historians have put it, designed to create "a climate of terror" among the region's Black communities.[27]

And yet the Supreme Court shrugged off the violence of lynching, using the same logic by which it dismissed discrimination in theaters and on railroads. Mob violence was beyond the scope of Congress's authority because it, too, was private conduct. The first such ruling came in 1875, in a case called *United States v. Cruikshank*, arising out of the Colfax Massacre in Louisiana on Easter Sunday 1873. A veritable army of white men, many of them veterans of the Confederate army, massacred dozens of Black people in a bitter election dispute. Historians have called it the last battle of the Civil War. But the Supreme Court ruled that the federal government lacked the authority to prosecute the offenders because the mob was a private group, not a state. "The Fourteenth Amendment," wrote Chief Justice Morrison Waite, "adds nothing to the rights of one citizen as against another." If state officials were involved in their capacity as government employees, then their conduct implicated the Constitution. But if they took off their uniforms and acted as private citizens, or if they simply looked the other way as the white mob did its terrible business, then their behavior, no matter how violent and destructive, was beyond the Constitution's purview.[28]

As a young man at Atlanta University, Johnson raged at the sickening drumbeat of lynchings and at the nation's supposed inability to intervene. The "only way to stop this lynching business," Johnson concluded in the early 1890s, was "to take a hand in it." If a "few white men were found strung up," he said bitterly, "the South would come to see" that lynching was "not such funny business after all." Even a youthful Johnson, however, understood that violence was not a practical tactic. Whites greatly outnumbered Black people in most of the South, and the resources of the white community made overt physical resistance futile.[29]

And so, after his near-lynching in 1901, James Johnson did what many Black people seeking greater freedoms would do in the first two centuries of American history. He moved north. It was the third time in a century that members of his family had relocated to escape dangerous political conditions. Moving north was not merely flight; it offered a chance to regain some of the political power that Jim Crow had stolen in places like Jacksonville. In time, migration would lead Johnson to the NAACP. Eventually, it would bring him to the American Fund. But at the turn of the century, he had a very different strategy. Migration, Johnson hoped, might alter the political landscape of the nation and thereby change the calculus of the ballot box. In particular, it might press the Republican Party, the party of Lincoln and the party of Johnson's childhood, to attend once again to Black voters. In New York, Johnson would become part of the effort to reconnect the Republican Party to its emancipatory roots—an effort that began in the patronage empire of Booker T. Washington.

Greatest American Game

Johnson found in New York a Black community where he could thrive. Not since his youth had he lived in a place where the possibilities for African Americans were as wide. He took up residence at the Hotel Marshall on West 53rd Street, at the heart of what he called "Negro Bohemia." The Marshall was home both to the city's leading Black artists and musicians and to its rising Black political class. Johnson entered a mixed-race world of Broadway musicals, writing lyrics alongside his brother Rosamond. He also met the patronage manager for the New York branch of Booker T. Washington's powerful Tuskegee network, a man named Charles Anderson.[30]

For Johnson, Anderson represented a new hope for advancement through politics after a decade of decline in the South. Anderson was the key figure in the Black wing of the city's Republican Party. Johnson recalled him as a "cold" and "calculating" player in the hard game of politics; Anderson, he continued, was "an astute politician, keen in his study of men and the uses to be made of them." Charlie Anderson was on intimate terms with the bosses of the state's white Republican leadership. He was close to party elites like Secretary of War Elihu Root, and even the new president of the United States, Theodore Roosevelt, who had been elevated suddenly by William McKinley's assassination. Anderson functioned as a vital intermediary between the Tuskegee machine and the Republican Party. He also worked as Booker T. Washington's enforcer. A fierce Tuskegee loyalist, Anderson operated behind the scenes to punish Washington's critics in the Black community. He got them fired from government jobs. He placed bad stories about them in the newspapers. "I can bet on my friends," he liked to say, "and they can bet on me."[31]

To place such bets, Anderson needed talented friends. Johnson fit the bill. He already knew Washington from a speech the Black leader had given in Jacksonville to mark Emancipation Day in 1898. Johnson was also connected to the Tuskegee machine through the Johnson family friend and newspaperman T. Thomas Fortune, who was a leading figure in Washington's network. And so, when Anderson established the New York City Colored Republican Club to support Roosevelt in the 1904 presidential election, he asked Johnson to serve as the club's vice president. Johnson agreed, and soon became an enthusiastic supporter of Republican politics. The "big guns of the campaign," Johnson later recalled, "boomed" in the club's meeting room. Black musicians came down the street from the Hotel Marshall to perform. Johnson and his brother even wrote a campaign tune, which Roosevelt himself proclaimed "bully good."[32]

Most of all, Johnson learned about the art of politics, the "greatest American game," as he came to call it. From inside the Republican machine he saw the force of "political loyalty" in the "vast army of actual and prospective holders of political jobs, from street cleaner up." Roosevelt's reelection in 1904 catapulted Anderson to the important (and lucrative) post of collector of internal revenue for Wall Street and the New York waterfront. Johnson, in turn, took over the presidency of the Colored Republican Club. He had become a consequential figure in Washington's circle.[33]

In his new position, Johnson put into practice Charlie Anderson's lessons about loyalty. An increasingly bitter fight in Black politics was breaking out between Washington and his younger rival, W. E. B. Du Bois. Johnson knew Du Bois, too. They had met in 1904, shortly after Johnson read Du Bois's searing 1903 book, *The Souls of Black Folk*. The two men had much in common. Born three years apart, they were college-educated Black Americans dedicated to equal rights. Johnson had "been much impressed" by Du Bois's book, at least privately, notwithstanding its uncompromising criticisms of the Tuskegee strategy of accommodation. *The Souls of Black Folk* accused the Tuskegee power brokers of speeding "the disfranchisement of the Negro," accelerating the "status of civil inferiority for the Negro," and reducing aid to the "higher education of Negro youth." Du Bois charged that Booker T. Washington promoted a fantasy of economic progress without political strength. Du Bois, by contrast, insisted on the priority of political rights. He contended that there could be little progress in civil rights (including economics) without the protections afforded by political power.[34]

Johnson kept his admiration for Du Bois private. He demurred when

Du Bois invited him to join the Niagara Movement, an organization established in 1905 as a rebuke to Tuskegee's more cautious strategies. And Washington rewarded Johnson's loyalty. Within a year, Anderson arranged to have Johnson appointed to the Consular Service, a merit position with a civil service rank that seemed likely to offer a secure position for a Black officeholder even if the political winds changed. Secretary of State Philander Knox appointed Johnson to the post of U.S. consul in a backwater Venezuela harbor town known as Puerto Cabello. A congratulatory letter from Washington graced the festivities at Johnson's farewell dinner in May. Johnson, it seemed, had been confirmed as a solid Tuskegee man.[35]

Venezuela meant respite from the racial insults so common in life in the United States. The diplomatic post also came with new status in the Black coalition of the Republican Party. During stints back in Washington, Johnson was now invited into the informal "Black Cabinet," a small group of leaders and political appointees who advised Republican presidents—first Roosevelt and then William Howard Taft—on questions touching the nation's Black community. Anderson and Washington were the group's unofficial leaders, and Johnson soon became a key member.[36]

After two years of service in Puerto Cabello, Johnson sought a transfer and promotion. Roosevelt raised the prospect of a plum job on the French Riviera, but Secretary of State Root recommended against it; the appointment of a Black man to so desirable a post, he said, "simply could not be done." Instead, the State Department transferred Johnson to Corinto in Nicaragua, a moderately more important post, where Johnson had a front row seat for the landing of American marines during the civil war that soon broke out.[37]

In 1910 Johnson married the urbane Grace Nail, the daughter of an influential Black family with real estate holdings in Harlem. Again, he sought a transfer to a more cosmopolitan setting. The tropical climate of Corinto irked Johnson, and Grace's family thought it unsuitable for her. Charlie Anderson met with the president personally to lobby on Johnson's behalf, and by early 1912 Johnson told Grace he was "quite sure" he would get a promotion. As the year progressed, however, the transfer became mired in what he called the "political tangle" of the three-way presiden-

*Johnson as U.S. consul with a sentry in Central
America, between 1909 and 1912.*

tial race between Taft, Theodore Roosevelt, and the Democratic nominee, Woodrow Wilson. Wilson's victory in November sealed his fate. Taft issued a lame-duck promotion, but the new secretary of state, William Jennings Bryan, canceled it and told Johnson that he should be grateful to have a job at all. Johnson resigned.[38]

Johnson later remembered that his dislike of Woodrow Wilson "came nearer to constituting keen hatred for an individual than anything I have ever felt." Wilson's election, he believed, served as "a signal" to the white South that "the country had been turned over not only to the Democratic Party in general, but to the South in particular." Federal buildings, Johnson wrote, had once been "the only place in the South where a Negro could pretend to share in the common rights of citizenship." But with Wilson's assumption of the presidency, newly emboldened Democratic appointees changed that. Johnson complained that the Democrats' postal service appointees in the South "cut 'Jim Crow' windows" into the side of federal buildings to force Black customers "to get their mail, without coming into the post office." Black post office customers "had to stand in sun or rain until the last white person on the inside had been served." The Capitol witnessed new segregation, too. In 1917 Johnson was denied a meal at the Supreme Court's cafeteria. Two years later he protested the whites-only policy at the public restaurant in the Library of Congress.[39]

Beginning in the fall of 1914, Johnson channeled his anger at Wilson and the Democrats through a weekly column in the *New York Age*, the newspaper edited by T. Thomas Fortune. The paper was squarely in the Tuskegee camp; indeed, by 1914 Washington had quietly become the newspaper's majority owner. Fortune, in turn, had become the informal dean of Black journalism. Yet leadership in the Black community was changing. Fortune left the paper in the same year Johnson arrived, and though the older man was replaced by another adherent to the gospel of Tuskegee, Booker T. Washington's empire grew fragile. Washington himself was increasingly hobbled. A malicious accusation associated him with a white woman in New York. Physically weakened and aging, he died in 1915.[40]

With Fortune and Washington out of the way, Johnson could write and speak his mind more freely. And in his new position, he developed an idea about the place of journalism and public opinion in Black America. Black papers, he wrote, were "not primarily newspapers." They were not the purveyors of truth for truth's sake, or at least not only that. They were "race papers," and as such they functioned as "organs of propaganda" by which the Negro could fight for what Johnson called the "right to contend for his rights." As Johnson saw it in 1915, the way to accomplish equality for Blacks was to produce propaganda promoting the power of the party of Lincoln and tearing down the party of Wilson.[41]

In editorial after editorial, Johnson excoriated Wilson's Democrats. Johnson condemned his old nemesis, William Jennings Bryan, as "better fitted to be the teacher of the infant class in a large Sunday school" than to serve as secretary of state. "A Democratic vote cast in Maine," Johnson asserted in the *Age*, "is an endorsement and a strengthening of Democratic practices in Mississippi." Any Black voter who thought about adopting an independent stance between the parties, he announced, was "a lost sheep."[42]

In 1916, Johnson came out strongly for the Republican presidential nominee, Charles Evans Hughes. His friend Du Bois called on African Americans to reject both major parties and throw their vote to Eugene Debs, the Socialist candidate. But Johnson vocally supported the Republican nominee. In part, Johnson genuinely admired Hughes's work as associate justice on the Supreme Court. Hughes had penned the opinion in *Bailey v. Alabama*, a case in which the Court had overruled an Alabama law establishing criminal punishments for farm laborers who quit a job before the end of their contracts. Hughes wrote that the criminal enforcement of such contracts was a new slavery in violation of the Thirteenth Amendment. Most of Johnson's energy for the 1916 campaign, however, stemmed from his hatred of Wilson rather than from any special love for Hughes. In a civil rights conference at Amenia, New York, in the fall, Johnson said that "it was the duty of every colored man" to oppose Wilson, even if he had kept the U.S. out of the world war. In early October, Johnson urged a "solid Negro vote" to oppose the "Solid South" of the Democratic Party. Even if "you feel the Republican Party has done little for us," he pleaded, "tell in the name of God, what we are to expect from" the Democrats. On questions of race, Johnson wrote bitterly, Wilson was a "man of timidity, of indecision, of inaction, and of cowardice." Johnson told his old patron Charlie Anderson that defeating Wilson was "the most vital question that has confronted the colored voters of the United States in twenty years."[43]

It was not to be. Early election returns seemed to be headed in the Republican candidate's direction. But late results from western states turned the tide for Wilson. Hughes and the Republicans lost.

For Johnson, however, electoral loss came with a silver lining. The election seemed to bring new signs of progress for Black voters in the Republican Party. Hughes arranged for Johnson to appear on the platform at Madison Square Garden in his final campaign rally. Just before Election Day, the would-be president sat down with Johnson to talk about Black communities' concerns. Surely these were signs of recognition by the Republican leadership of the growing power of Black voters. The key, as Johnson saw it, was the fast-growing migration to the North. As Black populations grew in northern cities, they would garner increasing political clout. In the North, after all, African Americans could vote on the same basis as white Americans. The Black vote might now be a deciding factor in elections in some important northern states. Here was "real political power," Johnson wrote hopefully, not something to "be traded for a mess of pottage." The future of Black politics, Johnson concluded, lay "with colored voters in Northern and Border States."[44]

Four years later Johnson's hopes seemed to come to fruition in the election of Warren Harding. Johnson attended the Republican National Convention in Chicago in July 1920 as a member of the party's National Advisory Committee. Harding called on Johnson personally for advice and guidance. Twice Johnson traveled to Ohio to sit on Harding's porch and talk politics. The Ohioan, Johnson conceded privately, was "a man of very little imagination and seemingly of very little human sympathy." Harding was reluctant to speak publicly in defense of Black voting rights, to take a strong stance in opposition to lynching, or even to condemn discrimination in the federal civil service. The candidate's key advisors in the Republican Party believed that doing any of these things would cost Harding more white votes than the Black votes it might win. On the other hand, the party's 1920 platform included a plank that declared lynching "a terrible blot on our American civilization." No such anti-lynching provision had appeared on the 1916 platform. Here was more evidence that the Republicans were beginning to heed what Johnson saw as the new electoral calculus of northern migration. "The Republican Party would increase its chances of national success," Johnson argued, if it won the "pivotal states in the North where the Negro holds the balance of power." Harding himself seemed to bend toward the party's Black constituency when he held a public "Colored Voters Day" in his hometown of Marion at the height of the campaign season. His eventual statement on lynching was arguably stronger than the position that appeared in the party platform. So pronounced was Harding's gesture to Black voters that Democratic Party operatives spread rumors that his great-grandmother had been Black. A century later DNA testing would disprove the claim. But Harding's moderate stance for civil rights had gone just far enough to make the rumors plausible.[45]

When Harding won by a landslide, Johnson was ecstatic. The party of Lincoln swept the electoral college votes of every border state save Kentucky, which Harding lost by a hair. Republicans picked up an astounding sixty-three seats in the House of Representatives and ten seats in the Senate, turning slim majorities in each chamber into commanding positions. The entire federal government would be in the hands of the Republican Party. And in the weeks after the election, Johnson turned to thinking about what African Americans should get from the new Republican-controlled federal government. First on his list was an anti-lynching bill. Such a bill had been part of the Republican Party platform. Harding had personally offered support for the legislation, at least in principle. And the new Black voting bloc in the North had helped deliver him the election. With unified Republican government for the first time in a decade, federal anti-lynching reform seemed certain to follow.[46]

Explode the Rape Myth

Johnson took up the cause of federal anti-lynching legislation in a new role with the National Association for the Advancement of Colored People.

Founded in 1909 after a race massacre in Abraham Lincoln's hometown of Springfield, Illinois, the NAACP aimed to be a new and more militant organization for the defense of Black Americans. Du Bois, whose Niagara Movement had combined with prominent white progressives to form the organization's base, served as the group's publicity director and editor of its monthly journal, *The Crisis*. Initially, Johnson had declined to join the new organization out of loyalty to Booker T. Washington. Yet Johnson had earned Du Bois's continuing respect, and when Washington died in 1915, the NAACP welcomed Johnson into the fold. By the end of the next year, the organization appointed him as its field director, where his job was to organize new local chapters, especially in the South. ("I find it difficult to think of any other field which would allow me so large an opportunity for the advancement of the race," he wrote to NAACP president Joel Spingarn.) NAACP insiders celebrated; it was a "coup d'état," they said, to convert a loyalist from the very heart of Tuskegee.[47]

Traveling through the South as NAACP field director afforded Johnson a new view of Jim Crow, and in particular a new view of lynching. Building on his thinking about Black journalism and race propaganda, Johnson came to believe that the problem was a crisis of public opinion.

He concluded that lynching was like the problems with which students of public opinion and propaganda like George Creel and Walter Lippmann were grappling. Johnson shared his theory at an NAACP conference on lynching held in Carnegie Hall in the spring of 1919. The "whole problem," Johnson proclaimed, "rests upon public opinion." Any campaign against lynching, no matter what the method, would require confronting the fundamental outlook of white Americans. The candid truth of the matter, Johnson asserted, was that deep down "public opinion in the United States"—white opinion, anyway—"was not actually against lynching." Many white Americans were "horrified at the very thought of lynching," to be sure. But it was also true that "they do not condemn it." Deep in their unconscious, even those white people who professed to believe lynching was wrong also "feel that somehow or other perhaps it was the only thing that could be done under the circumstances." The reason was that the "American public has had grafted upon its mind," Johnson concluded, "the idea that the lynching of Negroes and the crime of rape invariably go together."[48]

Rape supplied the script for the lynch mob. But the rape narrative, Johnson noted, was a "distortion and misrepresentation." Lynching was not actually "a punishment for the crime of rape." It was really an assertion of white dominance. An NAACP study in 1918 proved as much, showing that only a small fraction of lynchings involved even an allegation of rape. The fact that lynch mobs targeted women as well as men was evidence of the same point. Johnson pointed out bitterly that the light skin color of many African Americans served as silent testimony that the real problem of interracial rape worked in the reverse direction. White men had been sexually exploiting Black women for centuries. Yet in the realm of public opinion, such facts seemed to make little or no difference. As Lippmann noted, scripts and stereotypes could exist almost without regard to fact. What mattered was that the rape myth had a hold on the popular imagination. It served as one of the stock ideas by which public opinion organized the chaotic experience of the world. As Johnson saw matters, the rape myth had been established by the "well directed propaganda" of white supremacy.[49]

In April 1920, the NAACP's executive secretary, a white progressive named John Shillady, resigned after being beaten by a mob during an investigative trip to Texas. Johnson assumed the post. As the first Black person to hold the organization's highest executive office, he determined to lead the NAACP in a project of counter-propaganda, one that would smash the mold of the conventional rape storyline. He would, as one NAACP organizer put it, "explode the rape myth" and rewrite the script of southern lynching. Like his recent acquaintance Roger Baldwin, who was formulating a parallel public opinion strategy of his own, Johnson knew that he would need money and resources for such an ambitious program. But his first attempt began in the U.S. Congress.[50]

Johnson's effort to alter America's lynching narrative commenced in earnest when Congressman Leonidas Dyer of Missouri introduced an anti-lynching bill into the new 67th Congress in 1921. Dyer's uncle, David Dyer, was the federal judge who had struck down St. Louis's residential segregation initiative as unconstitutional in 1916. The next year, Congressman Dyer's district in St. Louis had served as shelter for Black refugees streaming across the Mississippi to escape the East St. Louis race riots. Now Dyer proposed to make killings by mobs of three or more people a federal offense. With the NAACP's active encouragement, and with Johnson deeply involved, the bill proposed penalties for counties in which lynchings took place and prison sentences for state officials implicated in such killings. Dyer's bill also authorized federal protection for those charged with state crimes who had reason to fear that they would be lynched before the resolution of their case.[51]

For nearly the next year and a half, Johnson spent most of his working days in the Capitol. The House Judiciary Committee amended the bill around the edges, but under Johnson's watchful eye Dyer's bill retained its basic core. He lobbied representatives and senators, reminding them time and again of the increasingly important Black vote in their districts and in their states. Some refused to meet. But he was buoyed by the fact that many Republicans opened their doors to welcome him. He coordinated letter-writing campaigns and successfully fended off late-stage efforts to dilute the bill. All in all, Johnson said, the campaign for the Dyer bill represented "the greatest concerted action I have yet seen the colored people take."[52]

Dyer's bill touched off a ferocious struggle in the House of Representa-

Johnson at the head of the NAACP's annual convention, Detroit, 1921, with the anti-lynching bill in the balance.

tives. If enacted, it promised, as President Harding urged in his message to the new Congress, to "wipe the stain of barbaric lynching" from the American scene. But southern Democrats took up a bitter fight against the bill. And to do so, they turned to the conventional storyline of the lynch mob and sketched lurid scenes from the script of the rape myth. James Paul Buchanan of Texas opened the debate by raising "the crimes of the rape fiend." There was "not one spot of earth" in which the lynch mob would not avenge the "pitiless horror" of violated white womanhood, Buchanan spat. James F. Byrnes of South Carolina, who would later serve as a justice on the U.S. Supreme Court and as Truman's secretary of state, insisted that rape was responsible for "most of the lynchings in America." The real lawlessness, Byrnes asserted, was not lynching at all but the anti-lynching bill proposed by Dyer and the Republicans, which Byrnes insisted violated the Constitution by encroaching on the prerogatives of state criminal law.[53]

In graphic language, white southerners summoned fantastical visions of fearsome Black devils and innocent white women. What if "your wife or your daughter be criminally assaulted by an African brute," a fevered James Benjamin Aswell of Louisiana asked. "Thinking men," he continued, "recognize that rape or attempted rape is the primary cause of the mob spirit," and any bill put forward to stop such mobs was nothing more than an effort to protect "the assaulters of women"; to pass such a bill, he raved, would be "to sacrifice the fairest of God's creatures" to the "lust" of the "beast." Representative Finis Garrett of Tennessee drew applause from his Democratic colleagues when he urged that the bill's title be amended to read "A bill to encourage rape."[54]

Congressman John Tillman of Arkansas won still more applause when he pronounced that "the most dangerous and deadly animal living is not the man-eating tiger of the jungle, nor the blood-thirsty lion of the desert, nor the hooded cobra of India, not the diamond rattlesnake of the western plains, but the lewd brute"—the "black criminal" who "would defile or pollute" the "pure girlhood or womanhood" of "a million sweet-faced Virginias" singing innocently on their way to school. Patrick Drewry of Virginia conjured a vision of "the good wife, bleeding and choking," who with her final breath tells her husband "that a fiend in human form attacked her while she, singing in her home, was preparing for his home-coming." No laws, Drewry fumed, could stop the vengeance that would inevitably flow when "her tender body had been outraged." Representative William Larsen of Georgia explained why: "When a virtuous female has been raped and ruined by a black brute, would you have her suffer further humiliation by being dragged before the court and the curious public?"[55]

Despite the sensational and hate-filled fantasies spinning out on the floor of the House, the Dyer bill moved forward. Johnson rallied Republican legislators by marshaling statistics about lynching that showed Democrats' lurid fantasies to be untrue. Congressman Dyer announced on the floor of the House that the rape myth "was as far from the truth as many of the other extravagant statements that have been made." In January 1922, the House moved toward a vote. Johnson reported back to the NAACP from Washington that he was "pouring" the organization's literature into the offices of the bill's supporters ("as much of our dope as they will hold"). Southern Democrats threw procedural obstacles in the way, but the Republican majority overcame them. Johnson even hoped the Republicans might be joined by "a number of Northern Democrats." As word of the bill's progress spread, the capital city's Black community began to appear in the galleries above the House floor. By late January, more than five hundred African Americans filled the galleries as the debate entered its final and ugliest phase.[56]

Congressman Thomas Sisson of Mississippi, an arch advocate of Jim Crow, viciously attacked the Dyer bill and announced that it would not stand regardless what Congress did. "We are going to protect our girls and womenfolk," he howled to cheers from his fellow white southerners. "When these black fiends keep their hands off the throats of the women of the South then lynching will stop, and it is never going to stop until that crime stops." Rising from his chair, Sisson declared, "I would rather the whole black race of this world were lynched than for one of the fair daughters of the South to be ravished and torn." Pandemonium broke out in the House chamber. Henry Allen Cooper, Republican of Wisconsin, leapt to his feet. "It is the first time," he exclaimed, "that I have heard mob law openly advocated in the Congress of the United States." The gallery went wild. "Does the gentleman advocate rape?" Sisson shot back. The chair tried in vain to quiet the crowd. "Sit down, niggers," the Mississippian sneered at the gallery.[57]

In the end, it was votes that counted, and the Republicans had the votes. On January 26, 1922, the House passed the Dyer bill by a margin of 231 to 119. Johnson had won.[58]

When the bill moved over to the Senate, the NAACP faced a greater challenge. The old rule of the filibuster meant that a blocking coalition of senators could defeat legislation unless two-thirds of the Senate voted to move forward. The Republican majority was five votes short of being able to win the day by itself. Even worse, key Republicans in the Senate doubted that Congress possessed the authority to enact Dyer's anti-lynching bill. Harkening back to cases like *United States v. Cruikshank* in 1875 and the *Civil Rights Cases* in 1883, the powerful senator William Borah of Idaho observed that the Supreme Court had limited Congress's power. The Court had ruled that the Fourteenth Amendment authorized Congress to prohibit discrimination or unlawful force by state officials, but not by private actors. Congress, Borah warned, could not prohibit private violence.[59]

Johnson remained undeterred. Such constitutional objections, he noted, had a curious feature. Constitutional lawyers' readings of the Fourteenth Amendment seemed to reflect the same kinds of habit of mind that had produced the rape myth. The Constitution's text did not by itself mandate the limits imposed by the Supreme Court. State actors lurked behind the ostensibly private lynch mobs of the South; law enforcement officers were often deeply and even principally involved. Moreover, at other times in American history, the Supreme Court had identified broad unspecified power in the federal government when the occasion seemed to demand it. Congress's power over immigration, which had produced an Emergency Immigration Act in May 1921, was one example. Congress's unwritten authority over fugitive slaves in the mid-nineteenth century had been another.[60]

Johnson asked a further question. Why did the state action doctrine seem so salient to constitutional lawyers, while other provisions of the Fourteenth Amendment fell out of view? Section 2 of the amendment was a case in point. Section 2 provided that any state denying voting rights to male citizens twenty-one years of age or older would lose representation in the Congress and the electoral college proportional to the size of the disfranchised population. There was no doubt that the Jim Crow constitutions of the South disfranchised many hundreds of thousands of Black men, and perhaps as many as 1 or 2 million. Yet neither Congress nor the Supreme Court had reduced the representation of any Jim Crow state. The conventions of constitutional law—the basic scripts for the meaning of the Fourteenth Amendment—omitted this problem altogether.[61]

Johnson gathered favorable opinions on the bill's constitutionality from Harding's attorney general, Harry Daugherty, as well as eminent Republicans like Elihu Root and former attorney general George Wickersham. Bouncing back and forth between the White House, the Republican National Committee, and Capitol Hill, Johnson argued that the constitutional objections were little more than "hair-splitting and sophistry," the result of "a maze of judicial decisions" that had as their real goal the nullification of the Fourteenth Amendment. Johnson argued moreover that objections to the bill overlooked the political gains to be won by the Republican Party for cementing the loyalty of Black voters.[62]

For all his work, however, Johnson could neither dislodge the constitutional storyline about state action, nor change the basic calculus of the Senate filibuster. In September, when a key cloture vote fell short, the Senate put off consideration of the Dyer bill until the lame-duck session after November's midterm elections. Johnson and the NAACP had counted on the leverage of the election to pressure senators to vote for the bill. The prospect of Black votes in the North in November, they had hoped, would yield success for civil rights in Congress after decades of failure. Postponement seemed to threaten a year and a half of work. And so Johnson cast about for one last trick to put the bill over the top. The opportunity arrived in the form of a new propaganda strategy—and a way to finance it.

Johnson joined the founding board of directors of the American Fund for Public Service in the very weeks during which the Dyer bill began to languish. He and Roger Baldwin had gotten to know one another after Baldwin approached Johnson in early 1920 to serve on the Executive Committee at the new ACLU. Two years later, in the spring of 1922, Baldwin brought Charles Garland's gift to Johnson's attention. A puzzled Johnson could not quite believe that Garland "simply did not want the money." It seemed too good to be true. But he told Baldwin that he was "in favor of accepting Mr. Garland's gift along the lines which he lays down," at least "in a general way." By July, the Fund was in place, and Johnson realized that at least some of Garland's million dollars might be spent in the work of reshaping public opinion on lynching.[63]

As if on cue, a publicity expert named Edward L. Bernays proposed to Johnson and the NAACP that they initiate a last-ditch publicity campaign to rescue the Dyer bill. The NAACP, Bernays recommended, should disrupt the conventional storyline of lynching by drawing on the propaganda strategies pioneered during the war.[64]

By 1922, Bernays's work was fast becoming the stuff of legend. The nephew of Sigmund Freud twice over (his mother was Freud's sister, his father's sister was Freud's wife), Bernays's life project was to establish the new field of public relations as an amalgamation of Freudian ideas about the subconscious, on the one hand, and the growing field of crowd psychology, on the other. As a young publicity flack on Broadway in the 1910s, he rescued a Broadway play facing obscenity charges by assembling a group of experts to testify to the play's value in the fight against venereal disease. During the war, he took his talents to the Committee on Public Information, where he worked with Creel to shape the country's wartime propaganda efforts. After the war, Bernays returned to the marketplace with new sophistication in the workings of the mass mind. When hairnet manufacturers looked to increase their sales, Bernays organized an effort to make long hair fashionable. Later in the 1920s, Bernays would launch his most famous campaign when he engineered an effort on behalf of the American Tobacco Company to encourage women to smoke cigarettes. Hundreds of fashionably dressed young women marched down Fifth Avenue smoking "Torches of Freedom" quietly paid for by American Tobacco. Bernays refused to let his own wife smoke, citing what he thought were obvious health risks. But when American Tobacco's green packaging on its Lucky Strikes brand proved off-putting to female consumers, Bernays crafted a campaign to make green the stylish color of the moment. Bernays's "Green Ball" for New York's high society was the go-to party of the season, financed once again by American Tobacco.[65]

Bernays borrowed shamelessly from Lippmann, Wallas, and their forerunners, Le Bon and Tarde, in the study of crowd psychology. Channeling their ideas about the workings of the mind in mass society, Bernays came to think that the buzzing confusion of the modern world was too much for people to comprehend. What the modern mind craved, Bernays believed, was simplicity. The mind, he liked to say, was "a logic-proof compartment" whose walls were made up of social scripts—straightforward conventions for making sense of the goings-on around us.[66]

Bernays was quick to see a powerful implication for politics, too. The workings of the mass subconscious, it seemed, were proof of democracy's impossibility. In a world of complexity, he believed, the "active energy of the intelligent few" would powerfully shape the ideas of the "public at large." Culture elites, Bernays insisted, inevitably determined "the organized habits and opinions of the masses," for it was culture elites who shaped the frames and templates into which people organize the maelstrom of experience. The men who built the mental circumstances in which people made sense of their lives were the real rulers of the world. They formed what

Where electoral politics failed, public opinion beckoned; Johnson's NAACP turned to publicity man Edward Bernays around the time he was becoming famous for selling cigarettes to women.

Bernays called "an invisible government which is the true ruling power of our country." They and they alone directed "the group and the herd" and operated what Bernays called "the basic mechanisms of social change." Echoing Lippmann, Bernays held that public relations men were the secret administrators of modern life, crafting and re-crafting the stereotypes by which the modern mind comprehended reality.[67]

As Bernays saw it, the "mysterious alchemy of public opinion" could be turned to virtuous works as easily as to cigarettes and smut. The NAACP had asked for his help in 1920 when they held their annual conference in a southern city for the first time. The Atlanta conference that year was one of Bernays's first publicity jobs after coming out of Creel's wartime CPI. He took to it with enthusiasm, promising to "dramatize" the NAACP's goals and "concentrate attention" on the organization. Focusing on prominent leaders in churches, politics, and education who would be "stereotypes for ideas that carried weight," Bernays helped produce a conference that he believed "had its definite effect in building up the racial consciousness and solidarity of the Negroes."[68]

Now, two years later, as Bernays watched Johnson struggle to sell the Dyer bill to the American public, he offered his services once again. Writing to the organization's vice president, Arthur Spingarn, Bernays proposed a "plan to secure public support for the passage of the Dyer bill" by "awakening the public to the necessity for its passage." It would, he said, be a classic "public relations campaign." He urged the creation of a national "Anti-Lynching Committee" made up of prominent Americans who would stand for the "moral law and order issue." Simultaneously, he urged that the NAACP take a full-page advertisement in daily newspapers with the goal of "crystallizing public opinion." Thousands of copies of the advertisement could be made and distributed separately with letters to opinion leaders around the country. The NAACP might thereby disrupt and remake the scripts by which so many white Americans tried to make sense of the horrors of lynching.[69]

The difficulty was money. The campaign would have to begin immediately if it were to save the Dyer bill. An effort of six to eight weeks, Bernays projected, would cost the NAACP $3,000 in his fee, plus an additional $4,000 to $5,000 in advertising costs and letter-writing expenses. The dollar amounts were not astronomical, to be sure. But given the NAACP's budget, such a campaign was entirely out of the question. When Johnson took the helm of the organization in 1920, he found its budget in crisis. The NAACP had no reserves in the bank and $4,000 in expenses each month. Fieldwork took up one-third of the organization's $50,000 annual budget, but the chapters contributed only $25,000 each year, leaving a huge shortfall to be filled by private fundraising. Johnson observed that the organization operated on a "very, very, very narrow margin." That was being generous. In reality, it didn't operate on a margin at all.[70]

In September, the NAACP proposed to the American Fund that one of its very first grants be for Bernays's anti-lynching campaign. Johnson orchestrated the application, but in view of his role as a member of the Fund board, he arranged for Arthur Spingarn of the NAACP's legal committee to apply for the fund. Spingarn wrote to Roger Baldwin proposing a $10,000 grant for support of what Spingarn (appealing to the Fund's desire to support dissenting causes) called "the most unpopular cause in America." Johnson chimed in to urge that such a grant might create a "revolution in public sentiment." Bernays's campaign aimed to supply the "uninformed American people such facts" as to disrupt an otherwise "insistent public opinion" and substitute a new body of public opinion in its place.[71]

Baldwin did not take much convincing. The board, he wrote in the same year, was "anxious to help stop lynching and will consider any realistic application." The Fund's directors unanimously agreed and made a grant to the NAACP of $2,500, conditional on the organization raising an additional $2,500. Johnson personally guaranteed the last $300 of the matching funds to ensure release of the money. In December and January, when Bernays's campaign ran over budget, the Fund kicked in an additional thousand dollars. In March, with the NAACP's coffers drained yet again by the costs of the anti-lynching campaign, the Fund loaned the organization another $3,000, which the Fund soon converted to an outright gift.[72]

All told, the Fund contributed $7,365, and the money was used just as Bernays had prescribed. Full-page advertisements ran in late November under the banner headline "The Shame of America." The ads appeared in the *New York Times*, the *Chicago Daily News*, the *Atlanta Constitution*, the *Washington Post*, the *Kansas City Journal*, the *Kansas City Star*, the *San Antonio Express*, and *The Nation*. The ads insisted that "the cause of lynching" was not rape, a claim the NAACP backed up with careful statistics. Twenty-eight people, screamed the subhead, had been publicly burned. The ads counted more than 3,000 lynched in thirty years. Writing back to New York from the Capitol, Johnson reported that the message and the prominence of its publication had caused "a sensation here among our people."[73]

The Senate reconvened days later, but in that forum the Johnson-Bernays campaign proved to be too late to alter the outcome for the Dyer bill. Democrat Oscar Underwood of Alabama, the minority leader, told majority leader Henry Cabot Lodge of Massachusetts that the Democrats would prevent all Senate action in the lame-duck session if the anti-lynching measure were put to a vote. Lodge (whose own reelection fight was now safely over) promised not to press the anti-lynching bill to a decision. The Dyer bill adventure had come to a bitter end.[74]

Johnson and the NAACP were devastated. "I do not believe you can understand the pressure under which I work," a demoralized Johnson confided to a friend. Close colleagues worried that Johnson might "break down unless he takes a much-needed rest soon." The blow was doubly difficult for Johnson because Republicans like Borah from the party of Lincoln and Emancipation had betrayed the cause by refusing to break the filibuster. Responsibility for lynching, he now charged, "rests equally with the Republican majority" as with "the lynching tactics of the Democrats." The "failure of the United States Senate" to even consider the measure, Johnson continued, was "a license to mobs to lynch unmolested." Johnson bitterly noted Harding's lukewarm support, and that of his attorney general, too. Indeed, newspapers around the country reported a rumor that the Dyer bill's defeat had been prearranged and planned all along. The *Atlanta Constitution* asserted that Republican leaders had "never seriously considered passing the proposed anti-lynching law." The Louisville *Courier-Journal* opined that the Republican Party was secretly "not at all displeased with the result of the filibuster." An irate W. E. B. Du Bois concurred. Republicans, he wrote in the NAACP's magazine, *The Crisis*, "never intended to pass the Dyer Bill, unless they could do so without effort, without a fight, and without appearing publicly to defend the rights of the Negro race." Johnson concluded that the "century-old attempt at government of, by and for the people" now "stands before the world convicted of failure."[75]

Neither political party, it seemed, could be trusted; if Black voters forgave the Republican Party for abandoning the Dyer bill, Johnson seethed, "we deserve disfranchisement now and forever." The failure of the Dyer anti-lynching bill touched off the historic move of African American voters away from the Republican Party. Du Bois asked whether "any Negro voter in the future" could support either major party "without writing himself down an ass?" In 1924, Johnson urged NAACP members to support northern Democrats and to abandon the unreliable Republican Party. Four years later he refused to serve as the Republican candidate for Congress in Harlem. "My fervor as a Republican partisan had for some time been cooling off," he remembered, "until now it was quite cold." Indeed, as the 1920s progressed, Johnson concluded that the partisan politics of the ballot box were a lost cause. America's "greatest game" was simply unavailable for the cause of Black equality. "As the national political condition now exists," he explained in 1928, "any involvement of the Association on a definite partisan basis would do the organization irretrievable harm." Writing the next year in H. L. Mencken's *American Mercury*, Johnson said that "in the political game played on the national gridiron," the Black voter had no role save one. The Negro, Johnson fumed, "is the ball." The fate of the Dyer bill, like Roger Baldwin's initiative and referendum project in St. Louis a decade before, had revealed electoral politics to be a dead end.[76]

The bill's collapse also revealed an NAACP in disarray. The demands of the Dyer bill had taken up virtually all of Johnson's time. The expense of the effort left the organization in financial crisis.[77]

And yet a new kind of politics rose from the ashes of the Dyer bill. Bernays's campaign for the NAACP had failed to win the Senate floor. But it touched American public opinion, even in (or perhaps especially in) white circles. The *Sun Francisco Call* described the NAACP program as "the most amazing advertisement ever paid for and printed in any newspaper." The progressive editors at *The Outlook* magazine reported that in the wake of the publicity Johnson orchestrated around the Dyer bill, many whites in the South were "coming to feel a sense of shame for their long endurance of this crime against democracy and humanity." Du Bois saw the same unexpected but happy consequence. "On one single day," he wrote of the NAACP's full-page advertisements, a lone organization of only a few thousand members and no great wealth had "made five million intelligent Americans think about lynching." The NAACP had "reached the unreached"—it had captured the attention of "white people who knew and cared little about lynching," and it had dislodged (even if just slightly) the inevitability of the rape myth. "Was it worth it?" Du Bois asked. The answer seemed clear to him. "Propaganda depends on advertising," and given the effects of advertising on public opinion, "we ought to have spent ten times that amount and we shall."[78]

Johnson agreed. Writing to Baldwin in 1924, Johnson noted that the number of lynchings had declined precipitously after the NAACP advertising effort. By the NAACP's count, sixty-one lynchings in 1922 had become twenty-eight in 1923, and then only three to that point in 1924. In traditional political terms, the NAACP's efforts seemed to have accomplished very little. The collapse of the Dyer bill combined with the Republicans' poor showing in the 1922 midterm elections had essentially ended the prospect of anti-lynching legislation. Yet even then, lynchings had plummeted. The lesson, Johnson concluded, was clear. The publicity Bernays had designed around the Dyer bill effort had done work outside the formal political system. It had changed public opinion sufficiently as to alter the shape of the problem.[79]

The American Fund, which had financed the anti-lynching advertisements, now emerged to support such efforts. In December and then again the following March, Johnson wrote Roger Baldwin seeking funds to help the NAACP's work. Together, Johnson suggested, the NAACP and the American Fund could give new facts to an "uninformed American people." Baldwin told Johnson that all the directors recognized the "hard sledding" that the NAACP had endured over the previous two years. And so new money from the Fund began to replenish the NAACP's nearly empty accounts. The loan of $3,000 in March (forgiven a year later) supported the organization's general operations. Another $1,500 in June paid for a move to bigger offices near Union Square. The total for the year amounted to 10 percent of the NAACP's annual budget.[80]

Johnson's lesson was much like the one Baldwin had learned in St. Louis on the eve of the First World War. The game of electoral politics offered few routes forward; legislative efforts like the anti-lynching bill were out of reach for the foreseeable future. Yet "agitation for a federal anti-lynching law," as one observer noted, had produced a "flux in social consciousness." What Johnson needed was more ways to reshape basic ideas about race, more ways to alter public opinion. His connection with the new American Fund seemed to provide a path.[81]

James Weldon Johnson and W. E. B. Du Bois (pictured here at middle and left, respectively, in a 1917 march against the East St. Louis massacre) won a grant from the Fund to support studies of Black public schools in the South. Published in The Crisis *beginning in 1926, the studies laid the groundwork for a theory of school cases as a mass organizing strategy.*

8

Educate the Masses

*I was surprised at learning that giving away money,
if it is done at all judiciously, is a difficult job.*
—JAMES WELDON JOHNSON

Distributing the American Fund's money turned out to be harder than any of the directors had guessed, and capitalism was part of the problem. Rapid stock market growth overwhelmed the directors' plan to spend Charles Garland's million in a few short years. The Dow Jones Industrial Average increased in value by nearly a third in the year and a half after the Fund opened for business. The Fund's own holdings fared even better. By 1926, the half-million dollars in First National Bank shares donated by Garland had nearly tripled in value. "The stock," Baldwin later remarked, "increased faster than we could give away income and principal."[1]

A greater difficulty was Johnson's mounting frustration at the Fund's ad hoc policy with respect to grant applications for Black causes. Standard operating procedure at the Fund was for Anna Marnitz, a fashionable single woman who commuted from her parents' apartment in the Bronx to serve as the Fund's part-time stenographer and secretary, to send Johnson all applications relating to the protection of racial minorities. Johnson reviewed applications from the cash-strapped would-be editors of Harlem magazines and from educators at industrial-education schools modeled on Booker T. Washington's Tuskegee Institute. Eccentric pamphleteers sought funding for screeds about American racial politics. Black people who had run afoul of the law in one way or another petitioned for assistance. Distinguished scholars and organizations applied, too. The historian Carter Woodson sought support for his Association for the Study of

Negro Life and History. The National Urban League, founded by Roger Baldwin's aunt Ruth and run by prominent Black Cornell graduate Eugene Kinckle Jones, asked the Fund to finance its programming. The sociologist E. Franklin Frazier sought a grant to support studies at the Atlanta School of Social Work on white racism as a psychiatric pathology. A who's who of Black leaders—including W. E. B. Du Bois, Howard University's Alain Locke, and Philadelphia lawyer Sadie Alexander—applied for funds to endow a Negro Foreign Fellowship Foundation to support Black college students who wanted to study abroad. Requests came in from Cleveland to support a Black theater and from Pittsburgh to support the city's Black press.[2]

The Fund supported some of these proposals and rejected others, but to Johnson the decisions seemed to lack rhyme or reason. Woodson received a modest grant; Frazier did not. Sometimes a principle emerged. The Fund rejected industrial education for Black youth, which Johnson and the directors disdained for its compromises with Jim Crow. Grants of several thousand dollars at a time and a few modest loans went to projects connected to the Urban League's work with Black workers. But mostly the Fund's directors had no plan, at least not for grants to support race-related causes. As early as the spring of 1924, Johnson was beginning to wonder if he was well matched with his fellow American Fund directors. He was the Fund's only Black director. But after two years of debate and experimentation, Johnson hit upon the first of several ideas that ultimately altered the trajectory of the Fund. Working closely with Du Bois, Johnson pitched a project about Jim Crow America that the two men described as a critical precondition to bridging the gap between Black communities and the American labor movement: creating an empowered and educated Black population capable of knowing and defending its rights. Du Bois and Johnson called for the American Fund to underwrite a study of Black schools as an initial foray into the vast project of changing the segregated South.[3]

Cash Value

Remaking Black schools appealed to Johnson in part because his family had treated education as a great equalizer. Education produced uplift. It offered connections to literature and to culture. Johnson had become principal at Jacksonville's Stanton Normal School as a young man because he viewed education as the path of progress.

Stanton Normal's story traced the arc of Black schooling in the postwar South. The school had been established in 1868, three years before Johnson's birth, when Black people in the area—nearly all of them ex-slaves—established an informal educational association. Like freedpeople across the South, they prioritized education for their children. Scraping together their meager funds, they managed to acquire a lot in downtown Jacksonville. The Freedmen's Bureau financed the building of a schoolhouse on the lot, as it did in towns throughout the former Confederacy, and named it after the recently retired secretary of war, Edwin Stanton. In a pattern that would recur for decades in towns across the South, the school's name left the impression that the Freedmen's Bureau or some northern philanthropist had paid for the entire school. In truth, freedpeople only months removed from slavery had borne much of the cost themselves.[4]

Johnson's mother became a teacher at Stanton in the 1870s. As Johnson remembered, she taught her sons to think of education as a way of life, not merely a way of "making a living." Freedpeople with few resources other than their own willpower also sought out education nearly everywhere across the South. The first group of "contraband slaves," who fled from their owners for the safety of Union lines in 1861, had immediately formed a school at Fort Monroe in Northern Virginia; a Black missionary teacher named Mary Peake taught a class of fifty students there before the war was six months old. By the end of the war's first year, dozens of Black teachers were convening informal schools for people moving from slavery to freedom. Literacy followed the Union army. Freedmen's schools appeared in Florida beginning in 1862 at Fernandina and in 1864 in Jacksonville, where a missionary teacher named Esther Hawks held mixed-race classes in a confiscated meeting hall of the white Odd Fellows fraternal order. In the middle of 1865, Freedmen's Bureau officials in Florida counted ten schools for Black students, a number that tripled by year's end.[5]

Free public schools for children in the South were a direct result of the freedpeople's enthusiasm for education; "public education for all at public expense was, in the South," Du Bois observed, "a Negro idea." In Johnson's home state, the first real system of public schools found its roots in the radical state constitution of 1868. By 1869, four years after Appomattox,

153 Black schools in the state enrolled 7,000 children. Across the South, freedpeople insisted on getting education for themselves and their children. Black political conventions held in the immediate aftermath of the war expressed the sentiment with force. "Whereas Knowledge is power, and an educated and intelligent people can neither be held in, nor reduced to slavery," resolved the Colored People's Convention of the State of South Carolina in 1865, "we will insist upon the establishment of good schools for the thorough education of our children." For decades, Johnson and countless others recounted stories of "old men and women" who went to night school, fathers who labored, and mothers who "toiled over wash-tub and cook-stove to keep children in school," securing education whenever the "opportunity was available." No sacrifice, Johnson wrote on one occasion, "was considered too great."[6]

In the decades after Johnson's graduation from Stanton Normal, however, Black education faltered. Johnson saw how schooling looked in rural Black communities when he spent the summer of 1891 teaching in a tiny Georgia cotton-farming community thirty miles south of Atlanta. "In all of my experience," he reflected forty years later, "there has been no period so brief that has meant so much in my education for life as the three months I spent in the backwoods of Georgia." He taught fifty students at five cents per pupil in a "shanty of a church," with not a single desk for the students nor a blackboard for the teacher. He lived in a crude two-room shack hosted by a sharecropper family, with no privacy except a simple sheet hung to divide the space. His students, he recalled fondly, were "willing and teachable." But the conditions under which his teaching took place were nothing like Stanton Normal in Jacksonville. Johnson came away from Georgia convinced, as he put it the next year in a student address at Atlanta University, that "education of the masses, above all else" was the vital need of the Black community.[7]

Johnson's time in the Georgia schoolhouse led him to believe that segregation was not just a reflection of white supremacy but also one of its central pillars. To be sure, even at the height of radical Reconstruction, when Republicans supported by Black voters controlled state governments, southern states typically separated public schools by race. Separate education indeed offered certain advantages for Black southerners;

James Johnson, at right, as principal at the Stanton School in Jacksonville.

among other things, separate classrooms created job opportunities for Black teachers. Yet from early on, some Black statesmen had objected. Hiram Revels, the first Black member of the United States Senate, warned that separate schools would too easily be relegated to second-class status. Revels's prediction soon proved accurate. After Reconstruction ended in the late 1870s, a new round of state constitutions flatly prohibited mixed-race public schools and set the stage for an all-out assault on freedpeople's education.[8]

For one thing, separation meant physical vulnerability. In 1869, an unidentified arsonist burned down Esther Hawks's school at the Jacksonville Odd Fellows hall. The Hawks school would turn out to be the last integrated classroom in the city for nearly a century. Night-riding vandals destroyed Black schools across the South. The Klan assaulted teachers, including a Black teacher whipped and driven out of Weakley County, Tennessee, in 1869, and a Virginia teacher forced to flee her schoolhouse through a window to escape a gang armed with "guns and pistols" in 1872. In Mississippi, one observer would later write, groups of Klansmen "ordered teachers to quit, forced school directors to resign, and ordered county superintendents to step down." By one estimate, the Klan burned or otherwise destroyed 256 schools used by Black students. Departure of U.S. forces from the South made things worse. In Georgia, Brigadier General Davis Tillson reported that "in almost every case . . . the withdrawal of troops has been followed by outrages on the freed people; their school houses have been burned" and "their teachers driven off or threatened with death."[9]

A subtler form of assault was just as damaging to the education of Black schoolchildren. Having separated Black schools from white, state governments found it that much easier to starve them of resources. From the end of Reconstruction to the first decade of the twentieth century, southern school districts reduced the ratio of Black school funding to white school funding by half. By 1898, Johnson's Florida spent twice as much on white schools as it did on Black ones, in both absolute and per-pupil terms.[10]

Segregation, combined with the successful disfranchisement of Black voters, ensured that funding disparities worsened after the turn of the twentieth century when southern states began to increase their overall school budgets. In the three years between 1902 and 1905 alone, funding at public

Burning a freedmen's schoolhouse in Memphis, Tennessee, in 1866.

schools in the former slave states increased by 75 percent. Little of the new spending went to Black schools. To the contrary, as Black educator and sociologist Horace Mann Bond observed, white officials raided Black school budgets to increase spending on white schools without raising taxes. In Florida, per-pupil funding in Black schools dropped from $4.63 to $3.11 between 1890 and 1910, while white schools' funding on a per-pupil basis increased from $9.42 to $11.58. Spending in Florida's Black schools slid from half of what it was in white schools to a mere quarter. The academic year in Black schools contracted by nine days during the same period, while the white school year gained twelve days. Florida's schools spoke the language of Jim Crow loud and clear, and Florida's Black families understood the message. The share of Black school-age children attending classes fell for the first time since the Civil War.[11]

Johnson's Jacksonville was not immune from the grim march of education inequities. Writing in 1915 about a new plan to issue bonds for school construction, Johnson observed that city officials had allocated nearly all of it to the construction of white schools. Johnson cited school funding disparities in state after state. In North Carolina, the ratio of Black school expenditures to white school expenditures dropped from 1.05 between 1880 and 1885 to 0.40 between 1906 and 1910. In 1914, Louisiana schools spent $16.60 on each white student, but only $1.59 on each Black student. South Carolina spent $9.65 for every white student, and a mere $1.09 for Black ones. The budgets of Alabama, Georgia, and Mississippi featured similar inequities.[12]

Teacher pay scales diverged, too. As principal of the Stanton School in Jacksonville, Johnson earned less than half what a white principal would have earned. White teacher salaries in Florida doubled between 1890 and 1910, increasing substantially faster than the national average. Black teacher salaries in the same period fell by as much as 50 percent. Teacher salaries of $60 and $100 each year amounted to less than what many cotton-field workers took home, less than a seventh of the salary of letter carriers in the postal service, and merely a quarter of the typical earnings of a Black pastor.[13]

The diminutive William N. Sheats, known as "Florida's little giant of education," did as much as anyone to call Du Bois and Johnson's American

A typical Black school in the Jim Crow South, photographed by Horace Mann Bond.

Fund study into existence. For as the state superintendent of education, he had nearly succeeded in shattering Black Floridians' education dreams.

Sheats became superintendent a year before Johnson took the job of principal at Stanton Normal. Education for white students, he believed, was the path to prosperity in the New South. Sheats's idea of education for Black students, by contrast, aimed to accommodate them to their subordination. He proposed to turn "the vast number of idle, absolutely worthless negroes" into "industrious and self-supporting" people—or at the very least "to fit them for residence among the white population" as a subordinate class.[14]

Segregation was a crucial ingredient in this poison cocktail of paternalism and white supremacy. The state's 1885 constitution provided that "white and colored children shall not be taught in the same school." Sheats claimed credit for the provision and put it to work, successfully lobbying the state legislature for a law criminalizing the teaching of mixed groups of white and Black students in the same school building, even in private schools. In 1896, he induced a county sheriff to arrest seven teachers and two patrons, all white, for violating what was known as the Sheats Law at an American Missionary Association school for training Black teachers in the small town of Orange Park, about fourteen miles upriver from Jacksonville. The Orange Park School boasted of teaching Black and white students alike "on the very spot where, less than a generation ago, gangs of slaves toiled under the overseer's lash." Sheats disdained the entire project as a "vile encroachment" upon the "social and moral system"; the real plan of these "fanatical equalitists," he warned, was undoubtedly "miscegenation" and race-mixing. A state court eventually struck down the Sheats Law as unconstitutional for technical reasons. But the damage was done. The Orange Park School never regained its footing, limping along until an arsonist burned its chapel building in 1911.[15]

Johnson joined in the protests against Sheats's attacks on Black education. He supported the Orange Park missionaries during the Sheats Law controversy and delivered a commencement address at the struggling school. Two years after the Orange Park episode, Johnson became president of a Black organization of teachers known as the Florida State Teachers Association, succeeding an Oberlin graduate named Thomas DeSaille Tucker, who served as president of the State Normal College for Negroes in Tallahassee. In 1901, when Sheats fired Tucker from the Tallahassee school and replaced him with a graduate of Booker T. Washington's Tuskegee Institute, Johnson became the most important Black educator in the state. He had not yet turned thirty years old, and he had already begun to redirect his life to New York. But there was little even an older man could have done to alter the trajectory of Black education. Johnson's autobiography, published in 1936, barely mentioned his tenure as president of the Teachers Association; it made no reference to the assault on the Orange Park School or to the firing of his predecessor. It seems possible that Johnson omitted these parts of his life history because he had failed utterly to fix them. By the end of Sheats's tenure as superintendent, Florida spent ten times more on white schools than on Black ones. Black people made up nearly half the state's population.[16]

Sheats understood that segregation was a valuable tool for diverting resources to white schools. Governor James Vardaman of Mississippi liked to say that "money spent for the maintenance of public schools for Negroes is robbery of the white man." The truth of the matter was the exact opposite. Du Bois labeled Jim Crow as "taxation without representation" for Black communities. Segregation allowed white governments to siphon money away from Black taxpayers.[17]

Vardaman's argument, which was commonplace in the white South, rested on the notion that Black residents paid few state and local property taxes because they owned little property. Johnson and others observed that this argument willfully misunderstood the way tax burdens work. Only rubes thought that the burden of a tax fell entirely on the person nominally paying it. Sophisticates understood that a landowner with property taxes was not necessarily the "one who really pays the taxes" (as Johnson put it) or at least not the only one who paid them. Renters typically paid landlords a rent that implicitly included a share of the tax due. Indeed, every person who rented from, worked for, or traded in goods and services with the property owner, Johnson explained, contributed to his tax obligations in the form of increased prices or decreased wages. The historian Carter Woodson agreed. The Black consumer and renter, Woodson insisted, paid into state coffers, even if their contributions were incorporated into the increased prices of the goods they bought or impounded into the reduced wages they earned. As Woodson saw it, Black residents often ended up paying more than their share, since when they did own property, white tax assessors frequently assigned unfairly high values to it. When Black schools received less in per-pupil funding than white schools, the result was a kind of theft from Black students.[18]

By the 1920s, leading Black intellectuals like Du Bois did the revolutionary rallying cry one better, calling the exploitation of Black education a kind of "double taxation" without representation. Since the era of the Stanton School in 1868, Black taxpayers had contributed their share of the tax dollars needed for public schools. But they had also raised additional private money to finance schools, either from their own communities or from outside philanthropists. Howard University's Alain Locke complained that "Negro education costs double and yields half." To prove the point, Horace Mann Bond showed that counties with higher percentages of Black people had higher racial disparities in school funding. Johnson's Florida illustrated the phenomenon. In 1910, counties in which Black people made up less than a quarter of the population provided white schools three times the per-pupil funding of Black schools. Counties in which Black people made up three-quarters or more of the population provided white schools nearly fourteen times the per-pupil funding of Black schools.

Three decades later, the Swedish sociologist Gunnar Myrdal explained the math. More Black students meant more Black school dollars to siphon into white schools. "If, for instance, there are twice as many Negroes as white children," he wrote in his landmark study of segregation in the South, "every dollar per pupil taken from the Negro group means two dollars per pupil added to the appropriation for the white group."[19]

Bond put the point more bluntly than the mathematical Swede. Not since auctioneers had put enslaved children on the block, Bond wrote furiously, had young Black people represented cash to white families in quite such a direct way. Across the South, the so-called Black Belt counties with large populations of Black children to exploit were the counties where slavery had taken hold most deeply. Now they featured the biggest school-funding inequalities. Quantifying the effects, Bond found that schools in the Deep South with the largest share of school-age Black children received only a fraction of what racial parity would have required, ranging from 21 percent in Mississippi and 28 percent in Georgia to 31 percent in Florida. By creating separate school systems, Jim Crow governments had stolen Black residents' tax dollars for white schools. Segregation, Bond concluded, meant that "Negro children" had "a definite cash value for every white school child."[20]

Out of Our Field

The NAACP's coffers were not much deeper than those of Black schools in the South. In 1923, Johnson appointed a special committee to "look into the finances of the Association," but the organization's financial difficulties were baked into its basic structure. As field secretary to the NAACP, Johnson had recruited new chapters and widened its membership. But maintaining far-flung operations was expensive, and new members were not wealthy enough to pay the dues required to support the national organization.[21]

The American Fund, by contrast, was still flush from the bull market of the 1920s. For its first year and a half, the Fund dispensed money without giving systematic thought to its approach. Baldwin and the board had established two main categories for which it would consider awards: aid to workers' movements, especially in the area of education and publishing, and protection for racial minorities. The board had also adopted an ad hoc guideline against self-dealing by its members: for organizations run by members of the board, the foundation only considered special projects, not subsidies for general operating costs. But for the most part the Fund operated in these early months with little by way of formal process or program.[22]

In 1924, the Fund moved to adopt a more systematic philosophy of giving. Board member Scott Nearing supported the move especially strongly. After being fired from the Wharton School for his radical politics (and then being canned again at the University of Toledo for his opposition to the war), Nearing had run for Congress as a Socialist against Fiorello La Guardia and lost. By the early 1920s, having weathered his Espionage Act trial relatively unscathed, Nearing was a committed socialist living what his biographer calls "a life of strenuous simplicity" and near self-subsistence on his small New Jersey farm. In April, Nearing distributed a memorandum to the board calling for a five-year program in which the American Fund would work for the economic transformation of the country. "What is most needed in the United States at the moment," Nearing argued, "is a carefully worked out and consistent propaganda for economic and social emancipation." Economic transformation would come not from the success of any one project, whether progressive or socialist, but from a new class consciousness that would change the minds of American workers. Nearing called on the Fund to establish its own Department of Research and Publicity alongside a cooperative publishing house and a monthly magazine on radical economics. He also advocated for further investments in worker education.[23]

Johnson saw the American Fund's priorities differently. In response to Nearing, Johnson issued his own five-year program for "the field of civil rights." At its heart was a simple idea, which was that the situation of Negro America was "sui generis." The Fund's agenda thus needed to be different for Black Americans than for its white working-class beneficiaries. The "battle for economic justice" was a valuable effort, Johnson conceded. But Black workers were not yet positioned to engage in class struggle. As Johnson put it, "the best way" to help a member of the Black working class was "to help him along the lines in which he is already working." Such work would include supporting Black sharecroppers who fell short in repaying their landlords at the end of the season. It would mean assisting Black parents in finding decent schools for their children. And it would involve backing Black communities' efforts to fight segregation in northern cities. Programs like these might seem less revolutionary than Nearing's socialist transformation. But Johnson suggested that only when the Black worker "acquires self-respect" would he be "able to fight the battle for economic justice."[24]

In Johnson's view, Black people were focused on things that white radicals took for granted—issues that had "long since passed out of the general radical program" proposed by advanced socialists like Nearing. Rights as basic as those achieved in the Magna Carta seven hundred years before, Johnson told the Fund's directors, were "still radical for American Negroes." That was the lesson of lynch mobs and massacres in East St. Louis and elsewhere. And so Johnson urged his radical white comrades at the Fund to treat aid to the Negro as "outside" the "general currents" of producers' movements, organized labor, and economic liberation. Such efforts, Johnson gently reminded his friends, "touch the Negro in hardly more than an indirect way." Black Americans had not yet, for the most part, entered the organized industrial workforce. Black people needed "elementary rights"—things like the right to vote and the protection of life and limb by ordinary law—before they could concern themselves with economic transformations.[25]

The chairwoman of the NAACP's board, a white socialist named Mary White Ovington, backed Johnson's efforts. The Garland Fund crowd, she suspected, seemed most likely to be interested in problems like peonage and sharecropping in southern agriculture. But Ovington joined Johnson in contending that the Fund should support the NAACP's efforts at legal defense in the courts, too. An endowed legal defense fund would be best of all. Ovington wanted Baldwin and other Fund directors to see, as she put it, that "the race problem is not just a piece of the class problem." Lifting up the working class would not automatically benefit Black Americans, Ovington wrote, because Black people were pariahs in the country's whites-only labor unions. Echoing Johnson, Ovington called on the American Fund to help the NAACP "carry out its own plans," to "assist in a battle that the oppressed themselves are waging."[26]

On behalf of the NAACP, Johnson and Ovington asked the American Fund for $50,000 for a legal defense fund to protect Black Americans from discriminatory laws and mob lynchings. When the Fund's directors demurred, a testy Ovington jabbed at Baldwin. "Perhaps what has happened is that you are now keenly feeling your power, that you enjoy it, and unlike Mr. Garland, you see no danger in it, but are more and more desirous of retaining it." If Ovington was onto something, the real obstacle was not Baldwin's psyche. The greater difficulty was that Baldwin and the American Fund's radical directors doubted that racial emancipation efforts fit into their project of social change.[27]

The directors of the American Fund came to the work of philanthropy with a variety of views. But in the early years of the Fund, its directors seemed certain of one thing. Except for Johnson, they uniformly opposed using their resources to support Black education.

Grants for children's education of any kind made little headway at the Fund. In late 1924, a memorandum for the board of directors openly suggested that education for young people was best thought of as outside the Fund's scope. The directors thus turned down grant applications ranging from experimental progressive schools to public school teachers' unions. Critics objected that the Fund's directors preferred more colorful radicalisms over the time-tested virtues of education for children. ("Education," one influential teachers' union leader appealed, "is perhaps the most important social enterprise in existence.") But Baldwin, in particular, rejected the idea that schools for children represented the kind of radical change the Fund should support. "Schooling, however free," Baldwin wrote to one disappointed applicant, "is not the major education that most children get." He doubted whether "any school methods now in effect" could "build the kind of character and intellect" capable of disrupting the influences of the mass-production world. Schools, Baldwin insisted, were essentially and ineradicably reactionary. What they actually did in the world was sustain the social systems in which they existed; in the United States, he believed, schools fostered and nourished the basic hierarchies of what Baldwin called "our authoritarian society." This, Baldwin concluded, was why giant philanthropic foundations like the Carnegie Corporation offered so much money to children's education. The American Fund's more modest resources were better used for less popular causes.[28]

Supporting education for Black children was even less appealing to many of the Fund's directors. By the early 1920s, Black schools were among the most prominent beneficiaries of the largest philanthropic foundations in the world. A survey of the education field for the American Fund's directors found that existing support for Black schools dwarfed the Fund's available resources. By 1909, the Rockefeller family had contributed $53 million to the General Education Board, which together with the Rockefellers' Southern Education Board placed $10 million into Black schools every year. The Phelps-Stokes Fund, the Carnegie Foundation, the Slater Fund, and the Laura Spelman Rockefeller Memorial Fund all made substantial grants in Black education. A fund established by Julius Rosenwald of the Sears, Roebuck company contributed millions more, helping to build 5,000 schools by the end of the 1920s. Rosenwald money contributed to the building of schools attended by 40 percent of the Black students in the country. The sheer size of these rich foundations threatened to make a mockery of any American Fund efforts in the same field. Annual grants from any one of the large foundations exceeded the total value of the American Fund. "There are already agencies in the field aiding Negro education," the Fund explained to a schools applicant from Huntsville, Texas.[29]

Black schools gained philanthropic support at a price. Northern philanthropic money went almost exclusively to institutions that promoted the paternalistic white supremacy of New South education reformers like Florida's William Sheats. The Peabody Fund, which had delivered $2.5 million to southern schools by the turn of the twentieth century, gave money only to segregated schools. (When schools were integrated, as they were during Reconstruction in Louisiana, Peabody directed financial support exclusively to private whites-only schools, reasoning that Black families already received support from taxpayers for education in the integrated public schools.) At the Slater Fund, general agent Jabez Lamar Monroe Curry (a Confederate army veteran) thought that the beneficiaries of Slater's largesse in Black schools were "stupid, indolent," and "shiftless" people "with a low tone of morality" and "strong racial peculiarities and proclivities."[30]

More genteel men like Roger Baldwin's uncle, William H. Baldwin Jr., took the lead in pressing Black educators toward the Booker T. Washington model of industrial-style education and political accommodation. As a trustee at Washington's Tuskegee Institute, the elder Baldwin worked closely with white educators, including Florida's Sheats, to create Black schools in the South that would accommodate the South's racial caste system and match the interests of industrial employers in cheap labor. Du Bois accused William of supporting Tuskegee to nurture a pliant pool of Black workers.[31]

Given how heavily Black schools in the South depended on the support of white school superintendents like Sheats and white northern philanthropists like William Baldwin Jr., it was often nearly impossible for Black schools to challenge Jim Crow. Leading southern Black educators therefore accommodated the patronizing forms of Jim Crow peddled by the big philanthropies. The writer Ralph Ellison, in his novel *Invisible Man*, would later scorch Black college presidents as subservient and ingratiating, but even in the 1920s Roger Baldwin condescended to what he called the "servile" attitude fostered in Black schools and colleges. "Negro education," he wrote of the decades-old joint venture of philanthropy and education, "is a little out of our field."[32]

For his part, Johnson had no more interest than Baldwin did in supporting Tuskegee-style industrial education. Such institutions had been the NAACP's foil from the organization's earliest days. Nonetheless, Johnson was at a loss for how to guide the Fund's resources toward projects for the Black working class.[33]

Just then, however, Johnson began to experiment with a new approach to his work at the Fund, one that catered more explicitly to its focus on industrial politics. Perhaps, Johnson suggested, the Fund could find a way to protect "the Negro as a minority group" by "helping the Negro to become as rapidly as possible an integral factor in the industrial and labor world." The Great Migration was making Black labor an important factor not only in southern cotton fields but also in the North's industrial centers. If the Fund would not support the NAACP's legal defense fund, it could at least finance surveys on the number of Black people in and out of organized labor. It could support research on the attitude of Black workers toward unions, and on the feelings of white workers toward Black ones. "Some method of educating the Negro in the modern labor ideas," Johnson proposed, "should be perhaps devised."[34]

In theory, Johnson's new initiative held promise. It catered to the labor interests of the Fund's radical white directors. But what exactly could the

Fund do to facilitate the organization of Black workers? White unions were almost entirely closed off to Black members. Black workers, many of them migrants or farmworkers, were too disorganized and too poor to do much about it.

Though Johnson could hardly have guessed it, solving the dilemma of how to organize Black workers alongside white ones—how to create working-class solidarities across racial divides—would preoccupy the Fund for nearly the next decade. But in the short run, Johnson and his colleagues at the NAACP offered a proposal that seemed modest in the moment, but which has reverberated through American democracy ever since. The best way to organize American labor, they suggested, was one that might have seemed counterintuitive at first, or even outright implausible. It was a path, moreover, that would defy the legacy of the vast philanthropic foundations. They proposed to transform Black education in the South.

Fasten Slavery Permanently

W. E. B. Du Bois first glimpsed the way forward. Schools for Black students in the South might draw the interest of white radicals like Baldwin if their purpose could be turned upside down. The prevailing model of industrial education for Black children attracted the support of wealthy northern capitalists. But what if education for the Black masses could become a path to organizing Black workers?

Schools had been of interest to Du Bois for decades. In 1901, while on the faculty at Atlanta University, he led a study of the Negro Common School, decrying the unjust funding of Black schools in the South and warning of efforts to reduce funding still further. (His 1911 update concluded that conditions had gotten worse, not better, in the intervening decade.) Du Bois's most famous book, *The Souls of Black Folk*, published in 1903, insisted that education would be central in "the social regeneration of the Negro." Six years later, the NAACP's founding platform demanded that states provide "a free and complete education" for Black students "as for all others." The inaugural issue of the NAACP's magazine, *The Crisis*, which Du Bois edited, singled out discrimination in schools as especially dangerous to democracy. "Human contact, human acquaintanceship, human sympathy," Du Bois wrote in the magazine's pages, "is the great solvent of human problems." Students separated by color, he contended, "grow up without learning the tremendous truth that it is impossible to judge the mind of a man by the color of his face." The NAACP's 1911 agenda led first and foremost with a commitment "to begin immediately a scientific study of Negro schools" and "to form a National Committee for the purposes of studying the problem of national aid to education."[35]

Most of all, Du Bois directed withering skepticism toward the idea that big philanthropy held a solution to the crisis of Black schools. In one sense, such a view was hardly surprising. Foundations like the Rockefeller General Education Board had financed the educational projects of Du Bois's rival, Booker T. Washington, while rejecting some of Du Bois's earliest efforts to study Black education. Throughout his career, Du Bois would tangle with the leading educational philanthropies. By the mid-1920s, for example, Du Bois had drawn the ire of the Rockefeller General Education Board and the Carnegie Corporation by engaging in a verbal war with the white president of Du Bois's alma mater, Fisk University, who was a recipient of Rockefeller and Carnegie money. But Du Bois's resistance to white philanthropists in Black education ran deeper. For Du Bois grasped that white money in Black schools went hand in hand with the projects of men who aimed to use education to repress equality rather than to further it.[36]

Thomas Jesse Jones was, for Du Bois, the most dangerous agent of northern educational philanthropy. Born in Wales and educated at Columbia University under the tutelage of the sociologist Franklin Giddings, Jones served as an assistant chaplain and instructor at the Hampton Normal School, an industrial school for Black students on the model of Booker T. Washington's Tuskegee. In 1910, Jones compiled statistics about Negro life for the decennial U.S. census. In 1912, the Phelps-Stokes Fund and the Rockefeller-financed General Education Board selected him to oversee a giant study of Black education jointly sponsored with the United States Department of Education. And in 1918 he helped establish the Commission on Interracial Cooperation, a group of white southerners and leaders of historically Black colleges. Jones hoped the Commission would serve as a counterweight to the growing influence of the NAACP in questions about race. In these capacities, Jones became a central figure in guiding philanthropic money to the Black South. Yet if few were as influential, none was more disliked by the Black educators who received his support. Carter Woodson called him "narrow-minded, short-sighted, vindictive and undermining."[37]

From the start, Jones championed Hampton's industrial education model, which he believed suited "the actual needs" of Black students. The right kind of education, Jones believed, would ameliorate what he called the "character failings inherent in the Negro race." Du Bois rejected everything about Jones's views. Speaking at a 1906 conference at Hampton, Du Bois had criticized Jones's theory of vocational education, condemning the Hampton model on its home turf. Jones retorted that Du Bois was motivated by "unfounded beliefs and hearsay evidence." Hampton never invited Du Bois back.[38]

Jones's two-volume 1917 report for the Department of Education called for "more adequate appropriations" to Black schools. But Jones specified that education for Black youth needed to be "wisely fitted" to what he saw as their limited abilities. More than further funding, he insisted, Black schools needed to be matched to the "mental, moral, and social" capacities of their students. With contempt, he mocked the "extravagant and high-sounding names" of Black schools. (He singled out Delaware's "High Educational College of Glory.") He derided them for teaching Greek and Latin to poor Black children, ridiculing what he disdained as a "childish love" for the classics. He scolded Black southerners for disliking industrial education, whose "real meaning," he said, had "been largely misunderstood by the colored people and their friends."[39]

Du Bois responded with a furious denunciation of Jones's report in the pages of *The Crisis*. "The General Education Board," Du Bois wrote, had "long ago surrendered to the white South by practically saying that the educational needs of the white South must be attended to before any attention is paid to the education of Negroes." Jones, said Du Bois, was not really aiming simply to stop "a silly desire to study 'Greek'" and substitute a more practical commonsense curriculum. Du Bois, Johnson, and Jones all knew that the ramshackle Black schools of the rural South were barely able to teach literacy let alone ancient languages. What Jones really wanted, Du Bois asserted, was to prevent Negroes from developing "a class of thoroughly educated men according to modern standards." Jones's industrial schools aimed to "deliberately shut the door of opportunity in the

Thomas Jesse Jones funneled Rockefeller money to Black schools whose form of "industrial" education he thought suited to the capacities of Black students.

face of bright Negro students." The reality was that Jim Crow governments used Black classrooms "as training schools for cheap labor and menial servants instead of for education," and did so under circumstances of "double taxation in the support of private school." Why, Du Bois asked, did Jones not have any Black coauthors on his report about Black schools? "In this very report," Du Bois observed, just as in running the school system itself, "the Negro was practically unrepresented." Here lay what Du Bois saw as "the weakness and sinister danger of Mr. Jones' report." The function of education in Jones's approach was to create a pool of "contented labor to be used only in an emergency." Du Bois asserted that Jones and the philanthropists aimed to maintain a reserve army of pacified Black labor "for keeping white union labor from extravagant demands."[40]

The sting of the influential Jones Report lingered, and in 1923 Du Bois set out to counter its baleful effects. In February, on a motion by Du Bois, the NAACP board of directors established a Committee on Education in Southern Schools to make education part of the organization's campaign for the year. A committee report followed in June, setting out the inequalities in school funding in the South. Throughout 1923, Du Bois stayed on topic, simultaneously publishing articles in *The Crisis* on the tragedy of Jim Crow schools, North and South alike. "Of all sorts of segregation and discrimination that meet the Negroes in the United States," Du Bois thundered, "that in the common public schools is most dangerous, most insidious, the most far reaching." The problem was that discrimination in elementary schools established "group hostility in those tender years of development when prejudices tend to become natural and instinctive." School discrimination, he wrote, "plants race prejudice in children during their most impressionable years."[41]

The real problem, as Du Bois saw it, was not separate schools as such. The "one thing worse than segregation," he cautioned, was "ignorance," and inexcusably underfunded schools were forcing ignorance on far too many. Philanthropists had stepped in to fill the void, at least in part. But Du Bois shined a bright light on the costs of relying on the apparent benevolence of the wealthy. Inequitable state funding, Du Bois observed, compelled Black educators "to go begging up and down the land, hat in hand, crawling to the door steps of the rich and powerful for the dole of knowledge." The experience of men like Thomas Jesse Jones, William H. Baldwin, and William Sheats demonstrated, moreover, that philanthropists had their own agenda, a mix of paternalistic white supremacy and capitalist self-interest. So long as they controlled the funding of Black schools, philanthropists would exert too much control over the content of the education that took place inside them. "We eternally damn the system that makes education depend upon charity," fumed Du Bois. Black educators like Locke and Woodson agreed with Du Bois that "education is not and should not be a private philanthropy: it is a public service and whenever it becomes a gift of the rich it is in danger."[42]

Philanthropists' effort to maintain a pool of docile labor in the South seemed to cut against the interests of most whites, too. "White laborers of the South will not allow the states to support decent common schools and high schools for Negroes," Du Bois wrote in *The Crisis*. But the same working-class voters who refused to fund public schools for Blacks, he observed, "sneer and yell and curse at black labor" because it "under-bids them." As early as 1903, Du Bois had questioned whether a nation could successfully industrialize when "one half of the labor class is completely unable to protect its rights." Now several decades later, Du Bois asserted that using the Negro worker "as a labor reservoir on starvation wage" blocked white workers from gains. The philanthropists' model of industrial education seemed designed to accomplish two ends at once, preserving white supremacy while maintaining cheap labor at the same time.[43]

The American Fund was a very different kind of foundation. In November 1924, Du Bois and Johnson approached the Fund with a proposal to reorganize the race problem in education and labor. Given his failed effort earlier in the year to gain financing for an NAACP legal defense fund, Johnson decided it was best that he not formally submit grant proposals on his own. (He voted on grants to the NAACP all the same.) Du Bois submitted the grant proposal under his name alone. But it was a joint production.

"Negroes," the request began, "form a large and increasingly important part of the laboring class in the United States." Under modern conditions, it was becoming impractical to promote the interests of the laboring class—to "deal with this class intelligently in the mass"—unless their children are being properly educated. But Black children were manifestly not able to find proper educations. "Today," Du Bois observed, "the average Negro child in the South is not being given an opportunity to learn even to read and write."[44]

Du Bois asked for an initial $5,000 grant and proposed to send agents into the field to study inequities in funding and conditions and to produce a series of studies to rebuff the pernicious Jones Report. "I believe that the seriousness of the situation," he wrote, "can only be brought to the conscience of the country by a careful investigation covering the South."[45]

Johnson followed up in a private letter to Baldwin supporting the application. "The large foundations," he observed to Baldwin, would not give Du Bois even "ten dollars to do anything." Two decades of feuding between philanthropists and Du Bois meant that no other foundation would undertake to assist Du Bois's study. Johnson doubted whether such foundations wanted to get to the bottom of the race problem. Du Bois's proposal, by contrast, was "for the specific purpose of showing up and breaking down the gross inequalities and injustices in the distribution of public school funds in the South." As Johnson saw it, the plan went "to the root of race conditions in that section."[46]

Baldwin was at first diffident. He was inclined not to fund the Du Bois application. "We are not entirely certain that we are the proper body to finance it," he wrote to Du Bois. Privately he reached out to the Rockefeller foundations and others to see if they would fund the proposal. "It concerns a matter really outside the scope of this Fund," he explained. The Slater Fund declined to offer any support. The Commission on Interracial Cooperation, which Thomas Jesse Jones had helped establish, belittled the proposal on the grounds that it would merely duplicate Jones's own 1917 report. Du Bois's project, said one commission member, would be "another superficial study ... adding insult to injury."[47]

Johnson defended the proposal, weighing in even though it was essentially his own application as much as it was his colleague and friend's. When the grant request failed to gain traction at a first meeting of the Fund's board, Johnson persuaded the directors to hold the application over to the next month's session. Du Bois used the intervening weeks to campaign for his grant. "It seems to me," he wrote Johnson, "that the trustees of the Garland Fund do not realize that unless certain investigations into the condition of the Negro are done by liberal agencies, we are bound to get all our information from unfair sources." The Bureau of Education was tainted by a bias in favor of the white South. Men like Jones aimed to make it appear "that only Hampton and Tuskegee have done anything toward Negro education" and that "Negro common schools in the South" were "improving so rapidly that there is no cause for alarm." The difficulty was that southerners could not tell the truth about Jim Crow. "No southerner, white or black, can attack the South and stay there." Without a new report prepared outside the auspices of compromised foundations such as the Phelps-Stokes Fund, Jones's report threatened "to settle matters for the next decade."[48]

At its heart, the Du Bois and Johnson proposal connected the financing of Black schools in the South to the labor problem in the North. White unions were increasingly hampered by the availability of cheap and unorganized Black labor. "If now the Garland Fund wishes to encourage organized labor among Negroes," Du Bois wrote to his friend, the Fund would have to "encourage intelligence among Negroes." Elementary education in the South was the place to start, and the "first step toward labor organization among Negroes" would be "to reveal the plight of the Negro common school."[49]

Still, Baldwin resisted. Old friends like L. Hollingsworth Wood, an ally from the ACLU and a white trustee at Fisk, encouraged Baldwin to vote against the proposal. The NAACP, urged Wood, would produce undue "antagonism on the part of the white South." But the new campaign by Johnson and Du Bois to connect Black education to labor organizing had a galvanizing effect on the American Fund board. Baldwin's closest ally on the board, Norman Thomas, described the project as "a valuable expenditure of money, the effect of which, although it may be irritating in some quarters, will be distinctly good." "This is one in which I believe," he affirmed.[50]

James Weldon Johnson and Grace Nail Johnson in the mid-1920s.

In May 1925, the American Fund board approved a $5,000 grant for Du Bois's study of Negro education in the South. ("We are willing to finance this," a grudging Baldwin told Du Bois.) The Fund board delegated oversight of the project to a committee consisting of Thomas and Johnson. Du Bois hired two assistants, Horace Mann Bond and the sociologist E. Franklin Frazier, to develop his observations on educational funding disparities. The three researchers worked with Black communities and teachers across the South. They collected statistics from local school boards. They gathered reports from school administrators. Photographers collected portraits of dilapidated schoolhouses.[51]

When Du Bois reported his findings to the Fund's board a year and a half later, he explained that his team had collected "a larger body of truth concerning Negro public schools in the South than has been gathered before." (Jones's rival study was the obvious reference.) Published versions of the research appeared in *The Crisis* beginning in September 1926 with a sixteen-page article about Black schools in Georgia. Du Bois's article drew the reader through the history of discrimination against Black schools in the state. He reviewed the legal framework of the state's Jim Crow education law. And he delivered pages of statistics detailing the systematic theft of funds from Black schools to pay for white ones. In county- and district-level statistics, Du Bois showed that it was local officials who did the dirty work of disparate funding. Local school officials used their discretion to siphon money from Black schools to white.[52]

Articles came out in *The Crisis* on Mississippi (December 1926), North Carolina (May and June 1927), South Carolina (December 1927), and Oklahoma (April and July 1928), each accompanied by damning statistics of discrimination and grim photographic documentation. Never before had the effects of race in American schooling been delivered to so wide an audience, let alone one made up of 30,000 Black readers.[53]

Du Bois's American Fund–sponsored project helped occasion a burst of new interest in education among Black leaders. At the NAACP, assistant executive secretary Walter White called for "nationwide agitation to launch a counter offensive" against school discrimination "in all northern and border states." Black educators like Kelly Miller at Howard cited growing segregation by race in northern and border-state schools as evidence against the argument of some white liberals that the color line was crumbling. Controversy proliferated over the exclusion of Black students from the best public schools in towns like Toms River, New Jersey, and cities like Philadelphia and Indianapolis. Outpourings of coverage followed in the Black press.

New Black constituencies for education appeared, too. In 1910, a mere 30 percent of school-age Black children attended school; by 1950 the share would be close to 70 percent. Black teachers became a more powerful voice, organizing themselves into new and more effective lobbying organizations. The Black-led Virginia Teachers' Association grew from 200 members in 1920 to 3,000 in 1930. Southern locales like Atlanta saw fresh organizing in the first half of the 1920s by Black families determined to resist the issuance of discriminatory school bonds, whose proceeds were to be allocated in such a way as to exacerbate already unequal school funding. Ever-greater disparities in school funding drew new attention. In Johnson's home state of Florida, William Sheats's long tenure led a group from Columbia University's Teachers College to describe Jacksonville-area colored schools in 1927 as so shockingly poor that they could "hardly be considered part of" the state's education system. A headline in the *Pittsburgh Courier* broadcast the news bluntly: "Negro Education in Florida Needs Help: Amazing Situation Revealed." Du Bois warned in the pages of *The Crisis* that failure to educate Black children risked "to fasten slavery permanently upon the colored people of the United States."[54]

The NAACP's appeal to the American Fund altered the outlook of both organizations. When Johnson had warned the directors of the Fund that efforts to protect Black people in America would need to be radically different from the strategies useful in supporting the labor movement, Mary White Ovington at the NAACP had called Johnson "hopelessly reactionary on labor and other problems." But now Johnson and Du Bois began to see ways in which the interests of the Black community and the labor movement might be aligned. "Our original faith in education," Johnson later recalled, may have been "almost childish." Now, he conceded to one correspondent, "the economic basis of the Negro's condition has not been sufficiently stressed." Education came to have new economic meaning for Johnson. "Day by day," he marveled, "negro education is bringing the economic problem to the fore."[55]

For Du Bois, the Fund helped propel a renewed economic radicalism. He had begun the decade with a series of articles in *The Crisis* arguing that education was critical to American democracy. In his American Fund studies of Black education, Du Bois offered a revised view. Education was vital, he now contended, because it opened up a path to economic flourishing and labor organizing for the Black community. The path was still inchoate, to be sure. In part he promoted more public money for Black schools and the Black teachers and students who worked and studied in them—money that would free schools from the cynical strategies of white donors. In part the idea was that educated people were better positioned to assert the kinds of rights crucial to economic success. And in part the idea was that only educated workers would be positioned to organize into unions. In each of these respects, however, the synthesis of education and labor augured a historic shift for Du Bois away from the middle-class orientation of the NAACP. For nearly his entire career, Du Bois had countered Booker T. Washington's insistence that economic questions came before political ones. Economic power, Du Bois had said, was nothing without the political might to protect it. Du Bois had criticized Thomas Jesse Jones, William H. Baldwin, and the big philanthropic foundations on the same ground: they had developed a theory of education organized around an economic vision of cheap labor. The radical directors of the American Fund, however, had pressed Du Bois and Johnson to develop an economic theory of their own.

"'Never let a nigger pick up a tool,'" Johnson recalled hearing white workers say. Engaging with Black education in 1924 and 1925 raised for Johnson the idea that the Garland Fund might combine its two main projects. The emancipation of American labor might be pursued by equipping Black Americans not only with the tools of industry but also tools for organizing.[56]

For the time being, however, a number of Johnson's comrades at the Fund remained unconvinced.

Clarence Darrow, right, and client Henry Sweet, far left, with the local legal team of Julian Perry and Thomas Chawke in Detroit, 1925.

9

First Victories

The Fund ought not, in our judgment, to sink its money into the bottomless pit of Negro associations.

LABOR ECONOMIST STUART CHASE TO THE
AMERICAN FUND FOR PUBLIC SERVICE, 1925

In August 1925, directors at the American Fund moved to end support for organizations focused on the interests of racial minorities.[1]

At a special meeting in the East 48th Street brownstone of *New Republic* editor Robert Morss Lovett, the directors assessed three years of eclectic grant making. They had made gifts to labor journalism and research. They had supported worker education and workers' health. They had helped to pay for campaigns in favor of birth control and in opposition to child labor. They had promoted the progressive wing of the labor movement and sustained the NAACP's anti-lynching and education study efforts. The Fund had kept its operating expenses extremely low; of $120,000 in spending the previous year, 95 percent had gone to beneficiaries and programs, and only 4.5 percent to overhead expenses. The Fund had made $100,000 in loans, a policy on which it would soon pull back after collecting overdue payments proved onerous.[2]

Yet to Roger Baldwin, no less than for James Weldon Johnson the year before, the group's track record seemed scattershot and ad hoc. The Fund's support for what the directors called "Work for the Negro" stood out to Baldwin (always the Fund's most active member) as anomalous. Grants like the one made three months earlier to W. E. B. Du Bois's studies of school inequality in the South seemed disconnected from the Fund's main work. The Fund, Baldwin contended, should focus on its principal mission, which for him was increasingly a mission of supporting the American labor movement, and especially its progressive wing. Along with allies like Lovett, Baldwin pressed a point that labor economist Stuart Chase made in a report drafted for the special August meeting. The board, Chase contended, ought no longer devote resources to what he saw as "the bottomless pit" of Black organizations like the NAACP.[3]

James Weldon Johnson opposed the idea, but he was out of town for the summer and in a poor position to intervene. In his place, Charles Garland made a rare appearance, at Baldwin's request, to support the new initiative. Garland had no formal role in the Fund's operations. But his wishes retained a certain moral authority among the directors. It mattered to them when he urged the group to focus exclusively on workers' organizations. And by the end of the evening the Fund seemed to have reached a new agreement. "The consensus of opinion," as the minutes of the meeting reflected, held that the Fund's mission was to attack economic exploitation. The labor movement was "the only force capable of accomplishing this and establishing a new free social order." The directors thus resolved to dedicate themselves exclusively to organizations that would increase the "militancy, efficiency and effectiveness" of the labor movement.[4]

Baldwin contended that the summer 1925 resolution proposed not so much to abandon Black Americans as to serve them in a different way. The American Fund's plan advanced one of the oldest and most widely held ideas about race and labor in the modern world. The idea was that economic exploitation, not racial discrimination, was the true source of the Black community's subordination. Class, not race, was the fundamental axis of oppression. Norman Thomas of the American Fund board put the point plainly not long after attending the Fund's special meeting. "What the Negro wants and needs," the Socialist Party leader asserted, "is what the white worker wants and needs, neither more nor less."[5]

Yet even as the brownstone summit seemed poised to divert the Fund's efforts away from racial minorities, new causes arose. Baldwin's ACLU planned one of them, though it soon took on a life of its own—the sensational Dayton, Tennessee, trial of John Scopes for teaching evolution in a public school classroom. A second, which followed the Scopes trial by a matter of weeks, was entirely unexpected. When Detroit authorities charged a Black doctor named Ossian Sweet with murder for defending his new home against a violent white mob, the Fund directors were drawn back into race questions. The Fund's money allowed America's best-known lawyer, Clarence Darrow, to handle both trials. And both episodes highlighted the utility of an institution about which the board had sharply divided views. Courts, the Fund's directors learned, could serve as tools in the struggle for public opinion.[6]

Thunder Bolt from a Clear Sky

The Fund's interest in courts began with a case out of the cotton-rich bottomlands on the Arkansas side of the Mississippi River.

A startling story had appeared in newspapers during the first week of October 1919. In Phillips County, Arkansas, in a remote Mississippi Delta region about halfway between Memphis and Little Rock, Black sharecroppers were said to be plotting revolution. The conspirators, said the papers, had developed a scheme to kill the county's white people and steal their land. Early accounts in the press reported that three stranded white men had accidentally stumbled upon the plotters on the night of September 30 when their car broke down near a small Black church in the tiny town of Elaine. A shadowy secret society called the Progressive Farmers and Household Union of America was meeting inside. Its aims were allegedly "a deliberately planned insurrection of the negroes against the whites"; its stark goal was purportedly the "killing of white people." True or not, the Black sharecroppers inside the church fired on the approaching white strangers, killing one. Two got away and sounded the alarm. Over the next two days, hundreds of armed white men turned out from the surrounding counties and from Delta towns in Mississippi and Tennessee, ostensibly to protect local whites from the revolutionary plot. On October 2, nearly six hundred soldiers from Camp Pike in Little Rock arrived to ensure the peace.[7]

The white press congratulated Phillips County for having put down the plot and for having done so with a supposedly admirable humanity. Blacks outnumbered whites in the county by nearly three to one; some estimates put the ratio closer to four to one. Rumors suggested that the alleged plot had involved hundreds of Black residents. In scale, it seemed to rival John Brown's violent insurrection at Harpers Ferry in 1859, or Nat Turner's slave rebellion in Virginia in 1831, or perhaps even the Haitian

Revolution of 1791. And yet according to press accounts from Elaine, a temperate response by the white community had brought peace to Phillips County at a cost estimated by the newspapers to have been two dozen Black deaths.[8]

But what had really happened? Johnson and the NAACP staff could hardly believe that the stories in the press were true. They knew only too well how misleading the propaganda of Jim Crow newspapers could be. From New York it was as hard for readers to tell what had taken place in Arkansas as it had been for Walter Lippmann to follow the events of the Russian Revolution two years before. The heavy fog of disinformation seemed to have spread from the Pittsburgh steel strike still underway. Here in Arkansas, once again, was a story at one remove, a story that came at arm's length through the mediating influence of the press.

Johnson and the NAACP responded by sending Walter White to investigate. Born in 1893 to light-skinned Black parents in Atlanta, White had a distinctive, though hardly singular, characteristic that was exceedingly useful in the investigation of lynchings and race riots. His skin color matched his name. "My skin is white, my eyes are blue, my hair is blond," he later wrote in the opening lines of his memoir. In 1916 and 1917, this white Black man had helped organize a campaign to protest Atlanta's decision to pay for a new white high school by eliminating an entire grade at the city's Black schools. Johnson noticed White's efforts and in 1919 invited the younger man to New York to join the NAACP staff, where White took on the dangerous job of investigating lynchings. His ability to pass made him an ideal choice for the work, though no one doubted that the work was dangerous nonetheless. John Shillady's race had not spared him a vicious beating in Texas. The NAACP published an account of the assault on Shillady in the same month it sent White down into Arkansas, armed with nothing more than manufactured credentials as a reporter for a cooperative Chicago newspaper.[9]

White did not stay long. Within a few days of his arrival in Phillips County, rumor spread that he was working for the NAACP. Some began to suspect that White might be Black himself (a "yellow nigger," they whispered). Plans for a lynch mob took shape, and after a friendly tip, White raced to catch a train back to the North. But White had been on the ground in Arkansas long enough to learn more than the white press had reported. A different story began to come out, one that was about the year's cotton harvest. Cotton prices in September 1919 during the run-up to the Elaine affair were higher than they had been since the Civil War. Where prices had recently been as low as twenty cents per pound, now cotton was selling for more than twice that, reaching as high as fifty cents per pound. Cotton bolls appeared in the fields like white gold. A typical sharecropper's harvest might yield five bales of five hundred pounds each. Such a harvest could be worth as much as $1,250, a small fortune in an era when a dollar a day was often the wage earned even by Black professionals. Sharecroppers had new hopes of breaking free from the cycles of debt and work that had kept them in peonage and poverty since the Civil War.[10]

Local white planters and merchants had their eyes on the harvest, too. For decades, they had arranged cotton production so as to place the risk of falling prices on the sharecroppers. But an exploitative economic arrangement for bust years in the cotton market now threatened to boomerang in a boom year. And so Phillips County's white planters decided to capture the profits from soaring cotton prices for themselves by refusing to pass along the higher market rates to their sharecroppers. Planters and merchants offered sharecroppers the previous year's low prices for their harvest. When sharecroppers balked and held out for higher prices, the white planters had openly threatened them in hopes of inducing discount settlements. And so, in late September the tenant farmers of the area around Elaine had gathered together in their modest wooden church to organize a union that would help them negotiate a fair market rate with the planters. Working with a local lawyer named U. S. Bratton, the union's members hoped that solidarity might win them some of the gains from the cotton market's sweepstakes.[11]

Walter White learned during his brief Arkansas sojourn that the three white men who had supposedly stumbled on the church had not actually had car trouble. They were a deputy sheriff and two associates who had set out deliberately to break up the sharecroppers' union meeting. Unprovoked, they had fired shots through the thin plank walls of the church to scatter the crowd. Women and small children were inside. But the sharecroppers were not entirely unprepared. Armed lookouts fired back and killed one of the white men. When the survivors sent out an alarm, a posse of armed white men materialized during the night. White's investigation showed that over the subsequent two days, the posse had not defended local planters; it had engaged in an indiscriminate slaughter. Roving white gangs killed something like one hundred Black people—later investigations would show the number to have been at least twice that figure—under the pretense of suppressing an imagined uprising. The idea of an insurrection was a big lie, a combination of fevered racism and lust for the riches blooming in the fields. But the violence was real. On October 2, the Camp Pike soldiers had set up machine-gun nests in the two closest towns. Their commander ordered the arrest of every Black person within a three-mile radius. By the end of the week eight hundred people had been rounded up and detained in the Elaine schoolhouse.[12]

Arkansas officials swiftly stepped in where the lynch mob and the army had left off. The governor deputized a committee of prominent local whites—the "Committee of Seven"—and authorized it to interrogate hundreds of Black sharecroppers about the goings-on. With no debate and with no apparent qualms, the interrogators subjected the detainees to brutal torture. With the help of whippings, an electrified torture chair, and suffocation-inducing drugs, the committee extracted dubious confessions from some of the Black people under detention. All-white grand juries quickly indicted 122 of them on charges of murder and conspiracy to murder. Not a single white person was arrested or charged, notwithstanding the murderous violence and the campaign of torture. Trials began a month later. Black people were excluded from the trial juries, too, though that was standard operating procedure; not one Black man had served on a Phillips County jury for at least three decades. Across three days of proceedings, with trials of an hour and less, white jurors returned speedy guilty verdicts for eleven defendants; a twelfth guilty verdict came a few days later. Judge Jimason Jackson handed out death sentences to each of the Elaine Twelve. Faced with grim prospects, most of the remaining 110 defendants pled guilty in return for sentences less than death.[13]

As court proceedings played themselves out, the white planters accomplished a crucial part of their plan. In some sense, it had been their mission all along. While much of the Black population of Elaine moldered in prison or lay dead in the canebrakes and sloughs of the Mississippi Delta, white planters seized the cotton in the fields. Poorer whites who had served in the murderous gangs now stole household property and livestock from the Black families who had fled their homes. The best contemporary estimate concluded that the "white lynchers of Phillips County" made off with "a cool million dollars" from the cotton crops of the eight hundred people who had been rounded up and the two hundred more lynched or left for dead. An undetermined further number lost thousands of dollars more in property stolen when they fled.[14]

When Walter White brought the real story back with him in late October, NAACP leaders reacted with indignation. Since East St. Louis in 1917, deadly race riots had broken out in Houston, Chicago, and Washington, D.C. Elaine seemed to bring the crisis to a fever pitch. Military weaponry had been deployed against defenseless citizens on the basis of a fabricated story of insurrection. Interrogators had tortured dozens. And a once-in-a-generation economic boon had been seized from poor Black members of the community and appropriated largely by the richest whites. W. E. B. Du Bois wrote to the *New York World* in late November to rebut its coverage of the episode. "There is not a civilized country in the world," he fumed,

When high cotton prices in 1919 meant white gold in the fields, Black sharecroppers in Arkansas were pushed off their farms and murdered by the hundreds; many of their bodies were never found.

"that would for a moment allow this kind of justice to stand." White published a fuller account of the dismal affair in early December. There was no conspiracy to massacre whites, he wrote in the pages of *The Nation*, only an effort to protest "vicious exploitation by unscrupulous landowners and their agents." Ida B. Wells-Barnett, who had been exposing the horrors of lynching for two decades, came to Phillips County and denounced national newspaper columns repeating the myth of an uprising to kill the white people of the county. Whites, she insisted, had slaughtered Blacks to seize their crops; "what they could not do lawfully," she said, "they did unlawfully with the aid of public sentiment and the mob."[15]

In all, the Elaine massacre, like the massacre of miners in Colorado six years earlier, was turning into another example of the pitched propaganda battle over economic exploitation and violence. In a mass society, the citizens would come to learn facts at one remove. Social conflict seemed once again to be turning into a contest over who could control the narrative.

But in the Arkansas cases, a new element appeared. As White had noted, Phillips County whites had not been satisfied with killing two hundred Black sharecroppers and seizing their crops, their livestock, and their personal property. The Jim Crow leaders of Elaine had gone a step further. They had taken the astonishingly brazen step of prosecuting surviving sharecroppers for the murder of the two white men who died during the terrorist rampage through the area's Black community. Few acts better captured the arrogance of white supremacy than Phillips County's extraordinary criminal prosecutions. Yet it was almost certainly a tactical error. The prosecution of the sharecroppers meant that the battle over the story of the Elaine riot would enter the courts, where it would leave the strict control of Jim Crow authorities.

Soon after the first sharecropper convictions in Elaine, a prominent Black lawyer in Little Rock named Scipio Africanus Jones realized that something had gone awry in several of the trials. The NAACP's most important ally in the state, Jones had been admitted to the bar in 1889, a few years before Johnson's admission to the Florida bar. Reviewing the cases, Jones saw that the jury verdicts against a half dozen of the defendants were legally defective. He set out to exploit the court's procedural mistake.[16]

The most prominent of the six defendants whose verdicts were amiss was a man named Ed Ware, probably the most successful Black sharecropper in the county and perhaps the state. Ware farmed 120 acres and owned more than one hundred chickens, not to mention a horse, a cow, and eight hogs. He drove his own Ford Model T. In the chaos of early October, while the Committee of Seven tortured Ware in an Arkansas jail, white plunderers took it all. His cotton vanished from the field. His car and his livestock disappeared, too, all of it lawlessly, but there was nothing he could do about it. From prison, Ware wrote his sorrow and his rage into lyrics. "And I just stand," went the anguished refrain, "and wring my hands and cry."[17]

Arkansas law offered Ware no path to recover his property. But Jones thought he could reverse Ware's conviction and those of five others. In his haste to reach guilty verdicts, Judge Jackson had not noticed that the jury verdicts failed to specify whether the defendants had committed murder in the first degree or the second. It was a mere technicality; the indictments charged murder in the first degree, and the juries had returned a verdict of "guilty as charged in the indictment." Few doubted that the all-white juries had meant to convict the defendants of first-degree murder. Yet previous decisions in the Arkansas Supreme Court had ruled that murder verdicts were only valid if they specified first degree or second. In March 1920, the Arkansas Supreme Court reversed the convictions as defective and ordered new trials.

Jones could do nothing to prevent a second set of trials, each of which produced a new round of guilty verdicts from juries that were just as all-white as the first had been. But astonishingly, Jones appealed successfully again. This time around, Judge Jackson had erred by refusing to let the defendants put on evidence of race discrimination in the jury selection.[18]

After reversal of the second round of convictions, the prosecuting lawyer for Phillips County put off the trial of Ware and the five others for two consecutive terms of the court. At the opening of each term, Jones reported on behalf of his clients that they were ready for trial. And under Arkansas law, the state's failure to prosecute a defendant for two consecutive terms of the court had the effect of quashing the indictments. By June 1923, there was no valid legal basis for holding Ware and the other five men. Jones moved for his clients' release. And the state released the men. In the midst of lynching and white supremacist terror, amid the outright theft of everything the sharecroppers owned and alongside lawless torture-filled interrogations, a subset of the formal rules of state law had consequences that ran in opposition to white supremacy. The courts had answered to a certain kind of reason. The passions of public opinion had not been able to dominate the legal process, at least not in its entirety. It was thin gruel. But in a grim world it was something.[19]

A second set of six defendants, led by a sharecropper named Frank Moore, soon became the focus of the NAACP in New York. Moore was said to be "the bravest man" on the local board of the Progressive Farmers and Household Union. The massacre had stripped his family of forty-two acres of cotton, fifteen acres of corn, and hundreds of dollars in household goods. After his arrest, interrogators whipped him "nearly to death" to make him implicate his fellow sharecroppers in the alleged "negro insurrection." But torture did not render his conviction unlawful. And by the time of Moore's trial, chastened prosecutors were ensuring that their all-white juries delivered verdicts without obvious procedural irregularities. The Arkansas Supreme Court therefore affirmed the death sentences handed out to Moore and his codefendants. In a desperate effort, Jones sought relief in the U.S. Supreme Court on the ground that the trial had been an unlawful courtroom lynching. It was a dubious argument. Just a few years before, in 1915, a Georgia jury had convicted a Jewish factory manager named Leo Frank on charges of rape and murder in a courtroom packed by a vengeful and threatening mob. Over the dissent of Justice Oliver Wendell Holmes Jr., who called the trial an example of "lynch law," the federal Supreme Court had let Frank's conviction stand. Jones's argument should have failed in light of the Frank case precedent. But it didn't.[20]

Membership at the high court had turned over substantially since its Frank decision. And this time Holmes's concerns about the pressure of irresistible public opinion prevailed. Writing for a Court majority, Justice Holmes agreed with the Moore defendants that their trial had been a mob in disguise. Recounting inflammatory articles about race war and insurrection in the Phillips County newspapers, and citing a lynch mob that had been turned back from the jail on the promise of convictions, Holmes observed that the courthouse had been "thronged" with a crowd threatening "dangerous consequences."[21]

Technically, all Holmes's opinion for the Court did was order the federal district court in Arkansas to hold hearings on the question of whether the trial in the Moore cases had in fact been a lynch mob by another name. But inside the NAACP the decision meant much more than that. One NAACP leader in Philadelphia called Holmes's opinion "a thunder bolt from a clear sky." According to Johnson, the case brought national attention to the conditions of sharecroppers across the Mississippi Delta. "Members of the Court," he wrote, "expressed amazement that such conditions as were cited could exist in the United States." Writing to the American Fund for Public Service in recognition of its continuing financial support, Johnson observed that the case "had a more far-reaching effect than the mere reversal of the decision of the lower court." Quoting influential constitutional lawyer Louis Marshall, Johnson celebrated that the Constitution now promised "a court that is not paralyzed by mob domination." When in January 1925 the last of the Arkansas sharecroppers were released from prison, Johnson and White issued a press release announcing that the moment "marks the entire victory of the NAACP in one of the most spectacular and bitterly fought contests ever waged for justice in America."[22]

And yet the courts had not really delivered an "entire victory." Nothing in the Court's decision reversed the theft by Phillips County whites of a million hard-earned dollars. Nothing in the case undid the crying economic exploitation of sharecropping. And nothing in the law even came close to addressing the ongoing theft of property from sharecroppers across the South, a theft licensed by the brutal violence with which whites in Arkansas had put down sharecroppers' efforts to organize and obtain market prices for the fruits of their labor.[23]

Johnson and White knew this, hyperbole to the contrary notwithstanding. Reviewing the Arkansas case, the two men reported to NAACP members that the "long and difficult fight" was only a start. They had managed to save "the lives of innocent men." They had done battle in the contest over public opinion, exploding the "lie that Negroes organized to kill white people." But "most important," they concluded, was the fact that an "entering wedge has been made in the fight" against the "sharecropping and tenant-farming" system of the South. *Moore v. Dempsey*, they proposed, was a beginning in the struggle against the economic exploitation of Black America.[24]

The Most Celebrated of Cases

The NAACP's partial win in *Moore v. Dempsey* helped occasion debate at the American Fund about the uses of law and the courts—and helped inspire what *Harper's Magazine* would later call Roger Baldwin's "most celebrated" case.[25]

Organized labor in America typically saw the courts as an adversary, not a friend. For much of the nineteenth century, courts had treated labor unions as criminal conspiracies. By the second half of the century, when unions were no longer unlawful as such, the courts deemed their most effective tactics illegal. The result was much the same: picketers and strikers were subject to arrest and criminal punishment. At the end of the century, courts turned the Fourteenth Amendment's guarantees of due process and equal protection of the laws into weapons of the employer class. Time and again, the courts struck down labor reform legislation on the ground that it unconstitutionally interfered with workers' rights to contract. Courts rejected laws setting maximum hours at work. They reversed laws establishing a minimum wage. They turned back hard-won prohibitions on "yellow dog contracts," by which employers banned their employees from joining labor unions.[26]

It was no wonder, then, that American labor and its left-leaning sympathizers resonated to Karl Marx's view of law and the courts. Marx asserted that the law merely pretended to advance equal rights while really protecting the property of the dominant social class. The law, he wrote in *The Communist Manifesto*, was simply the will of the bourgeois class "made into a law for all." American radicals in the Industrial Workers of the World agreed: "the capitalists control the courts of justice in America, and use them in their fight against organized labor." More cautious labor leaders like Samuel Gompers, who led the American Federation of Labor for four decades, came to share a similar sensibility after watching the courts strike down pro-labor legislative efforts as unconstitutional. The Knights of Labor, a labor organization with nearly a million members in the mid-1880s, was so distrustful of law and the courts that it barred lawyers from becoming members altogether. By the time of the Great Steel Strike in Pittsburgh in 1919, labor leaders professed "no faith that the courts... would be just."[27]

If the American labor movement embraced a role for the courts, it was as a mechanism for the production of martyrs. The trial of abolitionist John Brown for the failed slave insurrection at Harpers Ferry in 1859 supplied the model. Brown's trial, the speech he delivered in the courtroom, and his subsequent execution made him a "new saint awaiting his martyrdom," in Ralph Waldo Emerson's words. After the Civil War, a sequence of labor controversies created a new generation of saints. When Illinois executed four anarchists for police deaths in a bombing at a May 1886 rally for the eight-hour day, labor sympathizers labeled them the Haymarket Martyrs. (May Day celebrations around the world remember them to this day.) The trial of San Francisco labor leader Tom Mooney on charges of participating in a bombing on Preparedness Day in 1916 made "Free Tom Mooney" a cause célèbre slogan for decades. World War I radicalism trials yielded much the same effect; the mass trial of the Industrial Workers of the World in Chicago, the Espionage Act prosecution of Eugene Debs in Cleveland, and the draft law prosecutions of Emma Goldman and Alexander Berkman in New York produced successive rounds of new rallying cries for radicals. Roger Baldwin had assumed precisely this martyr role at his own 1918 conviction for refusing to participate in the wartime draft. The Civil Liberties Bureau had made full use of his dramatic statement to the federal court in Manhattan, reprinting and circulating its stirring call to patriotic civil disobedience. And as director of the American Fund for Public Service, Baldwin guided the Fund to invest in the ACLU's special Emergency Case Fund to defend radicals who found themselves the target of politicized prosecutions in the 1920s.[28]

None of this altered Baldwin's basic skepticism that courts, "dominated by a 'property' point of view," operated "for the benefit of the well-to-do and against the poor." The lesson of the war and its aftermath, he concluded, was that "government and law serve the strong."[29]

Yet the story of the Phillips County sharecroppers was difficult to explain if law was simply the rule of the strong. The Supreme Court's reversal of the Arkansas convictions would be hard enough to account for, but as Mary White Ovington put it to Baldwin, the lesson of the entire episode was that the sharecroppers themselves had sensed value in making recourse to the law, no matter that they surely knew it would be biased against them. "The Arkansas peons tried to get out of the clutches of their landlords," Ovington observed, by hiring a lawyer to handle their cases. Litigation may not have been the tactic of choice for white radicals. But lawyers and then courts had been the way Black sharecroppers in Arkansas attempted to resist their own exploitation. "For that reason," Ovington reasoned, it was "likely to be the best one for their sympathizers to pursue," too. "The Negro's reaction at present," she concluded, citing the Arkansas cases, "is not to arm and fight but to turn to the courts for protection." Who could say that either the Arkansas sharecroppers or the NAACP had been wrong to adopt such a strategy? The Arkansas cases demonstrated, she urged, that "the courts sometimes do protect."[30]

To be sure, as the NAACP's Ovington conceded to Baldwin, the Supreme Court had not addressed the cruel underlying economic exploitation of the sharecroppers. But by shining a light on conditions that would otherwise have remained outside public view, *Moore v. Dempsey* made an impression on even the Fund directors who were wariest of the law, people like economist Scott Nearing and (increasingly) Baldwin himself. The success of the NAACP in the courts thus encouraged the ACLU to consider, and the Fund to sponsor, a new effort: a case about the freedom of teachers in the nation's schools that would come to be known as the Scopes monkey trial.

In March 1925, the State of Tennessee enacted a statute making it a crime to teach evolution. The law prohibited the teaching of "any theory that denies the story of the Divine creation of man as taught in the Bible"; it barred, in particular, school instructors from teaching the view "that man has descended from a lower order of animals."[31]

Tennessee's new law immediately drew the attention of the Fund's directors. Some of their earliest civil liberties grants had gone toward defending socialist and progressive educators against political attack. In 1922 the Fund had awarded $5,000 to the Rand School of Social Science, a school on 15th Street in Manhattan run by the American Socialist Society. The award was ostensibly for educational purposes, but really it aimed to offset the costs of Rand's battle with New York State's notorious Lusk Committee, founded by the state legislature in 1919 to investigate revolutionary propaganda. At John Dewey's suggestion, the Fund made grants of nearly $7,000 to Henry Richardson Linville's Teachers Union, a progressive branch of the American Federation of Teachers, committed to "civil liberty in education." Like an American Fund specifically for educators, Linville's organization aimed to "free the minds of teachers everywhere from the oppression of economic and other forms of control."[32]

At the ACLU, Baldwin had established a Committee on Academic Freedom, chaired by Dewey and joined by Harvard Law School professor Felix Frankfurter and former Stanford University president David Starr Jordan. Norman Thomas from the American Fund's board served on Baldwin's ACLU committee, as did John Haynes Holmes, the Unitarian minister who had helped found both the NAACP and the ACLU. Linville, the president of the Teachers Union, joined too. The ACLU committee denounced "propagandists' efforts to distort education" and listed red scare laws, restrictive history textbook laws, and anti-evolution laws among its leading concerns.[33]

The ACLU's Committee responded quickly to the Tennessee law's enactment. "We are looking for a Tennessee teacher who is willing to accept our services in testing this law in the courts," read an ACLU press release the next month. The story that ensued is now familiar to students of American history and watchers of the classic play and film *Inherit the Wind*. A Tennessee newspaper reprinted the ACLU's press release. In turn, local businessmen in Dayton, Tennessee, persuaded a science teacher and football coach named John Scopes to stand trial under the law as a way to draw attention to their unheralded town. The rest was history, alternately as serious engagement and as media spectacle. The entire affair was anomalous. By Tennessee standards, Dayton was a liberal outpost, not a hot bed of anti-evolutionary sentiment; the leading local organizer of the case was a transplanted New York engineer working for a struggling coal mine. Scopes was not even really sure he had actually taught evolution in his science courses. It was no wonder that H. L. Mencken, the acerbic American journalist, described the proceedings as an extended farce.[34]

Less well known is the way the Scopes case emerged, as legal scholar Laura Weinrib has shown, out of a debate among leaders on the overlapping boards of the ACLU and the American Fund over the place of courts in progressive politics. With the NAACP's recent success in *Moore v. Dempsey* in mind, the ACLU sought out American Fund assistance for the early stages of the case. Better-established funding sources like the various Rockefeller-controlled foundations declined to have anything to do with the challenge to the Tennessee law. (Donating to the Scopes defense fund, explained the president of the Rockefeller Foundation, was "rather outside of Mr. Rockefeller's beat.") And so in mid-May, Helen Phelps Stokes of the ACLU board wrote to the Fund asking for a grant of $2,000 "to underwrite the defense" of Scopes until other sources of funding could be secured. The Fund directors readily assented, not so much because they had a special interest in the evolution controversy but because teachers' freedom of speech in the classroom had become a topic of great interest in the Fund's work defending radical teachers from the Lusk laws.[35]

The ACLU had two aims with the case. Baldwin and company hoped to get the case to the Supreme Court to establish a new principle on the freedom of teachers in public school classrooms—hopes that were buoyed in June when the Court ruled Oregon's mandatory public school attendance law unconstitutional. Secondly, the court challenge in Tennessee seemed poised to provide good publicity in the national public opinion battle over teachers' rights to offer heterodox ideas in the classroom. The ACLU staff, Baldwin later remembered, "knew we were in for fireworks when we landed a client." But the publicity soon took on a life of its own. Within a few short days a case that had been intended to establish a position that would be of use to the radicals of the Rand School got out of Baldwin's control. It became, as Baldwin recalled, "a setup to satisfy a publicity man's dreams."[36]

Whether the case was a good vehicle for advancing the projects of the American Fund was a different question. In mid-May, the aging Democratic Party leader, former secretary of state, and "Great Commoner" William Jennings Bryan offered to enter the case to defend the law; local Dayton prosecutors agreed, eager to enlist one of the country's most prominent critics of evolutionary theory. Clarence Darrow, Bryan's longtime antagonist in debates over evolution, quickly volunteered to serve as Scopes's lawyer. Baldwin opposed Darrow's involvement; as the country's celebrity trial lawyer, he would surely reduce the ACLU's control over the proceedings. But a wide-eyed Scopes eagerly agreed to Darrow's offer, and Baldwin could do little to intervene. The Scopes case promptly morphed from publicity boon to publicity circus. Newsreels captured every step of the proceedings, beginning with Bryan's entrance into town in a pith helmet and Darrow's much-hyped arrival at the Dayton train station. The publicity bonanza that followed brought a hucksterism of the kind a public relations man like Edward Bernays might have dreamed up. A new speaker's platform hastily erected on the courthouse lawn was matched by the new airstrip (Dayton's first) laid out in a nearby farm field. Banners and signs appeared all over town ("Read Your Bible" on the outside wall of the courthouse; "Where It All Started" at the drugstore where Dayton's boosters had dreamed up their scheme). A local booster club minted commemorative coins stamped with a monkey wearing a straw hat. Carpenters moved the jury box to make way for a microphone that broadcast the proceedings on live radio. Two hundred reporters rolled into town, matched by a ragtag army of evangelicals and proselytizers eager to seize the opportunity to spread ever more idiosyncratic versions of the old time religion. A live chimpanzee posed with curious tourists. Enterprising locals who were better entrepreneurs than scientists exhibited the supposed fossil remains of evolution's so-called missing link. Organ players, blind minstrel singers, and carnival barkers filled the streets. Viewing Scopes's white southern jury as impartial, Mencken sneered, would be "spitting in the eye of reason." The courtroom, Mencken charged, was packed with "morons." The entire South seemed to him an affront to a modern democracy. "Neanderthal man," he concluded, "is organizing in these forlorn backwaters of the land."[37]

From the carnival atmosphere of the trial's opening, to the final show-

Clarence Darrow arriving in Dayton, Tennessee, for the Scopes evolution trial in 1925.

down between Darrow and Bryan, in which the caustic atheist called Bryan himself to the stand and questioned the aging fundamentalist on the fine points of biblical literalism, the Scopes trial was a media spectacle. In the tumult and the chaos, the point of the Fund's sponsorship of the case was largely lost. Darrow had no interest in establishing a principle for the Supreme Court. He aimed to reveal religion as utterly fatuous and to leave science triumphant over superstition. Neither the Fund nor the ACLU had a stake in this particular fight. The Fund directors had no desire to see Scopes acquitted; to the contrary, Baldwin's goal was a guilty verdict that could be appealed in order to establish as a point of law that the federal constitution barred the State of Tennessee from controlling teachers' conduct in the classroom. In fact, the ACLU had much to lose from Darrow's arguments against religion, since the organization claimed to advance the rights of all speakers, including religious ones, and to represent the people against the powerful. Editors at the *New Republic* derided the Scopes case as "a trivial thing full of humbuggery and hypocrisy," arguing that the ACLU ought to have focused its efforts "not on the Supreme Court of the United States, but on the legislature and people of Tennessee." Liberal theologian Georgia Harkness told Baldwin that the trial had become "a disgrace to the country." At the very least, many agreed with law professor Felix Frankfurter that the entire affair had become "ludicrous."[38]

Ultimately no point of law was established. Scopes was duly convicted at trial and given a $100 fine, which no one thought Scopes himself would have to pay. The ACLU hoped that on appeal they might be able to revive the question of a constitutional right to academic freedom. The American Fund issued a new round of financing. But savvy justices on the Tennessee Supreme Court short-circuited the ACLU–American Fund project. Eager to bring an end to the circus-like affair in their backyard, the state's Supreme Court defended the power to enact anti-evolution statutes in public schools, but reversed Scopes's conviction on a technicality, ruling that the jury and not the trial judge ought to have handed down Scopes's fine. In an unusual addendum the court wrote that it saw "nothing to be gained by prolonging the life of this bizarre case." The state's prosecutors agreed and quietly dismissed the indictment. Scopes (and the ACLU) no longer had standing to bring the issue of academic freedom to the Supreme Court.[39]

Despite its whimper of an ending, the Scopes case accomplished something for the fledgling ACLU. Many years later, long after the Fund was defunct and after he had retired from the ACLU, Baldwin would describe the Scopes case as "the most famous of all our cases over the years." The publicity from Dayton had put the civil liberties organization on the national map. Scopes made new allies for the ACLU and established the organization as a protector of dissenting voices.[40]

The Scopes case also displayed the power and the danger of relying on the courts to do battle over public opinion. Somehow the American Fund, which had imagined itself as a champion of the underdog and the little guy against the dominant powers of the day, had ended up associated with Mencken's mockery of ordinary people in the South as rubes and dupes. This was hardly the democracy Baldwin and the radicals of the Fund had hoped to create. Going to the courts had unleashed powerful currents and swept the Fund's radicalism into unexpected eddies.

In an unanticipated sense, however, the Scopes case had reconnected the Fund's directors to one of its two core projects. The textbook Scopes was convicted of teaching had contained the standard dubious racial science of the day. Of the "five races or varieties of man," the text confidently asserted, the Caucasian was "the highest type of all . . . represented by the civilized white inhabitants of Europe and America." Nathaniel Shaler and Louis Agassiz had taught such things to generations of Harvard students, Baldwin included. It was commonplace in white circles, radical and otherwise. As W. E. B. Du Bois saw it, the Scopes monkey case revealed not an America divided between North and South, secular and evangelical, sophisticated and rube, but an America united in white supremacy, scientists and backwoods hicks alike. It was an America, Du Bois said, that Black people had known for three centuries: a land of "brutality, bigotry, religious faith and demagoguery," one that was "capable not simply of mistakes but persecution, lynching, murder and idiotic blundering."[41]

Nothing Except Power

In Detroit, blundering bigotry soon thrust racism back on the American Fund agenda.

Two months after the Scopes trial, on the evening of September 9,

1925, a crowd of white people, mostly men and boys, gathered on Garland Avenue, across the street from the home into which Dr. Ossian Sweet had moved the day before with his wife, Gladys. Sweet had watched such crowds before. A lynching near his boyhood home in Florida when he was five left him with traumatic memories. As a medical student at Howard University in Washington, D.C., he witnessed the brutal beating of a Black streetcar rider by a crowd of white thugs during the capital's 1919 race riots. He read in the NAACP's *Crisis* about the race riots in East St. Louis in 1917 and in Chicago and Arkansas in 1919. In Black papers like the *Chicago Defender*, he read about the fearsome destruction of the flourishing Black community of Tulsa, Oklahoma, in 1921, where white rioters had killed at least 150 people and destroyed more than 1,200 Black-owned homes.[42]

Now the white crowd had gathered for Sweet himself. Ever since 1917, when the Supreme Court had struck down racially restrictive zoning ordinances like the one Baldwin fought in St. Louis, white residents had sought new ways to keep Black people from living in their midst. Black migrants, however, kept coming. In 1925, more than half the total Black population in the North consisted of people born in the South, amount-

The Sweet family home on Garland Street in Detroit.

ing to around a million new arrivals. In Detroit, the census reported that the Black population had grown by more than 600 percent in the decade between 1910 and 1920, rising from 5,700 to 41,000. (Only Gary, Indiana, with its massive steelworks, witnessed a sharper increase.) By 1925 Detroit's Black population had increased twofold again. The reason was simple: jobs. The American automobile industry had taken root in the city and its suburbs. Chrysler occupied a factory on the city's east side, not far from the Dodge Brothers plant. General Motors turned out luxury Cadillacs at Detroit Assembly just to the west of downtown. Henry Ford's factory at Highland Park had essentially pioneered the entire industry, and now along the River Rouge he was building the largest industrial facility in the world, expected to employ a stunning 100,000 workers. Ford was as famous for his willingness to hire Black workers as he was for his hatred of labor unions, his antisemitism, and his factory's industry-leading $5-a-day wage.[43]

Often informal word of mouth sufficed to keep African Americans in the slum neighborhood known as the Black Bottom. The price of housing in booming Detroit's white neighborhoods helped, too. But white Detroit also resorted to violence. In 1925, neighborhood watch groups like Garland Avenue's "Waterworks Park Improvement Association" sprang up to keep Black residents out of predominantly white neighborhoods. That year alone, crowds of angry white neighbors had tried to chase new Black residents out of white neighborhoods no fewer than five times. Sweet knew of each incident. He was personally acquainted with at least two of the victims. He knew that months earlier, the chief surgeon at the hospital where he practiced medicine had been hounded from his home by a white mob that smashed through his front door and beat him and his wife. When Sweet moved into his new Garland Avenue home, purchased for his wife and their eighteen-month-old daughter, he came prepared. Two of his brothers accompanied him, along with seven friends, all Black. Sweet armed the group with a shotgun, two rifles, and six pistols, along with four hundred rounds of ammunition.[44]

Sweet's precautions proved warranted. At around 8 p.m. the first rock came through the window into the Sweets' bedroom. Soon rocks rained onto the roof. More windows broke. And then while Sweet, his wife, and a friend huddled in the downstairs kitchen, debating what to do, rifle shots rang out from the second floor. One of the men in Sweet's small company had fired across Garland Avenue, mortally wounding one white rioter and injuring another. Police soon entered the house and arrested Sweet and the others inside. Criminal charges for murder against the whole group soon followed.[45]

James Weldon Johnson learned of the Detroit case while trying, on doctor's orders, to get some exercise at a golf course in New Jersey. Almost immediately he understood that the Sweet controversy offered an opportunity to revisit the debate his colleagues in the American Fund had been having about support for Black causes. Just a year earlier, the American Fund had declined to endow the legal defense fund for the NAACP, preferring instead piecemeal support for particular projects. After the Scopes case spectacle, Johnson wondered whether the Detroit episode might lead the American Fund radicals to think differently. Johnson sent Walter White to investigate the case, just as he had in Arkansas six years before.[46]

Together, Johnson and White also reached out to Clarence Darrow, who had been brought more closely into the NAACP's orbit by his work for the Fund and the ACLU in the Scopes case. Johnson had come to like the irascible and charismatic lawyer. He had also drawn a different lesson from Darrow's involvement in the Scopes trial. Where Baldwin had been frustrated by Darrow's distractions from the free speech issue, Johnson had noticed that Darrow's client (as with so many Darrow clients) had been spared punishment. And so Johnson asked Darrow to represent the Sweet family. Darrow, for his part, had come to enjoy his renewed association with progressive politics after a decade working for wealthy clients. He agreed to represent the Sweets for a heavily reduced fee of $5,000.[47]

Johnson called upon Moorfield Storey, the first president of the NAACP, to approach the American Fund for help paying Darrow's fee and other Sweet case expenses. As Storey told the Fund, the unfolding developments in Detroit showed that the rights of Black Americans were central to the Fund's work. The Great Migration, Storey said, was fundamentally changing the nature of American society. Segregation and race relations in northern industrial cities were fast becoming the great issues of the day. The NAACP already had a case headed to the Supreme Court on the issue of racially restrictive covenants. Written by builders and owners into the deeds to their own homes, the covenants purported to prohibit the sale of a home to Black buyers, accomplishing privately what the Supreme Court had said racial zoning ordinances could not do publicly.* Now the Sweet case in Detroit seemed to present another vehicle for publicizing injustices in northern and border-state cities during the vast migration of Black people from South to North. "It is the dramatic focus," Storey continued, "of a situation that threatens to become general." For these reasons and more, Storey reasoned, the Sweet case "fit very closely in the program of the American Fund." The case "not only represents an attempt to accord protection" to the Black defendants, Storey concluded. The Sweet case was also about a great national issue of the day: the migration of Black people to cities and to the North. It was a case, as Storey put it, that put at issue a basic "principle of democracy."[48]

Johnson and Storey asked the Fund not only for $5,000 to pay Darrow's fee but also for an additional $20,000 to help seed the legal defense fund the NAACP had been struggling to establish. By the end of October, on the eve of the Sweet trial, the American Fund board came around. Baldwin and his colleagues granted both the NAACP's requests, subject to the condition that its award for the legal defense fund amount to $1 for every $2 the NAACP raised from other sources, capped initially at a ceiling of $15,000. American Fund advisor and progressive Wall Street lawyer L. Hollingsworth Wood applauded the work as "of fundamental importance in our American life."[49]

Darrow's involvement guaranteed that the trial playing out in Detroit would draw national attention. Darrow's strategy was to call as many of the Sweet family's white neighbors as he could. He started with an easy question: Why were you outside on Garland Avenue that night? Then the questions became more pointed. Hadn't the police estimated the crowd at between 150 and 200 people? Hadn't stones broken the house's glass windows before the gunfire began? Don't you object to Black people in your neighborhood? The witnesses seemed determined to deny all of Darrow's leading questions. But under pressure they began to give way. Yes, some conceded, they were opposed to Black residents on Garland Avenue. Yes,

---

* In *Corrigan v. Buckley*, decided in May 1926, the Court ruled unanimously that the enforcement of private discriminatory covenants in Washington, D.C., raised no issue of federal civil rights law.

they had joined the Improvement Association to keep Negroes out of their neighborhood. A thirteen-year-old witness admitted that teenagers had been throwing stones at the house. When one of the witnesses slipped and inadvertently characterized the crowd outside the house as having been large, Darrow went in for the kill. "You kind of forgot," he led the wavering witness, "you were to say 'a few people,' didn't you?" The answer came back with reluctant candor: "Yes, sir." It would become the trial's iconic moment.[50]

The presiding judge—an Irish American Democrat named Frank Murphy—insisted on racial equality in his courtroom. Some Detroit politicians drew their support from the resurgent Klan and the neighborhood improvement associations. Klan membership in Detroit had shot upward from 3,000 to 22,000 between 1921 and 1924 as whites reacted to the new Black migrants from the South. Yet Murphy had been elected to his judgeship by an unusual coalition of white ethnics and newly arriving Black voters. His conduct at the trial reflected the integrity that had won him support among the Black people in his constituency. The defendants, he instructed the jury, were legally and morally innocent if, at the time the shots were fired from the house, they believed danger was "actual and imminent." Moreover, he told them, "race and color" and circumstance were relevant to whether the defendants reasonably believed they were in danger. The Sweet defendants would have been within their rights, Murphy ruled, to take into account the racial circumstances, and the jury was warranted in doing the same. Walter White later wrote to Murphy to praise him for "the absolute fairness with which you conducted the recent trial."[51]

Unfazed by the all-white jury in the case, Darrow plumbed the depths of racism in Detroit. The neighborhood witnesses, Darrow announced, had lied when they denied throwing stones, when they minimized the size of the crowd, and when they claimed not to oppose Blacks moving onto their block. "I think every one of them lied," Darrow said candidly. And why had they lied? Was there "any question of their hatred and malice" against the defendants "because they were black"? Was there any question that the crowd was "there to drive them out" of their home? The hatred of the crowd had reappeared on the witness stand to finish the job and send the Sweets to prison. The mob on Garland Avenue was now asking a Detroit jury to act as the Arkansas jury had acted after the Elaine massacre and to become part of what Darrow called "the mob psychology which permeates crowds, through prejudice and feeling." Darrow had no doubt that the jury, too, had prejudice. "I am not blaming you; I am just stating a fact which is deeper than anything you gentlemen know of." And so Darrow challenged the jurors: "Put yourselves in that house on the corner," he dared them, "with a black skin and a white mob in front of you."[52]

The trial ended the day after Thanksgiving when a deadlocked jury reported its inability to reach a verdict. Judge Murphy declared a mistrial. In April 1926 the prosecutor began a series of new trials, now (at Darrow's insistence) trying each defendant one at a time beginning with Ossian Sweet's younger brother, Henry, who some believed had fired the offending rifle shots. Trial testimony proceeded as it had the first time. In his closing statement, Darrow again charged the white witnesses with a conspiracy of deception. "They have lied, and lied, and lied," he said. Again he insisted to an all-white jury that it, too, was racist: "Now, gentlemen, I say you are prejudiced." How could they not be, growing up in the United States of America, where the feeling of prejudice was "a part of your life long training." And Darrow redoubled his condemnation of racism in American life. "I believe the life of the Negro race," he concluded, "has been a life of tragedy, of injustice, of oppression. The law has made him equal, but man has not." Darrow exhorted the jurors to be better men and to live up to the principle of the law.[53]

In the courtroom as Darrow finished his argument, James Weldon Johnson "broke down and wept." There were few dry eyes among the Sweet allies when Darrow was done. And after three and a half hours of deliberation, the jury returned with a verdict of not guilty. The ordinarily formal and reserved Johnson hugged Darrow. The acquittal, Johnson wrote in *The Crisis*, marked "the end of the most dramatic court trial involving the fundamental rights of the Negro in his whole history in this country."[54]

Thanks to Darrow and the American Fund, the NAACP had won yet another victory in court. The Detroit prosecutor abandoned the other ten cases. And as Johnson explained in his address to the NAACP's annual conference in 1926, cases like Sweet's had helped put the courts front and center on the organization's agenda. "The Negro," Johnson explained, "has reached the point in his development where nothing vitally counts, except power." As Johnson saw it, insisting on civil rights in the courts was now a leading means for exercising the power that lay at Black Americans' disposal. "The courts," Johnson said, "are the most advantageous arena in which we can contend for the fulfilment of the guarantees that are ours in the constitution and the common laws of the land." To be sure, the courts often meant a "long and tedious" process, one that required "courage, tenacity, patience, and money," but Johnson insisted that "each time we win a court decision," the NAACP built "a bulwark for the protection of our rights of citizenship."[55]

Johnson and White announced that the case was a landmark because Darrow had won not by skirting the truth of the matter but by insisting "that race prejudice was at the bottom of all this trouble." That was why the outcome "meant much to Negroes." Victory on these terms meant that the race riots of the preceding decade would no longer be tolerated. The NAACP would defend African American migrants who defended themselves. At least sometimes the courts would go along. And indeed, the fiercely violent response to migration that had begun in East St. Louis in 1917 came to a temporary close on the Sweets' front lawn in Detroit. Johnson couldn't know that the Sweet trials would indeed mark a pause in the era of racist pogroms, at least not yet. But already he sensed the trials' importance. The key to the Detroit episode, he told NAACP members, was that "the Negroes themselves" had shown that they were "willing to fight for justice," and not only with weapons like the Sweet family's rifles but with a much more effective tool, too. "The most effective weapon," Johnson insisted, was dollars. With dollars the American Negro would vindicate the principle that "he who would be free, himself must strike the blow."[56]

The American Fund had supplied early ammunition for the Sweet case. And the case's outcome soon led it to supply more. When the NAACP raised far more than the amount it needed to earn the Fund's matching grant, the Fund redoubled its original $15,000 contribution, offering to match every additional $2 raised by the NAACP with $1 of its own. In all, including the American Fund's contributions, the NAACP raised $76,000, more than enough to cover what White estimated to be nearly $38,000 in fees and costs to defend the Sweet trials. With new optimism, Johnson thanked the American Fund for laying "a foundation for a Legal Defense Fund" and called for a new "Million Dollar Fund" for the NAACP's efforts. An endowment for the organization, he now insisted, was "possible and feasible," and the "recent effort for a legal defense fund" was proof.

"When the right of a negro to purchase and occupy a home and defend it against a mob was on trial," Johnson concluded, "we mobilized not only the faith, the courage, the determination, and the intelligence of the race and its friends, but also the money."[57]

A further payoff from the Sweet case would become apparent only years later. Frank Murphy, the presiding judge in both Sweet trials, stood not only for racial egalitarianism in the courtroom but also for a new kind of electoral politics, one that relied on a cross-race coalition of ethnic whites and working-class Blacks. The same mixed-race working-class coalition that made Murphy a judge in the early 1920s won him the Detroit mayor's office in 1930 over an opponent openly supported by the Klan. Murphy sealed his victory with the promise of what he called a "new deal" for Detroit. In 1932, Mayor Murphy would campaign for Franklin Roosevelt to be president on the platform of an expanded New Deal for the nation. Observers credited Murphy with nearly doubling the Democratic Party vote tally in Detroit's Black wards, which historically had voted Republican. Roosevelt won the state with 52 percent of the vote, becoming the first Democrat to take the state's electoral college votes since Grover Cleveland in 1892. Four years later, the swiftly expanding New Deal coalition swept Murphy into the governor's mansion. Three years after that, Roosevelt would make him his attorney general, and the year after that, Roosevelt appointed him to the U.S. Supreme Court. Some would later say that of all the justices on the Court in the entire twentieth century, Murphy was the most favorable toward the American Fund's two great causes: the labor movement and racial minorities. All this was in the future. But in the Sweet trials, where Murphy first came to national attention, the American Fund had helped produce a glimpse of a world to come.[58]

The Fund's culture program drew on James Weldon Johnson's experiences in the arts and letters during the first decade of the century, when he joined with his brother Rosamond (right) and impresario Bob Cole (left) to form Cole & Johnson Brothers, a trio who wrote, performed, and recorded popular songs like "Under the Bamboo Tree" and "Congo Love Song."

10

Capturing the Captors

I do not care a damn for any art that is not used for propaganda.
—W. E. B. DU BOIS, 1926

In December 1925, on the heels of the first Ossian Sweet trial in Detroit, James Weldon Johnson hosted an intimate dinner for Clarence Darrow at his Harlem home. Just a few months after Darrow's star turn in the Scopes evolution trial, the NAACP had invited the famous lawyer to New York for a mass meeting to raise money for the new legal defense fund—and to activate the terms of the American Fund's matching grant.[1]

The evening at Johnson's home gathered figures from the rapidly expanding world of Harlem culture. The young Black polymath Paul Robeson was there. A star college athlete, recently graduated from Columbia Law School, Robeson had paid for his legal education with summers in the American Professional Football Association, forerunner to the National Football League. Now turned to acting and music, Robeson was coming off starring roles in *All God's Chillun Got Wings* and *The Emperor Jones*, two buzzy plays about race in America by Eugene O'Neill, and he was soon to embark on what would be a successful concert tour singing Black spirituals. As the evening progressed, Darrow read aloud from his own autobiographical novel, which had just come out in a new edition. Robeson delivered a rendition of Johnson's poetry. Johnson later remembered the event as among the most memorable gatherings he and his wife, Grace, ever hosted.[2]

No one at the Johnson home that night doubted the power of literature, popular culture, and the arts to influence politics. The guests at Johnson's soiree were participants in the worlds of art and story and information to which observers like Walter Lippmann and Upton Sinclair had attributed so much power during and after the war. They were producers of ideas and images that bid to organize modern life.

So, as it turned out, was the American Fund on whose board Johnson served. Using what ultimately amounted to one-third of the Fund's total resources, the Fund's directors financed a culture program designed to intervene in the struggle for the catchphrases, images, and ideas with which Americans thought about basic social questions. In a world of dueling propaganda campaigns, it would not be sufficient merely to defend the rights of the kinds of people the Fund aimed to support; it would not be enough to defend Black criminal defendants like the Sweet family or the Arkansas sharecroppers, nor would it suffice to champion the rights of teachers like Scopes. To alter the world, the Fund's directors would need to finance a positive program of communication. They would need to help convey ideas and information that Americans would not otherwise encounter. Sometimes this meant forms of cultural expression that sought to break conventions and stereotypes. At other times, the Fund supported the distribution of basic information that existing media and cultural institutions seemed unlikely to impart.

Either way, challenges arose. One difficulty, which Johnson faced in his own literary career, was the age-old problem of reconciling art and politics. A second was the new and looming cultural power of Soviet communism.

Fascinating Perils

Johnson knew firsthand some of the ways popular culture could disrupt social conventions. But he had also seen popular culture entrench a society's worst stereotypes.

Living back in Jacksonville during the summer of 1914, after Woodrow Wilson and William Jennings Bryan had pushed him out of the State Department, Johnson had tried his hand at screenplay writing. With his hometown bidding against a little-known California town called Hollywood to become the center of the American film industry, Johnson wrote six short scenarios. The Lubin Manufacturing Company, a leading early film production firm, purchased one for a decent fee, quickly producing and distributing it as a short film. Johnson sold two more scenarios that summer. It seemed as if he had identified a lucrative new opportunity. His wife's family congratulated him warmly on the success of his new venture in the world of the photoplay, as early films were known.[3]

But there was a problem. Moving pictures depicting Black characters were almost uniformly degrading. Film production companies relied on Jacksonville for the Black actors and southern settings needed to create so-called minstrel films. Ever since the Edison company had produced a short film in 1894 depicting Black children in minstrel-like sequences, crude stories of Black life in the South had been among the most marketable products for film production companies. Such films adopted the most hateful stereotypes of nineteenth-century minstrel shows. Lubin had distributed its first minstrel-themed film, *Cake Walk*, in 1898. A few years later, a Lubin-produced film called *Who Said Watermelon?* featured two Black women ravenously consuming melons for the amusement of white onlookers. A stream of films followed, most of them featuring Black actors in blackface, all of them confirming the foundational conventions of Jim Crow. The characters stole. They lied. They adopted a foolish pomposity. They were parodies of a people.[4]

Critics denounced such films for planting "the seed of savagery in the breasts of those whites who even in this enlightened day and time are not any too far from barbarism." A Black columnist in the *New York News* described the supposedly comedic shorts as "caricatures of the black race." Worst of all, the columnist continued, was "the gruesome thought that members of our own race" were helping to produce such films. "Let us say," he concluded, "that the pittance they earn is as vile as the pieces of silver Judas threw into the Potter's field."[5]

Johnson's screenplays for Lubin involved precisely the kinds of stories the Black press decried. His first scenario was titled *Aunt Mandy's Chicken Dinner*; like each of the three screenplays he sold, it bore the subtitle *A Darkey Comedy*. Lubin released it in 1914 as *Mandy's Chicken Dinner*, featuring a love triangle between three Black characters played for ridicule and laughter. In the story, one suitor stole a chicken and tried to pin the theft on the other; predictable high jinks ensued in a fashion that portrayed the Black characters as hapless and stupid.[6]

Reactions in the Black press to Johnson's photoplay were swift and severe. The *Chicago Defender* called it "disgusting," "raw," and "vile." William Foster, a Black film producer based in Chicago with an outpost in Jacksonville, singled out the picture as especially "degrading and making the race ridiculous from every viewpoint." Moving pictures on such topics, Foster complained, "only appeal to the ignorant class and race-hating whites." Seeing his work on-screen, Johnson was horrified, too. When he and his wife, Grace, watched it in the theater, he later remembered, they "were so disappointed in it" as to be "actually ashamed." He had become a participant in the production of the same demeaning stereotypes he spent much of his adult life trying to overcome. Johnson never wrote a screenplay again. A year later, when D. W. Griffith's blockbuster film *The Birth of a Nation* came out in theaters, Johnson condemned it for its vicious racist stereotypes. The film, he wrote in the *New York Age*, was "an outrage on a race."[7]

To Johnson's good fortune, few outside his family knew he had written a minstrel show screenplay. Lubin acquired photoplay scenarios as work-for-hire; Johnson's film appeared on-screen without attribution and without so much as a screen credit at the film's end. Not even Foster, whose film production company tried to produce work that would reflect the dignity of Black life, seems to have connected Johnson to the dreadful film. The editors at the *Chicago Defender* never made the connection. Johnson's reputation survived unscathed.

But Johnson had learned a lesson. Popular culture imposed powerful pressures to adapt to the preexisting views of an audience—to what Lippmann and George Creel would soon be calling the stereotypes and catchphrases of the culture.

Johnson had first addressed the politics of the arts in September 1917, when he attended a conference in Bellport, Long Island, hosted by Lippmann's old organization, the Intercollegiate Socialist Society. Coming just two months after the East St. Louis race riots had left more than a hundred Black people dead, Johnson's session addressed "American Democracy and the Negro." But when Johnson stood up, he spoke not about electoral politics or court cases. Taking up a race man's twist on public opinion's role in democracy, he chose as his subject Black people's contributions to American culture and ideas.[8]

The conventional story, Johnson observed, was that the Black community was a "beggar under the nation's table waiting to be thrown the crumbs of civilization." But the truth of the matter, he asserted, was very different. "The Negro," Johnson contended, "has helped to shape and mold and make America." He was "a creator as well as a creature," and "a giver as well as a receiver." Of all the contributions to literature and the arts made by Americans, Johnson stated, those of Black artists stood out as the most distinctive. "The only things artistic in America that have sprung from American soil, permeated American life, and been universally acknowledged as distinctively American," he announced, have been "the creations of the American Negro."[9]

The "folk-art creations of the Negro" were Johnson's lead example; he listed Black folklore such as the Uncle Remus stories, along with dance and music, both secular and sacred. The Negro spiritual, for example, had gained widespread acclaim ever since the Fisk Jubilee Singers had brought the spirituals on tour from Fisk University in the 1870s. Even more influential was the "lighter music" produced by African American artists like Johnson and his brother—"our national medium for expressing ourselves musically in popular form," as he characterized it. Johnson held up ragtime as "the only artistic production sprung from American soil that is known the world over" as a "distinctive American product." Ragtime, Johnson later urged, had become the popular mode for America's musical expression. Who could say "that it does not express the blare and jangle and the surge, too, of our national spirit?"[10]

Johnson returned to the point when he joined the board of the American Fund. "No people that has produced great literature and art," he wrote in 1922, "has ever been looked upon by the world as distinctly inferior." For the rest of the decade, Johnson published anthologies of Black poetry and spirituals to show the African roots of American popular culture, gathering the cultural contributions of African Americans from the earliest days of slavery to urban Harlem in the twentieth century.[11]

Johnson's colleague at the NAACP, W. E. B. Du Bois, shared his friend's commitment to using cultural accomplishments to prove the genius of Black America. Even as the two men crafted their proposal about children's school studies in the South for the American Fund, Du Bois asserted that "a revival of art and literature" would be crucial in what he called "the immediate program of the American Negro." In Du Bois's words, Black artists' contributions to American life were the "singular spiritual heritage of the nation."[12]

Du Bois doubled the number of poems and short stories he published in *The Crisis* during the 1920s. Covers of the magazine featured stylish images of dignified men and beautiful women. The "great mission of the Negro to America and the modern world," Du Bois announced in 1922, "is the development of Art and the appreciation of the Beautiful." He inaugurated an influential literary competition at *The Crisis*. The National Urban League's magazine, *Opportunity*, established a rival competition.[13]

In the outpouring of Harlem arts and letters that followed, the Fund was a modest but not insubstantial player. Its education grants helped sustain *The Crisis*. The Fund subsidized *The Messenger*, a magazine edited by a young socialist named A. Philip Randolph. With a nudge from James Weldon Johnson, the Fund made grants to support the poet Claude McKay, whose verse and novels offered candid accounts of the Black experience from the Caribbean to Harlem. The poet Langston Hughes and, later, the novelists Ralph Ellison and Richard Wright published their work in publications supported by Fund grants.[14]

Just as important as such small grants was the way the Fund connected debates taking place uptown and downtown. During his service at the Greenwich Village–based Fund, Johnson took a lead role in engaging a question that roiled the Harlem arts scene. The precocious intellectual Alain Leroy Locke stood for one side of the debate. Born in Philadelphia in 1885, Locke graduated from Harvard in 1907 and went on to be the first Black Rhodes scholar from the United States before joining the faculty of Howard University's philosophy department. In 1924, Locke helped mark Harlem's coming of age by organizing a grand, one-hundred-person literary dinner at the Civic Club, in the same space where the Fund met each month. The next year, Locke edited a widely celebrated special issue of *The Survey*, an influential progressive magazine, documenting the spirit of the evening, with essays, poems, and art by Du Bois, Johnson, and a dozen others, including poets Hughes and McKay. Black workers featured prominently in an essay by Charles S. Johnson of the National Urban League. And in Locke's view, the "New Negro" of Harlem had made a choice. The

The cover of Alain Locke's special Harlem issue of Survey Graphic, *March 1925.*

New Negro chose beauty and aesthetic ideals over the propaganda—"pro-Negro as well as anti-Negro"—that had burdened Black art in the past.[15]

Du Bois, who had once struck some of the same notes, took an opposing view at the next annual NAACP conference. The art of Black America could not afford to pursue beauty over politics. "I do not care a damn," he bluntly told the attendees, "for any art that is not used for propaganda." Scholars have excavated the Locke–Du Bois debate ever since. But the two men's views arose out of a shared understanding of the underlying problem. Catchphrases and stereotypes had locked the Black image into narrow confines, reflecting and reproducing a system of oppressive public opinion. Langston Hughes made a similar point sharply in the pages of *The Nation* that same year. American culture had created a small set of standardized stereotypes for the Black figure. The obstacle "standing in the way of any true Negro art in America," Hughes asserted, was "the desire to pour" artists' representation of the race into the caricatures of Jim Crow, into what he called "the mold of American standardization."[16]

In the choice between beauty and propaganda, it fell to Johnson to identify a third mode of cultural expression, one he hoped would break the suffocating molds Hughes had identified. Ever since his screenplay disaster, Johnson had ached to find a form of Black cultural expression that would, as he put it, be capable of "expressing the imagery, the idioms, the peculiar turns of thought, and the distinctive humor and pathos, too, of the Negro" while not being weighed down by the history of Black dialect and minstrelsy.[17]

In 1927, Johnson published a slim but powerful volume of poems titled *God's Trombones*. The book's introduction announced the demise of the dialect tradition. "Traditional Negro dialect as a form for Aframerican poets," he asserted, "is absolutely dead." In its place, Johnson drew on a sermon language he called a "fusion of Negro idioms with Bible English." In the cadences of Black preachers, Johnson proposed, one could hear the "old African tongues," now "saturated with the sublime phraseology of the Hebrew prophets and steeped in the idioms of King James English." Johnson titled his new collection *God's Trombones* because the trombone played a continuous chromatic scale. "Like the human voice or the violin," Johnson observed, the trombone was capable of doing what the two binary notes of humor and pathos in traditional dialect could not: express a full range of notes to match the full, limitless range of the Black experience.[18]

Thoughtful readers instantly appreciated the significance of Johnson's accomplishment. The poet Countee Cullen said that Johnson had found "a medium with a latitude capable of embracing the Negro experience." The editors of the *Washington Eagle*, a Black paper, reported that "you put the slim book aside with a gasp at the immensity of it." Reading Johnson, they said, was like walking "with God on the parapets of infinity." The *Baltimore Afro-American* crowed that Johnson had "not descended

The Angel Gabriel on Judgment Day, *from Johnson's 1927 poetry volume,* God's Trombones, *by Harlem Renaissance artist Aaron Douglas.*

into dialect" and yet had "managed to convey" the original tones of the Black preacher in a form that was at once sublime and authentic. Hughes called Johnson's work "a folk synthesis of genuine beauty" and praised it for showing how to move away from the "quaintness of dialect" while preserving "Negro idioms and flavor."[19]

Johnson had come as close as anyone to crafting an artistic form that inverted what Du Bois had called the double consciousness of the Black experience. Du Bois had proposed that to be Black in America was to have the experience of "looking at one's self through the eyes of others, of measuring one's soul by the tape of a world that looks on in amused contempt and pity." Johnson's sly idea was to reverse the process. If white audiences could be drawn into a Black cultural form that was free of the minstrel legacy, then one would witness, as Johnson put it, "the paradox of the captor becoming the willing slave of the captive." A century earlier, the German philosopher Hegel had observed that slaves had a paradoxical power over their masters; the latter could not exist without the former. The identity of the master, Hegel had observed, was in this symbolic respect inextricably beholden to the slave. Now Johnson saw a similar dynamic in American popular culture. "The Negro," Johnson noted wryly, "drags his captors captive."[20]

Culture for the New Masses

Johnson's electric idea made him an intermediary between Harlem debates and the culture world of the American Fund left.

For the Fund's liberals and radicals, white and Black alike, capitalism twisted the conventions of working-class culture much as Jim Crow distorted Black life. The basic patterns of American popular culture—its ways of telling stories, its orientation toward uplift, its reverence for the robber baron elite—seemed to have been shaped by the logic of capital. The spirit of Horatio Alger, the late nineteenth-century author of popular books about young men who pulled themselves up by their own pluck and ingenuity, dominated the cultural landscape even as the chasm between the haves and have-nots grew wider. Such stories of "smug little morals," as the critic Mark Van Doren described them, substituted images that were vivid for facts that were true.[21]

The Fund's culture program supported writers and artists whose work, like that of Johnson, Locke, and Du Bois in Harlem, aimed to break the Procrustean beds of conventional cultural expression. Working-class American culture, asserted the Fund, was like the Black cultural traditions with which it overlapped. It was unexpectedly capacious. It contained resources for resistance to the dulling uniformity of mainstream culture. It promised to liberate the imagination.[22]

The Fund had made cultural grants from its earliest months. It supported the flourishing Christian socialist magazine *The World Tomorrow*, which advocated the platform of nonviolent change associated with the pacifist Fellowship of Reconciliation. Grants and loans went to *Pax*, the magazine of the Women's International League for Peace and

Freedom, and to the *New Republic*, which Lippmann had founded and where Fund director Robert Morss Lovett was on staff. The Fund issued grants to more radical publications, too, including a Spanish-language anarchist newspaper called *Cultura Obrera*, the Industrial Workers of the World's printing house, and the Communist Party newspaper, the *Daily Worker*. A Soviet literary and political magazine titled *Novyi Mir* received modest loans from the Fund in 1925, breaking from the Fund's usual policy against supporting foreign projects. Between 1924 and 1926, the Fund sponsored a labor-oriented Speakers Service Bureau based in Washington, D.C., and Minnesota, adapting George Creel's wartime strategy to the dissemination of ideas about the labor movement.[23]

In the mid-1920s, substantial grants—totaling $33,400—also went to a fledgling monthly called *New Masses*. The magazine's editors aimed to carry on the artistic and literary legacy of the prewar magazine *The Masses*, which had been shut down by the Wilson administration in 1917. The new magazine was staffed by youthful stars of the New York literary scene. Cartoonist Art Young, whose startling send-ups of plutocrats and warmongers had provoked the Wilson administration, joined the novelist John Dos Passos on the magazine's editorial board. The essayist and critic Edmund Wilson, only recently removed from service in a medical unit on the Western Front, played a lead role. So did playwright Eugene O'Neill. Old hands from *The Masses* took part as well, editor Max Eastman among them. But *New Masses* promised to dedicate itself to "creative youth," "artistic rebelliousness," and "experimentation," and to present itself to working-class and middle-class readers alike as "a symbol of hope and of liberation." It would eschew orthodox Marxism, its early editors assured the Fund, and revive instead an updated version of the old "satirical spirit" of the original. Taking Alain Locke's position in the Harlem debate with Du Bois, the editors committed themselves to "the highest standard of art and literature"; standards of beauty, they asserted, were "deeply human" and always better than crude propaganda. The magazine invested in art forms that aimed to be young and vital, forms based in popular culture like slang, vaudeville, moving pictures, and radio. Each issue would "strike its roots strongly into American reality." Black poets like Langston Hughes and Claude McKay wrote on working-class themes in its pages. Fund support for the magazine began with start-up financing in 1925 and commenced in earnest with the new magazine's first issue in 1926.[24]

Grants went to theatrical groups, fiction writers, and film producers. Awards in 1926 and 1927 to support a textile workers strike in Passaic, New Jersey, helped finance a landmark labor film documenting the strike. Wide-angle shots captured crowds of strikers demanding a rollback of wage cuts; close-ups delivered vivid representations of what strike organizers called "the real happenings" on the picket lines and in the relief kitchens. The resulting seven-reel film, *The Passaic Textile Strike*, mixed documentary footage with a melodrama drawn from the life of a textile-worker family.[25]

A similar grant to Max Eastman supported the early stages of an epic documentary film of the Russian Revolution. Narrated by Eastman, the film used astonishing archival footage from the revolution itself to offer an anti-Stalinist account of the events of 1917. After a decade of internal

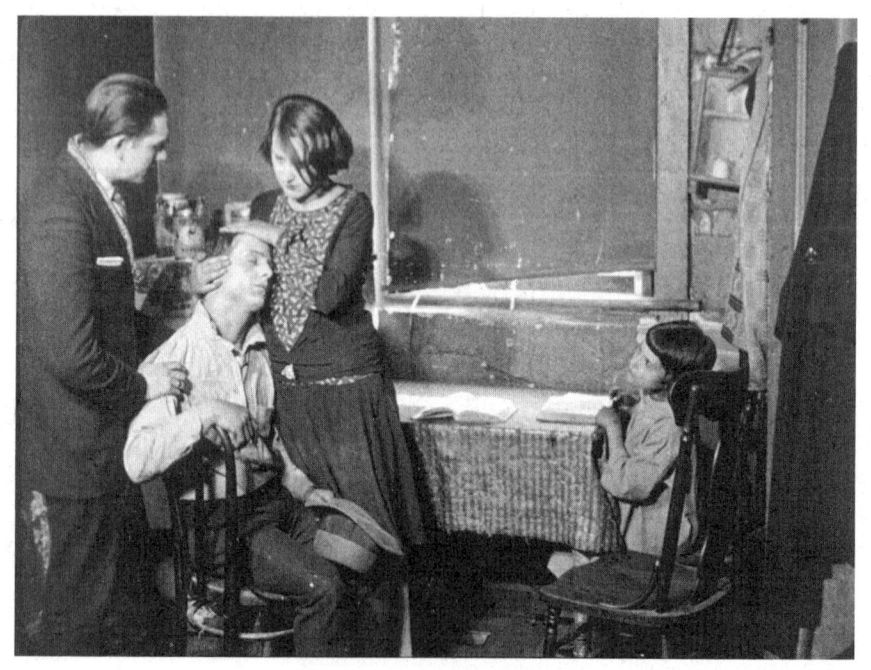

A still from The Passaic Textile Strike, *the innovative 1926 silent film made by and for striking wool mill workers in New Jersey.*

bickering among the producers, the documentary came out in theaters to critical acclaim in 1937 as *Tsar to Lenin*. New York's *Herald Tribune* called it "history in the making" in a way that had "never before been brought to the screen."[26]

The Fund's directors rejected more proposals for arts and culture projects than they accepted. They turned down the immigrant theater director Elia Kazan and the Black playwright Garland Anderson, both of whom would later emerge as artists of the first rank. The Fund turned away experimental theater applications from promising new drama troupes, declined to fund an art gallery proposal from Art Young, and dismissed many more. The culture program, for all its ambition, presented a persistent dilemma. The problem was that cultural productions needing philanthropic support were, almost by definition, unlikely to reach a large audience. Artistic projects that could reach an audience had commercial prospects; they did not need the American Fund. But if the goal of the culture program was to change society, then financing projects with no audience was like throwing money into the wind.[27]

The Fund's support for a news organization known as Federated Press offered one path to solving the paradox of financing culture efforts. Established in Chicago in the wake of the Pittsburgh steel strike in 1919, Federated Press aimed to be a news syndication service that would break through capitalists' control of newspaper and magazine coverage. The Press would serve to distribute the labor movement's stories. Soon it had one hundred affiliated newspapers in the United States and several more abroad. In 1925, the syndication service boasted bureaus in Chicago, New York, and Washington, from which it circulated stories to 150 papers and to individual subscribers who received the Press's supplemental weekly newsletter.[28]

Federated Press reporters in 1920 had covered the open warfare at Matewan, West Virginia, that pitted hundreds of striking coal miners against the coal operators' private militia of 2,000 gunmen. Once the Fund's support for the Press began in 1923, many of its articles covered events in which the Fund was involved. Though such articles rarely mentioned the Fund by name, the Press distributed stories about the NAACP's Supreme Court victory in the sharecropper case arising out

THE FEDERATED PRESS BULLETIN

OFFICIAL ORGAN OF THE FEDERATED PRESS LEAGUE

Vol. 6—No. 15   CHICAGO, ILL., SATURDAY, JAN. 12, 1924   Price 5 Cents

BITUMINOUS WAGE CONFERENCE MEETS
Operators at Cleveland Agree to Include Penna. With Ohio, Indiana and Illinois in Contract

Open Shop Negligence Ends In Fatal Explosion at Rockefeller Plant

Federated Press distributed news stories about labor and capital from a labor point of view.

of the Arkansas massacre. A correspondent for the Press named Esther Lowell reported on the Sweet trials in Detroit in 1925. Lowell and her journalist husband toured the South writing about Black workers in 1927 and 1928; the American Fund financed their trip and Federated Press distributed their stories.[29]

Supporting a syndication service like the Press proved far more cost effective than propping up radical newspapers. In all, the Fund made grants of just over $81,000 to Federated Press between 1923 and 1932. Each year in the mid-1920s, the Fund's money amounted to nearly a third of the Press's annual operating budget. Subsidizing Federated Press, moreover, allowed the Fund's directors to respond directly to the concerns that had helped inspire the Fund in the first place. Upton Sinclair had argued to the founding directors in the fall of 1922 that the "main trouble with our situation at the present time" was that "the people do not get the facts." For Sinclair, the Fund would be a way to support the dissemination of political information to the people—to ensure that "the facts are got to them." For Sinclair's purpose, Federated Press was an ideal institution. It required relatively modest sums to meet its budget. It leveraged its influence through a network of existing labor and left newspapers around the country, papers with their own distribution channels and their own lists of subscribers.[30]

The Fund's engagement with a labor movement radio station illuminated the mix of opportunities and risks that shadowed the Fund's cultural program. In early 1927, the Chicago Federation of Labor set up a pioneering labor movement radio station, WCFL, and put out a call for the establishment of labor stations around the country. Fund director Norman Thomas, who had recently been refused access to the airwaves on local New York stations, responded with an effort to acquire a radio station for the Socialist Party in New York City. Known as "Debs Memorial Radio" and using the call sign WEVD for the initials of the late socialist leader Eugene Victor Debs, Thomas brought the radio station plan to his fellow directors at the Fund for financing in late 1927. WEVD was deeply connected in the world of the Fund. Roger Baldwin sat on the board of the fledgling radio endeavor; so did Fund director Robert Morss Lovett and former Fund director Sidney Hillman. The new radio initiative proposed to establish a nonpartisan broadcast that would give voice to the "radical and labor movements" on the nation's new airwaves.[31]

The Fund had already begun to consider establishing a broadcasting station of its own, apart from Thomas's WEVD. Working-class Americans were acquiring ever-cheaper radio receivers at an astonishing rate; starting at essentially zero in 1920, by 1930 somewhere between one in two and one in three working-class urban families had a radio. The Radio Act of 1927, in turn, was reshaping the landscape of what new listeners could hear. Where the early days of the airwaves had been a cacophony of small broadcasters, the act empowered the federal government to allocate the broadcasting band to large general broadcasters, many of them affiliated with the National Broadcasting Company. Smaller broadcasters—the act's new Federal Radio Commission called them "propaganda stations"—lost out on the theory that big broadcasters and their general programming better suited the law's requirement that the radio band be distributed in the public interest.[32]

With radio ever more important, and with the new federal commission favoring large commercial broadcasters, the Fund championed the project of a "Free Speech Radio Station," one that would give preference to the voices of what an ACLU report, written for the Fund's directors, called "minority movements." The ACLU report did not mean racial minorities in particular, though they were included; the ACLU meant dissidents of all kinds, encompassing the voices of labor, socialist, and working-class organizations.[33]

Citing its own radio plans, the American Fund declined to participate in the first round of fundraising for WEVD. Thomas and the Socialist

Eugene Victor Debs Radio (WEVD), pictured here in an ad from 1942, put labor news and commentary on the airwaves.

Party were nonetheless able to raise start-up money from the International Ladies' Garment Workers Union and several other unions with deep connections to the Fund. And for a time, the station lived up to its billing. "Political and social justice," explained the managing director, "is one of the great objectives of Station WEVD." Programming included a "Jewish Hour," a news show called *Labor Looks at the Week*, and reports on labor conditions and strikes from around the country. Federated Press ran a show in 1929, as did the Socialist-backed Rand School.[34]

The experience of WCFL in Chicago, however, soon led Baldwin to conclude that a Fund-sponsored radio station would not attract enough listeners unless it emphasized music and entertainment over labor or radical content. The "serious stuff," Baldwin told Upton Sinclair, had to be "fed in small doses in between." Without what Baldwin called "commercial appeal," radical radio seemed to its critics like an echo chamber.[35]

WEVD's own path followed as Baldwin predicted. By the early 1930s, it became a station that offered entertainment nearly all the time—what one radio scholar describes as "musical programs, vaudeville, and sports and foreign language programs"—with a modest hour or two each day reserved for labor content. Most of all, Debs Radio lacked a secure financing structure. Refusing to run advertisements, it was reliant on the voluntary support of labor unions. But as WCFL in Chicago was learning, unions had financial challenges of their own.[36]

In 1931, continuing financial difficulties led Debs Memorial Radio and WEVD back to the Fund in an effort to reorganize itself as an "open forum for all minority groups"—a place where "dissident minority viewpoints" could broadcast their ideas. The Fund pledged support in principle, but the station concluded that the open forum concept was unworkable. WEVD sold itself instead to the *Jewish Daily Forward*. Over the years, the station limped on, merging eventually with the Jehovah's Witnesses' radio broadcasting station. The call sign WEVD survived until 2003.[37]

The Vanguard

For all its creativity and perseverance, the Fund's culture program sailed headlong into a storm that nearly sank the American left in the 1920s.

In 1923, shortly after the Fund's formation, the Communist International in Moscow ordered all the Communist factions of the U.S. to consolidate into a single Workers Party of America. From nearly the start, the Workers Party followed Soviet orders to enforce a new orthodoxy in what had been a fractured and discordant world of American communism. Two decades earlier, Lenin had proposed that "a party of a new type" could serve as the "vanguard of the proletarian struggle." Now "Bolshevization" was the first order of business, which meant centralization and a disciplined adherence to the Party line. The American branch of the Communist Party took up the effort with the zeal of a convert.[38]

If the Communist program roiled the American left in the 1920s, it posed special challenges to the heterodox amalgam of left and liberal causes in and around the American Fund. Roger Baldwin had thought it vital to include a Communist voice in the Fund's operations. He had included his old comrade William Z. Foster from the 1919 steel strike on the Fund's board to ensure what Baldwin hoped would be a diverse array of left and liberal perspectives.

Yet Baldwin had intended for Communist influence to remain limited. He believed that one Party member on the board was enough. ("One only, all alone," Baldwin insisted.) When Foster missed Fund board meetings because of Party commitments, his fellow board members refused to seat the proxies he sent in his place. Baldwin publicly criticized the Soviets for their political prisoners, excoriated Party apparatchiks in America for authoritarian tactics, and opposed the appointment of any further Party members to the board. As late as 1926 Baldwin pressed to expand the anti-Communist contingent on the board and resisted further funding for Communist projects. The Party, in turn, attacked the Fund as a counter-revolutionary outfit, ridiculing the directors as "a terrible bunch." Party insiders singled out Baldwin and the Socialist leader Norman Thomas for special derision.[39]

Communist influence, however, proved hard to contain. For one thing, the Party in the 1920s had committed itself to a policy of quietly taking control of liberal and labor organizations to expand its power. Foster was a leading practitioner of the art of "boring from within," as it was known in party circles. At the same time, labor union failures in the face of a concerted anti-union offensive by American employers in the first half of the 1920s had demoralized the main currents of the American left. Baldwin, for one, began to worry that the Communist Party might be the only energetic radical organization still standing. Inside the Fund, the appeal of Communist efforts grew.[40]

Communist influence led the directors in 1925 to break their rule against supporting enterprises outside the United States. In one of the Fund's most unusual efforts, it extended more than $33,000 to a Soviet agriculture experiment one thousand miles east of Moscow. Russian Reconstruction Farms, as the operation was known, aimed to spark a new era in cooperative farming. Soviet collectivization and Ford Motor Company farm machinery, according to the program's publicity efforts, promised to "end hunger in the world forever." The model farm sought to be "an example to all in Russia and a constructive token of friendship and good will for all men to see." But the experiment was doomed from the start. Its chief opponent on the board, Norman Thomas, had tried to say so, but his fellow directors voted in favor. Before long, the Soviet farm collapsed in a heap of rusted tractors, leaving the Fund's loans in default.[41]

A second sign of the Party's influence was Vanguard Press. The Fund had first pursued the idea of a publishing house in 1922 when Upton Sinclair urged it to establish a publisher to keep his own books in print. The Fund turned him down. But the possibility of establishing a publishing house intrigued the board. Within a few years, a business plan was on the table. Named to evoke Lenin's "vanguard of the proletariat," the Fund's publishing idea set out to produce "books in the Vanguard of thought for the Vanguard of humanity." Among other things, the Press would serve as an outlet for research supported by the Fund, especially when such research produced works that were "of a sort that regular publishers are not prepared to handle," either because they were too radical, or because demand was too low—or both, as often proved to be the case.[42]

In its role as sole shareholder in Vanguard Press, the American Fund laid out more than $100,000 in 1925 and 1926 to get the Press running and another $65,000 combined across the subsequent two years. American Fund directors Norman Thomas, Roger Baldwin, Morris Ernst, and Scott Nearing took seats on the publishing house board, as did directors Elizabeth Gurley Flynn and Clinton Golden for a time.[43]

The Press published pocket sized volumes with cheap bindings on timely topics. Early titles featured subjects like labor unions and monetary policy. A "What Is" series boasted titles such as *What Is Mutualism?*, *What Is Co-operation?*, and *What Is the Single Tax?* (the latter a reference to the land tax theory of nineteenth-century American radical Henry George, whose book *Progress and Poverty* Vanguard put back in print). The new house reprinted a classic book on sex (Edward Carpenter's *Love's Coming of Age*) and published a new one on birth control (Mary Ware Dennett's *Who's Obscene?*). It published a summary of Darwin's *Descent of Man* in a series called "Great Books Made Easy." An "A, B, C" series printed primers on the sciences and philosophy. The novelist James T. Farrell's "Studs Lonigan" trilogy cast a harsh light on social conditions for poor Irish Catholics in Chicago. Theodor Geisel, writing under the pen name Dr. Seuss, published his first children's books with Vanguard, including the classic story *The 500 Hats of Bartholomew Cubbins*.[44]

Closer to the heart of its project, Vanguard published a new English translation of the Russian anarchist Peter Kropotkin's pamphlets, as well as Lenin's *The State and Revolution* bound together with Lenin's *Imperialism*. Another series curated titles on American imperialism, mostly in Latin America. Vanguard made a standing offer to liberal organizations to go half in on the publication of books of "permanent educational value."[45]

In the middle of 1926, Scott Nearing, who chaired the Fund's Research Committee from his subsistence farm in New Jersey, proposed that the Fund partner with its own publisher to produce a series on Soviet Russia. As Nearing conceived it, the series would aim to spread the word about conditions on the ground in the new Soviet regime—"to answer the question," he wrote to Vanguard Press, of "what is actually happening in the Soviet Union."[46]

From the beginning, Nearing promised objectivity. The series required a director, he said, who was "not officially committed or biased," but who was "sincerely interested in the social experiments" of the Soviets. It was crucial, he continued in a letter to the skeptical Norman Thomas, that the studies not be "propaganda in any sense." He wanted, he tried to assure Thomas, exactly what Thomas himself had endorsed: a "picture" of the "actual working of the system in Russia."[47]

But Nearing's increasing adherence to the Soviet line compromised his ability to insist on the objectivity to which he purported to commit. Long a heterodox Marxist, Nearing joined the Party officially in 1927. To oversee the Vanguard Press series on Russia, Nearing tapped Jerome Davis, a sociologist at Yale University whose work with the YMCA in Moscow during the revolution of 1917 had instilled in him a deep interest in Soviet affairs. Davis, who would soon be fired from his untenured Yale post for his radical views, mixed heroic defenses of academic freedom and support for the most deserving groups, on the one hand, with lapses of judgment, on the other. He served on the advisory board of the ill-fated Russian Reconstruction Farms, and by the early 1930s, he was minimizing Stalin's murderous show trials. Davis asserted unapologetically that "a measure of dictatorship" might be required as the U.S. transitioned to its own revolutionary era.[48]

Anti-Communist critics on the Fund board, Norman Thomas chief among them, objected to the design of the Russian Studies series. Anything overseen by Nearing and Davis, one critic protested, would appeal only to readers who were already true believers. Roger Baldwin shared the critics' concerns, at least in part. Looking at a list of proposed authors for the studies—a list that included Nearing himself—Baldwin told Davis that he doubted the series would yield unbiased research.[49]

As it happened, Baldwin soon wrote a volume of his own for Vanguard Press, one that he would later regret.

In late 1926, after a grueling year running the ACLU and the Fund, he was exhausted. His separation from his wife, Madeleine Doty, became permanent, and Baldwin experienced what he described to Doty as "depressions"; "life," he confided, "really didn't seem worth living." His doctor identified a heart condition and prescribed rest. And so Baldwin planned a leave of absence and a season of European travel. The point was to get away from work, but Davis asked him if he would visit the Soviet Union and write a volume on civil liberties and free expression there; Baldwin demurred, recommending Harvard's Zechariah Chafee instead. But Davis persisted and proposed to pay for his travel out of the Vanguard–American Fund joint venture. Baldwin agreed and extended his European travels to include the Soviet Union.[50]

From the start of his trip, he heard from the ship crew what he later remembered as "weird tales of what was going on in Russia." At a prison in the Georgian Republic of the USSR, political prisoners laughed at him outright when he told them he was studying civil liberty under the Soviets. A guide who spoke too candidly soon disappeared. And writing to his mother from Moscow, Baldwin reported that the country seemed "completely controlled"; former professional classes and elites were beset by "fear and repression." But such experiences had only a modest effect on Baldwin's estimation of the new social experiment he was studying. For one thing, the city's working class seemed, he believed, to be "really free, in the saddle bossing the whole show," like nowhere else in the world. As he later recalled, he thus "made allowances" for what he felt certain was a "noble experiment." An atmosphere of intimidation and anxiety, Baldwin concluded, "was a trifle against the vastly greater liberties of the people won by the Revolution."[51]

The resulting Vanguard Press book, *Liberty Under the Soviets*, published in 1928, offered a credulous account of life in Bolshevik Russia. Baldwin conceded forthrightly "the facts of universal censorship of all means of communication and the complete suppression of any organized opposition to the dictatorship or its program." No civil liberty existed "for opponents of the regime." But the repressions were worthwhile, he asserted, because they were necessary for and outweighed by the "basic economic freedom" that the revolution afforded to workers and peasants.[52]

The shortsightedness of Baldwin's version of Soviet conditions was remarkable most of all because it contradicted one of his most basic tenets. Baldwin believed that civil liberties were indispensable to achieving social change "with a minimum of violence." He said so at the time, and nothing in the Soviet case exempted it from this basic underlying principle. But Baldwin was hardly alone in his blinkered account. American liberals and labor union leaders touring Russia in the mid-1920s produced an outpouring of unrealistic accounts. Columnists at the *New York Times* and *The Nation* praised the Soviet order. The philosopher John Dewey's *Impressions of Soviet Russia*, published in 1929, did the same. An American Fund insider named Jim Maurer, long a labor leader in Pennsylvania, led a tour for a contingent of the American Federation of Labor that reported "progress and hope."[53]

Some saw more clearly. The anarchist Alexander Berkman, who helped Baldwin translate documents for the book, called him naive. Emma Goldman, whom Baldwin had known since his St. Louis days and who had been disillusioned with the Soviet experiment for the better part of a decade, delivered an unsparing critique.[54]

Such criticisms led Baldwin to add a corrections page to a later edition. But the corrections did not fundamentally alter Baldwin's upbeat assessment. Indeed, Baldwin had anticipated the problem. "My bias," he told Davis before beginning the project, "is pro-Soviet." The "economic and political experiment in Russia," he said, was of such "overwhelming importance" he was willing to make "civil liberties a quite secondary issue."[55]

Baldwin would rue his assessment before the next decade was out. *Liberty Under the Soviets*, he later noted, "became to me a mockery, and an epitaph for the burial of a misplaced faith." Baldwin, as the critic Dwight Macdonald observed, had glossed "over unfavorable evidence with the varnish of faith." Events, Baldwin soon admitted, "proved my judgment wrong."[56]

Shares of First National Bank of New York, shown here in its offices at 88–96 Broadway in lower Manhattan, were the Fund's principal asset.

11

Money Haters and Tax Lawyers

Political agitation . . . must be conducted without public subvention.
—JUDGE LEARNED HAND, 1930

The American Fund used the fruits of a Wall Street fortune to attack capitalism and inequality. Board members sometimes rolled their eyes in wry amusement. The irony was palpable. But critics were less charitable.

Charges of hypocrisy came from all sides, ranging from congressional committees and the conservative press to disappointed applicants and disgruntled leftists. The critics charged that Roger Baldwin and the Fund—"capitalist angels of left wing propaganda," one skeptic sneered—used money as a paradoxical "antitoxin to the capitalist system." They were "money haters," as the *New York Tribune* called them, who willingly relied on capitalism's riches when it suited them to do so.[1]

The Fund's directors answered the charge of inconsistency with a story of their own. They insisted that the only responsible path—the only strategy supported by principle and practicality alike—was to leave no resource unused, no tool idle in the campaign to change the country for the better. Critics were unmollified. But they would have been nearly apoplectic had they known that, behind the scenes, the Fund's leaders were assiduously exploiting and even expanding the legal privileges afforded to great fortunes by the modern tax code.

Accumulations of wealth had long taken advantage of special legal privileges for charities and inheritance. Since the Middle Ages, wealthy Englishmen had relied on the common law of charitable trusts to allow them to extend their influence far beyond their natural lives. In the nineteenth-century United States, new bodies of law afforded further advantages to accumulations of money that wealthy people sought to dedicate to some cause. Organizations like the post–Civil War Peabody and Slater funds for the education of freedmen gained exemption from state taxes. Charitable institutions like the Massachusetts General Hospital won immunity from lawsuits.[2]

The modern income tax reproduced the law's long-standing special treatment of charitable organizations. When Congress in 1894 enacted the first peacetime income tax, the law exempted organizations "conducted solely for charitable, religious, or educational purposes." The Supreme Court struck down the tax as unconstitutional, but few voiced opposition to the exemption. After the Sixteenth Amendment to the Constitution, ratified in 1913, overrode the Supreme Court decision, Congress passed a new income tax law with an exemption for nonprofit "religious, charitable, scientific, or educational" organizations, as well as any nonprofit "civic league or organization" that was "operated exclusively for the promotion of social welfare."[3]

Tax increase legislation during the First World War deepened the emerging subsidy system for such privately endowed institutions by adding tax deductibility to tax exemption: a 1917 law passed by Congress allowed taxpayers to deduct the value of contributions to religious, charitable, scientific, and educational organizations. Wartime tax authorities at the Treasury Department, moreover, departed from nineteenth-century precedents in the law of charitable trusts to construe the new exemptions and deductions broadly.[4]

The law of charitable trusts had limited the use of tax-exempt institutions to form political influence organizations. The idea, articulated most prominently by Massachusetts's Supreme Judicial Court, was that the law did not subsidize its own critique. The leading case arose after Francis Jackson of Boston died in 1861, leaving $10,000 in a charitable trust to be used by prominent abolitionists "for the preparation and circulation of books, newspapers, the delivery of speeches, lectures, and such other means, as, in their judgment, will create a public sentiment that will put an end to negro slavery." A second bequest left $5,000 in a charitable trust to be used by equally prominent woman's rights movement leaders "to secure the passage of laws granting women . . . the right to vote; to hold office; to hold, manage, and devise property; and all other civil rights enjoyed by men." In the case of *Jackson v. Phillips*, brought by the estate's heirs to challenge the validity of the will, Justice Horace Gray ruled the first trust permissible, but the second void. Gray, who would later serve on the U.S. Supreme Court, reasoned that the laws of Massachusetts had always disfavored slavery as "contrary to natural right and the principles of justice, humanity and sound policy." Women's subordinate status, by contrast, was deeply rooted in the law, and "overthrowing or changing" the laws, he wrote for the court, could not be "a charitable purpose."[5]

Later generations of lawyers would puzzle over Gray's view that changing the law of slavery was more charitable than altering the law of coverture. But the tax law emerging after the world war abandoned the effort to parse Justice Gray's old distinctions. The commissioner of revenue affirmed that associations formed to sway public sentiment "in favor of prohibition on the sale of intoxicating liquors" could be tax exempt, even if "propagandist" in their methods. The commissioner upheld the tax-exempt status of the National Rifle Association, a corporation established, among other things, to "encourage legislation" for the establishment of gun ranges and to persuade the public of the importance of rifle practice as a means of national defense.[6]

Tax exemptions and deductions, however, generated controversy from the start. Such advantages offered what amounted to a subsidy for certain kinds of enterprises over others. Looked at one way, such tax subsidies effectively took money from the public fisc. Absent the relevant exemption or deduction, funds would have been collected by the government in the form of taxes. Tax-preferred status, by contrast, gave that same money to private actors and let them, rather than democratically elected public officials, decide what to do with it. As critics noted pointedly at the time, such tax advantages allowed people with money to substitute their own judgments for the decisions of accountable public officials. Special tax benefits were functionally identical to government expenditures, except that wealthy private individuals (not elected representatives) directed the spending according to their own definitions of the social welfare. Tax exemptions and deductions were, in this view, a glaring democratic failure, giving those with wealth and power a novel kind of control over public resources.⁷

Postwar concern with the private manipulation of public opinion helped produce certain new constraints on such tax privileges. In April 1919 the Treasury Department pivoted back toward Justice Gray's old rule in *Jackson v. Phillips*, denying exempt status to "associations formed to disseminate controversial or partisan propaganda." As the Treasury now saw matters, Congress had aimed to "foster education in the broadest sense," not to support organizations aiming to foment the rivalry of "one class against another." The tax code, it reasoned, ought not "encourage the dissemination of ideas" that inured "to the profit" of one group but to the detriment of another. Deductibility and exemption were, the solicitor of internal revenue observed in 1922, acts of "extraordinary grace" by the sovereign collectivity, to be extended with caution.⁸

The 1919 propaganda rule led the commissioner of internal revenue to disallow the deductibility of contributions to an organization with close ties to the American Fund: the League for Industrial Democracy, an organization run by Fund director Norman Thomas and dedicated to advocating public ownership of economic enterprise. The American Fund had more than a passing interest in the question, since it made $40,000 in grants to the league between 1922 and 1931, and donated $21,000 more to the organization's magazine, *Labor Age*. But the U.S. Board of Tax Appeals took the view that donations to the league ought not be tax deductible, citing the league's advocacy of "drastic political and economic changes." The influential Court of Appeals for the Second Circuit in New York reversed the decision, but soon revised its view and adopted the new Treasury position in a case involving another American Fund beneficiary, Margaret Sanger's American Birth Control League. Echoing Horace Gray's judgment on the charitable status of women's rights campaigns, Judge Learned Hand reasoned that Sanger's "political agitation" about birth control laws was "outside the statute" and therefore had to be "conducted without public subvention."⁹

In all, by the 1920s the prospects seemed dim that the American Fund would benefit from the special tax privileges of the new income tax code. The Fund had attracted its share of controversy. The directors, after all, made grants to Thomas's League for Industrial Democracy and to Sanger's birth control advocacy group. If the commissioner of internal revenue had deemed the Fund's beneficiaries too controversial and divisive, surely the Fund itself would not qualify for the tax code's special favor.

Roger Baldwin and the Fund's leadership set out to exploit the subsidies of the new tax system nonetheless. And with meticulous attention to bookkeeping, accounting detail, and savvy financial management, the radicals of the Fund managed to accomplish precisely that.

By a combination of good luck and tax planning, the money in the Fund's coffers had evaded taxation for decades. The 1920 Garland bequest itself, occasioned by the death of James A. Garland Jr. in 1906, had escaped the tax man's scythe by a hair. The death came mere months before Massachusetts's first estate tax went into effect. And though young Charles lived in Massachusetts, his father, James, had lived and died in Rhode Island, which had no estate tax at all. At the federal level, Congress enacted an estate tax in 1916. Charles came into his inheritance four years later, but the terms of the act excluded the estates of people whose deaths had preceded its enactment, even when the estate's distribution came later.[10]

Baldwin entrusted his friend and colleague Walter Nelles, the civil liberties lawyer who represented both the ACLU and the American Fund, with carrying on the Garland family's sterling record of tax avoidance. Under Nelles's care, and with an eye toward achieving favorable tax treatment, the Fund's Delaware corporate charter committed the foundation to "the wellbeing of mankind," using words the Rockefeller foundations had adopted in the previous decade. Likewise, the Fund's mission statement committed it to "charitable, benevolent, and public educational activities," modeling itself on language drawn straight from the text of the tax law.[11]

Nelles and Baldwin even crafted a formal exchange of scripted letters with Garland in 1922 exclusively for purposes of tax avoidance. The text, shaped by Baldwin and Nelles to mimic the preferred terminology of the federal government's tax regulations, called on the directors of the Fund not to use the money "to the advantage of one individual as opposed to another," or to the benefit "of one group as opposed to another," or "one class" as "opposed to another." In a press statement on the day of the Fund's incorporation, Nelles released a paragraph from Garland stating that "every person is an integral part of society" and that his money should be put "to the advantage of all." At the first board meeting of the

Fund, Baldwin memorialized Garland's request that the Fund not "arouse antagonism and controversy." For the next two decades, the Fund's publicly available annual reports reproduced the 1922 letter.[12]

The tax authorities were suspicious nonetheless—and for good reason, at least as a matter of tax law. The anodyne terms of the Fund's corporate documents belied the class and race vision of its early funding decisions, which ranged from support for striking coal miners to uncompromising demands for anti-lynching legislation. The Fund board was made up of men and women who saw society and its ills in the explicit terms of conflict among groups, if not class warfare. It was no surprise, then, when in May 1924, the Office of the Commissioner for Internal Revenue decided that the Fund was ineligible for exemption under the tax code. In the commissioner's official view, the Fund financed controversial propaganda rather than educational efforts.[13]

Baldwin and the Fund's officers sprang into action to establish eligibility for tax advantages. They retained prominent New York tax lawyer Nicholas Kelley, an advisor to the Fund on legal and accounting matters since its inception. Kelley's mother, Florence, had long been an influential labor reformer. As a young woman she had served as translator for Karl Marx's comrade and coauthor Friedrich Engels. She served as the nation's first factory inspector, cofounded the NAACP, and directed the National Consumers League, where she worked with Louis Brandeis in defense of wage and hours laws for women workers. The older Kelley had even applied for and received money from the Fund for causes ranging from labor legislation and workers' health to anti-militarism and NAACP legal defense efforts.[14]

The younger Kelley channeled his mother's socialist passions into a precocious interest in federal tax law. After Harvard Law School and a stint practicing law at the Cravath firm in New York, he opened a law practice specializing in the new income tax. Kelley served as counsel in some of the most important tax-exemption matters of the decade, and for the American Fund he helped craft a theory that had not yet been tested.[15]

In Kelley's view, the denial of tax-exempt status to propaganda organizations applied to charities and educational organizations, but not to a separate category in the code for civic leagues dedicated to promoting social welfare. Properly understood, Kelley argued, the American Fund was not a charity; it offered no alms to people in need. Nor was it an educational organization; it did no teaching, at least not on its own. As Kelley saw it, the Fund was exempt as a civic league.[16]

Kelley's theory had a downside. Contributions to tax-exempt charities were deductible for the donor; contributions to tax-exempt civic leagues were not. But for the Fund, deductibility was of little importance compared with exemption. Garland, whose remaining money was tied up in trusts, had little use for a deduction for his initial large contribution, and in any event no record remains in the American Fund archives of any effort on his part to take such a deduction. Though Baldwin had hoped early on that he might solicit further donations for the Fund, he had quickly abandoned the effort. The key for the Fund was therefore to achieve the tax exemption that Kelley's theory promised.[17]

Nicholas Kelley, the Fund's tax lawyer and son of a prominent socialist, helped design a new category of tax-exempt influence foundations.

After a year of lobbying, Kelley prevailed. The Bureau of Internal Revenue gave in. The commissioner did not share his reasons with the Fund, and the bureau's records on the matter are incomplete. It seems that the bureau had decided under pressure of Kelley's advocacy that denying the American Fund its exemption would cost more than it was worth. Deciding the case against the Fund would have required the bureau to decide which civic league organizations supported the social welfare and which did not. But what was the social welfare, and who was to define it? The bureau's decision in the Fund case abandoned the effort altogether, stipulating that it would not try to police the distinction between education and propaganda, at least not with respect to organizations claiming a civic league exemption.[18]

The effects for the Fund were substantial. At the 1920s corporate tax rate of 12.5 percent on net income, the Fund could have owed more than $100,000 in taxes for the seven years from 1922 up to the stock market crash of 1929. Tax exemption meant that this money, which otherwise would have been subject to appropriation by Congress, was left to the control of the American Fund. Economically speaking, the effect was the same as if the Congress had appropriated money to the control of a small cadre of socialists, labor radicals, civil rights advocates, and heterodox liberals, whose views otherwise had little prospect of gaining success in the political process.[19]

The civic league exemption, however, was hardly restricted to the American Fund. To the contrary, the Fund's political enemies swiftly took up the same tax advantages. Other organizations soon qualifying for the exemption included the Military Training Camps Association, an organization dedicated to "perpetuating the system of military instruction camps," "supporting a sound military policy," and promoting "loyalty to the country." The American Legion, founded in the wake of the war as a conservative and ultra-patriotic association of veterans, also qualified as a tax-exempt civic league promoting the social welfare. Such organizations were implacable opponents of the American Fund and its beneficiary organizations. Left to their own devices, they would undoubtedly have pressed for the same subsidies, and they would almost certainly have succeeded. But it is an irony nonetheless that the exemption the American Fund had helped to establish applied to them all. Worse still, at least from the perspective of the Fund, subsidies like the tax exemption offered special privileges not in proportion to the righteousness of a cause but in proportion to the sheer size of the sums dedicated to it. The implications were ominous. It was the adversaries of the Garland Fund who had the money to take advantage of the tax code. The beneficiaries of the Fund's efforts, by contrast, were among the poorest and most downtrodden people in America.[20]

PART III
AMERICAN REVOLUTIONARIES

Elizabeth Gurley Flynn addressing striking textile workers in Paterson, New Jersey, June 1913.

12

Nothing in Common

Sabotage is to the class struggle what guerrilla warfare is to the battle.
—ELIZABETH GURLEY FLYNN, 1913

Most people, at most times, in most places accommodate themselves to the world as it is. A few, with active minds and unusually energetic ambitions, try to reform it—to nudge it closer to its ideals.

Elizabeth Gurley Flynn was one of the still smaller number of people who aim to smash the world and remake it fresh. Her thrilling, fearless, and dangerous idea was that the world the bosses had made could be torn down and rebuilt by and for those they exploited. "The existing order of society," she insisted, turned virtuous citizens into victims and delivered victory to the wicked. But behind the status quo, Flynn insisted, lay the possibilities of a world as it could be.[1]

In the second decade of the twentieth century, Flynn's fiery determination propelled her into the front ranks of a now-lost world of American labor radicalism. She became one of the most recognizable members of the Industrial Workers of the World, which she joined shortly after its formation in 1906, when she was still a teenager. The Wobblies, as they were known, were America's most electric labor union. For decades, the American labor movement had been dominated by the American Federation of Labor, which organized skilled craft workers—some 2.5 million members by the early twentieth century, most of them white men of Northern European descent. The Wobblies, however, offered a different model for worker solidarity. Red-hot ambition and charismatic appeal aimed to make up for more modest membership numbers. Calling for one big union, the IWW proposed an avowedly revolutionary worker movement. They aimed to organize all workers, including the lowliest laborers, not merely those in the AFL's skilled trades. The Wobblies announced that their unions were open to all who toiled, regardless of race. They promised to defend the interests of laborers in the short term, to demand higher wages and better conditions in the coal mines and the lumberyards. But they kept relentless attention on the revolution in which the producing classes would claim their rightful share of the world's resources.[2]

For a decade and more, the sheer energy and determination of the IWW placed it on newspaper front pages across the United States. But the IWW rose to national attention for another reason as well, one that resonated with Flynn because it was particularly uncompromising and dangerous. The Wobblies preached sabotage and violence.

Historians sympathetic to the IWW have denied that Flynn or the union's other leading figures believed in or practiced violence. They have downplayed the Wobblies' spirited adoption of this most basic of revolutionary tactics. And understandably so. In later decades, America's most widely admired activists in labor and civil rights would reject the use of lawless violence. They would describe it as an inarticulate substitute for effective mobilization. Lawless violence, they would say, is a desperate gambit of the weak and confused.[3]

In the 1920s, after the crest of anarchic labor violence had broken, Flynn turned to the world of the American Fund in an effort to identify a more creative way forward. In her role as a director at the Fund, she would midwife a new radicalism of nonviolence and democratic change. In the end, others in and around the Fund board would carry the project forward. Flynn would get sick. She would go away for years to convalesce. Her views would change and harden. She would become tragically and unforgivably embedded in mid-century Stalinism. Yet for a crucial moment during the Fund's heyday, the embers of a fading Wobbly revolution would help spark a vital new conception of the labor movement, one whose promise would neither burn itself out in inchoate conflagration nor sacrifice itself to the cruel calculations of Soviet tactics.

To understand all that was at stake in the Fund's support for a constructive new labor movement, to make sense of its undimmed and undaunted ambitions for the future, we need to know the real, unvarnished version of its past. We need a clear-eyed view of two bloody decades in which a slight young woman based in the Bronx became one of the country's most outspoken advocates of using political violence to make a better world.

A Rebel Girl Smashes the Chains

Elizabeth Gurley Flynn was born in 1890 in Concord, New Hampshire, the first of four children of Annie Gurley, an Irish immigrant, and Tom Flynn, a laborer and itinerant civil engineer.[4]

Both sides of Elizabeth's family featured Irish rebels—"immigrants and revolutionists," as she liked to say. Her paternal great-grandfather, Paddy Flynn, had led a detachment of French troops in the failed 1798 rebellion planned by the famed Irish nationalist Wolfe Tone. Paddy Flynn's son (Elizabeth's paternal grandfather) had joined an abortive 1837 invasion of British Canada led by Irish dissidents in upstate New York.[5]

A generation later, Elizabeth's father redirected the rebellious spirit of his forebears to protest not the tyrannical British, but the autocratic power of American bosses. In 1875, while working in Maine's granite quarries, he joined together with other stone cutters protesting the ten-hour day. He advocated the doctrines of Henry George, the economist whose single-tax proposal for landowners galvanized the American left in the 1880s. In 1900, Tom Flynn voted for Socialist Party presidential candidate Eugene Debs and began attending party meetings.[6]

Elizabeth often felt that her mother suffered in her garrulous father's shadow; Elizabeth's sister Kathleen recalled that their mother "got things done" while their father "talked loud and long." But Annie Gurley Flynn was a strong and independent spirit in her own right. After immigrating to the United States in 1877, she took part in women's suffrage meetings led by Susan B. Anthony and Elizabeth Cady Stanton. After her father died, she helped raise her younger brothers who became leather and metal workers and joined the Knights of Labor, the large labor organization that boasted nearly 1 million members at its height in the mid-1880s. Annie worked as a tailor to earn wages for the family. She read widely about politics and economics and supported Irish nationalist causes. Elizabeth later remembered drinking "a burning hatred of British rule with our mother's milk." Her mother, she recalled, "despised informers, detectives, and anyone who had ever worn a British uniform."[7]

During Elizabeth's childhood, the Flynn family moved frequently while Tom looked for work. In 1895, the Flynns left Concord for the nearby mill town of Manchester, where Tom ran for the position of city engineer. When he lost, they relocated to Cleveland, Ohio, where Tom took the young Elizabeth on long walks down Euclid Avenue, the city's famous "millionaire's row," then boasting one of the greatest concentrations of wealth in the world. Elizabeth walked past the palace of John D. Rockefeller, the richest of the Gilded Age robber barons. Her father pointed out the mansion belonging to Mark Hanna, millionaire industrialist, U.S. senator, and advisor to President William McKinley.[8]

After a year, the family moved again, this time to the factory town of Adams, Massachusetts, home to the giant mills of the Berkshire Cotton Manufacturing Company. In Adams, a young Elizabeth began to draw on her parents' radicalisms. She raged against the Spanish-American War instigated by Hearst and Pulitzer and the yellow press—"the ruinous path of imperialism," she later called it.[9]

Flynn chafed at the bleak conditions in the mill towns of her childhood. "The gray mills in Manchester," she later remembered, had "stretched like prisons" along the banks of the Merrimack River. Fifty percent of the workers were women earning a dollar a day. They "lived in antiquated corporation boarding houses," she observed, and rushed to the factories in predawn darkness only to return home after sunset. In the town of Adams, recurrent slow periods at the mill reduced workers' meager piece-rate wages. Factory shutdowns came and went according to market cycles with neither rhyme nor reason, cutting off workers' wages altogether. Young employees suffered gruesome injuries, too. They had hands with three fingers gone, and heads scalped after hair got caught in unguarded machinery. Amid the suffering and the poverty, Flynn noted, mill owner William Brown Plunkett drove "a fine carriage with beautiful horses." He was the richest man in town. When President McKinley came to Adams in 1899 to lay the cornerstone for a new mill building, he visited Plunkett—but not the mill workers.[10]

When Elizabeth was ten, her parents moved the family yet again, this time to a tenement apartment in the Bronx. Photographs of Elizabeth around that time reveal a sober and resolute child, her facial expression betraying a hint of sadness. For a child with solemnity beyond her years, the structure of American life seemed topsy-turvy. People like Rockefeller, Hanna, and Plunkett possessed vast wealth. Most people, however, had next to nothing and led lives of poverty and suffering. As Flynn saw it, power and resources seemed to flow to the least deserving. Virtue was at odds with reward.

The bookshelves of the Flynn family apartment offered explanations for the world outside. Annie Flynn read aloud to her children from Edward Bellamy's novel *Looking Backward*, in which the narrator looks back from the year 2000 on the squalid tenements, dangerous factories, and bloody labor struggles of the late nineteenth century. Elizabeth fell in love with the book's alluring idea that the cruelties of industry might give way to a better society in which each person contributed according to their capacities and received fair shares of society's bounteous product. Elizabeth loved equally the utopian romance novel *News from Nowhere*, in which the English socialist William Morris conjured a future in which self-directed creativity replaced the viciousness of the wage system. The Russian anarcho-communist Peter Kropotkin's *An Appeal to the Young* added an uncompromising call to action. No one in the modern world, Kropotkin asserted, was free from complicity in workers' exploitation—not the schoolmaster who trained pupils to become capitalists, not the engineer whose inventions immiserated labor, not even the doctor, whose prescriptions were merely a temporary dressing for the gaping wounds of sickness and ill health among the poor. Kropotkin "struck home," Flynn later recalled. She felt as if the Russian radical was speaking to her "personally" in her family's "shabby poverty-stricken Bronx flat."[11]

Feminist volumes in Annie Flynn's collection reaffirmed Elizabeth's sense that injustice was embedded deep in the structures of social life. Mary Wollstonecraft's *A Vindication of the Rights of Woman* encouraged her to reconsider the spurious traditions of family life that had produced woman's "slavish dependence" on man. The German socialist August Bebel's book *Women and Socialism* called monogamous marriage a kind of prostitution and blamed private property for restricting women's naturally "free and unhampered" sex instinct. The British sexuality theorist Edward Carpenter offered a liberating defense of freedom in marriage and sex. Charlotte Perkins Gilman's *Women and Economics* asked why the sex relation was also an economic relation in which women depended for their subsistence on their husbands. British physician Havelock Ellis's *Studies in the Psychology of Sex* asserted the morality of women's sexual pleasure and desire. From these books, Elizabeth concluded that "the only justification for a man and woman being together is their mutual desire."[12]

The role of wife and mother held little appeal for Flynn. As an adult, she would learn that throughout her childhood her father had kept a secret family in Boston. Perhaps her father's longtime affair and revelations about his second family influenced her. But one way or another, she grew to doubt that the modern world left room for romantic connections based in anything other than pleasure. "The hurriedness of the present age," she later told audiences, "gets the spark of love wandering."[13]

Married love was only one of the conventions against which Flynn chafed. A newspaper clipping pasted prominently into her teenage scrapbook announced that "the history of progress is written in one word: Disobedience." The reading list of her youth centered around the idea that society's basic rules and institutions were not natural but invented. The fundamental units of social life—private property, marriage, women's subordination to men, capitalism—were chosen pieces of the social landscape, not bedrock features of human existence. They could be discarded and new institutions put in their place. People could make different choices. Man-made structures could be taken apart and reassembled in new form. Writers like Wollstonecraft, Bellamy, Morris, and Kropotkin encouraged their readers to imagine worlds of possibility in which the organizing principles of the existing order were turned upside down. Even "relations between the sexes" could change, Bebel contended; they had changed before, and they were, he observed, "bound to change again," for nothing was eternal, "either in nature or in human life."[14]

The teenage Flynn drank such radical ideas in gulps. Her parents introduced her to the most famous radicals of the day. She met the anarchist Emma Goldman and her lover and comrade, Alexander Berkman, who had just been released after fourteen years in prison for the failed assassination of the industrialist Henry Clay Frick. Goldman and Berkman recommended further volumes. Flynn read Karl Marx and Friedrich Engels's *Communist Manifesto*, where she encountered the call for a "total social change" that would leave no injustice of class or sex unaddressed. She devoured Engels's *Origin of the Family*, which catalogued the many forms of family life and sex relations in human history. Monogamous marriage and the forced role of wife and mother would not have to be Flynn's fate. They were, she read, mere artifacts of a particularly exploitative way of organizing the world.[15]

In all her reading, one set of implications seemed starkest. Rules about what belongs to whom undergirded the most basic norms of conventional morality. Mostly we can do as we please with what's ours. Mostly we can't with what's not. But Flynn concluded that capitalism had corrupted these fundamental moral ideas. If what rightly belongs to Jones or Murphy has been wrongly allocated by the law to Rockefeller, then protecting Rockefeller's property rights will magnify and multiply the underlying injustice. As Flynn came to see the world she lived in, the basic operations of conventional law and morality laundered society's most outrageous injustices. Morality and law disguised grave injustice with an unearned veneer of righteousness. Exploitation and inequality, as Flynn put it, turned morality into an accomplice in the real crime of the modern world, which was the vast gap separating the haves from the have-nots, the bosses from the workers, the unfathomably rich from the utterly destitute.

Flynn was onto something, of course. The wealthiest 1 percent of American households possessed a growing share of the nation's wealth, amassing nearly half the nation's assets by the early twentieth century; the bottom 90 percent owned merely a fifth of what the top 1 percent could claim, even as the top 1 percent added to its treasure chests by sweeping in between 20 and 25 percent of the nation's earnings each year. As Flynn saw it, the class exploitation reflected in such realities reached deep into social life. It turned even the most intimate and loving relations into mechanisms of exploitation. Virtually from the cradle, parents accommodated children to society as it was, preparing their children (as a rebellious sixteen-year-old Flynn put it) "to become the facile tools of our capitalistic masters." Teachers in schools, Flynn declared, "dictate to us what we shall learn, what morals we shall practice, what system of government we shall support, and what system of economics we shall follow." Schools passed along "perverted notions of conventionality and morality." All of society, it seemed, was geared to produce "chains of superstition in a man's mind."[16]

Mental chains were precisely what Elizabeth Gurley Flynn set out to break when she began, at the age of sixteen, to deliver lectures as a young speaker on the radical soapbox circuit. Her first public speech, sponsored by her father, came at the Harlem Socialist Club on West 125th Street. She was naturally gifted at delivering searing lectures, and with Tom's help, she was soon speaking in halls and on street corners around the city and across the Northeast.[17]

Flynn's favorite topics were socialism and sex. "The wage-working classes the world over are victims of society," she said. She told crowds in Harlem and Newark and Philadelphia that the "industrial autocracy" of the Rockefellers and the Carnegies had not only produced long hours and low pay, it had betrayed even the supposedly sacred precinct of the family. A half century earlier, abolitionists had emphasized slavery's destruction of the family. Now Flynn leveled the same critique at wage-slavery. She scandalized audiences by championing "free love"—free love "at all costs," as she put it, since the alternative was a "slave love" dominated by the "rude hand of capitalism." In the modern industrial world, she insisted, there was "no real home or love." "Tired people," she said, "had no time for love." Husbands and fathers who were exploited at work came home tired and downtrodden, where they abused wives and children as they themselves had been abused in the mill. Marriage under capitalism was legalized prostitution. Flynn called for the abolition of "loveless marriages," "unwelcome childbearing," and "household drudgery." Was a woman's place, she asked, "in the home"? In truth, Flynn scoffed, the "claimed sacredness of home" had gone to "naught before the rude hand of capitalism." Poverty wages for men made wives and daughters "absolutely dependent" upon husbands and fathers. Women's work in the home, she demanded, should be rewarded by a salary of its own.[18]

Content was only part of Flynn's success as a speaker. In her age, beauty, and sex she represented the idea that there could be something better than a grim world of industrial squalor. The attractive and energetic teenager captured audiences and won the attention of newspapers. The press dwelled on what one friend called her "crystal blue eyes" and "soft brown hair." She was a "wisp of a girl, slim and sweet faced," too, gushed one reporter. The novelist and editor Theodore Dreiser interviewed her and wrote a glowing story about the "Irish beauty" who "electrified" her audiences. Dreiser dubbed her the "East Side Joan of Arc," and the label stuck.[19]

Often the only woman in a crowd, Flynn chose a standard uniform that emphasized her distinctiveness. She typically wore a full-length skirt and bright white shirtwaists buttoned at the neck with a flowing red or green tie. She mixed seriousness of purpose and forceful energy with otherworldly beauty in the drab and soot-covered industrial city streets. The men in her audiences, reporters noted, were usually rapt, keeping "their eyes on her slim, tapering fingers as she gestured." It wasn't only men who noticed. At an outdoor rally in 1906, Emma Goldman remarked on her "beautiful face and figure."[20]

Critics in the press conceded Flynn's appeal, but were less charitable

Elizabeth Gurley Flynn, portrait, 1906.

in their assessment. Flynn was a "clear and present danger," as the *Los Angeles Times* put it, a "she-dog of anarchy." The police were watching, too. Flynn was arrested for the first time in 1906, soon after she entered the soapbox circuit, when a crowd grew too large along Broadway at 38th Street. Police found the sixteen-year-old Flynn speaking from a packing box, with a big red flag of radical solidarity flying above two American flags. Passersby grew angry at the conjunction of the flags. Others stopped to gawk at the socialist messages on the banner behind the speaker. Theaters let out for the evening, and the crowd swelled. Traffic snarled. Police arrested Flynn and her father and three others when they began to offer a socialist pamphlet for sale. The charge was failure to obtain a permit for the event. Flynn and her father were released at 2 a.m. A judge the next day told Flynn to go back to school. The principal at Morris High School was willing to have her back; her parents urged her to go. But Flynn dropped out and turned full-time to speaking and organizing.[21]

The publicity around Flynn's arrest—the first of ten in her lifetime—burnished her public image and helped make her one of the most popular speakers on the American left. Just months removed from her first speech in the Harlem Socialist Club, Flynn traveled around the country delivering energetic speeches in union halls and working-class neighborhoods. Crowds stopped to listen to, marvel at, and sometimes jeer the fierce teen. In Philadelphia, she gave what the city's leading evening newspaper described as a "stunning speech" from atop a tree stump that had been dragged into the middle of a major intersection in the industrial neighborhood north of the city's downtown. Some three hundred people stood "spellbound" and "hypnotized," the newspapers wrote the next day; the enchanted crowd, one writer gushed, seemed to follow her every emotion with eagerness, frowning when she frowned, laughing when she smiled, and growing "terribly earnest when she became merely moderately so." People braved rain and weather to hear her, and as one reporter wrote, "the crowds did not disperse until her last word was uttered." In New Jersey, observed another newspaper's beat writer, Flynn won over hecklers by "sheer force of her personality." She spoke in Pittsburgh, Cleveland, Cincinnati, and Chicago. Everywhere she went, observers recorded enthralled crowds.[22]

Flynn's early speeches offered a big critique, delivered in glittering generalities and with few specifics. Echoing the radical texts on her family's bookshelves, she promised that an end to private property would liberate love and family affection, breaking the shackles that turned intimate life into its own domain of disappointment and exploitation. But Flynn had little to say, at least at first, about how liberation would arrive. She energized audiences by telling stories in which listeners could recognize their own lives and see their own frustrations. But she had no account, except in the most general terms, of how the injustices she decried might be overcome. The exhortations of Marx, Engels, and Kropotkin were distant abstractions. Women's suffrage, for which Flynn mustered only modest enthusiasm, seemed like no answer, either. Voting rights for women in western states like Wyoming and Colorado had not undone the injustices in the family and the marketplace. Women, she believed, tended to vote with their class, reaffirming the very forms of economic exploitation that trapped them in subordinate positions at home.[23]

Flynn longed for the thrill of a bold movement with a sense of urgency, one that would resonate with her urge to disobey. The Wobblies soon supplied the comrades for whom she yearned—along with a strategy as dangerous as it was exhilarating.

Sabotage

Flynn first took note of the Industrial Workers of the World in early 1906, when Idaho officials arranged for the arrest of William "Big Bill" Haywood on charges of assassinating Frank Steunenberg, the state's former governor, in a dynamite blast at the gate to his home.[24]

Haywood, who had helped found the IWW at a Chicago convention the year before, was the outsized, one-eyed secretary treasurer of the Western Federation of Miners. Born in Salt Lake City in 1869, he spent a childhood in the mining camps of the Utah Territory, where life was punctuated by violence: fighting, murders, and shootings, he recalled, were virtually an everyday phenomenon. The massacre of 150 Arapaho and Cheyenne by American soldiers at Sand Creek in Colorado in 1864 was still a subject of recent memory. So was Mormon settlers' massacre of

120 emigrants on a wagon train headed for California a few years earlier. "Hardly a week passed," Haywood later recalled, without a fistfight between him and some new boy who mocked him for his missing right eye, which he lost in a youthful accident involving a knife and a slingshot. His first boss whipped him. Haywood fought back and then walked off the job. The mines in which he soon went to work were rough and dangerous places. Dreadful conditions led to deadly cave-ins, accidents, and explosions. Brawls, murders, and unexplained dynamite blasts took lives when the mines themselves did not.[25]

Haywood witnessed and participated in a level of industrial violence that is hard to imagine more than a century later. In strikes at Coeur d'Alene, Idaho, and at Cripple Creek, Colorado, in 1892, sheriffs' deputies fired on striking miners, touching off open battles. In the Leadville, Colorado, strike of 1896, miners torched the boss's mine. In 1899, strikers in Idaho dynamited an ore mill employing scab labor and wrecked a train carrying strikebreakers, leading Governor Steunenberg to call on President McKinley to send federal troops. Martial law in the state led to the arrests of 1,200 striking miners. A few years later Haywood shot a deputy three times while defending himself in a Denver brawl. Another Western Federation officer shot and killed two strikebreakers and was sentenced to life in prison. Dozens of deaths arose out of the infamous conflict known as the "Labor Wars" in Colorado in 1903 and 1904, including sixteen strikebreakers who died when the cage in which they were riding mysteriously fell in a deep mining shaft. A few months later, Western Federation strikers dynamited a train depot near Cripple Creek, which mine operators had been using to bring in nonunion labor. Thirteen strikebreakers died in an explosion that wrecked the station house.[26]

Coal-mine operators and western state authorities deployed ferocious violence, too. As the miners saw it, capital usually struck first. Bosses took extraordinary measures to prevent unions from forming, and stopped at almost nothing to break those that managed to gain traction. Pinkerton thugs threatened and beat union organizers. Labor spies reported back on union activities. Employers fired union members, kidnapped and murdered strike leaders, and ransacked union halls. Mine operators cooperated with state officials to arrest hundreds of union miners and ship them by boxcar out of state, threatening them with death if they returned. As-

Ruins of a rail station in Colorado's Cripple Creek mining district, splintered by a 1904 bombing connected to the Western Federation of Miners, predecessor to the IWW.

sociations of mine owners planted dynamite bombs as pretexts for calling in the militia.[27]

Mine owner violence was so extreme, so regular a part of miners' lives, that Haywood and the tough, independent-minded miners of the Western Federation developed a homegrown radical idea. What if the real trouble in the mines, the problem at the root of decades of bloody clashes, was the mine operators' putative property rights in the mines they called theirs? The mine owners, the union proposed, had appropriated for themselves coal and ore that was the product not of the owners' labor but of the miners' grinding toil. Maybe the mines ought to belong to the workers.[28]

In June 1905, after years of skirmishes, Haywood and the western miners joined together with dissident metalworkers, longshoremen, brewers, and railroad laborers to launch the Industrial Workers of the World. The organization's founding convention in Chicago, Haywood declared, would be "the Continental Congress of the working class." The new organization would take up arms in what it called "the irrepressible conflict between the capitalist class and the working class."[29]

For two decades, the labor movement's main organization, the American Federation of Labor, had served as an umbrella organization for unions that divided workers by trade or craft. In the brewing industry, for example, steam engineers, barrel makers, and deliverymen each had their own unions, organized separately, even though they all worked in the same industry, or for the same employer. Machinists belonged to the International Association of Machinists—even if they worked alongside typesetters in the International Typographical Union. Members of the United Brotherhood of Carpenters and Joiners organized separately from the Machine Wood Workers' Union and the Furniture Workers' International. Plumbers belonged to one union and steamfitters to another. And so on. Each body of workers assembled separately by trade in discrete unions to protect their own particular trade prerogatives. Divisions among workers did not end with the boundaries between crafts. Trade unions typically aimed to exclude lower-status labor of all kinds. The AFL bitterly opposed Asian immigration from its very earliest days. AFL unions supported immigration restrictions on European workers, too. And while the national organization purported to resist whites-only policies in its member unions, most unions—and nearly all their local chapters—excluded Black workers, often explicitly in their organizational charters.[30]

The IWW set about to establish an organization that would be based on the lowest-status workers, not one that would exclude them. Leading labor radicals of the day took part. Eugene Debs was at the founding meeting. So was the testy Daniel DeLeon, longtime editor, polemicist, and leader of the Socialist Labor Party. Lucy Parsons, the mixed-race anarcho-socialist widow of labor martyr Albert Parsons, who had been executed for participating in the 1886 Haymarket bombing in Chicago, attended as an honored guest. Together, unionists and leaders of the American left created in the IWW a new union that opened its doors wide "to every man that earns his living either by his brain or his muscle," as Haywood put it in the convention's opening remarks. An open-door policy would embolden any and all to join. Low dues would encourage even the lowest on the economic scale—those most likely to be hired as strikebreakers—to become members. The IWW, moreover, organized workers by industry rather than by craft. Mine workers, or brewery workers, or railroad workers, joined together with all those in their respective industries in solidarity, not divided by job title among carpenters, machinists, typesetters, and plumbers. Industrial unions would match modern industrial conditions. Capital had assembled itself on a new and larger industrial scale; "the trust is the natural development of industrial progress," wrote the organization's newspaper. Now industrial unions would take the same step on the labor side, allowing labor to operate at a scale matched to the actual conditions of the working class. With an organizational structure suited to the modern economy, the IWW would rescue labor "from the slave bondage of capitalism." The IWW would "put the working class in possession of the economic power" and "the means of life." The "machinery of production and distribution" rightly belonged to labor, not capital. Workers would at last come into "posession of the full value of the product of their toil."[31]

The Wobblies' slogan—"One Big Union"—meant actively organizing across race, nationality, and sex. The IWW welcomed all workers, "regardless of color, creed, nationality, sex or politics." Racial divisions among the working class, in particular, seemed to Haywood and the new union's leadership as counterproductive as the divisions between trades. "Leaving the Negro outside your union," the editors of the *Industrial Worker* reminded its readers, "makes him a potential, if not an actual scab." (If the capitalist "hires the Negro to take our places when we strike," asked Wobbly journalist Justus Ebert, "why, then, should we bar the Negro" from the union?) Capital exploited without regard to race and nationality; the IWW message was that labor should organize itself in the same way. Racial prejudice, lamented the *Industrial Worker*, kept "workers fighting each other, while the boss gets the benefit."[32]

The crucial divide in the modern economy, Haywood insisted, was that between labor and capital. The IWW therefore insisted that "the colored worker, man or woman, is on an equal footing with every other worker." The Wobblies organized racially integrated unions on the Philadelphia waterfront and (precariously) in the timber industry of the South. They recruited Japanese and Chinese laborers in western timber, agriculture, and mining. They organized Mexican workers in Arizona's mines and

California's fields. Critics derided the IWW (in the words of one contemporary observer) as a "horde of hobos and unskilled laborers" who refused to work. Socialist critics of the IWW disdained them as the "bum brigade" and "the slum proletariat." But openness to the most marginalized in American industry was a hallmark of the organization. At a moment when the labor movement sought to sustain itself by reactionary exclusion, the IWW's brand of solidarity operated by inclusion.[33]

Flynn was immediately taken by the bravado of the Wobs. Her parents' socialist friends, she wrote, seemed "stodgy" by comparison to the "more militant" and "more youthful" IWW. Here at last were labor radicals whose actions lived up to the unstinting language of the radical texts on her parents' shelves. Haywood's defiance of the status quo matched Flynn's infatuation with disobedience. When Eugene Debs and Daniel DeLeon came through New York supporting Haywood and the IWW cause in the summer of 1906, Flynn signed up. She joined the organization's "Mixed Local" No. 179, made up of New York workers from an assortment of industries. Within weeks, Wobbly leaders recruited her to speak at rallies in upstate New York and in Bridgeport, Connecticut. In the fall of 1907, she traveled to Chicago to represent Local 179 at the national convention. At the invitation of a handsome IWW organizer named Jack Jones, Flynn headed to the Mesabi iron range in Minnesota in 1907 to organize the miners who supplied ore to U.S. Steel. Organizing and speaking among the iron miners, she fell in love with Jones, whom she found "youthful and vigorous" with "deep blue eyes." The two married within weeks. (Wobbly leader Vincent St. John later recalled that Flynn "fell in love with the West and the miners and she married the first one she met.") Flynn became pregnant at age seventeen. The couple's first child died after a premature birth. A second child—a boy named Fred—was born in 1910. Jones expected Flynn to stay home and care for their infant. But Flynn continued to travel and organize. The couple soon split. Fred grew up largely in his grandmother's care in the Flynn family apartment in the Bronx while his increasingly famous mother traveled the IWW circuit.[34]

The IWW reached between 15,000 and 40,000 members in its first decade, though the exact numbers were always contested. Compared to the 1.5-million-member AFL, the organization was tiny. But organizers like

Flynn and Haywood attracted attention out of proportion to their union's membership because of the startling clarity of their message.[35]

Labor, they asserted, was at war with capital. The old AFL aimed to negotiate with its enemy, but such collaboration was a kind of treason in a war of the producing classes against the exploiting class. As the preamble to the IWW's constitution put it, the "working class" and the bosses had "nothing in common." IWW leaders said candidly that they would lead their forces in what they called a "war of the classes"—a "merciless class war between labor and capital, between exploited and exploiter." At its best, wrote Walker Smith, editor of the *Industrial Worker*, "a labor union" was "essentially an army of occupation," holding on to enemy territory and claiming it for its own.[36]

The war metaphor inspired what the IWW called "direct action" against the forces of capital. Justus Ebert explained direct action as "industrial action directly by, for, and of the workers themselves." The editors of the *Industrial Worker* defined it as "any effort made directly for the purpose of getting more of the goods from the boss." Most of all, direct action meant something other than political efforts through government. The western miners had watched as governors of both political parties, Democrats and Republicans alike, sided with the bosses and called out the militia to suppress strikes. In Colorado, years of work with elected officials came to naught in 1899 when the state supreme court struck down as unconstitutional a law capping the number of hours mining firms could expect from their workers. Direct action promised to meet power with power, bypassing the unreliable institutions of the state.[37]

Flynn's first engagements in IWW direct action were avowedly peaceful. When the IWW sent her to work as an organizer in Missoula, Montana, in the fall of 1909, the Wobblies had just started one of the first of the raucous organizing struggles known as "Free Speech Fights." Beginning in Missoula and then spreading to Spokane, Fresno, San Diego, and elsewhere, IWW organizers adopted a crude but ingenious tactic. Wobblies stood in the streets in the center of town. They spoke out against exploitative local employers in industries like lumber and mining. In Missoula and elsewhere they condemned crooked employment agencies, too, for funneling vulnerable migratory laborers to ruthless employers. As police carted away one soapbox speaker, another stepped up to deliver the message. Wobblies filled the jails in twenty-six towns across the American West.

The small-town jails were overwhelmed. Flynn telegraphed Haywood for reinforcements. "Don't go to law—go to jail!" was the slogan of the day. As Flynn recalled, "IWW floaters began to pour in with every freight train." Hiring no lawyers and demanding separate jury trials whenever possible, the organization sent dozens and even hundreds of members to jail for violating city ordinances against radical labor speech on the streets. "I never saw so many men want to break into jail," Flynn joked. Arrested again in Spokane, Flynn protested the jail conditions "so vigorously," remembered a local lawyer, that the local police soon regretted arresting her in the first place. Missoula authorities released her. A Spokane jury acquitted her of all charges.[38]

Difficulties with the strategy of free speech fights soon emerged, however. For one thing, local authorities learned that leaving IWW speakers alone deprived the group's events of their propaganda value. IWW speech fights anticipated and helped inspire Walter Lippmann's 1913 suggestion that sophisticated statesmen did not repress speech so much as let speakers tire themselves out. It was the man "forbidden to speak on the streets of San Diego"—the IWW man—who was dangerous, not the anarchist allowed to talk until blue in the face. In Denver, where future Wilson propaganda director George Creel was mayor, authorities foiled an IWW free speech event simply by saying "go ahead, boys, speak as much as you like." Repression of free speech, not free speech itself, posed the real danger to the established order.[39]

Even when authorities fell into the IWW trap and made mass arrests, the free speech fights proved to be of limited value in advancing Wobbly aims. Losing dozens of local leaders for days and even weeks at a time was costly; arrests, wrote the editor of the main IWW newspaper, took "active members off the firing line." And while street-corner speaking was crucial to organizing migrant workers in the intermountain West, speech fights were exhausting and at best only indirectly connected to organizing workers at the point of production. The speech fights spurred efforts by others, to be sure; Roger Baldwin later claimed that his World War I–era civil liberties campaign was inspired in part by the Wobblies' free speech carnivals. But the speech fights were also a distracting and expensive sideshow, redirecting workers' attention away from the struggle over control of industry.[40]

By 1913, the editors of the *Industrial Worker* observed that the "mass passive resistance strikes" of the speech fights had "about reached their limit." A new tactic presented itself. Now, the paper concluded, "is the time to use sabotage."[41]

There is "little doubt," as one leading historian of political and industrial violence concludes, that the IWW's predecessor organization, the Western Federation of Miners, "used bombings and assassinations as organized tools." The miners' union almost certainly assassinated Idaho's former governor Frank Steunenberg, though whether Haywood himself was involved is less clear.[42]

The WFM's use of force was tightly connected to its homegrown revolutionary ambitions for the basic social order of the American West. The WFM had seen force bring its revolution to fruition, at least for a time. Like the French Communards who saw in the fleeting Paris Commune of 1871 a symbol of the possibility of socialist revolution, western miners had managed to seize control of remote mining communities for just long enough to turn their vision of social life into the fact of the matter. Hard-to-reach mining settlements in remote locations and hardscrabble conditions could tip from company towns to union strongholds, especially when a few local officials and merchants allied with the miners, which they sometimes did. When gold and silver refinery workers went out on strike in Colorado City in early 1903, for example, sheriffs' deputies patrolled the town alongside WFM pickets to keep out the strikebreakers. Small populations in places like Colorado City reduced the availability of surplus labor. Single roads in and out of town allowed picket lines to keep nonunion labor away from shuttered smelters and empty mines. Mine owners in such situations retained formal title to their mines, to be sure. But labor solidarity transferred to the workers the effective power to decide what was whose for the time being. The solidarity of western miners' unions could undo the property relations of the formal legal system. Whose property was it, after all, if the union effectively decided who could go in and out?[43]

As for the IWW itself, most modern historians of American labor have sought to minimize the place of violence and sabotage. The union's most distinguished late twentieth-century historian insisted that the Wobblies "did not carry bombs." Another widely cited scholar claimed improbably that Haywood and his fellow advocates of industrial warfare "could have served as a model for Gandhi and Martin Luther King." An otherwise commendable biography of Flynn insists that she "viewed violence as counterproductive" and blames the AFL for violence that broke out during Flynn's organizing drives. Such sanitized histories reflect the historical moment of their authors more than their subjects, a moment in which advocates of social change had sworn off violence. But such accounts are themselves products of a brutal if cathartic reversal for Flynn and the IWW during and after the First World War, one in which they would at last disown violence. In truth, the IWW was heir to the WFM's violent legacy. Flynn and the Wobblies' other key organizers, as journalist Louis Adamic observed, were "veritable evangelists of sabotage."[44]

At a steel worker strike at McKees Rocks, Pennsylvania, for example, a secret committee of IWW strike leaders vowed in 1909 to kill a company guard for every striker killed in the skirmishing. (With characteristic bravado, Haywood later boasted that the ratio had actually been three to one.) At least thirteen people died in the fighting at McKees Rocks.[45]

The IWW's position on violence became a matter of public notoriety after the *Los Angeles Times* building blew up in September 1910 in a spectacular dynamite explosion that killed twenty-one people on the paper's staff and made national headlines for months. In the spring of 1911, authorities arrested brothers James and John McNamara—leaders of the International Association of Bridge and Structural Iron Workers—and charged them with the crime. At first, leaders in the AFL, the Socialist Party, and the IWW alike defended the McNamaras and insisted on the brothers' innocence. They blamed the *Times* for carelessly setting off a natural gas explosion. Clarence Darrow, ever the celebrity lawyer for the left, raced to Los Angeles to represent the brothers. But the McNamaras were guilty. Not even Darrow could get them off. The *Times*' editors had been critical of striking bridge and iron workers in Los Angeles, and the bombing turned out to be the culmination of a yearslong campaign of dynamite attacks by the McNamaras at dozens of anti-union firms across the country. When the McNamaras confessed, the mainstream of the labor movement disowned them and condemned the violence in which they had been engaged. "The McNamaras have betrayed labor," said the AFL's Samuel Gompers.[46]

Virtually alone among labor organizations and left-leaning political parties, the IWW stood stalwart behind the dynamiters even after they admitted to having arranged the bombing. Technically, the McNamaras' union—the Bridge and Structural Iron Workers—was part of the AFL. But the IWW did not scruple the difference. "I am with the McNamaras and always will be," announced Haywood, who defended the brothers in a widely publicized rally at Cooper Union in New York. The IWW newspaper *Solidarity* raged against mainstream labor's abandonment of these warriors in the battle against capital. "The IWW will decline to join in this unholy medley of condemnation," its editors opined, refusing to "meekly apologize for those . . . who occasionally strike back." The "capitalist sowed the wind," the paper's headlines screamed. "Let the blood be upon the heads of our masters!" Another IWW founder described the McNamaras as "the John Browns" of the coming revolution.[47]

The Socialist Party expelled Haywood and the other IWW members over their defense of the bombing, purging all members who advocated "crime, sabotage, or other methods of violence as a weapon of the working class." Victor Berger of Wisconsin, America's first Socialist congressman, condemned the IWW as lawless anarchists: "I for one do not believe in murder as a means of propaganda," he said. "I do not believe in theft as a means of expropriation"—nor, Berger added in a swipe at the Wobblies' rowdy free speech affairs, "in a continuous riot as a free-speech agitation." DeLeon went out of his way to castigate Haywood's Cooper Union address. Even the indomitable Eugene Debs broke with the Wobblies. Debs, who had helped found the organization in 1905, now condemned it as standing "for anarchy."[48]

After Los Angeles, an isolated IWW embraced violence as a tactic ever more explicitly. Haywood scorned the Socialists' pretenses of peace; their disavowal of violence, he said, was a betrayal of the McNamaras and of all Wobblies who went on trial for strike-related violence. Flynn, as one of the union's chief spokespeople, followed close behind.[49]

IWW strikes became more violent in the wake of the *Times* bombing, not less. A 1912 organizing drive among Black and white timber workers in Louisiana produced a riot and shootout in the tiny town of Grabow, leaving at least two union members and a deputy dead; Wobblies boasted that more dead deputies would have been counted if the Lumber Trust had not rushed the bodies away to hide just how many thugs it had hired to rough up the union. At Lawrence, Massachusetts, where a successful 1912 textile workers' strike brought new national attention to the IWW, Flynn, Haywood, and organizer Joseph Ettor offered exhortations to passive resistance. But their words came amid strikers' destruction of machinery and violent demonstrations against nonunion replacement workers. Authorities arrested Ettor, along with Wobbly organizer Arturo Giovannitti and striker Joseph Caruso, and charged them with the murder of a Lawrence resident killed during a clash between strikers and the state militia. The three were soon acquitted, but as soon as he was free, Giovannitti published an article defiantly defending the use of force.[50]

The lesson of Lawrence seemed to be that in certain situations, a little violence could help propel a strike to success. A year later, at the Durst Ranch in Wheatland, California, shooting broke out between striking IWW-affiliated agricultural workers and state officials, killing three workers, a deputy sheriff, and a district attorney. In Paterson, New Jersey, where the IWW led a strike that gained national attention, union-side vandals stoned dozens of strikebreakers' homes. Bombs exploded near nonunion laborers' residences. "I don't say violence should *not* be used," Flynn responded in a deliberately obscure circumlocution. Her view, she continued, was that "strike agitators should only advocate violence when they are absolutely certain that it is going to do some good." In all, Paterson witnessed 1,800 arrests, 5 deaths, and 20 injured policemen; rival socialists blamed Haywood for the violence.[51]

In 1914, IWW-affiliated dissidents in the WFM dynamited the miners' hall in Butte, Montana; Giovannitti, fresh off his acquittal on the murder charges in Lawrence, offered his approval. In 1916, deaths marred a strike in Minnesota's Mesabi Range in which Flynn was taking a lead part. The IWW had sent her there to renew the IWW effort to organize in the mines on which U.S. Steel relied. Strikers responded to orders to disperse by raining debris and firing shots onto police and nonunion workers. Later that same year, some three hundred Wobblies traveling to a free speech fight in Everett, Washington, were met by gunfire from anti-union vigilantes; before the fighting ended, five workers and two vigilantes lay dead, with fifty more injured on both sides combined. On the eve of U.S. entry into the war in early 1917, 275 striking Wobblies burned an icehouse in Kenosha, Wisconsin.[52]

Bursts of industrial violence were hardly confined to IWW conflicts; given the modest membership of the Wobblies, their conduct was only a small fraction of the labor unrest of the era. But the Wobblies gave violence its most striking articulation. "The worker," Haywood proclaimed in 1911, should "use any weapon which will win his fight." Wobbly papers echoed the point: "Whatever means are necessary will be employed," advised the editors of *Solidarity*, whose weekly column of news briefs was titled "Stray Bullets" and whose news roundup was bylined "A Western Rifleman." Cartoons in the organization's publications routinely featured images like the IWW as "a bomb underneath capitalism's July 4 bandstand." A history of the IWW by Flynn's friend Vincent St. John candidly asserted that the organization aimed "to use any and all tactics that will get the results sought with the least expenditure of time and energy."[53]

When the U.S. Commission on Industrial Relations headed by Frank Walsh called IWW leaders to testify before it, the IWW leaders stated their views without reservation. In 1914, St. John, who had organized workers on the Mesabi Range with Flynn in 1907 and 1908, told the commissioners that the Wobblies would destroy property and use violence whenever doing so advanced the interests of the workers. The exchange between St. John and William O. Thompson, counsel to the commission and a sympathizer with labor, was so extraordinary that Chairman Walsh leapt in to clarify its meaning:

Mr. Thompson. Then, the criterion of your action on a strike is whether or not the proposed action will gain the point of the strike?

Mr. St. John. That is the only one.

Mr. Thompson. Would that same reasoning apply to questions of violence against persons?

Mr. St. John. Certainly.

Chairman Walsh. Please turn this way, Mr. St. John, and speak a little louder; this is a difficult place to hear.

Mr. Thompson. I understood he said yes.

Mr. St. John. I said certainly.[54]

And again:

Mr. Thompson. In other words, your general policy is that whatever violence is necessary to carry the point, and if violence will carry the point, they must use it to gain the point?

Mr. St. John. Most assuredly; yes.

Mr. Thompson. Yes.

Chairman Walsh. What is the answer?

Mr. St. John. Most assuredly; yes.[55]

St. John was quick to add that violence was often not a smart tactic. But under questioning he qualified the point by agreeing that fending off strikebreaking laborers was "certainly" an occasion in which such violence would be warranted. As everyone at the commission understood, such battles between strikers and their would-be replacements had been the principal source of violence in the labor wars.[56]

Summoning John Brown and "the old abolitionists," Seattle-based IWW organizer James Thompson avowed to the Commission that he "not only" believed "in the destruction of property" but in "the destruction of human life if it will save human life." Under questioning, Haywood danced around the issue, insisting not implausibly that the most gruesome violence and the real lies were by the bosses. As for labor's use of force, he cited the success of peaceful strikes that had shut down mills and of nonviolent protests that had forced the release of prisoners from the jails. Here, too, was a kind of force, exerted by the power of labor acting as a united body. "I believe in that kind of violence," he affirmed. But Haywood added a vital and revealing exception: "When the workers are organized," he concluded, "it matters not to me what becomes necessary."[57]

Flynn's efforts with the IWW connected her to another violent radical movement. At the Lawrence strike in 1912 she met and fell in love with a man named Carlo Tresca, an Italian anarchist a decade her senior, who had fled to America in 1904 with Italian authorities in hot pursuit. In the United States, he became the roguish and dashing editor of an unruly succession of heterodox Italian-language anarchist newspapers. He was, as Roger Baldwin later remembered, a hearty and generous man, "overflowing with good will, romantic in his crusades" and with "a genius for friendship." In Flynn's words he was "hot headed"—a man of passions for causes, comrades, and lovers, seemingly always in the middle of the action.[58]

Tresca and the IWW held a common appeal for Flynn. Where many on the socialist left aimed for modest reforms or advocated gradual strategies, Tresca imagined the possibility of revolution by what Flynn later called a cataclysmic "splurge of violence." Tresca, who as Flynn noted idealized the violent Italian anarchist and revolutionary Errico Malatesta, seemed willing to do more than imagine such conduct. In 1914, he led gangs of striking waiters and hotel workers into the streets where they smashed restaurant windows and stormed hotels. (Tresca dubbed his bands of strikers "flying brigades" to evoke mobile military units.) Police clubbed Tresca and arrested him. But he was quoted in the papers: "I believe in violence, but only in violence when it advances the cause of labor." The worker's use of force in the service of his class, Flynn likewise insisted, was always justified, even if it was typically unwise.[59]

It fell to Flynn, as a self-described "jawsmith" for the Wobblies, to voice the IWW position on violence for audiences of workers. Flynn's stump speech on the subject began with the proposition that violence had been a "reaction against oppression" for all of history. To be sure, violence could sometimes be a sign of weakness, as it usually was in the AFL strikes that employed it. But in the end, the "ethics of the IWW," as Flynn saw it, approved "any and all means" that would advance the revolutionary project of seizing the means of production. Echoing Haywood and St. John at the Commission on Industrial Relations, Flynn adopted the position that the only test of a tactic's righteousness was its success in bringing about the working-class revolution. In this sense, Flynn and the IWW had no particular strategic vision at all—only a willingness to use whatever tactic was likely to work. Labor, she said in her rally remarks on violence, was "not committed to any creed" except a "spirit" ready to "do or die" for labor.[60]

Mostly Flynn promoted not violence but the related idea of sabotage, an idea IWW organizers began espousing around the time of the McKees Rocks strike, and whose virtue was in part its ambiguous relationship to violence and destruction. As a tactic, sabotage came out of the syndicalist strand of the French labor movement, where radicals had adopted the neologism "sabotage" to evoke the wooden clogs, or "sabots," worn by workers and thrown into the machinery to stop production. Haywood and William Z. Foster had both spent time in Europe in 1910 and returned with enthusiasm about the possibilities for a new kind of direct action. But the turn to sabotage also came out of a distinctly American resistance to scientific management in increasingly large industrial firms. Sabotage, wrote Wobbly editor Walker Smith, was "the best method to combat the evil" of modern managerial strategies for increasing productivity. Managers wielding ostensibly scientific theories of human engineering had adopted the "speed-up" and divided the production process into mindless tasks. Sabotage, Smith concluded, was "the only effective method of warding off the deterioration of the worker that is sure to follow the performance of the same monotonous task minute after minute, day in and day out."[61]

Flynn delivered one of the Wobblies' most influential definitions of sabotage in speeches during the Paterson strike of 1913. A fellow IWW organizer named Frederick Sumner Boyd had been arrested after calling for the city's silk workers to engage in acts of destruction in the mills. Flynn began her defense of Boyd with a defiant declaration of independence from the compromised moral principles of capitalist society. She would not, she announced, "attempt to justify sabotage on any moral ground" because workers' justification was self-evident. "If the workers consider that sabotage is necessary," she said, "that in itself makes sabotage moral. Its necessity is its excuse for existence." All that was necessary to understand the righteousness of sabotage, she continued, was to understand "the concept of class struggle." Where the strike was akin to "open battle," sabotage was labor's guerrilla warfare. In its simplest form sabotage was "the withdrawal of efficiency," by slacking or otherwise interfering with production. It was "not physical violence," at least not exactly or exclusively. In one fashion, it was the provision of labor at a "quality and speed proportional to the payment offered by the employer." Sabotage was the refusal of train engineers to deliver strikebreakers and soldiers to a struck mill or mine. It was the adulteration of delicate textiles like silk. It was the covert slipping of a machine belt to gain a half day off from otherwise grueling hours.[62]

Flynn was careful to add that the distinction between sabotage and violence did not mean that she deprecated the latter. Sabotage and violence were simply tactics appropriate for different conditions. She urged striking miners to hold on to their guns—to "exercise their constitutional right to bear arms."[63]

Flynn's position on violence became, for a time, even more extreme than that of her Wobbly comrades. When Lexington Avenue anarchist Arthur Caron killed himself and three others with the dynamite intended for John D. Rockefeller Jr., Flynn went out of her way to rally sympathy for the dead anarchists. Caron had hoped to avenge the Colorado miners and their wives and children killed at Ludlow earlier in the year. But most IWW leaders, including Haywood, disowned him. Spokesperson Joseph Ettor announced that the IWW disapproved of "dynamiting or setting off bombs or taking human life," except in self-defense.[64]

Flynn took a different tack. She championed Caron at the memorial service convened by anarchists at Union Square—and offered baseless speculation that the bomb had been planted by an undercover detective. Writing privately to her friend Mary Heaton Vorse, she explained that she "felt it would be a disgrace for all of us to remain silent after Ettor's repudiation of Caron." If Caron was in fact guilty, she continued, his act "was a natural consequence of the treatment he received" in the cruel world he protested. Caron, she wrote in an IWW newspaper article, had been arrested and beaten, hooted at and pelted with rocks and mud by the thugs and forces of capital. Who, Flynn asked rhetorically, was really responsible for the explosion? Who had taught Caron violence? In fact, she asked, wasn't "the psychology of violence" a "very natural result of police brutality and mob lawlessness"? Flynn expanded her comrade Ettor's self-defense right to encompass nearly all labor violence. And Flynn observed that St. John's testimony at the Commission on Industrial Relations just weeks earlier had supported violence explicitly. The true IWW principle, she concluded, was that violence was neither right nor wrong in the abstract. It was "either necessary or unnecessary, effective or useless," as each particular context required. "Circumstances alone determine" the propriety of violence, she wrote, and there was "no reason" why after

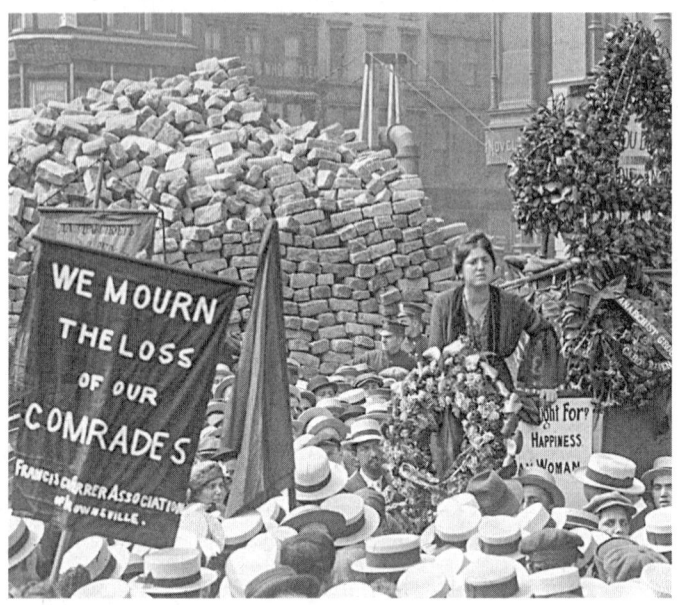

Flynn rallied crowds on Union Square in 1914 in an ill-considered defense of Arthur Caron, the clumsy bombmaker who blew up an apartment building (above) and killed himself with dynamite intended for the Rockefellers. The pictured speaker, historically identified as Flynn, is probably Flynn's ally the anarchist Becky Edelsohn. Flynn's lover, the bearded editor and organizer Carlo Tresca, is visible to Edelsohn's right, with New York police close behind.

defending the McNamaras the IWW should "now spit on the mangled corpses" of Caron and his comrades.[65]

Together with Tresca, Flynn emerged from the Caron episode in 1914 as the Wobblies' most uncompromising defender of violent tactics. And she carried the message out into the field. In the short-lived New York City waiters' strike, she and Ettor championed sabotaging the food served to restaurant and hotel guests; their meals were "one-fifth poison anyway," Flynn quipped, "and one-fifth seasoned sauces for covering tainted food." When she returned to the Mesabi Range in 1916, now accompanied by her Italian anarchist lover, she and the IWW preached the gospel of industrial sabotage anew. Strikers reportedly damaged mining equipment, destroyed railroad bridges, and spiked roads to shred the tires on mining company guards' vehicles.[66]

In the end, sabotage and violence were not merely figments of the bosses' propaganda. Social scientist Stuart Chase, who in the 1920s would become an influential figure in a new kind of nonviolent unionism, was right when he observed that "the employer, through his gunmen or his government," had "more often started the actual fisticuffs." But as Chase also noted, "after the first shot, there is little to choose between the parties in the belligerency." Labor had "replied with the utmost enthusiasm and vigor."[67]

What made the Wobblies' use of force so alluring to Flynn and to many others of her generation was that it aimed to make visible the violence disguised in everyday life. Properly understood, wrote Ettor, the real criminals of American life were the "industrial pirates" of capitalism, who ravaged the country and took it for themselves. The products of labor belonged rightly to the workers who made them. The so-called forces of "law and order" were therefore in actuality "as desperate and brutal a crew as ever scuttled a ship or quartered a man." Their property was theft. Indeed, even the bosses' claims to own the factory, the mill, and the mine was a kind of robbery. As Flynn told rally-goers, "the importation of strike-breakers" was "an act of force" because it violated the union workers' claims to the machinery of production. Seen this way, the IWW's use of force was simple self-defense. What made violence wrongful was the exploitative arrangement of the world by the bosses for the bosses. It was their distorted rules of property that properly counted as violence, not the necessary and righteous efforts of the IWW.[68]

The great difficulty with championing violence, however, was that it invited ferocious reprisals by the assembled forces of the status quo, regardless of which side had started the fight. The Wobblies' socialist critics countered angrily that the IWW had not fully thought through the implications of its tactics. From across the Atlantic, German socialist Karl Kautsky called the IWW "a mere child's disease of the labor union." Closer to home, Roger Baldwin dismissed violence as the work of "misguided idealists." Norman Thomas deprecated "the self-defeating methods of violence." Other American leftists objected that "appeals to violence" obscured "understanding of the real development of things." The anarchists' reliance on "propaganda of the deed" had not worked in Europe. It had been a strategic disaster at Haymarket. It had backfired after Ludlow in Caron's disastrous attempt on the life of Rockefeller. Sabotage was merely a new spasmatic iteration of the same old idea. The IWW, said socialist Robert Hunter in 1914, "could hardly have devised a method of propaganda" that "served more completely to defeat their purpose."[69]

The Espionage Act and the wave of wartime repression brought Hunter's prediction to fruition more quickly than Flynn could have imagined.

The IWW Does Not Believe in Violence

On July 31, 1917, vigilantes in Butte, Montana, lynched an IWW organizer named Frank Little, hanging him from a railroad trestle on the outskirts of town.

Little, who had been arrested alongside Flynn in the free speech fights at Missoula and Spokane in 1909, had been a target for state authorities and employers for years. Where Flynn was acquitted in Spokane, Little had been sentenced to thirty days in the local jail. When the Spokane judge asked him what he had been doing at the time of his arrest, he replied, "Reading the Declaration of Independence." The "hobo agitator," as Little was known among the Wobblies, was famous across the labor West for his energy and bravery. Mine operators had kidnapped him in Duluth in 1913 while he was agitating for unionization on the Mesabi Range. Little counted four other kidnappings in his career as a Wobbly speaker. And with the U.S. declaration of war in April 1917, Little emerged as an outspoken opponent of enlistment in the military. In Butte, he urged striking miners to stay out of what he called the capitalists' war. Anti-IWW vigilantes promptly seized him from his bed in the middle of the night and hanged him.[70]

Out of caution and pragmatism, the general executive board of the IWW declined to take a public position on the war in the spring of 1917. But few doubted the organization's real views. In the months before American entry into the conflict, Flynn had delivered speeches castigating patriotism and demanding to know why "the workers of the world" should fight the Kaiser to defend "the rule of Rockefeller and Morgan." Stray expressions of anti-war sentiment appeared through 1917 in the IWW magazine *Solidarity* and elsewhere in Wobbly literature. Haywood and his comrades, moreover, tried to seize the opportunity to organize workers during the period of increased wartime demand.[71]

The domestic political repression against which Roger Baldwin and the Civil Liberties Bureau fought, and for which World War I would become infamous, targeted the IWW regardless of its official protestations of restraint. Flynn called it a "wave of hysteria and mob violence." Nationalistic vigilante groups, often backed by local employers, ransacked IWW offices in Kansas City, Detroit, Seattle, and Duluth. Chicago war boosters raided the organization's headquarters in the city in May, seizing records and papers. In the first days of July, the Loyalty League in Jerome, Arizona, rounded up IWW labor agitators and banished them to the California desert. A week later, the sheriff of Bisbee, Arizona, broke up a strike by more than a thousand white and Mexican miners. Nearly two thousand deputized Arizonans rounded up twelve hundred miners in the early-morning hours, many of them citizens and many of them complying with the conscription law; citing the "Universal Law" of necessity—an inverted version of the same logic the Wobblies themselves had cited in resorting to violence—the town sheriff shipped the miners by railcar to the Mexican border and warned them not to return.[72]

Competing to outdo the vigilantes, governors from eight western states asked the White House to establish concentration camps to hold Wobblies for the duration of the war. State agencies initiated criminal investigations of the organization. In Tulsa, the arrest of seventeen local IWW leaders resulted in a near-lynching when a crowd seized them from the jail, whipped them, tarred and feathered them, and banished them from the city.[73]

The Wilson administration, for its part, did its best "to put the IWW out of business," in the words of one U.S. attorney. President Wilson declined the governors' request to create IWW concentration camps. But federal troops patrolled western mines and railways. In Spokane, where the army learned of an impending labor action in the timber industry, military officials detained local Wobbly leadership and held them under military authority until the strike threat passed. Meanwhile, the Department of Justice initiated a strategy of investigations and prosecutions that aimed to put an end to the IWW once and for all. In August 1917, President Wilson set in motion an investigation of the IWW led by federal judge J. Harry Covington in Washington, D.C.[74]

On September 29, federal authorities arrested Flynn and Tresca at Flynn's apartment in the Bronx. A local cop who had known Flynn from the neighborhood when they were children accompanied Justice Department officers to make the identification.[75]

Three weeks earlier, the Justice Department had coordinated simultaneous raids of IWW offices in Chicago, Fresno, Seattle, Spokane, and every other city with a significant IWW presence. Authorities had raided the homes of IWW leaders, too. On September 28, a federal grand jury in Chicago issued a single massive indictment naming every leading IWW figure, 165 people in all, including Haywood, Flynn, St. John, Ettor, and Giovannitti. The indictment charged each of them with more than one hundred violations of four different federal criminal laws. Separate grand juries indicted regional union officials in Fresno, Omaha, Sacramento, and Wichita. The Espionage Act charges alone were punishable by up to twenty years in prison.[76]

At Haywood's instruction, Wobbly leaders around the country surrendered to federal arrest and prepared for a mass trial before Judge Kenesaw Mountain Landis, a stern man and a staunch conservative. Flynn, however, objected to Haywood's plan. She pressed for a strategy like the old free speech fights in Spokane and Missoula. If every defendant sought a severance, she contended, the IWW would tie the government's "dragnet strategy up in knots." The government, moreover, had little or no individualized evidence against most of the defendants. Previous efforts at prosecution, after all, had mostly failed, producing acquittals and mistrials for Haywood in Idaho in 1907, Flynn in Missoula in 1909, and Ettor and Giovannitti in Lawrence in 1912. As Flynn saw it, acquittals in individual cases would be much-needed victories for the organization.[77]

Haywood refused to go along. Perhaps he thought that a single spectacular trial for all the defendants in solidarity with one another would produce a propaganda coup. Maybe he believed that he was more likely to be acquitted if jurors were distracted by a hundred less deeply involved codefendants. Whatever his motive, Flynn thought his approach dubious at best and suicidal at worst. Flouting Haywood's authority, she wrote an extraordinary private letter to President Wilson, asking that her case be severed from the cases against defendants who had actively participated in the IWW during the war. The only possible basis for her indictment, she told Wilson, was the sabotage pamphlet she had written after the Paterson strike. But Flynn distanced herself from the pamphlet's content, which she now said had been limited to the "times" and "conditions" of the Paterson controversy. She had been meaning, she continued, to rewrite it. Prosecutors in Chicago acceded to Flynn's request for a severance. Ettor, Giovannitti, and Tresca petitioned for and received severances, too.[78]

By the time the Chicago trial began in the spring of 1918, a hundred and one defendants were still on the docket. The cumbersome mass trial lasted for five months. But the jury deliberated for less than an hour before returning guilty verdicts on four charges for each of the remaining defendants. Judge Landis sentenced Haywood and fourteen others to twenty years in prison. Vincent St. John, whose testimony at the Industrial Relations Commission had been the most uncompromising, received twenty years despite having left the IWW two years before the war began.[79]

Prosecutions of the organization's regional leaders in Chicago, Sacramento, and Wichita produced similar if less spectacular outcomes. In all, 184 Wobbly leaders were tried and prosecuted in 1918 and 1919. Immigration officials identified dozens more as alien anarchists, citing IWW support for sabotage and the destruction of property. The Bureau of Immigration shipped more than three dozen Wobblies across the country from Seattle to Ellis Island for deportation.[80]

Haywood remained out of prison until the Court of Appeals for the Seventh Circuit in Chicago affirmed the Chicago convictions, at which point he jumped his bond, disappeared, and fled to the Soviet Union to live out the final decade of his life. (His labor allies back in the United States spent years trying to recoup their $15,000 in forfeited security bonds.) With war fever abating, and to avoid the risk of embarrassing acquittals, the government quietly dropped its case against Flynn and the handful of separate IWW defendants. Prosecutors had proven their point; wartime repression had achieved its goal. The IWW's membership plunged from 100,000 strong at its height in 1917 to a mere 15,000 by 1921, a third of the organization's size at its founding.[81]

Too late, the wartime IWW had scrambled to erase its earlier commitments to sabotage and destruction. Where the prewar IWW had styled itself an army in the class war, with flying brigades, bombs, and tactics suited for industrial battle, the wartime Wobblies struggled desperately (if implausibly) to present themselves as a simple bread-and-butter union. The Wobbly journalist Justus Ebert helped set the process in motion in his 1918 account of the IWW. "Nothing is further from the truth," he now insisted, than the interpretation of "direct action" as "violence, dynamiting and lawlessness." Retroactively redefining terms, he asserted that the "violence that the IWW commits is the violence of passive resistance." In the Chicago trial itself, lawyer George Vanderveer contended in his opening statement that "the IWW does not believe in violence." Not long before, sabotage and revolutionary rejection of the status quo had been the core of the IWW ethic; now Vanderveer denied all allegations of disloyalty. On his account, the old radical IWW, which had avowed incessant class war and denied the common humanity of the working class and the employer class, now prided itself on offering efficient labor to wartime employers. ("There was never better service rendered" than by the IWW's unions, Vanderveer said.) For his part, Haywood claimed no memory of his prewar radicalism. He denied any opposition to the war and boasted of his cooperation in employers' wartime production. The once revolutionary IWW speaker J. T. "Red" Doran now contended that his motive in organizing for the Wobblies had always been "to get eight hours and more pork chops," not to support overturning the means of production.[82]

IWW publications suddenly stopped advocating sabotage. Gone were images of the black cat and wooden shoes that had long been symbols of the saboteur. Gone was advocacy of the destruction of employer property. On May 4, 1918, the IWW's General Executive Board made the new posture official by disavowing violence and sabotage. The organization, announced the board in a bit of revisionist history, "does not now, and never has believed in or advocated either destruction or violence as a means of accomplishing industrial reform."[83]

Flynn had not been on trial, but she turned away from violence as a strategy more conspicuously than any of her comrades. The fiery speaker who had once rallied the most aggressive factions of the IWW, Flynn now spoke out about the nonviolent work of Mohandas Gandhi in India. "Gandhi," she said, was "showing the possibilities in passive resistance." If it could work "in the Far Eastern empire," she added, "it could be worked here." Even Flynn's anarchist lover Tresca suddenly disowned violence, in hopes of avoiding deportation back to Italy.[84]

The war's closing months and aftermath witnessed one final paroxysm of left-labor violence, this time without the guiding theoretical force of the IWW's prewar vision. In September 1918, just days after Judge Landis sentenced Haywood to twenty years in prison, a bomb destroyed the entrance of the federal courthouse in Chicago, killing four people and shattering windows a block away. In April 1919, postal officials discovered thirty bombs in packages addressed to some of the nation's most prominent men. The anarchists responsible for the mail bombs had targeted Judge Landis along with J. P. Morgan Jr. and John Rockefeller, the Supreme Court's Oliver Wendell Holmes, and half a dozen current or former members of Congress. Only one person suffered injuries in the campaign: the package directed to former U.S. senator Thomas Hardwick of Georgia exploded in the hands of Ethel Williams, the senator's Black maid. She lost both her arms at the wrists. On June 2, anarchists detonated bombs simultaneously in seven cities, destroying the D.C. home of Attorney General A. Mitchell Palmer and nearly killing his neighbor, the young assistant secretary of the navy Franklin Roosevelt. Other than the anarchist who accidentally blew himself up on Palmer's front step, this time a seventy-year-old night patrolman named William Boehner in New York was the lone casualty. A year later, in April 1920, two gunmen murdered a paymaster and a guard outside a Boston-area shoe factory and made off with almost $16,000; Massachusetts authorities attributed the killing to an anarchist cell. In September of that year, a bomb exploded on Wall Street and killed thirty-eight people in what was almost certainly another act of anarchist terror.[85]

In attack after attack, the purposive action of the IWW's prewar period, with its imaginative inversion of the basic morality of the capitalist world, had gone haywire. IWW leaders disowned some of the bombings, though they were mostly in prison or on the run. But given their open experiments with violence just a few short years earlier, they were in no position to object. Loose revolutionary language about violence had escaped from their control. Sabotage and violence, in the words of Louis Adamic, had lost their "social vision and purpose." Adamic, the closest student of the phenomenon, wrote that the spasmodic violence of the postwar moment was a demoralizing "menace" to the "national character."[86]

Only at Centralia, Washington, did the demoralized and leaderless IWW become actively involved in a postwar outbreak of violence. A remnant IWW group, apparently acting in self-defense, fired desperate and foolish shots from an IWW union hall, killing four American Legion veterans in a parade on Armistice Day 1919. Legionnaires and others lynched one Wobbly the next day; seven IWW men were later convicted of murder and sentenced to long prison terms. Even if the Centralia episode was an isolated event, postwar state governments dealt the IWW a final and decisive blow nonetheless. Twenty states and two territories, including the jurisdictions in which the IWW had been most engaged, criminalized what Flynn had for years preached: "the doctrine" (in the words of the Idaho law) "which advocates crime, sabotage, violence, or unlawful methods of terrorism" as a strategy of industrial reform. The laws, as one student of "criminal syndicalism" legislation observed, aimed squarely at the practices Flynn and her comrades had advocated. The power of the state had crushed what remained of the "revolutionary industrial union known as the Industrial Workers of the World."[87]

For Elizabeth Gurley Flynn, the most prominent former Wobbly not in prison or in exile, the end of the IWW's heady vision was a deep and abiding blow. For the next decade her health would slowly decline. But in the 1920s, in one last burst of creative energy, Flynn found ways to draw on elements of the IWW to recraft radicalism for a new landscape. If violence and sabotage were quixotic invitations to repression, Flynn would look elsewhere to identify subtler ways to end exploitation and alter the world.

One path beckoned with some urgency. Hundreds of radicals, many of them her former comrades, languished in American prisons. Defending them would bring Flynn into contact with a very different cadre of institution-builders organized around the new American Fund for Public Service. There she found a heterodox group of industrial unionists dedicated to channeling revolutionary energies into practical institutions—a group better suited than the otherworldly revolutionaries of the IWW to engaging with a modern mass industrial society. At the table of the American Fund, Flynn would pull further away from the clumsiest features of the IWW. Alongside Roger Baldwin, James Weldon Johnson, and others, her distinctive contribution would be to adapt the brilliant creativity of the Wobblies to the postwar world.

Labor union innovator Sidney Hillman, pictured here in 1922, during his service on the American Fund's founding board of directors.

13

Industrial Democracy

Brookwood became the mecca, the center of inspiration and courage for those who had a vision of a new world.

—FANNIA M. COHN OF THE INTERNATIONAL
LADIES' GARMENT WORKERS UNION, 1936

"I certainly dislike intensely to apply to the Garland Fund," wrote Elizabeth Gurley Flynn to Roger Baldwin in November 1922. She had "tried very hard," she added, "not to ask rich people for money." Nonetheless, as one of the very first applicants for support from the American Fund for Public Service, Flynn wrote Baldwin seeking help with the defense of a pair of Italian immigrant anarchists whose names were Nicola Sacco and Bartolomeo Vanzetti.[1]

If Flynn came to the Fund reluctantly, the escalating demands of the Sacco and Vanzetti case—which was fast becoming one of the greatest legal defense causes of the century—overcame her hesitations. Before long, the Fund became a vital institutional supporter of the Sacco Vanzetti Defense Committee. And in July 1924, Flynn cemented the bond between the two efforts by joining the Fund's board of directors.[2]

Flynn was a natural fit. For one thing, her appointment to the seat on the board opened up by social worker Mary McDowell's resignation ensured that there would continue to be at least one woman director at the Fund. A simultaneous nomination of *Nation* editor Freda Kirchwey increased the number of women on the Fund's board to two. Four years removed from ratification of the Nineteenth Amendment's prohibition on sex discrimination in voting, a modest women's representation on the board seems to have mattered to the Fund's male directors. In 1928, Clarina Michelson's appointment would briefly create a period of three women directors.³

More important to many of the directors was that Flynn was one of the few prewar IWW organizers still active in the labor movement. Baldwin noted that he nominated Flynn as "an ex-IWW" for her "spirit of revolt." She had been a "close colleague" for years, he later recalled. Rumors swirled that the two carried on a brief love affair. She was "a personal friend," Baldwin confessed, and he admitted affection as well as admiration for her. "One's heart sometimes dictates one way and one's mind sometimes the other," Flynn wrote Baldwin. The rumors would resurface years later when the two parted ways over Flynn's middle-age adherence to the Stalinist party line. In the meantime, however, Baldwin was glad to substitute Flynn's fierce outlook for that of the staid social worker McDowell.⁴

The American Fund's support for the Sacco and Vanzetti campaign allowed Flynn to gain unexpected mainstream support for some of the most uncompromising parts of her old world of labor radicalism. But the world of the Fund also swung her work in a new direction. The Fund connected Flynn to a new and fast-emerging kind of labor union, one to which the Fund was committing an ever-greater share of its fortune. In industries such as men's clothing and ladies' garments, labor organizers like founding American Fund director Sidney Hillman set out to alter the basic arrangements of economic life just as fundamentally as Flynn's old Wobbly comrades. Hillman and company aimed to build a movement and a set of institutions capable of giving workers a say in administering the giant institutions of the mass-production economy. As Flynn joined the Fund's monthly meetings in the bustling dining room of the Civic Club in Greenwich Village, her fellow directors were working to vindicate the project Hillman and others called industrial democracy.⁵

Sacco and Vanzetti

After the Chicago trial of 1918 and the smaller trials that took place around the country, virtually all Flynn's IWW friends were in prison. One thousand radicals rotted in federal prisons. Nearly a thousand more became prisoners in 1919, including a wave of radicals convicted under the newly enacted state criminal syndicalism laws. The Department of Labor deported more than 250 aliens, including Emma Goldman and Alexander Berkman, for holding anarchist views. A steady drumbeat of Espionage Act convictions continued—nearly two per day for a year after Armistice. In the first weeks of 1920, Attorney General A. Mitchell Palmer's dragnet raids produced 10,000 more arrests, scooping up thousands of citizens along with the anarchist and radical aliens who were ostensibly the intended targets.[6]

Flynn would later recall "the hurry and horror of it all." The arrests, jailings, and deportations, she said, seemed like a "hideous nightmare."[7]

But Palmer's recklessness united a wide coalition of critics—and offered Flynn a new political opportunity. She took up work alongside Baldwin's National Civil Liberties Bureau, helping the NCLB produce a long pamphlet defending the people she called political prisoners. Three days before Baldwin headed to prison himself in November 1918, the NCLB made Flynn a loan to create an organization focused exclusively on securing the release of political prisoners. Flynn called it the Workers Defense Union. The organization, she later said, was "like a godchild of the Civil Liberties Bureau." Where the Wobblies had fomented organizational schisms and produced bitter disagreements, the WDU served as what Flynn called a "united front" of labor organizations and liberal reformers. No fewer than 163 joined the WDU in the winter of 1918–19, ranging from progressive unions in the AFL to the remnants of the IWW. Socialist Party chapters joined together with the Harlem Professional League, the Hebrew Butchers Union, and the Hungarian Workers Council, not to mention the United Brotherhood of Carpenters and the International Ladies' Garment Workers Union. More organizations followed in the months and years thereafter. Flynn found offices for the WDU in a back room at the socialist-leaning Rand School of Social Science on East 15th Street. "I often felt I, too, was in jail," Flynn joked about the windowless storeroom. But it was an apt space from which to launch a campaign on behalf of imprisoned radicals.[8]

By January 1919, Flynn estimated there were 1,500 labor and political prisoners in the United States, and she worked (in her words) "day and night" to build a united front effort in their defense. She commuted early each morning from her family's apartment in the Bronx, where she now lived with Carlo Tresca, to the WDU's downtown office. Ella Reeve Bloor, a founding member in 1919 of the American Communist Labor Party, staffed the office with her. The WDU posted bail for Flynn's friend Vincent St. John. (St. John's conviction, Flynn said, was "the crowning outrage of the war.") WDU causes included the ailing Eugene Debs, who got nearly 1 million votes in 1920 as the Socialist Party candidate for president while inside a federal prison. Flynn advocated on behalf of a prominent midwestern socialist named Kate Richards O'Hare, convicted under the Espionage Act after an anti-war speech in North Dakota. The WDU took up the cause of anti-war hero Tom Mooney, who had been convicted of orchestrating the deadly preparedness day bombing in San Francisco in 1916. The WDU lobbied Attorney General Palmer and his replacement, the corrupt and soon-disgraced Harry Daugherty. They petitioned President Wilson and his successor Warren Harding directly, urging amnesties for the entire class of political prisoners and pressing for individualized releases, too.[9]

Flynn's striking accomplishment with the WDU was to marshal a wide array of liberals and progressives behind imprisoned radicals whose views had been anathema only a few months before. The organization widened

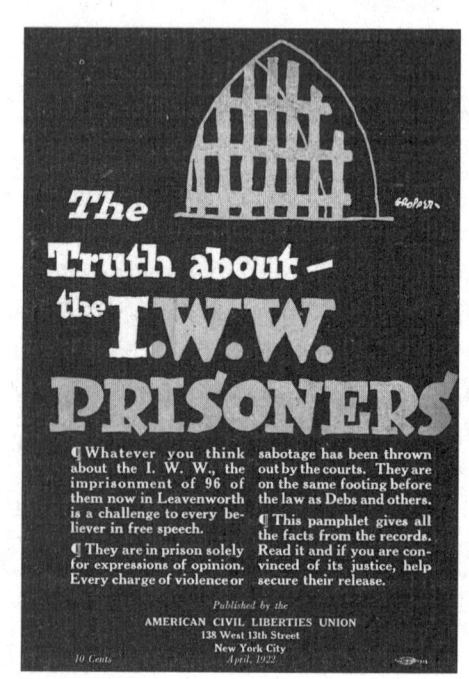

Flynn, the former Wobbly, began to work closely with the ACLU in its postwar campaigns on behalf of political prisoners.

its base of support still further by drawing attention to the awful conditions in which prisoners lived. Flynn lambasted the Labor Department for, at one point in 1920, holding 170 men in a single room. Emaciated prisoners fell sick, with little water and poor ventilation. The food for those being held on Ellis Island awaiting deportation, Flynn wrote, "sounds nice, but tastes like hell"; the daily prison menu, she continued, contained "a lot of swell names for swill." Flynn agitated for better healthcare for detainees, including a former Wobbly whose appendicitis operation in prison had gone badly awry. When prisoners got out, Flynn helped them find new clothing and other necessities.[10]

Most of all, Flynn turned her big-tent coalition to fight the deportations that shipped hundreds of alien radicals across the Atlantic. She organized a successful pressure campaign to persuade Secretary of Labor William Wilson to require individualized evidence of support for sabotage or the destruction of property before deporting an alien, a rule change that staved off deportation for several dozen Wobblies from the Pacific Northwest. (Ironically, Flynn would have flunked the test for aliens in light of her advocacy of sabotage and violence in the 1910s.) Flynn and Bloor assisted Wobblies rendered stateless by deportation. And over the opposition of the remnants of the IWW itself, Flynn's WDU helped broker clemency deals that released IWW prisoners. The IWW, still following the logic of its disastrous Chicago trial tactics, insisted that individual deals were betrayals of the cause. The WDU rejected such purity politics.[11]

In all, Flynn's efforts for political prisoners reunited the fractious forces of American left-liberal circles into a united front unlike anything seen since before the war. The WDU put Flynn in close contact with Clarence Darrow as well as Frank Walsh, who had led the Commission on Industrial Relations inquiry into the Ludlow massacre. Defense work at the WDU connected Flynn to the founder of the New York Civic Club, Frederic Howe, whom she persuaded to quit his post as Commissioner of Immigration for the Port of New York in protest against the conditions of confinement for alien detainees. Flynn even prevailed upon George Creel, Woodrow Wilson's wartime propagandist, to weigh in on behalf of an IWW prisoner in 1921. In a move drawn from Creel's flair for publicity, Flynn sponsored a Children's Crusade that brought the children of imprisoned radicals to protest outside the White House. James Weldon Johnson's wife, Grace, joined in Flynn's efforts. So did the libertarian but temperamentally conservative ACLU lawyer Albert DeSilver and his progressive colleague Walter Nelles. At Harvard Law School, Zechariah Chafee, Felix Frankfurter, and Dean Roscoe Pound joined Flynn in condemning the Palmer Raids. The WDU, it seemed, had found a voice in the big-tent world of the Fund, one that gave Flynn more reach than she had ever known in her years as a fire-breathing Wobbly.[12]

Success came with costs, to be sure. Flynn and her allies had not chosen the field on which they fought; playing defense had been forced on them by repressive government policies. Even worse, the amnesty effort was one that some forward-thinking statesmen had quietly decided was in the government's interest, too. Norman Thomas grasped the core of the difficulty when he observed in a private note to Flynn that deporting radicals had become "singularly inexpedient" for the incoming Harding administration. Clumsy deportations and imprisonments had galvanized the government's critics in a common cause. Releasing prisoners, as Walter Lippmann's writings had anticipated, allowed the government a simple path to defusing the energy of its critics. In 1920, the Justice Department recommended that President Wilson release or reduce the sentences of two hundred Espionage Act prisoners; Wilson agreed. On Christmas Day in 1921, President Warren Harding pardoned a physically failing Eugene Debs. And two years later, on Christmas Day in 1923, Calvin Coolidge (president since Harding's sudden death that August) released the last of the Espionage Act prisoners, including the remaining IWW convicts. Likewise, the number of political deportations fell by nearly 90 percent in 1922, dropping from an all-time high of 446 in 1921 to mere single digits annually by 1926. Espionage Act prosecutions ended. Ten years later, when Franklin Roosevelt granted full amnesty to the World War I Espionage Act felons, restoring their political and civil rights, the point was clear. Strategic retreat had drained most of the political significance from the cause of the wartime prisoners. The release of radical prisoners counted as a victory of sorts for Flynn and the WDU. But it was also a crisis for her coalition.[13]

The new cause for Flynn's defense efforts arose out of the April 1920 shooting and killing of the paymaster and guard outside a shoe factory in South Braintree, Massachusetts. Two men seized the paymaster's cash boxes and leapt into a car driven by two or three others, making off with nearly

$16,000 in cash. Three weeks later, Boston authorities arrested Italian anarchists Nicola Sacco and Bartolomeo Vanzetti on a streetcar while the two were trying to retrieve an automobile thought to have been involved in the crime. At the time of their arrest, Sacco and Vanzetti carried loaded pistols and a large quantity of ammunition, including shotgun shells like those used in a similar crime in December. Under questioning they lied about their anarchist affiliations. State officials charged them with murder.[14]

Outside an isolated circle of Italian immigrant anarchists, Flynn was among the first to take an interest in Sacco and Vanzetti. Tresca alerted her to the case within days of the men's arrests. Flynn's WDU issued a bulletin about the developing case in May. Flynn personally looked into the still-obscure matter a few months later while on a lecture tour for the WDU. Tresca, meanwhile, used his anarchist connections to put her in touch with the Sacco-Vanzetti Defense Committee, a small group of immigrants from the Italian anarchist community of Massachusetts. The group was skeptical of outsiders. But they welcomed Flynn once they recognized her from the IWW's Lawrence strike of 1912. Indeed, it soon turned out that Flynn had worked personally with Nicola Sacco during the IWW's 1912 textile strike in Lawrence, where Sacco contributed to the legal defense of IWW organizers Ettor and Giovannitti. Two years later, after the errant 1914 explosion that destroyed the Lexington Avenue apartment rather than its intended target at the Rockefeller estate, Flynn had publicly defended bombmaker Arthur Caron and others with loose connections to Sacco. Two years after that, in 1916, Sacco had organized Massachusetts fundraisers to support Flynn and Tresca's unionizing efforts on the Mesabi Range in Minnesota.[15]

After Flynn visited the two men in October 1920, one in a Dedham jail, the other in a dank Charlestown prison, the WDU began a publicity drive that touched off seven years of efforts. The defense of Sacco and Vanzetti became one of the most widely publicized campaigns of the twentieth century, more prolonged than the spectacular Scopes evolution trial in Tennessee, and more global in its reach than either the Ossian Sweet case in Detroit or the Elaine massacre cases out of Arkansas. The Sacco and Vanzetti episode, as historians would later observe, was most comparable to the Dreyfus Affair of two decades before, when the military conviction of a Jewish officer in the French army split France in two, locking the partisans of each side into a yearslong controversy.[16]

Flynn quickly brought in Baldwin's ACLU, then only a year old, which pledged to join with her in organizing a publicity campaign of public meetings and lectures. Together with an artist named Art Shields from the old *Masses* magazine, Flynn published a pamphlet titled *Are They Doomed*, which used striking photographs and crime-scene drawings to craft the narrative that Sacco and Vanzetti partisans would tell for years to come. In Flynn and Shields's telling, a "good shoemaker" (Sacco) and a "poor fish peddler" (Vanzetti) had been framed by a corrupt and prejudiced legal system. They were innocent victims, wrote Shields, of "persecution, intrigue, race prejudice, and third-degree police methods." By the time the two men's trial began in May 1921, Flynn had spoken on the men's behalf throughout New England and the mid-Atlantic and distributed some 50,000 copies of the Workers Defense Union pamphlet.[17]

With each passing stage of the case, the clumsiness of the prosecution effort lent credence to Flynn's story. During the trial, police led Sacco and Vanzetti manacled through the streets to the courthouse each day, where the two defendants sat through the proceedings in an iron cage placed in the middle of the courtroom in full view of the jurors. The unscrupulous prosecutor openly insinuated that the defendants' alien status and political views were evidence of their guilt; the jurors' loyalty to the United States, he implied, required that they vote to convict. And convict they did, on July 14. The judge, an aging and reactionary New Englander named Webster Thayer, conveyed contempt for the defendants just as clearly when he entered judgment against them. "Did you see what I did with those anarchistic bastards the other day?" he crowed to friends.[18]

The crude prejudice of the legal system helped make the names Sacco and Vanzetti a rallying cry for liberals across the United States and around the world. Progressive editors at magazines like *The Nation* and the *New Republic* leapt to the defense of the two men. By 1922, the typically cautious American Federation of Labor took up the cause, calling for a new trial in its annual meeting in Cincinnati despite Samuel Gompers's notorious disdain for anarchist radicalism. Two years later, the AFL platform condemned the men's trial as "a ghastly miscarriage of justice" and defended Sacco and Vanzetti as "defenseless victims of race and national prejudice and class hatred."[19]

Flynn knew full well, however, that the two men were hardly the poor shoemaker and fish peddler her publicity materials described. Thanks to Tresca, she understood from the beginning that Sacco and Vanzetti were part of a tight-knit cell of militant Italian anarchists who supported the violent overthrow of the existing social order. Sacco and Vanzetti were believers in the ideas of Italian-born anarchist Luigi Galleani, who preached the use of dynamite to bring down capitalism. Galleani's followers aimed to carry out the plan. Murderous robberies like the one in South Braintree—"expropriations" or "propaganda of the deed," as they called it—expressed the group's violent disdain for the basic rules of society. And where the Wobblies had retreated from the use of force in the face of the government's overwhelming advantage, Sacco, Vanzetti, and their Galleanisti comrades had led the way in taking the government's suppression of radicalism as an occasion for violent revenge.[20]

The tiny circle of Massachusetts-based anarchists had been involved in bombings going back at least as far as the 1914 Lexington Avenue blast. During the war they initiated a campaign of violence astonishing for its breadth and determination. A Galleanisti bomb killed ten detectives in a Milwaukee police station after police there suppressed an anti-war riot in 1917; another dynamite bomb nearly killed the prosecutor who later charged eleven local anarchists with the crime. In Philadelphia, dynamite shredded the homes of the president of the chamber of commerce, the acting superintendent of police, and a justice on the state supreme court in December 1918; miraculously, no one was killed. Two months later, the premature detonation of a bomb during a textile workers' strike in Lawrence, Massachusetts, killed four of Sacco and Vanzetti's comrades. In late April 1919, the same circle of anarchist militants launched the mail bomb campaign that sent thirty dynamite packages to prominent people around the country. On June 2, members of the cell planted the bomb that destroyed the house of Attorney General A. Mitchell Palmer, accidentally blowing one of the two men's closest comrades to pieces in the process. The same cell set off bombs in six other cities nearly simultaneously. The cart-drawn bomb that killed more than three dozen on Wall Street in September 1920 had served as a punctuation mark to the Galleanisti terror campaign.[21]

It was not lost on Flynn that the Galleanisti had targeted, among others, the Wobblies' principal enemies. Mail bombs went to Judge Kenesaw Mountain Landis, who had presided over the Chicago IWW trial, and Frank Nebeker, the prosecutor in the trial. In one sense, the bombings of 1919 and 1920 were the last blasts in a strategy of violent revolution that had begun with the Western Federation of Miners and former governor Frank Steunenberg in Idaho—a strategy in which Flynn's IWW had played a leading role.[22]

Yet Flynn's campaign for the two Italians put on display American radicalism's 1920s transition to a new, nonviolent chapter. The WDU aimed to distance itself from Sacco and Vanzetti's radical project and most of all to separate itself from their violent means. By suppressing the men's politics and insisting on their innocence, Flynn made sure from early on that the defense campaign focused on the particulars of the case and kept away from the tainted history of militant anarchist violence. "I can see nothing but disaster for Sacco and Vanzetti," she told the men's lawyer, Fred Moore, "if you attempt to make them the pivot around which the class struggle in America is to swing." Obscuring their deep involvement in domestic terrorism, Flynn crafted an image of Sacco and Vanzetti perfectly designed for a united front campaign of progressive forces: liberal critics, labor unions, and radicals alike.[23]

The difficult question for Flynn was what broader purpose such a united front strategy of legal defense might serve. She had always believed that the law was a form of class control, an embodiment of the power of the elite. Law could not offer a viable way to undo injustice; the law *was* injustice. For a decade and more, she and Haywood and the Wobblies had said as much. They had condemned the law as an instrument of capitalist exploitation and openly entertained violent extralegal tactics. In their own trial in Chicago, the Wobblies had refused the legal advantages of separate proceedings and had rejected all talk of compromise. Flynn's legalistic defense of Sacco and Vanzetti by comparison seemed to be compromised from the start, its ambitions curbed by compliance with the basic rules of the system it purported to attack. The energy and rebelliousness of the Wobbly moment seemed to have been sapped from the project. "I am," Flynn confided in Baldwin as early as 1922, "quite discouraged."[24]

I Shall Not Leave This Platform

Sidney Hillman, leader of the Amalgamated Clothing Workers union, or ACW, was not discouraged at all. Still in the middle stages of his meteoric rise from obscurity to power, Hillman took a seat as an inaugural member of the American Fund's board of directors in 1922. Formally, he served only a year in the role. But his influence lived on through members of his brain trust who remained on the board for the rest of its existence, giving Hillman as powerful a role as any director in the Fund's history in shaping the fate of Garland's million-dollar gift.

By any reasonable measure, Hillman was an unlikely candidate to become one of the most powerful men in America. A socialist refugee from a hard-luck family of Lithuanian rabbis, he immigrated to the United States in 1907 at the age of twenty, speaking no English. Migration for Hillman had been more necessity than choice. Arrested by czarist authorities for his activities with the Jewish workers' league known as the Bund, and then again for organizing on behalf of the Menshevik faction of socialist revolutionaries, he spent months in Russian prisons. When Czar Nicholas II dissolved the Russian parliament and cracked down again on revolutionaries in 1906, Hillman was forced to flee with little more than a fake passport and the clothes on his back. Yet by the 1930s, the impoverished refugee would maneuver himself to the forefront of an American labor movement that was achieving previously unimaginable successes. So great was his talent at creating new ways to organize American workers that in 1944, President Franklin Roosevelt would issue a famous standing order to his aides in the search for a vice presidential running mate. "Clear it with Sidney," the president said of proposed nominees.[25]

In 1922, Hillman's rising authority in union circles led Roger Baldwin to invite him to serve as a founding director at the American Fund. Hillman soon expanded his influence by proposing that the board add two close colleagues from his clothing workers union. Self-educated former miner and machinist Clinton Golden served as general organizer for Hillman's ACW beginning in the summer of 1923. Labor economist Leo Wolman functioned as the ACW's director of research while holding teaching posts at the New School for Social Research and Columbia University. By 1924, both men held seats on the American Fund board. Hillman himself stepped back from the Fund, pleading the press of business, but he and his comrades became the single most influential force in the otherwise fractious world of the American Fund. Baldwin counted himself among their leading supporters. Norman Thomas did, too. The ACW itself rarely required support; membership dues financed a labor empire whose autonomy Hillman jealously guarded. (The ACW sought and received one $77,500 loan from the Fund for a cooperative housing project in 1925; unlike many Fund borrowers, Hillman's union repaid the debt in full.) But all told, the Fund made at least $340,000 in outright grants to organizations and causes allied with Hillman's ACW and its model of industrial unions, a figure that amounted to a fifth of the Fund's total outlays over the course of its existence.[26]

Hillman's gift was his ability to translate radical passions into practical power. What Hillman and the world of the ACW proposed was nothing less than a new social order for labor and capital, one that would be achieved by marshaling the revolutionary energies of the IWW without the Wobblies' foolhardy and unsustainable excesses. Hillman's ACW aimed to exercise economic power amid industrial peace, not industrial war.

Hillman first emerged as a leader in the garment trades in September 1910, when seventeen seamstresses walked off the job at Hart, Schaffner, and Marx in Chicago to protest a reduction in the piece rates.

For years, fierce competition in the decentralized underworld of the garment and clothing industries had made the so-called needle trades a site of bitter and recurring labor strife. Low profit margins and ease of entry into the business yielded unhealthy working conditions and poverty wages. Strikes were more common in needlework than anywhere except construction and mining. And as in so many American industries, garment worker strikes often featured violence on all sides. As the strike at Hart, Schaffner spread across the city, from firm to firm, the usual brutish conduct followed. "Huskies" working for employers took up stations outside exits and entrances, brandishing clubs and threatening to "beat a merry tune on the skulls" of the strikers. Picketing workers answered back with threats of their own. "In the dead of the night," reported one contemporary account, "homes were entered" and "scabs dragged from their beds and beaten." A "secret night committee" of strikers "prowled after dark, spreading alarm" among would-be strikebreakers. The streets outside contested shops soon became sites of pitched battles between strikers, the police, and company security. Strikers shot a replacement worker and killed a security guard. Employers' goons killed a striker. And so it went. A seamstress strike over reductions in the piece rate had lifted the lid on a boiling cauldron of pent-up fury about basic labor arrangements.[27]

Amid the chaotic strike, Hillman seized the moment. When conservative AFL-affiliated union bosses with the United Garment Workers negotiated an inadequate deal that failed to protect future union organizing at the firm, Hillman led a group of insurgent workers who denounced the new contract as a betrayal of the rank and file. Still learning to speak English, Hillman took to the stage at the crucial strikers' meeting to denounce the supposed agreement. The AFL's aging captains and their outdated leadership, he asserted, had never effectively represented the tens of thousands of new immigrants who made up the mass of workers in the garment trades. The deal, he announced, was a kind of treason.[28]

Hillman's denunciation carried the day. The contract was scratched. The strike resumed. Hillman had humiliated the fading UGW and rejuvenated the strikers. And crucially, he had come to the attention of the leading progressives in the city. He impressed Jane Addams at the Hull House settlement. He got to know Clarence Darrow, who was soon to head to Los Angeles for the McNamara brothers' bombing trial. Partly under the influence of Addams and Darrow, and partly channeling old socialist habits he'd developed with the Mensheviks, Hillman helped negotiate a new kind of settlement agreement, one that marked what Hillman called "a new principle" in the resolution of the divisive battle between labor and capital.[29]

Under the terms of Hillman's proposed agreement, striking employees would be allowed to return to their jobs regardless of their union membership, and regardless of any charges that they had engaged in violence on the picket lines. Just as importantly, the Hart, Schaffner, and Marx agreement established what Hillman called an "arbitration machinery" to resolve existing disputes over wages, rates, and working conditions, and to adjudicate future grievances, too. Here was the heart of Hillman's vision. He would fiercely defend the right of labor to strike. He would stand up for union power. And he would also put in place systems to preserve that power over time. The "Board of Arbitration" set up by the agreement would include an employer arbitrator, a neutral arbitrator, and (crucially) an arbitrator chosen by the union. Labor arbitration gave workers a place at the table. Where once industry had been ruled by the arbitrary fiat of the employer—where once it had been a brutal state of nature—now the arbitration mechanism replaced the rule of the bosses with a rule of law for a durable system of peaceful dispute resolution.[30]

Not everyone saw the agreement as a panacea. At the rowdy meeting to review Hillman's proposed deal, a group affiliated with the IWW protested the arrangement. They charged that it represented a treasonous collaboration with the capital class—a betrayal of the foundational IWW principle that labor and capital had nothing in common. But Hillman seized the floor and beat back the opposition. "You can run over my dead body but I shall not leave this platform," he cried. "You may take my life, but you shall not repudiate this agreement while I live." The strikers ratified the deal.[31]

Hillman was hardly alone in pressing for a new unionism. Jane Addams and the progressives at Hull House had helped Hillman identify arbitration as the crucial mechanism. Louis Brandeis—the lawyer-reformer and future justice on the Supreme Court who counseled the young Roger Baldwin on social reform—had been among the first to make arbitration a model for labor relations when he helped establish the 1910 "Protocols of Peace" for the International Ladies' Garment Workers Union in New York City. Around the same time as Hillman's Chicago triumph, the new model for governing labor and capital spread from New York and Chicago to the needle trades in Baltimore, Boston, and Rochester. Hillman himself moved from Chicago to New York to serve briefly in 1914 as chief clerk to the Protocols of Peace arbitration machinery for the ILGWU and its 50,000 members. By December, Hillman returned to Chicago to become the first president of the new Amalgamated Clothing Workers, which grew to some 90,000 members in only a few years.[32]

What made the new unionism so popular was that it embraced a model of labor-capital relations that imagined worker and employer not as implacably opposed but as bound together with shared mutual interests. Labor, Hillman asserted, could not "survive on a negative attitude toward industry." The IWW path, he believed, was a dead end, and Haywood he called a "pathetic figure." Workers themselves were necessarily "interested in the success of the business enterprise in which they find employment." "The American worker," reasoned Hillman, "knows that he has a good deal to lose if his business is mismanaged." If employers prospered, Hillman went on, workers "may secure a share of that prosperity, and if they don't, it is we that may have to close shop." The reverse was also true. "The business enterprise cannot really do well unless it recognizes the legitimate claims of labor."[33]

Hillman's great life project—at once inspired and contradictory—was to transform American capitalism while adopting a practical attitude toward its existing institutions. He derided radicals who failed to connect their ideas to mechanisms of influence. He admired the Wobblies' ability to rally the downtrodden. He respected the charisma of strike leaders like Flynn and Haywood. But without power, he asked, "What earthly use is their radicalism?" The IWW, he asserted, promised far more than it could deliver. IWW organizers, he charged, left town after a strike was over. They did not do the ongoing hard work of organizing required to maintain worker power. For Hillman, abandoning the IWW's desperate short-term tactics did not also require abandoning transformative goals. When, in 1914 and 1915, Hillman and like-minded unionists split off from the United Garment Workers to establish the dissident Amalgamated Clothing Workers, they aimed to create what Hillman's close associate the labor economist David Saposs called "an industrial union with a radical phi-

Amalgamated Clothing Workers strikers on the picket line in 1915.

losophy." Saposs, who would soon become a fixture in the circles around the American Fund for Public Service, boasted that the ACW combined a sustainable focus on business stability "with industrial unionism and a belief in the overthrow of the capitalist order."[34]

Embedding revolutionary goals in durable institutional foundations was how the working class would gain a voice in the direction of the economy. As Hillman saw it, the prospect of cooperation plus a machinery for the resolution of disputes offered labor the chance to lead the firms at which they worked. After giving employers "all the fight" he could deliver, and after forcing the bosses "to recognize the status of labor," Hillman promised to put his union's know-how to work in helping firms achieve their "productive strength." Power to run the mass-production economy, Hillman contended, was real revolutionary power. At least it was power "that might be called revolutionary," he told a reporter in 1919. "We are making progress toward a complete change in the control of the industry," he continued. "By gradually increasing our power, and our responsibility in the industry, we are preparing to be ready to conduct it when the day for complete industrial democracy arrives." For Hillman, "nothing less than industrial democracy" would suffice—and no such democracy was "possible without a genuine and definite transfer of power."[35]

If the American Fund's circle and Hillman's new unionism had been a Venn diagram, the intersection between their sets, at least in the Fund's most active years in the middle of the 1920s, would have been nearly complete. Clinton Golden and Leo Wolman, who served on the Fund board while organizing and directing research at Hillman's ACW, exemplified the pattern and spread the clothing workers' new gospel. The "brute strength and bare hands" of the Wobblies, Golden asserted, had led only to the "riot sticks of the constabulary." Real industrial democracy, he insisted, required workers capable of assuming the mature responsibilities that came with control.[36]

David Saposs, who like Lippmann and Upton Sinclair studied propaganda and public opinion in the Pittsburgh steel strike after the war, won American Fund grants to write a book excoriating the IWW and championing Hillman's ACW as the unionism of the future. John Brophy, who led the dissident AFL coal miners of United Mine Workers' District 2 in central and western Pennsylvania, relied on American Fund grants to advocate for progressive unionism and teach about the virtues of nationalizing the coal industry. (At least one of Brophy's grants was carefully routed through Baldwin's future wife, Evelyn Preston, lest its New York leftist origins undermine his work.) Hillman's legal advisor at the ACW, Max Lowenthal, was a regular participant in the world of the American Fund and helped oversee the Fund's studies of the courts' role in labor strikes. The editor of the ACW's magazine, Joseph Schlossberg, was on the National Committee of the ACLU and supported key American Fund initiatives.[37]

Such men powerfully dissented from the conventional organizing structures of American capitalism in the 1920s. They supported public ownership of utilities and nationalization of key industries like the railroads. They advocated socialist foundations for the economy.

But their pragmatic new unionism also connected them to a broad swath of the professional middle classes. Hillman's ethic of law-bound labor-management cooperation found a comfortable home in the Wilson administration's wartime efforts to maintain labor peace for the sake of military-industrial production. More generally, the new unionism entailed a perilous relationship between progressive labor, on the one hand, and cutting-edge efforts at managerial efficiency, on the other. Since at least the first decade of the twentieth century, a generation of managerial administrators had proposed to reengineer the mass-production workplace. Frederick Winslow Taylor of Philadelphia's Midvale Steel was the most famous of such managers, instituting stopwatch studies to standardize even the most complex industrial tasks into one best way. The key reform, Taylor told Congress in 1912, was "the deliberate gathering in" by management "of the great mass of traditional knowledge, which in the past has been in the heads of the workmen." New frontiers of efficiency beckoned, but only once the information "acquired through years of experience" by employees—the "physical skill and knack of the workman"—had been pulled up into the minds of managers. Once the managerial revolution had relocated the active intelligence of the industrial firm, firms would be able to replace scarce craftsmen with far less expensive semiskilled machine operators.[38]

Scientific management, as Taylor called his reforms, had been a scourge of American labor since its early articulation in the first decade of the century. With the workman's knowledge now in the manager's head, engineers of Taylor's scientific approach dreamed of rationalizing the deployment of human resources in such a way as to eliminate both the need for and the power of the unions. Bill Haywood, the Wobbly leader, derided such managers, whose brains (if they had any, he wisecracked) were under their workmen's sturdy caps. Gompers denounced Taylorism in 1911 at the AFL's annual convention, and the labor organization would issue periodic condemnations for the next decade. Machinists and other industrial workers walked off the factory floor in protest of stopwatches and cameras. Congress's Commission of Industrial Relations heard from workers that they objected to "being reduced to a scientific formula."[39]

The new unionists adopted a different posture. In scientific management, they saw a tool labor might use to exercise power in the modern economy. Rationalization would smash the arbitrary autocracy of the foreman at the traditional industrial firm. Even more, rational planning might become the foundation of a dramatically more democratic form of economic life—one in which labor's expertise would have a role to play.[40]

Crucially, here was a path to industrial democracy that might satisfy unions' fractious constituencies, too. As the social scientist, Hillman ally, and Fund insider Stuart Chase observed, scientifically managed mass production held out the prospect of increased productivity and increased worker pay to match. The managerial revolution, it seemed, might raise union members' standard of living. The rationalization of the mass-production firm would mean simultaneous opportunities for democratic control and for material gain.[41]

Otto S. Beyer, a member of the scientific management–focused Taylor Society and a regular participant in the new unionist world of the American Fund, captured one version of the new unionist vision in a widely copied plan for the Baltimore & Ohio Railroad. Beyer, who would come to be known as "the father of labor-management cooperation" and who was a bête noire of the Fund's left wing, laid out a program that provided union recognition and increased wages in return for workers' participation in making the company more productive. Efficiency and union strength went together, according to Beyer, because only a labor voice in management would entice workers to participate. The security of being represented would assure workers that sharing labor-saving knowledge would not cost them their jobs.[42]

Organizers at Hillman's ACW similarly proposed that scientific management could bring "increased wages" and "shorter hours" while giving workers a "voice and vote in the shop." The American Fund's Clinton Golden endorsed the same idea and suggested that identifying waste in capitalism's allocation of industrial resources would help gather support for proposals to nationalize industry.[43]

Hillman's new unionism presented what historian David Montgomery would later call the "paradoxical marriage of progressive unionism and scientific management." Skeptics have long charged that the managerial revolution of a Taylor or a Beyer was a poisoned chalice for labor—that it displaced workers from control over the conditions of their work. Only control at the level of the shop floor, the skeptics contended, could mean real industrial democracy. But such critics rarely had an account of how such older forms of worker control could survive in the era of mass production—nor of how older approaches to worker control could offer the material prosperity that mass production afforded. Higher living standards turned on productivity gains, and productivity gains meant a constant disruption of the shop floor and its labor arrangements.[44]

The great achievement of progressive unionists around Hillman and the American Fund was to grasp the nature and scale of the problem and to begin to build solutions. In the mass economy, they saw that prosperity and control could be accomplished together, but only if control were relocated to a collective democratic process. Joint labor-capital control of a rationally managed economy might bring new efficiency, higher living standards, and industrial democracy, all together in one interwoven and mutually supportive package.

Excitement around this synthetic idea—the magical concept of industrial democracy—brought the new unionists of the 1920s to the Civic Club. It led them to gather around the American Fund's table, where conversations commenced (cautiously at first) between union stalwarts from Hillman's world and human resources engineers like Beyer. And it sparked the enthusiasm of Fund members, including Baldwin. Fund directors Norman Thomas and Robert Morss Lovett, for example, ran the League for Industrial Democracy, which had been established in 1905 as the Intercollegiate Socialist Society by American Fund founder Upton Sinclair. (It was the League whose tax case paralleled that of the Fund.) By the 1920s the

League served as a node in the extended new unionist world. Its affiliated journal, *Labor Age*, became the house organ of the industrial democracy project. Both became substantial beneficiaries of Fund grants.[45]

Industrial democracy flourished at the Fund in no small part because the Fund's resources offered a safe harbor during lean years for the labor movement. A mix of rising wages in certain sectors and anti-union employer offensives across the economy meant that there was precious little labor organizing to do in the 1920s. From a high of 5 million members in 1920, union membership in the United States fell to three and a half million by 1924, eventually dropping to less than 3 million at the end of 1933. During the 1920s the number of American union members fell every year save one even though the size of the paid civilian labor force increased by a quarter across the same period. Hillman's Amalgamated Clothing Workers did better than most. But even the ACW could not avoid the carnage. From 177,000 members in 1920, the ACW dropped to 134,000 in 1923 and then to 100,000 by 1930. In all, one-third fewer clothing industry workers belonged to unions at the end of the decade than had at its beginning.[46]

In a bleak decade for labor, Hillman's circle needed a way to nurture the spirit of the new unionism even in the absence of organizing opportunities. One path stood out. Hillman's closest advisors embraced what they called workers' education as training to "help the student bring about a better social order." For his part, Hillman had always believed that a dynamic model of continual education was indispensable to the work of organizing an industrial union. "The Activity," he called it. What Hillman meant was that only a continual process of learning would be able to maintain the energy and collective solidarity of the new kind of union he was building. In the managed mass-production economy, the skilled worker's intimate control over the production process was no longer available as a way of sustaining class solidarity. In the age of the machine operative, the workers (like Lippmann's citizens) would have to do industrial democracy at one remove. The difficulty was that the bureaucracy that industrial democracy required was not costless. It risked sapping the collective energies that maintained workers' power. For Hillman, an iterative process of learning—in his socialist youth he would have called it dialectical—offered a basis for achieving democratic control of industry while maintaining class solidarity. Learning would be a way of making concrete the structures on which workers' prosperity and voice depended.[47]

Brookwood

Brookwood Labor College, a now mostly forgotten institution in Katonah, New York, was the largest single beneficiary of the Fund's largesse. And it was at Brookwood, during the lowest ebb of labor's 1920s, that a generation of organizers and labor intellectuals gathered to hash out the spirit of the new unionism.[48]

Founded in 1921, while Roger Baldwin and Charles Garland were working out the arrangements for the American Fund, Brookwood arose out of the energies and vision of a thirty-six-year-old pacifist textile organizer and former Dutch Reformed minister named Abraham Johannes Muste. In later decades, after Brookwood fell victim to its own success, when the labor movement was near the height of its mid twentieth-century power, A. J. Muste would become one of America's most influential pacifists. In the 1940s, he would help found the Congress of Racial Equality, an early nonviolent civil rights organization, where he mentored key civil rights figures like James Farmer and Bayard Rustin. Martin Luther King Jr. would credit Muste as an inspiration for his own practice of nonviolent resistance. And by the time of his death in 1967, Muste would be a leading participant in protests against the Vietnam War. Historians remember him as the "American Gandhi."[49]

In the years immediately following the First World War, Muste was at the leading edge of the new unionism. In 1919, Muste left the church behind and threw himself into supporting the nationwide postwar strike wave. In Lawrence, Massachusetts, where seven years earlier Flynn and the Wobblies had fought for textile strikers, more than 17,000 workers had walked out in protest when the American Woolen Company cut workers' weekly hours from fifty-four to forty-eight without adjusting hourly wages upward. Traveling to Lawrence shortly after the strike began, Muste found the so-called 54–48 strikers—now nearly 30,000 of them—struggling with virtually no leadership to create a unified strike force. Workers came from nearly two dozen nationalities. The IWW had virtually disappeared after its 1912 victory; organizers like Flynn had simply decamped, leaving no enduring organizational infrastructure. After only a week off the job, Lawrence strikers appointed Muste, with essentially no labor experience, to head their strike committee.[50]

Muste understood the violent legacy of the IWW at Lawrence. ("A considerable amount of violence" had taken place, he recalled.) The peace had been breached again during the 1919 strike when Galleanisti anarchists dynamited American Woolen. They bungled the job and killed four of their own, but the police took no chances, mounting a machine-gun nest at a major intersection near the picket lines. Deputies swarmed the streets and beat strikers. Muste himself was beaten, arrested, and charged with disorderly conduct. The Lawrence strike seemed likely to go the way of so many strikes across the country in that grim year.[51]

At Lawrence, however, Muste introduced a new element. During the war he had left his church and become a pacifist. Now his anti-war pacifism "found expression," he said, in "the general industrial and labor situation." Muste took to strike meetings and urged the strikers to resist the dangerous appeal of anarchist elements goading them to attack the police. Such strategies, he predicted, would collapse just as IWW had failed. From a strictly practical perspective, he observed sensibly, there was no way to "destroy all the machine guns in the United States," or even all the machine guns in Lawrence and its neighboring towns. Violence played into the hands of the bosses—and would discredit the strike in the process.[52]

Muste's pacifism was no utopian delusion. Conflict, Muste believed, was essential to human life; it was inevitable and constant. But conflict did not necessarily mean violence, and violence was a distraction. For one thing, it reproduced itself, tipping disputes onto what Muste called "a kind of an inclined plane" toward more of the same. Most of all, the "resort to violence," Muste said, "always tends to be, in its way, evasion." Violence created "a relationship of thing to thing rather than human being to human being." It suppressed rather than resolved the underlying problems that had produced it.[53]

What Muste understood was that the alternative to violence was not surrender. The alternative was to design a strategy for success in a world in which employers were far better positioned than unions to deploy decisive force. At a crucial strike meeting, one striker articulated the point memorably. The bosses "can't weave wool with machine guns," he said; "we'll keep our arms folded and there will be no wool." The image of folded arms had come from the Wobblies in 1912. Now Muste made the phrase a slogan of nonviolent direct action. "What we must do," he explained, "is smile as we pass the machine guns and the police."[54]

A. J. Muste, at left, developed a strategy of industrial democracy and nonviolent resistance in the face of police repression at a 1919 textile strike in Lawrence, Massachusetts, right.

After sixteen hard-fought weeks of folded arms and nonviolent smiles, American Woolen capitulated. The fifty-four-hour week became a forty-eight-hour week while weekly pay remained constant. The result was stunning. Virtually everywhere across the country, in industries from steel to textiles, in cities from Boston to Seattle, unions had lost their strikes in 1919. Muste and the workers of Lawrence had succeeded.[55]

In the strike's aftermath, Muste formed the Lawrence workers into a union of its own, the Amalgamated Textile Workers, built in the image of Hillman's ACW. The parallels were more than nominal. Hillman and the Amalgamated Clothing Workers had provided strategic advice and financial support to Muste and the Lawrence strikers through the course of 1919. The ATW committed itself to a radicalism that the old AFL rejected. As Muste said, the Lawrence textile workers "held a good deal of the revolutionary philosophy and orientation" that had mobilized the IWW. The new union's constitution promised a "future in which the workers would control their destiny and the present class control would be ended." But the ATW brought ambitions for workers' control together with mechanisms for meeting their ongoing material wants in ways that the swaggering Wobblies had not. Muste's textile union adopted the industrial union structure Hillman favored, with its systems for the arbitration of labor grievances and cooperation with management in the control of the firm.[56]

A year after the Lawrence strike, Muste folded the ATW into Hillman's larger union. And a year after that, in 1921, he founded Brookwood Labor College.[57]

Wealthy friends connected to Muste through the interfaith pacifist organization Fellowship of Reconciliation provided the campus: a fifty-three-acre estate amid the horse farms and country mansions of Katonah, about fifty miles north of New York City. Labor unions and others dissatisfied with the prevailing orthodoxy of the American labor movement provided the energy. Roger Baldwin was among the founding supporters, along with leaders at the Women's Trade Union League, the Illinois and Pennsylvania branches of the AFL, the International Association of Machinists, and the International Timber Workers Union, all of them from dissident factions of the AFL.[58]

The new labor college's aim was partly practical. Its founders intended to help train labor leaders who would be able to deliver better wages and working conditions to their members. An early American Fund memo explained that Brookwood would provide "full and honest information" to workers "about matters of vital concern"—practical knowledge about everything from labor conditions, unemployment, and the union movement, to judicial injunctions against strikers and the work of legislatures.[59]

More ambitiously, the college aimed to create a generation of organizers who would capitalize on the steps toward industrial democracy Muste had taken at Lawrence in 1919 and that Hillman had begun to envision at the ACW. Brookwood offered its students no degrees; no accrediting body approved its curriculum. Instead, it offered training and networking to students eager to bring new ideas to the work of organizing and running unions.

At the American Fund, Baldwin and his colleagues believed that knowledge did more than provide information. Education shaped the consciousness and identity of its holders. Such were the lessons of Lippmann's studies of the newspapers and Upton Sinclair's broadsides against the commercial press. The news blackout in the Pittsburgh steel strike in 1919 had shown much the same thing. In Europe, social theorists such as the jailed Italian communist Antonio Gramsci and the English civil libertarian Norman Angell were developing some of the same ideas. Education and the press not only imparted facts to people, they created people's perceptions of the world. The American Fund's directors likewise hoped that a new approach to labor education would, in Scott Nearing's words, "instill into workers the knowledge and qualities" that would equip them to lead a struggle for "emancipation" and a "new world order." The right kind of education offered a new path toward fundamental social transformation, one that avoided the pitfalls of violent revolutionary confrontation. Baldwin described himself as having a "passion for the education of the masses in revolutionary ideas." The results, he believed, would be transformative. Once workers "understood their powers and mission," he wrote, they might even "unite to destroy the State, monopoly, and private property." At the very least, properly educated workers, as one 1923 Fund memo put it, would be "more effective" in exercising the power of labor in a mass democracy. Rather than educate workers to lift themselves "out of their class," the Fund proposed to educate workers to emancipate themselves and democratize the institutions of economic life.[60]

Brookwood aimed to teach future labor leaders, as Muste put it, "how to think, not what to think." The school's founding documents described a world in need of "a new social order" and claimed that change was "already on the way." Labor education, Muste and his colleagues contended, would hasten history's march into the future. Learning would both speed the revolution along ("hasten its coming") and "reduce to a minimum" the violence and destruction such social transformation would entail. Education might even "do away entirely with a resort to violent methods." The college, its leaders made clear, did not teach "the proposition that a violent revolution is . . . imminent in America," nor that the organizers of the working class should devote their "energies to preparing for such a revolution." Change was possible without the use of force so long as there was "increasing emphasis on workers' education" in combination with increased union strength. "Power without intelligent direction," Muste said, was "as helpless as theoretical knowledge without organized power."[61]

Brookwood's students were typically union members whose locals had identified them as future organizers and leaders. Affiliated unions usually paid the tuition for their members, if tuition was paid at all. Beginning in the 1923–24 academic year, the American Fund supplied about half the annual Brookwood budget, largely through grants and scholarships. In 1925 and 1926, James Weldon Johnson arranged American Fund support to establish NAACP-Brookwood scholarships, too, in hopes of organizing the increasingly large numbers of nonunionized Black workers in American industry. Many of the school's students, especially at first, came from the garment trades in New York City. Others came from the coal mines of the Midwest, or the construction trades and the railroads. There were needle trades workers—pocket sewers and pants basters and button-hole seamstresses, many of them recruited by Clinton Golden, who became Brookwood's field director soon after being appointed to the American Fund board. With a salary underwritten by the Fund, he took to the lecture circuit on behalf of the college, identifying new students at union halls around the country. Back in Katonah, socialists lunched with communists who dined with old-line trade unionists. Under Muste's moderating influence, faculty and students set ideological differences aside, at least for a time. One former Wobbly from the hardscrabble world of western

Fund insider David Saposs teaches labor economics to union organizers on the porch at Brookwood.

mines found the place "altogether enchanting"; in spirit, he remembered, "Brookwood was a labor movement in microcosm—without bureaucrats or racketeers—with emphasis on youth, aspiration, ideals."[62]

Nineteen students convened in the college's first year in 1921, and between thirty and fifty each year thereafter for more than a decade. One-third of the students were women. (Fannia Cohn, a prominent leader at the ILGWU, served on Brookwood's Advisory Committee.) A smaller number of Brookwood students were Black, including Floria Pinkney at the garment workers union, among others. The college announced that it "tolerates no discrimination as between white and colored." Foreign students attended, too, including a number from Europe and Latin America, and at least one from as far away as Japan. Students' schooling levels varied widely. Half had no more than a grade school education. Their backgrounds ranged widely, too. As Muste recalled, "some were orthodox and devout church members" from rural areas. Others arrived reading Marx, attending Eugene O'Neill plays on Broadway, and going to "avant garde dances in Greenwich Village on weekends."[63]

Brookwood offered a liberal arts curriculum with a new unionist twist. Muste taught a course on the history of civilization. Hillman's aide David Saposs—a former student of the Wisconsin economist John Commons—taught a course on labor history. There were courses on government, public speaking, writing, comparative labor movements, labor journalism, and more. Sociology instructor Arthur Calhoun taught popular courses on Marxism. On the right wing of the college, Otto Beyer of the Baltimore & Ohio Railroad Plan taught a course with Stuart Chase titled "Labor's Responsibilities in Production." Hillman's aide Leo Wolman served as an advisor. ACW magazine editor Joseph Schlossberg and Hillman ally John Brophy served as two of the school's founding directors.[64]

Alongside classes on Marx and the B&O Plan, Brookwood hosted programs in music (which Muste loved) and theater. Calhoun helped direct a course in Labor Dramatics, from which came the Brookwood Players: a traveling theater troupe that put on skits and short plays in union halls and at labor conventions across the Northeast and into the Midwest.[65]

The curriculum and indeed the entire school embraced a big idea about the future of labor. Brookwood "thinks of the labor movement," stated the school's first course announcement, "as a practical instrument by which workers achieve higher wages, shorter hours, and better conditions of work." But labor was not only an instrument for short-term improvements in workers' welfare. Labor, Brookwood's faculty and directors asserted, was "a great social force." Properly understood, the Brookwood view was that the labor movement had "as its ultimate goal" the achievement of a "good life for all men in a social order," one that was "free from exploitation and based upon control by the workers."[66]

Brookwood promised an education that would be up to the task of democracy under modern conditions. As a machinists union spokesman put it, Brookwood was "a means of combating the insidious propaganda being distributed to the public by capitalistic influences through the press and the public schools." Labor education would, one of Brookwood's chroniclers said, serve as a counterweight to the "powerful agencies of education and propaganda" that aimed to keep "the masses of unorganized workers . . . ignorant or hostile to labor." Here was an approach to education that aimed to be free of the pervasive distortions identified by critics like Lippmann at the end of the war. Muste endorsed training organizers and negotiators "not with prejudices" and "superstitions," and not merely with "opinions or hot air," but instead with a "willingness to seek out the facts and to base judgment and action on the facts."[67]

The spirit of Brookwood pressed beyond the technical fixes that Lippmann had identified. Where Lippmann had imagined a class of experts who might stand above the warring stereotypes of secondhand propaganda campaigns, Muste and Brookwood, like Hillman and the ACW, proposed to equip the masses of working-class Americans with an institutional structure that would empower them to participate in deciding the great issues of the day. When Hillman championed a dynamic process of education and learning as the heart of union solidarity ("The Activity"), he was operationalizing an educational program associated most closely with Muste's friend and former teacher John Dewey, the influential philosopher and educator at Columbia University.[68]

Dewey, who helped shape the American Fund education program, asserted that societies were democratic when they allowed all people to achieve what he called "self-realization" on a free and equal basis. A society dedicated to the "good of all its members on equal terms" needed to have a form of education that gave individuals "a personal interest" and an understanding of the social relationships in which they found themselves, along with at least the modicum of control that such an understanding would bring. For Dewey, democratic education meant inculcating a flexibility of the mind—it required "continuous readjustment" to train students to meet "new situations" in novel and responsive ways. Education for democracy, Dewey explained, entailed "the continuous reconstruction of experience," by which he meant study of (and reflection on) the world for the "purpose of widening and deepening" understanding. Democratic education was how lives of flourishing and self-realization might be achieved.[69]

Education in the right spirit nurtured "habits of mind" that loosened the rigid bonds of entrenched prejudices and arbitrary traditions. Schools, Dewey observed, had "always been a function of the prevailing type of organization of social life." But the goal of education was not "to adjust individuals to social institutions" by fitting them "into present arrangements and conditions." Existing arrangements in the world were not stable enough for such an approach. To the contrary, imposing change as if from outside the communities affected invited violent disruption. Education done right, by contrast, might "secure social changes," and do so "without introducing disorder." For Dewey, as for Muste, the effort was to find pathways to social transformation that avoided violent cataclysm, both because it was good to reduce the human harm that violence caused, and because violence, as Muste put it, evaded vital underlying questions about how human beings were to live together.[70]

Dewey had been a strong supporter of labor since watching Eugene Debs's American Railway Union in the Pullman strike in Chicago in 1894. He thrilled at the solidarity of the strikers, unified around "a common interest." The famous Laboratory School at the University of Chicago, which he founded two years later, was (in the words of his biographer) "an experiment in education for industrial democracy." It was crucial, in Dewey's conception, that democracy extend to people's work. "What does democracy mean," he asked, "save that the individual is to have a share in determining the conditions and the aims of his own work?" For the worker, Dewey's colleague Horace Kallen elaborated, education "integrates all his relationships." The more such integration might "become a function of the day-to-day habit of work," Kallen continued, the more "industrial democracy" would come into being.[71]

Brookwood modeled itself specifically on the Deweyan ideas of dynamic understanding and participation. "In the Laboratory School," Dewey had said, "the child comes to school to do." Norman Thomas echoed the idea for the Fund board. One might as well "talk of learning to swim out of water," he remarked, as try to learn by traditional methods of instruction and rote memorization. Learning by doing, as Thomas saw it, would inoculate students against the herd behavior endemic to modern democracies. It would, he hoped, equip students (in terms inspired by Dewey) to "form new and more adequate social groupings" in which they might escape the "unreflective crowd action" of the mass public.[72]

Dewey himself admired and actively supported Brookwood through financial contributions and fundraising appeals. Muste's labor college, he wrote in the *New Republic*, was "truly educational" in the best democratic sense: it led its students "to think" and "to think for themselves." Powerful special interests—what Dewey called "the big power trusts"—had come to "control education both in public and private schools"; they had "prepared and colored and censored textbooks" and shaped the sensibility of schools that aimed to accommodate their students to the world as it was. Brookwood, by contrast, stood for the "broad, free and generous way" of education that Dewey had helped to craft. "No activity," he continued, "can be more important than that of a labor college giving to workers themselves the vision of a new world."[73]

In 1926, Flynn explained that the Fund's policy was to avoid "any partisan group" (by which she meant official Communist Party and Socialist Party organizations) and also to skirt groups that had "gained trade union support" (by which she meant the AFL). Such policies were often honored in the breach, but they expressed a goal, even if one imperfectly achieved.[74]

Brookwood, where Muste welcomed students and teachers with "right tendencies" as well as "left" ones, almost perfectly embodied the Fund's aspiration to chart a heterodox middle path. A full 20 percent of the Fund's expenditures across the two decades of its existence went to labor education, with the overwhelming lion's share going to educational programs on the Brookwood and Muste model. Baldwin and the Fund's board appointed ACW ally Stuart Chase to supervise the Fund's labor education grants. Under Chase's watchful eye, programs with ACW sympathies flourished. Brookwood alone received more than half the American Fund's spending on workers' education, some $213,000 in all. In Chase's view, "the workers' education enterprises" worth funding were made up of "groups of militant trade union members" dissatisfied with the "inertia and apathy" of the mainstream labor movement and eager to pursue "a larger and broader program of militant activity." Baldwin agreed; the Fund, he wrote in 1923, should favor institutions that would "instill into the workers the knowledge and qualities" that would support "the struggle for the emancipation of their class."[75]

In this, the Fund helped propel a surge in labor education. Before 1918, only three institutions in the United States identified themselves as dedicated to workers' education. By 1924, Chase found no fewer than eighty labor education organizations around the country, enrolling some 20,000 workers. Every time a strike failed, a new labor school seemed to pop up: the Baltimore Labor College, the Boston Trade Union College, the Colorado Committee for the Promotion of Workers Education, the Denver Labor College, the Southern School for Women Workers, and the Work People's College in Duluth among them. The Fund supported all of these, along with labor colleges in Newark, Philadelphia, Pittsburgh, Portland, Rochester, and Seattle, as well as labor libraries in Philadelphia and Manhattan, and labor education efforts by urban labor federations in New York, Passaic, and Salem, not to mention similar efforts by state labor federations in Colorado and Wyoming. In Arkansas, the Fund supported Commonwealth College, a faction-plagued left-leaning school with roots in the Llano agricultural commune favored by Charles Garland. (Citing Dewey, Baldwin hoped that Commonwealth and its associated colony might yield lessons on how cooperative environments could alter the "bundles of habits" that make up the human psyche.)[76]

The American Fund increased its commitment to labor education in 1924 and 1925, when it made donations for the socialist Rand School in New York, the Communist-run Workers School of New York City, and the educational programs of progressive districts in the United Mine Workers. William Z. Foster's Trade Union Education League received funding, though that was curtailed when Foster refused to allow Stuart Chase to audit the TUEL's books on the Fund's behalf. Most significantly, in 1928 the American Fund entered into an exceptional commitment to provide $100,000 to Brookwood over the next ten years—a commitment that the

Fund managed to keep despite the catastrophic effects of the stock market crash of 1929 on its resources. New interest in workers' education, Norman Thomas said in 1925, was "one of the most heartening things" in an otherwise bleak decade in the American labor movement.[77]

One project the Fund declined to support, however, was the workers' education offshoot of Samuel Gompers's American Federation of Labor. The so-called Workers' Education Bureau, founded in 1921 as the educational wing of the AFL, was committed to promoting "responsible" labor organizations. It applied to the Fund in 1922 for $10,000. The Fund directors tabled the application at first, and then rejected the WEB proposal outright. The Fund, Baldwin explained, aimed to support radical education efforts, not "those which take the point of view of the old-line labor movement."[78]

Gompers was furious. In a story carried on the front page of the *New York Times*, he charged that the Fund was a revolutionary organization in disguise as a respectable foundation—a "pro-Soviet, pro-Communist" group of "red propagandists," as he told the *Times* reporter. Gompers's broadside against the Fund singled out Sidney Hillman. As Gompers well understood, his feud with the Fund was a skirmish in the larger battle between Hillman's new unionism and the old AFL.[79]

For her part, Elizabeth Gurley Flynn (who was no ally of Gompers) was ambivalent about the industrial democracy of the Brookwood cadre and Hillman's Amalgamated Clothing Workers. She sometimes cast dissenting votes against ACW projects. The new unionists celebrated the efficiency of modern manufacturing and cheered the prosperity that mass production might bring; men like Muste and Hillman championed labor-capital cooperation. Flynn's Wobbly comrades, by contrast, had denounced modern management techniques as a new tyranny. For Haywood and the IWW, sabotage had been one last desperate effort to derail the Taylorist remaking of the world of work. And Haywood had been right, in his way. Achieving a voice for labor through the efficient management of the industrial firm, no matter how successful, could, in some respects, be a kind of soulless enterprise, far removed from the ecstatic thrill of the IWW's rapturous dreams of worker revolution.[80]

But if the big-tent world of the Sacco and Vanzetti campaign and the Fund lacked the self-immolating purity of the Wobblies, it offered its own subtle inspiration. At the end of the decade, a young man named Myles Horton came through Brookwood Labor College. Horton was an intense and tireless student from the mountains of eastern Tennessee who had come to New York to study with the theologian Reinhold Niebuhr at Union Theological Seminary. Horton was determined to set up a school back in Appalachia to educate organizers for the hardscrabble communities in which he had grown up. In an appeal for what he called the Southern Mountains School, Niebuhr described Horton's goal as an educational center "to train radical labor leaders who will understand the need of both political and union strategy." Education, Niebuhr continued, would be "one of the instruments for bringing about a new social order."[81]

Horton's school, soon renamed the Highlander Folk School, came out of the world of Brookwood and the Garland Fund. Niebuhr was an occasional advisor on grant applications at the Fund. Norman Thomas would serve on Highlander's inaugural board of directors. Roger Baldwin and John Dewey offered their support. Like Brookwood, the school would strike its own course, between the hidebound AFL and self-destructive

Highlander Folk School in Tennessee; the school's founder, Myles Horton, is seated on the grass at center.

critics on the left. (As Niebuhr put it, the school would do what "neither A. F. of L. nor Communist leadership" could accomplish.) Highlander's instructor on labor unions had trained at Brookwood. By 1936, Highlander was applying alongside Brookwood for a joint grant from the Garland Fund. By then the Fund's resources had nearly been depleted; no money was forthcoming. But Highlander had become a southern Brookwood. After Brookwood closed in 1937, the Tennessee school would become the training ground for the Congress of Industrial Organizations' southern organizing campaigns. It was at Highlander in 1955 that Montgomery, Alabama, resident and activist Rosa Parks attended a workshop on the significance of the Supreme Court's decision in *Brown v. Board of Education*. A few months later, she refused to give up her seat on a segregated Montgomery bus. Working in the tradition of Brookwood's racially integrated labor education program from the 1920s, Highlander hosted civil rights figures like Martin Luther King Jr., John Lewis, and Diane Nash.[82]

At Highlander, civil rights efforts were a natural outgrowth of labor organizing. Horton believed that one could not emancipate the American working class without undoing the oppression of Black people, and vice versa. The new unionists at the American Fund had glimpsed the same idea at Brookwood. And in 1925 and 1926, the race question surged to the fore of the Fund's deliberations in a way that reshaped the future of American democracy.

14

The Messenger

The masses of Negroes in the United States have all along been workers.
—JAMES WELDON JOHNSON, DECEMBER 1924

A. Philip Randolph in Harlem, 1911.

In the summer of 1925, as Ossian Sweet was getting ready to move into his new house in Detroit, and while the Garland Fund was deciding whether to continue to fund Black organizations or to focus exclusively on the labor movement, a man named A. Philip Randolph approached the Fund to propose that its two projects—race and class—might go together.[1]

A meticulously dressed soapbox socialist from the street corners of Harlem, the thirty-six-year-old Randolph was known best, where he was known at all, as editor of a struggling radical magazine called *The Messenger*. At a precarious moment for the magazine, with its fragile finances near collapse, Randolph brought a novel experiment to the Fund. He proposed a Black labor union. And not just any Black labor union. Randolph envisioned a union that would organize the 12,000 railroad sleeping-car porters employed by the mighty Pullman Company, maker and operator of the luxury passenger cars that graced the nation's most profitable rail corridors.[2]

In the fall of 1925, Randolph and the Brotherhood of Sleeping Car Porters persuaded the Fund's directors that helping workers required supporting the Black workers whom most white labor unions excluded. The Fund's grant helped revive Randolph's foundering career and connected him to the most forward-thinking segments of the workers' organizations around Brookwood Labor College and Sidney Hillman's Amalgamated Clothing Workers. In turn, Randolph drew the American Fund into a decade-long battle at Pullman that propelled him into leadership roles in labor and civil rights for a half century to come. Randolph persuaded the directors of the American Fund that its two missions were one. Defending Black people's interests helped the workers' movement. Fighting labor exploitation required confronting Jim Crow.[3]

The Most Dangerous Negro in America

Asa Philip Randolph's father, James, was born a year before the end of the Civil War in a northern Florida town named for Thomas Jefferson's Virginia plantation, Monticello. The wealthy Virginian Edmund Randolph, a delegate to the 1787 Constitutional Convention and Jefferson's second cousin, had owned James's forebears as slaves. During Reconstruction, James attended a school run by white Methodist missionaries, where he showed an early aptitude. At age twenty, he was ordained a pastor by the African

Methodist Episcopal Church and took the pulpit in a tiny community of churchgoers in the town of Baldwin (no relation to Roger), west of Jacksonville. There James Randolph met Elizabeth Robinson, a thirteen-year-old parishioner. They married a year later and moved to a new congregation eighty miles south in Crescent City. In 1887, Elizabeth bore a son, James Jr. A second son, Asa, followed in 1889.[4]

When Asa Randolph was two years old, his family moved to Jacksonville proper, where his father found a marginally better post serving several area congregations. If the Jacksonville where James Weldon Johnson grew up in the 1870s had been home to a thriving Black community, the city in the 1890s was a much less welcoming place. Randolph's family lived not in the once-thriving LaVilla community of Black middle-class residents like the Johnson family, but in a gritty industrial area near the harbor. Where Johnson's childhood was populated by white and Black people, Randolph's neighborhood, as he later recalled, was "completely segregated." At the end of his street lay the city's railroad yards, where Black men performed dangerous low-status labor handling freight cars and shoveling coal. It was, Randolph said, "the toughest part of town."[5]

The Randolph family had "no money of any consequence," as Randolph put it, but they always managed to get by. James's ministry, which expanded to include three Jacksonville-area congregations, yielded small, in-kind gifts of food—bags of sweet potatoes or perhaps part of a hog—and occasional meager cash offerings. Mostly the family lived off modest returns from the pastor's second job as a tailor, repairing clothes and cleaning and dyeing suits. As soon as they were old enough, Asa and his older brother James took jobs delivering newspapers. At the age of twelve, Asa began working at a nearby pharmacy wholesaler, delivering medication to pharmacies. A job at a local fertilizer factory came next, where he earned seventy-five cents a day. His brother took work at a fish market, and Asa tried a grueling job in railroad maintenance. One way or another, labor for wages was a constant. And always with the same pattern, as Randolph later recalled: "all Negro help, but white bosses."[6]

The Randolphs of Jacksonville made up for penury with a painstaking formality, what Randolph later described as a kind of proletarian respectability. "Our household," Randolph recounted, "was respected for its moral standards." No liquor crossed the threshold. His mother forbade card games. Instead, the Randolph family home was a world of service and of learning, "a home of ideas," Randolph remembered, "in the sense of placing the emphasis upon ideas as against things." James Sr., who had not been able to pursue formal education after his elementary school years with the missionaries, sent his boys to the Cookman Institute across town, which offered a mix of Black teachers and white Methodist instructors from the North. James Sr. impressed upon his boys "that we could be whatever we wanted to be," as Randolph later remembered. "We were," their father told them, "as good as any boys living."[7]

The Randolph family's ethic of respectability reflected a deep race pride—"a deep racial devotion," as James Sr. put it, a sense that "we were a part of a race" and that membership in the race meant service to it. Randolph later remembered his father telling stories of racial progress and uplift, "always pointing out," in the words of the Ethiopian Prophecy in Psalm 68, "that Ethiopia would someday stretch forth its hands unto God." In the Randolph household, the great biblical figures—Moses, Jesus, Peter, Paul, and even God—were not white, as they were so often pictured in publishers' books, but instead "colored or swarthy." James Sr. spent "hours, frequently, night and day, talking" to his boys of the Black heroes who populated the race's history. He sought out books on the bishops of the African Methodist Episcopal Church, on the lives of leaders like Frederick Douglass and Toussaint L'Ouverture, and about slave rebels like Nat Turner and Denmark Vesey. While Elizabeth listened approvingly with her knitting or sewing, James Sr. "told us about Africa, especially Egypt and Ethiopia, their ancient history and glory," about Hannibal and the Carthaginian armies of North Africa who had dealt defeat after defeat to the Romans in antiquity. Randolph's father, the future labor leader later recalled, "was highly race conscious," and he wanted his children to be that way, too.[8]

Avoiding race consciousness in the Jim Crow South would have been hard. Decades later, Randolph remembered watching white customers casually humiliate his father, who could do little to defend himself or his boys from their barbs. But Randolph knew in his bones that his father was the moral better and intellectual superior of the men who sneered at him.[9]

One day, when Asa was only three, Jacksonville authorities arrested a Black man named Reed and charged him with the murder of a local white man. Rumors spread through the Black community of a plan by local whites to break into the county jail, seize Reed, and lynch him. Neighbors gathered at dusk outside the Randolph family's modest picket fence and resolved to do what they could to defend the man. As night fell, James Sr. took one of the guns the family kept hidden in the house and went off into the darkness. Elizabeth—whom Randolph recalled proudly as "a deadly marksman"—sat on the porch all night with a shotgun across her lap, guarding the boys. The white mob soon arrived at the jail. But James Sr. and the Black men of Jacksonville had gotten there first, forcing a standoff until the state police arrived to disperse the contending sides. Decades later, Randolph would recall the family lore about the episode as powerful inspiration. The story was "more revolutionary," as he later put it, "than sitting down and reading Karl Marx."[10]

Four years after delivering the valedictory address for his graduating class of the Cookman Institute (topic: "What I would like to see young Negroes do"), Asa Randolph left Jacksonville for New York. The words of a kindly coworker at the Jacksonville fertilizer factory rang in his ears. "I wouldn't plan to spend too much time here," the older man had said. There was no place in Jim Crow Jacksonville for him to go.[11]

Randolph's trip north was different from the Johnson brothers' journey to Broadway a decade earlier. James Weldon Johnson never forgot the insult of the Jim Crow rules that kept him out of the first-class car. Asa Randolph, by contrast, could not even dream of buying a ticket for the expensive first-class coach. Class barred him from the costly seats just as decisively as race did. Instead, Asa worked for his trip north, laboring belowdecks in the pantry of a steamship, where he washed dishes until his hands cramped. For five days he stayed in the bowels of the vessel, sleeping with the "real ship people," as he remembered them. From his bunk he watched as the lowliest workers of the ship's crew shot craps, played poker, fought, and slept. These men, mostly but not all Black, performed the hardest work on the boat. They shoveled coal into the furnace, prepared the food, cleaned the dining room, and swabbed the decks. It was, Randolph later remembered, "a hard experience" for even the toughest of the men, and "it was like Hades to me."[12]

Organizing workers like those with whom he had journeyed north would soon become Randolph's animating cause—and his life's work for the next sixty years, a project that connected his father's injunctions to serve the race with the new felt imperatives of industrial-age New York.

Living in a spare room for which he paid $1.50 a week, Randolph found work as an elevator operator in an all-white apartment building at 148th Street. From nearly the moment of his arrival, he turned the service ethic of his father's ministry toward uplift and self-organization efforts among his fellow workers. He worked as a porter at the Consolidated Gas Company on Amsterdam Avenue, where he urged other Black employees to agitate for better jobs, not only sweeping and washing but also supervising and bookkeeping. He was briefly a waiter on the *Paul Revere*, a steamer carrying well-heeled passengers between New York and Boston, until the steward caught him organizing the kitchen help. An acquaintance later recalled that Randolph would do nearly "anything to make a living, down to scrubbing floors," but he rarely lasted long in any one job. Sometimes he would quit as soon as he had earned enough money to live for a few weeks. Just as often, he would be fired, as he told his biographer years later, for "sowing seeds of discontent" among his co-workers about their working conditions and pay.[13]

In 1912, Randolph began taking evening classes at the City College of New York on 138th Street, one of "the hottest beds of radicalism in New York City," he later recalled. In this new setting, Randolph encountered stories about economic exploitation in history, stories that crowded up alongside the racial and religious narratives of his youth. In a straw poll that fall, nearly as many of Randolph's fellow students voted for Eugene Debs, the Socialist candidate, as voted for Woodrow Wilson. Debs's socialism appealed to Randolph. He soon joined the campus chapter of Upton Sinclair's Intercollegiate Socialist Society and participated in campus protests on behalf of striking textile workers in Lawrence and Paterson. At lectures and rallies, he encountered new heroes, not the Black historical figures of his father's stories but people like Debs as well as Big Bill Haywood and Elizabeth Gurley Flynn. He began to go by a more formal, grown-up moniker: A. Philip Randolph. And he began reading Marx and Engels, whose writings he gulped down as eagerly, he later recalled, as young readers consumed stories like *Alice in Wonderland*.[14]

Randolph's fascination with the radical social world of New York found unexpected support in his 1914 marriage to a widow six years his senior. Lucille Green was a successful Black entrepreneur and a recent graduate of the hairdressing school run by millionaire cosmetics queen Madam

Fury over a 1914 massacre at Rockefeller-owned mines near Ludlow, Colorado, (above) led American robber barons to a new generation of massive philanthropic and public relations efforts on behalf of unrestrained capitalism. In the aftermath, a small group of progressives, including Roger Baldwin (at left in 1919), quietly began searching for an endowment of their own to do battle with the giant foundations in the mass politics of public opinion.

> ...ON SINCLAIR
> ...ASADENA
> CALIFORNIA
>
> December 2, 1920
>
> Mr. Charles Garland,
> Buzzards Bay, Mass.
>
> Dear Comrade:
>
> You must have had letters from ten thousand cranks in the last week. I will be number ten thousand and one. I don't know whether I have ever met you but doubtless we have each heard of the other by now. I want to congratulate you upon the very fine propaganda stunt you have pulled off; it beats any of mine. You will, however, recognize the fact that I have given a good deal of time to propaganda stunts, and you may not mind if I suggest some schemes for carrying yours on. The late

When a young Cape Cod heir named Charles Garland rejected his million-dollar inheritance with much fanfare, the writer Upton Sinclair reached out to him by letter from Pasadena (above) to propose an alternative propaganda stunt: accept the money and establish a foundation.

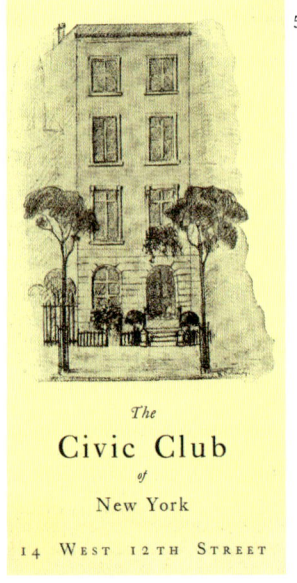

Garland Will Accept That Million

Charles Garland of Massachusetts has changed his mind and will accept the million dollars left him by his father, but says he will keep only $500 of it, to improve his farm. The illustration shows Garland and "April Farm," his three-room abode at North Carver, Mass.

The
Civic Club
of
New York

14 WEST 12TH STREET

After months of lobbying, Garland (pictured in this 1922 newspaper photograph at left) agreed. The resulting American Fund for Public Service, led by Roger Baldwin, typically met monthly over lunch at the Civic Club, a racially integrated social club on West 12th Street (pictured in 1920s membership pamphlet at right).

Baldwin assembled a board of directors including NAACP leader James Weldon Johnson, pictured here during his service on the Fund board.

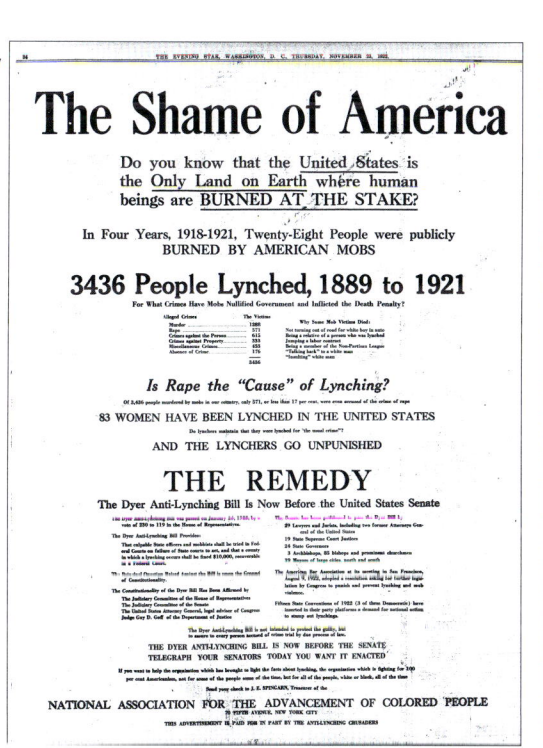

One of the Fund's first grants financed iconic full-page anti-lynching advertisements (left) in newspapers around the country. Soon thereafter, Johnson and W. E. B. Du Bois (together at right) won a Fund grant to study Black schools in the South. They described schools as a tool of discriminatory government spending; better schools, they asserted, would redirect resources to Black communities while empowering them in political and economic struggle.

TWELVE MEN CONDEMNED BY THE COURT.

Early victories in courtrooms followed hard on the heels of Congress's failure to enact anti-lynching legislation in 1922. Elaine massacre defendants in Arkansas whose convictions were overturned by the U.S. Supreme Court in 1923.

The Fund financed an ACLU team led by Clarence Darrow in the Scopes evolution trial (left) and paid Darrow's fees in the successful defense of Ossian Sweet (right), a Detroit doctor charged with murder for defending his family against white rioters angry that the family had moved into a white neighborhood.

The Fund's culture program sought to alter public opinion about race and capitalism in popular culture; it took up filmmaking, a radio station, book publishing, and magazines. Early issues of New Masses magazine aimed for avant-garde modernist art and radical opinion.

An eclectic group of grant recipients included Alice Hamilton (above), whose studies of workers' health helped make her the first woman on the Harvard faculty. The Daily Worker, a Communist newspaper that repeatedly failed to repay loans from the Fund, published cartoons like the one above right depicting J. P. Morgan Jr.'s control over democracy.

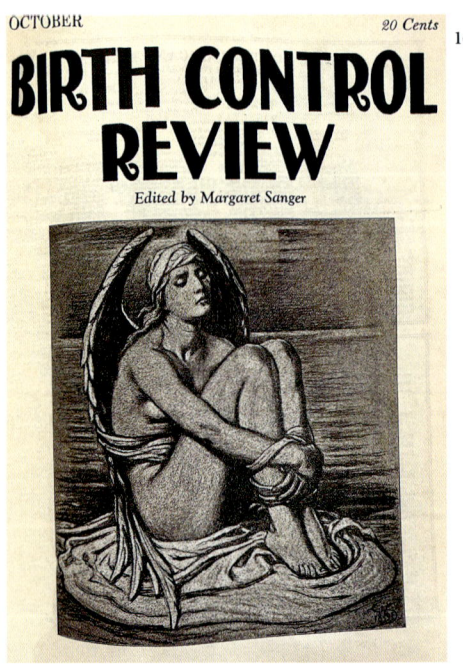

Grants went to the parts of Margaret Sanger's Birth Control League dedicated to freeing women's sexuality from the bonds of involuntary motherhood; much larger grants went to Vanguard Press, which published books on labor and economics with gorgeous endpapers like the one at left.

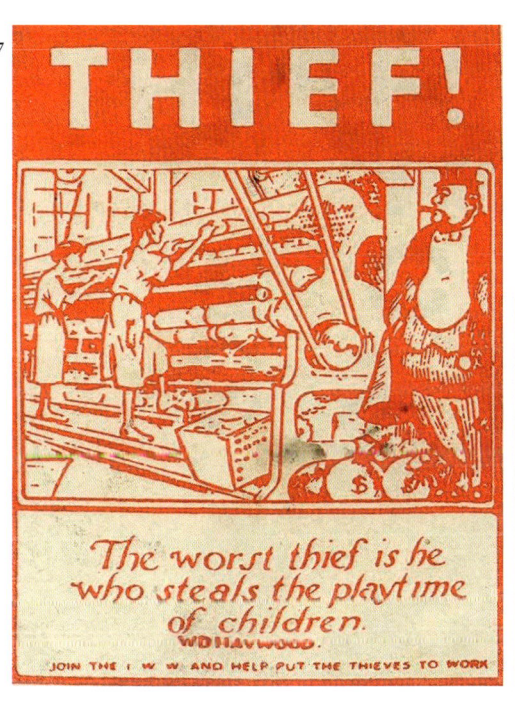

Elizabeth Gurley Flynn came to the Fund's board of directors from the Industrial Workers of the World, a radical labor union that during its heyday in the 1910s charged capitalism with turning morality upside down.

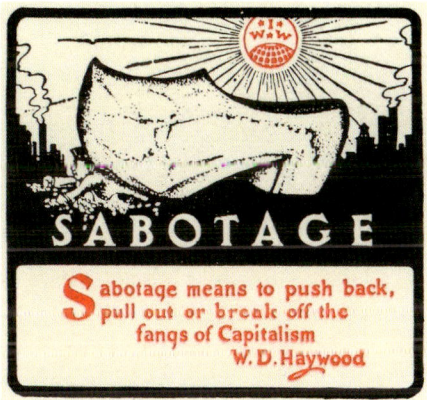

The Fund's principal project soon became a coalition of innovative labor organizations that included the League for Industrial Democracy, represented here by its magazine Labor Age. *The League rejected violence and resisted Communist influence, instead supporting institutions of economic democracy while helping the Fund win advantages in the modern tax code.*

The campaign to defend anarchists Nicola Sacco and Bartolomeo Vanzetti (above left) channeled the prewar IWW's fiery energies into the new heterodox world of the American Fund. Sidney Hillman of the Amalgamated Clothing Workers (below) served on the Fund's founding board and appointed lieutenants to do the same for two decades. A. Philip Randolph, pictured above right with the chairman of the U.S. Railway Mediation Board, worked with Hillman allies in the early stages of organizing one of the Fund's favorite unions, the Brotherhood of Sleeping Car Porters.

Brookwood Labor College, led by pacifist A. J. Muste (pictured above teaching on the college's campus in the Hudson Valley), offered history, economics, and strategy courses to labor union members; the Fund provided half the college's annual budget during the key 1920s years in which Brookwood helped develop a new conception of industrial democracy.

Among Brookwood's central projects was cross-race labor organizing; unidentified students pictured here at spring gradation in the mid-1920s.

Radical Group Makes Million Wall St. Profit

Public Service Fund Established by Garland, 'Money Hater,' Doubles the Endowment by Investments

Bank Stock Value Jumps

'Joke on Baker,' President of First National, Says Director Norman Thomas

As the Fund's holdings in the stock market grew by leaps and bounds in the 1920s, newspapers like the New York Herald Tribune and Fund directors such as Norman Thomas (headline at left) remarked on the irony. The Fund plowed its earnings into causes like the Passaic Textile strike of 1926; in the image above, Elizabeth Gurley Flynn leads a dramatic teach-in for Passaic strikers on how to use gas masks to combat police tear gas while walking the picket lines.

W. E. B. Du Bois, pictured in the offices of the NAACP magazine, The Crisis, worked closely with Fund director James Weldon Johnson on a large NAACP grant application in 1929 and 1930 to attack Jim Crow.. Omission of the magazine from the final grant helped propel Du Bois out of the organization he had founded two decades earlier.

Board member and lawyer Morris Ernst, at far left while defending a novel against obscenity charges, specialized in labor disputes and the defense of writers, including James Joyce. Ernst devised a strategy by which the Fund's increasingly divided board of directors approved the big NAACP grant.

After the 1931 arrest of nine young Black men and boys in Scottsboro, Alabama, the Fund supported defense efforts by both the NAACP and its Communist rivals; four of the Scottsboro defendants shown here in 1933.

With the Fund's resources dwindling after the 1929 stock market crash, civil rights lawyers Charles Hamilton Houston (seated at right) and his protégé Thurgood Marshall (standing at left) adapted the Fund's NAACP campaign to changed conditions, winning victories against unequal and segregated education systems on behalf of clients like Donald Murray (seated center) of Maryland.

The Fund's industrial democracy projects came to center stage in 1937 in a wave of sit-down strikes and in the epic Battle of the Overpass at Ford's giant River Rouge factory. United Auto Workers leader Walter Reuther (above, center, and below, center) and his brothers Roy (below, left) and Victor (below, right) were all connected to the Fund's Brookwood Labor College and drew on strategies developed there in the 1920s and early 1930s.

When the Supreme Court pivoted to uphold the New Deal's labor laws in 1937, its big switch propelled the sleeping car porters' union (pictured above in a 1936 parade) to its first contract with the giant Pullman Company. By contrast, New Deal programs in agriculture led to the eviction of tenant farmers in the Mississippi Delta. The Fund used some of its last resources to support the Southern Tenant Farmers Union (pictured below protesting in Washington).

In 1939, the U.S. Senate confirmed Felix Frankfurter (center with pocket handkerchief) to the Supreme Court despite controversy over his connections to the Fund's world; Elizabeth Dilling, one of the Fund's loudest critics, ducks away in the background.

Texas Congressman Martin Dies of the House Un-American Activities Committee (above left at an outdoor radio-broadcast rally) emerged as one of the Fund's most implacable foes, attacking it as a central hub in a left-wing conspiracy. The heterodox alliances of the Fund's interwar world collapsed in 1940 when the Nazi-Soviet Pact led the ACLU to expel Elizabeth Gurley Flynn (above right) because of her membership in the Communist Party. The Fund closed its doors the next year.

WHY SHOULD WE MARCH?

15,000 Negroes Assembled at St. Louis, Missouri
20,000 Negroes Assembled at Chicago, Illinois
23,500 Negroes Assembled at New York City
Millions of Negro Americans all Over This Great Land Claim the Right to be Free!

The Fund's accounts ran dry as American entry into World War II approached. But Fund beneficiaries like A. Philip Randolph and Charles Hamilton Houston carried forward its efforts to create a better world for working-class people of all races. Randolph's March on Washington Movement in 1941 (above) and Houston's successful 1944 case at the Supreme Court on behalf of Black railroad worker Bester Steele were culminations of the Fund's programs.

C. J. Walker. The couple had no children. Theirs was a kind of marriage of convenience, though animated by a mutual affection. They called one another "Buddy." Just as important, it seems, was that Lucille's money allowed Randolph to focus on politics. Lucille, moreover, introduced Randolph to Chandler Owen, a Black student at Columbia Law School with radical inclinations to match Randolph's. The men—both born in 1889, both migrants from the South with few connections in the city—quickly became inseparable partners on the Harlem radical scene. Owen introduced Randolph to the sociology of Lester Ward, a leading critic of free-market economics. Randolph shared his views on Marx. Long days at the New York Public Library led to evenings at public lectures by men like Morris Hillquit, leader of the city's Socialist Party. Late-night bull sessions at the Randolphs' apartment often followed.[15]

Lucille's income soon financed both men as they plunged into a small but growing world of street-corner socialism in Harlem. The "Lenin and Trotsky" of Lenox Avenue, as some began to call them, fell in with a crowd of brilliant Black socialists. Cyril Briggs, a Nevis-born journalist, was founder of an organization known as the African Blood Brotherhood. Wilfred Domingo was a Jamaican-American socialist and writer. Lovett Fort-Whiteman was a would-be actor taking classes at the socialist Rand School downtown. Though only in his thirties, Hubert Harrison from St. Croix served as the elder statesman of the group, arguing for a socialism that put "race first," as he wrote in 1917. (One member of the Harlem radical crowd dubbed Harrison "the Black Socrates"—partly because of his logically compelling polemics, but mostly because, as the poet Claude McKay observed, Harrison's massive head resembled the ancient busts at the Metropolitan Museum.) Randolph and Owen brushed shoulders with a young Jamaican Black nationalist named Marcus Garvey and later claimed to have hosted the 1916 rally that introduced Garvey's United Negro Improvement Association to the city's burgeoning Black populace. They connected with Virgin Islands–born labor organizer Frank Crosswaith, who organized Black needle-trades workers for the International Ladies' Garment Workers Union.[16]

In January 1917, Randolph and Owen established a magazine that aimed to focus the unsettled energy of Harlem's emerging Black radicalism. *The*

Messenger began as the house organ for the Headwaiters and Sidewaiters Society of Greater New York, a rare Black workers' organization. Their arrangement with the Society foundered after only a few months when the editors used the magazine's pages to accuse the headwaiters of exploiting the sidewaiters, who performed the menial tasks in a restaurant dining room. When the headwaiters objected, the two men moved their office next door and rebranded the magazine as an independent monthly. Lucille provided money to keep the journal afloat. The Socialist Party offered support, too, in return for the editors' endorsement of Morris Hillquit's mayoral campaign that fall.[17]

The Messenger, its editors announced on the cover of each issue, was "the only radical Negro magazine in America." In truth, it was the most successful entrant in a wartime profusion of Black radical publications, alongside new publications like Briggs's *Crusader*, Harrison's *Voice*, Marcus Garvey's *Negro World*, and Domingo's *Emancipator*. As a publication, *The Messenger* stood out as the best of the group. In its conception, *The Messenger* was the uptown counterpart to Greenwich Village's *The Masses*. Both publications combined striking art and poetry with contemporary fiction and radical politics. Like *The Masses*, the Harlem magazine opposed American entry into the war. According to *The Messenger*, phenomena like lynching, segregation, and disfranchisement made President Wilson's so-called war for democracy a "sham," a "mockery," and a "rape on decency and a travesty on common justice." Randolph and Owen reserved special venom for Black supporters of the war—so-called Old Crowd Negroes, whom they excoriated as "me-too-boss, hat-in-hand, lickspittling" supporters of Wilson's Jim Crow war. Even W. E. B. Du Bois, whose 1917 decision to close ranks with the White House in support of the war effort had astonished the two younger men, drew the magazine's ire.[18]

Du Bois's support for the war led Randolph and Owen to attack his most influential ideas. In 1903, Du Bois had written that the "Negro race, like all races" would be saved, if it was to be saved at all, "by its exceptional men"—its "aristocracy of talent and character" or its "Talented Tenth," as Du Bois put it most memorably. Randolph and Owen wrote that Du Bois's aristocracy lacked the "necessary racial and social and economic militancy" to bring about the liberation of the great, impoverished masses of the race. Race discrimination was only one part of the system that subordinated the masses of Black people. A talented tenth might win new rights for a lucky few to buy first-class railcar tickets. But such gains would do little for those working in the bowels of a steamship. Indeed, the fundamental "problem of the twentieth century," asserted *The Messenger* in 1920, was not "the color-line," as Du Bois had famously proposed. The fundamental problem, in Randolph's and Owen's view, was economic power and the accompanying distributions of "wealth and knowledge." The pages of *The Messenger* made the case for a revolutionary politics of race and class that Randolph and Owen believed more fundamental than either the NAACP's critique of Jim Crow or the American Federation of Labor's defense of unions. Randolph and Owen endorsed the Industrial Workers of the World and called the Bolshevik revolution "the greatest achievement" of the century. The time was ripe, they added, "for a great mass movement among negroes." In the absence of such a movement among workers of all races, capital would exploit racial divisions. Editorial

A medallion of interracial labor solidarity appeared in early issues of The Messenger.

cartoons drove the point home, depicting white and Black labor fighting over scraps while capital gorged on the profits.[19]

Randolph and Owen focused relentlessly on what they depicted as the double oppression of the Black worker. It was, they wrote, class and race working together that subordinated Black communities. Lynching was a product of capitalist exploitation in conjunction with race prejudice. For one thing, Randolph observed, Black people were not lynching's only victims; by his estimate, lawless mobs had taken 1,000 white lives in the late nineteenth and early twentieth centuries, Leo Frank's in Georgia among them. Moreover, Randolph insisted, race prejudice itself needed to be explained. Racism had a history and an origin story. And as Randolph saw it, racism was rooted in the economic interests of the owners of capital.[20]

Randolph and Owen's electric radicalism attracted interest in white progressive circles downtown. Roger Baldwin, then directing the wartime Civil Liberties Bureau, wrote a letter helping the men drum up subscriptions. The socialist Mary White Ovington, serving as chairwoman of the NAACP board, offered praise. Herbert Seligmann, who had been on the front lines with Walter Lippmann in France before moving on to publicity work for the NAACP, applauded *The Messenger*'s focus on the economic roots of racism.[21]

Wartime federal authorities took note, too—but they were more skeptical. Agents of the Bureau of Investigation began to keep tabs on Randolph's speaking engagements. In August 1918, after a Socialist Party event to rally support among Black workers in Cleveland, federal authorities arrested Randolph and Owen and charged them with violating the Espionage Act. A federal judge dismissed the charges, but the two men were now in the government's sights. Postmaster General Albert Burleson suspended *The Messenger*'s mailing privileges, just as he had suspended *The Masses* the year before. On the floor of the Senate, Senator James Byrnes of South Carolina charged that *The Messenger*'s editorial staff aimed to lead a revolutionary campaign of violence. A 1919 report by Attorney General Palmer concluded that it was "by long odds the most dangerous of all the Negro publications."[22]

In Harlem circles it became a commonplace that J. Edgar Hoover and Woodrow Wilson believed Randolph and Owen to be "the most dangerous Negroes in the United States." The epithet stuck because the men wore it as a badge of pride.[23]

For all the heated wartime rhetoric, radicalism's rapid postwar decline cooled *The Messenger*'s fire. Randolph and Owen boasted that their columns would radicalize 12 million Black Americans. But their magazine never exceeded its 1919 peak circulation of 26,000—impressive for a radical journal, to be sure, though at a scale wholly inadequate to launch a revolution. By the early 1920s, the magazine's circulation had fallen to 5,000. Owen estimated privately that only one-third of the readership was Black. The magazine, which ran an $11,000 annual operating deficit, equivalent to 40 percent of its annual budget, entered the 1920s like a variation on the old riddle about newspapers. It was a magazine about Black radicalism for white middle-class reds.[24]

Two controversies shattered radical Black Harlem as the new decade began. The first was over communism. A few men like Cyril Briggs and Lovett Fort-Whiteman threw themselves into the new Communist Party, established in Chicago late in the summer of 1919. Randolph and most Harlem radicals, however, broke the other way. Already in 1922 and 1923, Randolph had come to think that "Negro Communists are a menace." He called them "disruptionists," followers of a Party line that repeatedly undermined the efforts of the organizers and advocates who had been working with the Black masses for years. The principal problem, as Randolph put it, was that the Communists tried to leap too far and too fast without preparing the ground. Black laborers, he found, had not yet "even grasped the fundamentals and necessity of simple trade and industrial unionism." Talk of an American Bolshevism was therefore badly counterproductive and grossly irresponsible. The Party's efforts were more likely to "confuse the aims and ideals of the New Negro" than to galvanize morale for the struggle ahead.[25]

Randolph and Owen also broke with Marcus Garvey, whose United Negro Improvement Association had produced the second divisive controversy of the day. In 1916, when Randolph had invited Garvey to deliver his first lecture to an American audience, the newly arrived Jamaican struck him as "one of the greatest propagandists of his time." Garvey and Randolph continued to cooperate after American entry into the war, advocating self-determination for African states. But in the early 1920s, Randolph's view of Garvey and his bombastic Black nationalism dimmed. When Garvey met with a leader of the Ku Klux Klan to discuss their shared interest in a new exodus of Black Americans to Africa, simmering exasperation boiled over into contempt. The pages of *The Messenger* condemned Garvey's "erratic rampage" and "groundless braggadocio," his "sheer folly" and "foolish" behavior. Owen, in particular, attacked Garvey's far-flung business enterprises, including the ill-fated Black Star Line, whose promises to carry passengers and cargo around the Black Atlantic world were belied by a fleet of broken old vessels. Garvey, Owen charged, was a "consummate liar" and a "notorious crook."[26]

Garvey and his supporters answered back. In September 1922, someone mailed Randolph a package containing a severed human hand. "Listen Randolph," the accompanying note threatened, "watch your step or else." The package was signed "K.K.K." Randolph was certain that Garvey had sent it.[27]

Resolving to eliminate Garvey, Randolph and Owen aligned themselves with more conservative Black leaders whom they had lambasted just a few years before. "Garvey Must Go," rang out the headlines of *The Messenger*. Along with seven prominent Black New Yorkers, including James Weldon Johnson's father-in-law the Black real estate entrepreneur John Nail, Owen appealed to the Justice Department. Despite the fact that the same department had conducted hostile investigations of *The Messenger* and its editors, Owen seized on accounting irregularities at the Black Star Line and urged the attorney general to try Garvey on federal mail fraud charges. Owen and Randolph cheered Garvey's 1923 conviction, enthusiastically supporting his imprisonment and deportation to Jamaica.[28]

Fierce opposition to Communists and back-to-Africa nationalists drew on a common thread. Randolph's singular temperamental virtue was perseverance in incremental struggle. As Randolph once put it, he never adhered strictly "to any particular school of thought." He aimed to make better lives for Black people out of the basic ingredients of the worlds they had already made. Briggs, Domingo, Harrison, and Fort-Whiteman had looked for ways to call down the thunderclap of revolution, much like Flynn's Wobblies. Randolph, too, knew what it was to thrill to the energy of sudden upheaval. But where the bright flames of his fellow Black wartime radicals burned out before they could leave a mark, Randolph carried a steadier torch. "Each triumph," Randolph elaborated, "creates fresh hope and new faith," making new room for social transformations to come.[29]

In the near term, *The Messenger* stumbled. The poet Langston Hughes, whose work appeared in the magazine, complained that its editorial policy had become "God knows what." Randolph's friend and partner Owen despaired and decamped for Chicago to make money. Lucille's business income allowed *The Messenger* to limp along. But at the age of thirty-six, Randolph had lost his constituency.[30]

Just when all seemed lost, Randolph walked into a new if improbable opportunity, one that would lead him to embrace the American Fund's new unionism—and cause the Fund directors to think differently about their mission.

Upon the Shoulders of Black Abolitionists

Randolph's first impression of the American Fund was dim. Writing in *The Messenger* in 1921, he declared that the young Garland's unusual decision to reject his inheritance was "not laudable intellectual martyrdom" but the "symptom of a simpleton." Less charitably, Randolph called the foundation "irrefutable evidence" that its donor was "a mental nut."[31]

The brash Randolph applied for support from the Fund regardless. Writing to Baldwin in 1922, Randolph asked the Fund for an emergency loan, which the Fund issued, and followed up with a grant request for *The Messenger* amounting to $10,000. The magazine, he told them, encouraged Black readers to join unions. James Weldon Johnson "heartily" recommended that the Fund approve. *The Messenger*, he explained in a memo to the rest of the Fund board, was "the only magazine" that was "specifically interested in the Negro as a part of the labor world." Its pages brought "modern ideas about economics and industry" to a Black readership, which Johnson concluded was "sadly needed and vitally important." To be sure, Johnson explained, he himself was "not absolutely in accord" with the revolutionary socialism that had been "the policy of *The Messenger* magazine." Sometimes, Johnson noted, he had "directly opposed" Randolph's editorial positions. But Johnson and Randolph shared common Jacksonville roots. And Johnson insisted that *The Messenger* was "unique in its field" for connecting "organized labor and the Negro."³²

When the Fund voted on Randolph's project, the directors expressed hesitation about the bookkeeping and internal management of the magazine. Such concerns were standard fare at the Fund; they would turn down dozens of proposals on similar grounds in the years to come. In Randolph's case, they directed him to clean up his magazine's operating deficit before seeking further support. In the meantime, they approved a modest grant of $500 plus additional matching funds targeted to new subscriptions. Randolph reacted furiously. The grant, he charged, was too small. Its requirement that he repay the Fund's emergency loan before the grant money would issue struck him as especially outrageous. A scandalized Randolph invoked the perverse rules of the Jim Crow South: "If the Negro will learn to swim first," said white southern officials, "then he may go into the water." The Fund's posture seemed to be the same: "If you show you don't need us, then we will give you help." But *The Messenger* needed help now. The white directors at the Fund, Randolph felt, had disrespected his Harlem

The Fund began to support Randolph's magazine in 1923.

operation. Johnson tried to smooth the rift. But he also suggested that the younger man needed to reorganize the way he did business if more generous support were to be forthcoming. Randolph's books, Johnson noted candidly, were a wreck. He could not properly account for his magazine's revenues and expenses. For five years he had been running his operation on a shoestring, relying on subventions from Lucille to make ends meet.[33]

What happened next helped alter the life trajectory of the man who would become the most influential Black union organizer in the twentieth century. An indignant Randolph realized that like it or not, if he desired to access the resources of the Fund for *The Messenger*, he would have to draw closer to the new unionist world.

Johnson and Baldwin sent labor economist Stuart Chase to Harlem to work with Randolph on his account books and to consult on organizing strategies. Before long, the Fund drew Randolph into close working contact with the New York wing of Sidney Hillman's new unionist cadre and the fledgling labor community of Brookwood College.[34]

Randolph's budding relationship with the New York labor intellectuals marked a notable departure for American labor. For a generation and more, the main organizations of the American labor movement had proceeded as whites-only enterprises. As *The Messenger* noted angrily, the International Association of Machinists and the four great railroad brotherhoods—the Brotherhood of Locomotive Engineers (1863), the Order of Railway Conductors (1868), the Brotherhood of Locomotive Firemen (1873), and the Brotherhood of Railway Trainmen (1883)—all "by constitutional decree or general policy" forbade "the enrollment of Negro members." At the turn of the century, twenty-four of the largest unions, representing half of all union members in the country, explicitly excluded Black workers from membership. Du Bois estimated that another quarter of the labor movement barred Black members as a matter of informal practice. Even Debs, for whom Randolph had great admiration, had belonged to the all-white Locomotive Firemen.[35]

The migration of Black people from South to North was fast scrambling the labor market. But in the near term it meant, as *The Messenger* put it, that "the problems of the Negro worker" were "increasing not diminishing." On the railroads, the white labor brotherhoods now demanded contracts that effectively ended the hiring of new Black employees. Novel contractual terms on promotion and seniority precluded the advancement of Black employees, which soon caused the number of Black brakemen, switchmen, flagmen, and yardmen on the nation's railroads to dwindle. At the same time, thousands of Black workers excluded from unions stood ready to serve as a reserve army of strikebreaking labor, often self-consciously pursuing the only path available to them for gaining industrial employment. Employers appealed to Black replacement workers to crush postwar strikes in steel and meatpacking, and many Black workers willingly filled the role. White workers, in the words of Black sociologist Kelly Miller, were "the ones who lynch and burn." The labor movement's Jim Crowism seemed counterproductive and illogical. It offered employers a ready weapon for crushing labor. Yet Miller concluded along with many others that "there is nothing in the white working class" with which the Black worker could make common cause. The fictional Black worker in Claude McKay's 1928 novel *Home to Harlem* captured Black labor's characteristic response: "I'll scab through hell to make mah living."[36]

Randolph's own organizing efforts had run headlong into the racism of white labor. When Randolph formed the United Brotherhood of Elevator and Switchboard Operators for employees of the city's apartment build-

Randolph, standing at right, and the staff of The Messenger *in the magazine's office.*

ings in 1917, the AFL-affiliated and white-dominated Elevator Operators and Starters Union claimed jurisdiction and pushed him out. The short-lived National Brotherhood Workers of America, which Randolph joined in 1919, was unceremoniously thrown off docks along the East Coast by AFL-affiliated unions of white longshoremen. And when Randolph and Owen supported Frank Crosswaith's Trade Union Committee for Organizing Negro Workers in its efforts to funnel Black members into the ranks of existing white unions, few labor organizations outside the needle trades showed interest. Randolph coined a name for the giant labor federation: the "American Separation of Labor," he called it. The "present AFL," he concluded, "is the most wicked machine for the propagation of race prejudice in the country."[37]

In the middle of the 1920s there were no more than 50,000 to 80,000 Black union members, as compared to three and a half million white ones. Fewer Black workers belonged to all American labor unions combined than had belonged to the Knights of Labor in the 1880s, even though the total Black population had increased by 60 percent in forty years. Even in the relatively integrated United Mine Workers, Black union numbers fell precipitously from a peak of 20,000 men at the turn of the century to a mere 5,000. In 1925, Black workers made up 16 percent of the paid labor force but only between 1 and 2 percent of labor union members.[38]

In early June 1925, a tall, well-dressed man named Ashley L. Totten stopped Randolph on Seventh Avenue and asked if he would speak to a group of his fellow porters on the Pullman Company's famous railroad sleeping cars.[39]

The porters, with their starched uniforms and attentive service, did the work that gave Pullman cars their reputation for luxury and elegance. The porters made beds, shined shoes, tended to luggage, and served food. All of them were men. Nearly all were Black. For years, a small group of porters had tried with little success to press for higher wages and better working conditions through Pullman's company union, the Employee Representation Plan. And though he didn't say so in that initial meeting, Totten was looking for someone to organize the Pullman Company porters into a union. The right man would be an outsider to the company, someone who could not be fired in retaliation for organizing. Randolph fit the bill, and his June speech hit the right notes. At a secret summit in the Harlem home of porter William H. Des Verney later that month, the porters group asked Randolph to lead a new porters union. Lacking other opportunities and running a $10,000 annual deficit at his struggling magazine, the idea appealed. Randolph dedicated articles in the July and August issues of *The Messenger* to the cause of the Pullman porters. And on August 25, at the Elks Hall in Harlem, Randolph held the first public meeting of a new organization, dubbed the Brotherhood of Sleeping Car Porters. The crowd was some 500 people. It was, the *Amsterdam News* reported, "the greatest labor mass meeting ever held of, for, and by Negro working men."[40]

The session was a labor union conclave like few others. Members were barred from speaking individually so as to protect them as much as possible from Pullman reprisals. The meeting instead took the form of a church revival, a larger version of the services Randolph's father had held in Jacksonville churches. Meetings in the months to come adopted a dynamic structure of call and collective response, as porters, their wives (soon to be organized as the "Women's Auxiliary"), and fellow travelers cheered speeches against the quiet outrages of employment at Pullman and joined in songs of solidarity.[41]

Over the next year, in porter revivals all along a nationwide circuit from Chicago to St. Paul, Omaha, Kansas City, St. Louis, Seattle, Oakland, Los Angeles, New Orleans, Washington, Boston, Buffalo, and Detroit, Randolph and a small team of organizers adapted and transformed the industrial democracy project of the new unionists at the American Fund. Randolph aimed for what the Wobblies' unstinting vision of class war had disdained: cooperative industrial democracy, or what he called the "serious business of workers' control of industry." Through collective bargaining and contracts, he pursued rights for the porters that even the giant Pullman Company would have to respect, rights to better wages and hours along with recognition of the Brotherhood as a guarantee that the porters would gain the dignity of a say in the direction of their work lives.[42]

The goal was more easily articulated than accomplished. The Pullman Company had been a legendary employer of Black labor for more than half a century. George Mortimer Pullman, the firm's founder, established the company soon after the Civil War to build and service a higher class of railroad sleeping cars. In a widely circulated but apocryphal story, Pullman's prototype car, the "Pioneer," had been added to President Lincoln's funeral train. The company solidified its ties to the Great Emancipator by hiring Lincoln's son, Robert Todd Lincoln, as its lawyer. When Pullman died in 1897, the younger Lincoln took over as president of the company. Since its earliest years, the company had hired Black people as porters and maids for its cars. How better, said Pullman, to set thousands of formerly enslaved people on the path to freedom? The company supported charitable institutions in the Black community on Chicago's South Side. A Pullman Porters Benefit Association provided sick benefits to employee members and death benefits to their families. The Black press praised the company as "the greatest benefactor of our race."[43]

In many respects, the porters formed the aristocracy of the Black working class. Travel and connections to national networks of information conferred status on Pullman porters, as did their encounters with famous and wealthy rail passengers. Wages, though modest, exceeded those of most jobs available to Black workers. Indeed, the porters made an inauspicious vehicle

Advertisement for the Pullman Car dining service, 1894.

for Randolph's incremental socialism for one more reason, too. It was the Black porters on the Pullman cars who had subverted the great 1894 strike of Debs's all-white American Railway Union. Forming an organization called the Anti-Strikers Railroad Union and declaring loyalty to Pullman, the porters and their Black friends filled the jobs of the Jim Crow strikers.[44]

Yet for all the ostensible benevolence of the Pullman Company toward its Black workers, life as a Pullman porter featured galling indignities. Pullman generally refused to hire Black workers to jobs in its construction and repair shops, and the company outright prohibited Black workers from serving as conductors. Outside of special circumstances like the 1894 strike, Pullman hired Black employees only as porters and maids, a practice that stretched back to the 1860s, when George Pullman believed that recently freed slaves—men "trained as a race by years of personal service," as he put it—would serve as highly desirable figures in a very particular servile role in the emerging mass economy, fulfilling mostly white passengers' every need in the supposed age of free labor.[45]

Porters were paid substantially less than white conductors, often for work that was substantially more difficult. Where conductors started at $155 per month, new porters received $67.50. Tips increased the porters' take-home pay, by $58 per month on average, but were uncertain and made the porters more vulnerable to degrading treatment by their passengers. Standard pay, meager as it was, required a monthly minimum of 11,000 miles, sometimes the equivalent of nearly four hundred hours, or eight round-trip runs between New York and Chicago. Scheduling delays beyond the porters' control could mean missing the monthly mileage minimum and incurring pay penalties. Idle time in the station went unpaid, as did preparation for the runs. Porters in the first ten years of service purchased their own uniforms; all porters had to buy meals on the road and keep themselves supplied with basic equipment like shoe polish. Total monthly costs reduced a typical porter's take-home compensation by $33. A porter in the middle of the 1920s could expect to net around $95 each month, around half what the U.S. Bureau of Labor Statistics estimated was required to maintain a working-class family with three children.[46]

All this made the porters ripe for organizing. They were hardly versed in the new unionist language of industrial democracy, at least not at first. But their desire for dignity at work was not so far removed from the new unionists' aims of worker control through collective bargaining. Randolph, who dressed in a suit and tie every day, and who held himself ramrod straight, intuitively understood the respectability politics of the porters from his own meticulous upbringing. The Pullman Company's supposed paternalism compromised the dignity of the porters at every turn. The run from New York to Miami took forty-nine hours—but included only three hours of rest, with no berth for sleeping. Pullman officials exercised arbitrary power over porters by allocating the most profitable runs with the highest tips to porters who were most loyal to the company. Indeed, the flip side of Pullman's self-styled benevolence was an elaborate system of control and surveillance by an extensive internal network of company spies and stoolpigeon employees. Workers who caused trouble soon found themselves out of a job. The Pullman Employee Representation Plan, founded in 1920, offered a thin pretense of representing the workers before company officials while serving mostly, in one porter's words, as "a smoke screen" for what Randolph called the deeply rooted "feudalism of the company." The company union, announced *The Messenger* in 1926, was a mere "substitute for the real struggle," which was for "a fair share of the product" and for a form of "industrial democracy" that would guarantee fairness for the future. The autocracy at Pullman, Randolph protested in 1926, treated its porters "like slaves." Echoing the Supreme Court's infamous *Dred Scott* decision, Randolph told the porters that the unorganized Pullman porter had "no rights which the Pullman Company is bound to respect."[47]

Randolph turned to the Garland Fund in a confidential letter a month after the Brotherhood's first mass meeting. The unionization of Pullman's porters, he wrote to Baldwin and Flynn, was proceeding in secrecy. No porter knew whether any other was a member for fear that loose lips and company spies might destroy the campaign before it even got underway. "The entire movement," Randolph elaborated, rested "upon *The Messenger*," which could keep up a "constant educational agitation" among the porters without requiring members to make themselves vulnerable to firing by spreading word of the movement themselves. A grant from the Fund, Randolph said, would allow him to distribute copies of the magazine to the 12,000 porters.[48]

The application was a godsend to James Weldon Johnson. The NAACP leader had supported Randolph's earlier proposals. At the end of 1924, moreover, Johnson had urged his colleagues at the Fund to finance a study of Black workers, their attitudes toward unions, and unions' attitudes toward them. The Fund awarded $1,000 to Charles S. Johnson, research director at the National Urban League, to perform such a survey, which was still underway as the Pullman campaign began. Now the new application from Randolph seemed like a golden opportunity to counter efforts at the Fund to promote support for labor groups over aid to Black organizations. Randolph's Brotherhood intended to be both.[49]

At Johnson's insistence, and curious to learn more, the Fund directors appointed a two-person committee to gather information, naming Johnson to serve along with the newest member of the Fund board, H. H. Broach, an energetic vice president of the electrical workers union. In October, Johnson and Broach reported back. On the strength of what Johnson hoped might become "a strong link between organized labor and the Negro," the Fund made the first of what would soon become several grants to the Brotherhood. A second, larger grant in January 1926 allowed Randolph to expand the scale of the campaign. The porters' effort, Randolph told the directors, was "the most important move to organize Negro workers that has ever been made in this country"—and "the most promising," too. Most white unions, Randolph observed, barred Black members. The unique position of the porters was that racially exclusive hiring practices at Pullman allowed unionization to proceed without confronting the challenge of white union racism. The all-Black porters might become a model for Black organizing. "The struggle in which the Pullman porters are now engaged," he wrote, "is a great educational campaign which will carry the gospel of unionism to millions of negro workers who are now either entirely ignorant of this great movement or have false and distorted ideas of it or look upon it disinterestedly as a thing apart from their lives." Moreover, Randolph continued, such a campaign "will carry not only the gospel of unionism but of industrial democracy," one that, if successful, would "stimulate organization of hundreds of thousands of workers of the same race in other industries."[50]

With new money, Randolph hired technical experts with Brookwood connections to conduct a massive survey for the campaign. Economists from a Hillman-affiliated research consultancy called The Labor Bureau, joined by David Saposs from the Brookwood faculty, drafted a sprawling report on living conditions, wages, and attitudes toward labor unions among the porters. Johnson told Flynn it was "one of the most valuable results of the whole movement." The Labor Bureau documented higher wages at Pullman's rivals and detailed the better pay and conditions afforded to white Pullman conductors. It presented case studies of porters' lives and assembled statistics about the entire workforce of 12,000 porters. It assessed the profitability of the Pullman Company, its revenue and dividends, its soaring stock price and its healthy balance sheet, and concluded that ample resources were available to reduce the porters' working hours while increasing their monthly take-home pay.[51]

Momentum gathered and endorsements followed from the downtown Civic Club, where the Garland Fund directors held their meetings, and from progressives and labor leaders as well as the leadership of the NAACP. Columnists from the Fund-supported Federated Press wrote favorable stories on the porters' campaign. A socialist retreat in Pennsylvania's Pocono Mountains (itself supported by the Garland Fund) hosted Brotherhood organizer Frank Crosswaith for a weekend of training. Even the whites-only railway engineers put in a good word for the porters. Pullman executives raised pay to try to blunt the movement. But the union's membership numbers swelled. Randolph recorded 2,371 paid members in December 1925, which became 3,417 in February of the next year and 4,072 in April. The company fired union members when it could find them. (Des Verney, who had been among the porters to first approach Randolph, was fired before 1925 was out.) But Randolph now believed there were too many Brotherhood members for Pullman to fire them all.[52]

In the summer and fall of 1926, Randolph sought money for publicity work and research. Given the "almost insurmountable barriers . . . against the admission of Negroes into existing unions," he argued once more, the Pullman porters offered the best hope for a labor beachhead into the Black working class. The Brotherhood, as Crosswaith put it in *The Messenger* that November, would be "the first great attempt to introduce Negro workers to the cause of Industrial Democracy." Collective bargaining with Pullman—what Randolph called the "recognition of our movement"— would be the mechanism for achieving a democratic say in the basic conditions of the porters' work. "With the recognition of our economic rights, privileges, and power," Randolph explained in the pages of *The Messen-*

ger, the Brotherhood would "develop the initiative and ability to write our own economic contracts." And it was the contract that would turn humiliating and servile working conditions into a respectable independence. Contracts would entail responsibilities, to be sure. They would require the Brotherhood to "supply a high quality of service to the company and the public, to insist upon efficiency, industry, reliability, courtesy, sobriety and intelligent cooperation on the part of our members with the company." That was the workers' side of the deal in Hillman's new unionist formulation. But it was also the workers' ticket to the benefits of economic gains. "A group of workers without a wage agreement," as Randolph put it, was "like a man without a house or a piece of land." Such a person had no claim on improvements to the property and therefore no say in what improvements were to be made. "Under the industrial democracy of the collective bargaining regime," by contrast, Brotherhood members would "have a fundamental interest" in Pullman's good fortunes. "Our welfare as well as that of the public," Randolph explained, would be involved.[53]

The logic was pure Hillman. Industrial democracy by contract was not at odds with the interests of the Pullman Company, insisted Randolph. To the contrary, union participation in the governance of the firm would be to the company's advantage, and to the union's, too. It would allow the company to draw more effectively on the resources of its employees and allow the employees to share in the resulting upside. Randolph imagined an industrial world transformed, one in which "the development of moral and intellectual competence" among the porters would constrain Pullman to "extend a welcome hand" in the mutual enlightened self-interest of all involved.[54]

But Randolph's new unionism also gave Hillman's a twist. His vision of industrial peace and democracy was a project of race emancipation, too. The rights that a contract afforded had special significance for Black labor because a contract stood for rights that could be enforced. "The writing of our own economic contracts," Randolph asserted in *The Messenger*, "will usher the Negro into the final cycle of race freedom." Collective labor contracting, he contended, was "the final road to freedom of all oppressed peoples."[55]

By late 1926, Randolph's push to democratize Pullman embraced a further distinctive feature of the new unionism. The IWW, which Randolph had endorsed during his fiery Harlem radical days in the 1910s, had insisted that things like contracts, law, and the state were the puppets of capital. The AFL insisted that only direct economic power could lift the unions. By contrast, Hillman and his circle of innovative union intellectuals borrowed from their socialist roots to embrace the use of the state and the law to advance labor's ends. Political democracy, they asserted, advanced industrial democracy, and vice versa. Randolph now glimpsed in the porters' distinctive situation a novel way to use law and the state to organize the Black workers who historically had been the most difficult workers to organize. The Brotherhood, he wrote, would "avail ourselves of the machinery of government."[56]

The strategy of turning to government had much to recommend it. As the porters well remembered, the one significant break from company control over the porters had come during the war, when the United States Railroad Administration assumed emergency operation of railroads, including the Pullman Company's cars. A porter named Frank Boyd, who worked the long run from Chicago to Seattle, filed a grievance with the wartime Board of Railway Wages and Working Conditions to demand higher wages. Emboldened porters in Chicago and New York supported him. The next year, with the war controls still in place, the federal director general of railroads responded by issuing sweeping wage increases and new limits on the company's exploitative working conditions. As Boyd recalled, the 1919 order had "stirred the conscience of the porters as never before."[57]

More generally, a long history of federal government involvement in labor relations on interstate railroads meant that labor organizing took place in a different legal environment on the rails than in mills and factories. The Erdman Act of 1898, drafted in the wake of Debs's Pullman strike, authorized employees on railroads to ask the federal government to resolve disputes with their employers over wages, hours, or working conditions. The act and its 1913 successor conferred no coercive authority; arbitration under the legislation required the consent of employers and unions alike. But weaker railroad unions found it in their interest to invoke the government arbitration boards, even when the railroads declined to participate, in hopes that the act would induce federal officials to intervene. With the expiration of wartime controls, the Transportation Act of 1920 reinstated the system of voluntary arbitration. More importantly, the

1920 legislation established a new Railroad Labor Board with the power to recommend wage rates and working conditions. Crucially, the new Labor Board had the further authority to hold elections among the workers to decide which of two or more rival organizations was the proper representative of employees—a vital question in cases where company unions vied with the railway unions for the workers' allegiance. Six years later, in 1926, the Railway Labor Act established a presidential Emergency Board, which the president of the United States could invoke when labor disputes threatened to interrupt the movement of trains.[58]

Historians have long critiqued the Railway Labor Act and its predecessors for merely reaffirming the status quo. A century ago, left critics like American Fund director and Party leader William Z. Foster lambasted the act as "class collaboration," aligning traitorous labor leaders with the employers' goals of conciliation and arbitration.[59]

Randolph saw the railway labor system differently. He saw it as a mobilizing opportunity. The processes of the labor law, however anemic, held out hope for government recognition of the Brotherhood. The 1926 act, in particular, prohibited "interference, influence, or coercion" by a carrier in its employees' choice of a bargaining representative. Here was the kind of initially modest intervention that Randolph hoped would have large downstream effects. The act, he wrote in *The Messenger*, created a "system in which each party has rights which the other is bound to respect." Such a system, Randolph believed, offered "the promise of industrial peace." Incremental improvements might lead to revolutionary changes.[60]

Beginning in the summer and fall of 1926, the Garland Fund–supported Brotherhood launched a relentless, single-minded pursuit of its rights under the federal railway labor law. Randolph petitioned the Mediation Board created by the new Railway Act, asking it to resolve a dispute between Pullman and its porters over wages and working conditions. The company maintained its policy of ignoring the porters union. But now the Mediation Board's gears began to turn. In the spring of 1927, Mediation Board officials arrived at Brotherhood headquarters in Harlem to decide whether Randolph's union was the proper representative of the porters. The report drafted by The Labor Bureau, which had gathered masses of information about membership and much more, seemed decisive on the question. And in June, the federal board handed Randolph his first victory, affirming the Brotherhood as the porters' lawful representative.[61]

Randolph assured readers of *The Messenger* that the federal government's recognition would force Pullman to the table. In truth, however, the Railway Labor Act's voluntary structure gave neither the union nor the federal government the authority to force the company to do anything. And so, in September, with a new round of $10,000 in support from the American Fund, Randolph opened two further fronts in the legal campaign.[62]

First, the Brotherhood petitioned the Interstate Commerce Commission to investigate and prohibit tipping on interstate railroads. Working with union-side labor lawyer Donald Richberg, himself an author of the Railway Labor Act, the Brotherhood contended that tipping constituted a hidden charge for the rail-riding public. The practice, Richberg asserted, created incentives for discriminating between passengers who offered what were effectively bribes and passengers who did not. Tipping posed safety risks, too, since porters usually received tips only if they stayed on to their passengers' destinations, often several sleep-deprived days' travel away. Second, Richberg filed a lawsuit seeking to enjoin Pullman from carrying out elections for the company union, charging that such elections violated the Railway Labor Act by interfering with the workers' free choice of a bargaining representative.[63]

In the pages of *The Messenger*, Randolph crowed that the new moves at the Interstate Commerce Commission and in the courts were "destined to bring the company to terms." The union was that much closer, he said, to what he called the "Emancipation of the Pullman Porter from Industrial Slavery."[64]

By the fall of 1927, the Brotherhood had helped produce a substantial reorientation for both Randolph and the Garland Fund. Where Randolph had once endorsed the wild-eyed IWW, now he waded in the main currents of the American labor movement. To be sure, mass mobilizing remained crucial; Randolph and his comrades planned "a big, monster mass meeting" to take place even as their legal strategy unfolded. But Randolph and the porters sought the kind of legitimacy and authority that only more established labor institutions, despite their glaring racial exclusions, could deliver.[65]

More importantly in the near term, the new unionist ideas of the American Fund circle had combined with the Brotherhood's experience under federal labor relations law to turn Randolph's strategic vision toward the opportunities afforded by the state. Randolph had once protested the "entire warp and woof and fabric of American law"; he had scorned the law for its "spirit of inequality, injustice, and prejudiced administration." By the mid-1920s, however, he was fast becoming a champion of law and the state as tools of self-advancement and organizing. The "civil rights of an individual," he now insisted, might be rooted in social mobilization, but they would need to manifest "through law, legislation, executive orders, ordinances and court decisions." And where once he had pressed for revolution, now the special double problem of race and class led him back to his characteristic incrementalism. "The Negro's present plight," he later explained, required staying alert to the long-term goal of what he called "social justice" even as the immediate fight for "racial justice" proceeded. As if to mark the new attitude, *The Messenger*'s pages embraced the gradualism of the British Fabian socialists, Sidney and Beatrice Webb, whose latest book appeared in the magazine's reviews section. And he developed a new incremental view of change in history. Tactics such as the Interstate Commerce Commission petition would "so strengthen us," as Brotherhood official Milton Webster wrote to Randolph in September, "that the next step will not be so difficult." Randolph concurred: "we can't plant a seed and have it flower tomorrow; we must continue to nourish that seed with water in order to reap and enjoy the fruit in the future." As he later explained it, "every historical epoch has its roots in a preceding epoch." The "New Negro radicals" of the day "stood upon the shoulders of the civil rights fighters of the Reconstruction era." They, in turn, "stood upon the shoulders of the black abolitionists." Each generation built piece by piece on the work of another. "These are the interconnections of history," Randolph explained.[66]

The Garland Fund had changed, too. Directors who had voted to stop supporting what they had referred to as "Work for the Negro" in August 1925 now reversed their view in light of Randolph's successes with a group that had previously been resistant to unionization. At a nadir for American labor, Randolph and his comrades made progress in helping "open the way," as he put it, to unionizing the more than 100,000 "unorganized colored workers" on the railroads, not to mention the "hundreds of thousands of workers of the same race in other industries." As Randolph observed to the Fund, organized labor had shown a "general attitude" of hostility on the part "of the masses of our white fellow citizens toward the Negro." The "unorganized Negro worker," he continued, had famously been put to use "by the employing interest of the country," which was "eager to break down the standards of life" organized labor sought to establish. As Roy Lancaster, a senior figure among the porters, told Johnson in October, the Brotherhood's successes would help wake up "the entire Negro race to a realization of the need of economic organization as the first requisite to a solution of the so-called Negro problem." Victory for the porters might even awaken racist white labor unions to the new militancy of the Black working class. The day was at hand, Lancaster celebrated, "when the Negro race will no longer be labeled 'the scabs' of American labor."[67]

In September 1927, when the Interstate Commerce Commission determined that the Brotherhood's complaint had sufficient merit to move ahead, Randolph and the porters seemed on the cusp of success. Two federal agencies—the Railway Labor Board and now the commerce commission—had recognized the legitimacy of the all-Black union he had helped to create barely two years before. The progressive unionists around the Garland Fund had offered their support. The giant AFL seemed poised to sweep the Brotherhood into its powerful fold.[68]

And then it all very nearly collapsed, for Randolph and for the Fund alike.

A Quitter Never Wins

Randolph's position was far more precarious than his encouraging words to the porters let on. The tipping petition to the Interstate Commerce Commission was a long shot at best, and one that was unpopular among porters skeptical that eliminating the passenger tips on which they relied would redound to their benefit. In early March, the commission dismissed the Brotherhood's complaint. "We are referred to no law which prohibits tipping of Pullman porters," explained the commission majority. In his public reactions, Randolph tried to emphasize the dissenting opinion signed by three commissioners. But the outcome, he later admitted, tasted like "the bitter fruit of disappointment."[69]

As a last resort, Randolph turned to the never before used Emergency Board provision of the Railway Labor Act, which aimed to prevent service interruptions on the nation's railroads. Randolph told the porters that the Emergency Board provision would force Pullman to "bow to the verdict of law and reason." No less an authority than Richberg, who had authored the provision, assured him it would be possible. "Our immediate program," Randolph wrote in *The Messenger*, "is to proceed with the creation of an emergency." Doing so, however, required credibly threatening a work stoppage capable of bringing trains to a halt. In April, Randolph informed the Mediation Board that more than 6,000 porters—over half the entire workforce—had authorized the union to call a strike. But Edwin P. Morrow at the federal Mediation Board determined that this was not enough. The board, he explained, would not recommend to President Calvin Coolidge that he appoint an Emergency Board until the porters actually walked off the job.[70]

The board's posture put Randolph in a bind. As the Pullman Company suspected, and as Morrow surmised, Randolph had grave doubts about how many porters would really strike when doing so meant putting their jobs at risk. Running out of alternatives, a desperate Randolph announced a strike date of June 8 and called in all the support he could muster. Allies like James Weldon Johnson telegraphed the Mediation Board urging appointment of an Emergency Board to avert the strike threat. The Pullman Company persuaded Morrow, however, that the strike threat was a sham and that no more than 600 of the 12,000 porters would walk off the job. No real emergency loomed.[71]

His bluff called, Randolph turned to William Green, who took over the giant AFL and its Jim Crow unions after Samuel Gompers's death in 1924. Randolph now asked the labor leader to help his union save face. Would Green write a letter, Randolph asked, advising that "conditions were not favorable" and recommending that the strike be put off? Such a missive would serve as cover for the Brotherhood. Pulling back from the strike would be costly, but Randolph was sure that a strike effort would destroy the union he had spent three years building. Green agreed. He wrote the public letter Randolph requested. Randolph, in turn, called off the porters' strike.[72]

The results were as dire for the Brotherhood as they were humiliating for Randolph. The Mediation Board's decision, he lamented, had "created a let-down and widespread gloom among the porters." The legislation on which he had relied had turned out, in his words, "to have no tooth in it." Without an agenda for the porters' next move, *The Messenger* ceased publication. Internal bickering at the porters union broke out into charges and countercharges of incompetence and even embezzlement. The editors at the Black newspaper the *New York Age* dismissed Randolph as a charlatan. ("A. Piffle Randolph," they called him.) Communist critics accused Randolph of selling out to the counterrevolutionary, whites-only AFL. Membership in the Brotherhood plummeted. From as many as 7,300 members in late 1927, the union's ranks fell by half in 1929. By 1933, Randolph counted only 658 members. The hope that the porters would rally Black labor seemed dead.[73]

Yet despair was premature. The perpetually energetic Randolph thought so, anyway. "A winner," he liked to say, "never quits and a quitter never wins." For all the frustrations of 1928, Randolph's Brotherhood had persuaded well-placed people at the American Fund that civil rights efforts and labor organizing were complementary rather than rivalrous. This was no small thing. Without support for the Brotherhood of Sleeping Car Porters, the man who became a great leader for Black emancipation and economic equality might have fallen out of public life. The March on Washington Movement of World War Two would not have proceeded, nor would the March on Washington of 1963, at least not in the same way; Randolph led the former and helped create the latter. Without the American Fund, the Brotherhood, which a decade later would become the nation's flagship Black labor union, might have suffocated. And without the Brotherhood, the Fund's assault on Jim Crow, with its controversial project of school equalization, might never have begun.[74]

W. E. B. Du Bois, Nina Du Bois, and
James Weldon Johnson (left to right) in 1930.

15

Millennia Don't Just Happen

*The largest group of unorganized workers in America . . .
are in the twelve millions of colored people.*
— THE AMERICAN FUND'S COMMITTEE
ON NEGRO WORK, 1929

For a moment, it seemed like the Fund's accounts would run dry before it had the chance to regroup from Randolph's defeat.

Across the first four full years of its operation, the American Fund had given away nearly $800,000 and made an additional half a million dollars in loans, most of which was still outstanding. By the beginning of 1927, the Fund's pledges of future support to organizations like Brookwood Labor College and the publishing house Vanguard Press exceeded its liquid assets by $120,000. And so the Fund began preparations to wind down. A "tapering-off" committee prepared a plan for staged reductions in the support for existing beneficiaries like Federated Press and the Brotherhood of Sleeping Car Porters, as well as for legal defense efforts by the ACLU and the NAACP, the IWW's General Defense Committee, and the Communist-backed International Labor Defense. The tapering committee paid special attention to gradually weaning the Workers' Health Bureau, an organization closely connected to the International Ladies' Garment Workers Union and dedicated to developing a health program for the labor movement. Applications from new organizations, the Fund decided, would no longer be entertained.[1]

The directors seemed as exhausted as their coffers. The preternaturally optimistic Baldwin suffered from what his daughter, decades later, would call a period of "blackness or depression." Despairing for progressive and radical movements, Baldwin took a leave from the ACLU and spent most of 1927 on his trip through Europe and the Soviet Union. James Weldon Johnson remained active in Fund business, but took a leave of absence from the NAACP to concentrate on his writing. For her part, Flynn suffered a catastrophic sequence of blows. In 1925 she learned that her longtime lover, the anarchist Carlo Tresca, had been having an affair with her younger sister, Bina. A devastated Flynn tried to throw her energies into the textile workers' strike in Passaic, traveling to and from the city multiple times each week to rally the workers. The strike ended in demoralizing failure. Her campaign for Nicola Sacco and Bartolomeo Vanzetti had stalled; in August 1927, Massachusetts authorities would execute the two anarchists. Years of effort seemed to have come to nothing. It was too much. Traveling west on a speaking tour and exhausted by a half decade of futility and heartache, Flynn collapsed. A bacterial strep infection reached her heart. She nearly died.[2]

But if the end of the Fund seemed to have come into view, the stock market once again didn't see it, at least not yet. To the surprise and sometimes the amusement of the American Fund's directors, capitalism continued to generate new resources for its own subversion. In early 1927, the Fund's shares in the First National Bank of New York, which made up the largest portion of its assets, sold at $2,400 per share. Within a year, the share price had risen to $3,700. A year after that, in January 1929, shares sold for $5,300, and over the next nine months wild market exuberance propelled share prices to a peak of $8,050 per share, an astonishing growth of 335 percent over two and a half years, far greater than even the ballooning Dow Jones Industrial Average. "For a time," journalist Dwight Macdonald later quipped in the *New Yorker*, it looked as if Garland "would never be able to unburden himself of his wealth." Baldwin, recharged from his European tour, joked about the Fund's "new and ill-gotten wealth." Morris Ernst, the Fund's ebullient treasurer, cracked wise about the "dreary effects" of First National Bank's "unearned increments."[3]

By early 1928, Ernst estimated that the Fund would soon have more than $600,000 in discretionary funds after accounting for existing pledges. And so the directors of the American Fund opened a contentious debate about how to spend a new round of unexpected riches.[4]

At stake was a momentous proposal by James Weldon Johnson and the NAACP to spend the Fund's newly earned money on a legal campaign against Jim Crow. The proposed campaign promised to attack a wide array of white supremacist mechanisms in the American South, ranging from jury discrimination and voting rights, to segregation in public accommodations and housing. Its principal focus would be school equalization.[5]

A newly strengthened Communist wing of the Fund, however, objected. The Fund's left-most cohort charged that the NAACP put the formal appearance of equality over real fairness: legal equality rather than the actual thing itself. The Fund's progressive industrial democrats shared with their left-wing comrades a common commitment to economic emancipation and working-class mobilization. Both groups began with the same fundamental question. They both asked how it was possible to organize the working class in a nation divided by race. But the two factions offered rival answers. The Fund's progressives arrived at school equalization and civil rights to vindicate the efforts that had led them to support A. Philip Randolph's work for industrial democracy. The Fund's Communist bloc, by contrast, rallied behind a very different notion, a wild, implausible, impractical, infuriating, and astounding theory first articulated on the other side of the Atlantic by Lenin and then made into orthodox Soviet doctrine by Stalin. The NAACP's famous legal campaign against Jim Crow began in a great confrontation over the idea that a substantial part of the Deep South ought to be its own Black country.

The Black Belt

By 1928, the board had divided into warring camps—what the directors called left and right blocs.[6]

Still swerving left in the fellow-traveler posture he had adopted in his ill-measured book on civil liberties among the Soviets, Roger Baldwin increasingly aligned himself with a quietly growing Communist left on the Fund board. Scott Nearing, who had gone a step further than Baldwin and joined the Party in 1927, did the same. Nearing chafed at the centrist politics of the Fund's industrial democracy advocates. Temperament pushed him out of the Party before long; he could not abide ideological orthodoxy. But he remained solidly on the left of the Fund.[7]

Surreptitious tactics filled out the board's new left with more reliable Party believers. In 1926, William Foster announced that he would resign from the Fund board. The board's designated Communist had missed meetings repeatedly, and his unauthorized practice of sending Party functionaries to vote in his place had rankled others on the board. Relying on Foster's departure, the directors appointed Benjamin Gitlow, one of the original founders of the American branch of the Party and its vice presidential candidate in 1924 and again in 1928. Gitlow's role at the Fund was, in theory, to replace Foster as the Party member on the board. For convenience, though, the Fund placed him in a new seat pending Foster's departure. When Foster then reneged on his promise for nearly a year, he temporarily doubled the board's Communist faction. A year later, Robert W. Dunn, a veteran of Muste's American Textile Workers Union, joined the board to take a seat opened by the resignation of Robert Morss Lovett. Unbeknownst to most, but well understood by insiders Foster and Gitlow, Dunn had secretly joined the Party. Dunn's membership would not be known publicly until after his death in 1977, but in the meanwhile

William Z. Foster (left) and Ben Gitlow (right), the Communist candidates for president and vice president, at a Madison Square Garden campaign rally in 1928, during Gitlow's service on the Fund board and shortly after Foster had stepped down.

he reliably did the Party's bidding. The Communist contingent solidified its power in 1928 when the three Party members then on the board (Dunn, Gitlow, and Nearing) combined with Baldwin and Flynn to elect Clarina Michelson, a Boston heiress turned Communist functionary, to the seat finally opened by Foster's departure.[8]

The Fund suddenly had four members of the Communist Party. Adding Baldwin, and with Flynn participating remotely as she convalesced, the left wing of the Fund consisted of six people, which amounted to fully half the board after Fund director H. H. Broach—a close ally of Clinton Golden and a reliable vote for the Fund's industrial-democrat wing—stepped down in June 1928 to become president of the electrical workers union. For nearly a decade, "boring from within" had been Foster's preferred strategy for expanding Communist Party influence in progressive organizations. In a textbook instance of the gambit, the Party was now suddenly on the verge of capturing leadership of the Fund.[9]

The result was what Baldwin called a "fundamental antagonism" among board members. Fund director Freda Kirchwey felt herself caught between the obstreperous opposition of the Communists, on the one hand, and "peeved" liberals on the other, who were annoyed that she did not vote in lockstep with them. The rift, which Ernst described as a "bloc system" on the board, now haunted the organization's deliberations and threatened its most basic operations. Thomas complained that the "Communist bloc" voted "as a unit" and obstructed the board's deliberations. When Broach resigned, his seat went unfilled because the board was too badly split to agree on a new director. Rancor prevented the filling of open seats in 1929 and in 1931, too. The Fund's partisan split meant that Michelson would be the last director ever appointed to the organization.[10]

The root of the problem was not inside the board. The difficulty, as Baldwin observed, was external. Even as the exuberant stock market delivered an unexpected windfall, internecine Communist struggles 5,000 miles away in Moscow threatened to pull the Fund apart.[11]

The first clue that Soviet battles would cause collateral damage in the American Fund came at Passaic, the strike whose collapse had been such a blow for the ailing Flynn. The strike had broken out when 15,000 barely organized textile workers shut down the spinning machines in the city's woolen mills after a 10 percent wage reduction. Adopting the official Party strategy of a "united front from below," a Communist group led by an immigrant and recent Harvard Law School graduate named Albert Weisbord swooped in to support the strikers. Working closely with Flynn, Weisbord's United Front Committee combined with the American Fund to make the strike into what was, for its time, the high point of the Fund's heterodox, new unionist approach to labor action. Passaic workers struck not by trades but as an amalgamated, mass-production industrial union. A. J. Muste and carloads of students from Brookwood Labor College created a strike relief fund, organized a clothing drive, and urged nonviolence, putting Brookwood theory into practice. Sidney Hillman's Amalgamated Clothing Workers lined up behind the strikers and contributed 20,000 pounds of food relief. The Garland Fund approved loans and appropriations of more than $30,000 for strike relief, publicity, research, and legal defense, with Flynn serving as a go-between with the strikers. Flynn arranged the Fund grant for the innovative silent film *The Passaic Textile Strike*, combining fictionalized melodrama with documentary footage. In May 1927, the directors made available an additional $60,000 to provide a bail fund for strikers arrested on the picket lines. Further sums paid the salary of an organizer and underwrote the ACLU's legal defense of the picketers. The Garland Fund supported a study of the striking workers' health and paid for a survey of the Passaic textile industry by William Jett Lauck, one of the labor economists who had just finished a similar report for the Pullman porters.[12]

Suddenly, word from Moscow dismantled the strike. The Communist International decided that Weisbord's United Front Committee had violated the Party's cardinal rule against dual unionism. Ever since its Second Congress in 1921, the Comintern had instructed its American subsidiary that revolution would best be advanced by working with existing unions. Moscow now decided that this meant operating within the AFL-affiliated United Textile Workers. Soviet officials ordered the strike leadership in New Jersey to stand down and to turn the strike over to the weak, barely existent local UTW. Weisbord reluctantly complied and the UTW rapidly capitulated to the city's employers for nothing more than an informal assurance that wages might be restored on a piecemeal basis. The city's mills quickly fired the most militant of the strikers. "Passaic was great while it lasted," Flynn mourned, but now that it was over, it was "hard to know when" there would be another opportunity like it. The whole experience, she told a friend, left her "tired and empty."[13]

Matters worsened the next year, in 1928, when the Sixth Congress of the Communist International renounced the united front line that Comintern officials had just enforced against Weisbord and Flynn. Announcing that a "revolutionary upsurge" was about to accompany a new "third period" in the history of postwar capitalism, the Comintern declared that the united front line was out and that dual unionism (the strikers' sin at Passaic just two years before) was back in. Separate partisan organizations pursuing a sectarian Communist Party program were now the order of the day. In Russia, the 1928 about-face served Stalin's ruthless ascent to power; the move helped him condemn his rival Nikolai Bukharin for deviating to the right. But across a continent and an ocean, the new doctrine hit the Fund's left wing as an object not from Marx but from Mars.[14]

Ironies abounded. From the moment of the Fund's formation, critics had accused it of being a creature of Soviet communism. Such charges, which would continue for decades after the Fund's work was over, were badly exaggerated. For its first six years, the Fund had been dominated by a progressive center made up of anti-Communist socialists like Norman Thomas, eclectic leftists like Baldwin, and non-Communist new unionists from Sidney Hillman's world. The directors had financed some Communist-run projects, to be sure. More often, Party-sponsored projects ran into resistance from directors in the Fund's progressive center, which often included the liberal editors Lewis Gannett and Freda Kirchwey. Yet now, as the Fund prepared to spend its stock market windfall, partisan machinations echoed deadly Party struggles in Moscow. The new Comintern line, and its hard turn to the left, blocked the Fund from being able to make decisions one way or another.[15]

While serving on the American Fund board, Foster and Gitlow shuttled back and forth to Soviet Russia, competing as rivals for the favoritism of the congresses and plenums that made official Communist policy for affiliated parties around the world. Foster had returned from Moscow shortly before the Fund was opened in 1922. He went again in 1925, staying this time for four months. Gitlow traveled to Russia in the spring of 1927. Foster was there again in 1928 when Stalin launched the final stages of his seizure of power, returning to the United States to implement the Communist International's new order that affiliated parties renounce their erstwhile allies in social democratic and trade union circles in favor of the new hard line. The next year, in 1929, Gitlow returned to Moscow yet again in an unsuccessful effort to gain the Soviets' continued support, only to find that this time he had been tagged for counterrevolutionary deviations from the Party line.[16]

The new hard policy dealt a sharp blow to the political alliances of the American Fund world. Across the left, Party members broke with the innovative labor institutions that counted themselves among the Fund's principal beneficiaries. Foster complied with the new orthodoxy even though it contradicted the boring from within tactics he had espoused since the Pittsburgh steel strike in 1919—tactics he had used to good effect at the American Fund itself. Gitlow followed the new line, at least for a time, despite his ouster from the Party. Socialist labor institutions like Brookwood were now anathema to the Communists. Progressive unions of the kind that drew support from the Fund were now right-wing errors. Party members quit the progressive caucus of the United Mine Workers and split bitterly with Hillman's Amalgamated Clothing Workers. For those hewing to the Party line, cooperation with the social democrats, progressives, and liberals of the American Fund was now out of the question. Failure to walk in lockstep with the latest diktat from the Soviets meant betrayal of the revolution, or so said the apparatchiks.[17]

No issue put the new Soviet line in sharper relief than Stalin's 1928 policy on the Black working class—and none created as acute a problem on the American Fund board. For years, American organizers in the Party had urged Black workers to "force open the union doors" at AFL-affiliated trade unions. Communists had endorsed the fight against lynching alongside groups like the NAACP. Now, however, the Communist International's Sixth World Congress swerved to adopt a theory pressed by Stalin and embraced by his loyalists. Black America, theorized the Comintern, was not an oppressed *racial* minority—it was "an oppressed *national* minority." To an outsider, the difference might have seemed slight. But within the Party the implications were crucial. "The Party," as the Comintern's

Executive Committee put it, "must come out openly and unreservedly for the right of Negroes to national self-determination in the southern states." In the slogan that soon emerged, the Party would support the "right of self-determination of the Negroes of the Black Belt."[18]

The Black Belt thesis, which applied to a sickle-shaped region stretching from Virginia south and west to Texas, was disastrously ill-conceived—even "suicidal," as W. E. B. Du Bois put it. There was, to be sure, an intermittent tradition of Black nationalist separatism in the United States. Marcus Garvey had led its latest and most grandiose iteration just a few years before. But Garvey had always been divisive among Black American radicals, and in any event, as the closest observers noted, mass migration to the North was undermining the demographics on which the Black Belt thesis relied.[19]

The five Black delegates from the United States at the Sixth Congress were all veterans of A. Philip Randolph's world of Harlem radicalism. Now in Moscow in 1928, all but one objected to the extravagant self-determination thesis. Objections, however, were pointless at best and deadly at worst. When Lovett Fort-Whiteman, one of the Black delegates

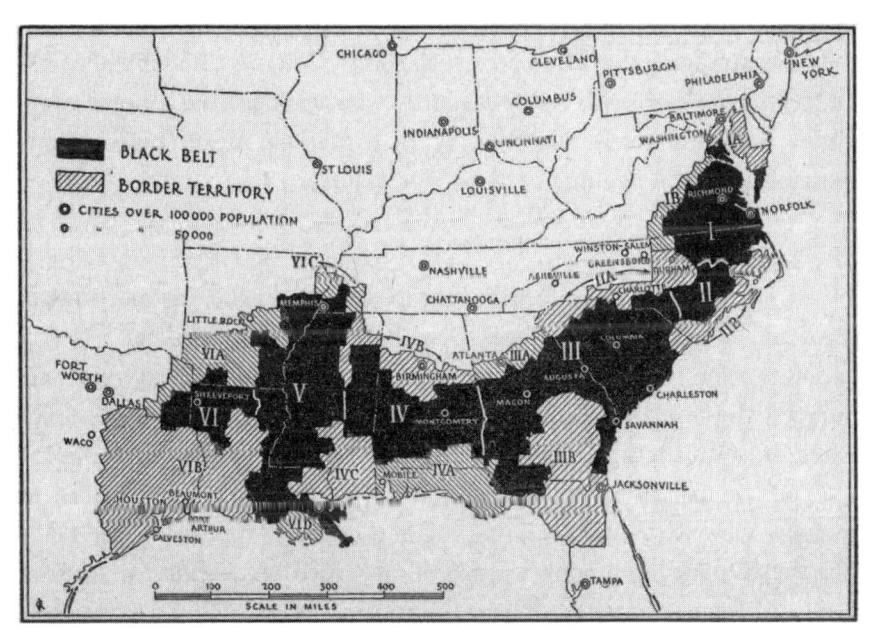

The Black Belt as drawn by the Comintern in 1928.

to the Sixth Congress and head of the Party-backed American Negro Labor Congress, resisted the new orthodoxy, Soviet authorities stripped him of his leadership posts. Continued objection led Soviet authorities to put Fort-Whiteman on trial for counterrevolutionary agitation, where he was sentenced to a life of internal exile, dying of starvation and blunt force trauma in a Siberian labor camp in 1939. An influential Black member of the Party named James Ford, who may later have had a role in betraying Fort-Whiteman's counterrevolutionary heresy to authorities, spluttered when he first heard the 1928 Black Belt policy. The self-determination thesis "would be of great importance" if the Party "had any serious contact with the Negro masses and any influence among them," he complained. But because "we have practically no Negro party members," Ford doubted the value of the idea. Ford estimated that there were merely fifty Black members out of a total Party membership in the United States of 15,000. Gitlow's ally Jay Lovestone, who led the American branch of the Party, observed that the Comintern thesis would keep it from increasing its numbers among Black Americans. When Gitlow complained, however, an ally at the Sixth Congress warned him that those not falling "in line" would be "severely condemned as deviators" and accused of "neglecting work among the Negro masses." Sure enough, the Party faithful expelled him from his leadership position for traitorous right-wing deviations. In the Russian saying that circulated at the Sixth Congress, dissenters would be treated as "*khvostists*"—the laggards who walk behind a horse's tail. Gitlow had little notion what the cryptic expression meant, but everyone understood that it couldn't be good.[20]

When Dunn, Gitlow, Michelson, and Nearing appeared at meetings of the Fund in late 1929, the Black Belt thesis of Black self-determination had swept the field on the Communist left. The Fund's Party members pursued the line and adopted the new intransigent tactics of the Sixth Congress with the single-minded relentlessness that was rapidly making the Party notorious among liberals and on the left. Nearing signed on to the new view with the special fervor of a convert, appending the Black Belt thesis to his latest book, a study of race titled *Black America*. Most of Nearing's book (printed in 1929 by the Fund's Vanguard Press) advanced a forceful if unoriginal account of the economics of racism in America. But

Nearing's introduction embraced the self-determination thesis, describing "the subject race of more than twelve million American Negroes" as suffering from the same form of colonial oppression as Filipinos and the peoples of Latin American countries. In the South, Nearing awkwardly contended, Jim Crow made the United States an imperial power.[21]

The analogy might have been more effective if more Black workers in the South had desired independence, or if self-determination wouldn't also have entailed separation from the huge wealth of the United States (wealth to which Black Americans had contributed untold sums under slavery and after). The American Fund's entire left wing nonetheless dedicated itself to supporting the Communists' new efforts. Hastily formed front groups arose to fulfill Moscow's sudden turn against cooperating with established unions. The organizations were essentially empty shells, with few if any members. But they deluged the Fund with applications seeking support for wildly ambitious programs to organize Black workers. The so-called National Textile Workers' Union approached the Fund about a major campaign to organize mills in the South, promising to concentrate on Negro organizers and asking for $26,000. A National Industrial Auto Workers Union appeared three days later, asking for $15,000 and assuring the Fund that it would pursue equality for Negro workers.[22]

The left wing of the board finally pressed the Fund into action when the Communists' new textile union commenced a clumsy organizing effort in Gastonia, North Carolina. At the giant Loray Mill, which employed 3,500 workers, scientific management techniques had combined with grueling hours, bad conditions, and low wages to set the textile workforce on edge. After management fired one-third of its workforce while aiming to maintain production levels through what workers called "the stretch out," a strike began. The Party-backed NTWU raced to the scene, led in part by Alfred Weisbord from the Passaic strike. But Weisbord and other organizers ran headlong into the refusal of white workers to make common cause with Black ones. (An artless rope separating the union hall into white and colored sections aimed to split the difference between Moscow's insistence on racial integration and the racist attitudes of local whites.) The strike stumbled—until the inept vengefulness of the police gave the bungling strike organizers a new cause. A picket-line clash on June 7, 1929, led to a shoot-out that left striker Ella May Wiggins and chief of police Orville Aderholt dead.[23]

In the murder prosecution of sixteen strikers that followed, the Communist-run International Labor Defense harkened back to Elaine, Arkansas, in 1919, to Sacco and Vanzetti outside Boston in 1921, and to Ossian Sweet in Detroit in 1925. The organizers on trial, they insisted, were the latest labor martyrs. The American Fund, for its part, delivered $20,000 for the trial and subsequent appeals. When all sixteen defendants (thirteen men and three women) were convicted of murder, the Fund provided additional bail money for their release pending appeal, only to lose most of it ($28,000 in all) when five of the convicted strikers jumped bail on a ship to Europe, heading to the Soviet Union.[24]

The forfeited bail money, combined with irregularities in the use of American Fund money by ILD lawyers, infuriated the Fund's non-Communist progressives and led them to oppose a barrage of new grant applications sponsored by the Party faithful. Dunn and Michelson submitted a recommendation for financing new, non-AFL unions affiliated with William Z. Foster's Trade Union Unity League (itself a clumsy remaking for the Comintern's new position of Foster's old Trade Union Educational League). Baldwin pressed James Weldon Johnson to support a proposal from A. Philip Randolph's old Harlem rival Cyril Briggs at the Communist-backed American Negro Labor Congress, a group that promised "militant mass Negro organization . . . under the leadership of the Negro proletariat." Party official J. Louis Engdahl, one of the architects of the Black Belt self-determination thesis, submitted an implausibly ambitious proposal for a long-term civil rights project in the Black community. In different circumstances, the Fund's progressives might have welcomed a new campaign in what Engdahl called "the struggle against lynching, segregation, discrimination, Jim Crowism, and other forms of white oppression against the Negro workers and farmers in the United States." But Engdahl's front organization, like Briggs's Congress, did not even begin to have the institutional capacity to carry out the struggles it proposed. Meanwhile, Nearing lobbed Party-supported attacks at the Fund's industrial democracy efforts for being insufficiently militant.[25]

That so few of the Party's late 1920s proposals received support was due in part to the costly flight of the fugitive Communists at Gastonia. But it was also due to the persistent progressive core of the Fund board, which combined increasingly hard-earned outrage at the Party's unreliable antics with a powerful alternative vision of cross-race labor organizing.

Gathering a bare majority of the directors, the progressive wing of the Fund designed a project that was mindful of the Pullman porters' experience, perhaps even a little chastened by A. Philip Randolph's ongoing struggles. Theirs would be an institutional effort to gain the rights Black workers needed, and the capacities they would require, to defend their own organizing in the mass-production world. In contrast to their Party-affiliated comrades, the Fund's progressives set out to develop a project that would reflect nearly a decade of experience in democratic labor organizing under the actually existing conditions of modern America.

A Revolution in Economic Life

Despite the surreptitious increase in its Communist membership, the Fund board still boasted a majority coalition of liberals, socialists, and industrial democrats. Now dubbed the "right wing" of the Fund by Gitlow and others, the Fund's old guard would have been squarely on the left almost anywhere else in the United States. The group included columnist Lewis Gannett, who had only recently left the staff of *The Nation* magazine, and who served on the executive board of the League for Industrial Democracy, where Norman Thomas held the post of codirector. Clinton Golden of the Brookwood faculty and the Amalgamated Clothing Workers remained on the Fund's board. So did Freda Kirchwey, whose editorial work at *The Nation* often featured the new unionism.[26]

Yet the margins for the Fund's social democratic majority had deteriorated even as its Communist wing grew. Hillman was long gone. His replacement, the labor economist Leo Wolman, had stepped down, too, and when Wolman's successor H. H. Broach departed to lead the electrical workers, the original Hillman seat lay empty. For a time, Flynn had developed into a reliable vote for heterodox new unionist efforts, much to the frustration of her sometime comrades on the left. But poor health diminished her influence. In 1929, nursing her spirits in Portland, Oregon, Flynn resigned from the board altogether. Baldwin, who had once been an enthusiastic supporter of the Brookwood circle, had swerved left. Golden remained a stalwart Brookwood supporter, but as field director for the school he spent increasing amounts of time out of town recruiting students.[27]

It fell to Morris Ernst to rally the Fund's faltering majority and co-opt the energy of the Black Belt thesis for the Fund's core project of industrial democracy. It was Ernst—the director most outraged by the ILD's support for the Gastonia bail jumpers—who emerged as the tactician for the American Fund's progressive center.[28]

Appointed treasurer in 1923, and serving as a director since 1925, Ernst had been born in 1888 to a German Jewish merchant family in Alabama. His parents relocated when he was a small child to New York, where Ernst grew up at the margins of the city's Jewish elite. He was small in stature, standing five feet six inches. But he made up for his size with what he called a "glandular optimism." At a time when Harvard imposed strict quotas on Jewish applicants, the powers in Cambridge turned Ernst away, claiming that he had failed the entrance examinations. (Ernst kept the rejection letter as inspiration for the rest of his life.) Upon graduating from his second-choice school, Williams, he used money from an uncle to establish a small Brooklyn-based shirt-making company, which he sold for a profit before taking a job as a manager in a midsized furniture manufacturing firm with connections to his wife's family.[29]

Mid-level business jobs barely engaged Ernst's prodigious energies. In 1910, he enrolled in the night program at New York Law School, where he found his calling. After graduating in 1912 and establishing a firm with two other young Jewish lawyers, Ernst won the Retail Jewelers' Association of Greater New York as a client. The National Jewelers Board of Trade soon hired him to serve as its general counsel. Before long he was doing lucrative work representing dozens of small businesses (most of them Jewish-owned) in the city's diamond district. Commercial law supplied an income, but it too failed to exhaust Ernst's capacities. He soon began advising Roger Baldwin on ACLU-related problems. The two men made an unusual match. Ernst called the frugal Baldwin "the dictator" and joked that the more abstemious man had attended the "hair-shirt school." Baldwin described Ernst—who was a regular at the 21 Club and at the Algonquin Hotel's boozy literary salons—as a "hail-fellow" man of "enormous nervous energy." Their common indefatigability united them, however, and Ernst soon became the lawyer for Garland Fund–affiliated publications like the socialist-inclined *Labor Age* of the Brookwood circle and the increasingly Communist-influenced *New Masses*. He served as counsel to the Fund's publisher, Vanguard Press, as well as liberal-progressive magazines such as *The Nation*, the *New Republic*, and the *New Yorker*. He successfully defended Fund beneficiaries Mary Ware Dennett and Margaret Sanger against criminal indictments when their birth control work resulted in prosecutions under New York's nineteenth-century laws on sex education and reproductive health.[30]

What made Ernst so valuable as a lawyer to ambitious ethnic businessmen of the jewelry trade and left-liberal activists alike was that he had little reverence for law as such. Lawlessness, he believed, was the real American way, notwithstanding the customary nostrums to the contrary from the Chamber of Commerce and the bar associations. The pure American types, he wrote, were not lawyers, nor even law men, but instead "the Gambler, the Competitor," and "the Rugged Individual." Such figures defied the law, Ernst observed, rather than "meekly submit" to "the sanctity of a legal halo." As Ernst saw it, Walter Lippmann's theory of the taboo—the idea that censorship laws were clumsy and counterproductive—stood for a general point. Americans, Ernst insisted, were not "overawed by laws." The Constitution was not sacred; it was, rather, a "declaration of an adventure with life."[31]

Adventure, above all, was the thing. In Ernst's practice, he was a risk-taking operator with little interest in the fine points of procedure. His most famous cases, beginning in the late 1920s, turned attention-getting risks into big rewards, both for clients and for Ernst himself. Ernst designed a creative mechanism by which cash-strapped publishers could retain him to defend books against censorship on obscenity charges. Publishers would pay him a share of the proceeds for every book sold—but only if he won. In 1932, he arranged for publication by Random House of a book that had been banned in the United States. Its author was an Irish writer named James Joyce and the book's title was *Ulysses*. In return for a contingent royalty on each copy sold, Ernst defended the book against the censors. He won—and earned riches and a modicum of fame for the rest of his life.[32]

Paying clients allowed Ernst to turn his law practice into what he called "a Robin Hood venture," using lucrative cases to subsidize his work on liberal causes. For Ernst in the 1920s, that usually meant labor cases.[33]

Given that "labor was the essential contributor to wealth," Ernst once wrote, those who did the work ought to "have a sort of first claim on the income of the land." Yet in the modern world, the opposite seemed closer to the truth. A "few of the people," he continued, "own most of the machines and the oil wells." The United States, Ernst noted, had become the richest nation on earth—but it also seemed to have "the longest breadlines." Most gallingly, the giant industrial firms of the American economy operated openly, even brazenly, as outright autocracies, dominating the lives of millions of working people while denying them a say in basic decisions.[34]

The beginning of a solution presented itself for Ernst in 1920, when he represented New York–area silk manufacturers in negotiations with striking workers belonging to A. J. Muste's Amalgamated Textile Workers

Morris Ernst, the lawyer who navigated the Fund's NAACP litigation grant through the badly split board of directors.

Union. Fresh off his startling success in Lawrence, Muste pressed not only for wages and working conditions but also for institutional mechanisms that would give the union a voice in the firm's operations. In a landmark agreement to end the strike, Muste and Ernst established a joint trade council, made up of both employees and managers, which was empowered to establish labor standards for the industry. The agreement, moreover, adopted a system of labor arbitration by which the silk manufacturers and Muste's union agreed to resolve their disputes.[35]

For Ernst, the promise of deals like the 1920 silk agreement lay not so much in the particulars of its wage and hour arrangements but in their vision of a mass-production economy in which workers and unions had a say. Here was the kind of innovative industrial democracy arrangement pioneered by Hillman's Amalgamated Clothing Workers. The idea was to create institutions like arbitration and the trade council that could channel workers' voices, serving as democratic opening wedges into the power wielded by the large-scale firms of the modern world.

Within the year, Ernst switched sides to represent Muste's ATW and other progressive industrial unions in pounding out arbitration and trade council arrangements with the textile firms that had once been his clients. Ernst's work for the ATW aimed for what, echoing Hillman's circle of labor intellectuals, he called "industrial peace." Industrial arbitration seemed to him, as it had seemed to Hillman and Muste, to hold out the promise of a novel participatory mode of social organization: a way of refashioning democracy for the age of managers and giant industrial corporations. Writing in the *Columbia Law Review* in 1921, Ernst argued that old institutions like the courts and the common law were badly outmoded for the challenges of the modern world. Procedural delay, litigation expenses, lack of expertise, and hostility toward labor doomed old-fashioned judges to irrelevance or worse. Instead, Ernst championed a system of impartial arbitrators ("chairmen," he called them) to be jointly selected by employees and employers. Parallel legislative bodies like the trade council of the silk industry contract of 1920 would settle basic questions of trade policy. The crucial innovation was to undo employers' autocratic control over industry.[36]

As Ernst saw it, a new democratic peace in labor relations would be part of a more "general movement" of the age that was "wiping out" certain antisocial private property rights in the name of the collective good.

Workmen's compensation statutes, inheritance taxes, excess profit taxes, tenement house regulations, and rent control laws—each of these progressive institutions substituted what Ernst called "industrial rights" for the old power of private property.[37]

When asked what drew him to connect the cause of industrial democracy to the rights of Black people, Ernst cited his Judaism. "I was tagged as a member of a minority group," he recalled, and "this made me identify with people pushed around." The explanation, however, only went so far. It was closer to the truth to say that industrial democracy commitments gave Ernst and his progressive colleagues at the American Fund a distinctive vantage on the value of civil rights work.[38]

Ernst had first given sustained thought to the special burdens of Black workers while serving with James Weldon Johnson on the Fund committee charged with supporting A. Philip Randolph's efforts for the Pullman porters. Ernst appeared at Randolph's rallies in the early months of the campaign. Soon he was a regular speaker at porters' events. Randolph even made Ernst an honorary member of the Brotherhood of Sleeping Car Porters, one of few white people to earn the privilege. "I still cherish my honorary membership card," he wrote a Brotherhood official a decade later.[39]

The Pullman porters' experience led progressives around the Fund to be skeptical of separatist strategies of racial uplift. Marcus Garvey's entanglements with the Klan had persuaded Randolph years before the Black Belt thesis emerged that separatism was a treacherous compromise with Jim Crow. The Pullman problem confirmed it. Even in a virtually all-Black workforce like the porters, racial division had hampered organizing. Animosity from the all-white conductors' union undermined the porters' efforts; further tensions with the all-white railroad brotherhoods exacerbated the situation. But if racial rifts plagued the porters union, workforces made up of people from different races suffered more acutely. For industrial unions, in particular, which organized across different occupations, interracial solidarity was indispensable. Industrial unions needed to be able to organize the highly skilled artisan aristocrats (mostly white) together with the unskilled workers (disproportionately Black). Unions that were exclusively white, Randolph admonished, offered merely the "illusion of strength and security," and they could not even begin to accomplish the industry-wide coverage that increasingly seemed vital. White workers would only be able to unionize successfully if they were in solidarity with the Black workers who could replace them. "Negro workers as strike breakers," Randolph said, were the fatal flaw of the whites-only approach to organized labor.[40]

For Black workers, segregated labor unions almost always lacked what Randolph called the "contact and influence" to deliver good jobs, leaving them with the dirtiest and most dangerous work in an industry. Separate Jim Crow unions for Black labor, Randolph added, attached a "stigma of racial inferiority to Negro workers." Segregation was an "affront" to the "sense of self-respect" of Black workers, establishing a "category of second-class trade union membership." Randolph contended that "Negro workers would suffer" if they tried to stand alone. They would be helpless before the "economic juggernauts" of the modern economy.[41]

By the mid-1920s, much of radical Harlem had come to see Jim Crow not merely as a manifestation of racial hatreds (the conventional old NAACP view), and not exclusively as a smokescreen for the underlying economic interests of capital (the socialist view). Theirs was a view that linked interracial solidarity to labor unity but identified each as significant in its own right. Black socialist organizer Frank Crosswaith attributed the weakness of the American labor movement to what he called the "tragedy of segregation." In Randolph's similar view, overcoming racial subordination was a vital step toward labor strength. If "the principle of social equality" was part of the Black emancipation project, he argued, it was a crucial labor goal, too. "We desire," he wrote in 1923, "as much contact and intercourse—social, economic and political—as is possible between the races." The point, he was quick to add, was not a "belief in the inferiority or superiority of either race." Nor was the goal integration for its own sake, or even the elimination of racism. The goal of integrated unions and contact across race lines was to give labor a democratic voice, which was, Randolph insisted, "the only sure guarantee of social progress."[42]

Randolph connected civil rights to the problem of industrial democracy when he applied his ideas about contact to the question of school equality. Writing in *The Messenger*, Randolph described racial segregation in the schools as a strategy of class division. Jim Crow in education, he wrote, "prevented the unity of class." Segregation in public schools, he continued, was "in the interests of the segregator." A version of this point was conventional in socialist thinking at the time, even clichéd. Capitalism's institutions supported the interests of owners. But Randolph added a new dimension. Drawing on the literature on social psychology and herd behavior he found so interesting, Randolph reasoned that imitation and sociability were wellsprings of modern social life. A principal problem with segregation was that it cut off the masses of Black people from the great bulk of the white population, interrupting the social interactions necessary for the formation of habits of reciprocal imitation. Segregation, Randolph concluded, was thus "a direct blow at the very life of the race," since economic opportunity could "only be achieved through contact." At the same time, segregation inured to the economic disadvantage of all working people, regardless of race; its effect was to prevent the "laboring masses" from combining "for the achievement of a common benefit."[43]

As treasurer, Ernst was the first on the American Fund board to see that the Fund would have more resources than anyone had expected. Ernst had tended not to assert himself in the Fund's operations, but he was only biding his time. The standard operating procedure of the Fund, as he saw it, had been to make indiscriminate grants to virtually any application that garnered the support of one or two members of the board, often because of some personal connection or professional interest. The result, Ernst believed, had been a wasteful ad hockery, without a rational plan.[44]

With the new windfall, Ernst set out to reorganize the process by which the Fund distributed its largesse. Overriding Baldwin's suggestion that the Fund resume its earlier approach of entertaining applications from all comers, Ernst proposed that the Fund "adopt a definite policy" of its own. The board agreed, and for the first time, Ernst took up the reins as a leader of the Fund's increasingly narrow progressive majority.[45]

To navigate the Fund's warring blocs, Ernst devised an ingenious arrangement to sustain the power of the progressive caucus and to channel it into the kind of civil rights work that Randolph had pioneered. Ernst divided the board into committees (he sometimes called them subcommittees), each responsible for a distinct field of interest, and each empowered to spend a sum of money set aside by the full Fund board. At the May 1929 meeting, the board adopted a version of Ernst's plan. Without anyone on the left wing of the Fund noticing until it was too late, Ernst arranged for the Committee on Negro Work to operate more effectively than the others by making it the only subcommittee not split between the progressive and left-wing factions. Each of the other subcommittees reproduced the same structural divide that blocked the Fund's operations more generally. The Committee for Organizing the Unorganized was split down the middle, two-to-two, with social democrats Golden and Thomas set against the Party members Gitlow and Michelson. The Committee on Civil Liberties grouped Dunn and Michelson with their sometimes-ally Baldwin—but Ernst sat on the committee, too. The Labor Education Committee combined Golden and Kirchwey for the progressives with Nearing for the hard left. The committee overseeing the Fund's research on imperialism was a mass of contending factions: Dunn, Nearing, and Baldwin worked alongside liberals Gannett and Johnson.[46]

Alone among all the committees, the Committee on Negro Work was made up of members of the same faction: Ernst, Gannett, and Johnson, all three from the Fund's congenial, progressive core. Time and again in the 1920s, the Communists had outfoxed the liberals by boring from within and co-opting leftist organizations. But this time Ernst had outmaneuvered them. Thus composed, the committee swiftly seized the opportunity Ernst had created. Before the other committees had even met, Ernst and Johnson produced a report recommending a giant grant to the NAACP. If made, the grant promised to be twice the size of any gift the Fund had ever awarded. It would use fully half the Fund's unexpected stock market gains. Taking stock of the Fund's efforts to date, the report reviewed the Fund's halting attempts to jump-start the labor movement. It surveyed the group's work with Black organizations. And taking up Randolph's idea from the Brotherhood of Sleeping Car Porters, the committee proposed that these two projects—labor and civil rights—be combined into a single effort.[47]

Johnson was the June 1929 report's principal author. Working closely with Walter White at the NAACP, he opened with the observation that "the largest group of unorganized workers in America" was also "the most significant and at present most ineffective bloc of the producing class." Johnson's claim was that "the twelve million colored people" were a reserve army of the nonunionized. Thanks to Jim Crow and the ubiquitous lynch mob, this group had barely even begun to benefit from basic civil rights of speech and protest of the kind the ACLU defended for organized labor. "Civil liberties in the coal baronries"—places like Ludlow, Colorado, or the coal company towns of Pennsylvania and West Virginia—flourished "compared to civil liberties among the Negroes of the South." What followed from this fact, according to Johnson and White, is worth quoting in full: "the largest single contribution which this Fund could make to the release of the creative energies of the producing class in America would be to finance a large-scale, widespread, dramatic campaign to give the Southern Negro his constitutional rights, his political and civil equality." Here was a fundamental point. Basic civil rights against lynching and discrimination, along with crucial mechanisms of democratic voice in politics, would be mechanisms for the emancipation of the working classes. Striking was dangerous enough for white strikers, who faced retaliatory firing and picket-line violence. Without achieving basic legal protections, Black workers faced that same violence and more, with even less recourse to the courts. Johnson and White went a step further. The defense of Black civil rights, they asserted, would give rise to "a self-consciousness and self-respect," which would in turn "effect a revolution in the economic life of this country." Civil rights for Black Americans were a precondition for labor's voice in the control of industry.[48]

If Johnson and White were right, they explained, then empowering the Black worker was "bound up with all the major problems in which this Fund is interested: the problems of labor; wages and income, democracy, wealth and privilege," and more. None of these issues could be understood let alone resolved without reference to "the plight of the Negro." That was the lesson of the Sweet case, where the Fund's support for the rights of a Black family in rapidly integrating Detroit had struck a blow for Black migrants' rights to participate in the economic life of the city. The Pullman porters case weighed on the men's minds, too, for though the porters' effort had not been "a dead loss," it had also not been "as successful as had been hoped." Donating money to "Negro labor organizations," they explained, seemed insufficient, in part because the field of such organizations had grown too vast. In any event, "the Negro does not dare organize today," Johnson and White continued, and "mere money" could "do little" to change that brute fact. The Committee on Negro Work therefore proposed a campaign run by the NAACP that would aim to alter the situation, "creating a psychological atmosphere favorable to bold, aggressive action." The campaign would be the very opposite of the Black Belt thesis. It would take advantage of all that the Fund and its members had learned about democratic change in the age of mass industry. And unlike the proposals of the Communist left, it would be doable.[49]

In all, the Committee on Negro Work initially called for between $214,000 and $229,000 to finance the NAACP campaign they had in mind, a figure equivalent to seven times the annual budget of Brookwood and four times the annual budget of the NAACP. The program would consist of "equal rights in the public schools, in the voting booths, on the railroads, and on juries . . . and the right to own and occupy real property." Citing Du Bois's school studies, Johnson, Ernst, and Gannett's report contemplated simultaneous school equalization suits in eleven southern states, all accompanied by an aggressive campaign run by an "expert publicity ser-

Walter White, around the time of the Fund's 1930 grant to the joint NAACP-Fund committee.

vice" to win a radical change in public opinion. Next would come suits to enforce voting rights, to roll back segregated railroad cars, to overturn racially restrictive covenants in home sales, and to end race discrimination in jury selection. The American Fund, suggested the Committee, should make this sweeping "campaign for the Negro its major field in allotting the remainder of its funds."[50]

The Committee on Negro Work had the advantage of being first—but Ernst and Johnson had actually gotten too far ahead of their colleagues. The Fund board heard the committee's pitch, but put off decisions until after the summer of 1929, when the other committees were expected to have finished their work.[51]

As the summer rolled by, more growth in the value of First National Bank shares emboldened the Committee on Negro Work still further. At the NAACP, Walter White proposed to Johnson a "spectacular dramatization" of the disfranchisement problem by challenging the legality of the election results for one or more U.S. senators from the South. White suggested a large-scale study of arrests in large cities to dispel the myth of Black criminality. Neither proposal went ahead, but after Ernst reported yet another new high-water mark for the Fund's stock market holdings in late September, Johnson raised the Committee on Negro Work's grant recommendation to more than $300,000. Basic civil rights, the committee asserted in its revised report, were the foundation of "any real economic independence." Muste weighed in to help with "educational activities" and to build a "ground work of economic knowledge" for Black workers.[52]

In a race to stay ahead of the other committees, White hastily gathered together budgets from the previous NAACP legal fights in the Arkansas peonage case and the Sweet case in Detroit. He rehearsed earlier litigations like the successful challenge to racially restrictive zoning in Louisville and the organization's winning case against whites-only Texas primary elections in the 1927 Supreme Court decision *Nixon v. Herndon*. In the revised proposal, the committee earmarked resources for school funding equalization suits, voting rights cases, railroad desegregation cases, jury service cases, and residential segregation cases. Black civil rights in Haiti and the Virgin Islands made the new, expanded list of projects for the committee's proposal. The animating idea was action to upend the psychological environment shaping the behavior of Black labor. The worker, said the committee, must come to hold "a new belief in salvation by economic reform achieved by himself. He must have a new sense of his own power." A vast publicity and propaganda campaign would accompany the litigations. The revised recommendation suggested a tripling of the print run of *The Crisis* and between $20,000 and $30,000 in spending on publicity and advertising. In all, the Committee on Negro Work's optimistic revised request totaled $314,000.[53]

Kindergarten Propositions

The Fund's fortunes tumbled when the market crashed. Even as Ernst, Gannett, Johnson, and White put the finishing touches on their ambitious recommendation, the boom market of the 1920s came to an end. Over two days at the end of October—Black Monday, October 28, and the next day—the Dow Jones Industrial Average plunged 29 percent from its September high. The slide was just beginning. Shares in the First National Bank of New York dropped in value by nearly 40 percent by the end of November. With the Fund's assets in apparent free fall, Baldwin suggested putting off consideration of further grants. Ernst acknowledged that it was virtually impossible to value the Fund's holdings because there seemed to be "no present market for the stock."[54]

The market's collapse reined in the NAACP's ambitions. When the Fund directors met on November 8 to block out some basic decisions, the board took a preliminary vote not on the revised $314,000 proposal but on a slimmed-down $100,000 grant. Gitlow was absent, distracted by tumult in the Party. Johnson recused himself because of his leadership role at the NAACP. By a narrow 5–4 vote, the board approved.[55]

Ominously, the NAACP program had squeaked through over the unanimous opposition of the board's left wing. Baldwin immediately protested that "so large a project" should not be decided on "so narrow a vote," urging that the directors consult "Negro leaders" not "connected with the Advancement Association." Another round of committee revisions was still to come, with one final vote of the Fund board. For the next stage, Gitlow would be back in the board's voting pool. If Johnson recused himself again, the board would split evenly between its left and right blocs and the grant would fail.[56]

With crucial grant money now doubly uncertain because of the markets and the votes, Johnson, White, and Du Bois took over from Ernst in pressing the case for a grant that would fuse civil rights to labor. In part, the NAACP officials adapted their arguments to meet the American Fund's priorities. They knew what the industrial democracy progressives of the Fund wanted to hear.[57]

The fusion of labor and civil rights, however, had a deeper history in the early NAACP than many observers would later understand. Since at least the Arkansas sharecropper massacre of 1919, the organization had found itself immersed in advocating for Black workers. Johnson's years-long membership on the American Fund board had helped orient the NAACP leader to labor questions. His Harlem mentorship of the young socialist writer Claude McKay had helped, too, as had his early Jacksonville connection to Randolph. One way or another, Johnson had spent the 1920s closer to the question of labor than any NAACP director before him, and closer than any of his successors for at least three-quarters of a century. It was Johnson who had signed a "united front" pledge on behalf of the NAACP with Cyril Briggs's Communist-affiliated African Blood Brotherhood and an array of Harlem socialists in 1923. It was Johnson who in 1925 had urged the American Fund to provide start-up support for Frank Crosswaith and his Trade Union Committee for Organizing Negro Workers. Johnson's NAACP had arranged Fund-sponsored scholarships for Black labor organizers at Brookwood. Johnson had joined A. Philip Randolph and Crosswaith at rallies to unionize Black elevator operators in 1924 and 1925. And Johnson had won the NAACP's endorsement for Randolph's Pullman porters in 1926 and then again at the federal Railway Mediation Board in 1928. At the decade's end, Johnson offered accolades on the book jacket for Nearing's Communist-inspired *Black America*, praising the book for excavating "the economic basis of the Negro's condition." The great difficulty, Johnson quipped darkly, was that "the white working masses" were as averse to Black membership in their unions as the "white bourgeoisie" was to Black guests at their dinner parties.[58]

Critics on the Fund's left charged that the civil rights organization had "no labor program," that its proposals were a transparent tactic to win Fund money for pure civil rights purposes. But in 1922, the NAACP had conditioned support for a proposed progressive third party of farmers and workers—the so-called Conference for Progressive Political Action—on the party's endorsement of Black workers' industrial emancipation. (A takeover by the Communist Party hobbled the CPPA effort.) Two years later, the NAACP proposed to the American Federation of Labor that the two organizations form a joint Interracial Labor Commission to bring workers together across racial lines. (The idea met a cool reception.) Endorsements of Black labor organizing became standard set pieces of the NAACP's 1920s conventions, as did condemnations of white labor union exclusivity. Annual reports recorded protests against discrimination in government employment, attacks on Jim Crow in the upholsterers' union, and fights on behalf of Black railway trainmen and steamship stewards. After floods on the Mississippi River in 1927, NAACP officials documented the abuse of Black workers on the levees.[59]

For his part, Du Bois had been an on-again-off-again socialist since at least his formal membership in Debs's Socialist Party in 1910. Under his stewardship, *The Crisis* ran articles in the 1920s condemning "the present method of control and distribution of wealth" as "desperately wrong." Du Bois penned editorials on unemployment, railway unions, and "The Negro and Organized Labor." Columns demanded that economic radicals find room for Black concerns, championed Sacco and Vanzetti, denounced peonage, and condemned the disfranchisement of the Black working class. In 1929, Du Bois pored over a new study of union demographics showing that of the 2.5 million Black people in the paid labor market outside of agriculture, a mere 66,000 belonged to traditional labor organizations. That same year, the NAACP officially demanded that the AFL "include Negroes" in its "program for unionizing [the] South," adding that the "labor problem in the South" could "never be satisfactorily adjusted when Negroes are excluded from unions." Sharp declines in the number of lynchings allowed the organization's annual review to announce that the NAACP was "able to give greater attention to barriers set up by labor unions and employers in industry." Du Bois now listed "industrial democracy" among the organization's "five major aims," right after the abolition of lynching and the achievement of "political freedom."[60]

Connections to American Fund circles linked Du Bois to the world of the industrial democracy intellectuals. At the end of 1929, he became vice chairman of the League for Independent Political Action, an organization that included Norman Thomas and A. J. Muste along with philosopher John Dewey. Du Bois's school studies, which the Fund had supported in the mid-1920s, drew further attention to the labor and economic dimensions of Jim Crow, promoting the idea that educating Black workers would empower them as industrial citizens. NAACP officials said that segregation in the schools was an economic issue for the further reason that, as Du Bois's school studies had helped show, public schools allocated tax dollars unequally because of race. As new federal funding made its way to public schools, the NAACP's Committee on Discrimination in the Expenditure of Public School Funds lobbied the Hoover administration to condition such funds on equality requirements that would funnel money to Black communities. The committee had limited success. But leading NAACP figures observed that the prospect of increased federal support for state-run schools created added reason to demand that states treat schools equally.[61]

For the members of the Fund's Committee on Negro Work, the choice between revolutionary and incremental change was illusory. "We all want to see the millennium," White explained, "but millennia don't just happen." They took "years of preparation and of hard, unremitting work." This hardly meant that economic transformation was out of reach. The "Negro in America," White contended, would serve as "the vanguard" for such change. But the reality of weak unions, racial divisions, and practically nonexistent support for Communist schemes meant that altering the country's economic arrangements would require engaging the world as it was. "Legal action" such as "the Arkansas Riot Cases," White said, was a viable strategy for attacking "economic exploitation through peonage in the lower South." The proposals of the left wing, in contrast, were nonstarters.[62]

By January, the Committee on Negro Work and the Fund's left-wing group were locked in a race to capture the Fund's rapidly diminishing assets. "Delay is prejudicing us," Ernst warned. White reminded Ernst to emphasize the value of the association's legal work in fighting economic exploitation.[63]

In a rare act of cooperation, White and Du Bois set aside their growing mutual dislike to work overtime on demonstrating the NAACP's labor credentials and its organizational track record. Du Bois produced a long memorandum on the "parallel between the pronouncements of the Negro radicals and, on the other hand, the pronouncements and things actually accomplished by the NAACP." Another report ticked off the dozens of articles on labor and the economy appearing in *The Crisis*—articles, Du Bois said, that had "played no inconsiderable part in creating labor consciousness among Negroes and recognition of the part in labor played by the Negro worker." A third rehearsed the NAACP's labor activities from the previous decade.[64]

Du Bois went to the heart of the case. "The Negro problem," he wrote in a draft recommendation for the committee, "is not simply a question of the uplift and advancement of Negro Americans." Civil rights

Du Bois, pictured with the staff of The Crisis *in its offices, helped formulate the NAACP's grant proposal only to see the association and the Fund cut his magazine out of the final award.*

questions were, "for historical and economic reasons," involved in nearly every facet of the Fund's work. The major problems were familiar: "labor, wages and income, democracy, wealth and privilege, education, war and peace, and a dozen others," and all of them were "involved in this problem of the rights and status of 12 million black Americans." Du Bois continued, "Unless Negroes learn of the aims and ideals of white labor and unless the white labor world comes to know the problems of colored labor, each by insidious propaganda may be pitted against each other in suicidal strife." A "campaign of education among American Negroes," on the other hand, he told Johnson, might lead "the race into industrial democracy and emancipation from their present peonage." The money for such a campaign, Du Bois's draft recommendation explained, would "hammer home and fix in court decisions the fundamental rights of black laborers." Du Bois concluded with the further point that "the NAACP is without doubt the only agency fitted to do this work." The left's supposed rival organizations were little more, he implied, than hollow front groups.[65]

For their part, the Fund's far left tried to undo the effects of Ernst's canny committee arrangements. The left faction insisted successfully that Nearing be added to the Committee on Negro Work on the theory of better late than never. (Nearing's recent book on Black labor lent him valuable expertise; his long service on the Fund board lent him a modicum of respect even across the growing partisan divide.) In February, Dunn and Michelson proposed merging the Committee on Negro Work with the Committee on Civil Liberties, on which they sat with Baldwin and Ernst. The ploy was a transparent attempt to subvert the NAACP grant and win the Fund's money for Communist projects. Because Ernst served on both committees, and because Nearing now held a seat on the Committee on Negro Work, the result of such a merged committee would have been a four-to-three committee margin in favor of the Fund's left. "There are issues involving Negro and white workers which should be considered jointly by the two committees," Dunn and Michelson urged.[66]

Ernst accepted the freethinking Nearing into the Committee on Negro Work. The prospect of combining with Party zealots Dunn and Michelson, by contrast, loomed as a disaster. The alternative that soon emerged, which was little better, was for Michelson to take Nearing's spot on the

Negro Work committee. With the Party now threatening the plans carefully laid for what seemed likely to be the Fund's last big grant, Ernst, Johnson, and White resolved to press to the finish line.[67]

As its divisions came to the fore, the Fund appeared headed for a breakdown. By an acrimonious 6–5 margin, with the leftists all voting no, the Fund barely approved an otherwise ordinary grant to the progressive socialists at the League for Industrial Democracy. The Committee on Nominations proposed to appoint a slate of progressive industrial relations specialists to the two empty director's seats, only to run into a buzz storm of left opposition.[68]

Inside the Committee on Negro Work, cooperation with Clarina Michelson quickly proved hopeless. Michelson, Ernst noted, "frankly disbelieved in the utility of any work in the fields suggested in the Committee's original report." The three original committee members pressed on without her. The final committee recommendation, written by Gannett and edited substantially by Ernst and Johnson, made one last pitch for a campaign of civil rights and school equalization conceived as a tool for supporting Black workers. For eight years, the committee observed, since the American Fund's founding in 1922, the directors had supported "trade-union organization work." Labor organizing had been one of the Fund's charter missions. But given the poor prospects for unions in the 1920s, such efforts had yielded less than was desired, and the lesson seemed clear. "To put money into the salaries of union organizers and into the rent of union headquarters, at this stage," the committee asserted, "would be like pouring money down a sink." Indeed, if a "really promising organization" appeared in the field today, it would not need the Fund's money. Union dues would make such a fledgling organization viable in the near future, if not right away, and in the meanwhile the old-line AFL was better positioned to sort the viable unions from the sure losers. The AFL could support start-up organizing with a chance to succeed; in any event, the committee added, "our money" would not make a difference. Supporting Communist organizations seemed no more promising, given their well-documented "record of splits in the party." Combined with "the ineffective personnel of its Negro organizations," factional infighting meant that the Party had "no immediate hope of the stability and effectiveness which should be conditions of our support." In all, grants to the present array of scattered and demoralized labor organizations would be, the committee concluded, "worse than a gamble."[69]

The great contrast, the committee suggested, was the Fund's "contributions to the campaign of the Civil Liberties Union." Support to the ACLU had substantially "aided subsequent organizing efforts" by defending the labor movement's leaders against politically motivated prosecutions. What "the mass" of Black workers needed, Ernst added, was "simpler and more elementary than even those rights." Johnson had made the point years before, when he urged his fellow directors to remember that Black Americans were still looking for their Magna Carta. Violent repression, lynching, and exclusion from basic civil rights were barriers to solidarity. Terror prevented Black workers from asserting themselves. Quoting Nearing's recent book, the committee elaborated the point:

Negro wage workers... carry the normal burden of workers under capitalism. In addition... American Negroes must constantly pay the penalty for their blackness. They are exploited as a race.... The clear line is drawn against the American Negro in every sphere of life.

Now the Fund and the NAACP could do for Black workers what the ACLU, with the Fund's help, aimed to do for white workers: vindicate the basic "kindergarten propositions" about freedom and civil liberty that would allow people to speak out and strike when conditions warranted:

Just as, at a certain stage in the labor movement of the North, the most effective outside support appeared in the field of civil liberties, helping give labor the courage and the opportunity to fight its own way, so we believe that the Negro and the Negro labor movement can be helped most by an energetic and dramatic program to assist the kindergarten propositions—assumed as axiomatic by the white workers even in feudal Pennsylvania—that Negroes have equal rights to go to school, to walk and ride in the streets, to live where they want to when they can afford it, to vote and to sit on juries. Here is the field where our help can be strategically effective—really revolutionary.

The aim of a big grant to the NAACP, concluded the Committee on Negro Work, was "to establish conditions and a psychology" that would "put the Negro laborer, industrial and agricultural, on an equal basis as regards organization with white labor." Black workers faced obstacles "which the white laborer does not face," and the goal of the grant would be to alter those "precedent conditions" before tackling the otherwise insuperable subsequent problem of creating the conditions for an "outburst of Negro organization."[70]

To mobilize such a project, the committee report harkened back to Walter Lippmann's ideas about information in modern democracies, and to the lessons that had run through Du Bois's mid-1920s debates with Alain Locke over propaganda and politics. Ernst, Gannett, and Johnson contended that "the maximum effectiveness" of the lawsuits could "be gained only through dramatization in a spectacular way," which in turn required "an intelligent and extensive propaganda campaign" capable of focusing "public attention upon the association's work." The recommendation therefore included a propaganda effort aimed at "bombarding the public mind" with the facts of Jim Crow. NAACP publicity director Herbert Seligmann, a veteran of propaganda efforts in 1919's red summer, during the Dyer anti-lynching bill controversy of 1922, and in the Sweet case in 1925, proposed a campaign of newspaper advertisements on the model of the anti-lynching ads that he and Edward Bernays had used to great effect during the Dyer episode.[71]

One late suggestion came in from Freda Kirchwey in Florida, where she was caring for her dying seven-year-old son Jeffrey, stricken with tuberculosis. "Sure, I'm with you and Morris on the Negro work," she wrote to Lewis Gannett during a brief reprieve from the heartache: "Vote me for the program." Kirchwey reported that she was "strong for the scheme." But what, she asked, about the "exclusion of" and "restrictions surrounding" Black members in the trade unions? Could legal actions be initiated to assert this "real issue of civil liberty" for Black workers? At the very least such a proposal "might help mitigate the wrath of the Communists in the Fund." Ernst, she recalled, doubted that any such action would be possible. Unions were private associations, he had reasoned, with no constitutional obligation not to discriminate. "Perhaps, damn it all," Kirchwey concluded, "there's nothing to be done" except "beg" the American Federation of Labor "to be nice."[72]

Gannett's draft initially took up Kirchwey's idea and proposed that $5,000 be set aside for "legal action for damages against labor unions which discriminate against Negro workers." But Ernst had no appetite for suing the labor movement, and Johnson did not protest. The committee's final recommendations, which Ernst, Gannett, and Johnson submitted to the Fund directors in May 1930, recommended the same slimmed-down $100,000 budget the Fund had tentatively approved in November. The proposal allocated most of the money to school equalization suits, and added $25,000 for the legal defense of people who might be targeted by southern state authorities for their participation in the NAACP's campaign. The recommendation included no money for challenging discrimination by Jim Crow labor unions.[73]

The Committee on Negro Work anticipated that its recommendations would "meet large objections from some members of the Board." Baldwin lobbied board members not to support "the proposed test cases involving Negro rights." On May 28, 1930, when at last the final vote was scheduled, the board's entire left wing cycled through parliamentary maneuvers designed to sabotage the grant. Michelson moved that Committee on Negro Work funds be set aside for legal defense efforts under the auspices of the Communist-run International Labor Defense. With crucial funding for the NAACP at stake, and with the Fund otherwise evenly split, Johnson declined to recuse himself. There was no rule requiring recusal, and even if the left wing spluttered angrily, they lacked a majority to force him out. With Johnson's vote, the Fund's progressives beat back the left-wing motion, six to five. A sequence of desperate motions to derail the NAACP grant followed. Baldwin proposed to set the money aside for legal defense work. Dunn moved that it be sent to the Communist-backed American Negro Labor Congress. Nearing would have used it to finance a new workers' school in the Black Belt. But the Fund's bare majority of social democrats and liberals held fast and defeated each motion in turn.[74]

With the obstacles cleared away, the recommendation of the Committee on Negro Work came to a vote. The Fund adopted it by the now familiar six-to-five margin. Baldwin, Dunn, Gitlow, Michelson, and Nearing voted no. As Gitlow recounted to Flynn, in the "big fight" between "the so called left and the right wing of the Board," the social democratic right wing had won out over the Communist Party's best efforts. The Committee on Negro Work was discharged. "Their work," the Fund's minutes recorded, "was finished." And a much broader effort had commenced.[75]

Garland Jailed For 60 Days in 'Love Farm' Case

Pleads Nolo Contendere to Charge Involving a Girl Whose Baby Died of Suffocation Last Fall

He and Wife Reconciled

Tells Judge Women Members of Cult Have Deserted Him and Goes to Prison

Special to the New York Herald Tribune
ALLENTOWN, Pa., April 15.—Charles

Charles Garland Indicted in Allentown; Associates in April Farm Colony Disappear

Special to The New York Times.

ALLENTOWN, Pa., April 5.—A Le- Rupp, former Pennsylvania Demo-

GARLAND COLONY IS DENOUNCED

Master in Report Calls It Communistic

Twelve Adults, Three Children Living on the Farm

Charter for Scheme Is Refused

Special Dispatch to the Globe
ALLENTOWN, Penn, Jan 3—An at-

Baby's Death Brings Garland 'Farm' Inquiry

Allentown, Pa., Authorities Begin Investigation of the Young Millionaire's 'April Association' There

FREE-LOVE PROJECT DENIED BY GARLAND

Colony Has No Definite Theory as to Marriage, No Iron Rule, He Asserts.

Special to The Washington Post.
Allentown, Pa., Jan. 10 (By A.

LOVE COLONY BABY'S DEATH STARTS HUNT FOR ITS GRAVE

DARROW, FAMOUS LAWYER IN EVOLUTION CASE IN TENNESSEE, MAY ENTER LEHIGH LAWSUIT

Warrant For Garland

GARLAND GIVES BAIL ON CHARGE GROWING OUT OF BABY DEATH IN LOVE COLONY

LEHIGH COUNTY SOCIAL EXPERIMENT NOT MAKING MUCH HEADWAY SINCE VISIT BY SHERIFF

Allentown, Jan. 12.—Deserted by

Garland, Love Farm Cultist, Sued by Wife

Garland Seized In 'April Farm' Dead Baby Quiz

Bettina Hovey, Named as Infant's Mother, and 3 Women Flee Colony as Sheriff Arrests Its Rich Founder

Radical Is Granted Bail

Millionaire, Who Financed Scopes Defense, Seeks Darrow as Counsel Jan. 23

A media frenzy descended on the Garland commune in January 1926; headlines from the Boston Globe, *the* Chicago Daily Tribune *(bottom center), the* New York Herald Tribune *(including second from top at right), the* New York Times, *the* Reading Eagle *(bottom left and lower center), and the* Washington Post.

16

Radical Enterprises

*Mr. Garland doesn't believe in any of the three
M's ... Morals, Marriage and Money.*
—NEW YORK AMERICAN, 1926

Into the second half of the 1920s, Charles Garland had generally kept busy in the orchards of April Farm, the relocated commune he had established outside Allentown, Pennsylvania, in 1924. The arrangement worked, at least for a while. Visitors marveled at Garland's capacity to work long days in the field. In between farm projects, he played with the children from his on-again, off-again marriage, who now numbered four. He gave them rides in the sidecar of his motorcycle and set them on his lap to drive the farm's prized tractor. He was, his children later remembered, a magical bedtime storyteller.[1]

Beneath the bucolic surface of the Pennsylvania countryside, however, April Farm was balanced precariously between Garland's remaining income and his increasingly erratic mental health. Residents had come to the farm because of their dissatisfaction in the world, not because of their capacities for good judgment, and certainly not because of any inclination for agricultural labor. Garland himself, as he had noted in 1920, had been singled out by the luck of an unearned inheritance rather than by any special merit or qualities of leadership.[2]

In July 1925, Garland's latest lover at April Farm, a woman named Bettina Hovey, gave birth to a daughter in the farmhouse. The baby was not well. Decades later, residents of the farm still remembered hushed tones and sadness surrounding the birth. At three months old, the infant died in her crib. The Lehigh County coroner found that the child had succumbed from lack of oxygen, smothered by blankets while she slept. But newspapers circulated lurid rumors of a murder at what they charged was a free-love colony. Soon the story was picked up in the New York press, which was eager to reprise the tale of the discontented heir.[3]

April Farm's immediate neighbors offered generous words about its residents, despite the commune's unusual arrangements. But local authorities grew suspicious, and attention in the newspapers prompted them to act. In January, an unsympathetic Lehigh County district attorney used the occasion of the infant's death to charge Garland with the crime of adultery. The commune leader's divorce from the socialite Mary Wrenn, it turned out, had not yet been finalized when Bettina became pregnant. Locals speculated that Clarence Darrow would represent Garland. Instead, the Fund's lawyer, Walter Nelles, took a train out from the city to help him submit a plea of nolo contendere, accepting a sentence of sixty days in the Lehigh County jail and a $500 fine.[4]

The infant's death and Garland's subsequent imprisonment dealt a blow to the already shaky April Farm. After a failed apple crop, morale soured. Longtime residents began to resent new members for treating time on the farm like a vacation. "They ate, slept, sat under a tree philosophizing and didn't work," remembered one resident who soon left in disgust. The free-love tenets of the community produced personal jealousies and romantic conflict, too. A new arrival from the nearby anarchist colony at Stelton, New Jersey, tried to put the April Farm community on firmer footing. He soon gave up, complaining that the farm had attracted "misfits, failures, and the generally disgruntled and unhappy." Outside critics pounced. The *New York Daily Mirror* ran a sensation-mongering twelve-part series, focusing on lurid tales of sexual scandal, complete with drawings of beautiful, young, and dissolute comrades wasting away amid agrarian abundance gone to seed. Attention in the press led to scrutiny by opportunistic red-hunters in Congress, too. At House hearings on militarism and the Communist threat, Representative John Philip Hill of Maryland charged that Garland had been sent to prison "for running a free-love farm after the Soviet Russian type." The characterization was uncharitable and misleading, but not entirely wrong. It came as no surprise when later that year, Pennsylvania officials rejected April Farm's application for a charter to establish a school for orphans, citing the farm's failure to live up to the "moral standards of this Christian nation."[5]

The Hearst newspaper empire disseminated a full-page exposé of the famous heir's difficult year.

Garland turned disillusioned and bitter. He was, he told his soon-to-be ex-wife, Mary, indifferent to whether they divorced or not. Legal categories like marriage, he complained, had "ceased to have moral significance." The law, he said, was a "wolf in sheep's clothing," which in a grim mixed metaphor he urged be lashed to a millstone and "cast into the sea."[6]

The real difficulty was that Garland was spiraling into an untreated depression that would eventually leave him a shell of his former self. Fellow residents at April Farm wrote darkly of "unfortunate circumstances" in his personal life. His mother, Marie Tudor, commented that she found him "confused in a fog most of the time," "battling at ideas, pure and abstract," and unable (as she put it) to "listen to his own soul." His children, though young, intuited the same problem. Even when surrounded by people, he seemed emotionally isolated. He was, his daughter Mary remembered, "the saddest person I ever met," the kind of person, as his son Jay would later note, who loved mankind but could not connect with people.[7]

A troubled Garland soon proved unable to hold off the grifters and parasites who angled to take advantage of his money: leeches who visited for a summer idyll, playing at utopianism on his dime only to leave when the weather changed. A cooperative community could not survive under such conditions. In 1930, April Farm's residents packed their belongings and left. Garland stayed on for a time, but his commune—a place he had hoped might serve as a model for a better way of life—splintered under the burden of shirked tasks and spurned love interests.[8]

April Farm's loss was the Communist Party's gain. Through an intermediary, the Party acquired the farm and turned it over to Ella Reeve Bloor, who had defended political prisoners with Elizabeth Gurley Flynn at the Workers Defense Union after the end of the war. Better known in leftist circles as "Mother Bloor," the now-aging radical had helped found the American branch of the Party at the watershed 1919 Socialist convention in Chicago. Weeks later, she had celebrated with Roger Baldwin upon his release from prison. With the transfer of Garland's farm, her world touched Baldwin's once more. For the next two decades, Bloor used the old April Farm property as a retreat for Party organizers.[9]

Meanwhile, Bloor's son, a Communist militant named Harold Ware, seized the opportunity of Garland's declining condition to exploit his remaining wealth. Tanned, charming, and wiry, with an abiding love of the farming life, Ware had been responsible for the American Fund's outlandish, ill-fated effort to support Russian Reconstruction Farms, the Soviet agricultural experiment that aimed to inaugurate a modern era in collective farming. It had been Ware who assured the Fund's directors that Soviet collectivism and Ford Motor Company farm machinery would end hunger. No less a figure than Lenin had seemed to agree; shortly before his death, and just a few years before the entire endeavor fell to pieces, he had cited Ware in the pages of *Pravda* as an agricultural genius.[10]

Back in the United States, Ware became one of the Soviet Union's early spies, ingratiating himself with American officials and channeling information on American agriculture to Moscow. With the advent of Roosevelt's New Deal in 1933, Ware expanded his role to serve as handler for some of the best-placed Party members in the American government.

Ware worked with the director of the underground section of the Party in the United States, a shadowy figure known as Josef Peters, who had been a U.S. delegate to the crucial Sixth Congress of the Comintern with special responsibility over the Black Belt question. Together, Ware and Peters established a secret cell of Washington government officials. Alger Hiss, whose later conviction on perjury charges would divide the nation, was almost certainly an early member. The Ware Group soon expanded to a network of sixty or seventy agents spread out among at least seven secret cells. Whittaker Chambers, who would later renounce his Soviet ties and expose the clandestine operation, ran a secret Party apparatus parallel to Ware's. Chambers and Ware were the Soviet Union's most prized intelligence assets in the United States.[11]

Baldwin later felt that he "never could reconcile" what he knew of Ware with the man's "exposure as a Soviet agent." But in the 1930s, Ware

Harold Ware, pictured here shortly before his death in a 1935 car accident, tried with partial success to turn the Fund's dwindling resources toward Soviet espionage and efforts to organize U.S. farmworkers.

and a fellow Party member named Lement Harris sustained their efforts by siphoning what was left of Charles Garland's trust income. They also convinced Garland to petition for grants from the by-then badly reduced accounts of the American Fund. Garland had no formal say in the Fund's operation. But Baldwin and his codirectors felt a moral obligation to take his inclinations into account, thus making the pliable Garland a convenient device for drawing down what remained of the Fund's resources.[12]

The first signs of the Garland heir's new affiliation came when he intervened in the fight over the NAACP litigation campaign grant. Gifts "to left wing radical activities," he told the board, had his "entire support and sympathy." If money was going to support organizing among Black workers, he favored the Party's efforts in the Black Belt, newly energized by the fateful 1928 resolutions of the Sixth Congress in Moscow. In the field of workers' education, Garland preferred the Communist-backed Workers' School in New York City. Clinton Golden, while serving as Brookwood Labor College's field director, had described the Workers' School as fanatically ideological. Its fevered propaganda, he had warned, mostly seemed to befuddle its immigrant worker students. Nonetheless, Garland urged the American Fund's directors to finance "the most radical of the enterprises which the Fund is asked to aid." Support for groups like the NAACP and Brookwood, he charged, amounted to the sponsorship of "right wing movements."[13]

By nearly any standard, of course, the organizations Garland critiqued as "right wing" were dramatically left of center in the politics of the United States in the early 1930s. They consisted of attempts by progressive labor unions to jump-start industrial democracy and efforts by leaders of the Black community to liberate Black Americans. Only in the overheated jargon of the Party did such projects count as right-wing deviations from a revolutionary line. But Garland was in deep.[14]

In 1934, Ware appointed Garland to a titular position running the office of a new front organization called Farm Research, Inc. Applying for American Fund grants under Garland's signature, Ware and Harris won support for Ware's Farm Research and for Harris's Farmers' National Committee for Action. The two men procured additional grants for the

Farmers' National Weekly, a Communist-affiliated newspaper that disseminated stories about foreclosures and sharecroppers' unions, as well as more modest sums for a so-called Farmers' Unity Council and an Alabama Farmers' Union. In 1934, again with Garland's signature, they even concocted an elaborate ruse to employ the Fund to smuggle Soviet money into the country without Russian fingerprints. Ware and Harris proposed that Moscow repay the Fund's old loan to Russian Reconstruction Farms using Amtorg, a Soviet trading corporation and industrial espionage vehicle in the United States, as a go-between. The Fund's role in the scheme would be to funnel the repaid loan money (disguised as a grant) to Harris's Party-backed Farmers' National Committee. The anti-Communists on the Fund board—Norman Thomas and James Weldon Johnson most of all, now joined by disillusioned ex-Party member Ben Gitlow—shut the idea down. To give money to Harris, sneered Gitlow, was to "give it for Communist Party wrecking activities in the agricultural field." Thomas always balked at money for Party operations. Laundering Moscow gold was a step too far.[15]

Ware's role ended suddenly in 1935 when he was killed in a car accident in Pennsylvania. Garland blamed a drowsy delivery truck driver. Whittaker Chambers and Ware's closest friends ruefully cited the dead spy's love of fast cars. Either way, Chambers took over the Ware Group cell. Lement Harris assumed the deceased farm expert's role harvesting Garland's money.[16]

The Party obtained decent yields from Ware's and Harris's efforts, at least by one measure. From 1934 to 1941, fully two-thirds of the Fund's new gifts went to Party-run organizations in agriculture. In some of those years, every new gift went to groups sponsored by Ware or Harris and endorsed by Garland. At the end of 1935, Garland asked to have the Fund's remaining assets released back to him so that he could distribute them as he saw fit. The board gently turned him down.[17]

In more important respects, however, Ware and Harris had effectively taken control of an organization in the process of shutting down. After issuing an average of $220,439 in grants per year for the first eight years of its operation, the Fund's new gifts after Ware's and Harris's arrival (and after the market crash of the Great Depression) averaged only $16,000 annually. In the Fund's final year, 1941, its grant to the late Harold Ware's front organization—its only new gift for the year—totaled a whopping $1,900.[18]

The directors' regular monthly meetings ceased. Correspondence dried up. By the time Ware and Harris had begun to take advantage of the diminished Garland, long before the Fund formally wound itself down, Baldwin was already arranging to deposit the American Fund's papers in archives at the New York Public Library. "This Fund," Baldwin wrote the library in 1932, "has practically ceased operations after ten years' work in giving away something like two million dollars to various progressive and radical enterprises."[19]

If the Fund's story had stopped here, its record might not have been worth the effort. Scott Nearing certainly thought so. The Fund, concluded the discontented director as he quit the board in 1930, was an "object lesson in the futility and iniquity of private giving." Grants, he said, had made the Fund's beneficiaries into "permanent beggars." Private philanthropy seemed to Nearing nothing more than "institutionalized poverty made tolerable," or at least made tolerable for the comfortable classes. Baldwin was not so critical, but he seemed resigned to having presided over a foundation whose accomplishments were modest, in no small part (as Nearing added) because of the relative weakness of its main beneficiaries in the labor movement.[20]

For Johnson, the Fund's future hung in the balance. It had promised a potentially transformative grant for a project substantially of his making. But would it be able to meet its new $100,000 commitment to Johnson's NAACP? The crash on Wall Street quickly put the payments on hold and cast the entire effort into question.

Ironically, however, the Great Depression that drained the Garland Fund's accounts also transformed its legacy. Ideas incubated by the Fund had failed to fledge in the hostile environment of the 1920s. But some of them began to thrive in the altered politics of a new decade. Economic crisis invigorated the Fund's leading experiments. Efforts to build an industrial democracy in a nation split by race moved from the radical wings to center stage in the theater of American law and politics.

In some respects, it was dumb luck. The world had changed in ways that gave the Fund's work new meaning. Yet there was something else, too. Out of the wide and chaotic array of projects bidding for support, the Fund had singled out institutions that proved capable of taking up new roles when crisis came. Over the next decade and beyond, the NAACP and A. Philip Randolph would alter the structure of race relations. Sidney Hillman's new unionism would reshape the labor movement and form the modern Congress of Industrial Organizations. The ACLU would become a standard-bearer for a new law of free speech. Here were organizations and people the Fund had nourished and sometimes sustained. When liberals and the left united in the so-called Popular Front of the mid-1930s, the Fund even scraped up a few more dollars for a significant new project among the tenant farmers of the cotton fields. Some of the Fund's successes were still years away. But now, at the dawn of the new decade, leaders of the social movements propelling such transformations convened to decide on first steps for the Fund's new legal campaign. The work on which they embarked would vindicate ideas that had circulated in the Fund's world for years—and alter American democracy in the process.

PART IV
OUTSIDERS ON THE INSIDE

*Nathan Margold, seated center in front row, at the
NAACP's 1932 conference in Washington, D.C.*

17

A Way of Action

Segregation irremediably coupled with discrimination . . .
represents the very heart of the evils . . . against
which our campaign should be directed.
—THE MARGOLD REPORT, APRIL 1931

James Weldon Johnson launched the NAACP's attack against Jim Crow on Tuesday, July 8, 1930. The occasion was a New York gathering of the old American Fund crowd, now convened as a combined Joint Committee with leaders from the NAACP. Johnson was joined by Walter White, attending in his role as the NAACP's acting secretary during the senior man's leave. From the Fund, Roger Baldwin and Lewis Gannett appeared. Johnson kept Morris Ernst apprised of the group's progress from afar.[1]

The plan of the Joint Committee was to bring suits on behalf of taxpayers challenging the unequal apportionment of school funds. Such suits would aim "to force equal if separate accommodations for Negroes and whites." And they would commence in the seven "worst states" in the Deep South: South Carolina, Georgia, Mississippi, Louisiana, Florida, Alabama, and Arkansas. Johnson understood that attacking Jim Crow in the courts would require working with people who could move not only in the Fund's circle but also in the corridors of power. It would require technicians, too, people with the professional training to navigate institutions of forbidding complexity. Until now, the Fund had aimed principally to alter ways of thinking; in an inhospitable political and economic climate, it spent most of its money on publications, research, publicity, and education. But only so many minds could be changed. The Fund had supported efforts to defend against criminal prosecutions in the great political trials of the age: the sharecroppers of Elaine, Arkansas; Ossian Sweet in Detroit; Sacco and Vanzetti in Massachusetts; the Communists in Gastonia; and Scopes in Tennessee, among others. But as Elizabeth Gurley Flynn found, defensive legal efforts could accomplish only so much. The new campaign proposed not to defend people from the rules but to change the rules.[2]

The project also raised an abiding question. Was attempting to revise the law a way to change the world?

The distinctive answer offered by the Garland Fund group emerged in 1930 and 1931 in unexpected fashion. Starting with a star faculty member at Harvard Law School, the project would take inspiration in the canyons of the American Southwest, where a cluster of Jewish immigrant lawyers joined the efforts of Native tribes challenging centuries of settler land theft in Arizona and New Mexico. It would exhume a forgotten legal idea from an old case arising out of San Francisco's Chinatown. It would dive into the institutional underpinnings of the Deep South. In the process, it would fundamentally revise the campaign Johnson had planned, remaking the future of American law along the way.[3]

But first Johnson needed a lawyer.

The Public and Its Government

The opening order of business, Johnson told the Joint Committee, was "a full-time, competent lawyer," someone who would be "attached to the national office" of the NAACP to lead the Joint Committee's assault on "unequal and inequitable distribution of public-school funds as between the races." Such a lawyer would need first to map out a detailed blueprint of the campaign, identifying legal theories and plotting out strategies. Ideally, the same person would then conduct the litigation. To find a person who could accomplish both tasks, the committee turned to Felix Frankfurter.[4]

Frankfurter was no radical. He was a professor at Harvard Law School. In 1939, he would be nominated to the Supreme Court by Franklin Roosevelt and confirmed by the Senate. As a justice, he would play a crucial role in deciding cases that arose out of the Fund's efforts, including the *Brown v. Board of Education* case that was a culmination of the NAACP's legal campaign.[5]

When Johnson and the Joint Committee reached out to him in 1930, Frankfurter had already burned a path through American law as a man whose energies and ambition matched his dazzling smarts. Born to Jewish parents in Vienna in 1882, Frankfurter immigrated to the United States at the age of eleven. He spoke no English when he arrived on Manhattan's Lower East Side and began middle school at P.S. 25, but the new language came quickly to a precocious child who wanted nothing more than to succeed in his new surroundings. By force of sheer determination and intelligence, the boy propelled himself forward. In 1897, he skipped high school entirely to enroll at City College. Frankfurter was part of the cohort of immigrant students making the college into what some called the "Harvard of the Proletariat." In a school filled with Catholic and Jewish strivers from Eastern and Southern Europe, Frankfurter thrived, graduating near the top of his class and delivering an honorary commencement address. He was nineteen years old. For a year, he worked in the city's energetic new Tenement House Department as a health and safety inspector. And in 1903, Frankfurter left New York to study law at the real Harvard—the Harvard of the bourgeoisie—in Massachusetts.[6]

Frankfurter excelled in law school. The school's dean, James Barr Ames, called him "the most able man" to graduate from the school in years. As a young lawyer, Frankfurter willed himself into the center of the surging progressive generation of the American legal profession, doing so with such success that before long the world of law reform began to orbit substantially around him. When Wall Street law firms spurned him because of his religion ("this is a good time to change your name, Frankfurter," one hiring partner advised), he joined the office of Henry Stimson, then the U.S. attorney for the Southern District of New York, where he prosecuted clients of the white-shoe law firms that had balked at hiring him. Most of all, he fell in love with the ethic of government service. Here was a path that rewarded his energy and intellect, one that seemed clear of Wall Street's crude barriers of class and religion.[7]

When Stimson went to Washington to become William Howard Taft's secretary of war, Frankfurter followed him to serve as a special assistant in charge of the Bureau of Insular Affairs, which managed the United States' overseas colonies. He supported Theodore Roosevelt in the presidential election of 1912, helped found the *New Republic* magazine along with progressives Herbert Croly, Walter Lippmann, and Walter Weyl in 1914, and joined the Harvard Law School faculty that same year. During the war, Frankfurter served as a special assistant to Secretary of War Newton Baker and counsel to the Wilson administration's Mediation Commission, where his job was to resolve labor disputes in defense industries and keep wartime production running. In 1919 he returned to Cambridge to resume the faculty post at Harvard that he would retain for the next two decades.[8]

Frankfurter's energies helped to create a new space in American law between the progressive modernizing energies of a new generation and the powerful institutions of the old one. At Harvard and in the Justice Department, the War Department, and the White House, Frankfurter would make himself a trusted envoy with valued connections in the world of progressive and occasionally radical politics. If Roger Baldwin brought Brahmin connections and an elite pedigree to the movements of outsiders and underdogs, Felix Frankfurter delivered the progressive energies of an

Felix Frankfurter in 1917 on the Harvard Law School faculty.

immigrant outsider to the inner sanctums of the establishment. Baldwin was an insider at home in the world of the dissenters. Frankfurter was the outsider who made his way into the establishment's holiest shrines.

Baldwin and Frankfurter met in 1917 while they were working on opposite sides of the wartime conscientious objector controversy. Frankfurter was an official of the Wilson administration; Baldwin was a civil society agitator for the American Union Against Militarism. From the start, their interactions produced a trust born of mutual recognition. The administrator thanked the agitator for his "peculiar helpfulness," which Frankfurter assured Baldwin "has been constantly borne in mind, and presented where it should be presented." Frankfurter promised that "the thing will work out all right." And in part it did, when Frankfurter helped broker a quiet executive branch arrangement to expand the definition of those eligible for conscientious objector treatment.[9]

The war drew Frankfurter more deeply into labor and civil liberties progressivism. As Newton Baker's chief aide for labor problems during the war, Frankfurter worked to win fellow Jewish immigrant Sidney Hillman's endorsement of the war in return for assurances of federal government support for Hillman's Amalgamated Clothing Workers. (The war, Hillman's theretofore equivocating communications department now blasted out, was a campaign for "labor's democratic rights.") When his wartime labor role in the government brought him to the copper-mining town of Bisbee, Arizona, he excoriated the Phelps Dodge Corporation for forcibly shipping more than a thousand striking miners into the New Mexico desert on railroad boxcars. (Characteristically, he expressed contempt for the IWW organizers at Bisbee, too.) During the postwar strike wave, Frankfurter drafted legal briefs with Hillman's lieutenant Leo Wolman (soon a central figure in the Garland Fund world) and sent younger colleagues and former students to help craft legal positions for the ACW.[10]

Frankfurter condemned the Palmer Raids. His blistering 1920 account of illegal practices at the Justice Department, signed by a dozen other prominent lawyers including his Harvard colleague Zechariah Chafee, castigated the government's "continued" and "fruitless" assault upon the Constitution. (Swinburne Hale, the New York lawyer who was soon to marry Charles Garland's mother, was among the report's signatories.) At the Workers Defense Union, Elizabeth Gurley Flynn urged wider distribution of the document; crediting it to Frankfurter, she called it "our pamphlet." Frankfurter, in turn, joined Flynn on the founding National Committee of Baldwin's new ACLU. Such connections had consequences. In 1921 a group of disgruntled Harvard alumni pressed the university to fire him. Frankfurter emerged unscathed, but his friend Chafee avoided being sacked only after an unprecedented formal trial at the Harvard Club of Boston acquitted him by a narrow margin.[11]

Frankfurter's connections to the world around Baldwin grew stronger in the early years of the Garland Fund. Beginning in 1922, he advised the Fund directors on grant applications from labor groups. When the railroad brotherhoods requested support for a study of the Supreme Court's labor cases, the directors rejected them on Frankfurter's recommendation. The Fund turned to the Harvard professor for advice on fighting court injunctions in the ongoing battle between railroad shop craft workers and the giant Pennsylvania Railroad Company; the fight initiated a decade of Garland Fund support for studies of the use of injunctions in strikes. The Fund relied on Frankfurter for advice on grant requests in connection with the case of Tom Mooney, the San Francisco labor leader jailed for the bombing of a Preparedness Day parade in 1916. As a wartime government official, Frankfurter had shaped the policy of President Wilson's Mediation Commission on the Mooney episode, work that had led the aging Theodore Roosevelt to blast him as a Bolshevik. It was not the last time the future justice's work with the Fund would intersect with his official duties.[12]

Beginning in 1923, Frankfurter served as the Fund's outside counsel in the Sacco and Vanzetti affair, working closely in an improbable partnership with Flynn. Frankfurter had disdained Flynn's Wobblies during the war, and the feelings had been mutual. Yet together, Flynn (the labor radical) and Frankfurter (the ambitious progressive) cooperated to manage the anarchists' legal team, helping among other things to broker loans from the Garland Fund to the Sacco-Vanzetti Defense Committee. Frankfurter also won support from the Fund for a volume of essays on the Supreme Court's minimum wage decisions. The Fund subsidized a free speech brief that Frankfurter drafted on Baldwin's behalf, successfully appealing Baldwin's conviction in New Jersey for illegal picketing. In 1926, Frankfurter litigated on behalf of the striking Passaic textile workers, representing the Communist-run and Garland Fund–supported United Front Committee in its battle against an injunction obtained by the industry bosses.[13]

Frankfurter approached the Fund with proposals of his own. He suggested an experimental public health program in Soviet Russia for the prevention of epidemics. It was Frankfurter who prompted the ACLU to establish a National Committee for the Legal Defense of the Chinese—a committee the Fund helped support. Marking his membership in the Fund's inner circle, Frankfurter sent greetings and well-wishes to Flynn for a dinner in her honor hosted by Baldwin and James Weldon Johnson. In 1928, Frankfurter joined a Boston committee for A. Philip Randolph's Brotherhood of Sleeping Car Porters, urging the Pullman Company to come to the negotiating table. And in 1929 he joined the Legal Committee of the NAACP. As Baldwin later recalled, Frankfurter was a "constant advisor and critic," sending "endless useful suggestions for lawyers, law points, and tactics."[14]

Yet if Frankfurter was in the world of the American Fund, he was only halfway of it. Where the men and women of the Fund's board fought to remake the world root and branch, the ambitious Frankfurter pruned its limbs to climb its heights.[15]

The Fund's world was made up of heterodox refugees from the repression of wartime dissent and its red scare aftermath. Many of its key figures were suited by temperament and politics to the roles of organizer and critic. Not so for Frankfurter. As Walter Nelles observed with a note of resentment, Frankfurter represented the "orthodox legal point of view" by comparison to the Fund's eclectic radicalism. He coveted and won government positions of trust and accountability—positions unattainable by his Fund compatriots.[16]

On the other hand, Frankfurter and the labor intellectuals around the Garland Fund agreed on certain things about modern democracy and its troubles. Frankfurter shared his friend Walter Lippmann's sense that mass society fundamentally changed the character of democratic self-government. Addressing problems at a modern scale placed new pressure on the channels by which people (voters) came to know things about their world. In Lippmann's formulation, liberty now turned on a system of production for the news that was ill-suited to meet democracy's imperatives. Baldwin's postwar disillusionment had followed the same path when he denied there was any such thing as a public, except perhaps what Lippmann had derided as a "phantom."[17]

Such ideas made sense of the world to Frankfurter. As a young lawyer, he castigated propagandists—men like Edward Bernays—as "professional poisoners of the public mind." Frankfurter's most ambitious book, *The Public and Its Government*, delivered as lectures at Yale in 1930, was deeply indebted to Lippmann's ideas. Borrowing from Graham Wallas, Frankfurter proposed that the "Great Society, with its permeating influence of technology, large-scale industry, progressive urbanization, accentuation of groups and group interests" was the characteristic problem for modern government. Where "popular rule" had been expected by some "to work miracles almost automatically," now it was clear that no such miracles would come to pass. Now we knew that democracy was "dependent on knowledge" far "beyond all other forms of government." Yet "chain newspapers, cheap magazines, the movies, and radio"—the institutional forms of the modern press—furnished countless "opportunities for arousing passions, confusing judgment, and regimenting opinion."[18]

With Sidney Hillman and his comrades of the Garland Fund circles, Frankfurter also believed that modern democracy rested on an economic foundation of security and independence for the working classes. "Freedom from economic constraint of want," he said at one speech, "was as important as freedom from [the] political constraint of kings and tyrants." Avoiding "a permanent, servile class" was crucial to what a youthful Lippmann had called "the economic foundations of democracy."[19]

Yet if Hillman and the labor intellectuals of the Fund championed a version of industrial democracy that demanded power and control for the working classes and their representatives, Frankfurter's attention to economics was rooted in a different idea. For him, the problem with squalor, want, and exploitation was that they spilled over into undesirable and even violent revolutionary impulses. Hillman hoped to take the energy produced by economic exploitation and harness it for a labor movement that might remake the foundations of American capitalism. Frankfurter, by contrast, worried that grueling social conditions, "if unattended," as he confided in one conversation in the fall of 1917, would "give rise to radical movements," or, as he said in a 1920 speech, dangerous "social unrest."[20]

Given his training and career, it was striking how little faith Frankfurter professed in the power of law to remedy modern social problems. The law's clumsy institutions, he often said, were insufficient to sustain substantial social improvements. Perhaps, in an earlier and simpler time, law might have supplied a form of government adequate to the social conditions of the age. Frankfurter liked to say that for Abraham Lincoln, law had been a complete "ministry of justice"; it had offered an all-encompassing system of social adjustment to the human problems of the day. But Frankfurter believed that law lacked the capacities necessary to do the kind of justice appropriate to the twentieth century. Part of the problem was that courts and judges carried antiquated social views. Decisions like *Lochner v. New York*, in which the Supreme Court in 1905 struck down a law setting a maximum-hours rule for wage workers, showed that judges obstructed vital social reforms. Frankfurter spent his entire career opposed to the error of *Lochner*-ism. Yet the deeper difficulty, as he saw it, was that regardless of how judges saw the world, law was by its nature ill-suited to accomplish what modern social problems required. Judges could do little more than set a narrow set of basic ground rules. They lacked professional training in economics and social work. Their mechanisms for gathering facts about the world were unwieldy. They employed no army to back their rulings, and no battalions of managers and social workers to do the complex work of putting their rulings into practice.[21]

"Law seldom works with the whole of a problem," Frankfurter wrote in scrawled notes for a speech on the role of the Supreme Court. It would not solve what he called the "negro problem," nor could it settle the issue of free speech. At best, all law could do was address "partial aspects of a problem." Law was a mere "partial layer" of any complex social situation, "a fragment" with a "necessarily partial effect" on the whole problem. Putting the point in Lippmann's terms, Frankfurter told his 1930 lecture audience at Yale that trying to manage a mass society exclusively with the tools of the law was a fool's errand, bound to fail—and likely to pull the legitimacy of the law down with it.[22]

Where law fell short, modern administration rose in its place. The kind of work Frankfurter had done at Bisbee and in labor mediation could be generalized. "The answer to the defects of democracy," he told his Yale audience, "is not the denial of the democratic idea." It was instead the creation of government offices staffed by people with "devotion, intelligence, and technical equipment." The Garland Fund's characteristic strategies—what Frankfurter called "agitation and advocacy"—had their place. They were valid "instruments of education, means for making effective the findings of knowledge and the lessons of experience." But ultimately the work of agitators like those at the Fund would have to give way to "the quiet, detached, laborious task of disentangling facts from fiction." Someone would need to extract "reliable information from interested parties" and make sensible judgments about technical policy problems. Only what he dubbed the "scientific study" of society's problems would allow democracy to "feed on knowledge and reality"—to "reach the mind rather than to exploit feeling."[23]

Frankfurter's model of administrative government was at once a solution to democracy's modern crisis and a threat to the practice of democracy itself. Frankfurter protested that he did not mean to create "a new type of oligarchy," a "government by experts." The "power which must more and more be lodged in administrative experts," he insisted, also had to be "properly circumscribed." The expert, he liked to say (quoting an Irish journalist), "should be on tap, but not on top." The flaw, however, was that Frankfurter had no theory of how the expert (once tapped) might be kept from coming out on top. In unguarded moments, Frankfurter admitted as much. "The art of governing," he said, "has been achieved best by men to whom governing is itself a profession."[24]

In the summer of 1930, when the Garland Fund's agitators reached out to him, the Harvard professor had a man in mind for whom the slow, hard work of the art of governing was becoming a vocation. Frankfurter identified a former student named Nathan Margold as the person to direct the new legal campaign.[25]

Powers of the Hualapai

Margold was a small man of quiet intensity and star-crossed fortunes. He was unfailingly gracious, with a gentle manner that helped him gain people's trust. Most of all, he was an inspired legal technician at a moment when the upheavals of the Great Depression were creating opportunities to reengineer the law from the ground up. By a mix of accident and determination, Margold found himself in a rare position to redraw not one but two different fields of the law. In both fields, his training and his experience led him to be far more interested in the allocation of power than the establishment of rights.

Born in Romania in 1899, Margold had immigrated to New York as a child. His early years followed along the same tracks Frankfurter had traveled two decades before. After public school in Brooklyn, Margold enrolled at City College in 1916 and then Harvard Law School in 1920 with a short army stint in between. Graduating with highest honors, he joined the U.S. Attorney's Office for the Southern District of New York, which hired him on the basis of a strong recommendation from Frankfurter, a veteran of the same office a decade earlier. As U.S. Attorney Emory Buckner noted, Margold even shared his law school mentor's diminutive size. In 1927, Frankfurter and another bantam-sized protégé, James Landis, arranged to hire Margold to the Harvard faculty as a lecturer in anticipation of a tenured faculty position.[26]

Margold's charmed run was sidetracked when the university's antisemitic president, A. Lawrence Lowell, fired him after his first year. There was a politics to the rejection; for a decade, Frankfurter had angered the university's Brahmin class. But Lowell removed Margold from the faculty because of the same Jewish quotas that had blocked Morris Ernst from admission to Harvard College a decade earlier. Frankfurter, the Law School's first Jewish professor—and fifteen years later still the only Jew on its faculty—had filled the unwritten law faculty quota of one. A furious

Nathan Margold in the early 1930s.

Margold drafted a detailed account of his meeting with Lowell and sent it to every member of the Harvard faculty. Frankfurter called for a faculty revolt; when most of his colleagues demurred, there was nothing to be done except make a record for posterity of Lowell's behavior.[27]

If Ivy League antisemitism strengthened the bond between teacher and former student, what most appealed to Frankfurter about Margold was not the younger man's strikingly similar life path. Nor was it his charisma. As even some of Margold's strongest supporters conceded privately, Margold was not as assertive or instantly impressive as some of Frankfurter's student favorites. Learned Hand called Margold "sweet and charming." Buckner, who said that Margold had "a fine character," added that he "is not a pusher," which Frankfurter certainly was. The thing that distinguished the young lawyer from his peers, what made him exceptionally talented in Frankfurter's eyes, was a feel for turning his teacher's ideas about administration into solutions for grave injustices that the theoretical existence of legal rights had utterly and damningly failed to redress. Law hardly mattered if it was not enforced. Margold would make power in action (instead of rights on paper) a crucial feature of his work for the American Fund. He would help make power an organizing principle of the early years of the NAACP litigation campaign that followed. Improbably, it was an idea that this Eastern European immigrant first worked out not for the NAACP but for the federal law of Native peoples.[28]

In 1929, the Institute for Government Research—a founding unit of the influential Brookings Institution—approached Frankfurter seeking help in developing a legal strategy to advocate on behalf of Native American peoples in the Southwest. Frankfurter urged them to hire Margold, who had resumed his law practice in New York. Based on Frankfurter's endorsement, the institute asked Margold to draft legislation to resolve Indians' land claims against the federal government.[29]

In one respect at least, Margold was an anomalous choice. A generation of Native leaders and advocates had arisen in the 1910s and 1920s to organize against what was a historic low point for Native communities in the United States. The Society of American Indians, founded in 1911 by Native men and women educated at Indian boarding schools, established a pan-Indian campaign to push for improved conditions for Native people. In 1924, with the Society's support, the Indian Citizenship Act extended U.S. citizenship to all Indians born within the territorial limits of the country. Two years later, a new lobbying organization known as the National Council of American Indians persuaded the Senate Committee on Indian Affairs to launch an investigation of the corrupt land allotment system and the forced assimilation of the Indian boarding schools. Other Native leaders, some of them organizing in the Mission Indian Federation established in California in 1919, demanded a more radical vision of liberation and tribal sovereignty.[30]

Neither immigrant Brooklyn nor the Manhattan U.S. Attorney's Office had prepared Margold to think about the ferment in the laws relating to American Indians. Harvard Law School had offered no course on Indian law. Nonetheless, Margold threw himself into the law of Native peoples. Perhaps his simmering anger at antisemitism in Cambridge fueled his interests in the mistreatment of other tribes. In truth, conditions on the ground for Native Americans would have been motivation enough. In the Dawes Allotment Act, enacted by Congress in 1887, the federal government had subdivided reservations into 160-acre parcels to be held privately by heads of households rather than collectively by tribes. Land not allocated into allotments was opened for sale and economic development. Commercial interests quickly swooped in to repurpose reservation lands for mining, railroads, and white settlement. Neglect, chicanery, and deception by federal officials abounded. During the half century after the Dawes Act, tribal land holdings fell from 138 million acres to 52 million acres. Native population levels in the continental United States reached an all-time low, falling to 240,000. Conditions, as an influential Brookings study from 1928 documented, were grim. "An overwhelming majority of Indians," the report concluded flatly, were "extremely poor."[31]

Armed with the reports spearheaded by the National Council, on the one hand, and the Brookings Institution, on the other, Margold took up the problem of land claims. Over months, he drafted a bill that aimed, as he told a Senate subcommittee, to dispose "finally and speedily" of "the whole problem of tribal claims." It would be nearly two decades before Congress passed the bill, but Margold's draft turned out to be an early step toward reversing the allotment-era assault on Native communities.[32]

Drafting the claims commission bill connected Margold to an energetic sociologist named John Collier, who with support from the American Fund was promoting land claims commissions as a path back to economic independence for Native peoples. Collier hired Margold to help at his organization, the American Indian Defense Association, and before long he concluded that Margold's legal knowledge was a "gold mine to the Indian cause." At the dawn of what Collier called "a new epoch" in the law of Indian land claims, Margold designed a plan for the Klamath tribe in Oregon to assume control of lands held in trust by the federal government. In Montana, he worked to increase the compensation owed to the Salish and Kootenai peoples of the Flathead Reservation.[33]

Margold did not stop there. As a volunteer, he took on the cause of twenty Pueblo tribes near Taos and Santa Fe. For decades, Margold observed, Mexican and U.S. settlers had "helped themselves" to healthy portions of the Pueblo lands in New Mexico. The U.S. government, charged by law with serving as guardian to the Indian tribes, had betrayed them instead. The government had done "nothing to remove the encroachers." Indeed, the government had encouraged them. The result was "impoverishment of the Indians and the crumbling of their civilization." Settlers had come "in time to regard themselves and to be regarded as the true owners" of Pueblo lands. Legislation in 1924 had promised to resolve the issue. But in the litigation that ensued, federal officials charged with representing the Pueblos had followed the usual deceitful course, declining a promising appeal to the Supreme Court and putting thousands of acres of the Pueblos' lands at risk. In December 1930, with Margold's assistance, the Pueblos initiated their own separate lawsuits in a last-ditch effort to secure their claims to the lands on which they had lived and relied for longer than anyone could remember. "The only hope of saving the lands of these tribes," Collier noted, "is through the way of action marked out by Margold."[34]

By early 1931, Margold was deeply immersed in the problem of Indian land claims. He testified in the Senate on the question. He wrote magazine essays describing the Pueblos' "distressing and deplorable condition" and excoriating the government for leading them to "judicial slaughter."[35]

Above all, Margold came to see things in Indian country according to lessons from Frankfurter's teachings. The administration of Indian law had sharply diverged from the letter of Indian law. Frankfurter, following his senior colleague Roscoe Pound, had taught his students that there was a gap between the law in action and the law on the books. But for the law of the Pueblos in the American Southwest the space between law and reality was a vast canyon. Treaties and statutes going back centuries purported to guarantee Indian claims to land. But the so-called rights established by treaties and laws barely mattered if the men who supposedly managed land on Indians' behalf sought instead to drive them out of existence. Legal doctrine had given way to murderous administration.[36]

Another Frankfurter recommendation, a few years later, would put Margold in a position to alter the corrupt tradition of federal Indian administration. In 1933, with Franklin Roosevelt in the White House, Frankfurter recommended his student for the position of solicitor in the Department of the Interior, one of the most powerful offices in the government for making federal Indian law. Margold got the job. As an administrator of the law, Margold was in a position to help remake it. Drawing on the work of Native activists and leaders, he took part in a seismic rearrangement of the federal law of Native peoples, one that delivered a modicum of power rather than another bitter dose of hollow legal rights.[37]

Two watershed reports served as vessels for Margold's work at Interior. Each ran in striking parallel to his blueprint for an NAACP campaign. Coming out of his late 1920s work at Brookings, both reports were drafted, as a formal matter, after his work for the NAACP was complete. But they illuminate the strategic vision of his program to attack Jim Crow. As Margold saw matters, the parallel projects of remaking federal Indian law and assaulting Jim Crow shared the same basic underlying structure.

The first Indian law report was a long, passionate opinion on the land claims of the Hualapai people who had lived for centuries along the south bank of the Colorado River near the Grand Canyon. Ever since the discovery of gold in the Hualapai ancestral homelands in the 1860s, treasure-seekers had put pressure on Hualapai holdings. Wagons appeared. Federal forts followed, with still more wagons close behind. An 1866 cession by Congress to the Atlantic and Pacific Railroad threatened the historic range of Hualapai lands. In 1874, after a short but violent period of hostilities, the U.S. Army forced the Hualapai off their land into exile at a parched reservation in the Colorado River lowlands. Nine years later, after escaping the reservation, and in return for ceding all other claims, the surviving Hualapai in 1883 accepted a reservation on the south side of the river near Peach Springs. But by the early twentieth century, officials of the Atchison, Topeka and Santa Fe Railroad (successor to the Atlantic and Pacific) had seized control of the crucial water source at the springs. In a crowning touch, President Herbert Hoover's Justice Department had entered into a treacherous consent decree in 1931 in which it purported on behalf of the Hualapai to cede Peach Springs to the railroad in return for other land and vague assurances of continued access to water.[38]

By the time Margold drafted his opinion on the matter in 1934, the dispute between railroad interests and Native people over Peach Springs had been going on for years. Throughout the 1920s, Native leaders in Hualapai country like Fred Mahone of the Mission Indian Federation had insisted that the railroad was no better than a squatter on tribal land. Now Margold and the Department of Interior took their side.[39]

Margold's opinion began with the proposition that the railroad's land claims were subordinate to the prior interests of the tribe. The Hualapai, Margold explained, enjoyed a historic "right of occupancy" at Peach Springs, one that long predated the railroad's claims. Nothing in the 1866 cession nor in the subsequent tribal reservation arrangement relinquished the Hualapai's historic interest in the land at Peach Springs. Not even the Justice Department's supposed consent decree in 1931 gave the railroad valid title, Margold concluded, because the consent decree had expressly

The contested Peach Springs Trading Post on Hualapai tribal land in Arizona, around the end of the First World War.

rested on the fraudulent assertion that the railroad already held valid title to Peach Springs, which it did not.[40]

Most of all, Margold's opinion offered a scathing denunciation of the craven management of Hualapai land rights by the United States government. He condemned the army's forcible internment of the Hualapai at the barren Colorado River reservation, where "climate and conditions" had killed many with dismaying speed. His predecessors in the Interior Department, he continued, had offered "ill-considered" and "utterly inexcusable" opinions approving the shameful 1931 consent decree—opinions that aimed merely to "justify the action already taken." The previous attorney general, in turn, had "blithely" approved the decree in a secret opinion, a "disgraceful" performance that left, as Margold saw it, a black mark on his reputation. Margold was adamant. The "settled government policy" on the question of Native land rights—which was to say, the law governing the matter—made clear that many decades of Hualapai cultivation and hunting had created legal rights in the land at Peach Springs. Yet still the tribe had been displaced. The corrupt enforcement of the law had vanquished the law as it had been written in the books. At least it had done so until the law in the books found powerful advocates of its own.[41]

The second of Margold's Interior Department reports came out two weeks after the Hualapai opinion. Drafted principally by his assistant solicitor, Felix Cohen, this second legal opinion carried the Hualapai memorandum's focus on power over rights to its logical conclusion. Cohen's father, a Jewish immigrant from Minsk named Morris Raphael Cohen, had attended City College with Frankfurter before becoming the first Jew to graduate from Harvard with a doctorate in philosophy. Morris and Frankfurter were so close that the philosopher named his son after his lawyer friend. Joining the faculty back at City College, Morris served as a legendary teacher and mentor to hundreds of students, one of the first of whom was Nathan Margold.[42]

Now two decades later, Morris's son Felix developed an idea for solving the problem Margold had diagnosed in the law of the Hualapai. If the problem for the Hualapai was corrupt management of Native peoples' interests by the United States, Cohen proposed to recognize greater authority in the tribes to govern themselves. Titled "Powers of Indian Tribes," the resulting document, styled as a formal opinion of the solicitor of the Interior Department and signed under Margold's name, asserted that the "most basic principle of all Indian law" was "the principle that those powers which are lawfully vested in an Indian tribe" were the "inherent powers of a limited sovereignty which has never been extinguished." Tribal authority, Cohen and Margold concluded, arose not merely out of powers granted to tribes by acts of Congress. Just as vital was the "inherent power" of Native peoples whose sovereignty over tribal affairs long predated the U.S. government.[43]

Together, the Hualapai opinion and the "Powers of Indian Tribes" report were quintessential products of the Frankfurter school of thinking about law. During the period between the enactment of the Dawes Act and the 1930s, the congressional architects of Indian law had aimed to assimilate Indians to a U.S. culture of rights. In the management of the Dawes Act, however, corruption and chicanery had dominated the rights the act purported to guarantee. Margold and Cohen drew a lesson. Legal rights mattered little without the power to enforce them. Native activists had been making the point to no avail for decades. But better late than never, the two men moved to reorder federal Indian law with this basic insight in mind. The "Powers of Indian Tribes" report reimagined federal Indian law not around who owned what, but around who had the authority to decide who owned what. Legal rights to land, as such, could only accomplish so much. What mattered more was establishing a system of administration that would shift control over Indian affairs into Indian hands, out of the hands of outside managers. In Margold's project, the people trusted to look out for Native interests would first and foremost be the Native tribes themselves.[44]

There was an irony in this. The authors of the report, Margold and Cohen, were not Indians, let alone members of the Hualapai or Pueblo communities of the Southwest. Native leaders like Mahone at the Mission Indian Federation advocated more far-reaching conceptions of Native sovereignty; future critics coming out of the National Council of American Indians would excoriate Margold for failing to consult Native people in his work. Nonetheless, the result was an important shift within the federal government toward empowering new kinds of Indian sovereignty.[45]

In 1934, Margold and his staff at Interior, along with John Collier, drafted the Indian Reorganization Act, which as the centerpiece of the so-called Indian New Deal ended the catastrophic Dawes allotment system and increased the legal authority of tribal governments across the country. Like Margold's memoranda from earlier in the same year, the act aimed to create power instead of rights. It authorized new tribal constitutions, restored to tribes certain powers in the administration of collective claims to land and minerals, and gave tribes broad authority to negotiate with local and state governments. The Indian New Deal vested tribes with the power to regulate the affairs of tribe members; to "cultivate native arts and crafts"; and to establish tribal councils and determine their rules and procedures. Tribal government proved no panacea, to be sure; the act controversially reserved certain powers to the federal administrators, blunting the full extent of tribal authority. Yet the point of Margold's intervention, like that of the Native activists before him, was clear. One way or another, administrative control was destiny.[46]

Seven years later, in 1941, during what would become his final year in the solicitor's post at Interior, Margold would win the Hualapai land case at the Supreme Court. In *United States v. Santa Fe Pacific Railroad Company*, a unanimous opinion joined by Margold's teacher Frankfurter upheld the Hualapai's collective tribal land claims to Peach Springs, citing the "aboriginal possession" and "nomadic tribal occupancy" outlined in Margold's 1934 report and championed by Hualapai activists. The case would go on to become a landmark decision for indigenous land claims around the world.[47]

The Hualapai opinion and the Margold-Cohen report on the power of Indian tribes amounted to a philosophy of law in the world. They stood for the Frankfurterian idea that administrative power dominated legal rights. And therein lay a puzzle for future historians. The NAACP–American Fund campaign on which Margold embarked after first turning to federal Indian law has come down to history as the paradigmatic campaign for legal rights. It stands as a climax of twentieth-century liberal legalism, the project through which American liberals learned to love the courts and celebrate the rights courts assert. Understood as such, observers ever since have alternately celebrated the campaign as a liberal triumph, or castigated it as a fool's errand. But either way this story turns out to be wrong. The Margold blueprint was not a guide, naive or otherwise, to the establishment of new rights; instead, the report was a strategy for navigating power in the institutions where authority resides.

Evil Eye and Unequal Hand

Margold's Indian work reshaped the law—but at first it also sorely tested the patience of NAACP officials.

Enthusiasm had run high for Margold's appointment as director of the joint legal campaign of the NAACP and the American Fund in the fall of 1930. Based on Frankfurter's recommendation, Charles Hamilton Houston, the vice dean at Howard Law School, asked Margold to lunch in September. Houston, who was another of Frankfurter's prized students, knew Margold from law school. The two served together as editors of the *Harvard Law Review*. In the spring term of 1923, while Houston was earning a graduate degree, he and Margold had even enrolled in the same section of Frankfurter's course Administrative Law, a new class designed to study institutional questions arising in the modern state.[48]

Houston came away from his lunch with Margold reminded that his fellow editor was "a remarkable man." Writing to Walter White at the NAACP, he called Margold an "indefatigable" lawyer with "an unusual mind." Margold seemed so energized to direct the Joint Committee legal campaign, Houston added, that he was willing to take the work for a lower fee than he would ordinarily require. A month later, White and Johnson met Margold over another lunch to impress upon him that work for the Joint Committee meant taking direction from the NAACP first and the Garland Fund second. Margold apparently agreed, and in October he entered an agreement with the Joint Committee to do the legal work on behalf of its campaign. An NAACP press release soon made it official. Nathan Margold would serve as the director of a "national legal campaign for Negro rights."[49]

For two months after signing on to direct the campaign, however, the NAACP's new lawyer was so engrossed in the Pueblo cases and in drafting the claims commissions bill for Brookings that he had little time for the organization's campaign. White and Johnson were dismayed at the delays. But when Margold at last turned to strategizing the Joint Committee's legal campaign in the first weeks of 1931, his Indian law efforts guided him through Jim Crow's legal thickets.[50]

The Joint Committee had asked him to design a campaign that would feature, first and foremost, school funding equalization cases. Such lawsuits aimed to put the lie to *Plessy v. Ferguson*'s duplicitous separate-but-equal standard, under which state-mandated separation of the races was permitted so long as the separate facilities purported to be equal. The Garland Fund had helped publicize the outrageous inequality in southern schools, going back all the way to the Du Bois studies of Black elementary schools. The Fund's Committee on Negro Work, and its successor the Joint Committee, believed that successful school cases would redirect tax dollars toward Black schools. Operating parallel equal schools, moreover, would be expensive; the cost of a true "dual school system" would be "so prohibitive as to speed the abolishment of segregated schools" altogether. Or so Johnson and many at the NAACP hoped.[51]

Sympathetic critics of the plan lobbed objections. Broadus Mitchell, an economist at Johns Hopkins University, wrote Morris Ernst to warn that any rights the NAACP achieved would give way to "all sorts of ways of evading the law, even when clearly and expensively established." Striking a Frankfurterian note, Mitchell warned Ernst that "so many matters lie within the discretion of administrative officers that your purpose would be defeated" even if "technically you had won." W. E. B. Du Bois amplified the critique. Frustrated by the American Fund's omission of a set-aside for *The Crisis* in its big NAACP grant, Du Bois warned Margold that institutional intransigence in the South would render any work he did pointless. "The real discrimination," Du Bois said, "comes in the administration of these general laws." The core of the problem for Mitchell (and increasingly for Du Bois as well) was that absent what he called "social progress" and "economic competence," mere legal rights would "have no meaning."[52]

As a close Frankfurter student, Margold grasped the complaint. Administration, he readily agreed, mattered more than formal legal rights. Economic power might matter more, too. But Margold saw something that more doctrinaire socialist critics like Mitchell had overlooked. Administration and economics were not outside forces. There was a law of administration. Legal rules and institutions constructed the authority of administrative officials. The law determined, or at least powerfully shaped, who could call themselves the solicitor of the Interior Department and what it meant to do so. The power of local school boards, by the same token, was built by the tax laws and the election rules that funded them and decided on their memberships. One can't tell who holds an office, or what the office does, without some law governing who decides.[53]

The law of administration therefore seemed to Margold a sensible place to begin a campaign of social change like the one the Joint Committee contemplated. Mitchell even conceded as much when he wrote the introduction to a 1931 ACLU study of civil rights titled "Black Justice." If "the Negro has been oppressed" because of economic exploitation, Mitchell observed, "the other way around" was also true: "he is economically servile because he has been oppressed." One route to disrupting the interactive cycle of economic exploitation and racial oppression might be as good as another. What was needed was a plausible starting point.[54]

For Margold, the real problem with the Joint Committee's initial plan of action was not its choice to use law but its failure to account for the legal foundations of the fierce resistance it was about to encounter. The scandal of the government's administration of Indian affairs—like his own experience of discrimination at the hands of the Harvard administration—had taught Margold that adversaries would not simply give way in the face of meritorious claims. With this in mind, he turned at last to drafting a plan for the NAACP and its Joint Committee. What he came up with would serve as the most famous, and in some ways least well understood, model for legal change in the twentieth century.

The law of racially separate education seemed straightforward. In a case called *Gong Lum v. Rice*, decided in 1927, the Supreme Court had formally upheld racial segregation in public schools. The case arose when a Mississippi grocery store owner named Jeu Gong Lum sent his two daughters to the local public school for white children. Lum and his daughters were of Chinese descent, though his daughters were U.S. citizens by birth. School officials sent the girls home, citing the Mississippi law prohibiting "colored" children from attending white schools. According to Chief Justice (and former president) William Howard Taft, Mississippi's decision to bar the girls from the white school was "within the discretion of the state in regulating its public schools." Separate education, Taft explained, was a "question which has been many times decided to be within the constitutional power of the state Legislature to settle." The Fourteenth Amendment, which guaranteed the equal protection of the laws to all persons, did not require integration. It merely required equality. The *Gong Lum* plaintiffs had not pressed the equality question because they had no interest in attending schools set aside for Black children, equal or otherwise. Chinese families in Mississippi turned to private religious schools or moved out of state after being rebuffed at the white schools; the Lum family relocated to Arkansas. Still, as Du Bois's Garland Fund studies had helped illuminate, the obvious inequalities in white and Black schools lurked as a gaping legal vulnerability for Jim Crow after *Gong Lum*. The Joint Committee aimed to exploit it.[55]

Margold, however, offered an objection of his own. Drawing on Du Bois's and Mitchell's recent observations about the difficulties the litigation campaign would face, he took them a step further. The mechanisms of school inequality, Margold observed, were intensely situation specific. They varied widely from place to place and changed over time. Some southern states discriminated by allocating resources unequally to counties based on whether they were predominantly white or Black. Others delegated authority to the county level, where white county officials presided over unequal allocations to school districts with predominantly white or predominantly Black populations. At other times, funding discrimination arose in school boards' local division of funds among the schools in a given district.[56]

There was not one Jim Crow. There were many. It followed that many different suits (a "multiplicity of suits," in Margold's words), both in kind and in number, would be necessary to advance the project contemplated by the NAACP and the Joint Committee. As Margold surveyed the problem, he concluded that the sheer number of cases would be downright "appalling." Separate suits would be required "against each officer charged with the duty" of making the funding decisions. To make matters worse, the most extreme funding disparities existed in school districts where local officials divided funds among schools. But those would also be the most labor-intensive and expensive lawsuits to bring. Such suits would entail detailed factual inquiries into the conditions of each school at issue. They would require hundreds or thousands of different proceedings against officials across thousands of local school districts. There were more than 15,000 school districts in southern states in 1930. (NAACP officials estimated 45,000 districts in the United States altogether; the real number was more than twice that.) An effort to challenge the equality of even a tiny fraction of the districts would be prohibitively costly. Worse still, such suits "would have to be brought year after year," since each case would address only the wrongful distribution of a given year's school budget. The next year's budget seemed likely to require an entirely new case and an entirely new analysis of the myriad ways in which the district had shortchanged Black students and their teachers. The Joint Committee had contemplated seven suits, one each for South Carolina, Georgia, Mississippi, Louisiana, Florida, Alabama, and Arkansas. But Margold contended that a mere seven suits "would barely cause a ripple on the surface of the vast sea of litigation required." It would take dozens, perhaps hundreds, or even thousands of court cases to make a sizable splash. Any smaller effort might merely "fritter away" the modest Garland Fund grant on "sporadic attempts" at equalization in one place for a single school year. In all, relying on the suits contemplated by the Fund's grant, as one historian later put it, would be like "trying to empty a swimming pool with an eyedropper." Such lawsuits would establish no new proposition of law to undermine Jim Crow. Each Pyrrhic victory would exert no force beyond the specific judgment obtained, if indeed judgments could be obtained. Even litigation wins, Margold warned, would leave "wholly untouched the very essence of the existing evils."[57]

Margold saw that he did not need to choose between attacking the law of segregation, on the one hand, or administration, on the other. Attacking the legal institutions that lay behind segregation was the real challenge. Far-flung school districts with their brick-and-mortar buildings and their thousands of flesh-and-blood officials would do their damnedest to defend the racial hierarchy in the South. Targeting the institutional structures of Jim Crow thus offered an enticing opportunity, not least because they relied heavily on the law for support. It was law that defined states, counties, towns, and school districts in such a way as to ensure that they were controlled by white communities. Law identified the offices of the school board and distinguished the school principal from the school janitor, not to mention people who were "colored" from people who were not. Even something so basic as the shape of districts in the South, which were distinctively large compared to other regions, had been formed by the law to accommodate the creation of racially separate schools.[58]

In his Indian law efforts, the priority of administrative law over formal legal rights would lead Margold to press for tribal sovereignty in the management of their own affairs. A parallel idea circulated in Communist circles in the form of self-determination for the Black Belt. The difficulty, as critics of the Black Belt thesis ranging from Du Bois to Randolph had noted, was that Black oppression had arisen from radically different historical and legal roots than Native exploitation. For Black Americans, there was no viable legal path to a separate sovereignty, and no popular constituency that wanted one. Margold's task—what he needed to do to advance the NAACP–American Fund effort—was to find another way to intervene in the administrative structure of Jim Crow.[59]

The strategy Margold hit upon reached back not to the *Gong Lum* case of 1927 but to a different Supreme Court decision involving people of Chinese descent. The now obscure 1886 case known as *Yick Wo v. Hopkins* arose when two San Francisco laundry owners were arrested for operating without the permit required by a city ordinance. Lawyers for the laundry owners, Yick Wo and Wo Lee, pointed out that city officials enforced the ordinance selectively to keep people of Chinese descent out of the laundry business. The Supreme Court agreed and decided that discriminatory administration was just as unconstitutional as discriminatory laws. Writing for the Court, Justice T. Stanley Matthews explained that the "denial of equal justice is still within the prohibition of the Constitution" even if it was administered by "an evil eye and an unequal hand" rather than being formally expressed in a statutory enactment.[60]

As Margold saw it, Jim Crow schooling posed the same administrative inequality the Court had rejected in *Yick Wo*. The southern states imposed segregation "under conditions which enable its officers" to provide facilities "in the colored schools" that were "grossly inferior to those provided in the white schools." The result was "segregation irremediably coupled with discrimination." Such segregation was plainly unconstitutional.[61]

In this respect, as historians would later note, Margold's proposed campaign went further than the Joint Committee had contemplated. The Joint Committee had planned to challenge Jim Crow only indirectly, leaving its basic legal framework in place while forcing southern states to live up to their promises of a purportedly equal segregation. Margold, by contrast, proposed that separating students on the basis of race was necessarily unconstitutional given the actually existing way Jim Crow worked. He proposed to "challenge the constitutional validity of segregation" as a practice because it was invariably, like laundry permit enforcement, accompanied by discrimination as administered. Segregation arising out of "administrative action," Margold wrote in his report's peroration, "is just as much a denial of equal protection of the laws" as segregation "by express statutory enactment." The "evil eye" and the "unequal hand" of administration, as the Court had called it in the *Yick Wo* case, was no more permissible in Jim Crow than it had been in the anti-Chinese laws of the nineteenth-century West.[62]

The Margold Report drew on the Chinese discrimination case with the same goal its author would seek in his opinions on Indian tribal powers. It was crafted to attack the legal administration behind Jim Crow and thereby develop an institutionally durable approach to ending oppression. Margold's *Yick Wo* strategy was not designed to attain integration for its own sake, though later historians would make the mistake of thinking so. Margold's point was that so long as schools were separate, Black schoolchildren and Black teachers would constantly be vulnerable to cheating by white school districts and their officials. The legal efforts to defend against backsliding would be unending. Thousands of white officials would continue to prefer white schools over Black ones; challenging them would be like Sisyphus pushing the boulder. At a single school for all children, by contrast, it would be much harder to treat Black students differently than white ones. Unifying the South's schools, Margold proposed, would thus do for Jim Crow what the institutional arrangements of Margold's early Indian law work aimed to do for Native peoples. Like giving Indian tribes more power, the idea of *Yick Wo* was to alter the institutional and administrative arrangements of oppression—to rearrange the legal structure of schools in such a way as to allow the power of the NAACP's lawsuits to be more effectively applied.[63]

To emphasize the point, Margold and Walter White added a new dimension to the Joint Committee's program of Black emancipation, one that was explicitly about the political power of Black people in the South. When Margold arrived on the NAACP legal team he found already underway an effort to fight against the disfranchisement of Black voters. After the death of prominent German Jewish lawyer and longtime NAACP director Louis Marshall, Margold took over the case. In March 1932, he argued the appeal in *Nixon v. Condon* at the Supreme Court, an update to the *Nixon v. Herndon* case from 1927, which had struck down Texas's state law prohibition on Black voters in Democratic Party primaries. Now Margold argued that a revised system, in which the Texas branch of the Democratic Party excluded Black voters on its own, also violated the Constitution. By a bare majority, the justices agreed with Margold and the NAACP. *Nixon v. Condon* was a small victory, to be sure; further machinations by the Texas Democratic Party would mean that the right to vote in the state's primaries would have to await the 1944 decision in *Smith v. Allwright*; Black voting rights in the South more generally would require decades of further protest and litigation, culminating in the Voting Rights Act of 1965. That the all-white primary case would be the first use of the American Fund's money in a case at the Supreme Court—that ultimately it would be the only such use during Margold's tenure with the NAACP— was fitting, not anomalous. Margold's blueprint for educational equalization adopted a parallel strategy. It targeted the legal power to adopt separate schools, for the separation of schools made resource inequalities easier to accomplish. The crucial thing, as Du Bois and Broadus Mitchell had pointed out in their critiques of the legal campaign's earliest formulations, was the management of authority. Margold agreed.[64]

Margold summed up the core of his approach in May 1932 in Washington at the twenty-third annual conference of the NAACP. Delegates from twenty-six states and the District of Columbia attended. Organization leaders White, Du Bois, Houston, and Ovington were all there. Together, the group made a Saturday visit to Harpers Ferry for a ceremony at the site of John Brown's rebellion. The next morning, on a cool Sunday, they traveled to Frederick Douglass's home in Anacostia for a violin recital by Joseph Douglass, grandson of the great abolitionist. Evening session speakers included Du Bois and White along with philosopher John Dewey and the journalist George Schuyler, a longtime figure in A. Philip Randolph's radical Harlem. Senators Robert La Follette, Arthur Capper, and Robert Bulkley appeared and spoke. The conference's theme was "The Struggle for Jobs and Economic Opportunity." Du Bois called for a new direction for the organization, emphasizing the need for a "positive economic program." The conference's chair, Walter White, promised to attack "the economic barriers in the path of the Negro."[65]

At a closely watched session of the conference, in what veteran NAACP publicity man Herbert Seligmann called "a sensational speech," Margold told the assembled national leaders of the organization that it would be impossible to carry out the campaign Walter White and James Weldon Johnson had first proposed. With White in the audience, Margold called their plan impractical "unless we have a world of money at our command and could sue year after year in dozens and dozens of communities." The alternative, Margold urged, was to "strike directly at the heart of the situation." Southern states should be forced to admit Black children into white schools, and not "on the old theory" of a "right to intermingle" that the Supreme Court had rejected in the *Gong Lum* case. That was a theory, Margold said, "which we cannot press," if only because the court had rebuffed it so recently. The better idea, as Margold conceived it, was the *Yick Wo*–inspired argument that drew on Frankfurter's approach to law, what Margold now called "a right to equality" in the administrative law of schools.[66]

Out of this foundational idea of attacking the administrative foundations of the Jim Crow regime came a plan of lawsuits against school districts in the South. But ever since, critics have leveled the charge that the white Harvard graduate Margold had made a grave mistake. Du Bois, soon on his way out at the NAACP and embittered at having been left out of the Garland Fund's grant, turned against the solution he had helped to design. Margold's plan, he charged, substituted a flimsy right to integrated schooling for the more important goal of a decent education. Du Bois, who would later express different views, ungraciously omitted to notice that Margold's strategy, responding in part to Du Bois's own exhortations, was designed not to achieve integration as such but to take account of the administration of southern governments and to recapture what Horace Mann Bond had called the "cash value of Negro children." By attending to institutional structure, Margold aimed to advance the project of recouping Black people's own tax dollars.[67]

Important traces of the Garland Fund's abiding interest in labor remained in Margold's plan, too. In particular, the blueprint revived the Committee on Negro Work's plan to desegregate labor unions. Where Morris Ernst had understandably worried that suing white labor unions would fracture the progressive labor movement coalition, Margold proposed an attack not on unions' private membership rules but on state laws banning integrated private associations. In Virginia, labor unions were white not merely because they excluded Black workers on their own accord; the law required segregated unions, at pain of a $5,000 fine or up to twelve months in jail. Margold proposed to attack the state's Jim Crow labor law alongside its separate and unequal schools.[68]

If there was a difficulty in Margold's plan, it was connected to a crucial difference between his proposed campaign for the NAACP and his work on Indian law. In the Hualapai lands case, and in his work with Felix Cohen on the powers of Indian tribes, Margold concentrated on empowering Indian peoples in the ongoing defense of their own interests. The Fourteenth Amendment, by contrast, seemed to offer no plausible analog to self-determination. Nor could Margold do more than gesture toward how the American Fund coalition of race liberals and union radicals might engineer a legal attack on the labor movement. Margold's enduring contribution was to have focused the NAACP plan of attack on questions of power and administration, and to have adapted it to the existing institutions of the American South. Yet even as he was finishing his report, events upended the world in which the Fund and the NAACP aimed to intervene.

Charles Hamilton Houston with local NAACP president Virginia McGuire at an anti-lynching protest in Washington, D.C., 1934.

18

Scottsboro and After

The I.L.D. has made it impossible for the Negro bourgeoisie in the future to be as complacent and supine before racial injustices as it was prior to Scottsboro.
—CHARLES HAMILTON HOUSTON
AT HOWARD UNIVERSITY, 1935

On March 25, 1931, in the town of Paint Rock, Alabama, population 320, an armed posse of white men pulled nine Black boys and young men, ages thirteen to twenty, off a freight train. The posse was responding to reports of a fight between white vagrants and a "bunch of Negroes" two stations back down the line. Unexpectedly, they found two young white women aboard the train, not much older than the nine. The women, ages eighteen and twenty-one, reported that they had been raped. Within hours, officials charged the nine youths with the crime. Amid fevered calls for a lynching party, the state of Alabama held four hasty trials in early April in the nearby county seat of Scottsboro. No trial lasted more than a day. Whites-only juries voted to convict all nine defendants, sentencing eight of them to die by electric chair. The case against the youngest defendant, thirteen-year-old Roy Wright, ended in mistrial when jurors insisted on execution even though the prosecutor had requested life imprisonment on account of the boy's age.[1]

The Scottsboro travesty, and the controversy that ensued, derailed Nathan Margold's finely wrought legal campaign. The Communist Party almost immediately saw the arrests for the outrage they were. Even before the sham trials were complete, the Party-backed International Labor Defense issued public statements denouncing the proceedings. Front groups like the League of Struggle for Negro Rights, run by Fund director Clarina Michelson and favored by Charles Garland, orchestrated mass public protests within weeks. Hundreds gathered at the end of April near 140th Street and Lenox Avenue in Harlem, where clashes with police led to arrests and beatings. In mid-May, a Harlem protest march of two hundred Communists snowballed as it proceeded through the streets to become, as one Scottsboro case chronicler puts it, a "crowd of three thousand" that "had fallen into step" to protest the impending Alabama executions. The *Daily Worker* called the episode a new Sacco and Vanzetti. Soon the ILD was making common cause with the defendants' families and rallying Black churches in Alabama and nearby Tennessee. Rallies and protests unfolded in cities across the country, as the ILD escorted grieving family members to share their stories with audiences Black and white. On the verge of rolling out its long-planned legal campaign, by contrast, the NAACP was caught in a vise between the moral urgency of the Alabama show trials, on the one hand, and its caution about being associated with nine accused rapists, on the other. Walter White chose the latter path. It was a mistake from which his reputation would never quite recover.[2]

For the next year and a half, Margold pressed on as best as he and the NAACP could manage amid the turmoil of the ongoing Scottsboro controversies. He assisted in the association's challenge to Texas's whites-only primary elections and contributed his expertise to a suit to overturn Black disfranchisement in Louisiana. But the association's stumbling effort to defend the Scottsboro Nine, combined with the Communist Party's energetic support for the young men's exoneration, produced a crisis for the NAACP's legal strategy. In the meanwhile, uncertainty about whether the cash-starved Garland Fund would be able to meet its grant promise put a pause to the campaign's work. A frustrated Margold left the NAACP for the Interior Department in early 1933, returning to the Indian law questions and the Hualapai cases that had become his passion.[3]

Margold's replacement, his old Harvard classmate and friend Charles Hamilton Houston, seemed by temperament and professional training likely to carry forward his predecessor's program. The two men had been favorite students in Felix Frankfurter's administrative law course. But at the crucial moment of the education campaign's takeoff, Houston drew lessons from the Scottsboro episode and the Communists' success. Emerging as one of a number of restless young militants pushing the NAACP toward mass politics, Houston recast the legal campaign Margold had designed. Staked to a substantial share of the American Fund's dwindling resources, he went all in on the Fund's bet that lawsuits could be a winning strategy in the era of mass mobilizing.[4]

Tactics for Mass Pressure

In most respects, Charles Hamilton Houston was an unlikely leader for mass politics. He was born in 1895 in Washington, D.C. His father, William, was a lawyer and a clerk in the pension office at the War Department. Both of William's parents (Charles's paternal grandparents) had escaped from slavery. Charles's mother, Mary, was a sought-after hairdresser for the wives of Washington's political elite. Her free Black father (Charles's maternal grandfather) had purchased her mother from slavery in South Carolina.[5]

In Washington, the family lived in what Houston's biographer Genna Rae McNeil calls a "respectable part of town for educated blacks," where Charles was "brought up as the best." As a boy he attended the city's finest public schools for Black students, including M Street High School, later renamed for the poet Paul Laurence Dunbar, one of the United States' only all-Black college preparatory high schools with a classical curriculum. After finishing at M Street at the age of fifteen, Houston enrolled at Amherst College, where he was the only Black student in his class, and for a time, the only Black student in the entire college. He graduated Phi Beta Kappa.[6]

Two years later, upon the country's 1917 entry into the war, he signed up for a new army training program for Black officers. Some NAACP members resisted the idea of separate officer training; segregated training for officers, they said, capitulated to Jim Crow. Houston supported the separate program. The army, he reasoned, would be segregated either way, and if there were to be Black officers, then segregated officer training would be required, at least for the time being. But for a year and a half, until the war's end, the Jim Crow program for which he had volunteered inflicted on him a train of white supremacist insults. Racist white officers railroaded Black enlisted men into unjust courts-martial. (As an officer, Houston was pressed into the quixotic role of representing the Black enlistees.) Commanders forced talented Black officers into demeaning and often dangerous positions. Jim Crow took root in the camps of the Western Front, filling them with racial indignities and deadly discriminations. If the German enemy was not danger enough, armed white soldiers posed a threat. One evening in 1918 in Vannes, France, a lynch mob of white enlisted men and two white officers formed, cornering Houston and two other Black officers on the town plaza. It was time, the mob screamed, to "put a few" of these army "niggers" in "their place." Quick thinking and good luck saved the three men that night. Houston made up his mind "that I would never get caught again without knowing something about my rights." If "luck was with me, and I got through this war," he resolved, "I would study law and use my time fighting for men who could not strike back." "I felt damned glad," he fumed after the war, "I had not lost my life fighting for this country."[7]

Houston enrolled in Harvard Law School in the fall of 1919, where he distinguished himself, eventually graduating twenty-second in a class of over two hundred men. The first Black student to be elected to the *Harvard Law Review*, Houston served on volume 35 along with Nathan Margold. Both men had sought out Felix Frankfurter, the phenom of the Harvard faculty, and the two Frankfurter students came to admire one another. Houston's encomiums in 1930 had helped Margold secure the position directing the NAACP's campaign. Margold, in turn, praised Houston as a brilliant lawyer with a "superlative" character and "unusual tact and personal charm." Frankfurter agreed. He remembered Houston, who wrote a doctoral thesis on the functions of due process in American administrative law, as one of his finest students.[8]

After a year studying law in Spain, Houston set out to replicate Frankfurter's Cambridge workshop for young progressive lawyers, but to do so for Black lawyers in the nation's capital. "There must be Negro lawyers in every community," Houston wrote while still enrolled in Frankfurter's course, and "the great majority" of them "must come from Negro schools." Surveying the nation's Black lawyers, Houston concluded that the need was desperate. After exhaustive efforts, he identified "no more than 100" Black lawyers engaged in full-time law practice in the South, and fewer than 1,000 in the country as a whole. There was one Black lawyer for every 90,000 Black people in the South, as compared to a national average among whites of one lawyer for every 695 people. "Experience has

Volume 35 of the Harvard Law Review. *Charles Hamilton Houston, the first Black editor, stands second from the right in the top row; Nathan Margold, one of only a handful of Jewish editors, sits second from the right in the second row.*

proved," Houston wrote, "that the average white lawyer, especially in the South, cannot be relied upon to wage an uncompromising fight for equal rights for Negroes."[9]

To bring his vision to life, Houston accepted a faculty position at the Howard University law school while practicing law alongside his father. The elder Houston had attended Howard when it was a mediocre night school with a poor reputation among lawyers in the white-dominated bar. For the next decade, first as a professor and then as the school's presiding vice dean, Houston modernized and upgraded the institution, shutting down its night program in 1930 and turning the school into a first-rate educational program with national stature. Change produced grumbling. The night program had been popular among working-class Black men who had to hold jobs during the day to make ends meet. But Houston pressed on. His Howard colleague William Hastie, a fellow graduate of Amherst and Harvard Law School and a second cousin of Houston's, later recalled that Houston was committed to preparing "the professional cadres needed to lead successful litigation against racism." When enrollment numbers declined because of new academic standards, Houston traveled to Black colleges around the country recruiting the best and brightest. The pitch he offered was alluring. He was creating a laboratory for social change. The "Negro lawyer," Houston explained in 1929, "must be trained as a social engineer." Even more than that, Black America's subordinate social condition meant that "the Negro lawyer must be prepared to anticipate, guide and interpret his group." The Black lawyer would have to manage his community's advancement.[10]

The American Bar Association accredited Houston's Howard as an ABA-approved law school in 1931. That same year the American Association of Law Schools admitted the institution to membership. Houston's assembly line of social engineers for the race had begun to roll.[11]

The eight Alabama convictions in April 1931 scrambled Houston's plans for technocratic legal engineering. Scottsboro, Houston said to a Howard group in 1935, "introduced the Negro to the possibilities and tactics of mass pressure." It "changed the emphasis of the Negro question from a race issue to a class issue." And it raised the expectations of Black communities. "Nobody who ever sent a telegram of protest" about the Alabama cases, Houston came to believe, was ever "going to tolerate the system and the oppression" of white supremacy in the same way. Scottsboro in this sense was an opportunity, but it was one that pressed Houston to develop strategies unlike any of the technocratic social engineering tactics he and Margold had learned from Frankfurter.[12]

Almost immediately, the Alabama travesty exacerbated the split that the NAACP grant had opened in the world of the American Fund. When the Communist-backed lawyers with the ILD gained an early advantage over the NAACP, the Party poured abuse on moderates and reformers. Adopting the Comintern's intransigent post-1928 line, and nursing wounds from the Party's defeat in the Garland Fund grant showdown of 1930, hardliner Clarina Michelson lashed out at her fellow Fund director James Weldon Johnson and at NAACP leaders White and Du Bois. Penning flyers and pamphlets for the Party's Agitprop Department, Michelson condemned the "treachery of the Negro Reformists," denouncing the NAACP for what she characterized as "servile cringing to the white ruling class oppressors." The civil rights organization, she charged, was trying to "stem the mass movement on behalf of the boys" and had nothing more to offer them "than the empty promises of a sly slave owner." Michelson smeared Norman Thomas and the Socialist Party, too, accusing them of being "equally treacherous as the NAACP." Charles Garland, under Communist influence until the end of the decade, weighed in to urge that the Fund redirect support for the NAACP to front groups like the obscure League of Struggle for Negro Rights. The conduct of the NAACP in the Scottsboro case, he asserted, "has been anything but advanced or radical."[13]

Lingering bitterness over the American Fund's NAACP grant helped explain the Party's efforts to embarrass the NAACP around Scottsboro. Writing to liberal white southerner Will Alexander, and copying James Weldon Johnson, Walter White recalled that "under party orders" Michelson and her fellow Communists on the Fund board had "fought bitterly to the very end" to defeat the Fund's NAACP grant and win it over for the ILD and Party fronts. Du Bois, who rarely agreed with White, concurred. Despite a growing affinity for the NAACP's critics, he derided the ILD's conduct as designed to promote the Party without regard to the interests of the Scottsboro defendants, a tactic he condemned as "too despicable for words." The Communists, Du Bois fumed, "want these lads murdered."[14]

The American Fund managed to skirt Scottsboro's fierce intramural controversies, even though its big 1930 grant had contributed to the hostilities. Not hamstrung like the NAACP by the worry that the unknown (and potentially unreliable) rape defendants might harm their reputation in other battles, the Fund's directors jumped in and offered financial support to whatever organization could best support the defense effort. Already at the end of March 1931, the Committee on Civil Liberties at the Fund voted to release money for the Scottsboro cause to both the Communist-backed ILD and the NAACP. A special meeting of the Fund directors later entrusted $5,000 to Morris Ernst's care to be "disbursed at his discretion" to support the Alabama defendants. Baldwin, though feeling "caught in the middle of it" between "the Communists and the NAACP," acted as a go-between. Baldwin even helped engineer a creative division of labor in which the NAACP pursued schools cases while the ILD used the Scottsboro cases to fight for the criminal procedure rights of Black defendants.[15]

The American Fund's role as a broker among the Scottsboro defendants' supporters helped sustain the cases' biggest successes. The ILD hired longtime Garland Fund advisor Walter Pollak to handle the appeal of seven convicted Scottsboro defendants at the Supreme Court. (The eighth, Eugene Williams, had won on appeal at the Alabama Supreme Court because of his age at the time of the alleged crime.) Pollak, a Harvard-trained lawyer from a Jewish family in New York, had served on a Fund committee studying labor injunctions in the middle of the 1920s. In 1925 he had represented Fund director Ben Gitlow before the Supreme Court in his losing appeal on criminal anarchy charges for advocating the violent overthrow of the government. Now in *Powell v. Alabama*, decided in 1932, Pollak successfully persuaded the Supreme Court to recognize a constitutional right to effective assistance of counsel in criminal prosecutions. Citing the defendants' farcical trial, the court reversed all seven convictions. Three years later, Pollak represented two of the Scottsboro defendants, Clarence Norris and Haywood Patterson, in a second round at the Supreme Court. This time, in *Norris v. Alabama* and *Patterson v. Alabama*, he won reversal of their convictions because of the state's exclusion of Black jurors from the jury pool in the retrials following the *Powell* case. Later that same year, when the defendants' allies formed a new Scottsboro Defense Committee, the group resembled a virtual reunion of the American Fund's heady early meetings. Fund directors Baldwin, Robert Morss Lovett, and Norman Thomas took part, along with Fund beneficiaries like Walter White and A. Philip Randolph. Communists from the ILD now joined, too, abandoning their sectarian attacks in favor of the Comintern's new Popular Front stance of uniting with liberals in order to build a coalition against the Soviet Union's fascist enemies.[16]

Houston, for his part, was an early adopter of something like the Garland Fund's middle ground between the NAACP old guard and the insurgent ILD. Though he carried himself as a buttoned-up lawyer and served as a member of the NAACP National Legal Committee, Houston admired the brash politics of the ILD and the Communists, even if their tactics sometimes chafed. A decade earlier, as a law student, and still stinging from the vicious discrimination of his wartime service, Houston had broken out of the Harvard mold by inviting Marcus Garvey to speak to a small group of students. In Houston's view, Garvey's United Negro Improvement Association, then at the height of its fame, was "a black man's dream," teaching the "simple dignity of being black." In the early 1930s,

Houston became friendly with the ILD's national secretary, an iconoclastic Black lawyer named William "Pat" Patterson, who helped persuade the Howard law dean that Scottsboro had "caught the imagination of Negroes as nothing else within a decade."[17]

Scottsboro's mobilization of mass-protest politics led Houston to revise the model of professional training at Howard. Where once he had envisioned technocratic social engineers on the Frankfurter model, now he assembled something more like A. J. Muste's Brookwood Labor College, combining institutional design with mass movement energies. Houston's Howard would do for race emancipation what Muste's Brookwood aimed to accomplish for labor. Guest speakers like Clarence Darrow came through, not because of their technical skills, but because they had moved things in the world. Houston led his students on parade as part of the ILD's mass Scottsboro protests. He made donations to the ILD. He orchestrated protests at federal agencies to demand attention to race discrimination in the distribution of federal money. It was the Communist Party, Houston argued, not the NAACP, and certainly not the NAACP's legal campaign, that had energized "the masses" of Black people "with a sense of their raw, potential power." NAACP leaders, he told the *Amsterdam News* soon after the *Powell v. Alabama* decision, seemed "to think that justice for the Scottsboro boys can be obtained in Alabama without outside pressure," and that the Communists' connection to the boys' cases "hurts the boys chances" of surviving. "I disagree," Houston stated flatly. "What sort of justice did the boys obtain in Alabama," he asked, before the ILD "entered the case?"[18]

The Communists at the ILD spat at Houston's generosity. When Houston defended basic civil rights, he was startled to find the ILD attacking him as one of the "agents of capitalism," trying to trick "the Negro people to put their faith in the courts" while currying favor with "the lynch bosses of Virginia." In December 1934, American Fund director Clarina Michelson's civil rights organization—really no more than a Party front—defamed Houston as one of the group's "Uncle Toms of the year." The prize was a bandanna.[19]

Nathan Margold's 1933 resignation highlighted unresolved issues in the American Fund's basic arrangement with the NAACP. The Fund's hotly contested May 1930 vote had purported to award $100,000 to a Joint Committee of the Fund and the NAACP. But the vote proved less conclusive than the grant's supporters had expected. From the spring of 1931 onward, the liberal contingent of the Fund board waged continuing skirmishes with the Fund's left wing over the release of money for the NAACP grant, fights that were made more bitter by the Fund's plunging Depression-era stock market assets. Squabbles over the NAACP's failure to make payments on a separate 1929 loan further delayed grant disbursements. ("I do not see," wrote an exasperated White in response to an American Fund dunning notice, "how it is humanly possible to comply with your request.") By early 1932, White acceded to the Fund's directive that the NAACP pause "all work on our plans pending word from the Garland Fund," testily reminding the Fund's left-wing directors that "the Association would not have employed Mr. Margold . . . had not the definite pledge been made for this program of work by the Fund."[20]

Holding the purse strings to the Joint Committee grant meant that the American Fund's directors retained ongoing power over the NAACP campaign. Over the next few years, the Fund required new votes of the board to release payments on the grant, even for small disbursements such as reimbursing Margold's expenses. In July 1933, with the legal campaign lacking a director, a badly divided Fund authorized the release of $10,000 for the 1934–35 fiscal year. Roger Baldwin now voted yes, leaving the Communists Dunn and Gitlow in dissent, with Michelson not voting. Sympathetic directors like Johnson, Gannett, and Kirchwey pressed at the time to commit to another $10,000 in the following year, but they could make no assurances, in part because Baldwin switched back to the left-wing position and resisted any promises for future funding. When Baldwin urged the NAACP to replace Margold with another white lawyer, the organization could do little but listen. Walter White offered the position to the talented Columbia professor Karl Llewellyn, who after sizing up the situation astutely declined on the grounds that he was "not the best person" to do the job.[21]

Walter White had all along seen Houston as the "ideal person" for the role, someone whom Frankfurter had endorsed as "one of the most brilliant and able students at Harvard within his memory." Among other things, White told Baldwin delicately, hiring a Black lawyer "would enable us not only to secure a man who would have all the intellectual and legal background necessary"—it would allow the Joint Committee to retain a lawyer "who will have a definite personal interest which would cause him to do the job better and less expensively." Margold concurred, calling Houston an "exceptionally able lawyer" and noting how poorly the Alabama courts had treated the ILD's northern white defense lawyers in the Scottsboro cases. Baldwin bowed to Houston's choice. On October 26, 1934, the Joint Committee signed a contract with Houston to serve as the new special counsel of the NAACP with authority over the Garland Fund legal campaign.[22]

The campaign Houston inherited was a shriveled relic of the $100,000 effort the Fund had approved in 1930, let alone the $300,000 juggernaut the Committee on Negro Work had contemplated in 1929. White mourned that the program—"cut down to the matters of schools and Jim Crow traveling accommodations"—was "far from what was originally promised and is a severe disappointment to us." It was "a pity," he observed to Houston, "that the stock market crash reduced the assets of the Fund to the extent that they will not be able to give us the full sum for this superb fight." By the time Houston arrived as special counsel, the Fund's net assets had fallen to a measly $52,000, plus whatever it was able to recover from $228,000 in unpaid loans. Lack of money, in turn, meant lack of results. Three years after Margold had finalized his campaign blueprint, White and the NAACP could claim little by way of progress, merely an ad hoc smattering of preliminary investigations scattered around the country. The campaign's docket was a far cry from the all-out attack on Jim Crow that the American Fund and the NAACP had contemplated.[23]

With a vitality that belied the Fund's evaporating grant money, however, Houston injected the mass energy of the Scottsboro Nine into the NAACP legal campaign. For months, young left-leaning militants, some of them supported by the American Fund, had been trying to turn the Black civil rights organization toward the mass politics of industrial democracy. Howard University economist Abram Lincoln Harris Jr. led the group. A longtime participant in Brookwood Labor College conferences and a speaker at the 1932 NAACP conference on jobs and economic opportunity, Harris had been a grant recipient from the American Fund for his landmark 1931 study, *The Black Worker: The Negro and the Labor Movement*. Harris and the other young delegates urged the NAACP to make the Black worker "conscious of his relation to white labor"—and to make the white worker, in turn, understand that "the purposes" of the labor movement could not "be achieved without full participation from the Negro worker." The group, which had first assembled at A. J. Muste's Brookwood for a Workers Education Conference for Negroes, featured the militants Harris, Ralph Bunche, and George Schuyler in sometimes tense dialogue with senior figures Du Bois, Johnson, and White.[24]

Organized in 1934, a Committee on the Future Plan and Program, with Harris as its chair, urged the NAACP to commit itself to a Brookwood-style program of organizing, workers' education, research, and publications. The organization's goal, Harris announced, should be to "lay the intellectual basis for united action between white and black workers." Harris, like his senior comrade A. Philip Randolph, condemned the idea of a "separate Negro group economy"; economic separatism, he insisted, could hardly sustain the desperately poor Black masses, eager for jobs in white-owned mass industries. Instead, Harris's *Report on Future Plan and Program* called for "the building of a labor movement, industrial in character, which will unite all labor, white and black." An inconclusive planning conference at board chair Joel Spingarn's Troutbeck estate in Amenia, New York, had reunited the restless dissenters and surfaced sharp disagreement between them and the association's "old guard."[25]

As special counsel, Houston channeled the views of the restive militants

By 1930, a million and a half Black workers were in industrial occupations—but only 4 percent of them belonged to labor unions.

into the legal effort. He continued to believe, as he always had, that Black Americans were "too conservative to rush into any radical, revolutionary program." The Black Belt self-determination thesis, in particular, held no appeal for him. Yet from his vantage, the ILD and its allies on the left had displayed admirable courage and ingenuity in mounting what he called "mass resistance and mass struggle." Echoing Harris's assessment, Houston proposed that the association and its legal campaign aim to "unite" Black Americans "with the 'poor white.'" (His cousin William Hastie concurred, urging the association "to get lined up right on vital economic issues.") Houston's diagnosis of the subordination of Black communities started not with segregation per se but with the economic problems of people like Black cotton farmers in Alabama. He placed the "integration of Negro workers into industry and the protection of their rights" at the core of what it meant to support Black communities. "The Communists," he noted, had "made it impossible for any aspirant to Negro leadership to advocate less than full economic, political and social equality, and expect to retain the respect and confidence of the group."[26]

Houston told a Howard University audience the next year that the ILD had "introduced the Negro to the possibilities and tactics of mass pressure." The Communists, he continued, had "changed the emphasis of the Negro question from a race issue to a class issue." For Houston, the point seemed to be confirmed days later when the U.S. Supreme Court handed down its Scottsboro decisions in *Norris v. Alabama* and *Patterson v. Alabama*. American Fund money supported both the ILD's successes and Houston's litigation campaign. Houston believed that neither project could thrive on its own. In the worlds connected by the Fund, class, race, and civil liberties would be fellow travelers.[27]

The Cost of Skin Pigmentation

When Houston assumed the role of special counsel with the NAACP in October 1934, he unveiled a newly streamlined Joint Committee campaign that aimed to merge institutional engineering with the mass power of the ILD's social mobilization. Putting the "lessons" of the Scottsboro cases and the ILD lawyers high on the agenda, he announced that the "aims of this program" were "to arouse and strengthen the will of the local communities to demand and fight for their rights." He would, he wrote, focus exclusively on "the issue of discrimination in education"; it was, he believed, far more "acute" a difficulty than Jim Crow inequalities in public transportation. Depression-era federal funds were being funneled into "building and repairing school buildings" and making "payment of teachers salaries." To capture the Black community's share of school resources was, for this reason among others, both an education project and an economic one that communities would mobilize to achieve. The key, as Houston saw it, was to support and energize "the local will to struggle" by lending "a hand in contests already undertaken or proposed by the local communities themselves, rather than to precipitate a struggle on a community which does not want it."[28]

Houston proposed to start by returning to the school funding problem with which the Committee on Negro Work project had begun, and which Margold had set aside. As he put it, the "center of the attack"—what he called "the foundation work" for the campaign—would be "in the deep South," where the "most flagrant" inequalities existed. He added that the attack should start "as low in the elementary grades as possible." This was where Du Bois had focused in the American Fund–supported studies of the mid-1920s, and with good reason. Elementary school education involved the largest gross sums and touched the largest numbers of people. It supported the greatest share of Black educators. But a note of worry crept into Houston's report. "These suits," he conceded, "will probably be the most expensive and the hardest to handle." That was why Margold had discouraged equalization suits despite the Committee on Negro Work's enthusiasm. And Margold had not been wrong about the grave difficulties such suits faced. What Houston's strategy would have to do was find a way to take account of his classmate's institutional insights while tapping the public passions that Scottsboro had opened up. For Houston, that meant rallying public opinion, and especially Black public opinion, behind the campaign.[29]

While traveling to recruit students for Howard Law School in 1934, Houston used a simple movie camera to film the glaring differences between white and Black schools in the rural South. "Motion pictures," Houston contended, "humanize and dramatize the discrimination which Negroes suffer." The statistics and photographs Du Bois had collected a decade earlier now came to life in a thousand feet of film reels, which the NAACP produced as a three-reel, thirty-minute motion picture documentary screened for NAACP chapters around the country. Houston's camera dwelled longest on a school near Rock Hill, South Carolina, not far from the spot where Houston's maternal grandfather had purchased the freedom of Houston's grandmother eighty years earlier. But he traveled across the entire South, some 25,000 miles between 1934 and 1936, making photographic studies of schools in Wise County, Virginia, on the Eastern Shore of Maryland, and on the streets of Baltimore. George Schuyler, A. Philip Randolph's old comrade at *The Messenger*, contributed photographs taken on a long drive across the South. The men usually drove, Houston noted, because of the indignity and squalor of Jim Crow rail transportation—what he discreetly called the "inconvenience and infrequency of southern trains" and "the general facilities of travel."[30]

Investigations into school inequalities produced a new round of articles in *The Crisis*, now edited by Roy Wilkins after Du Bois's embittered departure. The weekly Black press covered the story, too. An NAACP speakers service sent out dozens of lecturers in a miniature version of George Creel's wartime "Four Minute Men." In November 1936, White's special assistant, Juanita Jackson, a graduate of the University of Pennsylvania, orchestrated a publicity coup in the form of an evening radio broadcast with Edward R. Murrow of CBS. Murrow gave Walter White nine minutes of airtime, which White used to attack the galling "differences in school buildings and equipment," "unequal teachers salaries," and shorter school years that separated white schools from Black ones. Jackson reported afterward that the "comments are simply pouring in" from listeners Black and white around the country.[31]

All these efforts, as Houston put it in 1936, were designed "to undergird" the legal campaign in education "with just as wide public support as possible"—to mobilize something like the support the ILD had generated around the Scottsboro cases by, as White and Houston emphasized for the American Fund board, "getting over to the masses of people, white as well as colored, the significance of our fight against educational inequalities."[32]

Public opinion and support in the Black community also mattered because the campaign needed alternative funding sources. Houston asked the American Fund for an additional $15,000 in January 1936 to support what he predicted would be a "ten year fight" against Jim Crow. Allies on the American Fund board scraped together the votes to release $10,000.

But when the directors proved unwilling to meet the full request, Houston and White looked elsewhere for financial support. The "Negro fraternities and sororities," in particular, White explained, seemed likely to provide "substantial financial assistance in the work." So too might "Negro church organizations, teachers' associations on a national scale, labor unions, and fraternal orders."[33]

In all, Houston and White felt that by the mid-1930s the NAACP's fortunes seemed to be "on the upturn." The funding equalization strategy garnered support in Black communities, which Houston felt had grown tired of communism ("and the other isms," he added) in the wake of Scottsboro. The NAACP's Black constituency, Houston said, seemed to be "ready and hungry" for a campaign to bring greater funding to its own institutions.[34]

The difficulty was that Margold's creative and forceful alternative to suing school districts faced daunting challenges of its own. Privately, Houston thought it implausible that an obscure 1886 decision about Chinese laundries in San Francisco had secretly rendered Jim Crow illegal without anyone noticing. The critique was not entirely fair, but it had the virtue of realism. Moreover, if the Margold approach solved one problem, it created others. Many NAACP constituencies did not want a sudden conversion to integrated institutions, even if one could be achieved in law. Back in 1930, James Weldon Johnson had reminded the Committee on Negro Work to "be careful not to confuse unequal . . . distribution of public school funds with separate schools." The two presented "distinct issues," he said, in no small part because separate schools typically supported separate jobs. Black teachers were reluctant to adopt integration if that meant abolishing the institutions in which they worked. And on this score, the experience in northern school districts was not encouraging. In Baltimore, Detroit, and Chicago, white officials shut Black teachers out of employment, even in what were supposedly integrated schools. Margold's implicit integration mandate threatened to make the problem general, with little consideration for how such an outcome would alter the economic foundations of the Black middle class.[35]

Houston and Margold both found themselves pursuing the legal work of the association as a way of advancing the economic well-being of Black communities. At the association's request, Margold spent much of 1932 drafting local, state, and federal bills that proposed to ban racial discrimination in employment by government contractors. A Black lawyer named John P. Davis, who was one of the most outspoken members of the younger generation, raised money from the association to investigate discriminatory funding and employment disparities at the Tennessee Valley Authority. Association lawyers investigated efforts to intimidate Black railroad workers in Illinois and to run Black tenant farmers off land in Oklahoma. Houston was soon able to report to the Joint Committee on the association's progress in safeguarding $100 million in federal education money against racial discrimination by winning an amendment to the Senate version of a federal education spending bill. An American Fund grant supported the effort.[36]

In Houston's conception, the legal campaign over education in the courts was an economic cause like the battle for federal education funds or the fight for government jobs. Establishing rights to some kind of equality in learning, he argued, would "ultimately change the whole relation of the Negro to the South." With "better education," Houston insisted, a person was "bound to become more active and insistent on his rights." Education, he told a gathering of the National Bar Association in 1935, was "symbolic of all the more drastic discriminations which Negroes suffer in American life." Educational subordination, he continued, reflected the "inferior position" of Black communities, which they were expected to accept "without protest or struggle"—"economically exploited, politically ignored and socially ostracized."[37]

To maintain community support while avoiding the impossible costs of the original Committee on Negro Work plan for school equalization suits, Houston focused the equalization campaign on discrete pieces of school funding. He proposed to attack "differentials in teachers salaries in the South."[38]

The association's new investigations of school funding disparities found that Black principals, teachers, and supervisors still earned far less than their white peers. In Louisiana, Black educators earned on average thirty cents for every dollar earned by their white peers. In South Carolina the rate was thirty-five cents, in Georgia, thirty-four. Across the South as a whole, Black principals, teachers, and supervisors earned a mere forty-seven cents, on average, for every dollar to their white counterparts. In nineteen southern states, the association estimated, the "cost of skin pigmentation to colored teachers" reached "the tremendous total of between seven and eight million dollars annually." To be sure, teacher compensation inequalities were small compared to overall funding disparities; in South Carolina, the state spent only nineteen cents per Black student for every dollar on white students. But suing over teacher salary disparities had a crucial if technical administrative advantage over suing for school funding inequalities more generally. Racial inequalities appearing on the face of public salary schedules were far easier to attack than discrimination in discretionary school funding decisions. Moreover, after litigation, salary discrimination would be far easier to monitor and manage against backsliding. "There are," concluded Swedish social scientist Gunnar Myrdal a few years later in his influential study of race in the United States, "few major cases of racial wage discrimination so clear-cut and so pronounced as that found in the teaching profession in the South."[39]

Gibbs v. Broome, filed by Houston in 1937, was an early case brought under the American Fund grant. William B. Gibbs Jr., the Black principal at the Rockville Colored Elementary School in Montgomery County, Maryland, became an NAACP client when he contacted the association in October 1936 to volunteer as a plaintiff. Gibbs earned a lower salary than comparable white principals in the state's schools, in substantial part because of a statutory schedule that set white educators' minimum salaries substantially higher than those of Black educators. Houston and his NAACP colleagues sued the Montgomery County schools, contending that Gibbs's salary, like that of other Maryland teachers, failed to satisfy the old *Plessy v. Ferguson* requirement of separate but equal. As White described the *Gibbs* case to the American Fund in 1937, it had "vast importance both to education and labor." The suit challenged the "traditional and firmly fixed policy of the South to impose a wage differential on Negroes regardless of qualifications and ability." A successful challenge, as White saw things, would be "a great contribution toward removing the economic foundation for the perpetuation of race prejudice in the South," not least because the "payroll for education is the largest payroll of any single industry in the country." When a state court judge in Maryland allowed the Gibbs suit to go forward, the county school board moved quickly to settle the case, agreeing to a deal that equalized teacher pay and yielded Black teachers in the county more than $30,000 in additional annual compensation.[40]

A cascade of teacher pay cases followed in school districts across the South. Teachers in Brevard County, Florida, spoke up for equalization. Inquiries poured in from Alabama, Kentucky, Tennessee, and Virginia, where teachers asked about the possibility of bringing similar suits. In some states, like the Carolinas, efforts stumbled. But elsewhere the momentum grew. Houston reported to the American Fund that "the Negro teachers" of Virginia raised "$1,600.00 toward the costs of a fight for equalization of teachers salaries." Cases proceeded fastest in Maryland's other counties: Calvert County, Frederick County, and elsewhere. In 1939, a federal suit filed by NAACP lawyers against the board of education in Anne Arundel County yielded victory in the form of a ringing opinion by federal district court judge William Chesnut. A Republican appointee from the Hoover administration, Judge Chesnut ruled that Black schoolteacher Walter Mills had been "unconstitutionally discriminated against in the practice of his profession" by the county school board's distinction between "white and colored teachers." Declaring victory in a circular to its branches, the association called the win "a precedent" that would "break down the age-old tradition of paying Negroes less than other citizens." It was "another step in our program to secure 'equal pay for equal work.'" A year later, the U.S. Court of Appeals for the Fourth Circuit affirmed the reasoning of the *Mills* case in *Alston v. School Board of Norfolk*, upholding the claims of Black schoolteacher Melvin Alston and the Norfolk Teachers' Association.[41]

Community involvement was both a reason to pursue the salary cases and a crucial factor in their success. As one NAACP insider put it, salary equalization would "build up interest in the Association." It was a bread-and-butter strategy to regain the confidence battered by the Scottsboro episode—a way of "giving a material benefit to Negroes in general." State teachers' associations, in turn, provided vital support to the suits. In Maryland and Virginia, Black teachers established funds to support plaintiffs who put their jobs at risk as a result of leading the fight for fair pay. Black women, who made up 75 percent of Black teachers in the South, were especially active, including South Carolina teacher Septima Poinsette Clark, later associated with the Brookwood-inspired Highlander Folk School in Tennessee, and Lillie Jackson in Baltimore, whose daughter Juanita had arranged the association's radio broadcast.[42]

In all, the NAACP won twenty-seven of thirty-one salary equalization cases between 1939 and 1947. Black educators' salaries, which had hovered near 50 percent of white teachers' salaries in 1930, began a slow march to 65 percent in 1945 and 85 percent in 1950. Throughout the salary campaign, Houston and his team framed their efforts as a mass tactic to develop labor rights. In 1937, when Houston attended A. Philip Randolph's National Negro Congress, he proposed to the delegates that the school funding campaign was "tied to all the other struggles being waged for equal rights." Success in the anti-lynching fight would, he said, "free Negroes from physical terrorism and make it safe for them to protest." Winning rights at the ballot box would do the same, since Houston was adamant that courts were not the only way to fight Jim Crow, and in the end not even the best way. Most of all, Houston told the congress, labor rights to fair salaries would not only "wipe out the differentials in teachers' salaries," it would also "give real security of tenure in teaching positions." Myrdal, writing in 1944, agreed that a rise in the economic status of Black teachers would have dramatic effects. As Virginia educator Luther Porter Jackson put it, "the striving for equal salaries" was "a bid for economic democracy."[43]

Yet the salary cases posed a problem that had animated the world of the American Fund for a decade and a half, one that A. J. Muste had encountered at Brookwood and that Sidney Hillman faced at the Amalgamated Clothing Workers. Engaging the interests of a community was not the same as disrupting the systems in which it was embedded. Winning the hearts of Black teachers was not the same as bringing down Jim Crow.

As a matter of constitutional law, cases like *Gibbs* reaffirmed *Plessy v. Ferguson*, rather than attacking it. As White saw the matter, the teacher salary cases played into the tendency of "too many Negro educators" who preferred "separateness with all its attendant disabilities and inequalities." Such "separateness," White suggested indelicately, appealed to some Black teachers because it allowed them "to escape the competition which they would have to meet in a non-segregated scholastic life." Said this way, the point was clumsy and too harsh; Black teachers in Detroit were already learning that integrated schools would often exclude them from jobs without any competition at all. But the underlying tension was real. As James

Weldon Johnson and the Committee on Negro Work had put it to the American Fund in 1929 and 1930, segregation itself was an institutional mechanism for perpetuating the South's social hierarchy, and not only as a symbol. The political economy of separate schools facilitated unequal treatment, sustaining funding inequalities and institutional disparities. White told the American Fund that the "ultimate goal" of the salary cases was "to make segregated schools" so expensive as to "bankrupt the states which maintain separate school systems" and force them "eventually to abolish segregation." In some ways, the salary campaign organized local communities for action. On other dimensions, White worried, salary reform did not subvert Jim Crow so much as entrench it.[44]

Outstanding Accomplishment

Thurgood Marshall first touched the world of the American Fund in November 1934 when the Fund and the NAACP put him on retainer at Houston's request.[45]

Marshall was born in 1908 in Baltimore to William Canfield Marshall, a railroad porter and club steward, and Norma Williams Marshall, a teacher in the state's segregated Black schools. His unusual name—"Thoroughgood," later changed to Thurgood at his request when he was in grade school—came from a grandfather reputed to have used two names to draw two veterans' pensions. He spent his childhood in a mix of classroom misbehavior, on the one hand, and odd jobs, on the other. He worked as a delivery boy. He diluted whiskey as a Prohibition-era bootlegger's assistant. He served wealthy patrons as a private railroad dining car attendant. At school, where he lurched from leading the debate team to indifference and mischief, a creative teacher assigned him to memorize the Constitution as punishment for school misdeeds. "If you don't think that's terrible," Marshall liked to say, "just you try memorizing the Constitution sometime."[46]

The University of Maryland was whites-only, and Marshall deemed the state's only public college for Black students badly inadequate. He worked another sequence of part-time jobs to pay his way through Lincoln University, a small private school across the state line in the Pennsylvania countryside. He graduated with honors in 1930, despite run-ins with the school's disciplinary officials for fraternity hazing and a reputation for pranks like leading a cow into the university president's office. Deciding on law school, he applied first to the University of Maryland's law school at College Park. The school was cheap and nearby, and Marshall was a well-qualified student, but the university's president rejected the application because Marshall was Black. His mother, Norma, pawned her engagement and wedding rings so that Thurgood could commute to the more expensive Howard Law School in Washington.[47]

It was Howard, in Marshall's recollection, that first inspired him to set his sights on important things, and it was Charlie Houston who was responsible. The commuter kid emerged as the star student at Houston's newly reorganized training ground for Black social engineers. Marshall graduated first in his class. Houston arranged a scholarship for graduate studies with Frankfurter at Harvard, but Marshall declined and entered private practice in Maryland, living with his new wife, Vivian, in his parents' modest home. Almost immediately, however, Houston drew the fledgling lawyer into the world (and increasing workload) of the NAACP and its American Fund legal campaign. The next summer, Marshall joined Houston as he drove around North Carolina recruiting law students and documenting elementary school inequalities. The two men took turns behind the wheel, one driving Marshall's "little old beat up '29 Ford" while the other pounded out notes on a portable Remington typewriter in the passenger seat. Marshall smoked cigarettes the whole way.[48]

Marshall's social and family connections to Maryland schoolteachers proved useful in the salary equalization cases. "I was drafting plans," Marshall noted at the time, "to force Maryland to pay black teachers, my momma included, the same money as it paid white teachers." Houston made for a stern taskmaster. Marshall and his colleagues called the older man "cement drawers" and "iron shoes" because of his perfectionism. Marshall, by contrast, was disheveled and ribald, always a storyteller. But the two made a good match, and with Houston as a mentor and a model, Marshall found an inner drive. As local counsel in Maryland, Marshall built public support behind the Joint Committee program, covering "almost the entire state of Maryland personally inspecting Negro schools, taking contrasting pictures between white and Negro schools in the same localities," and "holding rallies to explain the various aspects of the campaign to local citizens." When Marshall's private practice in Baltimore faltered in the face of Depression economy pressures, Houston eagerly arranged with the American Fund for Marshall to join the NAACP staff full-time in New York at $200 per month. "I don't know of anybody I would rather have in the office," Houston told him.[49]

Before long, Thurgood Marshall was carrying around a battered, blue-backed copy of the American Fund's Margold Report. He "often referred" to it in the New York office, NAACP lawyer Jack Greenberg later recalled. "I had it for years," Marshall remembered. But Marshall was less enthralled by long-term strategy than his mentor Houston was—and far less than Margold had been. For Marshall, the 1931 strategy document was "not a blueprint" but a two-hundred-page lawyer's armory, stocked with doctrinal weapons he might use for whatever the fight of the moment required. "We took them as they came," Marshall said of his cases. "We tried our cases one by one. We had no plan, because you couldn't make a plan." There were too many constraints: money, time, and viable plaintiffs chief among them. For Marshall, taking cases as they came partly meant focusing on Maryland, not so much because it offered strategic legal advantages as because it was close to where he lived and where he had family connections. Fatefully, responding to the cases that came in the door also meant taking cases arising out of higher education, and in particular a category of controversies that Margold and the Joint Committee had not even considered: graduate and professional schools.[50]

In the first years of the 1930s, state university systems in the South featured graduate and professional schools for white students, but not for Black students. An NAACP study of seventeen states found that in fields like dentistry, journalism, law, medicine, nursing, pharmacy, sciences, and veterinary medicine, the South's public colleges boasted thousands of white students and not a single Black one.[51]

In 1933, however, a student named Thomas Hocutt applied to the pharmacy school at the University of North Carolina. When the school advised him that it did not accept Black students, Hocutt sued the school and got in touch with Walter White at the NAACP, who connected him with Houston and William Hastie at Howard. The case fizzled when the conservative Black president of North Carolina College for Negroes refused to release Hocutt's college transcript, thus providing the university an independent ground for rejecting his application. But Houston took note of the Hocutt case. It had been, he observed, "conceived and started by local citizens on their own initiative." The graduate and professional school cases were well positioned to avoid the pitfalls Margold had identified. There were no fact-intensive questions about the relative costs of the schools in question. Southern states had no graduate or professional schools for Black students at all. Jim Crow graduate schools could hardly be separate but equal if they did not exist. The cases were thus conceptually even crisper than the salaries suits, since salaries in states like Maryland were set on a discretionary case-by-case basis even though subject to racially unequal statutory minimums.[52]

For Marshall, the professional school cases were personal, too. The "sonsabitches" at the University of Maryland law school, he liked to say of himself, had "turned away the guy who finished number one at a better law school—Howard." Marshall set out to see if the sonsabitches would turn away Donald Murray: Baltimore resident, 1934 graduate of Houston's alma mater Amherst College, and grandson of a prominent African Methodist Episcopal Church bishop. With Marshall's help, Murray applied to Maryland's law school in early 1935. He was eminently qualified, overqualified even. But the school promptly rejected him because of his race, and as Houston reported to the American Fund's Joint Committee in March, the "groundwork for a test case against the University of Maryland" was "underway." Following the committee's instruction to concentrate on the promising Maryland case, Houston and Marshall filed suit in April. At a short trial in June before state judge Eugene O'Dunne, the state conceded under Houston's cross examination that it was prepared to admit students of every race and ethnic group except Black ones. There being no alternative law school for Black students, Judge O'Dunne ordered the school to admit Murray for the fall school term.[53]

Murray's matriculation still would not have happened had it not been for a quiet, eleventh-hour American Fund subvention. A week before the beginning of the term in September, Murray told Marshall that he did not actually have the money to pay his tuition in the fall. Houston and Marshall scrambled to make arrangements lest their big victory fall flat. Working closely with Fund treasurer Morris Ernst, the two lawyers avoided the appearance of outside agitation by funneling American Fund money for tuition and fees through Carl Murphy, publisher of the *Baltimore Afro-American* weekly newspaper. With the Fund's disguised support, Murray graduated in June 1938.[54]

Success in Maryland encouraged others. While Murray was entering law school in September 1935, a man named Lloyd Gaines wrote Houston and Marshall from Missouri to ask for help with admission to his state's public law school. Gaines, who had attended school as a child in a one-room schoolhouse in northern Mississippi, had managed to graduate with a degree in history from Missouri's Lincoln University. Gaines, who knew "long before finishing high school" that he wanted to be a lawyer, decided on the University of Missouri for law school. Missouri had a scholarship law in place designed to defeat civil rights litigation by offering Black students financial support for out-of-state legal education. But Gaines objected. Arguing that out-of-state scholarships were inadequate to fulfill the state's constitutional obligation of equal protection, Houston and Marshall helped Gaines sue the university. Gaines's initial loss at trial in July 1936 became, for Houston, an opportunity for mass mobilizing. He orchestrated protests outside the state supreme court during the case's appeal. And when the state supreme court cited *Plessy v. Ferguson* to uphold the out-of-state scholarship scheme, Houston and Marshall petitioned the U.S. Supreme Court to hear the case.[55]

For the better part of a decade, the Joint Committee had argued to the Fund that its campaign would generate new forms of cross-racial class solidarity. But supporting the production of a new Black professional class seemed a far cry from the labor mobilization that the Fund had intended. The Fund's left wing gloated, while its center ate crow. Norman Thomas, who had been one of the campaign's fiercest defenders, wondered if the NAACP lawyers would not be better off "to safeguard the rights of Negro workers" more directly; the campaign for professional school admissions now seemed to him "too legalistic" in its approach. Houston tried to assure him that the legal team understood "the limitations" of "courts as an instrument of social change." The lawyers, he explained, "used the courts as dissecting laboratories" to extract truths about prejudice and racism "from hostile officials." Houston sought to explain "how we attempt to activate the public into organized forms of protest and support." Agreeing that cases "unrelated to supporting popular action" were "usually futile," he described a plan "to tour Missouri," using the *Gaines* case as an organizing tool to connect "with the general fight for equalization of teachers' salaries" in the state.[56]

The Fund's concerns about the graduate school cases came to a head in 1937 when the uncertain and dwindling flow of money seemed to dry up for good. By 1937, the American Fund had distributed over $28,000 to the NAACP legal campaign: $8,082.76 for Nathan Margold's salary and fees, plus two $10,000 disbursements in 1934–35 and 1935–36, respectively. Houston appealed to Charles Garland himself. Assuring Garland that the NAACP was interested in agricultural labor, he cited the Arkansas peonage episode and *Moore v. Dempsey* from a decade before. He professed sincere interest "in agriculture and work among tenant farmers." But Garland deferred to Roger Baldwin, who objected that the Fund lacked sufficient resources to meet the NAACP's request while making the new agricultural worker grants that had renewed Garland's interest in his once-spurned inheritance. "Our obligation to Mr. Garland," he explained, had produced a vote of the board "to reserve prospective funds for farm organization." A "windfall" might "change the situation," though Baldwin saw "no prospect of any" on the horizon. Ernst disagreed, but without Baldwin's support further funding was an uphill battle.[57]

Walter White protested, too. Some members of the American Fund had been skeptical from the start, he conceded. Indeed, "when the Joint Committee undertook its first case, nearly everybody—including some members of the Joint Committee itself—felt the campaign would produce little result." But by the middle of 1937 it seemed already "sufficient to say that the campaign has now won the confidence of the public." It would be "tragic" if "just when its effect is beginning to be felt on a regional scale it should be cut off from the necessary support to broaden its scope and effectiveness." White and Houston requested a "subsidy of $10,000" to "see all projects in hand through to the courts of last resort." In a long shot, they added that a larger $25,000 award would allow them to pursue "complementary legislation where necessary" alongside the court cases. For the "decade's fight against education discrimination, at least $100,000 is needed," they concluded. The ask was big, but it promised, they urged, to "save a generation of American citizens."[58]

An emergency meeting at Norman Thomas's home in late 1937 yielded one last thread—the Fund could not offer $10,000 (let alone $100,000), but Baldwin proposed that it "carry the University of Missouri case to the

United States Supreme Court if that became necessary," using a reserve account for "projects to which the fund had already submitted itself." Dunn and Michelson, representing the Communist left wing of the Fund, voted no; Charles Garland did, too, though his vote technically did not count. Baldwin, who was growing increasingly distrustful of the Party, voted yes, as did Thomas and the remaining directors. Less than a year later, in October 1938, the justices of the Supreme Court agreed to hear the *Gaines* case, scheduling arguments for November. The Fund's final NAACP subvention helped see the case through.[59]

With *Gaines*, the legal strategy initially conceived by the American Fund's Committee on Negro Work—refined by the Joint Committee, amended by Nathan Margold, transformed by Houston, and honed by Marshall—came before the Supreme Court for the first time. Houston, who had stepped down from the post of full-time special counsel for the NAACP in July, appeared to argue the case in the Court's new three-year-old building, with Marshall supporting from the counsel table. Some later reported that Justice James McReynolds of Tennessee, a Wilson nominee from 1914, turned his back on Houston when the lawyer rose to speak.

Lloyd Gaines, pictured around the time of the 1938 Supreme Court decision to hear his case.

(All agreed that McReynolds walked out of the courtroom before the arguments closed.) But other justices seemed far more sympathetic. Chief Justice Charles Evans Hughes, a stalwart of the Republican Party, asked the lawyer for the state whether he could "say that Negroes have equal educational opportunities in Missouri, when they are compelled to leave their own state?" Justice Harlan Fiske Stone, former dean at Columbia's law school in New York and a future chief justice, asserted pointedly that the "national point of view" was "opposed to racial discrimination." A new justice, Hugo Black, himself a Louisiana Democrat, interrupted counsel for the university to ask whether he really meant "to suggest" that money for out-of-state training "would be adequate compensation for loss of civil rights."[60]

A month later, on December 12, 1938, the Joint Committee's legal campaign won its first victory in the high court. The State of Missouri, Chief Justice Hughes's opinion observed, conceded its obligation "to provide negroes with advantages for higher education substantially equal to the advantages afforded to white students." The Court went further, ruling that the "obligation of the State to give the protection of equal laws can be performed only where its laws operate," that is, within the state itself. The obligation, Hughes continued, "cannot be cast by one State upon another, and no State can be excused from performance by what another State may do or fail to do." Missouri's out-of-state scholarship system, in other words, failed to meet its constitutional obligations. Justice McReynolds dissented, joined by his colleague Pierce Butler. But by a 6–2 margin, with one seat on the Court vacant, the justices delivered Gaines a victory.[61]

The *Gaines* case was a vindication of James Weldon Johnson's long efforts with the Fund, a product of nearly two decades of trial and error. Morris Ernst, for one, wrote to White that "Charles Houston's job is probably the outstanding accomplishment of the Garland Fund." The result, Ernst marveled, was not only a triumph in one case but a victory that reverberated "throughout the South." It was, Ernst remarked, "persistent engineering of a high social nature." "I do not know where else" the Fund could have spent its money, he concluded, to get such results short of "bloodshed" or "long-term martyrdoms."[62]

One person who agreed with Ernst was a young activist and Brookwood

College graduate named Pauli Murray. Born in Baltimore to mixed-race parents who were treated as Black, and raised in Durham, North Carolina, with her mother's extended family, Murray moved to New York in 1926 at the age of fifteen and fell in with the Garland Fund crowd. Living with an aunt, she enrolled in Hunter College, then the city's public women's college. Hunter, which was the "poor girl's Radcliffe" to match City College's "Harvard of the Proletariat," did for Murray what City College had done for A. Philip Randolph, Felix Frankfurter, Nathan Margold, and so many others. It introduced her to a world of radical democratic socialisms. She took up with the Black literary and radical world that James Weldon Johnson had helped create, counting as friends people like the writer Langston Hughes and the labor organizer Ella Baker, and attending lectures at the Harlem YWCA by Du Bois, Randolph, and the novelist Zora Neale Hurston. The Scottsboro affair radicalized her. Before long, she was enrolled in a course taught by Ben Gitlow's close ally, the purged Communist Jay Lovestone, and attending Brookwood classes in Katonah while teaching workers' education programs in the city.[63]

In late 1938, inspired by the *Gaines* case, Murray applied to graduate school in her home state at the University of North Carolina. Her white great-great-grandfather had been a trustee at the university and her great-grandfather had attended the school, but these facts seemed not to matter. Two days after the Supreme Court ruled in Gaines's favor, the University of North Carolina denied her application, explaining that "members of your race are not admitted" and offering the pathetic assurance that the state legislature was expected to create a new graduate program for Black students. Applying to the university's law school, she was turned down again for the same reason. From 1939 until 1941, she worked in labor and civil rights for the Southern Tenant Farmers Union, which Norman Thomas helped to establish, and for the League for Industrial Democracy. Both groups had substantial overlap with, and received support from, the Garland Fund.[64]

Strangely, if Lloyd Gaines had inspired Pauli Murray and many others, his own story came to an uninspired close. He had won his case. But after Gaines won, he disappeared. He had long been a prickly test-case plaintiff. He had asked repeatedly for money from the NAACP and put his case at risk by ignoring his studies at the University of Michigan graduate program into which Houston and Marshall had placed him while his lawsuit progressed. Gaines had briefly fallen out of contact once before, in mid-1938, when he moved residences without telling anyone. Now he disappeared completely. Some worried, as columnist Louis Lautier proposed in the *Afro-American*, that Gaines might have been "a victim of foul play." But Gaines's siblings believed he had simply moved away as he had the year before. ("I can look after myself ok," Gaines wrote in a final enigmatic letter to his mother.) Word spread that he had been bribed to leave Missouri. At the NAACP, Walter White heard that Gaines had been given $2,000 to move to Mexico City. One of Gaines's old teachers at Lincoln University spotted him in Mexico a decade later. Houston and Marshall were furious that Gaines seemed to have abandoned the case. In Baltimore, the *Afro-American* stated flatly that Gaines had "walked out" on his case and left his lawyers and his race in the lurch.[65]

Murray viewed Gaines's disappearance in a different light. In February 1940, just weeks before engaging in a Brookwood-style nonviolent protest against bus segregation in Virginia, Murray wrote to the *Afro-American* to question its "editorial criticism of Gaines's motives." His disappearance, Murray insisted, was not his fault, but the fault of Black leadership. In a better, more democratic, and fairer world, she asserted, Lloyd Gaines "could have been neither intimidated nor bought off." The problem was Black leaders, who had reacted to the Court's decision with "confusion and wide disagreement," some advocating integration, others equalization. If "Lloyd Gaines has failed," she offered as a curious conclusion, "his failure rests squarely upon the shoulders of the colored people."[66]

Whatever the merits of Pauli Murray's peroration, she reflected the long-standing divide in the American Fund's world about the strategy embodied in the Supreme Court's new departure. The graduate school cases were tactically brilliant, to be sure. Like the salary cases, they had isolated a crisp constitutional question without the endless complexities of measuring equality in local school districts. But if Gaines had disappeared from his own case, so had the class mobilization envisioned by the young militants of the NAACP, by the social democrats of the American Fund's progressive center, and by the radicals of its Communist left. The craft virtuosity of Houston and his team of lawyers, for all Houston's talk to the contrary, had developed a bloodless legal strategy about professional education through arid legal briefs and courtroom analytics. In doing so, Pauli Murray worried, they had left Gaines to struggle alone.

For a generation now, critics have amplified Murray's contention into a complaint that Houston crafted a strategy for Du Bois's old talented tenth, not the millions who made up the working class. In isolation, as a story about the professional school cases narrowly, the critique looks powerful. But the NAACP's education campaign was only one project among the many that spun out of the generative world of the American Fund, and only one among the several efforts that Houston himself was pursuing. As Pauli Murray's own youthful energies suggested, the Fund's labor movement projects were moving forward apace.[67]

Walter Reuther (left) and his fellow auto workers organizer Richard Frankensteen after being beaten on the bridge to Ford's giant River Rouge factory in May 1937.

19

Use This Weapon

Brookwood favors the sit-down strike.
—JOEL SEIDMAN, LABOR ECONOMIST, 1937

In 1933, the revolution about which Brookwood's students and faculty had been dreaming erupted into the open. American workers went on strike. In Philadelphia, 4,500 workers from the International Ladies' Garment Workers Union (ILGWU) left their posts in the city's dress industry. Sixty thousand workers struck at dozens of dress shops between New Jersey and Connecticut. Sidney Hillman's Amalgamated Clothing Workers of America went on strike at New York City's men's clothing firms. Amalgamated Clothing Worker locals followed in quick succession at manufacturers in Boston, Philadelphia, Rochester, and Buffalo. Cotton shirtmakers struck at dozens of small shops from Allentown to New Haven. In Reading alone, 10,000 hosiery workers stepped away from the mills. Silk dyers walked picket lines in Paterson. Los Angeles garment workers struck in October.[1]

At the American Fund, the directors had long waited for what Roger Baldwin called the "rebel spirit" of the working classes to emerge. Now, thanks to the economic dislocation of the Great Depression, a wave of labor unrest swept across heavy industry, too. In western Pennsylvania, 70,000 miners went out; one hundred thousand more followed from Alabama to New Mexico. The year 1933 witnessed more work stoppages than any year since the 1919 strike waves. Employers lost two and a half million person-days to strikes in August alone. Labor actions accelerated in the months thereafter. In 1934, nearly 2,000 work stoppages across the country involved some 1.5 million workers. Auto parts workers struck in Toledo; trucks idled when drivers struck in Minnesota. Longshoremen left cargo on the docks in San Francisco. Textile spindles went still from North Carolina to Maine.[2]

With 15 million people out of work and unemployment rates reaching 25 percent, the Depression supplied a jolt of energy to labor not seen since the war. What those energies would ultimately yield was hard to foresee in 1933 and 1934. Economic conditions did not dictate any one social response. In Europe, economic crisis produced fascisms. In America's Great Depression, by contrast, a different strand of social politics emerged, one that took its shape to an astonishing extent from the men and women who had found shelter and inspiration in the American Fund's creative workshop. Leading figures from the world of the Fund now crafted novel labor laws and fueled a movement, building the nearest thing to an economic democracy the United States had ever seen. Never before had this group known such prospects for power. As labor economist and Fund regular W. Jett Lauck put it, the Depression's dislocations seemed to afford "an opportunity which will never occur again for generations."[3]

If the American Fund supplied the NAACP with Nathan Margold's blueprint for litigation, it offered labor something different. The small American Fund provided a loose set of principles for a new industrial unionism, tested by a decade of debate and designed for the age of mass production in industries ranging from textiles and auto to rubber and electronics. Fusing technocratic institutional design to movement zeal, Brookwood's teachers and students—the social democratic progressives of the American Fund world—staffed the new Congress of Industrial Organizations. They swept into key posts in the New Deal's labor agencies. And they imprinted on the labor revolution of the 1930s the struggle that had divided Fund insiders for a decade: a contest between two visions of economic transformation, the legal-technocratic and the mass movement. On the one hand, the New Deal's Wagner Act reengineered the legal machinery of capitalism. On the other hand, new machinery would exert only as much force as the mobilized passions of working classes supplied.

Brookwood Unbound

The revolution began in Toledo. For ten years, Brookwood Labor College students and faculty had fairly leapt into action at the chance to participate in labor actions, few and far between though they were. Brookwood students, staff, and alumni had thrown themselves into the 1926 Passaic textile strike. Three years later, Brookwood graduates had organized mill workers in Gastonia, North Carolina. Now, in the Depression setting, Brookwood pressed progressive labor ideas into service for a new generation of strikes, beginning with one of the most important strikes of the era, the 1934 fight over a large Ohio auto parts company called Electric Auto-Lite.[4]

It was two Brookwood alumni, the labor organizers Ted Selander and Sam Pollock, who identified Toledo as the starting point for unionizing the automobile industry. Firms in the fast-growing Great Lakes city of 200,000 made crucial parts for the nation's leading automobile manufacturers. Electric Auto-Lite, in particular, was the nation's largest supplier of electric automobile starters, automobile lamps, and batteries, serving manufacturers like Ford as well as the secondary consumer market. Such firms were vulnerable to unionization because interruptions in production would cripple downstream production by the great auto manufacturers. Auto parts firms also faced huge pressure to keep costs low. By 1933, poor conditions and inadequate pay at the notoriously anti-union Auto-Lite had produced stirrings of discontent among workers. The classic problem of unionizing the modern mass-production sector was that the structure of modern firms did not match the American Federation of Labor's craft unions; the factory floor at Auto-Lite featured electricians working alongside machinists, carpenters, and hundreds of machine operators whose skills did not fall into any one of the AFL's jurisdictional buckets. The AFL chartered a special union local—Federal Labor Union No. 18384—to try to solve the problem by organizing the city's auto workers into a single union pool. By February, the AFL union led a walkout of some 4,000 employees at Auto-Lite and two Toledo subsidiaries. The short strike gained a 5 percent wage increase and vague commitments to negotiate a new contract with the union. When Auto-Lite refused to follow through, Local 18384 went out again in April. But this time Auto-Lite hired replacements and fired the strikers. Production continued nearly unabated. The first stirrings of Toledo labor seemed to have stilled.[5]

Selander and Pollock saw a way to rekindle the fading effort. The great obstacle to labor's leverage was the vast reserve army of the unemployed. In Toledo alone, more than 54,000 people received meager local unemployment relief; the unemployment rate in the city among non-farm wage workers was an astonishing 80 percent. So long as employers like Auto-Lite could hire the jobless to tend the machines, strikers would gain little traction. Teams of Brookwood graduates and students had thus turned to an innovative new project: organizing not only nonunion workers but also the unemployed workers to whom firms turned for replacement labor. In industrial cities around the country, a network of Brookwooders adopted the teachings of A. J. Muste. Identifying themselves as "Musteites," and working out of Brookwood-inspired labor colleges, they established Unemployed Leagues to foster solidarity in the regiments of the jobless. Pollock and Selander founded the Musteites' Toledo branch and named it the Lucas County Unemployed League. Working in conjunction with a new Muste effort known as the American Workers Party, the Unemployed League rallied the unemployed to join in solidarity with strikers rather than replace them. As Roy Howard of the Scripps-Howard newspapers observed, "it was nothing new" to see the unemployed "appear on the streets" to fight the police and "raise hell." It was altogether startling to see them appear "in the picket lines to help striking employees" rather than "going in and getting the jobs the other men had laid down."[6]

In late April, Louis Budenz, a Muste follower based in New York, arrived in Toledo to rally the unemployed and the strikers alike. Budenz was the able editor of the Brookwood-allied magazine *Labor Age*, formally published by the League for Industrial Democracy. Years later, he would rediscover Catholicism and join Senator Joseph McCarthy as one of the most notorious anti-Communists of the American right. But in the early 1930s, his brand of socialist labor radicalism made him a charter member of the American Fund world; the American Fund had supported his magazine for years. As the "organizational and strategic mastermind" of Muste's unemployed strategy, Budenz helped the Toledo leadership of Local 18384 direct the strike. Taking up the Brookwood-inspired idea of marshaling the energies of the unemployed, Budenz assembled hundreds of unemployed people at the Auto-Lite gates carrying the Unemployed League's rattlesnake banners bearing the slogan of the American Revolution: "Don't Tread on Me." No longer strikebreakers, the jobless had become allies on the picket lines, raising the strike action (one observer noted) "to a level of mass picketing and militancy far beyond the bounds ever contemplated by the old line craft unions" of the AFL. Muste himself arrived with a rousing

May Day speech to energize the mixed crowd of strikers and nearly 10,000 unemployed Toledo residents. When a local Court of Common Pleas judge issued an order that the picket line be disbanded, Muste called on the crowds to engage in nonviolent defiance. Muste's allies calmly cited their constitutional rights and informed the judge that they would disregard his order. Mass arrests ensued. But as in the free speech fights of the Wobblies twenty years before, enforcement overwhelmed city officials. Arrests filled the city's jail with hundreds of unemployed protesters. With each new round of arrests, those who were released to make room for new detainees resumed their service on the line.[7]

By late May thousands of picketers appeared outside the Auto-Lite plant each day. Auto-Lite guards gathered weapons and ammunition inside the factory as tensions grew on the streets outside. A six-day rolling fight known as the "Battle of Toledo" ensued. Strikers' picket lines trapped Auto-Lite managers, guards, and replacement workers inside the plant. Sherriff's deputies threw tear gas bombs into the crowd, which promptly tossed them back. Fusillades of bolts and iron bars from the strikebreakers inside the plant alternated with volleys of bricks from the crowds in the streets. Strikers smashed factory windows and lit fires. A thousand men from the Ohio National Guard arrived. They charged with bayonets and fired on the crowd, killing two and wounding fifteen more. Enraged strik-

Strikers flee tear gas and police at the Auto-Lite strike in Toledo, 1934.

ers overturned cars and set them aflame. Matters seemed like they might grow worse when workers at the Toledo Edison Electric Company threatened to strike, too, over the company's failure to meet their wage demands. Talk of a revolutionary general strike ricocheted through the city.[8]

In previous generations, such episodes of labor violence had been put down with force. The combined muscle of powerful employers and the heavy-handed state had smashed the workers. But in Toledo, Muste's Brookwood cadre organized the unemployed to expand the scale of the protest. Crushing it seemed impossible. The industrial union—even one established through a temporary AFL charter—was a unit of labor power adapted to the scale and structure of the large mass-production firms. And where strikes had fizzled time and again since the postwar labor actions of 1919, the strike at Auto-Lite soon proved a success. Auto-Lite recognized the union, rehired the strikers, and increased wages as the union had demanded. Other auto part firms in the city followed suit. For a month and a half, strikers in Toledo had risked their livelihoods and their lives in a battle over the industrial future. A glimmer of industrial democracy had emerged on the other side.[9]

Unions around the country replicated the Toledo model. And as they did, labor activists and intellectuals from Brookwood and other American Fund beneficiaries cheered, prodded, and (above all) organized.

American Fund veterans seemed to be in crucial leadership roles nearly everywhere as industrial unionization rolled across the American economy. Hillman allies and Brookwood figures led an organization drive in the shirt-making shops of the East Coast, became economic advisors to the powerful United Mine Workers, and helped found the Steel Workers Organizing Committee (SWOC) in 1936. Others helped propel the garment workers campaigns of the New Deal era or organized coal miners in a newly militant union at the Gallup mines in New Mexico. David Dubinsky's International Ladies' Garment Workers Union, which had received substantial American Fund support during its internal struggles with a Communist faction in the 1920s, supplied Brookwood-trained leaders for key campaigns in West Virginia steel mills and in Ohio rubber manufacturing. By the middle of the 1930s, Brookwood instructors, not content to teach when there was so much to do, held joint positions at Brookwood and with the clothing workers in the Midwest, organized progressive dissidents among the mine workers, and brought worker education inside the union halls of the ILGWU. In Seattle, a Brookwood graduate led efforts to organize the unemployed.[10]

In 1935, the surge of activism among industrial unions culminated in a breakaway union movement with American Fund figures in lead roles. At the AFL's annual conference, held in Atlantic City, tensions led to a fistfight between John L. Lewis of the mine workers and William "Big Bill" Hutcheson of the AFL's carpenters' union. Sidney Hillman joined together with Lewis and dissident AFL union leaders to establish the Committee for Industrial Organization, breaking with AFL leadership to pursue the industrial unionization he and the Fund had supported since its founding. Along with Lewis, the group included John Brophy of the mine workers and Dubinsky of the ILGWU, among others. It was an unwieldy crew. Hillman and his American Fund allies had helped finance Brophy's resistance to Lewis's power at the UMW. But the coalition held together. With Lewis's encouragement, Brookwood trustee and Fund-insider Brophy became the committee's director. The role was fitting. The new CIO, which broke off from the AFL completely in 1937 as the Congress of Industrial Organizations, was connected by a skein of intellectual and professional threads. Where the old-line AFL had settled for a familiar business unionism focused on incremental economic gains for its members, the young CIO set its sights on a revolutionary democratization of American industry. It drew with enthusiasm on a new political coalition of urban immigrants and organized workers to deploy the power of the state in the service of the working class. The CIO forged uneasy but productive alliances between former Wobblies and an educated managerial class made up of labor economists and lawyers. It smashed together the energies of radical unionism with the architectural design of progressive technocrats. And in each of these crucial respects, the new and tangled CIO world reproduced the debates of the American Fund and its principal labor beneficiaries.[11]

Affirmative Legal Action

If many Brookwood organizers took staff positions at the CIO, others suddenly found themselves remaking the law in which the labor movement operated. For a decade, the labor technicians in the Fund's world had debated how to reorganize the relationship between labor and capital. Now the Great Depression and the election of Roosevelt created an opportunity to do just that.

The American Fund's engagement with labor law went back to the weeks before its first 1922 gatherings when a massive strike of 400,000 railway shopmen broke out in the machine shops, sheet-metal facilities, and boiler assembly departments of the nation's railroads. The railway shopmen's strike was the first truly nationwide railroad labor stoppage in American history, covering more areas of the country and including more workers than either the violent strike of 1877 or the 1894 clash that had made Eugene Debs a household name. One hundred thousand workers walked out in the Chicago area alone, representing six different AFL craft unions. Shops were shuttered in Los Angeles, Denver, Knoxville, Memphis, and New York. It was, in the words of one historian, "the greatest strike of the decade."[12]

In the world of the Fund, the shopmen's strike drew attention to the skewed legal landscape of labor and capital. With the strikers threatening to bring the nation's rails to a halt, President Harding's corrupt attorney general, Harry Daugherty, sought and obtained from the federal courts an injunction ordering the striking shopmen to refrain from interfering with the rails. For decades, injunctions like the shopmen's strike order had broken the back of labor. According to Frankfurter, injunctions were "America's distinctive contribution in the application of law to industrial strife." Courts had issued such orders in some 6,500 labor disputes since 1880. By the 1920s, one in four labor disputes in the country was restricted or prohibited by a judicial injunction laying out authoritarian codes for union conduct. The 1894 injunction against Eugene Debs's American Railway Union during the great Pullman strike, for example, had barred the defendants from attempting to persuade employees "to refuse or fail to perform any of their duties"—an essential feature of any labor stoppage. A decade later, in an AFL-sponsored boycott of the Buck's Stove & Range Company, the courts of the District of Columbia issued an injunction barring Samuel Gompers and his colleagues from using the word "unfair" (or any similar word or phrase) in connection with the boycotted firm.[13]

The 1922 injunction in the railroad shopmen strike was broader still. Issued by Judge Herbert Wilkerson, who had taken Kenesaw Mountain

Landis's seat on the federal court in Chicago, the order enjoined the striking shopmen from an astonishingly long list of behaviors, ranging from annoying railroad employees on their way to or from work, to using "jeers" toward railroad employees "at any time or place," to "aiding or encouraging" loitering near railroad facilities. The order prohibited the use of "persuasion," "argument," or "rewards" to induce workers to quit, banned union visits to workers' homes, and made it illegal to give an interview to a newspaper urging workers to quit. The Wilkerson order swept so broadly as to effectively displace the basic rules governing people in their conduct with one another, substituting a code of industrial conduct devised by a single judge. Making matters worse, violations of what critics called "government by injunction" were dealt with as contempt of court in summary criminal trials. No jury of the strikers' peers acted as a check on the judge's power. Elizabeth Gurley Flynn fumed that the order violated the free speech clause of the Constitution. Baldwin said it contravened "the right of agitation of new ideas."[14]

For a generation, the principal strategy of labor unions in the courts had been defensive: to protect workers from the injunctions issued at the behest of employers. The "best thing the state can do for labor," wrote Samuel Gompers in 1901, "is to leave labor alone." The radical wing of the American Fund, which rarely agreed with Gompers, offered a left-wing version of the same defensive strategy. The injunction problem, fund director Scott Nearing proposed, was proof of "the conflict theory of the state." "It should be taken for granted," Nearing explained, "that the capitalist state is against labor."[15]

Urgent pleas for support throughout the 1920s had offered powerful evidence for Nearing's thesis. Requests for help from unions facing injunctions poured into the American Fund. Strikers jailed for contempt in Oklahoma and Kansas requested relief. The Wabash System of Shop Crafts asked for help fighting off the Wilkerson injunction. A new Injunction Defense Committee in Seattle applied for assistance fighting an injunction in a restaurant strike with connections to the Wobblies. In 1926 and 1927, the Fund supported the legal defense efforts of editors convicted of criminal contempt for publishing news articles about strikes in Michigan and Tennessee. Money went to the defense of members of the IWW's Agricultural Workers Industrial Union convicted of violating a Kansas injunction. As late as 1935, with its resources depleted, the Fund made an emergency grant to the striking United Anthracite Miners in Pennsylvania to fight an injunction issued on behalf of a notoriously anti-union coal operator.[16]

Fighting off labor injunctions one by one, however, proved an unending task. In the wake of the Wilkerson injunction, the American Fund became a gathering place for a small group of lawyers interested in pursuing a different, affirmative strategy toward the law.

In 1923, prominent New York socialist Morris Hillquit came to the Fund seeking support for a lawsuit against the Pennsylvania Railroad in the railway shopmen strike, now badly hobbled by the Wilkerson injunction. Hillquit and the 50,000 members of the Pennsylvania branch of the shopmen's union proposed to turn the law around and use it affirmatively on workers' behalf by enforcing the union's rights under the specialized body of law governing railroad labor. Hillquit contended that the Transportation Act of 1920, properly understood, required the railroad to bargain with the Federation as the workers' chosen representative and precluded the railroad from substituting its own company-sponsored union for the Federation.[17]

The Fund awarded Hillquit and the Pennsylvania shopmen $3,000 to pursue the theory through the courts beginning in the summer of 1923. In each of the next two years the Fund repeated the grant, until, in 1925, the suit met defeat in the Supreme Court in a unanimous opinion written by Chief Justice William Howard Taft. The shopmen's strike had long since been crushed. But the Fund and the shopmen had broached a new way of thinking about labor and the law.[18]

The shopmen's strike touched off a wave of experiments among progressive unionists in the affirmative use of the law. At the Fund's first meetings in 1922, Baldwin proposed a large-scale study to explore new ways of engaging the injunction problem. Walter Nelles, the Fund's Harvard-trained general counsel, took up the idea. Nelles, who was to join the Yale Law School faculty in 1928, turned the Fund's studies of the labor injunction away from the old, defensive approach. As he explained to Fund director Lewis Gannett, he was "not interested in doing a piece of propaganda for the labor movement." Nor, he told Baldwin, did he aim to "furnish evidence" for Nearing's ideas about class domination of the courts. Nelles's "primary concern" was more positive and practical. "What," he asked, do "we want law to do?"—what should labor law be?[19]

With generous support from the Fund, Nelles set out to develop such a vision drawing on the social democratic ideas of the progressive new unionist crowd. An electrifying article in 1923 shaped his thinking. Robert Hale, an economist at Columbia University, proposed that private property in the modern economy—the supposed guarantor of freedom and liberty—contained an irreducible coercive dimension. The right to exclusive possession of some piece of property—land or personal item— was also a power to coercively exclude others from its value. The property owner held not only a right to enjoy their asset but also a power to invoke the power of the state against anyone else who sought to enjoy it.[20]

Nelles took Hale's point and applied it to the law of capital and labor. In the labor bargain, a typical employer—Nelles called him "Bedford"— had the "right" to coercively exclude workers from the factory. He could, in other words, fire them. In turn, the worker—Nelles called him "Dobbins"—had a theoretical right to coercively exclude the employer from their labor power. They could quit. What mattered, however, was not the respective theoretical rights of employer and employee but their practical capacities in the world. Dobbins's power to quit his job and Bedford's practical capacity to fire his workers turned on countless interdependent considerations. Bedford would be able to exclude his workers if he could hire other Dobbinses in their place at equal or lower pay. Separating Bedford from more of his money, in turn, would require the workers to "organize a coercive power superior to Mr. Bedford's," by which they might "coerce the cooperation of many Dobbinses." Rights to work or to fire or to hire or to quit were, in Nelles's terms, "barren" until filled in by the practical capacities of the participants, which in turn were constituted by the legal powers afforded them.[21]

The question for a legal strategist of industrial democracy was thus not whether to avoid the law or not. The law's field would reach into the relations of labor and capital whether the labor movement liked it or not. The only question was which reciprocal coercions to permit and which to exclude, the coercions of capital or the coercions of labor? "The question," Nelles concluded in his study for the Fund, published in the *Yale Law Journal* in 1931, "is which coercive power (not of course right in any strict sense) will result in more peace, freedom and happiness." Where earlier critics of labor law like Gompers and Nearing had imagined the labor injunction as a tool in the inevitable conflict between labor and capital, Nelles's studies for the Fund reconceived the injunction problem as a question of institutional design and social engineering. The law of labor and capital would distribute power and resources in society. There was no avoiding the law's effects, no neutral place in which law and government could be held off. Law, Nelles wrote, conditioned life, shaped its opportunities and its structure. The only thing to do was to decide how best to arrange law to promote the democratic interests of all.[22]

To build an industrial democracy for the modern economy would require more than the defensiveness of the old labor radicals. It would require what Nelles, along with Morris Ernst and ACLU lawyer Arthur Garfield Hays, began to call "affirmative legal action." As a member of the League for Industrial Democracy, Nelles helped lead a seismic shift in the way progressive unions thought about the law, breaking down (as he wrote to the Fund in 1925) "the prejudice" against using the law that had

Arthur Garfield Hays, standing here with Darrow and the Scopes legal team in 1925, was the ACLU lawyer who crafted the Fund's proactive "affirmative legal action" plan to use the law to advance the interests of labor.

kept unions "on the defensive." Hillquit, the shopmen's lawyer in 1923, won injunctions in the cloak industry for the International Ladies' Garment Workers Union and in the Boston fur trade. Hays sought injunctions against coal operators in the mountains of western Pennsylvania. Stuart Chase and Leo Wolman at The Labor Bureau and ACLU lawyer Carol Weiss King prepared studies of injunctions with Fund support. Max Lowenthal, who numbered Hillman's Amalgamated Clothing Workers among his clients, served alongside Morris Ernst on a Fund committee for which Ernst drafted a massive manuscript listing affirmative legal actions labor unions might initiate against employers. In 1926, at Hays's suggestion, the Fund supported an emergency injunction on behalf of the Passaic textile strikers to bar the sheriff from shutting down a strike meeting. With Fund support, Vanguard Press published a book by League of Industrial Democracy member McAlister Coleman on "aggressive legal tactics for labor," which the ACLU summarized in a practical guide of quick-action advice for labor unions. Louis Budenz's *Labor Age* magazine sponsored forums on the labor injunction that emphasized the importance of aggressive litigation tactics in contrast to Gompers's old strategy of simple defiance. "Use This Weapon" was the title of Hays's contribution; others urged labor to brave the "jungle-land of the injunction."[23]

One person who shared the Fund's progressive, new unionist vision of affirmative labor law was Felix Frankfurter at Harvard. Of all Frankfurter's work alongside the Fund, his most sustained engagement was on the question of labor injunctions, a topic on which he was fast emerging as the nation's leading voice.[24]

Frankfurter had organized legal strategy for Hillman's Amalgamated Clothing Workers when it ran into blunderbuss injunctions in a bitter 1920 strike in Rochester. In collaboration with the Fund, he had defended the Communist organizer Albert Weisbord—a former student, as it happened—for violating an injunction in the Passaic strike.[25]

By the late 1920s, supported by a grant from the American Fund's Committee on Research and Publications, Frankfurter turned his attention to legislation that might eliminate the labor injunction from employers' arsenals in ordinary labor disputes. In 1928, Senator George W. Norris of Nebraska invited Frankfurter and Pullman porter lawyer Donald Richberg along with a small group of lawyers and labor economists to draft an anti-injunction bill for the Judiciary Committee. Frankfurter and Nelles, who had worked together on the injunction problem, shared little love for one another. Yet the proposal Frankfurter drew up adopted key features of the philosophy Nelles had been developing in his studies for the Fund. "Government authority," the bill's policy statement asserted, had helped "the owners of property to organize" as corporations and in other forms of association. The labor market was no natural space or level playing field; its basic rules had been built by the law. It was necessary, therefore, given "prevailing economic conditions," that workers have similar opportunities afforded by law for self-organization. Promising "full freedom of association," the bill prohibited the enforcement of the "yellow dog" contracts in which employees promised not to join a union, and stripped federal courts of the power to enjoin workers from striking, joining a union, or supporting strikers.[26]

The old guard at the AFL worried the bill did not do enough to remove courts from labor-capital conflict. But that was by design. Even as Frankfurter's co-drafter Richberg hashed out the bill's terms, he was representing A. Philip Randolph in an effort to enjoin Pullman's company union. The Pullman employee representation plan, argued Richberg, was a violation of the porters' right to choose their representatives freely. Frankfurter himself was simultaneously consulting on the Fund's affirmative legal action experiments. Earlier AFL versions of anti-injunction legislation had aimed to shut off courts' injunction power entirely. The bill tacked in a different direction. It began with a proposition much like the one Nathan Margold would soon come to in the NAACP campaign. Law wasn't merely about rights. Law was power. As Robert Hale had understood, law would inevitably shape the forces of labor and capital because it defined them. It allocated coercive power to them. The affirmative strategy was not only to hold off the grant of certain powers to the owners and the bosses but to channel the power of the state toward the workers and their unions as well.[27]

After two years of internal debate, when the AFL finally endorsed a version of the bill, Roger Baldwin and the American Fund world leapt into action to press the bill into law. Fund treasurer Morris Ernst testified on behalf of the anti-injunction legislation in the Senate. At the ACLU, Baldwin formed a new National Committee on Labor Injunctions made up of some 400 prominent Americans. Muste and Richberg were members, as was Frankfurter's collaborator on labor injunction matters, Nathan Greene; the executive committee included American Fund stalwarts like Baldwin, Wolman, Ernst, and Hays. Despite its diminishing resources, the Fund promptly approved grants to the Committee, awarding it $3,000 each year in 1930 and 1931 to promote the bill through pamphlets and agitation. When the November 1930 elections swung Congress toward the Democrats, the bill's success was essentially guaranteed. The Senate approved it, 75–5, and the House, 362–14. President Herbert Hoover signed the Norris–La Guardia Act into law on March 23, 1932.[28]

With astonishing speed, the Depression's economic crisis had pulled ideas from the American Fund orbit and turned them into legislation. Here was a whole new level of success for an organization that had spent nearly all its active life on the outs, defending dissidents and bemoaning the state of politics. Legislative accomplishment ("a notable change" in the law, the ACLU boasted) was a novel experience—and a harbinger of things to come.[29]

Franklin Roosevelt's election in November 1932 took the victory a step further. Frankfurter entered the inner circle at the White House. Sidney Hillman soon won Roosevelt's ear, too. With them came the labor lawyers and economists who had been quietly revolving in the Amalgamated Clothing Workers and American Fund orbits for a decade.[30]

In the ILGWU injunction case from the early 1920s against the cloak industry, the garment workers' victory had come before a New York State judge named Robert Wagner. A decade later, after winning reelection to the U.S. Senate in the Democrats' 1932 landslide, Wagner found himself helping to lead a new Democratic majority in Congress. He was now an insider with the new president. Since at least 1930 he had been a participant in Baldwin's National Committee on Labor Injunctions. In 1932 he had voted for the Norris–La Guardia anti-injunction act. Now, as the Roosevelt transition team debated how to intervene in the Depression-era economy, Wagner gathered a working group to draft recovery legislation. He called on Hillman. He drew in Fund advisor W. Jett Lauck to help design industrial policy. Frankfurter worked in parallel. And even as the transition team turned away (temporarily, as it happened) from Wagner's preferred Keynesian approach, with its focus on increased government spending to spur growth, the group around Frankfurter, Hillman, and Wagner pressed successfully to keep labor protections in the plan.[31]

The National Industrial Recovery Act, a centerpiece of the president's first one hundred days in office, fundamentally remade the basic structure of the still-sputtering American economy. The NIRA authorized the president and industrial agencies of his creation to work with industrial trade associations for the development of "codes of fair competition." Such codes would aim to prevent "destructive wage or price cutting" by setting wages, prices, and trade practices for entire industries. Freed from the pressure of market rivals, firms would be able to refrain from costly competition. Prices would rise. Wages would follow. The economy would be restored. Such was the theory, anyway. A skeptical Hillman rightly told his union lieutenants that the act had been designed by bankers and industrialists.[32]

The good news for labor, however, was that as labor's representative in the drafting process, Jett Lauck had ensured that there would be "safeguards" for unions, too. Section 7(a) of the NIRA guaranteed to labor the right of free self-organization. Like the Railway Labor Act of 1926, Section 7(a) provided that employees "shall have the right to organize and bargain collectively through representatives of their own choosing." And in the spirit of the Norris–La Guardia Act, workers were to be free from "interference, restraint, or coercion" in the selection of their representatives. The new law and its industrial codes made the notorious yellow dog contracts unlawful, too.[33]

Labor also had influence over the NIRA's administration. In Frankfurter's circles, where administration was thought to be everything, this seemed like a good arrangement. And at first it was. Hillman took a seat on the National Industrial Recovery Board and served on its Labor Advisory Board. When President Roosevelt established a National Labor Board to work out the mechanics of worker organizing and collective bargaining under 7(a), he appointed Senator Wagner as the chair and Hillman's associate Wolman as one of its members. William M. Leiserson, a longtime Hillman friend and arbitrator for labor disputes in the textile industry, rounded out the new unionist presence on the board. Leiserson, who had been on the staff of the Commission on Industrial Relations for Frank Walsh in 1914 and 1915, served as the board's influential secretary.[34]

With figures from the worlds of Hillman and the American Fund staffing the NIRA's labor agencies, the National Labor Board took steps toward a government-administered version of the managerial industrial democracy that Hillman and the Amalgamated Clothing Workers had been practicing for decades. When a labor dispute broke out between the Full Fashioned Hosiery Workers Union and Berkshire Knitting Mills, based near Reading, Pennsylvania, Wolman and Leiserson seized the opportunity to bring the new unionism to the New Deal. Their solution at Berkshire was for the firm to rehire the strikers, and for the Labor Board to hold an election by secret ballot among the workers to choose, by simple majority, an exclusive representative for collective bargaining with the employer.[35]

The "Reading Formula," as it came to be known, was an astonishing moment in the history of the labor intellectuals who had circulated around the American Fund. Leiserson and Wolman, men who came out of Hillman's new unionism and Brookwood Labor College, respectively, made majority rule and exclusive representation—the Reading Formula's key ingredients—centerpieces of American labor-capital relations. For progressive union leaders like Hillman and Joseph Schlossberg at the ACW, the Reading system seemed to vindicate the industrial democracy project they had pioneered. Wolman had based the Reading approach on Hillman's successes in Chicago. He had also drawn on the trajectory of the railroad labor system that A. Philip Randolph and Donald Richberg sought to exploit for the Brotherhood of Sleeping Car Porters. The 1920 Transportation Act had expressly permitted so-called minority unions; employees who rejected a majority union could file grievances and negotiate with management "by representatives of their own choice." In the view of union-side labor lawyers, economists, and organizers, however, the minority representation system of the 1920 act had been an opening wedge for the much-hated company unions. A splintered labor force, moreover, fractured the strength that a unified union could offer. In electoral politics, the critics of minority unions pointed out, elections did not produce rival governments alongside the majority. Accordingly, at the insistence of the railroad brotherhoods, Congress in the 1926 Railway Labor Act dropped the 1920 minority union provision and adopted an exclusive representation model in its place. Wolman and the Labor Board's interpretation of 7(a) under the NIRA meant that the new law applied exclusive representation and majority rule to industries across the economy. The Reading Formula, Wolman and Leiserson insisted, would vindicate workers' votes, channeling them through elected representatives into an industrial democracy of collective bargaining and arbitration.[36]

Yet the Reading majority rule split the world of the American Fund in two, dividing the group along its now-familiar radical and progressive axes. For the radical wing, Roger Baldwin insisted that majority rule and exclusive bargaining endangered the kinds of progressive union dissidents who had long been beneficiaries of American Fund support. For a decade, the Fund had offered aid to breakaway miners organized around John Brophy as they protested the autocratic rule of union boss John Lewis. Now, Baldwin objected, the industrial codes of the NIRA threatened to strengthen authoritarian union leaders like Lewis by squeezing out dissenting voices. A majority of the ACLU's National Committee agreed with Baldwin, calling on the National Recovery Administration to respect minority unions.[37]

Labor experts in and around the American Fund and the ACLU vehemently dissented. "The whole situation in the coal mines," Wolman complained to Baldwin, "is difficult enough without our attempting here to reach an agreement between rival unions." Lauck, who split his time between Lewis's UMW and Senator Wagner's policy group, defended the majority rule and exclusive representation system as indispensable to marshaling labor power. "If the Act is to be workable," he insisted, if industrial democracy were to be vindicated, the "majority must rule." Morris Hillquit, the senior statesman of socialist labor lawyers, protested that workers "can maintain living standards only through an all-inclusive organization with unified leadership." Amalgamated Clothing Workers secretary-treasurer Schlossberg, for his part, warned Baldwin that his "demand for the recognition of minority unions" was dangerous at best. "Under the guise of minority unions," he elaborated, employers would set up "dummy organizations for the purposes of disrupting bona fide unions." Minority unions would "open wide the gates for company unions"; they had "the enthusiastic approval of the employers for this demand" because "the working conditions in a plant cannot be controlled by the workers" without one union structure. "The class struggle," Schlossberg finished, "cannot be conducted successfully" with "divided worker ranks against united employers."[38]

In truth, the NIRA was a poor vehicle for class struggle, majority rule or not. To Hillman's dismay, the first industrial codes, for industries like cotton textiles, adopted a forty-hour week and a $10 minimum weekly wage. (Hillman had called for thirty-six-hour weeks at $18 per week.) In disputes at Weirton Steel in West Virginia and at the Budd Manufacturing Company in North Philadelphia, obstinate employers showed the world that the National Labor Board lacked the coercive authority to make Section 7(a) stick. Like the Pullman Company in the late 1920s, they simply defied the board's efforts to put in place orderly labor-capital relations. The Budd Company, like Pullman, stopped responding to the board altogether. In a desperate bit of affirmative lawyering, Labor Board lawyers tried to get the courts to force Weirton and Budd to participate in hearings. Frankfurter recommended against such suits for fear that losses would further delegitimate the board's authority. When the suits went down to defeat, the results were catastrophic for the NIRA. Lacking a trustworthy statutory mechanism for resolving their grievances, workers went back on strike at firms around the country. Employers, for their part, now openly defied the NIRA's toothless regulations. The act was in collapse, so much so that when the Supreme Court struck it down as unconstitutional on May 27, 1935, in *Schechter Poultry v. United States*, observers suggested that the Court had rescued Roosevelt from a political liability. The majority rule controversy came to an inconclusive pause.[39]

In 1934 and 1935, Senator Wagner surrounded himself with staff from his office and from the National Labor Board to design legislation that might replace the tottering NIRA. Brainstorming sessions, which were like conferences of the labor worlds stretching out from Brookwood and Frankfurter, aimed for nothing short of establishing a new industrial democracy. "Democratic self-government in industry," Wagner explained, required "workers participating" just as "democratic government in politics" required citizens "having the right to vote." Some believed that the bill would lift the economy by raising wages through collective bargaining and conferring new purchasing power on the working classes. Others hoped to achieve industrial peace; cascading Depression-era strikes might be replaced with orderly legal processes while the factories kept running. Wagner's circle of advisors aimed to accomplish this by enacting Wolman's Reading Formula into law: majority rule without company unions. This, Wagner contended, was the essence of industrial democracy.[40]

At the ACLU, however, Baldwin's opposition to the majority rule model grew more obstinate. Exclusive representation and majority rule, he pointed out, left Black workers at the mercy of Jim Crow unions. The NAACP agreed. Baldwin objected to the exclusion of agricultural workers from Wagner's new bill, too, an objection Charles Hamilton Houston shared because of its disproportionate effects on Black workers. Yet for Baldwin, the real complaint was one that ran headlong into a core feature of the new unionism that the Brookwood wing of the American Fund world had nurtured for more than a decade. Where Hillman, Muste, and their teams of labor economists and organizers looked to the state as a powerful tool for organizing mass-production industries, Baldwin suspected that expanding the state's apparatus would undermine labor's real power. At the heart of his opposition lay a sense, as an ACLU resolution put it in 1934, that workers' rights were enforceable by "economic power and organized labor alone." "Capitalist courts," as Dunn and Michelson put it, would never deliver class justice.[41]

The Wagner bill's supporters responded by drawing on the affirmative legal action ideas of the Hillman school—ideas, ironically, that Baldwin had helped to finance for a decade at the American Fund. Senator Wagner told Baldwin that he misunderstood the basic landscape of labor and capital. The radical dream of a labor movement that proceeded outside the law was impossible. As Nathan Margold had said to his left-leaning critics in 1931, working outside the law did not exist as an option because the law shaped the field of action. Law decided what belonged to whom. It decided which tactics were permitted and which were not. It managed the micro-mechanics of social interaction. State involvement, Wagner now explained, was thus inevitable, "whether we will it or not." The right strategy, Wagner protested, was to "direct the nature" of the law, to control it rather than pretend it could be ignored. At the Amalgamated Clothing Workers, Joseph Schlossberg made a more practical appeal. "By your opposition," he protested to Baldwin, "you unwittingly lined up with the employers and all reactionaries who opposed the bill."[42]

Franklin Roosevelt signed Wagner's labor relations bill into law on July 5, 1935. The new law, he announced, "defines, as a part of our substantive law, the right of self-organization of employees in industry for the purpose of collective bargaining." There was industrial democracy. The act, he continued, "provides methods by which the Government can safeguard that legal right," including establishment of "a National Labor Relations Board to hear and determine cases in which it is charged that this legal right is abridged or denied." That was enforcement power, which the Railway Labor Act had lacked. Under the Wagner law, Roosevelt said, the NLRB would "hold fair elections to ascertain who are the chosen representatives of employees." There were the majority rule and exclusive representation arrangements that Lauck, Leiserson, and Wolman had adapted from Hillman's clothing workers—arrangements fostered at Brookwood for a decade.[43]

Section 7 of the Wagner Act recognized a "right to self-organization," to "bargain collectively through representatives of their own choosing," and to engage in "concerted activities" for such collective bargaining "or other mutual aid." Section 8 enumerated unfair employer labor practices said to interfere with the rights guaranteed in Section 7, including coercion, domination, company unions, discrimination against union members, and refusal to bargain, all of which came under the jurisdiction of the new National Labor Relations Board, to which Brookwood faculty member David Saposs and American Fund director Clinton Golden (only recently resigned from his Brookwood post) were promptly appointed.[44]

The Wagner Act conjured a technocratic design for industrial democracy. Like Margold's 1931 report for the NAACP, it aimed to reassemble the relevant governing institutions in novel ways that would allow democracy to flourish. For Margold, the institutional architecture of equality had included school districts, states, and the courts. For the Wagner Act, a democratic architecture meant unions, employers, and a federal agency. If the institutions were different, the impulses ran parallel. The Wagner Act codified a system of union recognition, collective bargaining, and grievance arbitration astonishingly close to the new unionism Hillman had long envisioned for mass production industries. The ideas of the heterodox Brookwood circle seemed to have found a sturdy legal scaffolding.

Yet even in the moment of its apparent triumph, criticisms by Baldwin and the Communists planted seeds of doubt. Hillman's formula had combined the bureaucracy of industrial democracy, on the one hand, with the energies of a mass labor movement, on the other. His central idea—the central Brookwood idea—had been to maintain both at once, to hold on to architecture and mobilization at the same time. One without the other would either be empty managerialism or wasted passions. In the view of its left critics, the Wagner Act tipped too far toward the managerial. It created an elaborate structure not for industrial democracy or the redistribution of resources, but for what the first section of the act called the free "flow" of the "channels of commerce." The president had signaled the same idea in his signing day statement when he emphasized the Wagner Act's capacity to smooth out economic disruptions ("to remove one of the chief causes of wasteful economic strife," he said). The danger was that institutional structures would lull the energies of a movement that was nothing if not propelled by the fuel of solidarity. Muste had warned Wagner of exactly that. Orderly government management of labor disputes, even if in the name of a "square deal" for workers, he cautioned, would cool "the ardor" of the employees. "Labor spies and company agents" would worm their way into the workers' ranks. They would intimidate employees with threats of firings, layoffs, and closures. If the law was to support the worker, Muste charged, what it needed to do was to support unwaveringly the worker's only "real weapon"—"the right collectively to cease labor."[45]

Sit-Down Strike

American workers sat down in 1936. In January, workers at Firestone Tire & Rubber in Akron, Ohio, stopped work in their places to protest the suspension of a union worker. Production resumed when Firestone bosses agreed to reinstate the man with back pay, but copycat sit-down strikes soon followed at Firestone's rivals Goodyear and B. F. Goodrich. By the end of May, Goodyear complained that its Akron plants had been the target of nineteen sit-down strikes since February, nearly all producing what one Goodyear assessment called "substantial concessions on the part of management." Rolling sit downs continued around the city for the rest of the year. In November, in South Bend, Indiana, workers at the Bendix Corporation sat down on the job in their auto parts plant and won a new contract. A sit down at the Midland Steel Frame Company in Cleveland produced gains for workers building parts for Ford and Chrysler. In the middle of December, Detroit workers at the auto parts firm Kelsey Hayes struck inside the company's plant. And then, in the last days of the year, workers sat down on the job at the crucial Fisher Body plants making auto bodies for the entire run of General Motors vehicles: Buick, Cadillac,

Chevrolet, Oldsmobile, and Pontiac. Seven thousand workers put down their tools in the Fisher plant in Cleveland. Thousands of workers followed suit at two Fisher plants in Flint, with a number of smaller production sites coming right behind. Production for the largest manufacturing company in the world ground to a halt.[46]

The sit-down tactic had a special genius. A standard walkout handed control over the factory floor to management as its first act. The sit-down strike, by contrast, occupied the factory floor for the workers in a direct and forceful but nonviolent act. The picket line, always a flash point in strikes, gave way to a new battle line inside the plant. The tactical advantages were many. Factories were warm while picket lines could be cold. Strikers stayed in solidarity with one another, rather than separating at the end of each day. At the same time, the sit-down strike channeled the movement energies of an industrial revolution. Strikers in a sit-down action claimed the factory for their own.

For all these reasons, the sit-down tactic emerged in the United States as the movement's answer to labor law's new, potentially stifling order. The sit down was the energetic twin to the Wagner Act's cool architecture of industrial peace. Where the Wagner Act and the affirmative legal strategies of labor promised to smooth labor wars into an expert jurisprudence of conciliation, the sit-down strike was the guerrilla tactic that aimed to disrupt managerialism's seductive call. And like the new unionism's professional bureaucracies and labor intellectuals, the sit down was a distinctive product of debates from the American Fund world at places like Brookwood—debates that had nurtured both the dream of democratic peace and the ideals of worker revolution.

Brookwood and the American Fund's labor world took the erratic sit down tactic and turned it into a powerful strategy. Brookwood's curriculum adopted the writings of Richard Gregg, a member of Muste's pacifist Fellowship of Reconciliation. Gregg had been a labor lawyer during the railroad shopmen strike of 1922. He despaired of the recurrent bouts of violence in labor disputes. His life changed, however, when he encountered an article about Mohandas Gandhi in a Chicago bookstore. Leaving his life in the United States behind, he moved for three years to India to study Gandhian nonviolent resistance. In a stream of books on the subject, the most famous of which was the 1934 *Power of Non-Violence*, Gregg wrote about "mass non-violence" as a startlingly effective path for social change in the modern era. The crucial feature, Gregg wrote, was that "non-violent resistance acts as a sort of moral jiu-jitsu." It turned the tables on a stronger adversary by using the adversary's strength against him, illuminating the injustice of his power and causing him, in Gregg's words, "to lose his moral balance."[47]

The idea, of course, appealed to Muste, who had practiced a form of strategic nonviolence when his textile strikers at Lawrence in 1919 carefully kept "their arms folded" in the face of brutal sheriffs' deputies. Brookwood taught union organizers that the carefully controlled sit-down strike could work the "jiu-jitsu" effect Gregg described. Mass nonviolence could be turned, as indeed Gregg anticipated, to class struggle. In the best Brookwood tradition, the sit-down strike balanced revolutionary passions with real-world practicalities, all the while echoing the tactics of predecessors. The sit down borrowed the affirmative legal action tactic of progressive labor lawyers like Nelles and Frankfurter, who had aimed to co-opt the repressive law of labor relations and turn it in the workers' service. The sit downs likewise inverted the basic order of property rights, insisting on a subversive claim to ownership rights for workers in their jobs.[48]

Sit-down strikes resonated with the best dimensions of the Wobblies' gospel of sabotage, when Elizabeth Gurley Flynn and others had upended the moral world by imaginatively redefining what belonged to whom. Counterproductive labor violence had squandered the moral righteousness of Flynn's conceptual gymnastics. The practice of the sit-down strike, by contrast, took the creative energy of challenging the bosses' property rights and turned it in workers' favor. On a picket line, the striker was in a tactically disadvantageous position: an unfamiliar setting exposed to the public gaze and forced to fend off scabs and strikebreakers. Picket lines practically invited the use of force, which in turn set off a cycle of employer reprisals and state repression. On the line, as Gregg put it, the union was "snared in the same net of ideas and valuations" as the bosses. The sit down, by contrast, allayed strikers' fears about replacements. Scabs had nowhere to go. The sit down demanded that the employer decide whether to use force to displace the strikers. It fostered morale among the strikers, whose connections to one another on the shop floor could now be augmented by another, new solidarity. To be sure, the sit-down strike produced distinctive hardships as well. Food and medical care could be in short supply. Strikers inside a plant were separated from their families.

But such challenges were opportunities as well as dangers. The difficulties of the sit-down strike rewarded union leaders who combined effective preparation with derring-do. Careful planning and heroic moments of ingenuity linked the sit-down strikers to their organizers, to their comrades, and to their families on the outside. Laying claim to the factory floor necessitated practical structures of support that produced and reproduced working-class energies.[49]

The three Reuther brothers, with roots in the Detroit area and close connections to Brookwood, were as responsible as anyone in the United States for developing the logic of the sit-down strike and perfecting its release of the labor movement's pent-up energies.[50]

Victor, Roy, and Walter Reuther were born to the family of an oft-injured socialist laborer in West Virginia. As young men, the three had made their way to Detroit, where they threw themselves into socialist politics around the booming automobile industry. At Detroit City College (now Wayne State University) they founded a Social Problems Club, which they affiliated with the League for Industrial Democracy, to "discuss the prime issues of the day." The club's reading list was a veritable who's who of American Fund authors: Upton Sinclair, whose exhortations to Charles Garland had spurred the Fund's establishment; Scott Nearing and Norman Thomas, who served on the board; Stuart Chase, the labor economist on whose consulting services the Fund relied; Charles Beard, who served on Fund grant application committees; Harry Laidler of the League for Industrial Democracy; and Will Durant, the historian whose anarchist school received support from the Fund and interacted with Garland's April Farm commune.[51]

All three brothers soon developed connections to Brookwood. Perhaps the link came through League for Industrial Democracy circles or Clinton Golden's recruiting efforts. Maybe it came through an old elementary school friend of Walter's who spent time at Brookwood in the early 1930s. One way or another, Roy (the middle of the three brothers) enrolled at Brookwood in 1933 and became a Brookwood instructor in 1935. He taught classes at the Katonah campus and led a course on the problems facing labor unions in a Brookwood extension program for the United Automobile Workers in Detroit. At summer sessions for the UAW, he convened student discussions on the battle between industrial and craft unions. He taught about the dangers of company unions, the labor injunction, and the value of collective bargaining agreements. In early 1936, he invited Sidney Hillman to Brookwood to speak on industrial unionism.[52]

Victor, the youngest of the three, was in residence as Brookwood's "unofficial peace ambassador," speaking to union groups on the dangers of militarism and war. And Walter Reuther, the oldest, spoke at Brookwood in December 1935, not long after returning with Victor from an eighteen-month stay in the Soviet Union. Brookwood offered Walter a position as an instructor for the spring of 1936, either at Katonah or in one of two planned Brookwood–CIO joint ventures in Detroit and Pittsburgh. Walter accepted, but the rising mobilization of workers in the automobile industry soon led him to reconsider. It was precisely the wrong moment to be, as he put it, "running away from" the field of automobile labor. Workers' education had been labor's refuge for the depressed years of the 1920s, but now history called. Brookwood officials took the decision with grace, helping Walter secure a position on the UAW executive committee and promising "several thousand dollars in Brookwood scholarships for the autoworkers."[53]

With a small group of Brookwooders around them at the helm of Local 174 of the United Automobile Workers, Walter and Roy identified the Kelsey Hayes Wheel Company, which among other things supplied brakes for Ford, as a promising target for a well-prepared sit-down strike. In November 1936, the two brothers telegrammed Victor to rush back to the Motor City; "recent developments in auto," they reported, were transforming "our future work." Victor took a job as a punch press operator on the second shift at Kelsey Hayes. Former Brookwood students took positions on the day shift and signed on to handle publicity for the local. An early work stoppage on December 10 ended inconclusively. Four days later, at the shift change on December 14, five hundred workers stepped away from their machines. Work at the plant came to a halt. With the workers still inside, Walter and his wife, May Reuther, organized food relief for "the strikers inside the plant and their families outside." Kelsey Hayes managers tried to send in replacements ("pug uglies" in the strikers' lingo), but the striking workers repelled them, and this time Detroit police were reluctant to intervene. With the scabs dealt with, a revolutionary cell of Brookwooders crafted plans for the delivery of Christmas trimmings until, on Christmas Eve, a deal was struck. The sit-down strikers, as Victor remembered, "marched out into the glare of flash bulbs and cheers" with a victory. Local 174 had won a "general wage hike for all," doubling and even tripling their pay. A new shop steward system and shop committee provided the rudiments of industrial democracy on the factory floor.[54]

Brookwood's Detroit vanguard struck again at the end of the month in Flint, where Roy Reuther had been organizing workers in the Fisher Body plants of General Motors. Frank Murphy, the civil rights–friendly judge in the Ossian Sweet trials a decade earlier, had won election in November as Michigan's governor on a platform of supporting labor. The Reuthers had planned a new, bigger sit down once he was in office; they counted on him to restrain the police and National Guard. But events on the ground moved more quickly than careful planning allowed. With GM preparing to remove crucial equipment from one of two Fisher plants, Roy and the UAW local called for workers to sit down where they were. Victor hurried into the GM company town to join as an auxiliary union staffer. Walter raced back and forth from the west side of Detroit with reinforcements of pickets, supplies, and food. For six weeks, the strikers held out inside the Flint plants while UAW and CIO officials organized the vast logistics of the operation. Roy gave workers' education classes in the Brookwood style

Sit-down strikers at a General Motors Fisher Body plant in Flint, Michigan, 1937.

on the factory floor. Labor plays and songs by a new Fisher Body Union Orchestra evoked the Brookwood Players and filled out the Katonah influence on the culture of the strike.[55]

The Flint sit-down strike deployed all the rudimentary pieces of the new democracy of the postwar moment. With an eye to publicity, the union stretched a ladder to the occupied second floor at Fisher Two. While most of the food for the hundreds of sit-down strikers went in the front door past cooperative factory guards, the ladder became a symbolic passage for food to men inside. Celebrities came by to make deliveries in support of the strike and to have their picture taken on the famous ladder. Publicity specialists like Edward Bernays and Ivy Lee could not have designed a system with more flair. Strike committees inside the plant formed a kind of democratic government, dividing the work of "food, recreation, education, postal services, sanitation, grievances," and more. Rules prohibited littering or bringing liquor into the building and required daily showers and shifts in cleaning the plant. Workers' courts—called "Kangaroo Courts" in a measure of comic relief—enforced the rules. Outside the plant, in Flint proper, further committees established an ersatz welfare state, supporting families and the strikers, too, organizing picketing, transportation, food, entertainment, and strike relief.[56]

Here was industrial democracy at the scale of thousands, in the giant facilities of General Motors. GM's William Knudsen, soon to be named president of the company, protested that the sit-down strikers were "trespassers" and "violators of the laws of the land" in "illegal possession" of the plant. But lawyers for the union responded that the workers had "a property right in the job" itself. Citing the Wagner Act's protections for workers' right to organize, they insisted that the law, properly understood, recognized their rights to a say in the governance of the firms for which they worked. A local judge issued an injunction against the union, but its power soon diminished when CIO general counsel Lee Pressman uncovered the judge's substantial undisclosed investment in GM stock. And when Governor Murphy refused to send the National Guard in to evict the strikers despite the pressure of the injunction, workers in Flint and elsewhere understood full well that their claims to property in the factories in which they worked had been vindicated.[57]

Behind the great Flint strike stood the American Fund's heady mix of revolutionary ideas with practical organizing, built always around institutions designed to prevent thrilling gains from evaporating into evanescent wins. Joining the Reuther brothers at Flint in 1937 was Brookwood graduate Rose Pesotta, on loan from the ILGWU. Federated Press and *New Masses*, both of which had been sustained during the 1920s by American Fund grants, reported on the strike from the front lines. Longtime recipients of the Fund's largesse from the progressive wing of the UMW arrived at Flint to represent the CIO in the strike's crucial early days.[58]

Few in the group really practiced Gregg's power of nonviolence, not in the full sense of the idea, anyway. In a clash on January 11 known as the "Battle of the Running Bulls," local police used tear gas and fired live rounds in an effort to take back the plants for GM. Strikers inside the buildings responded with a barrage of bolts and metal from the roofs. Three weeks later, when the weary strikers had reached a crucial juncture, Walter and Roy led a detachment of crack union men from Detroit with military precision to take and hold a third GM plant. Strikers' committees resembled an army camp more than a pacifist meeting; defense squadrons, lookouts, and security details competed with theater and musical entertainments. But the strikers had achieved Gregg's central imperative. They had turned the strategic calculus in the workers' favor. (As Reinhold Niebuhr pointed out, Gregg himself maintained a studied ambiguity about whether nonviolence was strategically prudent or required as a matter of principle.) The sit-down strategy had allowed a modest fraction of the workforce to occupy both the operational and the moral high ground. It was the bosses and the police who would have to resort to the use of force. And in the setting of the auto industry in 1937, that advantage proved decisive. In February, GM and the union reached a deal. Secretary of Labor Frances Perkins, the first woman to serve in a presidential cabinet position, had declined Roger Baldwin's invitation to serve on the new American Fund board back in 1922 when she was between stints as a New York labor regulator. Now she joined with Governor Murphy to broker a settlement establishing a form of industrial democracy at GM. The firm promised not to interfere with worker organizing, not to sponsor a company union, and to engage in collective bargaining with the UAW exclusively for six months.[59]

In the most momentous industrial dispute of the New Deal era, members of the old American Fund world turned up at countless union meetings and behind innumerable assembly line machines. Intellectuals and organizers from the League for Industrial Democracy joined union leaders from the ACW and the CIO and instructors from Brookwood to turn the world on its head. Back in Katonah, Joel Seidman, who had been one of Roy Reuther's instructors at Brookwood, celebrated the success of a strategy he believed had been hatched on the college's wooded campus. "If a sit-down strike can force General Motors to engage in collective bargaining with the automobile workers," he told a skeptic, "then Brookwood favors the sit-down strike." Tucker Smith, now serving as the labor college's director, went further. "Two Brookwooders inside the plant organized a 'resident labor college,'" he marveled, a mere "twenty-four hours after the first great sit-down strike started." The educational director of the plant, the publicity director for the union, not to mention organizers in Detroit and Flint—all these people, Smith continued, were "Brookwood grads."[60]

Though he was not a graduate as such, it was Walter Reuther who used the strategic value of Brookwood's nonviolent direct action most spectacularly just a few months later at the overpass to Ford's massive River Rouge plant, the largest mass-production facility in the world. Perhaps the most iconic moment in American labor history could hardly have been better designed to maximize its publicity value. Inviting newsmen, clergy, and sympathetic congressional staffers from Senator Robert La Follette's Civil Liberties Subcommittee, Reuther dispatched one hundred members of UAW Local 174's Women's Auxiliary to distribute flyers championing "Unionism, Not Fordism." Reuther and his aides instructed the leafleteers to stay on the public property of the Miller Avenue right of way outside Ford's main entrance, Gate Four. With three union lieutenants, Reuther climbed the overpass for a photograph opportunity with the Ford Motor Company name in the background. Almost immediately, Ford guards began to beat the four union men. As if according to the Greggian script taught at Brookwood, Reuther declined to resist. "I didn't fight back," Reuther later explained. His resistance, just as Gregg had proposed, was moral, not physical. The nonresistant protest, Gregg had explained, "accepts blow after blow, showing no signs of fear or shrinking or resentment." The Ford thugs threw Reuther to the ground, kicked him, picked him back up and hit him some more, all before throwing him down the stairs off the rear side of the overpass, only to pummel him further on the first landing. Like Muste at Lawrence in 1919, Reuther kept his arms folded, "fists crossed over his forearms," as one observer recalled.[61]

Photographs of Reuther and his aides being beaten on the Ford bridge appeared in newspapers across the country the next day. At the Battle of the Overpass, the dashing, Christ-like Reuther—a man who might simply have become a labor college teacher had history gone a different way—became one of the most famous labor leaders in America.[62]

Less than a decade after his battle at Ford, Walter Reuther was elected president of the UAW, the nation's largest union, boasting roughly three-quarters of a million members. For three years he served as president of the CIO itself, before merging the CIO back into the AFL in 1955. He was "the most dangerous man in Detroit," according to American Automobile Manufacturers Association spokesman and future governor George Romney. He stood astride the nation's leading industry for a quarter century and presided over a vast mid-century elevation of American working-class living standards. In the 1950s and 1960s, he championed civil rights. Critics in the labor rank and file would come to resent him. They would blame him for betraying the bottom-up energies he and the Brookwood squadrons had tapped in 1936 and 1937. They would charge him with abandoning grass-roots democracy for an enervating, bureaucratized system of high wages and labor peace. But his legacy, like the legacy of the American Fund, turned out to be on both sides of an essential and inescapable conflict. The Fund had hosted debates among progressives, liberals, social democrats, socialists, and Communists. It had lived in a middle space between the revolutionaries and the technocrats. At its best, the world of the Fund had embodied Hillman's old idea of "The Activity," living on the knife's edge between a vital mobilization and a necessary institutionalization, between the sit downs and the Wagner Act. The Fund had supported both legal-technocratic systems and mass movements, aiming to foster a dynamic industrial order in which each would reinforce the other. The Fund's legacy in Detroit was not so much to have chosen one over the other, but to have moved a debate over democracy and capitalism, for at least a time, from the margins of American life to its center.[63]

The interracial Southern Tenant Farmers Union relied on some of the last grants from the American Fund to organize sharecroppers in the Mississippi Delta in the 1930s.

20

Switch in Time

Only power can effect the enforcement and adoption of a given policy, however meritorious it may be.
—A. PHILIP RANDOLPH, 1941

While Walter Reuther and the sit-down strikers fought pivotal battles in the industrial Midwest, the Supreme Court made a turn of its own, one with powerful ramifications for nearly two decades of Fund efforts.

For half a century, the Court had struck down laws aimed at improving the condition of labor. Maximum-hours laws, minimum-wage laws, laws banning injunctions in labor disputes, child labor laws, and so-called yellow dog contract laws barring employers from prohibiting union membership among their employees—these and more fell under the Court's scythe. Such reforms, in the justices' view, were unconstitutional violations of employers' and employees' rights to contract with their labor and their property as they saw fit. In 1935 alone, the Court reversed the National Recovery Act's industrial codes, blocked legislation protecting farmers against foreclosure, and knocked out the new federal retirement program for railroad workers. In 1936, the justices overturned state minimum-wage laws for women, cut the legs out from under the new federal agriculture law, and undid Congress's effort to remake the Depression-plagued coal industry. Many observers speculated that the Wagner Act would be among the next to fall.[1]

The Roosevelt administration attacked the Court with a thinly disguised contingency plan. "Court packing," as Roosevelt's winter 1936–37 initiative became known, aimed to save the New Deal by adding six FDR appointments to the nine-person Court. The plan would have changed the Court's voting composition decisively. But as the proposal began to wend its way through Congress, the justices changed course. In April and May 1937, the existing Court upheld the Wagner Act and other reform laws, blunting the pending Court-packing bill's momentum in the process. In a phrase coined in the *New York Post* that quickly spread around Washington that spring, the Court's abrupt turn was the "switch in time" that rescued the nine-member Court—the "switch in time that saved nine." The *Post*'s quip suggested that Justice Owen J. Roberts had altered his usual voting pattern in order to block the Roosevelt packing plan. Many at the time thought so, and many interpretations in the historical literature lean in the same direction, though there is evidence both ways.[2]

Whatever the reasons for the 1937 switch, the clash between the conservative Court and Roosevelt's electoral coalition was a culmination of nearly two decades of social mobilization in and around the orbit of the American Fund. Among the first cases in the Court's decisive year was a free speech case straight out of the radical wing of the Fund's world. Decided in early January, *De Jonge v. Oregon* reversed the conviction of an Oregon Communist named Dirk De Jonge who had been tried for taking part in a Communist Party meeting. ACLU lawyers seasoned by efforts on behalf of the Scottsboro defendants represented De Jonge and persuaded the high court, for the first time in its history, to strike down a law on the basis of the freedom of assembly guaranteed in the Constitution. The case rendered unconstitutional key parts of the criminal syndicalism acts that had been used to prosecute radicals after the war. In March and April the Court upheld a minimum-wage law for women workers and sustained the Wagner Act, delivering victories to the labor movement. The Wagner Act case, in particular, handed a win to the still-new Steel Workers Organizing Committee of the Committee for Industrial Organization, whose lead organizers were former Brookwood hands and American Fund figures. "No single decision in my experience more largely affected civil liberties," reflected Roger Baldwin, who had come around to support the new law. Finally, at the end of April, in *Herndon v. Lowry*, the Court reversed the conviction of Angelo Herndon, a twenty-five-year-old Black Communist radicalized in part by the Scottsboro prosecutions. Georgia authorities had charged Herndon with inciting insurrection for advocating self-determination in the Black Belt. Lawyers affiliated with Baldwin's ACLU persuaded the Court to reject the conviction on the grounds that it violated the freedom of speech guaranteed in the Constitution.[3]

The switch of 1937 altered the landscape in which labor, race, and civil liberties organizations had operated. Nowhere were the effects more visible than in the altered fate of the Fund's longtime beneficiary, the Pullman porters union.

Vanguard of the Black Workers

A. Philip Randolph's Brotherhood of Sleeping Car Porters had nearly expired after its humiliating defeat at the hands of the Pullman Company in 1928. Once 7,000 members strong, the union had shrunk by the early 1930s to 650 at best. The crucial Chicago branch, which according to Randolph was home to half the Brotherhood's membership, counted only 250. Most of the union's regional offices, in cities like Louisville, Pittsburgh, St. Louis, and Buffalo, closed altogether. At the New York headquarters, the electricity and the phones were turned off. Rent parties to raise funds for the office lease came up short, and the landlord evicted the group for failure to pay rent. Frustrations boiled over when the Brotherhood's most trusted organizer accused the frugal (if often disorganized) Randolph of corruption and mismanagement. With James Weldon Johnson's encouragement, the American Fund launched an inquiry into the union's affairs. A powerless Randolph submitted meekly. The inquiry ultimately came to nothing, but the Fund's directors demurred when Randolph tried one last time to gain American Fund support for his fight with Pullman's company-sponsored union.[4]

The Brotherhood's collapse left Randolph penniless. His wife's hair salon—long his source of financial support—fell on hard times, too. Randolph's usually impeccable suits developed a worn shine. His shirts were soiled. Mayor Fiorello La Guardia quietly noted that Randolph's shoes had holes. Reviewing the situation, the American Fund's favorite Black economist, Abram Harris, concluded glumly that the porters union was dead.[5]

The New Deal's labor laws, however, raised the Brotherhood from its grave. In 1934, Randolph joined with white railroad union leaders to lobby for amendments to the Railway Labor Act that granted Pullman porters the same collective bargaining rights soon to be embedded in the Wagner

Act. Five months later, the American Federation of Labor formally admitted the Brotherhood with an international charter, affiliating the porters with the giant labor federation on equal terms after a decade of delay. Union elections at Pullman the next May produced a resounding victory for the suddenly revived Brotherhood. Porters in sixty-six sleeping car terminals around the country—some 5,931 Pullman workers in all—voted for Randolph's union, as compared to 1,422 who voted for its rival, a hastily assembled successor to the old company union. Even then Pullman refused to negotiate in good faith, stonewalling Randolph's negotiating team while letting a challenge to the amended Railway Labor Act play itself out in the courts. Pullman officials were confident the company would win; the legal precedents were on its side, and the justices seemed to be, too. But when the Supreme Court switched, the Pullman Company lost.[6]

On March 29, 1937, the same day the Court reversed its position on minimum-wage laws, it upheld the new Railway Labor Act and its protections for worker organizing. The effects for Randolph were nearly in-

A. Philip Randolph (center) and the once-struggling Brotherhood of Sleeping Car Porters soon after their landmark contract with the Pullman Company.

stantaneous. Within three days, Pullman grudgingly agreed to bargain in earnest, after a decade of refusals and delay. Before the summer was out, the colossal Pullman Company entered into a historic collective bargaining agreement with the All-Black porters of the Brotherhood. The contract reduced monthly working hours from 400 to 240, provided for time-and-a-half overtime pay, and increased the minimum monthly wage by $12. The amount was fitting for a contract signed on the twelfth anniversary, to the day, of when the fledgling porters union, soon to be sustained by an American Fund grant, had first met at the Elks Hall in Harlem. The Brotherhood, Randolph crowed to Walter White, had resumed its role as "the vanguard of the black workers of America."[7]

One of the American Fund's last substantial grant efforts involved another piece of what was becoming the largest Black working-class mobilization since the days of Marcus Garvey. The Southern Tenant Farmers Union emerged from the same Arkansas cotton fields where white planters had killed two hundred Black sharecroppers in the Elaine massacre of 1919. A decade and a half later, in the midst of the Depression, falling cotton prices had further impoverished tenant farmers and sharecroppers, Black and white alike. One of the first laws Roosevelt signed as president, the Agricultural Adjustment Act of 1933, or AAA, aimed to increase crop prices and restrict output by empowering the Department of Agriculture to enter into agreements with farmers to remove acreage from production in return for cash payments. But if New Deal legislation had resurrected Randolph's porters union, it made things worse for the tenant farmers. In the Delta, the AAA led planters to evict their tenants and sharecroppers in order to capture the new federal money for themselves.[8]

American Fund director Norman Thomas, who traveled to Arkansas to see conditions for himself, helped found the tenant farmers union, or STFU, as an interracial group. In the organization's lore, the meeting's key moment came when a survivor of the Elaine massacre stood and called on his fellow farmers to work with one another regardless of race. ("Aren't we all brothers and ain't God the father of us all?" he said in union legend.) Invoking the values of the Declaration of Independence—"life, liberty, and the pursuit of happiness"—their program demanded the representation of dirt farmers in government agencies, fair distribution of government agricultural aid, and employment for farmers pushed off the land by drought and crop reduction schemes. Echoing the vision of the Wagner Act and the new unions of the industrial economy, the STFU called on landlords and planters to recognize the union as the collective bargaining representative of the tenant farmers. The union backed legal defense efforts for tenants facing evictions, planned test cases against planters in the courts, and arranged mass demonstrations.[9]

For Thomas, the union (which he described as "the most important development" in the modern history of the agricultural South) effectively reprised the outlook of the American Fund's most significant projects, from Brookwood and the new unionism, to Federated Press and the *New Masses*, to the NAACP and the Pullman porters. It pitted labor against the accumulated power of capital. It combined a civil liberties struggle against brutal sheriffs and squads of murderous deputies with a class struggle against landlords. Black sharecroppers who joined the union faced what observers called a "reign of terror," with night-riding Klansmen and cabins riddled with gunfire. Thomas himself was bum-rushed off a Delta stage by a sheriff and his goons—and threatened with more serious harm if he were ever to return. State troopers erected machine guns at a key crossroads just north of Elaine. The menacing reference to the 1919 massacre was lost on no one.[10]

Most of the American Fund's money had run out, but Thomas persuaded the directors to scrape together modest annual grants of more than $2,000 in each of the Fund's final six years in operation. The grants amounted to more than 10 percent of the union's yearly budget. In all, the Fund and allied organizations like the ACLU and the League for Industrial Democracy provided the STFU with three-quarters of its annual operating budget from 1935 into the early 1940s. The support helped the sharecroppers union grow to more than 25,000 members; the Fund's resources, one union member wrote to Charles Garland, had allowed the sharecroppers "to maintain the morale and solidarity of our ranks." Organizers added tenant farmer chapters in the bootheel of southeastern Missouri, in Mississippi, and in Oklahoma. A short STFU-sponsored strike increased the pay of wage laborers in the cotton fields. STFU protests at the Department of Agriculture in Washington gained better enforcement of tenants' rights to federal acreage reduction payments. Inspired by the sharecroppers union, a committee convened by Wisconsin senator Robert La Follette Jr. directed a harsh spotlight on heavy-handed anti-labor tactics by planters and industrial bosses alike.[11]

The varying strands of New Deal–era Black labor mobilization, ranging from the Pullman porters to the STFU, came together in a group known as the National Negro Congress, or NNC, first proposed at a May 1935 conference at Howard University. The conference, which took up "The Position of the Negro in Our National Economic Crisis," had assembled an eclectic mix of liberals and leftists. The NAACP's Young Turks were there; labor economists Abram Harris and Charles Wesley, whose book on Black labor had just been published by Vanguard Press, played lead roles. The splintered old guard of the organization came, too. W. E. B. Du Bois attended the Howard sessions, having just quit the NAACP. So did NAACP lawyer Charles Hamilton Houston. Norman Thomas sent prepared remarks on the sharecroppers union. Communists like American Fund director Robert Dunn took part as well, thanks to the new line from Moscow encouraging coalition building with liberals and socialists—a line that would be made official that summer when the Comintern's Seventh World Congress announced the Popular Front policy to help defeat the Nazi threat.[12]

The NNC that emerged from the Howard conference was like a reunion of the big-tent coalition of the American Fund from before the radicalizing turn of the Communists in 1928 and the crack-ups over the NAACP litigation grant and the Scottsboro affair that had followed. The now-revived A. Philip Randolph became the congress's titular leader, ratifying his place as the most prominent Black labor leader in the country. On a day-to-day basis, the young Black lawyer John P. Davis, who had recently completed his NAACP-supported study of discrimination at the TVA, directed the organization. A former student of Felix Frankfurter at Harvard Law School, Davis's sympathies had veered toward the Communist Party during Scottsboro, though he had worked with Houston and Walter White on a 1934 trip through the South documenting discrimination in government relief work. With Davis at the rudder, the NNC coordinated with American Fund director Clinton Golden and the CIO Steel Workers Organizing Committee to promote the interests of Black workers in steel mills. NNC organizers joined in the CIO's automobile industry drive, too, since Black workers made up a substantial share of the workforce at Ford's

River Rouge plant. Construing the labor cause broadly, the NNC lobbied in favor of anti-lynching legislation and advocated for the five Scottsboro defendants still in prison. The congress's local councils orchestrated consumer boycotts against businesses that discriminated against Black workers, coordinated a "Jobs for Negroes" campaign, and arranged rent strikes against slumlords.[13]

For his part, Randolph carried the spirit of the upstart NNC to the annual conventions of the old-line AFL. Under the Brotherhood's new international charter, Randolph served as a vice president of the giant labor federation. Using his position, he led picketers outside the convention's hotels demanding an end to whites-only unions. On the convention floor, he worked with CIO official and longtime American Fund insider John Brophy to press for the eponymous "Randolph Resolution," which would have excluded unions with Jim Crow membership rules from the federation. Racial divisions among the laboring classes, Randolph told convention-goers, were a self-inflicted wound. "Fools and Cowards Cut Their Own Throats," read the picket line signs outside the Atlantic City convention hall in the fall of 1935.[14]

For as long as the Popular Front continued, Randolph fit happily at the head of the NNC. Mixing themes of class and race liberation, Randolph's words to the NNC's first annual convention at the Eighth Regiment Armory in Chicago in February 1936 stressed the vital importance of economic liberation for the Black masses. In the face of 15 million unemployed Americans and what he called "the collapse of capitalist prosperity," Randolph urged industrial unions in the new CIO style as the next step in "the struggle" by Black workers "against exploitation." Randolph demanded a Bill of Rights for Black people, including voting rights, anti-lynching legislation, unemployment insurance, and nondiscriminatory labor unions. The message was quintessential Popular Front. A decade earlier, Randolph had lambasted Communist influence and had willingly testified to Congress about the Communist threat. Now he denounced what he called "red scare" tactics and defended the NNC's Communist Party members as "sincerely fighting for race rights."[15]

For all the efforts at unity in mobilizing Black labor, internecine struggles of the kind that had nearly wrecked the American Fund in 1930 persisted just beneath the surface. At the STFU, a Communist Party takeover of the union's erstwhile ally Commonwealth College soon proved to be the boll weevil in the union's cotton fields. Party-affiliated faculty and staff at the Fund-supported labor college in Arkansas launched a wild, hamfisted effort to capture the STFU from its socialist leadership. A disturbed Commonwealth student even fired shots in a failed attempt to assassinate STFU leader H. L. Mitchell during a campus visit. Mitchell expelled the Commonwealth contingent from the union and barred Party members from STFU meetings, but a Fund-orchestrated merger between the STFU and a CIO union of cannery and agricultural workers soon reproduced the problem. Party members took control of the cannery union and diverted its joint efforts with the sharecroppers' organization to pursuing Party efforts like the ill-fated Black Belt thesis. The STFU hemorrhaged members until Mitchell pulled the union out of the CIO in early 1939.[16]

Mutual suspicion between the Communists and other constituencies simmered at the NNC, too. Memories of Scottsboro-related infighting had led Walter White to keep the NAACP formally outside the NNC's new coalition. And behind the scenes, Communists at the NNC quietly sought to replicate earlier efforts at the American Fund to bore from within and cement control of the group. Davis pressed the NNC toward the Communist line at every turn, staffing its key positions with Party faithful. Preoccupied by the negotiations between the Brotherhood and Pullman and lulled by the Popular Front's promises of cooperation, Randolph did not object.[17]

Matters came to a head after the Nazi-Soviet Pact of August 1939 ended cooperative relations between Communists and their erstwhile allies on the left. Stalin ordered U.S. Communists to turn away from a united fight against fascism and to support the new Soviet alliance with Hitler. At the NNC's third meeting in April 1940—held somewhat improbably in an auditorium of the Department of Labor in the nation's capital—Davis swerved to follow the new line by orchestrating a resolution condemning Roosevelt's opposition to German aggression. Randolph objected, but it was Davis who had done the day-to-day organizing work for the congress, and it was Davis who had prepared for the moment. In a room packed with Davis's people, the resolution passed in a landslide over Randolph's protests. When it came time for his remarks, Randolph criticized the Soviets for joining with the Nazis, only to watch the crowd leave its seats and head angrily for the exits in protest. Ralph Bunche, who took Randolph's side in the schism, estimated that only one-third of the audience remained in the auditorium by the speech's end. Yet if Davis had won the meeting, he had killed the NNC. As Bunche saw it, Davis's "Negro Congress dug its own grave," not least by driving off the leader who made the NNC a broad coalition rather than a fringe effort. Randolph soon announced that he would not stand for reelection at the Negro Congress, and the Popular Front of the Black working class came crashing to an end. "I consider the Communists," he said, "a definite menace and a danger to the Negro people and labor." Those who followed the Party line, he added, were "living in a fool's paradise."[18]

Power Plays

On June 18, 1941, A. Philip Randolph and Walter White walked into the White House to meet with Franklin Roosevelt.

Two decades before, when the American Fund began, such a meeting would have been astonishing. To be sure, Black leaders had visited the White House since at least the Civil War, when Frederick Douglass met twice with Abraham Lincoln. In 1901, Theodore Roosevelt had invited Booker T. Washington to dinner, though backlash among white southern critics had been vicious. In 1925, Randolph was part of a delegation of Black leaders who urged Calvin Coolidge to pass anti-lynching legislation. In 1940, with a new world war in the offing, Randolph, White, and other prominent Black Americans had met in the Oval Office to press Roosevelt on integrating any future wartime military.[19]

Two things made the June meeting stand apart. Its subject matter was one; the topic for the day was the status of Black workers. The second difference was that the president needed something from Black leaders, not the other way around. Roosevelt requested the meeting because Randolph had promised to bring 100,000 protesters to Washington on July 1, just two weeks hence, to demand a place for Black workers in the booming defense economy. The march, which Randolph had been organizing for months, risked embarrassing the U.S. before the world. Perhaps white residents of the Jim Crow capital city would meet protesters with violence in an ugly reprise of 1919. Maybe the marchers would embarrass the nation just as it was aiming to take a new leadership role in world affairs. Either way, the president hoped to head off the momentum of what Randolph had come to call the March on Washington Movement.[20]

Randolph's campaign for Black employment got underway near the end of 1940. Reflecting on the as yet unsuccessful efforts to integrate the defense industries, Randolph decided that decorous requests, as he told one of his aides, were "not going to get us anywhere." What Black Americans needed, Randolph decided, was a mass movement to raise the stakes, a movement of "10,000 Negroes to march on Washington in protest," right down Pennsylvania Avenue.[21]

Ever since five hundred unemployed men in a rabble known as Coxey's Army had arrived in Washington demanding economic relief after the Panic of 1893, protest marches in the capital had been a way to draw the nation's attention. In 1932, a so-called Bonus Army of 20,000 Depression-era veterans seeking an advance on pension bonuses had helped usher President Herbert Hoover out of office; his clumsy efforts to clear their encampment went badly awry, killing two veterans and an infant and injuring many more. Now, in the winter of 1940–41, Randolph traveled the country urging audiences of Pullman porters to think that another march might be possible. The effort would be a gamble, to be sure. From the start, his aides at the Brotherhood of Sleeping Car Porters had raised questions about whether they could actually assemble 10,000 protesters. But Randolph pressed on, demanding that Black workers get their due for supporting "the cause of national defense and national unity." There could be no such unity, he continued, "where one tenth of the population" was denied its "basic rights as American citizens." Gaining those rights would require a show of strength. "Only power," he told the newspapers all around the country, would make a difference. "Virtue and rightness" could only go so far. "Power and pressure are at the foundation of the march of social justice and reform," a foundation that rested in the "organized masses" united for a specific and concrete purpose. "We must fight for it," Randolph's statement concluded, "and fight for it with gloves off."[22]

To carry on the battle, a March on Washington Committee established in the spring of 1941 included White of the NAACP and Randolph's old comrade Frank Crosswaith from radical Harlem, along with several Black churchmen. In a new addition to the ranks of Black leadership, a trio of Black labor union leaders joined the committee, representing the Blasters and Drillers union, the Laundry Workers, and the American Federation of Teachers. "Nothing counts," Randolph announced in the official call for the march, "but pressure, more pressure and still more pressure." Stumping for the protest before receptive audiences that spring, Randolph raised his ambitious goal for the demonstration's headcount by a factor of ten. "When 100,000 Negroes march on Washington," he cried, the nation would wake up to the oppression of the Black working-class masses.[23]

Randolph's efforts received little support from his old allies at the diminished NNC. Following the line dictated by Stalin after the Nazi-Soviet Pact, the Communist Party opposed efforts to enlist Black labor in a wartime economy that was mobilizing against Germany. When the Nazis turned on Stalin and Germany invaded Russia in late June, the Communist line changed—but its position on Randolph's march remained the same. Suddenly American Communists criticized the march for a new reason; protest threatened America's capacity for war against a Germany with which the Soviets were now at odds.[24]

Roosevelt hoped to stop the march for more straightforward reasons. Mass protests threatened to disrupt military preparation and production. Drawing attention to the U.S.'s system of racial segregation, moreover, undermined the messaging of a war against Nazism. Through his wife, Eleanor, the president implored Randolph and White to call it off. He enlisted Randolph's old labor movement ally Sidney Hillman to jawbone defense contractors into hiring Black workers. But Randolph and White demanded more than goodwill. They insisted on nothing less than an executive order making discrimination in defense industries unlawful.[25]

The big question as spring turned into early summer was whether Randolph would really be able to deliver on his promised protest. In 1928, the Pullman Company had called his strike bluff; Randolph had been humiliated. But this time proved different. When Randolph demanded an executive order at the June 18 White House meeting, Roosevelt at first demurred. "Questions like this can't be settled with a sledge hammer," the president pleaded. But the invitation to the Oval Office and now his revealing choice of words suggested otherwise. The march was precisely the forceful tool that would settle the question. Randolph answered that the march could not be called off unless he and White came away with an order banning discrimination in the defense economy.[26]

Executive Order 8802 came out a week later, just in time to forestall the march. "There shall be no discrimination in the employment of workers in defense industries or government," announced the order, "because of race, creed, color, or national origin." Under the terms of 8802, moreover, it was the "duty of employers and of labor organizations to provide for the full and equitable participation of all workers." To implement its rule against discrimination, the order established a new administrative body—a Committee on Fair Employment Practice—to hear complaints of discrimination and to redress valid grievances.[27]

Playing a hand of his own making, Randolph had caused the president of the United States to fold. The *Amsterdam News* called him "the man of the hour" and ranked him alongside Frederick Douglass as one of the greatest Black leaders in American history. Du Bois praised the effort and its results as "most astonishing." Journalist Lerone Bennett Jr. would later call it "one of the most brilliant power plays ever executed by a Negro

A. Philip Randolph (left) with Eleanor Roosevelt und Fiorello La Guardia, pictured here at a Madison Square Garden rally for fair employment in 1946.

leader." Editors at another Black newspaper said that Randolph's success had confirmed the wisdom of his basic strategy. "Only mass action can pry open the iron doors" that had been closed to "America's black minority."[28]

In the spring and summer of 1941, Charles Hamilton Houston was busy mounting a parallel campaign, one with similar goals but a different method.

As the Depression economy gave way to a wartime boom, many of the largest American unions posed obstacles to Black workers as formidable as those set by defense industry employers. To be sure, Black wage earners were rallying to the banner of the labor movement in numbers not seen for generations. Black workers made up as much as a quarter of the CIO in 1940—between 300,000 and 500,000 members out of 2 million— even though nearly 90 percent of the U.S. population identified as white. Unions had welcomed Black members in industries like mining, auto, steel, garments, and textiles. Persistent Jim Crowism in labor unions, however, helped keep vast swaths of the industrial economy lily-white. The construction trades, the electrical workers union, the carpenters union, and the plumbers union were notoriously still whites-only. The railroad brotherhoods continued to bar Black members. So did the boilermakers, the shipbuilders, and the pulp and paper workers. The list went on.[29]

From the start, designers of the joint NAACP–American Fund litigation campaign had discussed targeting Jim Crow labor unions alongside unequal schools, discriminatory teacher salaries, and Jim Crow railroads. American Fund director Lewis Gannett's initial 1930 draft for the NAACP grant had proposed, among other things, lawsuits challenging racially exclusive unions. Gannett's fellow director Freda Kirchwey had affirmed the idea. Nathan Margold's influential report the next year had sketched out a strategy for suing white labor unions in states where the law authorized or even required racial exclusivity.[30]

Margold had offered to help think through the labor problem when Houston assumed control of the NAACP–American Fund joint litigation project in 1934. As both men understood, the task of taking on Jim Crow labor was more urgent now that the New Deal had empowered unions. Roosevelt's collective bargaining laws gave exclusive collective bargaining authority to the union that won a majority vote of the workers. The Wagner Act and the amended Railway Labor Act thus gave unions new legal power to exclude minority workers from jobs in union shops. Houston offered a grim one-liner to describe FDR's collective bargaining arrangements. "NRA," he said, did not mean National Recovery Administration. It meant "Negro Robbed Again."³¹

As early as 1935 and 1936, Black railroad workers reached out to Houston to complain that they were being frozen out of work by discriminatory collective bargaining agreements. Black shopworkers at the Missouri Pacific wrote him, as did Black freight handlers in New York harbor. The difficulty, as Houston and White explained it to the American Fund's joint committee in June 1937, was that "Negro transportation workers are gradually being eliminated." White union member majorities at a given workplace, the NAACP leaders continued, could vote for their own Jim Crow union "to represent all the workers in the shop." On the rails, such votes left Black workers utterly unrepresented. Powerful old railroad worker unions like the Brotherhood of Locomotive Firemen had barred Black members for decades, going back to Eugene Debs's time in the union in the late nineteenth century. Whites-only unions, Houston continued, "naturally arrange working conditions so that no new non-union men"— which meant no Black men—"can be employed or promoted." A union shop meant a white shop. Houston concluded that the conjuncture of New Deal collective bargaining with whites-only unions would soon produce the "elimination of the Negro worker" from the nation's rails.³²

Houston had pitched the dwindling American Fund for money to pursue the unions after the Court's switch on the constitutionality of the New Deal. "Now that the National Labor Relations Act has been held constitutional," he wrote, "it becomes of utmost importance to see that it is not used as a weapon to exclude Negroes from jobs." As Houston described the problem to the Fund's directors, newly strengthened racist exclusions in unions threatened white workers' interests, too, at least in the medium to long term. If union representatives could exclude Black workers, Houston warned, collective bargaining laws would drive millions of Americans— the entire Great Migration workforce—into the ranks of the scabs. The decades-old pattern in which reserves of nonunionized Black workers thwarted union power would continue.³³

As it happened, the Fund turned Houston down, despite his powerful case. The Fund was managing the last of its resources. And such a grant, as Kirchwey had noted in 1930, was poison for the Fund's labor union constituencies.

The case for a campaign against the unions was sufficiently compelling, however, that Houston leapt at the chance to pursue it when the opportunity arose again. In 1939, Black railroad workers with the independent Association of Colored Railway Trainmen and Locomotive Firemen approached him for help defending their jobs in the face of new collective bargaining agreements from which they had been excluded. Now back in private practice in Washington, D.C., and freed from the coalitional constraints of the American Fund and the NAACP, Houston took on the work he had deferred. With Black railroad workmen's associations ready to foot the bill, he exhumed the labor union branch of the NAACP litigation campaign. A series of lawsuits followed, including two in Virginia on the rails at the port of Norfolk, and one in Memphis against the locomotive firemen and the Gulf, Mobile & Northern line. The most promising case, Houston thought, involved a courageous Black locomotive fireman from Alabama. As the cases made their way through the courts, Houston developed a strategy that would remake the basic legal architecture of race and labor.[34]

The law of race and employment in the United States in early 1941 was easily described. It permitted employers and unions to make decisions about hiring, layoffs, promotion, and firing on whatever basis they chose. Employers and unions could include or exclude people because of their race—or for essentially any reason at all. The law's name for the basic principle was "employment at will." Bosses could do as they pleased, so long as their contracts with workers and unions permitted. There were precious few exceptions to the stark at-will rule, confined mostly to government employment and government contractors.[35]

The Wagner Act did not expressly change the situation with respect to race. The NAACP had lobbied Congress to add a prohibition on race discrimination into the act, but the association had been unable to overcome objections from powerful southern Democrats and recalcitrant AFL interests. Houston thus had good reason in 1940 and 1941, as his biographer writes, to focus his "primary attention" on Black workers and on labor union racism. Here was the next question now that the Wagner Act was up and running. Two decades earlier, the NAACP had found success in the courts after the Senate rejected its anti-lynching bill; in *Moore v. Dempsey*, overturning the legal lynching of the Arkansas sharecroppers, the Supreme Court had done what the elected branches would not.[36]

Even as Houston prepared to launch his effort in the courts, however, Randolph voiced a rival claim about how the problem of Black industrial labor should be approached. As Randolph saw it, lawsuits offered no solution. The situation of the "colored fireman," he noted, was indeed in crisis. But no judge, he predicted to a convention of Black railroad workers in early 1941, would "compel railroads to employ a Negro." Legal action would not "prevent the railroads and the white firemen's union from making secret and collusive contracts, perhaps even unwritten contracts, to the effect that only white men will be employed as firemen." The speech's climax laid out Randolph's claim in candid terms. "The power of the colored firemen," he concluded, "like all workers, white or black, does not inhere in the law, but in their own self-organization." Law "confers rights," he said, "but not power." Law could "be the source of rights," but he insisted that "organization is the source of power." Rights that were "granted by the law may be nullified by power." The result, Randolph said, was that "the organization of Negro firemen into an all-embracing labor union, is their only hope and salvation."[37]

Randolph gave voice to an enduring criticism of law and the courts, a worry that had haunted the American Fund's engagement with Black rights and labor for two decades. Similar critiques had swirled around the Fund's legal defense campaigns, its Scopes case funding, and its role in the defense of Ossian Sweet in Detroit. Critics had assailed its NAACP litigation program. Legal rights, in this view, were a weak substitute for the power of mass organizing.

In practice, however, Randolph did not really believe that mobilizing the passions of the masses could build sustainable power on its own. Randolph himself had always mixed fiery organizing campaigns with a cool and savvy use of law and the state. As leader of the Brotherhood of Sleeping Car Porters in the 1920s he had adapted Sidney Hillman's new unionist tactics, deploying the Railway Labor Act to create focal points for organizing the energies of the Pullman porters. In the 1930s, he had used the collective bargaining regime of the New Deal labor laws and the Court's 1937 switch to propel the porters union into a position of power.

Affirmative legal action on behalf of labor had become one of Randolph's hallmarks. For him, power and law were looped together, each shaping the other. Movement politics and law in the Fund's world were supplements, not substitutes. They operated according to different rhythms and by reference to different logics. As the fever of mass movements receded, institutional structures and legal rights asserted themselves. The latter might sustain the victories of the former. Similar fusions of powerful energies with canny procedures had been Hillman's innovation at the Amalgamated Clothing Workers; his discipline (his "Activity," as he had dubbed it) helped turn the ACW into an early model for the CIO. Brookwood Labor College had carried the project forward in A. J. Muste's mixture of revolution and pragmatism. The Brotherhood of Sleeping Car Porters' fraternal rituals and their replicating of the Black church tradition served the same end, connecting a far-reaching program of change to sustainable institutions.[38]

The March on Washington effort itself offered a case in point. Some of Randolph's younger colleagues, including future civil rights leader Bayard Rustin, complained that he had called off the march prematurely and given in too soon. He had received too little from the White House, they charged, in return for standing down the reserve army of protesters he had so assiduously recruited. "Nothing tangible had been gained," one critic wrote. But Randolph had a reason for navigating the march as he did, and it wasn't only unhappy memories of overplaying his hand in the 1928 strike threat that had gone awry for the Pullman porters. He explained the point carefully so as not to be misread. "The purpose of the march," he answered critics like Rustin, was to accomplish a very particular goal—"a specific and definite thing." The movement had not been designed to raise the zeal of the masses merely for the sake of creating energy to no end. Such tactics, Randolph scoffed, would lead to "a continuous state of sullen unrest and blind resentment among Negroes." A movement that did not take its victories when they appeared would be unable to sustain the passions it mobilized. Had the movement gone ahead and marched despite having gained the desired concession of the president's order, it would have lost credibility within its own ranks and destroyed its position at the negotiation table. "Such a strategy," Randolph told his youthful detractors, "would have promptly and rightly been branded as a lamentable species of infantile leftism," an "appeal to sheer prima donna dramatics." The reference, drawn from Randolph's younger days in radical Harlem, was not lost on his restive audience. In 1920, Lenin had attacked those who rejected tactical alliances as suffering from an infantile disorder. Now Randolph deployed the charge of immature tantrums to insist that movements needed to nurture and sustain their energies. Having been stoked, the combustible ardor of the masses of Black workers needed to be conserved so that it might be available as a source of power in the days to come. Power, after all, would not be a onetime affair. The struggle would go on. And with the prospect of power seemingly within reach, Randolph refused to let the new strength of Black workers dissipate in a mad conflagration.[39]

The energies of Randolph's movement dwindled nonetheless. After a series of wildly successful rallies in the summer of 1942, including one at Mad-

Randolph's March on Washington Movement mobilized to relieve Black workers of the burdens of discrimination in employment, housing, and the Jim Crow armed forces.

ison Square Garden that drew 20,000 people, the March on Washington Movement had a harder and harder time articulating its reason for being. Randolph seemed to want to maintain the movement's vigor to preserve the pressure it could exert on the wartime federal government. But at the Fair Employment Practices Commission, a lack of effective enforcement authority had begun to take a toll. Hearings on the railroad worker situation had been scheduled for January 1943, only to be scrapped by the White House during the run-up to the 1942 midterm elections. When the hearings proceeded in September 1943, with Houston now serving as assistant counsel to the committee, they produced findings and an order purporting to end employment discrimination on the basis of race at twenty railroads and in seven unions. The railroads, however, refused to comply, claiming that chaos and disruption would follow in the wartime economy. The FEPC referred the railroad case to Roosevelt, but he shied away from the controversy by delegating the question to a committee chaired by a white North Carolina judge who was inclined to kill it. The FEPC process and the movement that had set it in motion seemed to have ground to a halt.[40]

Houston's lawsuits on behalf of Black railroad workers picked up steam as the engine of Randolph's mass movement sputtered. Houston's leading client, Bester William Steele, was a veteran locomotive fireman in Alabama at the Louisville and Nashville Railroad Company. For more than three decades, Steele had done the dirty, dangerous, and grueling work of shoveling coal into engine furnaces, sometimes as much as twenty tons of it in a single day. Still, it was a good job. It paid well, and Steele's seniority had allowed him to select desirable routes.[41]

A 1941 collective bargaining agreement changed all that. Using its power under the amended Railway Labor Act, the all-white Brotherhood of Locomotive Firemen had set its sights on the jobs held by Steele and his fellow Black firemen across the South. The Southeastern Carriers Conference Agreement, negotiated between the Brotherhood of Locomotive Firemen and the rail carriers, was what one FEPC staffer called the "ultimate in all discriminatory agreements." Stripping employees like Steele of their seniority rights, the agreement's structure threatened to edge Black firemen out of their jobs entirely.[42]

Suing a white railroad brotherhood and a southern railroad company required courage and careful judgment. With good jobs in short supply during the Depression, gangs of white railroaders had already tried to

Bester William Steele, pictured here in a 1945 photograph, challenged efforts by the railroads and by all-white labor unions to push him out of his job as a locomotive fireman.

circumvent seniority rules by violence; one railroad labor expert in 1943 reported ten Black firemen murdered and twice that number beaten on lines along the Mississippi River. The NAACP identified lynchings of Black railroad workers as far north as Illinois. And the Railway Labor Act offered little protection; unlike its Wagner Act cousin, it contained no protections from employers who retaliated against workers for organizing.[43]

Southern courts posed obstacles, too. Having failed to persuade a state trial court that the contract violated the rights of his client, Houston appealed to the Alabama Supreme Court, where he was the first Black lawyer to appear in at least twenty-nine years and where a virulent segregationist named Lucien D. Gardner presided as chief justice. Some said Houston was the first Black lawyer ever to make an appearance before the state high bench. To no one's surprise, the court gave short shrift to the Black railroad workers' interests. Asserting that "freedom of individual enterprise" was "one of the cornerstones of our form of government," the chief justice ruled for a unanimous court that the membership rules of a union were up to its members. (The fact that many southern states banned interracial associations went unmentioned.) Likewise, a railroad was free, in Gardner's words, to "continue the policy of having only white engineers." That was the basic principle of employment at will. In case anyone had missed the case's significance, Alabama's Gardner dropped the free enterprise facade and went to the heart of the matter. Turning to the Supreme Court's 1896 decision in *Plessy v. Ferguson*, he noted that courts had upheld "laws permitting, and even requiring" the separation of the races. "Legislation," he asserted, quoting directly from the *Plessy* opinion, "is powerless to eradicate racial instincts." Quoting from *Plessy* again, the Alabama chief justice warned ominously that any attempt to undo the South's system of racial subordination would "only result in accentuating the difficulties" at issue.[44]

Houston had already begun to make incursions against the increasingly archaic *Plessy* doctrine Gardner invoked. The *Gaines* case in 1938 had limited southern states' ability to decide for themselves what counted as equal. A year later, in an elaboration of the structure of the constitutional law switch, the Court had gone out of its way to signal new willingness to strike down racist laws. And when the *Steele* case arrived at the Court in 1944, Houston won another victory, this time in a Court remade by Roosevelt appointments. Houston's teacher Felix Frankfurter, the longtime advisor to the NAACP and the American Fund, was now on the Court. So was Frank Murphy, who had presided over the Sweet trials as a judge in Detroit in 1925 and then sided with the sit-down strikers as governor in 1937. By 1944, Roosevelt had appointed eight of the nine justices, including its chief, Harlan Fiske Stone.[45]

Significantly, Roosevelt's wartime administration had intervened on its own motion to take Houston's side—though with an important twist. The core of Houston's argument was that the new collective bargaining agreement, sanctioned by the Railway Labor Act, had deprived Steele of his rights to property without due process of law. For the Roosevelt administration, this argument cast too broad a net. If the Wagner Act structure of democratically elected exclusive bargaining representatives was unconstitutional because it violated the rights of workers who were not union members, the entire New Deal labor regime might come undone. Solicitor General Charles Fahy thus drew out a narrower argument, one that had been buried in Houston's brief at the Alabama high court. The real problem, contended Fahy, was that the white locomotive firemen's brotherhood, in its role as exclusive bargaining representative at the Louisville & Nashville railroad, had a duty under the Railway Labor Act to serve the railroad's workers "as a whole, and not merely for the benefit of certain portions of it." The statute said no such thing, at least not explicitly. But in Fahy's account, the statute carried the obligation nonetheless, not least because otherwise a wartime Court would be faced with a grave constitutional question about the basic organization of the American labor force.[46]

In a decision issued on December 18, 1944, the high court adopted Fahy's position and sided unanimously with Houston and his client Bester Steele. According to the Court, unions were not required to admit Black workers. But they were obliged to treat fairly all workers within the bargaining units they represented, whether the workers were union members or not. Writing for Frankfurter and five other justices, Chief Justice Stone articulated a wholly new protection for minority workers in American industry. Citing the 1886 *Yick Wo* case from San Francisco's Chinatown that Nathan Margold had seized on a decade before, and now adding a reference to the *Gaines* decision of 1938, the Court condemned race discrimination in labor relations as obviously unfair; discriminatory provisions were, in the Court's terms, "irrelevant and invidious."[47]

Charles Hamilton Houston, pictured a few years before he argued and won Steele's case at the Supreme Court.

Justice Murphy joined his colleagues but would have gone further. The same day it decided *Steele*, the Court announced its disgraceful decision in *Korematsu v. United States*, upholding the collective internment of people of Japanese ancestry living on the West Coast. Murphy issued a ringing *Korematsu* dissent. And in a forcefully worded concurrence in *Steele*, Murphy insisted on stronger legal protections for Black workers. The labor movement's favorite justice took the view in Steele's case that the Railway Labor Act vested the white union with the authority of the law. If New Deal labor legislation gave unions the power to serve as exclusive bargaining representatives, Murphy reasoned, such unions were carrying out a power delegated to them by the government. It followed for Murphy that such a union's conduct had to adhere to the constitutional rules against race discrimination applicable to the government. "The Constitution voices its disapproval," Murphy thundered, "whenever economic discrimination is applied under authority of law against any race, creed or color. A sound democracy cannot allow such discrimination to go unchallenged." Murphy seemed to say that unions could not exclude Black members any more than the government could lawfully disadvantage citizens on the basis of their race. With *Korematsu* lurking in the background, Murphy pilloried the Court for relying on "legal niceties" to avoid his more forceful conclusion.[48]

Houston and his clients were exuberant. The victory, Houston wrote in a long private memorandum, was "the culmination of five years of effort." The ruling, he observed, was applicable to any similarly situated Black railroad worker under the Railway Labor Act, and the principle of fair representation extended to all Black workers covered by the National Labor Relations Act. Houston offered praise in particular for Justice Murphy's "stirring concurrence," which he commended for confronting "the question of racial discrimination head-on." In the press, Houston announced plans to sue every railway company that was party to the Southeastern Carriers Conference Agreement at issue in Steele's case, and to seek injunctions against the Brotherhood of Locomotive Firemen "if it attempts to bargain just for its members to the exclusion of Negro employees of the craft." Houston predicted that some 4,000 Black firemen were ready to sue.[49]

Houston was hardly alone in his praise for the outcome. The *Pittsburgh*

Courier called it a "thunderous decision" that would produce "a new bill of rights for the Negro in American Labor." A few weeks later, a *Courier* columnist opined that the principles of *Steele* and its companion case went "to the very roots of economic conditions affecting the lives of hundreds of thousands of Negroes of current and future generations." No "greater steps forward" had been made for the Black worker, proposed the *Courier*, since Emancipation.[50]

Yet to treat *Steele* as an unalloyed triumph was to overlook the stark limits of the Court's holding in the case—and the obstacles that still stood in the way of Black workers like Bester Steele. Columnist Marjorie McKenzie in the *Courier*, who took note of the Japanese internment case decided the same day, cautioned that "the fundamental issue of open membership in labor unions is still before us"; the "vigorous language of Mr. Justice Murphy's concurring opinion," McKenzie continued, was, "after all, not the opinion of the court." Courts, moreover, were notoriously cumbersome forums for the resolution of employment questions, as Houston was among the first to observe. Houston's teacher Felix Frankfurter defended the justices' cautious approach in the case as a virtue. But in a public letter to the *Washington Post* in early 1945, Houston scored his teacher's conception of the judicial process as inadequate ("too hazardous, too cumbersome, too expensive and too slow") for providing the relief workers deserved. By the time of the Court's 1944 decision in Steele's dispute, the case itself had already run two and a half years and had not yet yielded any actual relief on the job. The case had already cost more than $2,500. But Houston noted that Steele only earned "between $250 and $300 a month" in what was one of the highest-paying jobs a Black worker could get. The litigation would have been impossible for most Black employees, and even Steele could not have proceeded without the financial backing of his independent Black union. Making matters still worse, court calendars were "now dangerously clogged," adding delay to expense. In all, Houston concluded, the legal process could not be counted on to help the Bester Steeles of the world.[51]

Houston's remarks proved prophetic. It would be another four years before Bester Steele's case came to trial. Only in 1951, a full decade after Houston had filed suit, and a year after Houston's own death by heart attack, did Steele, the railroad, and the union reach a settlement that vindicated Steele's claims. In the meanwhile, the all-white locomotive firemen's union continued to insist that railroads across the South comply with the revised seniority terms of the Southeastern Carriers Conference Agreement, daring Black firemen to sue. Few did. As the dispute drifted on, technological changes like the spread of diesel engines and the rise of the trucking industry cut the ground out from under railroad firemen, Black and white alike.[52]

All in all, the ups and downs of the *Steele* case might have confirmed Randolph's critique of trying to change the world by changing the law—if not for one crucial piece of the story.

Houston had not really expected more than what he got for his client Bester Steele, even though he sometimes expressed a wish otherwise. But Houston had concluded that a campaign in the courts was worthwhile anyway. He had initiated the legal campaign first contemplated in the American Fund not as a criticism of Randolph's FEPC project, and not even as an alternative to it, but in support of it. Until the *Steele* decision, Houston noted in December 1944, "both the railroads and the union" had ignored the FEPC's orders. "Now that the United States Supreme Court has spoken," Houston predicted, doing so would be just that much harder. Houston's strongest defense of the *Steele* case was not that it would by itself vindicate Black workers' interests against railroads and Jim Crow unions, but that it would, as he applauded, put "a legal base under a large part of the F.E.P.C. work." The litigation, the movement, and the federal government were parts of the same structure. For the collective bargaining process, Houston predicted moreover that Justice Murphy's concurring opinion would be the next step. "The ground work," he said, invoking one of his favorite metaphors, "has now been laid so that in the near feature we will be in position to challenge the right of the railroad unions to represent the craft or class at all as long as it excludes Negroes from membership."[53]

For all his cautions about relying on legal change to the exclusion of mass mobilizing, Randolph was entirely in agreement. Shortly before *Steele* was filed, Randolph spoke highly of the "favorable repercussions" that victory in the railroad lawsuits would have. The case, he said, would serve "as a warning to white railroad labor that black railroad labor is awakening, both as to its rights and power." Randolph's lieutenant at the Brotherhood of Sleeping Car Porters, Milton Webster, agreed. A "favorable decision from the Supreme Court," Webster told a group of Black railroad workers in 1941, "will be helpful and should be encouraged," even if in itself it "will not solve the problem." Writing privately to Houston, Randolph praised him as "one who has demonstrated your loyalty to your people" by pursuing the institutional basis of what Randolph called "economic democracy" in the postwar world.[54]

Randolph and his lieutenants expressed hesitation about the campaign that led to *Steele* in part because of worry that an obligation of fair representation might do more than obligate unions to treat nonwhite workers with dignity and respect. Such a duty, they feared, might weaken unions by allowing disgruntled workers of all kinds to challenge democratically ratified collective bargaining deals. The company influence that New Deal labor laws had tried hard to hold off might creep back in through complaints surreptitiously supported by employers opposed to the union. Dissidents would be able to hold up union actions and pry into union decision-making. And indeed, over time such things came to pass. A pro-employer right-to-work movement seized on *Steele* not to make unions better but to disable them. *Steele* was no panacea.[55]

But neither Houston nor Randolph had contemplated that their work would yield a final solution for all time. Randolph's march had made the Court's *Steele* decision possible by making the issue of Black employment salient and by pressuring the Roosevelt administration to intervene on the side of the Black workers. The *Steele* decision, in turn, sustained the FEPC's efforts in a feedback loop of mutual support. Houston hoped *Steele* would contribute to extending Roosevelt's wartime order into a permanent institution that would last beyond the end of the war. Employment discrimination, he believed, was too complex and widespread for the slow, cumbersome, and expensive courts. As a good Frankfurter student, Houston believed that a long-term solution to the problem required the managerial capacities of an administrative agency, and his efforts alongside Randolph were not in vain. Though the federal FEPC was allowed to expire in the war's aftermath, states established their own FEPCs. Beginning with New York in 1945, and spreading across the North, the Midwest, and the West, state fair employment laws prohibited race-based employment discrimination by employers and unions alike. Empowered by the new fair employment laws, state courts in the North vindicated Houston's gloss on the *Steele* decision by striking down collective bargaining agreements that made membership in a whites-only union a condition of employment. In Kansas and California, state supreme courts extended Justice Murphy's concurring opinion by prohibiting unions from excluding people from membership on the basis of their race. When the merged AFL-CIO banned race discrimination in its unions in 1955, Randolph described the rule as an extension of *Steele* and as the realization of *Brown v. Board of Education*, decided the previous year. Just as no public school could mandate segregation, nor could any union local exclude Black workers. In 1964, the Civil Rights Act, passed by Congress and signed into law by President Lyndon Johnson, resolved the question of employment discrimination by employers and unions nationwide. Movement passions had lodged themselves in the law. Altered legal institutions, in turn, had sustained the movement.[56]

Steele v. Louisville & Nashville Railroad and the 1940s March on Washington Movement were capstones to two decades of fractious debates and contested experiments at the American Fund for Public Service. Harkening back to a generation of efforts to shape Americans' ideas about labor and about race, Houston told the readers of the *Washington Post* that one of his goals had been, like Roger Baldwin's at the American Fund in 1922, to smash the bonds of old ideas. "The *Steele* decision," Houston predicted, "will influence and mold public opinion." The rise of state fair employment laws suggested he was right. For a generation, for nearly the entirety of the time between the two world wars, the Fund sustained experiments in industrial democracy for a racially divided nation. The Fund had financed publicity and propaganda and mass organizing. It had sponsored innovation in the affirmative use of the state by liberals and the labor left. It had helped transform the laws of labor and free speech for a modern democracy. It had remade the project of racial liberation. It had financed dozens of fights to make a better world. Its failures were many, and its triumphs were not final. But as Houston told his clients after *Steele* in December 1944, there were no final victories to be had. "The fight," he offered hopefully, "has just begun."[57]

21

A Rather Astonishing Fund

*Hypocrisy is necessary for progress . . . it tends to take
you from where you are to where you want to go.*

—ROGER BALDWIN, 1972

The Fund did not last long enough to celebrate Houston's success at the Supreme Court in the *Steele* case, or even to mark Randolph's triumph at the White House. The directors had discussed liquidating the Fund as early as 1932; in January of that year, a Morris Ernst motion to close up shop and donate the balance of its resources to the ACLU failed to pass in an evenly divided vote. By 1939, the American Fund had become so inactive that it all but ceased to function. The directors inadvertently over-

*The Brookwood Labor College drama troupe performed
the play* Sit-Down *in their final performance in 1937.*

looked its annual meeting that year. Baldwin confessed to Ernst that the Fund was "practically out of business."[1]

Some of the Fund's largest beneficiaries had already been shuttered. Brookwood Labor College closed its doors in 1937. The end for the labor college had begun five years earlier, when intransigence among Communist faculty and students caused a frustrated A. J. Muste to bar hyperfactional Party members from the faculty and the student body. ("If we are to preserve our institution," longtime Brookwood faculty member and American Fund regular David Saposs lamented, "we must have the right to protect ourselves.") Muste backtracked in the face of protests from Party loyalists at the American Fund. But he remained convinced that the Party would contrive either to capture the school for its own or destroy it. In 1933, he resigned. For four years, the school limped on, helped in part by the arrival of the Popular Front's truce on the left. The final show of the Brookwood Players was a Chautauqua-style theater production titled *Sit-Down*.[2]

James Weldon Johnson did not live to see the end of the Fund. He died in a railroad accident in 1938. Johnson and his wife, Grace, were struck by a train at an unguarded grade crossing while driving back to their home in Great Barrington during a rainstorm. Grace survived, but Johnson died from massive head injuries. More than 2,500 people packed Salem Methodist Church in Harlem for the funeral. New York mayor Fiorello La Guardia spoke. Du Bois was there along with Walter White and the Harlem literary set, including Langston Hughes, Claude McKay, and Carl Van Vechten. As Johnson's biographer described it, "a quarter-mile procession of automobiles followed the hearse to Brooklyn's Greenwood Cemetery."[3]

Elizabeth Gurley Flynn spent the better part of a decade, from 1927 to 1936, convalescing in the Pacific Northwest. Returning to New York in 1936, she resumed service on the ACLU's board of directors. The next year, Flynn joined the Communist Party, then still committed to a Popular Front cooperation with liberals and socialists in the fight against fascism. When the Nazi-Soviet Pact changed the posture of Communist parties around the world, Flynn fell in line. Anti-Communist directors at the Fund, including Morris Ernst and Norman Thomas, demanded that the civil liberties union denounce the Party and expel Flynn from the organization's board. Old allies from the Fund like Robert Morss Lovett objected that such an act of intolerance would violate the organization's basic principles. The ACLU board agreed with Ernst and Thomas and resolved to bar anyone from the union's governing committees who also belonged to a "political organization which supports totalitarian dictatorship."[4]

At an extraordinary trial at the City Club on West 44th Street in May 1940, stretching from 8 p.m. until 2:30 in the morning, a narrowly divided ACLU board voted to expel Flynn by a vote of 10–9. As the organization's executive director, Baldwin had no vote on the matter, but few doubted that he favored removing Flynn. Badly burned by the Nazi-Soviet Pact, Baldwin had turned decisively against his Popular Front alliances.[5]

Historians and observers ever since have been sharply critical of the ACLU's expulsion of Flynn. They have scorned it as an unprincipled effort to placate red-baiting critics. The view from the American Fund, however, offers a different picture. By 1940, Communists in and around the Fund had tried repeatedly to wrest control of the organization's money, and by the Fund's final years they had partly succeeded. Party faithful had smashed Brookwood and broken the National Negro Congress. They had fought the Fund's majority over the NAACP litigation campaign grants. They had co-opted Commonwealth College and the tenant farmers union. The expulsion of Flynn was one of many expulsions of Communists from left organizations, and not the first. After years of tension, the Nazi-Soviet Pact had delivered the internecine struggle to the Fund's door. The resulting rancor destroyed what was left of the Fund's heterodox world.[6]

The pact also seemed to destabilize the fragile Charles Garland. Nearing forty years of age, the Fund's founding donor was still using his influence to direct small grants from its shrinking endowment to Communist-affiliated agricultural organizations. In December 1939, however, he suffered a catastrophic psychological collapse. Hospitalized at Bellevue in New York and then transported to a mental institution in Florida, he was, Baldwin reported to the Fund's directors, "beyond the reach even of his family." Over the course of the next year, Garland became one of the first American recipients of a new experimental treatment. Psychiatrists strapped two electrodes to the sides of his head and applied 110 volts of alternating current to induce seizures. Hospitals repeated the electroshock therapy procedure on Garland more than one hundred times. Just a few years later, psychiatrists would discover that overexposure to electric currents caused a brutal side effect called cognitive blunting. They would dramatically shorten the duration of the stimulus. But the alteration came too late for Garland, who emerged from his crude treatment a withdrawn and distant man.[7]

A broken Garland retreated to Mount Vernon, New York, for a quiet existence with his second wife. Life with their two young children, both born before his breakdown, was punctuated by occasional visits from the children of his first marriage. Garland took work as a machinist. Always a tinkerer and small-time inventor, in his spare time he built human glider contraptions consisting of wearable wings. He patented a windup toy fish for children's bathtubs. He drew up blueprints for a helicopter design. In a touch Cervantes's Don Quixote might have appreciated, he designed an impracticable windmill theoretically capable of withstanding high winds. Garland died, almost entirely forgotten, on a farm in New Hampshire in 1974.[8]

The American Fund officially wound itself down soon after its donor left the hospital in 1941. A final report documented Garland's initial gift of just under $1 million, as well as stock market returns from the 1920s that had doubled the available assets. Across nineteen years, the Fund had given away $1,857,000, while spending a mere $67,000 on administrative overhead. Ninety-five percent of the Fund's assets had gone to beneficiaries, a figure that compared favorably to the best-run (and much larger) foundations of its era, as well as to the giant foundations operating a century later.[9]

In June, Baldwin gathered with a rump group of directors to dissolve the Fund altogether. Garland joined in a final gathering at the Cooperative Cafeteria, an informal hangout near Union Square, and thanked Baldwin, as newspapers reported the next day, for doing "a wiser and better job than he himself could have done." Garland told the papers that the Fund "did as well as could be expected." Reflecting on the mixed left-liberal makeup of the board, Baldwin wrote that "on the whole, I doubt if a wiser arrangement could have been made for doing the job we set out to do." Echoing the late James Weldon Johnson, he added that "spending a million or two well" turned out to be "a tough job," one that seemed to Baldwin "hardest of all" for those "pioneering social causes" that might or might not survive to turn into important movements. Where twenty years before, newspapers had condemned the start-up foundation as a criminal enterprise, now the *New York Times* offered quiet praise for the Fund's "record of many good causes." Asked by another reporter about the Fund's important accomplishments, Morris Ernst did not hesitate. The Fund's great cause, he replied, was campaigns by and for Black Americans.[10]

In years to come, the Fund's directors and beneficiaries would offer similar, if more chastened, assessments of the Fund's body of work. Du Bois, who years before had predicted that the Fund would become "one of the main agencies for the emancipation of the American Negro," told readers in his newspaper column that by setting *Brown v. Board* in motion, the Fund had made "the impossible happen." Norman Thomas later recalled "a rather astonishing fund," one "I am glad to say I had some chance to help." (Thomas singled out the grants to the Brotherhood of Sleeping Car Porters and A. Philip Randolph as especially important contributions.) Lewis Gannett mused about whether the Fund had any impact, but credited it with moving history in *Brown v. Board* and with sustaining the labor movement through its bleak 1920s. Elizabeth Gurley Flynn, by then in the leadership ranks of the Communist Party, remembered the Fund's contributions to the defense of Sacco and Vanzetti, which she believed roused public opinion on behalf of labor during otherwise lean years for the movement.[11]

Later in life, Roger Baldwin looked back on his time with the Garland Fund with a mix of pride and regret. In a 1963 interview, he confessed that the directors had not always made good decisions; "we often merely gave blood transfusions to agencies already headed for the grave." Some years after that, as he neared ninety, Baldwin admitted that he did "not feel satisfied with our record of risk and compromises," suggesting that the Fund had "yielded too often to friendship and passing pressures." In an unfinished autobiography, he reflected further on an abiding ambivalence. "Temperamentally," he wrote, "I just don't like large wealth in private hands," even if it were "to be disposed by high-minded people." Baldwin wrote that he preferred "the role of government," even when it was "badly handled as it so often is," or at least "the collective decisions" of unions, cooperatives, and membership organizations that used "their own money" and were "dependent on their members' dues."[12]

Baldwin also elaborated more generously, and for good reason. The Fund's modest endowment had allowed its directors to put issues on the political agenda that elected officials had skirted time and again, and which unions and membership organizations alone could not sustain. In Baldwin's memory, this meant first and foremost Brookwood, with its "new experiments in labor education" and its new model for the labor movement. He recalled buzzy lunch hours of men and women at the interracial Civic Club. He remembered friends "in the thick of the labor and left movements" making grants for emergency legal defense in civil liberties cases, supporting struggles for Black liberation, providing strike relief funds to labor unions, and subsidizing research, magazines, and publications, all in a long-shot effort to shape a democratic public opinion. He remembered errors, to be sure. But ultimately, he affirmed, "I suppose we did quite a lot of good."[13]

Roger Baldwin retired as executive director of the ACLU in 1950. In January 1981, he received the Presidential Medal of Freedom. He died seven months later at the age of ninety-seven.[14]

A sketch of Roger Baldwin by artist Peggy Bacon in 1937, National Portrait Gallery, Washington, D.C.

Epilogue
Legacies

Garland's million has had a brilliant career—two, in fact—one in Wall Street, and the other on the road to kingdom come.
—ROGER BALDWIN, 1934

On May 20, 1954, three days after the Supreme Court ruled racially segregated public schools unconstitutional in the case of *Brown v. Board of Education*, the Associated Press ran a striking story, syndicated in newspapers around the country. Two and a half decades earlier, noted the AP's correspondent, "a man who believed no one should enjoy money he didn't earn" had "set in motion a chain of events which are changing American social history." In a phone interview, NAACP executive secretary Walter White said that the American Fund's early grants of nearly $30,000 had allowed the NAACP to launch "a broad frontal attack on the basic causes of discrimination." As Thurgood Marshall put it soon after the *Brown* case had been filed, the Fund's support had "formed the groundwork for the first attack," laying the foundation for a sequence of successful cases against Jim Crow. Felix Frankfurter, who had helped launch the campaign as an outside advisor, now played a crucial role as a justice helping behind the scenes to arrange a unanimous opinion.[1]

Other Fund projects bore fruit as well. Propelled by the CIO, labor union membership reached a historic high point. One in three workers in the paid labor market belonged to a union in the middle of the 1950s. Black Americans became more likely than white Americans to live in a union household, a correlation that held fast for the remainder of the twentieth century. And as unions grew, economic inequality shrank. The share of national income going to the top ten percent of earners in the population fell dramatically; having soared to near 50 percent around the time of the Garland Fund's founding, it dropped by almost twenty percentage points, nearing its lowest point in the twentieth century. During the 1920s the highest-earning 1 percent of Americans took in 20 percent of the nation's income. That share was cut in half by the time *Brown* was decided.[2]

The law of civil liberties and free speech began to change, too. Three years after *Brown*, the Supreme Court blunted the draconian speech laws that had sent Roger Baldwin and his friends to prison in the era of the First World War. For most of the 1920s, the U.S. Supreme Court had continued to uphold the criminal convictions of radical dissenters; Ben Gitlow's conviction for distributing a "Left Wing Manifesto" had been affirmed by the justices shortly before he became a Fund director. A 1957 decision in a case called *Yates v. United States*, however, dramatically narrowed the reach of the criminal law. Signaling a new era of protections for dissenting speakers, the Court treated advocacy of revolution as protected speech, foreshadowing later cases in which the justices would outlaw the old criminal syndicalism laws altogether.[3]

The behind-the-scenes work of the American Fund did not secretly and single-handedly undo the old Jim Crow, shrink economic inequality, or produce the new law of free speech, of course. How could it have? Great shocks like economic collapse and war fueled mid-century change. So did long-term demographic trends. But such upheavals don't determine history's path; they are the occasions in which people remake the world. And when crisis arrived, the ideas, institutions, and movements of the Fund's interwar workshop were ready to reshape America.[4]

A version of the American Fund's network of racial and labor liberals remained intact for decades. From the 1940s into the mid-1960s, Baldwin, Muste, and A. Philip Randolph were elder statesmen of the civil rights movement, supporting fundraising efforts for organizations like the influential civil rights group Congress of Racial Equality. The postwar ACLU board of trustees added Thurgood Marshall to its roster of civil libertarians. Walter Reuther, in turn, joined the board of the NAACP. A contribution from his United Auto Workers helped finance *Brown v. Board of Education* at the Supreme Court. The next year, when Highlander Folk School alumna Rosa Parks helped touch off the Montgomery bus boycott, the UAW would again provide vital support. The *Brown* decision itself sustained the boycott movement by providing crucial authority for a federal court order against the city's bus companies. In 1960, the old League for Industrial Democracy spun off Students for a Democratic Society, better known as SDS. Its Port Huron Statement in 1962, supported by Reuther's UAW, revived for a new generation the critique of persistent economic inequality, racial hierarchy, and distorted public opinion.[5]

When observers take up the story of *Brown*, they sometimes tell it as the Associated Press did in 1954. Celebratory accounts like the landmark 1975 book *Simple Justice* by journalist Richard Kluger start with Charles Garland's money and the story of Nathan Margold's early blueprint.[6]

Observers of late have not been as generous. They assert that the Fund's best-known campaigns settled for a limited set of legal rights where the real issue was brute power. The joint NAACP–American Fund campaign, charge the critics, substituted courthouse triumphs for transformative change. So did the ACLU, they say, by pursuing abstract ideas about the freedom to speak in a world where some people had the resources to make themselves heard, and others did not. Similar critiques attack Sidney Hillman's CIO for erecting labor union institutions said to have sapped the energies of working-class mobilization.[7]

What such critics omit is that the Fund helped invent the politics underlying their complaints. The Fund sustained the movements that made up the heart of what historians now call "the long civil rights movement"—a decades-long effort of class and labor mobilizing before the era of *Brown v. Board*. Historians of the long civil rights movement purport to offer a grassroots alternative to the story of court-ordered desegregation. But the Fund's two decades of efforts reveal the distinction as a false dichotomy. Social mobilizations and the litigation campaign came out of the same emancipatory project, figuring as complements to one another, not rivals. In the world of the Fund, the passions of movement politics were married to the technocratic architecture of the law, and vice versa. Theirs was the faith that neither worked without the other. Once mobilized, the energies of a mass movement needed to be lodged in institutions capable of sustaining successes over time. This was the logic of Hillman's theory of strikes coupled with collective bargaining. It was the function of A. Philip Randolph's rousing meetings with the Pullman porters, on the one hand, and the care with which he avoided reckless strikes and protests that would squander his followers' passions, on the other. It was the electricity of the sit-down strikes alongside the bureaucratic structure of the Wagner Act.[8]

Of the nearly $2 million the Fund gave away in its two decades of operation, over half went to labor movement efforts. The largest share went to social democratic magazines, news services, and publishers with connections to Hillman's new unionism—publications committed to undoing the disinformation Baldwin, Sinclair, and so many others had identified in the news media after World War I. Twenty percent of the Fund's grants went to workers' education, with Brookwood College at the top of the long list of worker school beneficiaries. Other large chunks of the Fund's grant money went to research, legal defense, and strike relief.[9]

In its heyday, the program of the American Fund's majority was to develop a basic vision of economic fairness for a nation fractured by race. From the middle of the 1920s into the 1930s, its initially scattered and ad hoc experiments centered increasingly on this project. Infused by the idea of industrial democracy, and committed to the concomitant belief that fairness could only be sustained by power, the Fund's program appeared in the debates of the League for Industrial Democracy, the catalog of Vanguard Press, and secret gatherings of the Black and white members of the Southern Tenant Farmers Union. The social democratic vision of the Fund underwrote free speech defenses of labor organizers. It sustained Du Bois and Johnson's study of the Black schools educating future movement participants. And it animated Nathan Margold's plan for a legal campaign against Jim Crow that put power and resources at its center. The same campaign that produced *Brown v. Board of Education* also anticipated its forgotten sibling, *Steele v. Louisville & Nashville Railroad*. The effort to close out state-mandated segregation also pressed for a fairer distribution of resources, both at once.

People and movements touched by the American Fund did more for twentieth-century American liberalism than all the money of the era's much larger and more famous foundations. And yet today, three-quarters of a century after its vision came to partial fruition, the Fund that linked together these famous movements has itself largely faded from memory. So has its vision of the twentieth-century rights revolutions it sponsored. At the U.S. Supreme Court, *Brown v. Board* has come to stand for the perverse proposition that a country shamelessly discriminating on the basis of race for two hundred years may now not take race into account, even to support those suffering from the costs of repression. Race blindness, as the proposition is called, is a notion completely disconnected from the American Fund–NAACP project with which *Brown* began. Likewise, the freedom of speech, which in its early twentieth-century origins was about lifting up democratic voices and promoting public discourse, now supports the rights of the richest and strongest to distort public opinion in the service of their own interest. Labor unions, meanwhile, have lost power and influence. Coming of age in a vision of democratizing capitalism, they are now caricatured as forms of oppression and constraint. In some ways, they find themselves just as awkwardly positioned for a twenty-first-century economy of automation, gig work, and mobile finance as the old trade unions were at the dawn of mass production.[10]

What explains the receding of the Fund's core projects since midcentury? James Weldon Johnson came close to the heart of the matter when he observed, just a few years before he died, that the world is "constantly shifting and changing." Margold's plan for remaking the administrative structure of Jim Crow schools became ill-suited to a changed world in which the problem was not the separate schools of the segregation era but rather the separate school districts of the age of white flight. Sidney Hillman's descendants in the labor movement underestimated the enervating effects of bureaucratic collective bargaining on movement energies. The architects of the Wagner Act did not anticipate the effects of global trade and deindustrialization; they had few answers when American employers renewed the anti-union campaigns of the 1920s. Charles Hamilton Houston and Bester Steele won their case at the Supreme Court—but the coal-fired steam locomotive gave way to the diesel engine and made firemen's jobs obsolete.[11]

After the organizers of the American Fund generation stepped aside, new challenges presented themselves in the struggle for transformative change and a decent, democratic society. How could it have been otherwise? The problems of a new generation are not rebukes to those who came before us so much as they are reminders that each generation needs to update the strategies it inherits.[12]

The men and women of the Fund faced obstacles specific to their time and place, but they confronted universal challenges, too. They worked to hold fractious coalitions together. They balanced reformist projects with transformative ones. They struggled to weigh pragmatism and principle, immediate results and long-term transformation. They worried that money could be a corrupting force. They worked through failure and mistake. In their final years they did their best to manage an increasingly opinionated donor. And they navigated the difficulties arising out of moving from outsiders to insiders.

They had breakthroughs, too. The Fund's directors found that a number of seemingly separate projects actually went together. Economic fairness was at risk in a world of racial exploitation and misinformation. Racial equality required an economic foundation and a public relations strategy. In turn, the public sphere of democratic communication faltered under conditions of grievous inequality and thrived when countervailing forces found meaningful voice. Omitting the American Fund's story from the history of twentieth-century movements has obscured much of what those seemingly separate movements were up to—and what they were up against. Far from a one-sided campaign for rights against state repression, theirs was, at least sometimes, a three-dimensional effort to produce institutions of racial equality, economic fairness, and free speech adequate to modern mass democracy.

The fading of the Fund's story from memory has been, in part, an artifact of the Fund's unavoidable and awkward dilemma: The Fund relied on wealth to attack inequality. Purporting to reject the Rockefeller model of using unwarranted riches to gain influence, the Fund launched an effort that drew on the very features of the world it claimed to decry.

The year the Supreme Court decided *Brown v. Board of Education* also witnessed an overhaul of the tax code. Congress's new treatment, passed in the summer of 1954, set the nonprofit categories as they come down to us today. Charitable organizations exempt from tax and eligible for tax-deductible donations came under section 501(c)(3) of the Internal Revenue Code. An amendment offered by Senator Lyndon Johnson of Texas excluded nonprofit organizations that participated in electoral campaigns. American Fund lawyer Nicholas Kelley's theory of tax-exempt civic leagues, which the Fund had helped pioneer in the 1920s, survived in a separate provision. Under section 501(c)(4), organizations are not eligible for tax-deductible donations. But they may engage in a broader range of political activities while remaining exempt from tax on their own income.[13]

Section 501(c)(4) carried forward what was fast becoming a new kind of activist wealth in American democracy. In 1934, when Congress first codified the Treasury Department's exemption for nonprofit organizations like the American Fund, there were two hundred private foundations in the United States, the combined assets of which amounted to less than $1 billion. In the half century thereafter, some 30,000 private foundations would spring up, many of them taking advantage of the model the Fund had pioneered. By 2023, more than 100,000 private foundations, deploying assets of $1.5 trillion, contributed $104 billion to charitable efforts alone. Section 501(c)(4), meanwhile, would go on to underwrite a vast network of lobbying organizations and think tanks. The mid-century legal framework and its American Fund precedent had established a regulatory architecture for what critics today label "dark-money" organizations—a "new world of nonprofit activity" capable of injecting increasingly large amounts of money into social causes, often while keeping secret the identities of their donors. Many pursue projects that would have been anathema to the directors of the American Fund. Wealthy donors like the Coors family, the Koch brothers, Richard Mellon Scaife, John Olin, the Bradley Foundation, and the DeVos Foundation put tax-preferred foundation money toward efforts to undermine precisely the kinds of labor union gains, civil rights protections, and institutions of democratic public opinion for which the Fund and its beneficiaries fought.[14]

Just as in the 1920s, many of the winners in our lopsided economy today have turned their wealth to bending the world toward their own vision of the good. Pursuing buzzy new models like "philanthrocapitalism" or "effective altruism," the wealthy have already begun to deliver basic public goods that were long, though not always, the province of government. From space exploration to public education, philanthropy and private enterprise sometimes seem to be bidding to displace democracy altogether. Our twenty-first-century world of robber baron donors cries out anew for limits on the influence of the moneyed few, limits of the kind Frank Walsh and the Commission on Industrial Relations proposed after the Ludlow massacre. The directors of the American Fund would have been among the first to say so.[15]

When presented with the opportunity to use money, however, the directors of the American Fund seized it, even if the critics charged hypocrisy. Baldwin later explained that he turned to wealth to subvert inequality because he believed that to disdain it was foolish. Refusing to use the power made available by the world in which he lived might have preserved the moral purity of the effort, but only at the unacceptable cost of unilateral disarmament in the fight to shape society. For better and worse, he and his fellow directors found truth in what observers have long noted about American life: it is distinctively susceptible to influence by forms of private power, whether interest group lobbyists or civic groups or philanthropic foundations. To be sure, the Fund eschewed many of the patterns set by the Rockefellers and the Carnegies. Baldwin chose a spend-down structure to ensure that the American Fund would not become a perpetual foundation on the model of its larger peers. During its lifetime, the Fund operated on a shoestring in order to maintain its scarce resources for grants. And unlike the giant philanthropies of the Roaring Twenties, the Fund mostly turned its resources over to the membership organizations that were among its principal beneficiaries. Leaders of the Fund's grant recipients served on its board of directors and turned it into a running dialogue among the mass social movements it sought to promote.[16]

The directors found that influence doesn't always require huge sums. The law of diminishing returns means that the first few dollars are typically more valuable than the ones that follow. For a foundation the size of the Fund, the point was crucial. Its resources were modest.[17]

In fact, it is quite possible that you are as rich as Charles Garland was, or nearly so. As I write this, 23 million people in the United States have a net worth nominally equal to or greater than the million dollars of Garland's much-discussed inheritance. A million dollars is not what it once was. But today nearly 150,000 Americans have assets worth more than $30 million, roughly equivalent after inflation to the amount given away by the American Fund's directors.[18]

Perhaps you are one of the lucky ones. If not, there is a good chance that you know someone who has such a fortune, and in time you may have one, too. What is such a person to do? Should they, like Garland, disown their money? Should they, à la Baldwin, Johnson, and Flynn, dedicate it to the cause of democracy? Should you? Are you more at ease with the world around us than they were with theirs?

In the end, the Fund's most distinguishing asset was not its money. If you don't have vast sums—if perhaps like a young heir a century ago you don't want them—the American Fund has left you something as well.

What made its money valuable was the network it convened. The Fund connected social movement leaders from overlapping and sometimes rival movements, from different backgrounds and with different outlooks. They were men and women. They were new immigrants, Great Migration participants, and proverbial *Mayflower* descendants, liberals and socialists, movement leaders and intellectuals. Some came from poverty. Others came from privilege. In all, they hailed from a sprawling, heterogeneous America that was just coming into existence, one whose future they set out to shape.

Charles Garland's inheritance and its story bequeath us today not any one Supreme Court decision, any one institution or law, and not even any one archetype for making change in the world. The deeper legacy of the American Fund is to have identified components of a compelling democratic vision—a vision of economic fairness, racial equality, and basic human freedoms. The Fund advanced that vision with modesty about the unearned influence of its wealth. Its leading figures were attentive to the conditions for organizing movements in the modern world. And they turned those movements into durable institutions. At once restless and strategic, they developed a creative politics that came together a century ago, in unlikely fashion, when a dissatisfied young man set out on a most unusual path.

The opportunity presents itself once more.

		Year			Total to Organization
	AFFILIATED SUMMER SCHOOLS	1921			20 —
	AGRICULTURAL WORKERS UNION OF ALABAMA	1937			500 —
	ALABAMA FARMERS UNION (Dists 7 & 8)	1937			300 —
	ALL AMERICA ANTI IMPERIALIST LEAGUE (See also Anti-Imperialist League of the United States)	1926			1000 —
	AMALGAMATED ASS'N OF STREET & ELECTRIC RY EMPLOYEES (Includes $300 loan to Consolidated Railway Workers which was cancelled)	1924			1700 —
	AMALGAMATED TEXTILE WORKERS OF PATTERSON & PASSIC	1925			550 —
	AMERICAN BIRTH CONTROL LEAGUE	1924 1925 1926-7 1927-8 1929		500 — 3542 — 7000 — 3000 — 2000 —	13452

First page of the American Fund for Public Service's grant ledger, 1922–1941.

Appendix A

Gifts, 1922-1941

COMPLETE LISTING OF AMERICAN FUND FOR PUBLIC SERVICE GIFTS, 1922-1941

Reconstructed from "Gifts—To June 30, 1941," box 8, AFPS Records, New York Public Library. Asterisks (*) indicate loans deemed uncollectible or bail forfeited.

	YEAR	ANNUAL GIFT	SUB-TOTAL	TOTAL TO ORG.
AFFILIATED SUMMER SCHOOLS	1931			30—
AGRICULTURAL WORKERS UNION OF ALABAMA	1937			500—
ALABAMA FARMERS UNION (Dists 7 & 8)	1937			900—
ALL AMERICA ANTI IMPERIALIST LEAGUE (See also Anti-Imperialist League of the United States)	1928			1000—
AMALGAMATED ASS'N OF STREET & ELECTRIC RY EMPLOYEES (Includes $200 loan to Consolidated Railway Workers that was canceled)	1926			1700—
AMALGAMATED TEXTILE WORKERS OF PATERSON AND PASSAIC	1925			880—
AMERICAN BIRTH CONTROL LEAGUE	1924	500—		
	1925	956.12		
	1926-27	7000—		
	1927-28	3000—		
	1929	2000—		13456.12

544   APPENDIX A: GIFTS, 1922–1941

	YEAR	ANNUAL GIFT	SUB-TOTAL	TOTAL TO ORG.
AMERICAN CIVIL LIBERTIES UNION				
National Office				
Affirmative Legal Action (pamphlet)			781.85	
Cornish case (loan canceled)	1928		500—	
Emergency Case Fund	1925	1796.02		
(for list of cases for	1926	3447.21		
which this money was used,	1927	5670.64		
see last page of this report)	1928	4946.20		
	1929	1686—		
	1930	1414.29		
	1931	1627.96	20588.32	
Contempt of Court Pamphlet	1925–28		360—	
Field Organizers	1930–32		5796.29	
Injunctions, Campaign Against	1930–31		3000—	
Indemnity Bonds. Test case re	1929		200—	
Louis Post Book	1922		500—	
Macklem Bail forfeited (uncol. loan)	1926		*750—	
Miser case	1926		500—	
Mooney Case—(see MOONEY CASE)				
Pamphlets	1931–32		542—	
Passaic cases (see PASSAIC STRIKE)				
Revolving Loan Fund (bal. canceled)	1934		1211.09	
Reactionary Organizations Inv. of	1923		1872.47	
National Mooney Billings Committee				
(see MOONEY CASE)				
Work in W. Virginia	1923		1000—	
West Va. Publicity Campaign				
on behalf of striking miners				
A.C.L.U. & L.I.D. (see League				
for Industrial Democracy)				
Total—National Office				37602.02
Northern California Branch	1926–27	1532.76		
Uncol. loan		*500.00		2032.76
Philadelphia Branch	1930		500—	
	1931		500—	1000—
Pittsburgh Branch (loan canc.)	1931			400—

APPENDIX A: GIFTS, 1922-1941 545

	YEAR	ANNUAL GIFT	SUB-TOTAL	TOTAL TO ORG.
ACLU (Cont'd)				41034.78
Southern California Branch				
General	1923	1000—		
	1924	1767.11		
	1925	2267.12		
	1926	2133.09		
	1927	1609.45	8776.77	
Richard Ford Case	1925		3500—	
Special Campaign	1926		5000—	
Total—So. Calif. Branch				17276.77
Total ACLU				58311.55
AM. COMMITTEE FOR CHINESE RELIEF	1925			2000—
AM. COMMITTEE FOR PROTECTION OF FOREIGN BORN	1936			150—
AM. EMPLOYERS OFFENSIVE, study of	1925		1494—	
	1926		1712.05	
	1927		1192.25	4399.30
AM. FEDERATION OF TEACHERS	1926			2000—
AMERICAN FOREIGN INVESTMENTS (See IMPERIALISM STUDIES)				
AM. INDIAN DEFENSE COMMITTEE	1931			500—
AM. LEAGUE AG. WAR & FASCISM	1935			2000—
AM. STUDENT DELEGATION TO RUSSIA	1926		350—	
part of loan to T. Dabney canceled	1934		205—	555—
ANTI-IMPERIALIST LEAGUE OF U.S. (See also All-America Anti-Imperialist League)	1930			813.49
AMERICAN SHOE WORKERS UNION				
Uncollectible loan	1937			*16448.48

APPENDIX A: GIFTS, 1922-1941

	YEAR	ANNUAL GIFT	SUB-TOTAL	TOTAL TO ORG.
ASSOCIATED TEXTILES, Inc. Uncollectible loan	1933			*40767.37
BALTIMORE LABOR COLLEGE	1928			389.27
BILLINGS, WARREN	1926-31	205—		
BLANCHARD, Paul—Survey & Conf. of Southern Ministers (See LEAGUE FOR INDUSTRIAL DEMOCRACY)				
BOSTON TRADE UNION COLLEGE	1925		1317.50	
	1927		382.50	1700—
BROCKTON DIST. SHOE WORKERS	1923		500—	
	1925		415—	915—
BROOKWOOD				
General budget				
Loan canceled	1923-24	7500—		
Appropriations	1923-24	6110—		
	1924-25	6268—		
	1925-26	10000—		
	1926-27	25000—		
	1927-28	25000—		
	1928-29	20000—		
	1929-30	20000—		
	1930-31	15000—		
	1931-32	15000—		
	1932-33	10000—		
	1933-34	10000—		
	1934-35	5000—		
	1935-36	5000—	179878—	
Special appropriations				
Boiler Repairs	1925		877.15	
Dependency Scholarships	1925-26		1972.50	
Extension Work	1928		1000—	
Library Fund	1923		1000—	
Research-Bloom manuscript	1926	500—		
Minority Viewpoint	1925-30	1100—		
Labor Org. Tech.	1925-26	2800—	4400—	
Scholarships for Negroes	1925	1000—		
	1926	1000—	2000—	

APPENDIX A: GIFTS, 1922-1941 547

	YEAR	ANNUAL GIFT	SUB-TOTAL	TOTAL TO ORG.
BROOKWOOD (special appropriations cont'd)				
Southern Group			100—	
Summer Institutes	1925	2355.85		
	1926	3000—	5355.85	
Tucker Smith Vacation Fund	1935		1000—	
Water System	1936		500—	
Spec. A.F.L. Investigation	1928		1751.50	199835—
BROTHERHOOD OF SLEEPING CAR PORTERS				
Org. & prep. of brief	1925-26		11200.00	
Bringing case before I.C.C.	1927-28		2724.56	
Organization work	1928		4000	17924.56
BUREAU OF INDUSTRIAL RESEARCH	1923-24			2841.44
BURLINGTON DEFENSE COMMITTEE	1935			800—
COHEN, Jacob (See Memphis Labor Review)				
COLORADO COMMITTEE FOR THE PROMOTION OF WORKERS EDUCATION	1929			1500—
COLO & WYO STATE FEDS OF LABOR	1925-26		2500—	
	1926-27		2500—	
	1927-28		750—	5750—
COMMITTEE ON COAL & GIANT POWER	1925		1500—	
	1926		5160—	
	1927		3340—	
	1928		4017.22	
	1929		3997.78	
	1930		992.50	19007.50
COMMITTEE ON MILITARISM IN EDUCATION				
Pamphlet	1925		5400—	
General (includes $800 loan cncld)	1926	5000—		
	1927	2000—	7000—	12400—

	YEAR	ANNUAL GIFT	SUB-TOTAL	TOTAL TO ORG.
CONFERENCE FOR PROGRESSIVE LABOR ACTION				
Educational Work in South	1929–30	3000—		
Educational Work	1930	1200—	4200—	
Pamphlets	1930		665.76	4865.76
COOPERATIVE GLOVE ASSOCIATION (Loan canceled)	1926			1000—
COOPERATIVE LEAGUE OF AMERICA	1924		1602.78	
	1926		1500—	3102.78
CULTURA OBRERA	1925			1075—
DABNEY, THOMAS (See Am. Student Delegation to Russia)				
DAILY WORKER	1924		1581.35	
Loan canceled	1929		6875—	
Uncollectible loan	1928		*4650.36	
Uncollectible loan	1925		*4500—	17606.71
DENVER LABOR COLLEGE	1924		1000—	
(Farmer Labor Summer School)	1925		1000—	
	1926		798.83	2798.83
DU BOIS, Dr. W. E. B. & Study of Negro Education in the South	1925–26			5000—
EASTMAN, MAX (Russian Film)	1934	100—		100—
EAST SIDE EDUCATIONAL CENTER (Uncollectible loan)	1935			*325—
EMERGENCY COMMITTEE FOR	1926		6520—	
STRIKERS RELIEF	1927		1000—	
	1928		1000—	8520—
EVANS, Mrs. Elizabeth Glendower See Sacco Vanzetti Case				
EQUITY PRINTING COMPANY (See Industrial Workers of the World)				

APPENDIX A: GIFTS, 1922-1941 549

	YEAR	ANNUAL GIFT	SUB-TOTAL	TOTAL TO ORG.
FARMERS EDUCATIONAL & COOPERATIVE UNION				
Louisiana Farmers—General	1937		700—	
Special—car	1937		250—	
" "	1940		300—	1250—
Southern Organizing Committee	1938		2500—	
	1939		2000—	4500—
(See also Alabama Farmers Union)				
FARMERS NATIONAL COMMITTEE FOR ACTION				
General Budget	1934-35	1050—		
	1935-36	1900—		
	1936-37	2500—	5450—	
Special Org. Campaign	1936-37		2000—	
Old debts of	1938		500—	7950—
Farmer National Committee				
Farmers National Weekly				
Farm Holiday News				
Farm Holiday Association				
FARMERS NATIONAL WEEKLY				
General Budget	1934-35	1750—		
	1935-36	3000—		
	1936-37	2500	7250	
Retirement of old debts	1937		1500—	8750—
FARM RESEARCH, INC.	1937		625—	
	1938		1500—	
	1939		1500—	
	1940		4300—	
	1941		1950—	9875—
FARMERS UNITY COUNCIL	1938		3500—	
(Lem Harris)	1939		1500—	
	1940		300—	5300—

550   APPENDIX A: GIFTS, 1922-1941

	YEAR	ANNUAL GIFT	SUB-TOTAL	TOTAL TO ORG.
FEDERATED PRESS				
General Budget	1923	12125—		
	1924	11334.55		
	1925	3500—		
	1926-27	3000—		
	1927-28	5000—		
	1928-29	5000—		
	1929-30	5000—		
	1930-31	4000—		
	1931-32	4000—	52959.55	
Economic Service	1922-23	910—		
	1923-24	3570—		
	1924-25	3570—		
	1925-26	3640—		
	1926-27	3640—		
	1927-28	3600—		
	1928-29	3600—	22530—	
Special appropriations				
Albert Coyle's Trip to Mexico	1926		549.64	
A.F. of L. Convention Report	1925		283.90	
British Strike Cables	1926		312.58	
Louis Budenz Trip	1926		321.29	
Labor News Letter	1929		3000—	
Promotion Work	1926	59.92		
	1928	1000—	1059.92	
Ziegler Investigations	1926		75—	
Shields-Lowell Southern Trip				
(See Shields-Lowell)				
Total-Federal Press				81091.88
FEDERAL LABOR UNION OF ST. THOMAS (Virgin Islands)	1923			100—
FELLOWSHIP OF YOUTH FOR PEACE	1925			88—
FERRER SCHOOL (See Modern School of Am)				
FURRIERS UNION (See Joint Board Furriers Union)				

APPENDIX A: GIFTS, 1922-1941

	YEAR	ANNUAL GIFT	SUB-TOTAL	TOTAL TO ORG.
GENERAL DEFENSE COMMITTEE				
Chicago—Publicity	1924		650—	
Relief	1925-26		2400—	
General	1928		2000—	
Calif. Branches-Sacramento Inj.	1923		500—	
" "—Burns Case	1925-26		662.40	
" "—Crim. Synd. Cases	1923		500—	6712.40
Centralia (See CENTRALIA CASES)				

GASTONIA CASES				
I.L.D.—Legal Defense	1929		20475.00	
Bail forfeited (includes $10,000 Beal, Pontiac)			*28747.03	Bail Fund
Int. Cash. Bail (uncollectible loan)			*3057.24	Bail Fund
A.C.L.U.—about $550 of A.C.L.U. Emergency Loan fund used for Gastonia cases				

GENERAL RELIEF COMMITTEE FOR TEXTILE WORKERS, PASSAIC (See Passaic Strike)				

GRECO-CARRILLO DEFENSE COMMITTEE (Loan canceled as uncollectible)	1928			*7513.96

HARRIS, LEMUEL (See Farmers Unity Council)				

IL MARTELLO	1924-25		2200—	
Book Shop (uncollectible loan)	1934		2500—	4700—

IL NUOVO MONDO	1926		10000—	
	1927		2000—	
Uncollectible loan	1935		*3592.92	15592.92

552   APPENDIX A: GIFTS, 1922-1941

	YEAR	ANNUAL GIFT	SUB-TOTAL	TOTAL TO ORG.
IMPERIALISM STUDIES				
First Series—Research & publication	1924	5147.47		
"American Foreign Investments" by	1925	2968.30		
R. W. Dunn, Research "Dollar	1926	3870.87		11986.64
Diplomacy" by Freeman & Nearing.				
Also Lauck study.				
Second Series				
Marsh, Jenks & Knight volumes	1925	3767.00		
on Bolivia, Cuba, and Santo	1926	13680.74		
Domingo	1927	2153.24		
	1928	3510.33		
	1929	181.63	23292.94	
Refund for books sold by Vanguard			−526.54	22766.40
Third Series				
Diffie, Rippy & Kepner volumes	1929	163.50		
on Porto Rico, Colombia & Banana	1930	2599.83		
Empire	1931	783.45		
	1932	1611.95		
	1933	232.73		
	1934	—		
	1935	1000.00		
	1936	232.54		
	1937	13.48	6637.48	
Refund for books sold by Vanguard			−299.41	6338.07
Total for all three series				41092.11
INDEPENDENT SHOE WORKERS UNION				
Uncollectible loan	1934			*2800—
INDUSTRIAL PIONEER				
(See Industrial Workers of the World)				
INDUSTRIAL ESPIONAGE STUDY	1924			1345—
INDUSTRIAL WORKERS OF THE WORLD				
Equity Printing Co. (uncol.loan)			*20007.79	
" " " (" ")			*3325—	
Industrial Pioneer	1926		1820—	
Miners of Wayne, Alberta, Can.	1926		500—	25652.79

APPENDIX A: GIFTS, 1922-1941

	YEAR	ANNUAL GIFT	SUB-TOTAL	TOTAL TO ORG.
INJUNCTION STUDY				
Labor Bureau & Walter Nelles	1923		1107.24	
	1924		2600—	
	1925		5000—	
	1926		1400—	
	1927		1160—	
	1928		4400—	15707.24
INTERNATIONAL COMMITTEE FOR POLITICAL PRISONERS	1925			1827.50
INTERNATIONAL LABOR DEFENSE				
New York City				
General expenses	1928		2000—	
Accorsi case	1929		1000—	
Bimba case	1927		500—	
Cheswick case	1928		350—	
Gastonia (See GASTONIA CASES)				
Kovacovich cases	1928		750—	
Michigan cases—legal exp.	1929		1000—	
" " —bail canceled	1933		*1879.27	
Passaic cases (See PASSAIC STRIKE)				
Pamphlets	1931		150—	
Woodlawn cases	1928		1250—	
Ziegler cases	1926		3000—	
Miscellaneous cases	1930		3500—	
Bail forfeited (Nat'l office & Branches)	1934		*1051.35	
Gastonia-see GASTONIA CASES				
Loan canceled as uncollectible	1934		*447—	
Misc. Loans canc'd as gifts	1934		2058.30	
Loss on Mich. bail			*620—	
Total I.L.D. New York, exclusive of Passaic & Gastonia cases			19555.92	
Pittsburgh Branch	1926		1500—	
Chicago Branch	1924		2500—	23555.92
INTERNATIONAL LADIES' GARMENT WORKERS UNION				
Loan canceled	1930			55945.72

	YEAR	ANNUAL GIFT	SUB-TOTAL	TOTAL TO ORG.
INTERNATIONAL PAMPHLETS	1930		1600—	
	1931		200—	
	1932		200—	
	1933		600—	
	1940		200—	2800—
INTERNATIONAL PUBLISHERS	1931		1000—	
	1934		1200—	
	1935		300—	
	1940		200—	
Loan canceled "Oil Imperialism" as uncollectible	1930		694.69	3394.69
INVESTMENT BANKERS, Study of	1925–26			988.07
JOINT AMNESTY COMMITTEE	1923			1000—
JOINT BOARD FURRIERS UNION	1940			*40000—
KING, Carol Weiss See: Macklem case Vajtauer case				
LABOR AGE (includes $500 loan canceled)	1923–24		1100—	
	1924–25		6315—	
	1926–27		6900—	
	1927–28		3600—	
	1928–29		2850—	20765—
LABOR BUREAU, INC. See- Injunction Study Directory of Labor Organizations Investment Bankers Study				
LABOR DEFENSE COUNCIL (Chicago) (See International Labor Defense)				
LABOR HERALD (See Trade Union Educational League)				
LABOR DEFENSE COUNCIL (England)	1924		500—	
LABOR ORGANIZATIONS, Directory of	1923			661.23

APPENDIX A: GIFTS, 1922-1941 555

	YEAR	ANNUAL GIFT	SUB-TOTAL	TOTAL TO ORG.
LABOR PRESS DIRECTORY	1924-26			821.85
LABOR RESEARCH ASSOCIATION				
Nearing Research Project	1929-33		3000—	
Facts for Workers	1929-30		750—	3750—
LADIES AUXILIARY—INTERNATIONAL	1926		4000—	
ASSOCIATIONS OF MACHINISTS	1927-28		2000—	6000—
LAUCK, William Jett				
Industrial Code Study	1924		600—	
Health Investigation, Passaic (See PASSAIC STRIKE)				
Loss on Lenox Bldg.—stock	1941		*15100.07	15700.07
LEAGUE FOR INDUSTRIAL DEMOCRACY				
General	1922-23		6400—	
Field Secretary's Salary	1923-24	3500—		
" " "	1924-25	3500—		
" " "	1925-26	3500—		
Field Sec's Sal & Trav. Exp.	1923-26	3000—		
Field Sec'y and Pamphlets	1926-27	3500—		
" " "	1927-28	2000—		
" " "	1928-29	1000—		
Pamphlets	1924-25	1000—		
"	1926	1000—		
"	1930	1500	23500—	
With Am. Civ. Lib. Union—Report on Infringement of Right to Organize in W. Va.	1925		600—	
Study of Newer Developments in Capitalism	1926-28		1900—	
Survey & Conf. of So. Ministers by Paul Blanchard	1926-27		1400—	
West Va. Pub. Campaign on behalf of striking miners (L.I.D. & ACLU)	1924-25		2266.61	36066.61
Committee on Coal & Super Power—(see this heading)				
Chicago Office	1930-31			4000—

	YEAR	ANNUAL GIFT	SUB-TOTAL	TOTAL TO ORG.
LEAGUE FOR MUTUAL AID (Loan canceled as gift)	1934			5000—
LIBERATOR Loan canceled	1922			500—
LINDSEY, Judge Ben	1925			1000—
LOUISIANA FARMERS UNION (See Farmers Educational and Cooperative Union)				
MISSOURI FEDERATION OF LABOR	1926			15000
MODERN SCHOOL ASSOCIATION	1922		500—	
	1924		500—	
	1926		2000—	3000—
MOONEY CASE				
Am. Civil Liberties Union	1929		70.25	
Tom Mooney Moulders Def. Com.	1924–26	1000—		
	1929	500—		
	1930	1000—		
	1935	1000—	3500—	
Nat'l Mooney Billings Def. Com.	1926–31		3300—	
No. Calif. M. B. Com. (loan canc'd)	1930		250—	
N.Y. Mooney-Billings com.	19–		30—	
Total Mooney Case				7150.25
NATIONAL ASSOCIATION FOR THE ADVANCEMENT OF COLORED PEOPLE New York City				
Anti-Lynching Campaign	1922–23		3365.50	
General	1923		1500—	
" Loan canceled	1924		2500—	
Defense Fund	1925–26		26552.80	
Legal Defense	1928		5000—	
Scholarship (see BROOKWOOD)				

APPENDIX A: GIFTS, 1922-1941   557

	YEAR	ANNUAL GIFT	SUB-TOTAL	TOTAL TO ORG.
NAACP (Cont'd)				
Joint Committee N.A.A.C.P.—	1931-33	8082.76		
A.F.P.S.	1934	10000—		
	1936	3500—		
	1937	6500—		
	1938	700—	28782.76	
Boston Branch	1923		500—	
				68201.06
NATIONAL ASSOCIATION FOR CHILD DEVELOPMENT (See Pioneer Youth)				
NATIONAL CHILD LABOR COMMITTEE	1925			2500—
NATIONAL CONSUMERS LEAGUE	1923-24			3948.84
NATIONAL COMMITTEE FOR UNITY OF AGRICULTURAL & RURAL WORKERS				
General	1934-35		2200—	
	1935-36		3000—	
	1936-37		5000—	
	1937		3850—	14050—
Subsequent appropriations see United Cannery, Agr., Packing & Allied Workers of A.				
NATIONAL FARM HOLIDAY NEWS	1937			2375—
NATIONAL MOONEY-BILLINGS COMMITTEE (See MOONEY CASE)				
NEW MASSES	1925-26		1500—	
	1926-27		17000—	
	1927-28		8000—	
	1928-29		2400—	
Uncollectible loan	1928		*3000—	31900—

APPENDIX A: GIFTS, 1922-1941

	YEAR	ANNUAL GIFT	SUB-TOTAL	TOTAL TO ORG.
NEWARK LABOR COLLEGE	1925			180—
NEW REPUBLIC (book subsidy) (balance due canceled in return for copies of the book)	1934			741.08
NEW STUDENT	1925		386.86	
	1926		333.06	719.92
NEW YORK CALL & LEADER	1923		44500—	
Loan canceled	1924		10000—	54500—
NEW YORK WOMEN'S TRADE UNION LEAGUE	1926			2500—
NORTHERN CALIFORNIA MOONEY BILLINGS COM. (See MOONEY CASE)				
NORTHERN STATES COOP. LEAGUE	1926			1000—
NORTHWESTERN UNIV. & GARRETT BIB. INSTITUTE STUDENTS				497.41
NOVY MIR—Loan canceled			500—	
Uncollectible loan	1935		*3000—	3500—
OPTIONAL MILITARY DRILL LEAGUE				250—
OKLAHOMA LEADER (stock written off)	1941			*20000—
OIL IMPERIALISM by Louis Fisher (See International Publishers)				
PAPER BOX MAKERS UNION	1927–28		2000—	
(loan canceled)	1929		1000—	3000—
PASSAIC CENTRAL LABOR UNION	1927–28			600—

APPENDIX A: GIFTS, 1922-1941 559

	YEAR	ANNUAL GIFT	SUB-TOTAL	TOTAL TO ORG.
PASSAIC STRIKE (1926) A.C.L.U. (also $1621.54 of A.C.L.U. Em. Case Fund used for Passaic cases)	1926		500—	
I.L.D.—Bail premiums paid Legal Expenses		3022.61 720.50	3743.11	
General Relief Committee, U.T.W. (uncollectible loan)	1927		*20000—	
Wm. Jett Lauck & Assistants— investigation of textile industry in Passaic	1926		5000—	
United Front Textile Workers	1925		818—	30061.11
Special Health investigation (See Workers' Health Bureau)				
PATERSON SILK WORKERS (Joint Committee)	1931			2000—
PENN FED. OF LABOR	1926-27 1927-28 1928		3818.30 3000— 1333—	8151.30
PENN SYSTEM FEDERATION #40 (loan canceled)	1923 1924 1925		3000— 2000— 2500—	7500—
PENNSYLVANIA FARMERS UNION	1937			105—
PEOPLES LOBBY	1928-29 1929-30		3000— 1800—	4800—
PEOPLES RECONSTRUCTION LEAGUE	1926			1000—
PERSONAL SERVICE FUND	1926			10000—

APPENDIX A: GIFTS, 1922-1941

	YEAR	ANNUAL GIFT	SUB-TOTAL	TOTAL TO ORG.
PHILADELPHIA LABOR COLLEGE				
General	1924-25	1000—		
"	1925-26	2570.55		
" Loan canceled	1926	1000—		
"	1926-27	2500—		
"	1927-28	1800—		
"	1929	440.25	9310.80	
Research			1200—	10510.80
PIONEER YOUTH OF AMERICA				
General	1925	5970—		
	1925-26	10000—		
	1926-27	9918.66		
	1928-29	7128.71	33017.37	
Salary of Educational Director	1925		1000—	
Camp Scholarships	1924		2500—	36517.37
PITTSBURGH EDUCATIONAL FORUM	1928			1700—
PITTSBURGH LABOR COLLEGE	1929			52—
POLISH PEOPLES PUB. CO. Uncollectible loan	1927			*3084—
POLITICAL PRISONERS DEFENSE & RELIEF COMMITTEE	1924			1500—
PORTLAND LABOR COLLEGE	1925	250—		
	1925-26	2400—		
	1926-27	2500—		
	1927-28	1050—	6200—	
POWER PUBLISHING COMPANY Loan canceled				1000—
PROGRESSIVE LIBRARY OF W. PHILA.	1926		1200—	
Uncollectible loan	1930		*2470—	3670—
PUBLISHING ENTERPRISE (*See* VANGUARD PRESS)				

APPENDIX A: GIFTS, 1922-1941   561

	YEAR	ANNUAL GIFT	SUB-TOTAL	TOTAL TO ORG.
RADICAL LIBRARY OF W. PHILADELPHIA	1925			1000—
RADIO BROADCASTING STATION	1925			600—
RAND BOOK STORE	1926			800—
RAND SCHOOL—EDUCATIONAL DEPT.	1922-23	5000—		
" " (Schol.)	1926-27	2500—		
	1927-28	2500—	10000—	
RESEARCH DEPT.	1923-24	3250—		
	1924-25	4800—		
	1925-26	6615—		
	1926-27	5861.73		
	1927-28	5300—		
	1928-29	4200—	30026.73	40026.73
REVOLUTIONARY AGE	1930 32			583.42
ROCHESTER LABOR COLLEGE	1923			78—
RUSSIAN RECONSTRUCTION FARMS Loan & stock canceled as uncollectible	1934			18097—
RUSSIAN STUDIES	1926			
	1927			
	1928			
	1929			
	1930			
	1932			15109.89
SACCO VANZETTI CASE				
Sacco-Vanzetti Def. Com. Loan Can'd	1922		400—	
" " App.	1925		2500—	
" " Uncol. loan	1927		*10000—	
Eliz. G. Evans	1926		1000—	13900—
SCOTTSBORO DEFENSE COMMITTEE Loan canceled as uncollectible	1941			*5000—

APPENDIX A: GIFTS, 1922-1941

	YEAR	ANNUAL GIFT	SUB-TOTAL	TOTAL TO ORG.
SEATTLE LABOR COLLEGE	1924-25		500—	
	1925-26		1000—	
	1926-27		1000—	
	1927-28		1000—	
	1930		1000—	
	1931-33		850—	5350—
SEATTLE UNION RECORD				
Uncollectible Loan	1929			*5000—
SHIELDS-LOWELL TRIP	1929		800—	
	1930		700—	
	1931		400—	
	1932		100—	2000—
SHORR, ISAAC (see Mahler Case)				
SHARE CROPPERS UNION				
General Budget	1936		2500—	
Convention Expenses	1936		200—	2700—
SOUTHERN FARM LEADER	1937			250—
SOUTHERN TENANT FARMERS UNION				
General Budget	1935	2000—		
	1936	2500—		
	1937	2500—		
	1938	2500—		
	1939	2000—		
	1940	320—	11820—	
Special Educational Work	1936		200—	
Convention Expenses	1937		300—	
Legal Fund	1937		500—	12820.00
SOUTHERN ORGANIZING COMMITTEE (See Farmers Educational & Cooperative Union of America)				
SOUTHERN SUMMER SCHOOL FOR	1926		500—	
WOMEN WORKERS	1927		2392.37	
	1928		329.67	
	1929		3000—	
	1930		3000—	
	1931		2858.70	12080.74

APPENDIX A: GIFTS, 1922-1941 563

	YEAR	ANNUAL GIFT	SUB-TOTAL	TOTAL TO ORG.
SPEAKERS SERVICE BUREAU	1924		2500—	
	1926		10000—	12500—
ST. PAUL TRADES & LABOR ASSEMBLY	1926			150—
SURVEY OF RADICAL ORGANIZATIONS	1923-25			694—
SPIVAK, JOHN (Uncollectible loan)	1937			*200—
TEACHERS UNION	1922		500—	
	1923		3172.50	
	1924-25		2000—	
	1925		1000—	6672.50
THEATRE UNION (Uncol. Loan)	1937			*505—
TRADE UNION COM. FOR ORGANIZING	1925		2435—	
NEGRO WORKERS	1926		600—	3035—
TRADE UNION EDUCATIONAL LEAGUE	1923		1500—	
Loan canceled	1930		900—	2400—
UNION HEALTH CENTER (ILGWU)	1926			10000—
UNITED ANTHRACITE MINERS (Loan canceled as uncollectible)	1936			*500—
UNITED FRONT TEXTILE WORKERS (See Passaic Strike)				
UNITED MINE WORKERS OF AMERICA				
District #2 (strike relief)	1922			2000—
" " (educational work)	1925	3700—		
	1926	2000—		5700—
District #12, Sub. Dist. 12,	1924-25	3844.43		
Educational Work	1925-26	4425—		
	1926-27	3300—		
District #17—W. Va.	1923	2000—		
Westmoreland County-Loan canc'd	1924	200—		21469.43

	YEAR	ANNUAL GIFT	SUB-TOTAL	TOTAL TO ORG.
UNITED CANNERY, AGRICULTURAL PACKING & ALLIED WORKERS OF A. (See also Nat. Com. for Unity of Ag. & Rural Workers)	1938 1939 1940		5000— 2000— 500—	7500—
UNITY HOUSE—Pt. of loan canceled	1934			6750—
VAJTAUER CASE	1925–26			1900—
VANGUARD PRESS Preliminary expense	1925 1926		1001.06 3409.19	
Total Preliminary expenses Vanguard Press	1926 1927 1928 1929 1930		4410.25 75000.00 25000.00 61043.12 7500.00 13500.00 186453.37	
Less proceeds of sale of V.P. Total outlay			−45000.00	141453.37
VIRGIN ISLANDS COMMITTEE	1924			160—
WABASH SYSTEM FEDERATION SHOP Crafts #13	1923			300—
WASHINGTON CONCILIATION COMMITTEE (see Centralia Cases)				
WEST VA. PUBLICITY CAMPAIGN (see League for Ind. Dem.)				
WHO'S WHO IN THE LABOR MOVEMENT & LIST OF RADICALS	1923 1924 1925 1926		964.76 3930.38 5419.72 25—	10339.86
WOMEN'S INTERNAT'L LEAGUE FOR PEACE & FREEDOM—For "Pax"	1925 1927 1928	2400— 1200— 1200—	4800— 143.16 400.01	5343.17

APPENDIX A: GIFTS, 1922-1941 565

	YEAR	ANNUAL GIFT	SUB-TOTAL	TOTAL TO ORG.
WOOD, L. HOLLINGSWORTH & ESTATE OF ALBERT DESILVER) (See Amalgamated Textile Workers of Paterson & Passaic)				
WORKERS EDUCATION STUDY	1924		200—	
	1925		7874.22	
	1926		2922.53	10996.75
WORKERS HEALTH BUREAU				
General Budget	1923	1500—		
	1924	5000—		
	1925	4557.16		
	1926	5222.45		
	1927	4644.75	20924.36	
Special Investigations				
Passaic Strike			4000—	
Coal & Automobile Studies			1118.53	26042.89
WORKERS INTERNATIONAL RELIEF	1929			1000—
WORKERS SCHOOL—General	1925	763.95		
"	1926	5000—		
"	1927	2500—		
"	1928	2500—	10763.95	
Library Fund	1926		1000—	
Books	1929		859.25	12623.20
WORKERS LIBRARY PUBLISHERS	1929		350—	
	1930		350—	
	1931		180—	880—
WORK PEOPLES COLLEGE—DULUTH	1924		250—	
	1925		1000—	1250—
WORLD TOMORROW	1922		1000—	
Includes $500 loan canceled	1923		1000—	
	1924		2000—	
	1925		2000—	
Loan canceled	1925		3000—	9000—

	YEAR	ANNUAL GIFT	SUB-TOTAL	TOTAL TO ORG.
WORLD WAR VETERANS	1923			1150—
WYO. CONF. OF METHODIST CHURCH	1925			300—
YOUNG WORKERS LEAGUE OF AM. (Superior, Wisc.)	1925 1926		1200 2000	3200—
YOUNG WORKERS LEAGUE (Chicago)	1926			1200—

Detailed Report of the Expenditure of $20,588.32 Emergency Case Fund of the American Civil Liberties Union [incomplete]

Aliquippa cases	300—	Hindu Deportation	100—
Bence	153—	I.L.G.W.U.	53.75
Bland	506.84	Laredo Lynching	150—
Borghi	150—	Lashkowitz, N. Dakota	500—
Brophy-Toohey	25—	Lawrence	750—
Bruno	125—	Lewis	35.80
Bruvold	105—	Loucas	150—
Burns	37—	Lynn	525—
Canter	23.27	Marion	500—
Centralia	450—	Minerich	250—
Charleroi, Pa.	100—	National Miners Relief Com.	100—
Cheswick Cases	1622.13	Neil, Joe (Kansas)	712.85
Chinese Committee	500—	Newark	100—
Clifford	399.22	Ohio	389.09
Colorado cases	712.85	Passaic	1621.64
Columbia Mine	175—	Phillips case	150—
Connors	100—	Ripley case	1248.36
Fackaberry	25—	Rowan case	443.50
Fall River	382—	Scheidel case	75—
Francis, Rothschild	371.02	Tresca case	150—
Gastonia cases	550—	West Va. & So. Dakota cases	200—
Ghose, Sailendra	500—	Whitney	678.50
Giletti	180—	Williams	50—
Godolpho	25—	Woodlawn	1250—
Greensboro Strike	50—		

Appendix B

Garland Fund Outlays, 1922–1941

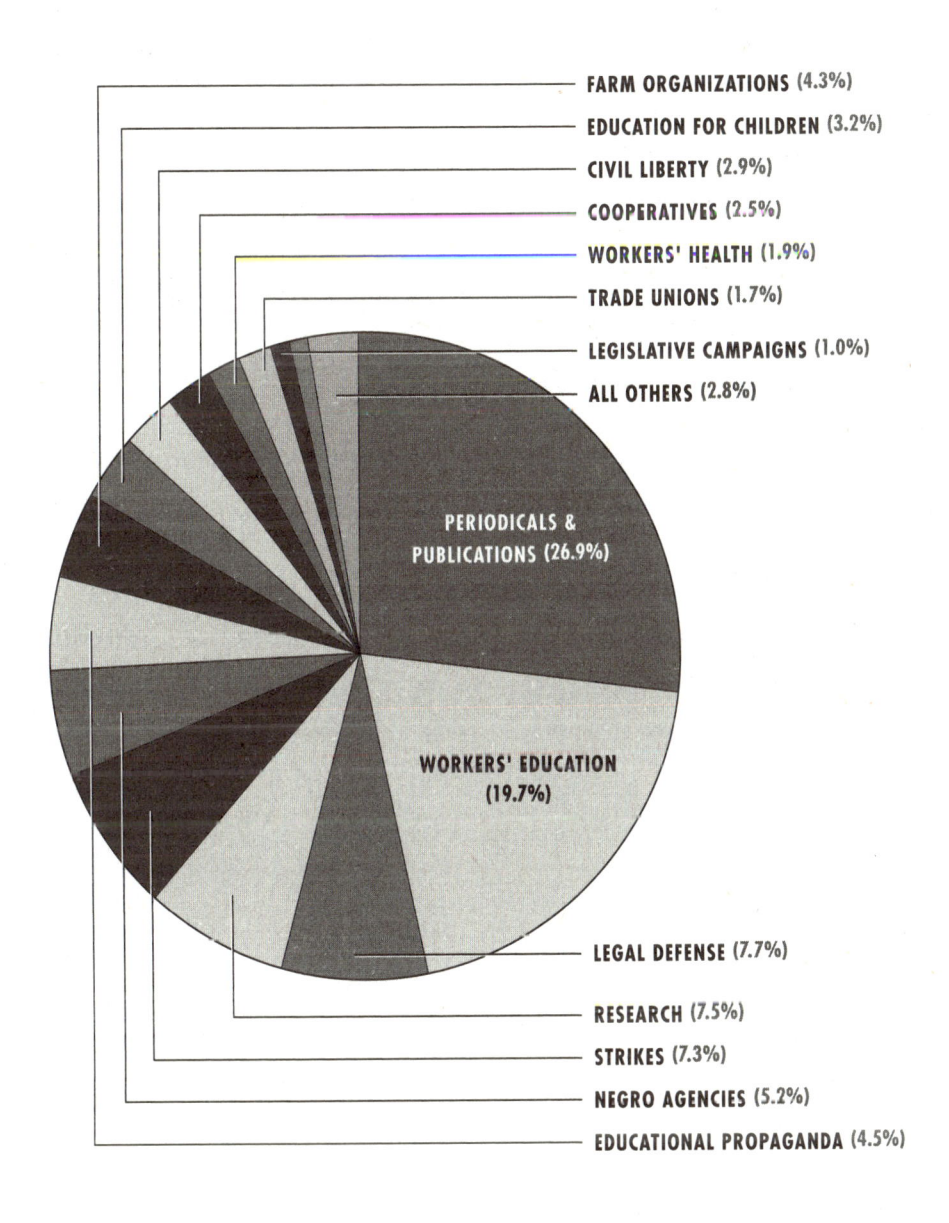

- FARM ORGANIZATIONS (4.3%)
- EDUCATION FOR CHILDREN (3.2%)
- CIVIL LIBERTY (2.9%)
- COOPERATIVES (2.5%)
- WORKERS' HEALTH (1.9%)
- TRADE UNIONS (1.7%)
- LEGISLATIVE CAMPAIGNS (1.0%)
- ALL OTHERS (2.8%)
- PERIODICALS & PUBLICATIONS (26.9%)
- WORKERS' EDUCATION (19.7%)
- LEGAL DEFENSE (7.7%)
- RESEARCH (7.5%)
- STRIKES (7.3%)
- NEGRO AGENCIES (5.2%)
- EDUCATIONAL PROPAGANDA (4.5%)

Appendix C

Board of Directors, 1922–1941

Communist Party members shaded in gray during their period of formal Party membership, secret or otherwise. Empty seats left blank.

Seat	1922	1923	1924	1925	1926	1927	1928
1	Baldwin	Baldwin	Baldwin	Baldwin	Baldwin	Baldwin	Baldwin
2	Foster	Foster	Foster	Foster	Foster		Michelson
3	Gannett	Gannett	Gannett	Gannett	Gannett	Gannett	Gannett
4	Hillman	Hillman	Wolman	Wolman	Broach	Broach	Broach
5	Johnson	Johnson	Johnson	Johnson	Johnson	Johnson	Johnson
6	Lovett	Lovett	Lovett	Lovett	Lovett	Dunn	Dunn
7	McDowell	McDowell	Flynn	Flynn	Flynn	Flynn	Flynn
8	Magnes	Magnes	Kirchwey	Kirchwey	Kirchwey	Kirchwey	Kirchwey
9	Nearing	Nearing	Nearing	Nearing	Nearing	Nearing	Nearing
10	Thomas	Thomas	Thomas	Thomas	Thomas	Thomas	Thomas
11	Ward	Ward	Golden	Golden	Golden	Golden	Golden
12					Ernst	Ernst	Ernst
13					Gitlow	Gitlow	Gitlow
Total	11	11	11	11	13	12	13

APPENDIX C: BOARD OF DIRECTORS, 1922–1941

Seat	1929	1930	1931	1932	1933	1934	1935
1	Baldwin	Baldwin	Baldwin	Baldwin	Baldwin	Baldwin	Baldwin
2	Michelson	Michelson	Michelson	Michelson	Michelson	Michelson	Michelson
3	Gannett	Gannett	Gannett	Gannett	Gannett	Gannett	Gannett
4							
5	Johnson	Johnson	Johnson	Johnson	Johnson	Johnson	Johnson
6	Dunn	Dunn	Dunn	Dunn	Dunn	Dunn	Dunn
7	Flynn						
8	Kirchwey	Kirchwey	Kirchwey	Kirchwey	Kirchwey	Kirchwey	Kirchwey
9	Nearing	Nearing					
10	Thomas	Thomas	Thomas	Thomas	Thomas	Thomas	Thomas
11	Golden	Golden	Golden	Golden	Golden	Golden	
12	Ernst	Ernst	Ernst	Ernst	Ernst	Ernst	Ernst
13	Gitlow	Gitlow	Gitlow	Gitlow	Gitlow	Gitlow	Gitlow
Total	12	11	10	10	10	10	9

Seat	1936	1937	1938	1939	1940
1	Baldwin	Baldwin	Baldwin	Baldwin	Baldwin
2	Michelson	Michelson	Michelson	Michelson	Michelson
3	Gannett	Gannett	Gannett	Gannett	Gannett
4					
5	Johnson	Johnson	Johnson		
6	Dunn	Dunn	Dunn	Dunn	Dunn
7					
8	Kirchwey	Kirchwey	Kirchwey	Kirchwey	Kirchwey
9					
10	Thomas	Thomas	Thomas	Thomas	Thomas
11					
12	Ernst	Ernst	Ernst	Ernst	Ernst
13	Gitlow	Gitlow	Gitlow	Gitlow	Gitlow
Total	9	9	9	8	8

Appendix D

Note on Language

In the text of this book, the American Fund for Public Service appears, as it did in the 1920s, alternately as the American Fund and the Garland Fund, and sometimes simply as the Fund. I quote writers and speakers using the terms they employed, including on several occasions the n-word, in order to convey truths from the past, including ugly ones, to readers in the present. It mattered to me that in as many instances as not, racial epithets as quoted here were deployed by champions of Black civil rights. When referring in my own language to racial and other demographic categories, I usually adopt conventions from the early twenty-first century in order to communicate with readers today. I capitalize the term "Black" when referring to historical people who identified with their African ancestry, largely out of respect for the book's James Weldon Johnson, who advocated more than a century ago for capitalization of the then-standard term "Negro." The Communist Party (or "the Party") is capitalized, but "communism" and "communist" as ideas and ideologies are not. In quoting historical actors or others referring to racial, demographic, or political categories, I try to replicate the capitalization practices they adopted.

Acknowledgments

When a book takes thirteen years and dozens of archives to complete, the debts accumulate and the interest compounds. Archivists and librarians are the hidden angel donors of history books, this one more than most. The New York Public Library, which holds the records of the American Fund for Public Service, decided more than ninety years ago to care for (and later to microfilm) the Fund's papers. Its commitment to the preservation and dissemination of knowledge makes research into the Fund's world possible. The intrepid Reuther Library at Wayne State in Detroit, whose deeply knowledgeable curators are an inspiration, maintains substantial collections relating to the Fund, as does the elegant Ransom Center at the University of Texas, where the Morris Ernst Papers offer unexpected treasures. The story of the Fund came together for me by connecting these principal repositories with materials spread among libraries around the United States, in particular the Beinecke Library at Yale, the Center for Oral History at Columbia's Butler Library, the Hoover Institution at Stanford, the Houghton Library at Harvard, the Library of Congress, the Moorland-Spingarn Center at Howard University, the National Archives, Princeton's Mudd Manuscript Library, the Schomburg Center in Harlem, the Sophia Smith Collection at Smith College, and the Tamiment Library at NYU, all of which host indispensable materials on the Fund and its people. The archives list in the endnotes offers a fuller accounting of the unexpected off-line spaces where traces of the Fund can be found. Thanks and respect to the archivists at all these institutions, who do the vital work of preserving our knowledge of the past. Special thanks also to the Mason Public Library in Great Barrington and the Scoville Memorial Library in Salisbury, Connecticut, whose reading rooms made for summer writing hideaways.

In New Haven, the Yale Law School's Lillian Goldman Library embodies the ideal of exquisite professionalism. I'm especially grateful to John Nann, who has been responding ably to reference questions for this project for as long as it has been around, as well as to Drew Adan, Julian Aiken, Alison Burke, Femi Cadmus, Kathryn James, Lora Johns, Maryellen Larkin, Fred Shapiro, Michael VanderHeijden, and the rest of the Goldman Library crew. Thanks, too, to Alieta-Marie Lynch, who dedicated her verve and intelligence to assisting with the book, not least with the table of gifts in Appendix A.

Over the years, an extended team of student research assistants joined me in digging into obscure corners as we searched for lost documents and hidden stories. Their energy buoyed my spirits and assured me that there was something worth saying in what we found. Many thanks to Dani Abada, Jessie Agatstein, Keerthana Annamaneni, Kossi Anyinefa, Ella Attell, Michael Avi-Yonah, Lina Bae, Rachel Baker, William Baldwin, Liz Beling, Kyle Bigley, Rachel Blatt, Sebastian Brady, Jordan Brewington, Zach Brown, Catherine Chen, Lauren Cho, Lulu Chua-Rubenfeld, Jordan Laris Cohen, Michael Cotter, Jordan Cozby, Josh Czaczkes, Charles Du, Claire Elliman, Berit Fitzsimmons, Jessie Garland, Joseph Goode, Larissa Jiminez Gratereaux, Owen Hathaway Hacker, Solange Hilfinger-Pardo, Ryan Howzell, Mason Hunter, Meenu Krishnan, Hilary Ledwell, Diana Lee, Aaron Levine, Gigi Liman, Ann Manov, Kiki Manzur, Michael Masciandaro, Joe Masterman, Marcella Michalek, Gillian Monsky, Abigail Moore, Michael Morse, Ako Ndefo-Haven, Kelly O'Reilly, Valerie Pavilonis, Jevon Potts, Zoe Rubin, Katharina Schmidt, Greg Schwartz, Abbey Shumsky, Emma Sokoloff-Rubin, Brandon Thompson, Spencer Todd, Tavi Unger, Ethan Wong, Victor Yu, Constance Zhang, and Ruth Zheng.

Two Yale Law School deans, first Robert Post and then Heather Gerken, offered unstinting support for the research that made this book possible. And after more than a decade of research and writing, it sometimes seems that nearly all my colleagues in the Law School and many in Yale's History Department have read and responded to one or another parts of the book. Special gratitude for beyond-the-call engagement to Akhil Amar, Jack Balkin, Laurie Benton, David Blight, Justin Driver, James Forman Jr., Glenda Gilmore, Amy Kapczynski, Jennifer Klein, John Langbein, Daniel Markovits, Sam Moyn, Mark Peterson, Robert Post, Claire Priest, Judith Resnik, Jed Rubenfeld, Paul Sabin, Reva Siegel, Jim Whitman, Gideon Yaffe, and Taisu Zhang.

ACKNOWLEDGMENTS

The University of Chicago Law School invited me to deliver its Fulton Lecture in 2016, back when the story's outlines had barely come into view. Since then, panels, talks, and workshops helped me work out various aspects of the story. Many thanks to the American Bar Foundation, the American Society for Legal History, Butler University, Carnegie Mellon University, Columbia Law School, Davenport College at Yale, Fordham Law School, Harvard Law School, Hiram College, the Knight Institute at Columbia, Lafayette College, New York University, Northwestern Law School, the Stanford Philanthropy and Civil Society Faculty Forum, the University of Albany, the University of Colorado, the University of Southern California, and Yale Law School, among others. I learned new things about the project at each and every session.

Colleagues, friends, and family around the country read parts of the book and pushed me to make it the best it could be. Among them are Maggie Blackhawk, Curtis Bradley, Tomiko Brown-Nagin, Blake Emerson, Eric Foner, Maeve Glass, Annette Gordon-Reed, Ariela Gross, Dan Hulsebosch, Daniel Judt, Laura Kalman, Jeremy Kessler, Michael Klarman, Alison LaCroix, Sam Lebovic, Jon Levy, Rebecca Lossin, Ken Mack, Christian McMillen, Maria Montoya, Bill Nelson, Farah Peterson, Kate Redburn, Rob Reich, Noah Rosenblum, Jeff Symonds, Mark Tushnet, Alex Zhang, and Susee Witt. Getting to learn from, argue with, and write alongside the generous and brilliant Megan Francis at the University of Washington has been one of the best parts of writing this book. Risa Goluboff has been teaching me about the world of the Fund in one way or another since the fall of 1995. Laura Weinrib talked through the project at a low moment in what sometimes seemed an overwhelming undertaking. (Thank you, Megan, Risa, and Laura!) The participants at a Columbia Law School conference on nonprofit law led by David Pozen and David Schizer helped me see the taxation story more clearly, as did helpful reads from nonprofit tax gurus Charles Dowling, Brian Galle, Lauren Libby, and Justin Zaremby. Elliot and Frani Gerson always asked about my latest research finds while I recharged my batteries during fishing retreats.

I am forever indebted to the knowledgeable, tough, and collaborative group of scholars who gathered in Atlanta to discuss the book at Georgia State University for Tim Lytton's manuscript conference in the spring of 2024. Eric Arnesen, Mia Bay, Joe Crespino, Mary Dudziak, Dan Ernst, Willy Forbath, Megan Francis, Martha Jones, Michael Kazin, Anthony

Michael Kreis, Nelson Lichtenstein, Paul Lombardo, Bill Novak, Pat Sullivan, John Thielman, Sasha Volokh, Jason Morgan Ward, and Laura Weinrib made up an all-star cast of readers and critics. Tim's conferences are legendary for a reason.

Near the start of my work, I had the good fortune to meet the late journalist Richard W. Cowen and his lovely family, including his gracious wife Constance. Inspired by Charles Garland's second April Farm commune, which was based not far from the Cowen family home in Allentown, Pennsylvania, Dick spent years researching Garland's life. As he and Connie downsized to an apartment, he handed over to me newspaper clippings, archival findings, and correspondence, all organized into dozens of binders. Many of the things Dick had in storage, including interviews with people who had since passed away, would have been impossible to replicate. His materials, which are cited in this book as the Richard Cowen Collection (RCC), are now held at Yale Law School's library.

I was lucky, too, to be able to sit with the Honorable José Cabranes, the late Norman Dorsen, and the indomitable Aryeh Neier to talk about their recollections of working with the astonishing and sometimes infuriating Roger Baldwin. Tim Rogan shared correspondence between Baldwin and journalist Dwight Macdonald. Josh Klein collected documents at the National Archives on the federal government's surveillance of Baldwin during World War One. John Henry Schlegel unearthed a Walter Nelles letter for the Fund about labor injunctions. Samantha Barbas and Joel Silverman shared insights and sources on Morris Ernst. Alejandro Lujan, the archivist at the Office of the Command Historian in the U.S. Army Special Operations Command, helped me trace Walter Lippmann's wartime propaganda work. At the last minute, after a serendipitous correspondence, Mike Gannett supplied the unpublished autobiography of his grandfather Lewis, who served on the Fund's board for its entire nineteen-year existence.

Virtually every one of the many images in the book was corralled by the indefatigable Andrina Tran, who directed a full scale campaign for permissions and high-resolution images that I couldn't possibly have managed on my own. Andrina and I were lucky that many people selflessly chipped in time and effort to give permissions and check their attics for old photographs, among them Eric Arnesen, Adrienne Berard, Stephanie Begen, Katherine Degn at Kraushaar Galleries, Juliette Hamilton, Karen

Cohen Holmes, Ellen Iseman of the Century Association, Jill Rosenberg Jones of the James Weldon Johnson Foundation, Tai Jones, Tony Pecinovsky at International Publishers, James B. Rogers, Constancia Dinky Romilly, Shaun Slifer at the Mine Wars Museum, and Adam Van Doren. At the Reuther Library, Kristen Chinery, Dan Golodner, Mary Wallace, and their colleagues were unsparingly generous with their time. Frederick Courtright arranged quotation permissions.

A special note of gratitude also to the lunch spots that sustained me during long days buried among archival boxes, notably 320 Coffee & Creamery in Detroit, Medici Roasting in Austin, the inimitable Sylvia's near the Schomburg in Harlem, and my much-loved Yorkside across from Sterling Library in New Haven.

At Simon & Schuster, my experience has been blessed by editorial wisdom and touched with some sadness. Writers today sometimes complain that great editors no longer exist. I had four. The late Alice Mayhew helped create the project. Her enthusiasm, sympathy, and instincts for big ideas and good stories shaped the book's DNA. Our regular lunches at Michael's in Midtown were a wonder. I was heartbroken that Alice passed before I managed to bring the book together, though I suspect she saw where the story was headed before I did. I'd like to think she would be proud of what we managed to accomplish. Bob Bender, who took over the project, was the first person to read the book as a whole. His good judgment influenced the manuscript's architecture, while his kind but firm encouragement kept me at the keyboard. Bob's retirement introduced me to Robert Messenger, whose deep knowledge of the world of New York intellectuals (left and right alike) was serendipitous good fortune for the manuscript. I treasured talking about old City College and its dueling subcultures, and Robert edited the entire manuscript with a shrewd sense for flow and staging. When Robert stepped back from publishing, I worried that at last my luck had run out. Megan Hogan, who carried the text to the finish line, has been a revelation, bringing an exquisite eye for prose as well as smarts about what the manuscript still needed. Working with her has been a joy. Johanna Li and Jennie Miller coordinated important publishing details and left me with a reassuring sense that things were well in hand. Lisa Healy managed the book's production with aplomb.

At the Wylie Agency, Andrew Wylie saw promise in Garland's curious story from the start. He and Jacqueline Ko have offered the consummate professionalism and zealous representation for which they are renowned.

Supporters closest to home propelled the book forward. My parents raised me in a community with a stray connection to the Garland Fund, though we didn't know it at the time. I'll always be grateful to have grown up in Philadelphia's Germantown, where people of many races, class backgrounds, and faiths modeled being rich in love, not money, even if the industrial structure of the New Deal was giving way around us. My extended family provided indispensable support; I can't wait to see all of you again On the Way to Cape May. My stepson Nick has shared good cheer, a big heart, and writerly chops of his own. Annie Paul gracefully co-parented two amazing boys. Gus and Teddy, you're the best. More than a decade ago, when I wrote a book about war and dedicated it to you, I said the next big one would be about peace. Well, boys, this is it. Also, I'm winning fantasy baseball next year.

Beverly Gage has held me together through thick and thin. These pages could not have been written without her love. She rooted for the project, and she knows the spot in Grove Street where she saved me from abandoning the book I'd always wanted to write. I dedicate it to her.

Notes

ARCHIVES AND ABBREVIATIONS

ABSP Arthur B. Spingarn Papers, 1850–1968, Library of Congress

ACLUA American Civil Liberties Union Archives, 1912–1950, Princeton University, Microfilm Scholarly Resources, Wilmington, Delaware

ACWA Amalgamated Clothing Workers of America Records, 1914–1980, Cornell University

AFPSR American Fund for Public Service Records, New York Public Library, Microfilm Scholarly Resources, Wilmington, Delaware

AFS-VDC Aldino Felicani Sacco-Vanzetti Collection, 1915–1977, Boston Public Library

AJMP Papers of A. J. Muste, Swarthmore Peace Collection, Swarthmore College

Am1919 American 1919 Race Riots Collection, 1919–1922, Beinecke Rare Books Library, Yale University

APRC A. Philip Randolph Collection, Schomburg Center for Research in Black Culture, New York Public Library

APRP Papers of A. Philip Randolph [microform], introduction by August Meier and John Bracey, 1889–1979, Library of Congress

ASW Anna Strunsky Walling Papers, Sterling Memorial Library, Yale University

AUAM Archives of the American Union Against Militarism, Swarthmore Peace Collection, Swarthmore College

BGP Benjamin Gitlow Papers, 1918–1963, Hoover Institution Archives, Stanford University

BLCR Brookwood Labor College Records, Walter P. Reuther Library, Wayne State University

BLCS Brookwood Labor College: Mark & Helen Norton Starr Collection, Walter P. Reuther Library, Wayne State University

NOTES—ARCHIVES AND ABBREVIATIONS

BSCPR Records of the Brotherhood of Sleeping Car Porters, Chicago Historical Society

CCOH Columbia Center for Oral History, Butler Library, Columbia University

CHHP Charles Hamilton Houston Papers, Moorland-Spingarn Research Center, Howard University

CHHPP Personal Papers, Writings, Documents by and about Charles Houston, Vice Dean of the Howard University School of Law, Moorland-Spingarn Research Center, Howard University

ChLAm The Church League of America Collection of the Research Files of Counterattack, Tamiment Library & Robert F. Wagner Labor Archives, New York University

CGP Clinton S. Golden Papers, Special Collections Library Repository, Penn State University Library

CMP Clarina Michelson Papers, Tamiment Library & Robert F. Wagner Labor Archives, New York University

DCAAA Documents from the Comintern Archives on African Americans, 1919–1929, Comintern Archives, Moscow, Russia, Microfilmed for the Schomburg Center

DKP Dorothy Kenyon Papers, Sophia Smith Collection, Smith College

EGF-B Elizabeth Gurley Flynn: Peter Martin and Roberta Bobba Materials, Tamiment Library, New York University

EGFP-NY Elizabeth Gurley Flynn Papers, 1896–1964, Tamiment Library, New York University

EGFP-W Elizabeth Gurley Flynn Papers, 1917–1923, Wisconsin Historical Society

EGP Emma Goldman Papers, New York Public Library

FBI Select Federal Bureau of Investigation Files

FFPH Felix Frankfurter Papers, Harvard Law School Library

FFPLC Felix Frankfurter Papers, Library of Congress

FKP Papers of Freda Kirchwey, Schlessinger Library, Radcliffe Institute, Harvard University

FRCP Frank R. Crosswaith Papers, Schomburg Center for Research in Black Culture, New York Public Library

FSCP Felix S. Cohen Papers, 1904–1992, Beinecke Library, Yale University

HBP Heber Blankenhorn Papers, 1884–1956, Walter P. Reuther Library, Wayne State University

NOTES—ARCHIVES AND ABBREVIATIONS

HRL Henry Richardson Linville Collection, Walter P. Reuther Library, Wayne State University

HWP Harry Weinberger Papers, 1915–1944, Sterling Library, Yale University

JBPC Papers of John Brophy, Special Collections of the University Libraries at the Catholic University of America

JBPS Jane Burr Papers, Sophia Smith Collecton, Smith College

JCP John Collier Papers, Sterling Library Manuscripts & Archives, Yale University

JPCC John and Phyllis Collier Collection, Walter P. Reuther Library, Wayne State University

JPLP Joseph P. Lash Papers, Franklin D. Roosevelt Library, Hyde Park

JWJP James Weldon Johnson and Grace Nail Johnson Papers, Beinecke Library, Yale University

KPEP Katherine Pollak Ellickson Papers, Walter P. Reuther Library, Wayne State University

LBM Lewis Browne Manuscripts, Lilly Library, Indiana University Bloomington

LGP Lewis Gannett Papers, 1891–1966, Houghton Library, Harvard University

LHWP L. Hollingsworth Wood Papers, 1903–1953, Haverford College

LKCP Lucy Kramer Cohen Papers, Beinecke Library, Yale University

LMAC League for Mutual Aid Collection, Walter P. Reuther Library, Wayne State University

LMCR Lubin Manufacturing Company Records, Rare Book Department, Free Library of Philadelphia

MDP Madeleine Doty Papers, Sophia Smith Collection, Smith College

MECP Merle Eugene Curti Papers, Wisconsin Historical Society

MHVP Mary Heaton Vorse Papers, Walter P. Reuther Library, Wayne State University

MLEP Morris Leopold Ernst Papers, Harry Ransom Center, University of Texas at Austin

MLP Max Lowenthal Papers, Archives and Special Collections, Elmer L. Anderson Library, University of Minnesota

MSC Modern School Collection, 1880–1982, Special Collections and University Archives, Rutgers University

NAACPP National Association for the Advancement of Colored People Records, Library of Congress, Proquest edition

NAACPLC National Association for the Advancement of Colored People Records, 1842–1999, Library of Congress

NLCR Negro Labor Committee Records, Schomburg Center for Research in Black Culture, New York Public Library

OSC Ossian Sweet Collection, Detroit Public Library

RAC Rockefeller Archive Center, Office of the Messrs. Rockefeller, Sleepy Hollow, NY

RBM-NARA Records of the Board of Mediation, Record Group 13, National Archives & Records Administration

RBMP Richard B. Moore Papers, Schomburg Center for Research in Black Culture, New York Public Library

RCC Richard Cowen Collection, Yale Law School

RCP Richard Cowen Papers, Walter P. Reuther Library, Wayne State University

RNBI Investigation of Roger Baldwin: Collected WWI Documents, National Archives & Records Administration

RNBP Papers of Roger Nash Baldwin (1885–1981), Seeley G. Mudd Manuscript Library, Princeton University

RNBPL Peggy Lamson Collection on Roger Baldwin, Mudd Manuscript Library, Princeton University

RPP Roscoe Pound Papers, Harvard Law School Library

RPSNH Rose Pastor Stokes Papers, 1879–1933, Sterling Memorial Library, Yale University

RPSNY Rose Pastor Stokes Papers, Tamiment Library & Robert F. Wagner Archive, New York University

RRC Roy Reuther Collection: Papers, 1924–1971, Walter P. Reuther Library, Wayne State University

RWDC Robert W. Dunn Collection, Walter P. Reuther Library, Wayne State University

SCVP Evelyn Shrifte Collection Relating to Vanguard Press, Special Collections Research Center, Syracuse University

STFUR Southern Tenant Farmers Union Records, 1934–1991, Southern Historical Collection, Wilson Library, University of North Carolina at Chapel Hill

NOTES TO PAGES 1-2   583

STLSSE St. Louis School of Social Economy, University Archives, Washington University in St. Louis

UMW2 United Mine Workers of America, District #2 Papers, 1927–1950, IUP Special Collections and University Archives, Indiana University of Pennsylvania

VPR Vanguard Press records, ca. 1925–ca. 1985, Rare Book & Manuscript Library, Columbia University

VRP Victor G. Reuther Papers, Walter P. Reuther Library, Wayne State University

WEBDBP W. E. B. Du Bois Papers, University of Massachusetts Special Collections and University Archives

PROLOGUE: A CURIOUS INHERITANCE

1. *tall, with dark hair*: "On Refusing a Million," *New York Times*, Nov. 28, 1920, 2. *deplored the postwar mob violence*: Charles Garland to Nicola, Dec. 18, 1919, RCC. *New Testament*: "Following Christ Garland Rejects Million Dollars," *Atlanta Constitution*, Nov. 30, 1920. *Tolstoy*: Roger Nash Baldwin interview with Richard Cowen [1978?], on file with author. *Russian Revolution*: "Millions Rejected by Garlands Is to Be Kept for Their Heirs," *Boston Globe*, Dec. 2, 1920, 14. *H. G. Wells*: "Man Who Won't Accept Inheritance of $1,000,000," *St. Louis Post-Dispatch*, Nov. 28, 1920, 5; see also Gloria Garrett Samson, *The American Fund for Public Service: Charles Garland and Radical Philanthropy, 1922–1941* (Greenwood Press, 1996) at 1; Lewis Browne, "Garland May Be Saint, Says Rabbi," *Washington Times*, May 2, 1923, 12; Lewis Browne, "Charles Garland's Experiment," typescript [1923], LBM.
2. *"system which starves"*: "Renounces Rights to Million-Dollar Gift," *Indianapolis News*, Nov. 30, 1920, 3; "Garland's Sons Turn Down Million Each," *Boston Daily Globe*, Nov. 23, 1920, 1; "On Refusing a Million: What Charles Garland Is Like and His Reasons for Rejecting a Fortune," *New York Times*, Nov. 28, 1920, 91; Samson, *American Fund*, 1.
3. *perplexed*: "Millions Rejected by Garlands," *Boston Daily Globe*; "Garland Fortune Will Be Continued in Trusteeship," *Arizona Republican*, Dec. 2, 1920, 2. *up and down the East Coast and as far away*: E.g., "Unusual Man in Limelight," *Los Angeles Times*, Dec. 7, 1920, 12; "Crazy? No, Just Dippy," *Los Angeles Times*, June 20, 1921, 11; "Giving Up Inheritance Due to Study of Tolstoi," *Baltimore Sun*, Nov. 24, 1920, 7; "Spurns Million for Hard Work 'as a Christian,'" *Chicago Tribune*, Nov. 23, 1920, 5; "Massachusetts Man Refuses Right to Million Dollar Legacy," *Arizona Republican*, Nov. 30, 1920, 1. *Jesus*: Margarite Marshall, "Garland Is Follower of Christ," *New York World*, Nov. 27, 1920, 1. *"honest toil"*: "Garland's Sons Turn Down Million Each," *Boston Daily Globe*. *jovial janitor*: "Sets Example for Garland; Janitor Will Accept Fortune, Work, Smoke Good Cigars and Have Auto," *New York Times*, Dec. 4, 1920, W-20. *comedian*: Richard Cowen, Garland Book, 73, RCC. *Bolsheviks*: Edward S. Martin, "Editor's Easy Chair," *Harper's Monthly Magazine*, Feb. 1921, 397–99. *sex and marriage*: Harold R. Hall, "Garland Would Drop Soul-Twin for New Love," *Boston Herald-American*, Jan. 24, 1922, 1; "Love for Love's Sake," *New York Tribune*, Jan. 24, 1922. *debutante wife*: "On Refusing a Million," *New York Times*; "Mrs. Charles Garland Willing to Be a Poor Man's Wife," *Baltimore Sun*, Nov. 25, 1920, 1. *Gossip columnists*: "Heir to a Million Gives Up $800,000," *New York Times*, July 24, 1922. *"depressing news"*: "'Depressing News,' Remarks H. G. Wells," *Boston Daily Globe*, Nov. 28, 1920, 13. Charles's younger brother, Hamilton, initially committed to following Charles's lead, but when Hamilton's birthday entitled him to his inheritance, he quietly accepted it. "Garland Brothers to Accept Millions," *Boston Daily Globe*, Jan. 10, 1922, 8.
4. *Upton Sinclair*: Upton Sinclair to CG, Dec. 2, 1920; Dec. 29, 1920; Jan. 8, 1921; Jan. 15, 1921; Upton Sinclair to Mrs. CG, Dec. 29, 1920, all in b. 5, JPCC; "Crank No. 1426," *Los Angeles*

Times, Jan. 29, 1921, 1–14. ***Sinclair recommended***: Upton Sinclair to CG, Jan. 10, 1922, b. 9, f. 13, RNBP. ***met on the Cape***: RNB, "A Memo on Charles Garland," Feb. 1975, b. 25, f. 1, RNBP. ***"promote the wellbeing"***: Delaware Certificate of Incorporation, Board of Directors Minutes, b. 5, r. 3, AFPSR.

5. ***"philosophical anarchist"***: Lucille Milner, *Education of an American Liberal* (Horizon Press, 1954), 51. ***"gamble"***: "How They'll Spend Fortune That Garland Spurned," n.d., r. 3, b. 5, AFPSR. ***"not reformers... law of percentages"***: RNB, Inserts [n.d., 1922?], Public Relations, 1922–1941, r. 3, b. 5, AFPSR.

6. ***"only result"***: "Mr. Garland and His Money," *New York Tribune*, July 31, 1922, b. I-C-196, f. 1, NAACPLC. ***nearly $2 million***: Report of the American Fund for Public Service, Inc. ... Summary of Nineteen Years, 1922–1941 (New York City, June 30, 1941). ***Rockefellers alone***: "The Spirit of Service," *Los Angeles Times*, Dec. 20, 1924, A4.

7. ***"golden transmission"***: Benjamin Stolberg, "Muddled Millions: Capitalist Angels of Left Wing Propaganda," *Saturday Evening Post*, Feb. 15, 1941, 9. ***"Red Revolutionary"***: Elizabeth Dilling, *The Red Network: A Who's Who and Handbook of Radicalism for Patriots* (self-published, 1934), 163. ***criminal enterprise***: "No Line of Merit in Garland Fund," *New York World*, July 29, 1922. ***"Free Love Fund"***: Dilling, *Red Network*, 163. ***"revolutionary"***: R. B. Spencer to William J. Burns, June 5, 1923 ("refer to Mr. Hoover"), FOIPA No. 1253953-001. ***J. Edgar Hoover ... "revolutionary"***: Department of Justice Journal Memorandum, American Fund for Public Service, Inc., Alleged Financing of Revolutionary Movements, DOJ 61-2149, Apr. 21, 1923, FOIPA Request No. 1222087-000, Mar. 20, 2014. ***"red network"***: Dilling, *Red Network*, 163; Martin Dies, *The Trojan Horse in America* (Dodd, Mead, 1940), 255; Special House Committee on Un-American Activities, *Investigation of Un-American Propaganda Activities in the U.S.* (Government Printing Office, 1938), 1.388–89, 527–28, 574; U.S. House of Representatives Special Committee on Un-American Activities, *Investigation of Un-American Propaganda Activities in the United States: Hearings Before a Special Committee on Un-American Activities* (Government Printing Office, 1939), 10.5990–991; House Un-American Activities Committee, *Hearings Before the Committee on Un-American Activities House of Representatives, Eighty-Second Congress, First Session, February 28 & March 9, 1951* (Government Printing Office, 1951), at 1883, 1891–1901; see also Special Committee to Investigate Communist Activities in the United States, *Hearings Pursuant to H. Res. 200 Providing for an Investigation of Communist Propaganda in the United States*, 71st Cong., 2nd Sess. (Government Printing Office, 1930) (Hamilton Fish Jr., chairman), *passim*. ***"parlor pinks"***: Press Release, American Federation of Labor (AFL), Apr. 13, 1923, reel 5, AFPSR.

8. ***"mixture of forces"***: ME to RNB, June 28, 1926, and Scott Nearing to RNB, May 28 [1926], 162.2, MEP; RNB, *The Reminiscences of Roger Baldwin, 1953–1954*, at 326 ("we were a mixed group ... to box the left compass"), CCOH.

9. ***During a decade***: Kevin Boyle, *Arc of Justice: A Saga of Race, Civil Rights, and Murder in the Jazz Age* (Henry Holt, 2004); Ann Douglas, *Terrible Honesty: Mongrel Manhattan in the 1920s* (Farrar, Straus & Giroux, 1995); Donald L. Miller, *Supreme City: How Jazz Age Manhattan Gave Birth to Modern America* (Simon & Schuster, 2014). ***"Mr. Garland's Million"***: "Radicals: Mr. Garland's Million," *Time*, June 30, 1941, 19. ***democratic conception of free speech***: Laura Weinrib, *The Taming of Free Speech: America's Civil Liberties Compromise* (Harvard University Press, 2016); Adam Hochschild, *American Midnight: The Great War, a Violent Peace, and Democracy's Forgotten Crisis* (Mariner Books, 2022); David Rabban, *Free Speech in Its Forgotten Years* (Cambridge University Press, 1997); Mark A. Graber, *Transforming Free Speech: The Ambiguous Legacy of Civil Libertarianism* (University of California Press, 1991); Louis Menand, *The Metaphysical Club: A Story of Ideas in America* (Farrar, Straus & Giroux, 2001). ***new generation of progressive labor unions***: Robert H. Zieger, *The CIO, 1935–1955* (University of North Carolina Press, 1995).

10. ***landmark decisions***: Brown v. Board of Education, 347 U.S. 483 (1954); Steele v. Louisville & Nashville Railroad, 323 U.S. 192 (1944). For the growing if still recessive literature on *Steele*, see Reuel Schiller, *Forging Rivals: Class, Law, and the Collapse of Postwar Liberalism* (Cambridge

University Press, 2015); Sophia Lee, *The Workplace Constitution from the New Deal to the New Right* (Cambridge University Press, 2014); Risa L. Goluboff, *The Lost Promise of Civil Rights* (Harvard University Press, 2007); David E. Bernstein, *Only One Place of Redress: African Americans, Labor Regulaions, and the Courts from Reconstruction to the New Deal* (Duke University Press, 2001); Deborah Malamud, "The Story of *Steele v. Louisville & Nashville Railroad*: White Unions, Black Unions, and the Struggle for Racial Justice on the Rails," in Lauren J. Cooper and Catherine L. Fisk, eds., *Labor Law Stories* (Foundation Press, 2005), 57–105; Risa Lauren Goluboff, "'Let Economic Equality Take Care of Itself': The NAACP, Labor Litigation, and the Making of Civil Rights in the 1940s," *UCLA Law Review* 52 (2005): 1393.

11. **elected Harding**: Robert C. Post, *The Taft Court: Making Law for a Divided Nation, 1921–1930* (Cambridge University Press, 2024), at 1:xxvi. **world-historic riches**: Ron Chernow, *Titan: The Life of John D. Rockefeller, Sr.* (Random House, 1998); Tom Metcalf, "Rockefeller Was Almost Three Times Richer Than Bezos," *Bloomberg Business Week*, May 21, 2019. **84 percent of the nation's wealth**: Emmanuel Saez and Gabriel Zucman, "Wealth Inequality in the United States Since 1913: Evidence from Capitalized Income Tax Data," *Quarterly Journal of Economics* 131/2 (May 2016): 519, 552. As I write this, the top 10 percent of Americans own around two-thirds of the nation's total wealth.

12. **few gains**: Frank Stricker, "Affluence for Whom?—Another Look at Prosperity and the Working Classes in the 1920s," *Labor History* 24 (1983): 5–33; Irving Bernstein, *The Lean Years: A History of the American Worker, 1920–33* (Houghton Mifflin, 1960), at 9, 128–30. **union membership**: Leo Wolman, "War Prosperity and Its Aftermath," in *Ebb and Flow in Trade Unionism*, ed. Wolman (NBER, 1936); Leo Troy, "Trade Union Membership, 1897–1962," *Review of Economics and Statistics* 47 (1965): 93–113. **scientific management**: David Montgomery, *The Fall of the House of Labor: The Workplace, the State, and American Labor Activism, 1865–1925* (Cambridge University Press, 1987), at 218–54. **lynch mobs**: Kidada Williams, "Regarding the Aftermath of Lynchings," *Journal of American History* 101 (2014): 856; Michael J. Pfeifer, "At the Hands of Parties Unknown? The State of the Field of Lynching Scholarship," *Journal of American History* 101 (2014): 832. **violence in the American West**: Beth Lew Williams, *The Chinese Must Go: Violence, Exclusion, and the Making of the Alien in America* (Harvard University Press, 2018). **disinformation and propaganda**: Megan Ming Francis, "The Battle for the Hearts and Minds of America," *Souls* 13 (2011): 46–71; Christopher Cappozola, *Uncle Sam Wants You: World War I and the Making of the Modern American Citizen* (Oxford University Press, 2008). **capacity of voters**: Walter Lippmann, *Public Opinion* (Macmillan, 1922).

13. **"safe for intolerance"**: RNB, Written for the *Yale Daily News*, n.d. [1927?], Series 3, Writings and Speeches, r. 22, RNBP.

14. **alchemists**: Elmer Peterson to AFPS, 1925, r. 32, AFPSR. **patent medicines**: Jeannette B. Trader to AFPS, 1929, r. 36, AFPSR. **tooth powders**: C. R. Holt to AFPS, 1926, r. 30, AFPSR. **"tired of Great Causes"**: F. Scott Fitzgerald, *The Jazz Age*, ed. E. L. Doctorow (New Directions, 1996) (1931), 5. **historians wondered**: Arthur S. Link, "What Happened to the Progressive Movement in the 1920s?," *American Historical Review* 64 (1959): 833–51; Daniel T. Rodgers, "In Search of Progressivism," *Reviews in American History* 10 (1982): 113–32. **"bonds of old institutions"**: RNB to Charles Garland, Apr. 12, 1922, r. 1, AFPSR; Samson, *American Fund*, 20. "This beats them all," said director Morris Ernst about the tooth powder application. Morris Ernst to EGF, Apr. 5, 1926, r. 30, AFPSR.

15. **accountants**: Auditor's Reports, r. 5, AFPSR. **tax code**: See chapter 11, below.

16. For critiques of the Fund and its world, see Weinrib, *The Taming of Free Speech*; Goluboff, *The Lost Promise of Civil Rights*; Derrick Bell, *Silent Covenants: Brown v. Board and the Unfulfilled Hopes for Racial Reform* (Oxford University Press, 2005); Megan Ming Francis, "The Price of Civil Rights: Black Lives, White Funding, and Movement Capture," *Law & Society Review* 53 (2019): 275; Christopher L. Tomlins, *The State and the Unions: Labor Relations, Law, and the Organized Labor Movement in America, 1880–1960* (Cambridge University Press, 1985). Unsparing accounts of the Fund include Samson, *American Fund*; Samantha Barbas, *The Rise and Fall of Morris Ernst, Free Speech Renegade* (University of Chicago Press, 2021); Francis, "Price

of Civil Rights"; and Richard Magat, *Unlikely Partners: Philanthropic Foundations and the Labor Movement* (Cornell University Press, 1998), 19-20. For an older, more affirmative assessment, see Merle Curti, "Subsidizing Radicalism: The American Fund for Public Service, 1921-41," *Social Service Review* 33 (1959): 274. In recent years, Megan Francis's powerful critique has bid to become the most influential account of the Garland Fund. Francis contends that the mostly white philanthropists of the Fund diverted the NAACP from its early anti-lynching mission toward an education effort that marginalized concern for Black lives. As we will see, the Francis critique, which aptly describes the effects of white philanthropists' aid to Black education in the period, overlooks the NAACP's astonishing 1920s success (with Fund support) in reducing the number of lynchings, understates James Weldon Johnson's substantial control over the Fund's grant making to Black organizations, and omits the brilliant interventions of A. Philip Randolph on the Fund's programming (see chapter 14). The evidence in what follows shows that the Fund nudged the NAACP toward a new working-class radicalism, while meanwhile the NAACP subtly co-opted the Fund for its own ends. For a fuller explanation, see my exchange with Francis in Megan Ming Francis and John Fabian Witt, "Movement Capture or Movement Strategy? A Critical Race History Exchange on the Beginnings of *Brown v. Board*," *Yale Journal of Law & the Humanities* 31 (2021): 520.

1: DEMOCRATIC FAITH

"my democratic thinking": RNB, *The Reminiscences of Roger Baldwin, 1953-1954* (1963), at 40, CCOH.
1 **born**: RNB, "Autobiography (1884-1920)," b. 20, f. 11, 30, RNBP. *"inescapable"*: Peggy Lamson, *Roger Baldwin: Founder of the American Civil Liberties Union* (Houghton Mifflin, 1976), 1. **Cushings**: Robert L. Duffus, "The Legend of Roger Baldwin," *American Mercury* 5 (1925): 408.
2. **Gold Coast . . . *"swanky dances"***: Robert C. Cottrell, *Roger Nash Baldwin and the American Civil Liberties Union* (Columbia University Press, 2000), 14-15; see also Emma Goldman, *Living My Life*, vol. 1 (Alfred A. Knopf, 1931), 486.
3. **outsized energy**: See Duffus, "Legend of Roger Baldwin," 408. **championed the causes . . . ACLU**: RNBP, "Autobiography (1884-1920)," b. 20, f. 11, RNBP; Lamson, *Roger Baldwin and the American Civil Liberties Union*, 90, 119. **short book**: RNB, *Liberty Under the Soviets* (Vanguard Press, 1928).
4. **Walden Pond**: RNB, "Autobiography," b. 20, f. 11, 14; Joseph P. Lash, interview with RNB, Oct. 6, 1971, I-C-2, JPLP. **canoes**: RNB to [Charlotte M. Ryman?], [n.d., fall 1912?], b. 14, f. 8, RNBP; Scott R. DeKins to RNB, Nov. 26, 1918, b. 11, f. 15, RNBP; RNB to Mary Bulkley, Sept. 9, [1942-1944?], b. 4, f. 30, RNBP; Marshall W. Cox, "I roomed with him, and I know," [n.d., 1959?], b. 5, f. 30, RNBP; RNB, Note on Eduard Lindeman, [n.d., 1953?], b. 9, f. 26, RNBP. **bird-watching**: RNB to CMR, May 21, 1899, b. 14, f. 7, RNBP; Ruth Baldwin to RNB, Jan. 20, 1925, b. 11, f. 4, RNBP; RNB, "Laurence Rich Gross," 1972, b. 7, f. 5. **domineering father**: Lamson, *Roger Baldwin and the American Civil Liberties Union*, 12.
5. **"Grand Duke" . . . "exuded authority"**: RNB, "Autobiography," b. 20, f. 11, 17, RNBP. **chronic affairs . . . three children**: Cottrell, *Roger Nash Baldwin*, 17-19.
6. **walled himself off**: Lucy Nash Baldwin to RNB, [n.d., 1923], b. 6, f. 1, RNBP; RNB to Mary Bulkley, Aug. 14, [1938?]; RNB to MB, Jan. 7, [1939?], all in b. 4, f. 30, RNBP. **child of his own**: Cottrell, *Roger Nash Baldwin*, 245. **"best money"**: Joseph P. Lash, interview with Herbert Baldwin, Oct. 26, 1971, JPLP. **penny-pinching**: "Memo for Mrs. Lamson on My Attitude Toward Money," Apr. 1974, b. 25, f. 2, RNBP; Dwight Macdonald, "In Defense of Everybody," *New Yorker*, July 11, 1953, 30. **underdogs**: RNB to Jerome Shestack, 1973, b. 15, f. 3, RNBP.
7. **searing event . . . would cry**: Joseph P. Lash, interview with RNB & Helen Manoni, Jan. 8, 1972, and with Helen Manoni, Oct. 31, 1971, b. 49, JPLP.
8. **"My parents"**: RNB, "The Roger Baldwin Story: A Prejudiced Account by Himself," 1979, 24, f. 10, RNBP, also in Woody Klein, ed., *Liberties Lost: The Endangered Legacy of the ACLU* (Praeger, 2006).

9. *Channing*: Jack Mendelsohn, *Channing: The Reluctant Radical* (Little, Brown, 1971), 29; Edward Bartlett Rugemer, *The Problem of Emancipation: The Caribbean Roots of the American Civil War* (Louisiana State University Press, 2009), 145–79; William Ellery Channing, *Memoir of William Ellery Channing: With Extracts from His Correspondence and Manuscripts* (W. M. Crosby & H. P. Nichols, 1860), 1:18. *pastor*: See Madeleine Hooke Rice, *Federal Street Pastor: The Life of William Ellery Channing* (Bookman Associates, 1961). *self-styled transcendentalists*: Andrew Delbanco, *William Ellery Channing: An Essay on the Liberal Spirit in America* (Harvard University Press, 1981); Daniel Walker Howe, *The Unitarian Conscience: Harvard Moral Philosophy, 1805–1861* (Wesleyan University Press, 1988), at 54. *secret committee*: John Stauffer, *The Black Hearts of Men: Radical Abolitionists and the Transformation of Race* (Harvard University Press, 2001), 240.
10. *same house*: RNB, "Autobiography," b. 20, f. 11, 7, RNBP. *Long Island Railroad . . . Washington*: Louis Harlan et al., eds., *The Booker T. Washington Papers*, vol. 3 (1972–1984), 528–29 n2.
11. *Washington founded*: Henry Allen Bullock, *A History of Negro Education in the South: From 1619 to the Present* (Harvard University Press, 1967), 79; Adam Fairclough, *A Class of Their Own: Black Teachers in the Segregated South* (Harvard University Press, 2007), 141. *"Atlanta Compromise"*: See Robert J. Norrell, *Up from History: The Life of Booker T. Washington* (Harvard University Press, 2009), 277–79; see also Jennings L. Wagoner Jr., "The American Compromise: Charles W. Eliot, Black Education, and the New South," in *Education and the Rise of the New South*, ed. Ronald K. Goodenow et al. (G. K. Hall, 1981), 26–20. *Tuskegee trustees*: James D. Anderson, *The Education of Blacks in the South, 1860–1935* (University of North Carolina Press, 1988), at 88. *"without strikes"*: Booker T. Washington, "Atlanta Exposition Address," in Jacqueline M. Moore, ed., *Booker T. Washington, W. E. B. Du Bois, and the Struggle for Racial Uplift* (Rowman & Littlefield, 2003), 127. *"separate but equal"*: Plessy v. Ferguson, 163 U.S. 537 (1896).
12. *"almost worship" . . . policies*: Eric Anderson and Alfred A. Moss, *Dangerous Donations: Northern Philanthropy and Southern Black Education* (University of Missouri Press, 1999), 64–65. *defended . . . backlash*: Robert Norrell Jr., "When Teddy Roosevelt Invited Booker T. Washington to Dine at the White House," *Journal of Blacks in Higher Education* 63 (2009): 70; Carl Schurz, "Can the South Solve the Negro Problem," *McClure's*, March 1904, 274. *Todd Lincoln*: Louis R. Harlan and Raymond W. Smock, *The Booker T. Washington Papers* (University of Illinois Press, 1972), 5:420, n1.
13. *"rich deposit"*: John Graham Brooks, *An American Citizen: The Life of William Henry Baldwin, Jr.* (Houghton Mifflin, 1910), 197; Anderson and Moss, *Dangerous Donations*, 72–74. *critics*: James D. Anderson, "Northern Foundations and the Shaping of Southern Black Rural Education, 1902–1935," *History of Education Quarterly* 18 (1978): 371, 376.
14. *met Washington . . . servant*: RNB, Reminiscences, 312–14. *donation*: Cottrell, *Roger Nash Baldwin*, 5. *John Brown*: Dwight Macdonald, "In Defense of Everybody II," *New Yorker*, July 18, 1953, 34.
15. *"worst and dirtiest"*: RNB to CMR, Apr. 18, 1898, b. 14, f. 6, RNBP.
16. *Shaler*: Nathaniel Southgate Shaler, *The Autobiography of Nathaniel Southgate Shaler* (Houghton Mifflin, 1909), 3, 13. *teachers*: RNB to George W. Pierson, Mar. 27, 1909, b. 16, f. 2, RNBP. *Agassiz*: Louis Menand, *The Metaphysical Club* (Farrar, Straus & Giroux, 2001), 101.
17. *most popular classes*: H. Phillip Bacon, "Fireworks in the Classroom: Nathaniel Southgate Shaler as a Teacher," *Journal of Geography* 54 (1955): 349, 350. *"immemorial savagery"*: Nathaniel Southgate Shaler, "The Negro Problem," *Atlantic Monthly*, Nov. 1884, 697. *less intellectual*: Nathaniel Southgate Shaler, *The Neighbor: A Natural History of Human Contacts* (Houghton Mifflin, 1904), 134. *"children"*: Shaler, "The Negro Problem," 698, 703.
18. *September 1906*: RNB, "A Memo on St. Louis," 1965, b. 14, f. 12, RNBP; RNB, "Autobiography," b. 20, f. 11, 12, RNBP. *"people good"*: Ibid., 25. *Brandeis*: Alfred Steinberg, "Sketch on Baldwin," [n.d.]; RNB, "Roger Baldwin Story"; "Memo for a Short Story of My Public Activities," 1960, all in b. 24, f. 6, RNBP. *"democratic experiment"*: RNB, "Memo for Jeff Hornback," Oct. 1964, b. 14, f. 12, RNBP. *"uplift"*: RNB, "Recollections of a Life in Civil Liberties," *Civil Liberties Review* 39 (1975): 41.

19. *city's population* . . . *"squalid and dirty"*: Walter S. Johnson, *The Broken Heart of America: St. Louis and the Violent History of the United States* (Basic Books, 2020), 181–215; James Neal Primm, *Lion of the Valley: St. Louis, Missouri* (Pruett, 1990), 357. *"begging girls"*: Robert H. Lauer and Jeanette C. Lauer, "Will a Private War on Poverty Succeed? The Case of the St. Louis Provident Association," *Journal of Sociology & Social Welfare* 10 (1983): 12, 19. *crowded with fights*: Lamson, *Roger Baldwin*, 30.
20. *"Whiskey Ring"*: Primm, *Lion of the Valley*, 318–24. *"been stealing elections"* . . . *"blacksmith-politician"*: "The Trial of Edward Butler for Bribery, Columbia, Missouri, November, 1902," in John D. Lawson, ed., *American State Trials* (Thomas Law, 1918), 492–94. *"Dark Lanterns"*: Julian S. Rammelkamp, *Pulitzer's Post-Dispatch, 1878–1883* (Princeton University Press, 1967), at 151. *"Big Cinch"*: "A 'Big Cinch' Bulwark," *St. Louis Post-Dispatch*, Jan. 26, 1911, 14; Johnson, *Broken Heart of America*, 176.
21. *poorest areas*: RNB, "Autobiography," b. 20, f. 11, 10, RNBP. *social worker*: Ibid., 22; RNB, "Roger Baldwin Story," 1979, b. 24, f. 10, RNBP; RNB, "St. Louis and Reform," [n.d.], b. 21, f. 1, RNBP; RNB, "Recollections of a Life in Civil Liberties," 41; RNB to F. W. Taussig, Oct. 2, 1940, b. 14, f. 16, RNBP. *uncle William*: RNB, "Memo for Jeff Hornback," Oct. 1964, b. 14, f. 12, RNBP. *called uplift*: See Booker T. Washington, *Up from Slavery: An Autobiography* (Doubleday, 1901), 62. *"right and wrong"*: James Alan O'Neal, "A Community of Freethinkers: A History of the Ethical Society of St. Louis, 1886–1996" (unpublished manuscript commissioned by the Ethical Society of St. Louis, 2006), at 65.
22. *probation officer*: RNB, "Recollections of a Life in Civil Liberties," 41; RNB, *Reminiscences*, 22. *2,000 children*: Cottrell, *Roger Nash Baldwin*, 27. *"result of conditions"*: Bernard Flexner and RNB, *Juvenile Courts and Probation* (Century Company, 1914), 8. *"protect and educate"*: Ibid., i–x.
23. *taught social work*: RNB, "American Education," *New York Call*, Oct. 31, 1918, b. 11, f. 14, RNBP. *Civic League . . . Missouri Conference*: RNB, "The Individual and the State: The Problem as Presented by the Sentencing of Roger N. Baldwin," Nov. 1918, b. 11, f. 17, RNBP; *Social Legislation*: "Committee for Social Legislation: Organized to Promote Legislation for Social Betterment in the Missouri General Assembly of 1909," b. 9, f. 2, RNBP. *"young, impetuous"*: Frances McLean to the National Association for Organizing Charity, Nov. 30, 1911, STLSSE.
24. *Folk*: Doris Kearns Goodwin, *The Bully Pulpit* (Simon & Schuster, 2013), 369; Johnson, *Broken Heart of America*, 200–201. *bribery and perjury*: Primm, *Lion of the Valley*, 390. *sentenced*: Ibid., 370. *"plain people"*: Ibid., 376. *"people can rule"*: Lincoln Steffens, *The Shame of the Cities* (McClure, Phillips, 1904), 23.
25. *never served . . . prison*: Primm, *Lion of the Valley*, 390–91.
26. *redeem the promise*: Thomas Cronin, *Direct Democracy: The Politics of Initiative, Referendum, and Recall* (Harvard University Press, 1989).
27. *People's Power League*: Lloyd Spoonholtz, "The Initiative and Referendum: Direct Democracy in Perspective, 1898–1920," *American Studies* 14 (1973): 43, 46. *"single-tax"*: Ibid., 48; "Charter Objections," *St. Louis Post-Dispatch*, Jan. 11, 1911, 10. *Bryan*: Calvin R. Ledbetter Jr., "Adoption of Initiative and Referendum in Arkansas: The Roles of George W. Donaghey and William Jennings Bryan," *Arkansas Historical Quarterly* 51 (1992): 199, 216. *Roosevelt championed*: "Roosevelt Defends Recall, Initiative and Referendum," *St. Louis Post-Dispatch*, Feb. 21, 1912, 1. *California and Oregon*: Spoonholtz, "Initiative and Referendum," 49–53. *twenty-two states*: Ibid., 48.
28. *Missouri enacted*: "Missouri Is Well Posted on the Referendum," *St. Louis Post-Dispatch*, Oct. 25, 1908, 2B; "Referendum Adopted; Blow to Corruption," *St. Louis Post-Dispatch*, Nov. 19, 1908, 4B. *municipal charter*: "New and Old Charter," *St. Louis Post-Dispatch*, Jan. 18, 1911, 10. *"only measure"*: "Broken Reed of the Referendum," *St. Louis Post-Dispatch*, Apr. 26, 1908, 2.
29. *"popular government"*: RNB, "St. Louis's Successful Fight for a Modern Charter," *National Municipal Review* 3 (1914): 720, 724.
30. *Pulitzer*: W. A. Swanberg, *Pulitzer* (Charles Scribner's Sons, 1967), viii. *Civil War*: James McGrath Morris, *Pulitzer: A Life in Politics, Print, and Power* (Harper, 2010), 44. *hotel brawl*: Ibid.,

64; Swanberg, *Pulitzer*, 3. **candidacy**: Glenn C. Altschuler, "Pulitzer's World," *Reviews in American History* 39 (2011): 464; Rammelkamp, *Pulitzer's Post-Dispatch*, 153–62.
31. **Pulitzer's formula**: James W. Markham, *Bovard of the Post-Dispatch* (Louisiana State University Press, 1954), xvii. **"fight for progress ... plutocracy"**: Joseph Pulitzer, "The Post-Dispatch Platform," *St. Louis Post-Dispatch*, Apr. 10, 1907, 1. **"new idea"**: Markham, *Bovard of the Post-Dispatch*, 21.
32. **The World**: Altschuler, "Pulitzer's World," 646. **Bly**: Paul Starr, *The Creation of the Modern Media: Political Origins of Modern Communications* (Basic Books, 2004), 256. **"force ... public opinion"**: W. A. Swanberg, *Citizen Hearst: A Biography of William Randolph Hearst* (Scribner, 1961), 222.
33. **Pulitzer Jr.**: Daniel W. Pfaff, *Joseph Pulitzer II and the Post-Dispatch* (Pennsylvania State University Press, 1991), 56. **surveyed ... "universal suffrage"**: "The Dregs of Citizenship," *St. Louis Post Dispatch*, Nov. 16, 1907, 4.
34. **"bridge arbitrary"**: Primm, *Lion of the Valley*, 422. **"people's bridge"**: RNB, "The Use of Municipal Ownership to Abolish Trans-Mississippi Freight and Passenger Tolls," *National Municipal Review* 4 (1915): 468, 469–70; **"longest bridge"**: Ibid., 468.
35. **"every device ... campaign message"**: RNB, "St. Louis's Successful Fight for a Modern Charter," 721; **"reach"**: RNB, "Outline of Paper on Preparation of Bills and Publicity Methods," [n.d., 1910–1917], b. 24, f. 4, RNBP; **"radical ... people"**: RND, "The Use of Municipal Ownership," 471–72.
36. **first initiative**: Johnson, *Broken Heart of America*, 252; Primm, *Lion of the Valley*, 435.
37. **Black population**: Ibid., 441. **1914 report**: Samuel Walker, *In Defense of American Liberties: A History of the ACLU* (Oxford University Press, 1990), 34, 385 n15. **"hardest"**: William A. Crossland [& RNB], *Industrial Conditions Among Negroes in St. Louis* (Washington University Press, 1914), also in b. 16, f. 24, RNBP. **less than $12**: Ibid., 27. **bricklayer ... painter**: "Wages and Hours of Labor," *Monthly Labor Review* 21 (U.S. Department of Labor, Sept. 1925), 54, 56, 70.
38. **early strategy discussions**: RNB, "A Memo on Julian W. Mack," June 1964, b. 9, f. 32, RNBP. **interracial groups**: Cottrell, *Roger Nash Baldwin*, 42–44. **won a fight**: RNB, "St. Louis and Reform," [n.d.], b. 21, f. 1, RNBP. **social work degree**: RNB to David F. Houston, Aug. 4, 1911; DFH to RNB, Aug. 26, 1911; RNB to DFH, Aug. 28, 1911, all in b. 16, f. 29, RNBP. **public school principals**: "Race Union Is Opposed," *St. Louis Star*, Mar. 9, 1909, 1; RNB to George W. Pieksen, Mar. 27, 1909, b. 16, f. 2, RNBP. See also RNB, Summary of the Investigation of Industrial Conditions Among Negroes in St. Louis with Recommendations for Action, 1914, b. 16, f. 24, RNBP.
39. **he predicted**: RNB to Booker T. Washington, Feb. 3, 1913, b. 16, f. 27, RNBP; RNB to Eugene K. Jones, Feb. 13, 1914, b. 16, f. 27, RNBP. **Baltimore ... Kentucky**: Benno C. Schmidt Jr., "Principle and Prejudice: The Supreme Court and Race in the Progressive Era. Part I: The Heyday of Jim Crow," *Columbia Law Review* 82 (2018): 444, 499–500; see also Committee on Housing on Negroes, "The Legal Segregation of Negroes in St. Louis," Jan. 1913, b. 16, f. 26, RNBP.
40. **Oklahoma ... purchasing property**: Spoonholtz, "Initiative and Referendum," 52.
41. **United Welfare Association**: Laurence Felix, "Segregation Constitutional?," *St. Louis Post-Dispatch*, Feb. 19, 1916, 6; Oscar Leonard, "Segregation Puts Property Above Manhood," *St. Louis Post-Dispatch*, Feb. 26, 1916, 6; Display Ad 45 [No Title], *St. Louis Post-Dispatch*, Feb. 20, 1916, A6; Small Property Owner, "Letters from the People: Evils Due to Race Prejudice," *St. Louis Post-Dispatch*, Feb. 2, 1916, 14. **"ordinance to prevent"**: Buchanan v. Warley, 245 U.S. 60 (1917). **"negro invasion"**: "United Welfare Ass'n Explains Its Attitude on Question of Segregation," *St. Louis Post-Dispatch*, Feb. 16, 1916, 4. **"let the Negro whip"**: Primm, *Lion of the Valley*, 412.
42. **aldermen**: Daniel T. Kelleher, "St. Louis 1916 Residential Segregation Ordinance," *Missouri Historical Society Bulletin* 26 (1970): 239, 241. **challenged**: Committee on Housing on Negroes, "The Legal Segregation of Negroes in St. Louis." **"Citizens' Committee"**: Letter of the Citizens' Committee Opposed to the Legal Segregation of Negroes, Jan. 25, 1916, b. 16, f. 27, RNBP; see also "Segregation Unamerican," *St. Louis Post-Dispatch*, Jan. 27, 1916, 14; Dr. Charles Henry

Phillips Jr., "Letters Sent to Post-Dispatch on Segregation Issue," *St. Louis Post-Dispatch*, Feb. 27, 1916, 8.
43. *"impossible"*: RNB to BTW, Feb. 3, 1913, b. 16, f. 27, RNBP. *special election*: "Segregation to Be Fought in Courts; Won by 34,000," *St. Louis Post-Dispatch*, Mar. 1, 1916, 1. *"instrument"*: Roland G. Usher, "Negro Segregation in St. Louis," *Gazette Times*, Mar. 18, 1916, 9. *"long run"*: RNB to *The Argus*, Mar. 2, 1916, b. 16, f. 27, RNBP.
44. *legal challenges*: "Segregation Being Argued," *St. Louis Post-Dispatch*, Apr. 10, 1916, 1; *Dyer*: "City Is Enjoined from Enforcing Segregation Laws," *St. Louis Post-Dispatch*, Apr. 17, 1916, 1; "Highest Court Hears Louisville Segregation Case," *St. Louis Post-Dispatch*, Apr. 11, 1916, 13; "Entire Supreme Court to Hear Segregation Arguments," *St. Louis Post-Dispatch*, Apr. 17, 1916, 3; "The Right to Occupy One's Property," *St. Louis Post-Dispatch*, Apr. 22, 1916, 10.
45. *"races . . . economic condition"*: Schmidt, "Principle and Prejudice," 505.
46. *November 1917*: Buchanan v. Warley, 245 U.S. 60 (1917).
47. *"Majorities"*: RNB to *Argus* Editor, Mar. 2, 1916, b. 16, f. 27, RNBP. *"democratic faith"*: RNB, "St. Louis and Reform," [n.d.], b. 21, f. 1, RNBP.
48. *fifty-five*: Charles L. Lumpkins, *American Pogrom: The East St. Louis Race Riot and Black Politics* (Ohio University Press, 2008), 190. *new and growing*: See Samuel Gompers, "East St. Louis Riots—Their Causes," *American Federationist* 24 (1917): 621, 623–24. *Black population*: Johnson, *Broken Heart of America*, 226; Lumpkins, *American Pogrom*, 71, 124. *Tensions*: Elliott M. Rudwick, *Race Riot at East St. Louis, July 2, 1917* (World Publishing, 1964), at 16–22. *"growing menace"*: W. E. B. Du Bois and Martha Greuning, "The Massacre of East St. Louis," *The Crisis*, Sept. 1917, 219. *Armour . . . "industrial standards"*: Gompers, "East St. Louis Riots," 621.
49. *Tensions burst*: Johnson, *Broken Heart of America*, 233–34; Lumpkins, *American Pogrom*, 97–99.
50. *July 1*: Johnson, *Broken Heart of America*, 235–40; Lumpkins, *American Pogrom*, 111–13; Malcolm McLaughlin, "Ghetto Formation and Armed Resistance in East St. Louis, Illinois," *Journal of American Studies* 41 (2007): 435, 463. *"shot down"*: "Race Rioters Fire East St. Louis and Shoot or Hang Many Negroes," *New York Times*, July 3, 1917, 1. *"man hunt"*: Du Bois and Greuning, "Massacre of East St. Louis," 221.
51. *mob with a rope*: Johnson, *Broken Heart of America*, 236. *"gutters"*: "Race Rioters Fire East St. Louis," 1. *"rope" . . . "fire"*: "To Conscientious Objector: Today—Yesterday," *Four Lights*, Aug. 25, 1917. *martial*: Lumpkins, *American Pogrom*, 122. *regiment*: "Race Rioters Fire East St. Louis," 1. *arm*: Lumpkins, *American Pogrom*, 125.
52. *massacred*: Lumpkins, *American Pogrom*, 128; Du Bois and Greuning, "Massacre of East St. Louis," 219. *souvenir hunters*: "The East St. Louis Riots," *Norfolk Journal and Guide*, July 7, 1917, 4. *$3 million*: Lumpkins, *American Pogrom*, 128.
53. *"Race Rioters"*: "Race Rioters Fire East St. Louis," 1. *"hunted down"*: "The Week," *The Nation*, Aug. 2, 1927, 111. *Jews in Russia*: "Illinois and Race Riots," *Los Angeles Times*, July 5, 1917, II4. *Wells*: Ida B. Wells, "The East St. Louis Massacre: The Greatest Outrage of the Century," in *The Light of Truth: Writings of an Anti-Lynching Crusader*, ed. Mia Bay (Penguin Press, 2014), 456. *Carnegie . . . "murder"*: "Roosevelt and Gompers Row at Russian Meeting," *New York Times*, July 7, 1917, 1, 4; also *The Works of Theodore Roosevelt* (C. Scribner's Sons, 1926), 4: 506–8.
54. *"people of East St. Louis"*: RNB, "East St. Louis—Why?" *The Survey*, Aug. 1917, 448.
55. *"Labor conquers" . . . "Liberty"*: Du Bois and Greuning, "Massacre of East St. Louis," 219. *Karch*: Charles Karch to Thomas Watt Gregory, July 23, 1917, Department of Justice Files, cited in Rudwick, *Race Riot at East St. Louis, July 2, 1917*, at 137; Thomas Watt Gregory to Woodrow Wilson, July 27, 1917; Wilson to Gregory, July 23, 1917, both in Arthur S. Link, ed., *Papers of WoodrowWilson*, vol. 43 (Princeton University Press, 1983), 297. *"Excited"*: Gompers, "East St. Louis Riots," 622.
56. *sequence of urban massacres*: Robert Whitaker, *On the Laps of Gods: The Red Summer of 1919 and the Struggle for Justice That Remade a Nation* (Three Rivers Press, 2008); Cameron McWhirter, *Red Summer: The Summer of 1919 and the Awakening of Black America* (St. Martin's Griffin, 2011). *riots*: Eric Ledell Smith, "The 1917 Race Riot in Chester, Pennsylvania," *Pennsyl-*

vania History: A Journal of Mid-Atlantic Studies 75 (2008): 171. **Houston**: Robert L. Zangrando, *The NAACP Crusade Against Lynching, 1909–1950* (Temple University Press, 1980), at 40.
57. *"lighting a fire . . . no peace"*: Norrell, *Up from History*, 344. **new ideas**: See Du Bois and Greuning, "The Massacre of East St. Louis," 219.
58. *"very simple"*: RNB, "Autobiography," b. 20, f. 11, 40, RNBP. *"very perfection"* . . . *"public opinion"*: RNB, "A Suggested Outline of Work on the Problems of Colored People in Cities," [n.d., Apr. 1913], b. 9, f. 44, RNBP.

2: WEAPONS OF TRUTH

"war fever": RNB, "Autobiography," b. 20, f. 11, 53, RNBP.
1. **submarine**: Rodney Carlisle, *Sovereignty at Sea: U.S. Merchant Ships and American Entry into World War I* (University Press of Florida, 2010), at 11–13; "Patrol Picks Up Survivors," *New York Times*, Mar. 19, 1917, 1.
2. *"He Kept"*: John Milton Cooper Jr., *The Warrior and the Priest: Theodore Roosevelt and Woodrow Wilson* (Harvard University Press, 1983), 307.
3. *"propaganda"*: Christopher Capozzola, *Uncle Sam Wants You: World War I and the Making of the Modern American Citizen* (Oxford University Press, 2008); David Greenberg, *Republic of Spin: An Inside History of the American Presidency* (W. W. Norton, 2016); David M. Kennedy, *Over Here: The First World War and American Society*, rev. ed. (Oxford University Press, 2004); Stephen Vaughn, *Holding Fast the Inner Lines: Democracy, Nationalism, and the Committee on Public Information* (University of North Carolina Press, 1980), xii.
4. **New York**: RNB, "Recollections of Theodore Schroeder," Nov. 1970, b. 14, f. 22, RNBP; Peggy Lamson, *Roger Baldwin: Founder of the American Civil Liberties Union* (Houghton Mifflin, 1976), 66. **American Union**: Lamson, *Roger Baldwin*, 67; see also Robert L. Duffus, "The Legend of Roger Baldwin," *American Mercury* 5 (1925): 408, 409.
5. **anti-war pamphlets**: AUAM to James P. Warbasse, May 27, 1916, r. 1, AUAM. **It targeted**: AUAM Statement, [n.d.], r. 1, AUAM. **news stories**: AUAM, "Work Since We Began in December," [n.d.], r. 1, AUAM. **publicity bureau**: Charles Hallinan to AUAM, May 12, 1917, r. 1, AUAM. **arranged hearings**: AUAM Release, May 6 [1916?], r. 1, AUAM. **public meetings**: Anti Preparedness Committee, Release on Receipt [n.d., early 1916?], r. 1, AUAM. **Posters**: "Democracy Controlling the Dogs of War" and "Lady Liberty: 'No Militarism Here,'" both in r. 1, AUAM. *"national referendum"*: AUAM Postcard, "National Referendum on Peace or War," [n.d., 1917?], r. 1, AUAM.
6. **Selective Service**: Selective Service Act, 40 Stat. 76, 77 (1917). **Espionage Act . . . *"United States"***: Espionage Act, 40 Stat. 217, 219 (1917). *"unmailable"*: Milwaukee Social Democratic Pub. Co. v. Burleson, 255 U.S. 407 (1921).
7. **Close friends**: Adrian Anderson, "President Wilson's Politician: Albert Sidney Burleson of Texas," *Southwestern Historical Quarterly* 77 (1974): 339, 340; **Gregory**: Thomas Watt Gregory to Woodrow Wilson, July 27, 1917, in Arthur S. Link, ed., *Papers of Woodrow Wilson* (Princeton University Press, 1983), 43:297. **Ku Klux Klan**: Thomas Watt Gregory, "Reconstruction and the Ku Klux Klan: A Paper Read Before the Arkansas and Texas Bar Associations," July 10, 1906, 2–3. *"intolerable burden"*: Ibid., 11.
8. *"intellectual reign"*: Harry N. Scheiber, *The Wilson Administration and Civil Liberties* (1960; Quid Quo Pro Books, 2013), 36. *"avenging Government"*: "All Disloyal Men Warned by Gregory," *New York Times*, Nov. 21, 1917, 3; **Debs**: Debs v. United States, 249 U.S. 211 (1919). **Chicago . . . IWW convictions**: Philip Taft, "The Federal Trials of the IWW," *Labor History* 3 (1962): 57; Earl Bruce White, "*The United States v. C.W. Anderson et al.*: The Wichita Case, 1917–1919," in *At the Point of Production: The Local History of the IWW*, ed. Joseph Robert Conlin (Greenwood, 1981), 143–64; Melvyn Dubofsky, *We Shall Be All: A History of the Industrial Workers of the World* (Quadrangle, 1969), 408. **Eastman . . . 2,000 people**: Geoffrey R. Stone, *Perilous Times: Free Speech in Wartime from the Sedition Act of 1798 to the War on Terrorism* (W. W. Norton, 2004), 146–70. **South Dakota**: R. Stewart to NCLB, Dec. 18, 1917; Richard F.

Pettigrew to NCLB, Dec. 23, 1917; RFP to Walter Nelles, May 20, 1918, all in r. 5, v. 37, ACLUA. *"rich man's war"*: Regner & Ringle to NCLB, Apr. 20, 1918, r. 5, vol. 37, ACLUA. *"Long Live"*: RNB to Henry J. Nelson, July 24, 1917, r. 5, vol. 36, ACLUA; *"business element"*: H. J. Trelease to Liberty Defense Union [?], Apr. 12, 1918, r. 5, vol. 36, ACLUA.

9. *post office*: Donald Johnson, *The Challenge to American Freedoms: World War I and the Rise of the American Civil Liberties Union* (University of Kentucky Press, 1963), 57; see also Zechariah Chafee Jr., *Free Speech in the United States* (Harvard University Press, 1941), 97–100. **Burleson refused**: Ibid., 42–43. *mailing privileges*: George P. West, "A Talk with Mr. Burleson," *The Public*, Oct. 12, 1917, 1. *"skipped a number"*: H. C. Peterson and Gilbert C. Fite, *Opponents of War, 1917–1918* (University of Wisconsin Press, 1957), at 97; *seventy-five separate*: John Fabian Witt, *Patriots and Cosmopolitans: Hidden Histories of American Law* (Harvard University Press, 2009), 191. *foreign-language*: Chafee, *Free Speech in the United States*, 299.

10. *"got into"*: Donald Johnson, "Wilson, Burleson, and Censorship in the First World War," *Journal of Southern History* 28 (1962): 48, 51–52. *"instant"*: West, "A Talk with Mr. Burleson," 1.

11. *"demon"*: Joseph Freeman, *An American Testament: A Narrative of Rebels and Romantics* (Farrar & Rinehart, 1936), 327. **established a team**: RNB, "Autobiography," b. 20, f. 11, 57–58, RNBP.

12. *"graveyard"*: Ibid., 59. **Wald resigned**: Crystal Eastman to AUAM, [n.d., June 1917?]; Crystal Eastman, [June 14, 1917], both in r. 1, AUAM.

13. *"there came"*: Witt, *Patriots and Cosmopolitans*, 193; John Haynes Holmes, *I Speak for Myself: The Autobiography of John Haynes Holmes* (Harper & Brothers, 1959), 189. *"Civil Liberties Bureau"*: Crystal Eastman, Executive Committee Meeting, [n.d., June 25, 1917]; Crystal Eastman, Executive Committee Meeting, Aug. 5, 1917; AUAM, "Dear Contributing Member," Aug. 1, 1917, all in r. 1, AUAM. *"civil liberties"*: Witt, *Patriots and Cosmopolitans*, 194–96; Christopher W. Schmidt, "The Civil Rights–Civil Liberties Divide," *Stanford Journal of Civil Rights & Civil Liberties* 12 (2016): 1.

14. **Bullard**: Arthur Bullard, Memorandum on Censorship, July 1916, b. 185, f. 220, Papers of Colonel E. M. House. *"loud"*: Arthur Bullard, *Mobilising America* (Macmillan, 1917), 25. *"conscript public opinion"*: Frank I. Cobb, "The Press and Public Opinion," *New Republic*, Dec. 31, 1919, 144.

15. **World opinion**: Charles Roetter, *The Art of Psychological Warfare, 1914–1945* (Stein and Day, 1974), at 50; also "Why Is a Censor?," *Current Opinion* 62 (1917): 408; "Press Comment on the Censorship Plan," *New York Times*, May 24, 1917, 2.

16. *"disaffection"*: U.S. Congress, *Espionage and Interference with Neutrality: Hearings Before the Committee on the Judiciary, House of Representatives, Sixty-Fifth Congress, First Session, on H.R. 291, April 9 and 12, 1917* (Government Printing Office, 1917), at 37. *"Weapons of Truth"*: Upton Sinclair to Woodrow Wilson, Oct. 22, 1917; WW to Joseph Patrick Tumulty, Oct. 30, 1917, both in *Papers of Woodrow Wilson*, vol. 44 (Princeton University Press, 1968), 467–72.

17. **Committee on Public Information**: James R. Mock and Cedric Larson, *Words That Won the War: The Story of the Committee on Public Information, 1917–1919* (Princeton University Press, 1939), at 11. **sensationalizing journalist**: George Creel, *Rebel at Large: Recollections of Fifty Crowded Years* (G. P. Putnam's Sons, 1947), 3. *"bread alone"*: George Creel, "Public Opinion in Wartime," *Annals of American Political and Social Science* 78 (1918): 185, 188–89; see also Norman Angell, *The Great Illusion: A Study of the Relation of Military Power in Nations to Their Economic and Social Advantage* (William Heineman, 1910). *"dramatized"*: Josephus Daniels's Diary, Apr. 11, 1917, in *Papers of Woodrow Wilson*, 22:39–40.

18. **75 million**: George Creel, *Complete Report of the Chairman of the Committee on Public Information* (Government Printing Office, 1920), 2. **official daily**: George Creel, *How We Advertised America: The First Telling of the Amazing Story of the Committee on Public Information That Carried the Gospel of Americanism to Every Corner of the Globe* (Harper & Brothers, 1920), 207–9; see also Robert A. Emery, "The Official Bulletin, 1917–1919: A Proto-Federal Register," *Law Library Journal* 102 (2010): 441; "Police Throughout Nation to Help in Apprehending Draft Delinquents," *Official Bulletin*, Nov. 30, 1917, r. 5, ACLUA; Mock and Larson, *Words That Won the War*, 92. **Content supplied**: Creel, *How We Advertised America*, 76. **coordinated** . . .

Four-Minute: Creel, *Complete Report of the Chairman*, 14–16, 22, 33–37, 40–42, 44, 47, 51, 72–73.
19. *four-minute speeches*: Creel, *Complete Report of the Chairman*, 29–30. *"catch-phrases"*: See Creel, *Public Opinion*, 188. *French 75*: Creel, *How We Advertised America*, 86.
20. *small team*: Ibid., 56.
21. *Jordan*: Peterson and Fite, *Opponents of War*, 4. *"Hang Dave"*: "Pacifists Riot and Are Rioted Against in East," *Chicago Daily Tribune*, Apr. 2, 1917, 1. *Bigelow*: NCLB, "The Outrage on Herbert S. Bigelow of Cincinnati, Ohio (October 28, 1917)," Mar. 1918, r. 5, ACLUA. *Praeger*: APR, "Lynching: Capitalism Its Cause; Socialism Its Cure," *The Messenger*, Mar. 1919, 8; Eugene Lyons, *Workers' Defense Bulletin* (Workers Defense Union, 1919), 6; Harry N. Scheiber, *The Wilson Administration and Civil Liberties* (Cornell University Press, 1960), 51. *Ellis . . . "leading white citizens"*: Peterson and Fite, *Opponents of War*, 91.
22. *164 instances*: NCLB, *War-Time Prosecutions and Mob Violence* (NCLB, 1918), 3. *German-Americans*: Ibid., 6–7. *American flags*: Ibid., 10–11. *patriotic groups*: Stone, *Perilous Times*, 156. *added manpower*: Homer S. Cummings and Carl McFarland, *Federal Justice: Chapters in the History of Justice and the Federal Executive* (Macmillan, 1937), 421.
23. *Bigelow's case*: Paul L. Murphy, *World War I and the Origin of Civil Liberties in the United States* (W. W. Norton, 1979), 165.
24. *awkwardly positioned*: Ibid., 166–67, see also NCLB, "The Outrage on Rev. Herbert S. Bigelow of Cincinnati, Ohio, October 28, 1917," Mar. 1918, b. 18, f. 16, RNBP; NCLB, "Mass Meeting on American Liberties in War Time: First Opportunity in New York to Hear Herbert S. Bigelow," 1918; NCLB, Dear Friend, Jan. 9, 1918, both in r. 1, v. 3, ACLUA.
25. *"intolerance"*: RNB to Harold Evans, Apr. 13, 1918, ACLUA, quoted in Johnson, *Challenge to American Freedoms*, 71. *"counteract unjust prejudices"*: Walter Nelles to C. N. Libby, July 28, 1918, r. 5, ACLUA.
26. *Western Front*: Clayton D. Laurie, "'The Chanting of Crusaders': Captain Heber Blankenhorn and AEF Combat Propaganda in World War I," *Journal of Military History* 59 (1995): 463, 547.
27. *Upper East Side . . . New Republic*: Ronald Steel, *Walter Lippmann and the American Century* (Atlantic Monthly Press, 1980), 3–12. *"peace without victory"*: Ibid., 109; Heinz Eulau, "Wilsonian Idealist: Walter Lippmann Goes to War," *Antioch Review* 14 (1954): 87, 94.
28. *the president's vision*: Walter Lippmann to Norman Angell, Mar. 1, 1917, in *Public Philosopher: Selected Letters of Walter Lippmann*, ed. John Morton Blum (Ticknor & Fields, 1985), 63, 112–13. *propaganda platoon*: Steel, *Walter Lippmann and the American Century*, 139–42; Heber Blankenhorn, *Adventures in Propaganda: Letters from an Intelligence Officer in France* (Houghton Mifflin, 1919), 6.
29. *salient . . . beyond enemy lines*: Laurie, "Chanting of Crusaders," 466–72.
30. *great success*: Ibid., 467. *assault*: Blankenhorn, *Adventures in Propaganda*, xii. *Patton . . . tanks*: Jon B. Mikolashek, *Blood, Guts, and Grease: George S. Patton in World War I* (University Press of Kentucky, 2019), at 62 ff.
31. *"hypnotized"*: Erich Ludendorff, *My War Memories: 1914–1918*, vol. 1 (Hutchinson, 1919), at 361. *"bitterly honest"*: Laurie, "Chanting of Crusaders," 468.
32. *"herd-instinct"*: Friedrich Nietzsche, *The Gay Science* (E. W. Fritsch, 1887), 169. *Le Bon*: Gustave Le Bon, *The Crowd: A Study of the Popular Mind* (Macmillan, 1896), 10–11. *"magnétisation"*: Gabriel Tarde and Elsie Clews Parsons, trans., *The Laws of Imitation* (Henry Holt, 1903), 77–78. *ideas*: Gabriel Tarde, *L'Opinion et la Foule* (Felix Alcan, 1901).
33. *taught at Harvard*: Steel, *Walter Lippmann and the American Century*, 26–30. *politics*: Graham Wallas, *Human Nature in Politics* (A. Constable, 1908), xiii. *"half-conscious"*: Ibid., 23. *"Great Society"*: Graham Wallas, *The Great Society: A Psychological Analysis* (Macmillan, 1914).
34. *"routineers"*: Walter Lippmann, *A Preface to Politics* (Mitchell Kennerley, 1913), 24. *"taboo . . . club"*: Ibid., 35–36.
35. *redirected the energies*: Ibid., 37. *"thousand avenues"*: Ibid., 127.
36. *"moral equivalent"*: Ibid., 49. *"disconcerting effect"*: Walter Lippmann, *Drift and Mastery: An Attempt to Diagnose the Current Unrest* (Mitchell Kennerley, 1914), xv–xvi.

37. *Lippmann's statesman could turn*: WL to Edward M. House, Apr. 12, 1917, in Blum, *Public Philosopher*, 65; WL to Woodrow Wilson, Feb. 6, 1917, ibid., 61; WL to WW, Apr. 3, 1917, ibid., 64.
38. **had opposed entry**: WL to Robert Dell, June 7, 1915, ibid., 28; WL to Joseph Lee, Jan. 8, 1918, ibid., 33. **cheerleader**: WL to Norman Angell, Mar. 1, 1917, ibid., 63; WL to WW, Feb. 6, 1917, ibid., 61; WL to WW, Apr. 3, 1917, ibid., 64.
39. **mole**: "Abstract from Report," Feb. 16, 1918, Military Intelligence Division Correspondence, 10434-8-16, b. 3295, RG 165, NARA. **inspector general**: Robert C. Cottrell, *Roger Nash Baldwin and the American Civil Liberties Union* (Columbia University Press, 2000), 65–66; RNB, "Recollections of a Life in Civil Liberties," *Civil Liberties Review* 1 (1975): 39, 62–63.
40. **charged**: Biddle to Director of Military Intelligence, Oct. 11, 1918, Military Intelligence Division Correspondence, 10902-13-86, b. 3762, RG 165, NARA; see also Donald Johnson, *The Challenge to American Freedoms: World War I and the Rise of the American Civil Liberties Union* (University of Kentucky Press, 1963), 26–54; Cottrell, *Roger Nash Baldwin*, 78.
41. *"perform any service"*: RNB to Local Board Number 129, Sept. 12, 1918, b. 6, f. 7, RNBP. **physical exam**: RNB, *The Reminiscences of Roger Baldwin, 1953–1954* (1963), at 68, CCOH; RNB to Hon. Francis G. Caffey, U.S. Dist. Atty, Oct. 9, 1918, b. 11, f. 12, RNBP.
42. *"good friends"*: RNB to Lucy Nash Baldwin, Oct. 31, 1918, b. 11, f. 20, RNBP. **attention:** "Pacifist Professor Gets Year in Prison," *New York Times*, Oct. 31, 1918, 11; "Baldwin Gets Year for Draft Act Defiance," *New York Call*, Oct. 31, 1918, b. 11, f. 14, RNBP. *"compelling motive"*: RNB, "The Individual and the State: The Problem as Presented by the Sentencing of Roger N. Baldwin" (AUAM, 1918), also in r. 1, AUAM. *"law makers"*: RNB to Hon. Julius M. Mayer, [n.d., Nov. 1918], b. 11, f. 12, RNBP.
43. *"the ends"*: "He Chose Words in Haste," *New York Times*, Nov. 1, 1918, 14, also in b. 11, f. 14, RNBP.
44. *"Abolitionist traditions"*: Oswald Garrison Villard to RNB, Nov. 13, 1918, b. 11, f. 17, RNBP.
45. *"swamped"*: RNB, "Autobiography," b. 20, f. 11, 53, RNBP.

3: THE LESS WE KNOW

"Private propaganda": Frank I. Cobb, "The Press and Public Opinion," *New Republic*, Dec. 31, 1919, 147.

1. **murderous violence**: JWJ, *Along This Way* (Viking, 1933), 342; Cameron McWhirter, *Red Summer: The Summer of 1919 and the Awakening of Black America* (St. Martin's Griffin, 2011), 13; William M. Tuttle Jr., *Race Riot: Chicago in the Red Summer of 1919* (Athenaeum, 1970), at 10, 30; Elizabeth Dale, *Fight for Rights: The Chicago 1919 Riots and the Struggle for Black Justice* (Library Press@UF, 2022). **20,000**: *Annual Report of the Attorney General of the United States for the Year 1919* (Government Printing Office, 1919), at 21. **enemy aliens**: U.S. Department of Justice, *Annual Report of the Attorney General of the United States* 27 (Office of the Attorney General, 1919). **Four million**: Adam Hochschild, *American Midnight: The Great War, a Violent Peace, and Democracy's Forgotten Crisis* (Mariner Books, 2022), 223. **Seattle ... coal mines**: Melvyn Dubofsky and Rhea Dulles Foster, *Labor in America: A History* (Harlan Davidson, 2010), 211–15. *"telephone operators" ... East Coast*: Hochschild, *American Midnight*, 223.
2. **Essex County Jail**: RNB to Hon. John J. Hanley, Dec. 17, 1918, b. 11, f. 12; RNB to Lucy Nash Baldwin, Oct. 31, Nov. 1, Nov. 3, 1918, b. 11, f. 20. **boasted**: RNB to Thomas Elliot, n.d. [1918–1919], b. 6, f. 7; "The Roger Baldwin Story: A Prejudiced Account by Himself" (1979), b. 24, f. 10, all in RNBP.
3. **lobby ... "behind bars"**: RNB to Albert DeSilver, Mar. 5, 1919, b. 11, f. 12, RNBP.
4. **courts-martial and long terms**: Donald Johnson, *The Challenge to American Freedoms: World War I and the Rise of the American Civil Liberties Union* (University of Kentucky Press, 1963), 52; see also RNB to Frederick P. Keppel, Dec. 5, 1917; F. P. Keppel to RNB, Aug. 27, 1918, both in r. 1, v. 10, ACLUA. **Selective Service**: RNB to Hon. Francis G. Caffey, U.S. Dist. Atty, NYC, Oct. 9, 1918, b. 11, f. 12, RNBP; RNB to Clerk of the U.S. Court, NYC, May 1, 1919, b. 11, f. 12, RNBP. **sometimes pleasurable**: RNB, editorial inserts to "Autobiography," [n.d.], b. 21, f. 1, RNBP.

NOTES TO PAGES 59-64   595

5. *"Tombs"*: RNB to LNB, Nov. 1, 1918, b. 11, f. 20, RNBP; New York State Senate, *Documents of the Senate of the State of New York: One Hundred and Thirty-Eighth Session, 1915* (J. B. Lyon, 1915), at 148. *"Yale man"* . . . *dining*: RNB to LNB, Oct. 10, 1918; RNB to LNB, Nov. 3, 1918, both in b. 11, f. 20, RNBP. *burlesque show*: Peggy Lamson, *Roger Baldwin: Founder of the American Civil Liberties Union* (Houghton Mifflin, 1976), 90.
6. *"cooker"*: RNB to LNB, Nov. 12, 1918, b. 11, f. 20, RNBP. *"long vacation"*: RNB to mother, Oct. 31, 1918, b. 11, f. 20, RNBP. *"extraordinarily decent"*: RNB to LNB, Oct. 10, 1918, b. 11, f. 20, RNBP. *"proud of you"*: [Frank Fenno Baldwin?] to RNB, Nov. 13, 1918, b. 11, f. 18, RNBP.
7. *retreat* . . . *"self-communion"*: L to RNB, Dec. 6, 1918, b. 11, f. 15, RNBP. *"quiet and seclusion"*: RNB to LNB, Oct. 27, 1918, b. 11, f. 20, RNBP. *cabins* . . . *"several years"*: RNB to LNB, Nov. 12, 1918, b. 11, f. 20, RNBP.
8. *modest pride*: RNB, *The Reminiscences of Roger Baldwin, 1953-1954* (1963), at 64-65, CCOH. *Mobs had assaulted*: "Thousands in Posse Hunt Draft Mobs," *Chicago Examiner*, Aug. 4, 1917, r. 5, ACLUA; NCLB, "Dear Friend," Jan. 9, 1918; NCLB, "To the Congress of the United States," Jan. 13, 1918, both in r. 1, v. 3, ACLUA.
9. *better strategies*: RNB to [N.T], [n.d.], b. 14, f. 28, RNBP. *"American public opinion"*: RNB to NCLB, Sept. 27, 1918, v. 43, ACLUA.
10. *Going undercover*: Rudolph W. Chamberlain, *There Is No Truce: A Life of Thomas Mott Osborne* (Macmillan, 1935), 238-41. *Nellie Bly*: Paul Starr, *The Creation of the Modern Media: Political Origins of Modern Communications* (Basic Books, 2004), 256. *four feet by* . . . *"top to toe"*: Thomas Mott Osborne, *Within Prison Walls: Being a Narrative of Personal Experience During a Week of Voluntary Confinement in the State Prison at Auburn* (D. Appleton, 1914), 41-60. *Bertillon*: Alphonse Bertillon, *Identification Anthropométrique: Instructions Signalétiques* (Imprimerie Administrative, 1893); Rebecca M. McLennan, *The Crisis of Imprisonment: Protest, Politics, and the Making of the American Penal State* (Cambridge University Press, 2008), 319-75.
11. *environments*: See Thomas Mott Osborne, "Common Sense in Prison Management," *Journal of the American Institute of Criminal Law and Criminology* 8 (1918).
12. *press conference*: See Osborne, *Within Prison Walls*.
13. *"cry of 'Fire'"*: Ibid., 135; *Calumet*: L. A. Scot Powe, "Searching for the False Shout of 'Fire,'" *Constitutional Commentary* 19 (2002): 345, 349-50. *"elemental brute* . . . *safety"*: Osborne, *Within Prison Walls*, 136.
14. *"no such thing as 'the criminal'"*: Thomas Mott Osborne, *Society and Prisons* (Yale University Press, 1916), 19; Osborne, *Within Prison Walls*, 136; Osborne, "Common Sense in Prison," 812; McClennan, *Crisis of Imprisonment*, 376-416.
15. *"true interests"*: Osborne, *Society and Prisons*, 163-64; also Thomas Mott Osborne, *Prisons and Common Sense* (J. B. Lippincott, 1924), 24.
16. *"really know"*: RNB, "The Seventh Tier Soviet," *The Liberator*, Dec. 1918, 10.
17. *"Seventh Tier Soviet"*: Ibid., 10-11; RNB to Hon. John J. Hanley, Dec. 17, 1918, b. 11, f. 12, RNBP. *Prisoners' Welfare League*: "Prison Welfare League Is Under Ban," May 1, 1919, b. 11, f. 14, RNBP.
18. *"mixed lot"*: RNB to LNB, Nov. 12, 1918, b. 11, f. 20, RNBP. *"packed"*: RNB to My Friends, May 26, 1919, b. 11, f. 12, RNBP. *"too interesting"*: RNB to Madeleine Z. Doty, [n.d., Mar. 1919?], b. 2, f. 9, MZDP.
19. *Bellair*: RNB to MZD, Mar. 31, 1919, b. 2, f. 9, MZDP; Harry Bellair to RNB, July 28, 1919; Harry Bellair, "Statement," [n.d., 1919?], both in b. 4, f. 8, RNBP. *"very unstable"*: Bernard Glueck to RNB, Sept. 24, 1919, b. 4, f. 8, RNBP. *"so effected"*: Harry Bellair to RNB, Aug. 13, 1919, b. 4, f. 8, RNBP.
20. *"Ain't it* . . . *solid ground"*: Harry Bellair to RNB, Aug. 13, 1919, b. 4, f. 8, RNBP.
21. *"fairy"*: George Chauncey, *Gay New York: Gender, Urban Culture, and the Making of the Gay Male World* (Perseus Books, 1994), 14. *"intermediate sex"*: Edward Carpenter, *The Intermediate Sex: A Study of Some Transitional Types of Men and Women* (Mitchell Kennerley, 1912), 18. *"conventionally masculine"*: Chauncey, *Gay New York*, 13.

22. **Taft**: Joseph P. Lash, interview with Phil Taft, Oct. 12, 1972, JPL. *"unfulfilled desires"*: RNB to [Mary Bulkley?], July 8, [1923?], b. 4, f. 30, RNBP. *"moral life"*: Johnson, *Challenge to American Freedoms*, 47. *"blade"*: Joseph P. Lash, interview with RNB, Sept. 29, 1971, b. 49, JPLP. **admired**: Joseph P. Lash, interview with Elsa Butler and William Butler, Dec. 5, 1971, b. 49, JPLP. *"inner repulsions"*: Ernest to Holmes, Nov. 16, 1949, b. 44, HRC-MEC, in Leigh Ann Wheeler, *How Sex Became a Civil Liberty* (Oxford University Press, 2013), 232 n54.
23. *"dramatic experiences"*: RNB to My Friends, July 31, 1919, b. 11, f. 12, RNBP. *"pleasurable experience"*: Editorial inserts to "Autobiography," [n.d.], b. 21, RNBP; see also RNB to My Friends, July 31, 1919, b. 11, f. 12, RNBP; RNB, Editorial inserts to "Autobiography," [n.d.], b. 21, RNBP.
24. *"toward freedom"*: RNB to My Friends, July 31, 1919, b. 11, f. 12, RNBP.
25. *Impressionability*: See Walter Lippmann, "Liberty and the News," *The Atlantic*, Dec. 1919, 779–87.
26. *Madeleine Doty*: RNB, A Memo on MZD for the files of Smith College, Oct. 1978, b. 6, f. 1, RNBP; also in b. 1, f. 4, MZDP; Robert C. Cottrell, *Roger Nash Baldwin and the American Civil Liberties Union* (Columbia University Press, 2000), 103. *"Maggie Martin"*: Madeleine Zabriskie Doty, *Society's Misfits* (Century Company, 1916), 9. *"No special"*: Ibid., 72. *"collective"*: Ibid., 3. *"self-control"*: Ibid., 101.
27. **sexual freedoms**: Chauncey, *Gay New York*, ch. 9. **Thomas**: RNB, A Memo on MZD for the files of Smith College, Oct. 1978, b. 6, f. 1, RNBP; also in b. 1, f. 4, MZDP. *"grim mockery"*: RNB, Marriage Vows, 1919, b. 1, f. 4, MZDP, also in b. 24, RNBP. *"charge my husband"*: Beulah Powers, "Hubby Pays Wife for Doing Housework in Happy Doty-Baldwin 50-50 Marriage," *New York Evening Mail*, Sept. 15, 1920, b. 1, f. 4, MZDP.
28. **affairs . . .** *"natural limit"*: RNB to MZD, July 27, 1921, b. 2, f. 9, MZDP. **dreaming**: RNB to MZD, Sept. 5, 1920, b. 2, f. 9, MZDP. *"walk . . . union"*: MZD, "Marriage," b. 24, f. 13, RNBP. **clashes**: RNB to MZD, July 9, 1925, b. 2, f. 9, MZDP; Lucy Nash Baldwin to RNB, [1923], b. 6, f. 1, RNBP; see also Cottrell, *Roger Nash Baldwin*, 112–16. **divorce**: RNB, A Memo on MZD for the files of Smith College, Oct. 1978, b. 6, f. 1, RNBP; also in b. 1, f. 4, MZDP; MZD to RNB, March 24, 1936, b. 6, f. 1, RNBP; MZD, "Marriage," b. 24, f. 13, RNBP; Frank Fenno Baldwin to RNB, Dec. 15, 1934, b. 3, f. 15, RNBP; RNB, *Reminiscences*, 154.
29. *"first-hand"*: RNB, untitled, [n.d., 1919? 1920?], b. 19, f. 6, RNBP. *"crowd"*: MZD, "Marriage," b. 24, f. 13, RNBP.
30. *"never understand"*: Benjamin David Diamond, "Conflicts Resolved: Roger Nash Baldwin and the Founding of the ACLU," 1974, b. 24, f. 11, RNBP, quoting RNB, *Reminiscences*, 103. **harvest fields . . . Texas**: RNB to MZD, Mar. 31, 1919, b. 2, f. 9, MZDP. *"most tense"*: RNB, untitled, [n.d., 1919? 1920?], b. 19, f. 6, RNBP. *"direct contact"*: RNB to Albert DeSilver, Aug. 12, 1919, b. 11, f. 8, RNBP. *"whole training"*: RNB to MZD, Mar. 31, 1919, b. 2, f. 9, MZDP.
31. **Chicago**: RNB, Recollections of Bill Haywood, Apr. 1962, b. 7, f. 14, RNBP; RNB, "Autobiography," b. 20, f. 11, 105. **skepticism**: William Haywood to RNB, Sept. 17, 1919, b. 19, f. 6, RNBP. **Cooks and Waiters**: RNB, *Reminiscences*, 105. *"They had guts"*: RNB, "Autobiography," b. 20, f. 11, 104–8.
32. **lead smelter . . . Ohio**: RNB, *Reminiscences*, 109–11. **first industrial wages**: RNB to LNB, Oct. 26, 1919, b. 3, f. 16, RNBP. **Pittsburgh**: RNB, *Reminiscences*, 110.
33. **Homestead**: Stuart Chase, "Violence in Labor Conflicts," in *American Labor Dynamics in the Light of Post-War Developments: An Inquiry by Thirty-Two Labor Men, Teachers, Editors, and Technicians*, ed. J. B. S. Hardman (Russell & Russell, 1928), 351; see also Philip Taft, "Violence in American Labor Disputes," *Annals of the American Academy of Political and Social Science* 364 (1966): 127, 129.
34. **Founded**: David Brody, *Labor in Crisis: The Steel Strike of 1919* (J. B. Lippincott, 1965), at 19. *"Industry"*: Ibid., 127.
35. **Gompers**: See Philip Taft, *The A. F. of L. in the Time of Gompers* (Harper & Brothers, 1957). **twenty-four unions**: Colston E. Warne, ed., *The Steel Strike of 1919* (D. C. Heath, 1963), xiii. **quarter-million workers**: Brody, *Labor in Crisis*, 113.
36. **told Baldwin . . . industrial spy**: RNB, "Autobiography," b. 20, f. 11, 108–9, RNBP. **Foster**: Ed-

ward P. Johanningsmeier, *Forging American Communism: The Life of William Z. Foster* (Princeton University Press, 2014), 3.
37. **ordinance ... Troopers shot**: Interchurch World Movement of North America, *Report on the Steel Strike of 1919* (Harcourt, Brace and Howe, 1920), at 236–41; William Z. Foster, *The Great Steel Strike and Its Lessons* (B. W. Heubsch, 1920), 98. **affidavits**: Interchurch World Movement of North America, *Public Opinion and the Steel Strike: Supplementary Reports of the Investigators to the Commission of Inquiry, the Interchurch World Movement* (Harcourt, Brace and Howe, 1921), 186–219. **"brutality"**: Mary Heaton Vorse, *Men and Steel* (Boni and Liveright, 1920), 66. **"third degree"**: Ibid., 70. **Wood**: Interchurch World, *Report on the Steel Strike*, 241.
38. **propaganda campaign**: Ibid., 242. **"independent investigation"**: Interchurch World Movement, *Public Opinion and the Steel Strike*, 92–93. **"firsthand news"**: John Dos Passos, *The Big Money* (Houghton Mifflin, 1933), 115.
39. **"practically at an end"**: Interchurch World, *Public Opinion and the Steel Strike*, 94. **"Pittsburgh"**: Ibid., 134. **"Laborers ... Crumbling"**: Ibid., 136. **"strike was lost"**: Ibid., 39.
40. **false**: See ibid., 92–101. **"dark towns"**: Vorse, *Men and Steel*, 99–101. **"blanket of silence"**: George Soule, "Civil Rights in Western Pennsylvania," in Interchurch World, *Public Opinion and the Steel Strike*, 220.
41. **propaganda specialist**: Interchurch World, *Public Opinion and the Steel Strike*, 306 n7. **"private propaganda"**: Cobb, "Press and Public Opinion," 147. **"marauding soldiers"**: Ibid., 145. **"publicity"**: Ibid., 144.
42. **called off**: Foster, *Great Steel Strike and Its Lessons*, 1; see also Robert K. Murray, "Communism and the Great Steel Strike of 1919," *Mississippi Valley Historical Review* 38 (1951): 445, 464. **unions' goals**: Brody, *Labor in Crisis*, 39.
43. **"covert surveillance" ... last report**: RNB, "Autobiography," b. 20, f. 11, 109–11, RNBP. **secretly tailing**: Col. Gordon Johnston & Capt. John B. Campbell to Intelligence Officer, U.S. Disciplinary Barracks, Fort Leavenworth, Kansas, May 3, 1920, Military Intelligence Division Correspondence, 10902-13, RG 165, NARA.
44. **"Pittsburgh district"**: Walter Lippmann, *Public Opinion* (Macmillan, 1922), 219.
45. **"romantic notion ... no public"**: RNB, "Where Are the Pre-War Radicals," *The Survey*, Feb. 1926, 560, also in b. 23, f. 1, RNBP. **"phantom"**: Ibid.; see generally Walter Lippmann, *The Phantom Public* (Brace, 1925).
46. **deep skepticism**: Ronald Steel, *Walter Lippmann and the American Century* (Atlantic Monthly Press, 1980), 257.
47. **"freedom of speech"**: U.S. Const., amend. 1. **advance of publication**: William Blackstone, *Commentaries on the Laws of England: A Facsimile of the First Edition of 1765–1769* (University of Chicago Press, 1979), at 4:150–53. **"main purpose"**: Patterson v. Colorado, 205 U.S. 454, 462 (1907). **three opinions**: Schenck v. United States, 249 U.S. 47 (1919); Debs v. United States, 249 U.S. 211 (1919); Frohwerk v. United States, 249 U.S. 204 (1919). **"stringent"**: Schenck, 249 U.S., at 52. **"clear and present"**: Ibid., 47.
48. **Chafee ... lobbied**: See Zechariah Chafee Jr., "Freedom of Speech in War Time," *Harvard Law Review* 32 (1919): 932–73; Gerald Gunther, "Learned Hand and the Origins of Modern First Amendment Doctrine: Some Fragments of History," *Stanford Law Review* 27 (1975): 719–73; Mark DeWolfe Howe, ed., *Holmes-Laski Letters: The Correspondence of Mr. Justice Holmes and Harold J. Laski, 1916–1935*, vol. 1 (Harvard University Press, 1963), at 142–65. **"social interest"**: Chafee, "Freedom of Speech in War Time," 958. **"at best"**: Learned Hand to Oliver Wendell Holmes Jr., June 28, 1918, in Howe, *Holmes-Laski Letters*, 114; see generally Thomas Healy, *The Great Dissent: How Oliver Wendell Holmes Changed His Mind and Changed the History of Free Speech in America* (Metropolitan Books, 2013).
49. **five Russian anarchists**: Richard Polenberg, *Fighting Faiths: The Abrams Case, the Supreme Court, and Free Speech* (Viking, 1987); Michael Willrich, *American Anarchy: The Epic Struggle Between Immigrant Radicals and the US Government at the Dawn of the Twentieth Century* (Basic Books, 2023), 253–92. **peroration**: Abrams v. United States, 250 U.S. 616 (1919); Robert C. Post, "Writing the Dissent in *Abrams*," *Seton Hall Law Review* 51 (2020): 21–39; Laura Weinrib,

"Power and Premises: The Contested Meanings of the *Abrams* Dissent," *Seton Hall Law Review* 51 (2020): 61–103. ***Abrams***: Jacob Abrams to RNB, Nov. 28, 1918, b. 12, f. 1, RNBP; RNB, "Autobiography," b. 20, f. 12, 392, RNBP. ***"Persecution . . . experiment"***: Abrams v. United States, 250 U.S. 630 (1919); Healy, *Great Dissent*.
50. ***pragmatism . . . "true"***: William James, *Pragmatism: A New Name for Some Old Ways of Thinking* (1907; Floating Press, 2008), 57. ***"hypothesis"***: Ibid., 205; see generally Louis Menand, *The Metaphysical Club* (Farrar, Straus & Giroux, 2001), 409–33; James T. Kloppenberg, "Pragmatism: An Old Name for Some New Ways of Thinking?," *Journal of American History* 83 (1996): 100.
51. ***James's theory***: Menand, *Metaphysical Club*, 428–31; Mark A. Graber, *Transforming Free Speech: The Ambiguous Legacy of Civil Libertarianism* (University of California Press, 1991), ch. 4. ***"sifted"***: Chafee, "Freedom of Speech in War Time," 958.
52. ***"worth resisting"***: Walter Lippmann, "The Basic Problem of Democracy," *The Atlantic*, Nov. 1919, 617.
53. ***artillery***: Creel, *How We Advertised America*, 86. ***Bullard***: Arthur Bullard, Memorandum on Censorship, July 1916, b. 185, f. 220, Papers of Colonel E. M. House. ***Dewey***: John Dewey, *The Public and Its Problems: An Essay in Political Inquiry* (Pennsylvania State University Press, 2012), 133. ***"adverse opinion"***: Harry Kalven Jr., "Ernst Freund and the First Amendment Tradition: Professor Ernst Freund and Debs v. United States," *University of Chicago Law Review* 40 (1973): 235, 242.
54. ***"institutions"***: Walter Lippmann to Oliver Wendell Holmes Jr., Nov. 18, 1919, in *Public Philosopher: Selected Letters of Walter Lippmann*, ed. John Morton Blum (Ticknor & Fields, 1985), 132–33. ***"can prevail"***: Walter Lippmann, *Liberty and the News* (Harcourt, Brace and Howe, 1920), 71.
55. ***"second, third"***: Lippmann, "Basic Problem of Democracy," 620.
56. ***Plato's cave***: Lippmann, *Public Opinion*, vii. ***"world outside"***: Ibid., 3. ***"messengers"***: Lippmann, *Liberty and the News*, 85. ***"habitual viewpoints"***: Lippmann, "Basic Problem of Democracy," 623. ***"catchwords"***: Ibid., 620. ***"stereotypes"***: Lippmann, *Liberty and the News*, 54–55. ***"buzzing confusion"***: Ibid., quoting William James, *The Principles of Psychology*, vol. 1 (Henry Holt, 1913), 488. ***"most part"***: Lippmann, *Liberty and the News*, 54–55.
57. ***favorite example***: Ibid., 39; Walter Lippmann and Charles Merz, "A Test of the News," *New Republic* (Special Suppl.), Aug. 4, 1920, 3. ***"quack"***: Lippmann, "Basic Problem of Democracy," 624.
58. ***"subsidiary phase . . . bricks"***: Lippmann, "Liberty and the News," 779. ***"arguing"***: Lippmann, *Public Opinion*, 86.
59. ***new orientation***: Lamson, *Roger Baldwin*, 123–24.
60. ***"two months"***: RNB to H. Austin Simons, Dec. 1, 1919, b. 11, f. 8, RNBP. ***casting about for funds***: RNB, Memorandum to the Persons Named in the Enclosed Prospectus, Mar. 23, 1922, Board of Directors Correspondence, r. 1, AFPS.

4: FREEDOM AND ECONOMICS

"sense of democracy": RNB, *The Reminiscences of Roger Baldwin, 1953–1954*, at 308, CCOH.
1. ***Jefferson***: Annette Gordon-Reed, *The Hemingses of Monticello: An American Family* (W. W. Norton, 2008), 629–54; Daniel Scott Smith, "Population and Political Ethics: Thomas Jefferson's Demography of Generations," *William & Mary Quarterly* 56 (1999): 591. ***attack on the slave system***: David S. Reynolds, *John Brown, Abolitionist: The Man Who Killed Slavery, Sparked the Civil War, and Seeded Civil Rights* (Knopf, 2005); John Stauffer, *The Black Hearts of Men: Radical Abolitionists and the Transformation of Race* (Harvard University Press, 2002). ***radicals consorted***: Christine Stansell, *American Moderns: Bohemian New York and the Creation of a New Century* (Henry Holt, 2000), 178. ***Black Panthers . . . Park Avenue***: Tom Wolfe, *Radical Chic & Mau-Mauing the Flak Catchers* (Farrar, Straus & Giroux, 1970); also Steve Fraser, *The Limousine Liberal: How an Incendiary Image United the Right and Fractured America* (Basic Books, 2016).

NOTES TO PAGES 81-85   599

2. *money*: Dwight Macdonald, "In Defense of Everybody—Part II," *New Yorker*, July 18, 1953, 29; see also RNB, Memo for Mrs. Lamson on My Attitude to Money, Apr. 1974, b. 25, f. 2, RNBP. *"tight wad"*: Peggy Lamson, *Roger Baldwin: Founder of the American Civil Liberties Union* (Houghton Mifflin, 1976), 149. *"hairshirt"*: Samantha Barbas, *The Rise and Fall of Morris Ernst: Free Speech Renegade* (University of Chicago Press, 2021), 58. *corrupting*: RNB, *The Reminiscences of Roger Baldwin, 1953-1954* (1963), at 332, CCOH. *"one thing" . . . barter*: Macdonald, "In Defense of Everybody," 29–30. *vulgar*: RNB, *Reminiscences*, 324. *fanatical track*: Oliver Jensen, "The Persuasive Roger Baldwin," *Harper's*, Sept. 1951, 52.
3. *inequality*: Thomas Piketty et al., "Distributional National Accounts: Methods and Estimates for the United States," *Quarterly Journal of Economics* 133 (2018): 553, 587; David Huyssen, *Progressive Inequality: Rich and Poor in New York, 1890-1920* (Harvard University Press, 2014); *six*: Commission on Industrial Relations, *Industrial Relations: Final Report and Testimony Submitted to Congress by the Commission on Industrial Relations Created by the Act of August 23, 1912*, vol. 1 (Government Printing Office, 1916), at 28, 80.
4. *resumed*: RNB to Albert DeSilver, Aug. 12, 1919, b. 11, f. 8, RNBP; Scott Nearing to RNB, May 5, 1919, b. 11. f. 17, RNBP; Robert C. Cottrell, *Roger Nash Baldwin and the American Civil Liberties Union* (Columbia University Press, 2000), 121.
5. *"freedom . . . labor"*: Laura Weinrib, *The Taming of Free Speech: America's Civil Liberties Compromise* (Harvard University Press, 2016), 82–145; Lamson, *Roger Baldwin*, 123–24; William A. Donahue, *The Politics of the American Civil Liberties Union* (Transaction Books, 1985), 31. *renamed*: Cottrell, *Roger Nash Baldwin*, 121. *National Committee*: National Committee of the American Civil Liberties Union, 1920, r. 16, vol. 120, ACLUA; Samuel Walker, *In Defense of American Liberties: A History of the ACLU* (Oxford University Press, 1990), 66–70. *"partisans"*: Weinrib, *Taming of Free Speech*, 125; also Charles Lam Markmann, *The Noblest Cry: A History of the American Civil Liberties Union* (St. Martin's Press, 1965), 38.
6. *"believe"*: RNB to Scott Nearing, Nov. 18, 1918, b. 14, f. 28, RNBP. *"parliamentary"*: Basil [Atkinson?] to RNB, Apr. 26, 1919, b. 12, f. 1, RNBP; see also Weinrib, *Taming of Free Speech*, 82–110.
7. *minimum wage*: Florence Kelley to RNB, Washington Minimum Wage Commission Secretary Job Offer, 1913, b. 10, f. 14, RNBP. *juvenile*: Bernard Flexner and Roger N. Baldwin, *Juvenile Courts and Probation* (Century Company, 1914). *"formulating"*: Mary Van Kleeck, "Sources of Power for Industrial Freedom: Introductory Statement," [n.d.], b. 19, f. 5, RNBP. *"getting"*: RNB, "Sources of Power for Industrial Freedom," [n.d.], b. 19, f. 5, RNBP. *"direct"*: RNB, Untitled, [n.d., 1919? 1920?], b. 19, f. 6, RNBP. *"organization"*: Norman Thomas, "What Is Industrial Democracy?" (League for Industrial Democracy, 1925); see also RNB, "Evie: For the Children," July 1978, b. 3, f. 14, RNBP; Robert Westbrook, "Schools for Industrial Democrats: The Social Origins of John Dewey's Philosophy of Education," *American Journal of Education* 100 (1992): 401, 407.
8. *"timid"*: RNB, "The Immorality of Social Work," *World Tomorrow*, Feb. 1922, 44–45; also in b. 23, f. 3, RNBP. *"underlying"*: RNB, "Social Work and Radical Economic Movements," *Proceedings of the National Conference of Social Work* 45 (1918): 396, 397.
9. *"socialize"*: RNB, "An Industrial Program After the War," *Proceedings of the National Conference of Social Work* 45 (1918): 426, 429. *"learn"*: Benjamin David Diamond, "Conflicts Resolved: Roger Nash Baldwin and the Founding of the ACLU," 1974, b. 24, f. 11, 15, RNBP.
10. *romantic notions*: RNB, "Where Are All the Pre-War Radicals?," *The Survey*, Feb. 1926, 560; also in b. 23, f. 1, RNBP. *"liberty"*: RNB, "Personal Liberty," *Annals of the American Academy of Political and Social Science* (1936), b. 22, f. 1, RNBP. *"speak"*: Kleeck, "Sources of Power for Industrial Freedom," b. 19, f. 5, RNBP. *"weapon"*: RNB, "Outline for Debate with Olgin," b. 24, f. 3, RNBP.
11. *"minority"*: RNB, *Reminiscences*, 192.
12. *set out*: Memorandum for Mr. Hoover, June 20, 1921, FBI FOIA 1218889-1, Cottrell, *Roger Nash Baldwin*, 127.
13. *"lid is on"*: RNB, "Freedom of Opinion," *Socialist Review* 9 (1920): 115. *"Critical"*: RNB, "The

Myth of Law and Order," in *Behold America!*, ed. Samuel D. Schmalhausen (Farrar & Rinehart, 1931), 658. *"campaign... rights"*: RNB, "Freedom of Opinion," 115.
14. *"budget to carry"*: [RNB], Suggestions for Reorganization of the National Civil Liberties Bureau, r. 16, vol. 120, ACLUA; also RNB, Memorandum to the Persons Named in the Enclosed Prospectus, Mar. 23, 1922, Board of Directors Correspondence, r. 1, AFPSR; Minutes of the National Committee [1920], r. 16, vol. 120, ACLUA.
15. *September 1913... "industrial democracy"*: Thomas G. Andrews, *Killing for Coal: America's Deadliest Labor War* (Harvard University Press, 2008), 252; George S. McGovern and Leonard F. Guttridge, *The Great Coalfield War* (Houghton Mifflin, 1972), 252–64.
16. *"little... society"*: Ron Chernow, *Titan: The Life of John D. Rockefeller, Sr.* (Random House, 1998), 574. *"open"*: George Creel, "The High Cost of Hate," *Everybody's Magazine* 30 (1914): 756; Commission, *Industrial Relations*, 1:83.
17. *"hastened"... wages*: Andrews, *Killing for Coal*, 247–51.
18. *Tensions... March*: Andrews, *Killing for Coal*, 255. *"death"*: Chernow, *Titan*, 577; see also McGovern and Guttridge, *Great Coalfield War*, 210–49.
19. *April 20... died*: Andrews, *Killing for Coal*; Chernow, *Titan*, 271–73.
20. *"call"*: Colorado State Federation of Labor, "Call to Arms," *International Socialist Review* 14 (1914): 720. *Ten Days War*: Chernow, *Titan*, 278–81.
21. *strike*: Chernow, *Titan*, 283–84.
22. *new foundation*: Raymond B. Fosdick, *John D. Rockefeller, Jr.: A Portrait* (Harper & Brothers, 1956), 120. *Franklin*: Randall G. Holcombe, *Writing Off Ideas: Taxation, Foundations, and Philanthropy in America* (Transaction, 2000), 4. *Girard's school*: Ibid., 140. *millionaires*: Olivier Zunz, *Philanthropy in America: A History* (Princeton University Press, 2014), 8. *$1 billion*: Chernow, *Titan*, 344. *net worth*: United States Department of Commerce, *Historical Statistics of the United States, Colonial Times to 1970* (Government Printing Office, 1975), at 224; Tom Metcalf, "Rockefeller Was Almost Three Times Richer Than Bezos," *Bloomberg*, May 21, 2019, bloomberg.com/news/articles/2019-05-21/john-d-rockefeller-was-almost-three-times-richer-than-bezos.
23. *Board*: Chernow, *Titan*, 485; Leonard P. Ayres, "The Seven Great Foundations," *Journal of Education* 72 (1910): 316. *Carnegie*: Ibid., 288–89. *Teaching*: Ibid., 340–41. *Sage*: Edward Devine, "The Russell Sage Foundation," *Charities and the Commons* (1907): 1055–56. *Six*: Henry S. Pritchett, "Should the Carnegie Foundation Be Suppressed?," *North American Review* 201 (1915): 554. *Rockefeller and Carnegie*: "Three Swollen Fortunes," *New York Sun*, Jan. 18, 1920; "Individual Benefaction," *New York Times*, Dec. 5, 1920, 26. *$2 billion*: "The Spirit of Service," *Los Angeles Times*, Dec. 20, 1924, A4.
24. *"era"*: "Philanthropy on a Colossal Scale," *New York Observer*, Mar. 7, 1910, 327. *"promote"*: Fosdick, *John D. Rockefeller, Jr.*, 121; Jonathan Levy, "Altruism and the Origins of Nonprofit Philanthropy," in *Philanthropy in Democratic Societies: History, Institutions, Values*, ed. Rob Reich, Chiara Cordelli, and Lucy Bernholz (University of Chicago Press, 2016), 38; J. G. Bright to Collector of Internal Revenue, May 1, 1924, r. 3, b. 5, AFPSR; see also Charles H. Johnson, June 28, 1929, c.160, MLEP. *"alms"*: Robert W. Bruer, "Business and Philanthropy," *Harper's*, June 1916, 81. *"evil"*: "Philanthropy on a Colossal Scale," 327.
25. *dead hand*: Julius Rosenwald, "The Burden of Wealth," *Saturday Evening Post*, Jan. 5, 1929, 12; Rob Reich, "On the Role of Foundations in Democracies," in Reich et al., *Philanthropy in Democratic Societies*, 69–70; *Jefferson*: Thomas Jefferson to James Madison, Sept. 6, 1789, Founders Online, National Archives, founders.archives.gov/documents/Madison/01-12-02-0248.
26. *gifts*: Commission, *Industrial Relations*, 1:81.
27. *originally*: Fosdick, *John D. Rockefeller, Jr.*, 120–21; Samuel Gompers, "The Rockefellers Condemned and Doomed by Themselves," *American Federationist* 22 (1915): 42–43. *"might"*: Chernow, *Titan*, 565. *objections... State*: Rob Reich, *Just Giving: Why Philanthropy Is Failing Democracy and How It Can Do Better* (Princeton University Press, 2020), 4–8; Zunz, *Philanthropy in America*, 20–21. Ironically, the New York charter may have been better than a federal one for advancing the Rockefeller goal of minimizing regulatory meddling. See Roberta Romano, *The Genius of American Corporate Law* (AEI Press, 1993).

28. *"wage slavery"*: Upton Sinclair, *The Jungle* (Doubleday, Page, 1906). *"upon a charge of murder"*: Chernow, *Titan*, 579. *"shoot him down"*: Fosdick, *John D. Rockefeller, Jr.*, 152–53. **Protesters**: Chernow, *Titan*, 579. **bomb exploded**: Beverly Gage, *The Day Wall Street Exploded: A Story of America in Its First Age of Terror* (Oxford University Press, 2009), 96–101; Thai Jones, *More Powerful Than Dynamite: Radicals, Plutocrats, Progressives, and New York's Year of Anarchy* (Bloomsbury, 2014); Michael Willrich, *American Anarchy: The Epic Struggle Between Immigrant Radicals and the US Government at the Dawn of the Twentieth Century* (Basic Books, 2023), 132–34. *"monster"*: Chernow, *Titan*, 579.
29. *"unjust"*: Chernow, *Titan*, 579; Albert F. Shenkel, *The Rich Man and the Kingdom* (Fortress Press, 1995).
30. **King**: Maria Montoya, "Making an American Workforce: The Rockefellers and the Legacy of Ludlow," in *Making an American Workforce: The Rockefellers and the Legacy of Ludlow*, ed. Fawn-Amber Montoya (University Press of Colorado, 2014), 189–96; Chernow, *Titan*, 581; Memorandum Regarding Appointment of W. L. Mackenzie King, RG 3, SG 3.1, subgrp 1, series 900, b. 21, f. 156, RAC.
31. *"extreme . . . employed"*: Howard M. Gitelman, *Legacy of the Ludlow Massacre: A Chapter in American Industrial Relations*, vol. 1 (University of Pennsylvania Press, 1988), 52.
32. *"Rockefeller Plan"*: Ibid., 190–91; Fosdick, *John D. Rockefeller, Jr.*, 163; Montoya, "Making an American Workforce"; W. L. Mackenzie King to John D. Rockefeller, Jr., Aug. 6, 1914, Office of the Messrs. Rockefeller, Business Interests, series C (FA312), b. 23, f. 212, RAC.
33. **Walsh**: Commission, *Industrial Relations*, 1:267–68; see also "Rockefeller Says He Tries to Be Fair," *New York Times*, May 21, 1915, 22; "Rockefeller Again Heckled by Walsh," *New York Times*, May 22, 1915, 6.
34. **James**: Jesse James, Jr., *Jesse James: My Father* (Buckeye, 1899), 144–45.
35. *"hammer"*: "Walsh Again Tilts with Rockefeller," *New York Times*, May 23, 1915, 15.
36. *"industrial despots"*: Commission, *Industrial Relations*, 1:80. *"entire country"* . . . *"industrial interests"*: Ibid., 1:83. *"psychological condition"*: Paul Kellogg, "Editorials," *The Survey*, Nov. 1914, 177. *"philanthropic trusts"*: Frank P. Walsh, "Perilous Philanthropy," *The Independent*, Aug. 23, 1915, 262–64.
37. **new regulations**: Commission, *Industrial Relations*, 8:7647. **dissolution**: Ibid., 1:269. **taxes**: Ibid., 1:221.
38. **local protests**: Alan Axelrod, *Selling the Great War: The Making of American Propaganda* (St. Martin's Press, 2009), 36. **pamphlets**: "Rockefeller Again Heckled by Walsh," 6; George Creel, "How 'Tainted' Money Taints," *Pearson's*, Mar. 1915, 296; Committee of Coal Mine Miners, "The Struggle in Colorado for Industrial Freedom," 1914, 2. *"premeditated fraud"*: Creel, "How 'Tainted' Money Taints," 289. *"poisoners"*: George Creel, "Poisoners of Public Opinion," *Harper's Weekly*, Nov. 7, 1914, 436–38. *"Poison Ivy"*: Upton Sinclair, *The Brass Check: A Study of American Journalism* (Upton Sinclair, 1920), 311. **a novel**: Upton Sinclair, *King Coal: A Novel* (Macmillan, 1917).
39. *"missed"*: "Gives Rockefeller Lesson in Finance," *New York Times*, Sept. 23, 1915, 1. **Plan**: Gitelman, *Legacy of the Ludlow Massacre*, 190.
40. **pensions**: "Meddlesome and Impudent Philanthropy," *Nashville Tennessean*, Nov. 26, 1912, 6. **Rockefeller Foundation charter**: Barry D. Karl and Stanley Katz, "The American Private Philanthropic Foundation and the Public Sphere, 1890–1930," *Minerva* 19 (1981): 236, 255.
41. *"imagine"*: Gitelman, *Legacy of the Ludlow Massacre*, 192. *"corrupted"*: Gompers, "The Rockefellers Condemned and Doomed by Themselves," 42–43. *"machinery"*: Commission, *Industrial Relations*, 8:7647. *"verbal"*: "An American Bernhardi," *American Federationist* 22 (1915): 747, 748. *"Most . . . philanthropic"*: Walsh, "Perilous Philanthropy," 262–64.
42. *"educate"*: RNB to Frank P. Walsh, Sept. 15, 1915, b. 13, f. 9, RNBP. *"faith"*: Commission, *Industrial Relations*, 8:7664. *"repugnant"*: Ibid., 8:7916.
43. *"no work"* . . . *"financed"*: RNB, "Social Work and Radical Economic Movements," *Proceedings of the National Conference of Social Work* 45 (1918): 396, 397. *"professional"*: Norman Hapgood, *Professional Patriots: An Exposure of the Personalities, Methods, and Objectives Involved in*

the Organized Effort to Exploit Patriotic Impulses in These United States During and After the Late War (Albert and Charles Boni, 1927), 22. *"sense"*: RNB, "Autobiography (1920–1931)," b. 20, f. 12, 338, RNBP.
44. *3 million members*: Greg Patmore, "A Tale of Two Employee Representation Plans in the Steel Industry: Pueblo, Colorado, and Sydney, Nova Scotia," in Montoya, *Making an American Workforce*, 125–52.

5: GARLAND'S MILLION

"meanest person": George M. Cohan quoted in "An Idealistic Young Man Who Refuses a Million Dollars," *Literary Digest*, Jan. 8, 1921, 46, 48.
1. *tutor*: Ellis Paxson Oberholtzer, *Jay Cooke: Financier of the Civil War* (George W. Jacobs, 1907), 2:202 n1. *clerk*: Henrietta M. Larson, *Jay Cooke: Private Banker* (Greenwood Press, 1968), 304; "Obituary: James A. Garland," *New York Daily Tribune*, July 28, 1900, 9.
2. *Cooke*: T. J. Grayson, "Salmon P. Chase and Jay Cooke: Financing the Civil War," in *Leaders and Periods of American Finance* (John Wiley & Sons, 1932), 234–65. *collapsed*: Jay Cooke & Company, "In the Matter of Jay Cooke & Co. in Bankruptcy: Notice to Creditors" (Allen, Lane & Scott's Printing House, 1873); Lewis, Trustee, v. United States, 92 U.S. 618 (1875). *Panic*: M. John Lubetkin, *Jay Cooke's Gamble: The Northern Pacific Railroad, the Sioux, and the Panic of 1873* (University of Oklahoma Press, 2006); Christopher P. Munden, "Jay Cooke: Banks, Railroads, and the Panic of 1873," *Pennsylvania Legacies* 11 (2011): 3–5.
3. *back to wealth*: Larson, *Jay Cooke*, 420; Oberholtzer, *Jay Cooke: Financier*, 2:537; *Poor's Directory of Railroad Officials, 1892* (Poor's, 1892), at 507; "Bar Harbor Is Happy," *New York Times*, July 13, 1895, 13. *Garland Jr.*: "James A. Garland Dead," *New York Times*, Sept. 14, 1906, 7; "Staked $10,000,000 for Love—and Lost Both," *Times-Dispatch*, Oct. 25, 1914, 6; Harvard University, *Class of 1893 Fourth Report* (Harvard University Press, 1910), 93–94. *Evelyn Nesbit*: Mosette Broderick, *Triumvirate: McKim, Mead & White: Art, Architecture, Scandal, and Class in America's Gilded Age* (Knopf, 2010), 473.
4. *father's estate*: James A. Garland Jr., The Will of James A. Garland Jr., Proved Feb. 7, 1907, Probate Record Book 894, Registry of Probate, Old Court House, Suffolk County, Boston, Mass.; "Mr. Garland and His Money," *New York Tribune*, July 31, 1922, I-C-196, NAACPLC; RNB, *The Reminiscences of Roger Baldwin, 1953–1954*, 326.
5. *In one week*: "$63,763,357 Given by Rockefeller in Wife's Memory," *New York Times*, Nov. 25, 1920, 1.
6. *Charles Garland*: "On Refusing a Million: What Charles Garland Is Like and His Reasons for Rejecting a Fortune," *New York Times*, Nov. 28, 1920, 91. *six feet*: Marguerite Mooers Marshall, "Why Young Garland Refuses a Million," *New York Evening World*, Nov. 26, 1920, 1. *"one can"*: Richard Cowen, Garland Book, 64, RCC.
7. *Tudor . . . O'Keeffe*: "Wife of Garland Says She Too Will Refuse a Fortune," *New York World*, Nov. 25, 1920; Helen Hoffman, "What's Wealth to Us Compared to Love?," *San Francisco Chronicle*, Apr. 24, 1921, 12; "Frederic Tudor," *Dictionary of American Biography* 19 (Dumas Malone ed., 1936), 47–48; "Giving Up Fortune, Mrs. Garland Weds," *New York Times*, May 26, 1912, 15; "Staked $10,000,000 for Love," 6; Roxana Robinson, *Georgia O'Keeffe: A Life* (Harper & Row, 1989), 359. *remarriage*: Tudor v. Vail, 195 Mass. 18, 20–22 (1908); also Marie Tudor Garland, *The Marriage Feast* (G. P. Putnam's Sons, 1920). *Kahlil Gibran*: Jean Gibran & Kahlil Gibran, *Kahlil Gibran: His Life and World* (Interlink Books, 1991), 314–15; Robin Waterfield, *Prophet: The Life and Times of Kahlil Gibran* (St. Martin's Press, 1998), 178.
8. *Harvard*: RNB and Corliss Lamont, "Harvard Heretics and Rebels," *Harvard Alumni Bulletin* (1936), b. 23, f. 3, RNBP. *handsome*: "On Refusing a Million," 91. *mental illness*: Jay Garland, interview with author, June 26, 2013; RNB to AFPS, Dec. 1939, r. 25, b. 39, AFPSR. *unusual mother*: "Morning World," July 20, 1922, r. 3, b. 5, AFPSR.
9. *"naturally speaking"*: William Blackstone, *Commentaries on the Laws of England* (Clarendon Press, 1766) (University of Chicago Press, 1979), 2:10. *"too great"*: Jeremy Bentham, *Theory of*

Legislation (Trubner, 1864), 122. *Mill:* Jens Beckert, *Inherited Wealth*, trans. Thomas Dunlap (Princeton University Press, 2008), 212. *"general prosperity":* Richard T. Ely, "The Inheritance of Property," *North American Review* 153 (1891): 54–56. *"self-respect":* Theodore Roosevelt, "Seventh Annual Message to the Congress," 1907, presidency.ucsb.edu/documents/seventh-annual-message-4.

10. *Roosevelt:* Ibid. *"plain account":* H. G. Wells, *New Worlds for Old* (Macmillan, 1908), 353. *"spirit":* Ibid., ch. 5; see also "The Spirit of Service," *Los Angeles Times*, Dec. 20, 1924, A4; *"monstrous . . . descent":* Wells, *New Worlds for Old*, 145–46; see also Robert L. Hale, "Coercion and Distribution in a Supposedly Liberal State," *Political Science Quarterly* 38 (1923): 470, 483.
11. *"question the justice" . . . "face the facts":* CG to RNB, Nov. 21, 1922, r. 1, AFPSR. *not accept:* "On Refusing a Million," 91. *"hands":* CG to RNB, Nov. 21, 1922, r. 1, b. 1, AFPSR. *"Private property":* "Garland's Sons Turn Down Million Each," *Boston Daily Globe*, Nov. 23, 1920, 1.
12. *"meanest man":* Cowen, Garland Book, 4, RCC. **hefty commission:** "Would He Accept Million? Sure, and Pay Commission," *New York World*, Nov. 26, 1920, 8. *H. G. Wells:* "Refusal of Million 'Depresses' Wells," *New York World*, Nov. 28, 1920.
13. *cautious editorial:* Edward S. Martin, "Easy Chair," *Harper's*, Feb. 1921, 397–400. *"most extraordinary":* "Why Young Garland Refuses a Million," *New York Evening Post*, Nov. 26, 1920, 3.
14. *Garland struggled:* "That Rejected Million," *New York Tribune*, Nov. 28, 1920, pt. 2, 1; CG to RNB, Nov. 21, 1922, r. 1, b. 1, AFPSR. *expensive farm:* "On Refusing a Million," 91; "Garland Tells Why He Rejected Money," *Providence Journal*, Nov. 30, 1920. *income:* RNB, interview with Richard Cowen, Dec. 10, 1976, 19, RCC. *truck drivers . . . runners:* "Would He Accept Million?," 8; also "Think Garland Should Use His Million in Good Works," *New York World*, Nov. 29, 1920, 6.
15. *drop in the bucket . . . legitimate:* "Garland Still Scorns Riches," *New York Sun*, June 18, 1921, 6.
16. *reached out:* Upton Sinclair to CG, Dec. 2, 1920; US to CG, Dec. 29, 1920, both in b. 5, JCP. *"weapon":* Woodrow Wilson to Joseph Patrick Tumulty, Oct. 30, 1917, in *Papers of Woodrow Wilson*, vol. 43, ed. Arthur Link (Princeton University Press, 1983), 467–72.
17. *"Dead Hand":* Anthony Arthur, *Radical Innocent: Upton Sinclair* (Random House, 2007), 177. *"invisible":* Adam Smith, *Wealth of Nations* (W. Strahan & T. Cadell, 1776); **bestseller . . . "National News":** Upton Sinclair, *The Brass Check: A Study of American Journalism* (Upton Sinclair, 1920), 436–38.
18. *"congratulate . . . honest weekly":* US to CG, Dec. 2, 1920, b. 5, JCP.
19. *ready reply & admired* **The Brass Check:** CG to US, Jan. 8, 1921, b. 5, JCP. *"dumbest . . . radical movement":* US to CG, Dec. 2, 1920, b. 5, JCP. *"daily newspaper":* US to CG, Jan. 10, 1922, b. 13, f. 9, RNBP.
20. *"honest newspaper . . . ironical spectacle":* US to Mary Garland, Dec. 29, 1920, b. 5, JCP.
21. *"trusteeship":* US to CG, Jan. 10, 1922, b. 13, f. 9, RNBP. *"vote of confidence":* RNB to US, Jan. 17, 1922, b. 14, f. 22, RNBP.
22. *coincidence . . . younger brother . . . Hale:* RNB, A Memo on Charles Garland, Feb. 1975, 3, b. 25, f. 1, RNBP; Peggy Lamson, *Roger Baldwin: Founder of the American Civil Liberties Union* (Houghton Mifflin, 1976), 148. *related:* "Frederic Tudor," *Dictionary of American Biography* 19, at 48.
23. *Mutual Aid Society:* Lamson, *Roger Baldwin*, 138.
24. *"pioneering":* Memorandum on Trust Fund, Mar. 4, 1922, r. 2, b. 2, AFPSR. *visited . . . "found":* RNB, *Reminiscences*, 325. *"fairly close":* RNB to US, Jan. 17, 1922, b. 14, f. 22, RNBP.
25. *Mary:* "On Refusing a Million," 91. *leaving him:* "Garland in Boston, Seeks Miss Conrad," *New York Times*, Jan. 24, 1922, 8; "Girls Sharing Life on Farm with Idealist as Wife Quits," *Boston American*, Oct. 16, 1922. *unusual ideas:* "Love Nest of Garland Open to Lovelorn," *Chicago Tribune*, Oct. 21, 1922, 13; "Soul Twin of Garland Would Share His Love with His Wife," *Austin Statesman*, Jan. 30, 1922, 5; "Never Again! Garland's Comment on Marriage," *New York Tribune*, Feb. 1, 1922, 2; "Garland Donates All His $1,000,000 to Art Liberals," *New York World*, July 19, 1922, b. I-C-196, NAACPLC; "Garland May Run Love Farm," *Boston Herald*, Oct. 17, 1922, 1. *"love two women":* "Garland in Amazing Triangle," *Boston Daily Advertiser*, Jan. 22, 1922, 1. *inheritance:* "Garland Will Take Million," *Boston Post*, Jan. 9, 1922, 1; "Garland Takes Millon He Formerly Refused," *New York Times*, Jan. 9, 1922, 2:3. *"no chances":* RNB, *Reminiscences*, 325.

26. *Delaware corporation*: Walter Nelles to RNB, June 25, 1922, r. 1, b. 1, AFPSR; RNB to Albert DeSilver, Harry Weinberger, JWJ, NT, and CG, June 3[?], 1922; WN to RNB, June 26, 1922; RNB to NT, Lewis Gannett, and Robert Morss Lovett, July 6, 1922; Memorandum for WN, May 8, 1922, all in r. 1, b. 1, AFPSR.
27. *"benefit"*: CG to RNB, July 15, 1922, r. 1, b. 1, AFPSR; see also Committee on Negro Work to AFPS, [n.d., early 1930], b. 1, f. 14, JWJP. *"distributed"*: CG to AFPS, Nov. 16, 1922, r. 3, b. 5, AFPSR.
28. *"freeing"*: RNB to CG, Apr. 12, 1922, r. 1, b. 1, AFPSR. *"pioneering causes"*: RNB, *Reminiscences*, 325. *"rigid rules"*: AFPS Board Meeting, Aug. 10, 1922, r. 3, b. 5, AFPSR.
29. *domestic. . . . "classes"*: Ibid. *"so new"*: Walter Nelles, Press Release, July 5, 1922, r. 3, b. 5, AFPSR.
30. *"dictate the direction" . . . "bound"*: Newspaper Enterprise Association Service, "How They'll Spend Fortune That Garland Spurned," [n.d.], r. 5, b. 8, AFPSR. *"not reformers"*: RNB, Inserts [n.d., 1922?], r. 5, b. 8, AFPSR.
31. *bowed out*: Charles Garland Correspondence, b. 25, JPCC. *his own projects*: See, e.g., Upton Sinclair, 1922, b. 5, r. 3, AFPSR; Recommendations Made by the Committee on Applications, Jan. 24, 1924, r. 1, AFPSR; Upton Sinclair to Merle Curti, Sep. 22, 1958, MECP. *"kingpin"*: Norman Thomas to Merle Curti, Apr. 22, 1958, MECP. *"persons of wide contact"*: RNB to CG, May 17, 1922, r. 1, b. 1, AFPSR.
32. *"intentionally mixed" . . . "left compass"*: RNB, *Reminiscences*, 326. *Among the first*: JWJ, *Along This Way* (Knopf, 1933); RNB to Persons Named in the Enclosed Prospectus, Mar. 23, 1922; Mary Ovington to JWJ, July 25, 1922, both in II-L-I, NAACPLC.
33. *founding National Committee*: Certificate of Incorp., Delaware, r. 3, b. 5, AFPSR; RNB to WN, Apr. 10, 1922, r. 1, b. 1, AFPSR; Gloria Garrett Samson, *The American Fund for Public Service: Charles Garland and Radical Philanthropy, 1922–1941* (Greenwood Press, 1996), at 19. *Walsh*: RNB to Persons Named in the Enclosed Prospectus, Mar. 23, 1922, II-L-I, NAACPLC, also in r. 1, b. 1, AFPSR. *Lovett*: Ibid., 43. *Gannett*: LG to RNB, Apr. 2, 1922; RNB to LG, Apr. 3, 1922, r. 1, b. 1, AFPSR. *Kirchwey*: RNB to Clinton S. Golden, June 10, 1924, r. 1, b. 1, AFPSR; RNB, *Reminiscences*, 326; "Starving Coal Miners First to Share Garland's Million," *New York Mail*, July 29, 1922, I-C-196, f. 1, NAACPLC.
34. *Hillman*: Steve Fraser, *Labor Will Rule: Sidney Hillman and the Rise of American Labor* (Free Press, 1991); Fraser, "Sidney Hillman: Labor's Machiavelli," in *Labor Leaders in America*, ed. Melvyn Dubofsky and Warren Van Tine (University of Illinois Press, 1987).
35. *Thomas*: W. A. Swanberg, *Norman Thomas: The Last Idealist* (Scribners, 1976); Samson, *American Fund for Public Service*, 36. *Nearing*: John A. Saltmarsh, *Scott Nearing: An Intellectual Biography* (Temple University Press, 1991), 121. *"errant"*: RNB, *Reminiscences*, 326. *"manufacture"*: Samson, *American Fund for Public Service*, 56.
36. *Foster*: Maurice Isserman, *Reds: The Tragedy of American Communism* (Basic Books, 2024), 33–76; Samson, *American Fund for Public Service*, 20–21. *Magnes*: Judah Magnes to AFPS, Dec. 1924; JM to RNB, [n.d., 1924?], both in b. 1, f. 1, AFPSR; Samson, *American Fund for Public Service*, 28–29. *"free"*: Ibid., 31. *Ward*: Ibid., 34.
37. *McDowell*: Lea D. Taylor, "The Social Settlement and Civic Responsibility: The Life Work of Mary McDowell and Graham Taylor," *Social Service Review* 28 (1954): 31–40; Samson, *The American Fund for Public Service*, 45; Arthur, *Radical Innocent*, 47.
38. *Ernst*: AFPS Board Meeting, Feb. 14, 1923, r. 3, b. 5, AFPSR; RNB to EGF, June 22, 1925, r. 1, b. 1, AFPSR; Samantha Barbas, *The Rise and Fall of Morris Ernst, Free Speech Renegade* (University of Chicago Press, 2021), 55. *Flynn*: RNB to EGF, June 10, 1924, r. 1, b. 1, AFPSR; see also EGF, *Rebel Girl: An Autobiography, My First Life (1906–1926)* (International Publishers, 1973), at 21. *Clinton Golden*: Thomas R. Brooks, *Clint: A Biography of a Labor Intellectual, Clinton S. Golden* (Atheneum, 1978).
39. *Lippmann . . . Frankfurter*: AFPS Committees [n.d.], r. 2, b. 2, AFPSR. *Dewey*: Members of Sub-committees, r. 3, b. 5, AFPSR; RNB to John Dewey, Oct. 3, 1922; John Dewey to RNB, Oct. 4, 1922, both in r. 10, b. 15, AFPSR. *Alice Hamilton*: Barbara Sicherman, *Alice Hamilton: A Life in Letters* (Harvard University Press, 1984), 266–67.

40. *"family . . . catholicity"*: RNB, *Reminiscences*, 326.
41. **Civic Club**: RNB to AFPS, July 18, 1922; RNB to AFPS, Aug. 4, 1922, r. 3, b. 5, AFPSR; **499 applications**: Merle Curti, "Subsidizing Radicalism: The American Fund for Public Service, 1921–41," *Social Service Review* 33 (1959): 274, 279.
42. **United Mine Workers**: WN to RNB, Oct. 5, 1922, r. 1, b. 1, AFPSR.
43. *"survey"*: RNB, Inserts [n.d., 1922?], r. 3, b. 5, AFPSR.
44. **Hindu immigrants**: ACLU Emergency Case Fund, b. 9, r. 5, AFPSR; Hardeep Dhillon, "The Making of Modern U.S. Citizenship and Alienage," *Law & History Review* 41 (2023): 1, 36 n150; Nayan Shah, *Stranger Intimacies* (University of California Press, 2012), 203–4; Patrick Weil, *The Sovereign Citizen* (University of Pennsylvania Press, 2013), 81. **Native peoples**: American Indian Defense Committee, in Complete Listing of American Fund Gifts to 1941, r. 5, AFPSR; RNB and Stuart Chase, *Survey of Enterprises in the Liberal, Labor and Radical Movements in the United States* (Prepared for the AFPS, 1924), 8–13. **Chinese Americans**: Forrest Bailey to AFPS, Dec. 27, 1927, and ACLU Emergency Case Fund, both in r. 5, b. 9, AFPSR. **unionizing**: AFPS, *First Report*. **against lynching**: Arthur Spingarn to AFPS, Sept. 19, 1922; JWJ to RNB, Oct. 2, 1922; RNB to AFPS, Dec. 1, 1922; RNB to JWJ, Jan. 26, 1923; Mary White Ovington to RNB, June 18, 1923, all in r. 10, b. 16, AFPSR.

6: FREE LOVE FARM

"a man extraordinary": Rabbi Lewis Browne, "Garland May Be Saint, Says Rabbi," *Washington Times*, May 2, 1923, 12.

1. **trust accounts**: Charles Garland to AFPS Directors, Nov. 16, 1922, r. 1, b. 1, AFPSR; also RNB, Memo on Charles Garland to Richard Cowen, Feb. 1975, b. 25, f. 1, RNBP. **earn $2,000**: U.S. Department of Labor, *Hours of Labor, May 15, 1921: Bulletin of the United States Bureau of Labor Statistics, No. 302* (Government Printing Office, 1921), at 68. **North Carver**: John Collier to CG, July 18, 1925, b. 25, f. 6, JPCC.
2. *"new moral world"*: John F. C. Harrison, *Quest for the New Moral World: Robert Owen and the Owenites in Britain and America* (Routledge, 1969). **Brook Farm**: Carl Guarneri, *The Utopian Alternative: Fourierism in Nineteenth-Century America* (Cornell University Press, 1991). *"complex marriage"*: Anthony Wonderley, *Oneida Utopia: A Community Searching for Human Happiness and Prosperity* (Cornell University Press, 2017).
3. **revival**: Timothy Miller, *The Quest for Utopia in Twentieth-Century America: Volume 1, 1900–1960* (Syracuse University Press, 1998); Robert S. Fogarty, *All Things New: American Communes and Utopian Movements, 1860–1914* (University of Chicago Press, 1990). **rejection of consumerism**: Laurence Veysey, *The Communal Experience: Anarchist and Mystical Communities in Twentieth-Century America* (University of Chicago Press, 1978); Arthur Eugene Bestor Jr., *Backwoods Utopias* (University of Pennsylvania Press, 1950). *"to demonstrate"*: Miller, *Quest for Utopia*, 99. **Modern School**: Paul Avrich, *The Modern School Movement: Anarchism and Education in the United States* (Princeton University Press, 1980). **Bethel College**: James R. Goff Jr., "Charles F. Parham and His Role in the Development of the Pentecostal Movement: A Reevaluation," *Kansas History* 7 (Autumn 1984): 3. **Burning Bush**: Edwin Smyrl, "Burning Bush," *Southwest Historical Quarterly* 50 (1947): 335. **Zion City**: Philip L. Cook, *Zion City, Illinois: Twentieth-Century Utopia* (Syracuse University Press, 1996). **Nevada Colony . . . Army of Industry**: Wilbur S. Shepperson, *Retreat to Nevada: A Socialist Colony of World War I* (University of California Press, 1966).
4. **Garland visited**: RNB to CG, Oct. 23, 1924, and CG to RNB, Oct. 24, 1924, both in r. 29, AFPSR. **dynamited stumps . . . chicken coop**: Caryl Frink, "Flapper Visits Garland's Love Farm," *New York American*, Oct. 27, 1922; Lewis Browne, "Garland May Be Saint, Says Rabbi," *Washington Times*, May 2, 1923, 12; Lewis Browne, "Seven Seeking New Creed of Life," *Washington Times*, May 3, 1923, 12; Lewis Browne, *Charles Garland's Experiment* [ms.], Browne mss., b. 10, Lilly Library, Indiana University, Bloomington. **south of Allentown**: *What Is April Farm?* [pamphlet, c. 1925], JPCC.

606   NOTES TO PAGES 118-127

5. *Pennsylvania location*: Paul Scott to RNB, n.d. [Spring / Summer 1925], r. 14, AFPSR. *nine or ten hours . . . "new social order"*: Browne, "Garland May Be Saint." *deeded April Farm*: *What Is April Farm?*, 1.
6. *conscientious objector*: Browne, "Seven Seeking New Creed." *Slovick*: Richard Cowen, Garland Book, 621, RCC; Melvyn Dubofsky, *We Shall Be All: A History of the IWW, the Industrial Workers of the World* (Quadrangle Books, 1969), 353–55. *from Stelton*: Bettina Hovey to Marie Tudor, Aug. 1, 1925, b. 2, f. 6, JPCC, and binder 9, RCC; Avrich, *Modern School Movement*, 288.
7. *"philosophical anarchists"*: Browne, *Charles Garland's Experiment* [ms.], 7. *"non-sectarian"*: *What Is April Farm?*, 4; *"experiment in social science" . . . "experimental work"*: Paul Scott to the Secretary of the Commonwealth of Pennsylvania, Aug. 21, 1925, binder 9, RCC. *"private property . . . gather together"*: *What Is April Farm?*, 2–4.
8. *sexual freedom*: Browne, *Charles Garland's Experiment* [ms.], 4. *"free-love colony"*: *New York World*, quoted in Cowen, Garland Book, 16, RCC. *"too closely tied . . . kills love"*: Browne, *Charles Garland's Experiment* [ms.], 4.
9. *"spiritual interpretation"*: CG, "Three Fables," *New Masses*, Oct. 1926, 25. *"interested in sex" . . . romantic partners*: Richard Cowen, interview with Roger Baldwin, Dec. 10, 1976, 19, 29–30, RCC; Richard Cowen, interview with Bettina Hovey, June 1978, in Cowen, Garland Book, 613, RCC. *"better selves"*: Browne, *Charles Garland's Experiment* [ms.], 4–5.
10. *packing house . . . irrigation*: Cowen, Garland Book, 482–83, RCC. *"beautiful . . . life"*: "Esther Walters [interview with Paul Avrich, 1972]," in Paul Avrich, *Anarchist Voices: An Oral History of Anarchism in America* (Princeton University Press, 1995), 251. *"easy-going"*: Richard Cowen, interview with Robert Urffer, 1989, in Cowen, Garland Book, 624, RCC; see also April Farms Incorporation Hearing Transcript, Nov. 5, 1925, 19–30, b. 21, f. 21, MSC. *Reporters found*: Caryl Frink, "Garland Provides Narrow Diet for Women on Love Farm," *New York American*, Oct. 30, 1922; Browne, *Charles Garland's Experiment* [ms.], 2, 7. *Fordson model*: Cowen, interview with Urffer, in Cowen, Garland Book, 624, RCC. *"poor but happy"*: "Accepted $1,000,000 Only to Give Away," *Baltimore Sun*, Jan. 11, 1922, 3; "Garland Takes Legacy Only to Give It All Away," *Chicago Daily Tribune*, Jan. 11, 1922, 2.
11. *"supremely happy"*: Browne, "Garland May Be Saint," 12.

7: THE USUAL CRIME

"grafted upon its mind": JWJ, Second Address, National Conference on Lynching, May 5, 1919, b. 77, f. 530, JWJP.
1. *"Death turned"*: JWJ, *Along This Way: The Autobiography of James Weldon Johnson* (Viking Press, 1933), 167; Jacqueline Goldsby, *A Spectacular Secret: Lynching in American Life and Literature* (University of Chicago Press, 2006), 170–71.
2. *not the first time*: JWJ, *Along This Way*, 85–86.
3. *Mary Turner*: NAACP, *Thirty Years of Lynching in the United States, 1889–1918* (NAACP, 1919), at 26; Julie Buckner Armstrong, *Mary Turner and the Memory of Lynching* (University of Georgia Press, 2011).
4. *"tough-looking lot"*: JWJ, *Along This Way*, 333–35.
5. *One hundred and eight . . . more than a thousand*: NAACP, *Thirty Years of Lynching*, 29; see also Equal Justice Initiative, *Lynching in America: Confronting the Legacy of Racial Terror* (EJI, 2015); Stewart Tolnay and E. M. Beck, *A Festival of Violence: An Analysis of Southern Lynchings, 1882–1930* (University of Illinois Press, 1995). *female reporter*: JWJ, *Along This Way*, 165–67.
6. *"son of a bitch"*: JWJ, *Along This Way*, 167. *"belonged to a race"*: JWJ, *Autobiography of an Ex-Coloured Man*, ed. Henry Louis Gates (Vintage Books, 1989), 187–88.
7. *formative event*: Goldsby, *Spectacular Secret*, 166. *6 million*: Isabel Wilkerson, *The Warmth of Other Suns: The Epic Story of America's Great Migration* (Random House, 2010).
8. *"ill-fitted"*: RNB, "Autobiography (1920–1931)," b. 20, f. 12, RNBP. *"soul of a poet"*: W. E. B. Du Bois, *Dusk of Dawn: An Essay Toward an Autobiography of a Race Concept* (Harcourt, Brace & World, 1940).

9. *Johnson was born*: JWJ, *Along This Way*, 3–19; see also Rebecca Scott and J. M. Hebard, *Freedom Papers: An Atlantic Odyssey in the Age of Emancipation* (Harvard University Press, 2005).
10. *born a free man*: JWJ, *Along This Way*, 4–6. *wintered there*: Joan D. Hedrick, *Harriet Beecher Stowe: A Life* (Oxford University Press, 1994), 340–41.
11. *"good town"*: JWJ, *Along This Way*, 45; Robert Cassanello, *To Render Invisible: Jim Crow and Public Life in New South Jacksonville* (University Press of Florida, 2013); Patricia Kennedy, *LaVilla, Florida, 1866–1887: Reconstruction Dreams and the Formation of a Black Community*, M.A. thesis (University of Florida, 1990), 49. *St. James Hotel*: JWJ, *Along This Way*, 15. *Stanton Normal*: Ibid., 12. *real estate*: Ibid., 291–92.
12. *Black middle class*: Barbara Ann Richardson, *A History of Blacks in Jacksonville, Florida, 1860–1895: A Socio-Economic and Political Study*, Ph.D. thesis (Carnegie Mellon University, 1975).
13. *Florida's constitution*: Jerrell Shoffner, "The Constitution of 1868," *Florida Historical Quarterly* 41 (Apr. 1963): 356–74. *city of Jacksonville*: Eugene D. Levy, *James Weldon Johnson: Black Leader, Black Voice* (University of Chicago Press, 1973), 58–59; Richardson, *History of Blacks in Jacksonville*, 54–197; Cassanello, *To Render Invisible*, 48–49; Larry Eugene Rivers and Canter Brown Jr., "'The Art of Gathering a Crowd': Florida's Pat Chappelle and the Origins of Black-Owned Vaudeville," *Journal of African American History* 92 (2007): 169–90.
14. *civil rights bill*: "A Bill to Be Entitled an Act to Protect all Citizens of the State of Florida in Their Civil Rights, and to Furnish the Means for Their Vindication," *Acts and Resolutions Adopted by the Legislature of Florida* (Hamilton Jay, State Printer, 1873), ch. 1947, no. 13, at 25.
15. *"land of black mammies"*: JWJ, *Along This Way*, 9.
16. *family piano*: Ibid. *"Roman Cities"*: Ibid., 37. *Fortune*: Ibid., 48; Alexander Shawn Leigh, "T. Thomas Fortune, Racial Violence of Reconstruction, and the Struggle for Historical Memory," in *Remembering Reconstruction*, ed. Carole Emberton, Bruce E. Baker, and W. Fitzhugh Brundage (Louisiana State University Press, 2017). *grandfather, Stephen*: JWJ, *Along This Way*, 40.
17. *age of five*: JWJ, *Along This Way*, 34–36; Levy, *James Weldon Johnson*, 12–13; Joe M. Richardson, "The Freedmen's Bureau and Negro Education in Florida," *Journal of Negro Education* 31 (1962): 460; Richardson, *History of Blacks in Jacksonville*, 142–48; Raphael O'Hara Lanier, *History of Negro Education in Florida*, Ph.D. thesis (Stanford University, 1928), 61–63; Irvin D. S. Winsboro and Abel A. Bartley, "Race, Education, and Regionalism: The Long and Troubling History of School Desegregation in the Sunshine State," *Florida Historical Quarterly* 92 (2014): 714–45. *Atlanta University*: Levy, *James Weldon Johnson*, 23–48; JWJ, *Along This Way*, 65–66, 121–22.
18. *young principal*: Richardson, *History of Blacks in Jacksonville*, 147–48; Levy, *James Weldon Johnson*, 53–56, 61–63. *Daily American*: JWJ, *Along This Way*, 137.
19. *songwriting, too*: Levy, *James Weldon Johnson*, 75–76; Stewart Lane, *Black Broadway: African Americans on the Great White Way* (Square One Publishers, 2015), 46–47. *"Lift Every Voice"*: Imani Perry, *May We Forever Stand: A History of the Black National Anthem* (University of North Carolina Press, 2018).
20. *Johnson would reflect*: JWJ, *Along This Way*, 44–45.
21. *Democrats swept*: Richardson, *History of Blacks in Jacksonville, Florida*, 192–217. *intermarriage*: "An Act Relating to the Intermarriage of White Persons with Persons of Color," ch. 3283, no. 65, in *Acts and Resolutions Adopted by the Legislature of Florida at Its Eleventh Session* (Charles E. Dyke, State Printer, 1881), 86. *poll tax*: Edward C. Williamson, "The Constitutional Convention of 1885," *Florida Historical Quarterly* 41 (1962): 116, 121–23. *Jim Crow law*: "An Act Requiring All Railroad Companies in This State to Furnish First Class Cars," in *Acts and Resolutions Adopted by the Legislature of Florida at Its First Session Under the Constitution of A.D. 1885* (Bowen, State Printer, 1887), at 116. *"first experience"*: JWJ, *Along This Way*, 64–65. *home rule*: Levy, *James Weldon Johnson*, 59. *registered voters*: Richardson, *History of Blacks in Jacksonville*, 216–19. *mixed-race education . . . streetcars*: Levy, *James Weldon Johnson*, 77; also Robert Cassanello, *To Render Invisible*, 26.
22. *state after state*: C. Vann Woodward, *The Strange Career of Jim Crow* (Oxford University Press,

1955); C. Vann Woodward, *Origins of the New South, 1877–1913* (Louisiana State University Press, 1951); J. Morgan Kousser, *The Shaping of Southern Politics: Suffrage Restriction and the Establishment of the One-Party South, 1880–1910* (Yale University Press, 1974); Plessy v. Ferguson, 163 U.S. 537 (1896). *private businesses ... beyond Congress's reach*: Civil Rights Cases, 109 U.S. 3 (1883); see also Hall v. DeCuir, 95 U.S. 485 (1878).
23. *"fury of the mob"*: JWJ, *Along This Way*, 158.
24. *2,805*: Tolnay and Beck, *A Festival of Violence*, 269–274. *5,000*: Michael J. Pfeifer, "At the Hands of Parties Unknown: The State of the Field of Lynching Scholarship," *Journal of American History* 101 (2014): 832, 841; Lisa D. Cook, "Converging to a National Lynching Database: Recent Developments and the Way Forward," *Historical Methods* 45 (2012): 57; Megan Ming Francis, "The Price of Civil Rights: Black Lives, White Funding, and Movement Capture," *Law & Society Review* 53 (2019): 275–309. *fewer than six*: Robert L. Zangrando, *The NAACP Crusade Against Lynching, 1909–1950* (Temple University Press, 1980), at 38.
25. *Florida*: EJI, *Lynching in America*, t. 1. *105 Black men*: NAACP, *Thirty Years of Lynching*, 35. *Georgia ... sixty-one*: Ibid. *Sam Hose*: Philip Dray, *At the Hands of Persons Unknown: The Lynching of Black America* (Random House, 2002), 3–6.
26. *Hilliard*: NAACP, *Thirty Years of Lynching*, 12; Amy Louise Wood, *Lynching and Spectacle: Witnessing Racial Violence in America, 1890–1940* (University of North Carolina Press, 2009), at 64. *Dade County*: NAACP, *Thirty Years of Lynching*, 13.
27. *"usual crime"*: Jonathan Markovitz, *Legacies of Lynching: Racial Violence and Memory* (University of Minnesota Press, 2004), 11. *one in four*: NAACP, *Thirty Years of Lynching*, 10. *eighty ... were women*: Walter White to Moorfield Storey, Oct. 19, 1922, NAACPP. *"relic of slavery"*: JWJ, "The Practice of Lynching: A Picture, the Problem, and What Shall Be Done About It," *Century Magazine*, Nov. 1927, 65–70. *"state-sanctioned terrorism"*: Tolnay and Beck, *Festival of Violence*, 14, 19.
28. *Colfax Massacre*: Charles Lane, *The Day Freedom Died: The Colfax Massacre, the Supreme Court, and the Betrayal of Reconstruction* (Henry Holt, 2008); Nicholas Lemann, *Redemption: The Last Battle of the Civil War* (Farrar, Straus & Giroux, 2006); United States v. Cruikshank, 92 U.S. 542, 554 (1875); Akhil Reed Amar, "Heller, HLR, and Holistic Reasoning," *Harvard Law Review* 122 (2008): 145, 181.
29. *"only way to stop"*: JWJ, *The Best Methods for Removing the Disabilities of Caste from the Negro: Lecture Written as a Student at Atlanta University*, n.d., b. 67, f. 294, JWJP.
30. *Hotel Marshall ... Charles Anderson*: Levy, *James Weldon Johnson*, 80–100; also Gilbert Osofsky, *Harlem: The Making of a Ghetto* (Harper & Row, 1966). *"Negro Bohemia"*: JWJ, *Along This Way*, 151.
31. *"cold" and "calculating"*: JWJ, "The Gentlemen's Agreement and the Negro Vote," *The Crisis*, Oct. 1924, 260 ff, b. 68, f. 314, JWJP; Irma Watkins-Owens, *Blood Relations: Caribbean Immigrants and the Harlem Community, 1900–1930* (Indiana University Press, 1996), at 75–76. *close to party elites ... "bet on my friends"*: Levy, *James Weldon Johnson*, 100.
32. *Emancipation Day in 1898*: Levy, *James Weldon Johnson*, 66–67. *"big guns" ... "bully good"*: JWJ, *Along This Way*, 218–19.
33. *"greatest American game"*: JWJ, *Along This Way*, 218–19.
34. *"much impressed"*: Levy, *James Weldon Johnson*, 104. *"disfranchisement"*: W. E. Burghardt Du Bois, *The Souls of Black Folk: Essays and Sketches* (A. C. McClurg, 1903), 51.
35. *Tuskegee man*: Levy, *James Weldon Johnson*, 104, 107; JWJ, *Along This Way*, 259–60, 313.
36. *racial insults*: Levy, *James Weldon Johnson*, 104–10. *"Black Cabinet"*: JWJ, *Along This Way*, 239, also 259–60.
37. *"simply could not"*: JWJ, *Along This Way*, 250. *Corinto*: Levy, *James Weldon Johnson*, 113.
38. *Grace Nail*: Levy, *James Weldon Johnson*, 114. *"quite sure" ... Johnson resigned*: P. C. Knox to President William Howard Taft, Dec. 21, 1911, b. 12, f. 270, JWJP; JWJ to GNJ, Apr. 6, 1912; JWJ to GNJ, Aug. 17, 1912; JWJ to GNJ, Aug. 31, 1912; JWJ to GNJ, Sept. 10, 1912; JWJ to GNJ, Oct. 31, 1912, all in b. 41, ff., 21–23, JWJP; JWJ to JEN, May 26, 1912, b. 42, f. 59, JWJP; JWJ, *Along This Way*, 251–60, 293.

39. *keen hatred . . . "get their mail"*: JWJ, *Along This Way*, 300–306. *cafeteria*: Levy, *James Weldon Johnson*, 165.
40. *weekly column*: Levy, *James Weldon Johnson*, 151 ff.; Emma Lou Thornbrough, *T. Thomas Fortune: Militant Journalist* (University of Chicago Press, 1972). *fragile*: Robert J. Norell, *Up from History: The Life of Booker T. Washington* (Harvard University Press, 2009); Louis R. Harlan, *Booker T. Washington: The Wizard of Tuskegee* (Oxford University Press, 1983), 320–21.
41. *"race papers"*: JWJ, "Do You Read Negro Papers?," *New York Age*, Oct. 22, 1914, in *The Selected Writings of James Weldon Johnson*, ed. Sondra Kathryn Wilson (Oxford University Press, 1995), 1:151. *equality for Blacks*: See, e.g., JWJ, "President Wilson and the Negro," *New York Age*, Dec. 24, 1914; JWJ, "Is This Civilization?," *New York Age*, Jan. 21, 1915; JWJ, "Abraham Lincoln," *New York Age*, Feb. 11, 1915; JWJ, "The Reasons Why," *New York Age*, Oct. 26, 1916, all in JWJP.
42. *"better fitted"*: JWJ, "Bryan Talks," *New York Age*, June 15, 1916. *"vote cast in Maine"*: JWJ, "Strange Gods," *New York Age*, Oct. 22, 1914. *"lost sheep"*: JWJ, "The Lost Sheep," *New York Age*, Nov. 19, 1914, all in JWJP; see also Wilson, *Selected Writings of James Weldon Johnson*, 203.
43. *came out strongly*: JWJ, "Hughes the Nominee," *New York Age*, June 15, 1916; Bailey v. Alabama, 219 U.S. 219 (1911). *"every colored man"*: Edward T. Ware to JWJ, Oct. 21, 1916, b. 22, f. 524, JWJP. *"solid Negro vote" . . . "name of God"*: JWJ, "Vote the Republican State Ticket," *New York Age*, Oct. 12, 1916, b. 69, f. 347, JWJP; JWJ, "Why Charles E. Hughes Should Be Elected," *New York Age*, Oct. 19, 1916; JWJ, [response to letter to the editor], *New York Age*, Aug. 10, 1916. *"man of timidity"*: JWJ, *New York Age*, Oct. 19, 1916, JWJP; Levy, *James Weldon Johnson*, 164–67; also JWJ to Charles Anderson, Oct. 22, 1916, b. 2, f. 22, JWJP.
44. *on the platform*: JWJ, *Along This Way*, 307; Richard B. Sherman, *The Republican Party and Black America from McKinley to Hoover, 1896–1933* (University of Virginia Press, 1973). *"real political power"*: JWJ, "The Frank Case Again," *New York Age*, Oct. 29, 1914. *"colored voters"*: J. E. Spingarn to JWJ [handwritten note in JWJ's hand], Aug. 17, 1916, b. 19, f. 454, JWJP.
45. *Harding called . . . "little imagination"*: JWJ to Pauleus Sannon, Aug. 26, 1920, b. 8, f. 185, JWJP; JWJ, *Along This Way*, 358; Randolph C. Downes, *The Rise of Warren Gamaliel Harding* (Ohio State University Press, 1970), 539–54; Levy, *James Weldon Johnson*, 208–9. *"terrible blot"*: Richard B. Sherman, "The Harding Administration and the Negro: An Opportunity Lost," *Journal of Negro History* 49 (July 1964): 151. *"increase its chances" . . . "Colored Voters Day"*: Sherman, *Republican Party and Black America*, 137–38, 142. *statement on lynching*: Claudine L. Ferrell, *Nightmare and Dream: Antilynching in Congress* (Garland, 1986), 107; Zangrando, *NAACP Crusade Against Lynching*, 57; Joshua Farrington, *Black Republicans and the Transformation of the GOP* (University of Pennsylvania Press, 2016), 14–17. *rumors*: JWJ, *Along This Way*, 391. *DNA testing*: Beverly Gage, "Our First Black President?," *New York Times Magazine*, Apr. 6, 2008.
46. *First on his list*: JWJ, *Along This Way*, 361–62; Levy, *James Weldon Johnson*, 242–43.
47. *more militant organization*: Patricia Sullivan, *Lift Every Voice: The NAACP and the Making of the Civil Rights Movement* (New Press, 2009); Megan Ming Francis, "The Battle for the Hearts and Minds of America," *Souls* 13 (2011): 46–71. *"so large an opportunity"*: JWJ to J. E. Spingarn, Nov. 5, 1916, JWJP. *"coup d'état"*: Levy, *James Weldon Johnson*, 184; JWJ, *Along This Way*, 309.
48. *"rests upon public opinion"*: JWJ, Second Address, National Conference on Lynching, May 5, 1919, b. 77, f. 530, JWJP.
49. *"distortion" and "well-directed propaganda"*: Ibid.; also JWJ, *Along This Way*, 329–30. *"crime of rape"*: JWJ, "The Practice of Lynching," 67. *study in 1918*: NAACP, *Thirty Years of Lynching*.
50. *"rape myth"*: Markovitz, *Legacies of Lynching*, 11.
51. *anti-lynching bill*: Ferrell, *Nightmare and Dream*, 107 ff. *David Dyer*: "City Is Enjoined from Enforcing Segregation Laws," *St. Louis Post-Dispatch*, Apr. 17, 1916. *Dyer's bill*: U.S. Congress, House, *To Protect Citizens of the United States Against Lynching in Default of Protection by the States*, H.R. 11279, 65th Congress, introduced in House, Apr. 9, 1918; U.S. Congress, House, *To Assure to Persons Within the Jurisdiction of Every State the Equal Protection of the Laws, and to*

Punish the Crime of Lynching, H.R. 13, 67th Congress, reported with an amendment in House, Oct. 31, 1921; JWJ, *Along This Way,* 365.
52. ***nearly the next year:*** JWJ, *Along This Way,* 362-73. *"concerted action":* Ibid., 365.
53. *"wipe the stain":* Zangrando, *NAACP Crusade Against Lynching,* 57. *"rape fiend":* 62 Cong. Record 458 (Dec. 17, 1921) (Rep. Buchanan, Texas). ***Byrnes of South Carolina:*** 62 Cong. Record 544-45 (Dec. 19, 1921).
54. *"wife or your daughter":* 62 Cong. Record 545 (Dec. 19, 1921) (Rep. Aswell, Louisiana). *"encourage rape":* 62 Cong. Record 548 (Dec. 19, 1921) (Rep. Garrett, Tennessee).
55. *"deadly animal":* 62 Cong. Record 1012 (Jan. 10, 1922) (Rep. John Tillman, Arkansas). *"bleeding and choking":* 62 Cong. Record 1307 (Jan. 17, 1922) (Rep. Drewry, Virginia). *"black brute":* 62 Cong. Record 1377 (Jan. 18, 1922) (Rep. Larsen, Georgia).
56. *"far from the truth":* 62 Cong. Record 787 (Jan. 4, 1922). *"pouring... as much of our dope":* JWJ to WW, Jan. 6, 1922, b. 24, f. 539, JWJP. *"Northern Democrats":* JWJ to WW, Jan. 25, 1922, b. 24, f. 539, JWJP. ***filled the galleries:*** Dray, *At the Hands of Persons Unknown,* 266.
57. *"protect our girls"... "mob law openly advocated":* 62 Cong. Record 1721 (Jan. 25, 1922). ***sit down:*** Sullivan, *Lift Every Voice,* 106.
58. ***had won:*** Zangrando, *NAACP Crusade Against Lynching,* 64.
59. ***Borah:*** Ferrell, *Nightmare and Dream,* 245-54; Levy, *James Weldon Johnson,* 256; Zangrando, *NAACP Crusade Against Lynching,* 64-66; *The Nation,* Dec. 22, 1922, 650; Magdalene Zier, "Crimes of Omission," *Stanford Law Review* 73 (2021): 777-819.
60. ***undeterred:*** JWJ, "Anti-Lynching Bill Sound," *New-York Tribune,* July 2, 1922, A4; Levy, *James Weldon Johnson,* 253-64.
61. ***Section 2:*** JWJ, "Regarding Negro Voters," *New York Tribune,* Dec. 23, 1923, A4; Levy, *James Weldon Johnson,* 255-56; JWJ to George B. Christian Jr., Sept. 11, 1922, Special Correspondence, 1910-1939: James Weldon Johnson, Sept.-Dec. 1922, NAACPP.
62. *"hair-splitting":* JWJ, "Anti-Lynching Bill Sound"; *Hearings Before the Committee on the Judiciary, Jan. 15 & 29, 1920, Segregation and Anti-lynching* (Government Printing Office, 1920), 45-46; Zangrando, *NAACP Crusade Against Lynching,* 60.
63. *"simply did not want":* JWJ, *Along This Way,* 386. *"in favor":* JWJ to RNB, July 20, 1922, r. 1, AFPSR. ***reshaping public opinion:*** JWJ to Moorfield Storey, Nov. 15, 1922, Special Correspondence, 1910-1939: James Weldon Johnson, Sept.-Dec. 1922, NAACPP.
64. ***last-ditch publicity campaign:*** JWJ, *Along This Way,* 356.
65. ***Bernays's work:*** Larry Tye, *The Father of Spin: Edward L. Bernays and the Birth of Public Relations* (Crown, 1998), 30-54; also Edward L. Bernays, *Crystallizing Public Opinion* (Boni & Liveright, 1923); John T. Flynn, "Edward L. Bernays: The Science of Ballyhoo," *Atlantic Monthly,* June 1932, 562, 566.
66. ***borrowed shamelessly:*** Tye, *Father of Spin,* 95-96; Edward L. Bernays, *Propaganda* (Liveright, 1928), 47. *"logic-proof":* Bernays, *Crystallizing Public Opinion,* 91.
67. *"intelligent few":* Bernays, *Propaganda,* 31. *"opinions of the masses" and "invisible government":* Ibid., 9. *"herd":* Bernays, *Crystallizing Public Opinion,* 124; also David Greenberg, *Republic of Spin: An Inside History of the American Presidency* (W. W. Norton, 2016), 167-68.
68. *"mysterious alchemy":* Bernays, *Crystallizing Public Opinion,* 104. ***Atlanta conference:*** JWJ, *Along This Way,* 356. *"concentrate attention... carried weight":* Bernays, *Propaganda,* 136-37.
69. *"plan to secure":* Edward L. Bernays to Arthur Spingarn, Sept. 11, 1922, ABSP; Bernays, *Crystallizing Public Opinion.*
70. ***Bernays projected:*** Bernays to Arthur Spingarn, Sept. 11, 1922, ABSP. ***budget in crisis:*** Sullivan, *Lift Every Voice,* 131. *"narrow margin":* Levy, *James Weldon Johnson,* 229.
71. *"most unpopular cause":* Arthur Spingarn to AFPS, Sept. 19, 1922, r. 10, AFPSR. *"revolution in public sentiment":* JWJ to RNB, Dec. 22, 1922, r. 10, AFPSR.
72. *"anxious to help":* RNB to Philander P. Claxton, Southern Cooperative League, r. 3, AFPSR. ***grant to the NAACP:*** Minutes of the Fifth Meeting of the Board of Directors of the AFPS, Oct. 11, 1922, in AFPS Correspondence, 1922, NAACPP. ***personally guaranteed:*** RNB to file, Nov. 18, 1922, r. 10, AFPSR; JWJ to RNB, Nov. 20, 1922, r. 10, AFPSR; also Walter White to

Moorfield Storey, Oct. 19, 1922, in NAACPP. ***additional thousand***: RNB to JWJ, Jan. 24, 1923, r. 10, AFPSR, and b. I-C-196, f. 1, NAACPLC. ***loaned***: Special Meeting of the Board of Directors, Friday, Mar. 30, 1923, in Collection A—Correspondence and Press Releases, NAACPP. ***converted***: RNB to NAACP, Mar. 1923, r. 16, and RNB to Charles Johnson, Sept. 11, 1928, r. 3, both in AFPSR.
73. ***Fund contributed***: Gifts to June 30, 1941, r. 5, AFPSR. ***ads appeared***: "The Shame of America," *New York Times*, Nov. 23, 1922. ***"sensation here"***: JWJ to Walter White, Nov. 23, 1922, b. 24, f. 539, JWJP.
74. ***bitter end***: Zangrando, *NAACP Crusade Against Lynching*, 69.
75. ***"pressure"***: Miles M. Jackson, "Letters to a Friend: Correspondence from James Weldon Johnson to George A. Towns," *Phylon* 29 (1968): 182, 197. ***"break down"***: Zangrando, *NAACP Crusade Against Lynching*, 69. ***"license to mobs"***: JWJ, "Open Letter to Every Senator of the United States," Dec. 13, 1922, b. 24, f. 539, JWJP. ***prearranged***: [Editorial], *The Nation*, Dec. 13, 1922, 649, 650. ***"never seriously considered"***: "Dyer Bill Abandoned," *Atlanta Constitution*, Dec. 6, 1922, 6. ***"not at all displeased"***: "Collapse of the Dyer Anti-Lynching Bill," *Louisville Courier Journal*, Dec. 9, 1922, 6. ***"never intended"***: W. E. B. Du Bois, "Opinion," *The Crisis*, Jan. 1923, 103. ***"convicted of failure"***: JWJ, "Memorandum from Mr. Johnson to Dr. Du Bois, 1923," in Wilson, *Selected Writings of James Weldon Johnson*, 2:39–41.
76. ***"deserve disfranchisement"***: JWJ, "Memorandum," 41. ***"down an ass"***: Du Bois, "Opinion," 105. ***support Northern Democrats***: Levy, *James Weldon Johnson*, 278. ***"cooling off"***: JWJ, *Along This Way*, 392. ***"greatest game"***: JWJ, *Along This Way*, 218–19; also James Weldon Johnson to Moorfield Storey, July 24, 1928, b. 20, f. 465, JWJP. ***"is the ball"***: JWJ, "A Negro Looks at Politics," *American Mercury*, Sept. 1929, 88–94.
77. ***crisis***: Richard C. Cortner, *A Mob Intent on Death: The NAACP and the Arkansas Riot Cases* (Wesleyan University Press, 1988), 25.
78. ***"most amazing advertisement"***: JWJ to RNB, Dec. 22, 1922, b. I-C-196, NAACPLC, and r. 10, AFPSR. ***"sense of shame"***: E. E. Miller, "What Southerners Think of the Dyer Bill," *The Outlook*, Dec. 6, 1922, 598–99. ***"one single day"*** . . . ***"and we shall"***: Du Bois, "Opinion," 104–6; also JWJ, "Memorandum," in Wilson, *Selected Writings of James Weldon Johnson*, 2:40–44. On the successes of the NAACP/Garland Fund publicity campaign, see Michael Weaver, "'Judge Lynch' in the Court of Public Opinion: Publicity and the De-Legitimation of Lynching," *American Political Science Review* 113 (2019): 293–310.
79. ***declined precipitously***: *Memorandum Regarding the Policy of the [American Public Service] Fund as It Relates to the Negro as a Minority Group*, May 15, 1924, r. 2, AFPSR. ***public opinion***: Francis, "The Battle for the Hearts and Minds of America," 63–71; Weaver, "'Judge Lynch' in the Court of Public Opinion,": 293–31.
80. ***"uninformed American people"***: JWJ to RNB, Dec. 22, 1922, b. I-C-196, NAACPLC. ***"hard sledding"***: JWJ to AFPS, Mar. 21, 1923, r. 16, AFPSR. ***loan of $3,000***: Three Thousand Dollar Loan, July 10, 1923, b. I-C196, f. 1, NAACPLC. ***forgiven***: Minutes of Thirty-Fourth Meeting . . . Jan. 23, 1924, and MWO to RNB, Apr. 2, 1924, both in b. I-C196, f. 1, NAACPLC. ***Another $1,500***: Gifts to June 30, 1941, r. 5, AFPSR; RNB to Mary White Ovington, June 21, 1923, r. 16, AFPSR.
81. ***"flux in social consciousness"***: "Mob Domination of a Trial as a Violation of the Fourteenth Amendment," *Harvard Law Review* 37 (1923): 247–50.

8: EDUCATE THE MASSES

a difficult job: JWJ, *Along This Way: The Autobiography of James Weldon Johnson* (Knopf, 1933).
1. ***nearly tripled***: Historical Share Price, First National Bank of New York, Global Financial Data, https://www.globalfinancialdata.com. ***"faster than"***: RNB, *The Reminiscences of Roger Baldwin, 1953–1954*, CCOH; also "Radicals Double Funds in Wall Street," *Evening Ledger*, Sept. 25, 1925, in RCC, binder 9.
2. ***mounting frustration . . . ad hoc***: JWJ to RNB, May 15, 1924, r. 2, AFPSR; Gloria Garrett Sam-

son, *The American Fund for Public Service: Charles Garland and Radical Philanthropy, 1922–1941* (Greenwood Press, 1996), at 77, 80–81. **Anna Marnitz:** Sixteenth Census of the United States: 1940, Manuscript Population Schedule, Ancestry.com; see also ARTSTOR.org for Marnitz gifts of handbag, belt, and goblet to the Metropolitan Museum of Art and the Brooklyn Museum. **would-be editors:** Looking Glass Publishing, 1925, r. 31, AFPSR; Wallace Thurman and Theophilus Lewis, Statement of Ownership, Control, Cost of Maintenance . . . for the Information of the AFPS, Dec. 1925, r. 31, AFPSR. *Eccentric pamphleteers:* Young Negroes Cooperative League, 1931, r. 35 AFPSR. **industrial-education:** Snow Hill Normal & Industrial Institute, 1922, r. 33, AFPSR. *afoul of the law:* E.g., JWJ to RNB, Mar. 7, 1924, r. 10, AFPSR. ***National Urban League . . . Eugene Kinckle Jones:*** National Urban League, 1922, r. 31, AFPSR; National Urban League, 1924–1926, r. 10, AFPSR. **Negro Foreign Fellowship:** Walter White, 1924, r. 33, AFPSR. ***Black theater:*** Playhouse Settlement, 1923, r. 32, AFPSR. ***Black press:*** Pittsburgh American, 1923, r. 32, AFPSR.

3. **Woodson:** Association for the Study of Negro Life and History, Inc., r. 28, AFPSR. **Frazier:** Atlanta School of Social Work, r. 28, AFPSR. *rejected industrial education:* E.g., Daytona Normal and Industrial Institute, 1922, r. 29, b. 47, AFPSR; also RNB to James H. Dillard, Dec. 4, 1924, r. 31, b. 49, AFPSR. **Urban League:** Trade Union Committee for Organizing Negro Workers, Feb. 10, 1926, r. 13, AFPSR; Preliminary Report on the Negro and Trade Unions, Feb. 1926, r. 13, AFPSR; National Urban League, r. 16, AFPSR; Minutes of the Ninety-Seventh Meeting of the AFPS, Feb. 26, 1930 (Urban League book, "The Negro and the Trade Unions"). *beginning to wonder:* JWJ to RNB, May 15, 1924, r. 2, AFPSR; RNB to JWJ, Aug. 27, 1926, r. 1, AFPSR.

4. *traced the arc:* Ronald E. Butchart, *Schooling the Freed People: Teaching, Learning, and the Struggle for Black Freedom, 1861–1876* (University of North Carolina Press, 2013).

5. *"making a living":* Eugene Levy, *James Weldon Johnson: Black Leader, Black Voice* (University of Chicago Press, 1973), 12; JWJ, *Along This Way* (Viking Press, 1933), 122. *"contraband slaves":* Henry Allen Bullock, *A History of Negro Education in the South: From 1619 to the Present* (Harvard University Press, 1967). *informal schools:* Joe M. Richardson, "The Freedmen's Bureau and Negro Education in Florida," *Journal of Negro Education* 31 (Autumn 1962): 460–67.

6. *"a Negro idea":* James D. Anderson, *The Education of Blacks in the South, 1860–1935* (University of North Carolina Press, 1988), 6 (quoting Du Bois, *Black Reconstruction*); Jarvis R. Givens, *Fugitive Pedagogy: Carter Woodson and the Art of Black Teaching* (Harvard University Press, 2021), 3; Kabria Baumgartner, *In Pursuit of Knowledge: Black Women and Educational Activism in Antebellum America* (New York University Press, 2019); Butchart, *Schooling the Freed People*; Donald G. Nieman, ed., *African Americans and Education in the South, 1865–1900* (Garland, 1994), at vii. **153 Black schools:** Sidney Johnston, *Florida's Historic Black Schools* (U.S. Department of the Interior, 2003), 11. *"Whereas Knowledge is power":* Heather Andrea Williams, *Self-Taught: African American Education in Slavery and Freedom* (University of North Carolina Press, 2005), 65–66; Christopher Span, "'I Must Learn Now or Not at All': Social and Cultural Capital in the Educational Initiatives of Formerly Enslaved African Americans in Mississippi, 1862–1869," *Journal of African American History* 87 (Spring 2002). *"old men and women" . . . "too great":* JWJ, "Since Lincoln Freed the Negro," *New York Tribune*, Feb. 11, 1934.

7. *"backwoods of Georgia" . . . "willing and teachable":* JWJ, *Along This Way*, 110–19. *"education of the masses":* Levy, *James Weldon Johnson*, 45.

8. **typically separated:** Adam Fairclough, *A Class of Their Own: Black Teachers in the Segregated South* (Harvard University Press, 2007), 56–95; Irvin D. S. Winsboro and Abel A. Bartley, "Race, Education, and Regionalism: The Long and Troubling History of School Desegregation in the Sunshine State," *Florida Historical Quarterly* 92 (2014): 714–45. **Hiram Revels:** Horace Mann Bond, *The Education of the Negro in the American Social Order* (Prentice-Hall, 1934), 53. **new round:** Mary E. Adkins, *Making Modern Florida: How the Spirit of Reform Shaped a New State Constitution* (University Press of Florida, 2016), 6–9.

9. **Hawks's school:** Leonard R. Lempel, "The Long Struggle for Quality Education for African Americans in East Florida," *Journal of Florida Studies* 1 (2018): 10, 13; Gerald Schwartz, "An Integrated Free School in Civil War Florida," *Florida Historical Quarterly* 61 (1982): 155. **Weakley**

NOTES TO PAGES 165-171   613

County . . . 1869: Fairclough, *Class of Their Own*, 51. **"guns and pistols"**: Ibid., 113. **"ordered teachers"** . . . **256 schools**: Ibid., 51. **"outrages . . . teachers driven off"**: Ibid., 49.
10. **by half**: Bond, *Education of the Negro*, 155; Bullock, *History of Negro Education*, 87. **spent twice the amount**: Robert A. Margo, *Race and Schooling in the South, 1880-1950: An Economic History* (University of Chicago Press, 1990), 17, 23-24; Thomas Everette Cochran, *History of Public School Education in Florida* (New Era, 1921), 197-99.
11. **increased by 75 percent**: Bullock, *History of Negro Education*, 114. **raided Black school budgets**: Horace Mann Bond, "A Negro Looks South," *Harper's Monthly Magazine*, June 1, 1931, 98, 108; J. Morgan Kousser, "Progressivism—for Middle Class Whites Only: North Carolina Education, 1880-1910," in Nieman, *African Americans and Education*, at 177-202; also Bond, *Education of the Negro*, 238-44. **in Florida**: Robert A. Margo, "Race Differences in Public School Expenditures," in Nieman, *African Americans and Education*, 203.
12. **Writing in 1915**: JWJ, "The Apportionment of Public School Funds in the South," *New York Age*, Mar. 11, 1915, b. 69, f. 344, JWJP; also Kousser, "Progressivism—for Middle Class Whites Only."
13. **As principal . . . teacher salaries**: Fairclough, *Class of Their Own*, 126-29; Howard N. Rabinowitz, "Half a Loaf: The Shift from White to Black Teachers in the Negro Schools of the Urban South, 1865-1890," *Journal of Southern History* 40 (1974): 565, 583.
14. **"little giant"**: Arthur O. White, "Booker T. Washington's Florida Incident, 1903-1904," *Florida Historical Quarterly* 51 (1973): 227-49. **"absolutely worthless"** . . . **"for residence"**: Arthur O. White, "Race, Politics and Education: The Sheats-Holloway Election Controversy, 1903-1904," *Florida Historical Quarterly* 53 (1975): 253, 255.
15. **"shall not be taught"**: J. Irving E. Scott, *The Education of Black People in Florida* (Dorrance, 1974), 8. **arrest seven teachers**: Joe M. Richardson, "'The Nest of Vile Fanatics': William N. Sheats and the Orange Park School," *Florida Historical Quarterly* 64 (1986): 393-406. **"very spot"**: Annual Report, July 1894, Orange Park Normal and Industrial School, Clay County Historical Archives, Green Cove Springs, Florida; T. S. Perry, "Normal School, Orange Park, Fla," *American Missionary* 48 (1894): 263. **"vile encroachment"**: Joe M. Richardson and Maxine D. Jones, *Education for Liberation: The American Missionary Association and African Americans, 1890 to the Civil Rights Movement* (University of Alabama Press, 2009), 31. **arsonist burned**: Richardson, "'Nest of Vile Fanatics,'" 405-6.
16. **joined**: Levy, *James Weldon Johnson*, 57. **Florida State Teachers Association**: JWJ, *Along This Way*, 145, 185. **fired Tucker**: Cochran, *History of Public School Education in Florida*, 24-26. **more than ten times**: Margo, *Race and Schooling in the South*, 10-17; Leonard R. Lempel, "The Long Struggle for Quality Education for African Americans in East Florida," *Journal of Florida Studies* 1 (2018): 10, 14.
17. **"robbery of the white man"**: Bond, *Education of the Negro*, 103. **"taxation"**: W. E. B. Du Bois, "Negro Education," *The Crisis*, Feb. 1918, 176.
18. **"really pays"**: JWJ, "The Importance of the Negro to the South," *New York Age*, Aug. 16, 1916, in Wilson, *Selected Writings of James Weldon Johnson*, 1:115-16. **every person**: JWJ, "The Apportionment of Public School Funds in the South," *New York Age*, Mar. 11, 1915, in Wilson, *Selected Writings of James Weldon Johnson*, 1:111-113. **theft from Black students**: Carter Godwin Woodson, *The Mis-Education of the Negro* (Associated Publishers, 1933), 28, 121; Givens, *Fugitive Pedagogy*, 94-125.
19. **"double taxation"**: Du Bois, "Negro Education," 176. **"costs double"**: Alain Locke, "Negro Education Bids for Par," *Survey Graphic*, Sept. 1925, 567. **higher percentages**: Bond, *Education of the Negro*, 95. **three times**: Margo, "Race Differences," 204. **"every dollar"**: Gunnar Myrdal, *An American Dilemma: The Negro Problem and Modern Democracy* (Harper & Brothers, 1944), 1:341.
20. **"cash value"**: Bond, *Education of the Negro*, 233.
21. **"look into the finances"**: JWJ to Arthur B. Spingarn, May 16, 1923, b. 19, f. 451, JWJP. **pay the dues**: Mary White Ovington to RNB, June 18, 1923, r. 31, b. 49, AFPSR; Sullivan, *Lift Every Voice*, 53-58.

22. *still flush*: Stuart Chase, AFPS Audit—1923, Jan. 8, 1924, r. 3, AFPSR (increase in market value). *without giving systematic*: Scott Nearing to RNB, Oct, 13, 1923, r. 1, AFPSR; RNB to CG, Nov. 29, 1924, r. 1, AFPSR; Scott Nearing to RNB and Lewis Gannett, Memorandum in re Fund Policy, Jan. 16, 1924, r. 2, AFPSR; Two Questions of Fund Policy, Proposed by Scott Nearing, Feb. 24, 1924, r. 2, AFPSR; ME, Memorandum, n.d. [1926?], r. 1, AFPSR. *two main categories*: RNB to AFPS Board of Directors, Dec. 19, 1922, r. 1, AFPSR. *guideline against self-dealing*: RNB to AFPS Board, Oct. 17, 1923, r. 1, AFPSR.
23. *moved to adopt*: RNB, Notice of Special Meeting, Apr. 3, 1924, r. 2, AFPSR. *Nearing*: Scott Nearing, *The Making of a Radical: A Political Autobiography* (Harper & Row, 1972); John A. Saltmarsh, *Scott Nearing: An Intellectual Biography* (Temple University Press, 1991); Stephen J. Whitfield, *Scott Nearing: Apostle of American Radicalism* (Columbia University Press, 1974). *"strenuous simplicity"*: John A. Saltmarsh, "Scott Nearing," in *American National Biography Online* (Oxford University Press, 2000). *five-year program*: Scott Nearing, *Consistent Educational Work Looking to the Establishment of a New World Order: A Five Year Program for the American Fund*, Apr. 3, 1924, r. 2, AFPSR. *"most needed"... education*: Nearing, *Consistent... Five Year Program*. Nearing beat the Soviets to the five-year plan idea by several years.
24. *"field of civil rights"*: Minutes of the Thirty-Seventh Meeting of the Board of Directors of the AFPS, Apr. 9, 1974, r. 3, AFPSR. *"sui generis"... "economic justice"*: Memorandum from James Weldon Johnson to Board of Directors, AFPS, Re: Policy of the Fund as It Relates to the Negro as a Minority Group, May 15, 1924, r. 2, AFPSR.
25. *"long since"... "elementary rights"*: Ibid.
26. *peonage*: Mary White Ovington to JWJ, July 25, 1922, AFPS Correspondence, 1922, b. II-L-1, NAACPLC. *"race problem"... "waging"*: Mary Ovington to RNB, May 19, 1924, b. 49, r. 31, AFPSR.
27. *legal defense fund*: Ibid. *"keenly feeling"*: Mary Ovington to RNB, May 28, 1924, r. 31, b. 49, AFPSR.
28. *the Fund's scope*: RNB, *A Few Questions Concerning Our Policy Which May Serve Members of the Board of Directors in Preparing Memos*, Dec. 1924, r. 1, AFPSR; also Committee on Applications, Apr. 2, 1924, r. 3, AFPSR. *"most important social enterprise"*: Henry B. Linville to EGF, Mar. 24, 1925. r. 33, AFPSR. *"Schooling"*: RNB to Harry Kelly [Ferrer School], July 31, 1923, r. 30, AFPSR. *like the Carnegie*: RNB to Charles J. Rhoades, 1924, r. 32, b. 51, AFPSR.
29. *prominent beneficiaries*: Anderson, *Education of Blacks in the South*, 153. *survey... $10 million*: The Labor Bureau, Inc.: Survey [1924], r. 4, AFPSR; also Interim Report on Survey of Organizations, Dec. 1922, r. 3, AFPSR. *$53 million*: Starr J. Murphy, "The Rockefeller Foundation," *The Survey*, Apr. 2, 1910, 54–55. *Phelps-Stokes... Rockefeller Memorial Fund*: Bullock, *History of Negro Education*, 84. *Rosenwald*: Olivier Zunz, *Philanthropy in America: A History* (Princeton University Press, 2012), 39. *"already agencies"*: AFPS to Houston Industrial Training School, 1923, r. 30, AFPSR; also J. Silas Harris [Negro National Educational Congress, Kansas City, Mo.] to AFPS, Apr. 23, 1925, r. 3, AFPSR.
30. The political scientist Megan Ming Francis has contended that the AFPS co-opted the agenda of the NAACP by pushing the civil rights organization away from anti-lynching work toward education efforts. See Megan Ming Francis, "The Price of Civil Rights: Black Lives, White Funding, and Movement Capture," *Law & Society Review* 53 (2019): 275–309. The critique is better applied to the larger foundations' grants toward Black education. For my response, see Megan Ming Francis and John Fabian Witt, "Movement Capture or Movement Strategy? A Critical Race History Exchange on the Beginnings of Brown v. Board," *Yale Journal of Law & the Humanities* 31 (2021): 520–46. Citations for the paragraph follow: *paternalistic white supremacy*: James D. Anderson, "Northern Foundations and the Shaping of Southern Black Rural Education, 1902–1935," *History of Education Quarterly* 18 (1978): 371–96; Eric Anderson and Alfred A. Moss, *Dangerous Donations: Northern Philanthropy and Southern Black Education* (University of Missouri Press, 1999); Donald Johnson, "W. E. B. Du Bois, Thomas Jesse Jones and the Struggle for Social Education, 1900–1930," *Journal of Negro History* 85 (2000): 71–95. *only to segregated... whites-only schools*: William P. Vaughn, "Partners in Segregation: Barnas Sears

and the Peabody Fund," *Civil War History* 10 (1964): 260-74; F. Bruce Rosen, "The Influence of the Peabody Fund on Education in Reconstruction Florida," *Florida Historical Quarterly* 55 (1977): 310; Earl H. West, "The Peabody Education Fund and Negro Education, 1867-1880," in Nieman, *African Americans and Education*, 407, 418. *"stupid, indolent"*: Roy E. Finkbein, "'Our Little Circle': Benevolent Reformers, the Slater Fund, and the Argument for Black Industrial Education, 1882-1908," in Nieman, *African Americans and Education*, 70, 77.

31. *More genteel*: Anderson, *Education of Blacks*, 88. *pliant pool*: Anderson, "Northern Foundations," 392; also Bertram D. Wolfe, *The Negro and Education*, b. I-C196, b. 11 (May-Dec. 1934), NAACPLC.
32. *scorch*: Ralph Ellison, *Invisible Man* (Random House, 1952) ("Dr. Bledsoe"). *"out of our field"*: RNB to WEBDB, Jan. 29, 1925, r. 7, AFPSR.
33. *Tuskegee-style*: WEBDB, Memorandum to JWJ, Jan. 15, 1925, r. 7, AFPSR. *resources toward projects*: See 1924 correspondence in reel 2, AFPSR.
34. *"labor world"* . . . *"devised"*: JWJ to AFPS, Dec. 17, 1924, r. 31, b. 49, AFPSR.
35. *1901 . . . study*: W. E. B. Du Bois, *The Negro Common School: Report of a Social Study Made Under the Direction of Atlanta University; Together with the Proceedings of the Sixth Conference for the Study of the Negro Problems, Held at Atlanta University, on May 28th, 1901* (University Press [Atlanta], 1901). *1911 update*: WEBDB, *The Common School and the Negro American: Report of a Social Study Made by Atlanta University Under the Patronage of the Trustees of the John F. Slater Fund, with the Proceedings of the 16th Annual Conference for the Study of the Negro Problems, Held at Atlanta University, on Tuesday, May 30th, 1911* (Atlanta University Press, 1911). *"social regeneration"*: WEBDB, *The Souls of Black Folk: Essays and Sketches* (A. C. McClurg, 1903). *"free and complete"*: Platform Adopted by National Negro Committee 1909, Minutes of the Meetings of the Board of Directors, NAACPP. *"Human contact"* . . . *"face"*: Quoted in Davison M. Douglas, *Jim Crow Moves North: The Battle over Northern School Desegregation, 1865-1954* (Cambridge University Press, 2005), at 195. *"scientific study"*: Minutes of Executive Committee Meeting Held at 3:00 p.m. on Jan. 3, 1911, Minutes of the Meetings of the Board of Directors, NAACPP.
36. *tangle with*: Matter of Du Bois Address, 1924-1925, b. 22, LHWP; David Levering Lewis, *W. E. B. Du Bois: The Fight for Equality and the American Century, 1919-1963* (Henry Holt, 1993), at 70, 143-50, 422-53.
37. *Born in Wales*: Johnson, "W. E. B. Du Bois, Thomas Jesse Jones and the Struggle," 71-95. *"narrow-minded"*: Carter Woodson, "Thomas Jesse Jones," *Journal of Negro History* 35 (Jan. 1950): 107-9; Givens, *Fugitive Pedagogy*, 106-110; Maribel Morey, *White Philanthropy: Carnegie Corporation's An American Dilemma and the Making of a White World Order* (University of North Carolina Press, 2021), 46-57; Khalil Anthony Johnson Jr., "Problem Solver or 'Evil Genius': Thomas Jesse Jones and the Problem of Indian Administration," *Native American and Indigenous Studies* 5 (2018): 37-69.
38. *"actual needs"* . . . *"hearsay evidence"*: Johnson, "W. E. B. Du Bois, Thomas Jesse Jones and the Struggle," 79, 85.
39. *"more adequate"* . . . *"mental, moral"*: Thomas Jesse Jones, *Negro Education; A Study of the Private and Higher Schools for Colored People in the United States*, 2 vols. (Government Printing Office, 1917), 1:xiii. *"high-sounding"*: Ibid., 1:12. *"childish love"*: WEBDB, "Negro Education," *The Crisis*, Mar. 1918, 173-74. *"largely misunderstood"*: Jones, *Negro Education*, 1:81.
40. *long ago surrendered*: Du Bois, "Negro Education," 177. *"silly desire"* . . . *"modern standards"*: Ibid., 174. *"deliberately shut"*: Ibid., 175. *"cheap labor"* . . . *"double taxation"*: Ibid., 176. *"practically unrepresented"* . . . *"sinister danger"*: Ibid., 178. *"contented labor"* . . . *"white union labor"*: Johnson, "W. E. B. Du Bois, Thomas Jesse Jones and the Struggle," 87 n2.
41. *Committee on Education*: Minutes of the Meeting of the Board of Directors, Feb. 14, 1923, 2, NAACPP. *inequalities in school funding*: Sullivan, *Lift Every Voice*, 130. *"most dangerous"* . . . *"tender years"*: WEBDB, "The Tragedy of 'Jim Crow,'" *The Crisis*, Aug. 1923, 169, 170. *"plants race prejudice"*: WEBDB, "The Negro and the Northern Public Schools," *The Crisis*, Mar. 1923, 205.

42. *"one thing worse"*: WEBDB, "Tragedy of 'Jim Crow,'" 171. *"begging"* . . . *"charity"*: WEBDB, "Gifts and Education," *The Crisis*, Feb. 1925, 151-52. *"a public service"*: WEBDB, *The Education of Black People: Ten Critiques, 1906-1960*, ed. Herbert Aptheker (Monthly Review Press, 1973), at 185; also Locke, "Negro Education Bids for Par," 568; Fairclough, *Class of Their Own*, 319-27; Jarod M. Scott, "Carter G. Woodson & Thomas Jesse Jones: A Comparative Study in Race and Philanthropy, 1915-1921," M.A. thesis (Clark University, 2003); also Marybeth Gasman, "W. E. B. Du Bois and Charles S. Johnson: Differing Views on the Role of Philanthropy in Higher Education," *History of Education Quarterly* 42 (2002): 493, 495.
43. *"will not allow"* . . . *"sneer and yell"*: WEBDB, "Gifts and Education," 151. *"one half"*: WEBDB, *Souls of Black Folk*, 143. *"labor reservoir"*: "Reflections of W. E. B. Du Bois on Education as a Force for Racial Progress," *Journal of Blacks in Higher Education* 2 (1993): 4-5.
44. *"form a large"* . . . *"read and write"*: WEBDB to AFPS, Nov. 9, 1924, r. 7, AFPSR.
45. *"seriousness"*: Ibid.
46. *"large foundations"* . . . *"the root"*: JWJ to RNB, Nov. 26, 1924, r. 10, AFPSR.
47. *"not entirely certain"*: RNB to WEBDB, Nov. 28, 1924, r. 7, AFPSR. *"outside the scope"*: RNB to James H. Dillard, Dec. 4, 1924, r. 7, AFPSR. *"another superficial study"*: T. J. Woofter Jr. to James H. Dillard, Dec. 15, 1924, James H. Dillard to RNB, Dec. 17, 1924, both in r. 7, AFPSR.
48. *defended the proposal*: JWJ to AFPS, Dec. 17, 1924, b. 49, f. 31, AFPSR. *next month's session*: Minutes of the Forty-Fifth Meeting of the Board of Directors of the American Fund for Public Service, Nov. 26, 1924, r. 5, b. 3, AFPSR. *"unfair sources"* . . . *"settle matters"*: WEBDB to JWJ, Jan. 15, 1925, WEBDBP, and r. 7, AFPSR.
49. *"encourage organized labor"* . . . *"reveal the plight"*: Ibid.
50. *"antagonism"*: L. Hollingsworth Wood to RNB, Jan. 17, 1925, r. 7, AFPSR. *"distinctly good"* . . . *"I believe"*: Norman Thomas to Board of Directors, AFPS, Mar. 25, 1925, r. 7, AFPSR.
51. *board approved*: Minutes of the Fifty-Second Meeting of the Board of Directors, AFPS, May 6, 1925, r. 3, AFPSR. *"willing"*: RNB to WEBDB, Jan. 29, 1925, r. 7, AFPSR; also RNB to WEBDB, May 7, 1925, r. 7, AFPSR. *Bond & Frazier . . . schoolhouses*: WEBDB, Preliminary Details of a Proposed Survey of Negro Common School Training in the Southern South, n.d. [Feb. 1925?], r. 7, AFPSR; WEBDB, *Report to the Directors of the American Fund for Social Service [sic] on a Study of Public Common School Education in the South for Negroes*, n.d. [Oct. 27, 1926]; WEBDB, Memorandum to the American Fund for Public Service, June 14, 1927, all in r. 7, AFPSR.
52. *"larger body"*: WEBDB, *Report to the Directors of the American Fund* [Oct. 27, 1926]. *in Georgia*: WEBDB, "The Negro Common School in Georgia," *The Crisis*, Sept. 1926, 248. *school officials*: Ibid., 253-60.
53. *Articles*: WEBDB, "The Negro Common School in Mississippi," *The Crisis*, Dec. 1926, 90-102; WEBDB, "The Negro Common School in North Carolina," *The Crisis*, June 1927, 117-18, 133-35; WEBDB, "South Carolina Negro Common Schools," *The Crisis*, Dec. 1927, 330-32; Horace Mann Bond, "The Negro Common Schools in Oklahoma," *The Crisis*, July 1928, 228, 242-46. *Black readers*: WEBDB, *Report to the Directors of the American Fund* [Oct. 27, 1926].
54. *"nationwide agitation"*: Douglas, *Jim Crow Moves North*, 188-89. *growing segregation*: Kelly Miller, "Is the Color Line Crumbling?," *Opportunity*, Sept. 1924, 284-85. *Controversies*: Levy, *James Weldon Johnson*, 282. *attending school*: Margo, *Race and Schooling*, 10. *Virginia Teachers' Association*: Fairclough, *Class of Their Own*, 316-17. *school bonds*: Joseph W. Newman, "Teacher Unionism and Racial Politics: The Atlanta Public School Teachers' Association," in *Education and the Rise of the South*, ed. Ronald K. Goodenow and Arthur O. White (G. K. Hall, 1981), 131, 134-35. *"hardly be considered"*: Arthur O. White, "State Leadership and Black Education in Florida, 1876-1976," *Phylon* 42 (1981): 168, 174. *"Needs Help"*: Winsboro and Bartley, "Race, Education, and Regionalism," 724. *"fasten slavery"*: Sullivan, *Lift Every Voice*, 124.
55. *"hopelessly reactionary"*: Levy, *James Weldon Johnson*, 185. *"almost childish"*: JWJ, *Negro Americans, What Now?* (Viking Press, 1934), 42-43. *"economic basis"*: JWJ to Jacob Baker

NOTES TO PAGES 187-194						617

[Vanguard Press], n.d. [1929?], b. 2, f. 33, JWJP. *"the economic problem"*: JWJ, "The American Negro," *The Times* (London), Apr. 22, 1930, 11.
56. *"Never let"*: JWJ, *Along This Way*, 355.

9: FIRST VICTORIES

"bottomless pit": Stuart Chase to AFPS, [n.d.], r. 4, b. 7, AFPSR.
1. *moved to end*: AFPS Board Meeting, Aug. 10, 1925, r. 3, b. 5, AFPSR.
2. *made gifts*: AFPS, *Report for the First Year* (AFPS, 1923), 6-12; see also "Survey of Organizations," Dec. 1922, r. 3, b. 5, AFPSR; RNB to AFPS, Dec. 19, 1925, r. 1, b. 1, AFPSR; Megan Ming Francis, "The Price of Civil Rights: Black Lives, White Funding, and Movement Capture," *Law & Society Review* 53 (2019): 275-309. *only 4.5 percent*: AFPS, Third Report, 1924-1925 (Feb. 1926), at 40-41, r. 5, b. 3, AFPSR. *loans*: Ibid., 10.
3. *scattershot*: RNB, "A Few Questions Concerning Our Policy Which May Serve Members of the Board of Directors in Preparing Memos," Dec. 1924, r. 2, b. 2, AFPSR. *"Work"*: Informal AFPS Board Meeting, Aug. 10, 1925, r. 3, b. 5, AFPSR. *studies*: WEBDB to AFPS, Nov. 9, 1924; RNB to WEBDB, Jan. 29, 1925; WEBDB, Proposed Survey, [n.d., Feb. 1925?], all in r. 7, b. 11, AFPSR. *allies*: RNB to AFPS, May 22, 1926, r. 1, b. 1, AFPSR. *"sink"*: Stuart Chase to AFPS, [n.d.], r. 4, b. 7, AFPSR.
4. *Garland . . . "effectiveness"*: Informal AFPS Board Meeting, Aug. 10, 1925, r. 3, b. 5, AFPSR. *Baldwin's request*: RNB to Charles Garland, Mar. 13, 1925, r. 1, AFPSR.
5. *"wants and needs"*: Quoted in Rod Bush, *We Are Not What We Seem: Black Nationalism and Class Struggle in the American Century* (New York University Press, 1999), 113.
6. *John Scopes*: Helen Phelps Stokes to AFPS, May 16, 1925, r. 20, b. 30, AFPSR. *Baldwin's ACLU*: RNB to Forrest Bailey, June 27, 1926, r. 44, vol. 298, ACLUA. *Darrow*: Moorfield Storey to AFPS, Oct. 22, 1925, r. 10, b. 16, AFPSR; RNB, *The Reminiscences of Roger Baldwin, 1953-1954* (1963), at 172, CCOH.
7. *Phillips County . . . "insurrection"*: Ware v. State, 252 S.W. 626 (Ark. 1920). *Camp Pike*: Ida B. Wells-Barnett, "The Arkansas Race Riot" (n.p., 1920), 1; Nan Elizabeth Woodruff, *American Congo: The African American Freedom Struggle in the Delta* (Harvard University Press, 2014), 86; Robert Whitaker, *On the Laps of Gods: The Red Summer of 1919 and the Struggle for Justice That Remade a Nation* (Three Rivers Press, 2008), 105.
8. *white press*: Whitaker, *On the Laps of Gods*, 97. *outnumbered whites*: Richard C. Cortner, *A Mob Intent on Death: The NAACP and the Arkansas Riot Cases* (Wesleyan University Press, 1988), 7; WW, "'Massacring Whites' in Arkansas," *The Nation*, Dec. 1919, 715. *deaths*: Woodruff, *American Congo*, 91; also Whitaker, *On the Laps of Gods*, 136.
9. *sending*: Cortner, *Mob Intent on Death*, 25. *characteristic*: WW, *A Man Called White: The Autobiography of Walter White* (Indiana University Press, 1948), 5. *"skin is white"*: Ibid., 3. *organize a campaign*: Ibid., 32. *vicious beating*: JWJ, *Along This Way* (Viking Press, 1933), 343. *un account*: NAACP, Statement, Aug. 23, 1919, b. 1, f. 8, Am1919. *Chicago newspaper*: Cortner, *Mob Intent on Death*, 26; WW, *Man Called White*, 49; also Robert L. Zangrando, *The NAACP Crusade Against Lynching, 1909-1950* (Temple University Press, 1980), at 85.
10. *rumor spread . . . train*: WW, *Man Called White*, 50-51. *cotton harvest*: WW, "'Massacring Whites,'" 715-16; see also Whitaker, *On the Laps of Gods*, 8-9. *fifty cents . . . small fortune*: Wells-Barnett, "Arkansas Race Riot," 9; WW, "'Massacring Whites,'" 716.
11. *For decades*: Risa L. Goluboff, *The Lost Promise of Civil Rights* (Harvard University Press, 2007), 51-80; Gerald David Jaynes, *Branches Without Roots: Genesis of the Black Working Class in the American South, 1862-1882* (Oxford University Press, 1986); Pete Daniel, *The Shadow of Slavery: Peonage in the South, 1901-1969* (University of Illinois Press, 1972). *exploitative*: Brittany Farr, "Breach by Violence: The Forgotten History of Sharecropper Litigation in the Post-Slavery South," *UCLA Law Review* 69 (2022): 674. *Hoop Spur*: Wells-Barnett, "Arkansas Race Riot," 7-9. *Bratton*: Ibid., 13; Whitaker, *On the Laps of Gods*, 9.
12. *deputy sheriff . . . big lie*: WW, "'Massacring Whites,'" 715. *one hundred . . . twice that figure*:

Gil Stockley, *Blood in Their Eyes: The Elaine Massacre of 1919*, rev. ed. (University of Arkansas Press, 2020), at 82–83; Woodruff, *American Congo*, 102–3. ***soldiers . . . schoolhouse***: Ibid., 86–88. ***eight hundred people***: Whitaker, *On the Laps of Gods*, 398.
13. ***"Committee of Seven"***: Ware v. State, 252 S.W. 626 (Ark. 1920), ***brutal torture***: Scipio A. Jones, "The Arkansas Peons," in *Twelfth Annual Report of the NAACP* (NAACP, 1922), 24. ***quickly indicted***: Woodruff, *American Congo*, 90. ***juries . . . guilty verdicts . . . less than death***: Whitaker, *On the Laps of Gods*, 72, 167, 175, 180.
14. ***seized the cotton***: Farr, "Breach by Violence," 722–24, n121. ***"white lynchers"***: Wells-Barnett, "Arkansas Race Riot," 24. ***eight hundred men***: Whitaker, *On the Laps of Gods*, 398. ***two hundred more***: Woodruff, *American Congo*, 91.
15. ***race riots***: See Cameron McWhirter, *Red Summer: The Summer of 1919 and the Awakening of Black America* (St. Martin's Griffin, 2011). ***"civilized country"***: David Levering Lewis, *W. E. B. Du Bois: The Fight for Equality and the American Century, 1919–1963* (Henry Holt, 1993), at 8. ***"vicious exploitation"***: WW, "'Massacring Whites,'" 715. ***"lawfully"***: Wells-Barnett, "Arkansas Race Riot," 12.
16. ***Scipio Africanus Jones***: Whitaker, *On the Laps of Gods*, 295–96; Cortner, *Mob Intent on Death*, 48–51.
17. ***Ware***: Wells-Barnett, "Arkansas Race Riot," 12. ***"just stand"***: Ibid., 5–6.
18. ***his haste***: Whitaker, *On the Laps of Gods*, 225. ***"guilty as charged"***: Banks v. State, 219 S.W. 1015 (Ark. 1920). ***March 1920***: Woodruff, *American Congo*, 98. ***jury selection***: Ware v. State, 252 S.W. 626 (Ark. 1920).
19. ***second round of convictions . . . clients' release***: Cortner, *Mob Intent on Death*, 162–65.
20. ***"bravest"***: Wells-Barnett, "Arkansas Race Riot," 33. ***"to death"***: Ibid., 17. ***"negro insurrection"***: Ware v. State, 252 S.W. 626 (Ark. 1920). ***Jones appealed***: See Cortner, *Mob Intent on Death*, ch. 7. ***Georgia jury***: Steve Oney, *And the Dead Shall Rise: The Murder of Mary Phagan and the Lynching of Leo Frank* (Pantheon Books, 2003). ***"lynch law"***: Frank v. Mangum, 237 U.S. (1915), 309, 350 (Holmes, J., dissenting).
21. ***"thronged"***: Moore v. Dempsey, 261 U.S. 86 (1923).
22. ***"thunder bolt"***: J. R. Maxwell to NAACP, Jan. 22, 1925, Correspondence and Press Releases on Trial of Arkansas Rioters, part 7, series A, NACCPP. ***"expressed amazement"***: JWJ to NAACP Board, Feb. 7, 1923, Monthly Reports, pt. 1, Reports of NAACP officers, 1918–1950, NAACPP. ***"far-reaching"***: JWJ to AFPS, Mar. 21, 1923, r. 16, b. 23, AFPSR. ***"entire victory"***: NAACP, "Special NAACP Release," Jan. 14, 1925, Correspondence and Press Releases on Trial of Arkansas Rioters, pt. 7, series A, NAACPP. For the NAACP and the *Moore v. Dempsey* decision as a path out of the dismal failure of anti-lynching legislation in the Senate, see Megan Ming Francis, *Civil Rights and the Making of the Modern American State* (Cambridge University Press, 2014), 126–63. On the case at the Supreme Court, see Robert C. Post, *The Taft Court: Making Law for a Divided Nation, 1921–1930* (Cambridge University Press, 2024), at 2:1025, 1039.
23. ***million hard-earned dollars***: Wells-Barnett, "Arkansas Race Riot," 24.
24. ***"long and difficult"***: WW to NAACP Donors, June 26, 1923, Fundraising Correspondence for Defendants in Arkansas Riot Case, pt. 7, series B, NAACPP. ***"innocent men . . . tenant-farming"***: WW to NAACP Donors, Nov. 20, 1923, pt. 7, series B, NAACPP.
25. ***"most celebrated"***: Oliver Jensen, "The Persuasive Roger Baldwin," *Harper's*, Sept. 1951, 47; also RNB, *Reminiscences*, 172.
26. ***courts as an adversary***: William E. Forbath, *Law and the Shaping of the American Labor Movement* (Harvard University Press, 1991); Mark V. Tushnet, *The NAACP Legal Strategy Against Segregated Education, 1925–1950* (University of North Carolina Press, 1987), at 7–8; Laura Weinrib, *The Taming of Free Speech: America's Civil Liberties Compromise* (Harvard University Press, 2016), 34–49. ***"yellow dog"***: Erdman Act of 1898, ch. 370, 30 Stat. 424 (1898).
27. ***"made into a law for all"***: Karl Marx and Friedrich Engels, *The Communist Manifesto*, ed. Eric Hobsbawm (Verso, 1998), 55. ***"capitalists control"***: General Defense Committee, 1925, r. 30, b. 47, AFPSR. ***Gompers***: See Clement Wood et al., *Don't Tread on Me: A Study of Aggressive Legal Tactics for Labor* (Vanguard Press, 1928), 36. ***barred lawyers***: Leon Fink, *Workingmen's*

Democracy: The Knights of Labor and American Politics (University of Illinois Press, 1985), 9. *"no faith"*: William Z. Foster, *The Great Steel Strike and Its Lessons* (B. W. Huebsch, 1920), 51.

28. *"new saint"*: Stephen B. Oates, *John Brown: To Purge This Land with Blood*, 2nd ed. (University of Massachusetts Press, 1984), 318. **Haymarket Martyrs**: Paul Avrich, *The Haymarket Tragedy* (Princeton University Press, 1984); Beverly Gage, *The Day Wall Street Exploded: A Story of America in Its First Age of Terror* (Oxford University Press, 2009). *"Free Tom Mooney"*: U.S. Congress Committee on the Judiciary, *Tom Mooney Hearings Before the United States House Committee on the Judiciary, Subcommittee No. 1 (Judiciary), Seventy-Fifth Congress, Third Session, on May 11, 17, 1938* (Government Printing Office, 1938), 76. **Civil Liberties Bureau**: AUAM, "The Individual and the State: The Problem as Presented by the Sentencing of Roger N. Baldwin," Nov. 1918, r. 1, AUAM. **Emergency Case Fund**: ACLU Emergency Case Fund Gifts, 1928–30, r. 17, b. 25, AFPSR; AFPS Board Meeting, Aug. 11, 1926, r. 3, b. 5, AFPSR.

29. *"dominated" . . . "strong"*: RNB to Hon. Francis G. Caffey, Oct. 1918, b. 111, f. 12, RNB.
30. *"Arkansas peons . . . protect"*: Mary Ovington to RNB, May 19, 1924, r. 31, b. 49, AFPSR.
31. *"any theory"*: Clarence Darrow and William J. Bryan, *The Word's Most Famous Court Trial: Tennessee Evolution Case: A Complete Stenographic Report of the Famous Court Test of the Anti-Evolution Act, at Dayton July 10 to 21, 1925, Including Speeches and Arguments of Attorneys* (National Book Company, 1925), 3.
32. **Rand School**: AFPS Board Meeting, Oct. 25, 1922, r. 3, b. 5, AFPSR. **Lusk**: Todd J. Pfannestiel, *Rethinking the Red Scare: The Lusk Committee and New York's Crusade Against Radicalism, 1919–1923* (Routledge, 2003); see also Weinrib, *Taming of Free Speech*, 151–55. **Dewey's suggestion**: John Dewey to RNB, Nov. 16, 1922, r. 13, b. 19, AFPSR. **grants of nearly**: AFPS, Gifts, r. 5, b. 8, AFPSR. *"in education" . . . "free the minds"*: Henry R. Linville to AFPS, Sept. 10, 1924, r. 13, b. 19, AFPSR.
33. **Committee on Academic Freedom**: See Richard Magat, "The Forgotten Roles of Two New York City Teachers in the Epic Scopes Trial," *Science & Society* 70 (2006): 541, 546. *"propagandists' efforts"*: Edward J. Larson, *Summer for the Gods: The Scopes Trial and America's Continuing Debate over Science and Religion* (Basic Books, 1997), 81.
34. *"Tennessee teacher"*: Ibid., 83. **extended farce**: Brenda Wineapple, *Keeping the Faith: God, Democracy, and the Trial That Riveted a Nation* (Random House, 2024).
35. **place of courts**: Weinrib, *Taming of Free Speech*, ch. 5. **sought out**: Helen Phelps Stokes to AFPS, May 16, 1925, r. 20, b. 30, AFPSR; AFPS Board Meeting, May 27, 1925, r. 3, b. 5, AFPSR. *"rather outside"*: Curtis, Fosdick, and Belknap to RNB, Sept. 21, 1925, r. 38, ACLUA. *"underwrite"*: Helen Phelps Stokes to AFPS, May 16, 1925, r. 20, b. 30, AFPSR.
36. **Oregon**: [RNB], "The Story of Civil Liberty: A Chronology of Leading Events," [n.d., 1944?], b. 16, f. 30, RNBP. *"fireworks . . . dreams"*: RNB, *Reminiscences*, 172.
37. *"Great Commoner"*: J. C. Long, *Bryan the Great Commoner* (D. Appleton, 1928); see also Lawrence W. Levine, *Defender of the Faith: William Jennings Bryan* (Oxford University Press, 1965), 329–30. **Darrow**: RNB, *Reminiscences*, 172. **Baldwin opposed**: Roger Cottrell, *Roger Nash Baldwin and the American Civil Liberties Union* (Columbia University Press, 2000), 156. **circus**: See Dwight Macdonald, "In Defense of Everybody—Part I," *New Yorker*, July 18, 1953, 38; Lucille Milner, *Education of an American Liberal* (Horizon Press, 1958), 163; John A. Farrell, *Clarence Darrow: Attorney for the Damned* (Doubleday, 2011), 367; Tom Arnold-Forster, "Rethinking the Scopes Trial: Cultural Conflict, Media Spectacle, and Circus Politics," *Journal of American Studies* 56 (2022): 142, 145. **Newsreels . . . train station**: Larson, *Summer for the Gods*, 145–46. **speaker's platform . . . "link"**: Larson, *Summer for the Gods*, 141–42. **Organ**: Ibid., 152. *"spitting"*: Ibid., 154. *"morons"*: Ibid., 165. *"Neanderthal"*: Ibid., 201.
38. **called Bryan**: Ibid., 4. *"trivial"*: Ibid., 202. *"Supreme"*: Ibid., 248. *"disgrace"*: Georgia Harkness to ACLU, Dec. 14, 1925, r. 38, ACLUA. *"ludicrous"*: FF to RNB, May 5, 1964, b. 3, f. 22, RNBP.
39. **$100 fine**: Cottrell, *Roger Nash Baldwin*, 156. **short-circuit . . . indictment**: Larson, *Summer for the Gods*, 221.
40. *"most famous"*: RNB, *Reminiscences*, 172.

41. *"five races"*: George William Hunter, *A Civic Biology: Presented in Problems* (American Book Company, 1914), 196. *Shaler* and *Agassiz*: Nathaniel Southgate Shaler, *The Neighbor: A Natural History of Human Contacts* (Houghton Mifflin, 1904); Louis Menand, *The Metaphysical Club* (Farrar, Straus & Giroux, 2001), 101, 116. *Baldwin included*: See RNB to George W. Pieksen, Mar. 27, 1909, b. 16, f. 2, RNBP. *"brutality"*: Farrell, *Clarence Darrow*, 375.
42. *Garland Avenue*: Kevin Boyle, *The Arc of Justice: A Saga of Race, Civil Rights, and Murder in the Jazz Age* (Henry Holt, 2004), 29. *watched... Black-owned homes*: Ibid., 22–23; Alfred Brophy, *Reconstructing the Dreamland: The Tulsa Riot of 1921* (Oxford University Press, 2002).
43. *struck down*: Buchanan v. Warley, 245 U.S. 60 (1917). *more than half*: Stewart E. Tolnay, "The African-American 'Great Migration' and Beyond," *Annual Review of Sociology* 29 (2003): 209, 211. *600 percent*: Boyle, *Arc of Justice*, 106. *Only Gary*: Mayor's Inter-Racial Committee, *The Negro in Detroit* (Detroit Bureau of Governmental Research, 1926), sec. 2, 4. *automobile industry... wage*: Boyle, *Arc of Justice*, 102–3.
44. *"Waterworks Park"*: Ibid., 159. *five times*: Ibid., 24. *chief surgeon*: Ibid., 25; also Moorfield Storey to AFPS, Oct. 23, 1925, I-C-196, NAACPLC; "Clarence Darrow Defends Detroit 'Rioters,'" *Chicago Defender*, Oct. 24, 1925, 3. *Sweet moved... ammunition*: Boyle, *Arc of Justice*, 26–28.
45. *first rock*: Ibid., 35–40; "1 Slain, 1 Shot When Negroes Fire at Crowd," *Detroit Free Press*, Sept. 10, 1925, 1.
46. *Johnson learned... sent*: JWJ, *Along This Way*, 382–83; Boyle, *Arc of Justice*, 197. *piecemeal support*: RNB to Mary White Ovington, June 21, 1923, r. 10, b. 16, AFPSR.
47. *Clarence Darrow*: Boyle, *Arc of Justice*, 385; Moorfield Storey to AFPS, Oct. 22, 1925, r. 10, b. 16, AFPSR. *reduced fee*: December Meeting NAACP, Monthly Reports, NAACPP; "Clarence Darrow Defends Detroit 'Rioters,'" 3; "Darrow Gets Delay of Trial," *Detroit Free Press*, Oct. 17, 1925, 11; "Race Riot Trial Opens: Darrow Aids 11 Negroes," *New York Herald Tribune*, Oct. 31, 1925, 5.
48. *Storey*: JWJ to Moorfield Storey, Sept. 12, 1925; JWJ to Moorfield Storey, Oct. 20, 1925, both in Meetings of the Board of Directors, Records of Annual Conferences, Major Speeches, and Special Reports, pt. 1, Special Correspondence, 1910–1939, JWJ correspondence, NAACPP. *Great Migration... "principle of democracy"*: Moorfield Storey to AFPS, Oct. 22, 1925, r. 10, b. 16, AFPSR.
49. *asked the Fund*: Ibid.; also JWJ to EGF, Oct. 27, 1925, r. 10, b.16 AFPSR. *granted both*: EGF to Storey, Oct. 29, 1925, I-C-196, NAACPLC, also in r. 10, b. 16, AFPSR; AFPS Board Meeting, Oct. 28, 1925, r. 3, b. 5, AFPSR. *"fundamental importance"*: L. Hollingsworth Wood to EGF, Oct. 27, 1925, r. 10, b. 16, AFPSR.
50. *Darrow's strategy*: "Darrow Bares Conspiracy in Sweet Case," *Chicago Defender*, Nov. 14, 1925, 3; "Heard Glass Crash in the Sweet Homes Before Shots Came," *New York Herald Tribune*, Nov. 8, 1925, 6; "Trial Transcript: The People v. Ossian Sweet, Gladys Sweet, et al. (1925)," Clarence Darrow Digital Collection, University of Minnesota. *teenagers*: Ibid., 744. *"kind of forgot"*: Ibid., 864; see also WW, *Man Called White*, 79.
51. *Murphy*: See Beth Tompkins Bates, *The Making of Black Detroit in the Age of Henry Ford* (University of North Carolina Press, 2012), 7. *Klan*: Ibid., 82. *"actual and imminent"*: Honorable Frank Murphy, "Charge to the Jury in the Case of *Michigan v. Henry Sweet*" (1926), Clarence Darrow Digital Collection. *"race and color"*: "Closing Argument of Clarence Darrow in the First Sweet Trial," in *People v. Ossian Sweet, Gladys Sweet, et al.* (1925), 30, Clarence Darrow Digital Collection. *"absolute fairness"*: WW to Judge Murphy, Dec. 4, 1925, pt. 5, group I, series D, Legal File, 1909–1939, NAACPP.
52. *"every one of them"*: "Closing Argument of Clarence Darrow in the First Sweet Trial," 30. *"hatred and malice"*: Ibid., 93. *"mob psychology"*: Ibid., 100. *"deeper than anything"*: Ibid., 28. *"Put yourselves"*: Ibid., 94.
53. *trial ended*: WW, *Man Called White*, 76–77. *"lied, and lied... man has not"*: "Trial Transcripts: Closing Arguments in the Henry Sweet Trial (2nd Sweet Trial)," 6, Clarence Darrow Digital Collection.

54. *"broke down"*: JWJ, *Along This Way*, 384. *acquittal*: WW, *Man Called White*, 79; "Henry Sweet Freed by Jury in 2nd Trial," *New York Age*, May 26, 1926, 1. *"most dramatic"*: JWJ, "Detroit," *The Crisis*, July 1926, 20.
55. *abandoned*: Boyle, *Arc of Justice*, 344. *"nothing . . . except power"*: JWJ, "NAACP, 17th Annual Conference Draft," b. 77, f. 521, JWJP.
56. *"race prejudice . . . strike the blow"*: [JWJ], "Victory in Sweet Case Completed," July 22, 1927, pt. 5, group I, series D, NAACPP.
57. *Fund redoubled*: JWJ to EGF, Jan. 5, 1926; EGF to JWJ, Jan. 8, 1926; MLE to NAACP, Mar. 10, 1928, both in I-C-196, NAACPLC. *offering to match*: Boyle, *Arc of Justice*, 307. *White estimated*: WW, *Man Called White*, 79. *"Legal Defense Fund"*: JWJ to EGF, Jan. 22, 1926, I-C-196, NAACPLC. *"Million Dollar Fund . . . money"*: JWJ, "NAACP, 17th Annual Conference Draft," b. 77, f. 521, JWJP.
58. *"new deal"*: Bates, *Making of Black Detroit in the Age of Henry Ford*, 7. *would campaign*: Ibid., 180. *of all the justices*: Sidney Fine, *Frank Murphy: The Washington Years* (University of Michigan Press, 1984).

10: CAPTURING THE CAPTORS

"do not care a damn": WEBDB, "Criteria of Negro Art," *The Crisis*, Oct. 1926, 296.
1. **December 1925**: JWJ, *Along This Way* (Viking Press, 1933), 379–80. *mass meeting*: "Clarence Darrow to Speak Here," press release, Dec. 1, 1925, and "Directions for Ushering and Canvassing the Darrow Mass-Meeting," [Dec. 13, 1925], both in Darrow Mass Meeting File, I-C-332, NAACPP. *matching grant*: Moorfield Storey to AFPS, Oct. 22, 1925; EGF to Moorfield Storey, Oct. 29, 1925; Storey to EGF, Nov. 2, 1925; JWJ to EGF, Nov. 24, 1925, all in r. 10, b. 16, AFPSR.
2. **Robeson**: "Robeson Back from London," *New York Times*, Dec. 23, 1925, 22; "Robeson to Sing for Nursery Fund: Benefit to Be Given in Greenwich Village Theatre Mar. 15," *New York Amsterdam News*, Mar. 11, 1925, 9; "Paul Robeson, Lawrence Brown Score Big New York Success with Negro Songs," *Pittsburgh Courier*, May 2, 1925, 1. *most memorable*: JWJ, *Along This Way*, 379.
3. **back in Jacksonville**: JWJ, *Along This Way*, 266–67. *State Department*: Eugene Levy, *James Weldon Johnson: Black Leader, Black Voice* (University of Chicago Press, 1973), 123. *hometown*: Ibid., 297. *Jacksonville, Lubin, & Hollywood*: Robert Jackson, *Fade In, Crossroads: A History of the Southern Cinema* (Oxford University Press, 2017), 26; "Foster Photoplay Co. Licensed in Florida," *Chicago Defender*, Apr. 11, 1914, 1; David Morton, "A Year-Round Playground Twenty-Seven Hours from Broadway: Re-Assessing Jacksonville's Legacy as an 'Almost Hollywood,'" *Florida Historical Quarterly* 98 (2020): 220; Richard Alan Nelson, "Movie Mecca of the South: Jacksonville, Florida, as an Early Rival to Hollywood," *Journal of Popular Film and Television* 8 (1980): 46. *wrote six short scenarios*: JWJ, *Along This Way*, 297–98; JWJ, "Aunt Mandy's Chicken Dinner: A Darkey Comedy," June 25, 1914, b. 74, f. 436, JWJP; JWJ, "The Black Billionaire," July 1914, b. 74, f. 437, JWJP; JWJ, "Do You Believe in Ghosts? A Darkey Comedy," b. 74, f. 441 & f. 442, JWJP. *congratulated him*: John E. Nail to JWJ, July 9, 1914, b. 40, f. 17, JWJP.
4. **crude stories**: Jacqueline Najuma Stewart, *Migrating to the Movies: Cinema and Black Urban Modernity* (University of California Press, 2005), 54, 57, 266. *hateful stereotypes*: Jackson, *Fade In, Crossroads*, 26; also Amy Louise Wood, *Lynching and Spectacle: Witnessing Racial Violence in America, 1890–1940* (University of North Carolina Press, 2009), at 134. *Cake Walk . . . consuming melons*: Stewart, *Migrating to the Movies*, 54.
5. *"seed of savagery . . . vile"*: Charlene Regester, "The African-American Press and Race Movies, 1909–1929," in *Oscar Micheaux and His Circle: African-American Filmmaking and Race Cinema of the Silent Era*, ed. Pearl Bowser et al. (Indiana University Press, 2001), 35.
6. **Aunt Mandy's**: JWJ, "Aunt Mandy's Chicken Dinner," June 25, 1914, b. 74, f. 436, JWJP; see also "The Tale of a Chicken," *Moving Picture World Magazine*, June 1914, 568; JWJ, "Do You Believe in Ghosts: A Darkey Comedy," in *The Essential Writings of James Weldon Johnson*, ed. Rudolph P. Byrd (Modern Library, 2008), 6.

7. *"disgusting . . . race-hating whites"*: Allyson Field, *Uplift Cinema: The Emergence of African American Film and the Possibility of Black Modernity* (Duke University Press, 2015), 227. *"vile"*: "States Theater Shows Colored Men Stealing Chickens," *Chicago Defender*, May 30, 1914, 1. *"degrading"*: "Foster, the Moving Picture Man, Returns," *Chicago Defender*, June 20, 1914, 4. *"ashamed"*: JWJ, *Along This Way*, 298. *"outrage"*: JWJ, *New York Age*, Apr. 1, 1915, b. 69, f. 344, JWJP.
8. *conference in Bellport*: Harry Laidler, *Preliminary Announcement of Autumn Conference of the Intercollegiate Socialist Society* . . . Sept. 18–24, 1917, Edwin Markham Correspondence, Hormann Library, Wagner College.
9. *"beggar"* . . . *"creations of the American Negro"*: JWJ, *Along This Way*, 327.
10. *"folk-art creations"* . . . *"lighter music"*: Ibid., 327–28. *"distinctive American product"*: JWJ, "James W. Johnson Replies to Criticisms of His Preface," *New York Tribune*, Apr. 9, 1922, C5. *Ragtime* . . . *"blare and jangle"*: JWJ, *Book of American Negro Poetry*, at xv; also JWJ, "Since Lincoln Freed the Negro," *New York Tribune*, Feb. 11, 1934, SM2.
11. *"No people"*: JWJ, *Book of Negro Poetry*, at vii. *anthologies*: JWJ and J. Rosamond Johnson, eds., *The Book of American Negro Spirituals* (Viking, 1925); JWJ & J. Rosamond Johnson, eds., *The Second Book of American Negro Spirituals* (Viking, 1926); JWJ, *Black Manhattan* (Knopf, 1930); also JWJ, "Negro Folk Songs and Spirituals," *The Mentor*, Feb. 1929, 50–52.
12. *"revival of art and literature"*: WEBDB, "The Immediate Program of the American Negro," *The Crisis*, Apr. 1915, 310–12; also WEBDB, "The Negro in American Literature," *Epworth Herald*, Jan. 28, 1928, 70–71. *"singular spiritual heritage"*: WEBDB, *The Souls of Black Folk: Essays and Sketches* (A. C. McClurg, 1903), 251.
13. *"great mission of the Negro"*: WEBDB, "Truth and Beauty," *The Crisis*, Nov. 1922, 7–9. *influential literary competition*: Jenny Woodley, *Art for Equality: The NAACP's Cultural Campaign for Civil Rights* (University Press of Kentucky, 2014), 71; Emily Bernard, "The Renaissance and the Vogue," in *The Cambridge Companion to the Harlem Renaissance*, ed. George Hutchinson (Cambridge University Press, 2007), 28–40; also David Levering Lewis, *W. E. B. Du Bois: The Fight for Equality and the American Century, 1919–1963* (Henry Holt, 1993), at 156–75.
14. *education grants*: Minutes of the Fifty-Second Meeting of the Board of Directors, AFPS, May 6, 1925, r. 3, AFPSR. *The Messenger*: Minutes of the Fifteenth Meeting of the Board of Directors, AFPS, Feb. 14, 1923, r. 3, AFPSR. *Claude McKay*: Personal Service Fund Gifts, 1923-1925, r. 11, AFPSR; Winston James, *Claude McKay: The Making of a Black Bolshevik* (Columbia University Press, 2022). *Hughes* . . . *Ellison* . . . *Wright*: The New Masses, r. 11, AFPSR; see also Christopher J. Lebron, *The Making of Black Lives Matter: A Brief History of an Idea* (Oxford University Press, 2016); David Levering Lewis, *When Harlem Was in Vogue* (Penguin, 1997).
15. *Locke*: See Jeffrey C. Stewart, *The New Negro: The Life of Alain Locke* (Oxford University Press, 2018), 92, 294; Abby Arthur Johnson and Ronald Maberry Johnson, *Propaganda and Aesthetics: The Literary Politics of Afro-American Magazines in the Twentieth Century* (University of Massachusetts Press, 1979); Arnold Rampersad, *The Art and Imagination of W. E. B. Du Bois* (Harvard University Press, 1976), 193; Bernard, "Renaissance and the Vogue," 34; Veronica Chambers and Michelle May-Curry, "The Dinner Party That Started the Harlem Renaissance," *New York Times*, Mar. 29, 2024, C8; Alain Leroy Locke, "Enter the New Negro," in *Survey Graphic: Harlem, Mecca of the New Negro*, Mar. 1925, 634. *"pro-Negro as well as anti-Negro"*: Alain Locke, "The Drama of Negro Life," *Theatre Arts Monthly* 10 (1926): 701; also Locke, "Enter the New Negro," 631.
16. *"do not care a damn"*: WEBDB, "Criteria of Negro Art," *The Crisis*, Oct. 1926, 296. *"standing in the way"*: WEBDB, "Krigwa Players Little Negro Theatre," *The Crisis*, July 1926, 134–36. *"mold of American standardization"*: Hughes, "Negro Artist and the Racial Mountain," 692.
17. *to find a form*: JWJ, *Book of American Negro Poetry*, xl–xli; JWJ, *The Autobiography of an Ex-Coloured Man* (Vintage Books, 1989), 20–21. *"expressing the imagery"*: Nathan Irvin Huggins, *Harlem Reniassance*, rev. ed. (Oxford University Press, 2007) (1971), 231; Gregory S. Carr, "Top

Brass: Theatricality, Themes, Theology in James Weldon Johnson's God's Trombones," *Theatre Symposium* 21 (2013): 54; Joseph Sorett, *Spirit in the Dark: A Religious History of Racial Aesthetics* (Oxford University Press, 2016), 114–38.

18. *"Traditional Negro dialect"* . . . *"fusion"*. . . . *King James English"*: JWJ, *God's Trombones*, ed. Henry Louis Gates Jr. (Penguin, 2008) (1927), 8-9. *"the human voice or the violin"*: Ibid., 7.

19. *"capable of embracing"*: Countee Cullen, "And the Walls Came Tumblin' Down," *The Bookman*, Oct. 1927, 221. *"slim book"*: *Washington Eagle*, May 27, 1927, b. 61, f. 224, JWJP. *"descended"*: *Baltimore Afro-American*, June 4, 1927, b. 61, f. 224, JWJP. *"folk synthesis"*: Langston Hughes, "200 Years of American Negro Poetry," *Transition* 24 (1966): 90, 93.

20. *"through the eyes of others"*: Du Bois, *Souls of Black Folk*, 3. *"paradox of the captor"*: JWJ, "Since Lincoln Freed the Negro," SM2. *Hegel*: Georg Wilhelm Friedrich Hegel, *The Phenomenology of Spirit*, trans. Terry Pinkard (Cambridge University Press, 2018). *"drags"*: JWJ, *Along This Way*, 328.

21. *"smug little morals"*: Mark Van Doren, "First Glance," *The Nation*, Mar. 28, 1928, 351; see generally Michael Denning, *The Cultural Front: The Laboring of American Culture in the Twentieth Century* (Verso, 1997), 242; Carol Nackenhoff, *The Fictional Republic: Horatio Alger and American Political Discourse* (Oxford University Press, 1994).

22. *dulling uniformity*. . . . *liberate the imagination*: The Fund's culture program was, in some respects, an actualized American version of the project of intellectual and culture work conceived around the same time by the imprisoned Italian Communist Antonio Gramsci. See Antonio Gramsci, *Prison Notebooks*, 3 vols., ed. Joseph A. Buttigieg (Columbia University Press, 1992), esp. vol. 1 §§ 44–61, and Denning, *The Cultural Front*, 51–64.

23. **Christian socialist magazine:** *World Tomorrow*, 1922-1926, r. 14, AFPSR. **Pax:** Gifts to June 30, 1941, 47, r. 5, AFPSR. **New Republic:** Minutes of the Board of Directors, Oct. 28, 1925, r. 3, AFPSR; *New Republic*, 1925, r. 24, AFPSR; Minutes of the Board of Directors, June 28, 1934, r. 4, AFPSR. **Cultura Obrera:** *Cultura Obrera*, r. 7, b. 11, AFPSR; Gifts to June 30, 1941, 9. **printing house:** Equity Printing Co., Gifts to June 30, 1941, r. 5, AFPSR, 21. **Daily Worker:** Gifts to June 30, 1941, r. 5, AFPSR, 13. **Soviet . . . Novyi Mir:** Gifts to June 30, 1941, 33, r. 5, AFPSR; Minutes of the Board of Directors, Oct. 22, 1930, r. 4, AFPSR; Novy Mir Publishing Co., 1925, r. 24, AFPSR. **Speakers Service Bureau:** Speakers Service Bureau, 1925, r. 13, AFPSR. The *Novyi Mir* grants were emblematic of both the Fund's struggles to get its loans repaid and the creative significance of some of its beneficiaries. Within a few years, the Fund was in litigation against the magazine's American representatives seeking repayment; decades later, the magazine would be a forum for Soviet dissidents like Aleksandr Solzhenitsyn. The Fund also made large grants to the socialist newspaper *New York Call*—grants that were soon rendered pointless by the paper's untimely collapse. Few of the Fund's culture program grants were so unproductive. See Minutes of the Board of Directors, Sept. 19, 1922, r. 3, b. 5, AFPSR; *New York Call*, 1922, r. 11, AFPSR; Norman Thomas, Memorandum on the *New York Call*, July 20, 1923, r. 3, AFPSR; Minutes of the Board of Directors of the AFPS, Aug 1, 1923, r. 3, AFPSR; *New York Call*, 1923-1924, r. 16, b. 33, AFPSR.

24. **New Masses:** "Radical Magazine Backed by $1,500,000," *New York Times*, Dec. 8, 1925; Gifts to June 30, 1941, 33, r. 5, AFPSR. *"creative youth, artistic rebelliousness"* . . . *"experimentation"* . . . *"symbol of hope"*: *New Masses*, 1926, r. 11, AFPSR. *"satirical spirit"*: *Liberator*, 1922, r. 31, AFPSR. *"highest standard"* . . . *"deeply human"*: Virginia Hagelstein Marquardt, "'New Masses' and John Reed Club Artists, 1926–1936: Evolution of Ideology, Subject Matter, and Style," *Journal of Decorative and Propaganda Arts* 12 (1989): 56–75. *"strike its roots strongly"*: Helen Langa, "'At Least Half the Pages Will Consist of Pictures': 'New Masses' and Politicized Visual Art," *American Periodicals* 21 (2011): 24–49. **Black poets:** E.g., Hughes, "Four Poems," *New Masses*, Dec. 1926, 10; McKay, "Song of New York," *New Masses*, May 1926, 15; see also Richard Wright, "Two Million Black Voices," *New Masses*, Feb. 25, 1936, 15. **start-up financing:** Gifts to June 30, 1941, 27, r. 5, AFPSR.

25. *theatrical groups*: Gifts to June 30, 1941, 44, r. 5, AFPSR (Theatre Union). *fiction writers*: Personal Service Fund Gifts, 1923–1925, r. 11, AFPSR (Claude McKay, Upton Sinclair). *film*

producers: Minutes of the Board of Directors, Feb. 25, 1937, f. 4, AFPSR (Share Croppers Film Committee); Share Croppers Film Committee, 1937, r. 24, AFPSR. *Passaic*: Gifts to June 30, 1941, 35, r. 5, AFPSR. *"the real happenings"*: Steven J. Ross, *Working-Class Hollywood: Silent Film and the Shaping of Class in America* (Princeton University Press, 1998), 162. *seven-reel film*: Ibid.; Kevin Brownlow, *Behind the Mask of Innocence* (Knopf, 1990), 498–508; Jacob A. Zumoff, *The Red Thread: The Passaic Textile Strike* (Rutgers University Press, 2021), 107–11; Steven J. Ross, "Struggles for the Screen: Workers, Radicals, and the Political Uses of Silent Film," *American Historical Review* 96 (1991): 333, 355–57; Barry Sabath, "The Passaic Textile Strike Comes to Screen" (1976), Brandon Collection, Museum of Modern Art Archives, New York.

26. *grant to Max Eastman*: Gifts to June 30, 1941, 14, r. 5, AFPSR. *astonishing archival footage*: "Russian Revolution in Films of That Period," *New York Post*, Mar. 8, 1937. *internal bickering*: Max Eastman for Russian Revolution Film, 1930, 1934, 1941, r. 26, AFPSR. *"history in the making"*: "Tsar to Lenin—Filmarte," *New York Tribune*, Mar. 9, 1937, 13; see also "The Screen: In re Revolution: Tsar to Lenin," *New York Times*, Mar. 9, 1937, 27. The Stalinist *Daily Worker*, which the American Fund had supported in its earlier years, accused Eastman of pro-Trotsky bias and demanded a boycott of any theater showing the film. See "Workers Protest Film Edited by Eastman," *Daily Worker*, Mar. 9, 1937, 9.

27. *Elia Kazan*: New Theatre League, 1936, r. 36, AFPSR. *Garland Anderson*: Minutes of the Board of Directors, Nov. 24, 1925, r. 3, AFPSR; Better Plays, Inc., 1928, r. 34, b. 54, AFPSR. *experimental theater applications*: Fred Eastman, 1926, r. 29, AFPSR; American Laboratory Theatre, r. 28, AFPSR; Raymond O'Neill, "The Strolling Players," 1924, r. 32, AFPSR; Workers' Dramatic League, 1925, r. 33, AFPSR. *art gallery*: Minutes of the Board of Directors, Apr. 28, 1926, r. 3, AFPSR. *commercial prospects*: E.g., God of Vengeance Case, 1925, r. 30, AFPSR.

28. *Federated Press . . . Chicago*: *Revolutionary Radicalism: Its History, Purpose and Tactics . . . Filed April 24, 1920, in the Senate of the State of New York*, 4 vols. (J. B. Lyon, 1920), 2:1990–99; Interchurch World Movement, *Public Opinion and the Steel Strike: Supplementary Reports of the Investigators to the Commission of Inquiry* (Harcourt, Brace, 1921), 89. *distribute the labor movement's stories*: David Montgomery, "Thinking About Workers in the 1920s," *International Labor & Working Class History* 32 (1987): 4, 16. *one hundred affiliated newspapers*: Jon Bekken, "'No Weapon So Powerful': Working-Class Newspapers in the United States," *Journal of Communication Inquiry* 12 (1988): 104–19.

29. *warfare at Matewan*: Art Shields, *On the Battle Lines, 1919–1939* (International Publishers, 1986), at 49–53; Philip Taft, "Violence in American Labor Disputes," *Annals of the American Academy of Political and Social Science* 364 (1966): 127, 137. *distributed stories . . . the Arkansas massacre*: Esther Lowell, Federated Press, Eastern Bureau, Jan. 15, 1925, NAACP Legal File, Arkansas Riots, 1920–1925, I-D-44, NAACPP. *Esther Lowell . . . Sweet trials*: Esther Lowell, "Negro Home Defenders Get Second Trial," Federated Press Eastern Bureau Sheet 2, No. 1718, Nov. 28, 1925, NAACP Legal File, Sweet Case, I-D-88, NAACPP. *Lowell and . . . [Art Shields] . . . toured the South*: Shields, *On the Battle Lines*, 170–91.

30. *radical newspapers*: Minutes of the Board of Directors, Jan. 17, 1923, r. 3, AFPSR. *just over $81,000*: Gifts to June 30, 1941, 17, r. 5, AFPSR. *"do not get the facts"*: Upton Sinclair to RNB, Nov. 25, 1922, r. 32, AFPSR.

31. *radio station, WCFL*: Nathan Godfried, *WCFL: Chicago's Voice of Labor, 1926–1978* (University of Illinois Press, 1997); also Lizabeth Cohen, *Making a New Deal: Industrial Workers in Chicago, 1919–1939* (Cambridge University Press, 1990), at 133–37. *radio station for the Socialist Party*: Elizabeth Fones-Wolf, *Waves of Opposition: Labor and the Struggle for Democratic Radio* (University of Illinois Press, 2006), 22. *"Debs Memorial Radio"*: WEVD Radio Station, 1927, r. 33, AFPSR; WEVD—Debs Memorial Radio Station, 1931, r. 20, AFPSR. *financing in late 1927*: WEVD to AFPS, Nov. 21, 1927, b. 6, f. 6, BGP. *"radical and labor movements"*: Robert Dunn to Forrest Bailey, Nov. [10?], 1927, and G. August Gerber to Robert Dunn, Dec. 2, 1927, both in WEVD Radio Station, 1927, r. 33, AFPSR.

32. *broadcasting station*: Radio Broadcasting Station, 1925, r. 12, b. 18, AFPSR. *had a radio*: Co-

hen, *Making a New Deal*, 133. **allocate the broadcasting band . . . "propaganda stations"**: Tim Wu, *The Master Switch: The Rise and Fall of Information Empires* (Random House, 2010), 82–83; also Fones-Wolf, *Waves of Opposition*, 15.
33. ***"Free Speech Radio Station" . . . "minority movements"***: Forrest Bailey to AFPS, Dec. 13, 1927, WEVD Radio Station, 1927, r. 33, AFPSR.
34. **declined to participate**: Minutes of the Board of Directors, Feb. 28, 1928; but see WEVD—Debs Memorial Radio, 1931, r. 20, AFPSR. ***ILGWU***: Fones-Wolf, *Waves of Opposition*, 22. ***"Political and social justice"***: Letter from WEVD Radio Station to undisclosed recipient, 1929, WEBDBP. ***"Jewish Hour" . . . Labor Looks at the Week . . . labor conditions . . . Federated Press . . . Rand School***: Fones-Wolf, *Waves of Opposition*, 22.
35. ***"fed in small doses"***: RNB to Upton Sinclair, May 27, 1930, r. 12, b. 18, AFPSR.
36. ***"musical programs"***: Cohen, *Making a New Deal*, 20. ***WCFL***: Nathan Godfried, "The Origins of Labor Radio: WCFL, the 'Voice of Labor,' 1925–1928," *Historical Journal of Film, Radio and Television* 7 (1987): 143, 157.
37. ***"open forum for all minority groups"***: Special Meeting of Board of Directors, June 17, 1931, r. 4, AFPSR. ***"dissident minority viewpoints"***: Fones-Wolf, *Waves of Opposition*, 22. ***sold itself***: Ibid.
38. **Communist factions**: Maurice Isserman, *Reds: The Tragedy of American Communism* (Basic Books, 2024), 42–46; Theodore Draper, *The Roots of American Communism*, rev. ed. (Transaction Press, 2003) (1957), 176–96. ***"party of a new type" & "Bolshevization"***: Isserman, *Reds: The Tragedy*, 67. ***"vanguard"***: V. I. Lenin, "What Is to Be Done?," in V. I. Lenin, *Collected Works* (Foreign Language Publishing House, 1961), 5:347, 372.
39. ***"One only"***: RNB, *The Reminiscences of Roger Baldwin, 1953–1954* (1963), at 329, CCOH. **refused to seat**: RNB to Foster, n.d. [late 1923/early 1924?]; Norman Thomas to RNB, Aug. 26, 1924; RNB to William W. Weinstone, Nov. 6, 1925; EGF to Foster, Oct. 1, 1926, all in reel 1, AFPSR. **political prisoners**: RNB, "To Our Friends," Feb. 13, 1927. ***party apparatchiks***: Robert C. Cottrell, *Roger Nash Baldwin and the American Civil Liberties Union* (Columbia University Press, 2000), 145–49. **opposed**: RNB to Board, June 22, 1925, reel 1, AFPSR. **expand the anti-Communist**: William Z. Foster to RNB, Dec. 4, 1926; RNB to William Z. Foster, Dec. 8, 1926, both in r. 1, AFPSR. **resisted further funding**: RNB to EGF, June 22, 1925, r. 1, AFPSR. ***"terrible bunch"***: Scott Nearing to EGF, Jan. 5, 1926, r. 1, b. 1, AFPSR.
40. ***"boring from within"***: Isserman, *Reds: The Tragedy*, 65–67; Trade Union Educational League, 1922, r. 33, AFPSR. **anti-union offensive**: Daniel R. Ernst, *Lawyers Against Labor: From Individual Rights to Corporate Liberalism* (University of Illinois Press, 1995); David Montgomery, *The Fall of the House of Labor: The Workplace, the State, and American Labor Activism, 1865–1925* (Cambridge University Press, 1987). **only energetic radical organization**: RNB to EGF, c. 5-17-26, r. 1, AFPSR ("healthy force").
41. **agriculture experiment**: Russian Reconstruction Farms, r. 21, AFPSR; Minutes of the Forty-Sixth Meeting of the Board, Dec. 17, 1924; Minutes of the Forty-Seventh Meeting of the Board, Jan. 7, 1925, and Minutes of the Fifty-Fifth Meeting of the Board of Directors, July 22, 1925, both in r. 3, AFPSR. ***"end hunger"***: [Harold Ware], "If You Could End Hunger in the World Forever?," r. 21, AFPSR. ***Norman Thomas***: Minutes of the Special Meeting of the Board, Mar. 7, 1934, r. 4, AFPSR. **default**: Russian Reconstruction Farms, r. 21, AFPSR.
42. **keep his own books in print**: Upton Sinclair, 1922, b. 5, r. 3, AFPSR. **publishing house**: Upton Sinclair, 1934, r. 32, AFPSR. ***"Vanguard of thought" & "regular publishers are not prepared"***: AFPS, Funding of Vanguard Press, b. 6, f. 5, BGP. **too radical**: *History of Vanguard Press*, c. 1980, typescript ms., SCVP.
43. **more than $100,000 . . . another $65,000 combined**: Gifts to June 30, 1941, at 21, 40, 46, r. 5, AFPSR.
44. **pocket-sized volumes**: R. J. Baker, Business Plans [Apr. 12, 1926], 1, b. 6, f. 5, AFPSR; "Vanguard Books Only 50 c Each," b. 6, f. 5, BGP; "Books at Cost Idea," n.d., b. 6, f. 5, BGP. **Early titles**: "A List for the Fall of 1928 of the Books of Macy-Masius Now Combined with the Vanguard Series," Vanguard Press, 1928, and "Vanguard Press Publications for Spring 1930," both in b. 4, SCVP. ***Studs Lonigan trilogy***: See Ann Douglas, "Studs Lonigan and the Failure of History in Mass

Society," *American Quarterly* 29 (1977): 487. **Dr. Seuss . . . 500 Hats of Bartholomew Cubbins:** Theodor Geisel, b. 53, VPR. For positive assessments of Vanguard's early work by Baldwin and Sinclair, see RNB, *Reminiscences of Roger Baldwin, 1953-1954*, at 328, and Upton Sinclair to Merle Curti, Sept. 22, 1958, MECP.

45. *"permanent educational value"*: Gloria Garrett Samson, *The American Fund for Public Service: Charles Garland and Radical Philanthropy, 1922-1941* (Greenwood Press, 1996), at 167; also John Tebbel, *Between Covers: The Rise and Transformation of Book Publishing in America* (Oxford University Press, 1987), 268-69.
46. *"actually happening"*: SN to Vanguard Press, June 9, 1926, r. 12, AFPSR.
47. *"not officially committed"*: Ibid. *"propaganda in any sense"*: SN to Norman Thomas, Aug. 25, 1926, r. 12, AFPSR.
48. *joined the party*: Harvey Klehr et al., *The Soviet World of American Communism* (Yale University Press, 1998), 334; also Scott Nearing, *The Making of a Radical: A Political Autobiography* (Harper & Row, 1972). *tapped Jerome Davis*: Scott Nearing to Jerome Davis, July 12, 1926, r. 12, AFPSR. *Davis*: Sheila Slaughter, "The Danger Zone: Academic Freedom and Civil Liberties," *American Academy of Political and Social Science* 448 (1980): 46, 55; Paul Hollander, *Political Pilgrims: Travels of Western Intellectuals to the Soviet Union, China, and Cuba, 1928-1978* (Oxford University Press, 1981), at 162-63. *"measure of dictatorship"*: Jerome Davis, *Capitalism and Its Culture* (Farrar & Rinehart, 1935), 519.
49. *appeal only to readers*: Morris Ernst to AFPS, June 15, 1926, r. 12, AFPSR. *doubted the series*: RNB to Jerome Davis, Sept. [26?], 1926, r. 12, AFPSR; also RNB to Jerome Davis, Sept. [?], 1926, and RNB to Jerome Davis, Oct. 5, 1926, r. 12, AFPSR.
50. *"depressions"*: Cottrell, *Roger Nash Baldwin*, 183-84. *Davis asked*: Jerome Davis to RNB, Sept. 22, 1926, r. 12, AFPSR. *recommending . . . Chafee*: RNB to Jerome Davis, Sept. [26?], 1926, r. 12, AFPSR.
51. *"weird tales"*: RNB, *Reminiscences of Roger Baldwin, 1953-1954*, at 385. *laughed at him*: Ibid., 387. *guide who spoke too candidly*: Ibid., 388. *"completely controlled"*: RNB to Lucy N. Baldwin, July 23, 1927, b. 3, f. 3, RNBP. *"in the saddle"*: Ibid. *"made allowances"*: RNB, *Reminiscences of Roger Baldwin, 1953-1954*, at 389-90. *"vastly greater liberties"*: Ibid., 393.
52. *"universal censorship"*: RNB, *Liberty Under the Soviets* (Vanguard Press, 1928), 2-3; see also RNB to Jerome Davis, Oct. 13, 1926, r. 12, AFPSR.
53. *"minimum of violence"*: Ibid., 3. *outpouring of unrealistic accounts*: Hollander, *Political Pilgrims*, 164. *philosopher John Dewey*: Robert B. Westbrook, *John Dewey and American Democracy* (Cornell University Press, 1991), 463-95. *"progress and hope"*: Quoted in Cottrell, *Roger Nash Baldwin*, 188.
54. *Berkman . . . naive*: RNB to William G. Nowlin Jr., Mar. 24, 1974, b. 4, f. 12, RNBP.
55. *"pro-Soviet"*: RNB to Jerome Davis, Sept. [?], 1926, r. 12, AFPSR.
56. *"became to me a mockery" & "proved my judgment wrong"*: RNB, *Reminiscences of Roger Baldwin, 1953-1954*, at 411, 405.

11: MONEY HATERS AND TAX LAWYERS

political agitation: Slee v. Commissioner, 42 F.2d 184, 185 (2nd Cir. 1930) (L. Hand, J.).
1. *Charges of hypocrisy*: E.g., Arnold Peterson to Roger Nash Baldwin, Sept. 15, 1924, r. 33, AFPSR; "A Lovely Inconsistency," *Boston Post*, Sept. 27, 1925; see also Walter S. Steele, "Subsidizing Red Radicalism," *National Republic*, Nov. 1930, 16-17; Elizabeth Dilling, *The Red Network: A Who's Who and Handbook of Radicalism for Patriots* (self-published, 1934), 17, 163-65; Martin Dies, *The Trojan Horse in America* (Dodd, Mead, 1940), 255; Scott Nearing, *The Making of a Radical: A Political Autobiography* (1972), 48-49; Gloria Garrett Samson, *The American Fund for Public Service: Charles Garland and Radical Philanthropy, 1922-1941* (Greenwood Press, 1996). *"capitalist angels"*: Benjamin Stalberg, "Muddled Millions," *Saturday Evening Post*, Feb. 15, 1941, 9-10. *"money haters"*: "Radical Group Makes Million Wall St. Profit," *New York Tribune*, Sept. 25, 1925.

2. *special legal privileges*: Boris I. Bittker and George Rahdert, "The Exemption of Nonprofit Organizations from Federal Income Taxation," *Yale Law Journal* 85 (1976): 299; Kenneth Liles and Cynthia Blum, "The Development of Federal Tax Treatment of Charities," *Law & Contemporary Problems* 39 (1975): 6; Elias Clark, "Limitation on Political Activities: A Discordant Note in the Law of Charities," *Virginia Law Review* 46 (1960): 439. *exemption from state taxes*: Randall J. Holcombe, *Writing Off Ideas: Taxation, Foundations, and Philanthropy in America* (Transaction Publishers, 2000), 4; J. S. Seidman, *Seidman's Legislative History of Federal Income Tax Laws* (Prentice-Hall, 1938). *immunity from lawsuits*: Olivier Zunz, *Philanthropy in America: A History* (Princeton University Press, 2012); McDonald v. Massachusetts General Hosp., 120 Mass. 495 (1876).
3. *"solely for charitable"*: An Act to Reduce Taxation, to Provide Revenue for the Government, and for Other Purposes, 28 Stat. 509, 556 (1894). *"exclusively for the promotion"*: Revenue Act of 1913, 38 Stat. 140, 172 (1913); see also Ellen P. April, "Churches, Politics, and the Charitable Contribution Deduction," *Boston College Law Review* 42 (2001): 843; Joseph J. Thorndike, "How the Charity Deduction Made the World Safe for Philanthropy," *Tax Notes*, Dec. 17, 2012; David Schizer, "Subsidizing Charitable Contributions: Incentives, Information, and the Private Pursuit of Public Goals," *Tax Law Review* 62 (2009): 221.
4. *deduct the value of contributions*: War Revenue Act of 1917, 60 Statutes at Large 300, 330, s. 1201 (1917). *Wartime tax authorities*: Thorndike, "How the Charity Deduction."
5. *"end to negro slavery" ... "charitable purpose"*: Jackson v. Phillips, 96 Mass. 539, 540 (1867).
6. *"propagandist"*: Oliver A. Houck, "On the Limits of Charity: Lobbying, Litigation, and Electoral Politics by Charitable Organizations Under the Internal Revenue Code and Related Laws," *Brooklyn Law Review* 69 (2003): 1.
7. *from the public fisc*: Robert L. Hale, "Coercion and Distribution in a Supposedly Liberal State," *Political Science Quarterly* 38 (1923): 470; "Deductions Allowed: Charitable Contributions," 1922 C.B. 142 (1922).
8. *"associations formed"*: Office of the Commissioner of Internal Revenue, *Regulations Relating to the Income Tax and War Profits and Excess Profits Under the Revenue Act of 1918* (Government Printing Office, 1919), art. 517 at 134. *"extraordinary grace"*: "Deductions Allowed: Charitable Contributions," 1922 C.B. 142 (1922).
9. *$40,000 in grants*: Gifts to June 30, 1941, 25–26, r. 5, AFPSR. *"drastic political"*: Bertha Poole Weyl v. Commissioner, 18 B.T.A. 1092 (Bd. of Tax Appeals, Feb. 11, 1930); see also Bureau of Internal Revenue, *Cumulative Bulletin No. 2, January–June 1920, Income Tax Rulings* (Government Printing Office, 1920), 153; American Association for Labor Legislation, 1920 C.B. 152, 154; Houck, "On the Limits of Charity," 10, 63; Philip Hamburger, "Liberal Suppression: Section 510(c)(3) and the Taxation of Speech" (2000), 48–49; "Section 214(A)—Deductions Allowed: Charitable Contributions," 1922 C.B. 142, 143. *reversed its view*: Weyl v. Commissioner of Internal Revenue, 48 F.2d 811 (2d Cir. 1931). *another American Fund beneficiary*: Gifts to June 30, 1941, 2, r. 5, AFPSR; *"political agitation"*: Slee v. Commissioner, 42 F.2d 184, 185 (2d Cir. 1930).
10. *Gurland bequest*: Will of James A. Garland Jr., July 19, 1906, Probate Record Books, vol. 894, Registry of Probate of Suffolk County, Boston, Mass. (1907). *Massachusetts ... Rhode Island*: Arthur W. Blakemore and Hugh Bancroft, *The Inheritance Tax Law: Containing All American Decisions and Existing Statutes with Supplement* (Boston Book Co., 1914), 587–88, 1094. *excluded the estates*: Revenue Act of 1916, 39 Stat. 756, 777 (1916).
11. *"wellbeing of mankind"*: Certificate of Incorporation, Delaware, in Board of Directors Meeting Minutes, 1922–1941, r. 3, b. 5, AFPSR; also RNB to Charles Garland, Mar. 26, 1922, r. 3, b. 5, AFPSR; RNB to Norman Thomas, Lewis Gannett, and Robert Morss Lovett, July 6, 1922, r. 3, b. 5, AFPSR. *Rockefeller*: Jonathan Levy, "Altruism and the Origins of Nonprofit Philanthropy," in *Philanthropy in Democratic Societies: History, Institutions, Values*, ed. Rob Reich, Chiara Cordelli, and Lucy Bernholz (University of Chicago Press, 2016), 35, 38; Raymond B. Fosdick, *John D. Rockefeller, Jr.: A Portrait* (Harper & Brothers, 1956), 121.
12. *scripted letters*: RNB to Walter Nelles, June 5, 1922, r. 3, AFPSR. *"advantage of one"*: Charles

Garland to AFPS, July 15, 1922, JWJP; Charles Garland to AFPS, July 20, 1922, r. 1, AFPSR; also AFPS, *Report for the Second Year Ending June 30, 1924* (New York, 1925), at 19–20. **"integral part"**: Richard Cowen, Garland Book, 218, RCC. **"arouse antagonism"**: Roger N. Baldwin, "Conference with Charles Garland, July 20, 1922," r. 1, AFPSR; see also Affidavit of Norman M. Thomas, May 1923, r. 1, AFPSR.

13. **ineligible for exemption**: Morris Ernst to RNB, May 13, 1924; Walter Nelles to RNB, May 12, 1924; and J. G. Bright to Collector of Internal Revenue, May 1, 1924, all in Treasurer's Correspondence, 1923–1933, r. 2, AFPSR.
14. **Florence Kelley**: Kathryn Kish Sklar, *Florence Kelley and the Nation's Work: The Rise of Women's Political Culture, 1830–1900* (Yale University Press, 1995); also Florence Kelley, *Notes of Sixty Years: The Autobiography of Florence Kelley*, ed. Kathryn Kish Sklar (Charles Kerr, 1986). **applied for ... and received**: People's Reconstruction League, 1926, r. 32, AFPSR; Minutes of the the Board of Directors, Apr. 25, 1923 (National Consumers League), r. 3, AFPSR; National Consumers League, 1924–25, r. 16, AFPSR; National Consumers League, 1924, r. 31, AFPSR; New Republic, 1925, r. 25, AFPSR; Minutes of the Board of Directors, Nov. 26, 1924, r. 3, AFPSR.
15. **The younger Kelley**: Nicholas Kelley Papers, New York Public Library. **tax-exemption matters**: Weyl v. Commissioner of Internal Revenue, 48 F.2d 811 (2d Cir. 1931). Kelley would go on to become one of the leading corporate lawyers of his day, representing Chrysler in labor disputes in the 1930s (see "Auto Wages Go Up," *Review of Reviews*, May 1934, 46) and becoming general counsel at Chrysler in 1937. His firm, Kelley, Drye, helped draft the anti-union Taft Hartley Act in 1947. See "Theodore Iserman, Lawyer, Dies, Helped Draft Taft Hartley Act," *New York Times*, Feb. 28, 1974, 40.
16. **tax-exempt status**: Merle Curti, "Subsidizing Radicalism: The American Fund for Public Service, 1921–41," *Social Service Review* 33 (1959): 274, 277–78. **Properly understood**: Lewis Gannett to Nicholas Kelley, Nov. 22, 1922, r. 3, AFPSR; NK to RNB, Nov. 24, 1922, Feb. 17, 1928, and Apr. 23, 1928, all in r. 3, AFPSR.
17. **remaining money**: Charles Garland to AFPS Directors, Nov. 16, 1922, r. 1, b. 1, AFPSR; also RNB, Memo on Charles Garland to Richard Cowen, Feb. 1975, b. 25, f. 1, RNBP. **further donations**: Walter Nelles, Press Release, July 5, 1922, r. 3, b. 5, AFPSR.
18. **Kelley prevailed**: Deputy Commissioner of Internal Revenue to AFPS, [date illegible] [1929]; Nicholas Kelley to Miss S. Gross, May 31, 1929; NK to JWJ, Aug. 20, 1929; NK to Anna Marnitz, Oct. 3, 1929; RNB to NK, n.d. [1929]; NK to Anna Marnitz, Jan. 22, 1930; John R. Kirk [Deputy Commissioner of Internal Revenue] to AFPS, July 6, 1938, all in r. 3, b. 5, AFPSR.
19. **tax rate of 12.5 percent**: Jack Taylor and Beth Kliss, "Corporation Income Tax Brackets and Rates, 1909–2002: Data Release," available at https://www.irs.gov/pub/irs-soi/02corate.pdf. Actual tax incidence would have turned on the Fund's decisions in managing its assets, which might have been different had the tax applied.
20. **"military instruction"**: Military Training Camps Association, Income Tax Rulings—Part I, 1926 C.B. 84. **American Legion**: "Section 231, Article 519: Civic Leagues," 1920 C.B. 210 (1920).

12: NOTHING IN COMMON

"guerrilla warfare": EGF, *Sabotage: The Conscious Withdrawal of the Workers' Industrial Efficiency* 4 (I.W.W. Publishing, 1915).
1. **"existing order"**: EGF, "The IWW Call to Women," *Solidarity*, July 31, 1915.
2. **Flynn**: Rosalyn Fraad Baxandall, *Words on Fire: The Life and Writing of Elizabeth Gurley Flynn* (Rutgers University Press, 1987); Rosalyn Fraad Baxandall, "Elizabeth Gurley Flynn: The Early Years," *Radical America* 8 (Jan.–Feb. 1975): 97; Helen Camp, *Iron in Her Soul: Elizabeth Gurley Flynn and the American Left* (Washington State University Press, 1995); Lara Vapnek, *Elizabeth Gurley Flynn: Modern American Revolutionary* (Westview Press, 2015). **The Wobblies**: Melvyn Dubofsky, *We Shall Be All: A History of the Industrial Workers of the World* (Quadrangle Books, 1969); also Eric Thomas Chester, *The Wobblies in Their Heyday: The Rise and Destruction of the Industrial Workers of the World* (Bloomsbury Academic, 2014); Peter Cole, *Wobblies on the*

Waterfront: Interracial Unionism in Progressive Era Philadelphia (University of Illinois Press, 2007); Philip S. Foner, *History of the Labor Movement, Volume 4: The Industrial Workers of the World, 1905-1917* (International Publishers, 1961); Ahmed White, *Under the Iron Heel: The Wobblies and the Capitalist War on Radical Workers* (University of California Press, 2022).

3. ***downplayed***: Dubofsky, *We Shall Be All*, 147 and *passim*, and Vapnek, *Elizabeth Gurley Flynn*, 53-69; also Joseph R. Conlin, "The IWW and the Question of Violence," *Wisconsin Magazine of History* 51 (Spring 1968): 316; Ronald Genini, "Industrial Workers of the World and Their Fresno Free Speech Fight, 1910-1911," *California Historical Quarterly* 53 (1974): 101; Philip Foner, Letter to the Editor, *The Nation*, [n.d., probably Mar. 1952], b. 1, f. 32, EGFP-NY. ***desperate gambit***: Louis Adamic, "Sabotage," *Harper's Weekly*, January 1931, 216, 226. For a re-revisionist account, see Beverly F. Gage, "Terrorism and the American Experience: A State of the Field," *Journal of American History* 98 (2011): 73; and Beverly F. Gage, "Why Violence Matters: Radicalism, Politics, and Class War in the Gilded Age and Progressive Era," *Journal for the Study of Radicalism* 1 (2007): 99. Very recently, an uptick in violence as a political tactic has produced a new surge in interest in IWW violence. See Rebecca H. Lossin, "No Interests in Common: Sabotage as Structural Analysis," *Journal for the Study of Radicalism* 15 (2021): 75; R. H. Lossin, "On Sabotage," *Verso Blog*, Feb. 15, 2021; Rebecca H. Lossin, "The Point of Destruction: Sabotage, Speech, and Progressive Era Politics," Ph.D. Diss., Columbia University, 2020.

4. ***born in 1890***: Legal and Financial Documents, f. 4, EGF-B.
5. ***"immigrants and revolutionists"***: EGF, *The Rebel Girl: An Autobiography, My First Life, 1906-1926* (International Publishers, rev. ed. 1973) (1955), at 23.
6. ***Tom Flynn***: Ibid., 43.
7. ***"got things done"*** . . . ***"burning hatred"***: Vapnek, *Elizabeth Gurley Flynn*, 9.
8. ***"millionaire's row"***: EGF, *Rebel Girl*, 32-34.
9. ***factory town*** . . . ***"ruinous path"***: Ibid., 33-35. Decades later, the future billionaire Warren Buffett would turn Berkshire Cotton into his famous holding company, Berkshire Hathaway.
10. ***"stretched like prisons"*** . . . ***"fine carriage"***: Ibid., 36.
11. ***"struck home"***: Camp, *Iron in Her Soul*, 11; also EGF, *Rebel Girl*, 47-48.
12. ***"slavish dependence"***: Mary Wollstonecraft, *A Vindication of the Rights of Woman* (A. J. Matsell, 1833) (1792), 8-9. ***"free and unhampered"***: August Bebel, *Women Under Socialism*, trans. Daniel DeLeon (New York Labor News, 1904), 343. ***"mutual desire"***: Stephen Charles Cole, "Elizabeth Gurley Flynn: A Portrait," Ph.D. thesis, Indiana University, 71.
13. ***secret family***: Baxandall, *Words on Fire*, 22. ***"spark of love"***: EGF, "Orange Men Interested," n.d., 1904-1905 Old Poetry Scrapbooks, EGFP-NY.
14. ***"Disobedience"***: 1904-1905 Old Poetry Scrapbooks, EGFP-NY. ***"between the sexes"***: Bebel, *Women Under Socialism*, 10.
15. ***famous radicals***: Camp, *Iron in Her Soul*, 10. ***"total social change"***: Friedrich Engels, Preface (1888), to Karl Marx and Friedrich Engels, *Manifesto of the Communist Party* (Whitehead Estate, 1919), 5. ***forced role***: 1904-1905 Old Poetry Scrapbooks, EGFP-NY.
16. ***top 1 percent***: Richard Sutch, "The One Percent Across Two Centuries: A Replication of Thomas Piketty's Data on the Concentration of Wealth in the United States," *Social Science History* 41 (2017): 587; Facundo Alvaredo et al., "The Top 1 Percent in International and Historical Perspective," *Journal of Economic Perspectives* 27 (2013): 3. ***"facile tools"***: EGF, "Education and the School System," in Baxandall, *Words on Fire*, 79 ff. ***"chains of superstition"***: "Miss Elizabeth Gurley Flynn, Girl Socialist" (Aug. 1908), 1904-1905 Old Poetry Scrapbooks, EGFP-NY.
17. ***first public speech***: Vapnek, *Elizabeth Gurley Flynn*, 15-16.
18. ***"victims of society"***: EGF, "Victims of Society," Jan. 1906, 1904-1905 Old Poetry Scrapbooks, EGFP-NY. ***"industrial autocracy"***: "Sleuths Listen to Miss Flynn," [1907?], EGFP-NY. ***"slave love"***: Camp, *Iron in Her Soul*, 12. ***"no real home"***: East Side Joan of Arc Lectures (1907), EGFP-NY. ***"loveless marriages"***: EGF, "Problems Organizing Women," *Solidarity*, July 15, 1916. ***"claimed sacredness"***: "Orange Men Interested," EGFP-NY.
19. ***"crystal blue eyes"***: Lucille Milner, *Education of an American Liberal: An Autobiography* (Hori-

zon Press, 1954), 272; at least one reporter called Flynn's eyes a "grave hazel"; see "Girl Socialist Sways Hearers: The East Side Joan of Arc Magnetizes Crowds at City Plaza," *Public Ledger* (Newark) [1908?], EGFP-NY. *"brown hair"*: "Crowd Magnetized by Wisp of a Girl," 1906–1907 Early Newspaper Clippings, 2, EGFP-NY. *"East Side Joan of Arc"*: EGF, *Rebel Girl*, 65.
20. *"their eyes"*: "Girl Socialist Sways Hearers," EGFP-B. *"beautiful face"*: Vapnek, *Elizabeth Gurley Flynn*, 17.
21. *"she-dog of anarchy"*: Baxandall, *Words on Fire*, 2; "Most Bloodthirsty Agitators Are the She-Dogs of Anarchy," *Los Angeles Times*, Mar. 15, 1908, III-1. **arrested**: Vapnek, *Elizabeth Gurley Flynn*, 7–8. **dropped out**: EGF, *Rebel Girl*, 63–64.
22. **ten arrests**: Cole, "Elizabeth Gurley Flynn: A Portrait," 24; Harbor Allen, "The Flynn," *American Mercury*, Dec. 1926, 427 (asserting fifteen arrests). *"stunning speech"*: "Girl's Plea for Socialism," *Bulletin* [Philadelphia], Aug. 1907, 1906–1907 Early Newspapers and Clippings, 9, EGFP-NY. *"terribly earnest"* & *"sheer force"*: "Girl Socialist Sways Hearers," EGFP-B. *"last word"*: "Miss Flynn Speaks in Rain," 1906–1907 Early Newspapers and Clippings, 9, EGFP-NY.
23. **Women's suffrage**: Baxandall, *Words on Fire*, 77, 95, 103, 135; Camp, *Iron in Her Soul*, 13; Vapnek, *Elizabeth Gurley Flynn*, 17–18.
24. **first took note**: EGF, *Rebel Girl*, 70; J. Anthony Lukas, *Big Trouble: A Murder in a Small Western Town Sets Off a Struggle for the Soul of America* (Touchstone, 1997).
25. **one-eyed secretary treasurer ...** *"Hardly a week"*: William D. Haywood, *Bill Haywood's Book: The Autobiography of William D. Haywood* (International Publishers, 1929), 12.
26. **violence**: Joseph R. Conlin, *Big Bill Haywood and the Radical Union Movement* (Syracuse University Press, 2002); Lukas, *Big Trouble*; Philip Taft, "Violence in American Labor Disputes," *Annals of the American Academy of Political and Social Science* 364 (1966): 127. **shot a deputy**: Haywood, *Bill Haywood's Book*, 145; Stuart Chase, "Violence in Labor Conflicts," in *American Labor Dynamics in the Light of Post-War Developments*, ed. J. B. S. Hardman (Russell & Russell, 1928), 349–56.
27. **usually struck first**: Haywood, *Bill Haywood's Book*, 58–61; Robert Hunter, *Violence and the Labor Movement* (Macmillan, 1914); Emma F. Langdon, *The Cripple Creek Strike: A History of Industrial Wars in Colorado* (Arno Press, 1969).
28. **so extreme, so regular**: Elizabeth Jameson, *All That Glitters: Class, Conflict, and Community in Cripple Creek* (University of Illinois Press, 1998), 75–76. **belong to the workers**: Ibid., 23, 161–96.
29. *"Continental Congress"*: Dubofsky, *We Shall Be All*, 81. *"irrepressible conflict"*: *Founding Convention of the IWW: Proceedings* (Merit Press, 1969), 6; Dubofsky, *We Shall Be All*, 78.
30. **main organization**: Philip Taft, *The AFL in the Time of Gompers* (Harper & Brothers, 1957). **opposed Asian immigration**: Beth Lew-Williams, *The Chinese Must Go: Violence, Exclusion, and the Making of the Alien in America* (Harvard University Press, 2018), 118–19; Ronald Takaki, *Strangers from a Different Shore: A History of Asian Americans* (Little, Brown, 1989), 200. **excluded Black workers**: Paul Frymer, *Black and Blue: African Americans, the Labor Movement, and the Decline of the Democratic Party* (Princeton University Press, 2008); Sophia Lee, *The Workplace Constitution from the New Deal to the New Right* (Cambridge University Press, 2014); C. H. Wesley, *Negro Labor in the United States, 1850–1925: A Study in Economic History* (Vanguard Press, 1927).
31. **opened its doors wide**: Dubofsky, *We Shall Be All*, 57–87. *"every man that earns"* & *"slave bondage"*: *Founding Convention*, 1. *"industrial progress"*: Foner, *History of the Labor Movement*, at 134. *"means of life"*: "Testimony of Mr. William D. Haywood, May 12, 1915," Commission on Industrial Relations, *Industrial Relations: Final Report and Testimony Submitted to Congress by the Commission on Industrial Relations Created by the Act of August 23, 1912* (Government Printing Office, 1916), at 11:10573. *"full value"*: *Founding Convention*, 1.
32. *"regardless of color"*: Foner, *History of the Labor Movement*, 4:122. *"Leaving the Negro"* & *"colored worker"*: Ibid., 4:124–25. *"hires the Negro"*: Justus Ebert, *The I.W.W. in Theory and Practice* (IWW, 1918), 67. *"fighting each other"*: Quoted in Philip Foner, "The IWW and the Black Worker," *Journal of Negro History* 55 (1970): 45, 47.

33. *"equal footing"*: Foner, *History of the Labor Movement*, 4:124-25. **Philadelphia waterfront**: Cole, *Wobblies on the Waterfront*. **the South**: Covington Hall, *Labor Struggles in the Deep South*, ed. David Roediger (Charles H. Kerr, 1999), 137-44. **western timber**: Dubofsky, *We Shall Be All*, 127-28. **Mexican workers**: Ibid., 184, 370-71. *"bum brigade"*: Ibid., 140.
34. *"stodgy"*: Baxandall, *Words on Fire*, 7. *"Mixed Local"*: Camp, *Iron in Her Soul*, 15. *"youthful and vigorous"*: Elsa Jane Dixler, "The Woman Question: Women and the American Communist Party, 1929-1941," Ph.D. thesis, Yale University, 1974, at 61. *"first one"*: EGF, *Rebel Girl*, 85. **premature birth**: Vapnek, *Elizabeth Gurley Flynn*, 27. **soon split**: Ibid., 34. **grandmother's care**: EGF, *Rebel Girl*, 123.
35. **between 15,000 and 40,000**: Commission on Industrial Relations, *Final Report and Testimony*, 11:1456, 10576; Paul Frederick Brissenden, *The IWW: A Study of American Syndicalism* (Columbia University, 1919), 352-56.
36. *"nothing in common"*: Justus Ebert, *Industrial Unionism: The Road to Freedom* (IWW, 1913), 6. *"merciless class war"*: IWW, *Jersey Justice at Work* (IWW, 1913). *"army of occupation"*: Walker C. Smith, "The Only Hope of the Working Class," *Industrial Worker*, Jan. 8, 1910, 1.
37. *"direct action"*: Methods and Tactics: Direct Action, b. 1, f. 2, EGFP-NY; "Woodsmen Should Wear the Wooden Shoe," *Industrial Worker* [Spokane], July 17, 1913; John Graham Brooks, *American Syndicalism: The IWW* (Macmillan, 1913), 128-29. *"workers themselves"*: Ebert, *I.W.W. in Theory and Practice*, 51. *"any effort"*: "Direct Action in Action," *Industrial Worker* [Spokane], Sept. 17, 1910, 2. **bypassing... the state**: Dubofsky, *We Shall Be All*, 139-57.
38. *"Free Speech Fights"*: "Call to Action by Gurley Flynn," *Industrial Worker* [Spokane], Nov. 10, 1909, 1; David Rabban, "The IWW Free Speech Fights and Popular Conceptions of Free Expression Before World War I," *Virginia Law Review* 80 (1994): 1055. **jails in twenty-six towns**: David M. Rabban, *Free Speech in Its Forgotten Years, 1870-1920* (Cambridge University Press, 1999), at 77. *"Don't go to law"*: EGF, Untitled Account of IWW 1909 Activities—Tragedy and Farce of McKees Rock and then Missoula, [n.d.], b. 1, f. 32, EGFP-NY. *"every freight train"*: EGF, Labor & the Law / The War on the Reds—The Struggle for Free Speech [n.d. 1924?], b. 1, f. 32, EGFP-NY. *"break into jail"*: Ibid. *"so vigorously"*: Benjamin H. Kizer, "Elizabeth Gurley Flynn," *Pacific Northwest Quarterly* 57 (1966): 110, 111. **Missoula authorities & Spokane jury**: EGF, *Rebel Girl*, 103-10.
39. *"streets of San Diego"*: Walter Lippmann, *A Preface to Politics* (Mitchell Kennerley, 1913), 262. *"go ahead, boys"*: Quoted in Haywood, *Bill Haywood's Book*, 276.
40. *"firing line"*: Walker C. Smith, "Law or Sabotage?," *Industrial Worker* [Spokane], June 26, 1913. **point of production**: Dubofsky, *We Shall Be All*, 196-97. **Baldwin... inspired**: RNB, Autobiography (1884-1920), b. 20, f. 11, RNBP.
41. *"reached their limit"*: P. Brankin, "Sabotage as First Resort," *Industrial Worker*, June 26, 1913; P. Brankin, "Sabotage as First Resort," *Industrial Worker*, July 10, 1913; see also "Law or Sabotage?" *Industrial Worker*, June 26, 1913.
42. *"little doubt"*: Gage, "Why Violence Matters," 105. **assassinated**: Lukas, *Big Trouble*.
43. **remote mining communities**: Dubofsky, *We Shall Be All*, 120-25 (Goldfield, Nevada). **Colorado City**: Lukas, *Big Trouble*, 222-23.
44. *"carry bombs"*: Dubofsky, *We Shall Be All*, vii, 147. *"Gandhi"*: Conlin, "IWW and the Question of Violence," 321. *"counterproductive"*: Vapnek, *Modern American Revolutionary*, 57. *"veritable evangelists"*: Louis Adamic, *Dynamite! The Story of Class Violence in America* (Viking, 1931), 376.
45. **kill a company guard**: Ebert, *I.W.W. in Theory and Practice*, 46. **three to one**: Haywood, *Bill Haywood's Book*, 241. **thirteen... died**: Taft, "Violence in American Labor Disputes," 133.
46. **Times building... yearslong campaign**: Graham Adams Jr., *Age of Industrial Violence, 1910-15: The Activities and Findings of the United States Commission on Industrial Relations* (Columbia University Press, 1966); John A. Farrell, *Clarence Darrow: Attorney for the Damned* (Random House, 2011), 206-81; Robert Ovetz, *When Workers Shot Back: Class Conflict from 1877 to 1921* (Brill, 2018), at 325-68. *"betrayed labor"*: Adams, *Age of Industrial Violence*, 18.
47. *"with the McNamaras"*: Quoted in Adams, *Age of Industrial Violence*, 19. *"unholy medley"*...

"*meekly apologize*" . . . "*sowed the wind*" . . . "*upon the heads*": Brooks, *American Syndicalism*, 161–62 (quoting *Solidarity*, Jan. 4, 1912). "*John Browns*": Frank Bohn, "Those Dynamiters Again," *New York Call*, Jan. 6, 1913.

48. "*crime, sabotage*" . . . "*murder*" . . . "*riot*": Brissenden, *IWW: A Study*, 278, 279. **DeLeon . . . castigate**: Daniel DeLeon, "That Haywood Speech," *Daily People*, Dec. 26, 1911; also Brissenden, *IWW: A Study*, 252. "*for anarchy*": Debs quoted in Haywood, *Bill Haywood's Book*, 279; see generally Gage, "Why Violence Matters," 106.
49. **Haywood scorned:** "Haywood and Others," *New York Times*, Dec. 23, 1911, 8.
50. **town of Grabow:** Hall, *Labor Struggles in the Deep South and Other Writings*, 137–44. **passive resistance:** Dubofsky, *We Shall Be All*, 227–52; Justus Ebert, *The Trial of a New Society* (IWW, 1913), 82, 115–17, 132; Ebert, *I.W.W. in Theory and Practice*, 53; William Cahn, *Lawrence 1911: The Bread and Roses Strike* (Pilgrim Press, 1980), 114, 135. **strikers' destruction . . . violent demonstrations:** Dubofsky, *We Shall Be All*, 246–48. **acquitted:** Conlin, *IWW and the Question of Violence*, 324. **defending the use of force:** Adamic, "Sabotage"; Foner, *History of the Labor Movement*, 4:160–61.
51. **Durst Ranch:** Dubofsky, *We Shall Be All*, 294–98. **Paterson:** Adams, *Age of Industrial Violence*, 88–90. "*don't say*": Quoted in Dorothy Gallagher, *All the Right Enemies: The Life and Murder of Carlo Tresca* (Rutgers University Press, 1988), 47. **1,800 arrests:** Adams, *Age of Industrial Violence*, 90. **rival socialists:** Haywood, *Bill Haywood's Book*, 278.
52. **miners' hall in Butte:** David Emmons, "An Aristocracy of Labor: The Irish Miners of Butte, 1880–1914," *Labor History* 28 (1987): 275, 302. **Mesabi Range:** David LaVigne, "Rebel Girls: Women in the Mesabi Iron Range Strike of 1916," *Minnesota History* 65 (2016): 90, 92–95. **Everett:** John Richardson, "Mill Owners and Wobblies: The Event Structure of the Everett Massacre of 1916," *Social Science History* 33 (2009): 183–215. **Kenosha:** "IWW Yearbook: 1917," IWW History Project, University of Washington.
53. "*any weapon*": Quoted in Robert Hunter, *Violence and the Labor Movement* (Macmillan, 1914), at vii–viii. "*Whatever means*" . . . "*Western Rifleman*": Linda J. Lumsden, *Black, White, and Red All Over: A Cultural History of the Radical Press in Its Heyday, 1900–1917* (Kent State University Press, 2014), at 132. "*bomb underneath*": Walker C. Smith, "Workers Should Declare Their Own Independence," July 3, 1913. **St. John:** EGF, *Rebel Girl*, 87–88. "*any and all tactics*": Brooks, *American Syndicalism*, 160.
54. "*I said certainly*": Commission on Industrial Relations, *Final Report and Testimony Submitted to Congress by the Commission on Industrial Relations Created by the Act of August 23, 1912* (Government Printing Office, 1916), at 2:1445–62.
55. "*Most assuredly*": Ibid., 2:1571.
56. **strikebreaking laborers:** Ibid.
57. "*old abolitionists*": *Final Report*, 5:4239. "*that kind of violence*": Ibid., 11:10592.
58. **Carlo Tresca:** Nunzio Pernicone, *Carlo Tresca: Portrait of a Rebel* (Palgrave Macmillan, 2005); Nunzio Pernicone, "Carlo Tresca and the Sacco-Vanzetti Case," *Journal of American History* 60 (1979): 535. "*overflowing*": *The Reminiscences of Roger Baldwin, 1953–1954*, 75, CCOH. "*hot headed*": EGF to Mary Heaton Vorse, July 5, 1914, MHVP; Vapnek, *Elizabeth Gurley Flynn*, 59; EGF, *Rebel Girl*, 152.
59. "*splurge*": EGF, *Elizabeth Gurley Flynn Speaks to the Court* (New Century Publishers, 1952), 9. **striking waiters:** Gallagher, *All the Right Enemies*, 45. "*believe in violence*": Pernicone, *Carlo Tresca*, 86.
60. "*jawsmith*": Baxandall, *Words on Fire*, 11. "*any and all means*": EGF, Violence [1915?], b. 1, f. 32, EGFP-NY.
61. "*sabots*" & "*only effective method*": Walker C. Smith, *Sabotage: Its History, Philosophy, and Function* (IWW, 1913), in *Direct Action & Sabotage: Three Classic IWW Pamphlets from the 1910s*, ed. Salvatore Salerno (Charles H. Kerr, 2014), at 57, 60, 64. **resistance to scientific management:** Mike Davis, "The Stop Watch and the Wooden Shoe: Scientific Management and the Industrial Workers of the World," in *Workers' Struggles, Past and Present: A "Radical America" Reader*, ed. James Green (Temple University Press, 1983), 83–100.

62. *"justify sabotage"* . . . *machine belt*: EGF, *Sabotage: The Conscious Withdrawal of the Workers' Industrial Efficiency* (I.W.W. Publishing Bureau, 1915), 2.
63. *"right to bear arms"*: Ibid., 19.
64. *anarchist Arthur Caron*: Paul Avrich, *The Modern School Movement: Anarchism and Education in the United States* (Princeton University Press, 1980), 184–200; Thai Jones, *More Powerful Than Dynamite: Radicals, Plutocrats, Progressives, and New York's Year of Anarchy* (Bloomsbury, 2014); "I.W.W. Bomb Meant for Rockefeller Kills Four of Its Makers, Wrecks Tenement and Injures Many Tenants," *New York Times*, July 5, 1914, 1. *Haywood, disowned*: EGF, "Lexington Avenue Bomb Explosion," *Solidarity* (Cleveland), July 18, 1914, 1. *"dynamiting"*: Ibid.
65. *championed Caron* . . . *"disgrace"*: EGF to Mary Heaton Vorse, July 17, 1914, MHVP. *"psychology of violence"* . . . *"Circumstances alone"*: EGF, "Lexington Avenue Bomb Explosion," 2.
66. *"poison"*: Allen, "The Flynn," 431. *Mesabi . . . 1916*: LaVigne, "Rebel Girls: Women in the Mesabi Iron Range Strike," 91–93.
67. *"actual fisticuffs"*: Chase, "Violence in Labor Conflicts," in Hardman, *American Labor Dynamics*, 349–56.
68. *"industrial pirates"*: Joseph Ettor, *Industrial Unionism: The Road to Freedom* (I.W.W., 1913), 14. *"act of force"*: EGF quoted in J. S. Apelman, "Elizabeth Gurley Flynn, Radical Activities," Jan. 27, 1922, in Department of Justice, Documents on Elizabeth Gurley Flynn, 1921–1922.
69. *"child's disease"*: John Graham Brooks, *American Syndicalism. The I.W.W.* (Macmillan, 1913), 74. *"misguided idealists"*: RNB, "Recollections of a Life in Civil Liberties," *Civil Liberties Review*, Spring 1975, 39, 43–44; Cottrell, *Roger Nash Baldwin*, 32. *"self-defeating"*: W. A. Swanberg, *Norman Thomas: The Last Idealist* (Charles Scribner's Sons, 1976), 73. *"real development"* . . . *"defeat"*: Hunter, *Violence and the Labor Movement*, 55.
70. *"Reading the Declaration"*: Arnold Stead, *Always on Strike: Frank Little and the Western Wobblies* (Haymarket Books, 2012), 44. *"hobo agitator"*: Dubofsky, *We Shall Be All*, 186. *kidnapped*: "Hell Is Popping in Minot, N.D.," *Industrial Worker* (Spokane), Aug. 21, 1913. *vigilantes*: Ralph Chaplin, *Wobbly: The Rough-and-Tumble Story of an American Radical* (University of Chicago Press, 1948), 210–11; Camp, *Iron in Her Soul*, 78.
71. *declined to take & anti-war sentiment & seize the opportunity*: Dubofsky, *We Shall Be All*, 354–58; Philip Taft, "The Federal Trials of the IWW," *Labor History* 3 (1962): 73. *fight the Kaiser*: EGF, "From Elizabeth Gurley Flynn," *The Masses*, Mar. 1916, 12.
72. *"mob violence"*: EGF, "Labor & the Law / The War on the Reds"; EGF, *Rebel Girl*, 229. *ransacked* . . . *"Universal Law"*: Dubofsky, *We Shall Be All*, 383–86.
73. *concentration camps*: Dubofsky, *We Shall Be All*, 394. *Tulsa*: Haywood, *Big Bill Haywood's Book*, 296; Taft, "Federal Trials," 57, 60.
74. *"out of business"*: Quoted in Dubofsky, *We Shall Be All*, 407. *Spokane*: Ibid., 402. *Covington*: Ibid., 406.
75. *arrested*: EGF, *Rebel Girl*, 233.
76. *simultaneous raids & Separate indictments*: Dubofsky, *We Shall Be All*, 406, 408. *indictment* . . . *165 people in all*: Philip Taft, "Federal Trials," 60 (the usual number given [166] is incorrect because one defendant was named twice). *up to twenty*. "An Act to Punish Acts of Interference with Foreign Relations," Statutes at Large 40, 217, s. 3 at 219; Sam Lebovic, *State of Silence: The Espionage Act and the Rise of America's Secrecy Regime* (Basic Books, 2023), 7.
77. *surrendered*: Vapnek, *Elizabeth Gurley Flynn*, 69. *old free speech fights*: See, e.g., Ronald Genini, "Industrial Workers of the World and Their Fresno Free Speech Fight, 1910–1911," *California Historical Quarterly* 53 (1974): 101, 106. *"dragnet strategy"*: Vapnek, *Elizabeth Gurley Flynn*, 69; also Baxandall, *Words on Fire*, 28–29. For a different, dimmer view of Flynn's loyalty and tactical judgment, see Dubofsky, *We Shall Be All*, 425–29.
78. *letter to President Wilson*: Camp, *Iron in Her Soul*, 80–81; Baxandall, *Words on Fire*, 28.
79. *guilty verdicts*: Chester, *Wobblies in Their Heyday*, 185–86; Dubofsky, *We Shall Be All*, 436–37. *despite having left*: Alexander Sidney Lanier to Warren Harding, Jan. 23, 1922, NY Mss L, E. G. Flynn 1922 to 1923, EGFP-W.
80. *184 Wobbly leaders*: Taft, "Federal Trials," 57–60. *to Ellis Island*: Statement of W. A. Blackwood,

I. W. W. Deportation Cases: Hearings Before a Subcommittee of the Committee on Immigration and Naturalization House of Representatives, Sixty-Sixth Congress, Second Session (Government Printing Office, 1920).

81. *affirmed*: Haywood v. United States, 268 F. 795 (7th Cir. 1920). *jumped his bond*: Taft, "Federal Trials," 75–76. *quietly dropped*: Vapnek, Elizabeth Gurley Flynn, 69. *membership plunged*: John S. Gambs, The Decline of the I.W.W. (Russell & Russell, 1966), 165–66.
82. *"Nothing is further"*: Ebert, The I.W.W. in Theory and Practice. *"does not believe"*: George F. Vanderveer, Opening Statement of Geo. F. Vanderveer, Counsel for the Defense of One Hundred and One Members of the Industrial Workers of the World in the Case of the U.S.A. vs. Wm. D. Haywood, et al. (I.W.W. Publishing Bureau, 1918), 75. *"service rendered"*: Ibid., 71. *"pork chops"*: Evidence and Cross-Examination of J. T. (Red) Doran in the Case of the U.S.A. vs. Wm. D. Haywood et al. (General Defense Committee, Chicago, June 28, 1918), 149.
83. *"destruction or violence"*: "Resolution Regarding Sabotage," Defense News Bulletin, May 4, 1918.
84. *Gandhi . . . "passive resistance"*: J. S. Apelman, "Elizabeth Gurley Flynn, Radical Activities," Memorandum in re Elizabeth Gurley Flynn, Feb. 19, 1923, Justice Department Documents on Elizabeth Gurley Flynn. *Even . . . Tresca*: Pernicone, Carlo Tresca, 219–20.
85. *September 1918*: "IWW Bomb Kills Four in Chicago," New York Times, Sept. 5, 1918, 1. *April 1919 . . . Ethel Williams*: Paul Avrich, Sacco and Vanzetti: The Anarchist Background (Princeton University Press, 1991), 140–41. *seven cities*: "Red Killed by Washington Bomb," New York Sun, June 4, 1919, 2. *paymaster and a guard*: Moshik Temkin, The Sacco-Vanzetti Affair: America on Trial (Yale University Press, 2009); Lisa McGirr, "The Passion of Sacco and Vanzetti: A Global History," Journal of American History 93 (2007): 1085. *thirty-eight people*: Beverly Gage, The Day Wall Street Exploded: A Story of America in the First Age of Terror (Oxford University Press, 2009).
86. *attack after attack*: Avrich, Sacco and Vanzetti, 136–37. *"social vision" . . . "menace"*: Adamic, "Sabotage," 226.
87. *Centralia*: Adamic, Dynamite, 292–305; Tom Copeland, The Centralia Tragedy of 1919: Elmer Smith and the Wobblies (University of Washington Press, 1993); Robert Tyler, Rebels of the Woods: The IWW in the Pacific Northwest (University of Oregon Press, 1967). *Twenty states*: Eldridge Foster Dowell, A History of Criminal Syndicalism Legislation in the United States (Johns Hopkins University Press, 1939), 21. *"advocates crime"*: Quoted at ibid., 150. *"criminal syndicalism" . . . "known as"*: Ibid., 21.

13: INDUSTRIAL DEMOCRACY

"Brookwood became the mecca": Cohn quoted in Cara Cook, ed., Brookwood Fifteenth Anniversary Review (Academy Press, 1936), 10.

1. *"dislike"*: EGF to RNB, Nov. 16, 1922, r. 17, b. 24, AFPSR.
2. *escalating*: EGF to Amleto Fabbri, July 8, 1926, r. 12, b. 18, AFPSR; Notice of Special Meeting, Nov. 11, 1924, r. 1, b. 1, AFPSR; see also Gloria Garrett Samson, The American Fund for Public Service: Charles Garland and Radical Philanthropy, 1922–1941 (Greenwood Press, 1996), at 127–28. *joining*: RNB to EGF, June 10, 1924; EGF to RNB, July 20, 1924, both in r. 1, b. 1, AFPSR.
3. *Freda Kirchwey*: AFPS to FK, June 10, 1924; Minutes of the Fortieth Meeting of the Board of the AFPS, July 9, 1924, r. 3, AFPSR. *Michelson's appointment*: Samson, American Fund for Public Service, 180–81.
4. *"ex-IWW"*: RNB, The Reminiscences of Roger Baldwin, 1953–1954 (1963), at 326, CCOH. *"spirit"*: Ibid., 301–2. *"colleague" & "friend"*: RNB, "Autobiography (1884–1920)," b. 20, f. 12, 126, RNBP. *"One's heart"*: Samson, American Fund for Public Service, 144. *parted ways*: Corliss Lamont, ed., The Trial of Elizabeth Gurley Flynn by the American Civil Liberties Union (Horizon Press, 1968); see also Joseph P. Lash interview with Helen Manoni, Oct. 16, 1972, JPLP. *substitute*: RNB to CG, June 10, 1924, r. 1, b. 1, AFPSR.
5. *Civic Club*: RNB to EGF, June 10, 1924; r. 1, b. 1, AFPSR; see also Lucille Milner, Education of an

American Liberal (Horizon Press, 1957), 67. **industrial democracy**: James Henle, "The New Partnership in Industrial Production: An Interview with Sidney Hillman," *The World*, July 27, 1919.

6. **comrades**: Melvyn Dubofsky, *We Shall Be All: A History of the Industrial Workers of the World* (Quadrangle/New York Times Book Company, 1969), 441–43. **deported**: "Writ Served on Emma Goldman for Deportation," *St. Louis Post-Dispatch*, Sept. 18, 1919, 1; "Emma Goldman and 250 'Reds' to Be Deported Today," *St. Louis Post-Dispatch*, Dec. 21, 1919, B5. **raids**: William Preston, *Aliens and Dissenters* (University of Illinois Press, 1994).
7. **"hurry"**: EGF, *Rebel Girl: An Autobiography, My First Life, 1906–1926* (International Publishers, rev ed. 1973) (1955), at 265.
8. **opportunity ... remnants of the IWW**: Ibid., 242–47. **Party chapters joined together**: EGF to Frederic C. Howe, July 22, 1919, EGFP-W. **"in jail"**: EGF, *Rebel Girl*, 245.
9. **1,500**: EGF, *Rebel Girl*, 242; also EGF to All Liberty-Loving Workers, May 12, 1920; EGF to Friend, May 14, 1920, both in EGFP-W. **"day and night"**: EGF, *Rebel Girl*, 265. **Bloor**: Ibid., 249. **St. John**: WDU, "Dear Friend," July 30, 1921, EGFP-W. **"crowning outrage"**: Frank P. Walsh to EGF, Jan. 16, 1922, EGFP-W.
10. **lambasted**: WDU, Deportees Held on Ellis Island to William B. Wilson, Feb. 24, 1920, EGFP-W. **"sounds nice"**: EGF to Frederic C. Howe, July 22, 1919, EGFP-W. **better healthcare**: Tomas Martinez to EGF, Oct. 17, 1921, and A. Gross to WDU, Jan. 11, 1922, both in EGFP-W.
11. **pressure campaign**: Helen C. Camp, *Iron in Her Soul: Elizabeth Gurley Flynn and the American Left* (Washington State University Press, 1995), 90–91. **clemency deals**: George Creel to Harry Weinberger, Apr. 26, 1921; Political Prisoners, [n.d., ca. July 14, 1921]; Workers Defense Union, "Dear Friend," July 30, 1921; Alexander Sidney Lanier to Warren Harding, Jan. 23, 1922; HW to WH, Jan. 27, 1922, all in EGFP-W. **betrayals**: Walter Nef to EGF, Nov. 25, 1922; HW to Frederick A. Blossom, Nov. 29, 1922; Workers' Prison Relief Committee to HW, Dec. 7, 1922; Harry Feinberg to HW, Dec. 11, 1922, all in EGFP-W.
12. **contact with ... Darrow**: HW to EGF, Aug. 19, 1921; Creel to Weinberger, Apr. 26, 1921, both in EGFP-W. **Howe**: EGF to Frederic C. Howe, July 22, 1919, EGFP-W; "Latest Dealings in the Realty Field," *New York Times*, Sept. 30, 1917, 14. **Children's Crusade**: EGF, *Rebel Girl*, 292–96. **wife, Grace**: Ibid., 280. **DeSilver**: Ibid., 246. **Nelles**: Ibid., 312. **condemning the Palmer Raids**: National Popular Government League, *Report upon the Illegal Practices of the United States Department of Justice* (National Popular Government League, 1920).
13. **"singularly inexpedient"**: Norman Thomas to Eugene Lyons, Jan. 6, 1920, EGFP-W. **Justice Department ... IWW convicts**: Geoffrey R. Stone, *Perilous Times: Free Speech in Wartime from the Sedition Act of 1798 to the War on Terrorism* (W. W. Norton, 2004), 230–332. **deportations fell**: Preston, *Aliens and Dissenters*, 352, n95. **full amnesty**: Sam Lebovic, *State of Silence: The Espionage Act and the Rise of America's Secrecy Regime* (Basic Books, 2023).
14. **authorities arrested**: Felix Frankfurter, "The Case of Sacco and Vanzetti," *Atlantic Monthly*, May 1927, pp. 409-10; also Frankfurter, *The Case of Sacco and Vanzetti: A Critical Analysis for Lawyers and Laymen* (Little, Brown & Co., 1927), 6–7. **charged them**: Moshik Temkin, *The Sacco-Vanzetti Affair: America on Trial* (Yale University Press, 2009), 9; Paul Avrich, *Sacco and Vanzetti: The Anarchist Background* (Princeton University Press, 1991).
15. **among the first**: Lara Vapnek, *Elizabeth Gurley Flynn: Modern American Revolutionary* (Westview Press, 2015), 82; see also Fred Moore to EGF, Aug. 18, 1920, b. 32, f. 6, AFS-VDC; WDU, Delegates' Meeting [Oct. 13?, 1920], b. 1, f. 9, EGFP-NY. **bulletin**: EGF to WDU Delegates, May 8, 1920, b. 1, f. 9, EGFP-NY. **welcomed Flynn**: EGF, *Rebel Girl*, 203. **with ... Sacco ... in Lawrence**: Anne F. Mattina and Dominique Ciavattone, "Striking Women: Massachusetts Mill Workers in the Wake of Bread and Roses, 1912–1913," in *The Great Lawrence Textile Strike of 1912: New Scholarship on the Bread and Roses Strike*, ed. Robert Farrant and Jurg Siegenthaler (Routledge, 2014), 153, 163. **Sacco contributed**: Avrich, *Sacco and Vanzetti*, 26. **Flynn ... defended**: EGF, "Lexington Avenue Bomb Explosion," *Solidarity* (Cleveland), July 18, 1914, 1. **organized ... fundraisers**: Avrich, *Sacco and Vanzetti*, 29; EGF, *Rebel Girl*, 307.
16. **Dedham jail**: EGF, *Rebel Girl*, 203; also Mary Heaton Vorse, Oct. 1920, b. 1, f. 9, EGFP-NY. **Dreyfus Affair**: Temkin, *Sacco-Vanzetti Affair*, xv.

17. *publicity campaign*: EGF, *Rebel Girl*, 306. *Doomed*: Art Shields, *Are They Doomed?* (Workers Defense Union, 1921); WDU Meeting, Mar. 19, 1921, b. 1, f. 9, EGFP-NY; see also EGF, *Rebel Girl*, 307. *"shoemaker"*: Ibid., 335. *"persecution"*: Shields, *Are They Doomed?*, 4.
18. *manacled*: EGF, *Rebel Girl*, 314-20. *"anarchistic bastards"*: Avrich, *Sacco and Vanzetti*, 3-4.
19. *Progressive editors*: "Sacco-Vanzetti—a Federal Lynching," *The Nation*, Sept. 22, 1926, 263; Elizabeth Glendower Evans, "New Light on a Bad Business: Fresh Facts in the Sacco-Vanzetti Case," *New Republic*, Dec. 26, 1923. *By 1922 . . . "ghastly miscarriage"*: EGF, *Rebel Girl*, 324-25.
20. *Galleani*: Eric Foner, "Sacco and Vanzetti," *The Nation*, Aug. 20, 1977, 138; Avrich, *Sacco and Vanzetti*, 26-29. *"expropriations"*: Nunzio Pernicone, "Carlo Tresca and the Sacco-Vanzetti Case," *Journal of American History* 60 (1979): 535-47. *"propaganda of the deed"*: Michael Willrich, *American Anarchy: The Epic Struggle Between Immigrant Radicals and the US Government at the Dawn of the Twentieth Century* (Basic Books, 2023), 28, 220-99; Foner, "Sacco and Vanzetti," 138.
21. *Lexington Avenue*: Avrich, *Sacco and Vanzetti*, 99. *bomb campaign*: Ibid., 104-5, 138. *April 1919*: Beverly Gage, *The Day Wall Street Exploded: A Story of America in Its First Age of Terror* (Oxford University Press, 2009), 27; Willrich, *American Anarchy*, 293-96. *Mitchell Palmer*: "Red Killed by Washington Bomb," *New York Herald*, June 4, 1919, 2; Stone, *Perilous Times*, 222.
22. *last blasts*: See Beverly Gage, "Why Violence Matters: Radicalism, Politics, and Class War in the Gilded Age and Progressive Era," *Journal for the Study of Radicalism* 1 (2007): 99-105.
23. *"nothing but disaster"*: Mary Anne Trasciatti, "Elizabeth Gurley Flynn, the Sacco-Vanzetti Case and the Rise and Fall of the Liberal-Radical Alliance, 1920-1940," *American Communist History* 15 (2016): 191, 203.
24. *"quite discouraged"*: EGF to RNB, Nov. 16, 1922, r. 3, b. 5, AFPSR.
25. *arrested . . . forced to flee*: Steven Fraser, *Labor Will Rule: Sidney Hillman and the Rise of American Labor* (Free Press, 1991), 11-14, 20; Steven Fraser, "Sidney Hillman: Labor's Machiavelli," in *Labor Leaders in America*, ed. Melvyn Dubofsky and Warren Van Tine (University of Illinois Press, 1987), 208-10. *"Clear it"*: Fraser, *Labor Will Rule*, 526-27.
26. *founding director*: RNB to Persons Named in the Enclosed Prospectus, Mar. 23, 1922, II-L-I, NAACPLC. *Clinton Golden*: Thomas R. Brooks, *Clint: A Biography of a Labor Intellectual, Clinton S. Golden* (Atheneum, 1978), 69. *Wolman*: Irving Bernstein, *Turbulent Years: A History of the American Worker, 1933-1941* (Houghton Mifflin, 1970), at 74. *seats*: RNB to CG, June 10, 1924, b. 1, f. 1, AFPSR. *stepped back*: Second Annual Meeting of the Members, May 28, 1924, r. 3, b. 5, AFPSR; see also RNB to Robert Morss Lovett, Sept. 28, 1923; RNB to Lewis Gannett, May 10, 1924; RNB to Leo Wolman, June 10, 1924, all in r. 1, b. 1, AFPSR. *leading supporters*: AFPS Board Meeting, Mar. 7, 1923, r. 3, b. 5, AFPSR; Samson, *American Fund for Public Service*, 68. *$77,500 loan*: AFPS Board Meeting, Mar. 15, 1925, r. 3, b. 5, AFPSR. *outright grants*: AFPS, *Final Report*, 2.
27. *fierce competition . . . Strikes were more common*: Fraser, *Labor Will Rule*, 26-41. *"Huskies" . . . killed*: Ibid., 52-53; see also N. Sue Weiler, "Walkout: The Chicago Men's Garment Workers' Strike, 1910-1911," *Chicago History* 8 (1979-1980): 238, 248; N. Sue Weiler, "The Uprising in Chicago: The Men's Garment Workers Strike, 1910-1911," in *A Needle, a Bobbin, a Strike: Women Needleworkers in America*, ed. Joan M. Jensen and Sue Davidson (Temple University Press, 1984).
28. *insurgent workers*: Fraser, *Labor Will Rule*, 40-76.
29. *progressives*: Ibid., 210. *"new principle"*: Amalgamated Clothing Workers of America, *The Clothing Workers of Chicago, 1910-1922* (Chicago Joint Board, 1922), at 59.
30. *"arbitration machinery"*: Ibid., 45. *"Board"*: Ibid., 57.
31. *meeting . . . "dead body"*: Fraser, *Labor Will Rule*, 65.
32. *"Protocols of Peace"*: Leon Stein, *Out of the Sweatshop: The Struggle for Industrial Democracy* (Quadrangle/New York Times Book Company, 1977), ch. 6; Melvin I. Urofsky, *Louis D. Brandeis: A Life* (Pantheon Books, 2009), 250; Graham Adams Jr., *The Activities and Findings of the United States Commission on Industrial Relations* (Columbia University Press, 1966), 119. *spread*: Bernstein, *Turbulent Years*, 75. *Clerk*: Fraser, *Labor Will Rule*, 81-82. *returned*: Ibid., 96.

33. *"negative attitude" & "claims of labor"*: Sidney Hillman, "Labor Attitudes," in *American Labor Dynamics in the Light of Post-War Developments: An Inquiry by Thirty-Two Labor Men, Teachers, Editors, and Technicians*, ed. J. B. S. Hardman (Russell & Russell, 1928), 292–96. *"pathetic figure"*: Fraser, *Labor Will Rule*, 234.

34. *"earthly use"*: Hillman, "Labor Attitudes," 292. *split*: Fraser, *Labor Will Rule*, 211. *"radical philosophy"*: David J. Saposs, *Left Wing Unionism* (International Publishers, 1927), 151. *"capitalist order"*: Ibid., 149.

35. *"all the fight"*: Hillman, "Labor Attitudes," 295. *"called revolutionary"*: Henle, "New Partnership in Industrial Production."

36. **Wolman**: Bernstein, *Turbulent Years*, at 74. *"brute"*: Brooks, *Clint*, 73–74.

37. *studied propaganda*: David G. Saposs, "The Mind of Immigrant Communities in the Pittsburgh District," in Interchurch World Movement of North America, *Public Opinion and the Steel Strike: Supplementary Reports of the Investigators to the Commission of Inquiry, the Interchurch World Movement* (Harcourt, Brace, 1921), 224. *grants*: AFPS Board Meeting, July 22, 1925, r. 3, b. 5, AFPSR. **Brophy**: John Brophy to Norman Thomas, b. 1, f. 2, JBPC; John Brophy to Evelyn Preston, Nov. 11, 1928, b. 1, f. 3, JBPC; Applications to AFPS from July to Sept. 1922; AFPS Board Meeting, June 13, 1928, both in r. 3, b. 5, AFPSR. **Lowenthal**: RNB, Memorandum for AFPS Regarding Application of Pennsylvania System Federation #90, [n.d., after Aug. 27, 1923?], r. 11, b. 17, AFPS. **Schlossberg**: Cletus E. Daniel, *The ACLU and the Wagner Act: An Inquiry into the Depression-Era Crisis of American Liberalism (Cornell Studies in Industrial and Labor Relations)* (Cornell University Press, 1980), 42.

38. *comfortable home*: Fraser, *Labor Will Rule*, 114–45. **Taylor**: Robert Kanigel, *The One Best Way: Frederick Winslow Taylor and the Enigma of Efficiency* (MIT Press, 1997); Mike Davis, "The Stop Watch and the Wooden Shoe: Scientific Management and the Industrial Workers of the World," in *Workers' Struggles, Past and Present: A "Radical America" Reader*, ed. James Green (Temple University Press, 1983), 83–100. *"deliberate gathering . . . workman"*: David Montgomery, *Workers' Control in America: Studies in the History of Work, Technology, and Labor Struggles* (Cambridge University Press, 1979), 115.

39. *Scientific management . . . scourge*: Davis, "Stop Watch and the Wooden Shoe," 86–95. *brains*: David Montgomery, *The Fall of the House of Labor: The Workplace, the State, and American Labor Activism, 1865–1925* (Cambridge University Press, 1987), at 45. **Gompers**: Philip Taft, *The A. F. of L. in the Time of Gompers* (Harper & Brothers, 1957), 299–300. *"reduced"*: Montgomery, *Fall of the House of Labor*, 248.

40. *tool labor might use*: David Montgomery, "Thinking About American Workers in the 1920s," *International Labor and Working-Class History* 32 (1987): 4–24; Steve Fraser, "Dress Rehearsal for the New Deal: Shop-Floor Insurgents, Political Elites, and Industrial Democracy in the Amalgamated Clothing Workers," in *Working-Class America: Essays on Labor, Community, and American Society*, ed. Michael H. Frisch and Daniel J. Walkowitz (University of Illinois Press, 1983), 212–55.

41. *pay to match*: Montgomery, *Fall of the House of Labor*, 421; John Fabian Witt, "Speedy Fred Taylor and the Ironies of Enterprise Liability," *Columbia Law Review* 103 (2003): 1–49.

42. **Beyer**: Ibid., 423; William Z. Foster, *The Watson-Parker Law: The Latest Scheme to Hamstring Railroad Unionism* (Trade Union Educational League, 1926), 13; see also Otto S. Beyer to RNB, Nov. 22, 1922, r. 3, b. 5, AFPSR. *"father"*: "Otto Beyer Dead," *New York Times*, Dec. 9, 1948, 33.

43. *"increased wages" . . . industry*: Montgomery, *Fall of the House of Labor*, 421–25.

44. *"paradoxical marriage"*: Ibid., 424. Montgomery was himself a skeptic, channeling the critique of men like Fund director William Z. Foster before him.

45. **Lovett**: AFL, Press Release, Apr. 13, 1923, r. 5, b. 8, AFPSR. **Thomas**: Norman Thomas to EGF, June 29, 1925, r. 1, b. 1, AFPSR. *substantial beneficiaries*: Gifts to June 30, 1941, 25–26, r. 5, AFPSR.

46. *lean years*: Irving Bernstein, *The Lean Years: A History of the American Worker, 1920–1933* (Houghton Mifflin, 1960). *rising wages in certain sectors*: Frank Stricker, "Affluence for Whom? Another Look at Prosperity and the Working Classes in the 1920s," *Labor History* 24 (1983): 5, 17. *5 million . . . same period*: Leo Troy, "Trade Union Membership, 1897–1962," *Review of*

Economics and Statistics 47 (1965): 93. **ACW:** Fraser, *Labor Will Rule*, 207; Leo Wolman, *Ebb and Flow in Trade Unionism* (National Bureau of Economic Research, 1936), 30.

47. **"help the student":** Lillian Herstein, "Realities in Worker Education," in Hardman, *American Labor Dynamics in the Light of Post-War Developments*, 379. **"The activity":** Fraser, *Labor Will Rule*, 112-13.

48. **largest single beneficiary:** AFPS, *Report for the Second Year Ending June 30, 1924* (New York, 1924), at 4; AFPS, *Report of the American Fund for Public Service, Inc., for the Three Years July 1, 1938 to June 30, 1941 and Summary of Nineteen Years, 1922-1941* (New York, 1941), at 2.

49. **Founded in 1921 ... "American Gandhi":** See Charles F. Howlett, *Brookwood Labor College and the Struggle for Peace and Social Justice in America* (Edwin Mellen Press, 1993); Leilah Danielson, *American Gandhi: A. J. Muste and the History of Radicalism in the Twentieth Century* (University of Pennsylvania Press, 2014); Jo Ann Ooiman Robinson, *Abraham Went Out: A Biography of A. J. Muste* (Temple University Press, 1981); Staughton Lynd, "A. J. Muste," in *The American Radical*, ed. Mary Jo Buhle et al. (Routledge, 2013), 266-67.

50. **strike wave ... strike committee:** AJM, *The Reminiscences of A. J. Muste* (1972), 333, CCOH; Lynd, "A. J. Muste," 263-64.

51. **"considerable amount":** Philip Taft, "Violence in American Labor Disputes," *Annals of the American Academy of Political and Social Science* 364 (1966): 127, 128. **machine-gun nest:** Danielson, *American Gandhi*, 71-72.

52. **"found expression":** AJM, *Reminiscences*, 356. **"destroy all":** Ibid., 381.

53. **"inclined plane ... human being":** Ibid., 295-96.

54. **"can't weave wool":** Ibid., 382. **"smile":** Nat Hentoff, *Peace Agitator: The Story of A. J. Muste* (Macmillan, 1963), 51.

55. **capitulated:** Lynd, "A. J. Muste," 263-64.

56. **Amalgamated Textile Workers:** Ibid., 64; AJM, *Reminiscences*, 423. **Hillman:** Danielson, *American Gandhi*, 73. **"revolutionary philosophy":** AJM, *Reminiscences*, 421.

57. **folded & founded:** Danielson, *American Gandhi*, 80-83; Howlett, *Brookwood Labor College and the Struggle*.

58. **campus:** Ibid., 84; Samson, *American Fund for Public Service*, 126. **Baldwin ... AFL:** Jonathan D. Bloom, "Brookwood Labor College, 1921-1933: Training Ground for Union Organizers," M.A. thesis (Rutgers University, 1978), 7-8.

59. **"full and honest":** Samson, *American Fund for Public Service*, 121.

60. **Gramsci & Angell:** Joseph A. Buttigieg, "On Gramsci," *Daedalus* 131 (Spring 2002): 67-70; Antonio Gramsci, *Prison Notebooks* (Columbia University Press, 1975), 1:137-69; Martin Ceadel, *Living the Great Illusion: Sir Norman Angell, 1872-1967* (Oxford University Press, 2009). **new approach:** Richard J. Altenbaugh, *Education for Struggle, the American Labor Colleges of the 1920s and 1930s* (Temple University Press, 1990), at 6; also Danielson, *American Gandhi*, 67. **"instill into ... emancipation":** Samson, *American Fund for Public Service*, 86. **"order":** Ibid., 109. **"passion":** Samson, *American Fund for Public Service*, 7. **"more effective ... their class":** AFPS, Press Release, Apr. 14, 1923, r. 5, b. 8, AFPSR.

61. **"how to think":** Samson, *American Fund for Public Service*, 80. **"new social order ... methods":** Ibid., 106. **"proposition":** Howlett, *Brookwood Labor College and the Struggle*, 33, n4. **"increasing emphasis ... organized power":** AJM, "Whither American Labor," *Labor Age* 15 (1926): 5, 6.

62. **typically union members:** Howlett, *Brookwood Labor College and the Struggle for Peace*, 56. **half the annual Brookwood budget:** Memorandum in re Brookwood Budget, Mar. 24, 1926, container 162.3, MLEP ($25,000 of Brookwood's $52,000 annual budget) ($32,000 annual budget in year the Fund gave $15,000); also Brookwood College Budget Committee, 1932, b. 3, f. 15, KPEP. **NAACP-Brookwood scholarships:** Eugene Levy, *James Weldon Johnson: Black Leader, Black Voice* (University of Chicago Press, 1973), 275; Report for October Meeting, 1925, NAACP Monthly Reports, NAACPP; see also WEBDB to JWJ, Jan. 15, 1925, r. 7, b. 11, AFPSR. **Golden:** Samson, *American Fund for Public Service*, 127. **"enchanting":** Len De Caux, *Labor Radical: From the Wobblies to CIO* (Beacon Press, 1970), 95-96.

63. **students convened:** Howlett, *Brookwood Labor College and the Struggle for Peace*, 56; Census

of Brookwood Students, Mar. 1927, b. 1, f. 1, BLCR. *Cohn*: Brookwood Educational Advisory Committee, b. 24, f. 16, BLCR. *Pinkney*: Report for October Meeting, 1925, NAACP Monthly Reports, NAACPP; A. J. Muste to JWJ, June 24, 1926, b. 10, r. 16, AFPSR. *"tolerates"*: Bloom, "Brookwood Labor College," 83. *Foreign . . . "weekends"*: Howlett, *Brookwood Labor College and the Struggle*, 56.

64. *Saposs & Wolman*: AJM to Sidney Hillman, Nov. 2, 1923, b. 15, f. 3, BLCR. *courses*: Brookwood AFPS Correspondence, 1924–1926, b. 22, f. 12, BLCR. *Calhoun*: Howlett, *Brookwood Labor College and the Struggle*, 69–70. *"Labor's Responsibilities"*: Fraser, *Labor Will Rule*, 221. *founding directors*: Bloom, "Brookwood Labor College," 7–8.

65. *Brookwood Players*: Arthur Levine, "Brookwood Remembered: An Unheralded Educational Experience," *Change: The Magazine of Higher Learning* 13 (1981): 38, 41; Howlett, *Brookwood Labor College and the Struggle*, 305–6; Bloom, "Brookwood Labor College," 76.

66. *"thinks . . . free from exploitation"*: James W. Robinson, "The Expulsion of Brookwood Labor College from the Workers' Education Bureau," *Labour History* 15 (1968): 64, 67.

67. *"insidious propaganda"*: Bloom, "Brookwood Labor College," 35. *"powerful agencies"*: Ibid., 97. *"prejudices"*: Hentoff, *Peace Agitator*, 66.

68. *"The Activity"*: Fraser, *Labor Will Rule*, 54, 112–13.

69. *"self-realization"*: John Dewey, "Self-Realization as the Moral Ideal," *Philosophical Review* 2 (1893): 652–64. *"good"*: John Dewey, *Democracy and Education: An Introduction to the Philosophy of Education* (Macmillan, 1916), 99. *"continuous readjustment"*: Ibid., 87. *"reconstruction"*: Bert MacLeech, "Workers' Education in the United States," Ph.D. thesis, Harvard University, 1951, 243–44.

70. *"habits" & "social changes"*: Dewey, *Democracy and Education*, 99. *"social life" . . . violent disruption*: Robert B. Westbrook, *John Dewey and American Democracy* (Cornell University Press, 1991), 109.

71. *"common interest"*: Robert B. Westbrook, "Schools for Industrial Democrats: The Social Origins of John Dewey's Philosophy of Education," *American Journal of Education* 100 (1992): 401, 408. *"experiment" . . . "work"*: Ibid., 412–13. *"integrates"*: Horace M. Kallen, *Education, the Machine, and the Worker: An Essay in the Psychology of Education in Industrial Society* (New Republic, 1925), 193.

72. *"swim . . . crowd action"*: Norman Thomas, *What Is Industrial Democracy?* (League for Industrial Democracy, 1925), 51–52; also MLE to AJM, Mar. 5, 1926, b. 31, f. 18, BLCR; Howlett, *Brookwood Labor College and the Struggle*, 14–16; Bloom, "Brookwood Labor College," 18; Westbrook, "Schools for Industrial Democrats," 114.

73. *"truly educational"*: John Dewey, "Labor Politics and Labor Education," *New Republic*, Jan. 9, 1929, 211–13. *"power trusts . . . generous way"*: John Dewey, "Freedom in Worker's Education," *American Teacher* 13 (1929): 1, 3. *"No activity"*: John Dewey, "Help for Brookwood," in *The Later Works of John Dewey, 1925–1953*, vol. 6, ed. Jo Ann Boydston (Southern Illinois University Press, 2008), at 328.

74. *"partisan group"*: EGF to H. H. Broach, Feb. 16, 1926, r. 1, b. 1, AFPSR.

75. *"right tendencies"*: Levine, "Brookwood Remembered," 41. *20 percent*: AFPS, *Final Report*, 2; AFPS, *Report for the Second Year*, 4–6; AFPS, *Third Report* (1925), 12. *Chase*: AFPS Board Meeting, Mar. 7, 1923, r. 3, b. 5, AFPSR. *Brookwood*: Total Amounts Appropriated in Various Fields, 2, AFPSR; Brookwood Gifts to 1941, r. 6, b. 10, AFPSR. *"workers' education"*: Report on Worker's Education Enterprises for AFPS, June 25, 1928, r. 2, b. 2, AFPSR. *"knowledge and qualities"*: RNB to Spencer Miller, Mar. 26, 1923, r. 33, b. 52, AFPSR.

76. *surge*: Stuart Chase, "The Labor Bureau, Inc.: Survey," 1924, r. 4, b. 7, AFPSR. *new labor school . . . Commonwealth College*: See AFPS Gifts, r. 5, b. 19, AFPSR; Covington Hall, *Labor Struggles in the Deep South & Other Writings*, ed. David Roediger (Charles H. Kerr, 1999), 223. *"bundles of habits"*: RNB to Alice Chown, Dec. 23, 1924, r. 29, AFPSR. Commonwealth's most famous student was Orval Faubus, who would go on to abandon his socialist roots and become a prominent leader of massive resistance to civil rights in his role as governor of Arkansas. See Megan Day, "There Once Was a Socialist College in the Rural South," *Jacobin*, June 14, 2021.

77. **Rand School**: AFPS Board Meeting, Oct. 25, 1922; Feb. 24, 1923; Mar. 25, 1925; May 27, 1925, all in r. 3, b. 5, AFPSR; RNB, Memorandum for AFPS, Apr. 23, 1926, r. 2, b. 2, AFPSR. **Workers School**: Gifts and Loans to Workers Party Organizations, Feb. 2, 1926, r. 3, b. 5, AFPSR; BG to Jay Lovestone, Sept. 29, 1926, b. 6, BGP. **TUEL**: AFPS Board Meeting, June 6, 1923, r. 3, b. 5, AFPSR. **audit**: Katheryn Fenn to RNB, July 31, 1928; RNB to KF, Oct. 31, 1928; KF to RNB, Jan. 8, 1929, all in r. 13, b. 19, AFPSR. **exceptional commitment**: MLE, Report on the Financial Condition of AFPS, Feb. 8, 1928, r. 3, b. 5, AFPSR, also in c. 162, MLEP; RNB, "Brookwood and the Garland Fund," 31. **"heartening"**: Thomas, What Is Industrial Democracy?, 16–17.

78. **"responsible"**: Workers' Education Bureau, 1922, r. 33, b. 52, AFPSR. **rejected**: Norman Thomas to WEBDB, [n.d., 1923], r. 33, b. 52, AFPSR; Samson, American Fund for Public Service, 70–71. **"old-line"**: RNB to Spencer Miller, Apr. 3, 1923, r. 33, b. 52, AFPSR.

79. **"pro-Soviet"**: "Gompers Says Fund Proves Itself Red," New York Times, Apr. 14, 1923, 15.

80. **Flynn**: AFPS Board Meeting, Mar. 25, 1925; Feb. 24, 1926, both in r. 3, b. 5, AFPSR. **sabotage**: Davis, "The Stop Watch and the Wooden Shoe," 86–95; Louis Adamic, Dynamite! The Story of Class Violence in America (Viking, 1931), ch. 32.

81. **Horton**: Frank Adams and Myles Horton, Unearthing Seeds of Fire: The Idea of Highlander (J. F. Blair, 1975), 15; John M. Glen, Highlander: No Ordinary School, 1932–1962 (University Press of Kentucky, 1988), at 10. **"radical labor"**: Myles Horton, The Long Haul: An Autobiography (Doubleday, 1990), 61–62.

82. **Niebuhr was an occasional advisor**: Memorandum of Meeting of the Committee on Brookwood, Jan. 13, 1933, b. 6, f. 4, BGP. **Thomas**: Ibid. **support**: Glen, Highlander, 15–16. **"neither A. F. of L."**: Horton, Long Haul, 61. **trained at Brookwood**: Glen, Highlander, 26. **joint grant**: Brookwood Grant Rejection, Dec. 1936, r. 36, b. 57, AFPSR. **training ground**: Adams and Horton, Unearthing Seeds of Fire, 100. **Rosa Parks**: Ibid., 148. **King**: Ibid., 123. **Lewis**: Ibid., 144.

14: THE MESSENGER

"all along been workers": JWJ to AFPS, Dec. 17, 1924, r. 10, b. 16, AFPSR.
1. **Randolph approached**: APR to EGF, Sep. 21, 1925, r. 6, b. 10, AFPSR.
2. **novel experiment**: APR to AFPS, Jan. 6, 1925, r. 6, b. 10, AFPSR; Eric Arnesen, "A. Philip Randolph: Emerging Socialist Radical," in Reframing Randolph: Labor, Black Freedom, and the Legacies of A. Philip Randolph, ed. Andrew E. Kersten and Clarence Lang (New York University Press, 2015), 45–76; Eric Arnesen, Brotherhoods of Color: Black Railroad Workers and the Struggle for Equality (Harvard University Press, 2001), 89–90; Jervis Anderson, A. Philip Randolph: A Biographical Portrait (Harcourt Brace, 1972).
3. **fall of 1925**: H. H. Broach and JWJ to EGF, Nov. 25, 1925, r. 6, b. 10, AFPSR.
4. **father**: Anderson, A. Philip Randolph, 25–30. **age twenty**: Ibid., 30–32. **Crescent City**: Paula F. Pfeffer, A. Philip Randolph, Pioneer of the Civil Rights Movement (Louisiana State University Press, 1990), 6.
5. **two years old**: Anderson, A. Philip Randolph, 33. **once-thriving**: Patricia Kennedy, "LaVilla, Florida, 1866–1887: Reconstruction Dreams and the Formation of a Black Community," M.A. thesis (University of Florida, 1990), 49; JWJ, Along This Way: The Autobiography of James Weldon Johnson (Viking Press, 1933), 45. **"completely segregated"**: APR, The Reminiscences of A. Philip Randolph (1972), 22–24, CCOH. **"toughest"**: Anderson, A. Philip Randolph, 35.
6. **"no money"**: APR, Reminiscences, 22–24. **Jacksonville-area**: Ibid., 22. **sweet potatoes**: Ibid., 48. **tailor . . . "white bosses"**: Ibid., 22–24. **pharmacy**: "A. Philip Randolph, Outline—Autobiography," b. 1, f. 1, APRC.
7. **"Our household"**: APR, "Vita," r. 32, b. 41, 22, APRP. **"home of ideas"**: Ibid., 24. **Cookman Institute**: APR, Reminiscences, 50–60; Anderson, A. Philip Randolph, 44–45. **"whatever we wanted"**: Ibid., 13. **"as good as"**: Ibid., 10.
8. **"racial devotion"**: APR, Reminiscences, 27. **"always pointing . . . colored"**: APR, "Vita," r. 32, b. 41, 13, APRP; see also Edward J. Blum and Paul Harvey, The Color of Christ: The Son of God and the Saga of Race in America (University of North Carolina Press, 2012). **"hours"**: Arnesen,

"Emerging Socialist Radical," 48–49. *sought out*: Ibid., 32. *lives of leaders*: Andrew E. Kersten, *A. Philip Randolph: A Life in the Vanguard* (Rowman & Littlefield, 2007), 5; Anderson, *A. Philip Randolph*, 39. *"about Africa"*: APR, "Vita," r. 32, b. 41, 13, APRP. *Hannibal*: Kersten, *A. Philip Randolph*, 5. *"race conscious"*: APR, Reminiscences, 18.
9. *casually humiliate*: APR, "Vita," r. 32, b. 41, 12–13, APRP; Anderson, *A. Philip Randolph*, 41.
10. *only three*: "Timely Action," *Florida Star*, July 14, 1892, 2; see also Margaret Vandiver, *Lethal Punishment: Lynchings and Legal Executions in the South* (Rutgers University Press, 2005), 149. *"deadly"*: APR, "Vita," r. 32, b. 41, 12–13, APRP. *"more revolutionary"*: Theodore Kornweibel Jr., *No Crystal Stair: Black Life and the "Messenger," 1917–1928* (Greenwood Press, 1975), at 29. A similar episode, which took place in 1890, and which James Weldon Johnson and others recorded, happened early enough in Randolph's life that the 1892 episode seems more likely to be the one about which he later talked. See JWJ, *Along This Way*, 140–41.
11. *valedictory address*: Anderson, *A. Philip Randolph*, 46. *"wouldn't plan"*: APR, Reminiscences, 23–24.
12. *never forgot*: JWJ, *Along This Way*, 64. *"real ship people"*: APR, Reminiscences, 60–62. *"like Hades"*: Anderson, *A. Philip Randolph*, 66.
13. *spare room*: Anderson, *A. Philip Randolph*, 55–56. *worked as a porter*: Cornelius L. Bynum, *A. Philip Randolph and the Struggle for Civil Rights* (University of Illinois Press, 2010), 50. *briefly a waiter*: Anderson, *A. Philip Randolph*, 66. *"scrubbing"*: Ibid., 65. *quit . . . "sowing"*: Ibid.
14. *"hottest beds"*: Ibid., 61. *straw poll*: Willis Rudy, *The College of the City of New York: A History, 1847–1947* (Arno Press, 1977), (1949), at 298–99. *joined*: Kornweibel, *No Crystal Stair*, 30; Bynum, *A. Philip Randolph and the Struggle for Civil Rights*, 64. *new heroes . . . Wonderland*: Anderson, *A. Philip Randolph*, 61–62. For Randolph's turn to socialism, see especially Arnesen, "Emerging Socialist Radical."
15. *1914 marriage*: Bynum, *A. Philip Randolph and the Struggle*, 59. *Owen introduced*: APR, Reminiscences, 102; John Seabrook interview with APR and Richard Parrish, May 1, 1975, r. 33, b. 42, APRP. *Long days*: Anderson, *A. Philip Randolph*, 76; Kornweibel, *No Crystal Stair*, 30.
16. *"Lenin and Trotsky"*: Ibid., 75; Manning Marable, "A. Philip Randolph and the Foundations of Black American Socialism," *Radical America* 14 (1980): 209, 215. *Briggs*: Anderson, *A. Philip Randolph*, 79. *Fort-Whiteman*: Glenda Elizabeth Gilmore, *Defying Dixie: The Radical Roots of Civil Rights, 1919–1950* (W. W. Norton, 2008), at 34. *Hubert Harrison*: APR, Reminiscences, 152. *"race first"*: Hubert H. Harrison, *The Negro and the Nation* (Cosmo-Advocate, 1917), 3; Arnesen, "Emerging Socialist Radical," 57; Adom Getachew, "A 'Common Spectacle' of the Race: Garveyism's Visual Politics of Founding," *American Political Science Review* 115 (2021): 1197–209. *"Black Socrates"*: Jeffrey B. Perry, *Hubert Harrison: The Struggle for Equality, 1918–1927* (Columbia University Press, 2021), at 750. *Claude McKay*: Anderson, *A. Philip Randolph*, 79. *Garvey . . . 1916 rally*: Anderson, *A. Philip Randolph*, 122–23; APR, Reminiscences, 130. *Frank Crosswaith*: Anderson, *A. Philip Randolph*, 140. *needle-trades*: Kornweibel, *No Crystal Stair*, 31–32. Anderson, *A. Philip Randolph*, 76.
17. *Headwaiters*: Anderson, *A. Philip Randolph*, 78. *Their arrangement*: Ibid., 81–82.
18. *"only radical Negro"*: APR, Reminiscences, 168. *"sham"*: Anderson, *A. Philip Randolph*, 98. *"lick spittling"*: Ibid., 98–101.
19. *"Negro race"*: WEBDB, "The Talented Tenth," in *The Negro Problem: A Series of Articles by Representative Negroes of Today*, ed. Booker T. Washington (James Pott, 1903), 31. *"necessary racial"*: Anderson, *A. Philip Randolph*, 102–3, also *The Messenger*, Nov. 1, 1919. *"problem of the twentieth century" . . . "wealth and knowledge"*: Quoted in Abby Arthur Johnson and Ronald Maberry Johnson, *Propaganda and Aesthetics: The Literary Politics of Afro-American Magazines in the Twentieth Century* (University of Massachusetts Press, 1979), 58. *made the case*: "Negro Workers: The A.F. of L. or I.W.W.," *The Messenger*, July 1919, 14. *"greatest achievement"*: Anderson, *A. Philip Randolph*, 89. *"mass movement"*: Joint Legislative Committee Investigating Seditious Activities, *Revolutionary Radicalism: Its History, Purpose and Tactics . . . Being the Report of the Joint Legislative Committee Investigating Seditious Activities, Filed April 24, 1920, in the Senate of the State of New York* (J. B. Lyon, 1920), 2:1477. *Editorial cartoons*: Ibid., 2:1505.

20. ***product of capitalist exploitation***: APR, "Lynching: Capitalism Its Cause; Socialism Its Cure," *The Messenger*, Mar. 1919, 9-12.
21. ***attracted interest***: Joint Legislative Committee, *Revolutionary Radicalism*, 2:1482. ***Seligmann***: Barbara Foley, *Spectres of 1919: Class and Nation in the Making of the New Negro* (University of Illinois Press, 2003), 24-25.
22. ***Agents***: U.S. Attorney Francis Caffey to U.S. Attorney General Harry Daugherty, [n.d.], r. 23, b. 28, APRP. ***arrested***: Frederick Coleman to APR, Aug. 10, 1971, r. 23, b. 28, APRP; Anderson, *A. Philip Randolph*, 106. ***Burleson***: Manning, "APR and the Foundations," 215. ***James Byrnes***: Kornweibel, *No Crystal Stair*, 86. ***revolutionary***: Joint Legislative Committee, *Revolutionary Radicalism*, 2:1477. ***"long odds the most dangerous"***: U.S. Senate, *Investigation Activities of the Department of Justice: Letter from the Attorney General Transmitting in Response to a Senate Resolution of October 17, 1919, a Report on the Activities of the Bureau of Investigation of the Department of Justice Against Persons Advising Anarchy, Sedition, and the Forcible Overthrow of the Government* (Government Printing Office, 1919), 172.
23. ***"most dangerous"***: Anderson, *A. Philip Randolph*, 83.
24. ***would radicalize***: Joint Legislative Committee, *Revolutionary Radicalism*, 2:1493. ***peak circulation***: APR to RNB, May 12, 1922, r. 10, b. 16, AFPSR; Kornweibel, *No Crystal Stair*, 54; ***one-third of the readership***: Anderson, *A. Philip Randolph*, 146; ***operating deficit***: Chase to AFPS, [n.d., 1924], r. 10, b. 16, AFPSR; Chase to AFPS, June 19, 1925, r. 10, b. 16, AFPSR.
25. ***Briggs . . . Fort-Whiteman***: Harvey Klehr et al., *The Soviet World of American Communism* (Yale University Press, 1998), 218; also Robert A. Hill, "Racial and Radical: Cyril V. Briggs, 'The Crusader' Magazine, and the African Blood Brotherhood, 1918-1922," in *The Crusader*, ed. Cyril B. Briggs (Garland Publishing, 1987). ***"a menace"***: Jeff Henderson, "A. Philip Randolph and the Dilemmas of Socialism and Black Nationalism in the United States, 1917-1941," *Race & Class* 20 (1978): 143, 154. ***"disruptionists"***: Arnesen, "A. Philip Randolph: Emerging Socialist Radical," 68. ***"even grasped"***: Marable, "Foundations of Black American Socialism," 219. ***"aims and ideals"***: Henderson, "Dilemmas of Socialism," 154.
26. ***"greatest propagandists"***: Marable, "Foundations of Black American Socialism," 217. ***"erratic rampage"***: Kersten, *A. Philip Randolph*, 22-23. ***"consummate liar"***: Marable, "Foundations of Black American Socialism," 219.
27. ***human hand***: Anderson, *A. Philip Randolph*, 131. ***"Listen Randolph"***: Kersten, *A. Philip Randolph*, 22-23. ***Garvey***: Anderson, *A. Philip Randolph*, 132.
28. ***"Garvey Must Go"***: Kornweibel, *No Crystal Stair*, 133. ***appealed . . . cheered***: Ibid., 141-42.
29. ***"any particular"***: ARP, "The Black Militants of the Sixties Stand upon the Shoulders of the Negro Radicals of the Twenties," r. 30, b. 37, APRP. ***"Each triumph"***: Arnesen, "A. Philip Randolph," 68.
30. ***"God knows"***: Kersten, *A. Philip Randolph*, 138-39; ***Owen despaired***: Anderson, *A. Philip Randolph*, 142-44.
31. ***"not laudable"***: Gloria Garrett Samson, *The American Fund for Public Service: Charles Garland and Radical Philanthropy, 1922-1941* (Greenwood Press, 1996), 2.
32. ***applied for support***: APR to RNB, May 12, 1922, r. 10, b. 16, AFPSR. ***"heartily" recommended***: JWJ to RNB, Jan. 9, 1923, r. 10, b. 16, AFPSR. ***"unique in its field"***: JWJ to RNB, Sept. 9, 1924, r. 10, b. 16, AFPSR.
33. ***500 plus . . . reacted furiously***: RNB to JWJ, Feb. 20, 1923 and JWJ to RNB, Jan. 9, 1923. ***smooth the rift***: JWJ to APR and Chandler Owen, Feb. 26, 1923. ***Randolph's books***: JWJ to AFPS, Sept. 24, 1923; RNB to APR, [n.d., early 1924], all in r. 10, b. 16, AFPSR.
34. ***to Harlem***: RNB to JWJ, Dec. 13, 1923, r. 10, b. 16, AFPSR; AFPS Board Meeting, May 28, 1924, r. 3, b. 5, AFPSR. Randolph also developed relationships with Chase's economist colleagues Jett Lauck and George Soule. Joseph Schlossberg and Charles Erwin, who served as administrators and editors at the Amalgamated Clothing Workers, moved into Randolph's world, too, as did Abraham Lefkowitz, a Brookwood founder who visited Harlem to speak to Randolph's followers about the New York Teachers' Union. Others who came into Randolph's orbit included Algernon Lee, director of education at the Rand School and American Fund beneficiary, as well as

labor journalist Benjamin Stolberg, who was yet another beneficiary of the Fund and a confidant of Brookwood College's A. J. Muste. See APR to AFPS Committee [JW] and H. H. Broach], [n.d., 1926], r. 6, b. 10, AFPSR; BSCP to AFPS, Aug. 4, 1926, r. 28, b. 45, AFPSR; APR, "The Brotherhood's Anniversary," *The Messenger*, Sept. 1926, 265; see also RNB to AFPS, Apr. 23, 1926, r. 2, b. 3, AFPSR; AFPS Gifts 1923–1925, r. 11, b. 17, AFPSR.

35. *"by constitutional decree"*: Ben Fletcher, "The Negro and Organized Labor," *The Messenger*, July 1923, 759. **twenty-four of the largest unions**: Eric Arnesen, "Up from Exclusion: Black and White Workers, Race, and the State of Labor History," *Reviews in American History* 26 (1998): 146; Bruce Nelson, *Divided We Stand: American Workers and the Struggle for Black Equality* (Princeton University Press, 2001), xxxi–xxxii; Ray Marshall, "The Negro and Organized Labor," *Journal of Negro Education* 32 (1963): 375, 375; Paul Frymer, *Black and Blue: African Americans, the Labor Movement, and the Decline of the Democratic Party* (Princeton University Press, 2008), 51. **Du Bois . . . another quarter**: Herbert Hill, "Myth-Making as Labor History: Herbert Gutman and the United Mine Workers of America," *International Journal of Politics, Culture, and Society* 2 (1988): 132, 139. **Even Debs**: Philip S. Foner and Ronald L. Lewis, eds., *The Black Worker During the Era of the American Federation of Labor and the Railroad Brotherhoods* (Temple University Press, 2019), 71.

36. *"problems of the Negro worker"*: [unsigned], "A United Negro Trades," *The Messenger*, July 1923, 757. **demanded contracts . . . dwindle**: CHH, Report to Joint Committee, May 4, 1937, r. 6, b. 9, ABSP, also in I-C-198, f. 5, NAACPLC. *"who lynch"*: Kelly Miller, *The Everlasting Stain* (Associated Publishers, 1924), 297. *"there is nothing"*: Anderson, *A. Philip Randolph*, 148. *"scab through hell"*: Claude McKay, *Home to Harlem* (Northeastern University Press, 2012), 32.

37. **United Brotherhood**: Anderson, *A. Philip Randolph*, 149. **short-lived**: Henderson, "Dilemmas of Socialism," 150. **Trade Union**: Kornweibel, *No Crystal Stair*, 187. *"American Separation of Labor"*: Bynum, *A. Philip Randolph and the Struggle for Civil Rights*, 113. *"most wicked"*: Henderson, "Dilemmas of Socialism," 150.

38. **Black union members**: Irving Bernstein, *The Lean Years: A History of the American Worker, 1920–1933* (Houghton Mifflin, 1960), 102–3. **16 percent**: Fletcher, "Negro and Organized Labor," 759.

39. **stopped Randolph**: William H. Harris, *Keeping the Faith: A. Philip Randolph, Milton P. Webster, and the Brotherhood of Sleeping Car Porters, 1925–37* (University of Illinois Press, 1977), 109.

40. **All of them were men**: APR, Reminiscences, 231. **secret summit**: Harris, *Keeping the Faith*, 35; A. Philip Randolph, "The Brotherhood's Anniversary," *The Messenger*, Sept. 1926, 263. **dedicated articles**: Harris, *Keeping the Faith*, 35–36. *"greatest labor mass"*: Anderson, *A. Philip Randolph*, 168.

41. **barred from speaking**: Harris, *Keeping the Faith*, 35–36. **call . . . response**: Ibid.; Cynthia Taylor, "Keeping His Faith: A. Philip Randolph's Working-Class Religion," in Kersten and Lang, *Reframing Randolph*, 77–99. *"Women's Auxiliary"*: Melinda Chateauvert, *Marching Together: Women of the Brotherhood of Sleeping Car Porters* (University of Illinois Press, 1998); Beth Tompkins Bates, "Mobilizing Black Chicago: The Brotherhood of Sleeping Car Porters and Community Organizing, 1925–1935," in *The Black Worker: Race, Labor, and Civil Rights Since Emancipation*, ed. Eric Arnesen (University of Illinois Press, 2007), 195, 209–10; Jack Santino, *Miles of Smiles, Years of Struggle* (University of Illinois Press, 1991).

42. **nationwide circuit**: BSCP to AFPS, Aug. 4, 1926, r. 28, b. 45, AFPSR. *"serious business"*: "A United Negro Trades," *The Messenger*, July 1923, 757. **pursued rights**: APR, "Pullman Porters Need Their Own Union," *The Messenger*, Aug. 1925, 254–56.

43. **company supported . . . "greatest benefactor"**: Eric Arnesen, *Brotherhoods of Color: Black Railroad Workers and the Struggle for Equality* (Harvard University Press, 2001).

44. **Anti-Strikers**: Foner and Lewis, *Black Worker*, 72.

45. **refused to hire**: Harris, *Keeping the Faith*, 3. *"trained as a race"*: Anderson, *A. Philip Randolph*, 159.

46. **$67.50**: BSCP to AFPS, Aug. 4, 1926, r. 28, b. 45, AFPSR. **Tips**: Labor Bureau, BSCP Skeleton Brief to AFPS, Dec. 1926, r. 6, b. 10, AFPSR. **Standard pay**: BSCP to AFPS, Aug. 4, 1926, r. 28,

b. 45, AFPSR. *own uniforms . . . three children*: Labor Bureau, BSCP Skeleton Brief to AFPS, Dec. 1926, r. 6, b. 10, AFPSR.

47. *49 hours*: BSCP to AFPS, Aug. 4, 1926, r. 28, b. 45, AFPSR. *company spies*: Frank Crosswaith, Brotherhood Notes 1925, [n.d., 1926?], b. 3, f. 1, FRCP. *"smoke screen"*: Arnesen, *Brotherhoods of Color*, 88. *"feudalism"*: Ibid., 89. *"substitute"*: Benjamin P. Chass, "Binding the Worker to His Job," *The Messenger*, July 1926, 211. *"like slaves"*: Arnesen, *Brotherhoods of Color*, 89.

48. *secrecy . . . "entire movement"*: APR to EGF, Sept. 21, 1925, r. 6, b. 10, AFPSR.

49. *urged*: JWJ to RNB, Nov. 26, 1924; JWJ to RNB, Dec. 17, 1924; Eugene Kinckle Jones to AFPS, Jan. 14, 1925; JWJ to RNB, Jan. 22, 1925, all in r. 10, b. 16, AFPSR.

50. *two-person committee*: JWJ to EGF, July 17, 1926, r. 6, b. 10, AFPSR; APR to Broach, Aug. 9, 1926, r. 6, b. 10, AFPSR. *reported back*: AFPS Board Meeting, Oct. 28, 1925, r. 3, b. 5, AFPSR. *"strong link"*: JWJ to RNB, Sept. 9, 1924, r. 10, b. 16, AFPSR. *larger grant*: AFPS Board Meeting, Jan. 6, 1926, r. 3, b. 5, AFPSR. *"most important"*: BSCP to AFPS, Jan. 6, 1926, r. 6, b. 10, AFPSR. *"The struggle"*: APR to AFPS, Jan. 6, 1925, r. 6, b. 10, AFPSR.

51. *experts with Brookwood*: See APR to AFPS Committee (JWJ and Broach), n.d., 1926, r. 6, AFPSR; Jessica Wang, "Local Knowledge, State Power, and the Science of Industrial Labor Relations: William Leiserson, David Saposs, and American Labor Economics in the Interwar Years," *Journal of the History of the Behavioral Sciences* 46 (2010): 371, 379. *sprawling report*: Labor Bureau to EGF, Oct. 9, 1926, r. 6, b. 10, AFPSR. *"most valuable results"*: JWJ to EGF, July 17, 1926, r. 6, b. 10, AFPSR. *documented*: Labor Bureau BSCP Skeleton Brief to AFPS, Dec. 1926, r. 6, b. 10, AFPSR.

52. *endorsements followed . . . railway engineers*: APR to AFPS Committee, [n.d., 1926], r. 6, b. 10, AFPSR. *Pocono*: "Statement by Mr. Frank Crosswaith," [Jan. 3, 1929], b. 3, f. 18, FRCP; Camp Tamiment, r. 17, AFPSR. *raised porters' pay*: BSCP to AFPSR, Aug. 4, 1926, r. 28, b. 45, AFPSR. *numbers swelled*: APR to AFPS, Jan. 6, 1925 (2,371); APR to EGF, Mar. 13, 1926 (3,417); and "Statement of Membership, March and April" (4,072), all in r. 6, AFPSR. *Des Verney . . . was fired*: AFPS Board Meeting, Dec. 9, 1925, r. 6, b. 10, AFPSR.

53. *"almost insurmountable"*: BSCP to AFPSR, Aug. 4, 1926, r. 28, b. 45, AFPSR. *"first great"*: Frank R. Crosswaith, "An Ex-Slave Who Fights for the Next Emancipation," *The Messenger*, Nov. 1926, 330. *"recognition of our movement"*: APR, "Our Next Step," *The Messenger*, July 1926, 217. *"economic rights" & "Our welfare"*: APR, "The State and Policy of the Brotherhood," *The Messenger*, June 1926, 185. *"group of workers"*: APR, "The Story of the Brotherhood of Sleeping Car Porters," [n.d.], r. 9, b. 10, APRP. Fund support for the Brotherhood produced a fierce but intramural dispute between Robert Vann of the *Pittsburgh Courier* and James Weldon Johnson, whom Vann accused of using the Garland money as a "slush fund" for advancing his favored Black groups. Johnson suspected that Vann had been paid to produce the controversy by agents of the Pullman Company. See Eugene Levy, *James Weldon Johnson: Black Leader, Black Voice* (University of Chicago Press, 1973), 285; AFPS-*Pittsburgh Courier* Controversy, Sept.-Oct. 1926 and Oct.-Nov. 1926, I-C-201, NAACPLC.

54. *"moral and intellectual"*: APR, "The State and Policy of the Brotherhood," 185.

55. *"our own economic contracts" . . . "final road"*: Ibid.

56. *"avail ourselves"*: APR to Milton Webster, Aug. 3, 1926, b. 1, f. 4, BSCPR.

57. *during the war*: Arnesen, *Brotherhoods of Color*, 58. *filed a grievance . . . "stirred"*: Frank Boyd, "Previous Struggles of the Pullman Porters to Organize," *The Messenger*, Sept. 1926, 283.

58. *Erdman Act*: See Benjamin Aaron et al., *The Railway Labor Act at 50: Collective Bargaining in the Railroad and Airline Industries* (Government Printing Office, 1977).

59. *status quo*: E.g., Christopher L. Tomlins, *The State and the Unions: Labor Relations, Law, and the Organized Labor Movement in America, 1880-1960* (Cambridge University Press, 1985), at 121-22. *"class collaboration"*: William Z. Foster, *The Watson-Parker Law: The Latest Scheme to Hamstring Railroad Unionism* (Trade Union Educational League, 1926), 2.

60. *"interference"*: Railway Labor Act, 45 Stat. 577, 578 (1926). *"system"*: APR, "The Abolition of the U.S. Railroad Labor Board," *The Messenger*, June 1926, 164.

61. *Brotherhood launched*: APR, "On to the New Railroad Labor Board!," *The Messenger*, June

1926, 189. *petitioned*: APR to AFPS, Sept. 27, 1927, r. 6, AFPSR; Roy Lancaster to JWJ, Oct. 19, 1926, r. 6, b. 10, AFPSR. *arrived at the Brotherhood & first victory*: Harris, *Keeping the Faith*, 94–95. *The report*: Labor Bureau, BSCP Skeleton Brief to AFPS Dec. 1926, r. 6, b. 10, AFPSR.

62. *assured readers*: APR, "The Mediation Board," *The Messenger*, Sept. 1926, 272–73. *new round*: APR to AFPS, Sept. 27, 1927; AFPS to BSCP, Sept. 30, 1927; BSCP to AFPS, Dec. 22, 1927, all in r. 6, b. 10, AFPSR.

63. *petitioned*: APR to AFPS, Sept. 27, 1927, r. 6, b. 10, AFPSR. *tipping . . . a hidden charge*: Petition, *Brotherhood of Sleeping Car Porters v. The Pullman Co.*, Before the Interstate Commerce Commission, Sept. 7, 1927, BSCP Correspondence, 2-9/1927, c. 166.8, MLEP; also APR to WW, Sept. 27, 1930; Henry T. Hunt to MLE, Aug. 26, 1930, both in r. 34, b. 54, AFSPR; APR to RNB, Dec. 28, 1926; BSCP to AFPS, Aug. 4, 1926, both in r. 28, b. 45, AFPSR; APR to Milton Webster, June 10, 1926, b. 1 f. 3, BSCPR; see also APR, "Our Next Step," *The Messenger*, July 1926, 217.

64. *"destined"*: APR to Roy Lancaster, Sept. 9, 1927, APRP. *"Emancipation of the Pullman Porter"*: E. J. Bradley to Donors, b. 2, f. 8, APRP.

65. *"monster mass meeting"*: APR to Milton Webster, Sept. 1927, r. 2, f. 6, BSCPR.

66. *"warp and woof"*: Michael Mann, "A. Philip Randolph: Radicalizing Rights at the Intersection of Class and Race," in *African American Political Thought*, ed. Melvin L. Rogers and Jack Turner (University of Chicago Press, 2021), 305. *"civil rights"*: Ibid., 299. *"present plight"*: Ibid., 301. *embraced*: Thomas Kirksey, "The Decay of Capitalist Civilization," *The Messenger*, July 1923, 766. *"so strengthen"*: Milton Webster to APR, Sept. 13, 1927, r. 2, f. 6, BSCPR. *"plant a seed"*: APR to MW, June 17, 1927, r. 2, f. 3, BSCPR. *"every historical"*: Mann, "A. Philip Randolph," 303.

67. *"Work for the Negro"*: Informal AFPS Board Meeting, Aug. 10, 1925, r. 3, b. 5, AFPSR. *"open the way"*: BSCP to AFPS, Aug. 4, 1926, r. 28, b. 45, AFPSR. *"general attitude"*: APR to AFPS, Sept. 27, 1927, r. 28, b. 45, AFPSR. *"first requisite"*: Roy Lancaster to JWJ, Oct. 19, 1926, r. 27, b. 44, AFPSR.

68. *sufficient merit*: APR to AFPS, Sept. 27, 1927, r. 6, b. 10, AFPSR.

69. *unpopular among porters*: Rienzi B. Lemus, "Rienzi Declares That Traveling Public, Not Pullman Co., Will Bear Brunt of Pullman Porter Wage Raise," *New York Age*, June 23, 1928, 3. *"referred to no law"*: U.S. Interstate Commerce Commission, *Interstate Commerce Commission Reports* (L. K. Strouse, 1928), 743; Interstate Commerce Commission, Publications of the Federal Government, b. 151, RG 287, NARA. *"bitter fruit"*: APR, "The Story of the Brotherhood of Sleeping Car Porters," r. 9, b. 10, BSCPR.

70. *"bow to the verdict"*: APR to Roy Lancaster, Aug. 12, 1927, APRP. *"immediate program"*: APR, "Our Next Step," 217. *informed the Mediation Board*: Harris, *Keeping the Faith*, 109; *actually walked off*: Mediation Board Memorandum, June 4, 1928, at 71, and Edwin P. Morrow to Samuel Winslow, Bd of Mediation, Mar. 20, 1928, both in C-107, pt. 1, RBMA.

71. *Morrow surmised*: Edwin P. Morrow to Samuel Winslow, Mar. 20, 1928, C-107, pt. 1, RBMA. *announced*: APR to John Marrinan, June 6, 1928, C-107, pt. 1, RBMA. *telegraphed*: JWJ to Mediation Board, June 7, 1928, C-107, pt. 1, RBMA. *persuaded*: Mediation Board Memorandum, June 4, 1928, C-107, pt. 1, RBMA.

72. *"conditions"*: APR, *Reminiscences of A. Philip Randolph*, 265; Marable, "Foundations of Black American Socialism," 6. Marable argues that Randolph had a failure of nerve. The evidence, including private correspondence on both sides, suggests otherwise. Crucially, some Brotherhood officials knew the strike needed to be called off before the telegram from Green arrived. See Harris, *Keeping the Faith*, 111–12; Anderson, *A. Philip Randolph*, 201–2; Kornweibel, *No Crystal Stair*, 196; Beth Tompkins Bates, *Pullman Porters and the Rise of Protest Politics in Black America, 1925–1945* (University of North Carolina Press, 2001); also APR, "Report at the Brotherhood of Sleeping Car Porters Convention (1968)," in *For Jobs and Freedom: Selected Speeches and Writings of A. Philip Randolph*, ed. Andrew E. Kersten and David Lucander (University of Massachusetts Press, 2014), 65, 68.

73. *"let-down"*: APR, "Story of the Porter—a Saga in Trade Unionism" and "Appeal to Mediation Board," BSCP 7th Biennial Convention, 1950, r. 5, b. 5, BSCPR. *"no tooth"*: APR, "The Story

of the Brotherhood of Sleeping Car Porters," r. 9, b. 10, BSCPR. *"A. Piffle Randolph"*: Harris, *Keeping the Faith*, 114–15. *Membership*: Ibid., 183.

74. *"quitter never wins"*: APR, "On to the New Railroad Labor Board!," *The Messenger*, June 1926, 189.

15: MILLENNIA DON'T JUST HAPPEN

"largest group": Committee on Negro Work to the AFPS, June 18, 1929, b. 42, LGP, also in later drafts in I-C-196, f. 2, NAACPLC, and r. 2, b. 2, AFPSR.

1. *gave away*: AFPS Press Release, Sept. 28, 1926, r. 5, b. 8, AFPSR. *"tapering-off"*: Committee on Tapering Off Report, Aug. 9, 1926, r. 2, b. 3, AFPSR; see also RNB to AFPS, Mar. 13, 1926, b. 6, BGP. *Workers' Health Bureau*: David Rosner and Gerald Markowitz, "Safety and Health on the Job as a Class Issue: The Workers' Health Bureau of America in the 1920s," *Science & Society* 48 (1984/1985): 466–82. *new organizations*: Memorandum re Future Handling of Fund [n.d., 1928?], r. 2, b. 3, AFPSR.

2. *"blackness or depression"*: Joseph P. Lash, interview with RNB, Oct. 6, 1971, I-C-2, JPLP. *Bina . . . Passaic*: Lara Vapnek, *Elizabeth Gurley Flynn: Modern American Revolutionary* (Westview Press, 2015), 89–93; see also Stephen Charles Cole, *Elizabeth Gurley Flynn: A Portrait*, Ph.D. thesis, Indiana University, 1991, 103–4, n33. *strep infection*: Ibid.; Vapnek, *Elizabeth Gurley Flynn*, 93–94.

3. *share values*: Memorandum of Morris Ernst Re: American Fund, Feb. 8, 1928, Treasurer's Correspondence, 1923–1933, r. 2, b. 2, AFPSR. *"unburden himself"*: Dwight Macdonald, "In Defense of Everybody—I," *New Yorker*, July 11, 1953, 53. *"ill-gotten wealth"*: RNB to AFPS, May 13, 1929, b.1, f. 2, CMP. *"dreary effects"*: MLE to AFPS, May 4, 1929, b. 1, f. 2, CMP.

4. *Ernst estimated*: AFPS Board Meeting, Feb. 8, 1928, r. 2, b. 3, AFPSR.

5. *momentous proposal*: Committee on Negro Work to AFPS, June 18, 1929, b. 42, LGP; see also Gloria Garrett Samson, *The American Fund for Public Service: Charles Garland and Radical Philanthropy, 1922–1941* (Bloomsbury, 1996), 207.

6. *warring camps*: Ben Gitlow to C. E. Ruthenberg, Feb. 23, 1926, b. 6, f. 3, BGP.

7. *increasingly aligned*: Ibid.; RNB, "The Need for Militancy," in *The Socialism of Our Times*, ed. Harry W. Laidler and Norman Thomas (Vanguard Press, 1929), 80–81. *joined the party*: John Saltmarsh, *Scott Nearing: An Intellectual Biography* (Temple University Press, 1991). *out of the party*: Harvey Klehr et al., *The Soviet World of American Communism* (Yale University Press, 1998), 334; also Scott Nearing, *The Making of a Radical: A Political Autobiography* (Harper & Row, 1972). Baldwin's left turn led him to ever greater skepticism about funding for the NAACP. See RNB, *Report to the Board of Directors of the American Fund, Allocation of Funds to Enterprises Already Aided*, May 22, 1926, r. 1, AFPSR.

8. *would resign*: EGF to William Z. Foster, Aug. 12, 1926; WZF to EGF, Aug. 28, 1926, both in r. 1, b. 1, AFPSR; Benjamin Gitlow to Jay Lovestone, Sept. 29, 1926, b. 6, BGP. *missed meetings*: RNB to William Weinstone, Nov. 11, 1925; RNB to WZF, Dec. 8, 1926; WZF to AFPS, Oct. 24, 1925, all in r. 1, b. 1, AFPSR. *directors appointed*: EGF to BG, Feb. 12, 1926, r. 1, b. 1, AFPSR, also in b. 6, BGP; EGF to WZF, Aug. 18, 1926, r. 1, b. 1, AFPSR. *reneged*: WZF to RNB, Dec. 4, 1926, r. 1, b. 1, AFPSR. *Dunn*: EGF to Robert Morss Lovett, Aug. 20, 1926, r. 1, b. 1, AFPSR. *Dunn's membership*: Klehr et al., *Soviet World of American Communism*, 187. *elected Clarina Michelson*: Clarina Michelson, Board of Directors Correspondence, r. 1, AFPSR.

9. *participating remotely*: Anna Morntiz to EGF, Apr. 26, 1927; JWJ to EGF, Feb. 16, 1928; Robert W. Dunn to EGF, Oct. 24, 1928, r.1, b. 1, AFPSR. *stepped down*: H. H. Broach to AFPS, June 1928, r. 1, b. 1, AFPSR. *become president*: "Broach, 37, Youngest International Union Chief, Is Chosen to Head 150,000 Electrical Workers," *New York Times*, 1929, 1. *"from within"*: Edward P. Johanningsmeier, *Forging American Communism: The Life of William Z. Foster* (Princeton University Press, 2014), 48.

10. *"fundamental antagonism"*: RNB to AFPS, May 5, 1929, r. 2, b. 3, AFPSR. *opposition*: [Norman Thomas, Clinton Golden, or Benjamin Gitlow] to EGF, June 9, 1930, b. 6, BGP. *"bloc system"*:

MLE to AFPS, May 4, 1929, c. 162, MLEP. *"Communist bloc"*: Norman Thomas to John Brophy, Nov. 17, 1928, b. 1, f. 3, JBPC.
11. *Baldwin observed*: RNB to AFPS, May 5, 1929, r. 2, b. 3, AFPSR.
12. *"united front from below"*: Kevin McDermott and Jeremy Agnew, *The Comintern: A History of International Communism from Lenin to Stalin* (Red Globe Press, 1996), 81. *urged nonviolence*: Charles F. Howlett, *Brookwood Labor College and the Struggle for Peace and Social Justice in America* (Edwin Mellen Press, 1993), 250–51. *20,000 pounds*: J. A. Zumoff, "Hell in New Jersey: The Passaic Textile Strike, Albert Weisbord, and the Communist Party," *Journal for the Study of Radicalism* 9 (2015): 125, 148. *$30,000*: AFPS Board Meeting, Aug. 11, 1926, r. 3, b. 5, AFPSR. *publicity*: AFPS Board Meeting, Apr. 28, 1926, r. 3, b. 5, AFPSR. *legal services*: RNB to AFPS, Apr. 28, 1926, r. 3, b. 5, AFPSR. *$60,000*: Special AFPS Board Meeting, May 17, 1927, r. 3, b. 5, AFPSR. *Lauck*: AFPS Board Meeting, Aug. 25, 1926, r. 3, b. 5, AFPSR.
13. *"Passaic was great"*: EGF to Mary Heaton Vorse, Dec. 23, 1926, b. 19, MHVP.
14. *"revolutionary upsurge"*: Bert Cochran, *Labor and Communism: The Conflict That Shaped American Unions* (Princeton University Press, 1977), 43; also Theodore Draper, *American Communism and Soviet Russia* (Transaction, 2003); Maurice Isserman, *Reds: The Tragedy of American Communism* (Basic Books, 2024); Harvey Klehr et al., *The Secret World of American Communism* (Yale University Press, 1995).
15. *creature of Soviet communism*: E.g., Press Release, American Federation of Labor (AFL), Apr. 13, 1923, r. 5, AFPS; also Samson, *American Fund for Public Service*, 94. *continue for decades*: Martin Dies, *The Trojan Horse in America* (Dodd, Mead, 1940), 255; Special House Committee on Un-American Activities, *Investigation of Un-American Propaganda Activities in the U.S.* (Government Printing Office, 1938), 1:388–89, 527–28, 574; U.S. House of Representatives Special Committee on Un-American Activities, *Investigation of Un-American Propaganda Activities in the United States: Hearings Before a Special Committee on Un-American Activities* (Government Printing Office, 1939), 10:5990–991; House Un-American Activities Committee, *Hearings Before the Committee on Un-American Activities House of Representatives, Eighty-Second Congress, First Session, February 28 & March 9, 1951* (Government Printing Office, 1951), at 1883, 1891–901. *Communist-run projects*: See, e.g, *Daily Worker*, Trade Union Educational League, and Workers' School entries in the AFPSR. *ran into resistance*: E.g., Scott Nearing to Norman Thomas, Nov. 11, 1922, and Norman Thomas to RNB, Aug. 26, 1924, r. 1, AFPSR; Scott Nearing to Norman Thomas, Aug. 25, 1926, r. 12, AFPSR; Hugo Gellert and Michael Gold to AFPS, Mar. 23, 1928, LGP; Norman Thomas to Ernst, Feb. 16 [1930?], c. 170.19, MLEP.
16. *Foster had returned*: Johanningsmeier, *Forging American Communism*, 160. *four months*: Benjamin Gitlow, *I Confess: The Truth About American Communism* (E. P. Dutton, 1940), 401. *Gitlow traveled*: Ibid., 413–15. *again in 1928*: Ibid., 387. *Moscow yet again*: Ibid., 560–62.
17. *sharp blow*: McDermott and Agnew, *The Comintern*; Jacob Zumoff, *The Communist International and US Communism, 1919–1929* (Brill, 2014). *Foster complied*: James R. Barrett, *William Z. Foster and the Tragedy of American Radicalism* (University of Illinois Press, 1999). *Gitlow followed & United Mine Workers*: Gitlow, *I Confess*, 387. *Brookwood . . . anathema*: John Dewey, "Labor Politics and Labor Education," *New Republic*, Jan. 9, 1929, 211–13. *split . . . with . . . ACW*: Draper, *American Communism and Soviet Russia*, 278–99.
18. *"open the union doors"*: Negroes of the World! [Fourth Congress], n.d. [1922], DCAAA. *fight against lynching*: Ibid. *"oppressed national minority"*: Harry Haywood and Nikolai Nasanov [aka Nassanoff], *The Tasks of the American Communist Party Regarding Negro Work*, Aug. 2, 1928, DCAAA. *"self-determination in the southern states"*: Jane Degras, ed., *The Communist International, 1919–1943* (Frank Cass, 1971), at 2:554. *"Black Belt"*: Theodore Draper and Beverly Tomek, "The Communist International and the Dilemma of the American 'Negro Problem': Limitations of the Black Belt Self-Determination Thesis," *Journal of Labor & Society* 15 (2012): 549; Harvey Klehr and William Thompson, "Self-Determination in the Black Belt: Origins of a Communist Policy," *Labor History* 30 (1989): 354, 358; Aziz Rana, *The Constitutional Bind: How Americans Came to Idolize a Document that Fails Them* (University of Chicago Press, 2024), 189–91.
19. *Black Belt thesis*: Glenda Elizabeth Gilmore, *Defying Dixie: The Radical Roots of Civil Rights,*

1919-1950 (W. W. Norton, 2008), at 61–66; Robin D. G. Kelley, *Hammer and Hoe: Alabama Communists During the Great Depression* (University of North Carolina Press, 1990), 13–14. ***"suicidal"***: W. E. B. Du Bois, "My Evolving Program for Negro Freedom," in *What the Negro Wants*, ed. Rayford W. Logan (University of North Carolina Press, 1944), 31, 61. ***grandiose iteration***: Adom Getachew, "A 'Common Spectacle' of the Race: Garveyism's Visual Politics of Founding," *American Political Science Review* 115 (2021): 1197–209.

20. ***Black delegates***: Cedric Robinson, *Black Marxism: The Making of the Black Radical Tradition* (University of North Carolina Press, 2000), 216. ***all but one objected***: Draper, *American Communism & Soviet Russia*, 345–48. ***Fort-Whiteman . . . labor camp***: Gilmore, *Defying Dixie*, 154. ***Ford . . . spluttered***: Klehr and Thompson, "Self-Determination in the Black Belt," 359–65. ***"great importance" . . . fifty Black members***: Statement by Com. Ford at Negro Commission—Aug. 3, 1928, DCAAA. ***Jay Lovestone***: Barrett, *William Z. Foster and the Tragedy of American Radicalism*, 157–58; Harold Cruse, *The Crisis of the Negro Intellectual* (William Morrow, 1967), 141; Zumoff, *The Communist International*, 356. ***"severely condemned . . . khvostists"***: Gitlow, *I Confess*, 481.

21. ***"subject race"***: Scott Nearing, *Black America* (Vanguard Press, 1929), 5.

22. ***desired independence***: Tomek, "Communist International," 557–58. ***National Textile Workers' Union . . . $26,000***: Eli Keller to AFPS, Oct. 18, 1929, Miscellaneous Correspondences, b. 42, LGP. ***National Industrial Auto Workers Union***: Philip Raymond to AFPS, Oct. 21, 1929, Miscellaneous Correspondences, b. 42, LGP.

23. ***"the stretch out"***: John A. Salmond, *Gastonia 1929: The Story of the Loray Mill Strike* (University of North Carolina Press, 1995), 13–23; Gilmore, *Defying Dixie*, 65–78; Theodore Draper, "Gastonia Revisited," *Social Research* 38 (1971): 3, 7–11. ***artless rope***: Gilmore, *Defying Dixie*, 80. ***June 7, 1929 . . . shoot-out***: Salmond, *Gastonia 1929*, at 72; Gilmore, *Defying Dixie*, 89; Patrick Huber, "Mill Mother's Lament: Ella May Wiggins and the Gastonia Textile Strike of 1929," *Southern Cultures* 15 (2009): 81.

24. ***murder prosecution . . . latest labor martyrs***: Salmond, *Gastonia 1929*, at 89–93. ***American Fund . . . $20,000***: Minutes of the Board of Directors of the American Fund for Public Service, Inc., June 19, 1929, r. 2, AFPSR. ***bail money***: Minutes of the Ninety-Second Meeting of the Board of Directors of the American Fund for Public Service, Inc., Wed., Sept. 25, 1929, Civic Club, b. 1, f. 2, CMP. ***jumped bail . . . to the Soviet Union***: Salmond, *Gastonia 1929*, at 167–68; also Minutes of the Ninety-Seventh Meeting of the Board of Directors of the American Fund for Public Service, Inc., Wed., Feb. 26, 1930, Civic Club, CMP.

25. ***non-Communist progressives***: Surety Company Bail Fund, r. 21 and 22, AFPSR. ***oppose . . . new grant applications***: Samantha Barbas, *The Rise and Fall of Morris Ernst: Free Speech Renegade* (University of Chicago Press, 2021), 133. ***Dunn and Michelson***: Suggested Report for the Committee on Organizing the Unorganized, Nov. 20, 1929, b. 1, f. 2, CMP. ***"militant mass Negro"***: RNB to JWJ, Jan. 3, 1930, and Program of the American Negro Labor Congress: Champion of the Rights of the 12,000,000 Oppressed Negroes in the United States, both in b. I-C-196, f. 3, NAACPLC. ***"struggle against lynching"***: J. Louis Engdahl [ILD] to AFPS, Jan. 8, 1930, r. 19, AFPSR. ***Nearing . . . attacks***: Ninety-Ninth Meeting of the Board of Directors, May 14, 1930, Civic Club, r. 4, AFPSR.

26. ***"right wing"***: Benjamin Gitlow [?] to EGF, June 9, 1930, b. 6, f. 3, BGP. Kirchwey's husband, Evans Clark, had helped found The Labor Bureau, with its cadre of progressive, Hillman-affiliated labor economists from the American Fund circle such as Stuart Chase, W. Jett Lauck, and George Soule.

27. ***social democratic majority***: See Appendix C, Board of Directors, 1922–1941. ***reliable vote . . . to the frustration***: Benjamin Gitlow [?] to EGF, June 9, 1930, b. 6, f. 3, BGP. ***Flynn resigned***: RVD to AFPS Board, Apr. 20, 1929, and RNB to EGF, May 7, 1929, both in r. 1, AFPSR. ***Baldwin . . . swerved left***: See RNB, *Liberty Under the Soviets* (Vanguard Press, 1928), and discussion above in chapter 10.

28. ***most outraged***: Samantha Barbas, *The Rise and Fall of Morris Ernst, Free Speech Renegade* (University of Chicago Press, 2021), 133.

29. ***born in 1888 . . . furniture manufacturing***: Ibid.; Joel Silverman, *The Legal Exhibitionist: Morris*

Ernst, *Jewish Identity, and the Modern Celebrity Lawyer* (Fairleigh Dickinson University Press, 2022).
30. **night program . . . ACLU-related**: Barbas, *Rise and Fall of Morris Ernst*, 29–49. **"the dictator"**: Ibid., 53. **"hair-shirt"**: Ibid., 58. **"hail fellow"**: RNB, *The Reminiscences of Roger Baldwin*, 1953–1954, at 130, CCOH. **Labor Age . . . liberal-progressive magazines**: Barbas, *Rise and Fall of Morris Ernst*, 79. **Mary Ware Dennett and Margaret Sanger**: Ibid., 85–124; Laura Weinrib, *The Taming of Free Speech: America's Civil Liberties Compromise* (Harvard University Press, 2016), 288–300.
31. **"the Gambler" . . . "legal halo"**: Morris Ernst, *America's Primer* (Putnam, 1931), 125. **"overawed . . . adventure"**: Ibid., 127.
32. **Ulysses**: Barbas, *Rise and Fall of Morris Ernst*, 154–58.
33. **"Robin Hood"**: Ibid., 79.
34. **"labor . . . first claim"**: Ernst, *America's Primer*, 71. **"machines . . . oil wells"**: Ibid., 21. **"breadlines"**: Ibid., 40, 50.
35. **represented . . . silk manufacturers . . . arbitrate**: Agreement (dated Apr. 10, 1920) between Manhattan Silk co., College Point, L.I., Smith & Kaufmann, inc., New York City . . . and Amalgamated Textile Workers of America, by New York Silk Ribbon Local Union, Queens Silk Ribbon Local Union . . . , Harvard Law School Library, Harvard University; also Barbas, *Rise and Fall of Morris Ernst*, 60.
36. **"industrial peace" & "chairmen"**: Morris Ernst, "The Development of Industrial Jurisprudence," *Columbia Law Review* 21 (1921): 155, 159.
37. **"general movement" & "industrial rights"**: Ibid., 160.
38. **"pushed around"**: Barbas, *Rise and Fall of Morris Ernst*, 130.
39. **serving with JWJ**: APR, Roy Lancaster, and Frank Crosswaith to AFPS Subcommittee on the BSCP, Nov. 18, 1927, c. 1631, MLEP; Brotherhood of Sleeping Car Porters Corr., Feb. to Sept. 1927, c. 166.8, MLEP; AFPS to BSCP, Sept. 30, 1927, r. 6, AFPSR. **appeared . . . honorary member . . . "cherish"**: Barbas, *Rise and Fall of Morris Ernst*, 130.
40. **treacherous compromise**: Cornelius Bynum, *A. Philip Randolph and the Struggle for Civil Rights* (University of Illinois Press, 2010), 149–52; also Eric Arnesen, "A. Philip Randolph: Emerging Socialist Radical," in *Reframing Randolph: Labor, Black Freedom, and the Legacies of A. Philip Randolph*, ed. Andrew E. Kersten and Clarence Lang (New York University Press, 2015), 63–68. **conductors' union**: APR, *Reminiscences of A. Philip Randolph*, 243–44, CCOH; William H. Harris, *Keeping the Faith: A. Philip Randolph, Milton P. Webster, and the Brotherhood of Sleeping Car Porters, 1925–37* (University of Illinois Press, 1977), 112, 199–201. **all-white railroad brotherhoods**: Arnesen, *Brotherhoods of Color*, 108. **industrial unions**: Raymond Wolters, *Negroes and the Great Depression: The Problem of Recovery* (Greenwood, 1970), 350–51. **"illusion of strength . . . as strike breakers"**: Address by APR at NAACP Annual Conference, June 27, 1956, b. 2, f. 1.
41. **"contact and influence" . . . "self-respect"**: APR, Racially Segregated Unions [n.d.], b. 2, f. 22, APRC; **"would suffer" . . . "economic juggernauts"**: APR, Black Unionism, b. 2, f. 9, APRC.
42. **"tragedy of segregation"**: Frank R. Crosswaith, "A Relic of Slavery or the Tragedy of Segregation?" [1923?], FRCP. **"principle of social equality" . . . "social progress"**: Memorandum re: A. Philip Randolph, July 8, 1942, Federal Surveillance of African-Americans, 1920–1984, Bureau File No. 100-55316.
43. **"unity of class" . . . "interests of the segregator"**: APR, "Segregation in the Public Schools," *The Messenger*, June 1924, 185–88, reprinted in *For Jobs and Freedom: Selected Speeches and Writings of A. Philip Randolph*, ed. Andrew E. Kersten and David Lucander (University of Massachusetts Press, 2014), 129, 131. **conventional**: Arnesen, "Emerging Socialist Radical," 63–68. **social psychology . . . formation of habits**: APR, "Segregation in the Public Schools," 131. **"through contact" . . . "laboring masses"**: Ibid., 133–34.
44. **more resources**: Morris Ernst, *Report on the Financial Condition of the American Fund for Public Service, Inc.*, Feb. 8, 1928, c. 162.6, MLEP; also "Radical Magazine Backed by $1,500,000," *New York Times*, Dec. 8, 1925, in b. 6, f. 3, BGP. **biding his time**: Morris Ernst, Memorandum

[n.d., 1926?], r. 1, AFPSR. *indiscriminate grants & wasteful ad hockery*: Morris Ernst to AFPS, May 4, 1929, c. 162.6, MLEP; RNB, Memorandum for Morris L. Ernst as Roger Baldwin's Proxy, Dec. 20, 1926, c. 163.1, MLEP.

45. *"definite policy"*: Morris Ernst, Report on the Financial Condition of the American Fund for Public Service, Inc., Feb. 8, 1928.
46. *"subcommittees"*: Morris Ernst to AFPS Board, May 4, 1929, r. 2, AFPSR; Memorandum, n.t., n.d. [Nearing? May 1929?], c.162.6, MLEP. *adopted . . . Ernst's plan*: Minutes of the Board of Directors of the American Fund for Public Service, May 14, 1929, r. 2, AFPSR. *only subcommittee not split*: Robert W. Dunn to Members of the Board of Directors of the AFPS, May 18, 1929, c. 163.3, MLEP. *other subcommittees*: Ibid.
47. *seized the opportunity*: Memorandum re the AFPS, Aug. 15, 1929, Walter White to JWJ, Sept. 16, 1929, Walter White to JWJ, Sept. 26, 1929, JWJ to Morris Ernst, Sept. 27, 1929, and Memorandum Draft, Sept. 1929, all in b. I-C-196, f. 2, NAACPLC. *giant grant*: Committee on Negro Work to the AFPS, June 18, 1929, b. 42, LGP (hereinafter "June 18 Report"). *labor movement . . . Black organizations . . . single effort*: Ibid.
48. *principal author*: "To the Directors of the American Fund for Public Service" [Sept. 1929 draft] and JWJ to Morris Ernst, Sept. 27, 1929, both in b. I-C-196, f. 2, NAACPLC. *"unorganized workers"*: June 18 Report, 1. *"twelve million"*: Ibid. *"coal baronries" . . . "Negroes of the South"*: Ibid. *"largest single contribution"*: Ibid. *"revolution in the economic life"*: Ibid.
49. *"all the major problems"*: June 18 Report. *Sweet case*: Ibid., 2. *"dead loss" . . . "psychological atmosphere"*: Ibid., 4. *would be doable*: Ibid.
50. *$214,000 and $229,000*: Ibid., 4. *"equal rights"*: Ibid., 2. *"expert publicity"*: Ibid., 3. *suits to enforce . . . jury selection*: Ibid., 3–4. *"campaign for the Negro"*: Ibid., 2.
51. *put off decisions*: Minutes of the Board of Directors AFPS, June 19, 1929, r. 2, AFPSR.
52. *Bank shares*: AFPS Financial Statement, June 1, 1929, r. 2, AFPSR; also Historical Share Price Data, First National Bank, Global Financial Data Database. *"spectacular dramatization"*: Walter White to JWJ, Sept. 16, 1929, b. I-C-196, f. 2, NAACPLC. *study of arrests*: Ibid. *new high-water mark*: Minutes of the Board of Directors AFPS, Sept. 25, 1929, r. 3, AFPSR. *more than $300,000 & "real economic independence"*: Committee on Negro Work to the Directors of the AFPS, Oct. 18, 1929, r. 2, AFPSR (hereinafter "October 18 Ernst Mark-Up Draft"). *"educational activities" . . . "economic knowledge"*: [A. J. Muste], Memorandum for Committee on Negro Work, Oct. 22, 1929, 2, 9, c. 169.1, MLEP.
53. *budgets*: WW to JWJ, Sept. 26, 1929, Morris Ernst to JWJ, Sept. 26, 1929, Arkansas Riot Cases, Oct. 3, 1929, all in b. I-C-196, f. 2, NAACPLC. *whites-only Texas primary*: Memorandum re the National Association for the Advancement of Colored People [1929?], and WW to Morris Ernst, Nov. 6, 1929, both in b. I-C-196, f. 2, NAACPLC. *revised proposal*: Report of the Committee on Negro Work, Oct. 18, 1929, 2–5, b. 42, LGP (hereinafter "October 18 Report"); see also same in b. I-C-196, f. 2, NAACPLC. *Haiti and the Virgin Islands*: October 18 Report, 3. *"salvation by economic reform"*: Ibid., 4. *tripling of the print run*: Ibid. *revised request totaled $314,000*: Ibid., 5.
54. *Shares . . . dropped*: Historical Share Price Data, First National Bank, Global Financial Data Database. *further grants*: RNB comments, Minutes of the Ninety-Third Meeting of the Board of Directors, Oct. 30, 1929, r. 3, AFPSR. *"no present market"*: Minutes of the Board of Directors of the AFPS, Nov. 8, 1929, r. 2, AFPSR.
55. *preliminary vote*: Minutes of the Board of Directors of the AFPS, Nov. 8, 1929, r. 2, AFPSR.
56. *"so large"*: RNB to Ernst, Nov. 11, 1929, c. 169, MLEP.
57. *adapted their arguments*: Memorandum, Jan. 20, 1930, ME to WW, Jan. 17, 1930, Richette Randolph to JWJ, Jan. 15, 1930, WW to JWJ, Jan. 9, 1930, WW to WEBDB, Jan. 6, 1930, WW to WEBDB, Jan. 6, 1930, The Crisis and the Labor Problem [n.d., Jan. 1930], A Letter to the Cleveland Conference for Progressive Political Action [n.d., 1930?], all in b. I-C-196, f. 3, NAACPLC; also Minutes of the 97th Meeting of the Board of Directors of the AFPS, Feb. 25, 1930, b. 1, f. 14, JWJP.
58. *McKay*: Eugene Levy, *James Weldon Johnson: Black Leader, Black Voice* (University of Chicago

Press, 1973), 311. *Randolph*: Ibid., 274-75. *"united front"* **pledge**: "Harassed Negro Turns on Foes: Colored Organizations Sign Concordat Establishing United Front Against Race Enemies," Apr. 8, 1923, DCAAA. *Crosswaith*: Bernard Eisenberg, "Only for the Bourgeois? James Weldon Johnson and the NAACP, 1916-1930," Phylon 43 (1982): 110-24. ***Brookwood scholarships***: E.g., Report of the Secretary for the October Meeting of the Board, 1925, NAACPP. ***elevator operators***: Elevator Operators Gain Sympathy and Support of Negro Leaders and Organizations [n.d.], b. 3, f. 20, FRCP. ***porters in 1926***: Levy, *James Weldon Johnson*, 275. ***Railway Mediation Board***: JWJ to Joseph Marrinan [telegram], June 7, 1928, Records of the Board of Mediation, Office of the Secretary, Wage and Representation Case Files, 1926-1935, b. 1195, RG 13, NARA. *"economic basis"* . . . *"white bourgeoisie"*: JWJ to Jacob Baker [n.d., 1929], b. 2, f. 33, JWJP.

59. ***"no labor program"***: Walter White to WEBDB, Jan. 23, 1930, WEBDBP. ***third party***: A Letter to the Cleveland Conference for Progressive Political Action, b. I-C-196, f. 3, NAACPLC. ***hobbled***: Isserman, *Reds: Tragedy of American Communism*, 65-66. ***joint . . . commission***: *Fifteenth Annual Report of the NAACP for the Year 1924* (NAACP, Jan. 1925), at 48-50; A Letter to the American Federation of Labor (1924), b. I-C-196, f. 3, NAACPLC. ***cool reception***: Walter White to JWJ, Jan. 9, 1930, b. I-C-196, f. 3, NAACPLC. ***white labor union exclusivity***: *Twenty-Fourth Annual Report of the NAACP for 1933* (NAACP, 1934), 29. ***government employment***: *Twenty-Third Annual Report of the NAACP for 1932* (NAACP, 1933), at 13-18. ***upholsterers' union***: *Twentieth Annual Report of the NAACP for 1929* (NAACP, Jan. 1930), at 23. ***railway trainmen***: *Twenty-Third Annual Report*, 17. ***steamship stewards***: *Thirteenth Annual Report of the NAACP for the Year 1922* (NAACP, Jan. 1923), at 41. ***on the levees***: *Twenty-Third Annual Report*, 8-12 ("the struggle for jobs and economic opportunity"). See generally Kenneth W. Mack, "Rethinking Civil Rights Lawyering and Politics in the Era Before Brown," *Yale Law Journal* 115 (2005): 256, 318-31.

60. ***on-again-off-again socialist***: David Levering Lewis, *W. E. B. Du Bois: Biography of a Race, 1868-1919* (Henry Holt, 1993), at 523-43; William P. Jones, "'Nothing Special to Offer the Negro': Revisiting the 'Debsian View' of the Negro Question," *International Labor and Working-Class History* 74 (2008): 212, 214. ***"distribution of wealth"***: WEBDB, "Socialism and the Negro," *The Crisis*, Oct. 1921, 245-46. ***editorials . . . Black working class***: The Crisis and the Labor Problem [n.d., Jan. 1930], b. I-C-196, f. 3, NAACPLC. ***of the 2.5 million Black people***: Lewis, *W. E. B. Du Bois*, at 251. ***"include Negroes"***: NAACP Press Release, Oct. 15, 1929, b. I-C-196, f. 2, NAACPLC. ***"barriers set up"***: *Twentieth Annual Report*, 4. ***"industrial democracy"* . . . *"five major aims"***: General Aims [n.d., Jan. 1930?], b. I-C-196, f. 3, NAACPLC.

61. ***League for Independent Political Action***: Lewis, *Du Bois*, 252-53. ***school studies***: See above, ch. 8. ***Public School Funds***: Minutes of the Meeting of the Board of Directors, Mar. 11, 1929, NAACPP. ***increased federal support***: Minutes of the Meeting of the Board of Directors, June 10, 1929, NAACPP; Memorandum for the Joint Committee of the NAACP and AFPS from Charles H. Houston, July 24, 1936, r. 23, AFPSR; Walter B. Hill [Richmond, Va] to Walter White, Jan. 18, 1935, b. I C 196, f. 12, NAACPLC; Levy, *James Weldon Johnson*, 209

62. ***"see the millennium"* . . . *"lower South"***: Walter White to Morris Ernst, Nov. 6, 1929, b. I-C-196, f. 2, NAACPLC.

63. ***"Delay"***: Morris Ernst to Walter White, Mar. 8, 1930, b. I-C-196, f. 4, NAACPLC. ***economic exploitation***: Walter White to Morris Ernst, Nov. 6, 1929, b. I-C-196, f. 2, NAACPLC.

64. ***"Negro radicals . . . actually accomplished"***: Walter White to WEBDB, Jan. 6, 1930, b. I-C-196, f. 3, NAACPLC. ***"labor consciousness"***: Walter White to JWJ, Jan. 9, 1930, b. I-C-196, f. 3, NAACPLC. ***labor activities***: Memorandum from Mr. White to Mr. Johnson, Jan. 9, 1930, b. I-C-196, f. 3, NAACPLC.

65. ***"Negro problem"***: [WEBDB?], Report Recommending Garland Fund Assistance for the NAACP, 1929, WEBDBP; also in Committee on Negro Work to the AFPS, June 18, 1929, b. 42, LGP. ***major problems . . . "suicidal strife"***: [WEBDB?], "Report Recommending"; ***"campaign of education"***: WEBDB to JWJ, Dec. 20, 1929, WEBDBP, also in c. 169.4, MLEP. ***"hammer home" . . . "only agency"***: [WEBDB?], "Report Recommending."

66. ***Nearing . . . added***: Minutes of the Board of Directors of the AFPS, Nov. 8, 1929, r. 2, AFPSR.

merging the committee: Robert W. Dunn, Clarina Michelson, and RNB to AFPS, Feb. 24, 1930, c. 169.4, MLEP. *"considered jointly"*: Robert W. Dunn, Clarina Michelson, and RNB to AFPS Board, Jan. 24, 1930, b. 6, f. 3, BGP.

67. *accepted . . . Nearing*: Memo re the AFPS, Aug. 15, 1929, b. I-C-196, f. 2, NAACPLC; Minutes of the Board of Directors of the AFPS, Nov. 8, 1929, r. 2, AFPSR. *Michelson*: Minutes of the Board of Directors of the AFPS, Jan. 3, 1930, r. 2, AFPSR.

68. *6–5 . . . League for Industrial Democracy*: Ninety-Ninth Meeting of the Board of Directors of the AFPS, May 14, 1930, r. 4, AFPSR. *industrial relations specialists . . . left opposition*: Annual Meeting of the Members of the AFPS, May 28, 1930, r. 4, AFPSR.

69. *"frankly disbelieved"*: Memorandum to the Directors of the AFPS, May 28, 1930, in b. 1, f. 14, JWJP ("May 28 Memorandum"), also in b. I-C-196, f. 4, NAACPLC, b. 9, f. 2, ABSP; c. 169.1, MLEP, and b. 42, BGP. *written by Gannett*: Walter White to Lewis Gannett, May 29, 1930, b. I-C-196, f. 4, NAACPLC; Committee on Negro Work, Memorandum for the AFPS, n.d., c. 169.1, MLEP. *"trade-union organization"*: May 28 Memorandum, 1. *"money down a sink"*: Ibid., 2. *"our money"*: Ibid. *"record of splits"*: Ibid. *"ineffective personnel"*: Ibid. *"no immediate hope"*: Ibid. *"worse than a gamble"*: Ibid., 3.

70. *"Civil Liberties Union"*: Ibid., 1–2. *"aided subsequent organizing"*: Ibid., 2. *Ernst added*: Memorandum for the American Fund for Public Service, May 1930, Original Copy with Corrections (Mr. Ernst), b. I-C-196, f. 4, NAACPLC. *their Magna Carta*: JWJ to RNB, May 15, 1924, r. 2, AFPSR. *"penalty for their blackness"*: May 28 Memorandum, 2 (quoting Nearing, *Black America*, 132 ["penalty of their blackness"]). *"kindergarten propositions"*: May 28 Memorandum, 2. *"really revolutionary"*: Ibid. *"a psychology" . . . "precedent conditions"*: Ibid., 17. *"outburst"*: Ibid., 2.

71. *"dramatization"*: Ibid., 17. *"bombarding the public mind"*: Ibid., 18. *newspaper advertisements*: Herbert Seligmann to Walter White, Mar. 22, 1930, b. I-C-196, f. 4, NAACPLC.

72. *"Vote me for the program" . . . "be nice"*: FK to LG, Feb. 5, 1930, c. 169.1, MLEP.

73. *Gannett's first draft . . . $5,000 . . . "against labor unions"*: Memorandum to the Directors of the American Fund for Public Service, from the Committee on Negro Work [n.d.], 1930, b. 9, f. 2, ABSP. *"included no money"*: May 28 Memorandum, 19. For continuing obstacles to suing sometime-allies in the labor movement, even late into the 1940s, see Risa L. Goluboff, *The Lost Promise of Civil Rights* (Harvard University Press, 2007), 222–23.

74. *"large objections"*: Memorandum for the American Fund for Public Service, May 1930, Original Copy with Corrections (Mr. Ernst), b. I-C-196, f. 4, NAACPLC. *"proposed test cases"*: RNB to Clinton S. Golden, Feb. 24, 1930, r. 1, AFPSR. *parliamentary maneuvers*: Minutes of the One Hundredth Meeting of the Board of Directors of the AFPS, May 28, 1930, b. 1, f. 2, CMP.

75. *adopted . . . voted no & "finished"*: Ibid. *"big fight"*: Benjamin Gitlow to EGF, June 9, 1930, b. 42, BGP.

16: RADICAL ENTERPRISES

"three M's": "Mr. Garland's Free Love Farm," *New York American*, May 23, 1926.

1. *relocated commune*: "What Is April Farm?," pamphlet [n.d., 1925?], b. 2, JPCC; CG to Lewis Browne, May 6, 1923, LBM. *work long days*: "Garland Makes His Farming Pay," *Daily Boston Globe*, Oct. 20, 1929, A7. *played with the children . . . storyteller*: Richard Cowen interviews with Peggy Garland and Jay Garland, n.d., in Richard Cowen, Garland Book, 946–62, RCC.

2. *erratic mental health*: Marie Tudor to Paul Scott, Sept. 21, 1925, binder 9—1925, RCC; Paul Scott to RNB, Aug. 21, 1928, r. 14, AFPSR. *Residents had come*: "Esther Walters [interview with Paul Avrich, 1972]," in Paul Avrich, *Anarchist Voices: An Oral History of Anarchism in America* (Princeton University Press, 1995), 251.

3. *baby not well . . . hushed tones*: Richard Cowen interview, RCC. *died in her crib*: "The Baby's Grave That Blighted Mr. Garland's Free Love Farm," *New York Daily Mirror*, May 23, 1926; Cowen, Garland Book, 13, RCC. *lurid rumors*: "Garland Gives Bail on Charge Growing out of Baby Death in Love Colony," *Reading Eagle*, Jan. 12, 1926, 1; Cowen, Garland Book, 650,

RCC. *New York press*: "Baby's Death Brings Garland 'Farm' Inquiry," *New York Herald Tribune*, Jan. 11, 1926, 18.

4. *generous words*: April Farms Incorporation Hearing Transcript, Nov. 5, 1925, 19–30, b. 21, f. 21, MSC. *crime of adultery*: "Charles Garland Indicted in Allentown," *New York Times*, Apr. 6, 1926, 1. *divorce*: "No Reconciliation Says Mrs. Garland," *Morning Call* (Allentown, Pa.), Apr. 18, 1926, 5; "Wife of Garland Sues for Divorce," *New York World*, June 10, 1926. *Darrow*: "Garland Seized in 'April Farm' Dead Baby Quiz," *New York Herald Tribune*, Jan. 12, 1926, 9. *Nelles*: Cowen, Garland Book, 713–14, RCC. *sentence*: "Garland Jailed for 60 Days in 'Love Farm' Case," *New York Herald Tribune*, Apr. 16, 1926, 10.

5. *failed apple crop*: Cowen, Garland Book, 710, RCC. *"ate, slept"*: "Esther Walters," in Avrich, *Anarchist Voices*, 251. *personal jealousies*: Richard Cowen interview with Roger Baldwin, Dec. 10, 1976, 29–30, RCC. *"misfits, failures"*: Paul Scott to Marie Tudor, Sept. 29, 1925, binder 9—1925, RCC. *twelve-part series*: "The Baby's Grave That Blighted Mr. Garland's Free Love Farm," *New York Daily Mirror*, May 23, 1926. *"Soviet Russian type"*: *Abolition of Compulsory Military Training at Schools and Colleges: Hearings Before the Committee on Military Affairs, House of Representatives*, 69th Cong., 1st Sess. (Government Printing Office, 1926), 199. *"moral standards"*: Cowen, Garland Book, 679, RCC.

6. *"ceased . . . wolf . . . sea"*: "Garland Divorced in Brief Hearing," *Philadelphia Inquirer*, Aug. 11, 1926.

7. *"unfortunate circumstances"*: Paul Scott to Anna Marnitz [AFPS], May 22, 1926, r. 14, AFPSR. *"confused"*: Cowen, Garland Book, 753–54, RCC. *"saddest person"*: Richard Cowen interview with Mary (Garland) Brubaker, Nov. 1982, RCC.

8. *packed . . . and left*: AFPS Minutes for Jan. 8, 1930, r. 2, AFPSR; Minutes of the Ninety-Sixth Meeting of the Board of Directors, Jan. 8, 1930, r. 3, AFPSR.

9. *Bloor*: Kathleen A. Brown, "The 'Savagely Fathered and Un-Mothered World' of the Communist Party, U.S.A.," *Feminist Studies* 25 (1999): 537. *retreat for party organizers*: *Hearings Before the Subcommittee to Investigate the Administration of the Internal Security Act and Other Internal Security Laws of the Committee of the Judiciary, United States Senate*, 83d Cong., 2d Sess., Oct. 13 and 28, 1954 (Government Printing Office, 1954), at 6–7.

10. *Ware*: *The Reminiscences of Roger Baldwin, 1953–1954*, at 331, CCOH; Hope Hale Davis, *Great Day Coming: A Memoir of the 1930s* (Steerforth Press, 1994), at 101; Lement Harris, *Harold M. Ware: Agricultural Pioneer, USA and USSR* (American Institute for Marxist Studies, 1978). *Soviet agricultural experiment*: Russian Reconstruction Farms, r. 21, AFPSR; Minutes of the Forty-Sixth Meeting of the Board, Dec. 17, 1924; Minutes of the Forty-Seventh Meeting of the Board, Jan. 7, 1925; Minutes of the Fifty-Fifth Meeting of the Board of Directors, July 22, 1925, all in r. 3, AFPSR. *end hunger*: [Harold Ware], "If You Could End Hunger in the World Forever?," r. 21, AFPSR. *Lenin*: Sam Tanenhaus, *Whittaker Chambers* (Random House, 1997), 92. *fell to pieces*: Russian Reconstruction Farms, r. 21, AFPSR.

11. *early spies*: Thomas L. Sakmyster, *Red Conspirator: J. Peters and the American Communist Underground* (University of Illinois Press, 2011), 74–87; Tanenhaus, *Whittaker Chambers*, 91–97; Harvey Klehr et al., *The Secret World of American Communism* (Yale University Press, 1995), 92.

12. *"never could reconcile"*: RNB, *Reminiscences*, at 382. *trust income*: RNB to Board of Directors of the AFPS, Dec. 21, 1939, c. 163.7, MLEP; RNB to AFPS, Mar. 13, 1941, b. 6, f. 3, BGP. *petition for grants*: E.g., CG to AFPS, Feb. 22, 1934, and CG to AFPS, Mar. 19, 1935, both in AFPSR and binder 41, RCC; Gloria Garrett Samson, *The American Fund for Public Service: Charles Garland and Radical Philanthropy, 1922–1941* (Greenwood Press, 1996), at 213. *moral obligation*: RNB to NT, Dec. 29, 1939, r. 25, AFPSR.

13. *"radical activities . . . right wing movements"*. CG to AFPS Board of Directors, Nov. 30, 1931, in b. 1, f. 14, JWJP, and also in BGP and r. 1, AFPSR.

14. *in deep*: RNB, *Reminiscences*, 331; RNB, Memo on Charles Garland to Richard Cowen [to Bettina Hovey?], Feb. 1975, and Richard Cowen interview with Roger Baldwin, Dec. 10, 1976, at 11, both in Roger Baldwin binder, RCC; Gardner Jackson, *The Reminiscences of Gardner Jackson*, 1955, at 406–7, CCOH.

15. ***titular position***: *Hearings Before the Committee on Un-American Activities House of Representatives, Eighty-Second Congress First Session, February 28 and March 9, 1951* (Government Printing Office, 1951), at 1883, 1891–901; Federal Bureau of Investigation, "Jay David Whittaker Chambers," Apr. 8, 1949, FOIPA No, 1222087-000; Cowen, Garland Book, 878–81, RCC. ***won support***: RNB to AFPS, Apr. 23, 1934, b. 6, BGP; Minutes of the Board of Directors, 2/25/37, r. 4, AFPSR. ***additional grants***: RNB, Memorandum for the Board on the Appropriation for Farm Organization Work, Mar. 26, 1935, b. 6, BGP; Minutes of the One Hundred Eighteenth Meeting of the Board of Directors, Apr. 3, 1936, r. 4, AFPSR. ***modest sums***: Farmers' Unity Council, 1938, r. 52, AFPSR; AM to CG, Apr. 19. 1937, r. 2, b. 4, AFPSR; Minutes of the Board of Directors, Sept. 29, 1937, r. 4, AFPSR. ***elaborate ruse***: RNB to AFPS, Feb. 28, 1934, b. 6, BGP; NT to RNB, Mar. 3, 1934, r. 23, AFPSR; RNB to AFPS Board of Directors, Feb. 28, 1934, b. 1, f. 14, JWJP. *"wrecking activities"*: BG to RNB, Feb. 23, 1940, b. 6, BGP. ***always balked***: Norman Thomas to RNB, Mar. 3, 1934, c. 163.5, MLEP.
16. ***truck driver***: Charles Garland to RNB, Aug. 24, 1935. ***fast cars***: Chambers, *Witness*, 332; Davis, *Great Day Coming: A Memoir of the 1930s*, at 108. ***Chambers took over***: Chambers, *Witness*, 378–79. ***harvesting Garland's money***: E.g., Farmers' Unity Council, 1938, r. 25, AFPSR; Gardner Jackson, *Reminiscences of Gardner Jackson*, 1955, at 406, CCOH.
17. ***new gifts***: Report of the American Fund for Public Service, Inc., for the Two Years Ending June 30, 1936 (Oct. 1936); *Report of the American Fund for Public Service, Inc., for the Two Years July 1, 1936 to June 30, 1938* (October 1938); *Report of the American Fund for Public Service, Inc. for the Three Years July 1, 1938 to June 30, 1941* (June 30, 1941), all in r. 3, b. 5, AFPSR. ***released back... turned down***: CG to RNB, Dec. 6, 1935; CG to Lewis Gannett, Dec. 13, 1935; RNB to CG, Dec. 13, 1935; and RNB to CG, Jan. 24, 1936, all in r. 2, b. 3, AFPSR.
18. ***whopping $1,900***: *Report... for the Three Years... 1938 to... 1941*, at 5.
19. *"practically ceased"*: RNB to Directors of the New York Public Library, Sept. 28, 1932, r. 3, AFPSR.
20. *"permanent beggars"*: Scott Nearing, *The Making of a Radical: A Political Autobiography* (Harper & Row, 1972), 48–49. ***relative weakness***: [SN], Memorandum, n.d. [May 1929], c. 162.6, MLEP.

17: A WAY OF ACTION

"heart of the evils": Nathan R. Margold, *Preliminary Report to the Joint Committee Supervising the Expenditure of the 1930 Appropriation by the American Fund for Public Service to the NAACP*, 93, b. I-C-200, NAACPLC.
1. ***Tuesday***: Committee on Negro Work, July 8, 1930, I-C-196, f. 5, NAACPL. ***Joint Committee***: AFPS Board Meeting, [May 28, 1930], b. 1, f. 2, CMP. ***Johnson was joined***: JWJ to AFPS, June 27, 1930, b. I-C-196, f. 5, NAACPL; Committee on Negro Work, July 8, 1930, b. I-C-196, f. 5, NAACPL. ***From the Fund***: AFPS Board Meeting, [May 28, 1930], b. 1, f. 2, CMP.
2. ***unequal apportionment***: Committee on Negro Work to AFPS, [early 1930], b. 1, f. 14, JWJP. ***supported efforts... Elaine***: JWJ to AFPS, Mar. 21, 1923, r. 16, b. 23, AFPSR. ***Ossian Sweet***: AFPS Board Meeting, Oct. 28, 1925, r. 3, b. 5, AFPSR. ***Sacco***: AFPS Meeting, July 7, 1926, r. 3, b. 5, AFPSR. ***Gastonia***: AFPS Board Meeting, June 19, 1929, r. 3, b. 5, AFPSR. ***Scopes***: AFPS Meeting, May 27, 1925, r. 3, b. 5, AFPSR.
3. ***distinctive answer... fundamentally revise***: For accounts of the Margold Report's significance, see Mark V. Tushnet, *The NAACP Legal Strategy Against Segregated Education, 1925–1950* (University of North Carolina Press, 1987), at 21–33; Risa Lauren Goluboff, *The Lost Promise of Civil Rights* (Harvard University Press, 2007), 177–78; Richard Kluger, *Simple Justice: The History of* Brown v. Board of Education *and Black America's Struggle for Equality* (Alfred A. Knopf, 1975, rev. ed. 2004), 126–38; Jack Greenberg, *Crusaders in the Courts: How a Dedicated Band of Lawyers Fought for the Civil Rights Revolution* (Basic Books, 1994), 56–61; Genna Rae McNeil, *Groundwork: Charles Hamilton Houston and the Struggle for Civil Rights* (University of Pennsylvania Press, 1983), 114–17; Patricia Sullivan, *Lift Every Voice: The NAACP and the Making of the Civil Rights Movement* (New Press, 2009), 156–57; Patricia Sullivan, "Prelude to Brown:

Education and the Struggle for Racial Justice During the NAACP's Formative Decades, 1909–1934," in *From the Grassroots to the Supreme Court: Brown v. Board of Education and American Democracy*, ed. Peter F. Lau (Duke University Press, 2004), 155–72; Leland B. Ware, "Setting the Stage for *Brown*: The Development and Implementation of the NAACP's School Desegregation Campaign, 1930–1950," *Mercer Law Review* 52 (2001): 631.
4. *"full-time"*: Committee on Negro Work Meeting, July 8, 1930, b. 42, LGP; Tushnet, *NAACP Legal Strategy*, 15.
5. *professor*: Brad Snyder, *Democratic Justice: Felix Frankfurter, the Supreme Court, and the Making of the Liberal Establishment* (W. W. Norton, 2022).
6. *Jewish parents*: Snyder, *Democratic Justice*, 9–16; Brad Snyder, *The House of Truth: A Washington Political Salon and the Foundations of American Liberalism* (Oxford University Press, 2017), 6.
7. *"most able"*: Snyder, *Democratic Justice*, 27. *"change your name"*: Ibid., 24.
8. *Frankfurter followed*: Snyder, *House of Truth*, 12. *supported Theodore Roosevelt*: Snyder, *Democratic Justice*, 44–54. *During the war*: Snyder, *House of Truth*, 167.
9. *"peculiar helpfulness"*: FF to RNB, Sept. 27, 1917, vol. 15, r. 2, ACLUA; Jeremy K. Kessler, "The Administrative Origins of Modern Civil Liberties Law," *Columbia Law Review* 114 (2014): 1083.
10. *"labor's democratic"*: Steven Fraser, "Sidney Hillman: Labor's Machiavelli," in *Labor Leaders in America*, ed. Melvyn Dubofsky and Warren Van Tine (University of Illinois Press, 1987), 213; Steven Fraser, *Labor Will Rule: Sidney Hillman and the Rise of American Labor* (Free Press, 1991), 116–20. *legal briefs*: FF to Sidney Hillman, 1919, b. 2, f. 35, ACWA.
11. *blistering 1920 account*: National Popular Government League, *Report upon the Illegal Practices of the United States Department of Justice* (National Popular Government League, 1920), 9. *"continued"*: Ibid., 3. *"fruitless"*: Ibid., 7. *Swinburne Hale*: Ibid., 9. *"our pamphlet"*: Workers Defense Union, Jan. 15, 1921, f. 9, EGF-B. *joined Flynn*: Snyder, *House of Truth*, 299. *fire him*: Snyder, *Democratic Justice*, 137–38. *unprecedented formal trial*: Peter H. Irons, "'Fighting Fair': Zechariah Chafee, Jr., the Department of Justice, and the 'Trial at the Harvard Club,'" *Harvard Law Review* 94 (1981): 1205, 1234.
12. *he advised*: Committee on Application for Funds Meeting, Nov. 9, 1922, r. 3, b. 5, AFPSR. *court injunctions*: FF to RNB, [n.d., Aug. 1923?], r. 11, b. 17, AFPSR. *Mooney*: RNB to FF, Feb. 18, 1924, r. 10, b. 15, AFPSR. *blast him*: Theodore Roosevelt to FF, Dec. 1917, FBI File on Felix Frankfurter, FOIA Request Files, FOIPA Request No. 1218885, release no. 255588.
13. *disdained Flynn's Wobblies*: Melvyn Dubofsky, *We Shall Be All: A History of the Industrial Workers of the World* (Quadrangle Books, 1969), 418. *cooperated*: EGF, *Rebel Girl: An Autobiography, My First Life (1906–1926)* (International Publishers, 1973), 330; AFPS Board Meeting, July 7, 1926, r. 3, b. 5, AFPSR; FF to EGF, July 1926, r. 12, b. 18, AFPSR. *won support*: Florence Kelley to EGF, Sept. 28, 1925; EGF to FK, Oct. 30, 1925, both in r. 24, b. 37, AFPSR. *successfully appealing*: Laura Weinrib, *The Taming of Free Speech: America's Civil Liberties Compromise* (Harvard University Press, 2016), 230–37. *litigated on behalf*: Anti–Felix Frankfurter pamphlet, 1939, FBI File on Felix Frankfurter, FOIA Request Files, FOIPA Request No. 1218885, release no. 255588.
14. *epidemics*: FF to Lewis Gannett, June 1, 1925, r. 30, b. 47, AFPSR. *Defense of the Chinese*: Forrest Bailey to AFPS, Dec. 27, 1927, r. 5, b. 8, AFPSR. *helped support*: AFPS Board Meeting, [n.d., Dec. 28, 1927], b. 1, f. 2, CMP. *well-wishes*: "Radicals Hold Dinner," *New York Times*, Feb. 15, 1926. *Boston committee*: FF to Frank Crosswaith, Mar. 19, 1928, b. 3, f. 18, FRCP. *Legal Committee*: NAACP Board Meeting, Nov. 11, 1929, NAACPP. *"constant advisor"*: RNB, *The Reminiscences of RNB, 1953–1954*, at 134 (1963), CCOH.
15. *pruned its limbs to climb*: Frankfurter's early trust-busting for Elihu Root in the U.S. Attorney's Office had aimed not to overturn capitalism but to rescue it from the robber barons. In the summer of 1917, when his wartime labor mediation role brought him to the copper-mining town of Bisbee, Arizona, where the Phelps Dodge Corporation and a posse of 2,000 armed deputies had forcibly shipped more than a thousand striking miners by railroad boxcar hundreds of miles into the New Mexico desert, Frankfurter's report excoriated the IWW threat to production with

the same force he mustered against the copper giants and mining titans. Frankfurter's efforts to find alternative service for conscientious objectors in the draft aimed not to defend the freedom of conscience but to protect the armed forces from needless and counterproductive controversies. (No commander, he pointed out, wanted reluctant soldiers in their ranks.) His 1920 criticisms of the Justice Department's raids openly disavowed what he called the "radical doctrines" of the raids' targets. In the Sacco and Vanzetti case, Frankfurter's professional critique of the proceedings came alongside contempt for the men's anarchist views. "Keep the radical connection," he said privately, "entirely out of the publicity." As an advisor to the Fund, he discouraged support for radical "agitation" about institutions like the Supreme Court, favoring "scientific" investigation by professionals instead. See generally Christopher Capozzola, "'The Only Badge Needed Is Your Patriotic Fervor': Vigilance, Coercion, and the Law in World War I America," *Journal of American History* 88 (2002): 1354; Kessler, "Administrative Origins," 1083; National Popular Government League, *Report upon the Illegal Practices of the United States Department of Justice*, 3; Mary C. Crawford to RNB, Sept. 13, 1926, b. 11, f. 4, AFS-VDC ("radical connection"); FF to RNB, Oct.17, 1922, r. 32, b. 50, AFPSR ("agitation").

16. *"orthodox"*: Walter Nelles to MLE and Scott Nearing, Mar. 31, 1924, r. 9, b. 13, AFPSR.
17. *Lippmann's formulation*: Walter Lippmann, *The Phantom Public* (Harcourt, 1925), 67. *"phantom"*: RNB, "Where Are the Pre-War Radicals," *The Survey*, Feb. 1926, 33, also in b. 21, f. 3, RNBP.
18. *"professional poisoners"*: Larry Tye, *The Father of Spin: Edward L. Bernays and the Birth of Public Relations* (Crown, 1998), 63. *"Great Society"*: Felix Frankfurter, *The Public and Its Government* (Yale University Press, 1930), 24. *"popular rule"*: Ibid., 126. *"dependent on"*: Ibid., 127. *"chain newspapers"*: Ibid., 128–29.
19. *"Freedom from"*: FF, Notes on Supreme Court Speech, [n.d.], b. 177, f. 9, FFP. *"permanent, servile class"*: Ronald Steel, *Walter Lippmann and the American Century* (Atlantic Monthly Press, 1980), 65–66.
20. *undesirable . . . impulses*: Harlan B. Phillips, *Felix Frankfurter Reminisces* (Reynal, 1960), 138. *"if unattended"*: Felix Frankfurter, "Social Unrest: Solution of Industrial Problems Rests upon the Application of Scientific Principles and Not upon Arbitrary Force," *Current Affairs* 10 (1920): 5, 11. *"social unrest"*: Ibid., 11.
21. *"ministry of justice"*: FF, Notes on Supreme Court Speech, [n.d.], b. 177, f. 9, FFP. *struck down*: Lochner v. New York, 198 U.S. 45 (1905).
22. *"seldom works"*: FF, Notes on Supreme Court Speech, [n.d.], b. 177, f. 9, FFP. *manage the great society*: Frankfurter, *Public and Its Government*, 1–35.
23. *"answer"*: Ibid., 129. *"devotion"*: Ibid., 133. *"agitation"*: Ibid., 153, quoting Graham Wallas, *Human Nature in Politics* (1915). *"instruments . . . parties"*: Ibid. *"scientific study"*: Ibid., 157. *"feed on"*: Ibid., 53.
24. *"new type"*: Ibid., 157–8. *"on tap"*: Ibid., 161. *"art of governing"*: Ibid., 160.
25. *man in mind*: FF to MLE, June 5, 1930, c. 168, MLEP; Tushnet, *NAACP Legal Strategy*, 15.
26. *highest honors*: Margold CV, [n.d., 1930], b. I-C-196, f. 6, NAACPL. *diminutive size*: Emory Buckner to Young B. Smith, Mar. 5, 1928, b. 186, f. 17, FFPH. *in anticipation*: NRM to FF, Feb. 17, 1927, b. 186, f. 17, FFPH.
27. *furious Margold*: NRM to Harvard Law School faculty, Feb. 1928, b. 186, f. 17, FFPH. *faculty revolt*: Faculty Meeting Account, Feb. 21, 1928; John M. Maguire to FF, Feb. 22, 1928; Thomas Reed Powell to RNB, Feb. 24, 1928, all in b. 186, f. 17, FFPH; see also Bruce A. Kimball and Daniel R. Coquillette, *The Intellectual Sword: Harvard Law School, the Second Century* (Belknap Press, 2020), 174–75.
28. *"sweet and charming"*: Learned Hand to FF, Jan. 19, 1927, b. 63, r. 39, f. 6, FFPLC. *"fine character"*: Emory R. Buckner to Young B. Smith, Mar. 5, 1928, b. 186, f. 17, FFPH.
29. *Frankfurter urged*: NRM to FF, Feb. 11, 1930, FFPH. *had resumed*: Margold CV to NAACP, Oct. 17, 1930, b. I-C-169, f. 6, NAACPL. *draft legislation*: John Collier to FF, Feb. 11, 1931, FFPH; Vine Deloria Jr. and Clifford M. Lytle, *The Nations Within: The Past and Future of American Indian Sovereignty* (University of Texas Press, 1984), 153; Harvey D. Rosenthal, "Evolution

of the Indian Claims Commission," in *Their Day in Court: A History of the Indian Claims Commission* (Garland, 1990), 47–109.
30. **leaders and advocates**: Ned Blackhawk, *The Rediscovery of America: Native Peoples and the Unmaking of U.S. History* (Yale University Press, 2023), 365–407; Deloria and Lytle, *Nations Within*, 37–54; Maggie Blackhawk, "Legislative Constitutionalism and Federal Indian Law," *Yale Law Journal* 132 (2021): 2205, 2237, n149. **Society of American Indians & National Council**: Hazel W. Hertzberg, *The Search for an American Indian Identity* (Syracuse University Press, 1971); P. Jane Hafen, "'Help Indians Help Themselves': Gertrude Bonnin, the SAI, and the NCAI," *American Indian Quarterly* 37 (2013): 199. **Mission Indian Federation**: Christian W. McMillen, "The Birth of an Activist: Fred Mahone and the Politicization of the Hualapai, 1918 to 1923," *American Indian Culture & Research Journal* 27 (2003): 33.
31. **no course**: Harvard Law School, *Course of Instruction 1897/9–1955/56*, HLS.LIBR. **sale and economic development**: Blackhawk, *Rediscovery of America*, 334. **holdings fell**: Ibid., 334. *"extremely poor"*: Ibid., 392; Donald T. Critchlow, "Lewis Meriam, Expertise, and Indian Reform," *Historian* 43 (1981): 325.
32. *"finally"*: U.S. Congress, Subcommittee on the Committee on Indian Affairs, *Survey of Conditions of the Indians in the United States: Indian Claims Against the Government*, Part 25, 72nd Cong., 1st Sess. (Government Printing Office, 1931), 13409, 13670.
33. **support from the American Fund**: Gifts to June 30, 1941, AFPS, f. 5. *"gold mine . . . new epoch"*: John Collier to FF, Feb. 11, 1931, b. 186, f. 17, FFPH. **designed**: U.S. Senate, *Klamath Indian Corporation: Hearings Before the Committee on Indian Affairs, 72nd Cong., 1st Sess. on S. 3588, a Bill for the Incorporation of the Klamath Indian Corporation, and for Other Purposes* (Government Printing Office, 1932), 2. **Montana**: Margold Materials, 1930, JCP.
34. **volunteer**: JC to FF, Feb. 11, 1931, b. 186, f. 17, FFPH. **twenty Pueblo tribes . . .** *"owners"*: Nathan Margold, "The Plight of the Pueblos," *The Nation*, Feb. 4, 1931, 121. *"only hope"*: JC to FF, Feb. 11, 1931, b. 186, f. 17, FFPH.
35. **testified**: Senate Committee on Indian Affairs, *Survey of Conditions of the Indians in the United States Part 20: Pueblo Lands Board* (Government Printing Office, 1931), 71. *"distressing"*: Margold, "The Plight of the Pueblos," 123.
36. **diverged from the letter**: Margold, *Survey of Conditions of the Indians in the United States*, 13670. Ironically, Frankfurter may have developed some of his theory of law and administration while working for Henry Stimson as chief legal advisor for colonial administration, a position that gave him authority over U.S. relations with Native peoples in the territories. See Maggie Blackhawk's forthcoming article "The Crisis in Colonial Administration," *American Historical Review* (forthcoming 2025), at n14, as well as Blackhawk's book project in process, *American Colonialism: A National Biography*.
37. **recommendation**: Bruce Allen Murphy, *The Brandeis/Frankfurter Connection: The Secret Political Activities of Two Supreme Court Justices* (Oxford University Press, 1982), 114. For a new and fascinating account of Margold's interaction with Collier and the influential funder Thomas Jesse Jones, one that came too late for me to develop here, see Khalil Anthony Johnson Jr., *Schooled: An Unsettling History of American Education* (University of North Carolina Press, forthcoming).
38. **Hualapai**: Christian W. McMillen, *Making Indian Law: The Hualapai Land Case and the Birth of Ethnohistory* (Yale University Press, 2007), 7. **Railroad threatened**: Ibid., 12. **Nine years**: Ibid., 42. **had entered**: Ibid., xiv.
39. **in Hualapai country**: McMillen, *Making Indian Law*, 104–22.
40. *"right of occupancy"*: Nathan Margold, *Memorandum to the Secretary*, 1934, b. 1500, f. 51, Department of the Interior, Office of the Secretary, Record Group 48, NARA. **cession**: United States v. Santa Fe Pacific RR, 314 U.S. 339 (1941). **supposed consent decree**: Margold, *Memorandum to the Secretary*, 121. **which it did not**: Ibid., 78.
41. *"climate"*: Ibid., 3. *"ill-considered"*: Ibid., 149. *"inexcusable"*: Ibid., 150. *"justify"*: Ibid., 149. *"blithely"*: Ibid., 150. *"settled"*: Ibid., 51.
42. **second**: McMillen, *Making of Indian Law*, 128. **from Minsk**: David A. Hollinger, *Morris Cohen and the Scientific Ideal* (MIT Press, 1975).

43. *"most basic . . . extinguished"*: "Powers of Indian Tribes," *Decisions of the Department of the Interior* 55 (1934): 14, 19; Deloria and Lytle, *Nations Within*, 158–61; McMillen, *Making Indian Law*, 128–29.
44. *aimed to assimilate*: Deloria and Lytle, *Nations Within*, 159; on the distinction between rights and powers, see Maggie Blackhawk, "Federal Indian Law as Paradigm Within Public Law," *Harvard Law Review* 132 (2019): 1787, 1845–49.
45. *more far-reaching & future critics*: E.g., Graham D. Taylor, *The New Deal and American Indian Tribalism: Administration of the Indian Reorganization Act, 1934–1945* (University of Nebraska Press, 1980); Vine Deloria Jr., "Laws Founded in Justice and Humanity: Reflections on the Content and Character of Federal Indian Law," *Arizona Law Review* 31 (1989): 203, 206–7, 213–14, 219–20; Blackhawk, "Legislative Constitutionalism," 2236–58; Elizabeth A. Reese, "The Other American Law," *Stanford Law Review* 73 (2021): 555, 563. *important shift*: Blackhawk, *Rediscovery of America*, 398–407.
46. *drafted*: Dalia Tsuk Mitchell, *Architect of Justice: Felix S. Cohen and the Founding of American Legal Pluralism* (Cornell University Press, 2007), 4. *"cultivate native arts"*: Taylor, *The New Deal and American Indian Tribalism*, at 102; Elmer R. Risco, *A Fateful Time: The Background and Legislative History of the Indian Reorganization Act* (University of Nevada Press, 2000). *administrative control*: Karen Tani, "States Rights, Welfare Rights, and the 'Indian Problem': Negotiating Citizenship and Sovereignty, 1935–1954," *Law & History Review* 33 (2014): 1, 15–16.
47. *"aboriginal possession"*: United States v. Santa Fe Pacific Railroad Company, 314 U.S. 339 (1941); McMillen, *Making Indian Law*, xiii, 177.
48. *lunch . . . served together*: CHH to WW, Sept. 3, 1930, b. I-C-196, f. 5, NAACPL. *spring term*: CHH, LLB 1922, SJD 1923, Harvard Law School Student Permanent Records, 14258, b. 30, Harvard University Archives; NRM, LLB 1923, Harvard Law School Student Permanent Records. *new class*: Official Register of Harvard University, vol. 19, March 27, 1922, 8, Harvard University Archives.
49. *"remarkable man"*: CHH to WW, Sept. 3, 1930, b. I-C-196, f. 5, NAACPL; also WW to RNB, July 8, 1933, r. 23, b. 36, AFPSR. *over another lunch*: Committee on Negro Work Meeting, Sept. 18, 1930, r. 23, b. 36, AFPSR. *legal work*: NRM to Fred C. Knollenberg, Oct. 21, 1930, b. I-C-196, f. 6, NAACPL. *"legal campaign"*: NAACP Press Release, Nov. 9, 1930, b. I-C-196, f. 6, NAACPL.
50. *little time*: NRM to WW, Dec. 16, 1930, b. I-C-196, f. 6, NAACPL. *dismayed*: WW to Joint Committee, Dec. 17, 1930, b. I-C-196, f. 6, NAACPL; WW to NRM, Apr. 2, 1931, b. I-C-196, f. 7, NAACPL. *first weeks*: NRM to WW, Dec. 19, 1930, b. I-C-196, f. 6, NAACPL.
51. *Du Bois studies*: WEBDB, *Report to AFPS on Public Common School Education in the South for Negroes*, [Oct. 27, 1926], r. 7, b. 11, AFPSR. *"dual school system"*: Committee on Negro Work to AFPS, [n.d., May 1930], b. I-C-197, f. 7, NAACPL; Tushnet, *NAACP Legal Strategy*, 13–14.
52. *Broadus Mitchell*: Joan Cook, "Broadus Mitchell, 95, Professor, Historian and Hamilton Authority," *New York Times*, Apr. 30, 1998, 11. *"all sorts of ways"*: Broadus Mitchell to MLE, June 10, 1930, b. I-C-196, f. 5, NAACPL. *"real discrimination"*: WEBDB to NRM, Nov. 20, 1930, b. I-C-196, f. 6, NAACPL. *"social progress"*: BM to MLE, June 10, 1930, b. I-C-196, f. 5, NAACPL.
53. *law of administration*: On the law of administration, see William J. Novak, *New Democracy: The Creation of the Modern American State* (Harvard University Press, 2022).
54. *"has been oppressed"*: Broadus Mitchell, "Foreword—by a Southerner," in *Black Justice* (ACLU, 1931), 5.
55. *"within the discretion"*: Gong Lum v. Rice, 275 U.S. 78 (1927); Stephanie Hinnershitz, *A Different Shade of Justice: Asian-American Rights in the South* (University of North Carolina Press, 2017); Adrienne Berard, *Water Tossing Boulders: How a Family of Chinese Immigrants Led the First Fight to Desegregate Schools in the Jim Crow South* (Beacon Press, 2016); Jeannie Rhee, "In Black and White: Chinese in the Mississippi Delta," *Journal of Supreme Court History* 19 (1994): 117.

56. *offered an objection*: NRM, Preliminary Report to the Joint Committee, 1931, at 92–93, b. I-C-200, NAACPL (hereinafter NRM, Preliminary Report).
57. *"multiplicity"*: Nathan Margold, *Address Before the Twenty-third Annual Conference of the NAACP* (1930). *15,000 school districts*: Laurence Kennedy et al., "The Decline in the Number of School Districts in the U.S.: 1950–1980," *Public Choice* 79 (1994): 1. *"year after year"*: NRM, Preliminary Report, 41. *"would barely"*: Ibid. *"fritter away"*: Ibid., 40. *"trying to empty"*: Kluger, *Simple Justice*, 133; see also JWJ, "Repealing Void Laws," *New York Tribune*, June 17, 1929, 16.
58. *shape of districts*: William Fischel, *Making the Grade: The Economic Evolution of American School Districts* (University of Chicago Press, 2009), 112.
59. **Du Bois**: David Levering Lewis, *W. E. B. Du Bois: The Fight for Equality and the American Century, 1919–1963* (Henry Holt, 2000), at 262–65. **Randolph**: APR, "Why I Would Not Stand for Re-Election for President of the National Negro Congress," in *For Jobs and Freedom: Selected Speeches and Writings of A. Philip Randolph*, ed. Andrew E. Kersten and David Lucander (University of Massachusetts Press, 2014), 186–89.
60. *"denial of equal"*: Yick Wo v. Hopkins, 118 U.S. 373 (1886); Gabriel J. Chin, "Unexplainable on Grounds of Race: Doubts About Yick Wo," *U. Illinois Law Review* 2008 (2008): 1359; also Robert L. Tsai, "Racial Purges," *Michigan Law Review* 118 (2020): 1127, 1135.
61. *"under conditions"*: NRM, Preliminary Report, 93. *"irremediably coupled"*: Ibid., 25, 93.
62. *"challenge"*: NRM, Preliminary Report, 93–94. *"administrative action"*: Ibid.; also Ware, "Setting the Stage for *Brown*," 42–43; *Yick Wo*, 118 U.S. at 374.
63. *to alter the institutional and administrative arrangements of oppression*: NRM, Preliminary Report, 29–38.
64. *Margold took over*: NRM to WW, Oct. 9, 1930, b. I-C-196, f. 6, NAACPL. **Nixon v. Condon**: Darlene Clark Hine, *Black Victory: The Rise and Fall of the White Primary in Texas* (University of Missouri Press, 1979; new ed. 2003), 154–60; Sullivan, *Lift Every Voice*, 163; Will Guzmán, *Civil Rights in the Texas Borderlands: Dr. Lawrence A. Nixon and Black Activism* (University of Illinois Press, 2015), 79.
65. *annual conference*: NAACP, *Twenty-Third Annual Report of the National Association for the Advancement of Colored People for 1932* (NAACP, 1933), 7–8, 37–38; Sullivan, *Lift Every Voice*, 155–58.
66. *"sensational speech"*: Herbert Seligmann, Press Release: Twenty-Third Annual Convention, 1932, at 2, 2580443511, NAACPP. *"unless . . . equality"*: NRM, Address Delivered Before the Twenty-Third Annual Conference of NAACP, Washington, D.C., May 20, 1932, NAACPP.
67. *critics have leveled*: Derrick Bell, "Law, Litigation, and the Search for the Promised Land," *Georgetown Law Journal* 76 (1988): 229, 233; Goluboff, *The Lost Promise of Civil Rights*; Megan Ming Francis, "The Price of Civil Rights: Black Lives, White Funding, and Movement Capture," *Law & Society Review* 53 (2019): 275. *flimsy right*: W. E. B. Du Bois, "Does the Negro Need Separate Schools?," *Journal of Negro Education* 4 (1935): 328–35. *"lush value"*: Horace Mann Bond, *The Education of the Negro in the American Social Order* (Prentice-Hall, 1934), 236.
68. *desegregate labor unions*: NRM, Preliminary Report, 217.

18: SCOTTSBORO AND AFTER

"made it impossible": Quoted in Genna Rae McNeil, *Groundwork: Charles Hamilton Houston and the Struggle for Civil Rights* (University of Pennsylvania Press, 1983), 120.

1. *March . . . execution*: Dan T. Carter, *Scottsboro: A Tragedy of the American South* (Louisiana State University Press, 2007), 4; see also James Goodman, *Stories of Scottsboro* (Vintage Books, 1994).
2. **Communist Party**: Carter, *Scottsboro*, 49. *favored*: CG to AFPS, Nov. 30, 1931, r. 1, b. 1, AFPSR. *protests . . . NAACP*: Carter, *Scottsboro*, 122, 59, 142, 49, 91, 172, 19, 53.
3. **Margold**: WW to NRM, May 13, 1931, f. 7; WW to LG, May 18, 1931, f. 7; NRM to WW, May 2, 1932, f. 9; NRM to WW, Mar. 25, 1933, f. 10; NRM to RW, Apr. 4, 1933, f. 10, all b. I-C-196, f. 6,

NAACPLC. ***whites-only primary***: NRM to WW, Oct. 9, 1930; Oct. 14, 1930; Oct. 21, 1930, all b. I-C-196, f. 6, NAACPLC. ***disfranchisement in Louisiana***: NRM to WW, May 2, 1932; WW to William T. Andrews, Sept. 14, 1931; H. W. Robinson to NRM, Oct. 1, 1931, all in b. I-C-196, f. 8–9, NAACPLC. ***uncertainty***: WW to MLE, May 31, 1932; WW to Anna Marnitz, June 8, 1932; WW to Robert W. Dunn, June 17, 1932; WW to AM, Sept. 2, 1932; WW to AFPS, Sept. 28, 1932; RNB to WW, Nov. 10, 1932; WW to RNB, Nov. 11, 1932; WW to Mr. Turner, Jan. 26, 1933, all in b. I-C-196, f. 9, NAACPLC; see also NRM to WW, May 2, 1932; RNB to WW, Nov. 10, 1932; WW to RNB, Nov. 11, 1932; Joint Committee Meeting, Sept. 27, 1932; WW to AFPS, Sept. 28, 1932; WW to AFPS, Sept. 2, 1932; RNB to NAACP, Oct. 2, 1931, all r. 23, b. 36, AFPSR. ***Margold left***: WW to NRM, Mar. 20, 1933; NRM to WW, Mar. 25, 1933; NAACP, "NAACP Legal Advisor to High Government Post," Mar. 24, 1933, all in b. I-C-196, f. 10, NAACPLC.

4. ***Harvard classmate***: NRM to WW, Oct. 22, 1934, b. I-C-196, f. 10, NAACPLC; WW to RNB, July 8, 1933, r. 23, b. 36, AFPSR. ***favorite students***: WW to RNB, July 8, 1933, b. I-C-196, f. 10, NAACPLC; CHH, LLB 1922, SJD 1923, Harvard Law School Student Permanent Records, 14258, b. 30, Harvard University Archives; NRM, LLB 1923, Harvard Law School Student Permanent Records; Official Register of Harvard University, vol. 19, March 27, 1922, 8, Harvard University Archives. ***substantial share***: WW to CHH, June 21, 1933, b. I-C-196, f. 10, NAACPLC; WW to CHH, Aug. 10, 1934, b. I-C-196, f. 11, NAACPLC; RNB to AFPS Board, June 12, 1933; RNB to WW, July 7, 1933, both in r. 23, b. 36, AFPSR.

5. ***Houston***: McNeil, *Groundwork*, 19–24; Kenneth W. Mack, *Representing the Race: Creating the Civil Rights Lawyer* (Harvard University Press, 2012), 42–43.

6. ***"respectable"***: Ibid., 25–45; see also Thomas Sowell, "Black Excellence: The Case of Dunbar High School," *Public Interest* (Spring 1974): 35.

7. ***army training program*** ... ***"not lost my life"***: McNeil, *Groundwork*, 35–45; Leland B. Ware, "Setting the Stage for *Brown*: The Development and Implementation of the NAACP's School Desegregation Campaign, 1930–1950," *Mercer Law Review* 52 (2001): 631, 634.

8. ***enrolled***: Ibid., 49–51. ***Law Review***: Editorial Board, *Harvard Law Review* 35 (1921): 68. ***admire one another***: CHH to WW, Sept. 3, 1930, b. I-C-196, f. 4, NAACPLC. ***"superlative"***: NRM to WW, Oct. 22, 1934, f. 11, NAACPLC. ***finest students***: WW to RNB, July 8, 1933, b. I-C-196, f. 10, NAACPLC; McNeil, *Groundwork*, 53.

9. ***Spain***: Ibid., 54. ***"There must be"***: Ibid., 53. ***"no more ... rights for Negroes"***: CHH, "The Need for Negro Lawyers," *Journal of Negro Education* 4 (1935): 49, 49–51.

10. ***Howard ... national stature***: Ware, "Setting the Stage for *Brown*," 633. ***night program ... "lawyer"***: McNeil, *Groundwork*, 72, 76, 81, 71; Mack, *Representing the Race*, 43–45.

11. ***ABA-approved law school***: McNeil, *Groundwork*, 75.

12. ***"introduced"***: Ibid., 120. ***"telegram"***: Ibid., 121.

13. ***"treachery ... NAACP"***: Clarina Michelson, "Next Step in Struggle for Freedom of the Nine Scottsboro Boys," [n.d.], b. 3, f. 15, CMP. ***Communist influence***: See Richard Cowen, Garland Book 361, 889, RCC. ***"anything but advanced"***: CG to AFPS, Nov. 30, 1931, r. 1, b. 1, AFPSR.

14. ***"party orders"*** ... ***"fought bitterly"***: WW to Will Alexander, Aug. 16, 1932, b. 24, f. 541, JWJP; also WW, "Report of the Secretary," Aug. 1931, NAACP Monthly Reports, NAACPP. ***"too despicable"***: WEBDB, "The Negro and Communism," *The Crisis*, Sept. 1931, 313–14.

15. ***Committee on Civil Liberties***: RNB to Civil Liberties Committee, Mar. 31, 1931, c. 163, MLEP. ***"disbursed"***: AFPS Board Meeting, Sept. 26, 1935, r. 4, b. 7, AFPSR. ***"caught"***: RNB, "Autobiography (1920–1931)," b. 20, f. 12, 238, RNBP. ***division of labor***: WW to AFPS, Sept. 13, 1933, r. 23, b. 36, AFPSR.

16. ***Pollak***: *NAACP Report for 1931* (NAACP, 1932); WW, "Report of the Secretary," July 1932, NAACP Monthly Reports, NAACPP; Richard Carver Wood, "W. H. Pollak Dies," *New York Times*, Oct. 3, 1940, 25. ***Eugene Williams***: Carter, *Scottsboro*, 170. ***labor injunctions***: AFPS Board Meeting, May 7, 1924, r. 3, b. 5, AFPSR. ***Gitlow***: Gitlow v. New York, 268 U.S. 652 (1925). ***Powell***: Powell v. Alabama, 287 U.S. 45 (1932); see also Patricia Sullivan, *Lift Every Voice: The NAACP and the Making of the Civil Rights Movement* (New Press, 2009), 163. ***Norris***: Norris v.

Alabama, 294 U.S. 587 (1935). *Defense Committee*: Scottsboro Defense Committee to Friend, Sept. 29, 1939, b. I-H-5, NAACPLC.
17. **Houston**: McNeil, *Groundwork*, 51. *"black man's dream"*: Ibid., 100. **Patterson**: Ibid., 105. *"caught the imagination"*: Ibid., 109.
18. **Guest speakers**: Ibid., 77. *"masses"*: CHH, "An Approach to Better Race Relations," National YWCA Convention, May 1934, r. 28, RPP. *"What sort of justice"*: McNeil, *Groundwork*, 110.
19. *"agents of capitalism"*: Ibid., 98. *"lynch bosses"* . . . *"Uncle Toms of the year"*: Ibid., 104.
20. **May 1930 vote**: AFPS Board Meeting, May 28, 1930, r. 4, b. 57, AFPSR. **release**: MLE to JWJ, Jan. 7, 1932, c. 163, MLEP. **Squabbles**: See AM to WW, June 6, 1932, r. 25, b. 29, ABSP; Robert Dunn to WW, June 15, [1932?], r. 25, b. 29, ABSP; LG to WW, June 13, 1932, b. I-C-196, f. 9, NAACPLC; RNB to NAACP, Oct. 2, 1931, r. 23, b. 36, AFPSR. *"not see"*: WW to AM, June 8, 1932, b. I-C-196, f. 9, NAACPLC. *"pending word"*: WW to MLE, Jan. 14, 1932, c. 163, MLEP. *"the Association"*: WW to Robert Dunn, June 17, 1932, r. 23, b. 36, AFPSR.
21. **July 1933**: RNB to AFPS, June 12, 1933; RNB to WW, July 7, 1933, both r. 23, b. 37, AFPSR. **Llewellyn**: WW to NRM, May 22, 1934, b. I-C-196, f. 11, NAACPLC. *"not the best"*: NAACP Board Meeting, May 14, 1934, Part 1: NAACP Minutes, NAACPP. Baldwin proposed his friend Whitney Seymour, a recent assistant solicitor general in the Hoover administration with civil liberties inclinations, or Nathan Greene, a labor law expert and coauthor of Frankfurter's book on labor injunctions. Baldwin's associate Walter Nelles and his Yale Law School colleague Charles Clark suggested Albert Levitt, a talented but erratic crusader in Connecticut politics. See WW to NRM, Oct. 14, 1933; NRM to WW, Oct. 18, 1933, both b. I-C-196, f. 10, NAACPLC; Walter Nelles to MLE, June 9m, 1930, b. I-C-196, f. 10, NAACPLC; also Charles E. Clark to James Marshall, June 11, 1930, r. 25, b. 29, ABSP.
22. *"ideal person . . . less expensively"*: WW to RNB, July 8, 1933, b. I-C-196, f. 10, NAACPLC; see also r. 23, b. 37, AFPSR. *"exceptionally able"*: NRM to WW, May 25, 1934, b. I-C-196, f. 11, NAACPLC. **Alabama courts**: WW to NRM, May 22, 1934, b. I-C-196, f. 11, NAACPLC. **October 26, 1934**: CHH, Memorandum to Joint Committee, Oct. 26, 1934, b. I-C-196, f. 11, NAACPLC; see also r. 23, b. 37, AFPSR.
23. **$300,000 juggernaut**: See MLE markup, Committee on Negro Work Memorandum, Oct. 18, 1929, r. 2, b. 3, AFPSR. *"cut down"*: WW to NRM, Sept. 5, 1933, b. I-C-196, f. 10, NAACPLC. *"pity"*: WW to CHH, June 21, 1933, b. I-C-196, f. 10, NAACPLC. **measly $52,000**: AFPS, Report for Four Years, 1930–1934, Summary of Twelve Years (AFPS, Nov. 1934). **preliminary investigations**: WW to Joint Committee, Dec. 17, 1930, b. I-C-196, f. 6, NAACPLC; NRM to WW, Mar. 31, 1931; NRM to WW, Apr. 13, 1931; WW to LG, May 18, 1931, all in b. I-C-196, f. 7, NAACPLC; NRM to WW, May 2, 1932, b. I-C-196, f. 9, NAACPLC.
24. **Harris**: AFPS Board Meeting, Feb. 26, 1930, r. 4, b. 7, AFPSR; Abram L. Harris and Sterling D. Spero, *The Black Worker: The Negro and the Labor Movement* (Columbia University Press, 1931). *"conscious . . . worker"*: Raymond Wolters, *Negroes and the Great Depression: The Problem of Recovery* (Greenwood, 1970), 225; Sullivan, *Lift Every Voice*, 174.
25. **year later . . . "all labor, white and black"**: Wolters, *Negroes and the Great Depression*, 314–15; Jonathan Scott Holloway, *Confronting the Veil: Abram Harris Jr., E. Franklin Frazier, and Ralph Bunche, 1919–1941* (University of North Carolina Press, 2002), 84–122.
26. *"conservative . . . mass struggle"*: CHH, "Approach to Better Race Relations," National YWCA Convention, May 1934, r. 28, RPP. *"unite"*: McNeil, *Groundwork*, 102. **cousin**: Ibid., 66. *"lined up"*: Wolters, *Negroes and the Great Depression*, 327. *"integration . . . group"*: CHH, "Approach to Better Race Relations," National YWCA Convention, May 1934, r. 28, RPP.
27. *"mass pressure"*: McNeil, *Groundwork*, 120. **decisions**: Patterson v. Alabama, 294 U.S. 600 (1935); Norris v. Alabama, 294 U.S. 587 (1935).
28. *"lessons . . . want it"*: CHH, Memorandum to Joint Committee, Oct. 26, 1934, b. I-C-196, f. 11, NAACPLC.
29. *"foundation work"*: Ibid. **Du Bois**: WEBDB, *Report to AFPS on Public Common School Education in the South for Negroes*, [Oct. 27, 1926], r. 7, b. 11, AFPSR; WEBDB to NRM, Nov. 20, 1930, b. I-C-196, f. 6, NAACPLC; WEBDB, "The Negro Common School in Georgia," *The Crisis*, Sept.

1926, 248; WEBDB, "The Negro Common School: Mississippi," *The Crisis*, Dec. 1926, 2. *"These suits"*: "NAACP Funds," *The Crisis*, Dec. 1926, 60.

30. *movie camera*: NAACP Board Meeting, Oct. 8, 1934, pt. 1: Meetings of the Board of Directors, NAACPP. *"Motion pictures"*: McNeil, *Groundwork*, 140; Rawn James Jr., *Root and Branch: Charles Hamilton Houston, Thurgood Marshall, and the Struggle to End Segregation* (Bloomsbury, 2010), 84. *thousand feet of film reels*: CHH, Memorandum to Joint Committee, July 24, 1936; WW to AFPS, Jan. 8, 1936, both in r. 28, b. 44, AFPSR. *screened*: [CHH], "Campaign Against Inequalities in Education," Oct. 15, 1937, b. I-C-196, f. 8, NAACPLC. *Rock Hill*: Joint Committee Report, Mar. 21, 1935, b. I-C-196, f. 12, NAACPLC. *not far*: McNeil, *Groundwork*, 22. *Wise County*: Ibid., 140; CHH, Memorandum to Joint Committee, July 24, 1936, b. I-C-200, f. 1, NAACPLC. *Schuyler*: GS to CHH, Feb. 8, 1936; CHH to George Schuyler, Feb. 15, 1936, both in b. I-C-197, f. 1, NAACPLC. *"inconvenience"*: Requisition for Travel Advance to CHH, July 19, 1935, b. I-C-196, f. 12, NAACPLC.

31. *embittered departure*: NAACP Board Meeting, June 11, 1934; NAACP Board Meeting, July 9, 1934, both in pt. 1: NAACP Minutes, NAACPP. *Creel*: See Alfred A. Cornebise, *War as Advertised: The Four Minute Men and America's Crusade, 1917–1918* (American Philosophical Society, 1984). *Juanita Jackson*: WW to Edward R. Murrow, Oct. 21, 1936; NBC to Juanita Jackson, Oct. 29, 1936, both in b. I-C-202, f. 4, NAACPLC. *attack*: Jackson to Murrow, Nov. 4, 1936, b. I-C-202, f. 4, NAACPLC. *"comments"*: Jackson to Murrow, Nov. 9, 1936, b. I-C-202, f. 4, NAACPLC.

32. *"undergird"*: WW to AFPS, Jan. 7, 1936, b. I-C-200, f. 1, NAACPLC. *"getting over"*: WW to CHH and Thurgood Marshall, Sept. 5, 1937, b. I-C-198, f. 7, NAACPLC.

33. *additional $15,000 . . . "fraternal orders"*: WW to AFPS, Jan. 7, 1936, b. I-C-200, f. 1, NAACPLC. *scraped together*: Robert W. Dunn to WW, Jan. 27, 1936, r. 27, b. 44, AFPSR.

34. *"other isms"*: CHH to WW, Sept.17, 1936, b. I-C-198, f. 2, NAACPLC. *"ready and hungry"*: CHH, Confidential Memorandum to Walter White, Sept. 17, 1936, b. I-C-198, f. 2, NAACPLC.

35. *"be careful"*: JWJ, Synopsis for Program Re Expenditure of the $100,000 Fund, June 27, 1930, b. I-C-196, f. 5, NAACPLC.

36. *local, state, and federal bills*: WW to NRM, Nov. 15, 1932; NRM to WW, Nov. 16, 1932; WW to NRM, Nov. 17, 1932, all in b. I-C-196, f. 9, NAACPLC. *Davis*: John P. Davis, *Report of the Chief Social and Economic Problems of Negroes in the TVA*, c. 169, MLEP; Sullivan, *Lift Every Voice*, 192–93. *progress in safeguarding*: CHH, Memorandum to Joint Committee, May 4, 1937, r. 6, b. 9, ABSP.

37. *"ultimately change"*: CHH, Memorandum to Joint Committee, Nov. 14, 1935, r. 27, b. 44, AFPSR. *"symbolic"*: McNeil, *Groundwork*, 134.

38. *"differentials in teachers salaries"*: CHH, Memorandum to Joint Committee, Oct. 26, 1934, b. I-C-196, f. 11, AFPSR.

39. *funding disparities*: Table 12: "Average Annual Salaries of White and Negro Teachers, Principals, and Supervisors," in b. I-C-198, f. 13, NAACPLC. *"cost of skin pigmentation"*: Thurgood Marshall, "To the Branches," Nov. 22, 1939, b. I-C-199, f. 1, NAACPLC. *"major cases"*: Gunnar Myrdal, *An American Dilemma: The Negro Problem and Modern Democracy* (Harper & Brothers, 1944), 1:320.

40. *Gibbs*: Mark V. Tushnet, *Making Civil Rights Law: Thurgood Marshall and the Supreme Court, 1936–1961* (Oxford University Press, 1994), at 22–23. *first suit*: CHH to MLE, Mar. 10, 1937, r. 27, b. 44, AFPSR; McNeil, *Groundwork*, 152–53. *"vast"*: WW to AFPS Board, June 22, 1937, b. I-C-200, f. 1, NAACPLC.

41. *Brevard & Maryland's other counties*: CHH, Memorandum to WW Re Developments in Equalization of Teachers Salaries Fights, Nov. 30, 1937, r. 27, b. 44, AFPSR. *"$1,600.00"*: CHH to RNB, Mar. 9, 1938, b. II-L-15, NAACPLC. *federal suit . . . "colored teachers"*: Mills v. Board of Education of Anne Arundel County, 30 F. Supp. 245 (D. Md. 1939). *"precedent"*: Thurgood Marshall, "To the Branches," Nov. 22, 1939, b. I-C-199, f. 1, NAACPLC. *Alston*: Alston v. Virginia High School League, Inc., 108 F. Supp. 2d 543 (W.D. Va. 1997).

42. *"build up"*: Mark V. Tushnet, *NAACP's Legal Strategy Against Segregated Education, 1925–1950*

(University of North Carolina Press, 1986), at 37. **Black women**: John A. Kirk, "The NAACP Campaign for Teachers' Salary Equalization: African American Women Educators and the Early Civil Rights Struggle," *Journal of African American History* 94 (2009): 529, 534–35. **Jackson**: Tushnet, *NAACP's Legal Strategy Against Segregated Education*, 45.

43. **salary equalization cases**: Kirk, "NAACP Campaign for Teachers' Salary Equalization," 533. **"tied... positions"**: CHH, "Campaign Against Inequalities in Education," Oct. 15, 1937, b. I-C-198, f. 8, NAACPLC. **Myrdal**: Myrdal, *An American Dilemma*. **"economic democracy"**: Kirk, "NAACP Campaign for Teachers' Salary Equalization," 532.

44. **"too many"**: WW to John W. Davis, Jan. 21, 1937, b. I-C-198, f. 4, NAACPLC. **institutional mechanism**: Committee on Negro Work Memorandum to AFPS, Oct. 18, 1929, r. 2, b. 3, AFPSR. **"ultimate goal"**: WW to Joint Committee, July 20, 1937, r. 27, b. 44, AFPSR.

45. **on retainer**: WW to AFPS, Nov. 14, 1934, c. 163, MLEP.

46. **Marshall was born**: Juan Williams, *Thurgood Marshall: American Revolutionary* (Random House, 1998), 21–24. **"Thoroughgood"**: Carl T. Rowan, *Dream Makers, Dream Breakers: The World of Justice Thurgood Marshall* (Little, Brown, 1993), 40. **misbehavior... "try memorizing"**: Ibid., 34–35. **bootlegger's assistant**: Ibid., 40–41.

47. **whites-only**: Ibid., 42–45. **leading a cow**: John Shattuck, "The Centennial of Thurgood Marshall," John F. Kennedy Presidential Library and Museum, Kennedy Library Forums, 2008, jfklibrary.org/events-and-awards/kennedy-library-forums/past-forums/transcripts/the-centennial-of-thurgood-marshall. **law school**: Rowan, *Dream Makers, Dream Breakers*, 45–46.

48. **Howard**: Roger L. Goldman, *Thurgood Marshall: Justice for All* (Carroll & Graf, 1992). **fledgling lawyer**: Ibid., 22. **"'29 Ford"**: Sullivan, *Lift Every Voice*, 229–230; Gilbert King, *Devil in the Grove: Thurgood Marshall, the Groveland Boys, and the Dawn of a New America* (HarperCollins, 2012): 42–43.

49. **"drafting plans"**: Carl T. Rowan, *Dream Makers, Dream Breakers*, 71. **"iron shoes"**: Ware, "Setting the Stage," 33. **"almost"**: CHH, Memorandum to Joint Committee, Sept. 28, 1936, b. I-C-200, f.1, NAACPLC. **"anybody"**: CHH to Thurgood Marshall, Sept. 17, 1936, b. I-C-200, f. 1, NAACPLC.

50. **"often referred"**: Jack Greenberg, *Crusaders in the Courts: How a Dedicated Band of Lawyers Fought for the Civil Rights Revolution* (Basic Books, 1994), 56. **"years"**: "The Reminiscences of Thurgood Marshall," in *Thurgood Marshall: His Speeches, Writings, Arguments, Opinions, and Reminiscences*, ed. Mark V. Tushnet (Lawrence Hill Books, 2001), 462. **"blueprint... plan"**: Ibid., 423.

51. **NAACP study**: Tushnet, *NAACP's Legal Strategy Against Segregated Education*, 34.

52. **Hocutt**: Ibid., 52–53; WW to AFPS, May 26, 1933, r. 27, b. 44, AFPSR. **"conceived and started"**: CHH, Memorandum to Joint Committee, Oct. 26, 1934, r. 27, b. 44, AFPSR.

53. **"sonsabitches"**: Rowan, *Dream Makers, Dream Breakers*, 46. **Murray... "groundwork"**: Sullivan, *Lift Every Voice*, 208–9; Rowan, *Dream Makers, Dream Breakers*, 51; Tushnet, *Thurgood Marshall*, 17; [CHH], Memorandum to Joint Committee, July 29, 1935, r. 6, b. 9, ABSPL.

54. **American Fund subvention**: Rowan, *Dream Makers, Dream Breakers*, 55. **through Carl Murphy**: Ibid.; Joint Committee Meeting, Nov. 14, 1935, r. 6, b. 9, ABSP.

55. **Gaines**: Rowan, *Dream Makers, Dream Breakers*, 71. **attended school... "high school"**: James W. Endersby and William T. Horner, *Lloyd Gaines and the Fight to End Segregation* (University of Missouri Press, 2016), 11–12; Crystal R. Sanders, *A Forgotten Migration: Black Southerners, Segregation Scholarships, and the Debt Owed to Public HBCUs* (UNC Press, 2024), 71–84. **Lincoln University**: University of Missouri to Lloyd Gaines, Sept. 18, 1935, b. I-C-196, f. 11, NAACPLC. **Missouri**: Tushnet, *NAACP's Legal Strategy Against Segregated Education*, 71–74. **cited Plessy**: Missouri ex rel. Gaines v. Canada, 305 U.S. 337 (1938).

56. **"safeguard"... "usually futile"**: CHH to RNB, June 28, 1937, b. II-L-15, NAACPLC; see also r. 27, b. 44, AFPSR. **"tour Missouri"**: CHH to AFPS, Mar. 9, 1938, b. II-L-15, NAACPLC.

57. **distributed over $22,000**: Joint Committee Receipts and Disbursements, Dec. 31, 1937, r. 27, b. 44, AFPSR; WW to AFPS Board, June 22, 1937, b. I-C-200, f. 1, NAACPLC. **appealed to Charles Garland... "tenant farmers"**: CHH to RNB, June 28, 1937, r. 27, b. 44, AFPSR.

"obligation . . . no prospect": RNB to CHH, July 7, 1937, b. II-L-15, NAACPLC. ***Ernst disagreed***: CHH to AFPS, June 25, 1937, b. II-L-15, NAACPLC.
58. ***White protested***: WW to AFPS Board, June 22, 1937, b. I-C-198, f. 8, NAACPLC; LG to MLE, [n.d., late Oct. or early Nov. 1937]; WW to RNB, Oct. 1, 1937, both in c. 168, MLEP. *"Joint Committee"*: CHH, Memorandum to Joint Committee, Oct. 25, 1937, b. I-C-198, f. 8, NAACPLC; also in b. I-C-200, NAACPLC.
59. *"carry"*: CHH, Memorandum to NAACP, Nov. 3, 1937, b. I-C-198, f. 9, NAACPLC. ***agreed to hear***: CHH to RNB, Oct. 16, 1938, b. II-L-15, NAACPLC.
60. ***Supreme Court***: Endersby and Horner, *Lloyd Gaines and the Fight to End Segregation*, 89. ***McReynolds***: Ibid., 113–15. *"say that . . . civil rights"*: Ibid., 113.
61. *"to provide" . . . victory*: Missouri ex rel. Gaines v. Canada, 305 U.S. 337 (1938).
62. *"Houston's job"*: MLE to WW, Dec. 16, 1938, c. 168, MLEP.
63. ***Murray***: Glenda Elizabeth Gilmore, *Defying Dixie: The Radical Roots of Civil Rights, 1919–1950* (W. W. Norton, 2008), at 254. ***raised in Durham***: Rosalind Rosenberg, *Jane Crow: The Life of Pauli Murray* (Oxford University Press, 2017), 30–31. ***Black literary***: Ibid., 36. ***enrolled in classes***: Ibid., 54.
64. *"not admitted"*: Ibid., 70. ***Southern Tenant***: Ibid., 78; AFPS Gifts, 42, r. 5, b. 7, AFPSR.
65. ***prickly test-case plaintiff***: Endersby and Horner, *Lloyd Gaines and the Fight to End Segregation*, 92–93. *"foul play"*: Ibid., 219–20. ***Gaines's siblings***: Ibid., 230. *"look after myself"*: Ibid., 233. ***bribed . . . Mexico City***: Ibid., 218. ***old teachers***: Ibid., 235. ***furious***: Ibid., 218. *"walked out"*: Ibid., 219.
66. *"editorial criticism . . . colored people"*: Pauli Murray, "Defends Lloyd Gaines," *Afro-American*, Feb. 3, 1940, 4 (letter to the editor).
67. ***critics***: Risa L. Goluboff's *Lost Promise of Civil Rights* (Harvard University Press, 2007) is the leading exemplar in the modern literature. It is the great trailblazing accomplishment of scholars like Goluboff to have put the NAACP campaign into conversation with questions of labor and class.

19: USE THIS WEAPON

"sit-down": Charles F. Howlett, *Brookwood Labor College and the Struggle for Peace and Social Justice in America* (Edwin Mellen Press, 1993), 302.
1. ***ILGWU***: "Philadelphia Dress Strike Ends," *New York Times*, May 12, 1933, 4; Irving Bernstein, *Turbulent Years: A History of the American Worker, 1933–1941* (Houghton Mifflin, 1970), at 85. ***dress shops***: Ibid., 87–88. ***Reading . . . Paterson***: Ibid., 174–75. ***Los Angeles***: Ibid., 161.
2. *"rebel"*: RNB, "The Myth of Law and Order," in *Behold America!*, ed. Samuel D. Schmalhausen (Farrar & Rinehart, 1931), 660. ***miners***: Daniel Lewis, "The Mine War in Pennsylvania," *The Nation*, Aug. 16, 1933, 176. ***more***: See Harry R. Rubenstein, "The Great Gallup Coal Strike of 1933," *New Mexico Historical Review* 52 (1977): 173, 189. ***year . . . thereafter***: Bernstein, *Turbulent Years*, 172–73. ***stoppages***: Ibid., 217.
3. *"opportunity"*: Melvyn Dubofsky, *The State and Labor in Modern America* (University of North Carolina Press, 1994), 104.
4. ***Toledo***: See Roy Rosenzweig, "The Radicals and the Jobless: The Musteites and the Unemployed Leagues, 1932–1936," *Labor History* 16 (1975): 52–77. ***Passaic***: Howlett, *Brookwood Labor College and the Struggle*, 250. ***Gastonia***: Richard J. Altenbaugh, *Education for Struggle: The American Labor Colleges of the 1920s and 1930s* (Temple University Press, 1990), at 257–59. ***Ohio***: Bernstein, *Turbulent Years*, 221.
5. ***two Brookwood alumni***: Philip A. Korth and Margaret Beegle, *I Remember Like Today: The Auto-Lite Strike of 1934* (Michigan State University Press, 1989), at 111; see also Ted Selander, "The 1934 Toledo Auto Lite Strike," June 3, 1984, available at libcom.org/article/1934-toledo-auto-lite-strike-ted-selander. ***Auto-Lite***: Korth and Beegle, *I Remember Like Today*, 39. ***Federal Labor Union No. 18384***: Bernstein, *Turbulent Years*, 220; see also Rosenzweig, "The Radicals and the Jobless," 66; Selander, "1934 Toledo Auto Lite Strike."

6. *"Museites"*: Rosenzweig, "Radicals and the Jobless," 52, 53. *colleges*: Ibid., 56. *Leagues*: Nat Hentoff, *Peace Agitator: The Story of A. J. Muste* (Macmillan, 1963), at 86. *Lucas*: Korth and Beegle, *I Remember Like Today*, 16. *American*: See Bernstein, *Turbulent Years*, 221. *"nothing"*: Ibid., 221.
7. *Budenz*: Ibid., 221; see also Korth and Beegle, *I Remember Like Today*, 110; Len De Caux, *Labor Radical: From the Wobblies to CIO* (Beacon Press, 1970), 150. *supported*: RNB, Memorandum for AFPS, Apr. 12, 1926, r. 1, b. 1, AFPSR. *"organizational"*: Rosenzweig, "Radicals and the Jobless," 57. *Federal*: Bernstein, *Turbulent Years*, 220. *"Don't Tread"*: Roy Rosenzweig, "Organizing the Unemployed: The Early Years of the Great Depression, 1929-1933," in *Workers' Struggles, Past and Present*, ed. James Green (Temple University Press, 1988), 170. *"level"*: Hentoff, *Peace Agitator*, 87. *Muste's allies*: Bernstein, *Turbulent Years*, 222.
8. *"Battle" . . . city*: Ibid., 222-24.
9. *proved a success*: Ibid., 227-29.
10. *shirt-making shops*: Ibid., 77 (Jacob Potofsky). *United Mine Workers*: Ibid., 28 (W. Jett Lauck); see also W. Jett Lauck to RNB, June 19, 1928, r. 18, b. 25, AFPSR. *Steel Workers Organizing Committee*: Thomas R. Brooks, *Clint: A Biography of a Labor Intellectual, Clinton S. Golden* (Atheneum, 1978), 158-85 (Clinton Golden); also Merlyn S. Pitzele, "C.I.O. Big Shot," *Saturday Evening Post*, Feb. 19, 1944. *garment workers*: Brookwood Educational Advisory Committee, b. 24, f. 16, BLGR (Fannia Cohn); also Women's Research Foundation to AFPS, 1925, r. 33, b. 52, AFPSR. *coal miners*: Robert H. Zieger, *The CIO, 1935-1955* (University of North Carolina Press, 1995), at 28 (Powers Hapgood); Rubenstein, "Great Gallup Coal Strike," 176. *Dubinsky*: Howlett, *Brookwood Labor College and the Struggle*, 296; see also RNB, Memorandum to AFPS, Mar. 27, 1925, r. 23, b. 36, AFPSR; Bernstein, *Turbulent Years*, 77-89. *clothing workers*: Dorothy J. Bellanca to Tucker P. Smith, Sept. 23, 1936, b. 32, f. 21, ACWA. *Seattle*: Irving Bernstein, *The Lean Years: A History of the American Worker, 1920-1933* (Houghton Mifflin, 1960), at 416.
11. *breakaway*: Zieger, *CIO*, 22-25. *Brophy*: Ibid., 28; John Brophy, *A Miner's Life* (University of Wisconsin Press, 1964), 247-55. *Organizations*: Ibid., 90.
12. *"railway shopmen"*: See RNB, "Who's Got Free Speech?," [1923], b. 22, f. 1, RNBP. *"greatest strike"*: Bernstein, *Lean Years*, 211.
13. *Daugherty*: Colin J. Davis, "Bitter Conflict: The 1922 Railroad Shopmen's Strike," *Labor History* 33 (1992): 433, 451. *"distinctive"*: Felix Frankfurter and Nathan Greene, *The Labor Injunction* (Macmillan, 1930), 53. *"refuse"*: In re Debs, 158 U.S. 567, 571 (1895). *"unfair"*: Gompers v. Buck's Stove & Range Co., 221 U.S. 418 (1911).
14. *"jeers"*: Felix Frankfurter and James M. Landis, "The Power of Congress over Procedure in Criminal Contempts in 'Inferior' Federal Courts: A Study in Separation of Powers," *Harvard Law Review* 37 (1924): 1010, app. II at 1101. *"government"*: "Democratic Party Platform," July 7, 1896, available at presidency.ucsb.edu/documents/1896-democratic-party-platform. *free*: EFG, "Labor and the Law / The War on the Reds—The Struggle for Free Speech," [1924?], b. 1, f. 32, EGFP-NY. *"right"*: RNB, "Who's Got Free Speech?," [1923], b. 22, f. 1, RNBP.
15. *"best thing the state can do"*: William E. Forbath, "Law and the Shaping of the American Labor Movement," *Harvard Law Review* 102 (1989): 1109, 1112, n3; William E. Forbath, *Law and the Shaping of the American Labor Movement* (Harvard University Press, 1991). *"conflict theory"*: Walter Nelles to RNB, Feb. 18, 1924, r. 9, b. 13, AFPSR. *"state is against labor"*: Scott Nearing, Memorandum re Injunction Study, Jan. 28, 1924, r. 9, b. 13, AFPSR.
16. *Oklahoma and Kansas*: Agricultural Workers Industrial Union to AFPS, June 5, 1924, r. 14, b. 21, AFPSR. *Wabash System*: Organizing the Unorganized [n.d., 1930?], b. 6, f. 3, BGP; AFPS Board Meeting, May 9, 1923, r. 3, b. 5, AFPSR. *Injunction Defense Committee*: Our House to AFPS, Feb. 7, 1925, r. 32, b. 50, AFPSR. *United Anthracite Miners*: AFPS Board Meeting, Mar. 27, 1935, r. 4, b. 7, AFPSR.
17. *Hillquit . . . Federation*: Morris Hillquit to WN, June 12, 1923; MH to N. P. Good, June 25, 1923, both r. 11, b. 17, AFPSR.
18. *awarded . . . through the courts*: RNB to N. P. Good, Sept. 27, 1923, r. 11, b. 17, AFPSR; AFPS Gifts, r. 5, b. 8, 35, AFPSR. *suit met defeat*: Pennsylvania Fed'n v. Pennsylvania R. Co., 267 U.S. 205 (1925).

19. *large-scale study*: AFPS Board Meeting, Sept. 27, 1922; RNB to Evans Clark, Sept. 28, 1922, both r. 3, b. 5, AFPSR; RNB to AFPS, Sept. 27, 1922, r. 9, b. 13, AFPSR. *Nelles*: Evans Clark to NT, Nov. 10, 1922; MLE to RNB, Oct. 15, 1923, both r. 9, b. 13, AFPSR; "Prof. Walter Nelles of Yale Law School: An Expert on Labor Injunction and Former Lawyer Here Is Dead at Age of 53," *New York Times*, Apr. 1, 1937, 23. *"interested" & "primary"*: Walter Nelles to Lewis Gannett, July 17, 1923, r. 9, b. 13, AFPSR. *"furnish"*: WN to RNB, Feb. 18, 1924, r. 9, b. 13, AFPSR. *"want law to do"*: Walter Nelles, "Review of Ethical Systems and Legal Ideals by Felix S. Cohen," *Columbia Law Review* 33 (1933): 763, 764; Laura Kalman, *Legal Realism at Yale, 1927–1960* (University of North Carolina Press, 1986), 40–41; Daniel Ernst, "Common Laborers? Industrial Pluralists, Legal Realists, and the Law of Industrial Disputes, 1915–1943," *Law & History Review* 11 (1993): 59–100.
20. *generous support*: AFPS Gifts, r. 5, b. 8, 21, AFPSR. *Hale*: Robert L. Hale, "Coercion and Distribution in a Supposedly Liberal State," *Political Science Quarterly* 38 (1923): 470–94; Barbara H. Fried, *The Progressive Assault on Laissez Faire: Robert Hale and the First Law and Economics Movement* (Harvard University Press, 1998).
21. *"Bedford . . . barren"*: Walter Nelles, "The First American Labor Case," *Yale Law Journal* 41 (1931): 165, 183–84.
22. *"peace, freedom and happiness"*: Ibid., 184.
23. *"affirmative legal action"*: WN to AFPS, Dec. 14, 1925, c. 170, MLEP; Arthur Garfield Hays to RNB, Oct. 1, 1925, r. 5, b. 9, AFPSR; MLE to NT, June 15, 1926, c. 162, MLEP. *member*: Grace Poole et al., *The American Labor Who's Who* (Hanford Press, 1925), 170. *"on the defensive"*: WN to AFPS, Dec. 14, 1925, c. 170, MLEP. *Hillquit*: Edwin E. Witte, "Labor's Resort to Injunctions," *Yale Law Journal* 39 (1930): 374, 376; Charles Kutz to AFPS, May 15, 1923, r. 11, b. 17, AFPSR. *King*: RNB to Carol Weiss King, [n.d.], r. 32, b. 50, AFPSR. *Lowenthal*: Steven Fraser, *Labor Will Rule: Sidney Hillman and the Rise of American Labor* (Free Press, 1991), 163; AFPS Board Meeting, Mar. 26, 1924, r. 3, b. 5, AFPSR. *"aggressive legal tactics"*: Clement Wood and McAlister Coleman, *Don't Tread on Me: A Study of Aggressive Legal Tactics for Labor* (Vanguard Press, 1928); see also Laura Weinrib, *The Taming of Free Speech: America's Civil Liberties Compromise* (Harvard University Press, 2016), 188; Forbath, *Law and the Shaping of the American Labor Movement*, 118–27. *"Use"*: Arthur Garfield Hays, "Use This Weapon," *Labor Age*, July 1926, 15–16. *"jungle-land of the injunction"*: John F. Gatelee, "Fight Them Intelligently," *Labor Age*, July 1926, 17.
24. *work alongside the Fund*: Felix Frankfurter to EGF, [July 1926], r. 12, b. 18, AFPSR; see also Gloria Garrett Samson, *The American Fund for Public Service: Charles Garland and Radical Philanthropy, 1922–1941* (Greenwood Press, 1996), at 169, 208. *injunctions*: Committee on Research and Publications Report, Oct. 17, 1929, r. 1, b. 1, AFPSR; see also Frankfurter and Greene, *Labor Injunction*.
25. *bitter 1920 strike*: Fraser, *Labor Will Rule*, 163. *defended . . . Weisbord*: Senate Judiciary Committee, *Hearings on Felix Frankfurter Nomination to Supreme Court*, 34, Part 3, Hearings, FFPH.
26. *eliminate the labor injunction*: Committee on Research and Publications Report, Oct. 17, 1929, r. 1, b. 1, AFPSR. *Norris*: Bernstein, *Lean Years*, 396. *little love*: WN to EGF, Sept. 9, 1925, r. 1, b. 1, AFPSR. *"Government . . . association"*: Frankfurter and Greene, *Labor Injunction*, 211.
27. *Richberg . . . was representing*: APR to Milton Webster, Dec. 22, 1926, b. 1, f. 6, BSCPR.
28. *National Committee on Labor Injunctions*: ACLU to Oswald Garrison Villard, Nov. 18, 1930, vol. 380, ACLUA. *grants*: AFPS Board Meeting, Feb. 25, 1931, r. 4, b. 7, AFPSR; AFPS Gifts, r. 5, b. 8, 35, AFPSR. *bill's success*: Bernstein, *Lean Years*, 416; see also Norris–La Guardia Act, 47 Stat. 70 (1932).
29. *"notable change"*: ACLU, *Sweet Land of Liberty, 1931–1932* (American Civil Liberties Union, 1932), at 16.
30. *Hillman*: Fraser, *Labor Will Rule*, 285–87.
31. *Wagner*: Forbath, "Law and the Shaping of the American Labor Movement," 1198–99. *working group*: Bernstein, *Lean Years*, 28; Fraser, *Labor Will Rule*, 285–87.
32. *Recovery Act . . . "fair competition"*: National Industrial Recovery Act, 48 Stat. 195 § 10(a) (1933). *"price cutting"*: 48 Stat. 195 § 4(b).

33. *"safeguards"*: Stanley Vittoz, *New Deal Labor Policy and the American Industrial Economy* (University of North Carolina Press, 1987), 89. *"right to organize"*: 48 Stat. 195 § 7(a). *"free from"*: Norris–La Guardia Act, 47 Stat. 70 (1932).
34. *Hillman took a seat*: Steven Fraser, "Sidney Hillman: Labor's Machiavelli," in *Labor Leaders in America*, ed. Melvyn Dubofsky et al. (University of Illinois Press, 1987), 284, 293–94. **Wagner as the chair**: Bernstein, *Turbulent Years*, 173. **Leiserson**: Fraser, "Sidney Hillman," 295; Jessica Wang, "Local Knowledge, State Power, and the Science of Industrial Labor Relations: William Leiserson, David Saposs, and American Labor Economics in the Interwar Years," *Journal of the History of the Behavioral Sciences* 46 (2010): 371–93.
35. *labor dispute . . . collective bargaining*: Vittoz, *New Deal Labor Policy and the American Industrial Economy*, 138; Bernstein, *Turbulent Years*, 174.
36. *"Reading Formula"*: Ibid., 175; Vittoz, *New Deal Labor Policy and the American Industrial Economy*, 139. **Brookwood**: Bernstein, *Turbulent Years*, 221. *"representatives of their own choice"*: Pennsylvania Fed'n v. Pennsylvania R. Co., 267 U.S. 206 (1925).
37. *radical wing & National Committee*: Cletus E. Daniel, *The ACLU and the Wagner Act: An Inquiry into the Depression-Era Crisis of American Liberalism* (Cornell University Press, 1980), 35–38. **aid to breakaway miners**: Applications for Assistance July to Sept. 1922, r. 3, b. 5, AFPSR
38. *"rival unions"*: Daniel, *ACLU and the Wagner Act*, 35. *"majority must rule"*: Bernstein, *Turbulent Years*, 28. *"maintain living standards"*: Daniel, *ACLU and the Wagner Act*, 38. *"recognition . . . class struggle"*: Ibid., 42–43.
39. *Hillman's dismay*: Fraser, *Labor Will Rule*, 294. **Weirton & Budd**: Dubofsky, *State and Labor in Modern America*, 127; Bernstein, *Turbulent Years*, 177–79. **struck it down**: A. L. A. Schechter Poultry Corp. v. United States, 295 U.S. 495 (1935).
40. *"self-government in industry"*: Christopher L. Tomlins, *The State and the Unions: Labor Relations, Law, and the Organized Labor Movement in America, 1880–1960* (Cambridge University Press, 1985), at 105. The prominence of Fund-world labor intellectuals in the formation of New Deal labor law was nothing short of astonishing. Leon Keyserling, Wagner's economic advisor in the Senate, had studied law at Harvard, as had the solicitor of the Labor Department, Charles Wyzanski, who owed his job to his Harvard mentor Frankfurter. At the National Labor Board, Leiserson brought his expertise from labor arbitration in the textile industry. Lauck from the UMW inner circle exerted influence. So did Wolman at the Amalgamated Clothing Workers and now serving on the National Labor Board. Heber Blankenhorn joined Wagner's group, too. Blankenhorn, who had spread propaganda in World War I with Walter Lippmann, who had countered employer propaganda in the Steel Strike of 1919, and who had written a book on labor's use of affirmative legal tactics with support from the Fund, now came on as a public relations staffer. Labor economist Isador Lubin, who had worked closely with Hillman until Roosevelt's election, contributed his views from the Bureau of Labor Statistics. At the Department of Labor, the former Brookwood instructor David Saposs offered a report critical of company unions. And at the Twentieth Century Fund, American Fund director Freda Kirchwey's husband, Evans Clark, launched a campaign on behalf of the Wagner Act's model.
41. *"economic power"*: Laura Weinrib, "Civil Liberties Outside the Courts," *Supreme Court Review* 2014 (2015): 297, 362. *"Capitalist courts"*: Robert W. Dunn and Clarina Michelson, "Labor Research Association, Why the Wagner Labor Dispute Bill Is Anti-Labor," 1935, b. 2, f. 8, CMP.
42. *"whether we will it"*: Robert F. Wagner to RNB, Apr. 5, 1935, vol. 780, ACLUA. *"your opposition"*: Joseph Schlossberg to RNB, May 14, 1935, b. 136, f. 16, ACWA.
43. *"defines"*: Franklin D. Roosevelt, "Statement on Signing the National Labor Relations Act," July 5, 1935, presidency.ucsb.edu/documents/statement-signing-the-national-labor-relations-act.
44. *"self-organization"*: National Labor Relations Act, 49 Stat. 449 § 157 (1935). *"concerted activities"*: 49 Stat. 449 § 157. **Saposs & Golden**: Wang, "Local Knowledge, State Power," 380; Thomas R. Brooks, *Clint*, 125–26.

45. *"flow . . . commerce"*: 49 Stat. 449 § 151. *"wasteful economic strife"*: Roosevelt, "Statement on Signing the National Labor Relations Act." *"square deal . . . collectively to cease labor"*: Tomlins, *State and the Unions*, 111.
46. **stopped work**: James Gray Pope, "Worker Lawmaking, Sit-Down Strikes, and the Shaping of American Industrial Relations, 1935–1958," *Law & History Review* 24 (2006): 45, 49–50. *"substantial concessions"*: Ibid., 54. **South Bend . . . Pontiac**: Bernstein, *Turbulent Years*, 523.
47. **Gregg**: Howlett, *Brookwood Labor College and the Struggle*, 303; Joseph Kip Kosek, "Richard Gregg, Mohandas Gandhi, and the Strategy of Nonviolence," *Journal of American History* 92 (2005): 1318–48. *"mass non-violence"*: Richard Gregg, *The Power of Non-Violence* (George Routledge, 1935), 22.
48. *"arms folded"*: AJM, *The Reminiscences of A. J. Muste* (1972), 382, CCOH. **best Brookwood tradition**: Howlett, *Brookwood Labor College and the Struggle*, 302.
49. *"net of ideas"*: Kosek, "Richard Gregg, Mohandas Gandhi, and the Strategy of Nonviolence," 1335 (citing Gregg, *Power of Non-Violence*, 151).
50. **Reuther brothers**: See Nelson Lichtenstein, *The Most Dangerous Man in Detroit: Walter Reuther and the Fate of American Labor* (Basic Books, 1995).
51. *"prime issues of the day"*: Victor Reuther, *The Brothers Reuther and the Story of the UAW: A Memoir* (Houghton Mifflin, 1976), 58. **reading list**: Ibid., 59–60.
52. **connections**: Lichtenstein, *Most Dangerous Man in Detroit*, 51. **Roy . . . . bargaining agreements**: Labor Problems and Sketch of American Labor Movement, Aug. 1936, series I, b. 1, RPP. **Hillman to Brookwood**; Roy Reuther to Sydney Hillman, Jan. 16, 1926, b. 83, f. 19, ACWA.
53. *"unofficial"*: Howlett, *Brookwood Labor College and the Struggle*, 183. **eighteen-month stay**: Lichtenstein, *Most Dangerous Man in Detroit*, 36, 50. **Smith . . . *"running away"***: Ibid., 51–52. *"several thousand"*: Ibid., 58.
54. **Local 174**: Reuther, *Brothers Reuther and the Story of the UAW*, 130. *"recent developments"*: Lichtenstein, *Most Dangerous Man in Detroit*, 67. **punch press operator**: Reuther, *Brothers Reuther and the Story of the UAW*, 133. **took positions**: Ibid., 135–39. *"strikers"*: Ibid., 136. *"plug uglies" . . . intervene*: Ibid., 70. *"marched . . . wage hike"*: Ibid., 140–41.
55. **Fisher Body**: Reuther, *Brothers Reuther and the Story of the UAW*, 147. **Murphy**: Ibid., 150, 158. **two Fisher plants . . . strike**: Ibid., 152–54; see also Howlett, *Brookwood Labor College and the Struggle*, 306.
56. **ladder . . . flair**: Reuther, *Brothers Reuther and the Story of the UAW*, 152–53. *"food"*: Jeremy Blecher, *Strike!* (PM Press, 1972), 215. **Rules**: Bernstein, *Turbulent Years*, 526.
57. *"trespassers"*: Bernstein, *Turbulent Years*, 528. *"property"*: Ibid., 539. **local judge . . . Murphy**: Ibid., 528–29.
58. **Brookwood graduate . . . on loan**: Reuther, *Brothers Reuther and the Story of the UAW*, 151 (Rose Pesotta). **reported on the strike**: Howlett, *Brookwood Labor College and the Struggle*, 103, 171–72 (Carl Haessler for Federated Press); Carl Haessler, "Behind the Auto Strike," *New Masses*, Feb. 2, 1937, 3–5. **progressive wing of the UMW**: John Brophy, *A Miner's Life* (University of Wisconsin Press, 1964), 268–69.
59. **Running Bulls**: Reuther, *Brothers Reuther and the Story of the UAW*, 157, 187–89. **crucial juncture**: Bernstein, *Turbulent Years*, 538–39. **Perkins**: Ibid., 540–45. **Baldwin's invitation**: RNB to Frances Perkins, Apr. 4, 1922, r. 1, b. 1, AFPSR.
60. *"sit-down strike . . . Brookwood grads"*: Howlett, *Brookwood Labor College and the Struggle*, 302.
61. **River Rouge . . . *"Fordism"***: Lichtenstein, *Most Dangerous Man in Detroit*, 83. **Gate**: Bernstein, *Turbulent Years*, 570–71. *"fight" & "fists"*: Lichtenstein, *Most Dangerous Man in Detroit*, 84. *"accepts blow"*: Gregg, *Power of Non-Violence*, 26.
62. **Battle of the Overpass**: Lichtenstein, *Most Dangerous Man in Detroit*, 85.
63. **elected president**: Reuther, *Brothers Reuther and the Story of the UAW*, 22. *"most dangerous man"*: Lichtenstein, *Most Dangerous Man in Detroit*, 320. **championed civil rights**: Nelson Lichtenstein, "Walter Reuther in Black and White: A Rejoinder to Herbert Hill," *New Politics* 7 (1999): 7.

20: SWITCH IN TIME

"Only power": Quoted in Jervis Anderson, *A. Philip Randolph: A Biographical Portrait* (Harcourt Brace, 1972), 248.

1. **struck down laws**: William E. Forbath, *Law and the Shaping of the American Labor Movement* (Harvard University Press, 1991); John Fabian Witt, *The Accidental Republic: Crippled Workingmen, Destitute Widows, and the Remaking of American Law* (Harvard University Press, 2004). **National Recovery Act**: Schechter Poultry v. United States, 295 U.S. 495 (1935). **protecting farmers**: Home Building & Loan Ass'n v. Blaisdell, 290 U.S. 398 (1934). **federal retirement program**: Railroad Retirement Board v. Alton Railroad Co., 295 U.S. 330 (1935). **minimum-wage laws**: Morehead v. New York ex rel. Tipaldo, 298 U.S. 587 (1936). **federal agriculture law**: United States v. Butler, 297 U.S. 1 (1936). **coal industry**: Carter v. Carter Coal Co., 298 U.S. 238 (1936). **observers speculated**: Alan Brinkley, *The End of Reform: New Deal Liberalism in Recession and War* (Knopf, 1995); William E. Leuchtenberg, *The Supreme Court Reborn: The Constitutional Revolution in the Age of Roosevelt* (Oxford University Press, 1996).

2. *"Court packing"*: Laura Kalman, *FDR's Gambit: The Court Packing Fight and the Rise of Legal Liberalism* (Oxford University Press, 2022). **upheld the Wagner Act and other reform laws**: NLRB v. Jones & Laughlin Steel Corp., 301 U.S. 1 (1937) (Wagner Act); West Coast Hotel v. Parrish, 300 U.S. 379 (1937) (minimum wage). **abrupt turn**: Dan E. Ho and Kevin M. Quinn, "Did a Switch in Time Save Nine?," *Journal of Legal Analysis* 2 (2010): 69. *"switch in time"*: John Q. Barrett, "Attribution Time: Cal Tinney's 1937 Quip, 'A Switch in Time'll Save Nine,'" *Oklahoma Law Review* 73 (2021): 229.

3. **conservative Court**: Bruce Ackerman, *We the People: Foundations* (Belknap Press, 1991); Leuchtenberg, *Supreme Court Reborn*; but see Barry Cushman, *Rethinking the New Deal Court: The Structure of a Constitutional Revolution* (Oxford University Press, 1998). **a culmination**: Drew Hansen, "The Sit-Down Strikes and the Switch in Time," *Wayne Law Review* 46 (2000): 49. **Oregon Communist**: De Jonge v. Oregon, 299 U.S. 353 (1937). **Steel Workers Organizing Committee**: Robert H. Zieger, *The CIO: 1935–1955* (University of North Carolina Press, 1995), at 63–65. *"No single decision"*: RNB, *The Reminiscences of Roger Baldwin, 1953–1954*, at 176, CCOH. **Black communist**: Herndon v. Lowry, 301 U.S. 242 (1937); Brad Snyder, *You Can't Kill a Man Because of the Books He Reads: Angelo Herndon's Fight for Free Speech* (W. W. Norton, 2025). SWOC organizers with close connections to the American Fund and Brookwood included beneficiary John Brophy and director Clinton Golden.

4. **shrunk ... to 650**: William H. Harris, *Keeping the Faith: A. Philip Randolph, Milton P. Webster, and the Brotherhood of Sleeping Car Porters* (University of Illinois Press, 1977), 183. **regional offices**: Jervis Anderson, *A. Philip Randolph: A Biographical Portrait* (Harcourt Brace, 1972). **electricity and the phones**: Theodore Kornweibel Jr., *No Crystal Stair: Black Life and the Messenger, 1917–1928* (Greenwood Press, 1975), at 271. **Rent parties ... evicted**: Eric Arnesen, *Brotherhoods of Color: Black Railroad Workers and the Struggle for Equality* (Harvard University Press, 2001), 93. **corruption**: Draft of Mr. Bagnall's Proposed Report of Committee [n.d., Jan. 1929], b. 3, f. 18, FRCP. **inquiry**: Brotherhood of Sleeping Car Porters, r. 17, AFPSR. **directors demurred**: Brotherhood of Sleeping Car Porters, r. 34, AFPSR. Baldwin briefly seized on Randolph's injunction effort at Pullman as a way of diverting money away from the joint NAACP–American Fund litigation program. But Randolph declined, telling Baldwin that the NAACP efforts were "far-reaching and vital." APR to RNB, Sept. 27, 1930, r. 34, AFPSR.

5. **penniless ... holes**: Anderson, *A. Philip Randolph*, 213–14. **union was dead**: Abram L. Harris and Sterling D. Spero, *The Black Worker: The Negro and the Labor Movement* (Columbia University Press, 1931), 460.

6. **lobby for amendments**: Arnesen, *Brotherhoods of Color*, 94. **formally admitted**: Harris, *Keeping the Faith*, 209. **resounding victory**: Ibid., 206–7. **confident**: Ibid., 209–10.

7. **upheld ... Railway Labor Act**: Virginian Railway Co. v. System Federation No. 40, 300 U.S. 515 (1937). **Within three days**: Anderson, *A. Philip Randolph*, 224. **historic ... agreement**: Arnesen, *Brotherhoods of Color*, 95. *"vanguard"*: Quoted in Anderson, *A. Philip Randolph*, 220.

8. *same Arkansas cotton fields*: Nan Elizabeth Woodruff, *American Congo: The African American Freedom Struggle in the Delta* (Harvard University Press, 2003), 152 ff.; Jason Manthorne, "The View from the Cotton: Reconsidering the Southern Tenant Farmers Union," *Agricultural History* 84 (2010): 20–45. *further impoverished*: "Wages in Cotton Picking in 1935," *Monthly Labor Review* 42 (1936): 180; Agricultural Adjustment Act of 1933, 48 Stat. 31 (1933). *worse for tenant farmers*: Jack Temple Kirby, *Rural Worlds Lost: The American South, 1920–1960* (Louisiana State University Press, 1987), at 60–65.

9. *Norman Thomas... helped found*: The Reminiscences of Norman Thomas, 45, CCOH; Robin D. G. Kelley, *Hammer and Hoe: Alabama Communists During the Great Depression*, rev. ed. (University of North Carolina Press, 2015) (1990), 157–75; David Eugene Conrad, *The Forgotten Farmers: The Story of Sharecroppers in the New Deal* (University of Illinois Press, 1965), 82–95. *"Aren't we all brothers"*: Manthorne, "Reconsidering the Southern Tenant Farmers Union," 21. *"life, liberty"*: STFU, A Program for Action, Southern Tenant Farmers' Union (1934), r. 1, STFUR. *representation... collective bargaining*: Ibid.; Donald H. Grubbs, *Cry from the Cotton: The Southern Tenant Farmers Union and the New Deal* (University of North Carolina Press, 1971), 67ff. *defense efforts... mass demonstrations*: STFU, Program for Action.

10. *"most important development"*: Norman Thomas, *The Plight of the Share-Cropper* (League for Industrial Democracy, 1934), 35. *"reign of terror"*: STFU, Black Terror in Arkansas, r. 3, STFUR; Conrad, *Forgotten Farmers*, 158. *bum-rushed*: Thomas, *The Plight of the Share-Cropper*, 36. *machine guns*: Woodruff, *American Congo*, 173.

11. *modest annual grants*: Gifts to June 30, 1941, 42, r. 5, AFPSR. *10 percent... yearly budget*: H. L. Mitchell and Howard Kester to AFPS, Dec. 24, 1936, r. 3, STFUR. *three-quarters of... budget*: Grubbs, *Cry from the Cotton*, 78–79. *25,000 members*: Conrad, *Forgotten Farmers*, 173. *"maintain the morale"*: Howard Kester to Charles Garland, Mar. 1, 1936, r. 1, STFUR. *"bootheel"*: Conrad, *Forgotten Farmers*, 77. *increased the pay*: H. L. Mitchell to Frank Morrison, Oct. 4, 1935, r. 1, STFUR. *protests at the Department of Agriculture*: Jerold Auerbach, "Southern Tenant Farmers: Socialist Critics of the New Deal," *Arkansas Historical Quarterly* 27 (1968): 113. *La Follette*: Grubbs, *Cry from the Cotton*, 97–98; Laura Weinrib, *The Taming of Free Speech: America's Civil Liberties Compromise* (Harvard University Press, 2016), 204–9.

12. *May 1935 conference*: Eric Arnesen, "The Making and Breaking of a Popular Front: The Case of the National Negro Congress," *Labor: Studies in Working-Class History* 20 (2023): 5; Erik S. Gelman, *Death Blow to Jim Crow: The National Negro Congress and the Rise of Militant Civil Rights* (University of North Carolina Press, 2012). *"Position of the Negro"*: Program, National Conference Under the Auspices of Joint Committee on National Recovery Social Science Division of Howard University, [May 18–20, 1935], WEBDBP. *Young Turks... Robert Dunn*: Ibid.; Beth Tompkins Bates, "A New Crowd Challenges the Agenda of the Old Guard in the NAACP, 1933–1941," *American Historical Review* 102 (1997): 340, 360; Raymond Wolters, *Negroes and the Great Depression: The Problem of Recovery* (Greenwood, 1970), 353–82. *Popular Front*: Maurice Isserman, *Reds: The Tragedy of American Communism* (Basic Books, 2024), 131–40.

13. *revived A. Philip Randolph*: Jeff Henderson, "A. Philip Randolph and the Dilemmas of Socialism and Black Nationalism in the United States, 1917–1941," *Race & Class* 20 (1978): 143, 155. *young... John P. Davis*: Gelman, *Death Blow to Jim Crow*, 9–18; Wolters, *Negroes and the Great Depression*, 373–76; Minutes of the Meeting of the Board of Directors, Oct. 8, 1934, NAACPP. *Clinton Golden... in steel mills*: Erik S. Gellman, "The Spirit and Strategy of the United Front: Randolph and the National Negro Congress, 1936–1940," in *Reframing Randolph: Labor, Black Freedom, and the Legacies of A. Philip Randolph*, ed. Andrew E. Kersten and Clarence Lang (New York University Press, 2015), 129–62. *automobile industry*: Henderson, "A. Philip Randolph," 155. *anti-lynching & Scottsboro*: A. Philip Randolph, "The Crisis of the Negro and the Constitution (1937)," in Elliott M. Rudwick and August Meier, *Negro Protest Thought in the Twentieth Century* (Bobbs-Merrill, 1965), 179–85. *local councils... rent strikes*: Bates, "New Crowd Challenges," 349.

14. *old-line AFL... led picketers*: Gellman, "Spirit and Strategy," 139. *John Brophy & "Randolph

Resolution": John Brophy–Sidney Hillman Correspondence, b. 68, f. 40, ACWA. *"Fools and Cowards"*: Quoted in Gellman, "Spirit and Strategy," 135–36.
15. *"capitalist prosperity"* . . . *"against exploitation"*: Resolutions of the National Negro Congress Held in Chicago, Ill., February 14, 15, 16, 1936 (NNC, 1936), at 3. *urged industrial unions*: Wolters, *Negroes and the Great Depression*, 360–61. *Bill of Rights for Black people*: Richard Wright, "Two Million Black Voices," *New Masses*, Feb. 25, 1936, 15. *"fighting for race rights"*: Gellman, "Spirit and Strategy," 138; Randolph, "Negro and the Constitution," 186–87. At his second presidential address in 1937, Randolph struck a mix of social democratic and liberal notes ranging from a defense of the freedom of speech without which "oppressed minority groups could hardly exist," to a rejection of the Black Belt thesis in favor of the principle that Black people had always been "an integral part of the American commonwealth." Voicing the language of Sidney Hillman's new unionism and recalling his own work with the Brotherhood, Randolph denounced company unions and embraced collective bargaining as the mechanism by which Black and white workers alike could free themselves "from economic bondage" and "express their voice." See APR, "The Crisis of the Negro and the Constitution," in Rudwick and Meier, *Negro Protest Thought in the Twentieth Century*, 186–87.
16. *takeover*: William H. Cobb and Donald H. Grubbs, "Arkansas' Commonwealth College and the Southern Tenant Farmers' Union," *Arkansas Historical Quarterly* 25 (1966): 293. *effort to capture*: Norman Thomas to H. L. Mitchell, May 14, 1936, r. 2, STFUR; National Committee on Rural Social Planning to H. L. Mitchell, Oct. 21, 1936, r. 3, STFUR. *attempt to assassinate*: Ibid.; Lowell K. Dyson, "The Southern Tenant Farmers Union and Depression Politics," *Political Science Quarterly* 88 (1973): 230, 238. *expelled*: Grubbs, *Cry from the Cotton*, 174–75. *Fund-orchestrated merger*: Ibid., 166–80; Gardner Jackson, The Reminiscences of Gardner Jackson, 1965, at 749–50, CCOH. *hemorrhaged members*: Manthorne, "View from the Cotton," 40; Grubbs, *Cry from the Cotton*, 187–90.
17. *NAACP formally outside*: Patricia Sullivan, *Lift Every Voice: The NAACP and the Making of the Civil Rights Movement* (New Press, 2009), 219–20. *bore from within*: Anderson, *A. Philip Randolph*, 234–35. *Preoccupied . . . did not object*: Andrew E. Kersten, *A. Philip Randolph: A Life in the Vanguard* (Rowman & Littlefield, 2007), 49–50.
18. *Pact*: Isserman, *Reds*, 176–77. *third meeting*: Anderson, *A. Philip Randolph*, 234–35; Arnesen, "Making and Breaking," 38–41; Gellman, "Spirit and Strategy," 130, 139. *"own grave"*: Quoted in Anderson, *A. Philip Randolph*, 238. *"a definite menace"*: A. Philip Randolph, "Why I Would Not Stand for Re-Election for President of the National Negro Congress (1940)," in Kersten and Lucander, *For Jobs and Freedom*, 187. Others in the crowd at the NNC convention saw things differently. The novelist Ralph Ellison, then a young Communist, reported sitting "through the address with a feeling of betrayal" as he watched "a leader in the act of killing his leadership." Quoted in Arnesen, "Making and Breaking," 40. With its hard turn to the party line now laid bare, and lacking Randolph's thousands of Pullman porters, the NNC became a paper-thin front group until it expired six years later.
19. *twice with Abraham Lincoln*: David W. Blight, *Frederick Douglass: Prophet of Freedom* (Simon & Schuster, 2018), 408–9, 436–37. *Booker T. Washington*: Deborah Davis, *Guest of Honor: Booker T. Washington, Theodore Roosevelt, and the White House Dinner That Shocked a Nation* (Atria, 2012); Robert J. Norrell, "When Teddy Roosevelt Invited Booker T. Washington to Dine at the White House," *Journal of Blacks in Higher Education* 63 (2009): 70. *1925 . . . delegation*: Kersten, *A. Philip Randolph*, 53–54. *to press Roosevelt*: Walter White, *A Man Called White: The Autobiography of Walter White* (Viking, 1948), 186–87; Doris Kearns Goodwin, *No Ordinary Time—Franklin and Eleanor Roosevelt, The Home Front in World War II* (Simon & Schuster, 1994), at 167–68.
20. *Roosevelt had requested*: Goodwin, *No Ordinary Time*, 248–52. *organizing for months*: Anderson, *A. Philip Randolph*, 247–48; James Forman, *The Making of Black Revolutionaries* (Macmillan, 1972), 30. *risked embarrassing*: Roger Daniels, *Franklin Roosevelt: The War Years, 1939–1945* (University of Illinois Press, 2016), at 333–35.
21. *campaign for Black employment*: Michael Mann, "A. Philip Randolph: Radicalizing Rights at

the Intersection of Class and Race," in *African American Political Thought*, ed. Melvin L. Rogers and Jack Turner (University of Chicago Press, 2021), 290-313. *"get us anywhere"*: Anderson, *A. Philip Randolph*, 247-48. *"10,000 Negroes"*: Ibid.

22. *five hundred unemployed*: Benjamin F. Alexander, *Coxey's Army: Popular Protest in the Gilded Age* (Johns Hopkins University Press, 2015). ***Depression-era veterans***: Paul Dickson and Thomas B. Allen, *The Bonus Army: An American Epic* (Walker Books, 2004). ***traveled the country***: Paula F. Pfeffer, *A. Philip Randolph, Pioneer of the Civil Rights Movement* (Louisiana State University Press, 1990), 47-49. *aides . . . raised questions*: Anderson, *A. Philip Randolph*, 247-48. *"national defense" . . . "gloves off"*: Ibid., 248-49.

23. ***March on Washington Committee***: Ibid., 249-50. *"more pressure"*: A. Philip Randolph, "Call to Negro America to March on Washington for Jobs and Equal Participation in National Defense," *Black Worker*, May 1941. *"100,000 Negroes march"*: Anderson, *A. Philip Randolph*, 251.

24. *old allies*: Ibid., 253; Henderson, "A. Philip Randolph and the Dilemmas," 157.

25. *hoped to stop*: Daniels, *Franklin Roosevelt*, 333-35. *implored Randolph*: Goodwin, *No Ordinary Time*, 248-52. *ally Sidney Hillman*: Anderson, *A. Philip Randolph*, 252; Steven Fraser, *Labor Will Rule: Sidney Hillman and the Rise of American Labor* (Free Press, 1991), 479. *insisted on*: David Leonhardt, *Ours Was the Shining Future: The Story of the American Dream* (Random House, 2023), 127-29.

26. *"sledge hammer"*: Goodwin, *No Ordinary Time*, 251.

27. *"no discrimination"*: Exec. Order No. 8802, *Code of Federal Regulations* 3 (1938-1943), 957.

28. *"man of the hour" . . . "most astonishing"*: Anderson, *A. Philip Randolph*, 262. *"power plays"*: Lerone Bennett Jr., *Before the Mayflower: A History of the Negro in America, 1619-1966* (Johnson, 1966), at 304. *"only mass action"*: Lucy G. Barber, *Marching on Washington: The Forging of an American Political Tradition* (Oxford University Press, 2004), 109 (quoting "Roosevelt's Executive Order," *Chicago Defender*, July 12, 1941, 14).

29. *a quarter*: Compare Robert Korstad and Nelson Lichtenstein, "Opportunities Found and Lost: Labor, Radicals, and the Early Civil Rights Movement," *Journal of American History* 75 (1988): 786, 787 (half million), with Robert H. Zieger, *The CIO: 1935-1955* (University of North Carolina Press, 1995), at 152-53, 420 n34 (300,000). *90 percent*: Bureau of the Census, *Sixteenth Census of the United States: 1940, Population* (Government Printing Office, 1943), 2:9. *mining . . . textiles*: Zieger, *The CIO*, 83-84. *persistent Jim Crowism*: Paul Frymer, *Black and Blue: African Americans, the Labor Movement, and the Decline of the Democratic Party* (Princeton University Press, 2008), 51. *railroad brotherhoods*: Arnesen, *Brotherhoods of Color*, 203-29. *boilermakers . . . paper*: Frymer, *Black and Blue*, 51.

30. *original 1930 draft*: Committee on Negro Work, Memorandum to the Directors of the AFPS, n.d. [1929-1930], b. I-C-197, f. 7, NAACPLC. *Kirchwey*: Freda Kirchwey to Lewis Gannett, Feb. 5, 1930, c. 169.4, MLEP. *Margold's influential*: Nathan Margold, Preliminary Report to the Joint Committee Supervising the Expenditure of the 1930 Appropriation by the American Fund for Public Service to the NAACP, 217-18, b. I-C-200, NAACPLC.

31. *offered to help*: Nathan Margold to Walter White, Oct. 22, 1934, b. I-C-196, f. 10, NAACPLC. *exclusive . . . authority*: Christopher Tomlins, *The State and the Unions: Labor Relations, Law, and the Organized Labor Movement in America, 1880-1960* (Cambridge University Press, 1985), at 99-147. *exclude minority workers*: Herbert Hill, *Black Labor and the American Legal System* (University of Wisconsin Press, 1977), 93-105; Deborah Malamud, "The Story of *Steele v. Louisville & Nashville Railroad*: White Unions, Black Unions, and the Struggle for Racial Justice on the Rails," in *Labor Law Stories*, ed. Lauren J. Cooper and Catherine L. Fisk (Thomson/West, 2005), 60-61; Melvyn Dubofsky, *The State and Labor in Modern America* (University of North Carolina Press, 1994), 129. *"Negro Robbed"*: Quoted in Genna Rae McNeil, *Groundwork: Charles Hamilton Houston and the Struggle for Civil Rights* (University of Pennsylvania Press, 1983), 96.

32. *railroad workers . . . to complain*: Charles H. Houston, Memorandum for the Joint Committee of the NAACP and AFPS from Charles H. Houston, July 24, 1936, and [Houston], Report to the Joint Committee AFPS and the NAACP, May 4, 1937, both in r. 6, b. 9, ABSP. *"gradually*

being eliminated": Walter White to the Trustees of the AFPS, June 22, 1937, b. I-C-200, f. 1, NAACPLC. *barred Black members*: Arnesen, *Brotherhoods of Color*, 203–29. *"arrange working conditions"* . . . *"elimination of the Negro worker"*: White to the Trustees, June 22, 1937.

33. *"as a weapon to exclude"*: White to the Trustees of the AFPS, June 22, 1937, b. I-C-200, f. 1, NAACPLC.
34. *approached him*: McNeil, *Groundwork*, 156. *series of lawsuits*: Ibid., 158–61; Arnesen, *Brotherhoods of Color*, 204–6; Charles H. Houston to Joseph Wady, July 21, 1942, b. 163-14, f. 7, CHHP.
35. *whatever basis*: John Fabian Witt, "Rethinking the Nineteenth-Century Employment Contract, Again," *Law & History Review* 18 (2000): 627–57; Jay Feinman, "The Development of the Employment at Will Rule," *American Journal of Legal History* 20 (1976): 118–35.
36. *NAACP had lobbied*: Dubofsky, *State and Labor*, 129; Risa L. Goluboff, *The Lost Promise of Civil Rights* (Harvard University Press, 2007), 202; Malamud, "Story of Steele," 61. *"primary attention"*: McNeil, *Groundwork*, 157.
37. *"compel railroads"* . . . *"secret and collusive"* . . . *"salvation"*: Report of Proceedings of the Conference for Locomotive Firemen, Mar. 28–29, 1941, b. 163-22, f. 22, CHHP; Malamud, "Story of Steele," 64.
38. *deploying the Railway Labor Act*: See ch. 14, above. *one of Randolph's hallmarks*: See Mann, "A. Philip Randolph: Radicalizing Rights at the Intersection of Class and Race," 292–99; Bynum, *A. Philip Randolph and the Struggle*, 111, 135. *"The Activity"*: Fraser, *Labor Will Rule*, 112–13. Randolph had reasons of his own to criticize Houston's turn to the courts. As an official in the AFL, Randolph was constrained by ties to white labor unions that would not welcome lawsuits. In private practice, Houston lacked any such constraint. Moreover, in the moment, Randolph aimed to draw Black railroad workers to his own new organization, one that aimed to replace Houston's railroad union clients with a union that would organize workers across the railroad industry, rather than at merely one or another railroad firm. "Our plans," Randolph explained to Houston, "are to try to organize all Colored Firemen into one Movement, on whatever Railroad they may be." A. Philip Randolph to Charles H. Houston, Nov. 5, 1941, b. 163-23, f. 5, CHHP.
39. *Rustin, complained*: Anderson, *A. Philip Randolph*, 259. *"Nothing tangible"*: Roi Ottley, "Negro Morale," *New Republic*, Nov. 10, 1941, 613–15. *"purpose"* . . . *"blind resentment"* . . . *"infantile leftism"*: Anderson, *A. Philip Randolph*, 259–60. *infantile disorder*: N. [Vladimir] Lenin, *Left Wing Communism: An Infantile Disorder* (Marxian Educational Society [Detroit], 1921).
40. *Madison Square*: Anderson, *A. Philip Randolph*, 264. *lack of effective enforcement authority*: Anthony S. Chen, *The Fifth Freedom: Jobs, Politics, and Civil Rights in the United States, 1941–1972* (Princeton University Press, 2009), at 32–87. *Hearings . . . scrapped*: McNeil, *Groundwork*, 164; Arnesen, *Brotherhoods of Color*, 193. *findings and an order*: Arnesen, *Brotherhoods of Color*, 195–98; McNeil, *Groundwork*, 165. *referred . . . to Roosevelt . . . to a halt*: Arnesen, *Brotherhoods of Color*, 200.
41. *locomotive fireman*: Reuel Schiller, *Forging Rivals: Race, Class, Law, and the Collapse of Postwar Liberalism* (Cambridge University Press, 2015), 41; Malamud, "Story of Steele," 57, 68–69. *seniority . . . desirable routes*: Ibid, 54–64.
42. *"ultimate"*: Arnesen, *Brotherhoods of Color*, 195.
43. *violence*: Alexa B. Henderson, "FEPC and the Southern Railway Case: An Investigation into the Discriminatory Practices of Railroads During World War II," *Journal of Negro History* 61 (1976): 173. *lynchings . . . Illinois*: Nathan R. Margold to Walter White, May 2, 1932, b. I-C-196, f. 9, NAACPLC; see also Bester William Steele to Arthur Lewis, Aug. 9, 1941, b. 163-23, f. 2, CHHP.
44. *first . . . twenty-nine years*: McNeil, *Groundwork*, 162. *Some said*: "First Negro Makes Oral Plea in Ala High Court," *Chicago Defender*, Dec. 4, 1943; Malamud, "Story of Steele," 75. *short shrift*: Steele v. Louisville & Nashville R.R. Co., 16 So.2d 416, 421, 245 Ala. 113, 121 (1944). *"only white engineers"*: Ibid. *"even requiring"*: Ibid., 121, 422. *"racial instincts"*: Ibid. *"accentuating the difficulties"*: Ibid.
45. *new willingness*: United States v. Carolene Products, 304 U.S. 144, 152 n4 (1938). *another victory*: Steele v. Louisville & Nashville R. Co., 323 U.S. 192 (1944). *Roosevelt appointments*: Kalman, *FDR's Gambit*, 266–67.

46. ***intervened***: Malamud, "Story of Steele," 85–86. ***due process***: Petition for Writ of Certiorari, *Steele v. Louisville & Nashville R. Co.*, Oct. Term, 1943, no. 826, Mar. 1944. ***labor regime***: Sophia Lee, *The Workplace Constitution from the New Deal to the New Right* (Harvard University Press, 2010), 46. *"as a whole"*: Brief for the United States as Amicus Curiae, *Tunstall v. Brotherhood of Locomotive Firemen* and *Steele v. Louisville & Nashville R. Co.*, Oct. Term, 1944, nos. 37 and 45 (November 1944), 11.
47. *"irrelevant and invidious"*: *Steele*, 323 U.S. at 203.
48. ***internment***: Korematsu v. United States, 323 U.S. 214 (1944); Ibid., at 233 (Murphy, J., dissenting). *"any race, creed or color"* . . . *"legal niceties"*: *Steele*, 323 U.S., at 208 (Murphy, J., concurring).
49. *"five years of effort"*: Charles Houston to the Association of Colored Railway Trainmen (ACRT), International Association of Railway Employees (IARE), Arthur Shores, Bester W. Steele, Tom Tunstall, and Thurgood Marshall, Dec. 20, 1944, b. 163-23, f. 14, CHHP. *"if it attempts"*: "4,000 Who Lost Jobs May Sue," *Pittsburgh Courier*, Jan. 6, 1945; also Goluboff, *Lost Promise*, 215.
50. *"thunderous decision"*: "High Court Decision Hailed as New 'Bill of Rights' for Negro in Labor," *Pittsburgh Courier*, Dec. 30, 1944. *"very roots"*: M. S. Stuart, "Southern Say-So: Charley Houston Fought Five Years to Win Railroad Brotherhood Cases," *Pittsburgh Courier*, Jan. 13, 1945. *"greater steps"*: Ibid.
51. *"fundamental issue"*: Marjorie McKenzie, "Pursuit of Democracy: NLRB Case and Not Rail Brotherhood Goes to Heart of Issue Facing Negroes," *Pittsburgh Courier*, Dec. 30, 1944. ***Frankfurter . . . defended***: Felix Frankfurter to E. Merrick Dodd, Mar. 7, 1945, and Felix Frankfurter to Merrick Dodd, Mar. 12, 1945, b. 184, ff. 12–13, FFPH; Malamud, "Story of Steele," 93. *"too hazardous, too cumbersome"*: Charles H. Houston, "'The Union and FEP': A Communication," *Washington Post*, Apr. 13, 1945, 8. On the choice between actions in the courts and administrative processes, see David Freeman Engstrom, "The Lost Origins of American Fair Employment Law: Regulatory Choice and the Making of Modern Civil Rights, 1943–72," *Stanford Law Review* 63 (2011): 1071.
52. ***Only in 1951***: Schiller, *Forging Rivals*, 255.
53. *"both"* . . . *"membership"*: Charles Houston to the ACRT, IARE, Arthur Shores, Bester W. Steele, Tom Tunstall, and Thurgood Marshall, Dec. 20, 1944, b. 163-23, f. 14, CHHP.
54. *"favorable repercussions"*: Report of Proceedings of the Conference for Locomotive Firemen, Mar. 28–29, 1941, b. 163-22, f. 22, CHHP. *"favorable decision"*: Ibid. *"demonstrated your loyalty"*: A. Philip Randolph to Charles H. Houston, Oct. 7, 1943, b. 163-12, f. 24, CHHP.
55. ***might weaken unions . . . disable them***: Frymer, *Black and Blue*, 95–96; Lee, *Workplace Constitution*, 122; Schiller, *Forging Rivals*, 249–50; David E. Bernstein, *Only One Place of Redress: African-Americans, Labor Regulations, and the Courts from Reconstruction to the New Deal* (Duke University Press, 2001), 63–65; Karl E. Klare, "The Quest for Industrial Democracy and the Struggle Against Racism: Perspectives from Labor Law and Civil Rights Law," *Oregon Law Review* 61 (1982): 158, 187, 197–98.
56. ***permanent institution***: McNeil, *Groundwork*, 195; Malamud, "Story of Steele," 96. ***states . . . FEPCs***: Arthur Earl Bonfield, "The Origin and Development of American Fair Employment Legislation," *Iowa Law Review* 52 (1967): 1043; William J. Collins, "The Political Economy of State-Level Fair Employment Laws, 1940–1964," *Explorations in Economic History* 40 (2003): 24. ***state courts***: Goluboff, *Lost Promise*, 204–14. ***prohibiting unions***: Betts v. Easley, 169 P.2d 831 (Kan. 1946), and James v. Marinship Corp., 155 P.2d 329 (Cal. 1944); see also Schiller, *Forging Rivals*, 48–80. ***true meaning***: APR, "Racially Segregated Unions" [n.d.], b. 2, f. 22, APRC. On the feedback loop between the *Steele* case and the FEPC, see Goluboff, *Lost Promise*, 204–6.
57. *"influence and mold"*: Charles H. Houston, "'The Union and FEP': A Communication," *Washington Post*, Apr. 13, 1945, 8. *"has just begun"*: Charles Houston to the ACRT, IARE, Arthur Shores, Bester W. Steele, Tom Tunstall, and Thurgood Marshall, Dec. 20, 1944, b. 163-23, f. 14, CHHP.

21: A RATHER ASTONISHING FUND

"Hypocrisy": RNB, interview with Joseph P. Lash, Mar. 7, 1972, b. 49, JPLP.
1. **Morris Ernst motion**: Minutes of the One Hundred Eighth Meeting, Jan. 13, 1932, r. 4, AFPSR; Anna Marnitz to Clarina Michelson, Jan. 22, 1932, r. 1, AFPSR. *"practically out of business"*: RNB to Morris Ernst, Dec. 7, 1939, container 163.7, MLEP.
2. **closed its doors**: Charles F. Howlett, *Brookwood Labor College and the Struggle for Peace and Social Justice in America* (Edwin Mellen Press, 1993), 302–6. **hyperfactional party**: Leilah Danielson, *American Gandhi: A. J. Muste and the History of Radicalism in the Twentieth Century* (University of Pennsylvania Press, 2014), 115; Nat Hentoff, *Peace Agitator: The Story of A. J. Muste* (Macmillan, 1963), 71–72; James W. Robinson, "The Expulsion of Brookwood Labor College from the Workers' Education Bureau," *Labour History* 15 (1968): 64, 68; Memorandum of Meeting of the Committee on Brookwood Held on Friday, Jan. 13, 1933, b. 6, f. 4, BGP. *"preserve our institution"*: [David J. Saposs], Re Communist Accusation That Brookwood Is Sectarian (Investigation by American Fund), May 9, 1932, b. 3, f. 14, KPEP. **backtracked**: AFPS [Clarina Michelson and Robert W. Dunn], Memorandum on Brookwood Labor College, n.d. [1932], b. 3, f. 14, KPEP; Memorandum of Meeting of the Committee on Brookwood Held on Friday, Jan. 13, 1933. **resigned**: Danielson, *American Gandhi*, 168–77; Statement of the Board of Directors of Brookwood, r. 89, b. 4, AJMP. **Sit-Down**: Howlett, *Brookwood Labor College and the Struggle*, 305–6; Tucker Smith to Merlin Bishop, Mar. 15, 1937, b. 52, BLCR. After Brookwood closed, Baldwin and his second wife, Evelyn Preston, who held a mortgage on the college's property, arranged with the Reuther brothers to transfer the college's books to UAW Local 174 in Detroit. See Brookwood Labor College—Smith, Tucker, 1936, b. 3, VRP; RNB to AFPS Board of Directors, Aug. 15, 1938, b. 1, LGP.
3. *"quarter-mile procession"*: Eugene Levy, *James Weldon Johnson: Black Leader, Black Voice* (University of Chicago Press, 1973), 345–47; "Thousands Attend Johnson Funeral," *New York Times*, July 1, 1938, 19.
4. **convalescing**: Lara Vapnek, *Elizabeth Gurley Flynn: Modern American Revolutionary* (Westview Press, 2015), 93–102; Helen C. Camp, *Iron in Her Soul: Elizabeth Gurley Flynn and the American Left* (Washington State University Press, 1995), 130–37. **joined the Communist Party**: Vapnek, *Elizabeth Gurley Flynn*, 107; Lara Vapnek, "The Rebel Girl Revisited: Rereading Elizabeth Gurley Flynn's Life Story," *Feminist Studies* 44 (2018): 13–42. **anti-Communist directors**: Samuel Walker, *In Defense of American Liberties: A History of the ACLU* (Oxford University Press, 1990), 129–33; Burt Neuborne, "Of Pragmatism and Principle: A Second Look at the Expulsion of Elizabeth Gurley Flynn from the ACLU's Board of Directors," *Tulsa Law Review* 41 (2006): 799–816. **objected**: Maxwell Geismar, "Preface to the Trial of Elizabeth Gurley Flynn by the American Civil Liberties Union," in *The Trial of Elizabeth Gurley Flynn by the American Civil Liberties Union*, ed. Corliss Lamont (Horizon Press, 1968). *"totalitarian dictatorship"*: Lamont, *Trial of Elizabeth Gurley Flynn*, 21, 45, Laura Weinrib, *The Taming of Free Speech: America's Civil Liberties Compromise* (Harvard University Press, 2016), 300–303. Flynn later claimed to have joined the party in 1926, and at least one biographer has concurred. See EGF, *Elizabeth Gurley Flynn Speaks to the Court* (New Century, July 1952), 11; Camp, *Iron in Her Soul*, 121–23. The early dating to 1926 would later become a convenient date for Flynn when she served as a leading party official. Internal American Fund evidence suggests that she was not yet formally affiliated with the party until her return to New York in the mid-1930s. See Benjamin Gitlow to EGF, June 9, 1930, b. 6, f. 3, BGP.
5. **vote of 10–9**: Lamont, *Trial of Elizabeth Gurley Flynn*, 176.
6. **scorned**: E.g., the sophisticated version in Weinrib, *Taming of Free Speech*, 300–303. **wrest control**: See above, chapter 16. **smashed Brookwood**: Danielson, *American Gandhi*, 115. **broken the National Negro Congress**: Arnesen, "Making and Breaking," 41. **fought the Fund's majority**: See above, chapter 15. **Commonwealth College and the tenant farmers union**: See above, chapter 20. **not the first**: See, e.g., Muste at Brookwood above in this chapter and H. L. Mitchell at the STFU in chapter 20; see also Steven Fraser, *Labor Will Rule: Sidney Hillman and the Rise*

of American Labor (Free Press, 1991), 202–3, on Hillman's mid-1920s break with William Z. Foster's Trade Union Educational League and the Amalgamated Clothing Workers' expulsion of party member (and soon-to-be Fund director) Ben Gitlow. Of the Fund's directors at the ACLU trial, Ernst voted in favor of the motion to expel Flynn. Robert Dunn, whose party membership was still secret, voted against it and remained a board member at the ACLU along with another secret Communist, Abraham J. Isserman.

7. *collapse & "beyond the reach"*: RNB to AFPS Board, Dec. 21, 1939, c. 163.7, MLEP; also b. 6, f. 3, BGP; r. 25, AFPSR; NT to RNB, Dec. 26, 1939, r. 25, AFPSR. *Bellevue . . . institution in Florida & electroshock*: Author interview with Jay Garland [youngest son of Charles Garland], June 26, 2013; Richard Cowen interview with Roger Baldwin, Dec. 10, 1976, at 46–47, RCC; Sally J. Ling, *Out of Mind, Out of Sight: A Revealing History of the Florida State Hospital at Chattahoochee and Mental Health Care in Florida* (Sally J. Ling, 2013), 93–94. *experimental treatment*: David Oshinsky, *Bellevue: Three Centuries of Medicine and Mayhem at America's Most Storied Hospital* (Doubleday, 2016), 227–29; Jonathan Sadowsky, "Beyond the Metaphor of the Pendulum: Electroconvulsive Therapy, Psychoanalysis, and the Styles of American Psychiatry," *Journal of the History of Medicine* 61 (2006): 1–25. *cognitive blunting*: Raheem Suleman, "A Brief History of Electroconvulsive Therapy," *American Journal of Psychiatry Residents' Journal* 16 (2020): 6.

8. *quiet existence*: Author interview with Jay Garland, June 26, 2013; RNB interview with Richard Cowen, Dec. 10, 1976, at 8, RNB binder, RCC; also "All Nations Were There at War Plant 'E' Ceremony," *Daily Worker*, Aug. 23, 1943, 5.

9. *final report*: *Report of the American Fund for Public Service, Inc., for the Three Years, July 1, 1938, to June 30, 1941*, and *Summary of Nineteen Years, 1922–1941* (New York, 1941), at 2, in r. 3, b. 5, AFPSR.

10. *final gathering*: Minutes of the Joint Meeting of the Members of the Board of Directors of the AFPS, Inc., June 18, 1941, c. 163.7, MLEP, r. 4, AFPSR (Robert Dunn, Clarina Michelson, and Norman Thomas attended along with Baldwin). *"wiser and better job"*: Ibid. *"as well as could be expected"*: Richard Cowen, Garland Book, 923, RCC. *"wiser arrangement"*: Peggy Lamson, *Roger Baldwin: Founder of the American Civil Liberties Union* (Houghton Mifflin, 1976), 149–50. *"many good causes"*: "Topics of the Times: One Fund Ends," *New York Times*, June 21, 1941, 16; also "$2,000,000 Spent, Garland Fund Dies," *New York Times*, June 20, 1941, 23. *empowerment of Black Americans*: "$1,000,000 Garland Fund Gone," *New York Herald Tribune*, June 20, 1941, 16.

11. *"main agencies"*: W. E. B. Du Bois, "The American Fund," *The Crisis*, June, 1926, 57. *"the impossible"*: W. E. B. Du Bois, "We Rejoice and Tell the World," *National Guardian*, May 31, 1954, 5; David Levering Lewis, *W. E. B. Du Bois: The Fight for Equality and the American Century, 1919–1963* (Henry Holt, 1993), 557; Justin Driver, *The Schoolhouse Gate: Public Education, the Supreme Court, and the Battle for the American Mind* (Pantheon, 2018), 248–50. *"rather astonishing"*: The Reminiscences of Norman Thomas, 1950–1965, part 2, 38, CCOH. *Gannett mused*: Lewis Gannett, 1891–1966: His Story (Michael R. Gannett ed., 2007), 64–71 (unpublished ms. on file with author). *Flynn . . . remembered*: Elizabeth Gurley Flynn, *The Rebel Girl: An Autobiography, My First Life, 1906–1926* (International Publishers, 1973) (1955), at 325–26, 330. Fund veterans also expressed various retrospective frustrations with the Fund's operations. Morris Ernst, who had chafed at Baldwin's penny-pinching, and whose late-career turn to anti-Communism led him to a friendship with J. Edgar Hoover, dismissed the Fund in his old age as having been made up of inept directors from the "hair-shirt school of thinking" whose mental blocks about the use of money led them to distribute Garland's money in amounts too small to make a difference. Scott Nearing, who had been one of Ernst's hair-shirters, offered the opposite complaint; the Garland Fund's undue generosity, he charged, had made radical organizations into "permanent beggars." Some former directors regretted too "scattered" an effort. Freda Kirchwey grew impatient at the log-rolling tactics required by the board's rival factions of liberals and leftists. Insiders at the Fund who turned from left to right in their politics were especially unsparing in their evaluations. Ben Gitlow, confessing error in his party adventures, testified

before the House Un-American Activities Committee that the Fund had routinely funneled money to Communist-backed projects, in part by providing loans or extending bail money and then allowing the beneficiaries to make off without repaying. See Samantha Barbas, *The Rise and Fall of Morris Ernst: Free Speech Renegade* (University of Chicago Press, 2021), 58 ("hairshirt"); Scott Nearing, *The Making of a Radical: A Political Autobiography* (Harper & Row, 1972), 48–49 ("permanent beggars"); Merle Curti, "Subsidizing Radicalism: The American Fund for Public Service, 1921–41," *Social Service Review* 33 (1959): 286–88, 295–96 ("scattered," Kirchwey and Gitlow). The historian Merle Curti, writing in 1959, noted the Fund's contributions to "workers' education and trade union organization" and praised the directors for their commitment to "experimental and radical approaches to the problem of improving social welfare." See Curti, "Subsidizing Radicalism," 274, 295.

12. *"blood transfusions"*: RNB, *Reminiscences*, 332. *"not feel satisfied"*: Lamson, *Roger Baldwin*, 150. *"large wealth"*: RNB, "Autobiography (1884–1920)," b. 20, f. 11, RNBP.
13. *"new experiments"*: RNB, *Reminiscences*, 328. *"thick of the labor"*: Ibid., 329. *"lot of good"*: Ibid. Baldwin singled out Vanguard Press, of whose books he said, "I have no doubt they did good." Ibid. Upton Sinclair agreed, asserting to Merle Curti that "those cheap little radical classics had an immense effect." Upton Sinclair to Merle Curti, Sept. 22, 1958, MECP.
14. *retired . . . died*: "Roger Baldwin, 97, Is Dead; Crusader for Civil Rights Founded the ACLU," *New York Times*, Aug. 27, 1981, A1 and D10.

EPILOGUE: LEGACIES

"the road to kingdom come": RNB, Garland's Million, typescript ms. 1934, p. 14, b. 5, RNBP.

1. *"set in motion"*: [James Marlow], "Charles Garland Gift Aided Battle Against Segregation," *Trenton Evening Times*, May 21, 1954, 23; also same with a tendentious headline as "NAACP's Real Beginning from White Man's Funds," *San Angelo Standard*, May 21, 1954. *"groundwork"*: Thurgood Marshall, "An Evaluation of Recent Efforts to Achieve Racial Integration in Education Through Resort to the Courts," for a Conference on the Courts and Racial Integration, Howard University, sponsored by the *Journal of Negro Education*, April 16–18, 1952, NAACPP. *crucial role*: Brad Snyder, *Democratic Justice: Felix Frankfurter, the Supreme Court, and the Making of the Liberal Establishment* (W. W. Norton, 2022), 548–69.
2. *One in three workers*: Leo Troy, "Trade Union Membership, 1897–1962," *Review of Economics and Statistics* 47 (1965): 93, 94. *more likely than white*: Henry S. Farber et al., "Unions and Inequality over the Twentieth Century: New Evidence from Survey Data," *Quarterly Journal of Economics* 136 (2021): 1325. *inequality shrank*: Emmanuel Saez and Gabriel Zucman, "Wealth Inequality in the United States Since 1913: Evidence from Capitalized Income Tax Data," *Quarterly Journal of Economics* 131 (2016): 519.
3. *uphold*: Gitlow v. New York, 268 U.S. 652 (1925); see also Geoffrey R. Stone, *Perilous Times: Free Speech in Wartime, from the Sedition Act to the War on Terrorism* (W. W. Norton, 2004), 237–38. *narrowed the reach*: Yates v. United States, 354 U.S. 298 (1957). *later cases*: Principally Brandenburg v. Ohio, 395 U.S. 444 (1969).
4. *don't determine history's path*: The parallel here is Max Weber's theory of ideas as the switchmen who decide the tracks along which the engine of history moves. See Max Weber, "The Social Psychology of World Religions," in *From Max Weber: Essays in Sociology*, ed. H. H. Gerth and C. Wright Mills (Oxford University Press, 1946), 280.
5. *Congress of Racial Equality*: RNB, AJM, and APR, "Dear Friends," Mar. 30, 1953, b. 5, f. 29, RNBP; August Meier and Elliott Rudwick, *CORE: A Study in the Civil Rights Movement* (Oxford University Press, 1973). *Thurgood Marshall*: Walker, *In Defense of American Liberties*, 68. *Reuther*: Nelson Lichtenstein, *The Most Dangerous Man in Detroit: Walter Reuther and the Fate of American Labor* (Basic Books, 1995), 315–16. *helped finance* **Brown . . . Montgomery**: Kevin Boyle, *The UAW and the Heyday of American Liberalism* (Cornell University Press, 1995), 121–22. *federal court order*: Browder v. Gayle, 142 F. Supp. 707 (M.D. Ala. 1956), affirmed by Gayle v. Browder, 3542 U.S. 903 (1956). *Students for a Democratic Society*: Boyle, *UAW and*

the Heyday, 159; Todd Gitlin, *The Sixties: Years of Hope, Days of Rage* (Bantam Books, 1987), 109–12; Students for a Democratic Society, *The Port Huron Statement* (SDS, 1962).

6. **Celebratory accounts**: Richard Kluger, *Simple Justice: The History of* Brown v. Board of Education *and Black America's Struggle for Equality*, rev. ed. (Vintage, 2004) (1975), 131–39.

7. **legal rights . . . brute power**: Risa L. Goluboff, *The Lost Promise of Civil Rights* (Harvard University Press, 2007); Michael J. Klarman, *From Jim Crow to Civil Rights: The Supreme Court and the Struggle for Equality* (Oxford University Press, 2004); Gerald N. Rosenberg, *The Hollow Hope: Can Courts Bring About Social Change?* 3rd ed. (University of Chicago Press, 2023) (1991); Derrick A. Bell Jr., "Serving Two Masters: Integration Ideals and Client Interests in School Desegregation Litigation," *Yale Law Journal* 85 (1976): 470; Megan Ming Francis, "The Price of Civil Rights: Black Lives, White Funding, and Movement Capture," *Law & Society Review* 53 (2019): 275. **abstract ideas about freedom**: Laura Weinrib, *The Taming of Free Speech: America's Civil Liberties Compromise* (Harvard University Press, 2016); Sam Lebovic, *Free Speech and Unfree News: The Paradox of Press Freedom in America* (Harvard University Press, 2016); Jeremy K. Kessler and David E. Pozen, "The Search for an Egalitarian First Amendment," *Columbia Law Review* 118 (2018): 1953; Genevieve Lakier, "The First Amendment's Real Lochner Problem," *University of Chicago Law Review* 87 (2020): 1243. **sapped the energies**: Christopher L. Tomlins, *The State and the Unions: Labor Relations, Law, and the Organized Labor Movement in America, 1880–1960* (Cambridge University Press, 1985); Karl E. Klare, "Judicial Deradicalization of the Wagner Act and the Origins of Modern Legal Consciousness, 1937–1941," *Minnesota Law Review* 762 (1978): 265; Katherine Van Wezel Stone, "The Post-War Paradigm in American Labor Law," *Yale Law Journal* 90 (1981): 1509; James B. Atleson, *Values and Assumptions in American Labor Law* (University of Massachusetts Press, 1983).

8. **"long civil rights movement"**: Jacquelyn Dowd Hall, "The Long Civil Rights Movement and the Political Uses of the Past," *Journal of American History* 91 (2005): 1233. See also Kenneth W. Mack, "Rethinking Civil Rights Lawyering and Politics in the Era Before Brown," *Yale Law Journal* 115 (2005): 256–354, which offers parallels to the account I offer here.

9. **two decades of operation**: See appendix A.

10. **not take race into account**: SFFA v. Harvard, 600 U.S. 181 (2023). **freedom of speech**: Robert C. Post, *Citizens Divided: Campaign Finance Reform and the Constitution* (Harvard University Press, 2014). **Labor**: Kate Andrias and Benjamin I. Sachs, "Constructing Countervailing Power: Law and Organizing in an Era of Political Inequality," *Yale Law Journal* 130 (2021): 546; Kate Andrias, Sharon Block, and Benjamin Sachs, "A New Path for Unionizing Uber and Lyft," *Commonwealth Beacon*, Dec. 2, 2023; Veena Dubal, "The Legal Uncertainties of Gig Work," in *The Oxford Handbook of the Law of Work*, ed. Guy Davidov, Brian Langille, and Gillian Lester (Oxford University Press, 2024); Cynthia L. Estlund, "The Ossification of American Labor Law," *Columbia Law Review* 102 (2002): 1527.

11. **"constantly shifting"**: JWJ, *Along This Way: The Autobiography of James Weldon Johnson* (Knopf, 1933), 389–90; Michelle Adams, *The Containment: Detroit, the Supreme Court, and the Battle for Racial Justice in the North* (FSG, 2025). **enervating effects**: Stone, "The Post-War Paradigm." **anti-union campaigns**: Kim Phillips-Fein, *Invisible Hands: The Making of the Conservative Movement from the New Deal to Reagan* (W. W. Norton, 2009), 87–114. **obsolete**: Reuel Schiller, *Forging Rivals: Race, Class, Law, and the Collapse of Postwar Liberalism* (Cambridge University Press, 2015).

12. **update the strategies**: For contemporary experiments in matching a new economic organizing program to the challenges of the twenty-first-century economy, see among others the project of establishing social and sectoral bargaining as an update to the industrial union model advanced first by the Wobblies and then picked up by the CIO in the heyday of the Fund. See Kate Andrias, "The New Labor Law," *Yale Law Journal* 126 (2016): 2; Kate Andrias and Benjamin I. Sachs, "The Chicken and Egg of Law and Organizing: Enacting Policy for Power Building," *Columbia Law Review* 124 (2024): 777–847; Andrias and Sachs, "Constructing Countervailing Power," 625–27.

13. **Charitable organizations**: Internal Revenue Code of 1954, Pub. Law 591, ch. 736, sect. 501(c)

(3), 1954, at 163. **Senator Lyndon Johnson:** Patrick L. O'Daniel, "More Honored in the Breach: A Historical Perspective of the Permeable IRS Prohibition on Campaigning by Churches," *Boston College Law Review* 42 (2001): 753. **organizations:** Internal Revenue Code of 1954, Pub. Law 591, ch. 736, s. 501(c)(4), at 163–64.

14. **Congress . . . codified:** Revenue Act, 48 Stat. 680, 700 s. 101 (1934); Revenue Bill of 1934, S. Rep 73-558, 73d Cong., 2d sess., Mar. 28, 1934, 26; To Provide Revenue, Equalize Taxation, and for Other Purposes, H. Rep. 73-1385, 73d Cong., 2d Sess., Apr. 30, 1934, 17, 26; Revenue Revision, 1934: Hearings Before the Committee on Ways and Means, H. Rep., Dec. 15–21, 1933, and Jan. 9–11, 1934, 73d Cong., 2d Sess. (1934), 177 ff. **two hundred:** Rob Reich, *Just Giving: Why Philanthropy Is Failing Democracy and How It Can Do Better* (Princeton University Press, 2020), 141–42. **half century thereafter:** Joint Committee on Taxation, *Historical Development and Present Law of the Federal Tax Exemption for Charities and Other Tax-Exempt Organizations,* Apr. 19, 2005, 20; Elizabeth Drew, *Politics and Money: The New Road to Corruption* (Macmillan, 1983), 10; Tevi Troy, "Devaluing the Think Tank," *National Affairs,* Winter 2012. **100,000 private foundations:** Reich, *Just Giving,* 142. **$1.5 trillion . . . $104 billion:** Giving USA, *Giving USA 2024: The Annual Report on Philanthropy for the Year 2023* (Giving USA Foundation, 2024), 33, 98. **501(c)(4):** David Pozen, "The Tax Code Shift That Is Changing Liberal Activism," *The Atlantic,* Nov. 27, 2018. **"dark-money":** Jane Mayer, *Dark Money: The Hidden History of the Billionaires Behind the Rise of the Radical Right* (Doubleday, 2016), 86, 94. **"new world of nonprofit activity":** Norman I. Silber, *A Corporate Form of Freedom: The Emergence of the Nonprofit Sector* (Westview Press, 2001), 143–65; also Daniel Schulman, *Sons of Wichita: How the Koch Brothers Became America's Most Powerful and Private Dynasty* (Grand Central Publishing, 2014). In 1973, an aide to President Richard Nixon would gleefully cite the value of such "tax-exempt refuges" for rolling back federal regulations on private economic activity. See Mayer, *Dark Money,* 94.

15. **winners in our lopsided economy today:** David Callahan, *The Givers: Money, Power, and Philanthropy in a New Gilded Age* (Knopf, 2017); Anand Giridharadas, *Winners Take All: The Elite Charade of Changing the World* (Knopf, 2018). **cries out anew:** Dana Brakman Reiser and Steven A. Dean, *For-Profit Philanthropy: Elite Power & the Threat of Limited Liability Companies, Donor-Advised Funds, & Strategic Corporate Giving* (Oxford University Press, 2023); Rob Reich, Chiara Cordelli, and Lucy Bernholz, eds., *Philanthropy in Democratic Societies: History, Institutions, and Values* (University of Chicago Press, 2016).

16. **purity:** Joseph P. Lash, interview with RNB, Mar. 12, 1972, b. 49, JPLP ("The world can't get along without hypocrisy."). On experimentalism as a rationale for philanthropies in democratic societies, see Reich, *Just Giving,* 160; on the argument for time-limited spend-down foundations, see ibid., 55–59; John Stuart Mill, "The Right and Wrong of State Interference with Corporation and Church Property," in John Stuart Mill, *Dissertations and Discussions,* vol. 1 (John W. Parker & Son, 1859), 1, 6; Ray D. Madoff and Rob Reich, "Now or Forever: Rethinking Foundation Life Spans," *Chronicle of Philanthropy,* Mar. 30, 2016.

17. **diminishing returns:** Brian Galle, "Charities in Politics: A Reappraisal," *William & Mary Law Review* 54 (2013): 1561, 1581–82; Richard L. Hasen, "Lobbying, Rent-Seeking, and the Constitution," *Stanford Law Review* 64 (2012): 191, 229.

18. **23 million people:** "Number of High Net Worth Individuals in the United States from 2017 to 2024," Statista, July 29, 2024, https://www.statista.com/forecasts/1478254/number-of-high-net-worth-individuals-usa. **more than $30 million:** Robert Frank, "The Ultra-Wealthy Just Gained $49 Trillion," CNBC, July 19, 2024, https://www.cnbc.com/2024/07/19/population-ultra-high-net-worth-wealth.

Photo Credits

INSERT IMAGES (BY NUMBER)

1: Prints and Photographs Division, Library of Congress, reproduction number LC-DIG-ds-10032.; 2: Madeleine Z. Doty Papers, Sophia Smith Collection, SSC- MS-00049, Smith College Special Collections, Northampton, Massachusetts; 3: John and Phyllis Collier Collection, Walter P. Reuther Library, Archives of Labor and Urban Affairs, Wayne State University, 4. John and Phyllis Collier Collection, Walter P. Reuther Library, Archives of Labor and Urban Affairs, Wayne State University; 5: John and Phyllis Collier Collection, Walter P. Reuther Library, Archives of Labor and Urban Affairs, Wayne State University; 6: James Weldon Johnson and Grace Nail Johnson Papers. Yale Collection of American Literature, Beinecke Rare Book and Manuscript Library, published courtesy of Jill Rosenberg Jones; 7: *Evening Star*, Washington, D.C., Nov. 23, 1922. Chronicling America: Historic American Newspapers, Library of Congress; 8: James Weldon Johnson and Grace Nail Johnson Papers. Yale Collection of American Literature, Beinecke Rare Book and Manuscript Library, published courtesy of Jill Rosenberg Jones; 9: drawn from Ida B. Wells-Barnett, *The Arkansas Race Riot* (Chicago, 1920), in the collections of Beinecke Rare Book and Manuscript Library, Yale University; 10: Pictorial Press / Alamy Stock Photographs; 11: *Detroit News* Collection, Walter P. Reuther Library, Wayne State University; 12: from the collections of the Beinecke Rare Book and Manuscript Library, Yale University; 13: Smithsonian Institution Archives, Science Service Records, Image #SIA2008-3287; 14: *Daily Worker*, Chicago, Ill., July 15, 1925, Serial and Government Publications Division, Library of Congress; 15: from George Bernard Shaw, *The Socialism of Shaw*, ed. James Fuchs (Vanguard Press, 1926), in the collections of Beinecke Rare Book and Manuscript Library, Yale University; 16: Manuscripts and Archives, Sterling Memorial Library, Yale University; 17: Industrial Workers of the World stickerette, Richard F. Brush Art Gallery, St. Lawrence University, via JSTOR.org; 18: Industrial Workers of the World political sticker, Richard F. Brush Art Gallery, St. Lawrence University, via JSTOR.org; 19: Marxists Internet Archive, https://www.marxists.org/history/usa/pubs/laborage/v11n09-oct-1922-LA.pdf; 20: Bettmann / Getty Images; 21: Prints and Photographs Division, Library of Congress, reproduction number LC-USZ62-97540; 22: Marianne Mather / *Chicago Tribune* / TCA; 23: Brookwood Labor College Papers, Walter P. Reuther Library, Archives of Labor and Urban Affairs, Wayne State University; 24: Brookwood Labor College Papers, Walter P. Reuther Library, Archives of Labor and Urban Affairs, Wayne State University; 25: American Labor Museum, Haledon, New Jersey, and Bettmann / Getty Images; 26: *New York Herald Tribune*, September 25, 1925; 27: Photographs and Prints Division, Schomburg Center for Research in Black Culture, The New York Public Library; 28: *New York Journal* American Photography Collection, Harry Ransom Center, University of Texas at Austin, published courtesy of Stephanie G. Begen, granddaughter of Morris Ernst; 29: Associated Press Photo / File; 30: Prints and Photographs Division, Library of Congress, reproduction number LC-DIG-ppmsca-09709; 31: Walter P. Reuther Library, Archives of Labor and Urban Affairs, Wayne State University; 32: Walter P. Reuther Library, Archives of Labor and Urban Affairs, Wayne State University; 33: Prints and Photographs Division, Library of Congress, reproduction number LC-DIG-ppmsca-08115, published courtesy of Brown Brothers / Lelands; 34: Harris & Ewing Collection, Prints and Photographs Division, Library of

PHOTO CREDITS

Congress, reproduction number LC-DIG-hec-38833; 35: Harris & Ewing Collection, Prints and Photographs Division, Library of Congress, reproduction number LC-DIG-hec-25815; 36: ND-41-120-03, Neal Douglass Photograph Archive (AR.2005.048). Austin History Center, Austin Public Library; 37: George Grantham Bain Collection, Prints and Photographs Division, Library of Congress, reproduction number LC-USZ62-96665; 38: A. Philip Randolph Papers, Manuscript Division, Library of Congress

IMAGES THROUGHOUT (BY PAGE NUMBER)

iv: Walter P. Reuther Library, Archives of Labor and Urban Affairs, Wayne State University; xxii: Alton H. Blackington Collection, Robert S. Cox Special Collections and University Archives Research Center, UMass Amherst Libraries; 12: Madeleine Z. Doty papers, Sophia Smith Collection, SSC- MS-00049, Smith College Special Collections, Northampton, Massachusetts; 15: Roger Nash Baldwin Papers, MC005, Public Policy Papers, Department of Special Collections, Princeton University Library; 21: Roger Nash Baldwin Papers, MC005, Public Policy Papers, Department of Special Collections, Princeton University Library; 34: *The Crisis*, September 1917, in Collection of the Smithsonian National Museum of African American History and Culture, Gift of Bobbie Ross in memory of Elizabeth Dillard; 38: Digital Collections, University of Minnesota Libraries; 46: Miriam and Ira D. Wallach Division of Art, Prints, and Photographs, New York Public Library; 52: LSE Archives, London School of Economics and Political Science; 57: Madeleine Z. Doty Papers, Sophia Smith Collection, SSC-MS-00049, Smith College Special Collections, Northampton, Massachusetts; 69: Prints and Photographs Division, Library of Congress; 71: William Z. Foster, *The Great Steel Strike and Its Lessons* (Huebsch, 1920), in Project Gutenberg; 80: Prints and Photographs Division, Library of Congress; 88: PhotoQuest / Getty Images; 92: Rockefeller & King: Colorado Fuel & Iron Industrial Bulletin, October 1915, Sterling Memorial Library, Yale University; 94: Prints and Photographs Division, Library of Congress; 98: Freda Kirchwey Papers, Schlesinger Library, Harvard Radcliffe Institute, and personal collection of Adam Van Doren; 100: Oil portrait by Walter William Ouless, 1902, after Walter William Ouless photograph, 1899, National Portrait Gallery, London; 104: Headline, *Boston Globe*, November 30, 1920; 114: Still from 1921 news reel, Collection of Kenny King / West Virginia Mine Wars Museum; 116: John & Phyllis Collier Collection, Walter P. Reuther Library, Archives of Labor and Urban Affairs, Wayne State University; 119: Alton H. Blackington Collection, Robert S. Cox Special Collections and University Archives Research Center, UMass Amherst Libraries; 121: *American Pictorial*, October 27, 1922, courtesy of the New York State Library; 124, 131, 140, 165, 184: James Weldon Johnson and Grace Nail Johnson Papers, Yale Collection of American Literature, Beinecke Rare Book and Manuscript Library; 147: Everett Collection Historical / Alamy; 153: The American Tobacco Company, 1929, Marilyn E. Jackler Memorial Collection of Tobacco Advertisements, Archives Center, National Museum of American History, Smithsonian Institution; 160: James Weldon Johnson and Grace Nail Johnson Papers, Yale Collection of American Literature, Beinecke Rare Book and Manuscript Library; 166: *Harper's Weekly*, May 26, 1866, Miriam and Ira D. Wallach Division of Art, Prints, and Photographs, New York Public Library; 168: Horace Mann Bond Papers, Robert S. Cox Special Collections and University Archives Research Center, UMass Amherst Libraries; 180: Phelps Stokes Fund Photograph Collection, Photographs and Prints Division, Schomburg Center for Research in Black Culture, The New York Public Library; 188: Labadie Photograph Collection, University of Michigan; 195: African-American men taken prisoner during the Elaine Massacre by U.S. Army troops sent from Camp Pike, G1595.09, Arkansas State Archives; 205: Looking Back at Tennessee Collection, accession 1988-017, Tennessee State Library and Archives; 208: Walter P. Reuther Library, Archives of Labor and Urban Affairs, Wayne State University; 216: Photographs and Prints Division, Schomburg Center for Research in Black Culture, The New York Public Library; 223: Beinecke Rare Book and Manuscript Library, Yale University; 225: from James Weldon Johnson, *God's Trombones: Seven Negro Sermons in Verse* (Viking Press, 1927), courtesy of the Beinecke Rare Book and Manuscript Library, Yale University; 228: *Passaic Textile Strike*, still image courtesy of the Library of Congress, Moving Image Research Center; 230: Federated Press Bulletin, January 12, 1924, courtesy of the

New York Public Library; 232: *The Weekly Newsmagazine of Radio Broadcast Advertising*, Nov. 9, 1942, Sterling Library, Yale University; 240: William J. Roege Photograph Collection, New York Historical; 247: Century Association Archives Foundation, New York, New York; 252, 261: Elizabeth Gurley Flynn Papers, Tamiment Library, Special Collections, New York University, permissions courtesy of International Publishers Co, Inc.; 265: Photograph by Schedin & Lehman. Courtesy of Special Collections, Pikes Peak Library District, image no. 192-6003; 280: *(top)* George Grantham Bain Collection, Prints & Photographs Division, Library of Congress, *(bottom)* Bettmann / Getty Images; 290: from *The Literary Digest*, vol. 74, no. 2 (July 8, 1922), from the collection at Sterling Memorial Library, Yale University; 294: American Civil Liberties Union, *The Truth about the I.W.W. Prisoners* (ACLU, 1922), from the collection of the Widener Library, Harvard University; 305: Courtesy of the Jacob Rader Marcus Center of the American Jewish Archives, Cincinnati, Ohio, at americanjewisharchives.org; 313: *(left)* Walter P. Reuther Library, Archives of Labor and Urban Affairs, Wayne State University, *(right)* Bettmann / Getty; 316: Walter P. Reuther Library, Archives of Labor and Urban Affairs, Wayne State University; 323: Wisconsin Historical Society Archives, Highlander Research and Education Center Records, M2019-039, box 93, folder 4; 325: Prints and Photographs Division, Library of Congress; 333: *The Messenger*, December 1920, courtesy of Sterling Memorial Library, Yale University; 338: May 1923 issue of *The Messenger*, from the Alice Dunbar-Nelson Papers, Special Collections, University of Delaware Library, Newark, Delaware (MS0113); 340: Frank Crosswaith Collection, Photographs and Prints Division, Schomburg Center for Research in Black Culture, The New York Public Library; 343: Prints and Photographs Division, Library of Congress; 356: W. E. B. Du Bois Papers, Robert S. Cox Special Collections and University Archives Research Center, UMass Amherst Libraries; 360: Bettmann / Getty Images; 365: James S. Allen, *The Negro Question in the United States* (International Publishers, 1936), from the collections of the PJ Mode Collection of Persuasive Cartography, Cornell University, reprinted courtesy of International Publishers, Co., Inc.; 372: author's collection, published courtesy of Stephanie G. Begen, granddaughter of Morris Ernst; 379: Prints and Photographs Division, Library of Congress; 385: Photographs and Prints Division, Schomburg Center for Research in Black Culture, The New York Public Library; 390: "Garland Jailed for 60 Days in 'Love Farm' Case," *New York Herald Tribune*, April 16, 1926, p. 10, "Love Colony Baby's Death Starts Hunt for Its Grave," *Reading Eagle*, Jan. 11, 1926, p. 1, "Garland Colony is Denounced," *Boston Globe*, Jan. 9, 1926, p. 1, "Baby's Death Brings Garland 'Farm' Inquiry," *New York Herald Tribune*, Jan. 11, 1926, p. 18, "Free Love Project Denied by Garland," *Washington Post*, Jan. 11, 1926, p. 17, "Garland Seized in 'April Farm' Dead Baby Quiz," *New York Herald Tribune*, Jan. 12, 1926, p. 9, "Charles Garland Indicted in Allentown," *New York Times*, Apr. 6, 1926, p. 1, "Garland, Love Farm Cultist, Sued by Wife," *Chicago Daily Tribune*, June 9, 1926, p. 1, "Garland Gives Bail," *Reading Eagle*, Jan. 12, 1926, p. 1; 395: New York American, May 23, 1926, from the microform collection of the Library of Congress; 397: from Ella Reeve Bloor, *We Are Many* (International Publishers, 1940): photo appears courtesy of International Publishers, Co., Inc.; 404: Scurlock Studio Records, Archives Center, National Museum of American History, Smithsonian Institution; 408: Harvard Law School Library, Historical & Special Collections; 415: Lucy Kramer Cohen Papers, Yale Collection of Western Americana, Beinecke Rare Book and Manuscript Library, published courtesy of Juliette Hamilton, granddaughter of Nathan Margold; 420: "Transportation Coast-to-Coast and San Francisco," Goodyear Tire & Rubber Company Records, Archives and Special Collections, University Libraries, The University of Akron; 434: Afro Newspaper / Gado, Getty Images; 439: Harvard Law School Library, Historical & Special Collections; 446: "In Industry to Stay," image in Abram L. Harris, *The Negro Worker: A Problem of Vital Concern to the Entire Labor Movement* (Progressive Labor Library Pamphlet No. 3), Morris Ernst Papers, University of Texas at Austin; 461: The Associated Press, New York, New York; 466: Walter P. Reuther Library, Archives of Labor and Urban Affairs, Wayne State University; 471: Photo history of the Toledo Auto-Lite Strike, Scrapbook, Toledo Lucas County Public Library; 478: Marianne Mather / *Chicago Tribune* / TCA; 493: photograph by Sheldon Dick for the U.S. Farm Security Administration / Office of War Information Black & White Photographs, Prints and Photographs Division, Library of Congress; 498: Louise Boyle / Southern Tenant Farmers Union Photographs, 1937 and 1982, Kheel Center, Cornell University, published courtesy of James Boyle Rogers; 502: Scurlock Studio Records, Archives Center,

PHOTO CREDITS

National Museum of American History, Smithsonian Institution; 511: Bettmann / Getty Images; 517: March on Washington Movement Flyer, AFL-CIO Information Department, Photographic Prints Collection, University of Maryland; 519: from *The Crisis*, Feb. 1945, Yale Collection of American Literature, Beinecke Rare Book & Manuscript Library; 521: Scurlock Studio Records, Archives Center, National Museum of American History, Smithsonian Institution; 527: Walter P. Reuther Library, Archives of Labor and Urban Affairs, Wayne State University; 532: Published with permission of Katherine Degn and Kraushaar Galleries, New York, New York

Index

Page numbers in *italics* refer to photo captions and epigraphs.

Abrams, Jacob, 75
Abrams v. United States, 75–77
ACLU (American Civil Liberties Union), 5, 108, 111, 112, 114, 115, 151, 184, 203, 245, 296, 307, 357, 362, 378, 388, 401, 411, *478*, 479, 504, 527, 534, 535
  Baldwin at, 2, 14, 24, 76, 83–85, 107, 108, 190, 201, 237, 298, 358, 370, 410, 480–81, 484–86, 500–501, 532
  "Black Justice" study of, 426
  Committee on Academic Freedom, 203
  critics of, 84
  De Jonge and, 500
  Emergency Case Fund, 201
  Flynn and, *294*, 298, 528–29
  National Committee on Labor Injunctions, 480–81, 484
  political prisoners and, *294*
  radio and, 231
  Sacco and Vanzetti and, 298
  Scopes trial and, 190, 202–7, 210
Adamic, Louis, 272, 288
Adams, MA, 256
Addams, Jane, 22, 40, 303, 304
Aderholt, Orville, 367
Adler, Felix, 22
administration, 412–14
  Du Bois and, 425
  Federal Indian Law and, 414–23
  Frankfurter and, 413–14, 423, 425
  Margold and, 425–26, 537
  segregation and, 429–30, 432, 433
advertising campaigns, 152, *153*
AFL (American Federation of Labor), 4, 33, 67–69, 96, 97, 111, 200, 238, 253, 254, 266, 268, 269, 272, 273, 277, 293, 303, 306, 313, 314, 320, 322–24, 333, 349, 364, 387, 389, 469, 473, 474, 480, 506, 514
  auto workers and, 469, 472
  CIO and, 473, 497
  Pullman porters and, 354, 355, 502
  NAACP and, 383, 526
  Randolph and, 341, 526, 673n38
  Sacco and Vanzetti and, 298
  Taylorism and, 308
  Workers' Education Bureau, 322
AFL-CIO, 497, 526
Africa, 328, 335–36
African Blood Brotherhood, 331, 382
African Methodist Episcopal Church, 326–27, 328, 458
African Methodist Episcopal Zion Church, 36
Agassiz, Louis, 19, 207
Agricultural Adjustment Act (AAA), 503–04
Agricultural Workers Industrial Union, 475
Agriculture, U.S. Department of, 503, 504
Akron, OH, 488
Alabama, 167, 405, 428, 519–20
Alabama Farmers' Union, 399
Alexander, Sadie, 162
Alexander, Will, 441
Alger, Horatio, 226
All God's Chillun Got Wings (O'Neill), 217
Alston, Melvin, 453
Alston v. School Board of Norfolk, 453
Aluminum Ore Company, 33
Amalgamated Clothing Workers of America (ACW), 111, 113, 300–302, 304–10, *305*, 313, 314, 317, 318, 320–22, 326, 362, 364, 369, 373, 409, 454, 467, 479, 481, 483, 484, 486, 487, 496, 516, 642n34, 667n40
Amalgamated Textile Workers (ATW), 313–14, 372–73
American Association of Law Schools, 440

American Automobile Manufacturers
    Association, 497
American Bar Association, 440
American Birth Control League, 7, 244
American Communist Labor Party, 294
American Expeditionary Force (AEF), 50, 72
American Federationist, 96
American Federation of Labor, *see* AFL
American Federation of Teachers, 203, 510
American Fund for Public Service (Garland
    Fund)
  accomplishments and legacy of, 400–401,
      497, 530–32, 533–41
  advisors to, 112–13
  aims of, 3–5, 7, 109–10, 115, 189–90, 245, 387
  amounts given by, 3, 357, 400, 460, 530, 536,
      676n11
  annual reports of, 8, 246
  archives of, 400
  critics and adversaries of, 3, 8, 174, 241,
      248–49, 535, 539, 586n16, 676n11
  directors of, 4, 6–9, *98,* 110–15, 162, 174,
      230, 241, 245–46, 291–92, 357, 540,
      568–69, 676n11
  diverse membership and shared beliefs in,
      4, 113, 541
  division into committees, 376–77, 386–87
  establishment of, 2–4, 109–15, 117, 122,
      245–47, 491, 530
  finances of, 3, 5, 8, 161, 171, 189, *240,*
      241–49, 322, 357–59, 361, 363, 376, 377,
      380, 381, 384, 398–400, 436, 437, 444, 445,
      640, 444, 445, 460, 504, 513, 530, 540
  first board meeting of, 245–46
  first grants by, 114–15, 155
  as forgotten, 536–38
  funding policies of, 109–10, 115, 171–72,
      234, 246, 376–77
  Garland's wishes and, 246, 398, 441, 460,
      461, 538
  grant ledger of, *542*
  incorporation of, 8, 109, 245
  list of gifts by, 543–66
  mission statement of, 245
  partisan split in, 361, 363, 364, 369, *372,* 376,
      377, 386, 391, 444, 461, 484, 505–7
  percentages of fund outlays, 567
  stock market holdings of, 3, 161, 322, 358,
      361, 363, 376, 377, 380, 381, 444, 445, 530
  tax treatment of, 245–49
  termination of, 400, 527–28, 530
  see also specific people and issues
American Indian Defense Association, 418

American Legion, 248, 288
American Mercury, 157
American Missionary Association, 131, 132, 169
American Negro Labor Congress, 366, 368, 390
American Professional Football Association, 217
American Protective League, 48
American Railway Union, 319, 344, 474
American Socialist Society, 202
American Textile Workers Union, 360
American Tobacco Company, 152
American Union Against Militarism, 40–41,
    43, 409
American Woolen Company, 311–34
American Workers Party, 470
Ames, James Barr, 407
Amherst College, 437, 458
Amsterdam News, 342, 443, 511
Amtorg, 399
anarchists, 52, 53, 91, 108, 118, 119, 201, 227,
    236, 238, 254, 257, 262, 270, 273, 277, *280,*
    282, 285, 287–88, 312, 394, 491
  Berkman, 201, 238, 258–59, 293
  Caron, 279–82, *280,* 297, 299
  Galleanisti, 299–300, 312
  Goldman, 91, 201, 238, 258–59, 261, 293
  Sacco and Vanzetti, *see* Sacco and Vanzetti
Anderson, Charles, 137–39, 142
Anderson, Garland, 229
Angell, Norman, 315
Anthony, Susan B., 255
antisemitism, 209, 370, 415–17, 426
Appeal to the Young, An (Kropotkin), 257
April, Joe, 117
April Farm, *116,* 117–22, *119, 121, 392,*
    393–96, *395,* 491
Are They Doomed, 298
Argot, Hester, 128
Arkansas, 208, 405, 428, 507
  sharecroppers and massacre in, 191–202,
      195, 212–13, 218, 229–30, 297, 368, 380,
      382, 406, 460, 515
Arkansas Supreme Court, 197, 198
Army, U.S., 419, 421
arts and culture, *216,* 217–33
  Black dialect and, 224–25
  capitalism and, 226
  commercial appeal and, 229
  communism and, 218, 233–34
  Du Bois and, 217, 221–23, 226, 227
  Federated Press and, 229–30
  film, 218–20, 224
  Harlem and, 127, 217, 221–23, *225,* 226
  Johnson and, 132, *216,* 217–22, 224–26

literature, 217, 221
Locke and, 222–23, *223*, 226, 227
New Masses and, 227–28
politics and, 218, 223
propaganda and, 217, 218, 223–24, 227
radio and, 232–33
Associated Press, 533, 535
Association for the Study of Negro Life and History, 161–62
Association of Colored Railway Trainmen and Locomotive Firemen, 514
Aswell, James Benjamin, 148
Atchison, Topeka and Santa Fe Railroad, 420
Atlanta, GA, 192
Atlanta Constitution, 156
Atlanta School of Social Work, 162
Atlanta University, *124*, 131–34, 136, 164, 177
Atlantic and Pacific Railroad, 419
Atlantic Monthly, 78
Aunt Mandy's Chicken Dinner (Johnson), 219
automobile workers, 209, 468, 491, 492, 497, 505, 512
   Black, 505–6
   at Electric Auto-Lite, 469–72, *471*
   at General Motors, 488–89, 493–96, *493*
   National Industrial Auto Workers Union, 367
   strikes by, 469–72, *471*, 488–89, 493–96
   United Auto Workers, 491–93, 495–97, 534, 535

Bacon, Peggy, *532*
Bailey v. Alabama, 142
Baker, Ella, 463
Baker, Newton, 409
Baldwin, Evelyn Preston, 67, 307
Baldwin, Frank, Jr., 16
Baldwin, Frank Fenno, 13–16, 20, 60
Baldwin, Lucy Cushing, 13, 15, 16, 60, 68
Baldwin, Roger Nash, xv, 2–4, 7, 8, *12*, 13–37, *15*, 96, 97, 101, 108, 146, 161, 162, 189, 190, 241, 289, 309, 339, 361, 363, 369–70, 376, 377, 381, 386, 390–91, 400, 405, 411, 444, 460–61, 467, 475, 526, 527, 528, *532*, 533, 534, 536, 539–40
   at ACLU, 2, 14, 24, 76, 83–85, 107, 108, 190, 201, 237, 298, 358, 370, 410, 480–81, 484–86, 500–501, 532
   American Fund established by, 2–4, 109–15, 117
   American Fund funding policies and, 171
   on American Fund's accomplishments, 531–32
   as American Fund's central figure, 24, 110–11
   American Fund terminated by, 530

   at American Union Against Militarism, 40, 43
   Bellair and, 63–65
   birth of, 13
   Black education and, 174, 176, 177, 184, 185, 187
   Bloor and, 396
   Brandeis and, 20, 75, 96, 304
   childhood of, 14–16, 18–19
   civil liberties as viewed by, 43–44, 238, 270, 359, 500
   at Civil Liberties Bureau, 43, 47–49, 54, 59, 60, 66, 67, 82–83, 97, 201, 283, 293, 334
   Communists and, 233–34, 237, 441, 461, 529
   courts and, 200–202, 204, 206, 207
   death of, 532
   democracy as viewed by, 13, 14, 26, 27, 36, 73–74, 81, 83–85, 96, 97, 207
   depression suffered by, 357–58
   draft noncompliance, arrest, and imprisonment of, 13–14, 55, 58–66, 75, 79, 201, 293, 396, 534
   Ernst and, 370–71
   family background of, 13
   Flynn and, 291, 292, 300, 529
   Frankfurter and, 408–10
   Garland and, 2, 107–9, 120, 311
   at Harvard, 13, 14, 16, 19, 20
   Hillman and, 301
   injunction problem and, 476, 480–81
   Johnson and, 127, 128, 151, 158, 368
   labor education and, 314, 315, 320–23
   Liberty Under the Soviets, 237–39
   Lippmann and, 54
   lynching and, 155
   majority rule model and, 484–86
   as manual laborer, 67–68, 79
   marriage to Evelyn Preston, 67, 307
   marriage to Madeleine Doty, *57*, 65–67, 237
   money habits and views of, 15–16, 81–82, 85, 676n11
   move to New York City, 40
   Mutual Aid Society founded by, 108
   Osborne and, 62–63
   Perkins and, 495
   race and, 19, 20, 29–31, 115, 173–74
   radio initiative and, 231, 232
   Randolph and, 337, 345
   in St. Louis, 20–24, *21*, 26, 28–32, 35–37, 40, 60, 61, 84, 115, 157, 158
   schools as viewed by, 174, 176, 177
   Scopes trial and, 206, 207
   Scottsboro case and, 441, 442
   sexuality of, 63–66

INDEX

Baldwin, Roger Nash (*cont.*)
  Soviet Union visited by, 237–39
  steel strike and, 58, 59, 68–73, 79, 82
  Taft and, 64
  taxes and, 245–47
  on Tresca, 277
  Vanguard Press and, 235
  violence as viewed by, 282
  voter initiative and referendum project of, 26, 28–30, 157
  Ware and, 397
  Wilson and, 39–40, 59, 60
  World War I and, 39, 54–56
Baldwin, William H., Jr., 17–19, 22, 89, 97, 175–76, 181
Baltimore, MD, 450
Baltimore Afro-American, 224–25, 459, 464
Baltimore & Ohio Railroad, 308
Battle of the Overpass, 497
Battle of the Running Bulls, 495
Beard, Charles, 491
Bebel, August, 257–58
Bellair, Harry, 63–65
Bellamy, Edward, 257, 258
Bendix Corporation, 488
Bennett, Lerone, Jr., 511–12
Bentham, Jeremy, 102
Berger, Victor, 273
Berkman, Alexander, 201, 238, 258–59, 293
Berkshire Cotton Manufacturing Company, 256
Berkshire Knitting Mills, 483
Bernays, Edward L., xv, 151–58, *153*, 205, 389, 412, 494
Bertillon, Alphonse, 61
Beyer, Otto S., 308, 309, 317
Bezos, Jeff, 89
B. F. Goodrich, 488
Bigelow, Herbert, 47, 48
Big Money, The (Dos Passos), 70–71
birth control, 7, 244, 371
Birth of a Nation, The, 220
Bisbee, AZ, 409, 413
Black, Hugo, 462
Black America (Nearing), 366–67, 382, 386, 388
Black Americans
  African emigration idea and, 336
  class and, 115, 172, 326, 333–34, 352, 440, 447, 504
  in Communist Party, 335, 366
  Communists' Black Belt thesis on, 364–68, *365*, 370, 374, 379, 397, 398, 447, 500, 507, 671n15
  Du Bois on experience of, 225

Northern migration of, 6, 29, 127, 136, 143, 176, 208–11, 214, 339, 513, 541
  political participation of, 130
  racial science and, 19–20, 207
  as voters, 41, 133, 137, 141–44, 146, 151, 156–57, 164, 166, 215, 430–31, 436
  voting rights of, 30, 130, 143, 150, 173, 359, 380, 430–31, 436, 506
  see also civil rights; racial violence; segregation
Black Belt self-determination thesis, 364–68, *365*, 370, 374, 379, 397, 398, 447, 500, 507, 671n15
Black Cabinet, 139
Black education, *160*, 161–87, *168*, 192
  Baldwin and, 174, 176, 177, 184, 185, 187
  Black teachers in, 165–67, 169, 186, 187
  Du Bois and, 162, 163, 167, 177–87, 189, 221, 536
  Florida and, 166–71, 186
  funding for, 166–67, 169–71, 174–83, 185–87, 355, 359, 379, 380, 384, 387, 390, 405, 406, 425–28, 431, 441, 448–51, 512
  graduate and professional, 457–65
  Houston on, 451
  industrial-style, 161, 162, 175–82, *180*
  Johnson and, 162–64, 167–69, 171–73, 176, 182–87, 221, 536
  Jones and, 178–83, *180*, 185, 187
  labor organization and, 162, 183–84, 186, 187
  NAACP and, 176–78, 181, 184, 185, 189, 586n16, 614n30
  philanthropic foundations and, 174–83, *180*, 187
  Sheats and, 167–69, 175–76, 181, 186
  taxes and, 167, 169–71, 175, 180, 425–26, 432
  vandalism of schools in, 165–66, *166*
  workers and, 162, 175–82
Black nationalism, 336, 365
Black newspapers, 141, 144, 162
Black Panthers, 81
Black professional class, 459
Black Star Line, 336
Blackstone, William, 102
Black Worker, The (Harris), 445
Black workers, 5, 17, 18, 173, 176–77, 182, 189, 230, 325, 335, 374, 381, 447, 459, 506
  in automobile industry, 505–6
  and combining of civil rights and labor efforts, 377, 378, 382–86, 388–90, 385–86
  education and, 162, 175–82
  employment discrimination and, 450–51, 510–12, 514, *517*, 518–26, *517*, 525

Ford and, 209
Harris on, 445–46
labor unions and, 32–33, 115, 162, 173, 176, 177, 183–84, 266, 267, 326, 338, 339–41, 346, 347, 352–53, 355, 364, 367, 374, 375, 382, 383, 389, 390, 398, 432–33, *446*, 486, 506, 512–14, 518–26
March on Washington Movement and, 508–11, 516–18, *517*
NAACP and, 377, 378, 382–86, 388–90
on railroads, 5, 327, 339–40, 383, 451, 513–15, 518–26, *519*, 673n38
sharecroppers, *see* sharecropping and peonage
as strikebreakers, 35, 340, 344, 353
wages of, 68, 182, 193, 343, 344
Blankenhorn, Heber, 49–50, 72, 73, 667n40
Bloor, Ella Reeve, 293–95, 396
Bly, Nellie, 27, 61
Boehner, William, 287
Bolshevism, 2, 233, 333, 335, 410
see also Russian Revolution
bombings
by Caron, 279–82, *280*, 297, 299
by Galleanisti, 299–300, 312
Haymarket, 201, 266, 282
mail bombs, 287, 299
by McNamara brothers, 272–73, 281, 303
Preparedness Day, 201, 294, 410
rail station, *265*
Wall Street, 287–88, 299
Bond, Horace Mann, 167, *168*, 170, 171, 185, 432
Bonus Army, 509
Borah, William, 149, 156
Boston Globe, 2, *104*, 392
Boyd, Frank, 349
Boyd, Frederic, Sumner, 278
Bradley, Joseph P., 133–34
Bradley Foundation, 539
Brandeis, Louis, 20, 75, 77, 96, 246, 304
Brass Check, The (Sinclair), 106, 107
Bratton, U. S., 193
Briggs, Cyril, 331, 332, 335, 336, 368, 382
Britain, 44
Broach, H. H., 346, 361, 369
Brook Farm, 117, 120
Brookings Institution, 416, 417, 419, 424
Brookwood Labor College, 291, 311, 314–24, *316*, 326, 339, 346–47, 357, 362, 364, 369, 370, 371, 379, 382, 398, 443, 445, 446, 454, 462–63, 468–73, 483, 485–87, 496, 497, 500, 504, 516, 531–32, 536, 642n34, 667n40
Brookwood Players, 317, 494, *527*, 528
closing of, 528

Communist faculty and students at, 528, 529
curriculum of, 317
democratic theory of, 318
Dewey and, 318–20
founding of, 314
heterodoxy of, 320
NAACP–American Fund scholarships at, 316
Reuther brothers and, 491–94, 496, 497
strikes and, 467, 469–72, 489–90, 492–93, 495, 496
students at, 315–16
Brophy, John, xv, 306–7, 317, 473, 484, 506
Brotherhood of Elevator and Switchboard Operators, 340–41
Brotherhood of Locomotive Firemen, 339, 513, 514, 518, 522
Brotherhood of Sleeping Car Porters, 326, 341–55, 357, 374, 377, 382, 411, 483, 501–3, *502*, 507, 509, 510, 513, 516, 531, 671n15
Brown, John, 17, 19, 81, 191, 201, 273, 276, 431
Browne, Lewis, 117
Brown v. Board of Education, 5, 324, 406, 526, 531, 533–38
Bryan, William Jennings, 25, 140, 141, 204–6, 218
Buchanan, James Paul, 147
Buckner, Emory, 415, 416
Buck's Stove & Range Company, 474
Budd Manufacturing Company, 485
Budenz, Louis, 470, 479
Bukharin, Nikolai, 363
Bulkley, Robert, 431
Bullard, Arthur, 44, 45, 77
Bunche, Ralph, 446, 507–8
Bund, 301
Bureau of Insular Affairs, 407
Bureau of Labor Statistics, U.S., 344, 667n40
Burleson, Albert, 41–43, 47, 77, 334
Butler, Edward, 22, 24, 27
Byrnes, James F., 147, 334

Cake Walk, 219
Calhoun, Arthur, 317
Calumet, MI, 62, 74
Campbell, Abraham, 129
Camp Pike, 191, 194
capitalism, 4–6, 9, 14, 91, 161, 200, 241, 257–60, 281, 305, 334, 358, 376, 412, 468, 497, 506, 537
culture and, 226
invisible hand of, 105
and nationalization of industry, 307, 309
Capper, Arthur, 431
Carnegie, Andrew, 3, 89, 96

Carnegie organizations, 89, 96, 174, 175, 178, 540
Caron, Arthur, 279–82, *280*, 297, 299
Carpenter, Edward, 64, 66, 235, 258
Caruso, Joseph, 274
censorship, 77, 78, 371
   post office and, 41–43, 54, 75, 334
   during World War I, 39–45, 60, 75, 77, 534
   see also free speech
Centralia, WA, 288
Chafee, Zechariah, Jr., 75–77, 79, 237, 296, 409, 410
Chambers, Whittaker, 397
Channing, William Ellery, 16–18, 20, 23, 26, 55–56, 76
charitable trusts and institutions, 242–43, 247, 538–39
   see also philanthropic foundations
Chase, Stuart, 189, 190, 281, 308, 317, 320–21, 339, 479, 491, 648n26
Chauncey, George, 64
Chawke, Thomas, *188*
Chesnut, William, 453
Chicago, IL, 58, 208, 343, 450, 474, 483
   Haymarket bombing in, 201, 266, 282
Chicago Daily Tribune, 392
Chicago Defender, 208, 219, 220
Chicago Federation of Labor, 230–31
Chinese immigrants, 411, 429–30
   in *Yick Wo* case, 429–30, 432, 450, 521
Christopher, Milton, 129
cigarettes, 152, *153*
CIO (Congress of Industrial Organizations and Committee for Industrial Organization), 5, 324, 401, 468, 473, 492, 493, 495, 496, 497, 505, 506, 516, 533, 535
   AFL and, 473, 497
   Black members of, 512
   Southern Tenant Farmers Union and, 507
   Steel Workers Organizing Committee, 472, 500, 505
Citibank, 100
City College of New York, 330, 407, 415, 421, 463
Civic Club, 222, 292, 295, 309, 347, 532
civil liberties, 534
   Baldwin's views on, 43–44, 238, 270, 359, 500
   in Soviet Union, 238–39, 359
   invention of phrase, 43–44
   Civil Liberties Bureau, 43, 47–49, 54, 59, 60, 66, 67, 82–83, 97, 112, 201, 283, 293, 334
civil rights, 130, 142, 311, 324, 326, 355, 359, 374, 377–80, 385–86, 388, 534–35, 539
   labor and, 377, 378, 382–86, 388–90, 385–86
   "long" movement for, 535

Civil Rights Act of 1964, 526
Civil Rights Cases, 133, 149
Civil War, 99, 128, 136, 163, 167, 193, 326, 508
Clark, Evans, 648n26, 667n40
Clark, Septima Poinsette, 453–54
class, 5, 73, 200, 215, 266–68, 286, 298, and *passim*
   American Fund and, 110, 246, 467
   Baldwin and, 79, 85, 97, 115
   Class struggle, *253*, 269, 278, 484, 490, 504
   culture and, 226–27, 231
   democracy and, 412
   Du Bois and, 187
   Frankfurter and, 412
   gender and, 257–59, 263
   labor education and, 315
   mass production and, 310
   NAACP and, 382–83, 445–47, 464
   race and, 172–73, 182, 190, 324, 326, 333, 340, 352, 359, 382, 440, 447, 459, 506, 535
   Randolph and, 329, 334, 352, 375–76
   Sacco and Vanzetti and, 300
   the state and, 200, 349–50, 475, 477–78, 485–86
   see also Black Americans, class and
class consciousness, 172
Cleveland, Grover, 215
coal miners, *see* miners
Cobb, Frank, 44, 72, 77
Cohan, George M., 99, 103
Cohen, Felix, 421–23, 433
Cohen, Morris Raphael, 421
Cohn, Fannia M., 291, 317
Cole, Bob, 132, *216*
Cole & Johnson Brothers, *216*
Coleman, McAlister, 479
Colfax Massacre, 136
Collier, John, 417–18, 422
Colorado coal miners' strike and Ludlow massacre, 86–88, *88*, 91–93, *92*, 95, 109, 196, 279, 282, 295, 378, 539
Colorado Fuel & Iron Company (CF&I), 86–88, 93, 95
Colored People's Convention of the State of South Carolina, 164
Columbia Law Review, 373
Columbia University, 186, 462, 477
Commission on Industrial Relations, 93–97, *94*, 111, 275–77, 279, 285, 295, 308, 482, 539
Commission on Interracial Cooperation, 178, 183
Committee for Industrial Organization, *see* CIO
Committee on Civil Liberties, 386, 441
Committee on Fair Employment Practice, 511

Committee on Negro Work, 357, 377–81, 384–91, 425, 432, 445, 448, 450, 451, 455, 461
Committee on Public Information (CPI), 38, 45–47, 74, 152, 154
Committee on Research and Publication, 479
Commons, John, 317
Commonwealth College, 321, 507, 529
Communist Manifesto, The (Marx and Engels), 200, 259
Communist Party, Communists, 14, 112, 120, 233, 257, 294, 320–22, 324, 335, 355, 359, *360*, 361–69, 377, 379, 383, 384, 396–97, 447, 470, 472, 487, 497, 500, 505, 676n11
   American Fund and, 3–4, 7, 234, 359–61, *360*, 363–64, 366–69, 386–89, 391, 399, 440–41, 461, 464, 505, 529, 677n11
   April Farm and, 394, 396
   arts and, 218, 233–34
   Baldwin and, 233–34, 237, 441, 461, 529
   Black, 335–36, 366, 500
   Black Belt thesis of, 364–68, *365*, 370, 374, 379, 397, 398, 447, 500, 507, 671n15
   Brookwood Labor College and, 528, 529
   Comintern, 362–68, *365*, 397, 440, 442, 505
   expulsion from Brookwood, 528
   expulsion from ACLU leadership, 528–29
   expulsion from STFU, 507
   Flynn and, 528, 531
   Garland and, 394, 396, 398–99, 529
   Gastonia workers and, 367, 368, 406
   Lement Harris and, 398–400
   Houston and, 442, 443
   labor unions and, 234, 362–64, 367
   NAACP and, 440
   National Negro Congress and, 505–7, 529
   Nazi-Soviet Pact and, 528, 529
   Popular Front, 401, 442, 505–7, 509, 528, 529
   Randolph and, 335, 355, 506–8
   Scottsboro case and, 435, 436, 443
   Southern Tenant Farmers Union and, 507, 529
   textile workers' strike and, 362–63
   Ware and, 396–400, *397*
   World War II and, 510
Conference for Progressive Political Action (CPPA), 383
Congress of Industrial Organizations, *see* CIO
Congress of Racial Equality, 311, 534
Consolidated Gas Company, 330
Constitution, U.S., 18, 42, 76, 136, 147, 150, 199, 371, 429, 431, 455, 475, 500, 522
Constitutional amendments
   First, 74, 76
   Thirteenth, 142
   Fourteenth, 133, 136, 149–50, 200, 426–27, 433
   Sixteenth, 242
   Nineteenth, 291
Constitutional Convention, 326
Cooke, Jay, Jr., 99
Cooke, Jay, Sr., 99
Cooke & Co., 99
Cookman Institute, 328, 329
Coolidge, Calvin, 296, 354, 508
Cooper, Henry Allen, 149
Coors family, 539
Corrigan v. Buckley, 211n
cotton, 167, 176, 191, 193–95, *195*, 401, 447, 503
courts, 190–91, 200, 207, 307, 352, 373, 405–6, 459, 460, 515, 523–25
   affirmative legal action and, 478–79, *478*, 486, 489, 490, 516
   Baldwin and, 200–202, 204, 206, 207
   class domination of, 476, 486
   Johnson on role of, 213–14
   labor unions and, 200–201
   liberal legalism and, 423
   Marx's view of, 200
   NAACP campaign and, 359
   public opinion and, 191, 207
   see also Supreme Court, U.S.; *specific cases*
corruption in government, 22–29, 31
Covington, J. Harry, 284
Coxey's Army, 509
Creel, George, xv, 45–47, *46*, 56, 74, 77, 78, 95, 105, 145, 152, 154, 220, 227, 270, 295, 449
crime, 61, 62, 66
criminal justice system
   juvenile, 23, 83–84
   prisons, 58, 61, 62, 66, 74
Crisis, 144, 156, *160*, 177–79, 181, 185–87, 208, 213, 222, 381, 383, 385, *385*, 425, 449
Croly, Herbert, 407
Crosswaith, Frank, 331, 341, 347, 375, 382, 509
crowd psychology, 51–54, 151–53, 376
   panic and, 61–62, 79
   Randolph and, 376
   see also propaganda; public opinion
Cullen, Countee, 224
Cultura Obrera, 227
culture, *see* arts and culture
Curry, Jabez Lamar Monroe, 175

Daily American, 132
Daily Worker, 227, 436
dark money, 539

Darrow, Clarence, xv, 217, 272, 295, 303, 394, 443
  Scopes defended by, 7, 191, 204–6, *205,* 217, *478*
  Sweet defended by, 7, *188,* 191, 210–14
Darwin, Charles, 235
Daugherty, Harry, 150, 294, 474
Davis, Jerome, 236–37
Davis, John P., 451, 505, 507–8
Dawes Allotment Act, 417, 422–23
dead hand, 90, 101, 105–6, 242–43
Debs, Eugene, 41, 74, 111, 141, 201, 231, 255, 266, 268, 273, 294, 296, 319, 330, 339, 344, 384, 474, 513
Debs Radio, 231–33, *232*
Declaration of Independence, 503
De Jonge, Dirk, 500
De Jonge v. Oregon, 500
DeLeon, Daniel, 266, 273
democracy, 3, 4, 9, 14, 24, 35–37, 58–59, 65, 73, 74, 79, 107, 114, 127, 152, 177, 318, 320, 332, 349, 378, 401, 411, 412, 497, 539
  Baldwin's views on, 13, 14, 26, 27, 36, 73–74, 81, 83–85, 96, 97, 207
  direct, 25–27, 31, 36
  education and, 187, 318–19
  Frankfurter on, 411–14
  free speech and, 79
  industrial, 114–15, 292, 306, 308–10, *313,* 319, 322, 342, 344–49, 359, 361, 368, 373, 374, 375, 382–84, 386, 398, 400, 412, 445, 472, 478, 483–87, 493–95, 526, 536
  labor unions and, 95
  newspapers and, 27
  wealth and, 82, 85–86, 90, 93–94, 96–97
Democratic Party, 22, 25–27, 41, 133, 140–43, 147, 148, 156, 157, 215, 269, 462, 481, 514
  Black voters and, 430–31
Dennett, Mary Ware, 235, 371
deportations of radicals, 285, 293, 295, 296
Depression, Great, 399, 400, 414, 448, 457, 467–69, 474, 481, 485, 499, 503, 509, 512, 518
DeSilver, Albert, 43, 67, 296
Des Verney, William H., 342, 347
Detroit, MI, 209, 450, 491, 492–93, 496, 497
  Sweet family in, 7, 191, 207–15, *208,* 217, 218, 230, 297, 326, 378, 380, 389, 406, 493, 515, 520
Detroit City College, 491
DeVos Foundation, 539
Dewey, John, 77, 84, 113, 203, 238, 318–21, 323, 384, 431
Dies, Martin, 4
Dillet, Etienne, 128

disinformation, 538
  and economic structure, 538
  see also propaganda
Domingo, Wilfred, 331, 332, 336
Doran, J. T. "Red," 286
Dos Passos, John, 70–71, 227
Doty, Madeleine, xv, *57,* 65–67, 237
Douglas, Aaron, *225*
Douglass, Frederick, 328, 431, 508, 511
Douglass, Joseph, 431
Dow Jones Industrial Average, 161, 358, 381
Dred Scott v. Sandford, 345
Dreiser, Theodore, 261
Drewry, Patrick, 148
Dreyfus Affair, 297
Dr. Seuss, 235–36
Dubinsky, David, 472, 473
Du Bois, Nina, *356*
Du Bois, W. E. B., xv, 7, 35, 36, 111, 127, 128, 142, 133, 156–58, *160,* 169–70, 176, 332, 339, *356,* 379, 382–86, *385,* 389, 425, 427, 431, 440, 446, 448, 449, 463, 505, 511, 528, 531
  arts and, 217, 221–23, 226, 227
  Black Belt thesis and, 365, 429
  on Black experience, 225
  Brown v. Board reaction of, 531
  education and, 162, 163, 167, 177–87, 189, 221, 536
  Elaine massacre and, 195–96
  Johnson and, 138–39, 144
  Margold and, 425, 432
  at 1932 NAACP conference, 431
  Scopes trial and, 207
  Scottsboro case and, 441
  The Souls of Black Folk, 138, 177
  Talented Tenth of, 332–33, 465
  Washington and, 138
Dunbar, Paul Laurence, 437
Dunn, Robert W., 360–61, 366, 368, 377, 386, 390–91, 444, 461, 486, 505
Durant, Will, 491
Durst Ranch, 274
Dyer, David, 31, 32
Dyer, Leonidas, 146
  anti-lynching bill of, 146–49, *147,* 151, 154, 156–58, 189, 246, 389

Eastman, Crystal, xv, 43–44
Eastman, Max, xv, 41–43, 106, 227
  Russian Revolution documentary of, 228–29
East St. Louis, IL, 32–33
  massacre in, 33–36, *34,* 41, 48, 58, 146, *160,* 173, 195, 208, 214, 220

East St. Louis Massacre, The (Wells), 35
Ebert, Justus, 267, 269, 286
economic inequality, 5, 6, 9, 82, 103, 104, 241, 259, 533–34
Edelson, Becky, *280*
education, 174, 314–15
  American Fund and, 161 ff., 311–24
  democracy and, 187, 318–19
  Dewey's views on, 319–20
  elementary school, 174, 448
  funding for, 166–67, 174–76, 182–83, 185, 186, 355, 359, 379, 380, 384, 387, 390, 405, 406, 425–28, 431, 448–51, 512
  graduate and professional, 457–65
  philanthropic foundations and, 89, 174
  school construction, 167
  segregation in, 426–33
  see also Black education; labor education; segregated schools; teachers
Education, U.S. Department of, 178, 179
Elaine massacre of sharecroppers, 191–202, *195*, 212–13, 229–30, 297, 368, 382, 406, 503, 504
Electric Auto-Lite, 469–72, *471*
Eliot, Charles, 91
Ellis, Havelock, 258
Ellis, J. H., 48
Ellison, Ralph, 176, 222, 671n17
Ely, Richard T., 102
Emerson, Ralph Waldo, 17, 107, 120, 201
Emperor Jones, The (O'Neill), 217
Engdahl, J. Louis, 368
Engels, Friedrich, 246, 263, 330
  The Communist Manifesto, 200, 259
  The Origin of the Family, 259
Erdman Act, 349
Ernst, Morris, xv, 112, 235, 358, 361, 370–74, *372*, 377, 379–82, 384–86, 388–90, 405, 415, 425, 432, 441, 458, 462, 478, 479, 481, 527, 528, 531, 676n11
  Baldwin and, 370–71
  censorship cases of, 371
  committees created by, 376–77, 386–87
  early life of, 370
  Judaism of, 374
  law as viewed by, 371, 373
  law practice of, 370–73
  NAACP and, *372*
  Randolph and, 374
Erwin, Charles, 642n34
Espionage Act, 41–42, 45, 47, 48, 54, 58, 59, 67, 74, 75, 75n, 82, 112, 172, 201, 282, 284, 293, 294, 296, 334

Ethical Culture movement, 22, 23
Ettor, Joseph, 274, 279, 281, 284, 285, 297
evolution case, *see* Scopes, John

Fahy, Charles, 520–21
Fair Employment Practices Commission (FEPC), 518, 524, 525
Farmer, James, 311
Farmers' National Committee for Action, 398, 399
Farmers' National Weekly, 399
Farmers' Unity Council, 399
Farm Research, Inc., 398
Farrell, James T., 235
fascism, 468, 507, 528
FBI (Federal Bureau of Investigation), 3–4, 85, 334
Federal Radio Commission, 231
Federated Press, 106–7, 229–30, *230*, 232, 347, 357, 495, 504
Fellowship of Reconciliation, 226, 314, 489
film industry, 218–20, 224
Firestone Tire & Rubber, 488
First Amendment, 74, 76
First National Bank of New York, 100, *240*, 358, 380, 381
Fisk Jubilee Singers, 221
Fisk University, 178, 184, 221
Fitzgerald, F. Scott, 8
Flint, MI, 493–95, *493*, 496
Florida, 130, 405, 428
  Black community in, 130, 133–35, 163, 166–71, 169–71, 186
  Jacksonville, *see* Jacksonville, FL
Florida State Teachers Association, 169
Florida Times-Union, 132
Flynn, Annie Gurley, 255–58, 268
Flynn, Bina, 358
Flynn, Elizabeth Gurley, xv, 85, 112, 235, 253–63, *261*, 289, 291–300, 305, 322, 330, 345, 347, 361, 369, 391, 406, 475, 540
  ACLU and, *294*, 298, 528–29
  arrests of, 262, 270, 284
  Baldwin and, 291, 292, 300, 529
  birth of, 255
  Caron defended by, 279–81, *280*
  childhood of, 256–58
  in Communist Party, 528, 531
  family background of, 255
  Frankfurter and, 409–11
  health problems of, 254, 288, 358, 361, 69, 528
  IWW and, 253, 254, 263, 268–70, 272, 274, 276–89, 292, *294*, 295–96, 300, 311, 336, 410, 490
  law and morality as viewed by, 259, 300

Flynn, Elizabeth Gurley (*cont.*)
  marriage and children of, 268
  marriage as viewed by, 257–60
  physical appearance and public image of, 260–62
  political prisoners defended by, 289, 292–95, *294*, 396
  Sacco and Vanzetti defended by, 291, 296–300, 358, 531
  speeches of, *252*, 260–63, 277, 278, *280*, 283, 287
  textile workers' strikes and, 297, 358, 361–63
  Tresca and, 276–77, *280*, 281, 284, 287, 293, 297–99, 358
  violence and sabotage as viewed by, 272, 277–81, 287–89, 295, 490
  Wilson and, 285
  Workers Defense Union of, 293–98, 300
Flynn, Kathleen, 255
Flynn, Paddy, 255
Flynn, Tom, 255, 256, 258, 260, 262, 268
Folk, Joseph, 24, 26
folklore, 221
Ford, Henry, 6, 209
Ford, James, 366
Ford Motor Company, 122, 209, 234, 396, 469, 492
  River Rouge plant of, *466*, 496–97, 505–6
Fortune, T. Thomas, 131, 138, 141
Fort-Whiteman, Lovett, 331, 335, 336, 365–66
Foster, William (film producer), 219–20
Foster, William Z. (Communist and Garland Fund director), xvi, 69–70, 72, 73, 112, 233–34, 278, 321, 350, 360, *360*, 361, 363–64, 368
Fourier, Charles, 117, 120
Fourteenth Amendment, 133, 136, 149–50, 200, 426–27, 433
Francis, Megan Ming, 586n16, 614n30
Frank, Leo, 334
Frankensteen, Richard, *466*
Frankfurter, Felix, xvi, 75n, 113, 203, 206, 296, 406–14, *408*, 415, 421, 424, 425, 438, 463, 474, 505, 521, 533, 655n15, 657n36, 667n40
  on administration, 413–14, 423, 425
  Baldwin and, 408–10
  childhood of, 407
  FDR and, 481
  Flynn and, 409–11
  Houston and, 436, 438, 440, 443, 444, 456, 520, 523, 525
  labor law and, 479–82, 485, 490
  law as viewed by, 412–13, 422, 432
  law career of, 406–8, *408*, 411–13

Lippmann and, 411, 413
Margold and, 414–16, 418, 421, 423–25, 438, 440
NAACP and, 411, 520
Native Americans and, 421–23
The Public and Its Government, 412
on revolutionary movements, 412
Sacco and Vanzetti and, 410
Weisbord and, 479
Franklin, Benjamin, 88
Frazier, E. Franklin, 162, 185
Freedmen's Bureau, 131, 163
freedpeople, 128, 163–65, *166*, 242, 343, 344
free speech, 5, 14, 55, 74–79, 84, 85, 111, 115, 410, 413, 475, 534, 535, 537
  beginnings of, 74–77, 500
  De Jonge v. Oregon and, 500
  democracy and, 79
  Herndon v. Lowry and, 500–501
  IWW fights for, 269–71, 273, 274, 282, 284, 471
  limits of, 74–79, 85
  power and, 87–97
  pragmatist theory of, 76–77
  and pursuit of truth, 77–78
  radio and, 231
  switch in time of 1937 and, 500
  teachers and, 203, 204, 206
  Yates v. United States and, 534
  see also censorship
French Revolution, 51
Freud, Sigmund, 151
Freund, Ernst, 77
Frick, Henry Clay, 68, 70, 258
Full Fashioned Hosiery Workers Union, 483

Gaines, Lloyd, 459–64, *461*, 520, 521
Galleani, Luigi, 299
Galleanisti, 299–300, 312
Gallup mines, 472
Gandhi, Mohandas, 272, 287, 311, 489
Gannett, Lewis S., xvi, *98*, 111, 363, 369, 377, 379, 381, 387, 389, 390, 405, 444, 476, 512, 531
Gardner, Lucien D., 519–20
Garland, Charles, xvi, *xxii*, 1, 9, 101–2, 117, 120, 174, 190, 321, 393–96, 398–400, 504, 529–30
  April Farm commune of, *116*, 117–22, *119*, *121*, 392, 393–96, *395*, 491
  American Fund wishes of, 246, 398, 441, 460, 461, 538
  arrest and imprisonment of, 394
  Baldwin and, 2, 107–9, 120, 311
  children of, 393–95, 530
  Communists and, 394, 396, 398–99, 529

death of, 530
electroshock therapy of, 529–30
at Harvard, 2, 103
inheritance and establishment of American Fund, 1–5, 8, 101, 103–15, 117, 122, 151, 161, 245–47, 337, 358, 460, 491, 530, 533, 535, 540, 541
machinist work of, 530
marriage as viewed by, 2, 102, 108–9, 395
marriages of, 2, 107–9, 393–95, 530
mental health of, 393, 395, 529–30
Sinclair and, 2, 105–8, 491
trusts and income of, 104–5, 117, 247, 393, 398
Wells and, 1, 2, 102–3
Garland, James Albert, Jr., 1, 100–101, 245
Garland, James Albert (called Albert), Sr., 99–101, *100*
Garland, Jay, 395
Garland, Marie Tudor, xviii, 2, 101, 102, 104, 108, 395, 409
Garland, Mary (daughter of Charles), 395
Garland, Mary Wrenn (wife of Charles), 2, 107–9, 393–95
Garland Fund, *see* American Fund for Public Service
garment workers, 302–4, 316, 317, 331, 341, 472–73, 512
  Amalgamated Clothing Workers of America, 111, 113, 300–302, 304–10, *305*, 313, 314, 317, 318, 320–22, 326, 362, 364, 369, 373, 409, 454, 467, 479, 481, 483, 484, 486, 487, 496, 516, 642n34, 667n40
  International Ladies' Garment Workers Union, 232, 291, 293, 304, 317, 331, 357, 467, 472, 473, 479, 481, 495
  strikes by, 302–3, *305*, 467, 468
  United Garment Workers, 303, 305
  see also textile workers
Garrett, Finis, 148
Garrison, William Lloyd, 55
Garvey, Marcus, 331, 332, 335–36, 365, 374, 442, 503
Gary, Elbert Henry, 6, 68
Gary, IN, 209
Gastonia, NC, 367, 368, 370, 406, 469
Gates, Bill, 89
Gates, Frederick T., 86
Geisel, Theodor (Dr. Seuss), 235–36
General Education Board, 89, 175, 178, 179
General Electric, 58
General Motors (GM), 488–89, 493–96, *493*
George, Henry, 25, 235, 255

Georgia, 125–26, 164, 166, 167, 171, 185, 405, 428, 500
German Americans, 47–48
Germany
  Nazi, 505, 507, 510, 528, 529
  in World War I, 44, 50, 53, 56, 74, 75n
Gibbs, William B., Jr., 452
Gibbs v. Broome, 452–54
Gibran, Kahlil, 101
Giddings, Franklin, 178
Gilman, Charlotte Perkins, 258
Giovannitti, Arturo, 274, 284, 285, 297
Girard, Stephen, 88, 89
Gitlow, Benjamin, xvi, 360, *360*, 361, 363–64, 366, 369, 377, 381, 390–91, 399, 442, 444, 463, 534, 676n11
God's Trombones (Johnson), 224–25, *225*
Golden, Clinton, xvi, 112, 235, 301, 306, 309, 316, 361, 369, 370, 377, 398, 487, 491, 505
Goldman, Emma, 91, 201, 228, 258–59, 261, 293
Goluboff, Risa L., 664n67
Gompers, Samuel, xvi, 4, 35, 68, 96, 272, 298, 308, 322, 354, 474, 475, 478, 479
Gong Lum v. Rice, 426–27, 429, 432
Goodyear, 488
Gould, Jay, 27
Gramsci, Antonio, 315
Grant, Ulysses S., 22
Gray, Horace, 243, 244
Great Depression, 399, 400, 414, 448, 457, 467–69, 474, 481, 485, 499, 503, 509, 512, 518
Great Migration, 6, 29, 127, 136, 143, 176, 208–11, 214, 339, 513, 541
Great Society, The (Wallas), 51
Great Society, Wallas's idea of, 51–53, 79, 85, 412
Green, William, 354
Greenberg, Jack, 457
Greene, Nathan, 481
Gregg, Richard, 489–90, 495, 496
Gregory, Thomas, 35, 41, 42, 47, 48, 77
Griffith, D. W., 220
guns, 243

Haiti, 192, 380
Hale, Robert, 477, 480
Hale, Swinburne, 108, 409
Hamilton, Alice, 113
Hampton Normal School, 178, 179, 183
Hand, Learned, 75–77, 79, 241, 244, 416
Hanna, Mark, 256, 257
Harding, Warren, 1, 5–6, 143, 144, 147, 150, 156, 294, 296, 474
Hardwick, Thomas, 287

Harkness, Georgia, 206
Harlem, 127, 161, 217, 221–23, *225*, 226, 227, 260, *325*, 326, 331, 332, 334, 335, 339, 342, 349, 350, 365, 368, 375, 382, 431, 436, 463, 503, 509, 517, 528
Harlem Professional League, 293
Harlem Socialist Club, 260, 262
Harpers Ferry, 17, 81, 191, 201, 431
Harper's, 90, 104, 200
Harriman, Job, 118
Harris, Abram Lincoln, Jr., xvi, 445–46, 501, 505
Harris, Lement, 398–400
Harrison, Hubert, 331, 332, 336
Hart, Schaffner, and Marx, 302–3
Harvard Law Review, 424, 438, *439*
Harvard Law School, 75, 113, 203, 246, 296, 362, 406–8, *408*, 415, 417, 438, 442, 505, 667n40
Harvard University, 2, 19, 49, 51, 91, 113, 207, 370, 410, 415
 antisemitism at, 415–17, 426
 Baldwin at, 13, 14, 16, 19, 20
 Garland at, 2, 103
 Jewish students and faculty at, 370, 421, *439*
Hastie, William, 439, 447, 457
Hawks, Esther, 163, 165
Hawthorne, Nathaniel, 120
Haymarket bombing, 201, 266, 282
Hays, Arthur Garfield, 478, *478*, 479, 481
Haywood, William "Big Bill," xvi, 67–68, 263–75, 277–79, 283–86, 300, 305, 308, 330
Headwaiters and Sidewaiters Society of Greater New York, 332
Hearst, William Randolph, 27
Hearst newspapers, 27, *121*, 256, *395*
Hebrew Butchers Union, 293
Hegel, Georg Wilhelm Friedrich, 226
Herndon, Angelo, 500
Herndon v. Lowry, 500–501
Highlander Folk School, 323–24, *323*, 454, 534
Hill, John Philip, 394
Hilliard, Robert, 135
Hillman, Sidney, xvi, 114, 231, *290*, 292, 300–310, 314, 322, 346, 349, 363, 369, 373, 409, 412, 472, 473, 481–83, 485, 486, 492, 497, 510, 535, 537
 Amalgamated Clothing Workers union of, 111, 113, 300–302, 304–10, *305*, 313, 314, 317, 318, 320–22, 326, 362, 364, 369, 373, 409, 454, 467, 479, 481, 483, 484, 486, 487, 496, 516, 642n34, 667n40
 arbitration and, 303–4, 314
 Baldwin and, 301
 FDR and, 481
 immigration to the U.S., 111, 301
 IWW and, 304, 305
 labor-capital cooperation promoted by, 303–7, 322
 new unionism of, 304–10, 322, 339, 348, 401, 483, 487, 515, 536, 671n15
 "The Activity" and, 310, 318, 497
Hillquit, Morris, 331, 332, 476, 479, 484
Hiss, Alger, 397
Hocutt, Thomas, 457–58
Holmes, John Haynes, 43, 96, 203
Holmes, Oliver Wendell, Jr., 74–77, 79, 198–99, 287
Home to Harlem (McKay), 340
Hoover, Herbert, 420, 481, 509
Hoover, J. Edgar, 4, 334–35, 384, 676n11
Horton, Myles, 323, *323*
Hose, Sam, 134–35
House Un-American Activities Committee, 4
Houston, Charles Hamilton, xvi, 7, 424, 431, *434*, 436–40, 442–43, *439*, 459, 486, 505, 512–14, 518, *521*, 537
 childhood of, 437
 death of, 523
 enslaved ancestors of, 437, 439
 Frankfurter and, 436, 438, 440, 443, 444, 456, 520, 523, 525
 Gaines case of, 461–64
 Gibbs v. Broome case of, 452–54
 Hocutt case and, 457–58
 law students recruited by, 438–40, 448, 456
 law training and practice of, 438, 442, *439*, 514, 673n38
 Margold and, 424, 436–37
 Marshall and, 456–57
 at NAACP, 444–54, 458–61
 National Negro Congress and, 505
 professional school cases and, 458–59
 railroad worker cases of, 513–14, 518–25, 527
 Randolph and, 524, 525, 673n38
 school funding cases and, 448–51
 school inequalities documented by, 448–49, 456
 Scottsboro case and, 435, 440, 443, 445
 teacher salary cases and, 451–54, 456, 458
 wartime service of, 437–38, 442
 White and, 444
Houston, Mary, 437
Houston, William, 437, 439
Hovey, Bettina, 393
Howard, Roy, 470
Howard Law School, 424, 439–40, 443, 448, 456–58

INDEX 697

Howard University, 222, 435, 445, 447, 505
Howe, Frederic, 295
Hualapai people, 419–23, *420*, 433, 436
  administration and, 421
Hughes, Charles Evans, 142, 462
Hughes, Langston, 222–25, 227, 337, 463, 528
Hull House, 22, 40, 303, 304
Human Nature in Politics (Wallas), 51
Hungarian Workers Council, 293
Hunter, Robert, 282
Hunter College, 463
Hurston, Zora Neale, 463
Hutcheson, William "Big Bill," 473
hypocrisy, 107, 241, *527*, 538–39

immigrants, 6, 17, 29, 30, 62, 68, 115, 150, 473, 541
  Chinese, *see* Chinese Immigrants
  Japanese, 522, 523
  in St. Louis, 21–22
  as workers, 266–68
Impressions of Soviet Russia (Dewey), 238
Indians, *see* Native Americans
industrial democracy, 114–15, 292, 306, 308–10, *313*, 319, 322, 342, 344–49, 359, 361, 368, 373, 374, 375, 382–84, 386, 398, 400, 412, 445, 472, 478, 483–87, 493–95, 526, 536
industrial unions, 5, 267, 302, 305–6, 310, 313–14, 335, 374, 468, 472, 473, 504, 506
Industrial Worker, 267, 269–71
Industrial Workers of the World (IWW; Wobblies), 14, 41, 64, 67–69, 85, 91, 112, 200, 201, 227, 253–54, 265–89, 292, 293, 295, 300, 302, 304, 306, 312, 316, 322, 333, 336, 342, 357, 409, 410, 473, 475, 655n15
  Agricultural Workers Industrial Union, 475
  Caron and, 279–81
  constitution of, 269
  critics of, 268, 282
  deportations of members of, 285
  end of, 288
  Flynn and, 253, 254, 263, 268–70, 272, 274, 276–89, 292, *294*, 295–96, 300, 311, 336, 410, 490
  founding of, 263, 265–66, 286
  free speech fights of, 269–71, 273, 274, 282, 284, 471
  Galleanisti anarchists and, 299–300
  Hillman and, 304, 305
  Industrial Relations Commission and, 275–77, 279, 285
  McNamara brothers and, 272–73, 281
  membership of, 268–69, 286

  prosecution and imprisonment of members of, 284–87, 292, 295, 296, 299, 300
  racial integration in, 267–68
  Randolph and, 348–49, 351
  slogan of, 267
  textile workers and, 274, 297, 311–14
  trial of, 119
  violence against, 282–84, 288
  violence and sabotage as tactics of, 254–55, 271–83, 285–88, 299, 300, 322, 490
  Western Federation of Miners and, *265*, 272
  Wilson administration and, 284, 285
  World War I and, 283–84, 286
industry, 6, 22, 35, 52, 67, 82, 84, 94, 257, 372
  mass production in, 3, 118, 174, 292, 306–10, 322, 362, 369, 373, 468, 469, 472, 486, 487, 496, 537
  nationalization of, 307, 309
  scientific management in, 278, 307–9, 322, 367
  inherited wealth, 102–4, 242
    of Garland, 1–2, 5, 8, 101, 103–8, 117, 122, 151, 161, 245–47, 337, 358, 460, 530, 533, 535, 540, 541
  socialism and, 102, 103
  taxes on, 95, 102, 245, 374
  Wells on, 102–3
Injunction Defense Committee, 475
Institute for Government Research, 416
Interchurch World Movement, 70–72
Intercollegiate Socialist Society, 220–21, 309, 330
Interior, U.S. Department of, 419–23, 425, 436
International Labor Defense (ILD), 357, 368, 370, 390, 435–36, 440–43, 445, 447, 449
International Ladies' Garment Workers Union (ILGWU), 232, 291, 293, 304, 317, 331, 357, 467, 472, 473, 479, 481, 495
Interstate Commerce Commission, 351–53
Invisible Man (Ellison), 176
Isham, John, 132

Jackson, Francis, 242–44
Jackson, Jimason, 194, 197
Jackson, Juanita, 449
Jackson, Lillie, 454
Jackson, Luther Porter, 454
Jacksonville, FL, 125–27, 129–33, *131*, 136, 165, 167, 186, 218–20, 327–29, 337–38, 342, 382
  Stanton School in, 131, *131*, *132*, 162–64, *165*, 168, 170
Jackson v. Phillips, 243, 244
James, Jesse E., 93
James, William, 76, 78
Japanese immigrants, 522, 523

Jefferson, Thomas, 81, 90, 106, 326
Jehovah's Witnesses, 233
Jesus Christ, 2, 103
Jewish Daily Forward, 233
Jewish people, 297, 374, 406, 407
   Harvard and, 370, 415–17, 421, 426, *439*
Jim Crow, *see* segregation
Johns Hopkins University, 425
Johnson, Charles S., 222, 346
Johnson, Grace Nail, 139, *184*, 217, 219, 220, 295, 528
Johnson, Helen, 128–31, 163
Johnson, James, 128–31
Johnson, James Weldon, xvi, 111, 115, 125–33, 151, *160*, 161, *184*, 189, 190, 192, 221, 289, 325, 329, 336, 354, *356*, 358, 359, 374, 377, 381–82, 386–90, 399, 400, 405–7, 411, 425, 432, 440, 441, 444, 446, 450, 454–55, 462, 463, 530, 537, 540, 586n16
   Anderson and, 137–39, 142
   at Atlanta University, *124*, 131–34, 136, 164
   Baldwin and, 127, 128, 151, 158, 368
   Black workers and, 172–73, 382
   Brookwood and, 316
   childhood of, 130–31, *131*, 327
   civil rights and, 378
   Committee on Negro Work and, 377–80
   consul position of, 139–40, *140*, 218
   courts as viewed by, 213–14
   culture and, *216*, 217–22, 224–26
   Darrow dinner hosted by, 217
   death and funeral of, 528
   Du Bois and, 138–39, 144, *356*
   education issues and, 162–64, 167–69, 171–73, 176, 182–87, 221, 536
   Elaine massacre and, 199
   family background of, 128
   God's Trombones, 224–25, *225*
   Harding and, 143
   Hughes and, 142–43
   at Intercollegiate Socialist Society conference, 220–21
   law practice of, 132, 196
   lynching and, 125–28, 134, 136, 144–46, *147*, 148, 149, 154–59
   Magna Carta and, 173
   Margold and, 424
   marriage of, 139
   at NAACP, 111, 125–27, 134, 136, 144–46, *147*, 148, 151, 154–57, 316
   newspaper column of, 141–42
   in New York, 137
   Randolph and, 337–39, 346, 382, 501
   Republican Party and, 136–39, 142–44, 146, 148, 150, 156–57
   screenplays of, 218–20, 224
   songwriting of, 132, 137, 138, *216*, 221
   as Stanton School principal, 162–63, *165*, 168
   as Stanton School student, 131, *131*, 132, 164
   Sweet case and, 210, 211, 213–15
   Washington and, 137–39, 144
   Wilson and, 140–42, 218
Johnson, Lyndon, 526, 538
Johnson, Rosamond, 132, 137, 138, *216*, 221
Jones, Eugene Kinckle, 162
Jones, Jack, 268
Jones, Scipio Africanus, xvi, 196–97
Jones, Thomas Jesse, 178–83, *180*, 185, 187
Jordan, David Starr, 47, 203
Joyce, James, 371
Judiciary Committee, 480
Jungle, The (Sinclair), 2, 91, 95, 112
Justice Department, U.S., 7, 35, 41–43, 48, 54, 59, 64, 73, 79, 284, 296, 336, 408, 409, 420
   see also FBI
juvenile justice, 23, 83–84

Kallen, Horace, 319
Kansas, 475
Karch, Charles, 35
Kautsky, Karl, 282
Kazan, Elia, 229
Keller, Helen, 91
Kelley, Florence, 246
Kelley, Nicholas, 246–48, *247*, 538
Kellogg, Paul, 40, 43
Kelsey-Hayes Wheel Company, 488, 492–93
Keyserling, Leon, 667n40
King, Carol Weiss, 479
King, Martin Luther, Jr., 7, 311, 324
King, William Lyon Mackenzie, 91–93, *92*, 97
King Coal (Sinclair), 95
Kirchwey, Freda, xvii, *98*, 111, 291, 361, 363, 369, 377, 389–90, 444, 512, 514, 667n40, 676n11
Kluger, Richard, 535
Knights of Labor, 200–201, 255, 341
Knox, Philander, 139
Knudsen, William, 494
Koch brothers, 539
Korematsu v. United States, 522, 523
Kropotkin, Peter, 108, 236, 257, 258, 263
Krutch, Joseph Wood, *98*
Krutch, Marcelle, *98*
Ku Klux Klan, 6, 41, 165, 212, 215, 336, 374, 504

INDEX

Labor, U.S. Department of, 293, 295, 507, 667n40
Labor Age, 244, 310, 371, 470, 479
Laboratory School, 319–20
Labor Bureau, The, 346–47, 479, 648n26
labor education, 310, 315, 318, 320–22, 536
  Brookwood Labor College, *see* Brookwood Labor College
  Highlander Folk School, 323–24, *323*, 454, 534
labor injunctions, 314, 410, 442, 473–81, 492, 494, 499, 522
labor law, 473–88, 499
  affirmative legal action, 478–79, *478*, 486, 489, 490, 516
  Frankfurter and, 479–82, 485, 490
  National Industrial Recovery Act, 482–85
  Nelles and, 476–80
  New Deal and, 5, 468, 483, 495, 501, 512–13, 515, 520, 522, 525, 667n40
  Norris-La Guardia Act, 480–82
  sit-down tactic and, 489
  yellow dog contracts and, 480, 482, 499
labor movement, 67, 111, 112, 115, 177, 190, 227, 253, 254, 266, 268, 292, 301, 310, 311, 314, 322, 351, 375, 412, 446, 465, 486, 531, 532, 536, 537
  Black education and, 162, 183–84, 186, 187
  Brookwood approach to, 317–18
  civil rights and, 377, 378, 382–86, 388–90
  Federated Press and, 106–7, 229–30, *230*, 232, 347
  in France, 278
  martyrs in, 201
  radio and, 230–33
labor relations and disputes, 474, 490
  arbitration in, 303–4, 314, 349, 373, 484, 487
  Beyer and, 308
  collective bargaining in, 342, 345, 347, 348, 482–85, 487, 495, 496, 504, 512–15, 518, 525–26, 535, 537
  Commission on Industrial Relations, 93–97, *94*, 111, 275–77, 279, 285, 295, 308, 482, 539
  government management of, 488
  Hillman and, 303–7, 322
  injunctions in, 314, 410, 442, 474–81, 494
  National Labor Relations Act (Wagner Act), 468, 485–89, 494, 497, 499–502, 504, 512–15, 519, 520, 522, 536, 537
  on railroads, government involvement in, 349–51
  Reading Formula and, 483–85
  Rockefeller Plan and, 92–97
  World War I and, 307, 408, 409

labor strikes, 7, 17, 58, 84, 85, 200, 232, 246, 272, 277, 278, 281, 285, 303, 305, 313, 344, 378, 409, 410, 475, 488, 535
  auto workers, 469–72, *471*, 488–89, 493–96
  Brookwood and, 467, 469–72, 489–90, 492–93, 495, 496
  Depression-era, 467–68, 485
  garment workers, 302–3, *305*, 467, 468
  miners, 264, 269, 271, 281, 283, 409, 467, 655n15
  miners, and Ludlow massacre, 86–88, *88*, 91–93, *92*, 95, 109, 279, 282, 295, 378, 539
  news articles about, 475
  picket lines and, 33, 70, 71, 82, 84, 85, 200, 228, 271, 302, 303, *305*, 312, 362, 367, 378, 410, 467, 470, 471, 489, 490, 493, 494, 506
  by Pullman porters, 319, 354, 474, 510, 516, 645n72
  by railway shopmen, 474–76, 479, *478*
  sit-down, 467, 488–95, *493*, 499, 520, 536
  steel worker, 14, 58, 59, 68–73, *69*, *71*, 74, 75, 77–79, 82, 83, 107, 109, 112, 114, 192, 201, 229, 272, 306, 314, 364, 667n40
  strikebreakers and scabs in, 35, 340, 344, 353, 490, 492, 513
  textile worker, 228, *228*, *252*, 274, 297, 299, 311–14, *313*, 330, 358, 361–63, 367–68, 410, 469, 479, 490
  unemployed and, 469–71
labor unions, 5, 6, 32, 35, 84–86, 92, 107, 114, 235, 292, 333, 387, 535, 537, 539
  Black education and, 162, 183–84, 379, 384, 387–89
  Black workers and, 32–33, 115, 162, 173, 176, 177, 183–84, 266, 267, 326, 338, 339–41, 346, 347, 352–53, 355, 364, 367, 374, 375, 382, 383, 389, 390, 398, 432–33, 446, 486, 506, 512–14, 518–26
  Communists and, 234, 362–64, 367
  courts and, 200–201
  craft, 266, 469
  democracy and, 95
  discrimination by, 339–40, 366, 389–90, 512–14
  employer offensives against, 234, 310
  industrial, 5, 267, 302, 305–6, 310, 313–14, 335, 374, 468, 472, 473, 504, 506
  interracial solidarity in, 177, 267, *333*, 374–75, 534
  majority and minority, 483–86
  membership numbers, 310, 341, 383, 533
  miners and, 86, 87, 95, 264–65, 271

labor unions (*cont.*)
- new unionism, 304–11, 317, 322, 324, 337, 339, 342, 344–45, 348, 351, 362, 369, 401, 477, 483, 486, 487, 489, 504, 515, 536, 671n15
- racism in, *see* racism
- scientific management and, 307–9, 322
- Soviet Russia and, 238
- steel mills and, 68–69
- yellow dog contracts and, 480, 482, 499

La Follette, Robert, Jr., 431, 496, 504–5
La Guardia, Fiorello, 172, 501, *511,* 528
Laidler, Harry, 491
Lancaster, Roy, 353
Landis, James, 415
Landis, Kenesaw Mountain, 119, 284, 285, 287, 299, 474–75
Larsen, William, 148
Lash, Joseph, 64
Laski, Harold, 75
Lauck, William Jett, 362, 468, 481, 482, 484, 487, 642n34, 648n26, 667n40
Laura Spellman Rockefeller Memorial Fund, 175
Lautier, Louis, 464
law, 406–8, 480, 515, 524
- Black lawyers and, 438–40, 519
- Ernst's view of, 371, 373
- Flynn's view of, 259, 300
- Frankfurter's view of, 412–13, 422, 432
- liberal legalism and, 423
- Margold's view of, 416, 486, 515, 516
- Randolph's view of, 352
- *see also* courts; labor law

Lawrence, MA, 274, 297, 299, 311–14, *313,* 330, 490
Lawson, John, 95
League for Independent Political Action, 384
League for Industrial Democracy, 244, 309–10, 369, 387, 463, 470, 478, 479, 491, 496, 504, 535, 536
League of Struggle for Negro Rights, 436, 441
Le Bon, Gustave, 51, 53, 54, 79, 152
Lee, Algernon, 642n34
Lee, Blair, 45
Lee, Ivy, 95, 494
Lefkowitz, Abraham, 642n34
Leiserson, William M., 482–84, 487, 667n40
Lenin, Vladimir, 233, 235, 236, 359, 396, 517
Lewis, John L., 324, 473, 484
Liberator, 106
Liberty Under the Soviets (Baldwin), 237–39
"Lift Every Voice and Sing" (Johnson and Johnson), 132

Lincoln, Abraham, 18, 102, 132, 137, 141, 143, 144, 156, 342–43, 413, 508
Lincoln, Robert Todd, 18, 343
Lincoln University, 455–56, 459, 464
Linville, Henry Richardson, 203
Lippmann, Walter, xvii, 49–54, *52,* 62, 65, 72–74, 76–79, 84, 85, 106, 111, 113, 145, 152, 153, 192, 218, 220, 227, 270, 296, 306, 310, 314, 318, 334, 389, 407, 411, 667n40
- Frankfurter and, 411, 413
- on taboo, 52–53, 371
- on two classes of statesmen, 52–53

literature, 217, 221
Little, Frank, 282–83
Llano del Rio, 118, 321
Llewellyn, Karl, 444
Lochner v. New York, 413
Locke, Alain, xvii, 162, 170, 181, 222–23, *223,* 226, 227, 389
Lodge, Henry Cabot, 156
Looking Backward (Bellamy), 257
Loray Mill, 367
Los Angeles Times, 35, 89, 262, 272–73
Louisiana, 136, 167, 405, 428, 436
Louisville and Nashville Railroad Company, 518
Louisville *Courier-Journal,* 156
L'Ouverture, Toussaint, 328
Lovestone, Jay, 366, 463
Lovett, Robert Morss, xvii, 111, 189, 190, 227, 231, 309, 360, 442, 528
Lowden, Frank O., 34
Lowell, A. Lawrence, 415–16
Lowell, Esther, 230
Lowenthal, Max, 307, 479
Lubin, Isador, 667n40
Lubin Manufacturing Company, 218–20
Lucas County Unemployed League, 470
Ludendorff, Erich, 50
Ludlow massacre, 86–88, *88,* 91–93, *92,* 95, 196, 279, 282, 295, 378, 539
Lum family, 426–27, 429, 432
Lusk Committee, 202–4
lynchings, 6, 17, 33, 35, 115, 126, 134–36, 143–59, 173, 192, 198, 208, 288, 328–29, 332, 334, 364, 368, 378, 383, 388, 438, 454
- Elaine massacre, 191–202, *195,* 212–13, 229–30, 297, 368, 382, 406, 503, 504
- Johnson and, 125–28, 134, 136, 144–46, *147,* 148, 149, 154–59
- legislation against, 7, 146–49, *147,* 151, 154, 156–58, 189, 246, 389, 506, 508, 515
- of Little, 282–83

INDEX

NAACP and, 7, 125–27, 134, 144–46, *147*, 148, 149, 151, 154–58, 189, 389, 515, 519, 586n16, 614n30
  public opinion on, 144–45, 151–58
  in Quitman, 126
  rape allegations in, 125, 135, 145–50, 155
  Washington protest against, *434*

Macdonald, Dwight, 239, 358
Madison Square Garden, 142, *360*, *511*, 517–18
Magna Carta, 173, 388
Magnes, Judah, xvii, 112
Mahone, Fred, 420, 422
Malatesta, Errico, 277
Mandy's Chicken Dinner (Johnson), 219
March on Washington (1963), 355
March on Washington Movement, 355, 508–12, 516–18, *517*, 525, 526
Margold, Nathan, xvii, *404*, 405, 414–33, *415*, 438, *439*, 463, 535
  Administration and, 425–26, 537
  antisemitism experienced by, 415–17, 426
  Collier and, 417–18
  Du Bois and, 425, 432
  early life of, 414–15
  Frankfurter and, 414–16, 418, 421, 423–25, 438, 440
  Gong Lum case and, 426–27, 429, 432
  government contract cases of, 450–51
  Houston and, 424, 436–37
  Indian land claims work of, 416–24, 426, 428–30, 433, 436
  law as viewed by, 416, 486
  at NAACP, 416, 419, 423–33, 435, 438, 444, 445, 457, 458, 460, 461, 468, 480, 487, 512, 536, 537
  NAACP resignation of, 436, 443, 444
  report by, *405*, 424–31, 432–33, 435, 437, 445, 448, 450, 457, 461, 480, 487, 512, 521, 535, 536, 537
  school funding issue and, 427–28, 448, 450
  Yick Wo case and, 429–30, 432, 450, 521
Marnitz, Anna, 161
marriage, 3, 66, 257–60
  Garland's views on, 2, 102, 108–9, 395
  racial intermarriage, 133
  utopian communities and, *116*, 117, 120, 122
Maryland, 452–53, 456–58
  Baltimore, 450
Massachusetts General Hospital, 242
Masses, 41, 42, 75, 227, 298, 332, 334
Maurer, Jim, 238
Mayflower, 13, 541

Marshall, Louis, 199, 430
Marshall, Norma Williams, 455, 456
Marshall, Thurgood, xvii, 7, 455–57, 461, 533, 534
  childhood of, 455
  Gaines and, 461, 463–64
  Houston and, 456–57
  at Howard Law School, 456
  law practice of, 456
  at Lincoln University, 455–56
  at NAACP, 455, 347
  professional school cases and, 458–59
  salary equalization cases and, 456
Marshall, Vivian, 456
Marshall, William Canfield, 455
Marx, Karl, 200, 227, 246, 263, 317, 329–31, 363
  The Communist Manifesto, 200, 259
Massachusetts, 242–43, 245
mass production, 3, 118, 174, 292, 306–10, 322, 362, 369, 373, 468, 469, 472, 406, 487, 496, 537
Matthews, T. Stanley, 429
McCarthy, Joseph, 470
McDowell, Mary, xvii, 112, 291, 292
McGee, Mineola, 34
McGuire, Virginia, *434*
McKay, Claude, 222, 227, 331, 340, 382, 528
McKees Rocks, PA, 272, 278
McKenzie, Marjorie, 523
McKinley, William, 137, 256, 264
McNamara, James and John, 272–73, 281, 303
McNeil, Genna Rae, 437
McReynolds, James, 461–62
Mencken, H. L., 157, 203, 205, 207
Mesabi Range, 268, 274, 275, 281–83, 297
Messenger, 222, 326, 331–39, *333*, *338*, *340*, 342, 345, 347–48, 350–52, 354–55, 375–76, 449
Michelson, Clarina, xvii, 291–92, 361, 366, *368*, 377, 386–87, 390–91, 436, 440–41, 443, 444, 461, 486
Michigan, 475, 493
  Detroit, *see* Detroit, MI
  Flint, 493–95, *493*, 496
Midland Steel Frame Company, 488
Midvale Steel, 307
Military Training Camps Association, 248
Mill, John Stuart, 102
Miller, Kelly, 185–86, 340
Mills, Walter, 453
miners, 58, 95, 246, 263, 268, 269, 271, 306–7, 378, 472, 473, 476, 484, 499, 512
  Brookwood and, 316–17
  in Cripple Creek, 264, *265*
  fire at party for, 62, 74

miners (cont.)
  labor unions and, 86, 87, 95, 264–65, 271
  Little and, 282–83
  strike in Colorado and Ludlow massacre, 86–88, *88*, 91–93, *92*, 95, 109, 196, 279, 282, 295, 378, 539
  strikes by, 264, 269, 271, 281, 283, 409, 467, 655n15
  United Mine Workers, 86, 87, 114, 306–7, 321, 341, 364, 472, 473, 484, 495
  violence and, 264–65, *265*
  Western Federation of Miners, 263–65, *265*, 271, 272, 274, 300
  in West Virginia, 114–15, *114*, 229
minstrel films, 219, 226
Mission Indian Federation, 417, 420, 422
Mississippi, 167, 171, 185, 199, 405, 426–28
Mississippi Delta, *498*, 503
Mississippi River, 383, 519
Mitchell, H. L., 507
Mitchell, Broadus, 425–27, 431
Modern School, 118
money, 1–6, 9, 81, 99–110, 241–42, 539–40, 540–41, and *passim*
  Baldwin (Roger) and, 15, 81–82, 531
  corruption and, 9, 104
  democracy and, 82, 93–96
  see also hypocrisy
Montgomery bus boycott, 534–35
Montgomery David, 309
Mooney, Tom, 201, 294, 410
Moore, Frank, 198–99
Moore, Fred, 300
Moore v. Dempsey, 198–203, 229–30, 460, 515
Morgan, J. P., 68, 89
Morgan, J. P., Jr., 287
Mormons, 263–64
Morris, William, 257, 258
Morrow, Edwin P., 354
Murphy, Carl, 459
Murphy, Frank, xvii, 212, 213, 215, 493–95, 520, 522–24, 526
Murray, Donald, 458–59
Murray, Pauli, xvii, 463–65
Murrow, Edward R., 449
music, 221
  Johnson brothers' songwriting, 132, 137, 138, *216*, 221
Musk, Elon, 6, 89
Muste, A. J., xvii, 7, 311–20, *313*, 322, 360, 362, 372–73, 380, 384, 443, 446, 454, 470–72, 481, 486, 488, 489, 516, 528, 354
  Lawrence textile strike and, 311–14, *313*, 496

Musteites, 470
Mutual Aid Society, 108
Mutual Welfare League, 62, 63
Myrdal, Gunnar, 171, 452, 454

NAACP (National Association for the Advancement of Colored People), 5, 7, 29, 35, 36, 83, 132, 173, 186, 190, 203, 214, 246, 333, 334, 347, 357, 358, 359, 364, 377, *379*, 380–86, 388–89, 398, 401, 405, 436–37, 442, 445, 486, 504, 505, 514, 534
  AFL and, 383
  American Fund joint campaign, 377, 379, *379*, 380–82, *385*, 386, 389, 390, 400, 405–7, 424–33, 440–41, 443–45, 447, 449–52, 456, 458–62, 505, 512, 529, 533, 535, 537
  Arkansas sharecropper case and, 192, 195, 196, 198–203, 229–30, 380, 382, 515
  arts and, 223
  Bernays and, 151–58, *153*
  Black education efforts and, 176–78, 181, 184, 185, 189, 586n16, 614n30
  Black workers and, 377, 378, 382–86, 388–90
  Brookwood and, 316
  Brown v. Board of Education and, 5, 406, 531
  Committee on Negro Work and, 379
  Committee on the Future Plan and Program of, 446
  Communists and, 440
  conferences of, *147*, *404*, 431–32
  Crisis, 144, 156, *160*, 177–79, 181, 185–87, 208, 213, 222, 381, 383, 385, *385*, 425, 449
  Ernst and, 372
  finances of, 154–55, 157, 158, 171
  founding of, 144
  Frankfurter and, 411, 520
  and fusion of labor and civil rights, 382
  Gaines case and, 459–64
  graduate and professional education cases and, 457–65
  Houston at, 444–54, 458–61
  Johnson at, 111, 125–27, 134, 136, 144–46, *147*, 148, 151, 154–57, 316
  labor and, 382–84, 389–90
  Legal Defense Fund, 173–74, 176, 182, 210, 211, 214, 217
  lynching and, 7, 125–27, 134, 144–46, *147*, 148, 149, 151, 154–58, 189, 389, 515, 519, 586n16, 614n30
  Margold at, 416, 419, 423–33, 435, 438, 444, 445, 457, 458, 460, 461, 468, 480, 487, 512, 536, 537
  Margold's resignation from, 436, 443, 444

Marshall at, 455, 457
National Legal Committee, 442
National Negro Congress and, 505, 507
school funding cases of, 425–28, 431, 441, 448–51, 512
Scottsboro case of, 436, 440–41, 443, 445
segregation and, 359, 375
Sweet case and, 210–11, 213, 214, 380, 389
teacher salary cases of, 451–54, 456, 458, 464, 512
Wagner Act and, 514
Nail, John, 336
Napoleon I, 128
Nash, Diane, 324
Nation, 34–35, 42, 98, 111, 196, 223–24, 238, 291, 298, 369, 371
National Bar Association, 451
National Broadcasting Company, 231
National Brotherhood Workers of America, 341
National Civil Liberties Bureau (NCLB), 43, 47–49, 54, 59, 60, 66, 67, 82–83, 97, 112, 201, 283, 293, 334
National Committee for Organizing Iron and Steel Workers, 69, 70
National Committee for the Legal Defense of the Chinese, 411
National Consumers League, 246
National Council of American Indians, 417, 422
National Football League, 217
National Guard, 87, 471, 494
National Industrial Auto Workers Union, 367
National Industrial Recovery Act (NIRA), 482–85, 499
National Industrial Recovery Board, 482
National Labor Board, 482–85, 667n40, 667n40
National Labor Relations Act (Wagner Act), 468, 485–89, 494, 497, 499–502, 504, 512–15, 519, 520, 522, 536, 537
National Labor Relations Board (NLRB), 487
National Municipal Review, 23
National Negro Congress (NNC), 454, 505–8, 510
National Recovery Administration, 484, 513
National Rifle Association, 243
National Textile Workers' Union, 367
National Urban League, 162, 222, 346
Native Americans, 263, 406, 416–17, 422, 429
citizenship for, 417
Dawes allotment system and, 417, 422–23
Hualapai, 419–23, 420, 433, 436
Indian Reorganization Act and, 422–23
Jim Crow and, 419, 425, 426, 430, 433
Margold's work on land claims of, 416–24, 426, 428–30, 433, 436

"Powers of Indian Tribes" report on, 421–22
Pueblo, 418–19, 422, 424
railroads and, 419, 420, 423
Nazi Germany, 505, 507, 510, 528, 529
Nearing, Scott, xvii, 111–12, 172, 173, 202, 235–37, 315, 359, 361, 368, 377, 386–87, 390–91, 400, 475, 476, 478, 491
Black America, 366–67, 382, 386, 388
Nebeker, Frank, 299
needle trades, *see* garment workers
Negro Common School, 177
Negro Foreign Fellowship Foundation, 162
Negro Labor Congress, 366
Nelles, Walter, xvii, 43, 49, 108, 245, 296, 294, 411, 476–80, 490
Nesbit, Evelyn, 100
New Deal, 5, 215, 396, 468, 472, 483, 495, 499, 501, 503, 505, 512–13, 515, 520, 522, 525, 667n40
New Harmony, 117
New Masses, 227–28, 371, 495, 504
New Mexico, 406, 409, 418, 472
New Republic, 49, 57, 72, 111, 189, 206, 227, 298, 320, 371, 407
News from Nowhere (Morris), 257
newspapers, 27, 106, 107, 192, 230, 256, 314–15, 412
Black, 141, 144, 162
Hearst, 27, 121, 256, 395
political parties and, 26
new unionism, 304–11, 317, 322, 324, 337, 339, 342, 344–45, 348, 351, 362, 369, 401, 477, 483, 486, 487, 489, 504, 515, 536, 671n15
New Worlds for Old (Wells), 102
New York, NY, 137
New York Age, 131, 141–42, 220, 355
New York American, 393
New York Call, 106
New York Central Railroad, 100
New York City Colored Republican Club, 138
New York Civic Club, 222, 292, 295, 309, 347, 532
New York Daily Mirror, 394
New Yorker, 358, 371
New York Herald Tribune, 229, 392
New York News, 219
New York Observer, 89
New York Post, 500
New York Public Library, 400
New York Society for Ethical Culture, 22
New York Stock Exchange, 99, 100
New York Sun, 49
New York Times, 2, 34, 55, 93, 238, 322, 392, 530
New York Tribune, 3, 115, 135, 241

New York World, 3, 41, 104, 195
Niagara Movement, 139, 144
Niebuhr, Reinhold, 7, 495
Nicholas II, Czar, 301
Niebuhr, Reinhold, 323–24
Nietzsche, Friedrich, 51
Nineteenth Amendment, 291
NIRA (National Industrial Recovery Act), 482–85, 499
Nixon v. Condon, 430–31
Nixon v. Herndon, 380, 431
NLRB (National Labor Relations Board), 487
nonviolent action, 7, 226, 254, 276, 281, 287, 300, 311–13, *313*, 362, 464, 471, 489–90, 495, 496
  see also violence
Norfolk Teachers' Association, 453
Norris, Clarence, 442
Norris, George W., 479
Norris-La Guardia Act, 480–82
Norris v. Alabama, 442, 447
North Carolina, 167, 185
  Gastonia, 367, 368, 370, 406, 469
North Carolina College for Negroes, 457–58
Northern Pacific Railroad, 99
Novyi Mir, 227
Noyes, John Humphrey, 117, 120

O'Dunne, Eugene, 458
O'Hare, Kate Richards, 294
O'Keefe, Georgia, 101
Oklahoma, 185, 208, 475
Olin, John, 539
Oneida Community, 117
O'Neill, Eugene, 217, 227, 317
Opportunity, 222
Orange Park School, 169
Oriental America, 132
Origin of the Family, The (Engels), 259
Osborne, Thomas Mott, 61–63, 65, 66, 74
Outlook, 157
Ovington, Mary White, 173–74, 186, 201–2, 334, 431
Owen, Chandler, 331–37, 341
Owen, Robert, 117

pacifism, 1, 7, 226, 311, 312, 314, 489, 495
Palmer, A. Mitchell, 287, 293, 294, 296, 299, 334, 409
panic, in human behavior, 61–62, 79
Panic of 1873, 99
Panic of 1893, 509
Paris Commune, 271
Parker, Theodore, 17

Parks, Rosa, 324, 534
Parsons, Albert, 266
Parsons, Lucy, 266
Passaic, NJ, 228, 358, 361–63, 367, 410, 469, 479
Passaic Textile Strike, The, 228, *228*, 362
Paterson, NJ, *252*, 274, 278, 285, 330
Patterson, Haywood, 442
Patterson, William "Pat," 443
Patterson v. Alabama, 442, 447
Patton, George S., 50
Paul Revere, 330
Pax, 226–27
Peabody Fund, 175, 242
Peach Springs, AZ, 420–21, *420*, 423
Peake, Mary, 163
Pennsylvania, 378, 467, 476
  McKees Rocks, PA, 272, 278
  Pittsburgh, see Pittsburgh, PA
Pennsylvania Railroad Company, 410
People's Power League, 25
Perkins, Frances, 495
Perry, Julian, *188*
Pesotta, Rose, 495
Peters, Josef, 397
Phelps Dodge Corporation, 409, 655n15
Phelps-Stokes Fund, 175, 178, 183
philanthropic foundations, 3, 88–97, 105, 110, 174, 177, 400, 539, 540
  Black education and, 174–83, *180*, 187
  critique of, 93–97, 110, 241–45, 531, 539
  education and, 89, 174
  tax deductions and exemptions for, 242–49, *247*, 538–39
  Walsh Commission and, 93–97, *94*
Phillips County, AR, sharecroppers and massacre in, 191–202, *195*, 212–13, 218, 229–30, 297, 368, 380, 382, 406, 460, 515
picket lines, 33, 70, 71, 82, 84, 85, 200, 228, 271, 302, 303, *305*, 312, 362, 367, 378, 410, 467, 470, 471, 489, 490, 493, 494, 506
Pinkney, Floria, 317
Pittsburgh, PA, 162, 492
  steel strike in, 14, 58, 59, 68–73, *69*, *71*, 74, 75, 77–79, 82, 83, 107, 109, 112, 114, 192, 201, 229, 306, 314, 364, 667n40
Pittsburgh Chronicle Telegraph, 71, *71*
Pittsburgh Courier, 186, 522–23
Pittsburgh Gazette Times, 71
Pittsburgh Leader, 71
Pittsburgh Press, 71
Plato, 78
Plessy v. Ferguson, 17–18, 31–32, 133, 425, 452, 454, 459, 520

Plunkett, William Brown, 256, 257
Pollak, Walter, 442
Pollock, Sam, 469–70
Popular Front, 401, 442, 505–7, 509, 528, 529
Port Huron Statement, 535
Post, Robert, 75n
post office
　bombs and, 287, 299
　censorship and, 41–43, 54, 75, 334
　segregation and, 140–41
Pound, Roscoe, 296, 418
poverty, 23, 29, 61, 103–5, 257, 260, 400
Powell v. Alabama, 442, 443
Power, theory and practice of, 6, 50, 53, 67, 82, 83, 85, 143, 164, 187, 213, 257, 269, 349, 478, 540
　education and, 164, 315, 318
　Frankfurter and, 414
　Hale and, 477, 400
　Hillman and, 302–05, 412
　Houston and, 443
　Lippmann and, 51–54, 73, 78–79
　Margold and, 414–23, 425, 433
　NAACP legal campaign and, 381, 384, 430, 536; *see also* Margold and
　nonviolence and, 489
　Randolph and, 333, 499, 509, 515–17
　see also rights (power versus)
Power of Non-Violence, The (Gregg), 489–90
Praeger, Robert, 47–48
pragmatism, 76–77, 84
Pravda, 396
Preparedness Day parade bombing (San Francisco), 201, 294, 410
presidential elections
　of 1904, 138
　of 1912, 30, 139–40
　of 1916, 39, 142, 143
　of 1920, 143
　of 1932, 215, 481
Pressman, Lee, 494
Preston, Evelyn, 67, 307
prisoners, political, 289, 292–95, 294, 396
prisons, 58, 61, 62, 66, 74
private property, 1–3, 103, 105, 257–58, 263, 315, 373–74
　April Farm and, 116, 120
　coercive dimension of, 477
Progressive Farmers and Household Union of America, 191, 198
progressivism, 20, 22, 23, 25, 26, 40, 83, 84

propaganda, 49, 54, 57, 77, 79, 115, 241, 389, 412
　American Fund and, 218, 226–34
　arts and, 221–26
　Black newspapers and, 141, 144
　culture and, 217, 218, 223–24, 227
　Du Bois and, 222–24
　Elaine massacre and, 196
　free speech and, 44–49, 56, 77–79, 84
　IWW and, 282
　Lippmann and, 49–54, 77–79
　Locke and, 222–23
　radio and, 231
　steel strike and, 70–74, 71, 77, 78, 82, 83, 192, 229, 306, 314
　tax code and, 244, 246–48
　in World War I, 38, 39–40, 45–47, 46, 49–50, 53–54, 56, 60, 72, 74, 95, 105, 151, 152, 227, 667n40
　Vanguard Press and, 236
Public and Its Government, The (Frankfurter), 412
public opinion, 49, 51, 52, 56, 60, 65, 85, 106, 112, 146, 411–12
　courts and, 191, 207
　on lynching, 144–45, 151–58
　stereotypes and catchphrases in, 56, 78–79, 218, 220, 223–24
　see also propaganda
Pueblo tribes, 418–19, 422, 424
Pulitzer, Joseph, 26–27, 45, 61, 256
Pulitzer, Joseph, Jr., 27
Pullman, George Mortimer, 342, 344
Pullman Company, 326, 343
　porters, of, 18, 319, 326, 341–55, 357, 362, 369, 374, 377, 378, 382, 411, 474, 479, 480, 483, 485, 501–5, 502, 507, 509, 510, 515, 516, 524, 531, 535–36, 645n72, 671n15

Quitman, GA, 126

race blindness, 537
racial discrimination, 517
　in employment, 450–51, 510–12, 514, 517, 518–26, 517, 525
　see also segregation
racial integration, 375, 508–09
　Black teachers and, 430, 434
　Baseball and, 131
　Education and, 165, 324
　Houston and, 447
　labor unions and, *see* labor unions, Black workers and

racial integration (*cont.*)
  radical versions of, 375
  theater and, 132, 175
  Margold and, 430, 432
racial science, 19–20, 207
racial violence, 6, 17, 18, 29, 36, 58, 135, 144, 173, 195, 208, 214
  East St. Louis massacre, 33–36, *34*, 41, 48, 58, 146, *160,* 173, 195, 208, 214, 220
  Elaine massacre of sharecroppers, 191–202, *195,* 212–13, 229–30, 297, 368, 382, 406, 503, 504, 515
  Sweet family and, 7, 191, 207–15, *208,* 217, 218, 230, 297, 378, 380, 389, 406, 493, 515, 520
  see also lynchings
racism, 19-20, 162, 194, 207–13, 439, 459, and *passim*
  capitalism and, 334
  labor unions and, 339–40, 366, 389–90, 513–14
radio, 230-33, *232*
Radio Act, 231
Railroad Labor Board, 350, 353
railroads, 17, 28, 99, 100, 307, 308, 316, 349, 410, 537
  Black passengers on, 18, 125, 133–35, 380, 512
  Native peoples and, 419, 420, 423
railroad workers, 499, 501, 512, 513–15, 518–26
  Black, 5, 327, 339–40, 383, 451, 513–15, 518–26, *519,* 673n38
  and government involvement in labor relations, 349–51
  locomotive firemen, 339, 514, 518, *519,* 520, 522–24, 537
  Pullman porters, 18, 319, 326, 341–55, 357, 362, 369, 374, 377, 378, 382, 411, 474, 479, 480, 483, 485, 501–5, *502,* 507, 509, 510, 515, 516, 524, 531, 535–36, 645n72, 671n15
  shopmen, 474–76, 479, 489
Railway Labor Act, 350–51, 353–54, 482, 483, 487, 501, 502, 513, 515, 518–22
Railway Mediation Board, 350, 354, 382
Randolph, A. Philip, xviii, 7, 222, *325,* 326–41, *340,* 345–46, 357, 359, 365, 368, 374–76, 382, 401, 431, 442, 446, 449, 454, 463, 499, *502, 511,* 515–16, 524, 534, 642n34, 671n15
  AFL and, 341, 526, 673n38
  Baldwin and, 337, 345
  Black Belt thesis and, 365, 429, 671n15
  Brotherhood of Elevator and Switchboard Operators formed by, 340–41
  childhood of, 327–29
  Communist Party and, 506–8
  education of, 328, 329
  Ernst and, 374
  Fair Employment Practices Commission and, 518, 524
  FDR and, 508, 510–11, 516, 527
  finances of, 331, 337, 339, 501
  Garvey and, 335–36
  Houston and, 524, 525, 673n38
  IWW and, 348–49, 351
  jobs held by, 330
  Johnson and, 337–39, 346, 382, 501
  law as viewed by, 352, 515, 516
  March on Washington Movement of, 355, 508–12, 516–18, *517,* 525, 526
  marriage of, 330–31
  Messenger magazine of, 222, 326, 331–39, *333, 338, 340,* 342, 345, 347–48, 350–52, 354–55, 375–76, 449
  "most dangerous" label applied to, 334–35
  move to New York, 329
  National Negro Congress and, 505–8, 510
  Pullman porters and, 326, 341–55, 357, 374, 377, 382, 411, 480, 483, 501–3, *502,* 509, 510, 515, 516, 531, 535–36, 645n72, 671n15
  racial integration and, 375–76
  railroad workers and, 515, 524–25, 673n38
  see also power, theory and practice of (Randolph and)
Randolph, Edmund, 326
Randolph, Elizabeth Robinson, 327–29
Randolph, James, Jr., 327
Randolph, James, Sr., 326–30, 342
Randolph, Lucille Green, 330–32, 337, 339, 501
Randolph Resolution, 506
Random House, 371
Rand School of Social Science, 202, 204, 232, 293, 321, 331, 642n34
Reading Eagle, 392
Reading Formula, 483–85
Reconstruction, 17, 41, 128, 129, 133, 134, 164–66, 175, 326, 352
Republican Party, 41, 130, 133, 138, 149, 150, 158, 164, 215, 269, 462
  Johnson and, 136–39, 142–44, 146, 148, 150, 156–57
Reuther, May, 492
Reuther, Roy, xviii, 491–93, 495, 496
Reuther, Victor, xviii, 491–93, 495
Reuther, Walter, xviii, 491–93, 495, 497, 499, 534, 535
  Ford guards' beating of, *466,* 496–97

Marshall at, 455, 457
National Legal Committee, 442
National Negro Congress and, 505, 507
school funding cases of, 425–28, 431, 441, 448–51, 512
Scottsboro case of, 436, 440–41, 443, 445
segregation and, 359, 375
Sweet case and, 210–11, 213, 214, 380, 389
teacher salary cases of, 451–54, 456, 458, 464, 512
Wagner Act and, 514
Nail, John, 336
Napoleon I, 128
Nash, Diane, 324
Nation, 34–35, 42, *98*, 111, 196, 223–24, 238, 291, 298, 369, 371
National Bar Association, 451
National Broadcasting Company, 231
National Brotherhood Workers of America, 341
National Civil Liberties Bureau (NCLB), 43, 47–49, 54, 59, 60, 66, 67, 82–83, 97, 112, 201, 283, 293, 334
National Committee for Organizing Iron and Steel Workers, 69, 70
National Committee for the Legal Defense of the Chinese, 411
National Consumers League, 246
National Council of American Indians, 417, 422
National Football League, 217
National Guard, 87, 471, 494
National Industrial Auto Workers Union, 367
National Industrial Recovery Act (NIRA), 482–85, 499
National Industrial Recovery Board, 482
National Labor Board, 482–85, 667n40, 667n40
National Labor Relations Act (Wagner Act), 468, 485–89, 494, 497, 499–502, 504, 512–15, 519, 520, 522, 536, 537
National Labor Relations Board (NLRB), 487
National Municipal Review, 23
National Negro Congress (NNC), 454, 505–8, 510
National Recovery Administration, 484, 513
National Rifle Association, 243
National Textile Workers' Union, 367
National Urban League, 162, 222, 346
Native Americans, 263, 406, 416–17, 422, 429
citizenship for, 417
Dawes allotment system and, 417, 422–23
Hualapai, 419–23, *420*, 433, 436
Indian Reorganization Act and, 422–23
Jim Crow and, 419, 425, 426, 430, 433
Margold's work on land claims of, 416–24, 426, 428–30, 433, 436

"Powers of Indian Tribes" report on, 421–22
Pueblo, 418–19, 422, 424
railroads and, 419, 420, 423
Nazi Germany, 505, 507, 510, 528, 529
Nearing, Scott, xvii, 111–12, 172, 173, 202, 235–37, 315, 359, 361, 368, 377, 386–87, 390–91, 400, 475, 476, 478, 491
Black America, 366–67, 382, 386, 388
Nebeker, Frank, 299
needle trades, *see* garment workers
Negro Common School, 177
Negro Foreign Fellowship Foundation, 162
Negro Labor Congress, 366
Nelles, Walter, xvii, 43, 49, 108, 245, 296, 294, 411, 476–80, 490
Nesbit, Evelyn, 100
New Deal, 5, 215, 396, 468, 472, 483, 495, 499, 501, 503, 505, 512–13, 515, 520, 522, 525, 667n40
New Harmony, 117
New Masses, 227–28, 371, 495, 504
New Mexico, 406, 409, 418, 472
New Republic, 49, 57, 72, 111, 189, 206, 227, 298, 320, 371, 407
News from Nowhere (Morris), 257
newspapers, 27, 106, 107, 192, 230, 256, 314–15, 412
Black, 141, 144, 162
Hearst, 27, *121*, 256, *395*
political parties and, 26
new unionism, 304–11, 317, 322, 324, 337, 339, 342, 344–45, 348, 351, 362, 369, 401, 477, 483, 486, 487, 489, 504, 515, 536, 671n15
New Worlds for Old (Wells), 102
New York, NY, 137
New York Age, 131, 141–42, 220, 355
New York American, 393
New York Call, 106
New York Central Railroad, 100
New York City Colored Republican Club, 138
New York Civic Club, 222, 292, 295, 309, 347, 532
New York Daily Mirror, 394
New Yorker, 358, 371
New York Herald Tribune, 229, 392
New York News, 219
New York Observer, 89
New York Post, 500
New York Public Library, 400
New York Society for Ethical Culture, 22
New York Stock Exchange, 99, 100
New York Sun, 49
New York Times, 2, 34, *55*, 93, 238, 322, *392*, 530
New York Tribune, 3, 115, 135, 241

New York World, 3, 41, 104, 195
Niagara Movement, 139, 144
Niebuhr, Reinhold, 7, 495
Nicholas II, Czar, 301
Niebuhr, Reinhold, 323–24
Nietzsche, Friedrich, 51
Nineteenth Amendment, 291
NIRA (National Industrial Recovery Act), 482–85, 499
Nixon v. Condon, 430–31
Nixon v. Herndon, 380, 431
NLRB (National Labor Relations Board), 487
nonviolent action, 7, 226, 254, 276, 281, 287, 300, 311–13, *313*, 362, 464, 471, 489–90, 495, 496
  see also violence
Norfolk Teachers' Association, 453
Norris, Clarence, 442
Norris, George W., 479
Norris-La Guardia Act, 480–82
Norris v. Alabama, 442, 447
North Carolina, 167, 185
  Gastonia, 367, 368, 370, 406, 469
North Carolina College for Negroes, 457–58
Northern Pacific Railroad, 99
Novyi Mir, 227
Noyes, John Humphrey, 117, 120

O'Dunne, Eugene, 458
O'Hare, Kate Richards, 294
O'Keefe, Georgia, 101
Oklahoma, 185, 208, 475
Olin, John, 539
Oneida Community, 117
O'Neill, Eugene, 217, 227, 317
Opportunity, 222
Orange Park School, 169
Oriental America, 132
Origin of the Family, The (Engels), 259
Osborne, Thomas Mott, 61–63, 65, 66, 74
Outlook, 157
Ovington, Mary White, 173–74, 186, 201–2, 334, 431
Owen, Chandler, 331–37, 341
Owen, Robert, 117

pacifism, 1, 7, 226, 311, 312, 314, 489, 495
Palmer, A. Mitchell, 287, 293, 294, 296, 299, 334, 409
panic, in human behavior, 61–62, 79
Panic of 1873, 99
Panic of 1893, 509
Paris Commune, 271
Parker, Theodore, 17

Parks, Rosa, 324, 534
Parsons, Albert, 266
Parsons, Lucy, 266
Passaic, NJ, 228, 358, 361–63, 367, 410, 469, 479
Passaic Textile Strike, The, 228, *228*, 362
Paterson, NJ, *252*, 274, 278, 285, 330
Patterson, Haywood, 442
Patterson, William "Pat," 443
Patterson v. Alabama, 442, 447
Patton, George S., 50
Paul Revere, 330
Pax, 226–27
Peabody Fund, 175, 242
Peach Springs, AZ, 420–21, *420*, 423
Peake, Mary, 163
Pennsylvania, 378, 467, 476
  McKees Rocks, PA, 272, 278
  Pittsburgh, see Pittsburgh, PA
Pennsylvania Railroad Company, 410
People's Power League, 25
Perkins, Frances, 495
Perry, Julian, *188*
Pesotta, Rose, 495
Peters, Josef, 397
Phelps Dodge Corporation, 409, 655n15
Phelps-Stokes Fund, 175, 178, 183
philanthropic foundations, 3, 88–97, 105, 110, 174, 177, 400, 539, 540
  Black education and, 174–83, *180*, 187
  critique of, 93–97, 110, 241–45, 531, 539
  education and, 89, 174
  tax deductions and exemptions for, 242–49, *247*, 538–39
  Walsh Commission and, 93–97, *94*
Phillips County, AR, sharecroppers and massacre in, 191–202, *195*, 212–13, 218, 229–30, 297, 368, 380, 382, 406, 460, 515
picket lines, 33, 70, 71, 82, 84, 85, 200, 228, 271, 302, 303, *305*, 312, 362, 367, 378, 410, 467, 470, 471, 489, 490, 493, 494, 506
Pinkney, Floria, 317
Pittsburgh, PA, 162, 492
  steel strike in, 14, 58, 59, 68–73, *69*, *71*, 74, 75, 77–79, 82, 83, 107, 109, 112, 114, 192, 201, 229, 306, 314, 364, 667n40
Pittsburgh Chronicle Telegraph, 71, *71*
Pittsburgh Courier, 186, 522–23
Pittsburgh Gazette Times, 71
Pittsburgh Leader, 71
Pittsburgh Press, 71
Plato, 78
Plessy v. Ferguson, 17–18, 31–32, 133, 425, 452, 454, 459, 520

INDEX

Revels, Hiram, 165
Richberg, Donald, 351, 354, 479–81, 483
rights, 538
  civil, *see* civil rights
  industrial, 374
  power versus, 85, 422–23, 477, 480, 486, *499*, 509, 515–16, 535
Roberts, Owen J., 500
Robeson, Paul, 217
Rockefeller, John D., Jr., xviii, *80*, 86, 91–92, *92*, 94, 287
  Caron's attempted assassination of, 279–82, *280*, 297, 299
Rockefeller, John D., Sr., 6, 86, 88–90, 256, 257
Rockefeller organizations, 183, 204, 245, 538, 540
  Rockefeller Foundation, 3, 88–96, *92*, 101, 183, 204
  Rockefeller General Education Board, 89, 175, 178, 179
  Rockefeller Plan for employee representation, 92–97
Rockville Colored Elementary School, 452
Rodakiewicz, Henwar, 101
Romney, George, 497
Roosevelt, Eleanor, 510, *511*
Roosevelt, Franklin, 13, 111, 215, 287, 296, 406, 419, 474, 481, 518
  Agricultural Adjustment Act signed by, 503
  Hillman and, 301
  March on Washington Movement and, 508–11, 525
  National Industrial Recovery Act and, 482–85
  National Labor Board and, 482–85
  National Labor Relations Act and, 486–88
  New Deal of, 5, 215, 396, 468, 472, 483, 495, 499, 501, 503, 505, 512–13, 515, 520, 522, 525, 667n40
  Randolph and, 508, 510–11, 516, 527
  Supreme Court and, 499–500, 520
  White and, 508, 510–11
  World War II and, 507
Roosevelt, Theodore, 18, 25, 35, 102, 137, 138–40, 407, 410, 508
Root, Elihu, 137, 139, 150, 655n15
Rosenwald, Julius, 175
Russia
  Czarist, 301
  German invasion of, 510
  see also Soviet Union
Russian Reconstruction Farms, 234–36, 396, 399

Russian Revolution, 1, 2, 4, 63, 75, 78, 82, 192, 236, 238, 333
  Eastman's documentary on, 228–29
Rustin, Bayard, 7, 311, 516

Sacco and Vanzetti, xviii, 7, 291, 292, 296–300, 322, 368, 383, 406, 436, 531
  Defense Committee, 291, 297, 410
  Flynn's support of, 291, 296–300, 358
  robbery and murders, 296–97, 299
Sage, Russell, 3, 89
  in St. Louis, 20–24, 26, 28–32, 35–37
St. John, Vincent, 268, 275–77, 279, 284, 285, 294
St. Louis, MO, 20–37, 39
  Baldwin in, 20–24, *21*, 26, 28–32, 35–37, 40, 60, 61, 84, 115, 157, 158
  Black population of, 29
  bridges of, 28, 32, 33
  segregation in, 29–32
St. Louis Post-Dispatch, 26–28, 30, 31, 33
St. Louis Star, 29–30
San Francisco Call, 157
Sanger, Margaret, 7, 244, 371
Saposs, David, xviii, 305–6, *316*, 317, 347, 487, 528, 667n40
Scaife, Richard Mellon, 539
Schechter Poultry v. United States, 485
Schlossberg, Joseph, xviii, 307, 317, 483, 484, 486, 642n34
schools, *see* education
Schuyler, George, 431, 446, 449
scientific management, 278, 307–9, 322, 367
Scopes, John, xviii, 7, 190, 202–7, 205, 210, 217, 218, 297, 406, *478*, 515
Scottsboro Boys, 7, 435–36, 440–43, 445, 447–50, 453, 463, 500, 505–7
  Defense Committee, 442
Sears, Roebuck, 175
Seattle, WA, 58
Sedition Act, 54, 75n
segregated schools, 5, 7, 133, 164–65, 175, 181, 185–86, 375–76, 384, 425–32, 450, 454–55, 537
  Brown v. Board of Education and, 5, 324, 406, 526, 531, 533–38
segregation, 5, 7, 17–18, 129–30, 132–36, 164, 166, 168–70, 173, 210, 226, 327, 332, 333, 359, 368, 375, 378, 405, 447, 455, 536
  administrative foundations of, 429–30, 432, 433, 537
  on buses, 464, 534–35
  Indian land law and, 419, 425, 426, 430, 433

segregation (*cont.*)
  in labor unions, 32–33, 173, 177, 266, 326, 339–41, 352–53, 375, 382, 383, 390, 432–33, 486, 506, 512–14, 518–21, 524
  Margold and, 405
  NAACP and, 359, 375
  at post offices, 141
  in railroad cars, 18, 125, 133–35, 380, 512
  residential, 29–31, 208, 210–11, 380
  in St. Louis, 29–32
  social interactions hindered by, 376
  Supreme Court and, 5, 17–18, 31–32, 133, 135, 141, 208, 210–11, 324, 406, 452, 454, 459, 520, 526, 531, 533–38
  World War II and, 510
  Yick Wo case and, 429–30, 432, 450
Seidman, Joel, 467, 496
Selander, Ted, 469–70
Selective Service Act, 41, 55, 59
Self-Culture Hall, 22–23
Seligmann, Herbert, 334, 389, 432
Senate Committee on Indian Affairs, 417
sex, 2, 3, 66, 109, 258, 371
  birth control and, 7, 244, 371
  see also marriage
sexual orientation, 64
Shaler, Nathaniel Southgate, 19–20, 207
sharecropping and peonage, 172, 173, 191–202, *195*, 218, 229–30, 380, 503
  Elaine massacre and, 191–202, *195*, 212–13, 229–30, 297, 368, 382, 406, 503, 504, 515
  Southern Tenant Farmers Union and, 463, 498, 503–5, 507, 529, 536
Sheats, William N., 167–69, 175–76, 181, 186
Sheats Law, 168–69
Shields, Art, 298
Shillady, John, 145–46, 192
Simple Justice (Kluger), 535
Sinclair, Upton, xviii, 45, *80*, 91, 95, 97, 105, 110, 218, 230, 232, 235, 306, 309, 314, 330
  "Dead Hand" series of, 105–6
  Garland's inheritance and, 2, 105–8, 491
  The Jungle, 2, 91, 95, 112
Sisson, Thomas, 149
sit-down strikes, 467, 488–95, *493*, 499, 520, 536
Sixteenth Amendment, 242
Slater Fund, 175, 183, 242
slavery, 16–17, 19, 81, 128, 131, 171, 221, 243, 326
  abolitionists and, 17, 55, 81, 129, 201, 242, 260, 276, 352
  Bailey v. Alabama and, 142

  formerly enslaved people, 128, 163–65, *166*, 242, 343, 344
  fugitive slaves, 150, 163
  Hegel on, 226
  in Houston's family background, 437, 439
  lynching and, 135
  slave insurrections, 17, 81, 191–92, 201, 328, 431
Slovick, James, 119
Smith, Adam, 105
Smith, Tucker, 496
Smith, Walker, 269, 278
Smith v. Allwright, 431
social democrats, 364, 369, 377, 390, 391, 464, 468, 477, 497, 536
socialism, 1, 14, 118, 172, 173, 202, 226, 246, 257, 277, 303, 307, 330, 331, 344, 349, 376, 497, 505, 528
  Flynn and, 260, 262
  inherited wealth and, 102, 103
Socialist Party, 41, 43, 74, 105, 111–12, 142, 172, 190, 231–32, 234, 255, 272, 273, 293, 294, 320, 330–32, 334, 383, 441
Society of American Indians, 416–17
Solidarity, 273, 275, 283
Soule, George, 642n34, 648n26
Souls of Black Folk, The (Du Bois), 138, 177
South Carolina, 164, 167, 185, 405, 428
Southeastern Carriers Conference Agreement, 518, 522, 524
Southern Education Board, 175
Southern Tenant Farmers Union (STFU), 463, 498, 503–5, 507, 529, 536
Soviet Union, 4, 14, 227, 254, 286, 322, 358, 359, 363–64, 366, 368, 394, 399, 442, 492
  agriculture in, 234–36, 396
  Baldwin's trip to, 237–39
  civil liberties in, 238–39, 359
  Nazi Germany and, 507, 510, 528, 529
  positive attitudes toward, 238–39
  public health program in, 411
  spies of, 396–99, *397*
  Vanguard Press and, 236–37
Spanish-American War, 27, 256
Speakers Service Bureau, 227
Spingarn, Arthur, 154, 155
Spingarn, Joel, 144, 446
Stalin, Joseph, 228, 236, 359, 363, 364
  Hitler's pact with, 507, 510, 528, 529
Stalinism, 254, 292
Standard Oil, 89, 91
Stanton, Edwin, 163
Stanton, Elizabeth Cady, 255

Stanton School, 131, *131*, 132, 162–64, *165*, 168, 170
State Department, U.S., 139–40, *140*, 218
State Normal College for Negroes, 169
Steele, Bester William, xviii, 518–26, *519*, 537
Steele v. Louisville & Nashville Railroad, 5, 520–26, 527, 536, 537
steel workers, 58, 209, 313, 472, 512
  labor unions and, 68–69
  Steel Workers Organizing Committee, 472, 500, 505
  strikes by, 14, 58, 59, 68–73, *69*, *71*, 74, 75, 77–79, 82, 83, 107, 109, 112, 114, 192, 201, 229, 272, 306, 314, 364, 667n40
Steffens, Lincoln, 24, 26
Stelton, NJ, 118, 119
Steunenberg, Frank, 263, 264, 271, 300
Stimson, Henry, 407, 657n36
stock market, 381
  American Fund's holdings in, 3, 161, 322, 358, 361, 363, 376, 377, 380, 381, 444, 445, 530
  crash of 1929, 5, 322, 399, 400, 445
  Dow Jones Industrial Average, 161, 358, 381
Stokes, Helen Phelps, 204
Stolberg, Benjamin, 643n34
Stone, Harlan Fiske, 462, 520, 521
Storey, Moorfield, 210–11
Stowe, Harriet Beecher, 129
strikes, *see* labor strikes
Students for a Democratic Society (SDS), 535
Studies in the Psychology of Sex (Ellis), 258
suffrage, *see* voting rights
Supreme Court, U.S., 20, 75, 113, 135, 142, 147, 149–50, 198, 215, 243, 304, 406, 410, 410, 413, 418, 442, 461, 476, 499, 534, 541
  Abrams v. United States, 75–77
  Bailey v. Alabama, 142
  Brown v. Board of Education, 5, 324, 406, 526, 531, 533–38
  Civil Rights Cases, 133, 149
  Corrigan v. Buckley, 211n
  De Jonge v. Oregon, 500
  Dred Scott v. Sandford, 345
  FDR and, 499–500, 520
  Gaines case, 461–62, *461*, 463, 464, 520, 521
  Gong Lum v. Rice, 426–27, 429, 432
  Herndon v. Lowry, 500–501
  Korematsu v. United States, 522, 523
  Lochner v. New York, 413
  minimum-wage laws and, 499, 500, 502
  Moore v. Dempsey, 198–203, 229–30, 460, 515

Nixon v. Condon, 430–31
Nixon v. Herndon, 380, 431
Norris v. Alabama, 442, 447
Patterson v. Alabama, 442, 447
Plessy v. Ferguson, 17–18, 31–32, 133, 425, 452, 454, 459, 520
Powell v. Alabama, 442, 443
Schechter Poultry v. United States, 485
  segregation and, 5, 17–18, 31–32, 133, 135, 141, 208, 210–11, 324, 406, 452, 454, 459, 520, 526, 531, 533–38
Smith v. Allwright, 431
Steele v. Louisville & Nashville Railroad, 5, 520–26, 527, 536, 537
  tax law and, 242
United States v. Cruikshank, 136, 149
United States v. Santa Fe Pacific Railroad Company, 423
Yates v. United States, 534
Yick Wo v. Hopkins, 429–30, 432, 521
Survey, 40, 222, *223*
Sweet, Gladys, 208
Sweet, Henry, *188*, 213
Sweet, Ossian, xviii, 7, 191, 207–15, *208*, 217, 218, 230, 297, 326, 368, 378, 380, 389, 406, 493, 515, 520
Symonett, Mary, 128

taboo, 52–53, 371
Taft, Phil, 64
Taft, William Howard, 90, 139–40, 407, 426, 476
taxes, 235, 242, 255, 374
  American Fund and, 241–49, 247
  Black education and, 167, 169–71, 175, 180, 425–26, 432
  deductions and exemptions in, 242–49, *247*, 538–39
  Garland bequest and, 245, 247
  income, 242, 244
  inheritance, 95, 102, 245, 374
  propaganda and, 244, 246–48
  property, 170
Tarde, Gabriel, 51–54, 56, 152
Taylor, Frederick Winslow, 307–9, 322
teachers, 169, 203, 259
  Black, 165–67, 169, 186, 187, 450, 451–56, 458, 464
  free speech and, 203, 204, 206
  salaries of, 167, 451–54, 456, 458, 464, 512
Teachers Union, 203
Tenement House Department, 407
Tennessee, 206, 475

INDEX

Tennessee Valley Authority (TVA), 451, 505
Terminal Railroad Association, 28
Texas, 430–31, 436
textile workers, 256, 468, 482, 484, 512
    Amalgamated Textile Workers, 313–14, 372–73
    American Textile Workers Union, 360
    National Textile Workers' Union, 367
    strikes by, 228, *228*, *252*, 274, 297, 299, 311–14, *313*, 330, 358, 361–63, 367–68, 410, 469, 479, 490
    United Textile Workers, 362
    see also garment workers
Thayer, Webster, 298
Thirteenth Amendment, 142
Thomas, Norman, xviii, 43, 66, 111, 184, 185, 190, 203, 231–32, 234–37, 244, 282, 296, 301, 309, 320, 322, 323, 361, 363, 369, 377, 384, 399, 441, 442, 459, 460, 461, 463, 491, 528, 531
    National Negro Congress and, 505
    Southern Tenant Farmers Union and, 503–5
Thompson, James, 276
Thompson, William O., 275–76
Thoreau, Henry David, 14, 20, 55, 120
Tillman, John, 148
Tillson, Davis, 166
Time, 5
Toledo, OH, 469–72, *471*
Toledo Edison Electric Company, 472
Tolstoy, Leo, 1, 103
Tone, Wolfe, 255
Totten, Ashley L., 341
Trade Union Committee for Organizing Negro Workers, 382
Trade Union Education League, 321, 368
Trade Union Unity League, 368
Transportation Act, 349, 476
Treasury Department, U.S., 22, 242, 244, 539
Tresca, Carlo, xviii, 276–77, *280*, 281, 284, 285, 287, 293, 297–99, 358
trials, *see* courts
Truman, Harry, 147
Tsar to Lenin, 229
Tucker, Thomas DeSaille, 169
Tudor, Marie (mother of Charles Garland), xviii, 2, 101, 102, 104, 108, 395, 409
Turner, Mary, 126
Turner, Nat, 191–92, 328
Tuskegee Normal and Industrial Institute, 17–19, 29, 137–39, 141, 144, 161, 169, 175–76, 178, 183

Ulysses (Joyce), 371
Uncle Remus stories, 221
Underwood, Oscar, 156
Unemployed Leagues, 470
unemployed workers, 469–71, 473, 506
    Coxey's Army, 509
Unitarianism, 16, 20, 23, 43, 56, 76
United Anthracite Miners, 476
United Auto Workers (UAW), 491–93, 495–97, 534, 535
United Brotherhood of Carpenters, 293
United Front Committee, 362, 410
United Garment Workers (UGW), 303, 305
United Mine Workers of America (UMW), 86, 87, 114, 306–7, 321, 341, 364, 472, 473, 484, 495
United Negro Improvement Association, 331, 335, 442
United States v. Cruikshank, 136, 149
United States v. Santa Fe Pacific Railroad Company, 423
United Steelworkers of America, 112
United Textile Workers (UTW), 362
United Welfare Association, 30
University of Chicago Laboratory School, 319–20
University of Maryland, 455, 456, 458
University of Michigan, 463
University of Missouri, 459–61
University of North Carolina, 457–58, 463
University of Toledo, 172
Urban League, 162
U.S. Steel, 268, 274
    workers strike, 14, 58, 59, 68–73, *69*, *71*, 74, 75, 77–79, 82, 83, 107, 109, 112, 114, 192, 201, 229, 306, 314, 364, 667n40
utopian communities, 117–18, 120
    April Farm, *116*, 117–22, *119*, *121*, *392*, 393–96, *395*, 491

Vanderveer, George, 286
Van Doren, Dorothy, *98*
Van Doren, Irita, *98*
Van Doren, Mark, *98*, 226
Vanguard Press, 235–38, 357, 371, 479, 505, 536
Van Vechten, Carl, 528
Vanzetti, Bartolomeo, *see* Sacco and Vanzetti
Vardaman, James, 169–70
Vesey, Denmark, 328
Vietnam War, 311
Vigilancia, 39
Villa, Pancho, 54
Villard, Oswald Garrison, 55, *98*

Vindication of the Rights of Woman, A (Wollstonecraft), 257
violence, 282, 315, 319
  American Fund critique of, 226, 281, 300, anarchists and, 91, 279, *280*, 287–88, 296–97, 299–300
  Brookwood critique of, 489–90, 496
  IWW's defense and use of, 254–55, 271–83, 288, 299, 300
  IWW switch on, 285–88, 288–89
  Muste's critique of, 7, 311, 312–13, 471, 490
  Socialist critique of, 273
  working class revolutionary use of, 277, 286
  World War I, during, 47–49, 60
  see also racial violence
Virginia, 433, 453, 514
Virginia Teachers' Association, 186
Virgin Islands, 300
Vorse, Mary Heaton, 70, 72, 279
voters
  Black, 41, 133, 137, 141–44, 146, 151, 156–57, 164, 166, 215, 430–31, 436
  initiatives and referendums of, 25–26, 28–30, 157
voting rights
  for Black Americans, 30, 130, 143, 150, 173, 359, 380, 430–31, 436, 506
  for women, 255, 263, 291

Wabash System of Shop Crafts, 475
wages, 29, 32, 35, 72, 200, 246, 260, 308–10, 378, 469, 472, 485
  of Black workers, 68, 182, 193, 343, 344
  minimum, 83, 200, 410, 499, 500, 502, 503
Wagner, Robert, xviii, 481–82, 484, 485, 488
Wagner Act (National Labor Relations Act), 468, 485–89, 494, 497, 499–502, 504, 512–15, 519, 520, 522, 536, 537
Waite, Morrison, 136
Wald, Lillian, 43
Walden Pond, 14
Walker, Madam C. J., 330–31
Wallas, Graham, 51–53, *52*, 78, 85, 152, 412
Wall Street, 82, 407
  crash of 1929, 5, 322, 399, 400
  Panic of 1873 and, 99
  see also stock market
Wall Street bombing, 287–88, 299
Walsh, Frank, 93, *94*, 111, 112, 275–76, 295, 482, 539
Walsh Commission (Commission on Industrial Relations), 93–97, *94*, 111, 275–77, 279, 285, 295, 308, 482, 539

Walters, Alexander, 36
Ward, Harry F., 112
Ward, Lester, 331
War Department, 408
Ware, Ed, 197
Ware, Harold, xix, 396–400, *397*
Washington, Booker T., 17–20, 22, 29–31, 36, 133, 137–39, 141, 161, 169, 175, 178, 187, 508
  Baldwin (Roger) and, 18–19, 20, 30, 31
  Baldwin (William) and, 17–18, 175–76
  Du Bois and, 138, 187
  Johnson and, 137–39, 144
Washington, D.C., 58, 208, 474
  March on Washington (1963), 355
  March on Washington Movement, 355, 508–12, 516–18, *517*, 525, 526
Washington Eagle, 224
Washington Post, 392, 523, 526
Washington Times, 117, 118
Wayne State University, 491
wealth, 81–82, 89, 103, 105, 242, 257, 259, 372, 540
  democracy and, 82, 85–86, 90, 93–94, 96–97
  philanthropy and, *see* philanthropic foundations
  taxes and, 242–49
  see also inherited wealth; money
Webb, Sidney and Beatrice, 352
Webster, Milton, 352, 524–25
Weinrib, Laura, 203
Weirton Steel, 485
Weisbord, Albert, 362, 363, 367, 479
Wells, H. G., 1, 2, 102–3
Wells-Barnett, Ida B., 35, 196
Wesley, Charles, 505
Western Federation of Miners (WFM), 263–65, *265*, 271, 272, 274, 300
West Virginia, 114–15, *114*, 229, 378, 472, 485, 491
WEVD, 231, 33, 232
Weyl, Walter, 407
Wharton School, 172
Whiskey Ring scandal, 22, 31
White, Walter, xix, 185, 192, *379*, 380–82, 384–85, 387, 405, 430, 432, 440, 441, 442, 446, 449, 450, 457, 460, 462, 464, 503, 505, 507, 528, 533
  Committee on Negro Work and, 377–80
  Houston and, 444
  Elaine massacre and, 192–96, 199
  FDR and, 508, 510–11
  March on Washington and, 509

White, Walter (*cont.*)
  on Margold, 424
  at NAACP conference, 431
  Scottsboro case and, 436
  Sweet case and, 210, 212, 214
  teacher salary cases and, 454
white supremacy, 135, 164, 168, 175, 181, 182, 196–98, 207, 359, 440
Who Said Watermelon?, 219
Wickersham, George W., 90, 150
Wiggins, Ella May, 367
Wilkerson, Herbert, 474–76
Wilkins, Roy, 449
Williams, Ethel, 287
Williams, Eugene, 442
Wilson, Edmund, 227
Wilson, William, 295
Wilson, Woodrow, xix, 35, 58, 93, 227, 294, 295, 296, 307, 330, 334–35, 409
  Baldwin and, 39–40, 59, 60
  censorship and, 40–44, 77
  in elections, 30, 39, 140, 142
  Flynn's letter to, 285
  speech strategy of, 44–47, 56, 77
  IWW and, 284, 285
  Johnson and, 140–42, 218
  racial violence and, 41, 48, 88
  World War I and, 39–40, 44, 45, 49, 56, 60, 68, 74, 75n, 77, 95, 105, 332, 408, 410
Wobblies, *see* Industrial Workers of the World
Wollstonecraft, Mary, 257, 258
Wolman, Leo, 113, 301, 306, 317, 369, 409, 479, 481–84, 487, 667n40
  Reading Formula of, 483–85
Women and Economics (Gilman), 258
Women and Socialism (Bebel), 257–58
Women's International League for Peace and Freedom, 226–27
women's rights, 243, 244, 257–58
  voting, 255, 263, 291
Women's Trade Union League, 314
women workers, 246, 256, 499
Wood, Leonard, 70
Wood, L. Hollingsworth, 184, 211
Woodson, Carter, 161–62, 170, 179, 181
workers
  education of, *see* labor education
  hours worked by, 68, 72, 200, 201, 246, 255, 269, 286, 309, 311, 313, 317, 342, 344, 345, 347, 349, 367, 373, 413, 484, 485, 499, 503
  immigration and, 266–68

  mass production and, 3, 118, 174, 292, 306–10, 322, 362, 369, 373, 468, 469, 472, 486, 487, 496, 537
  scientific management of, 278, 307–9, 322, 367
  wages of, *see* wages
  women, 246, 256, 499
  see also Black workers
Workers Defense Union (WDU), 293–98, 300, 396, 409
Workers' Education Bureau, 322
Workers Education Conference for Negroes, 446
Workers' Health Bureau, 357
Workers Party of America, 233, 234
Workers School of New York City, 321, 398
World Tomorrow, 42, 226
World War I, 5, 9, 37, 39–56, 60, 65, 68, 74, 75n, 82, 83, 89, 97, 111, 172, 201, 218, 227, 248, 272, 274–75, 283, 286, 287, 332, 335, 408
  Black army officers in, 437–38, 442
  Black support for, 332
  censorship during, 39–45, 60, 75, 77, 534
  conscientious objectors and, 43, 60, 82, 119, 409, 656n15
  draft during, 13–14, 41, 42, 54–55, 58, 59, 201
  IWW and, 283–84, 286
  labor disputes and, 307, 408, 409
  mob violence during, 47–49, 60
  propaganda during, 38, 39–40, 45–47, 46, 49–50, 53–54, 56, 60, 72, 74, 95, 105, 151, 152, 227, 667n40
  tax legislation during, 242
  veterans of, 509
  Wilson administration and, 39–40, 44, 45, 49, 56, 60, 68, 74, 75n, 77, 95, 105, 332, 408, 410
World War II, 50, 507, 508, 510, 512
Wright, Richard, 222
Wright, Roy, 435
Wyzanski, Charles, 667n40

Yale Law Journal, 477
Yale Law School, 476
Yale University, 236, 412, 413
Yates v. United States, 534
yellow dog contracts, 480, 482, 499
Yick Wo v. Hopkins, 429–30, 432, 521
Young, Art, 227, 229

Vindication of the Rights of Woman, A (Wollstonecraft), 257
violence, 282, 315, 319
  American Fund critique of, 226, 281, 300, 296–297, 299–300
  anarchists and, 91, 279, *280*, 287–88, 296–297, 299–300
  Brookwood critique of, 489–90, 496
  IWW's defense and use of, 254–55, 271–83, 288, 299, 300
  IWW switch on, 285–88, 288–89
  Muste's critique of, 7, 311, 312–13, 471, 490
  Socialist critique of, 273
  working class revolutionary use of, 277, 286
  World War I, during, 47–49, 60
  see also racial violence
Virginia, 433, 453, 514
Virginia Teachers' Association, 186
Virgin Islands, 380
Vorse, Mary Heaton, 70, 72, 279
voters
  Black, 41, 133, 137, 141–44, 146, 151, 156–57, 164, 166, 215, 430–31, 436
  initiatives and referendums of, 25–26, 28–30, 157
voting rights
  for Black Americans, 30, 130, 143, 150, 173, 359, 380, 430–31, 436, 506
  for women, 255, 263, 291

Wabash System of Shop Crafts, 475
wages, 29, 32, 35, 72, 200, 246, 260, 308–10, 378, 469, 472, 485
  of Black workers, 68, 182, 193, 343, 344
  minimum, 83, 200, 410, 499, 500, 502, 503
Wagner, Robert, xviii, 481–82, 484, 485, 488
Wagner Act (National Labor Relations Act), 468, 485–89, 494, 497, 499–502, 504, 512–15, 519, 520, 522, 536, 537
Waite, Morrison, 136
Wald, Lillian, 43
Walden Pond, 14
Walker, Madam C. J., 330–31
Wallas, Graham, 51–53, *52*, 78, 85, 152, 412
Wall Street, 82, 407
  crash of 1929, **5**, 322, 399, 400
  Panic of 1873 and, 99
  see also stock market
Wall Street bombing, 287–88, 299
Walsh, Frank, 93, *94*, 111, 112, 275–76, 295, 482, 539
Walsh Commission (Commission on Industrial Relations), 93–97, *94*, 111, 275–77, 279, 285, 295, 308, 482, 539

Walters, Alexander, 36
Ward, Harry F., 112
Ward, Lester, 331
War Department, 408
Ware, Ed, 197
Ware, Harold, xix, 396–400, *397*
Washington, Booker T., 17–20, 22, 29–31, 36, 133, 137–39, 141, 161, 169, 175, 178, 187, 508
  Baldwin (Roger) and, 18–19, 20, 30, 31
  Baldwin (William) and, 17–18, 175–76
  Du Bois and, 138, 187
  Johnson and, 137–39, 144
Washington, D.C., 58, 208, 474
  March on Washington (1963), 355
  March on Washington Movement, 355, 508–12, 516–18, *517*, 525, 526
Washington Eagle, 224
Washington Post, *392*, 523, 526
Washington Times, 117, 118
Wayne State University, 491
wealth, 81–82, 89, 103, 105, 242, 257, 259, 372, 540
  democracy and, 82, 85–86, 90, 93–94, 96–97
  philanthropy and, *see* philanthropic foundations
  taxes and, 242–49
  see also inherited wealth; money
Webb, Sidney and Beatrice, 352
Webster, Milton, 352, 524–25
Weinrib, Laura, 203
Weirton Steel, 485
Weisbord, Albert, 362, 363, 367, 479
Wells, H. G., 1, 2, 102–3
Wells-Barnett, Ida B., 35, 196
Wesley, Charles, 505
Western Federation of Miners (WFM), 263–65, *265*, 271, 272, 274, 300
West Virginia, 114–15, *114*, 229, 378, 472, 485, 491
WEVD, 231–33, *232*
Weyl, Walter, 407
Wharton School, 172
Whiskey Ring scandal, 22, 31
White, Walter, xix, 185, 192, *379*, 380–82, 384–85, 387, 405, 430, 432, 440, 441, 442, 446, 449, 450, 457, 460, 462, 464, 503, 505, 507, 528, 533
  Committee on Negro Work and, 377–80
  Houston and, 444
  Elaine massacre and, 192–96, 199
  FDR and, 508, 510–11
  March on Washington and, 509

White, Walter (*cont.*)
  on Margold, 424
  at NAACP conference, 431
  Scottsboro case and, 436
  Sweet case and, 210, 212, 214
  teacher salary cases and, 454
white supremacy, 135, 164, 168, 175, 181, 182, 196–98, 207, 359, 440
Who Said Watermelon?, 219
Wickersham, George W., 90, 150
Wiggins, Ella May, 367
Wilkerson, Herbert, 474–76
Wilkins, Roy, 449
Williams, Ethel, 287
Williams, Eugene, 442
Wilson, Edmund, 227
Wilson, William, 295
Wilson, Woodrow, xix, 35, 58, 93, 227, 294, 295, 296, 307, 330, 334–35, 409
  Baldwin and, 39–40, 59, 60
  censorship and, 40–44, 77
  in elections, 30, 39, 140, 142
  Flynn's letter to, 285
  speech strategy of, 44–47, 56, 77
  IWW and, 284, 285
  Johnson and, 140–42, 218
  racial violence and, 41, 48, 88
  World War I and, 39–40, 44, 45, 49, 56, 60, 68, 74, 75n, 77, 95, 105, 332, 408, 410
Wobblies, *see* Industrial Workers of the World
Wollstonecraft, Mary, 257, 258
Wolman, Leo, 113, 301, 306, 317, 369, 409, 479, 481–84, 487, 667n40
  Reading Formula of, 483–85
Women and Economics (Gilman), 258
Women and Socialism (Bebel), 257–58
Women's International League for Peace and Freedom, 226–27
women's rights, 243, 244, 257–58
  voting, 255, 263, 291
Women's Trade Union League, 314
women workers, 246, 256, 499
Wood, Leonard, 70
Wood, L. Hollingsworth, 184, 211
Woodson, Carter, 161–62, 170, 179, 181
workers
  education of, *see* labor education
  hours worked by, 68, 72, 200, 201, 246, 255, 269, 286, 309, 311, 313, 317, 342, 344, 345, 347, 349, 367, 373, 413, 484, 485, 499, 503
  immigration and, 266–68

mass production and, 3, 118, 174, 292, 306–10, 322, 362, 369, 373, 468, 469, 472, 486, 487, 496, 537
scientific management of, 278, 307–9, 322, 367
wages of, *see* wages
women, 246, 256, 499
see also Black workers
Workers Defense Union (WDU), 293–98, 300, 396, 409
Workers' Education Bureau, 322
Workers Education Conference for Negroes, 446
Workers' Health Bureau, 357
Workers Party of America, 233, 234
Workers School of New York City, 321, 398
World Tomorrow, 42, 226
World War I, 5, 9, 37, 39–56, 60, 65, 68, 74, 75n, 82, 83, 89, 97, 111, 172, 201, 218, 227, 248, 272, 274–75, 283, 286, 287, 332, 335, 408
  Black army officers in, 437–38, 442
  Black support for, 332
  censorship during, 39–45, 60, 75, 77, 534
  conscientious objectors and, 43, 60, 82, 119, 409, 656n15
  draft during, 13–14, 41, 42, 54–55, 58, 59, 201
  IWW and, 283–84, 286
  labor disputes and, 307, 408, 409
  mob violence during, 47–49, 60
  propaganda during, 38, 39–40, 45–47, 46, 49–50, 53–54, 56, 60, 72, 74, 95, 105, 151, 152, 227, 667n40
  tax legislation during, 242
  veterans of, 509
  Wilson administration and, 39–40, 44, 45, 49, 56, 60, 68, 74, 75n, 77, 95, 105, 332, 408, 410
World War II, 50, 507, 508, 510, 512
Wright, Richard, 222
Wright, Roy, 435
Wyzanski, Charles, 667n40

Yale Law Journal, 477
Yale Law School, 476
Yale University, 236, 412, 413
Yates v. United States, 534
yellow dog contracts, 480, 482, 499
Yick Wo v. Hopkins, 429–30, 432, 521
Young, Art, 227, 229

About the Author

John Fabian Witt is the Duffy Professor of Law and Professor of History at Yale University, where he teaches and writes about the history of American law. His *Lincoln's Code: The Laws of War in American History* was a finalist for the Pulitzer Prize and a winner of the Bancroft Prize.